c. Overall conclusion/financial reporting objective
Based on your role in the case and the above information, conclude on whether the financial reporting will be more aggressive or conservative or somewhere in between. Note that aggressive accounting tends to overstate net income/assets and present the company in the best light. Conservative accounting ensures that net income/assets are not overstated and that all pertinent information (positive or negative) is disclosed.

2. Identification and analysis of financial reporting issues

a. Issue identification
Read the case and look for potential financial reporting issues. To do this, you need to know the accounting principles and rules and have an understanding of the business and the business transactions. Issues are usually about deciding whether or not to **recognize** something (revenues, liabilities etc.), deciding how to **measure** financial statement elements (leave them as they are or write them down or off), or how to **present/disclose** these items in the financial statements (treat them as current or long term, debt or equity, discontinued or continuing operations, etc.).

b. Ranking issues
Focus on the more important issues. In other words, focus first on the issues that are material to the users of the information (those that are more complex and/or those that affect any of the key numbers or ratios identified above). You should identify right away what you consider to be material.

c. Analysis
The analysis should consider both qualitative and quantitative aspects. It should also look at the issue from different perspectives. For example, in a revenue recognition issue, should the revenue be recognized now or later? Consider only the relevant alternatives.

Qualitative:
- Each perspective must be supported by making reference to GAAP and accounting theory (including the conceptual framework). For example, recognize the revenue now because... or recognize it later because...

- Make sure the analysis is case specific—i.e. that it refers to the facts of the specific case.

- Make strong arguments for both sides of the discussion. If the issue is a real issue, there is often more than one way to account for the transaction or event.

- Make sure that the analysis considers the substance of the transaction from a business and economic perspective.

Quantitative:
- Calculate the impact of the different perspectives on key financial statement numbers/ratios. Would this decision be relevant to users?

- Calculate what the numbers might look like under different accounting methods, if they are relevant.

3. Recommendations
After each issue is analyzed, conclude on how the items should be accounted for. Your conclusion should be based on your role and the financial reporting objective that you identified earlier.

for *Intermediate Accounting,* Eighth Canadian Edition

Check with your instructor to find out if you have access to *WileyPLUS!*

Study More Effectively with a Multimedia Text

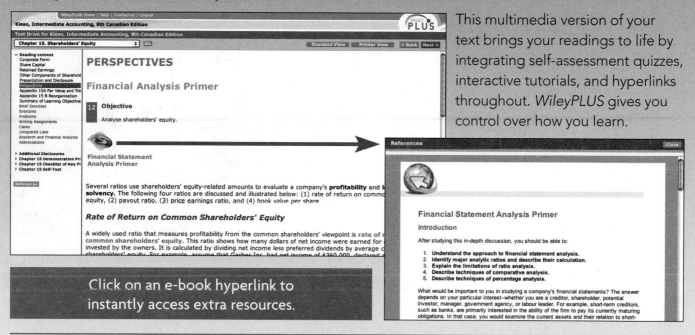

Click on an e-book hyperlink to instantly access extra resources.

This multimedia version of your text brings your readings to life by integrating self-assessment quizzes, interactive tutorials, and hyperlinks throughout. *WileyPLUS* gives you control over how you learn.

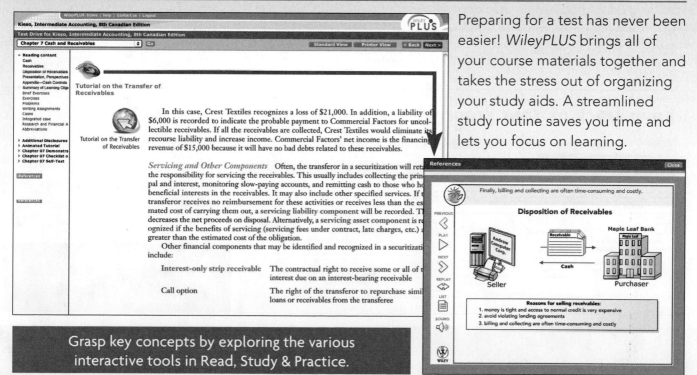

Grasp key concepts by exploring the various interactive tools in Read, Study & Practice.

Preparing for a test has never been easier! *WileyPLUS* brings all of your course materials together and takes the stress out of organizing your study aids. A streamlined study routine saves you time and lets you focus on learning.

John Wiley & Sons Canada, Ltd.

WILEY PLUS for *Intermediate Accounting*, Eighth Canadian Edition

Complete and Submit Assignments On-line Efficiently

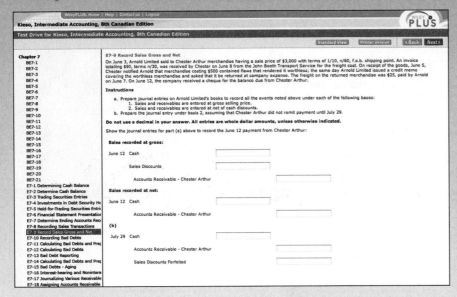

Your instructor can assign homework on-line for automatic grading and you can keep up-to-date on your assignments with your assignment list.

Your homework questions contain links to the relevant section of the multimedia text, so you know exactly where to go to get help solving each problem. In addition, use the Assignment area of *WileyPLUS* to monitor all of your assignments and their due dates.

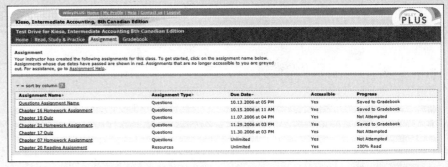

Keep Track of Your Progress

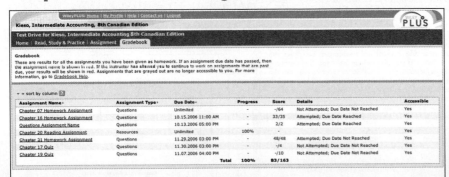

Your personal Gradebook lets you review your answers and results from past assignments as well as any feedback your instructor may have for you.

Keep track of your progress and review your completed questions at any time.

Technical Support: http://higheredwiley.custhelp.com
Student Resource Centre: http://www.wileyplus.com

For further information regarding *WileyPLUS* and other Wiley products, please visit www.wiley.ca

Intermediate Accounting

EIGHTH CANADIAN EDITION

Intermediate Accounting

Donald E. Kieso, PhD, CPA
KPMG Peat Marwick Emeritus Professor of Accounting
Northern Illinois University
DeKalb, Illinois

Jerry J. Weygandt, PhD, CPA
Arthur Andersen Alumni Professor of Accounting
University of Wisconsin
Madison, Wisconsin

Terry D. Warfield, PhD
Associate Professor
University of Wisconsin
Madison, Wisconsin

Nicola M. Young, MBA, FCA
Saint Mary's University
Halifax, Nova Scotia

Irene M. Wiecek, FCA
University of Toronto
Toronto, Ontario

John Wiley & Sons Canada, Ltd.

Library and Archives Canada Cataloguing in Publication
Intermediate accounting / Donald E. Kieso ... [et al.]. — 8th Canadian ed.

ISBN 978-0-470-83979-9 (v. 1)

ISBN 978-0-470-83980-5 (v. 2)

1. Accounting—Textbooks.   I. Kieso, Donald E.

HF5635.I573 2007   657'.044   C2007-900378-8

Production Credits
Editorial Manager: Karen Staudinger
Publishing Services Director: Karen Bryan
Marketing Manager: Aida Krneta
Developmental Editor: Daleara Hirjikaka
Editorial Assistants: Sheri Coombs, Pauline Ricablanca
Formatting: Emerson Group (Gail Ferreira Ng-A-Kien)
Cover and design: Interrobang Graphic Design Inc.
Cover Photo: Michael Ryan/Graphistock Photography/Veer
Printing and Binding: Quebecor World—Dubuque

References to the *CICA Handbook* are reprinted (or adapted) with permission from The Canadian Institute of Chartered Accountants, Toronto, Canada. Any changes to the original material are the sole responsibility of the author (and/or publisher) and have not been reviewed or endorsed by the CICA.

Printed and bound in the United States of America

2 3 4 5 QW 11 10 09 08

John Wiley & Sons Canada, Ltd.
6045 Freemont Blvd.
Mississauga, Ontario L5R 4J3
Visit our website at www.wiley.ca

Dedicated to our husbands
John and George

and to our children
Hilary
Tim
Megan
Nicholas, and
Katherine

for their support, encouragement, and tolerance
throughout the writing of this book;
and to the many wonderful students who have passed
through our Intermediate Accounting classrooms.
We, too, have learned from you.

ABOUT THE AUTHORS

Canadian Edition

Nicola (Nickie) M. Young, MBA, FCA, is a Professor of Accounting in the Sobey School of Business at Saint Mary's University in Halifax, Nova Scotia, where her teaching responsibilities have varied from the introductory offering to final year advanced financial courses to the survey course in the Executive MBA program. She is the recipient of teaching awards, and has contributed to the academic and administrative life of the university through chairing the Department of Accounting, membership on the Board of Governors, and the Pension and other Committees. Nickie was associated with the Atlantic School of Chartered Accountancy for over twenty-five years in a variety of roles, including program and course development, teaching, and program reform. In addition to contributions to the accounting profession at the provincial level, Nickie has served on national boards of the Canadian Institute of Chartered Accountants (CICA) dealing with licensure and education. For the last fifteen years, she has worked with the CICA's Public Sector Accounting Board (PSAB) as an Associate, as a member and chair of the Board, and as a chair and member of PSAB Task Forces.

Irene M. Wiecek, FCA, is a faculty member of the University of Toronto at Mississauga and is cross-appointed to the Joseph L. Rotman School of Management. She teaches financial reporting in various programs including the Commerce Program (Accounting Specialist) and the Master of Management & Professional Accounting Program (MMPA). The Associate Director of the MMPA Program for many years, she co-founded and is Co-Director of the ICAO/Rotman Centre for Innovation in Accounting Education, which supports and facilitates innovation in accounting education. Irene has been involved in professional accounting education for over twenty years both at the Institute of Chartered Accountants of Ontario and the CICA, teaching and developing case/program material in various programs including the ICAO School of Accountancy. She helped create and currently directs the CICA In-depth GAAP Program. In the area of standard setting, she is Chair of the Canadian Academic Accounting Association Financial Accounting Exposure Draft Response Committee (since 2002). Irene is a member of the CICA Qualifications Committee, which provides leadership, direction, and standards for admission into the CA profession. She is the recipient of the MMPA Faculty of the Year award for 2004 and 2006.

U.S. Edition

Donald E. Kieso, Ph.D., C.P.A., received his bachelor's degree from Aurora University and his doctorate in accounting from the University of Illinois. He has served as chairman of the Department of Accountancy and is currently the KPMG Emeritus Professor of Accountancy at Northern Illinois University. He has public accounting experience with Price Waterhouse & Co. (San Francisco and Chicago) and Arthur Andersen & Co. (Chicago) and research experience with the Research Division of the American Institute of Certified Public Accountants (New York). He has done postdoctorate work as a Visiting Scholar at the

University of California at Berkeley and is a recipient of NIU's Teaching Excellence Award and four Golden Apple Teaching Awards. Professor Kieso is the author of other accounting and business books and is a member of the American Accounting Association, the American Institute of Certified Public Accountants, and the Illinois CPA Society. He is the recipient of the Outstanding Accounting Educator Award from the Illinois CPA Society, the FSA's Joseph A. Silvoso Award of Merit, the NIU Foundation's Humanitarian Award for Service to Higher Education, the Distinguished Service Award from the Illinois CPA Society, and the Community Citizen of the Year Award from Rotary International.

Jerry J. Weygandt, Ph.D., C.P.A., is Arthur Andersen Alumni Professor of Accounting at the University of Wisconsin-Madison. He holds a Ph.D. in accounting from the University of Illinois. His articles have appeared in *Accounting Review, Journal of Accounting Research, Accounting Horizons, Journal of Accountancy*, and other academic and professional journals. Professor Weygandt is the author of other accounting and financial reporting books and is a member of the American Accounting Association, the American Institute of Certified Public Accountants, and the Wisconsin Society of Certified Public Accountants. He is the recipient of the Wisconsin Institute of CPAs's Outstanding Educator's Award and the Lifetime Achievement Award. In 2001, he received the American Accounting Association's Outstanding Accounting Educator Award.

Terry D. Warfield, Ph.D., is Associate Professor of Accounting at the University of Wisconsin-Madison. He received a B.S. and M.B.A. from Indiana University and a Ph.D. in accounting from the University of Iowa. Professor Warfield's area of expertise is financial reporting, and prior to his academic career, he worked for five years in the banking industry. He served as the Academic Accounting Fellow in the Office of the Chief Accountant at the U.S. Securities and Exchange Commission in Washington, D.C., from 1995–1996. Professor Warfield's primary research interests concern financial accounting standards and disclosure policies. He has published scholarly articles in *The Accounting Review, Journal of Accounting and Economics, Research in Accounting Regulation*, and *Accounting Horizons*, and he has served on the editorial boards of *The Accounting Review, Accounting Horizons*, and *Issues in Accounting Education*. Professor Warfield has served on the Financial Accounting Standards Committee of the American Accounting Association (Chair 1995–1996) and the AAA-FASB Research Conference Committee. Professor Warfield has received teaching awards at both the University of Iowa and the University of Wisconsin, and he was named to the Teaching Academy at the University of Wisconsin in 1995. Professor Warfield has developed and published several case studies based on his research for use in accounting classes. These cases have been selected for the AICPA Professor-Practitioner Case Development Program and have been published in *Issues in Accounting Education*.

PREFACE

The first Canadian edition of *Intermediate Accounting* made its appearance in 1982. In the 25 years since, it has changed, as have the many students who have used it. However, its goal has always been to help students understand, prepare, and use financial information by linking their accounting education with the "real-world" accounting environment. This continues to be the case with this new edition.

As always, we have aimed for a balanced discussion of concepts and procedures so that these elements reinforce one another. We have focused on the rationale behind transactions before discussing the accounting and reporting for those transactions. As with previous editions, we have thoroughly updated and revised every chapter to include coverage of all of the latest developments in the accounting profession and practice. In addition, we have included features to make all of this coverage even more understandable and relevant to today's accounting student. We have continued to refine the look of the text, added new pedagogical features and enhanced the technology package that accompanies the text, and we continue to emphasize the use of company data and examples so that students easily relate what they are learning to the real world of business.

Based on reviews by and feedback from intermediate accounting instructors and students from across the country, we have worked to help students prepare for the future, understand, and practise what they have learned. We strove to make the text as relevant for today's students as it was for those who used the first edition 25 years ago and are practising accountants today.

New Features

Helping Students Prepare for the Future

As Canada moves toward convergence of its GAAP and international standards, students need an increased understanding of the international reporting environment. To aid in building this awareness, we have introduced new sections comparing Canadian and international GAAP and discussing upcoming changes related to these differences. We also continue to feature marginal International Insights, marked with the icon shown here, to compare specific standards or terminology. The end of chapter material includes questions and cases that focus on international accounting.

 International Insight

Helping Students Understand

Today's classroom is a diverse one and, with this in mind, this text has undergone a review by an instructor of English as a Second Language, who implemented changes throughout. This is especially evident in the earlier chapters. This increased readability will help all students, no matter what their background may be, with the transition from introductory accounting to the more complex intermediate accounting course.

We have continued to refine the design of the text and have enhanced the four-colour design introduced in the seventh edition. Photos have been added to bring the opening stories to life and "infographics" have been redrawn for a more modern and colourful look.

Helping Students Practise

Student Website

In the seventh edition we introduced all-new cases to the end-of-chapter material. These included "Integrated Cases" that draw material from several chapters in order to help students build issue identification skills. In this edition we have increased their number, adding at least 20 more cases overall. Further, a new summary guiding students through the case study method now appears inside the front cover of this text. This is in addition to the full Case Study Primer available on the Student Website.

Analysis doesn't have to be just part of the cases though. Our new Digging Deeper feature asks students to look more closely at the results they obtain in the problems and exercises. For instance, they might then be asked to comment on results or determine how things might be different if one of the original variables were to change. Digging Deeper questions are identified using the icon shown here.

In addition to the changes in the chapters themselves, improvements have also been made in reordering the end of chapter material, cross referencing the brief exercises and exercises to the learning objectives, and the addition of a variety of new questions throughout.

Continuing Features

Many things have contributed to the success of Kieso over the quarter century. The following points outline just a few.

Real-World Emphasis

Since intermediate accounting is a course in which students must understand the application of accounting principles and techniques in practice, we strive to include as many real-world examples as possible.

Reinforcement of the Concepts

What Do the Numbers Mean?

Throughout each chapter students are asked "What Do the Numbers Mean?" and are presented with discussions applying accounting concepts to business contexts. This feature builds on the opening feature stories in making the accounting concepts relevant to students. Through current examples of how accounting is applied, students are better able to relate to and understand the material. In addition, a "Perspectives" section is present in most chapters. This section discusses the effect on the financial statements of many of the accounting choices made by corporate management, alerting students to look behind the numbers. Finally, the accounting equation appears in the margin next to key journal entries to help students understand the impact of each transaction on the financial position and cash flows of the company.

Integration of Ethics Coverage

Rather than featuring ethics coverage and problem material in isolation, we use an ethics icon to highlight ethical issues as they are discussed within each chapter. This icon also appears beside each exercise, problem, or case where ethical issues must be dealt with in relation to all kinds of accounting situations.

A Complete Package

Kieso continues to provide the most comprehensive and useful technology package available for the intermediate course. Its Student Website continues to expand with new tutorials on bad debts, bonds, and inventory methods. Also featured are a case primer, demonstration problems, expanded ethics coverage, and more. The site can be accessed at www.wiley.com/canada/kieso.

A key feature of every accounting package produced by John Wiley & Sons Canada, Ltd. is *WileyPLUS*. This on-line suite of resources that includes a complete multimedia version of the text will help your students come to class better prepared for lectures, and allows you to track their progress throughout the course more easily. They can take advantage of tools such as self-assessment quizzes and animated tutorials to help them study more efficiently. *WileyPLUS* is designed to provide instant feedback as students practise on their own. They can work through assignments with automatic grading or review custom-made class presentations featuring reading assignments, PowerPoint slides, and interactive simulations.

Currency and Accuracy

Accounting changes at a rapid pace—a pace that has increased in recent years. An up-to-date book is more important than ever. As in past editions, we have endeavoured to make this edition the most up-to-date and accurate text available. We have also ensured that new material subject to uncertainty has been vetted by subject matter experts.

The following list outlines the revisions and improvements made in the chapters of this volume.

Chapter 13 Current Liabilities and Contingencies

- Comparison of Canadian and international GAAP added
- Short section on measurement of current liabilities added
- Example added of vendor and purchaser entries for a sale/purchase with both sales tax and GST
- Discussion in the warranty section changed to include more of the wording in EIC 142
- Contingencies, Guarantees, and Commitments section reorganized for better flow
- Expanded formula and discussion of the "days payables outstanding" ratio

Chapter 14 Long-term Financial Liabilities

- Comparison of Canadian and international GAAP added
- New material on treatment of loans/notes (non-marketable) where interest rates are not equal to market rates
- New material on notes issued for property, goods, and services
- New section on imputing interest rates
- Updated material on issuance costs
- Debt extinguishment definition clarified
- Section on accounting for premiums and discounts—presentation versus bookkeeping

Chapter 15 Shareholders' Equity

- Comparison of Canadian and international GAAP added
- Updated material on income trusts
- Material on in-substance common shares (EIC 149) added
- Material added regarding presentation and disclosure from *CICA Handbook*, Section 1535 (Capital Disclosures) and 3251 (Equity), including the statement of changes in shareholders' equity

Chapter 16 Complex Financial Instruments

- Comparison of Canadian and international GAAP added
- Updated references to new *CICA Handbook*, Sections 3862 and 3863
- Expanded and clarified discussions on complex preferred shares, in-substance common shares, and debt with various settlement options

- Financial risks segment updated for terminology and definitions
- Information added on how to account for options on a company's own shares
- Journal entries streamlined for derivatives accounting
- Section expanded on differentiating the economics of hedging from hedge accounting
- Section on why special hedge accounting is necessary given symmetrical versus asymmetrical accounting for hedge transactions before Section 3865 is applied
- New Appendix C on fair value measurement including numeric example of Black Scholes options pricing model
- Small section added covering accounting for non-financial derivatives and executory contracts
- New paragraph on embedded derivatives
- Expanded end of chapter material to support the above

Chapter 17 Earnings per Share

- Comparison of Canadian and international GAAP added
- New section on contingently convertible notes
- Additional new end of chapter material

Chapter 18 Income Taxes

- Comparison of Canadian and international GAAP added
- Minor restructuring of material so that current income taxes are covered first, and then future taxes
- Increased coverage and emphasis on the tax basis of assets and liabilities
- Short section added on uncertain tax positions
- Carryforward period extended to 20 years
- Continued use of Allowance to measure future tax assets as IASB has indicated it will change to this method
- Intraperiod tax allocation extended to amounts recognized in OCI

Chapter 19 Pensions and Other Employee Future Benefits

- Comparison of Canadian and international GAAP added
- More emphasis placed on understanding the defined benefit plan cost components— i.e., the events that change the balances of the ABO and plan assets
- Change in terminology from using PBO (projected benefit obligation) to ABO (accrued benefit obligation) to conform more closely to the *CICA Handbook*
- Minor change in the structure of the chapter

Chapter 20 Leases

- Comparison of Canadian and international GAAP added
- Short section added on types of companies that are lessors
- Section added comparing a lessee's cash flows under a capital and an operating lease
- References added about determining lease variables in Excel
- Although no changes are expected in the standards over the life of this edition, references made throughout the chapter on the likely outcome of the IASB/FASB joint working group on leases that will affect lease accounting significantly on convergence to IFRS

Chapter 21 Accounting Changes and Error Analysis

- Comparison of Canadian and international GAAP added
- New *CICA Handbook*, Section 1506 on Accounting Changes, effective January 1, 2007
- Change in terminology from retroactive to retrospective
- "Impracticability" defined and the effects of impracticability on how a change in accounting policy is accounted for are clarified
- The "summary of accounting changes" illustration converted into a decision tree format
- Short section added on IFRS 1—First-time Adoption of International Reporting Standards

Chapter 22 Statement of Cash Flows

- Comparison of Canadian and international GAAP added
- Paragraph added on how organizations use technology to prepare cash flow statements
- Increased emphasis on how to interpret the cash flow statement
- Example provided on the effect of held-for-trading and available-for-sale investments on the statement of cash flows
- Short section added on distributable cash flows

Chapter 23 Other Measurement and Disclosure Issues

- Comparison of Canadian and international GAAP added
- Updated material on reporting requirements
- Expanded accounting for related party transactions
- Expanded discussion on accounting for private, small, and mid-sized entities
- Updated for changes in inventory accounting regarding interim financial reporting

Acknowledgments

We thank the users of our seventh edition, including the many instructors, faculty, and students who contributed to this revision through their comments and instructive criticism. Special thanks are extended to the reviewers of and contributors to our eighth edition manuscript and supplements.

Manuscript reviewers for this eighth edition were:

Wayne Campbell
Seneca College

Esther Deutsch
Ryerson University

Don Dougherty
Saint Mary's University

Helen Farkas
McMaster University

Ian Feltmate
Acadia University

George Fisher
Thomson Rivers University

Harold Greenspon
McGill University

Mary Heisz
University of Western Ontario

Wayne Irvine
Mount Royal College

Michael Kaine
Sheridan College

Doug Leatherdale
Georgian College

Bruce McConomy
Wilfrid Laurier University

David McConomy
Queen's University

Tom Pippy
Conestoga College

Morina Rennie
University of Regina

John Varga
George Brown College

Wendy Roscoe
Concordia University

Patricia Zima
Mohawk College

Don Smith
Georgian College

Appreciation is also extended to colleagues at the Rotman School of Management, University of Toronto and the Sobey School of Business, Saint Mary's University, who provided input, suggestions, and support, especially Joel Amernic and Dick Chesley, who have provided inspiration through many high-spirited debates on financial reporting theory and practice; Peter Thomas, for his professionalism and wisdom; Dan Segal, for his unique perspective on teaching the material and his contribution to the ever-expanding body of knowledge (including case material); and Laura Cumming, whose thoughtful reading of the text and problems provided excellent input.

It takes many people and co-ordinated efforts to get an edition off the ground. Many thanks to the team at John Wiley and Sons Canada, Ltd., who are superb: Editorial Manager Karen Staudinger, who has been an integral part of the last four editions; Karen Bryan, Publishing Services Director, for her incredible efforts over this and previous editions; Elsa Passera-Berardi, Media Editor, for managing this increasingly important aspect of the text; and Aida Krneta, Marketing Manager. The editorial contributions of David Schwinghamer, Zofia Laubitz, Laurel Hyatt, and Alison Arnot are also very much appreciated. A special thank you goes to Daleara Hirjikaka, our Developmental Editor, who dealt with us on an almost daily basis and kept everything on track.

We are particularly grateful to Cécile Laurin and Maria Belanger for all their help with the end-of-chapter material, through some especially trying times. Thanks also go to Helen Farkas, Patricia Zima, Andrea Chance, Miguel Minutti, Sibongile Mukandi, Gabriela Schneider, Ann Bigelow, Betty Mitchell, Shelley Coyle, Laura Cumming, Jo-Anne Ryan, and Tammy Morley, who contributed so much to the related supplements.

We appreciate the continuing co-operation of the accounting standards group at the Canadian Institute of Chartered Accountants and of Ron Salole, Vice-President of Standards. The Director and Principals of the Accounting Standards Board have been as open and helpful as possible in all our dealings with them. A special thank you is owed for this eighth edition to Ian Hague and Kate Ward. We also thank the CICA itself for allowing us to quote from their materials and Stantec Inc. for permitting us to use its 2005 Annual Report for our specimen financial statements.

Finally, on the occasion of the 25th anniversary of Kieso in Canada, we want to remember and thank Bruce Irvine and Harold Silvester who, through the first five editions of this text, set such a strong foundation. Their enthusiasm for intermediate accounting and their sharing of it with so many students set a high standard for us to follow.

If this book helps teachers instill in their students an appreciation of the challenges, value, and limitations of accounting, if it encourages students to evaluate critically and understand financial accounting theory and practice, and if it prepares students for advanced study, professional examinations, and the successful and ethical pursuit of their careers in accounting or business, then we will have attained our objective.

Suggestions and comments from users of this book are always appreciated. We have striven to produce an error-free text, but if anything has slipped through the variety of checks undertaken, please let us know so that corrections can be made to subsequent printings.

Irene M. Wiecek
TORONTO, ONTARIO
wiecek@rotman.utoronto.ca

Nicola M. Young
HALIFAX, NOVA SCOTIA
nicola.young@smu.ca

July 2007

BRIEF CONTENTS

CONTENTS

Tracking Points

Sears Canada credit card holders automatically enter a club: the Sears Club, whose members earn one point for every dollar they charge to their card. When they have collected a minimum 1000 points, they can redeem them for Sears Club Certificates, which are as good as cash at any Sears store. However, the points do have an expiry date and must be redeemed within 30 months.

Sears has a redemption rate that is average for the industry, says David Merkley, senior vice-president and chief financial officer at Sears Canada. Some customers redeem points for certificates but then don't cash the certificates, and then there are those who never redeem their points at all.

So how does Sears track and account for its potential obligation to these various point collectors? The liability that is inherent in the points program is tracked at the time of sale, Merkley explains. Sears keeps track of six-month, 12-month, 24-month, and 36-month rolling average redemption rates. The six-month figures are good for seasonal comparisons, since, for example, December is typically a busy time for point redemption. With the 24-month average, however, Sears can get a good estimate of how much will come back in the future by looking at past redemption patterns.

Sears tracks the sales that are charged to its credit card, which amount to approximately 55 percent of its total sales. Since these purchases collect points for the cardholder, a percentage of the sale is recorded in a liability account with the offset noted as a marketing expense. "As people use coupons to buy merchandise in the store, we then debit that liability account," Merkley says.

The expiry date allows for easy accounting of the current liability. "Canadian accounting allows you to bring that 'leakage' back into your income, but it does require that you have some means of quantifying it," Merkley says. Once the points have expired, Sears can debit the liability account for that amount and credit the income statement for the expense that had been set up 30 months earlier. ■

Current Liabilities and Contingencies

Learning Objectives

After studying this chapter, you should be able to:

1. Define liabilities and distinguish financial liabilities from other liabilities.
2. Define current liabilities, and identify and account for common types of current liabilities.
3. Explain the classification issues for short-term debt that is expected to be refinanced.
4. Identify and account for the major types of employee-related liabilities.
5. Account for common estimated liabilities.
6. Explain the recognition, measurement, and disclosure requirements for asset retirement obligations.
7. Identify the accounting and reporting requirements for contingent liabilities.
8. Identify the accounting and reporting requirements for guarantees and commitments.
9. Indicate how current liabilities and related items are presented and analyzed.
10. Compare current Canadian and international GAAP.

Preview of Chapter 13

This chapter explains the basic principles that underlie the accounting and reporting for current liabilities and asset retirement obligations and for contingent liabilities, commitments, and guarantees. The issues related to long-term liabilities are discussed in Chapter 14.

The chapter is organized as follows:

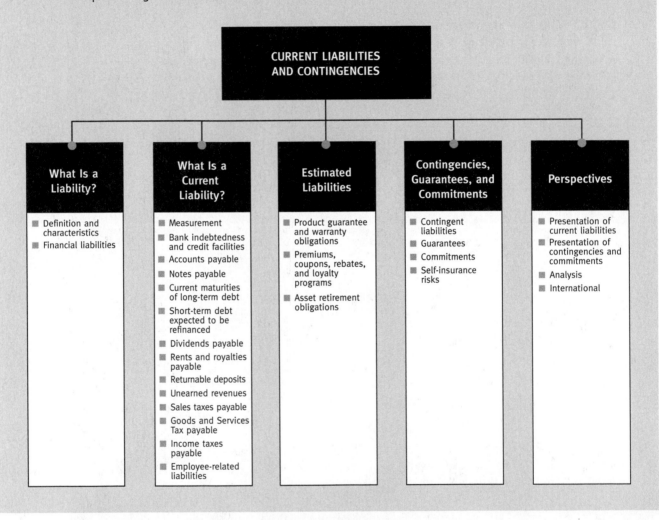

CURRENT LIABILITIES AND CONTINGENCIES

What Is a Liability?	What Is a Current Liability?	Estimated Liabilities	Contingencies, Guarantees, and Commitments	Perspectives
■ Definition and characteristics ■ Financial liabilities	■ Measurement ■ Bank indebtedness and credit facilities ■ Accounts payable ■ Notes payable ■ Current maturities of long-term debt ■ Short-term debt expected to be refinanced ■ Dividends payable ■ Rents and royalties payable ■ Returnable deposits ■ Unearned revenues ■ Sales taxes payable ■ Goods and Services Tax payable ■ Income taxes payable ■ Employee-related liabilities	■ Product guarantee and warranty obligations ■ Premiums, coupons, rebates, and loyalty programs ■ Asset retirement obligations	■ Contingent liabilities ■ Guarantees ■ Commitments ■ Self-insurance risks	■ Presentation of current liabilities ■ Presentation of contingencies and commitments ■ Analysis ■ International

WHAT IS A LIABILITY?

Underlying Concept

To be able to properly classify specific financial instruments, proper definitions are needed for assets, liabilities, and equities. The conceptual framework definitions are usually used as the basis for settling difficult classification issues.

The question "What is a liability?" is not easy to answer. For example, one might ask whether preferred shares are a liability or an ownership claim. The first reaction is to say that preferred shares are a legal ownership claim and should be reported as part of shareholders' equity. In fact, however, preferred shares have many characteristics of debt.[1] The

---

[1] This illustration is not just a theoretical exercise. In practice, there are several kinds of preferred share issues that have all the characteristics of debt instruments. They are reported as liabilities on the balance sheet even though they retain their legal status as equity. In some cases, the Canada Revenue Agency has even permitted the dividend payments to be treated as interest expense for tax purposes.

issuer (and in some cases the holder) often has the right to redeem the shares within a specified period of time, which makes the redemption similar to a repayment of principal. In addition, the dividend is often cumulative, making the return almost guaranteed and similar to interest. Preferred shares are only one of many financial instruments that may be difficult to classify.[2]

Definition and Characteristics

Section 1000 of the *CICA Handbook* defines **liabilities** as **"obligations of an entity arising from past transactions or events, the settlement of which may result in the transfer or use of assets, provision of services or other yielding of economic benefits in the future."**[3] In other words, a liability has three essential characteristics:

> **1 Objective**
> Define liabilities and distinguish financial liabilities from other liabilities.

1. It is an obligation to others that will be settled in the future by transferring or using cash or other assets, providing services, or giving up other economic benefits either on a date that can be determined, when some specified event occurs, or on demand.

2. The entity has little or no discretion to avoid the obligation.

3. The transaction or other event that creates the obligation has already occurred.[4]

Standard setters and preparers of financial statements use this definition to help them make classification decisions and decide whether or not particular items should be accounted for and reported as liabilities.

Financial Liabilities

A distinction is made between financial liabilities and those that are not financial in nature. **Financial liabilities** are contractual obligations to do either of the following:

1. To deliver cash or other financial assets to another party.

2. To exchange financial instruments with another party under conditions that are potentially unfavourable.[5]

Note that this definition requires the liability to be based on an obligation that is created by a contract. Liabilities that are created by legislation, such as income taxes payable, do not qualify as financial liabilities. In this chapter, most current liabilities are financial in nature, but if the obligation will be met by the delivery of goods or services (e.g., unearned revenue and warranty obligations), it is not considered a financial liability.

The distinction between financial and non-financial is significant because GAAP requires that certain financial liabilities be measured at their fair value rather than their historic (or amortized) cost. Some financial liabilities that historically have not been recognized in the financial statements now have to be recognized and measured at fair value. These are introduced in Chapter 16.

---

[2] *CICA Handbook* Section 3863, "Financial Instruments—Presentation," addresses the issues for distinguishing between financial liabilities and equity instruments. Chapter 16 provides a fuller discussion of this.

[3] *CICA Handbook*, Section 1000.32.

[4] *CICA Handbook*, Section 1000.33.

[5] *CICA Handbook*, Section 3855.19(c).

WHAT IS A CURRENT LIABILITY?

Objective 2
Define current liabilities, and identify and account for common types of current liabilities.

Because liabilities result in a future disbursement of assets or services, one of their most important features is the timing of when they are due. Obligations that mature in the short term place a demand on the entity's current assets—a demand that must be satisfied on time and in the ordinary course of business if operations are to continue. Liabilities with a distant due date generally do not result in a claim on the enterprise's current assets and are therefore categorized differently. This difference in timing and the impact on current assets is the reason for the division of liabilities into (1) current liabilities and (2) long-term liabilities.

The definition of a current liability is directly related to the definition of a current asset. Current assets are cash or other assets that it is reasonable to expect will be converted into cash, sold, or consumed in operations within a year from the balance sheet date or within a single operating cycle if the cycle is longer than a year. **Current liabilities** are described as including **"amounts payable within one year from the date of the balance sheet or within the normal operating cycle where this is longer than a year."**[6] In this definition the normal operating cycle is the same as the one that is used for current assets.

The **operating cycle** is the period of time between acquiring the goods and services for processing in operations and when cash is received from the eventual sale of the processed goods and services. Industries that manufacture products which go through an aging process and certain capital-intensive industries have an operating cycle of much longer than one year. On the other hand, most retail and service establishments have several operating cycles in a single year.

Measurement

Financial liabilities are recognized initially at their fair value. After acquisition, most of the financial liabilities that are discussed in this and later chapters are accounted for at their amortized cost, using the effective interest method.[7] This method is described in Chapter 14 rather than here as it is more appropriate for long-term instruments, the topic of the next chapter. Because current liabilities are short-term in nature, they are usually recorded in the accounting records and reported in financial statements at their full maturity value—the amount of cash that is payable in the future. This accounting is appropriate because the difference between the amortized cost of a current liability and its maturity value is not significant. The slight overstatement of liabilities that results from carrying current liabilities at their maturity value is accepted as immaterial.

Non-financial liabilities, on the other hand, are usually not payable in cash or other financial assets of a known amount. The way they are measured is different and depends on the specific liability. For example, unearned revenue is measured at the fair value of the goods or services to be delivered in the future; and warranty obligations are measured based on management's estimate of the cost of the goods or services to be provided in the future.

There are many different types of current liabilities. The following examples are covered next and in the order shown:

---

[6] *CICA Handbook*, Section 1510.05.

[7] *CICA Handbook*, Section 3855.71. At the intermediate level of accounting, the only liabilities that are designated as held for trading and later accounted for at fair value are derivatives, which are discussed in Chapter 16.

1. Bank indebtedness and credit facilities
2. Accounts payable
3. Notes payable
4. Current maturities of long-term debt
5. Short-term debt expected to be refinanced
6. Dividends payable
7. Rents and royalties payable
8. Returnable deposits
9. Unearned revenues
10. Sales taxes payable
11. Goods and Services Tax payable
12. Income taxes payable
13. Employee-related liabilities

Bank Indebtedness and Credit Facilities

A major element of a company's cash position is its bank indebtedness for current operating purposes and its **line of credit** or **revolving debt** arrangements that are related to this indebtedness. Instead of having to negotiate a new loan every time it needs funds, a company generally enters into an agreement with its bank that allows it to make multiple borrowings up to a negotiated limit. As previous borrowings are partly repaid, the company is permitted to borrow again under the same contract.[8] Because the financial institution commits itself to making money available to the borrower, the bank often charges an additional fee for this service over and above the interest that it charges on the funds that are actually advanced. Under such agreements, the financial institution also usually requires collateral and often sets restrictions on the company's activities or financial statement ratios.

While the amount of actual bank indebtedness is reported on the balance sheet, the total funds that the credit arrangement allows the company to borrow and any restrictions that are imposed by the financial institution are disclosed in the notes.

Borrowings and growth must be carefully managed! Maintaining close working relationships with customers, banks, suppliers, and other creditors is central to getting through the crunch. Based in British Columbia, **Pacific Safety Products Inc.** (PSP) enjoyed a 69-percent increase in sales in one year recently and, along with it, suffered the liquidity problems that often come with such success. The company's annual report indicated that one of PSP's major challenges during the year had been to manage its cash flow so that it could pay suppliers and thus ensure a continual flow of raw materials that were needed in the manufacturing process in order to meet customer orders on a timely basis.

PSP thus reported bank indebtedness of almost $3 million in its current liabilities at the company's year end. Providing details on the indebtedness, a note to the financial statements indicated a maximum operating line of credit of $3 million with the Bank of Nova Scotia, which was secured by accounts receivable, inventory, and an assignment of insurance. The note also reported that the company was not in compliance with the covenants imposed by the bank for the level of the current ratio and tangible net worth, but that the bank was allowing PSP to operate outside its covenants.

One year later, PSP reported sales that were only 75 percent of those reported for the preceding fiscal year, but its cash flow from operating activities was almost twice as high as in the earlier period! The uncollected receivables from one year earlier had been collected and this allowed the company to get over the cash crunch. Bank indebtedness was reduced to only $102,417, the operating line was reduced to $2 million, and the company was once again in compliance with the covenants imposed by the bank.

What
Do the
Numbers
Mean?

---

[8] *Emerging Issues Committee Abstract* EIC-101.

Accounts Payable

Accounts payable, or trade accounts payable, are balances that are owed to others for goods, supplies, or services purchased on open account. This means that evidence of the obligations' existence comes from regular invoices rather than from separate contracts for each transaction. Accounts payable arise because of the time lag between the receipt of goods and services and the payment for them. This period of extended credit is usually stated in the terms of sale and purchase—for example, 2/10, n/30 or 1/10, E.O.M.—and is commonly 30 to 60 days long.

Most accounting systems are designed to record liabilities for purchases of goods when the goods are received. Sometimes there is a delay in recording the goods and the related liability on the books, such as when waiting for an invoice. If title has passed to the purchaser before the goods are received, the transaction should be recorded when the title passes. Attention must be paid to transactions that occur near the end of one accounting period and the beginning of the next so that the record of goods and services received (the inventory or expense) agrees with the liability (accounts payable) and that both are recorded in the proper period. Chapter 8 discussed this cut-off issue in greater detail.

There is no real difficulty in measuring the amount of an account payable since the invoice received from the creditor specifies the exact amount of money that is necessary to settle the account. The only calculation that may be necessary is the amount of any cash discount. Again, refer to Chapter 8 for illustrations of the entries for accounts payable and purchase discounts.

Notes Payable

Notes payable are written promises to pay a certain sum of money on a specified future date and may arise from purchases, financing, or other transactions. In some industries, instead of the normal procedure of extending credit on an open account, notes (often referred to as trade notes payable) are required as part of the sale/purchase transaction. Notes payable to banks or loan companies are generally created by cash loans. Notes may be classified as short-term or long-term, depending on the payment due date. Notes may also be interest-bearing or non-interest-bearing (i.e., zero-interest-bearing). The accounting for such notes is shown next.

Interest-Bearing Note Issued

Assume that Provincial Bank agrees to lend $100,000 on March 1, 2008, to Landscape Corp. and the company signs a $100,000, four-month, 12% note. The entry to record the cash received by Landscape Corp. on March 1 is:

A   =   L   + SE
+100,000   +100,000

Cash flows: ↑ 100,000 inflow

March 1	Cash	100,000	
	Notes Payable		100,000
	(To record issue of four-month, 12% note to Provincial Bank)		

If Landscape Corp. has a December 31 year end but prepares financial statements semi-annually, an adjusting entry is required to recognize the interest expense and interest payable of $4,000 ($100,000 × 12% × 4/12) on June 30. The adjusting entry is:

A   =   L   +   SE
+4,000   −4,000

Cash flows: No effect

June 30	Interest Expense	4,000	
	Interest Payable		4,000
	(To accrue interest for four months on Provincial Bank note)		

At maturity on July 1, Landscape Corp. pays the note's face value of $100,000 plus the $4,000 of interest. The entry to record payment of the note and accrued interest is as follows:

July 1	Notes Payable	100,000	
	Interest Payable	4,000	
	Cash		104,000
	(To record payment of Provincial Bank note and accrued interest at maturity)		

A   =   L   + SE
−104,000   −104,000

Cash flows: ↓ 104,000 outflow

Zero-Interest-Bearing Note Issued

A zero-interest-bearing note, which was discussed in Chapters 7 and 9 from the perspective of the lender, may be issued instead of an interest-bearing note. Despite its name, a **zero-interest-bearing note *does* have an interest component**. The interest is just not added on top of the note's face or maturity value; instead, it is included in the face amount. The interest is the difference between the amount of cash received when the note is signed and the higher face amount that is payable at maturity. The borrower receives the note's present value in cash and pays back the larger maturity value.

To illustrate, assume that Landscape Corp. issues a $104,000, four-month, zero-interest-bearing note to the Provincial Bank on March 1. The note's present value is $100,000.[9] Landscape's entry to record this transaction is as follows:

March 1	Cash	100,000	
	Discount on Notes Payable	4,000	
	Notes Payable		104,000
	(To record issuance of zero-interest-bearing note to Provincial Bank)		

A   =   L   + SE
+100,000   +100,000

Cash flows: ↑ 100,000 inflow

The Notes Payable account is credited for the note's face value, which is $4,000 more than the actual cash that was received. The difference between the cash received and the note's face value is debited to Discount on Notes Payable. **Discount on Notes Payable is a contra account to Notes Payable and therefore is subtracted from Notes Payable on the balance sheet.** Illustration 13-1 shows the balance sheet presentation on March 1.

Current liabilities		
Notes payable	$104,000	
Less: Discount on notes payable	4,000	$100,000

Illustration 13-1

Balance Sheet Presentation of Discount

The discount amount, $4,000 in this case, represents the cost of borrowing $100,000 for four months. Accordingly, the discount is charged to interest expense over the life of the note. The accounting issues related to long-term notes payable are discussed further in Chapter 14.

Current Maturities of Long-Term Debt

Bonds, mortgage notes, and other long-term indebtedness that mature within 12 months from the balance sheet date—**current maturities of long-term debt**—are reported as current liabilities. When only part of a long-term obligation is to be paid within the next

---

[9] The bank discount rate that is used in this example to find the present value is 11.538%.

12 months, as in the case of a mortgage or of serial bonds that are to be retired through a series of annual instalments, **only the maturing portion of the long-term debt is reported as a current liability**. The balance is reported as a long-term liability.

Long-term liabilities that will mature in the next 12 months should not be included as current liabilities if they will be paid using assets that the company has accumulated for this specific purpose and has not reported as current assets. When current assets are not used or no other current liabilities are created in order to repay the maturing liability, it is incorrect to classify the liability as current.

There are other situations when maturing debt is not classified as a current liability. Examples include when the maturing debt is refinanced or retired by using the proceeds of a new debt issue or is replaced by issuing new shares. These circumstances are discussed in greater detail in the next section of this chapter.

A liability that is **due on demand** (i.e., callable by the creditor) or that will be due on demand within a year or operating cycle, if longer, is classified as a current liability. Liabilities often become callable by the creditor if there is a violation of a debt agreement. For example, most debt agreements require the borrower to maintain a minimum ratio of equity to debt, or as illustrated in the Pacific Safety Products situation above, specify minimum working capital requirements.

If an agreement is violated, the debt must be classified as current because it is reasonable to expect that current working capital will be used to satisfy the debt. The liability can only be classified as non-current if (1) the creditor waives the covenant (agreement) requirements, or (2) the violation has been cured within the grace period that is usually given in these agreements, **and** (3) **it is likely** that the company will not violate the covenant requirements within a year from the balance sheet date.[10]

Short-Term Debt Expected to Be Refinanced

Objective 3
Explain the classification issues for short-term debt that is expected to be refinanced.

Short-term obligations are debts that are scheduled to mature within one year from the date of an enterprise's balance sheet or within its operating cycle, if longer. However, within this category there exist **short-term obligations expected to be refinanced** on a long-term basis. This distinction is important as the latter are not expected to require the use of working capital during the next year or operating cycle.[11]

At one time, the accounting profession generally agreed with not including short-term obligations in current liabilities if they were "expected to be refinanced." Because the profession gave no specific guidelines, however, determining whether a short-term obligation was "expected to be refinanced" was usually based solely on management's **intent** to refinance the liability on a long-term basis. Classification was not clear-cut and the proper accounting was therefore uncertain. Take, for example, a company that might want a five-year bank loan but handles the actual financing with 90-day notes which it keeps renewing. In this case, is the loan long-term debt or a current liability?

Refinancing Criteria

To resolve these classification problems, authoritative criteria have been developed. Thus, a company is required to exclude a short-term obligation from current liabilities "to the

---

[10] *EIC-59* "Long-Term Debt with Covenant Violations" provides a more detailed discussion of the specific requirements.

[11] Refinancing a short-term obligation on a long-term basis means either replacing it with a long-term obligation or with equity securities, or renewing, extending, or replacing it with short-term obligations for an uninterrupted period that is more than one year (or operating cycle, if longer) from the date of the enterprise's balance sheet.

extent that contractual arrangements have been made for settlement from other than current assets."[12] A company must meet **both of the following criteria** in order to exclude amounts from the current liability category:[13]

1. The entity must **intend to refinance** the obligation on a long-term basis so that working capital will not be used during the following year or operating cycle, if longer.

2. The entity must **demonstrate an ability** to complete the refinancing. This could be demonstrated by either of the following:

   (a) actually refinancing the obligation by issuing a long-term obligation or issuing shares after the balance sheet date but before the financial statements are issued

   (b) entering into a financing agreement that clearly permits the refinancing on a long-term basis on terms that are readily determinable

If an actual refinancing occurs, the amount of the short-term obligation that is excluded from current liabilities cannot be higher than the proceeds from the new obligation or equity securities that are used to retire it. For example, assume that Montavon Winery has $3 million of short-term debt. It then issues 100,000 common shares after the balance sheet date but before the financial statements are issued, and intends to use the proceeds from the issue to liquidate the short-term debt at its maturity. If the net proceeds from the sale of the 100,000 shares total $2 million, only $2 million of the short-term debt can be excluded from current liabilities.

Another issue is the question of whether or not a short-term obligation can be excluded from current liabilities if it is paid off after the balance sheet date and then replaced by long-term debt before the balance sheet is issued. To illustrate, assume that Marquardt Limited pays off short-term debt of $40,000 on January 17, 2009, and issues long-term debt of $100,000 on February 3, 2009. Marquardt's financial statements dated December 31, 2008, are to be issued on March 1, 2009. Because the repayment of the short-term obligation occurred **before** funds were obtained through long-term financing, the repayment therefore **used existing** current assets and the short-term obligation is included in current liabilities at the balance sheet date. Illustration 13-2 shows this situation.

International Insight

The IAS 1 requirements are narrower: liabilities that are being refinanced and those that are due on demand because of violations of debt covenants are reported as current liabilities unless other arrangements have been completed by the balance sheet date.

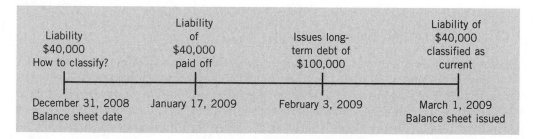

Illustration 13-2

Short-Term Debt Paid off after Balance Sheet Date and Later Replaced by Long-Term Debt

Dividends Payable

A cash **dividend payable** is an amount that a corporation owes to its shareholders because the board of directors has authorized a dividend payment. At the dividend declaration date, the corporation incurs a liability that places the shareholders in the position of creditors for the amount of dividends that was declared. Because cash dividends are normally paid within one year of the declaration (generally within three months in actual practice), they are classified as current liabilities.

---

[12] *CICA Handbook*, Section 1510.08.

[13] *EIC-122*, "Balance Sheet Classification of Callable Debt Obligations and Debt Obligations Expected to be Refinanced."

Underlying Concept

Preferred dividends in arrears create a probable future economic sacrifice, but the expected sacrifice does not result from a past transaction or past event. The sacrifice will result from a future event (the dividend declaration by the board of directors). Using a note to disclose the preferred dividends in arrears improves the predictive value of the financial statements.

Accumulated but undeclared dividends on cumulative preferred shares **are not recognized as a liability,** because **preferred dividends in arrears** are not an obligation until formal action is taken by the board of directors to authorize the distribution. Nevertheless, the company is required to disclose the amount of cumulative dividends that is unpaid, and this is usually done in a note to the financial statements.

Dividends that are payable in the form of additional shares **are not recognized as a liability**. Such stock dividends (discussed in Chapter 15) do not meet the definition of a liability, because they do not require future outlays of assets or services. In addition, the board of directors can revoke them at any time before they are issued. Undistributed stock dividends are generally reported in the shareholders' equity section because they represent a transfer of equity from retained earnings to contributed capital.

Rents and Royalties Payable

Rents and royalties payable are another type of current liability. This type of liability may be created by a **contractual agreement in which payments are conditional on the amount of revenue that is earned or the quantity of product that is produced or extracted**. For example, franchisees are usually required to pay franchise fees to the franchisor that are calculated as a percentage of sales; tenants in shopping centres may be obligated to pay additional rents on sales that are above a predetermined amount; and manufacturers may have licensing agreements that require them to pay the holder of a patent a royalty fee for each unit that the manufacturer produces.

Liabilities for expenses that are based on revenues earned or units produced are usually easy to measure. For example, if a lease calls for a fixed rent payment of $500 per month and 1% of all sales over $300,000 per year, the annual rent obligation amounts to $6,000 plus $0.01 of each dollar of revenue over $300,000. Or a royalty agreement may require the accrual of $1.00 per unit that is produced under the patented process, or the accrual of $0.50 on every barrel of oil that is extracted, with the accrued amount then paid to the owner of the mineral rights. As each additional unit of product is produced or extracted, an additional obligation, usually a current liability, is created.

Returnable Deposits

A company's current liabilities may include **returnable cash deposits** that are received from customers and employees. Deposits may be received from customers to guarantee the performance of a contract or service or to guarantee the payment of expected future obligations. For example, telephone companies often require a deposit from customers when they install a phone. Deposits may also be received from tenants to cover possible future damage to property. Some companies require their employees to make deposits for the return of keys or other company property. The initial classification of these items as current or non-current liabilities depends on the time between the date of the deposit and the end of the relationship that made the deposit necessary.

Unearned Revenues

A magazine publisher such as **Golf Digest** receives cheques from customers when magazine subscriptions are ordered, and an airline such as **Air Canada** usually sells tickets in advance for flights. For their part, retail stores increasingly issue gift certificates that can be redeemed for merchandise. In all these situations, the cash that is received is accounted for as an **unearned revenue**, a liability. In each case, the company has an obligation, based on the payment received in advance, to transfer assets or provide services in the future. Revenue is then recognized as the goods are delivered or the services are provided.

To illustrate, assume that the Rambeau Football Club sells 5,000 season tickets at $50 each for its five-game home schedule. The entry for the sale of the season tickets is:

Cash	250,000	
Unearned Football Ticket Revenue		250,000
(To record the sale of 5,000 season tickets)		

A   =   L   + SE
+250,000   +250,000

Cash flows: ↑ 250,000 inflow

As each game is completed, the following entry is made:

Unearned Football Ticket Revenue	50,000	
Football Ticket Revenue		50,000
(To record football ticket revenues earned)		

A   =   L   +   SE
      −50,000   +50,000

Cash flows: No effect

The balance in the Unearned Football Ticket Revenue account is reported as a current liability in the balance sheet. As revenue is earned, a transfer is made from unearned revenue to a revenue account on the income statement. Unearned revenue is material for some companies. In the airline industry, for example, tickets sold for future flights are a significant portion of total current liabilities. WestJet's unearned ticket revenue represented 34.8% of its current liabilities at September 30, 2006, up from 33.8% at December 31, 2005. At the same dates, Air Canada (a subsidiary of ACE Aviation Holdings Inc.) reported advance ticket sales equal to 23.9% and 23.6% of current liabilities, respectively. Illustration 13-3 shows specific unearned revenue (balance sheet) accounts and earned revenue (income statement) accounts that might be used in different industries.

Industry Type	Account Title	
	Unearned revenue	Earned revenue
Airline	Advance Ticket Sales	Passenger Revenue
Magazine publisher	Deferred Subscription Revenue	Subscription Revenue
Hotel	Advance Room Deposits	Room Revenue
Auto dealer	Unearned Warranty Revenue	Warranty Revenue

Illustration 13-3

Unearned and Earned Revenue Accounts

Sales Taxes Payable

Sales taxes on transfers of tangible property and on certain services must be collected from customers and remitted to the tax authority, usually a provincial or territorial government.[14] The balance in the Sales Taxes Payable account is the liability for sales taxes that have been collected from customers but not yet remitted to the appropriate government.[15] The following entry shows the accounting for a sale on account of $3,000 when a 4% sales tax is in effect:

---

[14] The rate of tax varies from province to province. In 2007 (when this text went into print), Alberta and the territories had no sales tax, while Ontario's rate was 8%, British Columbia's was 7%, and Saskatchewan charged 5%. The tax is usually applied to the sale amount, although in Quebec and Prince Edward Island it is applied to the selling price plus the GST.

[15] In New Brunswick, Newfoundland and Labrador, and Nova Scotia, the provincial retail sales tax has been combined with the federal Goods and Services Tax and named the Harmonized Sales Tax (HST). The 14% HST is administered for the most part by the Canada Revenue Agency and is accounted for on the same basis as the GST for the other provinces and territories.

A = L + SE	Accounts Receivable	3,120	
+3,120 +120 +3,000	Sales		3,000
	Sales Taxes Payable		120
Cash flows: No effect			

Goods and Services Tax Payable

Most businesses in Canada are subject to the Goods and Services Tax (GST). The GST is a tax, at a rate of 6% as of July 1, 2006, on the value added by each taxable entity. The amount that an entity must pay is determined by deducting its **input tax credit** (the GST the company paid on goods and services it purchased from suppliers) from the amount of GST the company collected, on behalf of the government, on sales to its customers.

Accounting for GST involves setting up a liability account—GST Payable—that is credited with GST charged on sales, and an asset account—GST Recoverable—that is debited for GST paid to suppliers. Normally, the amount that is collected on sales is higher than the amount paid on purchases, and a net remittance is therefore made to the Canada Revenue Agency (CRA). Since GST is also paid on purchases of capital assets, it is possible for the GST Recoverable account to have a larger balance. In these instances, a claim for reimbursement is made to the CRA.

Purchases of taxable goods and services are recorded by debiting the GST Recoverable account for the amount of GST and debiting the appropriate asset or expense account(s) for the purchase price. Since the GST paid is recoverable from the federal government, the GST is not included in the cost of the item(s) acquired. As an example, assume that Bateman Limited purchases merchandise for $150,000 plus GST of 6% ($9,000). The entry to record this transaction is as follows, assuming a perpetual inventory system is used:

A = L + SE	Inventory	150,000	
+159,000 +159,000	GST Recoverable	9,000	
	Accounts Payable		159,000
Cash flows: No effect			

If these goods are sold for $210,000 plus GST of 6% ($12,600), the sale entry is:

A = L + SE	Accounts Receivable	222,600	
+222,600 +12,600 +210,000	Sales		210,000
	GST Payable		12,600
Cash flows: No effect			

In many cases, GST and sales taxes are levied on the same sale and purchase. Assume, for example, that Smith Ltd. sells supplies to Jones Corp. for $1,000 and both a 7% provincial sales tax and 6% GST are charged on this amount. The entry made by each company follows:

Smith Ltd. (vendor company)		**Jones Corp.** (purchaser company)	
Accounts Receivable	1,130	Supplies Expense	1,070
Sales	1,000	GST Recoverable	60
Sales Taxes Payable	70	Accounts Payable	1,130
GST Payable	60	(To record purchase from Smith Ltd.)	
(To record sale to Jones Corp.)			

Notice that the purchaser includes the provincial sales tax charged in the cost of the goods or services purchased. The provincial sales tax, unlike the GST, is not recoverable by the purchaser.[16]

Because companies are permitted to offset the recoverable and payable amounts of GST, only the net balance of the two accounts is reported on the balance sheet. Note that until net credit balances are remitted to the Receiver General for Canada, they are reported as a current liability. A net debit balance, on the other hand, is reported as a current asset.

Income Taxes Payable

In Canada, federal and provincial income taxes are levied on a company's taxable income. Some business people consider the amount of income tax payable as an estimate because the calculation of income (and the tax payable on it) has to be reviewed and approved by the CRA. The meaning and application of numerous tax rules, especially new ones, are debatable and often depend on a court's interpretation. Using the best information and advice available, a business must prepare an income tax return at the end of its fiscal year and calculate the income tax payable that results from its operations of the current period.

Assume that Forest Ltd. determines, based on its taxable income for the year, that an income tax liability of $21,000 is payable, and assume that no accruals have been made during the year. Forest would make the following entry at year end:

Current Income Tax Expense	21,000	
Income Taxes Payable		21,000

$A = L + SE$
$+21,000 \quad -21,000$
Cash flows: No effect

Most corporations are required to make periodic tax instalments (payments) throughout the year based on the previous year's income tax or estimates of the current year's income tax. If Forest Ltd. had made $20,000 of tax instalments during the year, the entries for the instalments are summarized as follows:

Income Taxes Payable	20,000	
Cash		20,000

$A = L + SE$
$-20,000 \quad -20,000$
Cash flows: ↓ 20,000 outflow

Assuming the $21,000 tax liability from above, Forest Ltd. would then report an Income Taxes Payable balance of $1,000 in the current liabilities section of its year-end balance sheet ($21,000 − $20,000). Alternatively, if the company had made payments of $23,000, there would be a $2,000 debit balance in the Income Taxes Payable account ($23,000 − $21,000). This is reported as Income Taxes Receivable and is included with current assets.

An alternative approach that is often used charges (debits) the instalment payments to expense. When the tax return is completed at year end and the actual amount of tax for the year is known, the expense is then adjusted. This series of entries is as follows:

Instalment payments of $20,000			Instalment payments of $23,000		
Current Income Tax Expense	20,000		Current Income Tax Expense	23,000	
Cash		20,000	Cash		23,000

---

[16] In the provinces with a Harmonized Sales Tax (HST), the full 14% amount is treated as shown for the GST. In Quebec, as well, the Quebec Sales Tax paid by an entity is recoverable through a system of input tax refunds, similar to the input tax credits for the GST.

Income taxes per tax return: $21,000		Income taxes per tax return: $21,000	
Current Income Tax Expense 1,000		Income Taxes Receivable 2,000	
Income Taxes Payable	1,000	Current Income Tax Expense	2,000

Regardless of which series of entries is made, the resulting financial statements are identical.

If, in a later year, the CRA assesses an additional tax on an earlier year's income, Income Taxes Payable is credited and the expense is charged to current operations. However, if the additional tax was caused by an obvious arithmetic error that occurred when the amount of tax was originally calculated, the correction of the error is made through retained earnings if it is material.

It is common for there to be differences between taxable income **under the tax laws** and accounting income **under generally accepted accounting principles**. Because of these differences, the amount of income tax that is payable to the government in any specific year may differ substantially from the income tax expense reported on the financial statements that relates to income before taxes. Chapter 18 focuses on the problems of accounting for income tax and presents an extensive discussion of related issues that are both complex and interesting.

Unlike corporations, proprietorships and partnerships are not taxable entities. Because the individual proprietor and the members of a partnership, not the business itself, are subject to personal income taxes on their share of the business's taxable income, income tax liabilities do not appear on the financial statements of proprietorships and partnerships.

Employee-Related Liabilities

Objective 4
Identify and account for the major types of employee-related liabilities.

Amounts that are owed to employees for salaries or wages at the end of an accounting period are reported as a current liability called Salaries or Wages Payable. The following additional items that are related to employee compensation are also usually reported as current liabilities:

1. Payroll deductions

2. Compensated absences

3. Bonuses

Payroll Deductions

The most common types of **payroll deductions** are employee income taxes, Canada (Quebec) Pension Plan, employment insurance, and miscellaneous items such as other insurance premiums, employee savings, and union dues. Any amounts that have been deducted but not yet remitted to the proper authority by the end of the accounting period are recognized as current liabilities. This is also true for any matching amounts that the employer itself is required to pay.

Canada (Quebec) Pension Plan (CPP/QPP)   The Canada and Quebec pension plans are financed by the governments through a tax on both the employer and the employee. All employers are required to collect the employee's share of this tax. They deduct it from the employee's gross pay and remit it to the government along with the employer's share. Both the employer and the employee are taxed at the same rate, currently 4.95% each (2007) based on the employee's gross pay up to maximum contributory earnings of $40,200. This maximum amount is determined by subtracting the basic yearly exemption of $3,500 from the maximum amount of pensionable earnings of $43,700.

The maximum annual contribution for each of the employee and employer is therefore $1,989.90 in 2007.

Employment Insurance   Another payroll tax that the federal government levies is used for a system of employment insurance (EI). This tax is levied on both employees and employers. Employees must pay a premium of 1.80% (2007) of insurable earnings to an annual maximum contribution of $720 while the employer is required to contribute 2.52% or 1.4 times the amount of employee premiums. Insurable earnings are gross wages above a preset minimum and below a maximum amount of $40,000. Both the premium rates and insurable earnings are adjusted periodically.

Income Tax Withholding   Income tax laws require employers to withhold from each employee's pay the approximate amount of income tax that will be due on those wages. The amount of income tax that is withheld is calculated by the employer according to a government-prescribed formula or a government-provided income tax deduction table, and depends on the length of the pay period and each employee's wages, marital status, claimed dependents, and other permitted deductions.

Illustration   Assume a weekly payroll of $10,000 that is entirely subject to CPP (4.95%), employment insurance (1.80%), income tax withholdings of $1,320, and union dues of $88. The entry to record the wages and salaries paid and the employee payroll deductions is:

Wages and Salaries Expense	10,000	
Employee Income Tax Deductions Payable		1,320
CPP Contributions Payable		495
EI Premiums Payable		180
Union Dues Payable		88
Cash		7,917

A = L + SE
−7,917 +2,083 −10,000
Cash flows: ↓ 7,917 outflow

The required employer payroll taxes are recognized as compensation-related expenses in the same accounting period as the payroll is recorded. The entry for the required employer contributions is as follows:

Payroll Tax Expense	747	
CPP Contributions Payable ($495 × 1.0)		495
EI Premiums Payable ($180 × 1.4)		252

A = L + SE
+747 −747
Cash flows: No effect

The employer must send to the Receiver General for Canada the employees' income tax, CPP, and EI deductions as well as the employer's required contributions for CPP and EI. The entry to record the payment to the CRA for the payroll above is:

Employee Income Tax Deductions Payable	1,320	
CPP Contributions Payable ($495 + $495)	990	
EI Premiums Payable ($180 + $252)	432	
Cash		2,742

A = L + SE
−2,742 −2,742
Cash flows: ↓ 2,742 outflow

Until they are remitted to the government, these amounts are all reported as current liabilities. In a manufacturing enterprise, all payroll costs (wages, payroll taxes, and fringe benefits) are allocated to appropriate cost accounts such as Direct Labour, Indirect

Labour, Sales Salaries, or Administrative Salaries. This abbreviated and somewhat simplified discussion of payroll costs and deductions does not give a clear sense of the large volume of records and clerical work that is involved in maintaining a sound and accurate payroll system.

Compensated Absences

Compensated absences are absences from active employment for which employees are paid, such as statutory holidays and vacation. Employees have **vested rights** to these benefits. This means that the employer is legally required to pay the benefits even if the employee no longer works for the organization; thus, vested rights do not depend on an employee's continued service. For example, assume that you have earned four days of vacation as of December 31, the end of your employer's fiscal year. Because vacation pay is prescribed by law, your employer will have to pay you for these four days even if you resign from your job. In this case, your four days of vacation pay is a vested right and the costs are accrued by the company as expense **in the period in which the benefit is earned by the employee**.

Employers are required under provincial law to give each employee vacation equal to a specified number of days, or to pay them in lieu of the vacation. As a result, employers have an obligation for vacation pay that accrues as the employees work. This obligation—or liability—is usually satisfied by paying employees their regular salaries when they are absent from work while taking vacation.

Now assume that your vacation days **are not vested**, but that they can be carried forward to future periods if they are not used in the period when they are earned. If you continue to work for the company, you are entitled to the vacation days, but if you leave the company, you lose the right to them. Although the rights are not vested, they are accumulated rights and the company will have to honour the majority of those benefits that have been earned. **Accumulated rights** are rights that are not necessarily vested but can still be carried forward to future periods if they are not used in the period in which they are earned. In accounting for accumulated rights, the employer recognizes an expense and a liability for the cost of these compensated absences as they are earned by employees, but the estimated cost takes into account that, because of employee turnover, some of these benefits will never be paid.

Entitlement to **sick pay** varies greatly among employers. In some companies, sick pay vests and employees are allowed to accumulate unused sick time. They can take time off from work with pay even though they are not ill, or they will be paid for the unused sick days when they leave the company. In this case, an obligation exists to pay future amounts; therefore, **the estimated liability and expense are accrued** as the employees earn the benefit.

In other companies, employees receive sick pay only if they are absent because of illness, but the number of days they are entitled to accumulates with time. In this situation, it is very difficult to estimate in advance the expense that is associated with the benefits earned by the employees. As a result, no accrual is usually made. Because of measurement problems, most companies account for non-vesting sick pay on a pay-as-you-go basis.

In summary, an entity's expense and related liability for compensated absences is recognized in the year in which employees earn them as long as it is possible to reasonably estimate the amounts that are expected to be paid out in the future.

What rate should be used to accrue the compensated absence expense: the current rate or an estimated future rate? Most companies use the current rather than a future rate, which is less certain and raises issues about the discounting of the future amount. To illustrate, assume the following information for Amutron Limited that began operations on January 1, 2008:

- The company employs 10 individuals who are paid $480 per week.

- A total of 20 weeks of vacation is earned by all employees in 2008, but none is taken during the year.

- In 2009, the vacation weeks earned in 2008 are used when the current rate of pay is $540 per week.

The entry at December 31, 2008, to accrue the vacation pay entitlement earned by the employees is as follows:

Wages Expense	9,600	
Vacation Wages Payable ($480 × 20)		9,600

$$A = L + SE$$
$$+9,600 \quad -9,600$$
Cash flows: No effect

At December 31, 2008, the company reports a current liability of $9,600 on its balance sheet, and an expense of $9,600 for the benefits earned by employees in 2008 on its income statement. In 2009, the vacation time that is paid for (and was earned in 2008) is recorded as follows:

Vacation Wages Payable	9,600	
Wages Expense	1,200	
Cash ($540 × 20)		10,800

$$A = L + SE$$
$$-10,800 \quad -9,600 \quad -1,200$$
Cash flows: ↓ 10,800 outflow

In 2009, the vacation weeks are used and the liability is eliminated. Note that the difference between the cash paid and the reduction in the liability account is recorded as an adjustment to Wages Expense in the period when it is paid. This difference occurs because the liability account was accrued at the rate of pay in effect in the period when the benefit was earned. The cash paid, however, is based on the rate of pay in effect when the benefit is taken. If the future pay rates had been estimated accurately and used to calculate the accrual in 2008, then the cash paid in 2009 would have been the same as the liability.[17]

Bonus Agreements

For various reasons, many companies give a **bonus** to all or specific officers and employees. This amount is in addition to the regular salary or wage and may be a percentage of the employees' regular rates of pay, or it may depend on productivity increases or the amount of the company's annual profit. From the enterprise's standpoint, **bonus payments to employees** are considered additional compensation and are therefore an expense in determining the net income for the year.

To illustrate the entries for an employee bonus, assume that a company has income before bonuses of $100,000 for 2008 and that in January 2009 it will pay out bonuses of $10,700 related to 2008. An adjusting entry dated December 31, 2008, is made to record the bonus as follows:

International Insight

In Japan, bonuses to members of boards of directors and to the Commercial Code auditors are not treated as expenses. The bonuses are considered a distribution of profits and charged against retained earnings.

---

[17] Many companies have obligations for benefits payable to employees after they retire. The accounting and reporting standards for post-retirement benefit payments are complex and relate mainly to pensions and post-retirement health-care and life insurance benefits. These and other issues of employee future benefits are discussed in Chapter 19.

A =   L   +   SE
     +10,700   −10,700

Cash flows: No effect

| Employees' Bonus Expense | 10,700 | |
| Bonus Payable | | 10,700 |

The expense account appears in the income statement as an operating expense. The accrued liability, which is usually payable within a short time period, is included as a current liability on the balance sheet. In January 2009, when the bonus is paid, the entry is:

A   =   L   + SE
−10,700   −10,700

Cash flows: ↓ 10,700 outflow

| Bonus Payable | 10,700 | |
| Cash | | 10,700 |

It is important to be careful when calculating bonus amounts, especially if the formula specifies that the bonus is based on **after-tax** income. Because the bonus itself is a tax-deductible expense, simultaneous equations may have to be set up and solved to determine both the bonus and tax amounts.

ESTIMATED LIABILITIES

Objective 5
Account for common estimated liabilities.

Most liabilities that companies incur can be measured fairly accurately by the amount of cash (or the cash equivalent value of other assets) that the company must give up to discharge the obligation. However, some liabilities are more difficult to measure. Obligations from product guarantees and warranties, and obligations to provide premiums and price reductions in the future, **all relate to transactions of the current period** and must usually be estimated. Another example, referred to in Chapter 10, is the obligation related to asset retirements. Although asset retirement obligations are not usually **current** liabilities, the basic measurement and reporting requirements are covered in this chapter.

Product Guarantee and Warranty Obligations

A **warranty** or **product guarantee** is a promise made by a seller to a buyer to correct problems experienced with a product's quantity, quality, or performance. Guarantees are commonly used by manufacturers to promote sales. Automakers, for example, attract additional business by extending the length of their new-car warranty. For a specified period of time following the date of sale to the consumer, a manufacturer may promise to be responsible for all or part of the cost of replacing defective parts, to perform any necessary repairs or servicing without charge, to refund the purchase price, or even to double-your-money-back. Warranties and product guarantees result in future costs that are sometimes called "after costs" or "post-sale costs." They are often significant.

There can be two different situations with warranties:

1. **An embedded warranty.** In this case, the warranty is **provided with** the product or service, no additional fee is charged for it, and the amount that relates to the warranty cannot be separated from the product or service sales amount. The costs of honouring the warranty must be covered by the sales revenue that is received from sales of the product.

2. **Separate product.** In this case, the warranty is **sold separately** from the product or service, or the portion of the sales amount that is for the warranty can be determined. In these situations, the proceeds on the separate (or separable) sale of the product guarantee are used to cover the costs of later repairs and servicing.

As an example, consider the purchase of a plasma television and assume that it comes with a one-year warranty. At the time of purchase, it is common to also be offered the opportunity to purchase an extended warranty for an additional charge. The one-year warranty that is embedded in the sales price will usually be accounted for by the seller differently than the extended warranty product that is sold separately.

Warranty Embedded in Sales Price of Product

Although the future cost, due date of the obligation, and perhaps even the payee are not known, a liability is recognized in the accounts by the supplier **if (1) it is likely that future costs will be incurred as a result of the reported sales** and **(2) the amount can be reasonably estimated**. The liability amount is an estimate of all the costs that are likely to be incurred as a result of the warranty provisions after the product or service has been delivered. When the warranty is an integral and inseparable part of the sale, the accrual-based **expense warranty method** is used. Under this method, the warranty costs are estimated in advance and recognized as an operating expense **in the year of sale**, and a warranty liability is recognized for the estimated obligations that remain outstanding.

Illustration of Expense Warranty Method   Assume that Denson Machinery Corporation begins production of a new machine in July 2008, and sells 100 units for $5,000 each by its year end, December 31, 2008. Each machine is under warranty for one year and the company has estimated, from experience with a similar machine, that the warranty cost will probably average $200 per unit. To replace parts that are under warranty on machines that were sold in 2008, Denson incurs $4,000 in actual warranty costs in 2008 and $16,000 in 2009. Two equally valid series of entries could be made to record these events. Illustration 13-4 shows both approaches.

METHOD A		METHOD B	
1. Sale of 100 machines at $5,000 each, July–December, 2008			
Cash/Accounts Receivable 500,000		Cash/Accounts Receivable 500,000	
Sales	500,000	Sales	500,000
2. Recognition of estimated warranty expense at $200/unit for sales, July–December, 2008			
No entry		Warranty Expense	20,000
		Estimated Liability	
		under Warranty	20,000
3. Actual warranty costs incurred, July–December, 2008			
Warranty Expense	4,000	Estimated Liability	
Cash/Inventory/		under Warranty	4,000
Accrued Payroll	4,000	Cash/Inventory/	
		Accrued Payroll	4,000
4. Year-end adjusting entry to accrue outstanding warranty obligations at December 31, 2008			
Warranty Expense	16,000	No entry	
Estimated Liability			
under Warranty	16,000		
5. December 31, 2008, financial statement amounts reported			
Warranty Expense (I/S)	$20,000	Warranty Expense (I/S)	$20,000
Estimated Liability		Estimated Liability	
under Warranty (B/S)	$16,000	under Warranty (B/S)	$16,000
6. Actual warranty costs incurred, 2009			
Warranty Expense	16,000	Estimated Liability	
Cash/Inventory/		under Warranty	16,000
Accrued Payroll	16,000	Cash/Inventory/	
		Accrued Payroll	16,000

Illustration 13-4

Warranty Expense and Liability Entries

7. Adjusting entry, December 31, 2009, to adjust liability account to correct balance of $0			
Estimated Liability		No entry	
under Warranty	16,000		
Warranty Expense	16,000		

8. December 31, 2009, financial statement amounts reported			
Warranty Expense (I/S)	$0	Warranty Expense (I/S)	$0
Estimated Liability		Estimated Liability	
under Warranty (B/S)	$0	under Warranty (B/S)	$0
I/S: income statement B/S: balance sheet			

Under Method A, the actual warranty costs are charged to expense as they are incurred. At the end of the accounting period, a further expense and a liability are accrued for warranty costs to be incurred in the future on sales of the current period. Alternatively, with Method B the total expected warranty costs related to current period sales are charged to expense and the related obligation is recognized as a liability when the sales are recorded. As the actual warranty costs are incurred, the liability is then reduced. Either series of entries is acceptable: **both result in the same reported amounts on the income statement and the balance sheet**.

In situations where the warranty costs are immaterial or when the warranty period is relatively short, the product guarantee can be accounted for on a cash basis. Under the **cash method**, warranty costs are charged to expense as they are incurred; that is, they are charged **in the period when the seller or manufacturer honours the warranty**. No liability is recognized for future costs arising from warranties, and the expense is not necessarily recognized in the period of the related sale. If the cash basis is applied to the facts in the Denson Machinery Corporation example, $4,000 is recorded as warranty expense in 2008 and $16,000 as warranty expense in 2009, with the total sales being recorded as revenue in 2008. This method is required for income tax purposes.

Underlying Concept

Using the cash method when the costs are immaterial or the warranty period is short is a proper application of the materiality concept.

Warranty as a Separate Product

When an extended warranty or product maintenance contract is sold as a separate product or service, it is accounted for under a different method—the **sales warranty method**.[18] **The revenue on the sale of the extended warranty or contract is deferred** as unearned revenue and it is recognized in income over the life of the contract, generally on a straight-line basis. The revenue is unearned because the warranty seller has an obligation to perform services over the life of the contract. The costs of complying with the warranty or contract are recognized in expense as they are incurred.[19]

Illustration of Sales Warranty Method   To illustrate, assume that Hanlin Auto sells a car for $20,000. In addition to the regular warranty on the car (all repairs will be paid by Hanlin for the first 25,000 kilometres or two years, whichever comes first), Hanlin sells an extended warranty for $600 that protects the customer for an additional two years or 25,000 kilometres. The entry to record the automobile sale (with the embedded warranty) and the extended warranty sale on January 2, 2008, is:

---

[18] *EIC-142*, "Revenue Arrangements with Multiple Deliverables," indicates that this method is also appropriate when the warranty is embedded in the sales price of the product but it is separable, has stand-alone value, and its value can be objectively and reliably measured.

[19] *EIC-143*, "Accounting for Separately Priced Extended Warranty and Product Maintenance Contracts," CICA, December 17, 2003. Note that any incremental direct acquisition costs related to the sale of the contract, such as commissions, are deferred and amortized on the same basis as the revenue.

Cash	20,600	
Sales		20,000
Unearned Warranty Revenue		600

A   =   L   +   SE
+20,600   +600   +20,000

Cash flows: ↑ 20,600 inflow

The warranty that is embedded in the sale is accounted for under the **expense warranty method** explained previously. Hanlin thus makes a current year entry to recognize the estimated warranty expense and liability for the first 25,000 kilometres or two years. The **sales warranty method** is used for the extended warranty, and, in this case, no entries are needed until the third year. The entry to amortize the unearned revenue **on the extended warranty at the end of the third and fourth years** (using straight-line amortization) is as follows:

Unearned Warranty Revenue	300	
Warranty Revenue		300

A   =   L   +   SE
        −300   +300

Cash flows: No effect

Because the extended warranty contract does not start until after the regular warranty expires, no revenue is recognized on it until the third year. If the costs of performing services under the extended warranty contract are expected to be incurred in other than a straight-line pattern (as historical evidence might indicate), revenue is recognized over the contract period in the same pattern as the costs are expected to be incurred. In addition, if the costs of providing services under the contract are expected to be more than the remaining unearned revenue, a loss and related liability are recognized for any expected shortfall.[20]

Premiums, Coupons, Rebates, and Loyalty Programs

Many companies offer premiums and other benefits to customers on either a limited or continuing basis in return for box tops, certificates, coupons, labels, wrappers, or the accumulation of loyalty "points." The **premiums** may be silverware, dishes, a small appliance, toys, free transportation, or cash values against future purchases.[21] Customer **loyalty programs**, such as the one described for **Sears** in the chapter-opening vignette and the one offered by **Shoppers Drug Mart**, all promise future benefits to the customer in exchange for current sales.

    Printed coupons that can be redeemed for a cash discount on items purchased are extremely popular marketing tools, as is the cash rebate, which the buyer can obtain by returning the store receipt, a rebate coupon, and Universal Product Code (UPC label or bar code) to the manufacturer. **Contests** have also been widely used to get consumers' attention and their sales dollars, with the **Tim Hortons** "Roll Up The Rim To Win" promotion being one of the most successful contests in Canadian history. A wide variety of

Underlying Concept

Just as warranties do, obligations for most premiums and coupons meet the definition of a liability. In addition, the concept of matching means that the related expense is reported in the same period as when the revenue is recognized.

What Do the Numbers Mean?

---

[20] *EIC-143.*

[21] Premium plans that have been adopted widely include the frequent flyer programs that are used by all major airlines. On the basis of mileage or the number of trips accumulated, frequent flyer members are awarded discounted or free airline tickets. Airline customers can earn miles toward free travel by making long-distance phone calls, staying in hotels, and charging groceries and gasoline on a credit card. Those free tickets represent an enormous potential liability because when people use them they may displace paying passengers.

    When airlines first started offering frequent flyer bonuses, everyone assumed that they could accommodate the free ticket holders with seats that would otherwise be empty. That made the additional cost of the program so minimal that airlines did not accrue or report the small liability. But, as more and more paying passengers have been crowded off flights by frequent flyer awardees, the opportunity cost of the programs has grown enormously.

prizes are offered, including automobiles, vacations, major sporting events tickets, and sweepstake winnings!

The costs associated with these marketing tools are not inconsequential. For example, the Coupon Industry Association of Canada reports that Canadian consumers redeemed 100 million coupons in 2005, with an average value of $1.29 each. This represents a redemption rate of 2.9% of the coupons distributed by consumer packaged goods manufacturers to Canadian households, down from 4.7% in 2002.

With the life of many contests running a few months and the average coupon being valid for an average of 183 days, many companies have the practical problem of accounting for these marketing costs, as they affect more than one fiscal period. The accounting issue relates to the fact that while these promotions **increase current sales**, the associated costs are often incurred **in future periods**. That is, companies have existing obligations at the balance sheet date that will require them to give up economic benefits in the future; in other words, they have liabilities that must be recognized and reported. The matching concept also requires them to deduct those costs against the current period's revenue.

Source: Coupon Industry Association of Canada website at www.couponscanada.org

These premiums, coupon offers, frequent flyer miles, rebates, and prizes are made to stimulate sales, and their costs **are charged to expense** in the period that benefits from the premium or customer loyalty plan: the period of the sale. It is also important to estimate the cost of outstanding promotional offers related to past sales that will be presented for redemption in the future in order to properly show the **company's obligation or liability** on these offers. The cost of this type of program is charged to an expense account such as Premium or Loyalty Program Expense, and the outstanding obligations are included in a liability account such as Estimated Liability for Premiums, Estimated Liability for Coupons Outstanding, or Loyalty Program Liability.

The following example illustrates the accounting treatment related to a premium offer. In 2008, Fluffy Cakemix Corporation offered its customers a large non-breakable mixing bowl in exchange for $1.00 and 10 box tops. The mixing bowl costs Fluffy Cakemix Corporation $2.25, and the company estimates that 60% of the box tops will be redeemed. The premium offer results in the following transactions and entries in 2008:

1. Purchased 20,000 mixing bowls at $2.25 each:

A   =   L   +   SE
0   0   0

Cash flows: ↓ 45,000 outflow

Inventory of Premium Mixing Bowls	45,000	
Cash		45,000

2. Sold 300,000 boxes of cake mix at $1.50:

A   = L +   SE
+450,000   +450,000

Cash flows: ↑ 450,000 inflow

Cash	450,000	
Sales		450,000

3. Redeemed 60,000 box tops, receiving $1.00 per 10 box tops, and delivered 6,000 mixing bowls (60,000 ÷ 10):

A   = L +   SE
−7,500   −7,500

Cash flows: ↑ 6,000 inflow

Cash [(60,000 ÷ 10) × $1.00]	6,000	
Premium Expense	7,500	
Inventory of Premium Mixing Bowls		13,500
[Calculation: (60,000 ÷ 10) × $2.25 = $13,500]		

4. Adjusting entry made to recognize the estimated liability for outstanding premiums at the end of the period:

Premium Expense	15,000	
Estimated Liability for Premiums		15,000
Calculation:		
Total boxes sold in 2008	300,000	
Total estimated redemptions (60%)	180,000	
Box tops redeemed in 2008	60,000	
Estimated future redemptions	120,000	
Cost per premium: $2.25 − $1.00 =	$1.25	
Cost of estimated claims outstanding:		
(120,000 ÷10) × $1.25 =	$15,000	

$$A \;=\; L \;+\; SE$$
$$+15{,}000 \quad -15{,}000$$

Cash flows: No effect

The December 31, 2008, balance sheet of Fluffy Cakemix Corporation reports an inventory of premium mixing bowls of $31,500 as a current asset and an estimated liability for premiums of $15,000 as a current liability. The 2008 income statement reports a $22,500 premium expense among the selling expenses.

If the costs of such loyalty programs are really marketing expenses, the approach described above—similar to the expense warranty method described earlier—is a reasonable solution to the accounting for them. Increasingly, and as explained in Chapter 6, standard setters in Canada and internationally are beginning to interpret such award programs as revenue arrangements with multiple deliverables.[22] This means that, instead of accruing the estimated costs to match with current revenue, the better approach is to defer a portion of the revenue from the original transaction as unearned revenue and recognize it in the future as the obligation to supply the product or service to the customer is fulfilled by the entity. This approach is similar to the sales warranty method. Canadian practice is likely to change over time as situations which justify each of these approaches are identified.

Asset Retirement Obligations

In many industries, the construction and operation of long-lived assets means taking on obligations that are associated with the eventual retirement of those assets. For example, when a mining company opens up a strip mine, it may also make a commitment to restore the land on which the mine is located once the mining activity is completed. Similarly, when an oil company erects an offshore drilling platform, it may be legally obligated to dismantle and remove the platform at the end of its useful life.

The existing legal obligation that is associated with the retirement of a tangible long-lived asset and that results from its acquisition, construction, development, or normal operation must be recognized by the company **in the period when the obligation is incurred**, provided that a reasonable estimate can be made of its fair value.[23] This liability is known as an **asset retirement obligation (ARO)**, and the costs are added to the carrying amount of the associated asset. If the fair value cannot be reasonably estimated, this fact and the reasons for it must be reported.

6 Objective

Explain the recognition, measurement, and disclosure requirements for asset retirement obligations.

---

[22] As this text went to print, the International Financial Reporting Interpretations Committee (IFRIC) of the IASB was finalizing an interpretation on Customer Loyalty Programs (Draft Interpretation D20) expected to be issued late in 2007. The IFRIC's position is to allocate and defer the portion of the revenue from the transaction that relates to the entity's obligation to supply the award product or service in the future.

[23] *CICA Handbook*, Section 3110, "Asset Retirement Obligations."

Obligating Events

The following are examples of existing legal obligations that would require the recognition of a liability and asset cost. Note that the list is not exhaustive.

1. Decommissioning nuclear facilities

2. Dismantling, restoring, and reclaiming oil and gas properties

3. Certain closure, reclamation, and removal costs of mining facilities

4. Closure and post-closure costs of landfills

In order to benefit from these capital assets, the company generally has a legal obligation for the costs that are associated with their retirement. AROs occur in a variety of ways. For example, the obligation may arise from purchasing an asset before it is used (e.g., the erection of an oil rig), or it may increase over time through normal operations (e.g., a landfill or mine site that expands over time).

Measurement

The liability is initially measured at its fair value, which is defined as the amount that the company would need to pay to settle the ARO in an active market. Although active markets do not exist for many AROs, an estimate of the fair value should be based on the best information available. Such information would include the market prices of similar liabilities, if available. Alternatively, fair value can be based on estimates of the future costs discounted to their present value.

Recognition and Allocation

As explained in Chapter 10, the estimated ARO costs are added to the carrying amount of the related asset and a liability is recognized for the same amount. An asset retirement cost is recorded as part of the cost of the related asset because it is considered necessary in order to acquire and operate the asset, and to receive its future economic benefits. Because no future economic benefit is associated with the capitalized asset retirement costs in and of themselves, these costs are not recorded separately from the asset account.

Later, the ARO cost is amortized to expense over the related asset's useful life. While the straight-line method is acceptable, other systematic and rational allocations are also allowed.

Note that environmental cleanup costs that are required after such events as a major oil spill or accidental runoff of chemicals into a water table **do not result in an asset retirement obligation and addition to the cost base** of the underlying asset. These catastrophes do not result from the normal operations of the entity and therefore do not justify an increase in the asset's cost.

Illustration of Accounting for Initial Recognition of AROs

To illustrate the accounting for AROs, assume that on January 1, 2008, Wildcat Oil Corp. erected an oil platform off the Newfoundland coast. Wildcat is legally required to dismantle and remove the platform at the end of its five-year useful life. The total cost of dismantling and removal is estimated to be $1 million. Based on a 10% discount rate, the present value of the asset retirement obligation is $620,920 ($1 million × 0.62092). Wildcat makes the following entry to recognize the ARO:

A   =   L   + SE
+620,920   +620,920

Cash flows: No effect

	January 1, 2008	
Drilling Platform	620,920	
Asset Retirement Obligation		620,920

Over the asset's life, the retirement cost is allocated to expense. Using the straight-line method, Wildcat makes the following entries to record this expense:

December 31, 2008, 2009, 2010, 2011, 2012		
Amortization Expense ($620,920 ÷ 5)	124,184	
Accumulated Amortization		124,184

A   = L +   SE
−124,184   −124,184

Cash flows: No effect

In addition, because the liability is measured at its discounted cash flows, interest on the liability is accrued each period. An entry is made at December 31, 2008, to record the expense and the related increase or **accretion** in the carrying amount of the liability. The increase in the ARO liability is classified as an operating expense, but is reported as **accretion expense** rather than as interest expense.

December 31, 2008		
Accretion Expense ($620,920 × 10%)	62,092	
Asset Retirement Obligation		62,092

A =   L   +   SE
      +62,092   −62,092

Cash flows: No effect

On January 10, 2013, Wildcat contracts with Rig Reclaimers, Inc. to dismantle the platform at a contract price of $995,000. Wildcat then makes the following entry to record settlement of the liability:

January 10, 2013		
Asset Retirement Obligation	1,000,000	
Gain on Settlement of ARO		5,000
Cash		995,000

A   =   L   + SE
−995,000 −1,000,000 +5,000

Cash flows: ↓ 995,000 outflow

Subsequent Recognition and Measurement of AROs

CICA Handbook Section 3110 explains the accounting complexities that occur when the estimated amount of the obligation changes or additional costs and liabilities need to be recognized due to current operations. To summarize, the accretion expense for the interest element is calculated first. This is followed by an adjustment to the carrying amount of the Asset Retirement Obligation account for any increase or decrease in the cost estimates. This adjustment is also made to the book value of the long-lived asset to which it relates and, of course, to the amount of annual amortization.

Reporting and Disclosure Requirements

Most asset retirement obligations are long-term in nature and therefore are shown outside current liabilities. In addition to providing a description of the AROs and the assets they are associated with, companies also disclose the following:

1. Specific information about the assumptions that were used in determining the reported amounts

2. A reconciliation of the beginning and ending balances of the liability

3. The fair value of assets that are legally restricted for the purpose of eventually settling such obligations[24]

---

[24] *CICA Handbook*, Section 3110.21.

CONTINGENCIES, GUARANTEES, AND COMMITMENTS

Contingent Liabilities

Objective 7

Identify the accounting and reporting requirements for contingent liabilities.

A **contingency** is defined as an existing condition or situation involving uncertainty as to possible gain (**gain contingency**) or loss (**loss contingency**) and that will not be resolved until a future event or events occur or fail to occur.[25] As discussed in Chapter 5, **gain contingencies are not recorded** in the accounts. They are disclosed in the notes only when it **is likely** that a gain will be realized. As a result, it is unusual to find disclosures about contingent gains in the financial statements and the accompanying notes. On the other hand, it is not unusual to find **loss contingencies** reported. Any liability that is recognized in the accounts as a result of a loss contingency is, by definition, a **contingent liability**.

How likely it is that a future event will confirm the incurrence of a loss and liability can range from highly probable to only slightly probable. The terms **"likely," "unlikely,"** and **"not determinable"** are used in the following way to identify the range of probability outcomes:

> **Likely:** The chance of occurrence (or non-occurrence) of the future event is high.
>
> **Unlikely:** The chance of occurrence (or non-occurrence) of the future event is slight.
>
> **Not determinable:** The chance of occurrence (or non-occurrence) of the future event cannot be determined.[26]

A loss contingency is accounted for by a charge (debit) to expense **only if both the following conditions** are met:[27]

1. Information that is available before the financial statements are issued indicates that **it is likely** that a future event will confirm that an asset has been impaired or a liability has been incurred as of the date of the financial statements.

2. The loss amount can be **reasonably estimated**.

International Insight

In measuring the amount of provision to recognize, IAS 37 uses an "expected value" method that weights the possible outcomes according to their associated probabilities.

The first condition emphasizes that the likely existence of a liability must relate to events that occurred before the balance sheet date. The second criterion indicates that it has to be possible to make a reasonable estimate of the liability; otherwise, it cannot be accrued as a liability. The evidence that is used to determine a reasonable estimate of the liability may be based on the company's own experience, the experience of other companies in the industry, engineering or research studies, legal advice, or educated guesses by personnel who are in the best position to know. Often, **a range of possible amounts** may be determined. If a specific amount within the range is a better estimate than others, this is the amount that is accrued. If no particular amount is more likely than another, the bottom of the range is usually recognized, and the amount of the remaining exposure to possible loss is disclosed.

The table in Illustration 13-5 summarizes the accounting and reporting standards for contingencies.

---

[25] *CICA Handbook*, Section 3290.02.

[26] *CICA Handbook*, Section 3290.06.

[27] Loss contingencies that result in the incurrence of a liability are the more relevant ones for the discussion in this chapter. Loss contingencies that result in the impairment of an asset (e.g., the collectibility of receivables or a threat of expropriation of assets) are discussed more fully in other chapters of this textbook.

Probability	**Loss can be reasonably estimated?**	
	Yes	No
Likely	Accrue. Report exposure to loss in excess of amount accrued in Notes to Financial Statements*	Report in Notes to Financial Statements*
Not likely	Disclosure not required	Disclosure not required
Not determinable	Report in Notes to Financial Statements*	Report in Notes to Financial Statements*

*Disclose the nature of the contingency and either an estimate of the amount or the fact that an estimate cannot be made. *CICA Handbook* Section 3290.12, .15, and .22.

Illustration 13-5

Accounting and Reporting Standards for Loss Contingencies

As you would expect, using the terms "likely" and "unlikely" as a basis for determining the accounting for contingencies involves considerable judgement and subjectivity. Practising accountants often express concern over the diversity that exists in the interpretation of these terms. Current accounting practice for these situations relies heavily on the exact language that is used in responses that are received from lawyers—but the language of lawyers may be necessarily biased and protective rather than predictive. As a result, accruals and disclosures of contingencies vary considerably in practice. There is agreement, however, that general risks that are inherent in business operations, such as the possibility of war, strike, uninsurable catastrophes, or a business recession, are not contingent liabilities and are not reported in the financial statements.

Illustration 13-6 shows some common examples of loss contingencies and their usual accounting treatment.

Loss Related to	Not Accrued	May Be Accrued*
1. Risk of loss or damage of enterprise property by fire, explosion, or other hazards	X	
2. General or unspecified business risks	X	
3. Risk of loss from catastrophes assumed by property and casualty insurance companies including reinsurance companies	X	
4. Threat of expropriation of assets		X
5. Pending or threatened litigation		X
6. Actual or possible claims and assessments		X
7. Guarantees of indebtedness of others**		X
8. Agreements to repurchase receivables (or the related property) that have been sold		X

* Should be accrued when both criteria are met (likely and reasonably estimable).
** See also AcG-14, Disclosure of Guarantees

Illustration 13-6

Accounting Treatment of Loss Contingencies

Illustration 13-7 from the 2005 annual report of **Clearly Canadian Beverage Corporation** is an example of an accrual that relates to a loss contingency. It also includes a boilerplate disclosure (i.e., a statement that is made using almost the same words by many companies) about legal proceedings and claims that arise in the ordinary course of business operations.

Clearly Canadian Beverage Corporation
Note 16 Commitments and Contingencies [excerpts]

d)   Dispute with D. Bruce Horton and Continental Consulting Ltd.

In August 1999, a claim was filed against the company in the Supreme Court of British Columbia by D. Bruce Horton and his company, Continental Consulting Ltd. (Continental). Mr. Horton is claiming compensation from the Company for allegedly constructively dismissing him as an officer of the Company. Continental is claiming compensation from the Company alleging that the Company terminated its management agreement without cause. Mr. Horton and Continental are claiming an aggregate of CA $2,400,000 plus interest and costs. The Company does not accept Mr. Horton's and Continental's allegations, and has filed statements of defence and has further filed counterclaims against Mr. Horton and Continental for monies owed and damages. The Company has made an accrual based on its expected costs.

e)   Ordinary course business proceedings

The company is subject to various legal proceedings and claims that arise in the ordinary course of business. Management is of the opinion that such claims will not have a material adverse effect on the Company's future operations or financial position.

Litigation, Claims, and Assessments

The most common types of loss contingencies have to do with litigation, claims by others, and assessments.[28] The following factors, among others, must be considered in deciding whether a liability should be recorded as a result of pending or threatened **litigation** and actual or possible **claims** and **assessments**:

1. The **time period** in which the underlying cause of action occurred

2. The **probability** of an unfavourable outcome

3. The ability to make a **reasonable estimate** of the loss amount

To recognize a loss and a liability in the accounts, **the cause for litigation must have occurred on or before the date of the financial statements**. It does not matter that the company did not become aware of the existence or possibility of the lawsuit or claims until after the date of the financial statements. As long as management knows of the possibility before the statements are issued, it has a responsibility to evaluate whether the situation should be recognized or reported in the financial statements.

To evaluate the **likelihood of an unfavourable outcome**, management considers the nature of the litigation, the progress of the case, the opinion of legal counsel, the experience of the company and others in similar cases, and any company response to the lawsuit.[29]

Estimating the amount of loss from pending litigation, however, can rarely be done with any certainty. And, even if the evidence that is available at the balance sheet date does not favour the defendant, it is not reasonable to expect the company to publish in its financial statements a dollar estimate of the likely negative outcome. Such specific disclosures could weaken the company's position in the dispute and encourage the plaintiff to intensify its efforts. There is a fine line between a shareholder's right to know about potential losses and information that could hurt the company's interests.

---

[28] The CICA's *Financial Reporting in Canada, 2006 Edition* reports that in 2005 the four most common types of contingent losses disclosed by their sample of 200 Canadian companies were lawsuits (by 155 companies), environmental matters (by 26), contingent consideration (by 16), and possible tax reassessments (by 17).

[29] For some companies, litigation presents significant costs in employee time and legal fees, even if the outcomes are positive. For example, in 2003, U.S. giant Wal-Mart Stores Inc. reported that it was the target of 6,649 active lawsuits of all sorts (Associated Press).

These decisions are even more difficult in cases of **unfiled suits** and **unasserted claims and assessments**. With these, a company must first determine how likely it is that a suit will be filed or a claim or assessment will be asserted, and then, if it appears likely, how probable it is that the outcome will be unfavourable. For example, assume that a company is being investigated by the federal government for possible violations of anti-competition legislation, and that enforcement proceedings have begun. Such proceedings may be followed by private claims. In this case, the company must determine the probability of the claims being made and the likelihood of damages being awarded. If both are likely, if the loss can be estimated reasonably, and if the cause for action occurred on or before the date of the financial statements, a liability is accrued and a loss is recognized.

Guarantees

Closely related to the topic of contingencies are the requirements for all guarantor companies to disclose information about a variety of specific types of **guarantees** that they have provided. Instead of dealing with recognition and measurement issues, Accounting Guideline 14 "Disclosure of Guarantees" (AcG-14) supplements other disclosure requirements that relate to contingencies, contractual obligations, and financial instruments. The purpose of the expanded disclosures is to give readers better information about the entity's obligations and **particularly about the risks that are assumed as a result of issuing guarantees.**

> **8 Objective**
> Identify the accounting and reporting requirements for guarantees and commitments.

While many specific types of guarantees have been excluded, AcG-14 includes such guarantees as the following:

1. Contracts that require the guarantor company to make payments to another party in the event of a loss that has been caused by changes in a variety of variables that are associated with an asset, liability, or equity security of the guaranteed party

2. Performance guarantees

3. Some indemnification contracts (i.e., agreements to protect the guaranteed party from loss)

4. Some indirect guarantees of the indebtedness of others[30]

Specific examples of the above include a lessee's guarantee of the residual value of leased property under an operating lease, a standby letter of credit that guarantees another party's payment of a loan or performance of a duty under a contract, and an agreement to advance funds if a second entity's net income or working capital, for example, falls below a specified minimum.

AcG-14 requires the following disclosures:

- the nature of the guarantee, how it arose, and circumstances that require the guarantor to perform under the guarantee

- the maximum potential amount of future payments that the guarantor could be required to make, without any reduction for recoverable amounts

- the nature and extent of any recourse provisions or collateral held

- the carrying amount of the liability, if any

AcG-14 and this chapter do not address recognition and measurement issues for guarantees. These aspects are covered in the loss contingency standards and in the standards for the recognition and measurement of financial instruments. Illustration 13-8 presents

---

[30] AcG-14, par. 4(a).

RONA inc.'s note disclosure on guarantees that was reported in the company's interim financial statements for its third quarter ending September 24, 2006.

Illustration 13-8

Disclosure of Guarantees—
RONA inc.

Guarantees

In the normal course of business, the Company reaches agreements that could meet the definition of "guarantees" in AcG-14.

The Company guarantees mortgages for certain customers to an amount of $6,507. The terms of these loans extend until 2012 and the net carrying amount of the assets held as security, which mainly include land and buildings, is $15,336.

Pursuant to the terms of inventory repurchase agreements, the Company is committed towards financial institutions to buy back the inventory of certain customers at an average of 62% of the cost of the inventories to a maximum of $55,713. In the event of recourse, this inventory would be sold in the normal course of the Company's operations. These agreements have undetermined periods but may be cancelled by the Company with a 30-day advance notice. In the opinion of the management, the likelihood that significant payments would be incurred as a result of these commitments is low.

Commitments

Companies conduct business by entering into agreements with customers, suppliers, employees, and other parties. Although they are not liabilities at the balance sheet date, such **commitments** or **contractual obligations** commit the company and its assets into the future. While it would not be reasonable or desirable to require that companies disclose all of their outstanding contractual obligations, it is useful to have them highlight commitments that have certain characteristics. Disclosure is therefore required of the following significant commitments:

1. Commitments that involve a high degree of speculative risk when that risk is unusual for the type of business

2. Obligations to make expenditures that are abnormal for the size of the business and its usual operations

3. Commitments to issue shares

4. Contracts that dictate the level of a particular type of expenditure for a considerable period of time into the future[31]

Examples include major capital expenditure commitments, commitments to make lease payments, and major raw material purchase or sale agreements. Purchase commitments were discussed in Chapter 8.

Self-Insurance Risks

Companies may have a variety of uninsured risks. These include **non-insurance** (i.e., not having insurance for certain risks) or having **co-insurance** or **deductible clauses** in an insurance contract that result in only partial coverage of the risk. Some companies decide not to carry any coverage with an insurance company and to absorb potential losses

---

[31] *CICA Handbook*, Section 3280.01.

themselves, often referred to as **self-insurance**. Does this mean that such companies should report contingent liabilities for possible future losses?

The absence of insurance does not mean that a company can accrue a liability for the costs of potential and probable losses if no damages have been experienced at the balance sheet date. Fires, explosions, and other similar events that may cause damage to a company's property occur randomly and are unrelated to the company's activities. And, unlike an insurance enterprise that has contractual obligations to reimburse policyholders for losses, a company cannot owe such an obligation to itself. For these reasons, **no liability or loss is recognized until damage occurs**.

If a company is exposed to risks of loss because of an uninsured **past injury** to others, however, this amounts to an existing condition with uncertainty about the amount and timing of losses that may develop, and a contingency therefore exists. Thus, for example, if it can make a reasonable estimate of the liability, a company with a fleet of vehicles would have to accrue uninsured losses that could result from an actual injury to others or damage to the property of others if the injury or damage occurred before the date of the financial statements. However, if no injury or damage has actually occurred, such a company would not recognize a liability for **expected future injury** to others or damage to the property of others even if the amount of loss could be reasonably estimated.

PERSPECTIVES

Presentation of Current Liabilities

The current liability accounts are commonly presented as the first classification in the balance sheet's Liabilities and Shareholders' Equity section. In some instances, current liabilities are presented as a group immediately below current assets, with the total of the current liabilities deducted from the current assets total. Although this presentation is not seen often, it is an informative one that **focuses on the company's investment in working capital**.

9 Objective
Indicate how current liabilities and related items are presented and analyzed.

Within the Current Liabilities section, the accounts may be listed in the order of either their maturity or liquidation preference. Many companies list notes payable first (sometimes called commercial paper, bank loans, or short-term debt), regardless of their relative amounts, follow with accounts payable, and then end the section with the current portion of long-term debt. An excerpt from the December 31, 2006, balance sheet and notes to the financial statements of ClubLink Corporation is presented in Illustration 13-9. ClubLink is the largest owner, operator, and developer of member golf clubs in Canada. This excerpt is representative of the types of current liabilities that are found in the reports of many corporations.

Illustration 13-9

Balance Sheet Presentation of Current Liabilities

CONSOLIDATED BALANCE SHEETS

As at December 31 (thousands of dollars)	Reference	2006	2005
Current liabilities			
Accounts payable and accrued liabilities	5	$ 11,537	$ 11,730
Development capital assets costs to complete		780	3,707
Non-revolving long-term debt	7	8,776	6,713
Capital lease obligations	8	4,307	4,424
Prepaid annual dues and deposits		5,879	6,032
		31,279	32,606

5. Accounts Payable and Accrued Liabilities

(thousands of dollars)	2006	2005
Trade payables	$3,607	$ 3,741
Accrued payroll costs	2,112	2,799
Accrued interest	1,703	1,920
Accrued land lease rent	1,048	263
Accrued liabilities and other	3,067	3,007
	$11,537	$11,730

International Insight

IAS 37 has used the term "provisions" to refer to liabilities that have uncertainty about their timing or the amount of their future expenditure. It requires that companies report provisions separately and provide a reconciliation of the opening and closing balances of each class of provisions. It is likely that amendments to IAS 37 which are expected to take effect in 2008 will replace the term "provision" and use the general term "liability" instead.

In terms of disclosure, the entity should disclose enough supplementary information about its current liabilities so that readers can understand and identify the entity's current needs for cash. Such information includes identifying the major classes of current liabilities such as bank loans, trade creditors and accrued liabilities, taxes, dividends, deferred revenue, and future income taxes. Also, amounts owing to officers, directors, shareholders, and associated companies are reported separately from amounts that are owed to enterprises that the reporting entity deals with at arm's length. Secured liabilities and any assets that have been pledged as collateral are identified clearly. And finally, if the due date of any liability can be extended, details explaining this are disclosed.[32]

Presentation of Contingencies and Commitments

As Illustration 13-5 indicated, companies are required to disclose their contingent liabilities in a note when any of the following are true:

1. It is likely that a future event will confirm the existence of a loss but the loss cannot be reasonably estimated.

2. A loss has been recognized, but there is an exposure to loss that is higher than the amount that was recorded.

3. It is not possible to determine the likelihood of there being a future event that confirms the liability.

Companies are also required to report any significant contractual commitments that will result in future obligations that are unusual in nature or material in amount.

Illustration 13-10 provides excerpts from **Four Seasons Hotels Inc.**'s "Note 15. Commitments and contingencies," which is taken from the company's December 31, 2006, financial statements. This note identifies a variety of situations that involve future spending and uncertainty.

Illustration 13-10

Contingencies and Commitments Disclosure Example

---

14. Commitments and contingencies:

(a) Lease commitments:

The Corporation has entered into lease agreements for certain hotel properties and corporate offices for periods up to the year 2054.

(i) Future minimum lease payments for Four Seasons Hotel Vancouver and certain corporate offices (but exclusive of any contingent rentals, occupancy costs, and lease commitments relating to Four Seasons Hotel London, which is discussed below), are as follows:

---

[32] *CICA Handbook*, Section 1510.05 to .10.

2007	$ 4,824
2008	3,815
2009	3,206
2010	3,012
2011	2,780
Subsequent to 2011	20,266
	$37,903

(c) Guarantees, commitments and indemnifications:

(i) Guarantees and commitments:

As at December 31, 2006, the Corporation had provided certain guarantees in connection with properties under its management. These include guarantees in respect of four projects totalling a maximum of approximately $21,900, as well as a guarantee of $300 for relocation costs for certain employees. The Corporation has a lease guarantee in respect of Four Seasons Hotel Prague of approximately €0.9 million. To the extent it is called upon to honour any one of these guarantees, the Corporation generally has either the right to be repaid from hotel operations and/or has various forms of security or recourse to the owner of the property.

In addition, in 2006, the Corporation also had four other commitments totalling approximately $11,200 to four properties under its management. During 2005, the Corporation assigned its leases and sold the related assets of The Pierre. As part of the sale, in accordance with statutory provisions, the purchaser agreed to assume a portion of the Corporation's contribution history with a multiemployer pension fund for the unionized hotel employees (the "NYC Pension"). This permitted the Corporation to withdraw from the NYC Pension without incurring a withdrawal liability estimated at $10,700.

If the purchaser withdraws as a result of the lease cancellation by the landlord in certain circumstances in 2008 or 2011, the Corporation has agreed to indemnify the purchaser for that portion of the withdrawal liability relating to their assumption of the Corporation's contribution history. The amount of any potential future liability resulting from this indemnity is not determinable at this time as it would be based upon future events related to the NYC Pension.

If the purchaser withdraws from the NYC Pension prior to 2011 in any circumstances other than those described above and does not pay its withdrawal liability, the Corporation remains secondarily liable for its withdrawal liability up to an amount of $10,700. The Corporation has been indemnified by the purchaser for any such liability.

The Corporation believes that the likelihood of it being required to make a payment is remote, and no amount has been recorded as at December 31, 2006 in respect of a potential NYC Pension withdrawal liability.

The Corporation does not expect to fund any of these commitments during 2007. The Corporation's assessment of its potential liability for such matters could change as a result of, among other things, the associated risks and uncertainties.

(iii) Director and officer indemnification arrangements:

To the extent permitted by law, the Corporation and its subsidiaries indemnify individuals that are, or have been, directors or officers against certain claims that may be made against them as a result of their being, or having been, a director or officer at the request of the Corporation or its subsidiaries. The Corporation has documented these indemnification arrangements in agreements with each of its directors and certain of its senior officers. The Corporation has purchased directors' and officers' liability insurance that may be available in respect of certain of these claims.

(d) Other commitments and contingencies:

(i) In the ordinary course of its business, the Corporation is named as a defendant in legal proceedings resulting from incidents taking place at hotels owned or managed by it. The Corporation maintains comprehensive liability insurance and also requires hotel owners to maintain adequate insurance coverage. The Corporation believes such coverage to be of a nature and amount sufficient to ensure that it is adequately protected from suffering any material financial loss as a result of such claims.

(ii) A number of the Corporation's management contracts are subject to certain performance tests which, if not met, could allow a contract to be terminated prior to its maturity. The Corporation generally has various rights to cure any such defaults to avoid termination.

(iii) The Corporation is currently in dispute with the owner of Four Seasons Hotel Caracas (note 3(d)) over a variety of matters.

Analysis

Because the ability to pay current obligations as they come due is critical to a company's short-term financial health and continued existence, analysts pay particular attention to the current liabilities section of the balance sheet. As with most financial statement items, it is not the absolute dollar amount of the current liabilities that is important, but rather its relationship to other aspects of the company's position and results.

Current liabilities result from **both operating and financing activities**. Trade liabilities and other liabilities that **arise from operations**—such as payroll, rent, insurance, and taxes payable—are the most common. In addition, advances from customers are a source of operating credit, and it is important to distinguish them from other operating sources. Why? This liability requires the company to provide a service or product in the future rather than make a cash payment, and will therefore result in the recognition of revenue in the future. An increase in this category of liability predicts future revenues, not cash outflows.

Short-term notes and the current portion of long-term debt result **from financing activities**. The company must either generate operating cash flows to repay these liabilities or arrange for their refinancing. The refinancing, however, may come at a higher cost to the borrower than the original note or debt.

Identifying current liabilities separately from long-term obligations is important because it provides information about the company's liquidity. **Liquidity** refers to a company's ability to convert assets into cash to pay off its current liabilities in the ordinary course of business. The higher the proportion of "assets expected to be converted to cash" to "liabilities currently due," the more liquid the company. A company with higher liquidity is better able to survive financial downturns and has a better chance of taking advantage of investment opportunities that develop.

As indicated in earlier chapters of the text, basic ratios such as net cash flow provided by operating activities to current liabilities and the turnover ratios for receivables and inventory **are useful in assessing liquidity**. Three other key ratios are the current ratio, the acid-test ratio, and the days payables outstanding.

The **current ratio** is the ratio of total current assets to total current liabilities. The formula is shown in Illustration 13-11.

Illustration 13-11
Current Ratio Formula

$$\text{Current ratio} = \frac{\text{Current assets}}{\text{Current liabilities}}$$

The current ratio shows how many dollars of current assets are available for each dollar of current liabilities. Sometimes it is called the **working capital ratio** because working capital is the excess of current assets over current liabilities. The higher the ratio, the more likely it is that the company can generate cash to pay its currently maturing liabilities.

However, a company with a large amount of current assets that is made up almost entirely of inventory may have a satisfactory current ratio, but may not be very liquid. The current ratio does not show whether or not a portion of the current assets is tied up in slow-moving inventories. With inventories—especially raw materials and work in process—there is a question of how long it will take to transform them into finished goods, to convert the finished product into accounts receivable by selling it, and then collect the amounts that customers owe. Better information may be provided to assess liquidity by eliminating inventories and other non-liquid current assets such as prepaid expenses from the current asset ratio numerator. Many analysts prefer to use the resulting **acid-test** or **quick ratio**, shown in Illustration 13-12. This ratio relates quick assets such as cash, marketable securities, and receivables to total current liabilities.

Illustration 13-12
Acid-test Ratio Formula

$$\text{Acid-test ratio} = \frac{\text{Cash} + \text{Marketable securities} + \text{Net receivables}}{\text{Current liabilities}}$$

The current ratio and quick ratio are useful, especially when analyzing a company over time and when comparing it to other companies in the same industry.

The third ratio, the **days payables outstanding**, zeroes in on how long it takes a company to pay its trade payables—i.e., it determines the average age of the payables. **Trade payables** are amounts that the entity owes to suppliers for providing goods and services related to normal business operations; that is, they are amounts that result from operating transactions. When cash is managed well, the payment of payables is delayed as long as possible, but done in time to meet the due date. A trend where the age of the payables outstanding is increasing, particularly if it is above the normal credit period for the industry, may indicate liquidity problems for the company. Illustration 13-13 shows the formula for this ratio.

$$\text{Days payables outstanding} = \frac{\text{Average trade accounts payable}}{\substack{\text{Average daily cost of goods sold} \\ \text{or average daily cost of total} \\ \text{operating expenses}}}$$

Illustration 13-13

Days Payables Outstanding Formula

The formula provides a better result if all the suppliers that are represented in the payables amount (the numerator) provide the goods and services that are captured in the cost of goods sold amount (the denominator). If the trade accounts payable include the suppliers for most of the company's operating goods and services in addition to the inventory purchases, analysts prefer to use the "average daily cost of total operating expenses" as the denominator.

To illustrate the calculation of these ratios, partial balance sheet and income statement information is provided in Illustration 13-14 for **Shoppers Drug Mart Corporation**'s 52 weeks ended December 30, 2006.

Illustration 13-14

Selected Financial Statement Information

SHOPPERS DRUG MART CORPORATION

As at December 30, 2006 and December 31, 2005
(in thousands of dollars)

	2006	2005
Assets		
Current		
Cash	$ 62,865	$ 24,524
Accounts receivable	307,779	256,504
Inventory	1,372,124	1,216,549
Future income taxes (Note 4)	46,407	38,316
Prepaid expenses	32,248	29,018
	1,821,423	1,564,911
Liabilities		
Current		
Bank indebtedness	$ 134,487	$ 163,503
Commercial paper (Note 3)	503,550	469,850
Accounts payable and accrued liabilities	843,278	697,945
Income taxes payable	70,672	39,860
Dividends payable	25,797	21,343
	1,577,784	1,392,501

52 weeks ended December 30, 2006 and December 31, 2005
(in thousands of dollars, except per share amounts)

	2006	2005
Sales	$ 7,786,436	$ 7,151,115
Operating expenses		
Cost of goods sold and other operating expenses	6,958,361	6,430,933
Amortization	144,549	120,937
Operating income	683,526	599,245

The calculation of the current, acid-test, and days payables outstanding ratios for Shoppers Drug Mart is as follows:

$$\text{Current ratio} = \frac{\text{Current assets}}{\text{Current liabilities}} = \frac{\$1,821,423}{\$1,577,784} = 1.2$$

$$\text{Acid-test ratio} = \frac{\text{Quick assets}}{\text{Current liabilities}} = \frac{\$62,865 + \$307,779}{\$1,577,784} = 0.2$$

$$\text{Days payables outstanding} = \frac{\text{Average trade accounts payable}}{\substack{\text{Average daily cost of goods sold} \\ \text{or} \\ \text{Average daily total operating expenses}}}$$

$$= \frac{\dfrac{\$843,278 + \$697,945}{2}}{\dfrac{\$6,958,361}{365}} = \frac{\$770,612}{\$\ 19,064} = 40.4 \text{ days}$$

While a 1.2 to 1 current ratio and a 0.2 to 1 quick ratio appear low, it is difficult to make a definite statement about the company's liquidity. What amounts to an acceptable ratio depends on the industry and how it operates. In some industries, companies need significant amounts of current and quick assets compared to their current liabilities. In other industries, such as those that generate cash from cash sales or whose receivables and inventory turn over quickly, companies may be very liquid with low current and quick ratios. Shoppers Drug Mart, for example, is likely to convert its inventory to cash on a daily basis as customers pay cash or use credit cards such as Visa and MasterCard (credit card slips from these two companies are deposited daily as if they were cash). For these reasons, Shoppers Drug Mart is likely well able to meet its current liabilities as they fall due.

Shoppers Drug Mart's accounts payable are, on average, 40.4 days old. It appears that the company is not experiencing problems keeping up with payments as supplier credit terms are likely in the 30 to 45 day range. It is difficult to draw any definite conclusions about these numbers by themselves. They need to be compared with results from previous years, with credit policies, and with the numbers from other companies in the same industry.

International

Comparison of Canadian and International GAAP

Objective 10
Compare current Canadian and international GAAP.

In terms of what is covered at an intermediate accounting level, Canadian accounting standards on current liabilities, contingencies, and commitments are largely converged with those of the IASB. While there are differences in the details of some of the material addressed in the primary sources of GAAP and in the way some standards are applied, the general principles are similar. Illustration 13-15 sets out the major primary sources of Canadian GAAP in the *CICA Handbook* and the corresponding international GAAP for the topics covered in this chapter.

	Canada	International
Section 1510	Current assets and current liabilities	IAS 1 Presentation of financial statements IAS 19 Employee benefits
Section 3855	Financial instruments—recognition and measurement	IAS 39 Financial instruments—recognition and measurement
Section 3110	Asset retirement obligations	IAS 37 Provisions, contingent liabilities,
Section 3290	Contingencies	and contingent assets
AcG-14	Disclosure of guarantees	
Section 3280	Contractual obligations	IAS 1 Presentation of financial statements IAS 16 Property, plant and equipment

Illustration 13-15

Primary Sources of GAAP.

The following are examples of current differences:

Balance sheet classification. IAS 1 is more comprehensive than Section 1510. For example, IAS 1 requires current liabilities to be presented in order of liquidity on the balance sheet when this provides reliable and more relevant information; it also requires any breached long-term debt to be classified as a current liability unless it has been refinanced before the balance sheet date.

Asset retirement obligations. Here, the Canadian requirements are more comprehensive than those in IAS 37, and there are measurement differences for the liability.

Contingencies. Both sets are generally the same, although under IAS 37 a contingent liability that meets the recognition criteria is treated as a provision.

Disclosure of guarantees. IAS 37 addresses the recognition and measurement of non-financial guarantees as well as disclosure requirements, unlike AcG-14, which only deals with their disclosure.

In addition to the above differences, Canadian standards also do not identify specific requirements for "provisions"; instead, the Section 1000 definition of liabilities and general recognition principles are applied to this type of liability. For its part, IAS 37 specifically discusses their measurement, including when an expected value method and discounting should be applied. As this text went to print, changes were being proposed to IAS 37, the primary standard on non-financial liabilities and contingencies. The changes, which are not likely to be effective until 2008 or 2009, are not expected to eliminate any of the differences mentioned above.

Canadian standard setters have indicated, in general, that where there are differences the IFRS will be adopted at the changeover date to international standards. This is expected to occur in 2011.

Summary of Learning Objectives

1 Define liabilities and distinguish financial liabilities from other liabilities.

Liabilities are defined as obligations of an enterprise that are created by past transactions or events and may be settled through a transfer of assets, provision of services, or other yielding of economic benefits in the future. Financial liabilities are a subset of liabilities. They are contractual obligations to deliver cash or other financial assets to another party, or to exchange financial instruments with another party under conditions that are potentially unfavourable.

Student Website

Glossary

www.wiley.com/canada/kieso

KEY TERMS

accretion, 795
accumulated rights, 786

2 Define current liabilities, and identify and account for common types of current liabilities.

Current liabilities are obligations that are payable within one year from the balance sheet date or within the operating cycle if the cycle is longer than a year. The liquidation of a current liability is reasonably expected to require the use of current assets or the creation of other current liabilities. In practice, current liabilities other than borrowings are usually recorded in accounting records and reported in financial statements at their full maturity value. There are several types of current liabilities. The most common are accounts and notes payable, and payroll-related obligations.

3 Explain the classification issues of short-term debt that is expected to be refinanced.

An enterprise excludes a short-term obligation from current liabilities if the following conditions are met: (1) it intends to refinance the obligation on a long-term basis and (2) it demonstrates an ability to complete the refinancing by the time the financial statements are issued.

4 Identify and account for the major types of employee-related liabilities.

Employee-related liabilities include (1) payroll deductions, (2) compensated absences, and (3) bonus agreements. Payroll deductions are amounts that are withheld from employees and result in an obligation to the government. The employer's required contributions that have not yet been remitted are also included in this obligation to the government. Compensated absences earned by employees are company obligations that should be recognized as the employees earn the entitlement to them, as long as they can be reasonably measured. Bonuses that are based on income should be accrued as an expense and liability as the income is earned.

5 Account for common estimated liabilities.

Some liabilities cannot be measured precisely. When a company has an obligation to provide goods or services in the future and the obligation relates to revenue of the current period, for example, the obligation is estimated and reported as a liability and the expense is matched with the associated revenue. When the company later incurs the actual cost (or the reduced revenue) in future periods, the liability is then reduced.

6 Explain the recognition, measurement, and disclosure requirements for asset retirement obligations.

An asset retirement obligation (ARO) is an estimate of the costs that a company is obliged to incur when it retires certain assets. It is recorded as a liability and is usually long-term in nature. The liability is recognized at its fair value as the obligation is incurred and this fair-value amount is added to the cost of the long-lived tangible asset. Over time, the liability is increased for interest and the asset costs are amortized to expense. The obligation amount is also adjusted for changes in the estimate of the costs that are associated with retiring the asset, and it is increased when operations result in additional costs that become obligations. Companies must disclose information about the nature of the ARO and how it is measured, and they must provide a reconciliation that explains any changes from the opening balance of the account to its ending balance.

7 Identify the accounting and reporting requirements for contingent liabilities.

A loss contingency is accrued by a charge to expense and a credit to a liability if (1) information that is available before the issuance of the financial statements shows that it is likely that a liability has been incurred at the date of the financial statements, and (2) the loss amount can be reasonably estimated. If the existence of a liability is likely but it cannot be measured, or if its existence cannot be determined, it is reported in a note to the financial statements.

8 Identify the accounting and reporting requirements for guarantees and commitments.

Commitments, or contractual obligations, do not usually result in a liability at the balance sheet date. Information about certain outstanding commitments is reported at the balance sheet date. Because companies increase their risk by making a variety of financial and non-financial guarantees to outside parties, they are required to disclose information about these guarantees, even if it is unlikely that they will have to make payments under them.

9 Indicate how current liabilities and related items are presented and analyzed.

The current liability accounts are commonly presented as the first classification in the liability section of the balance sheet. Within the current liability section, the accounts may be listed in order of their maturity or in order of their liquidation preference. Additional information must be given about the current liabilities so that there is enough to meet the requirement of full disclosure. Loss contingencies that are likely but not measurable, or whose outcome cannot be determined, should be disclosed in notes to the financial statements. The nature of the contingency and an estimate of the possible loss should be reported. Commitments at year end that are significant in size, risk, or time are disclosed in a note to the financial statements. Three common ratios are used to analyze liquidity: the current, acid-test, and days payables outstanding ratios.

10. Compare current Canadian and international GAAP.

Canadian and international GAAP are substantially harmonized for the aspects of liabilities and contingencies that are covered at the intermediate level of accounting. The IFRS address measurement aspects of estimated liabilities and non-financial guarantees more fully than does Canadian GAAP. There are also some differences in classification and the terms that are used.

Brief Exercises

(LO 2) **BE13-1** Condo Corporation uses a periodic inventory system and the gross method of accounting for purchase discounts. On July 1, Condo purchased $40,000 of inventory, terms 2/10, n/30, FOB shipping point. Condo paid freight costs of $1,200. On July 3, Condo returned damaged goods and received credit of $6,000. On July 10, Condo paid for the goods. Prepare all necessary journal entries for Condo.

(LO 2) **BE13-2** Refer to the data for Condo Corporation in BE13-1. Assuming that Condo instead uses the net approach in accounting for its purchases, prepare all necessary journal entries for Condo.

(LO 2) **BE13-3** Storm Limited borrowed $50,000 on November 1, 2008, by signing a $50,000, three-month, 9% note. Prepare Storm's November 1, 2008, entry; the December 31, 2008, annual adjusting entry; and the February 1, 2009, entry.

(LO 2) **BE13-4** Refer to the data for Storm Limited in BE13-3. Assuming that Storm uses reversing entries, prepare the 2009 journal entry(ies).

(LO 2) **BE13-5** Kawaski Corporation borrowed $50,000 on November 1, 2008, by signing a $51,125, three-month, zero-interest-bearing note. Prepare Kawaski's November 1, 2008, entry; the December 31, 2008, annual adjusting entry; and the February 1, 2009, entry.

(LO 2) **BE13-6** Game Pro Magazine Ltd. sold 10,000 annual subscriptions on August 1, 2008, for $21 each. Prepare Game Pro's August 1, 2008, transaction entry and the December 31, 2008, annual adjusting entry.

(LO 2) **BE13-7** Nixil Limited conducts all its business in a province that has a 5% sales tax as well as the 6% GST, and both taxes are applied on the value of the product or service that is sold. Assume that all of Nixil's sales attract both types of tax. Prepare the summary journal entry to record the company's sales for the month of July, during which customers purchased $45,500 of goods on account.

(LO 2) **BE13-8** Refer to the data for Nixil Limited in BE13-7. Assume now that Nixil purchased $28,800 of merchandise inventory in July on which 6% GST was levied. Nixil uses the periodic inventory system. Prepare the summary entry to record the purchases for July and the subsequent entry to record the payment of any GST owing to the government.

(LO 2) **BE13-9** Gasaro Ltd. made four quarterly payments of $3,200 each to the CRA during 2008 as instalment payments on its estimated 2008 tax liability. At year end, Gasaro's controller completed the company's 2008 tax return, which showed income taxes of $20,000 for its 2008 income. Prepare a summary entry for the quarterly tax instalments and the year-end entry to recognize the 2008 income taxes. Identify any year-end balance sheet amount that is related to income taxes and indicate where it would be reported.

(LO 2) **BE13-10** Refer to the information about Gasaro Ltd. in BE13-9. Assume instead that the tax return indicated 2008 income taxes of $10,200. Identify any year-end balance sheet amount that is related to income taxes and indicate where it would be reported.

(LO 3) **BE13-11** At December 31, 2008, Fifa Corporation owes $500,000 on a note payable due on February 15, 2009. (a) If Fifa refinances the obligation by issuing a long-term note on February 14 and uses the proceeds to pay off the note due on February 15, how much of the $500,000 should be reported as a current liability at December 31, 2008? (b) If Fifa pays off the note on February 15, 2009, and then borrows $1 million on a long-term basis on March 1, how much of the $500,000 should be reported as a current liability at December 31, 2008?

(LO 4) **BE13-12** Zone Corporation's weekly payroll of $23,000 included employee income taxes withheld of $3,426; CPP withheld of $990; EI withheld of $920; and health insurance premiums withheld of $250. Prepare the journal entries to record Zone's payroll.

(LO 4) **BE13-13** Refer to the data for Zone Corporation in BE13-12. Assume now that the employer is required to match every dollar of the CPP contributions of its employees and to contribute 1.4 times the EI withholdings. Prepare the journal entry to record Zone Corporation's payroll-related expenses.

(LO 4) **BE13-14** Refer to the data for Zone Corporation in BE13-12 and BE13-13. Prepare Zone Corporation's entry to record its payroll-related payment to the CRA.

(LO 4) **BE13-15** At December 31, 2008, 30 employees of Tale Spin Inc. have each earned two weeks of vacation time. The employees' average salary is $600 per week. Prepare Tale Spin's December 31, 2008, adjusting entry.

BE13-16 Gargoyle Corporation provides its officers with bonuses based on income. For 2008, the bonuses total **(LO 4)** $450,000 and are paid on February 15, 2009. Prepare Gargoyle's December 31, 2008, adjusting entry and the February 15, 2009, entry.

BE13-17 Janvier Corp. provides at no extra charge a two-year warranty with one of its products, which was first sold in **(LO 5)** 2008. In that year, Janvier spent $63,000 servicing warranty claims. At year end, Janvier estimates that an additional $520,000 will be spent in the future to service warranty claims related to the 2008 sales. Prepare Janvier's journal entry to record the $63,000 expenditure, and the December 31 adjusting entry under Method A.

BE13-18 Refer to data for Janvier Corp. in BE13-17. Prepare entries for the warranty that recognize the full obligation **(LO 5)** at the time of sale, the $63,000 expenditure for servicing the warranty during 2008, and the adjusting entry required at year end, if any, under Method B.

BE13-19 Hill Corporation sells VCRs. The corporation also offers to sell its customers a two-year warranty contract. **(LO 5)** During 2008, Hill sold 15,000 warranty contracts at $93 each. The corporation spent $186,000 servicing warranties during 2008, and it estimates that an additional $1 million will be spent in the future to service the warranties. Hill recognizes revenue based on the proportion of costs incurred out of total estimated costs. Prepare Hill's journal entries for the sale of contracts, the cost of servicing the warranties, and the recognition of warranty revenue.

BE13-20 Klax Corp. offers a set of building blocks to customers who send in three UPC codes from Klax cereal, along **(LO 5)** with $2.00. The block sets cost Klax $1.50 each to purchase and $1.10 each to mail to customers. During 2008, Klax sold one million cereal boxes. The company expects 30% of the UPC codes to be sent in. During 2008, 120,000 UPC codes were redeemed. Prepare Klax's December 31, 2008, adjusting entry.

BE13-21 Kansara Corp. erects and places into service an off-shore oil platform on January 1, 2008, at a cost of $10 mil- **(LO 6)** lion. Kansara is legally required to dismantle and remove the platform at the end of its nine year useful life. The estimated present value of the dismantling and removal costs at January 1, 2008, using an 8% discount rate, is $410,000. Prepare the entry to record the asset retirement obligation.

BE13-22 Refer to the data for Kansara Corp. in BE13-21. Prepare any necessary adjusting entries that are associated **(LO 6)** with the ARO and the asset retirement costs at December 31, 2008.

BE13-23 Justice Inc. is involved in a lawsuit at December 31, 2008. (a) Prepare the December 31 entry assuming it is **(LO 7)** likely that Justice will be liable for $700,000 as a result of this suit. (b) Prepare the December 31 entry, if any, assuming it is not likely that Justice will be liable for any payment as a result of this suit.

BE13-24 Kohlbeck Corp. was recently sued by a competitor for patent infringement. Lawyers have determined that it **(LO 7)** is likely that Kohlbeck will lose the case and that a reasonable estimate of damages to be paid by Kohlbeck is $200,000. In light of this case, Kohlbeck is considering establishing a $100,000 self-insurance allowance. What entry(ies), if any, should Kohlbeck record to recognize this loss contingency?

BE13-25 Bakhshi Corporation shows the following financial position and results for the three years ended December **(LO 9)** 31, 2008, 2009, and 2010 (in thousands):

	2010	2009	2008
Cash	$ 650	$ 700	$ 600
Temporary investments	500	500	500
Accounts receivable	900	1,000	1,300
Inventory	4,900	4,600	4,000
Prepaid expenses	1,300	1,000	900
Total current assets	$ 8,250	$ 7,800	$ 7,300
Accounts payable	$ 1,550	$ 1,700	$ 1,750
Accrued liabilities	2,250	2,000	1,900
Total current liabilities	$ 3,800	$ 3,700	$ 3,650
Cost of goods sold	$15,000	$18,000	$17,000

For each year, calculate the current ratio, quick ratio, and days payables outstanding ratio, and comment on your results.

Exercises

(LO 1) **E13-1** **(Balance Sheet Classification of Various Liabilities)** How would each of the following items be reported on the balance sheet? If you identify an item as a liability, indicate whether or not it is a financial liability.

(a) Accrued vacation pay

(b) Income tax instalments paid in excess of the income tax liability on the year's income

(c) Service warranties on appliance sales

(d) A bank overdraft

(e) Employee payroll deductions unremitted

(f) Unpaid bonus to officers

(g) A deposit received from a customer to guarantee performance of a contract

(h) Sales taxes payable

(i) Gift certificates sold to customers but not yet redeemed

(j) Premium offers outstanding

(k) A royalty fee owing on units produced

(l) A personal injury claim pending

(m) Current maturities of long-term debts to be paid from current assets

(n) Cash dividends declared but unpaid

(o) Dividends in arrears on preferred shares

(p) Loans from officers

(q) GST collected on sales in excess of GST paid on purchases

(r) An asset retirement obligation

(s) The portion of a credit facility that has been used

(LO 2) **E13-2** **(Accounts and Notes Payable)** The following are selected 2008 transactions of Astin Corporation:

Sept. 1 Purchased inventory from Encino Company on account for $50,000. Astin records purchases gross and uses a periodic inventory system.
Oct. 1   Issued a $50,000, 12-month, 12% note to Encino in payment of Astin's account.
Oct. 1   Borrowed $50,000 from the bank by signing a 12-month, non-interest-bearing $56,000 note.

Instructions

(a) Prepare journal entries for each of the transactions.

(b) Prepare adjusting entries at December 31, 2008.

(c) Calculate the net liability, in total, to be reported on the December 31, 2008, balance sheet for the following:

1. The interest-bearing note

2. The non-interest-bearing note

(d) Prepare the journal entries for the payment of the notes at maturity.

(e) Repeat part (d) assuming the company uses reversing entries (show the reversing entries at January 1, 2009). Would the use of reversing entries be efficient for both types of notes?

(LO 2) **E13-3** **(Entries for Sales Taxes)** Stratton Corporation is a merchant and operates in the province of Ontario, where the PST rate is 8%. Stratton uses a perpetual inventory system. Transactions for the business for the month of March are as follows:

Mar. 1 Paid March rent to the landlord for the rental of a warehouse. The lease calls for monthly payments of $5,500 plus 6% GST.
3 Sold merchandise on account and shipped merchandise to Marvin Ltd. for $20,000, terms n/30, FOB shipping point. This merchandise cost Stratton $11,000.

Mar. 5 Granted Marvin a sales allowance of $500 (exclusive of taxes) for defective merchandise purchased on March 3. No merchandise was returned.

7 Purchased merchandise for resale on account from Tiller Ltd. at a list price of $14,000, plus applicable tax.

12 Made a cash purchase at Home Depot of a desk for the shipping clerk. The price of the desk was $600 before applicable taxes.

31 Paid the monthly remittance of GST to the Receiver General.

Instructions

(a) Prepare the journal entries to record these transactions on the books of Stratton Company.

(b) Assume instead that Stratton operates in the province of Alberta, where PST is not applicable. Prepare the journal entries to record these transactions on the books of Stratton.

(c) Assume instead that Stratton operates in the province of Prince Edward Island, where 10% PST is also charged on the GST. Prepare the journal entries to record these transactions on the books of Stratton.

(d) Assume instead that Stratton operates in the province of New Brunswick, where HST is 15%. Prepare the journal entries to record these transactions on the books of Stratton.

E13-4 (Liability for Returnable Containers) Diagnostics Corp. sells its products in expensive, reusable containers. **(LO 2)** The customer is charged a deposit for each container that is delivered and receives a refund for each container that is returned within two years after the year of delivery. When a container is not returned within the time limit, Diagnostics accounts for the container as being sold at the deposit amount. Information for 2008 is as follows:

Containers held by customers at December 31, 2007, from deliveries in:	2006	$170,000	
	2007	480,000	$650,000
Containers delivered in 2008			894,000
Containers returned in 2008 from deliveries in:	2006	$115,000	
	2007	280,000	
	2008	310,400	705,400

Instructions

(a) Prepare all journal entries required for Diagnostics Corp. for the reusable containers during 2008.

(b) Calculate the total amount that Diagnostics should report as a liability for reusable containers at December 31, 2008.

(c) Should the liability calculated in (b) be reported as current or long-term? Explain.

(AICPA adapted)

E13-5 (Income Taxes) Shikkiah Corp. began its 2008 fiscal year with a debit balance of $11,250 in its Income Taxes **(LO 2)** Receivable account. During the year, the company made quarterly income tax instalment payments of $8,100 each. In early June, a cheque was received from the CRA for Shikkiah's overpayment of 2007 taxes. The refunded amount was exactly as Shikkiah had calculated it would be on its 2007 income tax return. On completion of the 2008 income tax return, it was determined that Shikkiah's income taxes based on 2008 income were $37,800.

Instructions

(a) Prepare all journal entries that are necessary to record the 2008 transactions and events.

(b) Indicate how the income taxes will be reported on Shikkiah's December 31, 2008, balance sheet.

(c) Assume that the cheque from the CRA in early June is for $2,750. The difference arose because of calculation errors on Shikkiah's tax return. How would the difference be accounted for and where would it be shown on Shikkiah's financial statements?

E13-6 (Refinancing of Short-Term Debt) On December 31, 2008, Hattie Corporation had $1.2 million of short- **(LO 3)** term debt in the form of notes payable due on February 2, 2009. On January 21, 2009, the company issued 25,000 common shares for $38 per share, receiving $950,000 in proceeds after brokerage fees and other costs of issuance. On February 2, 2009, the proceeds from the sale of the shares, along with an additional $250,000 cash, are used to liquidate the $1.2 million debt. The December 31, 2008, balance sheet is issued on February 23, 2009.

Instructions

Show how the $1.2 million of short-term debt should be presented on the December 31, 2008, balance sheet, including the note disclosure.

(LO 3)   E13-7   (Refinancing of Short-Term Debt) On December 31, 2008, Zarle Corporation has $7.9 million of short-term debt in the form of notes payable that will be due periodically in 2009 to Provincial Bank. On January 28, 2009, Zarle enters into a refinancing agreement with the bank that will permit it to borrow up to 60% of the gross amount of its accounts receivable. Receivables are expected to range between a low of $5.7 million in May and a high of $7 million in October during the year 2009. The interest cost of the maturing short-term debt is 15%, and the new agreement calls for a fluctuating interest rate at 1% above the prime rate on notes due in 2010. Zarle's December 31, 2008, balance sheet is issued on February 15, 2009.

Instructions

Prepare a partial balance sheet for Zarle Corporation at December 31, 2008, that shows how its $7.9 million of short-term debt should be presented, including any necessary note disclosures.

(LO 4)   E13-8   (Compensated Absences) Mostel Limited began operations on January 2, 2007. The company employs nine individuals who work eight-hour days and are paid hourly. Each employee earns 10 paid vacation days and six paid sick days annually. Vacation days may be taken after January 15 of the year following the year in which they are earned. Sick days may be taken as soon as they are earned; unused sick days accumulate. Additional information is as follows:

Actual Hourly Wage Rate		Vacation Days Used by Each Employee		Sick Days Used by Each Employee	
2007	2008	2007	2008	2007	2008
$10	$11	0	9	4	5

Mostel Limited has chosen to accrue the cost of compensated absences at rates of pay in effect during the period when they are earned and to accrue sick pay when it is earned.

Instructions

(a) Prepare journal entry(ies) to record the transactions related to vacation entitlement during 2007 and 2008.

(b) Prepare journal entry(ies) to record the transactions related to sick days during 2007 and 2008.

(c) Calculate the amounts of any liability for vacation pay and sick days that should be reported on the balance sheet at December 31, 2007 and 2008.

(d) How would your answers to parts (b) and (c) change if the entitlement to sick days did not accumulate?

(LO 4)   E13-9   (Compensated Absences) Refer to the data in E13-8 and assume instead that Mostel Limited has chosen not to recognize paid sick leave until it is used, and has chosen to accrue vacation time at expected future rates of pay without discounting. The company uses the following projected rates to accrue vacation time:

Year in Which Vacation Time Was Earned	Projected Future Pay Rates Used to Accrue Vacation Pay
2007	$10.75 per hour
2008	$11.60 per hour

Instructions

(a) Prepare journal entry(ies) to record the transactions related to vacation entitlement during 2007 and 2008.

(b) Prepare journal entry(ies) to record the transactions related to sick days during 2007 and 2008.

(c) Calculate the amounts of any liability for vacation pay and sick days that should be reported on the balance sheet at December 31, 2007 and 2008.

(LO 4)   E13-10   (Payroll Tax Entries) The payroll of Auber Corp. for September 2008 is as follows: Total payroll was $495,000. Pensionable (CPP) and insurable (EI) earnings were $375,000. Income taxes in the amount of $90,000 were withheld, as was $9,000 in union dues. The employment insurance tax rate was 1.80% for employees and 2.52% for employers and the CPP rate was 4.95% for employees and 4.95% for employers.

Instructions

(a) Prepare the necessary journal entries to record the payroll if the wages and salaries paid and the employer payroll taxes are recorded separately.

(b) Prepare the entries to record the payment of all required amounts to the CRA and to the employees' union.

(c) For every dollar of wages and salaries that Auber commits to pay, what is the actual payroll cost to the company?

(d) Discuss any other costs, direct or indirect, that you think would add to the company's costs of having employees.

E13-11 **(Bonus Calculation and Income Statement Preparation)** The incomplete income statement of Pippen Corp. **(LO 4)** follows:

PIPPEN CORP.
Income Statement
For the Year 2008

Revenue		$10,000,000
Cost of goods sold		7,000,000
Gross profit		3,000,000
Administrative and selling expenses	$1,000,000	
Profit-sharing bonus to employees	_____?	_____?
Income before income taxes		_____?
Income taxes		_____?
Net income		$_____?

The employee profit-sharing plan requires that 20% of all profits remaining after the deduction of the bonus and income taxes be distributed to the employees by the first day of the fourth month following each year end. The income tax rate is 45%, and the bonus is tax-deductible.

Instructions

(a) Complete the condensed income statement of Pippen Corp. for the year 2008. You will need to develop two simultaneous equations to solve for the bonus amount: one for the bonus and one for the tax.

(b) Prepare the journal entry to record the bonus at December 31, 2008.

E13-12 **(Warranties)** Canoun Corporation sold 200 photocopiers in 2008 for $2,600 each, including a one-year **(LO 5)** warranty. Maintenance on each machine during the warranty period averages $380.

Instructions

(a) Prepare entries to record the machine sales and the related warranty costs under GAAP. Actual warranty costs incurred in 2008 were $18,000.

(b) Based on the data above and assuming that the cash basis is used, prepare the appropriate entries.

(c) Is the method in (b) ever acceptable under GAAP? Explain.

E13-13 **(Warranties)** Crowne Equipment Limited sold 500 Rollomatics on account during 2008 at $6,000 each. During **(LO 5)** 2008, Crowne spent $20,000 servicing the two-year warranties that are included in each sale of the Rollomatic. All servicing transactions were paid in cash.

Instructions

(a) Prepare the 2008 entries for Crowne using the expense warranty approach. Assume that Crowne estimates the total cost of servicing the warranties will be $120,000 for two years.

(b) Prepare the 2008 entries for Crowne assuming that the warranties are not an integral part of the sale. Assume that of the sales total, $150,000 is identified as relating specifically to sales of warranty contracts. Crowne estimates the total cost of servicing the warranties will be $120,000 for two years. Because the repair costs are not incurred evenly, warranty revenues are recognized based on the proportion of costs incurred out of the total estimated costs.

(c) What amounts would be shown on Crowne's income statement under parts (a) and (b)? Explain the resulting difference in the company's net income.

E13-14 **(Premium Entries)** Rani Corporation includes one coupon in each box of soap powder that it packs, and 10 **(LO 5)** coupons are redeemable for a premium (a kitchen utensil). In 2008, Rani Corporation purchased 8,800 premiums at $1.00 each and sold 110,000 boxes of soap powder at $5.00 per box. In total, 44,000 coupons were presented for redemption in 2008. It is estimated that 69% of the coupons will eventually be presented for redemption.

Instructions

(a) Prepare all the entries that would be made for sales of soap powder and for the premium plan in 2008.

(b) What amounts relative to soap powder sales and premiums would be shown on Rani's financial statements for 2008?

E13-15 **(Premiums)** Two independent situations follow:

1. In packages of its products, ITSS Inc. includes coupons that may be presented at retail stores to obtain discounts on **(LO 5)** other ITSS products. Retailers are reimbursed for the face amount of coupons redeemed plus 10% of that amount for

handling costs. ITSS honours requests for coupon redemption by retailers up to three months after the consumer expiration date. ITSS estimates that 60% of all coupons issued will eventually be redeemed. Information relating to coupons issued by ITSS during 2008 is as follows:

Consumer expiration date	12/31/08
Total face amount of coupons issued	$800,000
Total payments to retailers as at 12/31/08	$330,000

(a) What amount should ITSS report as a liability for unredeemed coupons at December 31, 2008?

(b) What amount of premium expense should ITSS report on its 2008 income statement?

2. Baylor Corp. sold 700,000 boxes of pie mix under a new sales promotion program. Each box contains one coupon that entitles the customer to a baking pan when the coupon is submitted with an additional $4.00 from the customer. Baylor pays $5.00 per pan and $1.00 for handling and shipping. Baylor estimates that 70% of the coupons will be redeemed even though only 250,000 coupons had been processed during 2008.

(a) What amount should Baylor report as a liability for unredeemed coupons at December 31, 2008?

(b) What amount of expense will Baylor report on its 2008 income statement as a result of the promotional program?

(c) Prepare any necessary 2008 journal entries to record the coupon liability and redemptions.

(AICPA adapted)

(LO 5) E13-16 (Warranties) Cranmore Corporation manufactures a line of amplifiers that carry a three-year warranty against defects. Based on experience, the estimated warranty costs related to dollar sales are as follows: first year after sale—2% of sales; second year after sale—3% of sales; and third year after sale—4% of sales. Sales and actual warranty expenditures for the first three years of business were:

	Sales	Warranty Expenditures
2007	$ 810,000	$ 6,500
2008	1,070,000	17,200
2009	1,036,000	62,000

Instructions

(a) Calculate the amount that Cranmore Corporation should report as warranty expense on its 2009 income statement and as a warranty liability on its December 31, 2009, balance sheet. Assume that all sales are made evenly throughout each year and that warranty expenditures are also evenly spaced according to the rates above.

(b) Assume that Cranmore's warranty expenditures in the first year after sale end up being 4% of sales, which is twice as much as was forecast. How would management account for this change?

(LO 6) E13-17 (Asset Retirement Obligation) Oil Products Limited purchases an oil tanker depot on July 2, 2008, at a cost of $600,000 and expects to operate the depot for 10 years. After the ten years, the company is legally required to dismantle the depot and remove the underground storage tanks. It is estimated that it will cost $75,000 to do this at the end of the depot's useful life.

Instructions

(a) Prepare the journal entries to record the acquisition of the depot and the asset retirement obligation for the depot on July 2, 2008. Based on an effective interest rate of 6%, the present value of the asset retirement obligation (i.e., its fair value) on the date of acquisition is $41,879.

(b) Prepare any journal entries required for the depot and the asset retirement obligation at December 31, 2008. Oil Products uses straight-line amortization. The estimated residual value of the depot is zero.

(c) On June 30, 2018, Oil Products pays a demolition firm to dismantle the depot and remove the tanks at a cost of $80,000. Prepare the journal entry for the settlement of the asset retirement obligation.

(d) Prepare the schedule to calculate the balance in the asset retirement obligation account for all years from 2008 to 2018, assuming there is no change in the estimated cost of dismantling the depot.

(e) Show how all relevant amounts will be reported on Oil Products Limited's financial statements at December 31, 2008.

(f) How would the accretion expense be reported on the statement of cash flows?

E13-18 **(Contingencies and Commitments)** Four independent situations follow. Answer the question at the end of **(LO 7)** each situation.

1. During 2008, Salt-n-Pepper Inc. became involved in a tax dispute with the CRA. Salt-n-Pepper's lawyers have informed management that Salt-n-Pepper will likely lose this dispute. They also believe that Salt-n-Pepper will have to pay the CRA between $900,000 and $1.4 million. After the 2008 financial statements were issued, the case was settled with the CRA for $1.2 million. What amount, if any, should be reported as a liability for this contingency as at December 31, 2008?

2. Toward the end of Su Li Corp.'s 2008 fiscal year, employer-union talks broke off with the wage rates for the upcoming two years still unresolved. Just before the new year, however, a contract was signed that gave employees a 5% increase in their hourly wage. Su Li had expended $1.2 million in wages on this group of workers in 2008. Prepare the entry, if any, that Su Li Corp. should make at December 31, 2008. Briefly explain your answer.

3. On October 1, 2008, the provincial environment ministry identified Jackson Chemical Inc. as a potentially responsible party in a chemical spill. Jackson's management, along with its legal counsel, have concluded that it is likely that Jackson will be responsible for damages, and a reasonable estimate of these damages is $5 million. Jackson's insurance policy of $9 million has a deductible clause of $500,000. How should Jackson Chemical report this information in its financial statements at December 31, 2008?

4. Etheridge Inc. had a manufacturing plant in Bosnia that was destroyed in the civil war. It is not certain who will compensate Etheridge for this destruction, but Etheridge has been assured by Bosnian governmental officials that it will receive a definite amount for this plant. The compensation amount will be less than the plant's fair value, but more than its book value. How should the contingency be reported in the financial statements of Etheridge Inc.?

E13-19 **(Financial Statement Impact of Liability Transactions)** The following is a list of possible transactions: **(LO 2, 4, 5, 7, 8)**

1. Purchased inventory for $80,000 on account (assume perpetual system is used).

2. Issued an $80,000 note payable in payment of an account (see item 1 above).

3. Recorded accrued interest on the note from item 2 above.

4. Borrowed $100,000 from the bank by signing a $112,000, six-month, non-interest-bearing note.

5. Recognized four months of interest expense on the note from item 4 above.

6. Recorded cash sales of $75,260, which includes 6% sales tax.

7. Recorded wage expense of $35,000. The cash paid was $25,000; the difference was due to various amounts withheld.

8. Recorded employer's payroll taxes.

9. Accrued accumulated vacation pay.

10. Signed a $2-million contract with Construction Corp. to build a new plant.

11. Recorded bonuses due to employees.

12. Recorded a contingent loss on a lawsuit that the company will probably lose.

13. Accrued warranty expense (assume expense warranty approach).

14. Paid warranty costs that were accrued in item 13 above.

15. Recorded sales of product and separately sold warranties.

16. Paid warranty costs under contracts from item 15 above.

17. Recognized warranty revenue (see item 15 above).

18. Recorded estimated liability for premium claims outstanding.

19. Recorded the receipt of a cash down payment on services to be performed in the next accounting period.

20. Received the remainder of the contracted amount and performed the services related to item 19 above.

Instructions

Set up a table using the format that follows and analyze the effects of the 20 transactions on the financial statement categories in the table. Use the following codes: increase (I); decrease (D); no net effect (NE).

Transaction	Assets	Liabilities	Owners' Equity	Net Income
1				

(LO 9)   E13-20   (Ratio Calculations and Discussion) Sprague Corporation has been operating for several years, and on December 31, 2008, presented the following balance sheet:

SPRAGUE CORPORATION
Balance Sheet
December 31, 2008

Cash	$ 40,000	Accounts payable	$ 80,000
Receivables	75,000	Mortgage payable	140,000
Inventories	95,000	Common shares (no par)	150,000
Plant assets (net)	220,000	Retained earnings	60,000
	$430,000		$430,000

Cost of goods sold in 2008 was $450,000, operating expenses were $54,000, and net income was $25,000. Accounts payable suppliers provided operating goods and services. Assume that total assets are the same in 2007 and 2008.

Instructions

Calculate each of the following ratios. For each ratio, also indicate how it is calculated and what its significance is as a tool for analyzing the financial soundness of the company.

(a) current ratio   (c) debt-to-total-assets ratio   (e) days payables outstanding

(b) acid-test ratio   (d) rate of return on assets

(LO 9)   E13-21   (Ratio Calculations and Analysis) Hood Limited's condensed financial statements provide the following information:

HOOD LIMITED
Balance Sheet

	Dec. 31, 2008	Dec. 31, 2007
Cash	$ 52,000	$ 60,000
Accounts receivable (net)	198,000	80,000
Marketable securities (short-term)	80,000	40,000
Inventories	440,000	360,000
Prepaid expenses	3,000	7,000
Total current assets	773,000	547,000
Property, plant, and equipment (net)	857,000	853,000
Total assets	$1,630,000	$1,400,000
Accounts payable	$ 220,000	$ 145,000
Other current liabilities	20,000	15,000
Bonds payable	400,000	400,000
Common shareholders' equity	990,000	840,000
Total liabilities and shareholders' equity	$1,630,000	$1,400,000

Income Statement
For the Year Ended December 31, 2008

Sales	$1,640,000
Cost of goods sold	(800,000)
Gross profit	840,000
Selling and administrative expense	(440,000)
Interest expense	(40,000)
Net income	$ 360,000

Instructions

(a) Determine the following:

1. Current ratio at December 31, 2008
2. Acid-test ratio at December 31, 2008
3. Accounts receivable turnover for 2008
4. Inventory turnover for 2008
5. Days payables outstanding for 2008
6. Rate of return on assets for 2008
7. Profit margin on sales

(b) Prepare a brief evaluation of the financial condition of Hood Limited and of the adequacy of its profits.

(c) In examining the other current liabilities on Hood Limited's balance sheet, you observe that unearned revenues have declined in the current year compared to the previous year. Is this a positive indicator about the client's liquidity? Explain.

E13-22 (Ratio Calculations and Effect of Transactions) Financial information for Carver Inc. follows: **(LO 9)**

CARVER INC.
Balance Sheet
December 31, 2008

Cash		$ 45,000	Notes payable (short-term)	$ 50,000
Receivables	$110,000		Accounts payable	32,000
Less: Allowance	15,000	95,000	Accrued liabilities	5,000
Inventories		170,000	Share capital (52,000 shares)	260,000
Prepaid insurance		8,000	Retained earnings	141,000
Land		20,000		
Equipment (net)		150,000		
		$488,000		$488,000

Income Statement
For the Year Ended December 31, 2008

Sales		$1,400,000
Cost of goods sold		
Inventory, Jan. 1, 2008	$200,000	
Purchases	790,000	
Cost of goods available for sale	990,000	
Inventory, Dec. 31, 2008	170,000	
Cost of goods sold		820,000
Gross profit on sales		580,000
Operating expenses		170,000
Net income		$ 410,000

Instructions

(a) Calculate the following ratios or relationships of Carver Inc. Assume that the ending account balances are representative unless the information provided indicates differently.

1. Current ratio
2. Inventory turnover
3. Receivables turnover
4. Average age of receivables (days sales outstanding)
5. Average age of payables (days payables outstanding)
6. Earnings per share
7. Profit margin on sales
8. Rate of return on assets

(b) For each of the following transactions, indicate whether the transaction would improve, weaken, or have no effect on the current ratio of Carver Inc. at December 31, 2008:

1. Writing off an uncollectible account receivable for $2,200
2. Receiving a $20,000 down payment on services to be performed in 2009
3. Paying $40,000 on notes payable (short-term)
4. Collecting $23,000 on accounts receivable
5. Purchasing equipment on account
6. Giving an existing creditor a short-term note in settlement of an open account owed

Problems

P13-1   The following are selected transactions of Ping Department Store Ltd. for the current year ending December 31:

1. On February 2, the company purchased goods having cash discount terms of 2/10, n/30 from Haley Limited for $50,000. Purchases and accounts payable are recorded using the periodic system at net amounts after cash discounts. The invoice was paid on February 26.

2. On April 1, Ping purchased a truck for $40,000 from Smith Motors Limited, paying $4,000 cash and signing a one-year, 12% note for the balance of the purchase price.

3. On May 1, the company borrowed $80,000 from Second Provincial Bank by signing a $92,000 non-interest-bearing note due one year from May 1.

4. On June 30 and December 31, Ping remitted cheques for $22,000 each as instalments on its current year tax liability.

5. On August 14, the board of directors declared a $15,000 cash dividend that was payable on September 10 to shareholders of record on August 31.

6. On December 5, the store received $500 from Jackson Players as a deposit on furniture that Jackson Players is using in its stage production. The deposit is to be returned to the theatre company after it returns the furniture on January 15.

7. On December 10, the store purchased new display cases for $9,000 on account. Sales tax of 5% and GST of 6% were charged by the supplier on the purchase price.

8. During December, cash sales of $83,500 were recorded, plus a 5% sales tax and 6% GST that must be remitted by the 15th day of the following month. Both taxes are levied on the sale amount to the customer.

9. Ping's lease for its store premises calls for a $2,500 monthly rental payment plus 3% of all sales. The payment is due one week after month end.

10. Ping is required to restore the area surrounding one of its store parking lots, at an estimated cost of $100,000, when the store is closed in two years. Ping estimates that the fair value of this obligation at December 31 is $84,000.

11. The corporate tax return indicated taxable income of $210,000. Ping's income tax rate is 25%.

Instructions

(a) Prepare all the journal entries that are necessary to record the above transactions when they occurred and any adjusting journal entries relative to the transactions that would be required to present fair financial statements at December 31. Date each entry.

(b) Identify the current liabilities that will be reported on the December 31 balance sheet, and indicate the amount of each one.

(c) Prepare the journal entries for transactions 7 and 8 above if the 5% sales tax is applied on the purchase or sale amount plus the GST.

(d) Why is the liabilities section of the balance sheet of primary significance to bankers?

(e) How are current liabilities related by definition to current assets?

P13-2   Bakshi Inc. financed the purchase of equipment costing $85,000 on January 1, 2008, using a note payable. The note requires Bakshi to make annual $32,389 payments of blended interest and principal on January 1 of the following three years, beginning January 1, 2009. The note bears interest at the rate of 7%.

Instructions

(a) Prepare the debt amortization schedule for the note over its term.

(b) Prepare the journal entry(ies) that are required for the year ended December 31, 2008, and the first instalment payment on January 1, 2009.

(c) Prepare the balance sheet presentation of the note at December 31, 2008 (include both the current and long-term portions).

(d) Prepare the balance sheet presentation of the note at December 31, 2009.

(e) Redo part (c) assuming that the equipment was purchased on July 1, 2008, and the payments are due beginning July 1, 2009.

P13-3   Starr Company Limited pays its office employees each week. A partial list follows of employees and their payroll data for August. Because August is the vacation period, vacation pay is also listed.

Employee	Weekly Pay	Vacation Pay to Be Received in August
Mark Hamud	$ 480	
Carrie Frisher	450	$ 900
Harry Fyord	110	220
Alexa Guinner	250	
Peter Cash	1,250	2,500

Assume that the income tax withheld is 10% of wages and that union dues withheld are 1% of wages. Vacations are taken the second and third weeks of August by Frisher, Fyord, and Cash. The employment insurance rate is 1.80% for employees and 1.4 times that for employers. The CPP rate is 4.95% for employee and employer.

Instructions

(a) Make the journal entries that are necessary for each of the four August payrolls. The entries for the payroll and for the company's payroll taxes are made separately.

(b) Make the entry to record the monthly payment of accrued payroll liabilities.

(c) Prepare the entry to accrue the 4% vacation entitlement that was earned by employees in August. (No entitlement is earned on vacation pay.)

P13-4   The following is a payroll sheet for Empire Import Corporation for the month of September 2008. The employment insurance rate is 1.80%, and the maximum annual amount per employee is $720. The employer's obligation for employment insurance is 1.4 times the amount of the employee deduction. Assume a 10% income tax rate for all employees, and a 4.95% CPP premium charged to both the employee and employer, up to an annual maximum of $1,989.90 per employee. Union dues are 1% of earnings.

Name	Earnings to Aug. 31	September Earnings	Income Tax Withholding	CPP	EI	Union Dues
B.D. Williams	$ 6,800	$ 800				
D. Prowse	6,300	700				
K. Baker	7,600	1,100				
F. Oz	13,600	1,900				

Instructions

(a) Complete the payroll sheet and make the necessary entry to record the payment of the payroll.

(b) Make the entry to record the employer's payroll tax expenses.

(c) Make the entry to record the payment of the payroll liabilities. Assume that the company pays all payroll liabilities at the end of each month.

(d) What is the total expense that the company will report in September 2008 relative to employee compensation?

P13-5   Henrik Inc. has a contract with its president, Ms. Sarrat, to pay her a bonus during each of the years 2008, 2009, and 2010. Assume a corporate income tax rate of 40% during the three years. The profit before deductions for bonus and income taxes was $250,000 in 2008, $308,000 in 2009, and $350,000 in 2010. The president's bonus of 12% is deductible for tax purposes in each year and is to be calculated as follows:

(a) In 2008, the bonus is to be based on profit before deductions for bonus and income tax.

(b) In 2009, the bonus is to be based on profit after deduction of bonus but before deduction of income tax.

(c) In 2010, the bonus is to be based on profit before deduction of bonus but after deduction of income tax.

Instructions
Calculate the amounts of the bonus and the income tax for each of the three years.

P13-6   Barbeau Corporation sells portable equipment with a two-year warranty contract that requires the corporation to replace defective parts and provide the necessary repair labour. During 2008, the corporation sells for cash 260 units at a unit price of $4,600. Based on experience, the two-year warranty costs are estimated to be $155 for parts and $185 for labour per unit. (For simplicity, assume that all sales occurred on December 31, 2008.) The warranty is not sold separately from the equipment, and no portion of the sales price is allocated to warranty sales.

Instructions
Answer (a) to (d) based on the information above.

(a) Record the 2008 journal entries, assuming the cash basis is used to account for the warranties.

(b) Record the 2008 journal entries, assuming the accrual basis is used to account for the warranties.

(c) What liability relative to these transactions would appear on the December 31, 2008, balance sheet and how would it be classified if the cash basis is used?

(d) What liability relative to these transactions would appear on the December 31, 2008, balance sheet and how would it be classified if the accrual basis is used?

Answer (e) to (h) assuming that in 2009 the actual warranty costs incurred by Barbeau Corporation were $21,400 for parts and $24,900 for labour.

(e) Record the necessary entries in 2009, applying the cash basis.

(f) Record the necessary entries in 2009, applying the accrual basis.

(g) Which method would you recommend to the company. Why?

(h) Assume that the warranty costs incurred by Barbeau Corporation in 2010 were substantially higher than estimated. How would the company deal with the discrepancy between the estimated warranty liability and actual warranty expense?

P13-7   Selamou Corporation sells televisions at an average price of $850 and they come with a standard one-year warranty. The company also offers each customer a separate three-year extended warranty contract for $90 that requires the company to perform periodic services and replace defective parts. The extended warranty begins one year after the purchase date. During 2008, the company sold 300 televisions and 270 extended warranty contracts for cash. Company records indicate that warranty costs in the first year after purchase average $25 per set: $15 for parts, and $10 for labour. Selamou estimates the average three-year extended warranty costs as $20 for parts and $40 for labour. Assume that all sales occurred on December 31, 2008, and that all warranty costs are expected to be incurred evenly over the warranty period.

Instructions
Answer (a) and (b) based on the information above.

(a) Record any necessary journal entries in 2008.

(b) What liabilities relative to these transactions would appear on the December 31, 2008, balance sheet and how would they be classified?

Answer (c) and (d) assuming that in 2009 Selamou Corporation incurred actual costs relative to 2008 television warranty sales of $4,410 for parts and $2,940 for labour.

(c) Record any necessary journal entries in 2009 relative to the 2008 television warranties.

(d) What amounts relative to the 2008 television warranties would appear on the December 31, 2009, balance sheet and how would they be classified?

Answer (e) and (f) assuming that in 2010 Selamou Corporation incurred the following costs relative to the extended warranties sold in 2008: $2,000 for parts and $3,000 for labour.

(e) Record any necessary journal entries in 2010 relative to the 2008 television warranties.

(f) What amounts relative to the 2008 television warranties would appear on the December 31, 2010, balance sheet and how would they be classified?

P13-8   Belle Limited sells a machine for $7,400 and it comes with a 12-month warranty agreement that requires the company to replace all defective parts and to provide repair labour at no cost to the customer. In 2008, sales occurred evenly throughout the year and resulted in 650 machines being sold in total. As a result of product testing, the company estimated that the warranty cost would be $370 per machine ($170 for parts and $200 for labour). The actual warranty costs were eventually incurred exactly as had been estimated, with half of the repairs occurring in 2008 and the other half in 2009.

Instructions

(a) Assuming that actual warranty costs are incurred exactly as estimated, what journal entries would be made under GAAP for the following?

1. The sale of machinery in 2008
2. The warranty costs incurred in 2008
3. The warranty expense charged against 2008 revenues
4. The warranty costs incurred in 2009

(b) Assuming that actual warranty costs are incurred exactly as estimated, what journal entries would be made if the cash basis were used for the following?

1. The sale of machinery in 2008
2. The warranty costs incurred in 2008
3. The warranty expense charged against 2008 revenues
4. The warranty costs incurred in 2009

(c) What amount, if any, is disclosed in the balance sheet as a liability for future warranty costs as at December 31, 2008, and December 31, 2009, under each method?

(d) Which method better reflects Belle Limited's income in 2008 and 2009? Why?

(e) Assume that the machine sold by Belle Limited undergoes technological improvements and management now has no past experience on which to estimate the extent of the warranty costs. The chief engineer believes that product warranty costs are likely to be incurred, but they cannot be reasonably estimated. What advice would you give on how to account for and report the warranties?

P13-9 To stimulate the sales of its Krusch breakfast cereal, Khamsah Corporation places one coupon in each cereal box. Five coupons are redeemable for a premium consisting of a child's hand puppet. In 2008, the company purchases 31,000 puppets at $1.50 each and sells 440,000 boxes of Krusch at $3.50 a box. From its experience with other similar premium offers, the company estimates that 32% of the coupons issued will be mailed back for redemption. During 2008, 105,000 coupons are presented for redemption.

Instructions

(a) Prepare the journal entries that should be recorded in 2008 relative to the premium plan, assuming that the company follows a policy of charging the cost of coupons to expense as they are redeemed and adjusting the liability account at year end.

(b) Prepare the journal entries that should be recorded in 2008 relative to the premium plan, assuming that the company follows a policy of charging the full estimated cost of the premium plan to expense when the sales are recognized.

(c) How would the accounts resulting from the entries in (a) and (b) above be presented on the 2008 financial statements?

P13-10 The Hernandez Candy Corporation offers a CD as a premium for every five chocolate bar wrappers that customers send in along with $2.00. The chocolate bars are sold by the company to distributors for 30 cents each. The purchase price of each CD to the company is $1.80; in addition, it costs 50 cents to mail each CD. The results of the premium plan for the years 2008 and 2009 are as follows (all purchases and sales are for cash):

	2008	2009
CDs purchased	250,000	330,000
Chocolate bars sold	2,895,400	2,743,600
Wrappers redeemed	1,200,000	1,500,000
2008 wrappers expected to be redeemed in 2009	290,000	
2009 wrappers expected to be redeemed in 2010		350,000

Instructions

(a) Prepare the journal entries that should be made in 2008 and 2009 to record the transactions related to the premium plan of the Hernandez Candy Corporation.

(b) Indicate the account names, amounts, and classifications of the items related to the premium plan that would appear on the balance sheet and the income statement at the end of 2008 and 2009.

(c) For each liability that you identified in (b), indicate whether its account is a financial liability. Explain.

P13-11   Paris Airlines is faced with two situations that need to be resolved before the financial statements for the company's year ended December 31, 2008, can be issued:

1. The airline is being sued for $4 million for an injury caused to a child as a result of alleged negligence while the child was visiting the airline maintenance hangar in March 2008. The suit was filed in July 2008. Paris's lawyer states that it is likely that the airline will lose the suit and be found liable for a judgement costing anywhere from $400,000 to $2 million. However, the lawyer states that the most probable judgement is $800,000.

2. On November 24, 2008, 26 passengers on Flight No. 901 were injured upon landing when the plane skidded off the runway. Personal injury suits for damages totalling $5 million were filed against the airline by 18 injured passengers on January 11, 2009. The airline carries no insurance. Legal counsel has studied each suit and advised Paris that it can reasonably expect to pay 60% of the damages claimed.

Instructions

(a) Prepare any disclosures and journal entries required by GAAP for the airline in preparation of the December 31, 2008, financial statements.

(b) Ignoring the 2008 accidents, what liability due to the risk of loss from lack of insurance coverage should Paris Airlines record or disclose? During the past decade, the company has experienced at least one accident per year and incurred average damages of $3.2 million. Discuss fully.

P13-12   In preparing Shoyo Corporation's December 31, 2008, financial statements, the vice-president, finance, is trying to determine the proper accounting treatment for each of the following situations:

1. As a result of uninsured accidents during the year, personal injury suits for $350,000 and $60,000 have been filed against the company. It is the judgement of Shoyo's legal counsel that an unfavourable outcome is unlikely in the $60,000 case but that an unfavourable verdict for approximately $225,000 is likely in the $350,000 case.

2. In early 2008, Shoyo received notice from the provincial environment ministry that a site the company had been using to dispose of waste was considered toxic, and that Shoyo would be held responsible for its cleanup under provincial legislation. The vice-president, finance, discussed the situation over coffee with the vice-president, engineering. The engineer stated that it would take up to three years to determine the best way to remediate the site and that the cost would be considerable, perhaps as much as $500,000 to $2 million or more. The engineering vice-president advocates recognizing at least the minimum estimate of $500,000 in the current year's financial statements, while the financial vice-president advocates just disclosing the situation and the inability to estimate the cost in a note to the financial statements.

3. Shoyo Corporation owns a foreign subsidiary that has a book value of $5,725,000 and an estimated fair value of $8.7 million. The foreign government has communicated to Shoyo its intention to expropriate the assets and business of all foreign investors. On the basis of settlements other firms have received from this same country, Shoyo expects to receive 40% of the fair value of its properties as final settlement.

4. Shoyo's chemical product division consists of five plants and is uninsurable because of the special risk of injury to employees and losses due to fire and explosion. The year 2008 is considered one of the safest (luckiest) in the division's history because there were no losses due to injury or casualty. Having suffered an average of three casualties a year during the rest of the past decade (ranging from $60,000 to $700,000), management is certain that next year the company will not be so fortunate.

Instructions

(a) Prepare the journal entries that should be recorded as at December 31, 2008, to recognize each of the situations above.

(b) Indicate what should be reported relative to each situation in the financial statements and accompanying notes. Explain why.

(c) Are there any ethical issues involved in accounting for contingencies?

P13-13   Mosaic Music Limited (MML) carries a wide variety of musical instruments, sound reproduction equipment, recorded music, and sheet music. MML uses two sales promotion techniques—warranties and premiums—to attract customers.

Musical instruments and sound equipment are sold with a one-year warranty for replacement of parts and labour. The estimated warranty cost, based on experience, is 2% of sales.

A premium is offered on the recorded and sheet music. Customers receive a coupon for each dollar spent on recorded music or sheet music. Customers may exchange 200 coupons plus $20 for a CD player. MML pays $34 for each CD player and estimates that 60% of the coupons given to customers will be redeemed.

MML's total sales for 2008 were $7.2 million: $5.4 million from musical instruments and sound reproduction equipment, and $1.8 million from recorded music and sheet music. Replacement parts and labour for warranty work totalled $164,000 during 2008. A total of 6,500 CD players used in the premium program were purchased during the year and there were 1.2 million coupons redeemed in 2008.

The accrual method is used by MML to account for the warranty and premium costs for financial reporting purposes. The balances in the accounts related to warranties and premiums on January 1, 2008, were:

Inventory of Premium CD Players	$ 39,950
Estimated Premium Liability	44,800
Estimated Liability for Warranties	136,000

Instructions

(a) MML is preparing its financial statements for the year ended December 31, 2008. Determine the amounts that will be shown on the 2008 financial statements for the following:

1. Warranty expense
2. Estimated liability for warranties
3. Premium expense
4. Inventory of premium CD players
5. Estimated premium liability

(b) Assume that MML's auditor determined that both the one-year warranty and the coupons for the CD players were, in fact, revenue arrangements with multiple deliverables that should be accounted for under the sales warranty method. Explain how this would change the way in which these two programs were accounted for in part (a).

(CMA adapted)

P13-14   Rodriguez Inc., a publishing company, is preparing its December 31, 2008, financial statements and must determine the proper accounting treatment for the following situations. The company has retained your group to assist it in this task.

(a) Rodriguez sells subscriptions to several magazines for a one-year, two-year, or three-year period. Cash receipts from subscribers are credited to Magazine Subscriptions Collected in Advance, and this account had a balance of $2.3 million at December 31, 2008. Outstanding subscriptions at December 31, 2008, expire as follows:

During 2009	$600,000
During 2010	500,000
During 2011	800,000

(b) On January 2, 2008, Rodriguez discontinued collision, fire, and theft coverage on its delivery vehicles and became self-insured for these risks. Actual losses of $50,000 during 2008 were charged to delivery expense. The 2007 premium for the discontinued coverage amounted to $80,000 and the controller wants to set up a reserve for self-insurance by a debit to delivery expense of $30,000 and a credit to the reserve for self-insurance of $30,000.

(c) A suit for breach of contract seeking damages of $1 million was filed by an author against Rodriguez on July 1, 2008. The company's legal counsel believes that an unfavourable outcome is likely. A reasonable estimate of the court's award to the plaintiff is in the range between $300,000 and $700,000. No amount within this range is a better estimate of potential damages than any other amount.

(d) Rodriguez's main supplier, Ball Ltd., has been experiencing liquidity problems over the last three quarters. In order for Ball's bank to continue to extend credit, Ball has asked Rodriguez to guarantee its indebtedness. The bank loan stands at $500,000 at December 31, 2008, but the guarantee extends to the full credit facility of $900,000.

(e) Rodriguez's landlord has informed the company that its warehouse lease will not be renewed when it expires in six months' time. Rodriguez entered into a $2-million contract on December 15, 2008, with Construction Company Ltd., committing the company to build an office and warehouse facility.

(f) During December 2008, a competitor company filed suit against Rodriguez for industrial espionage claiming $1.5 million in damages. In the opinion of management and company counsel, it is reasonably possible that damages will be awarded to the plaintiff. However, the amount of potential damages awarded to the plaintiff cannot be reasonably estimated.

Instructions

For each of the above situations, provide the journal entry that should be recorded as at December 31, 2008, or explain why an entry should not be recorded. For each situation, identify what disclosures are required, if any.

P13-15   Duggan Enterprises Ltd. sells a specialty part that is used in wide-screen televisions and provides the ultimate in on-screen clarity. To promote sales of its product, Duggan initiated a program with some of its smaller customers. In exchange for making Duggan their exclusive supplier, Duggan guarantees these customers to their creditors so that Duggan assumes the customers' long-term debt in the event of non-payment to the creditors. In addition to charging for parts, Duggan also charges a fee to customers who take the guarantee program, and bases the fee on the time frame that the guarantee covers, which is typically three years. In the current fiscal year, these fees amounted to $30,000 for the three-year coverage period.

Six months before Duggan's fiscal year end, one of its customers, Harrison Corp., began to experience financial difficulties and missed two months of mortgage payments. Harrison's lender then called on Duggan to make the mortgage payments. At its fiscal year end on December 31, 2008, Duggan had recorded a receivable of $15,000 related to the payments made by Duggan on Harrison's behalf. Harrison owes the lender an additional $30,000 at this point. The lender is contemplating putting a lien on Harrison's assets that were pledged as collateral for the loans but the collateral involves rights on development of new state-of-the-art three-dimensional television technology that is still unproven.

Instructions

(a) Prepare all required journal entries and adjusting entries on Duggan's books to recognize the transactions and events described above.

(b) Identify any disclosures that must be made as a result of this information and prepare the note disclosure for Duggan for the period ended December 31, 2008.

P13-16　Haida Corp. has manufactured a broad range of quality products since 1985. The following information is available for the company's fiscal year ended February 28, 2008:

1. The company has $4 million of bonds payable outstanding at February 28, 2008, that were issued at par in 1997. The bonds carry an interest rate of 7%, payable semi-annually each June 1 and December 1.

2. Haida has several notes payable outstanding with its primary banking institution at February 28, 2008. In each case, the annual interest is due on the anniversary date of the note each year (same as the due dates listed). The notes are as follows:

Due Date	Amount Due	Interest Rate
Apr. 1, 2008	$150,000	8%
Jan. 31, 2009	200,000	9%
Mar. 15, 2009	500,000	7%
Oct. 30, 2010	250,000	8%

3. Haida has a two-year warranty on selected products, with an estimated cost of 1% of sales being returned in the 12 months following the sale, and a cost of 1.5% of sales being returned in months 13 to 24 following sale. The warranty liability outstanding at February 28, 2007, was $5,700. Sales of warrantied products in the year ended February 28, 2008, were $154,000. Actual warranty costs incurred during the current fiscal year are as follows:

Warranty claims honoured on 2006–2007 sales	$4,900
Warranty claims honoured on 2007–2008 sales	1,100
	$6,000

4. Regular trade payables for supplies and purchases of goods and services on open account are $414,000 at February 28, 2008. Included in this amount is a loan of $23,000 owing to an affiliated company.

5. The following information relates to Haida's payroll for the month of February 2008. The company's required contribution for EI is 1.4 times that of the employee contribution and for CPP is 1.0 times that of the employee contribution.

Salaries and wages outstanding at February 28, 2008	$220,000
EI withheld from employees	9,500
CPP withheld from employees	16,900
Income taxes withheld from employees	48,700
Union dues withheld from employees	21,500

6. Haida regularly pays GST owing to the government on the 15th of the month. Haida's GST transactions include the GST that it charges to customers and the GST that it is charged by suppliers. During February 2008, purchases attracted $28,000 of GST, while the GST charged on invoices to customers totalled $39,900. At January 31, 2008, the balances in the GST Recoverable and GST Payable accounts were $34,000 and $60,000, respectively.

7. Other miscellaneous liabilities included $50,000 of dividends payable on March 15, 2008; $25,000 of bonuses payable to company executives (75% payable in September, 2008, and 25% payable the following March); and $75,000 in accrued audit fees covering the year ended February 28, 2008.

8. Haida sells gift cards to its customers. The company does not have a redemption date and customers can use their cards at any time. At March 1, 2007, Haida had a balance outstanding of $950,000 in its Unearned Revenues—Gift Cards account. The company received $225,000 in cash for gift cards purchased during the current year and $375,000 in redemptions took place during the year. Based on past experience, 15% of customer gift card balances never get redeemed. At the end of each year, Haida recognizes 15% of the opening balance of Unearned Revenues as earned during the year.

Instructions

(a) Prepare the current liability section of the February 28, 2008, balance sheet of Haida Corp. Identify any amounts that require separate presentation or disclosure under GAAP.

(b) For each item included as a current liability, identify whether the item is a financial liability. Explain.

(c) If you have excluded any items from the category of current liabilities, explain why you left them out.

(d) Assume that Haida Corp. is not in compliance with the debt covenants in the note payable due October 30, 2010, in item 2 above. How would this affect the classification of the note on the balance sheet?

(e) For a manufacturer such as Haida, how should the revenue from unredeemed gift cards be shown on the income statement as opposed to revenue from redeemed gift cards?

Writing Assignments

WA13-1   You are the independent auditor who has been contracted to audit ProVision Corporation's December 31, 2008, financial statements. ProVision manufactures household appliances. During your audit, you discover the following contingent liabilities:

1. ProVision began production of a new dishwasher in June 2008, and by December 31, 2008, had sold 100,000 units to various retailers for $500 each. Each dishwasher is sold with a one-year warranty included. The company estimates that its warranty expense per dishwasher will amount to $25. By year end, the company had already paid out $1 million in warranty expenditures. ProVision's income statement shows a warranty expense of $1 million for 2008.

2. ProVision's retail division rents space from Meadow Malls. ProVision pays a rental fee of $6,000 per month plus 5% on the amount of yearly retail profits that is over $500,000. ProVision's accountant, Burt Wilson, tells you that he has been instructed to increase the estimate of bad debt expense and warranty costs in order to keep the retail division's profits at $475,000.

3. ProVision's lawyer, Robert Dowski, informed you that ProVision has been cited for dumping toxic waste into the Salmon River. Cleanup costs and fines are estimated to be $3,330,000. Although the case is still being contested, Dowski is almost certain that ProVision will have to pay the fine and cleanup costs. No disclosure of this situation was found in the financial statements.

4. ProVision is the defendant in a patent infringement lawsuit filed by Heidi Golder over ProVision's use of a hydraulic compressor in several of its products. Dowski claims that, if the suit goes against ProVision, the loss may be as much as $5 million. However, Dowski advises you that he does not have enough information at this point to determine what might happen as a result of this action. Again, there is no mention of this suit in the financial statements.

As presented, you wonder if these items could make it difficult for you to issue an unqualified audit report. You know that you should flag these situations in your working papers.

Instructions

(a) In the form of a memorandum, address each of the above issues. The memo will be included in the audit working papers. Explain what led to the discovery of each problem, what the problem is, and what you advise your client to do (along with any appropriate journal entries) to ensure that the financial statements are in accordance with GAAP.

(b) Identify any issues that you consider unethical and suggest what should be done.

WA13-2   Antigonish Corporation includes the following items in its liabilities at December 31, 2008:

1. Accounts payable, $420,000, due to suppliers in January 2009

2. Notes payable, $1.5 million, maturing on various dates in 2009

3. Deposits from customers on equipment ordered from Antigonish, $250,000

4. Salaries payable, $37,500, due on January 14, 2009

5. Bonds payable, $2.5 million, maturing on July 1, 2009

Instructions

(a) What are the essential characteristics that make an item a liability?

(b) What distinguishes a current liability from a long-term liability?

(c) What distinguishes a financial liability from a non-financial liability?

(d) Indicate under what circumstances, if any, each of the liabilities listed above might be excluded from the current liabilities section of the December 31, 2008, balance sheet.

WA13-3   Eshkol Corporation reports in the current liability section of its balance sheet at December 31, 2008, short-term obligations of $15 million. The amount includes $11 million of the company's 12% long-term debt that matures in March 2009. Management has stated its intention to refinance the 12% debt so that no portion of it will mature during 2009. The financial statements are expected to be issued on March 25, 2009.

Instructions

(a) Assume that Eshkol Corporation issues $13 million of 10-year debentures to the public in January 2009 and that management intends to use the proceeds to liquidate the $11-million debt that matures in March 2009. Furthermore, assume that the debt that matures in March 2009 is paid from these proceeds before the issuance of the financial statements. Will this have any impact on the balance sheet classification at December 31, 2008? Explain your answer.

(b) Assume that Eshkol Corporation issues common shares to the public in January 2009 and that management intends to use the proceeds of this equity issue to entirely liquidate the $11-million debt that matures in March 2009. In this situation, should the $11-million debt that matures in March 2009 be included in current liabilities at December 31, 2008? Explain.

(c) Assume that the $11-million current portion of the long-term debt does not mature until August 2009. On February 15, 2009, Eshkol Corporation enters into a financing agreement with a commercial bank that permits Eshkol to borrow up to $15 million at the bank's prime rate of interest any time before 2010. Borrowings under this financing agreement mature three years after the funds are transferred. This agreement cannot be cancelled unless specific provisions are violated. No provision has been violated at March 25, 2009. Management intends to refinance the $11-million obligation under the terms of the financial agreement with the bank. How should the $11 million be classified on the December 31, 2008, balance sheet and what disclosures, if any, are required?

WA13-4   On February 1, 2009, one of Magen Manufacturing Limited's large storage tanks exploded. Windows in houses and other buildings within a one-kilometre radius of the explosion were severely damaged, and some people were injured. As at February 15, 2009 (when the December 31, 2008, financial statements were completed and sent for printing and public distribution), no lawsuits had been filed or claims asserted against the company as a result of the explosion. The company fully expects that it will be sued for injuries and damages. Because Magen Manufacturing was not insured for this type of casualty and the company will be considered at fault, it will have to pay for the damages from its own resources.

Instructions

Discuss the accounting treatment and disclosures that should be made for the casualty and contingent losses in Magen's financial statements for the year ended December 31, 2008.

WA13-5   Conduit Corporation has a bonus arrangement that gives each of the company's vice-presidents and other executives a $15,000 cash bonus if net income for the current year is at least $1 million more than the previous year's income. After noticing that the draft of the current year's financial statements reports an increase in net income of $950,000, Charles Dickinson, the VP Finance, meets with Don Street, the controller, to discuss the year's performance.

Dickinson mentions to Street that the estimate of warranty expense is currently recognized at $500,000 and that this is known to be a fairly "soft" estimate. He suggests that the estimate could be reduced by $25,000 and still be reasonable. Dickinson also draws attention to a $250,000 "most likely" estimate of a contingent loss that has already been recorded for some outstanding litigation. He thinks that the loss should be adjusted to $150,000, which would be the lower number in the range of possible outcomes. He suggests that, because of the uncertainty in estimating the size of the expected loss, Conduit Corporation could then disclose in a note the amount that has been recognized ($150,000) and the total additional exposure to loss.

Instructions

(a) Should Street lower his estimate of the warranty liability and the loss that has been recognized? Explain.

(b) What ethical issue is at stake? Is anyone harmed?

(c) Is Dickinson acting ethically? Explain.

Cases

Refer to the Case Primer on the Student Website to help you answer these cases.

Student Website

www.wiley.com/canada/kieso

CA13-1   Environmental accounting is one of the current trends in accounting that is the most controversial. It is not controversial in the sense that professionals disagree about whether it is important; rather, it is controversial because implementing an environmental accounting model would require accountants to go outside the traditional GAAP model. Environmental accounting is basically a form of social accounting that tries to measure the impact on the environment (usually negative) of running a business. It tries, for example, to evaluate the cost of polluting the air and water or of destroying rain forests.

Envirocompany Limited (EL) is a pulp and paper company that has been in operation for 50 years. Its shares trade on a major stock exchange. It is located in a small town in Northern Ontario and employs thousands of people. In fact, the town exists mainly because of the jobs created by EL. Its equipment is fairly outdated and pollutes the surrounding water and air with chemicals that have been shown to be carcinogens. The old equipment is part of the reason for the "success" of the company since it is all paid for and requires little maintenance. The employees tolerate the pollution because EL gives them good jobs and keeps the local economy going.

Last year, a new chairman of the board of directors was appointed to EL, Charles Champion. He first became aware of the size of the pollution problem before being appointed to the board and he felt that he would like to do something about it. He took this mission as a personal challenge. In the first year of his appointment, he commissioned several in-depth studies on how EL might reduce or eliminate the pollution. He wanted to be careful to protect himself and the other members of the board because directors were increasingly being held personally liable for the actions of companies.

Most studies pointed to the old machinery and recommended that it be replaced by new state-of-the-art equipment. Cost estimates ran into the millions of dollars and the board of directors felt that the company would not be able to survive that type of expenditure. One study proved that the company would not even be in business any more, given the cost of new environmentally friendly equipment, declining demand for un-recycled newsprint, and increasing competition from abroad. That study was quickly put away on a shelf.

Recent environmental studies had shown that the pollutants were seeping into the water table and finding their way south to major cities. The studies showed that there were increasing incidences of birth defects in animals and humans in the affected areas, including increases in sterility for certain aquatic and marine life. This caused several politicians to start grandstanding and calling for tighter pollution controls and steep fines.

Recently, there had been reports of people living downstream getting sick, apparently from the chemical pollutants from EL. One individual had threatened to sue, and EL's lawyers were privately acknowledging the potential for a class action suit. EL has insurance that would cover up to $1 million in damages.

Meanwhile, the accountants were struggling with how to account for the problem for the year-end statements. Champion has requested that two sets of financial statements be drafted. First, he would like to know how the problem should be reflected for the external statements that will be presented at the shareholders' meeting. Second, he would like a set of financial statements that looks at the problem from a broader, all-encompassing perspective that will help for management decision-making. Specifically, he wants to know if there is a liability, exactly what it is, and when it arose (or will arise), if at all.

Instructions

Analyze the issue from two perspectives. For your analysis of the external financial reporting, adopt the role of the company controller. For the other analysis, adopt the role of a university professor.

CA13-2   ABC Airlines (ABC) carried more than 11.9 million passengers to over 160 destinations in 17 countries in 2008. ABC is the descendant of several predecessor companies, including AB Air and BC Airlines. The amalgamated company was created in 1999. In the years that followed, the world airline industry slumped and caused many airline companies to go bankrupt or suffer severe financial hardship. ABC weathered the storm by going through a significant restructuring. One of the changes as a result of the restructuring was to have ABC employees take share options as part of their remuneration. This resulted in employees investing $200 million in the company.

In 2008, ABC was still suffering losses ($187 million in 2006 and $194 million in 2007) so the CEO announced a new restructuring plan that would hopefully put an end to the continuing losses (which were now partly due to increased competition and falling seat prices). The plan focused on three areas: improved network profitability, decreased overhead costs, and decreased labour costs. For the latter, employees were asked to accept reduced wages over a four-year period.

Just like most companies, the company is now concerned with increasing market share and maintaining customer loyalty. On the company's website, the following advertisement appears:

"Fly 5, Fly Free—Fly five times with ABC Airlines and its worldwide partners and earn a free trip. The more you fly, the more the world is within reach."

Free flights have been offered by ABC in the past through its well-publicized "Frequent Flyer Program." Under the program, customers earn points for flying with ABC and, once they accumulate enough points, they can then use them to take free flights. In the notes to the financial statements, ABC notes that the incremental costs of Frequent Flyer Points are accrued as the entitlements to free flights are earned. The accrual is included as part of accrued liabilities.

Excerpts from the 2008 financial statements follow (in millions):

Total assets (including current assets of $456.5)	$1,866
Current liabilities	765
Long-term debt	841
Preferred shares	289
Common shares	407
Deficit	(436)
Total liabilities and equity	$1,866

Instructions

Adopt the role of company management, and discuss the treatment of the "Fly 5, Fly Free" program for financial reporting purposes.

Integrated Cases

IC 13-1 Landfill Limited (LL) is a private company that collects and disposes of household garbage. Waste is collected and trucked to local disposal sites where it is dumped and then covered with topsoil. The disposal sites are owned by LL and were financed by debt from Bank Inc. at an average interest rate of 5%.

LL has several disposal sites that will be filled with garbage and later sold as industrial land. LL estimates that the sites will take 20 years on average to fill up. Varying amounts of garbage will be dumped each year. Salvage values are not known at the time although land normally holds its value unless toxic chemicals are found.

Government regulations require that the company perform capping, closure, and post-closure activities. Capping involves covering the land with topsoil and planting vegetation. Closure activities include drainage, engineering, and demolition. Post-closure activities include maintaining the landfill once the government has given final certification. It also includes monitoring the ground and surface water, gas emissions, and air quality. If the land is sold, the purchaser reduces the acquisition cost by an estimate of this cost. LL must also guarantee that the land is toxin free and if it is later found to contain toxins, LL will pay for cleanup.

In the past year, one of these landfill sites was sold. However, the company recently received notification from the purchaser's lawyers that high levels of toxins had been found leaking into the water table.

Obtaining new contracts, as well as keeping old contracts, depends on many factors. These include competitive bidding, the company's profile in the community, its past work performance, its financial stability, and having a history of adhering strictly to environmental standards. Financial statements are therefore relevant in the process of obtaining new contracts as they are examined by those who award the contracts.

Instructions

Adopt the role of the company auditor and discuss the financial reporting issues. Landfill Limited is one of your new audit clients this year.

Research and Financial Analysis

RA13-1   Stantec Inc.

Stantec Inc. is an Alberta-based company with more than 5,500 employees operating out of more than 60 locations in North America and the Caribbean. The company's 2005 Annual Report indicates that it "provides professional design and consulting services in planning, engineering, architecture, interior design, landscape architecture, surveying, and project management." Locate Stantec's 2005 financial statements at the end of this volume.

Instructions
Review the balance sheet and notes to the financial statements of Stantec Inc. and answer the following questions.

(a) What makes up the current liabilities reported at December 31, 2005? Be as specific as possible.

(b) What is the nature of the current liability "Billings in excess of costs and estimated earnings"? Why is it a current liability? Is it a financial or a non-financial liability?

(c) If Stantec does not borrow any additional funds during its year ended December 31, 2006, what amount would you expect to see reported as the current portion of long-term debt on the December 31, 2006, balance sheet? Explain.

(d) What restrictions, if any, have been imposed on the company by the banks and/or other suppliers of long-term credit?

(e) In note 9 to the financial statements, Stantec reports a provision for self-insured liabilities of $12.9 million. Investigate the reason for this liability. Explain why it is recognized as a liability even though the chapter indicates that provisions for self-insurance are not recognized as liabilities.

(f) Calculate Stantec's current ratio and quick ratio for each of the two years that are reported. Comment on the company's liquidity.

RA13-2   Canadian Tire Corporation, Limited

Instructions
Refer to the 2006 financial statements and 10-year financial review of Canadian Tire Corporation, Limited found on the Student Website or at www.sedar.com. Then answer the following questions.

(a) What makes up Canadian Tire's current liabilities? Suggest at least five different types of liabilities that are likely included in "Accounts payable and other."

(b) What were Canadian Tire's working capital, acid-test ratio, and current ratio for the two most recent years of data that are provided? How do these results compare with the measures for five years ago? Comment on the company's current liquidity in general, and compared to its liquidity five years ago. What role do the inventory and accounts receivable turnovers have in assessing liquidity in general, and for Canadian Tire specifically?

(c) What is the current portion of long-term debt? Explain clearly what makes up this amount. If the company does not borrow any additional long-term funds during 2007, how much would you expect to see on the 2007 balance sheet as the current portion of long-term debt? Explain clearly what would make up this amount.

(d) What types of commitments and contingencies has Canadian Tire reported in its financial statements? Identify which items are commitments and which are contingencies. What is management's reaction to the contingencies?

RA13-3   Danier Leather Inc. and Costco Wholesale Corporation

Danier Leather Inc. is a vertically integrated designer, manufacturer, and retailer of fashion leather and suede clothing and accessories for men, women, and children that operates mainly at shopping mall, street-front, and power centre locations. Costco Wholesale Corporation mainly sells a limited selection of items in a wide variety of product groups at close-to-cost prices in stripped-down big box stores. Its big box stores have a goal of selling very large volumes of merchandise with little credit risk, and achieving a high inventory turnover. The current asset and current liability sections of the 2006 and 2005 balance sheets of Danier Leather and Costco follow:

DANIER LEATHER INC.
(thousands of dollars)

	June 24, 2006	June 25, 2005
Assets		
Current Assets		
Cash	$ 11,833	$ 21,193
Accounts receivable	402	594
Income taxes recoverable	2,485	939
Inventories (Note 3)	32,348	29,031
Prepaid expenses	1,026	516
Assets of discontinued operations (Note 2)	–0–	23
Future income tax asset (Note 10)	529	159
	$ 48,623	$ 52,455
Liabilities		
Current Liabilities		
Accounts payable and accrued liabilities	$ 10,708	$ 8,170
Current portion, capital lease obligation	911	–0–
Future income tax liability (Note 10)	624	–0–
	$ 12,243	$ 8,170
Other information		
Revenue	$148,351	$166,350
Cost of sales	76,953	82,863
Selling, general and administrative expenses	78,796	77,215

COSTCO WHOLESALE CORPORATION
(thousands of dollars)

	Sept. 3, 2006	Aug. 28, 2005
Current Assets		
Cash and cash equivalents	$ 1,510,939	$ 2,062,585
Short-term investments	1,322,181	1,397,272
Receivables, net	565,373	529,150
Merchandise inventories	4,568,723	4,014,699
Deferred income taxes, and other current assets	264,866	234,295
Total current assets	$ 8,232,082	$ 8,238,001
Current Liabilities		
Short-term borrowings	$ 41,385	$ 54,356
Accounts payable	4,581,395	4,224,676
Accrued salaries and benefits	1,080,382	1,025,181
Accrued sales and other taxes	324,274	263,899
Deferred membership income	583,946	500,558
Current portion of long-term debt	308,523	3,225
Other current liabilities	899,286	688,642
Total current liabilities	$ 7,819,191	$ 6,760,537
Other information		
Revenue, net sales	$58,963,180	$51,879,070
Merchandise costs	52,745,497	46,346,961
Selling, general and administrative expense	5,732,141	5,061,339

Instructions

(a) Calculate the current and quick ratios for Danier Leather and Costco at their 2006 and 2005 year ends. Which company appears to have better liquidity? Explain the possible reason for this.

(b) Use calculations to estimate the number of days for each stage in the operating cycle of each company and then draw a timeline that shows the cash to cash **operating cycle** of both companies. The cycle includes the following stages: (1) from the receipt of goods from suppliers to the payment to suppliers (average age of payables or days payables outstanding), (2) from the receipt of goods from suppliers to the sale of merchandise (inventory turnover in days), and (3) from the sale of goods to the collection of cash from customers (accounts receivable turnover). What do these measures tell you about each company's cash flow?

(c) Which company do you think is more liquid? Why?

RA13-4 Loblaw Companies Limited and Sobeys Inc.

The financial statements of **Loblaw Companies Limited** for its 52 weeks ended December 31, 2005, and the financial statements for **Sobeys Inc.** for its 52 weeks ended May 6, 2006, are available on the Student Website or at www.sedar.com.

Instructions

(a) Calculate the current ratio and acid-test ratio for both companies at the end of the two most recent years that are reported. Comment generally on the results of these ratios. Is there anything particular about the industry that these companies operate in that might explain and justify ratios of this level?

(b) Calculate each company's (1) current cash debt coverage ratio, (2) cash debt coverage ratio, (3) receivables turnover ratio, (4) inventory turnover ratio, and (5) days payables outstanding, for the most recent year reported. Comment on each company's liquidity. Which company do you think is more liquid? Explain.

(c) What makes up the current portion of long-term debt at each company's most recently reported fiscal year end? Be specific. Does either company have long-term debt maturing in the next five years that will require significant cash flows in order to meet the amounts due? Explain.

RA13-5 Research Topics

There are many interesting company programs and other topics that relate to the definition, recognition, and measurement of liabilities. Examples include customer loyalty programs, retail gift cards, corporate restructuring obligations, air miles programs, product liability lawsuits, liability accruals on interim financial statements, and vendor rebates to customers.

Instructions

Choose one of the programs or other topics listed above. Research your choice using international and Canadian sources, and prepare a one-page summary of the liability recognition and measurement issues that are involved. If possible, identify any accounting standards that may help resolve the issues.

Gambling on Covenants

GREAT CANADIAN CASINOS

Great Canadian Gaming Corporation operates six casinos in B.C.'s Lower Mainland and on Vancouver Island. For the fourth quarter of 2005, the company reported a loss of $9.2 million, indicating that it might breach some of its financial covenants. One debt covenant involved the trust indenture for its bonds. It required Great Canadian Gambling to maintain (and not exceed) certain leverage ratios. If it failed to do so, it would trigger a technical default, which, on senior unsecured debt, could mean the bondholders would own the company, leaving the shareholders with nothing.

Great Canadian Gaming avoided this, however, negotiating with its lenders and bondholders to amend certain terms of its debt facilities. The company agreed to pay amendment fees, adjust its net debt-to-adjusted-EBITDA ratio, and increase the interest rate of its series A and series B notes for specific time periods. It agreed to increase the coupon on the bonds by 37.5 basis points, starting on April 1, 2006, until it had a net debt-to-adjusted-EBITDA ratio of 2.5 for two consecutive quarters. It would make no more new acquisitions until it could maintain this ratio.

The company announced an $80-million private equity placement, $50 million of which was provided by chief executive officer Ross McLeod. The 6.2 million units in this placement each consisted of one common share and one common share purchase warrant, at the price of $12.89 per unit. The company planned to use the proceeds from this placement to reduce debt and for general working capital purposes. In September 2006, the company announced a new $450-million bridge facility, the proceeds of which it used to redeem its series A and series B secured notes, creating a win-win situation for it and its bondholders. ■

Sources: Tavia Grant, "Great Canadian Private Placement Satisfies Covenants," *Globe and Mail*, March 28, 2006. Harry Koza, "Great Canadian Gambling Calls—Bondholders Win a Sweet Pot," *Globe and Mail*, September 1, 2006.

Long-Term Financial Liabilities

chapter 14

Learning Objectives

After studying this chapter, you should be able to:

1. Describe the procedures for issuing long-term debt.

2. Identify various types of long-term debt.

3. Explain the initial measurement of bonds/notes at their date of issuance.

4. Apply the methods of bond discount and premium amortization.

5. Value bonds and consideration in special situations.

6. Describe the accounting procedures for the extinguishment of debt.

7. Explain the issues surrounding off–balance sheet financing arrangements.

8. Indicate how long-term debt is presented and analyzed.

9. Compare current Canadian and international GAAP and understand which direction international GAAP is headed in.

After studying Appendix 14A, you should be able to:

10. Account for impairments on notes and loans receivable.

11. Distinguish between and account for debt restructurings that result in extinguishment or in debt continuation.

Preview of Chapter 14

Long-term debt and financial liabilities continue to play an important role in our capital markets because companies and governments need large amounts of capital to finance their growth. In many cases, the most effective way to obtain capital is by issuing long-term debt. This chapter explains the accounting issues that are related to long-term debt and financial liabilities.

The chapter is organized as follows:

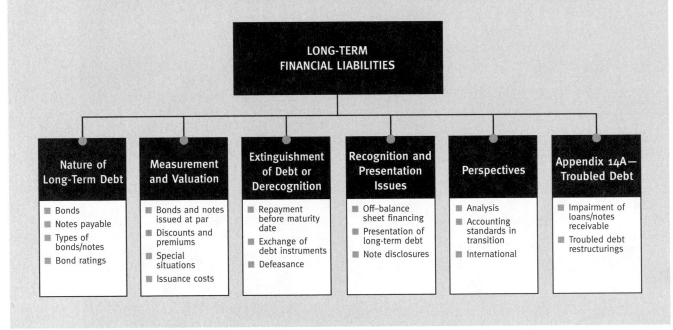

NATURE OF LONG-TERM DEBT

Objective 1

Describe the procedures for issuing long-term debt.

Long-term debt consists of obligations that are not payable within a year or the operating cycle of the business, whichever is longer, and will therefore require probable sacrifices of economic benefits in the future. Bonds payable, long-term notes payable, mortgages payable, pension liabilities, and lease liabilities are examples of long-term debt or liabilities.[1]

The process that leads to incurring long-term debt is often very formal. For example, the bylaws of corporations usually require that the board of directors and the shareholders give their approval before bonds can be issued or other long-term debt arrangements can be contracted.

Generally, long-term debt has various **restrictive covenants** (i.e., terms or conditions) that are meant to limit activities and protect both lenders and borrowers. The covenants and other terms of the agreement between the borrower and the lender are

---

[1] "Long-term debt" and "long-term liabilities" meet the definition of a financial liability in *CICA Handbook* Sections 3855 as they represent contractual obligations to deliver cash. These terms have the same meaning and are used interchangeably throughout the text.

stated in a bond indenture or note agreement. The details that are often found in the indenture or agreement include the following: the amount that the corporation is authorized to issue, the interest rate, the due date or dates, call provisions, property pledged as security, sinking fund requirements, working capital and dividend restrictions, and limitations on incurring additional debt.

Covenants to restrict the amount of additional debt are common. Additional debt increases the risk of insolvency and there is a limit to the amount of risk that creditors are willing to accept even though some lenders can tolerate more risk than others. Consider what happened to bondholders in the leveraged buyout[2] of **RJR Nabisco**. Solidly rated 9³/₈% bonds that were due in 2016 plunged 20% in value when management announced the leveraged buyout. The drop occurred because the additional debt that was added to the capital structure increased the probability of an eventual default.

What Do the Numbers Mean?

Bonds

Bonds are the most common type of long-term debt that companies report on their balance sheets. The main purpose of bonds is to borrow for the long term when the amount of capital that is needed is too large for one lender to supply. **By issuing bonds in $100, $1,000, or $10,000 denominations, a large amount of long-term indebtedness can be divided into many small investing units, which makes it possible for more than one lender to participate in the loan.**

A bond is created by a contract known as a **bond indenture** and represents a promise to pay both of the following: (1) a sum of money at a designated maturity date, and (2) periodic interest at a specified rate on the maturity amount (face value). Individual bonds are evidenced (proven to exist) by a paper certificate and they typically have a $1,000 face value. Bond interest payments are usually made semi-annually, but the interest rate is generally expressed as an annual rate.

An entire bond issue may be sold to an investment banker who acts as a selling agent that markets the bonds. In such arrangements, investment bankers may either underwrite the entire issue by guaranteeing a certain sum to the corporation, thus taking the risk of selling the bonds for whatever price the agent can get (which is known as **firm underwriting**), or the agent may sell the bond issue for a commission that will be deducted from the proceeds of the sale (known as **best efforts underwriting**). Alternatively, the issuing company may choose to place a bond issue privately by selling the bonds directly to a large institution—which may or may not be a financial institution—without the aid of an underwriter (which is known as **private placement**).

Notes Payable

The difference between **current** notes payable and **long-term notes payable** is the maturity date. As discussed in Chapter 13, short-term notes payable are expected to be paid within a year or the operating cycle, whichever is longer. **Long-term notes are similar in substance to bonds as both have fixed maturity dates and carry either a stated or implicit interest rate. However, notes do not trade as easily as bonds in the organized public securities markets, and sometimes do not trade at all.** Unincorporated and small corporate enterprises issue notes as their long-term instruments, whereas larger corporations issue both long-term notes and bonds.

Accounting for notes and bonds is quite similar. Like a bond, a note is valued at the present value of its future interest and principal cash flows, and any discount or

Underlying Concept

Even though the **legal form** of a note is different from a bond, the **economic substance** is the same as they both represent liabilities. They therefore receive substantially the same treatment from an accounting perspective, depending on the features that the specific note or bond carries.

---

[2] A leveraged buyout occurs when a group of individuals, often management, purchases the company. Debt is used to finance the acquisition and it is repaid from company cash flows.

premium is amortized over the life of the note, just as it is over the life of a bond. Calculating the present value of an interest-bearing note, recording its issuance, and amortizing any discount or premium will be shown for bonds in the next section. As you might expect, the accounting for long-term notes payable mirrors the accounting for long-term notes receivable, which was presented in Chapter 7.

Types of Bonds/Notes

Objective 2
Identify various types of long-term debt.

The following are some of the more common types of long-term debt that are found in practice. The more basic issues regarding bonds and notes will be covered in this chapter, while the more complex instruments will be discussed in Chapter 16.

Registered and Bearer (Coupon) Bonds   Bonds that are issued in the owner's name are called **registered bonds**. To sell a registered bond, the current certificate has to be surrendered and a new certificate is then issued. A **bearer** or **coupon bond**, however, is not recorded in the owner's name and may therefore be transferred from one owner to another by simply delivering it to the new owner.

Secured and Unsecured Debt   **Secured debt** is backed by a pledge of some sort of collateral. **Mortgage bonds/notes** are secured by a claim on real estate. **Collateral trust** bonds/notes are secured by shares and bonds of other corporations. Debt instruments that are not backed by collateral are **unsecured**—e.g., **debenture bonds**. **Junk bonds** are unsecured and also very risky, and therefore pay a high interest rate. These bonds are often used to finance leveraged buyouts.

Term, Serial, Perpetual, and Callable Bonds or Notes   Debt issues that mature on a single date are called **term bonds/notes**, and issues that mature in instalments are called **serial bonds/notes**. Serial bonds are frequently used by schools, municipalities, and provincial or federal governments. **Perpetual bonds/notes** have unusually long terms—i.e., 100 years or more. These are often referred to as century or millennium bonds, depending on the term. They will be discussed further in Chapter 16. **Callable bonds** give the issuer the right to call and retire the bonds before they mature.

Income, Revenue, and Deep Discount Bonds   **Income bonds** pay no interest unless the issuing company is profitable. **Revenue bonds** have this name because the interest on them is paid from a specified revenue source. **Deep discount bonds/notes**—which are also referred to as **zero-interest debentures, bonds, or notes**—have very little or no interest and therefore are sold at a large discount that basically provides the buyer with a total interest payoff (at market rates) at maturity.

Convertible and Commodity-Backed Bonds, and Bonds That May Be Settled in Common Shares   If bonds are convertible into other securities of the corporation for a specified time after they have been issued, they are called **convertible debt. Commodity-backed debt** (also called **asset-linked debt**) is redeemable in amounts of a commodity, such as barrels of oil, tonnes of coal, or ounces of rare metal. Certain bonds or other financial instruments give the issuer the option to repay or settle the principal in either cash or common shares. Since the issues for these types of financial instruments are more complex, they will be discussed in Chapter 16.

One of the more interesting recent innovations in the bond market is bonds whose interest payments are tied to changes in the weather. To understand how these weather bonds work, let's look at a bond issue by **Koch Industries**. Koch provides energy to utilities, distributors, and others around the country. It feels the heat financially when weather is colder than expected and the company has to buy energy in the open market to serve its clients. It can also experience losses if the weather is warmer than usual.

What Do the Numbers Mean?

To reduce the impact of the weather on its results, Koch structured a bond offering that is designed to deal with the problem. With Koch's bonds, if the weather is colder than normal, the interest rate drops half a percentage point for each one-quarter-degree decline in average temperature. Conversely, the rate goes up by half a percentage point if the weather is warmer by one-quarter of a degree. Investors even lose some of their original investment (principal) if weather deviates significantly from the average. However, certain investors like these risky bonds because they add diversification to their portfolios. Mother Nature, rather than economic factors, affects the bond value, which provides a new element of diversification.

Although weather bonds may sound unusual, more and more companies are issuing catastrophe-type bonds. For example, insurance companies are issuing bonds to protect themselves from catastrophes such as earthquakes and storms. Besides financial conditions, it seems that investors must now be concerned with meteorological matters as well.

Source: Adapted from Gregory Zuckerman and Deborah Lohse, "Weather Bonds Hedge against Mother Nature's Profit Effects," *Wall Street Journal*, October 26, 1999, p. C1.

Bond Ratings

There are many companies, including **DBRS**, **Moody's Investors Service**, **Fitch**, and **Standard & Poor's Corporation**, that assess credit ratings of company bonds and preferred shares. The bond quality designations and rating symbols of these firms are shown in Illustration 14-1.

Quality	Symbols	
	Moody's	Standard & Poor's/Fitch/DBRS
Prime	Aaa	AAA
Excellent	Aa	AA
Upper medium	A	A
Lower medium	Baa	BBB
Marginally speculative	Ba	BB
Very speculative	B, Caa	B

Illustration 14-1

Bond Quality Ratings

A credit rating is assigned to each new public bond issue and is a current assessment of the company's ability to pay the amounts that will be due on that specific borrowing. The rating may be changed up or down during the issue's outstanding life because the quality is constantly monitored. Note that institutional investors, such as insurance companies and pension funds, invest heavily in what are referred to as **investment grade securities**. Investment grade securities are high-quality securities (not speculative) and therefore only the first four categories qualify. **Because having an investment grade rating on a specific debt offering allows greater access to capital, there is pressure on a company to ensure that its debt instruments are rated investment grade.** Credit rating analysts review many business model and industry factors when they make their determinations. Trends in costs and revenues are especially important.

MEASUREMENT AND VALUATION

Bonds and Notes Issued at Par

When a note or bond is issued, it should be recognized at the fair value of the consideration that is received.[3] When bonds are issued on an interest payment date at **par** (i.e., at

3 Objective
Explain the initial measurement of bonds/notes at their date of issuance.

---

[3] *CICA Handbook*, Section 3855.55.

face value), no interest has accrued and there is no premium or discount. The accounting entry is made simply for the cash proceeds and the bond's face value. To illustrate, assume that a company plans to issue 10-year term bonds with a par value of $800,000, dated January 1, 2008, and bearing interest at an annual rate of 10% payable semi-annually on January 1 and July 1. If it decides to issue them on January 1 at par, the entry on its books would be as follows:

A   =   L   + SE
+800,000   +800,000

Cash flows: ↑ 800,000 inflow

Cash	800,000	
Bonds Payable		800,000

The entry to record the first semi-annual interest payment of $40,000 ($800,000 × 0.10 × 1/2) on July 1, 2008, would be:

A   = L +   SE
−40,000   −40,000

Cash flows: ↓ 40,000 outflow

Bond Interest Expense	40,000	
Cash		40,000

The entry to record accrued interest expense at December 31, 2008 (the year end), would be:

A =   L   +   SE
       +40,000   −40,000

Cash flows: No effect

Bond Interest Expense	40,000	
Bond Interest Payable		40,000

In Chapter 7, we discussed the recognition of a $10,000, three-year note issued at face value by Scandinavian Imports to Bigelow Corp. In this transaction, the stated rate and the effective rate were both 10%. The time diagram and present value calculation in Chapter 7 (see page 372) for Bigelow Corp. would be the same for the issuer of the note, Scandinavian Imports, in recognizing the note payable. Because the note's present value and its face value are the same ($10,000), no premium or discount is recognized. The issuance of the note is recorded by Scandinavian Imports as follows:

A   =   L   + SE
+10,000   +10,000

Cash flows: ↑ 10,000 inflow

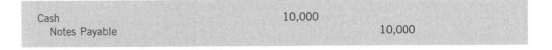

Cash	10,000	
Notes Payable		10,000

Discounts and Premiums

The issuance and marketing of bonds to the public does not happen from one day to the next. It usually takes weeks or even months. Underwriters must be arranged, the approval of the Securities Commission must be obtained, audits and the issuance of a prospectus may be required, and certificates must be printed. Frequently, the terms in a bond indenture are decided well in advance of the bond sale. Between the time when the terms are set and the time when the bonds are issued, the market conditions and the issuing corporation's financial position may change significantly. Such changes affect the bonds' marketability and, thus, their selling price.

A bond's selling price is set by the supply and demand of buyers and sellers, relative risk, market conditions, and the state of the economy. The investment community values a bond at the **present value of its future cash flows**, which consist of (1) **interest** and (2) **principal**. The rate that is used to calculate the present value of these cash flows is the interest rate that would give an acceptable return on an investment that matches the issuer's risk characteristics.

The interest rate that is written in the terms of the bond indenture (and is ordinarily printed on the bond certificate) is known as the **stated**, **coupon**, or **nominal rate**. This rate, which is set by the bond issuer, is expressed as a percentage of the bond's **face value**, also called the **par value**, **principal amount**, or **maturity value**. If the rate that is being used by the investment community (i.e., the buyers) is different from the stated rate, when buyers calculate the bond's present value, the result will be different from the bond's face value, and its purchase price will therefore also differ. The difference between the face value and the bond's present value is either a **discount** or **premium**.[4] If the bonds sell for less than their face value, they are being sold at a discount. If the bonds sell for more than their face value, they are being sold at a premium.

The interest rate that is actually earned by the bondholders is called the **effective yield** or **market rate**. If bonds sell at a **discount**, the **effective yield is higher than the stated rate**. Conversely, if bonds sell at a **premium**, the **effective yield is lower than the stated rate**. While the bond is outstanding, its price is affected by several variables, but especially by the market rate of interest. There is an inverse relationship between the market interest rate and the bond price. That is, when interest rates increase, the bond's price decreases, and vice versa.

To illustrate the calculation of the **present value of a bond issue**, assume that Discount Limited issues $100,000 in bonds that are due in five years and pay 9% interest annually at year end. At the time of issue, the market rate for such bonds is 11%. Illustration 14-2 shows both the interest and the principal cash flows.

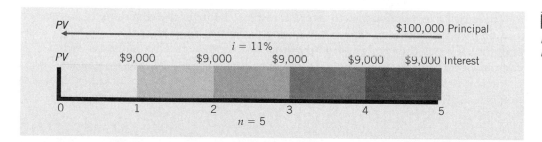

Illustration 14-2

Present Value Calculation of Bond Selling at a Discount

The actual principal and interest cash flows are discounted at an 11% rate for five periods as follows:

Present value of the principal: $100,000 × 0.59345	$59,345
Present value of the interest payments: $9,000 × 3.69590	33,263
Present value (selling price) of the bonds	$92,608

By paying $92,608 at the date of issue, the investors will realize an **effective rate or yield** of 11% over the five-year term of the bonds. These bonds would therefore sell at a

---

[4] Until the 1950s, it was common for corporations to issue bonds with low, even-percent coupons (such as 4%) to demonstrate their financial soundness. Frequently, the result was larger discounts. More recently, it has become acceptable to set the stated rate of interest on bonds in more precise terms (e.g., 6⁷/₈%). Companies usually try to match the stated rate as closely as possible to the market or effective rate at the time of issue. While discounts and premiums continue to occur, their absolute size tends to be much smaller, and often it is immaterial. A study conducted in the mid-80s documented that out of 685 new debt offerings, none were issued at a premium. Approximately 95% were issued either with no discount or at a price above 98. Now, however, zero-interest (deep discount) bonds are more popular, which causes substantial discounts.

discount of $7,392 ($100,000 − $92,608). Note that the price at which the bonds sell is typically stated as a percentage of their face or par value. For example, we would say that the Discount Limited bonds sold for 92.6 (92.6% of par). If Discount Limited had received $102,000, we would say the bonds sold for 102 (102% of par).

When bonds sell below their face value, it means that investors are demanding a rate of interest that is higher than the stated rate. The investors are not satisfied with the stated rate because they can earn a greater rate on alternative investments of equal risk. As they cannot change the stated rate, they therefore refuse to pay face value for the bonds and instead **achieve the effective rate of interest that they want** by lowering the amount invested in the bonds. The result is that the investors receive interest at the stated rate calculated on the face value, but they are essentially earning an effective rate that is higher than the stated rate because they paid less than face value for the bonds. Although notes do not trade as readily as bonds in stock markets, the same issues arise where the stated rate on the notes is different from the market rate at the date of issuance.

Objective **4**

Apply the methods of bond discount and premium amortization.

Straight-Line Method

If the $800,000 of bonds illustrated earlier were issued on January 1, 2008, at 97 (meaning 97% of par), the issuance would be recorded as follows:

A   =   L   + SE
+776,000   +776,000

Cash flows: ↑ 776,000 inflow

| Cash ($800,000 × 0.97) | 776,000 | |
| Bonds Payable | | 776,000 |

Because of its relationship to interest, discussed above, **the discount is amortized and charged to interest expense over the period of time that the bonds are outstanding. Under the straight-line method,**[5] the amount that is amortized each year is constant. For example, using the bond discount above of $24,000, the amount amortized to interest expense each year for 10 years is $2,400 ($24,000 ÷ 10 years) and, if amortization is recorded annually, it is recorded as follows:

A   =   L   +   SE
        +2,400   −2,400

Cash flows: No effect

| Bond Interest Expense | 2,400 | |
| Bonds Payable | | 2,400 |

At the end of the first year, 2008, as a result of the amortization entry above, the unamortized balance of the discount is $21,600 ($24,000 − $2,400).

If the bonds were dated and sold on October 1, 2008, and if the corporation's fiscal year ended on December 31, the discount amortized during 2008 would be only 3/12 of 1/10 of $24,000, or $600. Three months of accrued interest must also be recorded on December 31.

A premium on bonds payable is accounted for in much the same way as a discount on bonds payable. If the $800,000 of par value, 10-year bonds are dated and sold on January 1, 2008, at 103, the following entry is made to record the issuance:

A   =   L   + SE
+824,000   +824,000

Cash flows: ↑ 824,000 inflow

| Cash ($800,000 × 1.03) | 824,000 | |
| Bonds Payable | | 824,000 |

---

[5] Although the effective interest method is required under *CICA Handbook* Section 3855, the straight-line method has been used here. The straight-line method is valued for its simplicity and might be used by companies whose financial statements are not constrained by GAAP. A discussion of the effective interest method follows.

At the end of 2008 and for each year that the bonds are outstanding, the entry to amortize the premium on a straight-line basis is:

Bonds Payable	2,400	
Bond Interest Expense		2,400

$$A = L + SE$$
$$-2,400 \quad +2,400$$
Cash flows: No effect

Bond interest expense is increased by amortizing a discount and decreased by amortizing a premium. Amortization of a discount or premium under the effective interest method is discussed later in this chapter.

Some bonds are **callable** by the issuer after a certain date and at a stated price so that the issuing corporation may have the opportunity to reduce its debt or take advantage of lower interest rates. **Whether or not the bond is callable, any premium or discount must be amortized over the bond's life up to the maturity date because it is not certain that the issuer will call the bond and redeem it early.**

Bond interest payments are usually made semi-annually on dates that are specified in the bond indenture. When bonds are not issued on interest payment dates, **bond buyers will pay the seller the interest that has accrued from the last interest payment date to the date of issue**. By paying the accrued interest, the purchasers of the bonds are, in effect, paying the bond issuer in advance for the portion of the full six-month interest payment that the purchasers are not entitled to (but will receive) since they have not held the bonds during the entire six-month period. **The purchasers will receive the full six-month interest payment on the next semi-annual interest payment date.**

To illustrate, assume that $800,000 of par value, 10-year bonds, dated January 1, 2008, and bearing interest at an annual rate of 10% payable semi-annually on January 1 and July 1, are issued on March 1, 2008, at par plus accrued interest; the entry on the books of the issuing corporation is:

Cash	813,333	
Bonds Payable		800,000
Bond Interest Expense ($800,000 × 0.10 × 2/12)		13,333*
*Interest Payable might be credited instead		

$$A = L + SE$$
$$+813,333 \quad +800,000 \quad +13,333$$
Cash flows: ↑ 813,333 inflow

The purchaser is thus advancing two months of interest because on July 1, 2008, four months after the date of purchase, six months of interest will be received by the purchaser from the issuing company. The issuing company makes the following entry on July 1, 2008:

Bond Interest Expense	40,000	
Cash		40,000

$$A = L + SE$$
$$-40,000 \quad -40,000$$
Cash flows: ↓ 40,000 outflow

The expense account now contains a debit balance of $26,667, which represents the proper amount of interest expense: four months at 10% on $800,000.

The above illustration was simplified by having the January 1, 2008, bonds issued on March 1, 2008, at par. If, however, the 10% bonds were issued at 102, the entry on March 1 on the issuing corporation's books would be:

Cash [($800,000 × 1.02) + ($800,000 × 0.10 × 2/12)]	829,333	
Bonds Payable		816,000
Bond Interest Expense		13,333

$$A = L + SE$$
$$+829,333 \quad +816,000 \quad +13,333$$
Cash flows: ↑ 829,333 inflow

The premium would be amortized from the date of sale, March 1, 2008, not from the date of the bonds, January 1, 2008.

Effective Interest Method

A common method for amortizing a discount or premium is the **effective interest method**. This method is required under *CICA Handbook* Section 3855. Under the effective interest method, the steps are as follows:

1. Interest expense is calculated first by multiplying the **carrying value**[6] of the bonds/note at the beginning of the period by the effective interest rate.

2. The discount or premium amortization is then determined by comparing the interest expense with the interest to be paid.

Illustration 14-3 shows the formula for the calculation of the amortization under this method.

Illustration 14-3

Bond Discount and Premium Amortization Calculation

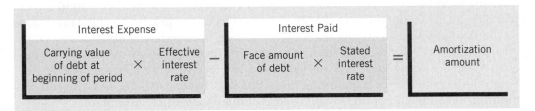

The effective interest method produces a periodic interest expense that is equal to a **constant percentage of the bonds' or notes' carrying value**.

Both the effective interest and straight-line methods result in the **same total amount of interest expense over the term of the bonds**.

Example: Bonds Issued at a Discount   To illustrate the amortization of a discount using the effective interest method, assume that Master Corporation issued $100,000 of 8% term bonds on January 1, 2008, that are due on January 1, 2013, with interest payable each July 1 and January 1. Because the investors required an effective interest rate of 10%, they paid $92,278 for the $100,000 of bonds, creating a $7,722 discount. The $7,722 discount is calculated as in Illustration 14-4.[7]

Illustration 14-4

Calculation of Discount on Bonds Payable

Maturity of bonds payable		$100,000
Present value of $100,000 due in 5 years at 10%, interest payable semi-annually [$100,000 × 0.61391]	$61,391	
Present value of $4,000 interest payable semi-annually for 5 years at 10% annually [$4,000 × 7.72173]	30,887	
Proceeds from sale of bonds		92,278
Discount on bonds payable		$ 7,722

[6] The book value, also called the carrying value, equals the face amount minus any unamortized discount, or plus any unamortized premium.

[7] Because interest is paid semi-annually, the interest rate that is used is 5% (10% × 6/12) and the number of periods is 10 (5 years × 2).

The five-year amortization schedule appears in Illustration 14-5.

Illustration 14-5

*Bond Discount
Amortization Schedule*

SCHEDULE OF BOND DISCOUNT AMORTIZATION
Effective Interest Method–Semi-Annual Interest Payments
5-Year, 8% Bonds Sold to Yield 10%

Date	Cash Paid	Interest Expense	Discount Amortized	Carrying Amount of Bonds
1/1/08				$ 92,278
7/1/08	$ 4,000[a]	$ 4,614[b]	$ 614[c]	92,892[d]
1/1/09	4,000	4,645	645	93,537
7/1/09	4,000	4,677	677	94,214
1/1/10	4,000	4,711	711	94,925
7/1/10	4,000	4,746	746	95,671
1/1/11	4,000	4,783	783	96,454
7/1/11	4,000	4,823	823	97,277
1/1/12	4,000	4,864	864	98,141
7/1/12	4,000	4,907	907	99,048
1/1/13	4,000	4,952	952	100,000
	$40,000	$47,722	$7,722	

[a] $4,000 = $100,000 × 0.08 × 6/12
[b] $4,614 = $92,278 × 0.10 × 6/12
[c] $614 = $4,614 − $4,000
[d] $92,892 = $92,278 + $614

The entry to record the issuance of Master Corporation's bonds at a discount on January 1, 2008, is:

Cash	92,278	
Bonds Payable		92,278

A = L + SE
+92,278   +92,278

Cash flows: ↑ 92,278 inflow

The journal entry to record the first interest payment on July 1, 2008, and amortization of the discount is:

Bond Interest Expense	4,614	
Bonds Payable		614
Cash		4,000

A = L + SE
−4,000   +614   −4,614

Cash flows: ↓ 4,000 outflow

The journal entry to record the interest expense accrued at December 31, 2008 (the year end), and amortization of the discount is:

Bond Interest Expense	4,645	
Bond Interest Payable		4,000
Bonds Payable		645

A = L + SE
+4,645   −4,645

Cash flows: No effect

Example: Bonds Issued at Premium If instead it had been a market where the investors were willing to accept an effective interest rate of 6% on the bond issue described above, they would have paid $108,530 or a premium of $8,530, calculated as in Illustration 14-6.

Illustration 14-6		
Calculation of Premium on Bonds Payable	Maturity value of bonds payable		$100,000
	Present value of $100,000 due in 5 years at 6%, interest payable semi-annually [$100,000 × 0.74409]	$74,409	
	Present value of $4,000 interest payable semi-annually for 5 years at 6% annually [$4,000 × 8.53020]	34,121	
	Proceeds from sale of bonds		108,530
	Premium on bonds payable		$ 8,530

The five-year amortization schedule appears in Illustration 14-7.

Illustration 14-7
Bond Premium Amortization Schedule

SCHEDULE OF BOND PREMIUM AMORTIZATION
Effective Interest Method–Semi-Annual Interest Payments
5-Year, 8% Bonds Sold to Yield 6%

Date	Cash Paid	Interest Expense	Discount Amortized	Carrying Amount of Bonds
1/1/08				$108,530
7/1/08	$ 4,000[a]	$ 3,256[b]	$744[c]	107,786[d]
1/1/09	4,000	3,234	766	107,020
7/1/09	4,000	3,211	789	106,231
1/1/10	4,000	3,187	813	105,418
1/1/10	4,000	3,162	838	104,580
1/1/11	4,000	3,137	863	103,717
7/1/11	4,000	3,112	888	102,829
1/1/12	4,000	3,085	915	101,914
7/1/12	4,000	3,057	943	100,971
1/1/13	4,000	3,029	971	100,000
	$40,000	$31,470	$8,530	

[a] $4,000 = $100,000 × 0.08 × 6/12
[b] $3,256 = $108,530 × 0.06 × 6/12
[c] $744 = $4,000 − $3,256
[d] $107,786 = $108,530 − $744

The entry to record the issuance of the Master Corporation bonds at a premium on January 1, 2008, is:

A = L + SE
+108,530   +108,530

Cash flows: ↑ 108,530 inflow

Cash	108,530	
Bonds Payable		108,530

The journal entry to record the first interest payment on July 1, 2008, and amortization of the premium is:

A = L + SE
−4,000   −744   −3,256

Cash flows: ↓ 4,000 outflow

Bond Interest Expense	3,256	
Bonds Payable	744	
Cash		4,000

As the discount or premium should be amortized as an adjustment to interest expense over the life of the bond, it results in a **constant interest rate** when it is applied to the carrying amount of debt that is outstanding at the beginning of any specific period.

Accruing Interest   In our examples up to now, the interest payment dates and the date when the financial statements were issued were the same. For example, when Master Corporation sold bonds at a premium, the two interest payment dates coincided with the financial reporting dates. However, what happens if Master wishes to report financial statements at the end of February 2008? In this case, as Illustration 14-8 shows, the premium is prorated by the appropriate number of months to arrive at the proper interest expense.

Interest accrual ($4,000 × 2/6)	$1,333.33
Premium amortized ($744 × 2/6)	(248.00)
Interest expense (Jan.–Feb.)	$1,085.33

Illustration 14-8

Calculation of Interest Expense

The journal entry to record this accrual is:

Bond Interest Expense	1,085	
Bond Interest Payable		1,085

$$A = L + SE$$
$$+1,085 \quad -1,085$$

Cash flows: No effect

If the company prepares financial statements six months later, the same procedure is followed to amortize the premium, as Illustration 14-9 shows.

Premium amortized (Mar.–June) ($744 × 4/6)	$496.00
Premium amortized (July–Aug.) ($766 × 2/6)	255.33
Premium amortized (Mar. Aug. 2008)	$751.33

Illustration 14-9

Calculation of Premium Amortization

The calculation is much simpler if the straight-line method is used. In the Master situation, for example, the total premium is $8,530 and this amount needs to be allocated evenly over the five-year period. The premium amortization per month is therefore $142 ($8,530 ÷ 60 months).

Special Situations

Deep Discount or Zero-Interest-Bearing Bonds/Notes (Marketable Securities)

As previously noted, financial liabilities should initially be recognized at fair value, which is generally the exchange value that exists when two arm's-length parties are involved in a transaction. If a zero-interest-bearing (non-interest-bearing) *marketable* security is issued for cash only, its fair value is the cash received by the security's issuer. The implicit interest rate is the **rate that makes the cash that is received now equal to the present value of the amounts that will be received in the future**. This rate would also equal the market rate of interest. The difference between the face amount of the security and the present value is recorded as **a discount and amortized to interest expense over the life of the note.**

To illustrate the entries and the amortization schedule, assume that your company is the one that issued the $10,000 three-year, zero-interest-bearing note to Jeremiah

5 Objective
Value bonds and consideration in special situations.

Company that was illustrated on page 373 in Chapter 7. Let's assume further that the note is marketable. The implicit rate that equated the total cash to be paid ($10,000 at maturity) to the present value of the future cash flows ($7,721.80 cash proceeds at the date of issuance) was 9%. Assume that the market rate of interest for a similar note would also be 9%. (The present value of $1 for three periods at 9% is $0.77218.) The time diagram that shows the one cash flow is as follows:

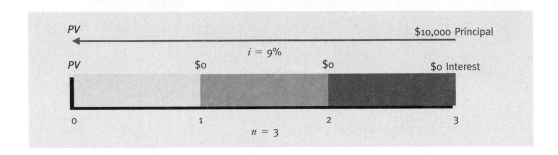

Your entry to record issuance of the note would be:

A = L + SE
+7,722   +7,722

Cash flows: ↑ 7,722 inflow

Cash	7,722	
Notes Payable		7,722

The discount is amortized and interest expense is recognized annually using the effective interest method. The three-year discount amortization and interest expense schedule is shown in Illustration 14-10.

Illustration 14-10
Schedule of Note Discount Amortization

SCHEDULE OF NOTE DISCOUNT AMORTIZATION
Effective Interest Method
0% Note Discounted at 9%

	Cash Paid	Interest Expense	Discount Amortized	Carrying Amount of Note
Date of issue				$ 7,721.80
End of year 1	$–0–	$ 694.96[a]	$ 694.96[b]	8,416.76[c]
End of year 2	–0–	757.51	757.51	9,174.27
End of year 3	–0–	825.73[d]	825.73	10,000.00
	$–0–	$2,278.20	$2,278.20	

[a] $7,721.80 × 0.09 = $694.96
[b] $694.96 – 0 – $694.96

[c] $7,721.80 + $694.96 = $8,416.76
[d] Adjustment to compensate for rounding

Interest expense at the end of the first year using the effective interest method is recorded as follows:

A = L + SE
+695   –695

Cash flows: No effect

Interest Expense ($7,722 × 9%)	695	
Notes Payable		695

The total amount of the discount, $2,278 in this case, represents the interest expense to be incurred and recognized on the note over the three years.

Non-Market Rates of Interest—Non-Marketable Loans

If the loans/notes do not trade on a market (i.e., when they are not securities) and the interest rate is a non-market interest rate, the situation must be analyzed carefully. The cash consideration that is given may not be equal to the fair value of the loan/note. Normally, in an arm's-length transaction, the loan would be issued with an interest rate approximating the market rate and therefore the consideration would approximate fair value. **If the loan is issued with an interest rate that is less than the market rate, this concession should be accounted for separately.**

In these cases, the entity must measure the value of the loan by discounting the cash flows using the market rate of interest (which is done by considering similar loans with similar terms). Any difference between the cash consideration and the discounted amount (the fair value of the loan) would be booked to net income unless it qualified for some other asset or liability.[8]

For example, assume that a government entity issues at face value a zero-interest-bearing loan that is to be repaid over five years with no stated interest. In doing this, the government is giving an additional benefit to the company beyond the debt financing. It is forgiving the interest that the company would normally be charged. Thus, the company is getting a double benefit—the loan and a grant for the interest that would otherwise be paid. The extra benefit would be accounted for separately as a government grant.

To illustrate, assume that to help a company finance the construction of a building, the government issues a $100,000, five-year, zero-interest-bearing note at face value when the market rate of interest is 10%. To record the loan, the company records a discount of $37,908, which is the difference between the loan's $100,000 face amount and its fair value of $62,092 ($100,000 × the present value factor for five years at 10% = $100,000 × 0.62092). The rest may be booked as a contra account to the related building account under government grant accounting since it relates to the construction of an asset. The issuer's journal entry is:

Cash	100,000	
Notes Payable		62,092
Building—Government Grant		37,908

A = L + SE
+62,092   +62,092

Cash flows: ↑ 100,000 inflow

The discount balance is subsequently amortized to interest expense using the effective interest method. The government grant credit balance is amortized to net income as the building is depreciated (in order to offset the costs) or the net value of the building (i.e., net of the government grant) is depreciated.[9] In this situation, the write-off of the discount and the amortization of the government grant are at different rates.

Notes Issued for Property, Goods, and Services

When a non-marketable debt instrument is exchanged for property, goods, or services in a bargained, arm's-length transaction, there are additional measurement issues. As with other transactions, it should be booked at fair value. But what is the fair value? If the issued debt is a marketable security, the value of the transaction would be easy to determine. If it is not, an attempt must be made to estimate the fair value. Normally, for monetary transactions we first try to measure the monetary asset or liability and, if this is not possible, we then attempt to value the non-monetary assets in the transaction. In this case, the note is a monetary liability and so we would try to value this first. The note could be valued using

---

[8] *CICA Handbook*, Section 3855.59.

[9] Note that the deferred credit could also initially be offset against the building assets account, resulting in a lower net book value.

a discounting technique. Similar to the previous example, the cash flows from the debt instrument could be discounted using a market rate of interest for similar debt with similar terms. If this is not possible, and if the fair value of the property, goods, or services is readily determinable, this latter value could then be used to value the transaction.

For example, assume that Scenic Development sold land having a cash sale price of $200,000 to Health Spa, Inc. in exchange for Health Spa's five-year, $293,860, zero-interest-bearing note. The $200,000 cash sale price represents the present value of the $293,860 note discounted at 8% for five years. The 8% interest rate is the market rate for a similar loan with similar terms. If both parties were to record the transaction on the sale date at the $293,860 face amount of the note, Health Spa's Land account and Scenic's sales would be overstated by $93,860 because the $93,860 is the interest for five years at an effective rate of 8%. Interest revenue to Scenic and interest expense to Health Spa for the five-year period would also then be correspondingly understated by $93,860.

The transaction could be measured by using a valuation technique to measure the value of the debt or alternatively by using the fair value of the land ($200,000). In this case, as we know the fair value of the land and we also know that the market rate is 8%, we can use either the land value or a discounting technique to measure the transaction. If either the fair value of the land or the market rate of interest were not known, we would have to determine or **impute** an interest rate. This will be discussed in the next section. Because the difference between the cash sale price of $200,000 and the face amount of the note, $293,860, represents interest at an effective rate of 8%, the transaction is recorded at the exchange date as follows:

```
A     =    L    + SE
+200,000   +200,000

Cash flows: No effect

A     =  L  +   SE
+200,000       +200,000

Cash flows: No effect
```

Health Spa, Inc. Books			Scenic Development Company Books		
Land	200,000		Notes Receivable	200,000	
Notes Payable		200,000	Sales		200,000

During the five-year life of the note, Health Spa annually amortizes a portion of the discount of $93,860 as a charge to interest expense. Scenic Development records interest revenue totalling $93,860 over the five-year period by also amortizing the discount. The effective interest method is required, although other approaches to amortization may be used if the resulting amounts are not materially different from those that result from the effective interest method.

If a higher interest rate was determined to be the market rate of interest, the land (and selling price) would be measured at a lower amount since there is an inverse relationship between the discount rate and the present value of the cash flows.

Imputed Interest for Notes

In note transactions, the effective market interest rate is either evident or it can be determined by using other factors in the exchange, such as the fair market value of what is given or received. But if a company cannot determine the fair value of the property, goods, or services that it has received and if the note has no ready market value, the problem of determining the present value of the note is more difficult. In such cases, to estimate the present value of a note, a company must use an approximate and appropriate interest rate that may be different from the stated rate (if there is one). This process of determining an approximate interest rate is called **imputation**, and the resulting interest rate is called the **imputed interest rate.**

In choosing the rate, one factor that affects the choice is the prevailing rate for similar instruments that have been issued by issuers with similar credit ratings. Other factors, such as restrictive covenants, collateral, the payment schedule, and the existing prime interest rate also play a part. Companies determine the imputed interest rate when they issue a note; any subsequent changes in prevailing rates are ignored.

Assume that on December 31, 2008, Wunderlich Company issued a promissory note to Brown Interiors Company for architectural services. The note has a face value of $550,000, a due date of December 31, 2013, and bears a stated interest rate of 2%, payable at the end of each year. The fair value of the architectural services is not readily determinable, and the note is not readily marketable. Based on the credit rating of Wunderlich Company, the absence of collateral, the prime interest rate at that date, and the prevailing interest on Wunderlich's other outstanding debt, an 8% interest rate is imputed as being appropriate in this circumstance. The time diagram for both cash flows is as follows:

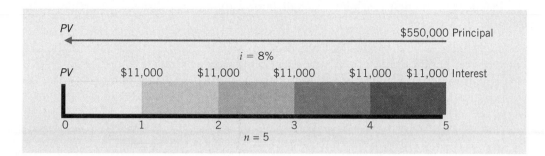

The note's present value and the imputed fair value of the architectural services are determined as in Illustration 14-11.

Face value of the the note		$550,000
Present value of $550,000 due in 5 years at 8% interest payable annually [$550,000 × 0.68058]	$374,319	
Present value of $11,000 interest payable annually for 5 years at 8% [$11,000 × 3.99271]	43,920	
Present value of the note		418,239
Discount on notes payable		$131,761

Illustration 14-11

Calculation of Imputed Fair Value and Note Discount

The issuance of the note and receipt of the architectural services are recorded as follows:

December 31, 2008		
Building (or Construction in Process)	418,239	
Notes Payable		418,239

A = L + SE
+418,239 +418,239

Cash flows: No effect

Illustration 14-12 shows the five-year amortization schedule.

SCHEDULE OF NOTE DISCOUNT AMORTIZATION
Effective Interest Method
2% Note Discounted at 8% (Imputed)

Date	Cash Paid (2%)	Interest Expense (8%)	Discount Amortized	Carrying Amount of Note
12/31/08				$418,239
12/31/09	$ 11,000[a]	$ 33,459[b]	$ 22,459[c]	440,698[d]
12/31/10	11,000	35,256	24,256	464,954
12/31/11	11,000	37,196	26,196	491,150
12/31/12	11,000	39,292	28,292	519,442

Illustration 14-12

Schedule of Discount Amortization Using Imputed Interest Rate

12/31/13	11,000	41,558ᵉ	30,558	550,000
	$55,000	$186,761	$131,761	

ᵃ $550,000 × 2% = $11,000
ᵇ $418,239 × 8% = $33,459
ᶜ $33,459 − $11,000 = $22,459

ᵈ $418,239 + $22,459 = $440,698
ᵉ Adjustment to compensate for rounding.

Payment of the first year's interest and amortization of the discount are recorded as follows:

A   =   L   +   SE
−11,000   +22,459   −33,495

Cash flows: ↓ 11,000 outflow

December 31, 2008		
Interest Expense	33,459	
Notes Payable		22,459
Cash		11,000

Issuance Costs

When bonds are issued, there are engraving and printing costs, legal and accounting fees, commissions, promotion costs, and other similar charges. For long-term financial liabilities, the entity has a choice to either recognize transactions costs in net income or add these costs to the carrying value of the debt[10] and amortize them over the life of the debt in a way that is similar to what is done for bond discounts.[11] Transaction costs include fees and commissions paid to agents, advisers, brokers and dealers, levies by regulatory agencies and exchanges and transfer taxes and duties. They do not include debt premiums/discounts, financing costs or internal administrative or holding costs.

To illustrate the accounting for the costs of issuing bonds, assume that Chipmunk Corporation sold $20 million of 10-year debenture bonds for $20,795,000 on January 1, 2009 (also the date of the bonds). Assume also that the costs of issuing the bonds were $245,000 and that the company chooses to expense these costs. The entries at January 1, 2009, and December 31, 2009, for the issuing of the bonds would be as follows:

A   =   L   +   SE
+20,550,000   +20,795,000   −245,000

Cash flows: ↑ 20,550,000 inflow

January 1, 2009		
Cash	20,550,000	
Bond Issue Expense	245,000	
Bonds Payable		20,795,000
(To record issuance of bonds)		

If the entity had chosen to amortize the cost, the amount would have been included as part of the carrying value of the debt and then amortized with the premium on the bond payable. Doing this effectively reduces the net amount that is received from the issue and increases the effective rate of interest.

---

[10] *CICA Handbook*, Section 3855.57. EIC Abstract 94 currently supports deferral of the costs. The costs would be added to the carrying value of the bonds.

[11] Debt issue cost is not considered an asset because it provides no future economic benefit.

EXTINGUISHMENT OF DEBT OR DERECOGNITION

Payment of debt is often referred to as **extinguishment of debt**. When debt is repaid or extinguished—i.e., when the obligation is discharged or cancelled or expires—it is **derecognized** from the financial statements.[12] If the bonds (or any other form of debt security) are held to maturity, **no gain or loss is calculated**. This is because any premium or discount and any issue costs will be fully amortized at the date the bonds mature. As a result, the carrying amount will be equal to the bond's maturity (face) value. And as the maturity or face value is also equal to the bond's market value at that time, there is no gain or loss.

From a financial reporting perspective, debt is considered to be extinguished when either of the following occurs:

1. The debtor discharges the liability by paying the creditor.

2. The debtor is legally released from primary responsibility for the liability by law or by the creditor.[13]

6 Objective

Describe the accounting procedures for the extinguishment of debt.

Repayment before Maturity Date

In some cases, debt is extinguished before its maturity date. The amount paid on extinguishment or redemption before maturity, including any call premium and expense of reacquisition, is called the **reacquisition price**. On any specified date, the bond's **net carrying amount** is the amount that is payable at maturity, adjusted for any unamortized premium or discount and cost of issuance. If the net carrying amount is more than the reacquisition price, the excess amount is a **gain from extinguishment**; conversely, if the reacquisition price exceeds the net carrying amount, the excess is a **loss from extinguishment**. At the time of reacquisition, the **unamortized premium or discount and any costs of issue that apply to the bonds must be amortized up to the reacquisition date**.

To illustrate, assume that on January 1, 2005, General Bell Corp. issued bonds with a par value of $800,000 at 97, due in 20 years. Bond issue costs totalling $16,000 were incurred and expensed. Eight years after the issue date, the entire issue is called at 101 and cancelled. The loss on redemption (extinguishment) is calculated as in Illustration 14-13 (straight-line amortization is used for simplicity).

Reacquisition price ($800,000 × 1.01)		$808,000
Net carrying amount of bonds redeemed:		
Face value	$800,000	
Unamortized discount ($24,000* × 12/20)		
(amortized using straight-line basis)	(14,400)	785,600
Loss on redemption		$ 22,400

*[$800,000 × (1 − 0.97)]

Illustration 14-13

Calculation of Loss on Redemption of Bonds

The entry to record the reacquisition and cancellation of the bonds is:

---

[12] *CICA Handbook*, Section 3855.45.

[13] *CICA Handbook*, Section 3855.46.

A   =   L   +   SE
−808,000   −785,600   −22,400

Cash flows: ↓ 808,000 outflow

Bonds Payable	785,600	
Loss on Redemption of Bonds	22,400	
Cash		808,000

What Do the Numbers Mean?

Note that it is often advantageous for the issuing corporation to acquire the entire outstanding bond issue and replace it with a new bond issue bearing a lower rate of interest. As an example, in June 2001, **Aliant Telecom Inc.** redeemed its 10.25% First Mortgage Bonds, Series AC, which were originally due in August 2006. The bonds were redeemed at 102% of the principal amount, plus $0.28 in accrued interest per $1,000 of principal. The premium of 2% was paid because the stated interest rate on the bonds was greater than the current market rate and holders therefore needed to be induced to part with the bonds.

Exchange of Debt Instruments

Underlying Concept

If the new debt is substantially the same as the old debt, the economic substance is that it is a continuation of the old debt, even though, legally, the old debt may have been settled.

The replacement of an existing issuance with a new one is called **refunding**. Generally, an exchange of debt instruments that have **substantially different terms** between a borrower and lender is viewed as an extinguishment of the old debt (and the issuance of a new one).[14] Alternatively, if the terms under the new debt are not substantially different, it is viewed as a **renegotiation or modification of the old debt**.

Professional judgement is applied in making this determination. The debt would be viewed as being substantially different when:

- the discounted present value of the cash flows under the new terms (discounted using the original effective interest rate) is at least 10% different from the discounted present value of the remaining cash flows under the old debt, or

- there is a change in creditor and the original debt is legally discharged.[15]

If the debt is considered settled, the liability and accounts related to the old debt are derecognized and a gain or loss results. The new debt is then recognized on the balance sheet.

Alternatively, if the debt is viewed as a **modification or renegotiation**, the debt is left on the balance sheet and a new effective interest rate is calculated that equates the cash flows under the new terms to the carrying value of the existing debt.[16]

Appendix 15A looks at modifications of debt instruments in more detail, focusing on when the debt is renegotiated under **troubled debt restructuring conditions**.

Defeasance

Occasionally, a company may want to extinguish or pay off debt before its due date but economic factors such as early repayment penalties may stop it from doing so. One option that the company has in this type of situation is to set aside the money in a trust or other arrangement and allow the trust to repay the original debt (principal and interest) as it becomes due according to the original agreement. To do this, the company must set aside sufficient funds so that the investment and any return will be enough to pay the principal and interest directly to the creditor. This is known as **defeasance**. If the creditor of the

---

[14] *CICA Handbook*, Section 3855.50.

[15] *CICA Handbook*, Section 3855.51.

[16] *CICA Handbook*, EIC Abstract 88.

original debt agrees to look to the trust for repayment and give up its claim on the company, this is known as **legal defeasance**. Since the company no longer has an obligation to the creditor, the debt may be derecognized.

In some cases, however, the company does not inform the creditor of the arrangement or the creditor does not release the company from the primary obligation to settle the debt. This version of the arrangement is often called **in-substance defeasance**. Does in-substance defeasance result in extinguishment of the debt on the company's books? In essence, if the trust is properly set up—e.g., the money is invested in low-risk or risk-free investments in an irrevocable trust—it can be argued that the debt has been prepaid and there is little risk to the company. On the other hand, the company still has the primary obligation. *CICA Handbook* Section 3855 does not permit derecognition of debt under in-substance defeasance arrangements.

RECOGNITION AND PRESENTATION ISSUES

The reporting of long-term debt is one of the most controversial areas in financial reporting. Because long-term debt has a significant impact on a company's cash flow, reporting requirements must be substantive and informative. One problem is that the definition of a liability and the recognition criteria in the *CICA Handbook* (Section 1000) are not precise enough to prevent the argument from being made that certain obligations do not need to be reported as debt.

Off–Balance Sheet Financing

Off–balance sheet financing is an attempt to borrow money in a way that results in the obligations not being recorded as debt on the balance sheet. It is an issue of extreme importance to accountants (as well as general management). **Because increased debt signals increased solvency risk, there is a reporting bias to keep low debt levels on the balance sheet**. From a user perspective, however, the amount of debt is very relevant and, in the interest of transparency, all debt should be recognized on the balance sheet.

7 Objective
Explain the issues surrounding off–balance sheet financing arrangements.

Different Forms

Off–balance sheet financing can take many different forms. Some examples follow:

1. **Non-consolidated subsidiaries.** Under present GAAP, a parent company does not have to consolidate a subsidiary company that is less than 50 percent owned where there is no control. In such cases, the parent therefore does not report the assets and the liabilities of the subsidiary. Instead, the parent only reports the investment in the subsidiary on its balance sheet. As a result, users of the financial statements might not understand that the subsidiary has considerable debt that the parent may ultimately be liable for if the subsidiary runs into financial difficulty. Investments were discussed in Chapter 9.

2. **Special purpose entities (SPE) or variable interest entities (VIE). A special purpose entity** or **variable interest entity** is an entity that a company creates so that it can perform a special project or function. For example, SPEs/VIEs might be formed to do the following:

   (a) Access financing. For example, companies sometimes set up SPEs/VIEs to buy assets such as accounts receivable or investments from the company. The company then sells the assets to the SPE/VIE in return for cash, thus obtaining financing. Investors invest in the SPE/VIE to benefit from the return on the assets and certain tax advantages. This process is known as a **securitization** of assets. In this way, the company essentially takes a pool of assets and turns it into securities. **Whether the company treats this as a sale or financing is discussed in Chapter 7.**

(b) Take on risk from the company. As in the example above, the sale of the receivables or investments eliminates price and cash flow risks for the company as it now holds cash instead of the more risky receivables or investments. The SPEs/VIEs provide a ready market for buying the assets.

(c) Isolate certain assets from other company assets. For example, the pension assets of company employees are often segregated in a trust fund or SPE. This arrangement allows greater security for the employees and the company gets certain tax advantages when it contributes money to the plan. Recognition of unfunded pension obligations is discussed in Chapter 19.

SPEs/VIEs thus serve valid business functions. **They only become problematic when they are used primarily to make a company's balance sheet look better— i.e., to disguise risk.**[17] As a general rule, these entities should be consolidated when the company is the main beneficiary of the SPE/VIE. Except for what has just been presented, the accounting for SPEs/VIEs is beyond the scope of this book.

3. **Operating leases.** Another way that companies keep debt off the balance sheet is by leasing. Instead of owning the assets, companies lease them. By meeting certain conditions, the company has to report only rent expense each period and provide a note disclosure of the transaction. Accounting for leases is discussed in Chapter 20.

The accounting profession's response to these off–balance sheet financing arrangements has been to tighten up the accounting guidance (for guarantees and SPEs) and also to mandate **increased disclosure (note) requirements**. This response is consistent with an efficient markets philosophy: the important question is not whether the presentation is off–balance sheet or not, but whether the items are disclosed at all.[18] The authors of this text believe that financial reporting would be enhanced if more obligations were recorded on the balance sheet instead of only describing them in the notes to the financial statements.

Presentation of Long-Term Debt

Current versus Long-Term

Objective 8
Indicate how long-term debt is presented and analyzed.

Companies that have large amounts and many issues of long-term debt often report only one amount in the balance sheet and support this (i.e., give details about the amount) with comments and schedules in the accompanying notes. Long-term debt that **matures within one year** should be reported as a **current liability**, unless it will be retired using something other than current assets.[19] If the debt is to be refinanced, the company must

---

[17] Two CICA guidelines deal with SPEs/VIEs: AcG 15 and AcG 12. These two pronouncements provide guidance to ensure that companies reflect the underlying economic substance of related-party transactions. They limit the potential for financial reporting manipulations and abuse relating to SPEs and securitizations.

[18] It is unlikely that the accounting profession will be able to stop all types of off–balance sheet transactions. Developing new financial instruments and arrangements to sell to customers is profitable for investment banking firms, especially where there is a demand for them. In the post-Enron era, however, many banks are discontinuing these types of products due to the now highly publicized negative connotations that are associated with them.

[19] *CICA Handbook*, Section 1510.06.

treat it as long-term unless the refinancing has occurred before the release of the financial statements or a refinancing agreement is in place.[20]

Debt versus Equity

As financial instruments become more and more complex, the line between what is debt and what is equity is becoming more blurred. As noted above, there is significant pressure on companies to watch their debt levels. The debt-versus-equity issue will be dealt with in Chapter 16 when more complex financial instruments are examined.

Note Disclosures

Note disclosures generally indicate the **nature of the liabilities, maturity dates, interest rates, call provisions, conversion privileges, restrictions imposed by the creditors, and assets designated or pledged as security**. Any assets that have been **pledged as security** for the debt should be shown in the assets section of the balance sheet. **The fair value** of the long-term debt should also be disclosed if it is practical to estimate it. Finally, disclosure is required of **future payments** for sinking fund requirements and maturity amounts of long-term debt during each of the next five years.[21] The purpose of these disclosures is to **aid financial statement users in evaluating the amounts and timing of future cash flows**. An example of the type of information that is provided is shown in the Stantec financial statements in Chapter 5.

PERSPECTIVES

The level of debt that a company holds is a very high-profile number. How much debt is the right amount? It depends. Some debt is good if it allows a company to take advantage of leveraging opportunities; however, too much debt increases the risk to the company. The higher the debt, the greater the risk that the company may not be able to repay it. Capital markets acknowledge this additional solvency risk by increasing the cost of capital and making it more difficult for companies with high debt levels to access additional capital.

In the hope of protecting themselves better, lenders insert covenants into lending agreements that require companies to manage their cash flow risks. Although debt holders assume that the covenants will protect them, covenants are often written in a way that can be interpreted (or misinterpreted) in different ways. Therefore, covenants may provide little or no protection. Note further that covenants normally refer to certain financial tests and ratios that the borrower must meet or the debt will become payable. **Because of this, the existence of restrictive covenants creates situations that encourage reporting bias.** This may create an environment in which the company feels forced to meet the test even if it means using aggressive accounting to do so.

Users of financial statements must be aware of the existence of covenants so that they understand the potential for misstating the financial statements. Whenever these conditions are important for having a complete understanding of the company's financial position and results of operations, they should be described in the body of the financial statements or the accompanying notes.

---

[20] *CICA Handbook*, EIC Abstract 122 requires the following: (1) the loan under the refinancing agreement must be for more than one year; (2) the company must be in compliance with all terms; and (3) the lender must be financially capable of honouring the agreement.

[21] *CICA Handbook*, Sections 3210 and 3861/3862.

Analysis

Long-term creditors and shareholders are interested in a company's long-run **solvency**, particularly its ability to pay interest as it comes due and to repay the face value of debt at maturity. Therefore, many debt agreements include covenants that stipulate that certain ratios be met. **Debt-to-total-assets and times interest earned** are two ratios that provide information about debt-paying ability and long-run solvency. Companies have a vested interest in making sure that they manage their debt levels in a way that does not weaken their solvency position. The **debt-to-total-assets ratio** measures the percentage of the total assets that is provided by creditors. It is calculated by dividing total debt (both current and long-term liabilities) by total assets, as shown in the following formula:

$$\text{Debt-to-total-assets} = \frac{\text{Total debt}}{\text{Total assets}}$$

The **higher the percentage** of debt to total assets, the **greater the risk** that the company may be unable to meet its maturing obligations.

The **times interest earned ratio** indicates the company's ability to meet interest payments as they come due. It is calculated by dividing income before interest expense and income taxes by interest expense:

$$\text{Times interest earned} = \frac{\text{Income before income taxes and interest expense}}{\text{Interest expense}}$$

To illustrate these ratios, we will use data from Stantec Inc.'s 2005 annual report, which disclosed total liabilities of $280.7 million, total assets of $628.8 million, interest of $0.571 million ($2 million less interest income), income taxes of $21.9 million, and net income of $40.6 million. Stantec's debt-to-total-assets ratio is calculated as follows:

$$\text{Debt-to-total-assets} = \frac{\$280.7}{\$628.8} = 44.6\%$$

Stantec's times interest earned ratio is calculated as follows:

$$\text{Times interest earned} = \frac{\$63.1}{\$0.571} = 110.5 \text{ times}$$

Stantec has a very moderate debt-to-total-assets percentage of 44.6%, and its interest coverage of 110.5 times is very safe. Note that when interest income is excluded, the ratio drops to 31.6—still a very safe number.

Accounting Standards in Transition

Historically we have used discount/premium accounts as contra/adjunct accounts when accounting for bonds and notes payable and sometimes receivables. These accounts are sometimes presented separately in financial statements as deferred costs/credits (but more often than not, they were presented with the bond/note payable/receivable itself on a net basis). Currently, GAAP is moving toward a model where there are no more deferred credits/debits on the balance sheet. Therefore, bonds/notes payable/receivable that are not classified as held for trading or available for sale, are measured on an ongoing basis at amortized cost on the balance sheet This calls into question whether we need to keep separate accounts for bookkeeping purposes to keep track of the discounts/premiums.

The CICA dictates recognition, measurement and presentation of financial statement elements and transactions in the financial statements but does not dictate how a company should do its bookkeeping. The company must decide how much or how little detail it needs to keep in its general ledger for decision making and information purposes, including tax and legal decisions/requirements. With respect to accounting for bonds and notes payable/receivable, a company may still choose to keep track of its premiums/discounts for bookkeeping purposes even though they present the bonds/notes on a net basis at amortized costs in the financial statements according to GAAP.

The text reflects this transition in GAAP. In chapters 7, 10, and 13, we have used the premiums/discount accounts in the bookkeeping journal entries as they relate to notes receivables/payables (while noting that for financial statements purposes, the amounts must be shown net). In chapters 9, 14, and 16 we have chosen to show the journal entries on a net basis. Both methods of bookkeeping are acceptable. As noted earlier, GAAP dictates the presentation on the financial statements (not the bookkeeping).

As we move forward, recording the journal entries on a net basis for financial reporting purposes will likely prevail.

International

The accounting standards in current Canadian GAAP for long-term debt are not significantly different from the IAS standards, especially as *CICA Handbook* Section 3855 was based on the International counterpart IAS 39 and *Handbook* Sections 3862 and 3863 mirror IAS 32 and IFRS 7 to a large extent. However, under IAS 39, transaction costs must be added to the measurement amount of the debt when it is initially recognized whereas under *Handbook* Section 3855, there is a choice allowing capitalization or expense. As noted in Chapter 9, there are no differential reporting options under the international standard nor does IAS 39 deal with related-party transactions.

9 Objective

Compare current Canadian and international GAAP and understand which direction international GAAP is headed in.

Canada	International
Section 3210: Long-term debt	
Section 3855: Financial instruments—recognition and measurement	IAS 39: Financial instruments: recognition and measurement
Section 3863: Financial instruments—presentation	IAS 32: Financial instruments: disclosure and presentation
Section 3862: Financial instruments—disclosures	IFRS 7: Financial instruments: disclosures

Illustration 14-14

Comparison of Canadian and International GAAP

The FASB is currently working on a liabilities and equity project as part of a larger review of financial instruments. The IASB is also re-examining the financial instruments standards. Both boards feel that the existing standards are too complex and would like to simplify and improve them. One of the long-term objectives relating to liabilities is to measure all financial instruments, including debt, at fair value, and require that gains and losses be recognized in net income. It is felt that the use of one measurement attribute will greatly simplify the accounting model.

Student Website

Glossary

www.wiley.com/canada/kieso

KEY TERMS

asset-linked debt, 838

bearer bond, 838

bond indenture, 837

callable bonds, 838

carrying value, 841

commodity-backed
    debt, 838

convertible debt, 838

coupon bond, 838

coupon rate, 841

debenture bonds, 838

debt-to-total-assets
    ratio, 858

deep discount
    bonds/notes, 838

defeasance, 854

discount, 841

effective interest
    method, 841

effective yield, 841

extinguishment
    of debt, 853

face value, 841

imputed interest rate, 850

income bond, 838

investment grade
    securities, 839

long-term debt, 836

long-term notes
    payable, 837

market rate, 841

maturity value, 841

mortgage bonds/notes,
    838

nominal rate, 841

off-balance sheet
    financing, 855

par value, 841

perpetual bonds/notes,
    838

premium, 841

present value of bond
    issue, 841

principal amount, 841

refunding, 854

registered bonds, 838

Summary of Learning Objectives

1 Describe the procedures for issuing long-term debt.

Incurring long-term debt is often a formal procedure. Corporation bylaws usually require the approval of the board of directors and the shareholders before bonds can be issued or other long-term debt arrangements can be contracted. Generally, long-term debt has various covenants or restrictions. The covenants and other terms of the agreement between the borrower and the lender are stated in the bond indenture or note agreement. Notes are similar in substance to bonds but do not trade as readily in capital markets, if at all.

2 Identify various types of long-term debt.

(1) Secured and unsecured bonds. (2) Term, serial, perpetual, and callable bonds or notes. (3) Convertible and commodity-backed bonds, and bonds that may be settled in common shares. (4) Registered and bearer (coupon) bonds. (5) Income, revenue, and deep discount bonds. The variety of types of bonds is a result of attempts to attract capital from different investors and risk takers and to satisfy the issuers' cash flow needs.

3 Explain the initial measurement of bonds/notes at their date of issuance.

The investment community values a bond at the present value of its future cash flows, which consist of interest and principal. The rate that is used to calculate the present value of these cash flows is the interest rate that provides an acceptable return on an investment that matches the issuer's risk characteristics. The interest rate written in the terms of the bond indenture and ordinarily appearing on the bond certificate is the stated, coupon, or nominal rate. This rate, which is set by the issuer of the bonds, is expressed as a percentage of the bond's face value, which is also called the par value, principal amount, or maturity value. If the rate used by the buyers differs from the stated rate, the bond's present value calculated by the buyers will differ from the bond's face value. The difference between the bond's face value and the present value is either a discount or premium.

4 Apply the methods of bond discount and premium amortization.

The discount (premium) is amortized and charged (credited) to interest expense over the period of time that the bonds are outstanding. Bond interest expense is increased by amortization of a discount and decreased by amortization of a premium. GAAP requires the effective interest method; however, in practice, the straight-line method is used where GAAP is not a constraint or where the results are not substantially different. Under the effective interest method, (1) bond interest expense is calculated by multiplying the bond's carrying value at the beginning of the period by the effective interest rate, and (2) the bond discount or premium amortization is then determined by comparing the bond interest expense with the interest to be paid.

5 Value bonds and consideration in special situations.

Bonds/notes may be issued with zero interest or for a non-monetary consideration. Measurement of the bonds and the consideration must reflect the underlying substance of the transaction. In particular, reasonable interest rates must be imputed. The fair value of the debt and of the non-monetary consideration should be used to value the transaction.

6 Describe the accounting procedures for the extinguishment of debt.

At the time of reacquisition, the unamortized premium or discount and any costs of issue that apply to the debt must be amortized up to the reacquisition date. The amount that is paid on extinguishments or redemption before maturity, including any call premium and expense of reacquisition, is the reacquisition price. On any specified date, the debt's net carrying amount is the amount that is payable at maturity, adjusted for unamortized premium or discount and the cost of issuance. Any excess of the net carrying amount over the reacquisition price is a gain from extinguishment; whereas the excess of the reacquisition price over the net carrying amount is a loss from extinguishment. Legal defeasance results in debt extinguishment. In-substance defeasance does not in itself result in extinguishment. If old debt is replaced by new debt, extinguishment occurs if the new debt has substantially different terms from the old debt.

7 Explain the issues surrounding off–balance sheet financing arrangements.

Off–balance sheet financing is an attempt to borrow funds in such a way that the obligations are not recorded. One type of off–balance sheet financing involves the use of certain variable interest entities.

8 Indicate how long-term debt is presented and analyzed.

Companies that have large amounts and many issues of long-term debt often report only one amount in the balance sheet and support this with comments and schedules in the accompanying notes. Any assets that are pledged as security for the debt should be shown in the assets section of the balance sheet. Long-term debt that matures within one year should be reported as a current liability, unless it will be retired without using current assets. If the debt is to be refinanced, converted into shares, or retired from a bond retirement fund, it should continue to be reported as non-current and accompanied by a note explaining the method to be used in its liquidation unless certain conditions are met. Disclosure is required of future payments for sinking fund requirements and maturity amounts of long-term debt during each of the next five years. Debt-to-total-assets and times interest earned are two ratios that provide information about debt-paying ability and long-run solvency.

9 Compare current Canadian and international GAAP and understand which direction international GAAP is headed in.

The international and Canadian standards are largely converged. Two exceptions relate to treatment of transaction costs (choice not allowed under international GAAP) and related-party transactions (no guidance given in the financial instruments standard). The IASB and FASB are working on a new standard to simplify accounting for financial instruments which would require all financial instruments to be valued at fair value with gains and losses to net income.

restrictive covenants, 836
revenue bonds, 838
secured debt, 838
securitization, 856
serial bonds/notes, 838
special purpose
  entity, 855
stated rate, 841
straight-line method, 841
term bonds/notes, 838
times interest earned
  ratio, 858
variable interest
  entity, 855
zero-interest debentures,
  bonds, or notes, 838

Appendix 14A

Troubled Debt

During periods of depressed economic conditions or other financial hardship, some debtors have difficulty meeting their financial obligations. During the late 1980s, bad energy loans and the rescheduling of loans between major banks and less developed countries, such as Argentina, Brazil, and Mexico, created a lot of uncertainty in the banking industry. Many companies had to restructure their debts or be bailed out of negative cash flow situations in some other way.

This appendix addresses the issues for **debtors** (those who owe the money) and **creditors** (those who loaned the money) in accounting for troubled debt. **In a troubled debt situation, the creditor usually first recognizes a loss on impairment.** Subsequently, either the loan terms are **modified** or the loan is **settled** on terms that are unfavourable to the creditor. The creditor continues to refine and recognize estimates of loss. In extreme cases, the creditor forces the debtor into bankruptcy in order to ensure the highest possible collection on the loan. The debtor recognizes a change in the debt only when there is a restructuring, foreclosure, or bankruptcy. Note that a restructuring of the debt could involve either of the following:

1. Settlement or extinguishment of the debt with new debt being issued

2. Modification of the terms of the old debt

   Illustration 14A-1 shows this continuum.

Illustration 14A-1

Usual Progression in Troubled Debt Situations

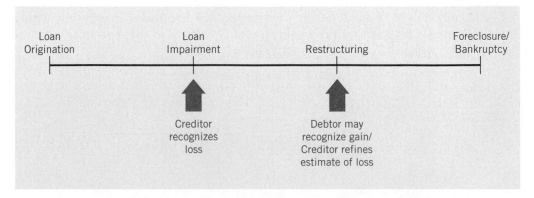

For the creditor, the major accounting issues for troubled debt situations are the **recognition** and **measurement** of the potential asset impairment. For the debtor, the major accounting issues are a bit more complex. It must be decided whether restructuring of the debt results in an extinguishment or settlement of the old debt (in which case the debt should be **derecognized**) or a modification of the old debt (with a resulting **remeasurement** of the cost of capital).

Impairment of Loans/Notes Receivable

Should the creditor wait until the loan becomes uncollectible, or should it record a loss earlier? As a general rule, losses should be recorded immediately if it is **likely** that the loss will occur and the loss is **measurable**.[22] More specifically, a loan is considered impaired when the lender **no longer has reasonable assurance of being able to collect the full amount of the principal and interest on a timely basis**.[23] Determining whether or not an entity's creditworthiness has deteriorated might be done by reviewing the following evidence:

10 **Objective**
Account for impairments on notes and loans receivable.

- financial statements evidencing liquidity problems

- independent credit reports

- a current default on a payment

- a failure to meet debt covenants

- a downgrading of credit status

- a decline in the market value of traded debt[24]

If a company is in receivership, bankruptcy, or liquidation, this may confirm the deterioration. More general factors, such as the state of the economy generally or in a specific industry sector, should also be considered.

Once loans are determined to be **impaired**, they should be **measured** at **estimated realizable amounts**, which generally means **discounting the expected future cash flows at the effective interest rate** inherent in the loans (the historical rate).[25] This approach is fine as long as both the amount and timing of the estimated cash flows can be **determined**. If this is not the case, the loan is measured at either of the following:

1. The fair value of any security underlying the loan

2. The observable market price for the loan

Illustration of Loss on Impairment

Assume that on December 31, 2008, Prospect Inc. issued a $500,000, five-year, zero-interest-bearing note to Community Bank. The note was issued to yield 10% (market rate) annual interest. As a result, Prospect received and Community Bank paid $310,460 ($500,000 × 0.62092) on December 31, 2008.[26] The following time diagram shows the factors that are involved:

---

[22] *CICA Handbook*, Section 3290 on contingencies.

[23] *CICA Handbook*, Section 3025.03.

[24] *CICA Handbook*, Section 3025.07.

[25] In theory, the market rate is a better choice for discounting since it reflects the current risk characteristics of the loan. The historical rate is recommended in *CICA Handbook* Section 3025.14 and .02(c) on the basis that most other assets and liabilities on the balance sheet are reflected at the historic rate.

[26] PV of $500,000 due in five years at 10%, with annual compounding.

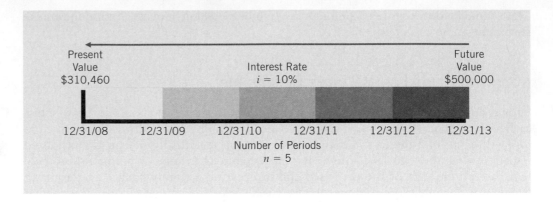

The entries to record this transaction on the books of Community Bank (the creditor) and Prospect Inc. (the debtor) are as in Illustration 14A-2.

December 31, 2008			
Community Bank (Creditor)		**Prospect Inc. (Debtor)**	
Notes Receivable	310,460	Cash	310,460
Cash	310,460	Notes Payable	310,460

Assuming that Community Bank and Prospect Inc. use the effective interest method to amortize discounts, Illustration 14A-3 shows the amortization of the discount and the increase in the note's amount over its life.

COMMUNITY BANK

Date	Cash Received (0%)	Interest Revenue (10%)	Discount Amortized	Carrying Amount of Note
12/31/08				$310,460
12/31/09	0	$ 31,046[a]	$ 31,046	341,506[b]
12/31/10	0	34,151	34,151	375,657
12/31/11	0	37,566	37,566	413,223
12/31/12	0	41,322	41,322	454,545
12/31/13	0	45,455	45,455	500,000
Total	0	$189,540	$189,540	

[a] $31,046 − $310,460 × 0.10
[b] $341,506 = $310,460 + $31,046

Unfortunately, during 2010, Prospect's business deteriorated due to increased competition and a weakening regional economy. After reviewing all available evidence at December 31, 2010, Community Bank determined that it was probable that Prospect would pay back only $300,000 of the principal at maturity. As a result, Community Bank decided that the loan was impaired, and that a loss should be recorded immediately. To determine the loss, first calculate the **present value of the expected cash flows discounted at the historical effective rate of interest**. This amount is $225,396. The following time diagram highlights the factors involved in this calculation:

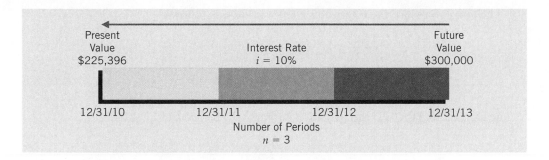

The loss due to impairment is equal to the difference between the present value of the expected future cash flows and the recorded carrying amount of the investment in the loan. Illustration 14A-4 shows this calculation.

Carrying amount of investment (12/31/10)*	$375,657
Less: Present value of $300,000 due in 3 years at 10% interest	
compounded annually ($300,000 x 0.75132)	225,396
Loss due to impairment	$150,261

*from Illustration 14A-3

Illustration 14A-4

Calculation of Loss Due to Impairment

The loss due to the impairment is $150,261, not $200,000 ($500,000 − $300,000); it is the former amount because, when the loss is recorded, it is measured at a present value amount, not an undiscounted amount.

The entry to record the loss is in Illustration 14A-5.

December 31, 2010

Community Bank (Creditor)		**Prospect Inc. (Debtor)**
Bad Debt Expense	150,261	No entry
Allowance for Doubtful		
Accounts	150,261	

Illustration 14A-5

Creditor and Debtor Entries to Record Loss on Note

A	=	L	+	SE
−150,261				−150,261

Cash flows: No effect

Community Bank (the creditor) debits Bad Debt Expense (or Losses) for the expected loss. At the same time, it reduces the overall value of its loan receivable by crediting Allowance for Doubtful Accounts. Interest would be recognized using the effective interest method at 10% (the historical rate) based on the $225,396 carrying value. Prospect Inc. (the debtor) makes no entry because it still legally owes $500,000. Illustration 14A-6 shows the amortization table for Community Bank.

COMMUNITY BANK

Date	Cash Received (0%)	Interest Revenue (10%)	Discount Amortized	Carrying Amount of Note
12/31/10				$ 225,396
12/31/11	$–0–	$22,540[a]	$22,540	247,936[b]
12/31/12	–0–	24,794	24,794	272,730
12/31/13	–0–	27,273	27,273	300,000[c]
Total	$–0–	$74,607	$74,607	

[a] 22,540 = $225,396 × 0.10   [b] 247,936 = $225,396 + 22,540   [c] Rounded

Illustration 14A-6

Schedule of Interest and Amortization (after Impairment)

ment buildings, but because of low occupancy rates it cannot meet its loan obligations.

allowance for doubtful accounts has been set up.[27] The entry to record this transaction on the books of Nova Scotia City Bank (the creditor) is as follows:

Real Estate	16,000,000	
Loss on Loan Impairment	4,000,000	
Note Receivable		20,000,000

A   =   L   +   SE
−4,000,000   −4,000,000
Cash flows: No effect

The real estate is recorded at its fair value, and a charge is made to the income statement to reflect the loss.[28]

The entry to record this transaction on the books of Union Trust (the debtor) is as follows:

Note Payable	20,000,000	
Loss on Asset Disposal	5,000,000	
Real Estate		21,000,000
Gain on Restructuring of Debt		4,000,000

A   =   L   +   SE
−21,000,000   −20,000,000   −1,000,000
Cash flows: No effect

Union Trust has a loss on the disposal of real estate in the amount of $5 million (the difference between the $21-million book value and the $16-million fair value). In addition, it has a gain on restructuring of debt of $4 million (the difference between the $20-million carrying amount of the note payable and the $16-million fair market value of the real estate).

To illustrate the granting of an equity interest (i.e., shares), assume that Nova Scotia City Bank had agreed to accept from Union Trust 320,000 of Union's common shares that have a market value of $16 million, in full settlement of the $20-million loan obligation. Assume also that the bank had previously recognized a loss on impairment of $4 million. The entry to record this transaction on the books of Nova Scotia City Bank (the creditor) is as follows:

Investment	16,000,000	
Allowance for Doubtful Accounts	4,000,000	
Note Receivable		20,000,000

A   =   L   +   SE
0
Cash flows: No effect

The shares that are received by Nova Scotia City Bank are recorded as an investment and at their market value on the date of the restructuring.

The entry to record this transaction on the books of Union Trust (the debtor) is as follows:

Note Payable	20,000,000	
Common Shares		16,000,000
Gain		4,000,000

A   =   L   +   SE
     −20,000,000   +20,000,000
Cash flows: No effect

---

[27] In reality, an impairment should likely have been set up when the bank first determined that a loss was likely and measurable. This would usually be done before the point when a loan is restructured or settled, as mentioned earlier in the chapter.

[28] According to *CICA Handbook* Section 3025.38, the creditor must decide whether the asset meets the criteria to be classified as held for sale. If it does, the asset is valued at its fair value less the costs to sell it.

Modification of Terms

In some cases, a debtor will have serious short-term cash flow problems that lead it to request one or a combination of the following modifications:

1. Reduction of the stated interest rate

2. Extension of the maturity date of the debt's face amount

3. Reduction of the debt's face amount

4. Reduction or deferral of any accrued interest

Under a **modification of debt**, the old debt still exists but with new terms. All existing deferred debits and credits (e.g., debt discounts and premiums, deferred financing costs, and deferred foreign exchange) continue to be deferred and amortized over the remaining debt. A new effective interest rate is imputed by equating the carrying amount of the original debt with the present value of the revised cash flows. If there are **substantial modifications**, however, **the transaction is treated like a settlement**. The modifications would be considered substantial in either of these two situations:

1. The discounted present value under the new terms (discounted using the original effective interest rate) is at least 10% different from the discounted present value of the remaining cash flows under the old debt.

2. There is a change in creditor and the original debt is legally discharged.[29]

If one of these conditions is met, the transaction is considered a settlement. Otherwise, it is treated as a modification.

When the economic substance is a **settlement**, the old liability is eliminated and a new liability is assumed. The new liability is measured at the present value of the revised future cash flows discounted at the currently prevailing market interest rate (as is done for the initial recording of a bond). The gain is measured as the difference between the current present value of the revised cash flows and the carrying value of the old debt.

Illustration

Assume that on December 31, 2008, Manitoba National Bank enters into a debt restructuring agreement with Resorts Development Corp., which is experiencing financial difficulties. The bank restructures a $10.5-million loan receivable issued at par (interest paid up to date) by doing all of the following:

1. It reduces the principal obligation from $10.5 million to $9 million.

2. It extends the maturity date from December 31, 2008, to December 31, 2012.

3. It reduces the interest rate from 12% to 8%. (The market rate is currently 9%.)

Is this a settlement or a modification? Has a substantial modification in the debt occurred? The test to establish whether this is a settlement or not involves the cash flows. The present value of both cash flow streams is calculated as follows, using the historic rate as the discount rate (for consistency and comparability):

Old debt: PV = $10,500,000 (since the debt is currently due)

New debt: PV = $9,000,000 (0.63552) + $720,000 (3.03735) = $7,906,572

---

[29] *CICA Handbook*, Section 3855.51.

The new debt's value differs by more than 10% of the old debt's value, so the renegotiated debt would therefore be considered a settlement, and a gain would be recorded through the following journal entry:

Note Payable—Old	10,500,000	
Note Payable—New		8,708,468
Gain		1,791,532

A = L + SE
−1,791,600 +1,791,600

Cash flows: No effect

Because it is new debt, it would be recorded at the present value of the new cash flows at the market interest rate ($9,000,000 × 0.70843) + ($720,000 × 3.243972).

Manitoba National Bank would record any loss on the same basis as an impaired loan (discussed earlier). That is, the recorded amount of the loan receivable would be reduced to the amount of the net cash flows receivable (but under the modified terms) discounted at the historical effective interest rate that is inherent in the loan.

If the test was not met and the debt was considered modified or exchanged, the debt would remain on the books at $10.5 million and no gain or loss would be recognized. As a result, no entry would be made by Resorts Development Corp. (debtor) at the date of restructuring. The debtor would **calculate a new effective interest rate**, however, in order to record interest expense in future periods. In this case, the new rate is calculated by relating the pre-restructure carrying amount ($10.5 million) to the total future cash flows ($11,880,000). The rate to discount the total future cash flows ($11,880,000) to the present value that is equal to the remaining balance ($10.5 million) is 3.46613%.

Based on the effective rate of 3.46613%, the schedule in Illustration 14A-7 is prepared.

RESORTS DEVELOPMENT CORP. (DEBTOR)

Date	Interest Paid (8%)	Interest Expense (3.46613%)	Reduction of Carrying Amount	Carrying Amount of Note
12/31/08				$10,500,000
12/31/09	$ 720,000[a]	$ 363,944[b]	$ 356,056[c]	10,143,944
12/31/10	720,000	351,602	368,398	9,775,546
12/31/11	720,000	338,833	381,167	9,394,379
12/31/12	720,000	325,621	394,379	9,000,000
	$2,880,000	$1,380,000	$1,500,000	

[a] $720,000 = $9,000,000 × 0.08
[b] $363,944 = $10,500,000 × 3.46613%
[c] $356,056 = $720,000 − $363,944

Illustration 14A-7

Schedule Showing Reduction of Carrying Amount of Note

Thus, on December 31, 2009 (the date of the first interest payment after the restructuring), the debtor makes the following entry:

December 31, 2009		
Notes Payable	356,056	
Interest Expense	363,944	
Cash		720,000

A = L + SE
−720,000 −356,056 −363,944

Cash flows: ↓ 720,000 outflow

A similar entry (except for different amounts for debits to Notes Payable and Interest Expense) is made each year until maturity. At maturity, the following entry is made:

A   =   L   + SE
−9,000,000   −9,000,000

Cash flows: ↓ 9,000,000 outflow

	December 31, 2012	
Notes Payable	9,000,000	
Cash		9,000,000

In this case also, Manitoba National Bank would account for the restructuring as an impaired loan.

Student
Website

Glossary

www.wiley.com/canada/kieso

KEY TERMS

creditor, 862

debtor, 862

loan foreclosure, 866

impairment, 862

troubled debt
  restructuring, 866

Summary of Learning Objectives for Appendix 14A

10 Account for impairments on notes and loans receivable.

An impairment loan loss is based on the difference between the present value of the future cash flows and the note/loan's carrying amount.

11 Distinguish between and account for debt restructurings that result in extinguishment or in debt continuation.

Restructured debt is considered settled when there is a new creditor or the value of the new debt is substantially different. When the old debt is considered settled, a gain or loss is recorded. When the new debt is considered to be a continuation of the old debt (modification or exchange), no gain or loss is recognized and a new effective interest rate is established that equates the carrying value of the old debt with the cash flows under the new arrangements.

Brief Exercises

Note: All assignment material with an asterisk (*) relates to the appendix to the chapter.

(LO 3) BE14-1   Branzei Corporation issues $500,000 of 11% bonds that are due in 10 years and pay interest semi-annually. At the time of issue, the market rate for such bonds is 10%. Calculate the bonds' issue price.

(LO 3) BE14-2   Capriati, Inc. issued an $800,000, four-year, 10% note at face value to Forest Bank on January 1, 2007, and received $800,000 cash. The note requires annual interest payments on each December 31. Prepare Capriati's journal entries to record the following:

 (a) The note issuance

 (b) The December 31 interest payment

(LO 3, 5) BE14-3   Montana Corporation issued a $110,000, four-year, zero-interest-bearing note to Sandford Corp. on January 1, 2008, and received $69,907 cash. The implicit interest rate is 12%.

 (a) Prepare Montana's journal entry for the January 1 issuance.

 (b) Prepare Montana's journal entry for the December 31 recognition of interest.

 (c) Assume that the effective interest of 12% had not been provided in the data. Prove the effective interest rate of 12% using a financial calculator or computer spreadsheet function.

 (d) Prepare the first three payments of an effective-interest amortization table for the note.

(LO 3, 5) BE14-4   Boitano Corporation issued a $50,000, four-year, 5% note to Johnson Corp. on January 1, 2008, and received a computer that normally sells for $41,077. The note requires annual interest payments on each December 31. The market interest rate for a note of similar risk is 13%.

 (a) Prepare Boitano's journal entry for the January 1, 2008, issuance.

 (b) Prepare Boitano's journal entry for the December 31, 2008, interest payment.

BE14-5 Kwanza Corporation issued a $140,000, four-year, zero-interest-bearing note to Salmon Corp. on January 1, 2008, and received $140,000 cash. In addition, the company agreed to sell merchandise to Salmon at an amount less than the regular selling price over the four-year period. The market interest rate for similar notes is 8%. Prepare Kwanza's January 1 journal entry. **(LO 3, 5)**

BE14-6 Plouffe Ltd. signed an instalment note on January 1, 2008, in settlement of an account payable of $40,000 owed to MacDonnell Ltd. Plouffe is able to borrow funds from its bank at 11%, whereas MacDonnell can borrow at the rate of 10%. The note calls for two equal payments of blended principal and interest to be made at December 31, 2008 and 2009. Calculate the amount of the equal instalment payments that will be made to MacDonnell Ltd. **(LO 3)**

BE14-7 Gandhi Limited issued $100,000 of 11% bonds on January 1, 2007. The bonds are due on January 1, 2011, with interest payable each July 1 and January 1. The bonds are issued at face value. Prepare the company's journal entries for the following: **(LO 3)**

(a) The January issuance

(b) The July 1, 2007, interest payment

(c) The December 31, 2007, adjusting entry

BE14-8 Assume that the bonds in BE14-7 were issued at 96. Assume also that Gandhi Limited records the amortization using the straight-line method. Prepare the journal entries related to the bonds for the following dates: **(LO 4)**

(a) January 1

(b) July 1

(c) December 31

BE14-9 Assume that the bonds in BE14-7 were issued at 101. Assume also that Gandhi Limited records the amortization using the straight-line method. Prepare the journal entries related to the bonds for the following dates: **(LO 4)**

(a) January 1

(b) July 1

(c) December 31

BE14-10 Story Corporation issued $700,000 of 9% bonds on May 1, 2008. The bonds were dated January 1, 2008, and mature on January 1, 2013, with interest payable each July 1 and January 1. The bonds were issued at face value plus accrued interest. Prepare the company's journal entries for the following: **(LO 4)**

(a) The May 1 issuance

(b) The July 1 interest payment

(c) The December 31 adjusting entry

BE14-11 On January 1, 2008, Qix Corporation issued $600,000 of 7% bonds that are due in 10 years. The bonds were issued for $559,229 and pay interest each July 1 and January 1. The company uses the effective interest method. Assume an effective rate of 8%. **(LO 4)**

(a) Prepare the company's journal entry for the January 1 issuance.

(b) Prepare the company's journal entry for the July 1 interest payment.

(c) Prepare the company's December 31 adjusting entry.

(d) Assume that the effective interest of 8% was not given in the data. Prove the effective interest rate of 8% using a financial calculator or computer spreadsheet function.

(e) Prepare the first three payments of an effective-interest amortization table for the bonds.

BE14-12 Assume that the bonds in BE14-11 were issued for $644,635 and the effective interest rate was 6%. **(LO 4)**

(a) Prepare the company's journal entry for the January 1 issuance.

(b) Prepare the company's journal entry for the July 1 interest payment.

(c) Prepare the company's December 31 adjusting entry.

(d) Assume that the effective interest of 6% was not given in the data. Prove the effective interest rate of 6% using a financial calculator or computer spreadsheet function.

(e) Prepare the first three payments of an effective-interest amortization table for the bonds.

(LO 4)   BE14-13   Izzy Corporation issued $800,000 of 8% bonds on November 1, 2007, for $919,020. The bonds were dated November 1, 2007, and mature in 10 years, with interest payable each May 1 and November 1. The company uses the effective interest method with an effective rate of 6%. Prepare the company's December 31, 2007, adjusting entry.

(LO 6)   BE14-14   On January 1, 2007, Uzbalis Corporation retired $590,000 (face value) of bonds at 98. At the time of retirement, the unamortized premium was $15,000. Prepare the corporation's journal entry to record the reacquisition of the bonds.

(LO 8)   BE14-15   At December 31, 2008, Land Corporation has the following account balances:

Bonds Payable—Due January 1, 2015	$922,000
Bond Interest Payable	80,000

Show how the above accounts should be presented on the December 31, 2008, balance sheet, and with the proper classifications.

Exercises

(LO 3)   E14-1   (Entries for Bond Transactions) Two independent situations follow:

1. On January 1, 2007, Simon Limited issued $400,000 of 10-year, 9% bonds at par. Interest is payable quarterly on April 1, July 1, October 1, and January 1.

2. On June 1, 2007, Graceland Inc. issued at par, plus accrued interest, $300,000 of 10-year, 6% bonds dated January 1. Interest is payable semi-annually on July 1 and January 1.

Instructions
For each of these two independent situations, prepare journal entries to record:

(a) The issuance of the bonds

(b) The payment of interest on July 1

(c) The accrual of interest on December 31

(LO 3, 4)   E14-2   (Entries for Bond Transactions—Effective Interest) Dion Inc. issued $1.6 million of 10%, 20-year bonds on January 1, 2007, at 102. Interest is payable semiannually on July 1 and January 1. Dion Inc. uses the effective interest method of amortization for a bond premium or discount. Assume an effective yield of 9.75%. (With a market rate of 9.75%, the issue price would be slightly higher. For simplicity, ignore this.)

Instructions
Prepare the journal entries to record the following. (Round to the nearest dollar.)

(a) The issuance of the bonds

(b) The payment of interest and related amortization on July 1, 2007

(c) The accrual of interest and the related amortization on December 31, 2007

(LO 3, 5)   E14-3   (Entries for Non-Interest-Bearing Debt) On January 1, 2008, Greene Inc. makes the following acquisitions:

1. Purchases land having a fair market value of $200,000 by issuing a five-year, non-interest-bearing promissory note in the face amount of $337,012.

2. Purchases equipment by issuing an eight-year, 6% promissory note having a maturity value of $275,000 (interest payable annually). The company has to pay 11% interest for funds from its bank.

Instructions

(a) Record Greene's journal entries on January 1, 2008, for each of the purchases.

(b) Record the interest at the end of the first year on both notes using the effective interest method.

(LO 3, 5)   E14-4   (Imputation of Interest) Two independent situations follow. Answer the questions at the end of each situation.

1. On January 1, 2008, Wright Inc. purchased land that had an assessed value of $380,000 at the time of purchase. A $580,000, non-interest-bearing note due on January 1, 2012, was given in exchange. There was no established exchange price for the land, and no ready market value for the note. The interest rate that is normally charged on a note of this type is 11%. Determine at what amount the land should be recorded at January 1, 2008, and the interest expense to be reported in 2008 related to this transaction. Discuss how the assessed value of the land could be used in this situation.

2. On January 1, 2008, Field Furniture Ltd. borrowed $5.2 million (face value) from Sinise Inc., a major customer, through a non-interest-bearing note due in four years. Because the note was non-interest-bearing, Field Furniture agreed to sell furniture to this customer at lower than market price. An 8% rate of interest is normally charged on this type of loan. Prepare the journal entry to record this transaction and determine the amount of interest expense to report for 2008.

E14-5 (Purchase of Land with Instalment Note) Dobson Ltd. issued an instalment note on January 1, 2008, in **(LO 3, 5)** exchange for land that it purchased from Samson Ltd. Samson's real estate agent had listed the land on the market for $120,000. The implied interest rate is 9%. The note calls for three equal blended payments of $43,456 that are to be made at December 31, 2008, 2009, and 2010.

Instructions

(a) Discuss how the purchase price of the land will be established.

(b) Using time value of money tables, a financial calculator, or computer spreadsheet functions, prove that the note will cost Dobson Ltd. 9% interest over the note's full term.

(c) Prepare an effective-interest amortization table for the instalment note for the three-year period.

(d) Prepare Dobson's journal entry for the purchase of the land.

(e) Prepare Dobson's journal entry for the first instalment payment on the note on December 31, 2008.

(f) From Samson Ltd.'s perspective, what are the advantages of an instalment note compared to a regular interest-bearing note?

E14-6 (Purchase of Equipment with Non-Interest-Bearing Debt) To meet customer demand for its product, **(LO 3, 5)** Abbott Inc. decided to purchase equipment from Central Ontario Industries on January 2, 2008, and expand its production capacity. Abbott issued an $800,000, five-year, non-interest-bearing note to Central Ontario Industries for the new equipment when the prevailing market interest rate for obligations of this nature was 12%. The company will pay off the note in five $160,000 instalments that are due at the end of each year over the life of the note.

Instructions

(a) Prepare the journal entry(ies) at the date of purchase. (Round to nearest dollar in all calculations.)

(b) Prepare the journal entry(ies) at the end of the first year to record the payment and interest, assuming that the company uses the effective interest method.

(c) Prepare the journal entry(ies) at the end of the second year to record the payment and interest.

E14-7 (Purchase of Computer with Non-Interest-Bearing Debt) Springfield Corporation purchased a computer **(LO 3, 5)** on December 31, 2007, paying $30,000 down and agreeing to make a further $75,000 payment on December 31, 2010. An interest rate of 10% is implicit in the purchase price. Sparrow uses the effective interest method and has a December 31 year end.

Instructions

(a) Prepare the journal entry(ies) at the purchase date. (Round to two decimal places.)

(b) Prepare any journal entry(ies) required at December 31, 2008, 2009, and 2010.

E14-8 (Imputation of Interest with Right) On January 1, 2007, Avery Inc. borrowed $500,000 from a major cus- **(LO 3, 5)** tomer through a non-interest-bearing note due in three years. As consideration for the non-interest-bearing feature, Avery agrees to supply the customer's inventory needs for the loan period at lower than the market price. The appropriate rate for imputing interest would be 8%.

Instructions

(a) Prepare the journal entry to record the initial transaction on January 1, 2007. (Round all calculations to the nearest dollar.)

(b) Prepare the journal entry to record any adjusting entries needed at December 31, 2007. Assume that Avery's sales of its product to this customer occur evenly over the three-year period.

E14-9 (Entries for Bond Transactions) On January 1, 2007, Aumont Inc. sold 12% bonds having a maturity value of **(LO 3, 4)** $500,000 for $537,907.37, which provides the bondholders with a 10% yield. The bonds are dated January 1, 2007, and mature on January 1, 2012, with interest payable on January 1 of each year. The company uses the effective interest method.

Instructions

(a) Prepare the journal entry at the date of issue.

(b) Prepare a schedule of interest expense and bond amortization for 2007 through 2009.

(c) Prepare the journal entry to record the interest payment and the amortization for 2007.

(d) Prepare the journal entry to record the interest payment and the amortization for 2009.

(LO 3) E14-10   (Information Related to Various Bond Issues) Austin Inc. has issued three types of debt on January 1, 2007, the start of the company's fiscal year:

1. $1-million, five-year, 12% unsecured bonds, with interest payable quarterly. The bonds were priced to yield 10%.

2. $22 million par of 10-year, zero-coupon bonds at a price to yield 12% per year

3. $19-million, 10-year, 10% mortgage bonds, with interest payable annually to yield 12%

Instructions

Prepare a schedule that identifies the following items for each bond: (1) the maturity value, (2) the number of interest periods over the life of the bond, (3) the stated rate for each interest period, (4) the effective interest rate for each interest period, (5) the payment amount per period, and (6) the present value of the bonds at the date of issue.

(LO 4) E14-11   (Entries for Bond Transactions—Straight-Line) Dion Inc. issued $1.6 million of 20-year, 10% bonds on January 1, 2007, at 102. Interest is payable semi-annually on July 1 and January 1. The company uses the straight-line method of amortization for any bond premium or discount.

Instructions

Prepare the journal entries to record the following:

(a) The issuance of the bonds

(b) The payment of interest and the related amortization on July 1, 2007

(c) The accrual of interest and the related amortization on December 31, 2007

(LO 4) E14-12   (Amortization Schedules—Straight-Line) Major Inc. sells 10% bonds having a maturity value of $2 million for $1,855,816. The bonds are dated January 1, 2007, and mature January 1, 2012. Interest is payable annually on January 1.

Instructions

Set up a schedule of interest expense and discount amortization under the straight-line method.

(LO 4) E14-13   (Amortization Schedule—Effective Interest) Assume the same information as in E14-12.

Instructions

Set up a schedule of interest expense and discount amortization under the effective interest method. (Hint: The effective interest rate must be calculated.)

(LO 4) E14-14   (Determine Proper Amounts in Account Balances) Three independent situations follow. Answer the questions at the end of each situation.

1. Winans Corporation incurred the following costs when it issued bonds: (1) printing and engraving costs, $25,000; (2) legal fees, $69,000; and (3) commissions paid to underwriter, $70,000. What accounting treatment could be given to these costs?

2. Gershwin Inc. sold $3 million of 10-year, 10% bonds at 104 on January 1, 2008. The bonds were dated January 1, 2008, and pay interest on July 1 and January 1. If Gershwin uses the straight-line method to amortize bond premium or discount, determine the amount of interest expense to be reported on July 1, 2008, and December 31, 2008.

3. Kenoly Inc. issued $600,000 of 10-year, 9% bonds on June 30, 2007, for $562,500. This price provided a yield of 10% on the bonds. Interest is payable semi-annually on December 31 and June 30. If Kenoly uses the effective interest method, determine the amount of interest expense to record if financial statements are issued on October 31, 2007.

(LO 4, 8) E14-15   (Entries and Questions for Bond Transactions) On June 30, 2008, Mischa Limited issued $4 million of 20-year bonds having a face value of 13% for $4,300,920, which provides a yield of 12%. The company uses the effective interest method to amortize any bond premium or discount. The bonds pay semi-annual interest on June 30 and December 31.

Instructions

(a) Prepare the journal entries to record the following transactions:

1. The issuance of the bonds on June 30, 2008

2. The payment of interest and the amortization of the premium on December 31, 2008

3. The payment of interest and the amortization of the premium on June 30, 2009

4. The payment of interest and the amortization of the premium on December 31, 2009

(b) Show the proper balance sheet presentation for the liability for bonds payable on the December 31, 2008, balance sheet.

(c) Answer the following questions:

1. What amount of interest expense is reported for 2008?

2. Will the bond interest expense that is reported in 2008 be the same as, greater than, or less than the amount that would be reported if the straight-line method of amortization were used?

3. What is the total cost of borrowing over the life of the bond?

4. Will the total bond interest expense for the life of the bond be greater than, the same as, or less than the total interest expense if the straight-line method of amortization were used?

E14-16 **(Entries for Retirement and Issuance of Bonds—Straight-Line)** On June 30, 2000, Autry Limited issued 12% bonds with a par value of $800,000 due in 20 years. They were issued at 98 and were callable at 104 at any date after June 30, 2007. **(LO 4, 6)**

Because of lower interest rates and a significant change in the company's credit rating, it was decided to call the entire issue on June 30, 2007, and to issue new bonds. New 10% bonds were sold in the amount of $1 million at 102; they mature in 20 years. The company uses straight-line amortization. The interest payment dates are December 31 and June 30 of each year.

Instructions

(a) Prepare journal entries to record the retirement of the old issue and the sale of the new issue on June 30, 2007.

(b) Prepare the entry required on December 31, 2007, to record the payment of the first six months of interest and the amortization of the bond premium.

E14-17 **(Entries for Retirement and Issuance of Bonds—Effective Interest)** Refer to E14-16 and Autry Limited. **(LO 4, 6)**

Instructions

Repeat the instructions of E14-16 assuming that Autry Limited uses the effective interest method. Provide an effective-interest table for the bonds for the inception of the bond to the date of the redemption. (Hint: it will be necessary to first calculate the effective interest rate on the 2000 and 2007 bonds.)

E14-18 **(Interest-Free Government Loans)** Grant Forest Products Limited needed to upgrade a burner at its sawmill in Timmins, Ontario, to comply with the new air pollution standards. The new burner, which is used to burn the scrap wood from the sawing operations, will not only reduce the amount of pollution, but will also supply heat for the plant facility, including the wood dryer. In order to encourage Grant Forest Products Limited in its compliance with the standards, the Province of Ontario extended an interest-free loan of $400,000 on December 31, 2008. The only conditions in obtaining the interest-free loan are that the loan proceeds be applied directly to the construction costs and that the loan be repaid in full on December 31, 2016. Grant Forest Products Limited borrowed the remaining funds from the bank for the construction of the burner and will be paying interest at the rate of 7% per year. **(LO 5)**

Instructions

(a) Discuss the issues related to obtaining the interest-free loan from the Province of Ontario.

(b) Prepare an amortization table for the loan using the effective interest method. Present the first three years of the loan.

(c) Prepare the entry on December 31, 2008, to record the interest-free loan.

(d) Prepare any adjusting journal entry that is necessary at December 31, 2009, the fiscal year end of the company, concerning any interest on the note.

E14-19 **(Entry for Retirement of Bond; Costs for Bond Issuance)** On January 2, 2003, Banno Corporation issued $1.5 million of 10% bonds at 97 due on December 31, 2012. Legal and other costs of $110,000 were incurred in connection with the issue. Banno Corporation has adopted the policy of capitalizing and amortizing the legal and other costs incurred by including them with the bond recorded at the date of issuance. Interest on the bonds is payable annually each December 31. The $110,000 in issuance costs are being deferred and amortized on a straight-line basis over the 10-year term of the bonds. The discount on the bonds is also being amortized on a straight-line basis over the 10 years. (The straight-line method is not materially different in its effect compared to the effective interest method.) **(LO 6)**

The bonds are callable at 102 (i.e., at 102% of their face amount), and on January 2, 2008, the company called a face amount of $850,000 of the bonds and retired them.

Instructions

(a) Ignoring income taxes, calculate the amount of loss, if any, that the company needs to recognize as a result of retiring the $850,000 of bonds in 2008. Prepare the journal entry to record the retirement.

(b) How would the amount of the loss calculated in part (a) differ if the policy for Banno Corporation had been to expense the costs of issuing the bonds at January 2, 2003? Assuming that Banno Corporation had followed this policy, prepare the journal entry to record the retirement.

(LO 6) **E14-20   (Entries for Retirement and Issuance of Bonds)** Hagman, Inc. had outstanding $6 million of 11% bonds (interest payable July 31 and January 31) due in 10 years. On July 1, it issued $9.3 million of 15-year, 10% bonds (interest payable July 1 and January 1) at 97. A portion of the proceeds was used to call the 11% bonds at 101 on August 1. The unamortized bond discount for the 11% bonds was $120,000 on August 1.

Instructions

Prepare the necessary journal entries to record the issue of the new bonds and the retirement of the old bonds.

(LO 6) **E14-21   (Entries for Retirement of Bonds)** George Inc. had bonds outstanding with a maturity value of $500,000. On April 30, 2008, when these bonds had a carrying value of $490,000, they were called in at 104. To pay for these bonds, the company had issued other bonds a month earlier and bearing a lower interest rate. The newly issued bonds had a life of 10 years. The new bonds were issued at 103 (face value of $500,000).

Instructions

Ignoring interest, calculate the gain or loss and record the retirement transaction.

(LO 8) **E14-22   (Long-Term Debt Disclosure)** At December 31, 2007, Reddy Inc. has three long-term debt issues outstanding. The first is a $2.2-million note payable that matures on June 30, 2010. The second is a $4-million bond issue that matures on September 30, 2011. The third is a $16.5-million sinking fund debenture with annual sinking fund payments of $3.5 million in each of the years 2009 through 2013.

Instructions

Prepare the note disclosure that is required for the long-term debt at December 31, 2007.

(LO 8) **E14-23   (Classification of Liabilities)** The following are various accounts:

1. Bank loans payable of a winery, due March 10, 2011 (the product requires aging for five years before it can be sold)

2. $10 million of serial bonds payable, of which $2 million is due each July 31

3. Amounts withheld from employees' wages for income taxes

4. Notes payable that are due January 15, 2010

5. Interest payable on a note payable. The note is due January 15, 2010, and the interest is due June 30, 2008.

6. Credit balance in a customer's account arising from returns and allowances after collection in full of the account

7. Bonds payable of $2 million maturing June 30, 2011

8. An overdraft of $1,000 in a bank account (no other balances are carried at this bank)

9. An overdraft of $1,000 in a bank account (other accounts are carried at this bank and have positive account balances)

10. Deposits made by customers who have ordered goods

Instructions

Indicate whether each of the items above should be classified on December 31, 2007, as a current or long-term liability or under some other classification. Consider each one independently from all others; that is, do not assume that all of them relate to one particular business. If the classification of some of the items is doubtful, explain why in each case.

(LO 8) **E14-24   (Classification)** The following items are found in a company's financial statements:

1. Interest expense (credit balance)

2. Gain on repurchase of debt

3. Mortgage payable (payable in equal amounts over the next three years)

4. Debenture bonds payable (maturing in five years)

5. Notes payable (due in four years)

6. Income bonds payable (due in three years)

Instructions

Indicate how each of these items should be classified in the financial statements.

*E14-25 (Impairments) On December 31, 2007, Moli Inc. borrowed $81,241 from Par Bank, signing a $125,000, five-year, non-interest-bearing note. The note was issued to yield 9% interest. Unfortunately, during 2008 Moli began to experience financial difficulty. As a result, at December 31, 2008, Par Bank determined that it was probable that it would receive only $93,750 at maturity. The market rate of interest on loans of this nature is now 11%. **(LO 10)**

Instructions

(a) Prepare the entry to record the issuance of the loan by Par Bank on December 31, 2007.

(b) Prepare the entry (if any) to record the impairment of the loan on December 31, 2008, by Par Bank.

(c) Prepare the entry (if any) to record the impairment of the loan on December 31, 2008, by Moli.

*E14-26 (Impairments) On December 31, 2006, Conchita Inc. signed a $2-million note to Sak City Bank. The market interest rate at that time was 12%. The stated interest rate on the note was 10%, payable annually. The note matures in five years. Unfortunately, because of lower sales, Conchita's financial situation worsened. On December 31, 2008, Sak City Bank determined that it was probable that the company would pay back only $1.2 million of the principal at maturity. However, it was considered likely that interest would continue to be paid on the full $2 million loan. **(LO 10)**

Instructions

(a) Determine the amount of cash that Conchita received from the loan on December 31, 2006.

(b) Prepare a note amortization schedule for Sak City Bank up to December 31, 2008.

(c) Determine the loss on impairment that Sak City Bank should recognize on December 31, 2008.

*E14-27 (Settlement of Debt) Nieland Inc. owes First Bank $245,000 plus $31,000 of accrued interest. The debt is a 10-year, 10% note. During 2007, Nieland's business deteriorated due to a faltering regional economy. On December 31, 2007, the bank agrees to accept an old machine and cancel the entire debt. The machine has a cost of $490,000, accumulated amortization of $294,000, and a fair market value of $220,500. The bank plans to dispose of the machine at a cost of $6,500. **(LO 11)**

Instructions

(a) Prepare the journal entries for Nieland Inc. and First Bank to record this debt settlement.

(b) How should Nieland report the gain or loss on the disposition of the machine and on the restructuring of debt in its 2007 income statement?

(c) Assume that instead of transferring the machine Nieland decides to grant the bank 15,000 of its common shares, which have a fair market value of $230,500. This is in full settlement of the loan obligation. Assuming that First Bank treats Nieland's shares as trading securities, prepare the entries to record the transaction for both parties.

*E14-28 (Term Modification—Debtor's Entries) On December 31, 2007, Morning Bank enters into a debt restructuring agreement with Evening Inc., which is now experiencing financial trouble. The bank agrees to restructure a $2-million, 12% note receivable issued at par by the following modifications: **(LO 11)**

1. Reducing the principal obligation from $2 million to $1.9 million

2. Extending the maturity date from December 31, 2007, to December 31, 2010

3. Reducing the interest rate from 12% to 10%

Evening pays interest at the end of each year. On January 1, 2011, Evening Inc. pays $1.9 million in cash to Morning Bank.

Instructions

(a) Discuss whether or not Evening should record a gain.

(b) Calculate the rate of interest that Evening should use to calculate its interest expense in future periods.

(c) Prepare the interest payment entry for Evening on December 31, 2009.

(d) What entry should Evening make on January 1, 2011?

(LO 11)   *E14-29   (Term Modification—Creditor's Entries) Assume the same information as in E14-28 above and answer the following questions related to Morning Bank (the creditor).

Instructions

(a) What interest rate should Morning Bank use to calculate the loss on the debt restructuring?

(b) Calculate the loss that Morning Bank will suffer from the debt restructuring. Prepare the journal entry to record the loss.

(c) Prepare the amortization schedule for Morning Bank after the debt restructuring.

(d) Prepare the interest receipt entry for Morning Bank on December 31, 2009.

(e) What entry should Morning Bank make on January 1, 2011?

(LO 11)   *E14-30   (Settlement—Debtor's Entries) Use the same information as in E14-28 above but assume now that Morning Bank reduced the principal to $1.6 million rather than $1.9 million. On January 1, 2011, Evening pays $1.6 million in cash to Morning Bank for the principal.

Instructions

(a) Can Evening record a gain under this term modification? If yes, calculate the gain.

(b) Prepare the journal entries to record the gain on Evening's books.

(c) What interest rate should Evening use to calculate its interest expense in future periods? Will your answer be the same as in E14-28 above? Why or why not?

(d) Prepare the amortization schedule of the note for Evening after the debt restructuring.

(e) Prepare the interest payment entries for Evening on December 31 of 2008, 2009, and 2010.

(f) What entry should Evening make on January 1, 2011?

(LO 11)   *E14-31   (Settlement—Creditor's Entries) Use the information in E14-28 and the assumptions in E14-30 above and answer the following questions related to Morning Bank (the creditor).

Instructions

(a) What interest rate should Morning Bank use to calculate the loss on the debt restructuring?

(b) Calculate the loss that Morning Bank will suffer under this new term modification. Prepare the journal entry to record the loss on Morning's books.

(c) Prepare the amortization schedule for Morning Bank after the debt restructuring.

(d) Prepare the interest receipt entry for Morning Bank on December 31, 2008, 2009, and 2010.

(e) What entry should Morning Bank make on January 1, 2011?

(LO 11)   *E14-32   (Debtor/Creditor Entries for Settlement of Troubled Debt) Langley Limited owes $137,300 to Fern Inc. on a 10-year, 11% note. Because Langley is in financial trouble, Fern Inc. agrees to accept some property and cancel the entire debt. The property has a book value of $55,000 and a fair market value of $82,500.

Instructions

(a) Prepare the journal entry on Langley's books for the debt settlement.

(b) Prepare the journal entry on Fern's books for the debt settlement.

Problems

P14-1   Four independent situations follow:

1. On March 1, 2009, Hannes Inc. issued $3 million of 9% bonds at 102 plus accrued interest. The bonds are dated January 1, 2009, and pay interest semi-annually on July 1 and January 1. In addition, Hannes incurred $27,000 of bond issuance costs.

2. On January 1, 2008, Rainer Ltd. issued 9% bonds with a face value of $500,000 for $469,280 to yield 10%. The bonds are dated January 1, 2008, and pay interest annually.

3. Czeslaw Building Inc. has several long-term bonds outstanding at December 31, 2009. These long-term bonds have the following sinking fund requirements and maturities for the next six years:

	Sinking Fund	Maturities
2010	$300,000	$100,000
2011	$100,000	$250,000
2012	$100,000	$100,000
2013	$200,000	—
2014	$200,000	$150,000
2015	$200,000	$100,000

4. In the long-term debt structure of Chico Inc., the following three bonds were reported: mortgage bonds payable, $10 million; collateral trust bonds, $5 million; bonds maturing in instalments, secured by plant equipment, $4 million.

Instructions

(a) For situation 1, calculate the net amount of cash received by Hannes as a result of the issuance of these bonds.

(b) For situation 2, what amount should Rainer report for interest expense in 2008 related to these bonds, assuming that it uses the effective interest method for amortizing any bond premium or discount?

(c) For situation 3, indicate how this information should be reported in Czeslaw's financial statements at December 31, 2009.

(d) For situation 4, determine the total amount of debenture bonds that is outstanding, if any.

P14-2 The following amortization and interest schedule is for the issuance of 10-year bonds by Bran Corporation on January 1, 2000, and the subsequent interest payments and charges. The company's year end is December 31 and it prepares its financial statements yearly.

Amortization Schedule

Year	Cash	Interest	Amount Unamortized	Book Value
Jan. 1, 2000			$5,651	$ 94,349
2000	$11,000	$11,322	5,329	94,671
2001	11,000	11,361	4,968	95,032
2002	11,000	11,404	4,564	95,436
2003	11,000	11,452	4,112	95,888
2004	11,000	11,507	3,605	96,395
2005	11,000	11,567	3,038	96,962
2006	11,000	11,635	2,403	97,597
2007	11,000	11,712	1,691	98,309
2008	11,000	11,797	894	99,106
2009	11,000	11,894	0	100,000

Instructions

(a) Indicate whether the bonds were issued at a premium or a discount and explain how you can determine this fact from the schedule.

(b) Indicate whether the amortization schedule is based on the straight-line method or the effective interest method and explain how you can determine which method is used.

(c) Determine the stated interest rate and the effective interest rate.

(d) Based on the schedule above, prepare the journal entry to record the issuance of the bonds on January 1, 2000.

(e) Based on the schedule above, prepare the journal entry or entries to reflect the bond transactions and accruals for 2000. (Interest is paid January 1.)

(f) Based on the schedule above, prepare the journal entry or entries to reflect the bond transactions and accruals for 2008. Bran Corporation does not use reversing entries.

P14-3   Samsa Inc. is building a new hockey arena at a cost of $3 million. It received a down payment of $500,000 from local businesses to support the project, and now needs to borrow $2.5 million to complete the project. It therefore decides to issue $2.5 million of 10-year, 10% bonds. These bonds were issued on January 1, 2005, and pay interest annually on each January 1. The bonds yield 11%. Any additional funds that are needed to complete the project will be obtained from local businesses. Samsa Inc. expenses all costs related to the issuance of bonds.

Instructions

(a) Prepare the journal entry to record the issuance of the bonds on January 1, 2005.

(b) Prepare a bond amortization schedule up to and including January 1, 2010, using the effective interest method.

(c) Assume that on July 1, 2008, the company retires half of the bonds at a cost of $1.2 million plus accrued interest. Prepare the journal entry to record this retirement.

(d) Assume that the costs incurred by Samsa Inc. to issue the bonds totalled $100,000. If Samsa Inc. chose to capitalize and amortize these costs by including them with the bond recorded at the date of issuance, how would this affect the amount of interest expense that is recognized by Samsa Inc. each year and over the 10-year term of the bonds in total, compared to its current accounting practice?

P14-4   In the following two independent cases, the company closes its books on December 31:

1. Merry Inc. sells $2 million of 10% bonds on March 1, 2007. The bonds pay interest on September 1 and March 1. The bonds' due date is September 1, 2010. The bonds yield 12%.

2. Dougherty Ltd. sells $6 million of 11% bonds on June 1, 2008. The bonds pay interest on December 1 and June 1. The bonds' due date is June 1, 2012. The bonds yield 10%. On October 1, 2009, Dougherty buys back $1.2 million worth of bonds for $1.4 million (includes accrued interest).

Instructions

For the two cases above, prepare all of the relevant journal entries from the time of sale until the date indicated (for situation 1, prepare the journal entries through December 31, 2008; for situation 2, prepare the journal entries through December 1, 2010). Use the effective interest method for discount and premium amortization (prepare any necessary amortization tables). Amortize any premium or discount on the interest dates and at year end. (Assume that no reversing entries were made.)

P14-5   Selected transactions on the books of Pleiades Corporation follow:

May 1, 2008	Bonds payable with a par value of $700,000, which are dated January 1, 2008, are sold at 105 plus accrued interest. They are coupon bonds, bear interest at 12% (payable annually at January 1), and mature on January 1, 2018. (Use an interest expense account for accrued interest.)
Dec. 31	Adjusting entries are made to record the accrued interest on the bonds and the amortization of the proper amount of premium. (Use straight-line amortization.)
Jan. 1, 2009	Interest on the bonds is paid.
April 1	Par value bonds of $420,000 are purchased at 103 plus accrued interest and are retired. (Bond premium is to be amortized only at the end of each year.)
Dec. 31	Adjusting entries are made to record the accrued interest on the bonds, and the proper amount of premium amortized.

Instructions

Prepare the journal entries for the transactions above.

P14-6   On April 1, 2009, Tenor Corp. sold 12,000 of its $1,000 face value, 15-year, 11% bonds at 97. Interest payment dates are April 1 and October 1, and the company uses the straight-line method of bond discount amortization. On March 1, 2010, Tenor took advantage of its favourable share prices to extinguish 3,000 of the bonds by issuing 100,000 shares. At this time, the accrued interest was paid in cash to the bondholders whose bonds were being extinguished. The company's shares were selling for $31 per share on March 1, 2010.

Instructions

Prepare Tenor Corp.'s journal entries to record the following:

(a) April 1, 2009: issuance of the bonds

(b) October 1, 2009: payment of the semi-annual interest

(c) December 31, 2009: accrual of the interest expense

(d) March 1, 2010: extinguishment of 3,000 bonds by the issuance of common shares (no reversing entries are made)

P14-7   Refer to P14-6 and Tenor Corp.

Instructions

Repeat the instructions of P14-6 assuming that Tenor Corp. uses the effective interest method. Provide an effective interest table for the bonds for two interest payment periods. (Hint: it will be necessary to first calculate the effective interest rate on the bonds).

P14-8   On December 31, 2009, Liz Limited acquired a computer software system from Careras Corporation by issuing a $500,000, non-interest-bearing note that is payable in full on December 31, 2013. The company's credit rating permits it to borrow funds from its several lines of credit at 10%. The system is expected to have a five-year life and a $50,000 residual value.

Instructions

(a) Prepare the journal entry for the purchase on December 31, 2009.

(b) Prepare any necessary adjusting entries related to amortization of the asset (use straight-line) and amortization of the note (use the effective interest method) on December 31, 2010.

(c) Prepare any necessary adjusting entries related to amortization of the software system and amortization of the bond on December 31, 2011.

P14-9   Yanzou Cosmetics Inc. purchased machinery on December 31, 2008, paying $140,000 down and agreeing to pay the balance in four equal instalments of $20,000 that are payable each December 31. An assumed interest rate of 10% is implicit in the purchase price.

Instructions

(a) Prepare the journal entries that would be recorded for the purchase and for the payments and interest on the following dates:

1. December 31, 2008   **4.** December 31, 2011

2. December 31, 2009   **5.** December 31, 2012

3. December 31, 2010

(b) From the perspective of the lender, what are the advantages of an instalment note compared to an interest-bearing note?

P14-10   On June 1, 2008, MacDonnell Corporation approached Shankman Corporation about purchasing a parcel of undeveloped land. Shankman was asking $240,000 for the land and MacDonnell saw that there was some flexibility in the asking price. MacDonnell did not have the necessary funds to make a cash offer to Shankman and proposed to give, in return for the land, a $300,000, five-year promissory note that bears interest at the rate of 4%. The interest is to be paid annually to Shankman Corporation on June 1 of each of the next five years. Shankman insisted that the note taken in return become a mortgage note. The amended offer was accepted by Shankman, and MacDonnell signed a mortgage note for $300,000 due June 1, 2013. MacDonnell would have had to pay 10% at its local bank if it were to secure the necessary cash for the land purchase. Shankmann, on the other hand, could borrow the funds at 9%. Both MacDonnell and Shankman have calendar year ends.

Instructions

(a) Discuss how MacDonnell Corporation would determine a value for the land in recording the purchase from Shankman Corporation.

(b) What is the difference between a promissory note payable and a mortgage note payable? Why would Shankman Corporation insist on obtaining a mortgage note payable from MacDonnell Corporation?

(c) Calculate the purchase price of the land and prepare an effective-interest amortization table for the term of the mortgage note payable that is given in the exchange.

(d) Prepare the journal entry for the purchase of the land.

(e) Prepare any adjusting journal entry that is required at the end of the fiscal year and the first payment made on June 1, 2009, assuming no reversing entries are used.

(f) Assume that Shankman had insisted on obtaining an instalment note from MacDonnell instead of a mortgage note. Then do the following:

1. Calculate the amount of the instalment payments that would be required for a five-year instalment note. Use the same cost of the land to MacDonnell Corporation that you determined for the mortgage note in part (a).

2. Prepare an effective-interest amortization table for the five-year term of the instalment note.

3. Prepare the journal entry for the purchase of the land and the issuance of the instalment note.

4. Prepare any adjusting journal entry that is required at the end of the fiscal year and the first payment made on June 1, 2009, assuming no reversing entries are used.

5. Compare the balances of the two different notes payable and related accounts at December 31, 2008. Be specific about the classifications on the balance sheet.

6. Why would Shankman insist on an instalment note in this case?

P14-11   Salsa Inc. developed a new sales gimmick to help sell its inventory of new automobiles. Because many buyers of new cars need financing, the company offered a low down payment and low car payments for the first year after purchase. It believes that this promotion will bring in some new buyers.

On January 1, 2007, a customer purchased a new $35,000 automobile, making a down payment of $3,000. The customer signed a note indicating that the annual interest rate would be 9% and that quarterly payments would be made over three years. For the first year, the company required a $400 quarterly payment to be made on April 1, July 1, October 1, and January 1, 2008. After this one-year period, the customer was required to make regular quarterly payments that would pay off the loan by January 1, 2010.

Instructions

(a) Prepare a note amortization schedule for the first year.

(b) Indicate the amount that the customer owes on the contract at the end of the first year.

(c) Calculate the amount of the new quarterly payments.

(d) Prepare a note amortization schedule for these new payments for the next two years.

(e) What do you think of Salsa Inc.'s new sales promotion?

P14-12   Mills Inc. issued 25-year, 9% mortgage bonds in the principal amount of $5 million on January 2, 1993, at a discount of $250,000. It then amortized the discount through charges to expense over the life of the issue on a straight-line basis. The indenture securing the issue provided that the bonds could be called for redemption in total but not in part at any time before maturity at 104% of the principal amount, but it did not provide for any sinking fund. On December 18, 2007, the company issued 20-year, 11% debenture bonds in the principal amount of $6 million at 102 and the proceeds were used to redeem the 25-year, 9% mortgage bonds on January 2, 2008. The indenture securing the new issue did not provide for any sinking fund or for retirement before maturity.

Instructions

(a) Prepare journal entries to record the issuance of the 11% bonds and the retirement of the 9% bonds.

(b) Indicate the income statement treatment of the gain or loss from retirement and the note disclosure that is required. Assume that 2008 income from operations is $3.2 million and that the weighted number of shares outstanding is 1.5 million and the income tax rate is 40%.

*P14-13   On January 1, 2008, Bostan Limited issued a $1.2-million, five-year, zero-interest-bearing note to NOG Bank. The note was issued to yield 8% annual interest. Unfortunately, during 2008 Bostan fell into financial trouble due to increased competition. After reviewing all available evidence on December 31, 2008, NOG Bank decided that the loan was impaired. Bostan will probably pay back only $800,000 of the principal at maturity.

Instructions

(a) Prepare journal entries for both Bostan and NOG Bank to record the issuance of the note on January 1, 2008. (Round to the nearest $10.)

(b) Assuming that both Bostan and NOG Bank use the effective interest method to amortize the discount, prepare the amortization schedule for the note.

(c) Under what circumstances can NOG Bank consider Bostan's note to be impaired?

(d) Estimate the loss that NOG Bank will suffer from Bostan's financial distress on December 31, 2008. What journal entries should be made to record this loss?

*P14-14   Jeremy Hill is the sole shareholder of Hill Inc., which is currently under bankruptcy court protection. As a debtor in possession, he has negotiated the following revised loan agreement with Vale Bank. Hill Inc.'s $500,000, 10-year, 12% note was refinanced with a $500,000, 10-year, 5% note.

Instructions

(a) What is the accounting nature of this transaction?

(b) Prepare the journal entry to record this refinancing (1) on the books of Hill Inc. and (2) on the books of Vale Bank.

(c) Discuss whether generally accepted accounting principles provide the information that would be useful to managers and investors in this situation.

*P14-15   Sandro Corporation is having financial difficulty and has therefore asked Botticelli National Bank to restructure its $3-million note outstanding. The present note has three years remaining and pays a current interest rate of 10%. The present market rate for a loan of this nature is 12%. The note was issued at its face value.

Instructions

For each of the following independent situations related to the above scenario, prepare the journal entry that Sandro and Botticelli National Bank would make for the restructuring that is described.

(a) Botticelli National Bank agrees to take an equity interest in Sandro by accepting common shares valued at $2.2 million in exchange for relinquishing its claim on this note.

(b) Botticelli National Bank agrees to accept land in exchange for relinquishing its claim on this note. The land has a book value of $1,050,000 and a fair value of $2.5 million.

(c) Botticelli National Bank agrees to modify the terms of the note so that Sandro does not have to pay any interest on the note over the three-year period.

(d) Botticelli National Bank agrees to reduce the principal balance down to $2.3 million and to require interest only in the second and third year at a rate of 9%.

*P14-16   Dionysus Inc. owes Salami Bank a $250,000, 10-year, 15% note. The note is due today, December 31, 2008. Because Dionysus Inc. is in financial trouble, Salami agrees to accept 60,000 shares of Dionysus' common shares, which are currently selling for $1.40; to reduce the note's face amount to $150,000; to extend the maturity date to December 31, 2012; and to reduce the interest rate to 6%. Interest will continue to be due on December 31 of each year. (Interest is still outstanding as at December 31, 2008.)

Instructions

(a) Prepare all the necessary journal entries on the books of Dionysus Inc. from the time of the restructuring through maturity.

(b) Prepare all the necessary journal entries on the books of Salami Bank from the time of the restructuring through maturity.

*P14-17   At December 31, 2007, Sioux Manufacturing Limited had outstanding a $300,000, 12% note payable to Teton National Bank. Dated January 1, 2005, the note was due on December 31, 2008, with interest payable each December 31. During 2008, Sioux notified Teton that it might be unable to meet the scheduled December 31, 2008, payment of principal and interest because of financial difficulties. On September 30, 2008, Teton sold the note, including interest accrued since December 31, 2007, for $280,000 to Osage Foundry, one of Sioux's oldest and largest customers. On December 31, 2008, Osage agreed to accept inventory that cost $240,000 but was worth $315,000 from Sioux in full settlement of the note.

Instructions

(a) Prepare the journal entry to record the September 30, 2008, transaction on the books of Teton, Sioux, and Osage. For each company, indicate whether the transaction is a restructuring of troubled debt.

(b) Prepare the journal entries to record the December 31, 2008, transaction on the books of Sioux and Osage. For each company, indicate whether this transaction is a restructuring of troubled debt.

*P14-18   Mildred Corp. owes Taylor Corp. a $110,000, 10-year, 10% note plus $11,000 of accrued interest. The note is due today, December 31, 2008. Because Mildred Corp. is in financial trouble, Taylor Corp. agrees to forgive the accrued interest and $10,000 of the principal, and to extend the maturity date to December 31, 2011. Interest at 10% of the revised principal will continue to be due on December 31 of each year.

Instructions

(a) Calculate the new effective interest rate for Mildred Corp. after the restructuring. (Hint: Use a financial calculator or computer spreadsheet function.)

(b) Prepare a schedule of the debt reduction and interest expense for the years 2008 through 2011.

(c) Calculate the gain or loss for Taylor Corp. and prepare a schedule of the receivable reduction and interest revenue for the years 2008 through 2011.

(d) Prepare all the necessary journal entries on the books of Mildred Corp. for the years 2008, 2009, and 2010.

(e) Prepare all the necessary journal entries on the books of Taylor Corp. for the years 2008, 2009, and 2010.

Writing Assignments

WA14-1   On January 1, 2009, Branagh Limited issued for $1,075,230 its 20-year, 13% bonds that have a maturity value of $1 million and pay interest semi-annually on January 1 and July 1. The bond issue costs were not material in amount. Three presentations follow of the balance sheet long-term liability section that might be used for these bonds at the issue date:

1. Bonds payable (maturing January 1, 2029)	$1,075,230
2. Bonds payable principal	
(face value $1,000,000, maturing January 1, 2029)	$ 97,220[a]
Bonds payable interest (semi-annual payment of $65,000)	978,010[b]
Total bond liability	$1,075,230
3. Bonds payable principal (maturing January 1, 2029)	$1,000,000
Bonds payable interest ($65,000 per period for 40 periods)	2,600,000
Total bond liability	$3,600,000

[a]The present value of $1 million due at the end of 40 (six-month) periods at the yield rate of 6% per period
[b]The present value of $65,000 per period for 40 (six-month) periods at the yield rate of 6% per period

Instructions

(a) Discuss the conceptual merit(s) of each of the three date-of-issue balance sheet presentations shown above.

(b) Explain why investors would pay $1,075,230 for bonds that have a maturity value of only $1 million.

(c) Assuming that, at any date during the life of the bonds, a discount rate is needed to calculate the carrying value of the obligations that arise from a bond issue, discuss the conceptual merit(s) of using the following for this purpose:

   1. The coupon or nominal rate

   2. The effective or yield rate at date of issue

(d) If the obligations arising from these bonds are to be carried at their present value and this is calculated according to the current market rate of interest, how would the bond valuation at dates after the date of issue be affected by an increase or a decrease in the market rate of interest?

WA14-2   Thompson Limited completed several transactions during 2008. In January, the company purchased under contract a machine at a total price of $1.2 million, payable over five years with instalments of $240,000 per year. The seller considered the transaction to be an instalment sale with the title transferring to Thompson at the time of the final payment.

On March 1, 2008, Thompson issued $10 million of general revenue bonds priced at 99 with a coupon of 10% payable July 1 and January 1 of each of the next 10 years. The July 1 interest was paid and on December 30 the company transferred $1 million to the trustee, Holly Trust Limited, for payment of the January 1, 2006, interest.

Due to the depressed market for the company's shares, Thompson purchased $500,000 in par value of its 6% convertible bonds for $455,000. It expects to resell the bonds when the price of its common shares has recovered.

As Thompson's accountant, you have prepared the balance sheet as at December 31, 2008, and have presented it to the company president. You are asked the following questions about it:

   1. Why has amortization been charged on equipment being purchased under contract? Title has not yet passed to the company and, therefore, the equipment is not yet our asset. Would it not be more correct for the company to show on the left side of the balance sheet only the amount that has been paid to date instead of showing the full contract price on the left side and the unpaid portion on the right side? After all, the seller considers the transaction an instalment sale.

   2. What is bond discount? As a debit balance, why is this not classified among the assets?

3. Bond interest is shown as a current liability. Did we not pay our trustee, Holly Trust Limited, the full amount of interest that is due this period?

4. The repurchased bonds (sometimes referred to as treasury bonds) are shown as a deduction from bonds payable issued. Why are they not shown as an asset since they can be sold again? Are they the same as bonds of other companies that we hold as investments?

Instructions

Answer these questions by writing a brief paragraph that justifies your treatment of the items in the balance sheet.

WA14-3

Part I. The appropriate method of amortizing a premium or discount on issuance of bonds is the effective interest method.

Instructions

(a) What is the effective interest method of amortization and what are the differences and similarities between it and the straight-line method of amortization?

(b) How is amortization calculated using the effective interest method? Why and how do amounts that are obtained using the effective interest method differ from amounts that are calculated under the straight-line method?

Part II. Gains or losses from the early extinguishment of debt that is refunded can theoretically be accounted for in three ways:

1. They can be amortized over the remaining life of old debt.

2. They can be amortized over the life of the new debt issue.

3. The can be recognized in the period of extinguishment.

Instructions

(a) Provide supporting arguments for each of the three theoretical methods of accounting for gains and losses from the early extinguishment of debt.

(b) Which of the above methods is generally accepted as the appropriate amount of gain or loss that should be shown in a company's financial statements?

Cases

Refer to the Case Primer on the Student Website to help you answer these cases.

 **Student Website**

www.wiley.com/canada/kieso

CA14-1 Pitt Corporation is interested in building a pop can manufacturing plant next to its existing plant in Montreal. The objective would be to ensure a steady supply of cans at a stable price and to minimize transportation costs. However, the company has been experiencing some financial problems and has been reluctant to borrow any additional cash to fund the project. The company is not concerned about the cash flow problems of making payments; instead, its real concern is the impact of adding long-term debt to its balance sheet.

The president of Pitt, Aidan Quinn, approached the president of Aluminum Can Corp. (ACC), its major supplier, to see if some agreement could be reached. ACC was anxious to work out an arrangement, since it seemed inevitable that Pitt would begin its own can production. ACC could not afford to lose the account.

After some discussion, a two-part plan was worked out. First ACC will construct a plant on Pitt's land next to the existing plant, and the plant will initially belong to ACC. Second, Pitt will sign a 20-year purchase agreement. Under the purchase agreement, Pitt will express its intention to buy all of its cans from ACC and pay a unit price that at normal capacity would cover labour and material, an operating management fee, and the debt service requirements on the new plant. The expected unit price, if transportation costs are taken into consideration, is lower than the current market price. If Pitt ends up not taking enough production in any specific year and if the excess cans cannot be sold at a high enough price on the open market, Pitt agrees to make up any cash shortage so that ACC can make the payments on its debt. The bank is willing to make a 20-year loan for the plant, taking the plant and the purchase agreement as collateral. At the end of 20 years, the plant will become Pitt's.

Instructions

Adopt the role of the controller and discuss the financial reporting issues. (Hint: Use first principles.)

CA14-2   The following is an excerpt from the second quarter report for **At Home Corporation (Excite@Home)**. Note that on August 27, 2001, the company announced that it had received a written notice from two of its holders of Convertible Notes in which the holders demanded payment of $50 million because the company had breached certain representations made on issuance of the notes. According to the company, if the notes were paid in cash, this would have a materially adverse impact on the company's liquidity and its ability to fund its operations.

---

5. Financing Transactions Convertible Note Financing

On June 8, 2001 we issued convertible notes and entered into related agreements with third party investors under which we received $100 million in cash financing. The notes do not bear interest and none of the conversion features discussed below resulted in an initial beneficial conversion feature requiring accounting treatment as a discount and amortization to interest expense. However, we incurred approximately $2 million of debt issuance costs that are being amortized to interest expense over the stated 5-year term of the notes through June 8, 2006. The notes are convertible at any time into shares of our Series A common stock at a rate of $4.38 per share, based on 110% of the weighted-average price of our Series A common stock on June 8, 2001. This conversion rate is subject to reduction as specified in the agreements upon the issuance of common stock in future equity transactions. The holders of these notes may elect to convert the notes at the original issuance price on each anniversary of the date of issuance starting on June 8, 2002, and therefore we have included the principal amount in current liabilities. The notes are also redeemable by us on the second, third and fourth anniversary of the date of issuance. At each such conversion or redemption date, as well as at maturity, we have the option of delivering the par amount in cash or Series A common stock at a rate of 95% of the average of the volume-weighted trading price of the common stock over the 10 trading days prior to each date of issuance, and the shares would be issued in eight equal instalments over an 80-day period. However, if we have not met specified conditions for redeeming the notes in stock, we may be obligated to pay cash rather than stock to satisfy these redemption obligations. In addition, we may elect to pay cash if redeeming the notes in stock results in an unacceptable level of dilution to our stockholders.

We are required to register the resale of the shares issuable upon conversion of the notes in accordance with timeframes specified in our registration rights agreement with the note holders. We are also required to maintain the listing of our Series A common stock on either the New York Stock Exchange, the Nasdaq National Market or the American Stock Exchange. We do not currently meet the Nasdaq continued listing requirement because our net tangible assets and stockholders equity are below the minimum thresholds and the bid price of our Series A common stock is currently less than the minimum $3.00 bid price required when such thresholds are not met. If we do not meet the continued listing requirements of one of these stock markets at any time after receiving a redemption notice from a note holder, if our Series A common stock were delisted, or if we fail to meet other specified conditions in our agreements with the note holders, the notes provide for acceleration of repayment in cash at that time. Our stockholders have approved a reverse stock split which would, if our board of directors elects to implement it, increase the trading price of our Series A common stock above $3.00, but we cannot assure you that this would result in a sustained increase above the minimum bid price requirements. In addition, events of default include failure to meet our payment obligations under these notes or our other outstanding debt obligations, failure to meet material provisions of the notes for a period of 30 days after receiving notice, or filing for bankruptcy. A default under these notes could result in the acceleration of the amounts due under our other outstanding convertible subordinated notes and debentures.

We have granted holders of these notes a security interest in $100 million of our assets that are not otherwise secured, as collateral for the outstanding amounts due under the notes. These notes are senior to our outstanding subordinated notes and debentures.

Instructions

Adopt the role of the company's auditor and discuss any financial reporting issues that are raised by the initial issue and the note holders' subsequent call to repay. Use current GAAP for your analysis. (Note that the company subsequently filed for bankruptcy protection and eventually closed its doors in 2002.)

IC14-3   **Great Canadian Gaming Corporation (GCGC)**, as the opening vignette of this chapter noted, has been criticized for its aggressive accounting by the independent research firm Veritas Investment Research.

In British Columbia, the provincial government helps casino operators expand by allowing casinos to keep an additional percentage of gambling revenues until the expansion has been paid for. For instance, if the casino operator spends additional funds on new slot machines, it can keep additional operating profits that would otherwise have been paid to the government. Sometimes, it takes many years for the casino to recoup such an investment. Casino companies also pay into a marketing fund of the provincial lottery corporation and these funds are used to advertise the casinos. GCGC capitalizes the amounts that it pays into the marketing fund.

As noted in the opening vignette, GCGC also has debt covenants that require the company to maintain certain leverage ratios. The following excerpts are from the company's financial statements for 2006.

Instructions

As an independent analyst, provide a critical analysis of the financial reporting issues related to the above.

e) Facility Development Commission

The Facility Development Commission ("FDC", formerly known as the Facility Development Improvement Fund) is a compensation component of the Company's Casino Operational Services Agreements ("COSAs") with the British Columbia Lottery Corporation ("BCLC"). FDC is earned (payable by BCLC to the Company) as a fixed percentage of gaming win, subject to the Company incurring sufficient Approved Amounts (a defined term in the COSAs and generally consists of approved capital or operating expenditures related to the development or improvement of gaming properties), and is paid weekly to the Company. Approved Amounts are reduced by the FDC receipts.

FDC is recorded as part of revenues on the statement of income (loss) when earned (when it is payable by BCLC to the Company), limited to the extent that sufficient Approved Amounts have previously been made by the Company (Note 3). If there is sufficient Approved Amounts, the FDC earned in any one period from BCLC is based on certain percentages of the win from gaming activities of that period at the Company's British Columbia casinos, community gaming centre and racetrack with slot machines. Currently, these FDC percentages range from 3% to 5% of the win from gaming activities (Note 15).

As at December 31, 2006, the Company has $350,445 (2005—$342,426) in Approved Amounts to be recovered by future FDC payments from BCLC. These Approved Amounts have not been reflected in these financial statements. Recovery of Approved Amounts requires that our operating agreements with BCLC remain in good standing.

f) Marketing fees to BCLC

The Company contributes between 0.5% and 1.5% of the gaming win in four of its BC casinos to BCLC as prepayment for marketing programs. The Company records the contribution to BCLC as a prepaid expense and expenses the prepayment based on confirmation of expenditures made by BCLC from this fund. In the event of and to the extent that the amounts contributed are not expended on marketing programs within the defined periods, the Company will be entitled to repayment of the contribution.

g) Capital reserve account

The Amended and Restated Operating Contract ("AROC") with the Nova Scotia Gaming Corporation ("NSGC") includes a provision for reimbursement of certain of the Company's qualifying expenditures under the Capital Reserve Account ("CRA").

The Company is required under the AROC to make contributions to the CRA equal to 5% of the annual gross operation revenues from the two Nova Scotia casinos.

Reimbursement of qualifying expenditures is received from the CRA, or if there is insufficient balance in the CRA, is recorded as a receivable from NSGC and recorded as a reduction in the historical cost of the related expenditures at the time approval is given by NSGC. According to the AROC, to the extent a receivable balance exists, the Company earns interest on the balance at a rate of prime plus 2% per annum. Management believes this interest rate to be the market rate of interest of a similar instrument with similar terms and conditions. As a result, the Company does not discount the receivable.

The replacement assets acquired using CRA funds are the property of the Company until the end of the AROC, at which time, the assets revert to NSGC.

h) Investments

The Company accounts for its investments in companies over which it has significant influence on the equity basis of accounting whereby the investments are initially recorded at cost and adjusted for the Company's share of income or losses of the investee companies.

Investments in companies which are not subject to significant influence are accounted for using the cost method whereby the investments are recorded at cost and earnings are recognized to the extent received or receivable.

When there is a loss in the value of an investment that is other than a temporary decline, the investment is written down to estimated realizable value.

i) Property, plant and equipment

Property, plant and equipment are recorded at cost less accumulated amortization and amounts approved under CRA. Amortization is expensed on a straight-line basis from the month the asset is put in use over the estimated useful lives of the assets at the following rates:

Land	not amortized
Buildings	20 to 40 years
Aircraft	20 years
Equipment	1 to 5 years
Enterprise Resource Planning systems	5 years
Leasehold improvements and interests	lesser of useful life or lease term

During the construction period of significant facilities, the Company capitalizes construction and overhead costs, including interest, directly attributable to the construction project. The costs of construction of the Company's gaming and ancillary facilities are classified as properties under development. When the property or portion thereof is substantially complete and ready for use, costs cease to be capitalized, are transferred from properties under development to their respective asset categories, and are amortized over the asset's estimated useful life.

j) Intangible assets

The Company's finite-lived intangible assets consist primarily of electronic gaming rights, operational service agreements, siteholder agreements and horseracing licences. Intangible assets are amortized over the estimated useful life ranging from five to twenty years. Judgment is used to estimate an intangible asset's useful life and is based on an analysis of all pertinent factors, including expected use of the intangible asset, contractual provisions that enable renewal or extension of the intangible asset's legal or contractual life without substantial cost, and renewal history. Changes in the estimate of an intangible asset's useful life are treated as a change in accounting estimate and are applied prospectively.

Intangible assets are tested for impairment consistent with the method described for long-lived assets below (Note 2(l)). The intangible assets impairment test had no impact on the Company's results for the years ended December 31, 2006 and 2005.

3. CHANGE IN ACCOUNTING POLICY

Effective September 30, 2006, the Company changed its accounting policy for the FDC and records FDC as revenues in the statement of income (loss) as it is earned (when it is payable by BCLC to the Company), limited to the extent that sufficient Approved Amounts exist. Approved Amounts to be recovered through future FDC payments from BCLC are disclosed in the notes to the consolidated financial statements (Note 2(e)).

The Company has elected to adopt the new accounting policy as it believes it more accurately reflects the nature of the current compensation arrangements with BCLC, provides better information on the cash flows of the Company and portrays property, plant and equipment on the balance sheet at amortized historical cost.

Previously, the FDC was accounted for as a form of government assistance upon approval by the BCLC of the Approved Amounts. Approved Amounts were recorded at the time of BCLC's approval as due from provincial gaming corporation on the balance sheet and reduced the cost of the related asset or operating expense. The due from provincial gaming corporation was recorded on a discounted basis using a discount rate that management believed to be the market rate of interest for a similar instrument with similar terms and conditions. The FDC received reduced the due from provincial gaming corporation receivable.

The accretive income recognized on the statement of income (loss) increased the due from provincial gaming corporation receivable.

The Company's former accounting policy for the FDC, while in accordance with Canadian generally accepted accounting principles, had increased in complexity, both in its application and in user understanding, and required significant management estimates, as a result of increases in the amount of the Company's capital expenditures and Approved Amounts. In considering these factors, management initiated a review of its accounting policy for FDC.

The Canadian Institute of Chartered Accountants Handbook Section on "Accounting Changes", effective January 1, 2007 with earlier adoption encouraged, requires where entities consider a voluntary change in accounting policies that the new policy result in more reliable and more relevant information about the effects of transactions on the entity's financial position, financial performance or cash flows.

The Company believes the new change in accounting policy for FDC is preferable to the prior method employed, and results in more reliable and more relevant presentation in the financial statements. The new policy does not require the significant management estimates inherent in the old policy. These estimates affected the determination of the due from provincial gaming corporation receivable, amortization expense, and accretive income.

This new accounting policy has been applied on a retrospective basis to prior periods, with the opening balance of retained earnings and other financial information and amounts disclosed in the financial statements adjusted and presented as if the new accounting policy had always been applied.

11. LONG-TERM DEBT

The Bridge Credit Facility was repaid and retired subsequent to the year-end. The Bridge Credit Facility and the Flamboro Promissory Note are shown as longterm debt on the balance sheet since they have been or will be repaid using proceeds from long-term debt issued subsequent to the year-end (Note 25(a)).

a) Bridge Credit Facility

On September 29, 2006, the Company closed on a $450,000 Bridge Credit Facility consisting of two tranches: a $250,000 non-revolving credit facility and a $200,000 revolving credit facility. This revolving credit facility replaced the Company's former $200,000 credit facility. The Bridge Credit Facility expires on October 1, 2007 and, among other covenants, requires the Company to maintain a Net Debt to Adjusted EBITDA (defined terms in the Bridge Credit Facility agreement) ratio of 4.25 or less, to be measured quarterly. Other covenants in the Bridge Credit Facility agreement include limiting the Company's ability to make investments, incur additional indebtedness or sell assets. The Bridge Credit Facility is guaranteed by the Company and its principal subsidiaries, and is secured by the Company's principal assets.

The interest rate for both tranches of the Bridge Credit Facility is based on the Company's Net Debt to Adjusted EBITDA ratio and is adjusted quarterly.

The initial advances under the Bridge Credit Facility bear interest at either the Toronto-Dominion Bank's Canadian prime rate or the Canadian banker's acceptance rate plus 1.50%. The maximum rate of interest occurs at a Net Debt to Adjusted EBITDA ratio of 4.25 and would be the prime rate plus 0.375% or banker's acceptance rate plus 1.875%. The interest rates otherwise determined by the Net Debt to Adjusted EBITDA ratio increase by 0.25% after 90, 180 and 270 days from September 29, 2006.

Amounts accrued or paid that are associated with the issuance of new debt instruments or establishment of new debt or credit facilities are deferred, included in prepaids, deposits, and other assets on the balance sheet, and are amortized on a straight-line basis over the term of the related debt to interest and financing costs, net on the statement of income (loss). Costs of $2,720 associated with establishing the Bridge Credit Facility are deferred and amortized over the expected term of the facility.

Subsequent to year-end, the Bridge Credit Facility was refinanced under a debt facility (Note 25(a)). As a result, the debt associated with the Bridge Credit Facility is shown as long-term debt on the balance sheet as at December 31, 2006.

Research and Financial Analysis

RA14-1   At Home Corporation (Excite@Home)

An excerpt follows from the December 31, 2000, financial statements of At Home Corporation, which is also known as Excite@Home. As noted in CA14-2, the company eventually went bankrupt in 2002. Its shares had traded as high as $100 per share in 1999.

Excerpt from note to 2000 financial statements:

9. Convertible Debt and Other Liabilities

Convertible Debt

On December 28, 1998 we issued $437 million principal amount of convertible subordinated debentures in a private offering within the United States to qualified institutional investors. The issue price was 52.464% of the $437 million principal amount due at maturity and issuance costs were $6.9 million, resulting in net proceeds to us of $222.4 million. The carrying amount, including accretion of original issue discount, of these convertible debentures was $243.5 million and $236.3 million as of December 31, 2000 and 1999, respectively.

The debentures mature on December 28, 2018, and interest on the debentures at the rate of 0.5246% per annum on the $437 million principal amount due at maturity is payable semi-annually commencing on June 28, 1999. The effective annual interest rate on the debentures, including accretion of original issuance discount and amortization of issuance costs, is approximately 4%. Each $1,000 debenture is convertible at the option of the holder at any time prior to maturity, unless redeemed or otherwise purchased, into 13.1 shares of our Series A common stock. No conversions of these debentures have occurred through December 31, 2000. At our option, we may redeem the debentures beginning in December 2003 for cash equal to the issue price plus accrued original issue discount and accrued interest.

On December 15, 1999, we issued $500 million principal amount of convertible subordinated notes in a private offering within the United States to qualified institutional investors. The net proceeds from this issuance were $485.7 million after deduction of issuance costs of $14.3 million. The notes mature on December 15, 2006 and bear interest at an annual rate of 4.75%. Each $1,000 note is convertible into our Series A common stock at a conversion price of $56.52 per share. No conversions of these notes have occurred through December 31, 2000.

We may redeem these notes beginning in December 2002 for cash equal to a redemption price that decreases ratably from 102.7% of the principal balance in December 2003 to 100% of the principal balance in December 2006, plus accrued interest.

Issuance costs related to our convertible debt were recorded as other assets and are being amortized by charges to interest expense ratably over the term of the debt.

Instructions

(a) Discuss the nature of the company's business. How does the company earn income? (Hint: Do an Internet search and use information from articles about the company.)

(b) What type of debt was issued on December 28, 1998? Why do you suppose that the company would issue the debt so that it receives proceeds of only 52.5% of the debt's face value?

(c) Propose a journal entry to record the debt. Assuming no debt was repaid the following year, propose the journal entry to record interest. For simplicity, assume that no value can be attributed to the conversion option.

RA14-2   Stantec

Refer to the financial statements of Stantec Inc. presented in Appendix 5B.

Instructions

Using ratio and other analyses, prepare an assessment of Stantec's solvency and financial flexibility.

RA14-3   George Weston versus Sobeys

Instructions

Access the financial information for George Weston and Sobeys either through the Student Website or SEDAR (www.sedar.com) and then answer the following questions.

(a) Calculate the debt-to-total-asset ratio and the times interest earned ratio for these two companies. Comment on the quality of these two ratios for both companies.

(a) What financial ratios do both companies use (look in the annual reports) to monitor and present their financial condition? Do both companies use the same ratios? Are the ratios calculated in the same way?

RA14-4   DBRS

DBRS is a large bond-rating agency in Canada.

Instructions

Access the agency's website at www.dbrs.com and answer the following.

(a) How does DBRS rate the debt of food retailer companies? In other words, what is its methodology?

(b) Which ratios are important in its analysis?

(c) What ratings has it given to George Weston and Sobeys?

(d) Comment on why the ratings in (c) might have been given.

(e) Is it possible to have different ratings on different debt instruments in the same company? Explain.

(Hint: Look at the DBRS list of rated companies or the S&P list of ratings.)

RA14-5   IASB/FASB Joint Projects

Go to the IASB or FASB website and review the status of the project on Liabilities and Equity and/or Financial Instruments.

Instructions

Discuss any major changes to GAAP that are being proposed.

RA14-6   First Quantum Minerals

First Quantum Minerals is a Canadian company whose shares trade on a Canadian exchange as well as the London, England, exchange.

Instructions

Go to the Student Website and look at the notes to the company's financial statements. Then answer the following questions.

Student Website

www.wiley.com/canada/kieso

(a) Which GAAP has been used to prepare the financial statements?

(b) At the end of the statements, there is a reconciliation to another GAAP. Which GAAP? Why do you think that the other GAAP is not IFRS?

(c) What are the merits of requiring foreign companies to use IFRS instead of allowing them to use their national GAAP with a reconciliation?

A Comfortable Investment

Since going public as an income trust in 2003, Sleep Country Canada has provided investors with a 30 percent increase in monthly distributions, along with significant growth in the market value of the fund's units.

"A good income trust is sold based on the strength and stability of its underlying business. The stronger, more stable the business, the greater its potential for making regular cash distributions to unitholders," says its chief financial officer, Vicki Jones. "Sleep Country is well-suited to an income trust because its operations are stable, as mattresses aren't a luxury or fashion item. Also, Sleep Country has low capital expenditure requirements. Those are two things that make an income trust attractive to investors."

However, following the federal government's decision in 2006 to progressively revoke an income trust's tax-free status until 2011, there is now much speculation about whether income trusts like Sleep County will continue to be attractive, "In 2011, Sleep Country Canada Inc., which is a corporation, and its subsidiaries will be taxed at the full federal and provincial rates," confirms Jones.

But for Sleep Country the tax hit will be less than it might be for other income trusts. "We are set up as a trust on corporation structure with a tax shelter built in between the trust and corporation of about $15 million, which roughly equates to about $5 million in cash tax," Jones explains. "Any earnings we have above $15 million are currently taxed at the full corporate rates. This is different than the newer structures, which generally have 100-percent shelter built in." ■

Shareholders' Equity

Learning Objectives

After studying this chapter, you should be able to:

1. Discuss the characteristics of the corporate form of organization.
2. Identify the rights of shareholders.
3. Describe the major features of preferred shares.
4. Explain the accounting procedures for issuing shares.
5. Identify the major reasons for repurchasing shares.
6. Explain the accounting for the reacquisition and retirement of shares.
7. Explain the accounting for various forms of dividend distributions.
8. Explain the effects of different types of dividend preferences.
9. Distinguish between stock dividends and stock splits.
10. Understand the nature of other components of shareholders' equity.
11. Indicate how shareholders' equity is presented.
12. Analyze shareholders' equity.
13. Compare current Canadian and international GAAP and understand which direction international GAAP is headed in.

After studying the appendices to this chapter, you should be able to:

14. Explain the accounting for par value shares.
15. Explain the accounting for treasury shares.
16. Describe the accounting for a financial reorganization.

Preview of Chapter 15

Capital markets are highly important in any economy that functions based on private ownership rather than government ownership. The markets provide a forum where prices are established, and these prices then become signals and incentives that guide the allocation of the economy's financial resources. More and more individuals and entities are investing in the capital marketplace (which includes the stock markets and exchanges, as well as other "arenas"). This chapter explains the various accounting issues for different types of shares or equity instruments[1] that corporations issue to raise funds in capital markets. The chapter also examines the accounting issues for retained earnings and other components of shareholders' equity.

The chapter is organized as follows:

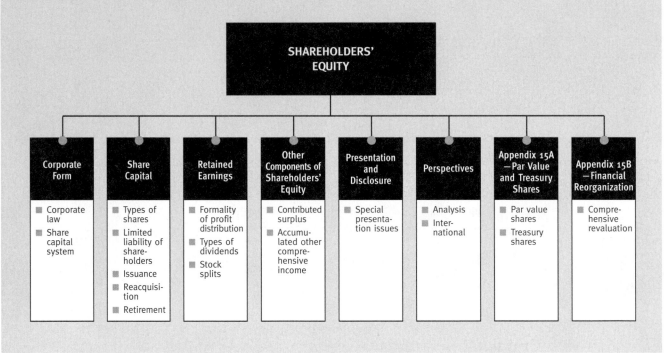

Owners' equity in a corporation is defined as **shareholders' equity** or corporate capital. The following four categories normally appear as part of shareholders' equity:

1. Common and/or preferred shares

2. Contributed surplus

3. Retained earnings (deficit)

4. Accumulated other comprehensive income[2]

---

[1] An equity instrument is "any contract that evidences a residual interest in the assets of an entity after deducting its liabilities," per *CICA Handbook* Section 3855.19(d). Most shares (including common and preferred shares) may be considered equity instruments; however, some preferred shares with debt-like features may be classified as financial liabilities. The latter will be discussed in Chapter 16.

[2] Non-publicly accountable companies must follow the new Handbook Section 1530, which is effective for years beginning on or after October 1, 2007. Public companies had to implement the new standard, along with the financial instruments and hedging standards, a year prior to this date.

The first two categories, **shares** and **contributed surplus**, form the **contributed capital**. The third and fourth categories, **retained earnings** and **accumulated other comprehensive income**, represent the enterprise's **earned** capital.

Contributed (paid-in) capital is the total amount that shareholders provide to the corporation for it to use in the business. **Earned capital** is the capital that is created by the business operating profitably. It consists of all undistributed income that remains invested in the enterprise. The distinction between paid-in capital and earned capital is important from both legal and economic points of view. Legally, there are restrictions on **dividend payouts**. These will be discussed later in the chapter. Economically, management, shareholders, and others want to see earnings for the **corporation's continued existence and growth**. Maintaining the level of contributed capital is also a goal.[3]

Many different meanings are attached to the word "**capital**" because the word is often used differently by various user groups. In corporate **finance**, for example, capital commonly refers to **sources of financing**. In **law**, capital is considered that portion of shareholders' equity that is required by statute to **be retained in the business for the protection of creditors**. Accountants use the word "capital" when referring not only to shareholders' equity but also to long-term assets (capital assets) or when referring to whether an expenditure should be treated as an asset (capitalized) or expensed. It is therefore important to pay careful attention to **the context** that the term is being used in.

THE CORPORATE FORM

Of the three **primary forms of business organization—the proprietorship, the partnership, and the corporation—**the dominant form of business is the corporate form. Although the corporate form has several advantages (as well as disadvantages) over the other two forms, its main advantage is that a corporation is a **separate legal entity** and, therefore, the entity's owners have **greater legal protection** against lawsuits. An additional important advantage is that incorporation involves the issue of shares, which gives **access to capital markets** for companies that choose to raise funds in this way.

Corporations may be classified by the nature of their ownership as follows:

1. **Public Sector Corporations:**

    (a) Government units such as municipalities, cities, and so on. No shares issued.

    (b) Government business enterprises such as Canada Post and liquor control boards (i.e., companies owned by the government and sometimes referred to as Crown corporations). Shares issued.

2. **Private Sector Corporations:**

    (a) Not-for-profit: companies whose main objective is something other than profit (such as churches, charities, and colleges). No shares issued.

    (b) For profit: companies whose main objective is to increase shareholder value and maximize profit. Shares issued.

    Private companies: companies whose shares are held by a few shareholders and are not available for public purchase. These entities are governed by shareholder agreements, which dictate who may hold the shares and how shareholder interests may or may not be transferred or disposed of. There are many private companies

---

[3] In Chapter 4, the concept of **capital maintenance** was discussed. The idea of creating shareholder value is based on at least retaining contributed capital and, ideally, causing it to grow through earnings. Note that the AcSB is moving away from the earned versus contributed distinction, since it is felt that income that is included as other comprehensive income is not really earned by the company nor is it contributed. It might be argued, however, that the income is indeed earned since management made decisions that resulted in these gains/losses.

1 Objective
Discuss the characteristics of the corporate form of organization.

International Insight

The North American and British systems of corporate governance and finance depend a lot on equity financing and the ownership of shares being widely spread out in highly liquid markets. The German and Japanese systems have relied more on debt financing, interlocking share ownership, banker/ directors, and worker/ shareholder rights.

in Canada, from small businesses to large corporate entities such as **McCain Foods** and **Maple Lodge Farms**.

Public companies: companies whose shares are available for purchase by the general public, normally through a stock exchange, such as the Toronto Stock Exchange, or stock market, such as the TSX Venture Exchange.[4] Public companies must follow GAAP,[5] securities laws that have been established by provincial securities commissions, corporations law, and finally rules established by the exchanges and markets that the companies trade on.

This book focuses on the for profit type of corporation operating in the private sector. Public sector entities and not-for-profit entities are generally covered in advanced accounting courses.

What Do the Numbers Mean?

Income or investment trusts (also called income or investment funds) have created a lot of interest in the last few years. **Sleep Country Canada** chose this legal form of organization when it went public. Legally, these funds are often set up as limited purpose **trust funds**. Their activities are limited and may be passive as normally they simply hold the shares of an operating company. Under the *Income Tax Act*, as long as the trust pays out its income to investors, the trust itself pays no income tax. They are most popular when the underlying operating company (the one whose shares are being held by the trust) produces steady cash flows, as this creates a steady cash flow to the investors. The investors then pay tax on the cash that they receive from the trust. The investors are referred to as "unitholders" and their liability is normally limited, but not as limited as the liability of a shareholder. It is important for the trustees of the trust (essentially the fund management) to ensure that the trust's insurance and other legal actions protect the unitholders adequately.

Income or investment trusts are special purpose entities (SPEs). Their special purpose is to invest in the shares of an operating company. In Canada, most of the earlier funds were in real estate (real estate investment trusts or REITs), however, many other industries followed in order to take advantage of the tax structure. There are a significant number of such trusts in Canada, including trusts for **Yellow Pages**, **Swiss Water Decaffeinated**, **Enbridge**, **Gateway Casino**, **Boston Pizza**, and **A&W**.

In 2006, the Canadian government announced that it planned to revoke the tax-free status of these entities, except for real estate investment trusts. The change in law will be phased in gradually and by 2011 most of these entities will no longer be exempted from taxes. Many observers predict that the number of trusts will fall from just under 300 to about 50 by then since it will be difficult for them to attract capital.

Corporate Law

Anyone who wants to establish a corporation must submit articles of **incorporation** to the provincial or federal government, depending on whether the person wants to do business in a specific province or across Canada. Once the requirements are properly fulfilled, the corporation **charter** is issued, and the corporation is recognized as a **legal entity** under the relevant business corporations act. While the provisions of most provincial business

---

[4] An "exchange" is a more formal marketplace that is more heavily regulated and uses a specific mechanism for pricing shares. Companies must meet certain requirements to be initially "listed" on the exchange, and then must continue to meet these ongoing requirements to remain listed. These requirements include numerous financial tests, such as asset and revenue levels. Stock "markets" use a different share pricing mechanism and are generally less heavily regulated. There is a wide range of types of stock markets. At the more formal end of the range is NASDAQ and at the less formal end are Alternate Trading Systems (ATS), which are unstructured, Internet-based platforms or marketplaces where interested buyers and sellers may meet and trade shares. The TSX is the senior exchange in Canada, whereas the TSX Venture Exchange deals with smaller, start-up companies.

[5] This is required under corporations law, which was discussed in Chapter 1 and gives GAAP legal status.

corporations acts are reasonably similar, there are some differences. Consequently, when legal aspects are discussed in this chapter, the discussion will only consider the *Canada Business Corporations Act* (CBCA).

The articles of incorporation specify such things as the **company name**,[6] place of **registered office, classes and maximum numbers of shares authorized**, restrictions of **rights to transfer shares, number of directors**, and any restrictions on the **corporation's business**. Once it has been incorporated, share certificates are prepared and issued to shareholders.

Share Capital System

A corporation's share capital is generally made up of a large number of units or shares. These shares may be organized into groups or **classes**, such as Class A shares versus Class B shares. Within a class, each share is exactly equal to every other share. The number of shares that are possessed determines each owner's interest. If a company has only one class of shares and it is divided into 1,000 shares, a person owning 500 shares has one half of the corporation's ownership interest, and a person holding 10 shares would have a one-hundredth interest.

Each share has certain rights and privileges that can only be restricted by provisions in the articles of incorporation. If there are no restrictive provisions, each share gives the following **basic or inherent rights**:

1. To share proportionately in **profits and losses**

2. To share proportionately in management (i.e., they give the **right to vote** for directors)

3. To share proportionately in the corporate **assets upon liquidation** of the corporation

The CBCA allows a corporation to assign a fourth right: this is the right to share proportionately in any new issues of shares of the same class. This right is known as a **preemptive right**.

The first three rights are expected in the ownership of any business; the last right may be used in a corporation to protect each shareholder's proportional interest in the enterprise. **The preemptive right protects an existing shareholder from the involuntary dilution of the shareholder's ownership interest**. What does this mean? It means that, without this right, the corporation would be able to issue additional shares without notifying the shareholders and at prices that were not favourable to the shareholders, which could result in the shareholders' specific percentage interest (the proportional ownership of the corporation) being reduced. Because the preemptive right that attaches to existing shares makes it inconvenient for corporations to make large issuances of additional shares, as they frequently do in acquiring other companies, many corporations have eliminated it.

The great advantage of the share system is that it makes it very easy to transfer an interest in a business from one individual to another. Individuals who own shares in a corporation may sell them to others **at any time** and **at any price** without obtaining the consent of the company or other shareholders. Each share is the personal property of the owner and may be disposed of at will.[7] For its part, the corporation is only required to maintain a list or **subsidiary ledger of shareholders**, which it needs as a guide to dividend payments, issuance of share rights, voting proxies, and similar elements. Because shares are so easily and frequently transferred, the corporation must update the subsidiary

2 Objective

Identify the rights of shareholders.

International Insight

In Canada and the U.S., shareholders are treated equally in their access to financial information. This is not always the case in other countries. For example, in Mexico, foreign investors and minority investors often have difficulty obtaining financial data. These restrictions are due to the habits of companies that for many years have been tightly controlled by a few shareholders and managers.

---

[6] Under the CBCA, the name must include the words "Incorporated," "Limited," or "Corporation," or their respective short forms, in either English or French.

[7] The company issuing the shares records a journal entry only when it first issues and sells the shares and when it buys them back. When shareholders buy and sell shares from each other, this is not recorded by the company.

ledger of shareholders periodically, generally before every dividend payment or share-holders' meeting. Major stock exchanges require controls over record keeping that are costly for the typical corporation. As a result, companies generally **outsource** this task to **registrars and transfer agents** that specialize in providing services for recording and transferring shares.

SHARE CAPITAL

Types of Shares

Common Shares

Underlying Concept

Common shares carry the risks and rewards of ownership.

In every corporation, there is one class of shares that represents the basic ownership interest. That class is called common shares. **Common shares** represent the **residual ownership interest** in the company, suffer the ultimate **risks** of loss, and receive the **benefits** of success. A common shareholder is not guaranteed annual dividends and is not guaranteed assets upon dissolution of the corporation. However, common shareholders generally **control** the corporation management through the **voting rights** attached to these shares.[8] They also tend to profit the most if the company is successful. If a corporation has only one authorized issue of capital shares, that issue is, by definition, common shares, and this is true even if the corporation's charter does not designate the shares as common.

Shares may be **in-substance common shares**.[9] These are shares that, even though they have the same characteristics as common shares, cannot be called common shares for legal purposes. The following should be considered when deciding whether to treat the instrument as common shares for financial statement purposes:

- Subordination: The shares do not have a preferred rank over other shares for dividend distributions or for the distribution of company assets upon windup of the company.

- Risks and rewards of ownership: The shares participate in the earnings/losses of the company and the appreciation/depreciation in value of the company.

- Obligation to transfer value: These shares have no obligation to transfer value. Given that they represent a residual interest in the company, they only have value if the company's net assets have value.[10]

Preferred Shares

Objective 3

Describe the major features of preferred shares.

In an effort to attract all types of investors, corporations may offer two or more classes of shares, with each class having **different rights or privileges**. In the preceding section, it was pointed out that each share of a particular issue has the same rights as other shares of the same issue and that there are three inherent rights in every share. By special contracts between the corporation and its shareholders, **some of these rights may be sacrificed by the shareholder in return for other special rights or privileges**. This creates special classes of shares, and because they have certain preferential rights, such shares are usually called **preferred shares**. In return for any special preference, the preferred shareholder is always required to sacrifice some of the basic rights of common share interests.

A common type of preference is to give the preferred shareholders a **priority claim on earnings and on assets (upon dissolution of the company)**, compared to the claims

---

[8] Shareholders who have voting rights elect the board of directors to make major decisions for them.

[9] *CICA Handbook*, EIC Abstract 149.

[10] Ibid.

of the common shareholders. This means that preferred shareholders are assured a dividend, usually at a stated rate, before any amount may be distributed to the common shareholders. They are also assured that if the company goes bankrupt, they rank before the common shareholders in terms of getting their money back. In return for this preference, the preferred shareholders may sacrifice the right to a voice in management or the right to share in profits beyond the stated rate.

Instead of issuing both common and preferred shares, a company may accomplish much the same thing by issuing two classes of shares, Class A shares and Class B shares. In this case, one of the issues is the common share and the other issue has some preference or restriction of basic shareholder rights. Illustration 15-1 is an excerpt about share classes from the notes to the financial statements of Four Seasons Hotels Inc.

What Do the Numbers Mean?

Illustration 15-1

Excerpt from the Notes to the Financial Statements of Four Seasons Hotels Inc.

---

11. Shareholders' equity:

(a)   Capital stock:

Authorized:
3,725,698
Variable Multiple Voting Shares ("VMVS"), entitling the holder to that number of votes that results in the aggregate votes attaching to the VMVS, representing approximately 65% of the votes attaching to the VMVS and the Limited Voting Shares ("LVS"), in aggregate, which, at December 31, 2005, was 16.09 votes (2004 – 16.07 votes) per VMVS. Changes in the number of votes attaching to the VMVS necessary to maintain this level will occur concurrently with the issue of additional LVS.

The VMVS rank equally with the LVS as to distributions on liquidation, dissolution or winding-up of FSHI. Dividends declared and paid on the VMVS are in amounts per share equal to 50% of the dividends per share declared and paid on the LVS, regardless of whether the number of votes attaching to the VMVS is further increased.

VMVS are convertible into LVS on a one-for-one basis at the option of the holder. The shares automatically convert into LVS upon any transfer outside of the family of Mr. Isadore Sharp, the Chief Executive Officer of FSHI, except a transfer of a majority of the shares to a purchaser who makes an equivalent offer to purchase all outstanding VMVS and LVS.

Unlimited
LVS, voting (one vote per share) and ranking equally with the VMVS as to distributions on liquidation, dissolution or winding-up of FSHI.

In this case, the existence of the VMVS allows the Sharp family to keep control of the company, as it will always have the majority of the votes.

Preferred shares may be issued with a dividend preference that is expressed as a **percentage of the par value or issue price**. Thus, holders of 8% preferred shares issued at $100 are entitled to an annual dividend of $8 per share. This share is commonly referred to as an 8% preferred share. The dividend may also be expressed as a **specific dollar amount** per share; for example, $8 per share. A preference as to dividends does not assure that dividends will be paid; it only means that the stated dividend rate or amount that applies to the preferred share must be paid before any dividends can be paid on the common shares.

Features of Preferred Shares   A corporation may attach whatever preferences or restrictions it desires to a preferred share issue, and in whatever combination, as long as the corporation does not specifically violate its incorporation law, and it may issue more than one class of preferred share. Some preferred share features include the quality of being:

1. **Cumulative**. Dividends on cumulative shares that are not paid in any given year are known as dividends in arrears and must be made up in a later year before any profits can be distributed to common shareholders. There is no liability, however, until the board of directors **declares** a dividend. According to common law custom, if the corporate charter is silent about the cumulative feature, the preferred share is considered cumulative.

2. **Convertible**. This feature allows the company or holder to exchange the shares for common shares at a predetermined ratio. Thus, the shareholder has the relative security of the preferred share yet may participate in the appreciation of the company by converting preferred shares to common shares.

3. **Callable/Redeemable**. The issuing corporation can **call** or redeem at its option (through its own choice) the outstanding preferred shares at specified future dates and at stipulated prices. The callable feature permits the corporation to use the capital that it has obtained through the issuance of such shares until the need has passed or having the issued shares is no longer advantageous. The existence of a call price or prices tends to set a ceiling on the market value of the preferred shares unless they are convertible into common shares. When a preferred share is called for redemption, any dividends in arrears must be paid.

4. **Retractable**. The holders of the shares can **put** or sell their shares to the company, normally after having given adequate notice, and the company must then pay the holders for the shares. The retraction option makes this instrument more attractive to the holders as it gives them more choice.

5. **Participating**. Holders of participating preferred shares share (at the same rate as common shareholders) in any profit distributions that are higher than the prescribed rate of the preferred share. That is, a 5% preferred share, if it is fully participating, will receive not only its 5% return, but also dividends at the same rate that is paid to common shareholders if the latter are paid amounts higher than 5% of par or stated value. Note that participating preferred shares are not always fully participating. That is, they can also be partially participating. For example, provision may be made that a 5% preferred share will be participating up to a maximum total rate of 10%, after which it ceases to participate in additional profit distributions; or a 5% preferred share may participate only in additional profit distributions that are in excess of a 9% dividend rate on the common share.

Preferred shares are often issued instead of debt because a company's debt-to-equity ratio has become too high. The issuing company may structure the instrument such that its legal form represents shares in hopes of avoiding treating the instruments as debt on the financial statements. Accounting for preferred shares can be complex because of their many and varied features and because accountants must account for the instruments in accordance with their economic substance as opposed to their legal form. Chapter 16 discusses the more complex aspects of these financial instruments.

Finally, issuances of common, preferred, or other shares may be made through **private placements**[11] as opposed to through the stock markets/exchanges. The difference between the two is that the company remains private if it has no shares that trade on a stock market/exchange and it would therefore not be subject to the same regulations as a public company.

---

[11] The term "private placement" refers to a situation where the shares are only offered privately to a select group of interested investors. In other words, they are not floated for sale on the stock exchange or market. Private placements are often directed at large institutional or individual investors.

Limited Liability of Shareholders

Those who own a corporation—the shareholders—contribute either property or services to the enterprise in return for ownership shares. **The property or service that has been invested in the enterprise is the limit on a shareholder's possible loss.** That is, if the corporation has losses that are so large that the remaining assets are not enough to pay creditors, the creditors have **no recourse** against the personal assets of the individual shareholders. This is unlike in a partnership or proprietorship, where the owners' personal assets can be accessed to satisfy unpaid claims against the enterprise. Ownership interests in a corporation are legally protected against such a contingency. The shareholders are thus said to have **limited liability**: they may lose their investment but they cannot lose **more** than their investment.

While the corporate form of organization gives the protective feature of limited liability to the shareholders, it also stipulates that the amount of the shareholders' investment that is represented in share capital accounts cannot be withdrawn unless all prior claims on corporate assets have been paid. This means that the corporation **must maintain this capital until dissolution of the corporation**. Upon dissolution, it must then satisfy all prior claims before distributing any amounts to the shareholders. In a proprietorship or partnership, the owners or partners may withdraw amounts whenever and at whatever amount they choose because all their personal assets can be accessed to protect creditors from loss.

Shares issued by corporations must be **without a nominal or par value** (according to the CBCA). This simply means that all proceeds from the issuance of the shares must be credited to the appropriate share capital account and become part of the shareholders' investment referred to above. In some provinces and in the United States, shares that have a fixed per-share amount printed on each share certificate are called **par value shares**.[12] Par value has only one real significance: it establishes the **maximum responsibility of a shareholder in the event of insolvency** (i.e., in jurisdictions where the concept of par value is legally allowed) or other involuntary dissolution. Par value is thus not value in the ordinary sense of the word. It is merely an amount per share that has been determined by the incorporators of the company and stated in the corporation charter or certificate of incorporation.

Issuance of Shares

Even though shares are equity instruments, they are exempted from *CICA Handbook* Section 3855, which deals with the recognition and measurement of financial instruments. They are covered instead by the following *CICA Handbook* Sections:

- 1535 Capital disclosures

- 3240 Share capital

- 3251 Equity

- 3862 Financial instruments—disclosures

- 3863 Financial instruments—presentation[13]

4 Objective

Explain the accounting procedures for issuing shares.

---

[12] *Accounting Trends and Techniques—2004* indicates that its 600 surveyed companies reported 655 issues of outstanding common stock, 570 par value issues, and 54 no-par issues; 6 of the no-par issues were shown at their stated (assigned) values. *Financial Reporting in Canada, 2005* (Toronto, CICA) Chapter 32 noted that out of 200 companies surveyed, 99.5% either made no reference to par or stated value or they indicated that the shares were without par or stated value.

[13] *CICA Handbook*, Section 3855.07(g).

In issuing shares, the following procedures are followed: First, the shares must be **authorized**. Next, shares are **offered for sale** and contracts to sell shares are entered into. Finally, amounts to be received for the shares are **collected** and the **shares are issued**.

Share Issue—Basic

Shares are sold for the price that they will bring in the marketplace. Normally the company will hire specialists (e.g., investment banking firms, underwriters) to value the shares[14] and help **promote and sell them**. As payment for their services, the underwriters take as commission a percentage of the total share consideration that is received from investors. The **net** amount that is received by the company becomes the credit to common or preferred shares. For example, assume that Video Electronics Corporation is organized with 10,000 authorized common shares. The only entry that is made for this authorization is a memorandum entry. There is no journal entry since there is no monetary amount involved in the authorization. If 500 shares are then issued for cash at $10 per share, the entry should be:

A   = L +   SE
+5,000   +5,000

Cash flows: ↑ 5,000 inflow

Cash	5,000	
Common Shares		5,000

Entries for preferred shares are the same as for common shares as long as the preferred shares are classified as equity.[15] As par value shares are relatively uncommon in Canada, the issues that are unique to them are covered in Appendix 15A.

Underlying Concept

Subscriptions receivable appear to meet the definition of an asset since they represent a future benefit to the company in terms of incoming cash. However, treating them as an asset results in the share capital increasing even though the shares are not yet issued. This does not provide transparent financial reporting.

Shares Sold on a Subscription Basis

Shares may also be sold, however, on a subscription basis. Sales of **subscribed shares** generally occur when new, small companies go public or when corporations offer shares to employees in order to have employees participate in the business ownership. When a share is sold on a subscription basis, its full price is not received immediately. Normally, only a **partial payment** is made, and the share is not issued until the full subscription price is received.

The journal entries for handling shares that are sold on a subscription basis are illustrated by the following example. Assume that Lubradite Corp. offers shares on a subscription basis to selected individuals, giving them the right to purchase 10 common shares at a price of $20 per share. Fifty individuals accept the company's offer and agree to pay 50% down and the remaining 50% at the end of six months. Lubradite's entries would be as follows:

A   = L +   SE
                    0

Cash flows: No effect

A   = L +   SE
+5,000   +5,000

Cash flows: ↑ 5,000 inflow

At date of issuance		
Subscriptions Receivable (10 × $20 × 50)	10,000	
Common Shares Subscribed		10,000
(To record receipt of subscriptions for 500 shares)		
Cash	5,000	
Subscriptions Receivable		5,000
(To record receipt of first instalment representing 50% of total due on subscribed shares)		

---

[14] The shares are valued using valuation models that include expected future cash flow or operating income from the company. This often results in pressure on the income numbers since a higher income results in a higher share price.

[15] Some of the more complex features of preferred shares that were noted earlier can make them like debt.

In Canada, whether the Subscriptions Receivable account should be presented as an asset or a contra equity account is a matter of professional judgement. In the United States, the SEC requires the latter treatment.

When the final payment is received and the shares are issued, the entries are:

Six months later		
Cash	5,000	
Subscriptions Receivable		5,000
(To record receipt of final instalment on subscribed shares)		

A　=　L　+　　SE
+5,000　　　　　+5,000

Cash flows: ↑ 5,000 inflow

Common Shares Subscribed	10,000	
Common Shares		10,000
(To record issuance of 500 shares upon receipt of final instalment from subscribers)		

A　=　L　+　　SE
　　　　　　　　0

Cash flows: No effect

Defaulted Subscription Accounts

Sometimes a subscriber is unable to pay all instalments and therefore defaults on the agreement. The question is what to do with the balance of the subscription account and the amount that has already been paid in. The answer is determined by the subscription contract, corporate policy, and any applicable law of the jurisdiction of incorporation. The possibilities include returning the amount already paid by the subscriber (possibly after deducting some expenses), treating the amount paid as forfeited and therefore transferring it to the Contributed Surplus account, or issuing fewer shares to the subscriber so that the number of shares issued is equivalent to what the subscription payments already received would have paid for fully.

For example, assume that a subscriber to 50 Lubradite common shares defaults on the final payment. If the subscription contract stated that amounts paid by the defaulting subscriber would be refunded, Lubradite would make the following entry when the default occurs, assuming that the refund was to be paid at a later date:

Common Shares Subscribed	1,000	
Subscriptions Receivable		500
Accounts Payable		500
(To record default on 50 shares subscribed for $20 each on which 50% had been paid)		

A　=　　L　+　　SE
　　　+500　　− 500

Cash flows: No effect

If the amount paid by the subscriber were forfeited, there would be a $500 credit to Contributed Surplus as this is a **capital transaction**.

Shares Issued with Other Securities (Lump Sum Sales)

Generally, corporations sell each **class of shares** separately so that they can determine the proceeds for each class and, ordinarily, even for each lot of shares in the class. Occasionally, however, two or more classes of securities are issued for a single payment or **lump sum**. It is not uncommon, for example, for more than one type or class of security to be issued in the acquisition of another company. The accounting problem in such **lump sum sales** is the allocation of the proceeds among the several classes of securities, or how to measure the separate classes of shares.

Two possible measurement techniques are used: (1) the **proportional method** and (2) the **incremental method**. These measurement techniques are often used in accounting, even for issues that are not lump sum share issues. The first method values each instrument and then proportionally allocates the value. The second method values one instrument (often the one that is easier to measure) and then allocates the rest of the amount to the other instrument. There is an example of this in Chapter 16 where the value of compound financial instruments is allocated to the different parts of the instrument. This same technique is used to bifurcate bundled sales as explained in Chapter 6 on pp. 311. Note that the labels are slightly different, i.e., the proportional method is essentially the same as the relative fair value method, and the incremental method is very similar to the residual value method.

Costs of Issuing Shares

Direct costs that are incurred to sell shares, such as underwriting costs, accounting and legal fees, printing costs, and taxes, should be reported as a reduction of the amounts paid in. **Issue costs** are therefore debited to Share Capital because they are **capital transactions**[16] rather than **operating transactions**.

Management salaries and other **indirect costs** related to the share issue should be expensed as they are incurred because it is difficult to establish a relationship between these costs and the proceeds that are received from the sale.[17] In addition, corporations annually incur costs for maintaining the shareholders' records and handling ownership transfers. These recurring costs, which are mainly registrar and transfer agents' fees, are normally charged to expense in the period in which they are incurred.

What Do the Numbers Mean?

Sometimes companies issue shares but do not receive cash in return (other than subscription sales). There is controversy in such cases about how this receivable should be presented on the balance sheet. Some argue that the receivable should be recorded as an asset like other receivables. Others argue that the receivable should be reported as a reduction of shareholders' equity. The SEC requires companies to use the latter approach because the risk of collection on these types of transactions is often very high. Canadian GAAP also supports this view unless there is substantial evidence that the company is not at risk for declines in the time value of the shares.[18]

Unfortunately, this issue surfaced with **Enron**. Starting in early 2000, Enron issued shares of its common stock to four "special purpose entities" and in exchange it received notes receivable. Enron then increased its assets and shareholders' equity, a move the company subsequently called an accounting error. As a result, Enron's 2000 audited financial statements overstated assets and shareholders' equity by $172 million. Enron's 2001 unaudited statements overstated them by $828 million. The $1-billion overstatement was 8.5% of Enron's previously reported equity as at June 30—a material amount.

Source: Adapted from Jonathan Weil, "Basic Accounting Tripped up Enron," "Financial Statements Didn't Add Up," and "Auditors Overlook Simple Rule," *Wall Street Journal*, November 11, 2001, p. C1.

Reacquisition of Shares

Objective 5
Identify the major reasons for repurchasing shares.

It is not unusual for companies to buy back their own shares. In fact, share buybacks now exceed dividends as a form of distribution to shareholders.[19] While corporations have varied reasons for purchasing their outstanding shares, some of the major ones are as follows:

---

[16] *CICA Handbook*, Section 3610.

[17] *CICA Handbook*, EIC Abstract 94 allows for costs that are direct and incremental to be treated as capital transactions.

[18] *CICA Handbook*, EIC Abstract 132.

[19] At the beginning of the 1990s, the situation was just the opposite; that is, share buybacks were less than half the level of dividends. Companies are extremely reluctant to reduce or eliminate their dividends because they believe that this action is viewed negatively by the market. On the other hand, many companies are no longer raising their dividend per share at the same percentage rate as increases in earnings per share, which effectively reduces the dividend payout over time.

1. **To increase earnings per share and return on equity.** By reducing shares outstanding and reducing shareholders' equity, certain performance ratios are often improved, such as earnings per share and return on equity.

2. **To provide shares for employee share compensation contracts or to meet potential merger needs.** Honeywell Inc. reported that part of its purchase of 1 million common shares was to be used for employee share option contracts. Other companies acquire shares to have them available for business acquisitions.

3. **To stop takeover attempts or to reduce the number of shareholders.** By reducing the number of shares that are held by the public, it is easier for the current owners and management to keep outsiders from gaining control or significant influence. When Ted Turner tried to acquire CBS, CBS started a substantial buyback of its shares. Share purchases may also be used to eliminate dissident shareholders.

4. **To make a market in the share.** By purchasing shares in the marketplace, a demand is created that may stabilize the share price or, in fact, increase it. Over the period 1997 to 2001, Nexfor Inc., a large North American producer of building materials, repurchased and cancelled 15.5 million shares for $122 million (representing 10% of the company's shares). The company commented that the shares were undervalued and represented a good deal.

5. **To return cash to shareholders.** In 2001, Methanex Corporation offered to purchase more than 29 million of its shares worth $175 million (approximately 18% of the total shares outstanding). Pierre Choquette, president and CEO of Methanex, commented: "These planned share repurchases are part of our commitment to return excess cash to shareholders. Our low-cost production facilities and leading market position combined with strong methanol pricing allowed us to generate almost $400 (U.S.) million in cash from operations over the past year. Our cash balance is currently in excess of $450 (U.S.) million and we have an undrawn $291 (U.S.) million credit facility."

6. **To create value for the shareholders.** If the company feels that the shares are trading at a value that is less than the company's perceived true value, it may buy back the shares as an investment. On October 25, 2006, Brick Brewing Co. Limited announced that it planned to buy back just over 1 million shares, representing 5% of its outstanding shares. The reason given was that the company felt that the current market price for the shares did not indicate the underlying value of the company and the buyback therefore amounted to an attractive investment at the time.

Some publicly held corporations have chosen to go private; that is, they decided to eliminate public (outside) ownership by purchasing their entire float of outstanding shares. This is often done through a **leveraged buyout**, which is when management or another employee group purchases the company shares and finances the purchase by using the company assets as collateral.

Once shares are reacquired, they may either be **retired** or held in the treasury for **reissue**. If they are not retired, such shares are referred to as **treasury shares**. Technically, a treasury share is a corporation's own share that has been reacquired after having been issued and fully paid. In Canada, the CBCA, with minor exceptions, requires that repurchased shares be cancelled and, if the articles limit the number of authorized shares, that the shares be restored to the status of authorized but unissued shares. While some provincial jurisdictions do allow treasury shares to exist, such shares remain relatively uncommon in Canada.[20] This is unlike the United States, where many companies hold treasury shares.[21] Appendix 15A briefly reviews the accounting for these shares.

---

[20] According to *Financial Reporting in Canada, 2005* (CICA: Toronto), only 13 out of 200 companies reported treasury shares (Chapter 32).

[21] *Accounting Trends and Techniques 2004* indicates that of its selected list of 600 companies, 398 carried common stock in treasury (and treated it as a contra equity account).

Retirement of Reacquired Shares

Objective 6
Explain the accounting for the reacquisition and retirement of shares.

When shares are purchased or redeemed by the issuing corporation, it is likely that the price paid will differ from the amount that was received for the shares when they were issued. As this is a **capital transaction**, any gains or losses are booked through equity (rather than through the income statement).

If the acquisition cost is greater than the original cost, then the acquisition cost should be allocated as follows:

1. First, to **share capital**, in an amount equal to the par, stated, or assigned value of the shares

2. Second, for any excess after the first allocation, to **contributed surplus**, to the extent that the contributed surplus was created by a net excess of proceeds over cost on a cancellation or resale of shares of the same class

3. Third, for any excess after the second allocation, to **contributed surplus** in an amount equal to the prorata share of the portion of contributed surplus that arose from transactions, other than those above, in the same class of shares

4. Last, for any excess after the third allocation, to **retained earnings**[22]

If the acquisition cost is less than the original cost, then the acquisition cost should be allocated as follows:

1. First, to **share capital**, in an amount equal to the par, stated, or assigned value of the shares

2. Second, for the difference after the first allocation, to **contributed surplus**[23]

For shares with **no par value** (i.e., for most shares in Canada), the assigned value is equal to the **average per share amount** in the account for that class of shares at the transaction date.[24] The difference between the stated or assigned value and the lower cost of acquisition is credited to contributed surplus and is seen as a contribution by the original shareholders that now accrues to the remaining shareholders.[25]

Applying the formulas noted above, in cases where the acquisition cost is **greater than the assigned cost**, this would normally result in debiting share capital (step 1) and retained earnings (step 4). Contributed Surplus would only be adjusted if there were a **prior balance** in the Contributed Surplus account that related to the shares that are being acquired.

To illustrate, assume that Cooke Corporation has the following in its shareholders' equity accounts:

Share capital:	
Class A, 10,500 shares issued and outstanding	$ 63,000
Class B, 50,000 shares issued and outstanding	100,000
Total share capital	163,000
Retained earnings	300,000
Total shareholders' equity	$463,000

---

[22] *CICA Handbook*, Section 3240.15.

[23] *CICA Handbook*, Section 3240.17.

[24] *CICA Handbook*, Section 3240.18.

[25] *CICA Handbook*, Section 3240.16.

On January 30, 2007, Cooke purchased and cancelled 500 Class A shares at a cost of $4 per share. The required entry is:

Class A Shares [500 ($63,000 ÷ 10,500)]	3,000	
Cash		2,000
Contributed Surplus*		1,000

*Average per share amount (assigned value) = $63,000 ÷ 10,500 = $6. Excess of assigned value over reacquisition cost = $6 − 4 = $2 per share for 200 shares.

A = L + SE
−2,000   −2,000

Cash flows: ↓ 2,000 outflow

On September 10, 2007, the company purchased and cancelled an additional 1,000 Class A shares. The purchase cost was $8 per share. The transaction is recorded as follows:

Class A shares [1,000 ($60,000 ÷ 10,000)]	6,000	
Contributed Surplus*	1,000	
Retained Earnings	1,000	
Cash		8,000

*Equals the whole amount of the excess from the above.

A = L + SE
−8,000   −8,000

Cash flows: ↓ 8,000 outflow

RETAINED EARNINGS

The basic source of **retained earnings**—earnings retained for use in the business—is income from operations. Shareholders assume the greatest **risk** in enterprise operations as shareholders' equity declines with any losses. In return, they also reap the **rewards**, sharing in any profits resulting from enterprise activities. Any income that is not distributed among the shareholders becomes additional shareholders' equity. Net income includes a considerable variety of income sources. These include the enterprise's main operation (such as manufacturing and selling a product), plus any secondary activities (such as disposing of scrap or renting out unused space), plus the results of extraordinary and unusual items. All lead to net income that increases retained earnings. The more common items that either increase or decrease retained earnings are expressed in account form in Illustration 15-2.

RETAINED EARNINGS

Debits	Credits
1. Net loss	1. Net income
2. Prior period adjustments (error corrections) and certain changes in accounting principle	2. Prior period adjustments (error corrections) and certain changes in accounting principle
3. Cash, property, and most stock dividends	3. Adjustments due to financial reorganization
4. Some treasury share transactions	

Illustration 15-2

Transactions That Affect Retained Earnings

Formality of Profit Distribution

Legality of Dividend Distribution

An enterprise's owners decide what to do with profits that are realized through operations. Profits may be **left in the business** for a future expansion or simply to have a margin of safety, or they may be **withdrawn and divided among the owners**. In a proprietorship or partnership, this decision is made by the owner or owners informally and requires no specific action. In a partnership, the partnership agreement would usually specify how profits or losses are to be shared. In a corporation, however, profit distribution (referred to as **dividends**) is controlled by certain **legal restrictions**. Not all shares carry the right to receive dividends.

First, no amounts may be distributed among the owners unless the **corporate capital is kept intact**. This restriction is based on the presumption that there have to be sufficient net assets or security left in the corporation to satisfy the liability holders after any assets have been distributed to shareholders as dividends. Various tests of **corporate solvency** have been used over the years. Under the CBCA, dividends may not be declared or paid if there are reasonable grounds for believing that (1) the corporation is, or would be after the dividend, unable to pay its liabilities as they become due; or (2) the realizable value of the corporation's assets would, as a result of the dividend, be less than the total of its liabilities and stated or **legal capital** for all classes of shares.

Second, distributions to shareholders must be **formally approved by the board of directors** and recorded in the minutes of the board's meetings. As the top executive body in the corporation, the board of directors must make certain that no distributions are made to shareholders that are not justified by profits, and directors are generally held personally liable to creditors if liabilities cannot be paid because company assets have been illegally paid out to shareholders.

Third, dividends must be in **full agreement with preferences created by the share capital contracts**. Once the corporation has entered into contracts with various classes of shareholders, the stipulations of such contracts must be followed.

Financial Condition and Dividend Distributions

Determining the proper amount of dividends to pay is a difficult financial management decision. Companies that are paying dividends are extremely reluctant to reduce or eliminate their dividends, because they believe that this action could be viewed negatively by the securities market. As a consequence, companies that have been paying cash dividends will make every effort to continue to do so.

Very few companies pay dividends in amounts equal to their legally available retained earnings. For instance, the board of directors of the **Bank of Montreal** announced a dividend on November 28, 2006, of 65 cents per share, which represented 50 percent of the 2006 earnings. The major reasons that companies have for limiting the dividend amount are as follows:

1. Agreements (bond covenants) with specific creditors that require all or a portion of the earnings to be retained in the form of assets in order to build up additional protection against possible loss.

2. The desire to retain assets that would otherwise be paid out as dividends, in order to finance growth or expansion. This is sometimes called internal financing, reinvesting earnings, or ploughing the profits back into the business.

3. The desire to smooth out dividend payments from year to year by accumulating earnings in good years and using such accumulated earnings as a basis for dividends in bad years.

4. The desire to build up a cushion or buffer against possible losses or errors in the calculation of profits.

Dividend policies vary among corporations. Some older, well-established firms take pride in a long, unbroken string of quarterly dividend payments.[26] They would lower or not declare the dividend only if they were forced to do so by a sustained decline in earnings

---

[26] Bank of Montreal and Bank of Nova Scotia have been paying dividends consistently since 1829 and 1833, respectively.

or a critical shortage of cash. Growth companies, on the other hand, pay little or no cash dividends because their policy is to expand as rapidly as internal and external financing permit. Investors in these companies hope that their share price will appreciate in value and that they will realize a profit when they sell their shares (i.e., they hope to benefit from capital appreciation).

Good business management means paying attention to more than just the legality of dividend distributions. **Economic conditions** also need to be considered and, most importantly, liquidity. Assume the following extreme situation:

Balance Sheet

Plant assets	$500,000	Share capital	$400,000
		Retained earnings	100,000
	$500,000		$500,000

The company has a retained earnings credit balance, and generally, unless the balance is restricted, the company can therefore declare a dividend of $100,000. But because all its assets are plant assets and used in operations, paying a cash dividend of $100,000 would require selling plant assets or borrowing.

Even if we assume a balance sheet that shows current assets, the question remains whether those cash assets are needed for other purposes.

Balance Sheet

Cash	$100,000	Current liabilities		$ 60,000
Plant assets	460,000	Share capital	$400,000	
		Retained earnings	100,000	500,000
	$560,000			$560,000

The existence of current liabilities implies very strongly that some of the cash is needed to meet current debts as they mature. In addition, day-by-day cash requirements for payrolls and other expenditures that are not included in current liabilities also require cash.

Thus, before a dividend is declared, management must consider the **availability of funds to pay the dividend**. Other demands for cash should also perhaps be investigated by preparing a cash **forecast**. A dividend should not be paid unless both the present and future financial position appear to justify the distribution. Directors must also consider the effect of inflation and replacement costs before making a dividend commitment. During a period of significant inflation, some costs that are charged to expense under historical cost accounting are understated in terms of **comparative purchasing power** (i.e., the amounts represent older dollars since the asset was purchased earlier when the dollars were likely worth more). Because these costs are not adjusted for inflation, income is therefore **overstated**.

The non-payment of dividends can also significantly impact a company. For instance, Torstar Corporation has Class B shares that are normally non-voting, but if the company does not pay dividends for eight consecutive quarters, the shares then have voting rights.

What Do the Numbers Mean?

Types of Dividends

There are basically two classes of dividends:

1. Those that are a return **on** capital (a share of the earnings)

2. Those that are a return **of** capital, referred to as **liquidating dividends**

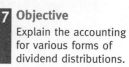

7 Objective

Explain the accounting for various forms of dividend distributions.

The natural expectation of any shareholder who receives a dividend is that the corporation has operated successfully and that he or she is receiving a share of its earnings. A liquidating dividend should therefore be adequately described in the financial statements. This type of dividend will be discussed in greater depth later in the chapter.

Dividends are commonly paid in cash but occasionally they are paid in shares or other assets. **Dividends generally reduce the total shareholders' equity in the corporation**, because the equity is reduced, either through an immediate or promised future distribution of assets. Stock dividends are different, however. When a stock dividend is declared, the corporation does not pay out assets or incur a liability. It issues additional shares to each shareholder and nothing more. Both types of dividends are discussed next.

Dividends—Cash

The board of directors votes on the declaration of dividends and if the resolution is properly approved, the dividend is declared. Before the dividend is paid, a current list of shareholders must be prepared. For this reason, there is usually a time lag between the declaration and payment. A resolution approved at the January 10 (**date of declaration**) meeting of the board of directors might be declared payable on February 5 (**date of payment**) to all shareholders of record on January 25 (**date of record**).[27]

The period from January 10 to January 25 gives time for any transfers in process to be completed and registered with the transfer agent. The time from January 25 to February 5 provides an opportunity for the transfer agent or accounting department, depending on who does this work, to prepare a list of shareholders as at January 25 and to prepare and mail dividend cheques.

To illustrate the declaration and payment of an ordinary dividend that is payable in cash, assume that on June 10 Rajah Corp. declared a cash dividend of 50 cents a share on 1.8 million shares and payable on July 16 to all shareholders of record on June 24. The following entries are required:

A　=　L　+　SE
　　+900,000　−900,000

Cash flows: No effect

A　=　L　+　SE
−900,000　−900,000

Cash flows: ↓ 900,000 outflow

At date of declaration (June 10)		
Retained Earnings (Cash Dividends Declared)	900,000	
Dividends Payable		900,000
At date of record (June 24)		
No entry		
At date of payment (July 16)		
Dividends Payable	900,000	
Cash		900,000

To have a ledger account that shows the amount of dividends declared during the year, the company can create and debit Cash Dividends Declared instead of debiting Retained Earnings at the time of declaration. This account is then closed to Retained Earnings at year end. Dividends may be declared either as a certain percent of par or stated value, such as a 6-percent dividend, or as an amount per share, such as 60 cents per share. In the first case, the rate is multiplied by the par or stated value of outstanding shares to get the total

---

[27] Determining the date of record is not always straightforward. It is generally the date prior to what is known as the ex-dividend date. Theoretically, the ex-dividend date is the day after the date of record. However, to allow time for the transfer of shares, stock exchanges generally advance the ex-dividend date by two to four days. Therefore, the party who owns the shares on the day prior to the expressed ex-dividend date receives the dividends, and the party who buys the stock on or after the ex-dividend date does not receive the dividend. Between the declaration date and the ex-dividend date, the market price of the shares includes the dividend.

dividend; in the second, the amount per share is multiplied by the number of shares out-standing. **Cash dividends are not declared and paid on treasury shares since the shares are owned by the company itself.**

Dividends in Kind

Dividends that are payable in corporation assets other than cash are called property dividends or **dividends in kind**. Property dividends may be merchandise, real estate, or investments, or whatever form the board of directors designates. Because of the obvious difficulties of dividing units and delivering them to shareholders, the usual property dividend is in the form of securities of other companies that the distributing corporation holds as an investment.

A property dividend is a non-reciprocal transfer of non-monetary assets between an enterprise and its owners. These dividends should be measured at the fair value of the asset that is given up[28] unless they are considered to represent a spin-off or other form of restructuring or liquidation, in which case they should be recorded at the carrying value of the non-monetary assets or liabilities transferred.[29] No gain or loss would be recorded in the second instance.

What Do the Numbers Mean?

When the U.S. Supreme Court decided that **DuPont**'s 23-percent investment in **General Motors** violated antitrust laws, DuPont was ordered to divest itself of the GM shares within 10 years. The shares represented 63 million of GM's 281 million shares then outstanding. DuPont could not sell the shares in one block of 63 million, nor could it sell 6 million shares annually for the next 10 years without severely depressing the value of the GM shares. At that time, the entire yearly trading volume in GM shares was not even 6 million shares. DuPont solved its problem by declaring a property dividend and distributing the GM shares as a dividend to its own shareholders.

The **fair value** of the non-monetary asset that is distributed is measured by the amount that could be realized if the asset were sold outright at or near the time of the declaration. This amount should be determined by referring to estimated realizable values in cash transactions of the same or similar assets, quoted market prices, independent appraisals, and other available evidence. Often a gain is recognized at this point (on the appreciation of the asset value just prior to the dividend).

Stock Dividends

If management wants to "capitalize" part of the earnings (i.e., reclassify amounts from earned to contributed capital) so that earnings are retained in the business on a permanent basis, it may issue a stock dividend. In this case, **no assets are distributed** and each shareholder has exactly the same proportionate interest in the corporation, and the same total book value, after the issue of the **stock dividend** as before the declaration. The book value per share is lower, however, because there are now more shares being held.

There is no clear guidance for how to account for stock dividends. The major issue is whether or not they should be treated in the same way as other dividends.[30] If they are treated like other dividends, they should be recorded by debiting Retained Earnings and crediting Share Capital. In terms of measuring the transaction, fair value would be used (measured by looking at the market value of the shares issued, at the declaration date).

---

[28] *CICA Handbook*, Section 3831.06.

[29] *CICA Handbook*, Section 3831.14. Note that if the transaction is with a controlling shareholder, then *CICA Handbook* Section 3840 applies.

[30] From a tax perspective, the CRA treats stock dividends received in the same way as other dividends. The dividends are measured at paid-up capital (legal capital, which is equal to the fair value for no par shares at the date of the dividend declaration).

Where the stock dividends give the option to the holder to receive them in cash or shares, the stock dividend is considered a non-monetary transaction under GAAP and **must** be treated as a regular dividend, valued at fair value.[31] Where there is no option to receive the dividend in cash, GAAP is silent; however, the CBCA states that for stock dividends, the declared amount of the dividend shall be added to the stated capital account. The CBCA does not allow shares to be issued until they are fully paid for in an amount not less than the fair equivalent of money that the corporation would have received had the shares been issued for cash. Therefore, if the company is incorporated under the CBCA, all stock dividends should be recorded as dividends and measured at fair value.

To illustrate a stock dividend, assume that a corporation has 1,000 common shares outstanding and retained earnings of $50,000. If the corporation declares a 10% stock dividend, it issues 100 additional shares to current shareholders. If it is assumed that the shares' fair value at the time of the stock dividend is $130 per share and that the shareholders had the option to take the dividend in cash but chose not to, the entry is:

A = L + SE
       0
Cash flows: No effect

At date of declaration		
Retained Earnings (Stock Dividends Declared)	13,000	
Common Shares		13,000

If the dividend is declared before it is distributed, then the journal entry would be a debit to Retained Earnings and a credit to Dividends Payable. Upon share issue, the journal entry would be a debit to Dividends Payable and a credit to Common Shares. Note that no asset or liability has been affected. The entry merely reflects a reclassification of shareholders' equity. No matter what the fair value is at the time of the stock dividend, each shareholder retains the same proportionate interest in the corporation. Illustration 15-3 proves this point.

Illustration 15-3

Effects of a Stock Dividend

Before dividend:	
Common shares, 1,000 shares	$100,000
Retained earnings	50,000
Total shareholders' equity	$150,000
Shareholders' interests:	
A — 400 shares, 40% interest, book value	$ 60,000
B — 500 shares, 50% interest, book value	75,000
C — 100 shares, 10% interest, book value	15,000
	$150,000
After declaration and distribution of 10% stock dividend:	
If fair value ($130) is used as basis for entry	
Shareholders' Common shares, 1,100 shares	$113,000
Retained earnings ($50,000 − $13,000)	37,000
Total shareholders' equity	$150,000
Shareholders' interests:	
A — 440 shares, 40% interest, book value	$ 60,000
B — 550 shares, 50% interest, book value	75,000
C — 110 shares, 10% interest, book value	15,000
	$150,000

---

[31] *CICA Handbook*, Section 3831, pars. .05 (f)(ii) and .06.

Note, in Illustration 15-3, that the total shareholders' equity has not changed as a result of the stock dividend. Also note that the proportion of the total shares outstanding that is held by each shareholder is unchanged.

Liquidating Dividends

Some corporations use contributed surplus as a basis for dividends. Without proper disclosure of this fact, shareholders may wrongly believe that the corporation has been paying dividends out of profits. We noted in Chapter 11 that companies in the extractive industries may pay dividends equal to the total of accumulated income and depletion. The portion of these dividends that is in excess of accumulated income represents a return of part of the shareholder's investment.

For example, assume that McChesney Mines Inc. issued a dividend to its common shareholders of $1.2 million. The cash dividend announcement noted that $900,000 should be considered income and the remainder a return of capital. The entry is:

	At date of declaration	
Retained Earnings	900,000	
Contributed Surplus	300,000	
Dividends Payable		1,200,000

$$A = L + SE$$
$$+1,200,000 \quad -1,200,000$$

Cash flows: No effect

In some cases, management may simply decide to cease business and declare a liquidating dividend. In these cases, liquidation may take place over several years to ensure an orderly and fair sale of all assets.

Effects of Dividend Preferences

The examples that now follow illustrate the effects of various dividend preferences on dividend distributions to common and preferred shareholders. Assume that in a given year, $50,000 is to be distributed as cash dividends, outstanding common shares have a value of $400,000, and 1,000 $6 preferred shares are outstanding (issued at $100,000). Dividends would be distributed to each class as follows, under the particular assumptions:

8 Objective
Explain the effects of different types of dividend preferences.

1. If the preferred shares are non-cumulative and non-participating:

	Preferred	Common	Total
$6 × 1,000	$6,000	$ 0	$ 6,000
The remainder to common	0	$44,000	44,000
Totals	$6,000	$44,000	$50,000

Illustration 15-4

Dividend Distribution, Non-Cumulative and Non-Participating Preferred

2. If the preferred shares are cumulative and non-participating, and dividends were not paid on the preferred shares in the preceding two years:

	Preferred	Common	Total
Dividends in arrears,			
$6 × 1,000 for 2 years	$12,000	$ 0	$12,000
Current year's dividend, $6 × 1,000	6,000	0	6,000
The remainder to common	0	$32,000	32,000
Totals	$18,000	$32,000	$50,000

Illustration 15-5

Dividend Distribution, Cumulative and Non-Participating Preferred, with Dividends in Arrears

3. If the preferred shares are non-cumulative and fully participating:[32]

	Preferred	Common	Total
Current year's dividend, $6	$ 6,000	$24,000	$30,000
Participating dividend—pro rata	4,000	16,000	20,000
Totals	$10,000	$40,000	$50,000

The participating dividend was determined as follows:

Current year's dividend: 　Preferred, $6 × 1,000 = $6,000 　Common, 6% of $400,000 = $24,000 (= a like amount) The 6% represents $6,000 on pref. shares/ $100,000	$ 30,000
Amount available for participation 　($50,000 − $30,000)	$ 20,000
Carrying value of shares that are to participate 　($100,000 + $400,000)	$500,000
Rate of participation 　($20,000/$500,000)	4%
Participating dividend: Preferred (4% of $100,000) Common (4% of $400,000)	$ 4,000 16,000
	$ 20,000

4. If the preferred shares are cumulative and fully participating, and if dividends were not paid on the preferred shares in the preceding two years (the same procedure that was used in example (3) is used again here to carry out the participation feature):

	Preferred	Common	Total
Dividends in arrears, 　$6 × 1,000 for 2 years	$12,000	$ 0	$12,000
Current year's dividend, $6	6,000	24,000	30,000
Participating dividend, 1.6% 　($8,000/$500,000)	1,600	6,400	8,000
Totals	$19,600	$30,400	$50,000

---

[32] When preferred shares are participating, there may be different agreements on how the participation feature is to be executed. However, if there is no specific agreement, the following procedure is recommended:

(a) After the preferred shares are assigned their current year's dividend, the common shares will receive a "like" percentage. In example (3), this amounts to 6% of $400,000.

(b) If there is a remainder of declared dividends for participation by the preferred and common shares, this remainder will be shared in proportion to the carrying value in each share class. In example (3), this proportion is:

Preferred $100,000/500,000 × $20,000 = $4,000
Common $400,000/500,000 × $20,000 = $16,000

Stock Splits

If a company has undistributed earnings over several successive years and has thus accumulated a sizeable balance in retained earnings, the market value of its outstanding shares is likely to increase. Shares that were issued at prices of less than $50 a share can easily reach a market value of more than $200 a share. The higher the share's market price, the harder it is for some investors to purchase it. The managements of many corporations believe that for better public relations, the corporation's shares should be widely owned. They wish, therefore, to have a market price that is low enough to be affordable to the majority of potential investors.

9 Objective
Distinguish between stock dividends and stock splits.

To reduce the market value of shares, the common device that is used is the stock split.[33] From an accounting standpoint, no entry is recorded for a stock split; a memorandum note, however, is made to indicate that the number of shares has increased.

Differences between a Stock Split and Stock Dividend

From a **legal** standpoint, a **stock split** is distinguished from a **stock dividend**, because a stock split results in an increase in the number of shares outstanding with no change in the share capital or the retained earnings amounts. As noted earlier, legally, the **stock dividend** may result in an increase in both the number of shares outstanding and the share capital while reducing the retained earnings (depending on the legal jurisdiction).

A stock dividend, like a stock split, may also be used to increase the share's marketability. If the stock dividend is large, it has the same effect on market price as a stock split. In the United States, the profession has taken the position that whenever additional shares are issued to reduce the unit market price, then the distribution more closely resembles a stock split than a stock dividend. **This effect usually results only if the number of shares issued is more than 20%–25% of the number of shares that were previously outstanding.**[34] A stock dividend of more than 20%–25% of the number of shares previously outstanding is called a **large stock dividend**.

In Canada, there is no specific GAAP guidance. In principle, it must be determined whether the large stock dividend is more like a stock split or a dividend (from an economic perspective). Professional judgement must be used in determining this.

Legal requirements must be considered as a constraint. As noted earlier, for instance, companies that are incorporated under the CBCA must measure any newly issued shares at market (including those issued as stock dividends). This means, therefore, that all stock dividends for such companies are to be treated as dividends and measured at market. On the other hand, in jurisdictions where legal requirements for stated share capital values are not a constraint, the following options would be available for stock dividends:

1. Treat as a dividend (debit retained earnings and credit common shares) and measure at either the market value of the shares or their par or stated value.

2. Treat as a stock split (memo entry only).

The SEC supports the second approach for large stock dividends of more than 25 percent. Illustration 15-8 summarizes and compares the effects of dividends and stock splits.

---

[33] Some companies use reverse stock splits. A reverse stock split reduces the number of shares outstanding and increases the price per share. This technique is used when the share price is unusually low. Note that a company's debt covenants or listing requirements might require that the company's shares trade at a certain level. A reverse stock split might help get the price up to where the company needs it to be.

[34] *Accounting Research and Terminology Bulletin No. 43*, par. 13.

Illustration 15-8

*Effects of Dividends
and Stock Splits*

Effect on:	Declaration of Cash Dividend	Payment of Cash Dividend	Declaration and Distribution of		
			(Small) Stock Dividend	(Large) Stock Dividend	Stock Split
Retained earnings	Decrease	0	Decrease[1]	Decrease[2]	0
Common shares	0	0	Increase	Increase	0
Contributed surplus	0	0	0	0	0
Total shareholders' equity	Decrease	0	0	0	0
Working capital	Decrease	0	0	0	0
Total assets	0	Decrease	0	0	0
Number of shares outstanding	0	0	Increase	Increase	Increase

[1] Generally equal to market value of shares.

[2] May be equal to par, stated value of shares or market value. Note that some companies may choose to interpret GAAP such that the dividend is treated as a stock split. In Canada, this is a matter of judgement and is governed by legal requirements regarding the value of stated capital and economic substance.

OTHER COMPONENTS OF SHAREHOLDERS' EQUITY

Contributed Surplus

Objective 10

Understand the nature of other components of shareholders' equity.

The term "surplus" is used in an accounting sense to designate the excess of net assets over the total paid-in par or stated value of a corporation's shares. As previously mentioned, this surplus is further divided between earned surplus (retained earnings) and contributed surplus. Contributed surplus may result from a variety of transactions or events, as Illustration 15-9 shows.

Illustration 15-9

*Transactions That May Affect
Contributed Surplus*

- Par value share issue and/or retirement (see Appendix 15A)
- Treasury share transactions (see Appendix 15A)
- Liquidating dividends
- Financial reorganizations (see Appendix 15B)
- Stock options and warrants (Chapter 16)
- Issue of convertible debt (Chapter 16)
- Share subscriptions forfeited
- Donated assets by a shareholder
- Redemption or conversion of shares

Accumulated Other Comprehensive Income

Accumulated other comprehensive income is the cumulative change in equity that is due to the revenues and expenses, and gains and losses that stem from non-shareholder transactions that are excluded from the calculation of net income. It is considered to represent earned income as well. Comprehensive income was discussed in Chapters 4 and 5.

PRESENTATION AND DISCLOSURE

Numerous disclosures are required under the *CICA Handbook*.[35] For example, basic disclosures include the amounts of authorized share capital, issued share capital, and changes in capital since the last balance sheet date.[36] In many corporations, there are restrictions on retained earnings or dividends and these should be disclosed. The note disclosure should reveal the source of the restriction, pertinent provisions, and the amount of retained earnings that is restricted, or the amount that is unrestricted.[37]

Restrictions may be based on maintaining a certain retained earnings balance, the corporation's ability to observe certain working capital requirements, additional borrowing, and other considerations. The example in Illustration 15-10 from the annual report of **Methanex Corporation** shows a note that discloses potential restrictions on retained earnings and dividends.

11 Objective
Indicate how shareholders' equity is presented.

Illustration 15-10

Excerpt from Methanex Financial Statements Regarding Restrictions on Retained Earnings

---

9. Capital stock:

(a) The authorized share capital of the Company is comprised as follows:
     25,000,000 preferred shares without nominal or par value; and Unlimited number of common shares without nominal or par value.

(b) Under covenants set out in certain debt instruments, the Company can pay cash dividends or make other shareholder distributions to the extent that shareholders' equity is equal to or greater than $850 million.

The following eements would normally be disclosed in note form:

1. The authorized number of shares or a statement noting that this is unlimited

2. The existence of unique rights (e.g., dividend preferences and the amounts of such dividends, redemption and/or retraction privileges, conversion rights, whether or not the dividends are cumulative)

3. The number of shares issued and amount received

4. Whether the shares are par value or no par value

5. The amount of any dividends in arrears for cumulative preferred shares

6. Details of changes during the year

7. Restrictions on retained earnings

Note that *CICA Handbook* Section 1300 allows enterprises that qualify for differential reporting (non-public companies where owners consent) to disclose the above information only for issued shares.

All companies must also disclose information about their objectives, policies, and processes for managing capital. They must also include summary quantitative data about what the company manages as capital and about any changes in capital.[38] The reason for requiring this disclosure is to give users of financial statements better insight into the way the company's capital is managed. An example of this type of disclosure taken from the *CICA Handbook*, Section 1535 appears in Illustration 15-11.

---

[35] *CICA Handbook*, Sections 1535, 3240, 3251, and 3862.

[36] *CICA Handbook*, Section 3240.02–.05.

[37] *CICA Handbook*, Section 3251.11.

[38] *CICA Handbook*, Section 1535.02.

Illustration 15-11

*Example of Required Capital
Disclosures*[39]

Facts

Group A manufactures and sells cars. Group A includes a finance subsidiary that provides finance to customers, primarily in the form of leases. Group A is not subject to any externally imposed capital requirements.

Example disclosure

The Group's objectives when managing capital are:

- to safeguard the entity's ability to continue as a going concern, so that it can continue to provide returns for shareholders and benefits for other stakeholders, and

- to provide an adequate return to shareholders by pricing products and services commensurately with the level of risk.

The Group sets the amount of capital in proportion to risk. The Group manages the capital structure and makes adjustments to it in the light of changes in economic conditions and the risk characteristics of the underlying assets. In order to maintain or adjust the capital structure, the Group may adjust the amount of dividends paid to shareholders, return capital to shareholders, issue new shares, or sell assets to reduce debt.

Consistently with others in the industry, the Group monitors capital on the basis of the debt-to-adjusted capital ratio. This ratio is calculated as net debt ÷ adjusted capital. Net debt is calculated as total debt (as shown in the balance sheet) less cash and cash equivalents. Adjusted capital comprises all components of equity (i.e., share capital, share premium, and retained earnings) other than amounts in accumulated other comprehensive income relating to cash flow hedges, and includes some forms of subordinated debt.

During 20x4, the Group's strategy, which was unchanged from 20x3, was to maintain the debt-to-adjusted capital ratio at the lower end of the range 6:1 to 7:1, in order to secure access to finance at a reasonable cost by maintaining a BB credit rating. The debt-to-adjusted capital ratios at 31 December 20x4 and at 31 December 20x3 were as follows:

	31 Dec 20x4 CU million	31 Dec 20x3 CU million
Total debt	1,000	1,100
Less: cash and cash equivalents	(90)	(150)
Net debt	910	950
Total equity	110	105
Add: subordinated debt instruments	38	38
Less: amounts in accumulated other comprehensive income relating to cash flow hedges	(10)	(5)
Adjusted capital	138	138
Debt-to-adjusted capital ratio	6.6	6.9

The decrease in the debt-to-adjusted capital ratio during 20x4 resulted primarily from the reduction in net debt that occurred on the sale of subsidiary Z. As a result of this reduction in net debt, improved profitability and lower levels of managed receivables, the dividend payment was increased to CU2.8 million for 20x4 (from CU2.5 million for 20x3).

Section 3862 of the *CICA Handbook* requires additional disclosures.

Illustration 15-12 provides an example of a shareholders' equity section on the balance sheet.

Illustration 15-12

*Example of Shareholders'
Equity Section*

FROST CORPORATION
Shareholders' Equity
December 31, 2008

Share Capital

Preferred shares, $7 cumulative, 100,000 shares authorized, 30,000 shares issued and outstanding	$ 3,000,000
Common shares, no par, stated value $10 per share, 500,000 shares authorized, 400,000 shares issued	4,000,000
Common stock dividend distributable, 20,000 shares	200,000

---

[39] *CICA Handbook*, Section 1535 illustrative examples.

Total share capital	7,200,000
Contributed surplus	990,000
Total paid-in capital	8,190,000
Retained Earnings	2,200,000
Accumulated Other Comprehensive Income	2,160,000
Total shareholders' equity	$12,550,000

Changes in shareholders' equity are often presented in a table in the notes to the financial statements. Illustration 15-13 shows the changes in shareholders' equity for **Imax Corporation**. Imax is a Canadian company whose shares trade on the TSX and NAS-DAQ. It has chosen to report under U.S. GAAP rather than prepare two sets of financial statements—one under Canadian GAAP and one under U.S. GAAP.[40] Note that changes in shareholders' equity are shown in a **separate statement** under U.S. and international GAAP. This is unlike in Canada, where companies thus far have never been required to produce a separate statement for such changes. Instead, the financial statements have generally included only a statement of retained earnings, and, as mentioned above, changes in share capital accounts are shown in the notes. With the adoption of *CICA Handbook* Section 1530 on comprehensive income and revised Section 3251 on equity, the requirement to include a statement of changes in shareholders' equity now exists in Canadian GAAP.[41]

International Insight

IAS 1 requires that a company present a separate statement for changes in all equity accounts. Canadian GAAP currently only requires a separate retained earnings statement and additional note disclosures.

Illustration 15-13

Example of Disclosures of Changes in Shareholders' Equity—Imax Corporation

IMAX CORPORATION
CONSOLIDATED STATEMENTS OF SHAREHOLDERS' EQUITY (DEFICIT)
In accordance with United States Generally Accepted Accounting Principles
(In thousands of U.S. dollars)

	Number of common shares issued and outstanding	Capital stock	Other equity	Retained earnings (deficit)	Accumulated other comprehensive income (loss)[(1)]	Total shareholders' equity (deficit)	Comprehensive income (loss)
Balance at December 31, 2002	32,973,366	$ 65,563	$ 1,542	$ (171,420)	$645	$ (103,670)	$ —
Issuance of common stock	6,328,392	50,046	—	—	—	50,046	—
Net income	—	—	—	231	—	231	231
Adjustment to paid-in-capital for non-employee stock options and warrants granted (note 17(c))	—	—	1,617	—	—	1,617	—
							$ 231
Balance at December 31, 2003	39,301,758	$115,609	$ 3,159	$ (171,189)	645	$ (51,776)	
Issuance of common stock	145,206	558	—	—	—	558	—
Net income	—	—	—	10,244	—	10,244	10,244
Adjustment to paid-in-capital for non-employee stock options and warrants granted (note 17(c))	—	—	182	—	—	182	—
Adjustment for exercise of non-employee stock options	—	114	(114)	—	—	—	—
Unrecognized actuarial loss on defined benefit plan (net of income tax recovery of $nil)	—	—	—	—	(1,584)	(1,584)	(1,584)
							$ 8,660
Balance at December 31, 2004	39,446,964	$116,281	$ 3,227	$ (160,945)	$ (939)	$ (42,376)	
Issuance of common stock	766,578	3,633	—	—	—	3,633	—
Net income	—	—	—	16,598	—	16,598	16,598
Adjustment to paid-in-capital for non-employee stock options granted (note 17(c))	—	—	291	—	—	291	—
Adjustment for exercise of non-employee stock options and warrants	—	1,760	(1,760)	—	—	—	—
Unrecognized actuarial loss on defined benefit plan (net of income tax recovery of $nil)	—	—	—	—	(1,189)	(1,189)	(1,189)
							$ 15,409
Balance at December 31, 2005	40,213,542	$121,674	$ 1,758	$ (144,347)	$ (2,128)	$ (23,043)	

---

[40] This choice is allowed by the OSC.

[41] *CICA Handbook* Section 3251.04 requires changes in equity for the period to be disclosed, including changes in retained earnings, accumulated other comprehensive income, contributed surplus, share capital, and reserves.

(1) Components of accumulated other comprehensive income (loss) consist of:

	As at December 31,		
	2005		2004
Unrecognized actuarial loss on defined benefit plan (net of income tax recovery of $nil)	$ (2,773)	$	(1,584)
Foreign currency translation adjustments	645		645
Accumulated other comprehensive income	$ (2,128)	$	(939)

(the accompanying notes are an integral part of these consolidated financial statements)

Special Presentation Issues

Preferred shares generally have no maturity date, and there is therefore no legal obligation to pay the preferred shareholder. As a result, preferred shares have historically been classified as part of shareholders' equity. Recently, more and more issuances of preferred shares have features that make the security more like a debt instrument (where there is a legal obligation to pay) than an equity instrument. As mentioned earlier, these will be covered in Chapter 16.

PERSPECTIVES

Analysis

Objective 12
Analyze shareholders' equity.

Several ratios use amounts related to shareholders' equity to evaluate a company's **profitability** and **long-term solvency**. The following four ratios are discussed and illustrated next: (1) rate of return on common shareholders' equity, (2) payout ratio, (3) price earnings ratio, and (4) book value per share.

Rate of Return on Common Shareholders' Equity

Student Website

Analyst Toolkit—
Financial Statement
Analysis Primer

www.wiley.com/canada/kieso

A widely used ratio that measures profitability from the common shareholders' viewpoint is **rate of return on common shareholders' equity**. This ratio shows how many dollars of net income were earned for each dollar invested by the owners. It is calculated by dividing net income less preferred dividends by average common shareholders' equity. For example, assume that Garber Inc. had net income of $360,000, declared and paid preferred dividends of $54,000, and had average common shareholders' equity of $2,550,000. Garber's ratio is calculated as follows:

$$\text{Rate of return on common shareholders' equity} = \frac{\text{Net income} - \text{Preferred dividends}}{\text{Average common shareholders' equity}}$$

$$= \frac{\$360,000 - \$54,000}{\$2,550,000}$$

$$= 12\%$$

As the calculation shows, because preferred shares are present, preferred dividends are deducted from net income to calculate the income available to common shareholders. Similarly, the carrying value of preferred shares is deducted from total shareholders' equity to arrive at the amount of common shareholders' equity used in this ratio.

When the rate of return on total assets is lower than the rate of return on the common shareholders' investment, the company is said to be trading on the equity at a gain. **Trading on the equity** describes the practice of using borrowed money at fixed interest rates or issuing preferred shares with constant dividend rates in hopes of obtaining a higher rate of return on the money used (this is sometimes also referred to as **leverage**). As these debt issues must be given a prior claim on some or all of the corporate assets, the advantage to common shareholders of trading on the equity must come from borrowing at a lower rate of interest than the rate of return that is obtained on the assets that have been borrowed. If this can be done, the capital obtained from bondholders or preferred shareholders earns enough to pay the interest or preferred dividends and to leave a margin for the common shareholders. When this occurs, trading on the equity is profitable.

Payout Ratio

Another measure of profitability is the **payout ratio**, which is the ratio of cash dividends to net income. If preferred shares are outstanding, this ratio is calculated for common shareholders by dividing cash dividends paid to common shareholders by net income available to common shareholders. Assuming that Troy Corp. has cash dividends of $100,000, net income of $500,000, and no preferred shares outstanding, the payout ratio is calculated as follows:

$$
\text{Payout ratio} = \frac{\text{Cash dividends}}{\text{Net income} - \text{Preferred dividends}}
$$

$$
= \frac{\$100,000}{\$500,000}
$$

$$
= 20\%
$$

For some investors, it is important that the payout be high enough to provide a good yield on the shares.[42] However, payout ratios have declined for many companies because many investors now view appreciation in the share value as more important than the dividend amount.

Price Earnings Ratio

The **price earnings (P/E) ratio** is an oft-quoted statistic that analysts use in discussing the investment potential of an enterprise. It is calculated by dividing the share's market price by its earnings per share. For example, assuming that Soreson Corp. has a market price of $50 and earnings per share of $4, its price earnings ratio would be calculated as follows:

$$
\text{Price earnings ratio} = \frac{\text{Market price of share}}{\text{Earnings per share}}
$$

$$
= \$50/\$4
$$

$$
= 12.5
$$

---

[42] Another closely watched ratio is the dividend yield: the cash dividend per share divided by the share's market price. This ratio gives investors some idea of the rate of return that will be received in cash dividends.

Book Value per Share

A much-used basis for evaluating net worth is the **book** or **equity value per share**. Book value per share is the amount that each share would receive if the company were liquidated **based on the amounts reported on the balance sheet**. However, the figure loses much of its relevance if the valuations on the balance sheet do not approximate the fair market value of the assets. **Book value per share** is calculated by dividing common shareholders' equity by the number of common shares outstanding. Assuming that Chen Corporation's common shareholders' equity is $1 million and it has 100,000 shares outstanding, its book value per share is calculated as follows:

$$\text{Book value per share} = \frac{\text{Common shareholders' equity less entitlement for preferred shares}}{\text{Number of shares outstanding}}$$

$$= \frac{\$1,000,000}{100,000}$$

$$= \$10 \text{ per share}$$

When preferred shares are present, an analysis of the covenants involving the preferred shares should be studied. If preferred dividends are in arrears, the preferred shares are participating, or if preferred shares have a redemption or liquidating value higher than their carrying amount, retained earnings must be allocated between the preferred and common shareholders in calculating book value.

To illustrate, assume that the following situation exists.

Shareholders' equity	Preferred	Common
Preferred shares, 5%	$300,000	
Common shares		$400,000
Contributed surplus		37,500
Retained earnings	0	162,582
Totals	$300,000	$600,082
Shares outstanding		4,000
Book value per share		$150.02

In the preceding calculation, it is assumed that no preferred dividends are in arrears and that the preferred is not participating. Now assume that the same facts exist except that the 5% preferred is cumulative, participating up to 8%, and that dividends for three years before the current year are in arrears. The common shares' book value is then calculated as follows, assuming that no action has yet been taken concerning dividends for the current year.

Shareholders' equity	Preferred	Common
Preferred shares, 5%	$300,000	
Common shares		$400,000
Contributed surplus		37,500
Retained earnings:		
Dividends in arrears (3 years at 5% a year)	45,000	
Current year requirement at 5%	15,000	20,000
Participating additional 3%	9,000	12,000
Remainder to common	0	61,582
Totals	$369,000	$531,082

Shares outstanding	4,000
Book value per share	$132.77

In connection with the book value calculation, the analyst must know how to handle the following items: the number of authorized and unissued shares; the number of treasury shares on hand; any commitments with respect to the issuance of unissued shares or the reissuance of treasury shares; and the relative rights and privileges of the various types of shares authorized.

International

Along with the rest of the GAAP relating to financial instruments, GAAP relating to shareholders' equity is also converting with international GAAP. Illustration 15-14 compares Canadian and international GAAP

> **13 Objective**
> Compare current Canadian and international GAAP and understand which direction international GAAP is headed in.

Canada	International
Section 1535: Capital Disclosure	IAS 1: Presentation of financial statements
Section 3240: Share capital	IFRS 7: Financial instruments: disclosures
Section 3241: Equity	

> **Illustration 15-14**
> *Comparison of Canadian and International GAAP*

The Canadian standards are essentially converged with the international. As mentioned in previous chapters, the IASB and FASB have are working on several projects to improve financial reporting in this area. These include the financial statement project and the project on liabilities and equity

Summary of Learning Objectives

1 Discuss the characteristics of the corporate form of organization.

The three main forms of organization are the proprietorship, partnership, and corporation. Incorporation gives shareholders protection against claims on their personal assets and allows greater access to capital markets.

2 Identify the rights of shareholders.

If there are no restrictive provisions, each share carries the following rights: (1) to share proportionately in profits and losses; (2) to share proportionately in management (the right to vote for directors); and (3) to share proportionately in corporate assets upon liquidation. An additional right to share proportionately in any new issues of shares of the same class (called the preemptive right) may also be attached to the share.

3 Describe the major features of preferred shares.

Preferred shares are a special class of share that possess certain preferences or features that common shares do not have. Most often, these features are a preference over dividends and a preference over assets in the event of liquidation. Many other preferences may be attached to specific shares. Preferred shareholders give up some or all of the rights normally attached to common shares.

 Student Website

Glossary

www.wiley.com/canada/kieso

KEY TERMS

accumulated other comprehensive income, 916

basic or inherent rights, 897

book value per share, 922

callable/redeemable (preferred shares), 900

capital maintenance, 895

common shares, 898

contributed (paid-in) capital, 895

convertible (preferred shares), 900

4 Explain the accounting procedures for issuing shares.

Shares may be issued on a subscription basis, in which case they are not considered legally issued until they are paid up. Shares may also be issued as a bundle with other securities, in which case the cost must be allocated between the securities. The incremental or proportional methods may be used to allocate the cost.

5 Identify the major reasons for repurchasing shares.

The reasons that corporations have for purchasing their outstanding shares are varied. Some major reasons are (1) to increase earnings per share and return on equity; (2) to provide shares for employee share compensation contracts or to meet potential merger needs; (3) to stop takeover attempts or to reduce the number of shareholders; (4) to make a market in the shares; or (5) to return excess cash to shareholders.

6 Explain the accounting for the reacquisition and retirement of shares.

If the acquisition cost of the shares is greater than the original cost, the difference is allocated to share capital, then contributed surplus, and then retained earnings. If the cost is less, the cost is allocated to share capital (to stated or assigned cost) and to contributed surplus.

7 Explain the accounting for various forms of dividend distributions.

Dividends are generally paid out of earnings or are a return of capital. Dividends paid out of earnings are normally cash, property, or stock dividends. They are recorded at fair value and debited to Retained Earnings. Dividends that are a return of capital are known as liquidating dividends and reduce contributed capital.

8 Explain the effects of different types of dividend preferences.

Dividends paid to shareholders are affected by the dividend preferences of the preferred shares. Preferred shares can be cumulative or non-cumulative, and fully participating, partially participating, or non-participating.

9 Distinguish between stock dividends and stock splits.

A stock dividend is a capitalization of retained earnings that generally results in a reduction in retained earnings and a corresponding increase in certain contributed capital accounts. The total shareholders' equity remains unchanged with a stock dividend. In addition, all shareholders retain their same proportionate share of ownership in the corporation. A stock split results in an increase or decrease in the number of shares outstanding. However, no accounting entry is required. Similar to a stock dividend, the total dollar amount of all shareholders' equity accounts remains unchanged. A stock split is usually intended to improve the shares' marketability by reducing the market price of the shares that are being split. Large stock dividends have the same impact on the markets as stock splits—i.e., the market price of the share declines—and professional judgement is therefore needed in deciding whether they should be treated as a stock split or dividend for accounting purposes. Measurement is also a matter of judgement. Care should be taken to ensure that legal requirements for stated legal capital are met.

10 Understand the nature of other components of shareholders' equity.

Contributed surplus is additional surplus coming from shareholder transactions. Accumulated other comprehensive income is accumulated non-shareholder income that has not been booked through net income.

11 Indicate how shareholders' equity is presented.

The shareholders' equity section of a balance sheet includes Share Capital, Contributed Surplus, Retained Earnings, and Accumulated Other Comprehensive Income. A statement of shareholders' equity is often provided.

12 Analyze shareholders' equity.

Common ratios used in this area are the rate of return on common shareholders' equity, payout ratio, price earnings ratio, and book value per share.

13 Compare current Canadian and international GAAP and understand which direction international GAAP is headed in.

The standards are essentially converged with international standards. In addition the IASB and FASB are continuing to work on a financial statements project as well as a liability and equity project.

Par Value and Treasury Shares

Objective **14**
Explain the accounting
for par value shares.

Neither par value shares nor treasury shares are allowed under the CBCA. As mentioned in the chapter, however, these types of shares are allowed under certain provincial business corporations acts and are common in the U.S. For this reason, they will now be discussed in greater detail in this appendix.

Par Value Shares

The par value of a share has no relationship to its fair market value. At present, the par value that is associated with most capital share issuances is very low ($1, $5, or $10). To show the required information for the issuance of par value share, accounts must be kept for each class of share as follows:

1. **Preferred or Common Shares**. These accounts reflect the par value of the corporation's issued shares. They are credited when the shares are originally issued. No additional entries are made in these accounts unless additional shares are issued or shares are retired.

2. **Contributed Surplus (Paid-In Capital in Excess of Par or Additional Paid-In Capital in the United States)**. This account indicates any excess over par value that was paid in by shareholders in return for the shares issued to them. Once it has been paid in, the excess over par becomes a part of the corporation's paid-in capital, and the individual shareholder has no greater claim on the excess paid in than all other holders of the same class of shares.

To illustrate how these accounts are used, assume that Colonial Corporation sold, for $1,100, 100 shares with a par value of $5 per share. The entry to record the issuance is:

A = L + SE
+1,100   +1,100

Cash flows: ↑ 1,100 inflow

Cash	1,100	
Common Shares		500
Contributed Surplus		600

When the shares are repurchased and cancelled, the same procedure is followed as was described in the chapter.

Treasury Shares

Treasury shares are created when a company repurchases its own shares but does not cancel them. Treasury shares may then be resold, and the *CICA Handbook* therefore recommends that the single-transaction method be used to account for them. This method treats the repurchase and resale as a single transaction. In this view, the repurchase of treasury shares is the first part of a transaction that is completed when the shares are later resold. Consequently, the holding of treasury shares is viewed as a transitional phase between the beginning and end of a single activity.

When shares are purchased, the total cost is debited to Treasury Shares on the balance sheet. This account is shown as a deduction from the total of the components of shareholders' equity in the balance sheet. An example of such disclosure follows:

15 Objective
Explain the accounting for treasury shares.

Shareholders' equity:	
Common shares, no par value; authorized 24,000,000 shares; issued 19,045,870 shares, of which 209,750 are in treasury	$ 27,686,000
Retained earnings	253,265,000
	280,951,000
Less: Cost of treasury shares	(7,527,000)
Total shareholders' equity	$273,424,000

When the shares are sold, the Treasury Shares account is credited for their cost. If they are sold at more than their cost, the excess is credited to Contributed Surplus. If they are sold at less, the difference is debited to Contributed Surplus (if it is related to the same class of shares) and then to Retained Earnings. If the shares are subsequently retired, the journal entries shown in the chapter would be followed.

Note also that dividends on treasury shares should be reversed since a company cannot receive dividend income on its own shares (dr. Dividends Payable, cr. Retained Earnings).

Summary of Learning Objectives for Appendix 15A

14 Explain the accounting for par value shares.

These shares may only be valued at par value in the common or preferred share accounts. The excess goes to contributed surplus. On a repurchase or cancellation, the par value is removed from the common or preferred share accounts and any excess or deficit is booked to contributed surplus or retained earnings as was discussed for no par shares.

15 Explain the accounting for treasury shares.

Treasury shares are created when a company repurchases its own shares and does not cancel or retire them at the same time—i.e., they remain outstanding. The single-transaction method is used when treasury shares are purchased. This method treats the purchase and subsequent resale or cancellation as part of the same transaction.

Appendix 15B

Financial Reorganization

Objective 16
Describe the accounting for a financial reorganization.

A corporation that consistently suffers net losses accumulates negative retained earnings, or a deficit. Shareholders generally presume that dividends are paid out of profits and retained earnings and therefore, a deficit sends a very negative signal about the company's ability to pay dividends. In addition, certain laws in some jurisdictions specify that no dividends may be declared and paid as long as a corporation's paid-in capital has been reduced by a deficit. In these cases, a corporation with a debit balance of retained earnings must accumulate enough profits to offset the deficit before it can pay any dividends.

This situation may be a real hardship on a corporation and its shareholders. A company that has operated unsuccessfully for several years and accumulated a deficit may have finally turned the corner. While the development of new products and new markets, the arrival of a new management group, or improved economic conditions may point to much improved operating results in the future, if the law prohibits dividends until the deficit has been replaced by earnings, the shareholders must wait until such profits have been earned, which can take quite a long time. Furthermore, future success may depend on obtaining additional funds through the sale of shares, but if no dividends can be paid for some time, the market price of any new share issue is likely to be low, assuming the shares can be marketed at all.

Thus, a company with excellent prospects may be prevented from accomplishing its plans because of a deficit, although present management may have had nothing at all to do with the years during which the deficit was accumulated. To permit the corporation to proceed with its plans might well be to the advantage of all interests in the enterprise; to require it to eliminate the deficit through profits might actually force it to liquidate.

A procedure that enables a company that has gone through financial difficulty to proceed with its plans without the encumbrance of having to recover from a deficit is called a **financial reorganization**. A financial reorganization is defined as a substantial realignment of an enterprise's equity and non-equity interests such that the holders of one or more of the significant classes of non-equity interests and the holders of all of the significant classes of equity interests give up some (or all) of their rights and claims on the enterprise.[43]

A financial reorganization results from negotiation and reaches its conclusion in an eventual agreement between non-equity and equity holders in the corporation. These negotiations may take place under the provisions of a legal act (e.g., *Companies Creditors Arrangement Act*) or a less formal process.[44] The result gives the company a fresh start and the accounting is often referred to as **fresh start accounting**.

---

[43] *CICA Handbook*, Section 1625.03.

[44] *CICA Handbook*, Section 1625.03, par. .15.

Comprehensive Revaluation

When a financial reorganization occurs, where the same party does not control the company both before and after the reorganization, and where new costs are reasonably determinable, the company's assets and liabilities should undergo a **comprehensive revaluation**.[45] This requires three steps:

1. The deficit balance (retained earnings) is brought to zero. Any asset writedowns or impairments that existed before the reorganization should be recorded first. The deficit is reclassified to Share Capital, Contributed Surplus, or a separately identified account within Shareholders' Equity.

2. The changes in debt and equity that have been negotiated are recorded. Often debt is exchanged for equity, reflecting a change in control.

3. The assets and liabilities are comprehensively revalued. This step assigns appropriate going concern values to all assets and liabilities as per the negotiations. The difference between the carrying values before the reorganization and the new values after is known as a **revaluation adjustment**. The revaluation adjustment and any costs incurred to carry out the financial reorganization are accounted for as capital transactions and are closed to Share Capital, Contributed Surplus, or a separately identified account within Shareholders' Equity. Note that the new costs of the identifiable assets and liabilities must not be greater than the entity's fair value if this is known.[46]

Entries Illustrated

The series of entries that follows illustrates the accounting procedures that are applied in a financial reorganization. Assume that New Horizons Inc. shows a deficit of $1 million before the reorganization is effected on June 30, 2008. Under the terms of the negotiation, the creditors are giving up rights to payment for the $150,000 debt in return for 100% of the common shares. The original shareholders agree to give up their shares.

1. **Restate impairments of assets that existed before the reorganization:**

Deficit	750,000	
Inventories (loss on writedown)		225,000
Intangible Assets (loss on writedown)		525,000

A = L + SE
−750,000   −750,000
Cash flows: No effect

Elimination of deficit against contributed surplus

Common shares	1,750,000	
Deficit		1,750,000

A = L + SE
0
Cash flows: No effect

2 and 3. **Restate assets and liabilities to recognize unrecorded gains and losses and to record the negotiated change in control:**

Plant Assets (gain on write-up)	400,000	
Long-Term Liabilities (gain on writedown)	150,000	
Common shares		550,000

A = L + SE
+400,000   −150,000   +550,000
Cash flows: No effect

---

[45] *CICA Handbook*, Section 1625.03, pars. .04 and .05.

[46] *CICA Handbook*, Section 1625, pars. .39 to .49.

Note that if there is no change in control, GAAP does not allow a comprehensive revaluation.

Disclosure

When a financial reorganization occurs, the following requirements must be fulfilled:

1. The proposed reorganization should receive the **approval** of the corporation's shareholders before it is put into effect.

2. The new asset and liability valuations should be **fair** and not deliberately understate or overstate assets, liabilities, and earnings.

3. After the reorganization, the corporation must have a zero balance of retained earnings, although it may have contributed surplus arising from the reorganization.

4. In the period of the reorganization, the following must be disclosed:
   (a) The date of the reorganization
   (b) A description of the reorganization
   (c) The amount of the change in each major class of assets, liabilities and shareholders' equity resulting from the reorganization

5. In subsequent reports, for a period of at least three years from the reorganization date, the following must be disclosed:
   (a) The date of the reorganization
   (b) The revaluation adjustment amount and the shareholders' equity account in which it was recorded
   (c) The amount of the deficit that was reclassified and the account to which it was reclassified
   (d) The measurement bases for the assets and liabilities that were revalued

Student
Website

Glossary

www.wiley.com/canada/kieso

KEY TERMS

comprehensive
   revaluation, 929
financial
   reorganization, 928
fresh start
   accounting, 928
revaluation
   adjustment, 929

Summary of Learning Objective for Appendix 15B

16 Describe the accounting for a financial reorganization.

A corporation that has accumulated a large debit balance (deficit) in retained earnings may enter into a process known as a financial reorganization. During a reorganization, creditors and shareholders negotiate a deal to put the company on a new footing. This generally involves a **change in control** and a **comprehensive revaluation** of assets and liabilities. The procedure consists of the following steps: (1) The deficit is reclassified so that the ending balance in Retained Earnings is zero. (2) The change in control is recorded. (3) All assets and liabilities are comprehensively revalued at current values so that the company will not be burdened with excessive inventory or fixed asset valuations in following years.

Brief Exercises

Note: All assignment material with an asterisk (*) relates to the appendices to the chapter..

BE15-1 Toby Corporation has four classes of shares: Class A, Class B, Series A, and Series B. How should Toby classify **(LO 2)** and present the different classes if the characteristics of each class are as follows?

> Series A shares – The shares are mandatorily redeemable and carry a dividend rate of 4%.
>
> Series B shares – The shares are cumulative and carry a dividend rate of $2 per share. They are subordinated to the Series A shares for dividend distribution.
>
> Class A shares – The shares are subordinated to both Series A and Series B shares for dividend distribution and participate in the earnings and losses of the company above a non-cumulative dividend of $0.50 per share. The shares have a voting right of one vote per share.
>
> Class B shares – The shares have a voting right of 10 votes per share. They are subordinated to both Series A and Series B shares for dividend and asset distribution and participate in the earnings and losses of the company.

*BE15-2 Shredder Limited issued 1,000 shares of no par value common shares for $60,400. Prepare Shredder's journal **(LO 4, 14)** entry if (a) the stock has no par value, and (b) the stock has a par value of $12 per share.

BE15-3 Belair Inc. sells 1,400 common shares on a subscription basis at $65 per share. On June 1, Belair accepts a 45% **(LO 4)** down payment. On December 1, Belair collects the remaining 55% and issues the shares. Prepare the company's journal entries.

BE15-4 Powerdrive Corporation issued 3,000 of its common shares for $70,000. The company also incurred $1,500 of **(LO 4)** costs associated with issuing the shares. Prepare the journal entry to record the issuance of the company's shares.

BE15-5 Marko Inc. has 41,000 common shares outstanding. The shares have an average cost of $20 per share. On July 1, **(LO 6)** 2007, Maverick reacquired 500 shares at $65 per share and retired them. Prepare the journal entry to record this transaction.

BE15-6 Rangers Corporation has 50,000 common shares outstanding, with an average value of $5 per share. On August **(LO 6)** 1, 2008, the company reacquired and cancelled 500 shares at $35 per share. There was Contributed Surplus of $2 per share at the time of the reacquisition (total $100,000). Prepare the journal entry to record this transaction.

BE15-7 Machines Inc. declared a cash dividend of $0.50 per share on its 2 million outstanding shares. The dividend was **(LO 7)** declared on August 1 and is payable on September 9 to all shareholders of record on August 15. Prepare all necessary journal entries for those three dates.

BE15-8 Millennium Inc. owns shares of Oakes Corporation that are classified as part of Millennium's trading portfolio. **(LO 7)** At December 31, 2008, the securities were carried in Millennium's accounting records at their cost of $750,000, which equalled their market value. On September 21, 2009, when the securities' market value was $1.7 million, Millennium declared a property dividend that will result in the Oakes securities being distributed on October 23, 2009, to shareholders of record on October 8, 2009. Prepare all necessary journal entries for the three dates.

BE15-9 On April 20, Rex Mining Corp. declared a dividend of $500,000 that is payable on June 1. Of this amount, **(LO 7)** $200,000 is a return of capital. Prepare the April 20 and June 1 journal entries for Rex.

BE15-10 Gren Football Corporation has 500,000 common shares outstanding. The corporation declares a 6% stock **(LO 7)** dividend when the shares' fair value is $35 per share (their carrying value is $20 per share). Prepare the journal entries for the company for both the date of declaration and the date of distribution.

BE15-11 Piggs Corporation has 200,000 common shares outstanding with a carrying value of $10 per share. Piggs **(LO 9)** declares a 2-for-1 stock split. How many shares are outstanding after the split? What is the carrying value per share after the split? What is the total carrying value after the split? What journal entry is necessary to record the split?

BE15-12 Lufia Corporation has the following account balances at December 31, 2008: **(LO 11)**

Common Shares Subscribed	$ 250,000
Common Shares—No Par Value	310,000
Subscriptions Receivable	80,000
Retained Earnings	1,340,000
Contributed Surplus	320,000
Accumulated Other Comprehensive Income	560,000

Prepare the December 31, 2008, shareholders' equity section of the balance sheet.

(LO 12)   BE15-13   Amilar Corporation has the following selected financial data:

	2008	2007
Net income	$ 720,000	$ 680,000
Total assets	5,136,000	4,525,000
Preferred shares, 4%, cumulative	600,000	600,000
Common shares	350,000	350,000
Retained earnings	2,786,000	2,190,000
Accumulated other comprehensive income	145,000	130,000
Total shareholders' equity	3,881,000	3,270,000
Cash dividends paid in the year	124,000	170,000
Market price of common shares	$97.46	$64.33
Weighted average number of common shares	80,000	80,000

There were no preferred dividends in arrears. Calculate the following ratios for 2008: (1) rate of return on common shareholders' equity, (2) payout ratio, (3) price earnings ratio, and (4) book value. Is Amilar Corporation trading on the equity?

(LO 15)   *BE15-14   Henderson Corporation has 750,000 shares outstanding. The shares have an average cost of $45 per share. On September 5, the company repurchases 1,500 of its own shares at $75 per share and does not cancel them. The shares are classified as treasury shares. On November 20, 2008, the company resells 1,000 of the treasury shares at $80 per share. Prepare the journal entries for the repurchase and subsequent sale of the treasury shares.

(LO 15)   *BE15-15   Use the information for Henderson Corporation in BE15-14. Assume now that the company resells the 1,000 treasury shares at $55 per share. Prepare the journal entries for the repurchase and subsequent sale of the treasury shares.

(LO 16)   *BE15-16   Truck Corporation went through a financial reorganization by writing down plant assets by $105,000 and eliminating its deficit, which was $144,000 before the reorganization. As part of the reorganization, the creditors agreed to take back 55% of the common shares in lieu of payment of the debt of $2.3 million. Prepare the entries to record the financial reorganization.

Exercises

(LO 4)   E15-1   (Recording Issuance of Common and Preferred Shares)   Vintage Corporation was organized on January 1, 2008. It is authorized to issue 100,000 preferred shares with a $7 dividend, and 4,000,000 common shares. The following share transactions were completed during the first year:

Jan. 10	Issued 500,000 common shares for cash at $25 per share.
Mar. 1	Issued 19,000 preferred shares for cash at $121 per share.
Apr. 1	Issued 29,000 common shares for land. The asking price for the land was $76,000; its fair value was $72,000.
May 1	Issued 120,000 common shares for cash at $12 per share.
Aug. 1	Issued 14,000 common shares to lawyers in payment of their bill of $18,000 for services rendered in helping the company organize.
Sept. 1	Issued 20,500 common shares for cash at $14 per share.
Nov. 1	Issued 1,200 preferred shares for cash at $130 per share.

Instructions
Prepare the journal entries to record the above transactions.

(LO 4)   E15-2   (Subscribed Shares)   Canway Inc. decided to sell shares to raise additional capital so that it could expand into the rapidly growing service industry. The corporation chose to sell these shares through a subscription basis and publicly notified the investment world. The offering was 30,000 shares at $24 a share. The terms of the subscription were 30% down and the balance at the end of six months. All shares were subscribed for during the offering period.

Instructions
Prepare the journal entries for the original subscription, the collection of the down payments, the collection of the balance of the subscription price, and the issuance of the shares.

(LO 4, 6)   E15-3   (Share Issuances and Repurchase)   Kao Corporation is authorized to issue 500,000 common shares. During 2008, the company took part in the following selected transactions:

1. Issued 5,000 shares at $35 per share, less $3,000 in costs related to the issuance of the shares.

2. Issued 2,000 shares for land appraised at $150,000. The shares were actively traded on a national stock exchange at approximately $46 per share on the date of issuance.

3. Purchased and retired 500 of the company's shares at $43 per share. The repurchased shares have an average per share amount of $40.

Instructions

(a) Prepare the journal entries to record the three transactions listed.

(b) When shares are repurchased, is the original issue price of those individual shares relevant? Explain.

*E15-4 (Shareholders' Equity Section) Radler Corporation's charter authorized 1 million shares of $11 par value common shares, and 300,000 shares of 6% cumulative and non-participating preferred shares, with a par value of $100 per share. The corporation engaged in the following share transactions through December 31, 2008: 300,000 common shares were issued for $3.6 million and 10,000 preferred shares were issued for machinery valued at $1,475,000. Subscriptions for 10,500 common shares have been taken, and 30% of the subscription price of $16 per share has been collected. The shares will be issued upon collection of the subscription price in full. In addition, 10,000 common shares have been purchased for $15 and retired. The retained earnings balance is $180,000 before considering the share repurchase transaction. **(LO 4, 11, 14)**

Instructions

(a) Prepare the shareholders' equity section of the balance sheet in good form.

(b) Repeat part (a) assuming the common shares and preferred shares are no par.

(c) Discuss the alternative presentations of the subscription receivable account. Would the presentation of the receivable affect the book value or the rate of return on shareholders' equity?

E15-5 (Correcting Entries for Equity Transactions) Rae Inc. recently hired a new accountant with extensive experience in accounting for partnerships. Because of the pressure of the new job, the accountant was unable to review what he had learned earlier about corporation accounting. During the first month, he made the following entries for the corporation's capital shares: **(LO 4, 11)**

May 2	Cash	192,000	
	Common Shares		192,000
	(Issued 12,000 common shares at $16 per share)		
10	Cash	600,000	
	Common Shares		600,000
	(Issued 10,000 preferred shares at $60 per share)		
15	Common Shares	15,000	
	Cash		15,000
	(Purchased and retired 1,000 common shares at $15 per share)		
31	Cash	8,500	
	Common Shares		5,000
	Gain on Sale of Shares		3,500
	(Issued 500 shares at $17 per share)		

Instructions

Based on the explanation for each entry, prepare the entries that should have been made for the capital share transactions. Explain your reasoning.

E15-6 (Equity Items on Balance Sheet) The following are selected transactions that may affect shareholders' equity: **(LO 7, 9, 10)**

1. Recorded accrued interest earned on a note receivable.

2. Declared a cash dividend.

3. Effected a stock split.

4. Recorded the expiration of insurance coverage that was previously recorded as prepaid insurance.

5. Paid the cash dividend declared in item 2 above.

6. Recorded accrued interest expense on a note payable.

7. Recorded an increase in the value of an available-for-sale investment that will be distributed as a property dividend. The carrying value of the available-for-sale investment was greater than its cost.

8. Declared a property dividend (see item 7 above).

9. Distributed the investment to shareholders (see items 7 and 8 above).

10. Declared a stock dividend.

11. Distributed the stock dividend declared in item 10.

12. Repurchased common shares for less than their initial issue price.

Instructions

In the table below, indicate the effect that each of the 12 transactions has on the financial statement elements that are listed. Use the following codes: increase (I), decrease (D), and no effect (NE).

Item	Assets	Liabilities	Shareholders' Equity	Share Capital	Cont. Surplus	Retained Earnings	Acc. Other Compr. Income	Net Income

(LO 7)   E15-7   (Preferred Dividends) The outstanding share capital of Millay Corporation consists of 2,000 shares of preferred and 5,000 common shares for which $250,000 was received. The preferred shares carry a dividend of $8 per share and have a $100 stated value.

Instructions

Assuming that the company has retained earnings of $90,000 that is to be entirely paid out in dividends and that preferred dividends were not paid during the two years preceding the current year, state how much each class of shares should receive under each of the following conditions:

(a) The preferred shares are non-cumulative and non-participating.

(b) The preferred shares are cumulative and non-participating.

(c) The preferred shares are cumulative and participating.

(LO 7)   E15-8   (Preferred Dividends) MacLeish Limited's ledger shows the following balances on December 31, 2008:

Preferred shares outstanding: 15,000 shares	$ 300,000
Common shares outstanding: 40,000 shares	3,000,000
Retained earnings	980,000

Instructions

Assuming that the directors decide to declare total dividends in the amount of $566,000, determine how much each class of shares should receive under each of the conditions that follow. Note that one year's dividends are in arrears on the preferred shares, which pay a dividend of $0.80 per share.

(a) The preferred shares are cumulative and fully participating.

(b) The preferred shares are non-cumulative and non-participating.

(c) The preferred shares are non-cumulative and are participating in distributions in excess of a 10% dividend rate on the common shares.

(LO 9)   E15-9   (Stock Split and Stock Dividend) The common shares of Hamilton Inc. are currently selling at $143 per share. The directors want to reduce the share price and increase the share volume before making a new issue. The per share carrying value is $34. There are currently 9 million shares issued and outstanding.

Instructions

(a) Prepare the necessary journal entries assuming that:

1. the board votes a 2-for-1 stock split.

2. the board votes a 100% stock dividend.

(b) Briefly discuss the accounting and securities market differences between these two methods of increasing the number of shares outstanding.

(LO 9)   E15-10   (Entries for Stock Dividends and Stock Splits) The shareholders' equity accounts of Chesterton Inc. have the following balances on December 31, 2008:

Common shares, 700,000 shares issued and outstanding	$10,000,000
Contributed surplus	3,200,000
Retained earnings	76,600,000

Common shares are currently selling on the Prairie Stock Exchange at $57.

Instructions

Prepare the appropriate journal entries for each of the following cases:

(a) A stock dividend of 5% is declared and issued.

(b) A stock dividend of 100% is declared and issued.

(c) A 2-for-1 stock split is declared and issued.

E15-11 (Dividend Entries) The following data were taken from the balance sheet accounts of Brenning Corporation on **(LO 7, 9)** December 31, 2008:

Current assets	$1,040,000
Investments—held to maturity	824,000
Common shares (no par value, no authorized limit, 500,000 shares issued and outstanding)	6,000,000
Contributed surplus	350,000
Retained earnings	1,840,000

Instructions

Prepare the required journal entries for the following unrelated items:

(a) A 5% stock dividend is declared and distributed at a time when the shares' market value is $57 per share.

(b) A 6-for-1 stock split is effected.

(c) A dividend in kind is declared on January 5, 2008, and paid on January 25, 2008, in bonds that were classified as held to maturity. The bonds have a carrying value of $100,000 (equal to cost) and a fair market value of $180,000.

*E15-12 (Shareholders' Equity Section) Bruno Corporation's post-closing trial balance at December 31, 2008, was as **(LO 11, 15)** follows:

BRUNO CORPORATION
Post-Closing Trial Balance
December 31, 2008

	Dr.	Cr.
Accounts payable		$ 310,000
Accounts receivable	$ 480,000	
Accumulated amortization—building and equipment		185,000
Accumulated other comprehensive income		100,000
Contributed surplus—common		1,460,000
Allowance for doubtful accounts		30,000
Bonds payable		300,000
Building and equipment	1,450,000	
Cash	190,000	
Common shares		200,000
Dividends payable on preferred shares (cash)		4,000
Inventories	360,000	
Investments—available for sale	200,000	
Land	400,000	
Preferred shares		500,000
Prepaid expenses	40,000	
Retained earnings		201,000
Treasury shares	170,000	
Totals	$3,290,000	$3,290,000

At December 31, 2008, Bruno had the following numbers for its common and preferred shares:

	Common	Preferred
Authorized	600,000	60,000
Issued	200,000	10,000
Outstanding	190,000	10,000

The dividends on preferred shares are $5 cumulative. In addition, the preferred shares have a preference in liquidation of $50 per share.

Instructions

Prepare the shareholders' equity section of Bruno's balance sheet at December 31, 2008.

(AICPA adapted)

(LO 5, 7) E15-13   (Participating Preferred and Stock Dividend) The following is the shareholders' equity section of Sakamoto Corp. at December 31, 2008:

Preferred shares,[1] authorized 100,000 shares; issued 25,000 shares	$ 750,000
Common shares (200,000 authorized, 60,000 issued)	1,800,000
Contributed surplus	1,150,000
Total paid-in capital	3,700,000
Retained earnings	2,470,500
Total shareholders' equity	$6,170,500

[1] The preferred shares have a $5 dividend rate, are cumulative, and participate in distributions in excess of a $3 dividend on the common shares.

Instructions

(a) No dividends were paid in 2006 or 2007. On December 31, 2008, Sakamoto wants to pay a cash dividend of $4 a share to common shareholders. How much cash would be needed for the total amount to be paid to preferred and common shareholders?

(b) The company instead decides that it will declare a 15% stock dividend on the outstanding common shares. The shares' market value is $105 per share. Prepare the entry on the date of declaration.

(c) The company decides instead to acquire and cancel 10,500 common shares. The current market value is $105 per share. Prepare the entry to record the retirement, assuming contributed surplus arose from previous cancellations of common shares.

(LO 5, 7, 11) E15-14   (Dividends and Shareholders' Equity Section) Feller Corp. reported the following amounts in the shareholders' equity section of its December 31, 2007, balance sheet:

Preferred shares, $8 dividend (10,000 shares authorized, 2,000 shares issued)	$200,000
Common shares (100,000 authorized, 25,000 issued)	100,000
Contributed surplus	155,000
Retained earnings	250,000
Accumulated other comprehensive income	75,000
Total	$780,000

During 2008, the company had the following transactions that affect shareholders' equity:

1. Paid the annual 2007 $8 per share dividend on preferred shares and a $3 per share dividend on common shares. These dividends had been declared on December 31, 2007.

2. Purchased 3,700 shares of its own outstanding common shares for $35 per share and cancelled them.

3. Issued 1,000 shares of preferred shares at $105 per share (at the beginning of the year).

4. Declared a 10% stock dividend on the outstanding common shares when the shares were selling for $45 per share.

5. Issued the stock dividend.

6. Declared the annual 2008 $8 per share dividend on preferred shares and a $2 per share dividend on common shares. These dividends are payable in 2009.

The contributed surplus arose from past common share transactions.

Instructions

(a) Prepare journal entries to record the transactions above.

(b) Prepare the December 31, 2008, shareholders' equity section. Assume 2008 net income was $450,000 and comprehensive income was $455,000.

(c) Prepare the statement of shareholders' equity for the year ended December 31, 2008.

E15-15 **(Comparison of Alternative Forms of Financing)** What follows are the liabilities and shareholders' equity **(LO 12)** sections of the balance sheets for Kingston Corp. and Benson Corp. Each has assets totalling $4.2 million.

Kingston Corp.		Benson Corp.	
Current liabilities	$ 300,000	Current liabilities	$ 600,000
Long-term debt, 10%	1,200,000	Common shares	2,900,000
Common shares		(145,000 shares issued)	
(100,000 shares issued)	2,000,000	Retained earnings	
Retained earnings		(Cash dividends, $328,000)	700,000
(Cash dividends, $220,000)	700,000		
	$4,200,000		$4,200,000

For the year, each company has earned the same income before interest and taxes.

	Kingston Corp.	Benson Corp.
Income before interest and taxes	$1,200,000	$1,200,000
Interest expense	120,000	–0–
	1,080,000	1,200,000
Income taxes (45%)	486,000	540,000
Net income	$ 594,000	$ 660,000

At year end, the market price of Kingston's shares was $101 per share; it was $63.50 for Benson's.

Instructions

(a) Which company is more profitable in terms of return on total assets?

(b) Which company is more profitable in terms of return on shareholders' equity?

(c) Which company has the greater net income per share? Neither company issued or reacquired shares during the year.

(d) From the point of view of income, is it advantageous to Kingston's shareholders to have the long-term debt outstanding? Why or why not?

(e) What is each company's price earnings ratio?

(f) What is the book value per share for each company?

*E15-16 **(Financial Reorganization)** The following account balances are available from the ledger of Yang Sheng **(LO 16)** Corporation on December 31, 2007:

Common Shares (20,000 shares authorized and outstanding)	$1,000,000
Retained Earnings (deficit)	(190,000)

On January 2, 2008, the corporation put into effect a shareholder-approved reorganization by agreeing to pass the common shares over to the creditors in full payment of the $260,000 debt, writing up plant assets by $135,600, and eliminating the deficit.

Instructions
Prepare the required journal entries for the financial reorganization of Yang Sheng Corporation.

*E15-17 **(Financial Reorganization)** The condensed balance sheets of Regina Limited follow for the periods immedi- **(LO 16)** ately before, and one year after, it had completed a financial reorganization:

	Before Reorg.	One Year After		Before Reorg.	One Year After
Current assets	$ 300,000	$ 420,000	Common shares	$2,400,000	$1,550,000
Plant assets (net)	1,700,000	1,290,000	Contributed surplus	220,000	
	–0–	–0–	Retained earnings	(620,000)	160,000
	$2,000,000	$1,710,000		$2,000,000	$1,710,000

For the year following the financial reorganization, the company reported net income of $190,000 and amortization expense of $80,000, and paid a cash dividend of $30,000. As part of the reorganization, the company wrote down inventories by $120,000 in order to reflect circumstances that existed before the reorganization. Also, the deficit, and any revaluation adjustment, was accounted for by charging amounts against contributed surplus until it was eliminated, with any remaining amount being charged against common shares. The common shares are widely held and there is no controlling interest. No purchases or sales of plant assets and no share transactions occurred in the year following the reorganization.

Instructions
Prepare all the journal entries made at the time of the reorganization.

Problems

P15-1   Onano Corporation's charter authorizes the issuance of 1 million common shares and 500,000 preferred shares. The following transactions involving share issues were completed. Each transaction is independent of the others.

1. Issued 5,300 common shares for machinery. The machinery had been appraised at $77,100, and the seller's book value was $62,200. The common shares' most recent market price is $15 a share.

2. Voted a $12 dividend on both the 25,000 shares of outstanding common and the 55,000 shares of outstanding preferred. The dividend was paid in full.

3. Issued 3,750 shares of common and 1,000 shares of preferred for a lump sum of $111,300. The common had been selling at $14 and the preferred at $65.

4. Issued 2,120 shares of common and 135 shares of preferred for furniture and fixtures. The common had a fair market value of $16 per share and the furniture and fixtures were appraised at $42,000.

5. Issued a $100,000, 8% bond payable at par and gave as a bonus 100 preferred shares, which at that time were selling for $68 a share.

Instructions
Prepare the journal entries to record the transactions.

P15-2   WDC is a public company whose shares are actively traded on the Toronto Stock Exchange. The following information relates to WDC Corporation:

January 1, 2008	The company is granted a charter that authorizes the issuance of 200,000 no par value common shares, and 100,000 no par value preferred shares that entitle the holder to a $3.00 per share annual dividend.
January 10, 2008	10,000 common shares are issued to the founders of the corporation for land that has a market value of $300,000.
March 10, 2008	3,000 preferred shares are issued for cash for $120 per share.
April 15, 2008	The company issues 100 common shares to a car dealer in exchange for a used vehicle. The asking price for the car is $6,500. At the time of the exchange, the common shares are selling at $60 per share.
August 20, 2008	WDC Company decides to issue shares on a subscription basis to select individuals, giving each person the right to purchase 200 common shares at a price of $65 per share. Fifty individuals accept the company's offer and agree to pay 10% down and the remainder in three equal instalments.
October 11, 2008	WDC issues 2,000 common shares and 400 preferred shares for a lump sum of $160,000 cash. At the time of sale, both the common and preferred shares are actively traded. The common shares are trading at $60 each; the preferred shares at $110 each.
December 31, 2008	WDC declares cash dividends totalling $18,000, payable on January 31, 2009, to holders of record on January 15, 2009.

Instructions
Prepare the general journal entries to record the transactions.

(CGA adapted)

P15-3   Polska Corporation's general ledger shows the following account balances (the average cost of Polska's shares is $30 per share), among others. The Contributed Surplus relates to the common shares.

Contributed Surplus	Common Shares	Retained Earnings
Balance $9,000	Balance $270,000	Balance $80,000

Instructions

Assuming that the above balances existed before any of the transactions that follow, record the journal entries for each transaction:

(a) Bought and cancelled 380 shares at $39 per share.

(b) Bought and cancelled 300 shares at $43 per share.

(c) Sold 3,500 shares at $42 per share.

(d) Sold 1,200 shares at $48 per share.

(e) Bought and cancelled 1,000 shares at $60 per share.

P15-4 Studio One Corp. had the following shareholders' equity on January 1, 2008:

Common shares, 200,000 shares authorized, 100,000 shares issued and outstanding	$ 250,000
Contributed surplus	350,000
Retained earnings	2,800,000
Total shareholders' equity	$3,400,000

The following transactions occurred, in the order given, during 2008:

1. Subscriptions were sold for 15,000 common shares at $28 per share. The first payment was for $12 per share.

2. The second payment for the sale in number 1 above was for $16 per share. All payments were received on the second payment except for 1,000 shares.

3. In accordance with the subscription contract, which requires that defaulting subscribers have all their payments refunded, a refund cheque was sent to the defaulting subscribers. At this point, common shares were issued to subscribers who had fully paid on the contract.

4. Repurchased 25,000 common shares at $30 per share. They were then retired.

5. Sold 3,000 preferred shares and 2,000 common shares together for $290,000. The common shares had a market value of $29 per share.

Instructions

(a) Prepare the journal entries to record the transactions for the company for 2008.

(b) Assume that the subscription contract states that defaulting subscribers forfeit their first payment. Prepare the journal entries for numbers 2 to 4 above.

P15-5 Transactions of Kalila Corporation are as follows:

1. The company is granted a charter that authorizes the issuance of 150,000 preferred shares and 150,000 common shares without par value.

2. The founders of the corporation are issued 10,000 common shares for land valued by the board of directors at $210,000 (based on an independent valuation).

3. Sold 15,200 preferred shares for cash at $110 per share.

4. Repurchased and cancelled 3,000 shares of outstanding preferred shares for cash at $100 per share.

5. Repurchased and cancelled 4,000 preferred shares for cash at $98 per share.

6. Repurchased for cash and cancelled 500 shares of the outstanding common shares issued in number 2 above at $49 per share.

7. Issued 2,000 preferred shares at $99 per share.

Instructions

(a) Prepare entries in journal form to record the transactions listed above. No other transactions affecting the capital share accounts have occurred.

(b) Assuming that the company has retained earnings from operations of $1,032,000, prepare the shareholders' equity section of its balance sheet after considering all the transactions above.

(c) Why is the distinction between paid-in capital and retained earnings important?

(d) How would the repurchase of the preferred shares differ if the preferred shares were retractable or callable/redeemable?

P15-6 Amado Limited has two classes of shares outstanding: preferred ($6 dividend) and common. At December 31, 2007, the following accounts and balances were included in shareholders' equity:

Preferred shares, 300,000 shares issued (authorized, 1 million shares)	$ 3,000,000
Common shares, 1,000,000 shares (authorized, unlimited)	10,000,000
Contributed surplus—preferred	200,000
Contributed surplus—common	17,000,000
Retained earnings	5,500,000
Accumulated other comprehensive income	250,000

The following transactions affected shareholders' equity during 2008:

Jan.	1	Issued 25,000 preferred shares at $25 per share.
Feb.	1	Issued 50,000 common shares at $20 per share.
June	1	Declared a 2-for-1 stock split (common shares).
July	1	Purchased and retired 30,000 common shares at $15 per share.
Dec. 31		Net income is $2,100,000; comprehensive income is $2,050,000.
Dec. 31		The preferred dividend is declared, and a common dividend of $0.50 per share is declared.

Instructions
Prepare the shareholders' equity section for the company at December 31, 2008. Show all supporting calculations.

P15-7 Perfect Pitch Inc. (PPI) is a widely held, publicly traded company that designs equipment for tuning musical instruments. Information pertaining to its shareholders' equity is as follows:

PERFECT PITCH INC.
Shareholders' Equity
December 31, 2007

Share capital	
Preferred shares, no par value, $8, cumulative, and participating	
(20,000 authorized; 1,000 issued and outstanding)	$100,000
Common shares, no par value	
(1,000,000 authorized; 40,000 issued and outstanding)	500,000
Contributed capital, preferred share retirement	20,000
	620,000
Retained earnings	280,000
Shareholders' equity	$900,000

The preferred share dividend was not paid in 2007.

Several transactions affecting shareholders' equity took place during the fiscal year ended December 31, 2008, and are summarized in chronological order as follows:

1. Exchanged 10,000 common shares for a prototype piano tuning machine. The machine was appraised at $110,000. On the transaction date, PPI's shares were actively trading at $10 per share.

2. Purchased and retired 10,000 common shares at $15 per share.

3. Paid the annual dividend on the preferred shares. The common shares were then paid a $2 per share dividend.

Instructions
Prepare journal entries for each of the three transactions.

*P15-8 Heinrich Corporation had the following shareholders' equity at January 1, 2008:

Preferred shares, 8%, $100 par value, 10,000 shares authorized,	
4,000 shares issued	$ 400,000
Common shares, $2 par value, 200,000 shares authorized,	
80,000 shares issued	160,000
Common shares subscribed, 10,000 shares	20,000
Contributed surplus—preferred	20,000
Contributed surplus—common	940,000
Retained earnings	780,000
	2,320,000
Less: Common share subscriptions receivable	40,000
Total shareholders' equity	$2,280,000

During 2008, the following transactions occurred:

1. Equipment was purchased in exchange for 100 shares of common. The shares' market value on the exchange date was $12 per share.

2. Sold 1,000 shares of common and 100 shares of preferred for the lump sum price of $24,500. The common shares had a market price of $14 at the time of the sale.

3. Sold 2,000 shares of preferred for cash at $102 per share.

4. All of the subscribers paid their subscription prices into the firm.

5. The common shares were issued.

6. Repurchased and retired 1,000 common shares at $15 per share.

7. Income for 2008 was $246,000.

Instructions

Prepare the shareholders' equity section for the company as at December 31, 2008. (The use of T accounts may help you organize the material.)

P15-9 The books of Passos Corporation carried the following account balances as at December 31, 2007:

Cash	$ 1,300,000
Preferred shares, $2 cumulative dividend, non-participating, 25,000 shares issued	750,000
Common shares, no par value, 300,000 shares issued	15,000,000
Contributed surplus (preferred)	150,000
Retained earnings	355,000

The preferred shares have dividends in arrears for the past year (2006). At its annual meeting on December 21, 2007, the board of directors declared the following: The current year dividends shall be $2 on the preferred and $1 per share on the common; the dividends in arrears shall be paid by issuing one share of common shares for each 20 shares of preferred held.

The preferred is currently selling at $80 per share and the common at $58 per share. Net income for 2007 is estimated at $77,000.

Instructions

(a) Prepare the journal entries that are required for the dividend declaration and payment, assuming that they occur at the same time.

(b) Could the company give the preferred shareholders two years of dividends and common shareholders a $1 per share dividend, all in cash? Explain your reasoning.

P15-10 Babluck Corp. has 5,000 preferred shares outstanding (no par value, $2 dividend), which were issued for $150,000; and 30,000 shares of no par value common, which were issued for $550,000.

Instructions

The following schedule shows the amount of dividends paid out over the last four years. Allocate the dividends to each type of share under assumptions (a) and (b). Express your answers in per share amounts and using the format that is shown.

		Assumptions			
		(a) Preferred, non-cumulative, and non-participating		(b) Preferred, cumulative, and fully participating	
Year	Paid-out	Preferred	Common	Preferred	Common
2006	$ 8,000				
2007	$ 24,000				
2008	$ 60,000				
2009	$126,000				

P15-11 Guo Limited provides you with the following condensed balance sheet information:

Assets		Liabilities and Shareholders' Equity		
Current assets	$ 40,000	Current and long-term liabilities		$100,000
Investments in ABC Company—		Shareholders' equity		
trading (10,000 shares)	60,000	Common shares[1]	$ 20,000	
Equipment (net)	250,000	Contributed surplus	110,000	
Intangibles	60,000	Retained earnings	180,000	310,000
Total assets	$410,000	Total liabilities andshareholders' equity		$410,000

[1]10,000 shares issued and outstanding.

Instructions

(a) For each transaction below, indicate the dollar impact (if any) on the following five items: (1) total assets, (2) common shares, (3) contributed surplus, (4) retained earnings, and (5) shareholders' equity. (Each situation is independent.)

1. The company declares and pays a $0.50 per share dividend.

2. The company declares and issues a 10% stock dividend when the shares' market price is $12 per share.

3. The company declares and issues a 40% stock dividend when the shares' market price is $17 per share.

4. The company declares and distributes a property dividend. The company gives one ABC share for every two company shares held. ABC is selling for $12 per share on the date when the property dividend is declared.

5. The company declares a 3-for-1 stock split and issues new shares.

(b) What are the differences between a stock dividend and a cash or property dividend?

P15-12 Some of the account balances of Vai Limited at December 31, 2006, are as follows:

$6 Preferred shares (no par, 2,000 shares authorized, 2,000 shares issued and outstanding)	$520,000
Common shares (no par, 100,000 shares authorized, 50,000 shares issued and outstanding)	500,000
Contributed surplus	103,000
Retained earnings	774,000
Accumulated other comprehensive income	22,350

The price of the company's common shares has been increasing steadily on the market; it was $21 on January 1, 2007, advanced to $24 by July 1, and to $27 at the end of the year 2007. The preferred shares are not openly traded but were appraised at $120 per share during 2007. Vai had net income of $154,000 during 2007.

Instructions

(a) Prepare the proper journal entries for each of the following:

1. The company declared a property dividend on April 1. Each common shareholder was to receive one share of Waterloo Corp. for every 10 shares outstanding. Vai had 8,000 shares of Waterloo (2% of the outstanding shares), and had purchased them in 2006 for $68,400. The shares were held for sale. The accumulated other comprehensive income relates only to these shares. The market value of Waterloo shares was $16 per share on April 1. The property dividend was distributed April 21 when the market value of the Waterloo shares was $18.50. The Waterloo shares stayed at a market value of $18.50 until year end.

2. On July 1, the company declared a 5% stock dividend to the remaining common shareholders. The stock dividend was distributed July 22.

3. A shareholder, in an effort to persuade Vai to expand into her city, donated to the company a plot of land with an appraised value of $42,000.

(b) Prepare the shareholders' equity section of Vai's balance sheet at December 31, 2007.

(c) How should Vai account for the difference in market value of the Waterloo shares between the date of declaration and date of distribution? Does the declaration of a property dividend create a financial liability?

P15-13 Ducat Corporation has outstanding $2 million no par value common shares that were issued at $10 per share. The balances at January 1, 2008, were $24 million in its retained earnings account; $5 million in its contributed surplus account; and $1.2 million in its accumulated other comprehensive income account. During 2008, the company's net income was $5.7 million and comprehensive income was $5.95 million. A cash dividend of 60 cents a share was paid on June 30, 2008; and a 6% stock dividend was distributed to shareholders of record at the close of business on December 31, 2008. You have been asked to give advice on how to properly account for the stock dividend. The existing company shares are quoted on a national stock exchange. The shares' market price per share has been as follows:

October 31, 2008	$31
November 30, 2008	33
December 31, 2008	38
Average price over the two-month period	35

Instructions

(a) Prepare a journal entry to record the cash dividend.

(b) Prepare a journal entry to record the stock dividend.

(c) Prepare the shareholders' equity section (including a schedule of retained earnings) of the company balance sheet for the year 2008 based on the information given. Write a note to the financial statements that states the accounting basis for the stock dividend and include separate comments on why this basis was chosen.

(d) Prepare a statement of shareholders' equity for the year 2008.

P15-14 Okanagan Inc. was formed on July 1, 2005. It was authorized to issue 300,000 shares of no par value common shares and 100,000 shares of cumulative and non-participating preferred stock carrying a $2 dividend. The company has a July 1 to June 30 fiscal year. The following information relates to the company's shareholders' equity account:

Common Shares

Before the 2007–08 fiscal year, the company had 110,000 shares of outstanding common issued as follows:

1. 95,000 shares issued for cash on July 1, 2005 at $31 per share

2. 5,000 shares exchanged on July 24, 2005, for a plot of land that cost the seller $70,000 in 1995 and had an estimated market value of $220,000 on July 24, 2005

3. 10,000 shares issued on March 1, 2006; the shares had been subscribed for $42 per share on October 31, 2005.

During the 2007–08 fiscal year, the following transactions regarding common shares took place:

October 1, 2007	Subscriptions were received for 10,000 shares at $46 per share. Cash of $92,000 was received in full payment for 2,000 shares and share certificates were issued. The remaining subscription for 8,000 shares was to be paid in full by September 30, 2008, and the certificates would then be issued on that date.
November 30, 2007	The company purchased 2,000 shares of its own common on the open market at $39 per share. These shares were restored to the status of authorized but unissued shares.
December 15, 2007	The company declared a 5% stock dividend for shareholders of record on January 15, 2008, to be issued on January 31, 2008. The company was having a liquidity problem and could not afford a cash dividend at the time. The company's common shares were selling at $52 per share on December 15, 2007.
June 20, 2008	The company sold 500 shares of its own common for $21,000.

Preferred Shares

The company issued 50,000 shares of preferred at $44 per share on July 1, 2005.

Cash Dividends

The company has followed a schedule of declaring cash dividends each year in December and June and making the payment to shareholders of record in the following month. The cash dividend declarations have been as follows since the company's first year and up until June 30, 2008:

Declaration Date	Common Shares	Preferred Shares
Dec. 15, 2006	$0.30 per share	$3.00 per share
June 6, 2007	$0.30 per share	$1.00 per share
Dec. 15, 2007	—	$1.00 per share

No cash dividends were declared during June 2008 due to the company's liquidity problems.

Retained Earnings

As at June 30, 2007, the company's retained earnings account had a balance of $690,000. For the fiscal year ending June 30, 2008, the company reported net income of $40,000.

In March of 2007, the company received a term loan from Manitoba Bank. The bank requires the company to establish a sinking fund and restrict retained earnings for an amount equal to the sinking fund deposit. The annual sinking fund payment of $50,000 is due on April 30 each year; the first payment was made on schedule on April 30, 2008.

Instructions

(a) Prepare the shareholders' equity section of the company's balance sheet, including appropriate notes, as at June 30, 2008, as it should appear in its annual report to the shareholders. (CMA adapted)

(b) Prepare the journal entries for the 2007–08 fiscal year.

(c) Discuss why the common shareholders might be willing to accept a stock dividend during the year rather than a cash dividend.

Writing Assignments

WA15-1   Algonquin Corporation sold 50,000 common shares on a subscription basis for $40 per share. By December 31, 2008, collections on these subscriptions totalled $1.3 million. None of the subscriptions have been paid in full so far.

Instructions

(a) Discuss the meaning of the account Common Shares Subscribed and indicate how it is reported in the financial statements.

(b) Discuss the arguments in favour of reporting Subscriptions Receivable as a current asset.

(c) Discuss the arguments in favour of reporting Subscriptions Receivable as a contra equity account.

(d) Indicate how these 50,000 shares would be presented on Algonquin's December 31, 2008, balance sheet under the method discussed in (c) above.

WA15-2   *CICA Handbook* Section 1000 defines various elements of financial statements.

Instructions

Answer the following questions based on Section 1000.

(a) Define and discuss the term "equity."

(b) What transactions or events change owners' equity?

(c) What are some examples of changes within owners' equity that do not change the total amount of owners' equity?

WA15-3   The directors of Amman Corporation are considering issuing a stock dividend. They have asked you to discuss this option by answering the following questions.

Instructions

(a) What is a stock dividend? How is a stock dividend distinguished from a stock split, both from a legal standpoint and from an accounting standpoint?

(b) For what reasons does a corporation usually declare a stock dividend? A stock split?

(c) Discuss the amount of retained earnings, if any, that should be capitalized in connection with a stock dividend.

(AICPA adapted)

*WA15-4   Henning Inc. is a medium-sized manufacturer that has been experiencing losses for the five years that it has been in business. Although the operations for the year just ended resulted in a loss, several important changes resulted in a profitable fourth quarter, and the company's future operations are expected to be profitable. The treasurer, Peter Henning, suggests that there be a financial reorganization to eliminate the accumulated deficit of $650,000.

Instructions

(a) What are the characteristics of a financial reorganization? In other words, what does it consist of?

(b) List the conditions that generally justify a financial reorganization.

(c) Discuss the propriety of the treasurer's proposals to eliminate the deficit of $650,000.

(AICPA adapted)

WA15-5   Other Comprehensive Income is a relatively new account on the income statement.

Instructions

From the perspective of the conceptual framework, discuss the validity of both this account and the Accumulated Other Comprehensive Income account.

Cases

Refer to the Case Primer on the Student Website to help you answer these cases.

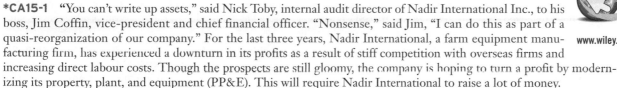

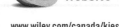
Student Website

www.wiley.com/canada/kieso

*CA15-1   "You can't write up assets," said Nick Toby, internal audit director of Nadir International Inc., to his boss, Jim Coffin, vice-president and chief financial officer. "Nonsense," said Jim, "I can do this as part of a quasi-reorganization of our company." For the last three years, Nadir International, a farm equipment manufacturing firm, has experienced a downturn in its profits as a result of stiff competition with overseas firms and increasing direct labour costs. Though the prospects are still gloomy, the company is hoping to turn a profit by modernizing its property, plant, and equipment (PP&E). This will require Nadir International to raise a lot of money.

Over the past few months, Jim has tried to raise funds from various financial institutions, but they are unwilling to lend capital. The reason they give is that the company's net book value of fixed assets on the balance sheet, based on historic cost, is not large enough to sustain major funding. Jim attempted to explain to bankers and investors that these assets are more valuable than their recorded amounts, especially since the company used accelerated amortization methods and tended to underestimate the useful lives of assets. Jim also believes that the company's land and buildings are substantially undervalued because of rising real estate prices over the past several years.

Jim's proposed solution to raise funds is a simple one: First, declare a large dividend to company shareholders that results in Retained Earnings having a large debit balance. Then, write up the fixed assets of Nadir International to an amount that is equal to the deficit in the Retained Earnings account.

Instructions

Adopt the role of the internal auditor and discuss the financial reporting issues.

CA15-2   Donald Young, controller for Centre Corporation, wants to discuss with the company president, Rhonda Santo, the possibility of paying a stock dividend. Young knows that the company does not have a huge amount of cash, but he is certain that Santo would like to give the shareholders something of value this year since it has been a few years since the company has paid any dividends. Young also is concerned that the company's cash position will not improve significantly in the near future. He feels that shareholders look to retained earnings and, if they see a large balance, they believe (erroneously, of course) that the company can pay a cash dividend.

Young wants to propose that the company pay a 100% stock dividend, as opposed to a cash dividend or a 2-for-1 stock split. He reasons (1) that the shareholders will receive something of value, other than cash; and (2) that retained earnings will be reduced by the stock dividend (as opposed to a split, which does not affect retained earnings) so shareholders will be less likely to expect cash dividends in the near future.

For her part, Rhonda is interested in setting up a program that would have the company make loans to top company executives so that they can purchase new shares that will be issued by the company. This way, there is again no impact on cash yet the executives can participate in increases (hopefully) in the company share price. If all goes well, they can sell the shares, pay back the loans, and keep the difference. The loans are also secured by the shares of the company. If the share prices decrease, the company would not necessarily enforce collection of the receivable.

Instructions

Adopt the role of the company auditor and discuss the financial reporting issues.

Integrated Cases

IC15-1　Sandolin Incorporated (SI) is a global, diversified firm whose shares trade on the major Canadian and U.S. stock markets. It owns numerous toll highways, several companies in the energy business, and an engineering consulting firm. Currently, its shares are trading at a 52-week high and its credit rating on all debt issues is AA. This is partly due to its revenues, which have doubled, and is also due to a recent restructuring. The restructuring is in the energy business and allows the company to position itself as a low-cost competitor in the industry. The restructuring involved laying off 5,000 employees and mothballing several oil and gas wells. The cost to extract oil and gas from the wells is presently too high. The company plans to retain the wells and work on new technology to reduce the extraction costs.

SI is in the process of putting together its annual financial statements and the VP Finance, Santos Suarez, is planning to meet with the company's auditors next week for a preliminary audit planning meeting. Santos is concerned about a phone call that he recently received from the government, as it was threatening legal action relating to the transportation part of the business. Among other things, SI owns a toll highway that stretches approximately 100 kilometres across a major urban centre. The road is very profitable since non-toll roads in the area are very congested and people use the toll road to commute. SI recently raised toll rates on the road and the government is claiming it is prohibited from doing this without government consent, which the government does not plan to give. Santos is concerned that if this news gets out, the credit rating and share price will suffer. SI believes that its contract allows it to change toll rates whenever it wants. SI's lawyers have reviewed the contracts and feel that SI's position is justifiable. The value of the toll road as a business is substantially less if the company loses the right to change the tolls.

While reviewing the company's dramatic increase in revenues, Santos became aware of a new type of transaction that the company has been entering into with increasing frequency in the past two months. As part of the energy business, SI employs a group of traders who make deals that reduce the company's exposure to fluctuating commodity prices. According to several e-mails between the traders, the deals are known as "round trip" trades. Several large trades involved purchases and sales with the same party for the same volume at substantially the same price. They have been treated as sales and account for 40% of the increase in revenues. The trader's position is that the company does make a commission on these deals, which adds up depending on the volume. The company never takes possession of the commodity that is being bought and sold.

Just before year end, the company acquired a mid-sized engineering firm. As part of the deal, the company issued shares to the vendor. The value of the issued shares was higher than the fair value of the engineering firm and the vendor gave SI a one-year note receivable for the difference. If profits from the engineering firm exceed a certain threshold—i.e., if the firm outperforms expectations—the note will not be paid. Currently, SI has recorded the note receivable as an asset.

Instructions

Adopt the role of Santos and analyze the financial reporting issues.

IC15-2　**Wallbridge Mining Company Limited (Wallbridge)** is in the business of locating and exploring mineral properties. Its shares list on the Toronto Stock Exchange and the company is audited by KPMG (Sudbury office). As the company is currently in its exploration stages it incurred losses of $1,880,537 on revenues of $297,109 in 2006 (which is down from the prior year loss of $4,376,017). The company's current Deficit is in excess of $17 million and cash outflows from operations were $1,184,723 in 2006.

Below is an excerpt from the notes to the financial statements for 2006:

(c) Mining interests:

The Company considers exploration costs to have the characteristics of property, plant and equipment. As such, the Company defers all exploration costs including acquisition costs, field exploration and field supervisory costs relating to specific properties until those properties are brought into production at which time exploration costs will be amortized on a unit-of-production basis based on proven and probable reserves or until the properties are abandoned, sold or considered to be impaired in value at which time an appropriate charge will be made.

The recovery of mining interest costs is dependent upon the existence of economically recoverable reserves, the ability of the Company to obtain the necessary financing to complete exploration, the development of future profitable production or the receipt of proceeds from disposition of such properties.

(vi) During the year, the Company issued common shares in return for property acquisitions as follows (refer to note 5):

• April 6, 2006	25,000 shares	$ 8,000	Drill Lake
• July 31, 2006	150,000 shares	$40,500	Pele Mountain
• December 31, 2006	200,000 shares	$82,000	Pele Mountain

In addition to the mining interests, the company also has several 100% interests in properties in the Sudbury area. The statements note that in order for the company to retain its rights to these properties, it must fulfill certain commitments and incur exploration expenditures. The commitments involve paying upfront amounts (in a combination of cash and shares) of several million dollars prior to production.

Instructions

Assume that you are a co-op student in KPMG's Sudbury office. The senior in charge of the audit has asked you to have a quick review of the financial statements of the company to determine any significant accounting issues.

Research and Financial Analysis

RA15-1 Canwest Global Communications Corp.

The **Canwest Global Communications Corp.** financial statements can be found on the Student Website.

Instructions

(a) The company has many different types of shares authorized, issued, and/or outstanding at the end of the 2006 year end. Prepare a chart that shows the following: name of share class, number of votes per share, rights in terms of dividends.

(b) Why would a company structure its capital in this way? Is there a need for the various classes of shares? Who owns the multiple voting shares? (Hint: Look at the Annual Information Form on www.sedar.com.)

(c) Calculate the average carrying value per share for the 2005 and 2006 year ends. Compare these values to the value that the company's shares are trading at. (Hint: Look at the Annual Information Form.)

RA15-2 Bank of Montreal versus Royal Bank of Canada

The **Bank of Montreal** and **Royal Bank of Canada** financial statements can be found on the Student Website.

Instructions

(a) What is the average carrying value of each company's common shares? Compare these values to market prices. What stock exchanges do these banks trade on?

(b) What is the authorized share capital of each company?

(c) Comment on how each company presents its common shares and shareholders' equity.

(d) Describe the changes (number of shares and price) in each company's common share accounts over the past three years. What types of activities are contributing to the changes?

(e) What amounts of cash dividends per share were declared by each company? What were the dollar amount effects of the cash dividends on each company's shareholders' equity?

(f) What is each company's rate of return on common shareholders' equity for the past two years? Which company gets the higher return on the equity of its shareholders?

RA15-3 Canadian Tire Corporation Limited

Instructions

Refer to the financial statements and accompanying notes and discussion of **Canadian Tire Corporation Limited** and answer the following questions.

(a) What are the issued and authorized shares for both classes of shares that the company has? What percentage of the authorized shares are issued?

(b) Compare the rights that are attached to each share. Are the class A shares more like preferred shares or common shares?

(c) Why does the company repurchase shares every year? How successful was it in achieving its objective in 2006?

(d) How did the company account for the excess of the amount paid on reacquisition over the carrying value of the shares? Recreate the journal entry.

(e) What was the average price of the shares at the beginning of the year? What were the shares repurchased at? Compare this with the market prices of the shares.

RA15-4   MDS INC.

The following is an excerpt from Note 10 to the financial statements of **MDS Inc.**:

Share Capital

Effective September 26, 2000, the Company declared a one-for-one stock dividend which has essentially the same impact as a two-for-one stock split. Information contained in this note pertaining to dividends, share repurchases, the stock option plan, the stock dividend and share purchase plan and the employee share ownership plan, has been adjusted to reflect the impact of the stock dividend. The tables contained in note 10a) present the number of shares issued, repurchased and converted based on the date of the actual transaction.

	Common	
(number of shares in thousands)	Number	Amount
Issued on conversion of Class A to Common	12,945	$ 22.2
Issued on conversion of Class B to Common	47,254	$317.9
Issued subsequent to conversions	9,676	442.6
Stock dividend	69,711	
Repurchases	(116)	(0.4)
Balance October 31, 2000	139,470	$782.3

The Statement of Retained Earnings is noted below:

Years Ended October 31

(millions of Canadian dollars) (restated note 2)	2000	1999	1998
Retained earnings, beginning of year	$324.1	$262.7	$237.6
Net income	110.3	81.9	44.3
Repurchase of shares and options (note 10)	(18.7)	(12.4)	(12.2)
Dividends	(10.3)	(8.1)	(7.0)
Retained earnings, end of year	$405.4	$324.1	$262.7

Instructions

Discuss the financial reporting issues for the stock dividend.

RA 15-5   Shaw Communications Inc.

On May 10, 2007, Shaw Communications Inc. ("Shaw") announced that it planned to implement a two-for-one stock split for its Class A Participating and Class B Non-Voting Participating shares subject to regulatory and shareholder approval.

Instructions

(a) Why might Shaw have declared a stock split?

(b) What impact did the stock split have on (1) total shareholders' equity, (2) total book value, (3) number of outstanding shares, and (4) book value per share?

(c) What impact did the split have on the shares' market value? What has since happened to their market price?

RA 15-6   Statements of changes in equity

International GAAP requires statements of changes in shareholders' equity. Canadian GAAP has historically only required statements of changes in retained earnings.

Instructions

Discuss why these differences occur. Obtain a copy of financial statements prepared under IFRS and compare the statements of changes in equity between the two.

RA 15-7   Impact of different legal systems on international GAAP

Companies from many countries have moved to, or are in the process of moving to, international GAAP. Evidence has shown that it is preferable to adopt IFRS on a wholesale basis (i.e., with no differences). This chapter shows how much the legal environment affects the accounting for shares. Different countries will have differing legal systems/environments, which may affect the accounting on a country by country basis.

Instructions

How should this be dealt with in your opinion?

Building on Complexity

 **Securities**

TD Securities' "structured finance" department focuses on the equity derivative business. Much of its clientele are institutional businesses looking for swaps, options, or customized derivatives. Todd Hargarten, vice-president and director of TD Securities Inc., describes his work with complex financial instruments as reactive, rather than proactive. "A lot of structured derivatives are bought, not sold," he says.

When working with corporate clients, Hargarten and his colleagues provide information on possible solutions to a business's situation. Often these structures are created for a specific large business, and while there may sometimes be solutions that apply broadly to different companies, in Canada that's rare, Hargarten says.

For their part, institutional investors make their own decisions. Most large pension plans have in-house expertise to develop their own product. By doing all the pieces themselves and breaking it down to a commodity, the pension funds are isolating the risk, Hargarten adds.

Retail demand for exposure to hot sectors also encourages the creation of structured products. For example, during the big days of telecom, some financial institutions offered a "custom telecom basket." This principal-protected, equity-linked note competed with bank-offered, equity-linked GICs. The main difference was the term; a note's term can be up to seven years, while a GIC is generally capped at five years. One limitation of these structured notes is that they are linked to the financial institution that created them, and brokers are therefore reluctant to push their competitor's branded product. As a result, these notes are limited in size, often ranging from $5 to $25 million.

Adding a bit more structure and flexibility to these instruments can become complicated. For example, covered call-writing funds were first developed in the early 1990s. Then principal protection was added. "Since then a lot of these structures morphed into other areas," Hargarten says. Indeed, as each year passes, the complexity of these and other financial instruments continues to increase. ■

chapter 16

Complex Financial Instruments

Learning Objectives

After studying this chapter, you should be able to:

1. Describe whether an instrument issued for financing purposes represents a liability, equity, or both.

2. Explain the accounting for the issuance, conversion, and retirement of convertible securities.

3. Understand what derivatives are and why they exist.

4. Explain the various types of financial risks, and how they arise.

5. Understand what options, forwards, and futures are.

6. Describe the recognition, measurement, and presentation issues for options, forwards, and futures.

7. Describe the various types of stock compensation plans.

8. Explain the differences between employee and compensatory option plans and other options.

9. Describe the accounting for compensatory stock option plans.

10. Compare current Canadian and international GAAP, and understand which direction international GAAP is headed.

After studying the appendices, you should be able to:

11. Understand how derivatives are used in hedging.

12. Explain what hedge accounting is and identify the qualifying hedge criteria.

13. Explain the difference between a fair value hedge and cash flow hedge.

14. Calculate the impact on net income of using hedge accounting for both types of hedges.

15. Account for stock appreciation rights plans.

16. Explain what performance-type plans are.

17. Understand the different fair value measurement options and models.

Preview of Chapter 16

Uncommon in the past, complex financial instruments are now used by companies in many different industries. Companies use these instruments in an effort to manage risk, gain access to pools of financing, and minimize the cost of capital and taxes. In response to this trend, the accounting profession has developed a new framework for dealing with these instruments in the financial statements. Earlier in the text, the accounting was discussed for basic financial instruments, including accounts and notes receivable/payable, investments, loans, and shares. This chapter focuses on complex financial instruments, such as hybrid and compound debt and equity instruments and derivatives, (which will be discussed separately). Since employee compensation plans often include such derivatives as stock options, these plans will also be discussed in this chapter.

The chapter is organized as follows:

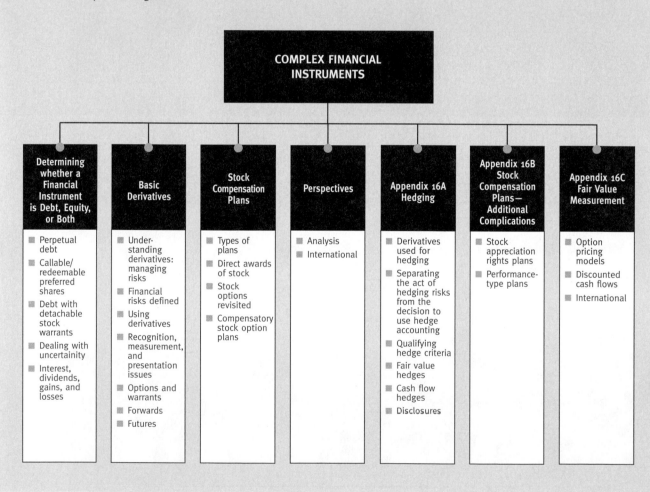

COMPLEX FINANCIAL INSTRUMENTS

Determining whether a Financial Instrument is Debt, Equity, or Both	Basic Derivatives	Stock Compensation Plans	Perspectives	Appendix 16A Hedging	Appendix 16B Stock Compensation Plans—Additional Complications	Appendix 16C Fair Value Measurement
■ Perpetual debt ■ Callable/redeemable preferred shares ■ Debt with detachable stock warrants ■ Dealing with uncertainty ■ Interest, dividends, gains, and losses	■ Understanding derivatives: managing risks ■ Financial risks defined ■ Using derivatives ■ Recognition, measurement, and presentation issues ■ Options and warrants ■ Forwards ■ Futures	■ Types of plans ■ Direct awards of stock ■ Stock options revisited ■ Compensatory stock option plans	■ Analysis ■ International	■ Derivatives used for hedging ■ Separating the act of hedging risks from the decision to use hedge accounting ■ Qualifying hedge criteria ■ Fair value hedges ■ Cash flow hedges ■ Disclosures	■ Stock appreciation rights plans ■ Performance-type plans	■ Option pricing models ■ Discounted cash flows ■ International

DETERMINING WHETHER A FINANCIAL INSTRUMENT IS DEBT, EQUITY, OR BOTH

Hybrid/combined instruments have more than one component including debt and equity (such as debt with detachable warrants) or may have the dual attributes of both debt and equity.[1] Examples include debt with detachable warrants or redeemable preferred shares. With these instruments, the main accounting complexity is in determining how to classify these instruments on the balance sheet. Are they debt? Are they equity? Or are they perhaps a bit of both? This is a **presentation issue** that in the end must be determined by examining the **economic substance** of the instrument. If they have components of both debt and equity, they may require bifurcation (i.e., splitting into debt and equity), which would also make the issue one of **measurement**. Whatever the classification that is chosen upon inception, this classification continues to be used until the instrument is removed from the balance sheet.[2]

Currently, the balance sheet is typically divided into at least three major elements: assets, debt, and equity. Since many users rely on the classification between debt and equity to assess liquidity and solvency, among other things, the classification issue is significant. As these types of instrument spread to an increasingly wide range of situations, financial statement preparers and analysts are therefore faced with the increasingly difficult task of classifying instruments that do not fit neatly into either the debt or equity category.

Recall from Chapters 14 and 15 the definitions of financial liabilities and equity instruments. A **financial liability** is any liability that is a contractual obligation to do either of the following:

1. Deliver cash or another financial asset to another party.

2. Exchange financial instruments with another party under conditions that are potentially unfavourable.

An **equity instrument** is any contract that evidences a residual interest in the assets of an entity after deducting all of its liabilities.

These definitions are critical in determining how to present the instruments.[3] Financial liabilities and equity instruments are covered by several *Handbook* sections. It is therefore important to ensure that you are dealing with the correct *Handbook* section. In deciding how to account for the instruments, do the following:

1. First look to Section 3863, which deals with the **presentation and classification** of financial instruments from the perspective of the issuer (financial liability versus equity instrument). You may have to bifurcate or split out the equity component of certain instruments.[4]

2. Then, for the financial liabilities, look to Section 3855, which deals with the **recognition and measurement** of financial instruments (except for equity instruments of the issuer). Financial liabilities that are held for trading are valued at fair value, with gains and losses booked to net income, and all other financial liabilities are measured at amortized cost using the effective interest method.[5]

1 Objective
Describe whether an instrument issued for financing purposes represents a liability, equity, or both.

Underlying Concept

In determining whether to classify the instrument as debt, consider the definition of a financial liability. In determining whether to classify it as equity, consider the definition of equity instruments.

Underlying Concept

Well-defined measurement tools help reduce measurement uncertainty. These tools ultimately help in preparing financial information that is more reliable.

---

[1] Instruments that have more than one component are sometimes referred to as **compound financial instruments**.

[2] *CICA Handbook*, Section 3863.10.

[3] *CICA Handbook*, Section 3863.11 and .13.

[4] Note that *Handbook* Section 3863 does not deal with measurement, however, it suggests methods that might be used to measure the debt and equity components. These will be looked at in this chapter.

[5] *Handbook* Section 3855 also deals with financial assets and equity instruments (of other entities). These were covered in other chapters in this text.

Illustration 16-1 shows an abbreviated decision tree that helps in determining how to analyze financial instruments for financial reporting purposes from the perspective of the issuer.

Illustration   16-1

Debt versus Equity

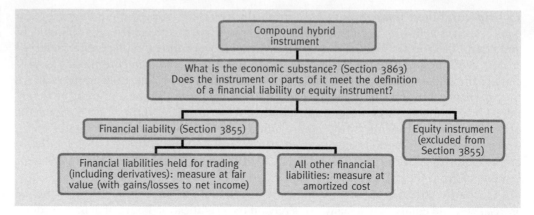

The **measurement** of compound/hybrid instruments is complicated by the fact that the economic value of these instruments can be attributed to **both** the debt and equity components (i.e., the instrument is neither 100% debt nor 100% equity, and instead is **part debt and part equity**). How should these two components be measured? We will review various types of instruments, noting first the nature of the instrument and then the accounting for it. The chapter will also present two measurement tools: the **incremental or residual method** and the **proportional method**. These tools may be used to allocate the value of an instrument between its debt and equity components.[6] Other measurement tools are presented in Appendix 16C.

Perpetual Debt

Underlying Concept

Perpetual debt is debt in legal form and, upon closer examination, is debt in its economic substance as well since it derives its value from the interest obligation.

Perpetual debt is debt that will never be repaid. Even though **legally, it is debt**, economically speaking, it is similar to equity because it represents permanent capital for the company. Should perpetual debt be presented as debt or equity? To determine this, we must take a closer look at how it derives its value. Traditional debt is valued by taking the present value of the principal and interest payments, discounted at market interest rates. Assume, for example, that Jiang Limited issues a $1,000, three-year bond that carries a coupon rate of 10%. If market rates are 10%, the value of the bond will be $1,000, calculated as in Illustration 16-2.

Illustration   16-2

Economic Value of a Three-Year Bond

Value of bond:		
PV annuity 3 years, 10%, $100	=	$ 249
PV $1,000, in 3 years, 10%	=	751
Aggregate fair market value		$1,000

Now assume that these bonds are 40-year bonds. Illustration 16-3 shows the calculation of the present value of the interest.

---

[6] Having stated this, note that Section 3855 prescribes that derivatives that are not accounted for as equity must always be valued at fair value. Derivatives will be covered in more detail in the following section.

Illustration 16-3

*Economic Value of a
40-Year Bond*

Value of bonds:		
PV annuity 40 years, 10%, $100	=	$ 978
PV $1,000, in 40 years, 10%	=	22
Aggregate fair market value		$1,000

Note that the value of the bond comes mainly from the interest and, as the life of the bond increases, the economic value that is attributed to the repayment of principal decreases significantly. Now assume that the bonds are perpetual bonds, which means that the principal of the bond will never be repaid. The value attributable to the present value of the principal will become smaller and smaller. **A perpetual bond's value is therefore driven solely by the contractual obligation to pay interest and, for this reason, despite the lack of obligation to repay the principal, it is a financial liability.**[7]

Callable/Redeemable Preferred Shares

Preferred shares have traditionally been treated as equity since they normally represent permanent financing. However, what if the shares have a fixed term and will be redeemed by the company at a set point in time? Although legally they are equity, these instruments, which are often called **term** or **mandatorily redeemable preferred shares**, meet the definition of a financial liability since there is an **obligation for the company to pay cash**. When the term expires, the company is obligated to buy back the shares from the holder. **These shares are therefore presented as liability on the balance sheet** and covered by Section 3855.

Sometimes, even though the shares do not have to be redeemed, the terms of the share agreement make redemption very likely. For instance, assume that Hope Inc. issued preferred shares that carry a dividend of 4%. According to the terms of the share agreement, the dividend rate will double in five years and again in 10 years. In this case, although the company is not contractually obligated to redeem the shares, the accelerating dividend will result in an unreasonably high cost of capital for the company, and Hope Inc. will therefore be compelled, from an economic point of view, to redeem them. In other words, **Hope has little or no discretion to avoid paying out cash and it could be argued that this obligation to deliver cash creates a financial liability.**[8] **Again, these shares would be presented as liabilities**.

If the holder has the right to require the issuer to redeem the shares for a fixed or determinable amount, the instruments are called retractable. Upon issuing retractable shares, the issuer creates a **contractual obligation to deliver cash—that meets the definition of a financial liability**. These instruments are recorded as liabilities and will be discussed further below.

What if a company issues preferred shares and there is a requirement to use its **best efforts** to repurchase a certain number of shares each year. Does this represent an obligation to the company? It really depends on the exact terms of the share agreement. If there is an **unavoidable** obligation to repurchase (i.e. mandatorily redeembable), then an obligation clearly exists. However, does "best efforts" represent an **unavoidable** obligation? Professional judgement must be applied in making this determination. If the company is required to use its best efforts to repurchase the shares **or** to continue to pay dividends,

---

[7] *CICA Handbook*, Section 3863.A3.

[8] *CICA Handbook*, Section 3863.14 and A4.

the instrument contains a liability element because either way, the company is obligated to pay cash.[9]

Redeemable shares are often used in tax and succession planning. Many small businesses are created and run by individuals who at some point decide that they would like to hand the company over to their children. One orderly way of doing this that minimizes taxes is through the use of redeemable preferred shares, sometimes referred to as **high/low preferred shares**. The business assets can be transferred to a new company, which makes it possible to take advantage of special tax provisions that minimize taxes, and the owner takes redeemable preferred shares as part of the consideration. The children then buy the common shares in the new company for a nominal amount, which allows them to benefit from subsequent increases in the company's value. This also gives them some or all of the voting control since the common shares would normally be voting shares.

The redemption amount of the preferred shares is set at the company's fair value at the time of the transaction. This means that the fair value is frozen for the individual at a point in time (which is why the label "estate freeze" is sometimes given to this type of transaction). All subsequent increases in value will go to the children through ownership of the common shares. The owner of the former company will eventually get his or her money out (which represents the fair value of the assets that he/she put in) of the new company at a future point by redeeming the preferred shares. This is a good example of yet another business reason to use complex financial instruments. Note that the redemption feature causes this instrument to be recorded as a (huge) liability since the company has an obligation to deliver cash upon redemption. Many small business owners are not happy with this accounting since it makes the company look highly leveraged when, in fact, the shares will normally not be redeemed in the short- or mid-term. Treating the shares as liabilities in the balance sheet may also cause the company to be offside on (i.e., to be failing to respect) pre-existing debt covenants. As a result of this, the CICA allows certain small businesses that qualify for differential reporting to treat these particular instruments as equity.[10]

Debt with Detachable Stock Warrants

Debt may be issued with a detachable warrant (an option to buy common shares of the company). The warrants give the holder the right to buy common shares at a fixed price (the **exercise** or **strike price**) for a specified period of time (the **exercise period**). Because the warrants are detachable or removable, there is often a market to buy and sell these instruments. **The warrants are equity instruments**[11] **and, therefore, the instrument is part debt and part equity. How much of the value of the instrument is due to the debt portion and how much is due to the warrant portion?**

The proceeds from the sale of debt with detachable stock warrants should be allocated between the two distinct and separable securities components that this instrument includes:[12]

---

[9] *CICA Handbook*, EIC Abstract 74 provides some guidance.

[10] *CICA Handbook*, Section 3863.36 and .37, and EIC Abstract 69.

[11] The definition of equity instruments may not appear to include options and warrants since they are only rights or obligations relating to a company's shares (not actual residual interests in the company); however, the appendix to *CICA Handbook* Section 3863.A2 specifically includes warrants and options as examples of equity instruments.

[12] *CICA Handbook*, Section 3863.16 and .18.

1. The note or financial liability portion

2. The warrant or equity instrument portion

There are various ways to measure these items and there is no prescribed way to measure the individual components. Two options are as follows:[13]

1. **Proportional method**: Determine the market values of similar straight debt (i.e., debt with no warrants) and tradable options or warrants. This is easier to do if there are existing markets for both these instruments as separate items. However, measurement of the debt portion can also be done by a PV calculation, discounting at the market rate for similar debt. Measurement of the option portion can be done using an options pricing model.[14] The components are then assigned these values. If the total is greater than or less than the instrument's issue price, the difference is pro-rated based on the respective market or fair values and is then allocated to each of the components.

2. **Incremental** or **residual method**: Value only one component (the one that is easier to value, which is often the debt component). The other component is valued at whatever is left.[15]

On August 22, 2002, **Orbital Sciences Corporation** issued four-year secured notes plus warrants. The debt was issued for net proceeds of $123.1 million (face value of $135 million). Each unit consisted of a $1,000 note plus a warrant to purchase up to 122.23 shares at $3.86 per share within four years. At the time of the agreement, the exercise price was 10% higher than the market value of the shares. The warrants were recorded based on their fair value of $28.8 million. Why did the warrants have value when the exercise price was actually greater than the fair value of the shares? This is because investors are willing to pay for the right to buy shares. **The value attributed to the warrant takes into account the possibility that the share price might increase in value over the exercise period.**

What Do the Numbers Mean?

In the case of Orbital, the warrants were valued at $28.8 million and, if the incremental method were used, the remaining value would therefore be attributed to the notes (after taking into account issue costs). A more complete example of these methods will be given later in this chapter using convertible debt as an illustration (see Illustrations 16-6 and 16-7).

Dealing with Uncertainty

Triggering Events

Certain preferred shares are redeemable or retractable if specific events occur. For example, preferred shares might become mandatorily redeemable if the company's shares are delisted from a stock exchange or perhaps if liquidity and solvency ratios fall to

---

[13] Although the *CICA Handbook* and Canadian GAAP do not mandate specific measurement techniques for bifurcation, Section 3863.21 and .22 and A7 to A9 refer to two possible ways to value the equity component: residual valuation (like the incremental method above) and option pricing valuation (like the proportional method above). The *CICA Handbook* presumes that the liability component may generally be valued with little measurement uncertainty by using discounting techniques and readily available information about interest (discount) rates.

[14] Calculation of this amount using an option pricing model is beyond the scope of this course and would generally be covered in a finance course. Appendix C provides a brief recap of option pricing models.

[15] These measurement techniques are not specific to convertible debt or compound instruments and may be used any time an element's total value needs to be allocated to its individual components. Recall from Chapter 6 the discussion about sales with multiple deliverables.

unacceptable levels. The "trigger" clause acts to protect the investors. When a clause like this exists, there is a risk that the company may have an obligation to redeem the shares and may therefore have a liability. In such cases, should the instrument be presented as a liability? On the one hand, it can be argued that as long as the triggering event has not occurred, the instrument should be classified as equity. Preferred shares by their nature are considered permanent capital. On the other hand, the triggering event may cause the company to have to pay out cash, which meets the definition of a financial liability. To decide the issue, contingency accounting comes into play.

Thus, if the triggering event is **probable or likely** when the instrument is first recognized, it makes sense to recognize the liability.[16] **Subsequently, the classification as either debt or equity remains the same until the triggering event occurs or fails to occur.**[17] At that point, a new assessment is made about whether the instrument represents a financial liability or equity.

Some financial instruments that are common shares or in-substance common shares require redemption in situations that are certain to occur—such as the death of the holder.[18] As in the discussion above, these instruments would not impose any obligation before the triggering event. Unlike the situation above, however, there is little uncertainty in this case. Are these instruments therefore equity-like since they represent residual interest in the company? Or are they debt-like since they impose an obligation? The instruments are generally treated as liabilities unless all of the following criteria are met:[19]

1. The instruments must be the **most subordinated** of all equity securities. In other words, they must be residual equity interests like common shares and therefore rank last in terms of priority for dividend payouts and asset distribution upon windup.

2. The **redemption feature must apply to all common shares** and in-substance common shares (thus proving that the shares are really a residual interest and do not have priority over any other shares).

3. The shares **must not have any preferential rights** (for instance, rights that cause them to rank more highly than common shares).

4. The **redemption event must be the same** for all the shares that the redemption feature applies to.

If all of these criteria are met, then **the instruments may be treated as equity**. In short, they are more equity-like because **they reflect a residual interest** in the company.

Settlement Options

Debt repayable in shares at the option of the issuer   Some debt instruments allow the issuing company to **repay the debt with either cash or shares**. These instruments have the **legal form of debt**; however, because there is no obligation to repay the principal in cash, they are not necessarily liabilities. On closer inspection, however, the obligation to pay interest does create a liability and so this instrument is a hybrid/combined instrument. **The interest portion is debt and the principal portion is equity**. How much should be allocated to each part? Once again, this is a **measurement issue** and the measurement technique or tool that was mentioned earlier (the incremental method) may

---

[16] *CICA Handbook*, Section 3863.14 and EIC Abstract 70.

[17] *CICA Handbook*, EIC Abstract 70.

[18] *CICA Handbook*, Section 3863.15.

[19] *CICA Handbook*, EIC Abstract 149. These instruments were discussed in Chapter 15 from the perspective of equity.

be used to allocate the carrying value between its debt and equity components when the debt is initially recognized. The present value of the interest payments is easily calculated by discounting the cash payments using the market rate of interest. The rest of the value may be attributed to the equity portion (and credited to shareholders' equity).

A further complexity may arise, depending on whether the settlement terms are specified in terms of a **dollar amount** or the **number of shares**. If the debt may be settled with a **fixed number** of shares, part of the instrument would be considered equity since the value of the settlement will vary depending on the value of the shares—it gives the holder some participation in the equity of the company. As noted above, the other part might be considered to be a liability if an obligation exists to pay interest. If, on the other hand, the contractual obligation represents a **fixed dollar amount** and may be settled using cash or a **variable number** of shares, this is still an obligation. The company owes the fixed amount and will distribute this fixed value only—whether it does this in cash or a variable number of shares. **The entire instrument would then be recognized as debt.**[20]

Retractable preferred shares   Some preferred shares have a retraction feature. **Retractable preferred shares** give the option to the holder of the instrument to force the company to redeem the instrument. Why would a company issue this type of share? There are at least two reasons:

1. The option gives more flexibility to the holder, so the company may be able to pay a lower dividend.

2. Alternatively, these shares might allow the company to gain access to a pool of capital that would not otherwise be available—i.e., to investors who are not willing to invest in straight debt or straight equity but would be willing to invest in this more flexible security.

When Great-West Lifeco merged with Canada Life, the company offered existing shareholders a choice for each Canada Life share that they held, and one of the choices included a retraction feature. Illustration 16-4 shows part of the news release that detailed these options.

Illustration 16-4

Example of Retraction Options

NEWS RELEASE

Great-West Lifeco and Canada Life Announce Results of Elections by Canada Life Shareholders

WINNIPEG AND TORONTO, July 7, 2003—Great-West Lifeco Inc. and Canada Life Financial Corporation today announced the proration calculations with respect to the elections made by holders of Canada Life common shares for consideration payable in connection with the combination transaction between Canada Life and Great-West Lifeco.

Under the terms of the transaction, Canada Life shareholders could elect to receive, in respect of each Canada Life share they held:
- $44.50 in cash (maximum cash to be paid limited to approximately $4.4 billion);
- 1.1849 common shares of Great-West Lifeco (maximum number of shares to be issued limited to approximately 56.0 million);
- 1.78 Great-West Lifeco Series E 4.80% non-cumulative 10-year soft retractable preferred shares (maximum number of shares to be issued limited to 24.0 million);
- 1.78 Great-West Lifeco Series F 5.90% non-cumulative perpetual preferred shares (maximum number of shares to be issued limited to 8.0 million); or
- a combination of these alternatives, subject to proration and maximum amounts noted

---

[20] *CICA Handbook*, Section 3863.11/.12 and EIC Abstract 164.

Notice that a shareholder could either take 1.78 Series E shares or 1.78 Series F shares. The Series E shares carry a lower dividend rate of 4.8 percent, which is presumably offset by the benefit of the retraction feature. How does a retraction feature affect the accounting? **Since the potential redemption is beyond the company's control, the company may have little or no possibility of choosing to avoid payment if the holder exercises the option for repayment. It has a contractual obligation to deliver cash.**[21] **As a result, this represents a financial liability.** Unlike the situation noted earlier, where there is a triggering event (and the company must assess how likely it is that the triggering event will occur), in the case of retractable instruments, the company would have no way of assessing how likely it is that the holders will exercise the retraction feature. Nonetheless, there is still a contractual obligation to deliver cash.

Illustration 16-5 shows an excerpt from a press release issued by **Brookfield Properties**. The company repurchased some of its own common shares and financed the repurchase by issuing new retractable preferred shares.

Illustration 16-5

Example of Retractable Preferred Shares

NEWS RELEASE

Brookfield Properties Announces Purchase of Additional Shares of BPO Properties

New York, April 25, 2003—Brookfield Properties Corporation (BPO: NYSE, TSX) announced today that it has acquired an additional 574,900 voting common shares of BPO Properties Ltd. (BPP: TSX) in a private transaction at a cost of C$27.00 per BPO Properties share. The transaction increased Brookfield's equity interest in BPO Properties from 87% to 92%.

A wholly-owned subsidiary of Brookfield acquired the additional shares by issuing C$15.5 million of retractable preferred shares. The preferred shares are retractable until April 25, 2005 for either cash or, at the option of the holder, 474,466 common shares of Brookfield and 94,893 common shares of Brookfield Homes Corporation, subject to certain adjustments.

The preferred shares would be treated as debt to the company since the option to "put" or present the shares to the company for "repayment" stays with the holder. Even though the shares may be "repaid" in either cash or shares, the option still stays with the holder, which means that the company may have little or no discretion to avoid paying out cash.

Objective 2

Explain the accounting for the issuance, conversion, and retirement of convertible securities.

Convertible debt   If bonds can be converted into other corporate securities during some specified period of time after their issuance, they are called **convertible bonds**. A convertible bond combines the benefits of a bond with the privilege of exchanging it for common shares **at the holder's option**. It is purchased by investors who want the security of a bond holding—guaranteed interest—plus the added option of conversion if the value of the common shares increases significantly.

Corporations issue convertible debt for two main reasons. One is the desire to raise equity capital without giving up more ownership control than necessary. To illustrate, assume that a company wants to raise $1 million at a time when its common shares are selling at $45 per share. Such an issue would require selling 22,222 shares (ignoring issue costs). By selling 1,000 bonds at $1,000 par, and with each bond being convertible into 20 common shares, the enterprise may raise $1 million by committing only 20,000 common shares.[22] Investors may be willing to take the bonds since they give the investors greater security (especially if the bonds are secured by company assets) yet allow them to participate in the company growth through the option to convert the bonds to common shares.

---

[21] *CICA Handbook*, Section 3863.14.

[22] In fact, the bonds would sell at a premium due to the embedded stock option.

A second, more common reason that companies have for issuing convertible securities is to obtain debt financing at cheaper rates. Many enterprises would have to issue debt at higher interest rates unless a convertible feature were attached. The conversion privilege entices the investor to accept a lower interest rate than would normally be the case on a straight debt issue. For example, Amazon.com at one time issued convertible bonds that paid interest at an effective yield of 4.75%, which was much lower than Amazon.com would have had to pay if it had issued straight debt. For this lower interest rate, the investor received the right to buy Amazon.com's common shares at a fixed price until the bonds' maturity.

There are reporting issues in the accounting for convertible debt at all of the following times:

1. Issuance

2. Conversion

3. Retirement

Convertible debt at time of issuance   As previously mentioned, the conversion feature on a convertible bond makes the instrument more valuable to an investor, and, therefore, the option feature itself has value. **The obligation to deliver cash under the bond represents a financial liability and the right to acquire the company's common shares represents an equity instrument.** Compound instruments must be split into their components and presented separately in the financial statements. Since the embedded option to convert to common shares is an equity instrument, that part of the instrument is presented as equity. The remaining component is presented as a liability.[23]

For example, assume that Bond Corp. offers three-year, 6% convertible bonds (par $1,000). Each $1,000 bond may be converted into 250 common shares, which are currently trading at $3 per share. Similar straight bonds carry an interest rate of 9%. One thousand bonds are issued.

Allocating the proceeds to the liability and equity components under the incremental or residual method involves valuing one component first (the bond) and then allocating the rest of the value to the other component (the equity component). The bond may be measured at the PV of the stream of interest payments ($1 million × 6% for three years) plus the PV of the bond itself ($1 million) all discounted at 9%, which is the market rate of interest. The remainder of the proceeds is then allocated to the option. This allocation is shown in Illustration 16-6.

Total proceeds at par	$1,000,000
Less:	
Value of bonds (PV annuity 3 years, 9%, $60,000 + PV $1,000,000, in 3 years, 9%)	(924,061)
Incremental value of option	$ 75,939

Illustration 16-6

Incremental Allocation of Proceeds between Liability and Equity Components

To place a value on the two securities using the proportional method, one would determine (1) the value of the bonds (as in the prior method) and (2) the value of the options, perhaps using an option pricing model such as the Black-Scholes model.[24]

---

[23] *CICA Handbook*, Section 3863.16.

[24] The Black Scholes option pricing model is a widely used measurement model that is used to value share options of companies whose shares are publicly traded. It will be discussed in Appendix 16C. Other measurement models such as binomial tree models may be used.

Illustration 16-7 shows the allocation between the bonds and options using the proportional method.

Illustration 16-7	Value of bonds (PV annuity 3 years, 9%, 60,000 + PV $1,000,000, in 3 years, 9%)	=	$924,061	92.7%
Proportional Allocation of Proceeds between Liability and Equity Components	Fair value of option using an option pricing model	=	72,341*	7.3%
	Aggregate fair market value		$996,402	100.0%

*estimated value (beyond scope of text)

The difference between the proceeds and the calculated fair value is then allocated back to the components based on their respective percentage values. The liability component would be valued at $927,000 ($1 million × 92.7%), and the equity component would be valued at $73,000 ($1 million × 7.3%).

The journal entry to record the issuance using the proportional method would be as follows:

A = L + SE
+1,000,000   +927,000   +73,000

Cash flows: ↑ 1,000,000 inflow

Cash	1,000,000	
Bonds Payable		927,000
Contributed Surplus—Conversion Rights		73,000

Underlying Concept

Note that the convertible debt is treated the same as the debt with detachable warrants. This is because the economic substance of the instruments is the same: they both have debt and give the holder the option to hold shares.

A = L + SE
      −985,942   +985,942

Cash flows: No effect

Convertible debt at time of conversion   If bonds are converted into other securities, the main accounting problem is to determine the amount at which to record the securities that have been exchanged for the bond. Assume that holders of the convertible debt of Bond Corp. decide to convert their convertible bonds before the bonds mature. The bond discount will be partially amortized at this point. Assume that the unamortized portion is $14,058. The entry to record the conversion would be as follows:

Bonds Payable	985,942	
Contributed Surplus—Conversion Rights	73,000	
Common Shares		1,058,942

This method, referred to as the book value method of recording the bond conversion, is the method that is most commonly used in practice.[25] Support for the book value approach is based on the argument that an agreement was established at the date that the bond was issued either to pay a stated amount of cash at maturity or to issue a stated number of shares of equity securities. Therefore, when the debt is converted to equity in accordance with the pre-existing contract terms, no gain or loss would be recognized upon conversion.[26] Any accrued interest that was forfeited would be treated as part of the new book value of the shares (and credited to Common Shares).[27]

[25] *CICA Handbook*, EIC Abstract 164 contemplates the use of the book value approach.

[26] An alternative approach that has some conceptual merit uses the market value to record the conversion. Under this method, the common shares would be recorded at market value (their market value or the market value of the bonds), the contributed surplus, bonds payable, and discount amounts would be zeroed out, and a gain/credit or loss/debit would result. Since the CBCA requires shares to be recorded at their cash equivalent value, legal requirements would tend to support this approach. The interesting question is whether the resulting gain/credit or loss/debit would be treated as an operating or capital transaction. If it were seen as arising from debt extinguishment, it would be an operating item (gain or loss) and recognized through the income statement. If it were seen as part of the process of issuing shares, it should be booked through equity. Alternatively, it could be prorated as are premiums that are associated with induced conversions.

[27] *CICA Handbook*, EIC Abstract 58.

Induced early conversions Sometimes the issuer wants to induce (cause) a prompt conversion of its convertible debt-to-equity securities in order to reduce interest costs or to improve its debt-to-equity ratio. As a result, the issuer may offer some form of additional consideration—known commonly as a sweetener—such as cash. This situation is referred to as an **induced conversion**. The additional premium should be allocated between the debt and equity components based on their fair values at the time of the transaction. The approach that is used should be consistent with the method that was used when the debt was originally recorded (i.e., the incremental method or the proportional method).[28]

Assume that Bond Corp. wants to reduce interest costs at some point during the life of the debt. It therefore offers an additional cash premium of $15,000 to the bondholders to convert, and at a time when the carrying amount of the debt was $972,476. Assume further that the **incremental or residual method** was used to allocate the issue price originally between debt and equity components, with the debt being measured at its discounted cash flows and the equity being valued as the residual amount. The bond's fair value at the conversion time is $981,462 (ignoring the conversion feature) due to lower market interest rates. The first step in the allocation of the premium is to determine the difference between the fair value and carrying value of the bonds:

$$\$981{,}462 - \$972{,}476 = \$8{,}986$$

Then the residual method would be used to allocate the premium between the debt and equity components (since this method was originally used):[29]

$$\$15{,}000 - \$8{,}986 = \$6{,}014$$

Thus, $8,986 would be treated as a debt retirement cost and $6,014 as a capital transaction similar to a redemption cost. The journal entry would be as follows:

Bonds Payable	972,476	
Expense—Debt Retirement Cost	8,986 (above)	
Contributed Surplus—Conversion Rights	75,939 (previously calculated)	
Retained Earnings	6,014 (above)	
Common Shares		1,048,415
Cash		15,000

A	=	L	+	SE
−15,000		−972,476		+957,476

Cash flows: ↓ 15,000 outflow

The shares are now valued at the total carrying value of the bonds, plus the option, as follows:

$$\$972{,}476 + 75{,}939 = \$1{,}048{,}415$$

Retirement of convertible debt The normal retirement of the liability component of convertible debt at maturity (its repayment) is treated the same way as non-convertible bonds, as explained in Chapter 14. The equity component remains in Contributed

---

[28] *CICA Handbook*, EIC Abstract 96.

[29] Note that if the proportional method were used to record the instrument when it was first recognized, it would make sense to use this method to allocate the premium. The value of the debt would be calculated (PV of cash flows) and the fair value of the option (using an option pricing model). This information would be used to determine the relative proportions that are attributable to the components.

Surplus. What happens, however, if the instrument is retired early and the company pays off the debt with cash? Assume that Bond Corp. decides to retire the convertible debt early and offers the bondholders $1,070,000 cash, which is the fair value of the instrument at the time of early retirement. The following journal entry would be booked:

$$
\begin{array}{lrl}
A & = & L & + & SE \\
-1,070,000 & & -972,476 & & -97,524
\end{array}
$$

Cash flows: ↓ 1,070,000 outflow

Bonds Payable	972,476	
Expense—Debt Retirement Cost	8,986	
Contributed Surplus—Conversion Rights	75,939	
Retained Earnings	12,599	
Cash		1,070,000

The amounts related to the instrument (including the bonds payable, any remaining discount, and the contributed surplus) are zeroed out and the loss is allocated between the debt portion and the equity portion. The portion allocated to the debt is the same as the amount in the previous example (i.e., the difference between the debt's carrying value and its fair value). If the residual method is used, the rest is allocated to the equity portion. Note that the fair value of $1,070,000 includes the fair value of the bond and the embedded option. The option is also removed from the books as it is seen as settled.

Convertible preferred shares   When convertible preferred shares are converted, Preferred Shares, along with any related amount in Contributed Surplus, is debited; Common Shares is credited.

Assume that Host Enterprises issued 1,000 shares of common upon conversion of 1,000 shares of preferred that was originally issued for a $200 premium. The entry would be:

$$
\begin{array}{lll}
A & = & L & + & SE \\
& & & & 0
\end{array}
$$

Cash flows: No effect

Preferred Shares	1,000	
Contributed Surplus—Conversion Rights	200	
Common Shares		1,200

If part of the original issue price of the preferred shares had been credited to the other Shareholders' Equity accounts, such as Contributed Surplus, then these accounts would be debited in the entry to record the conversion. Again, this follows the book value approach, which is acceptable as long as there are no legal requirements to record the common shares at fair value.

Settlement Amounts

Some debentures may be settled with assets other than cash, such as shares of another company. These instruments are known as **exchangeable debentures**. These instruments meet the definition of a liability since the definition includes an obligation to pay cash **or other assets**. The issue in this case is one of **measurement**. Since the value of the other assets may change with time, should the debt be continually remeasured?

Assume that Mantle Limited issued debentures that are exchangeable for shares of Gibraltar Inc., which Mantle is holding in its short-term investments as held for trading. **The economic value of the instrument changes as the value of the underlying shares changes and, therefore, the instrument (or part of it) must be remeasured continually.**[30] Note that the fact that Mantle owns the shares of Gibraltar does not change

---

[30] The option to exchange would be treated as a derivative and therefore measured at fair value with gains and losses booked to net income.

the fact that the carrying value of the debt must reflect the changing value of the Gibraltar shares. Owning shares provides economic protection against changes in the value of the liability. [31]

Interest, Dividends, Gains, and Losses

Once the determination is made to classify something in the balance sheet as debt, equity, or part debt and part equity, the related interest, dividends, gains, and losses must be consistently treated. **For instance, a term preferred share would be presented as a liability and, therefore, related dividends would be booked as interest or dividend expense and charged to the income statement (not to Retained Earnings).**[32]

If mandatorily redeemable or term preferred shares are issued at a discount or premium, the discount or premium is treated the same as if debt had been issued at a discount or premium. The liability is initially recognized at the net proceeds and the discount or premium is amortized to interest expense.[33]

Underlying Concept

Dividends would normally be debited to Retained Earnings; however, because the economic substance of a term preferred share is debt, dividends on term preferred shares are treated as interest or dividend expense.

BASIC DERIVATIVES

If you recall from previous chapters, **financial instruments** are contracts that create both a financial asset for one party and a financial liability or equity instrument for the other party.[34] Financial instruments can be primary or derivative. **Primary financial instruments** include most basic financial assets and financial liabilities, such as receivables and payables, as well as equity instruments, such as shares. The accounting issues for these instruments were covered in earlier chapters. **Derivative instruments**, on the other hand, are more complex. They derive (i.e., get) their value from an underlying primary instrument, index or non-financial item, such as a commodity (called the "underlying"), which is why they are called derivatives. Derivatives are defined as **financial instruments that create rights and obligations that have the effect of transferring, between parties to the instrument, one or more of the financial risks that are inherent in an underlying primary instrument. They transfer risks that are inherent in the underlying primary instrument without either party having to hold any investment in the underlying.**[35] They have three characteristics:

Objective 3
Understand what derivatives are and why they exist.

1. Their value changes in response to the **underlying instrument (the "underlying")**.

2. They require **little or no initial investment**.

3. They are settled at a **future** date.

Options, forwards, and futures are common types of derivatives. Accounting for these common types of derivative instruments will be discussed further in this chapter, along with examples. However, as a basic rule, derivatives are measured at fair value with gains and losses booked through net income. The notion of an **underlying** will be discussed in the context of these examples.

Sometimes the derivatives might be embedded in a compound financial instrument such that the instrument contains a host contract and the embedded derivative. Convertible

---

[31] Under *CICA Handbook* Section 3855, the shares would be revalued to market, and the gains and losses of both the debt and the investments would thus offset.

[32] *CICA Handbook*, Section 3863.23.

[33] *CICA Handbook*, EIC Abstract 69. For bookkeeping purposes, we may keep the discount/premium in a separate general ledger account.

[34] *CICA Handbook*, Section 3855.19.

[35] *CICA Handbook*, Section 3855.19.

debentures are one example of a combined financial instrument containing both a non-derivative host (the debt instrument) and an embedded derivative feature (which offers the option to convert to an equity instrument). **Embedded derivatives** that have economic characteristics that are not **closely related** to the host contract (i.e. are different or unrelated) should be separated out and accounted for as derivatives (i.e. measured at fair value with gain/losses to net income). In the convertible debenture example, the host is not considered to be closely related to the option since the host is debt-like and the option is equity-like. Another example might be a guaranteed investment certificate that pays the increase in value of a stock index instead of interest.

Understanding Derivatives: Managing Risks

Why do derivatives exist? In short, **they exist to help companies manage risks**. Companies currently operate in an environment of constant flux caused by volatile markets, new technology, and deregulation, among other things. This increases overall business risk as well as financial risk. The response from the financial community has been to develop products to manage some of these risks, with one result being the rise of derivatives. Recall from Appendix 5A the differing types of risks that a company faces. Managers of successful companies have always and will continue to manage risks to minimize unfavourable financial consequences and to maximize shareholder value. While managing risk helps keep uncertainty at an acceptable level (which may differ depending on the stakeholders), it also has its costs.

There are many layers of costs relating to the use of derivatives. Three categories of costs are as follows:

1. Direct costs

2. Indirect costs

3. Hidden or opportunity costs

Underlying Concept

As always, the benefits of entering into certain transactions, especially complex ones, must exceed the costs; otherwise, the company will be reducing shareholder value rather than creating it.

In order to enter into contracts such as insurance and derivative contracts, transaction costs are normally incurred, such as bank service charges, brokerage fees, and insurance premiums. These are the **direct**, visible costs that are charged by an intermediary or the other party to the transaction. Then there are **indirect**, less visible costs. The activity of researching, analyzing, and executing these transactions uses a significant amount of employee time. As managing risk sometimes results in limiting the potential for gain, there is also a **hidden cost**: the **opportunity cost. Use of too many complicated financial instruments increases the complexity of financial statements and therefore reduces their transparency and understandability.** Given the current climate, capital markets may penalize such companies with higher costs of capital and/or limit or deny access to capital. This latter aspect also represents a **hidden cost** to the company. Companies must consider all of the costs that are associated with derivatives and weigh them against the benefits.

The growth in use of derivatives has been aided by the development of powerful calculation and communication technology, which provides new ways to analyze information about markets as well as the power to process high volumes of payments. Thanks to these developments, many corporations are now using derivatives extensively and successfully.

What Do the Numbers Mean?

As shown in the graph that follows, the use of derivatives has grown steadily in recent years. Over U.S. $200 trillion in derivative contracts (notional amounts) were in play at the end of 2004. The chief players in the market for derivatives—large companies and various financial institutions—continue to find new uses for derivatives.

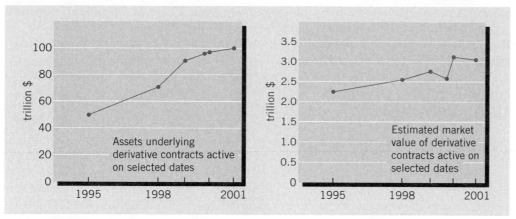

Source: Adapted from Daniel Altman, "Contracts So Complex They Imperil the System," *New York Times on the Web* (February 24, 2002).

However, as financial engineers develop new uses for derivatives—often by using increasingly complex webs of transactions that cover several markets—the financial system as a whole can be dramatically affected.

Financial Risks Defined

As mentioned above, companies use derivatives to manage risks, and especially financial risks. There are various kinds of financial risks, and they are defined in Section 3862 as follows:[36]

(a) **credit risk** The risk that one party to a financial instrument will cause a financial loss for the other party by failing to discharge (respect) an obligation.

(b) **liquidity risk** The risk that an entity will have difficulty meeting obligations that are associated with financial liabilities.

(c) **market risk** The risk that the fair value or future cash flows of a financial instrument will fluctuate because of changes in market prices. There are three types of market risk: **currency risk**, **interest rate risk**, and **other price risk**.

 (i) **currency risk** The risk that the fair value or future cash flows of a financial instrument will fluctuate because of changes in foreign exchange rates.

 (ii) **interest rate risk** The risk that the fair value or future cash flows of a financial instrument will fluctuate because of changes in market interest rates.

 (iii) **other price risk** The risk that the fair value or future cash flows of a financial instrument will fluctuate because of changes in market prices (other than price changes arising from **interest rate risk** or **currency risk**), whether those changes are caused by factors that are specific to the individual financial instrument or its issuer, or factors that affect all similar financial instruments being traded in the market.

Interest rate risk, other price risks, and currency risks are subsets of market risk. Therefore, there are only three main types of risks—credit, liquidity, and markets. It is important for companies and users of financial statements to identify and understand which risks a company currently has and how it plans to manage these risks. Keep in mind that derivatives often expose the company to additional risks. As long as the company

4 Objective
Explain the various types of financial risks, and how they arise.

---

[36] *CICA Handbook*, Section 3862.05A.

identifies and manages these risks, this is not a problem. **There is a problem, however, when stakeholders do not understand the risk profile of derivative instruments.** The use of derivatives can be dangerous, and it is critical that all the parties that are involved understand the risks and rewards associated with these contracts.[37]

Using Derivatives

Underlying Concept

Remember from finance courses that increased risk may bring the opportunity for increased rewards. Thus, some companies expose themselves to increased risks in order to maximize shareholder value.

An entity might use derivatives to reduce or offset various risks (normally referred to as **hedging**). It is also possible to enter into derivative contracts to create positions that are expected to be profitable.[38] Both are acceptable strategies and depend on the company's risk tolerance profile—i.e., the nature of the risks that the company can comfortably undertake and the amount of exposure to each risk that it is willing to accept. There are special optional accounting rules that a company can make use of when a derivative is used to hedge certain risk. Although hedging will be discussed in the body of the chapter, **hedge accounting** will be discussed in Appendix 16A due to its added complexity.

What types of business models and processes generate financial risk? Virtually all business models generate financial risks. The following are some examples:

- Any business that purchases commodities such as fuel, agricultural products, or renewable resources as inputs has a **market risk** associated with these inputs. These companies know that commodity prices vary significantly depending on supply and demand. This affects the company's profitability and may lead to volatile net income. Often, the commodities are priced in different currencies, which creates a **currency risk**.

- Likewise, any company that sells commodities has a **market risk**. Depending on the commodity pricing when the commodity is sold, the company might make more or less profit, which again can lead to volatile or unpredictable net income.[39]

- Companies that sell on credit have **credit risks**: the risk that the customer or other party (counterparty) may fail to make a payment.

- Companies that borrow money or incur liabilities increase **liquidity risk**: the risk that they will not be able to pay their obligations. Debt also creates **interest rate risk**.

- Companies that buy goods, finance purchases, create inventory, sell goods, and collect receivables have **market risks**: the risk that the value of the assets will change while the company is holding them.

Remember that derivative transactions may be an efficient way of managing these risks. Note that a company may rely on other tools to manage the risks, including internal controls (such as credit checks on customers to reduce or eliminate credit risk). Alternatively, a company may try to eliminate the risk in the first place; that is, by having a

---

[37] There are some well-publicized examples of companies that have suffered sizeable losses as a result of using derivatives, perhaps because they did not fully understand the possible effects of the contracts. For example, companies such as Showa Shell Sekiyu (Japan), Metallgesellschaft (Germany), Proctor & Gamble (United States), and Air Products & Chemicals (United States) have incurred significant losses from investments in derivative instruments. Companies sometimes suffer losses because of taking too much risk or because they do not understand the markets/positions taken. Another reason that a company may suffer losses when using derivatives is because of the timing of closing out the contracts/positions.

[38] When companies create positions that are expected to be profitable, there is often a risk of loss as well. Some refer to this as **speculating**.

[39] All business inputs have price risks associated with them. There is always a risk that prices to acquire the inputs will vary over time.

policy of selling only for cash (to eliminate credit risk) or perhaps using "just in time" inventory ordering (to reduce market risk). Derivatives are just one tool in managing risk.

Producers and Consumers as Derivative Users

McCain Foods Limited is a large producer of potatoes for the consumer market. Assume that McCain believes that the present price for potatoes is excellent, but that McCain will need two months to harvest its potatoes and deliver them to market. The company has **market risk** related to its inventory. Because the company is concerned that the price of potatoes will drop, it signs a contract in which it agrees to sell its potatoes today at the current market price, but for delivery in two months. This locks in the market price. Known as a forward contract, this type of contract reduces the **market risk** related to the potatoes (both in terms of price and cash flows).

Who would buy this contract? Suppose **McDonald's Corporation** is on the other side of the contract and it wants to have potatoes (for french fries) in two months and is worried that prices will increase.[40] McDonald's also has **market risk**. It therefore agrees to delivery in two months at the current fixed price because it knows that it will need potatoes in two months and that it can make an acceptable profit at the current price level. McDonald's is also managing its **market risk**.

In this situation, if the price of potatoes increases before delivery, you might conclude that McCain loses and McDonald's wins. Conversely, if prices decrease, McCain wins and McDonald's loses. However, the objective is not to gamble on the outcome. In other words, regardless of which way the price moves, both companies should be pleased because both have received a price at which they can make an acceptable profit. In summary:

- Both companies have existing risks because of the way they do business (their business model).

- Both seek to manage these risks.

- Both are using derivatives to reduce these risks.

- Both companies are seen to be hedging their risks because they are reducing uncertainty.

Commodity prices are volatile and depend on factors such as weather, crop disasters, and general economic conditions. For the producer of a product and its consumer to plan effectively, it makes good sense to lock in specific future revenues or input costs in order to run their businesses successfully. This is a key way to manage cash flows to limit the risk of going bankrupt.

Speculators and Arbitrageurs as Derivative Users

In some cases, instead of a company like McDonald's buying the contract, a **speculator** may purchase the contract from McCain. The speculator is not trying to reduce risk, however. Instead the objective is to maximize potential returns by being exposed to greater risks. The speculator is betting that the price of potatoes will increase and that the value of the forward contract will therefore also increase. The speculator, who may be in the market for only a few hours, will then sell the forward contract to another speculator or to a company like McDonald's. The speculator will never take delivery of the potatoes as this was never the intention. The goal was to generate a cash profit from trading in the derivative instrument itself. The difference between this transaction and the earlier hedging transaction is that in the earlier transaction the company was entering into a derivative to

---

[40] Why would one party think that prices will rise and the other that they will fall? The same information is rarely available to all parties. In most contract negotiations, therefore, there is information asymmetry, which leads to the parties expecting different outcomes.

reduce a pre-existing risk. In the case of the speculator, there is no pre-existing risk, just a desire to take on additional risk in the hope of increasing profits.

Another user of derivatives is an **arbitrageur**. These market players try to take advantage of inefficiencies in different markets. They try to lock in profits by simultaneously entering into transactions in two or more markets. For example, an arbitrageur might trade in a futures contract and at the same time in the commodity that underlies the futures contract, hoping to achieve small price gains on the difference between the two. Arbitrageurs exist because there is information asymmetry in different markets. This occurs when the same information is not available to all market participants in the different markets. Some markets are more efficient than others. The arbitrageurs force the prices in the different markets to move toward each other since they create demand and supply where previously there might not have been any, thus driving the prices either up or down.

Speculators and arbitrageurs are very important to markets because they keep the market liquid on a daily basis.

Non-financial Derivatives and Executory Contracts

Note that derivatives may be financial or non-financial. An example of a financial derivative might be a forward contract to buy U.S. dollars. An example of a non-financial derivative might be a futures contract to buy pork bellies. Even though Section 3855 deals with financial instruments (including financial derivatives), it also deals with certain non-financial derivatives that may be settled net in cash.[41] Thus commodities futures would be included under Section 3855.

It is not as simple as this, however. Many companies enter into contracts intending to take delivery of raw material as part of locking in supply. These contracts may be nothing more than purchase commitments. They are **executory contracts – contracts to do something in the future** (where no cash or product changes hands up front). Traditionally these contracts have not been recognized in the financial statements. The intent of Section 3855 was not to pick up these types of contracts. Unfortunately these types of contracts meet the definition of derivatives—their value changes with the value of the underlying (in this case the raw material); there is no investment up front and the contract will be settled in future.

Generally, as long as the company documents that a contract is for expected use, and it doesn't have a practice of "cash settling" similar contracts, it will not be accounted for as a derivative.[42]

Recognition, Measurement, and Presentation Issues

In Canada, up until 2003, there were no recognition and measurement principles for derivatives. As a result, many derivatives were not recognized in the financial statements. In March 2003, however, the CICA issued three Exposure Drafts on financial instruments, comprehensive income, and hedging. These Exposure Drafts became the new *CICA Handbook* Sections 3855, 1530, and 3865, respectively, with some modifications. The basic principles that were established in these proposed standards are as follows:

---

[41] If an instrument can be settled net in cash, it means that the option exists to take cash instead of delivery of the underlying product itself.

[42] The term "cash settling" refers to the practice of paying cash at the end of the contract as opposed to taking delivery or taking delivery and immediately selling the item for short-term profit taking purposes. The rules for non-financial derivatives are most complicated when the underlying material is fungible; i.e., readily convertible to cash.

(a) Financial instruments (including financial derivatives) and non-financial derivatives represent rights or obligations that meet the definitions of assets or liabilities and should be reported in financial statements.

(b) Fair value is the most relevant measure for financial instruments and is the only relevant measure for derivative financial instruments.

(c) Only items that are assets or liabilities should be reported as being these in financial statements.

(d) Special accounting for items that have been designated as being part of a hedging relationship should only be provided for qualifying items.[43]

Fair value is defined as the amount of consideration that would be agreed upon in an arm's-length transaction between knowledgeable, willing parties who are under no obligation to act.[44] Market prices are considered to provide the best evidence of fair value. Alternatively, valuation techniques may be used. Market values for many derivatives are readily available. However, derivatives on illiquid or unusual underlyings are often difficult to measure. Canadian accounting standards require that best efforts be used to estimate fair values except for some derivatives on equity securities when the equity cannot be reliably measured.[45]

We will now discuss three basic types of derivatives: options, forwards, and futures.

Options and Warrants

As discussed earlier in connection with convertible debt and debt with detachable warrants, **an option gives the holder the right to acquire or sell an underlying instrument at a fixed price (the exercise or strike price) within a defined term (the exercise period)**. For instance, a stock option to purchase shares of Four Seasons Hotels Inc. for a fixed price, on a specified date is a derivative instrument. The **underlying** is the shares; **i.e., this option derives its value from the share price of the underlying Four Seasons' shares**. If the share price goes up, the option is worth more. If it goes down, the option may become worthless.

The option allows the holder to protect himself against declines in the market value of the underlying shares but also allows the holder to participate in increases in the share value without having to hold the actual shares. Derivative instruments do not result in the transfer of the underlying (i.e., the shares in our example) at the contract's inception and perhaps not even when it matures. They also require a relatively low upfront investment (the cost of the option premium). The cost of the option is a fraction of the cost of the actual share itself. Before the end of the option period, the holder may sell the option to capture the value. The holder has the **right to exercise the option but is not obliged** to buy the shares at the exercise price. A recent example of the use of options in the capital marketplace is noted below.

On March 5, 2007, **Four Seasons Hotels Inc.** (Four Seasons) issued a Notice of Special Meeting and Management Information Circular about the privatization of the company. The privatization was to be effected by three large shareholders buying the shares that were held by the rest of the shareholders. The company would then be owned by these three large shareholders and taken private.

5 Objective
Understand what options, forwards, and futures are.

What Do the Numbers Mean?

---

[43] *CICA Handbook*, Section 3855.02.

[44] *CICA Handbook*, Section 3855.19(j).

[45] Embedded derivatives are beyond the scope of this text.

The company was started as a private company several decades ago by Isadore Sharp, who continued to retain control of the company after it went public. Four Seasons manages 74 luxury hotels and resorts in 31 countries and has several properties under development. The company has two main classifications of common shares: multiple voting shares, which are owned by the Sharp family through a company called Triples Holdings (Triples) and represent a controlling interest in the company, and subordinate/limited voting shares, which are held by the public.

At the time of the announcement, Kingdom Hotels International (Kingdom), owned by Prince Alwaleed owned 22% of the limited voting shares and Cascade Investment LLC (Cascade), owned by Bill Gates, owned 2% of the limited voting shares. Under the terms of the agreement, the purchasers offered $82 per share, which was priced to represent a premium of 28.4% in excess of the share price just before the announcement. The purchasers were represented by Kingdom, Cascade, and Triples.

The board of directors approved the deal, as did Triples (as controlling shareholder). All that remained for the completion of the transaction was a vote of the limited voting shares. The agreements required that 66.67% of these shareholders vote in favour (the majority of the minority). The vote was to be taken in April. Just before the vote, a major investor, Marisco Capital management LLC (which owned approximately 19% of the limited voting shares), announced that it would not vote in favour of the privatization and the share price began to fall.

As a result, there was heavy trading in derivative instruments that gave holders of the shares the right to sell the shares for $80 regardless of the outcome of the transaction. The holders of the Four Seasons shares, recognizing that the deal might not go through, were hoping to reduce their market price risk. Non-shareholders were speculating on the outcome of the deal. On the announcement that Marisco would not support the deal, the shares had slumped to $79.

A Framework for Options

Options may be purchased (**purchased options**) or written by a company (**written options**). If a company **purchases** an option, it will **pay a fee or premium and gain a right** to do something. If a company **writes** an option, it **charges a fee or premium and gives the holder/purchaser the right** to do something. The "right" in question may be either of the following:

1. A right to buy the underlying (a **call option**)

2. A right to sell the underlying (a **put option**)

   The framework is expressed in Illustration 16-8.

Illustration 16-8

A Framework for Options

A written option is riskier for the company because the writer has no control over whether it will be required to deliver something. The company is obligated to perform under the option. This is different from a purchased option, which gives the company the right but not the obligation to do something. Assume that a company writes or sells an option for $5 cash. **Because this creates an obligation for the company that has written the option, the option is accounted for as a liability.**[46]

An example of a purchase call option follows.

Illustration of a Purchased Call Option

Assume that Abalone Inc. purchases a **call option** contract on January 2, 2007, from Baird Investment Corp.[47] The option gives Abalone the option to purchase 1,000 Laredo shares (the underlying) at $100 per share (the exercise/strike price), and it expires April 30, 2007. For the right to receive any increases in the price of Laredo above the $100 strike price, Abalone pays a premium of $400.

At the time of the transaction, Laredo shares are trading at $100. If the price of Laredo shares increases above $100, Abalone can exercise the option and purchase the shares for $100 per share. Alternatively, Abalone may sell the option to someone else. Here, Baird has the **market risk associated with the shares**. Abalone has **market risk associated with the option** itself, or the $400. At worst, the option becomes worthless and Abalone loses the $400. If Baird has written the option without holding an investment in Laredo (a "naked" position), it will suffer a loss if the price of Laredo increases. If Baird holds shares in Laredo offsetting the option sold (a "covered call"), its profit on the investment will be limited to the difference between $100 and the price it paid for the shares plus the $400 premium received from Abalone. If Laredo's share price never increases above $100 per share, the call option is worthless and Abalone recognizes a loss equal to the initial price of the call option.

The following journal entry would be made at the acquisition date of January 2, 2007:

Derivatives—Trading	400	
Cash		400

A = L + SE
0

Cash flows: ↓ 400 outflow

6 Objective
Describe the recognition, measurement, and presentation issues for options, forwards, and futures.

The option premium is composed of two amounts: (1) the intrinsic value and (2) the time value. Illustration 16-9 shows the formula to calculate the option premium.

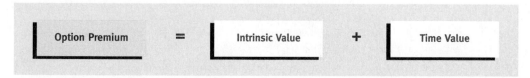

Illustration 16-9

Option Premium Formula

Intrinsic value is the difference between the market price of the underlying and the strike or exercise price at any point in time. It represents the amount that would be realized by the option holder if the option were exercised immediately. On January 2, 2007, the intrinsic value of the option related to the Laredo shares is zero because the market price is equal to the strike price of $100. **Time value** refers to the option's value over and above its intrinsic value. Time value reflects the **possibility that the option will have a fair value greater than zero because there is some expectation that the price of**

---

[46] *CICA Handbook*, Section 3855.A36(d). Note that options dealing with the company's own shares are presented as follows: written call options as equity per Section 3863.18 and.A2, written put options as debt per Section 3863.14, and purchased options as contra equity per Section 3863.07.

[47] Baird Investment Corp. is referred to as the **counterparty**. Recall that derivatives are financial instruments. Recall also that financial instruments are a contract between two parties. Counterparties frequently are investment bankers or other entities that hold inventories of financial instruments.

Laredo shares will increase above the strike price during the option term. As indicated, the option's value is $400.[48]

On March 31, 2007, the price of Laredo shares has increased to $120 per share and the intrinsic value of the call option contract is now $20,000. That is, Abalone could exercise the call option and purchase 1,000 shares from Baird for $100 per share and then sell the shares in the market for $120 per share. This gives Abalone a potential gain of $20,000 ($120,000 – $100,000) on the option contract.[49]

The options may be worth more than this due to the time value component; that is, the shares may increase in value over the remaining month. Assume the options are trading at $20,100. In addition, we must consider the original cost of the option. The entry to record this change in value of the option at March 31, 2007, is as follows:[50]

A = L + SE
+19,700   +19,700

Cash flows: No effect

Derivatives—Trading	19,700	
Gain		19,700[a]
[a]$20,100 − $400		

At March 31, 2007, the call option is reported in the balance sheet at its fair value of $20,100 and the net gain increases net income for the period. The options are "in-the-money"—that is, they have value.

On April 1, 2007, assuming the shares are still worth $120 and Abalone settles the option in cash rather than by taking delivery of the shares of Laredo, the entry to record the settlement of the call option contract with Baird is as follows:

A = L + SE
−100   −100

Cash flows: ↑ 20,000 inflow

Cash	20,000	
Loss	100[51]	
Derivatives—Trading		20,100

Illustration 16-10 summarizes the effects of the call option contract on net income.

Illustration 16-10

Effect on Income—Option

Date	Transaction	Income (Loss) Effect
March 31, 2007	Net increase in value of call option ($20,100 − $400)	$19,700
April 1, 2007	Settle call option	(100)
	Total net income	$19,600*
*This amount is net of $400 cost for the right to participate in the increase in the value of the shares.		

On April 1, 2007, Abalone could have taken delivery of the shares under the option contract. Assume that the shares will be designated as held for trading. The entry to record this is as follows:

---

[48] The value is estimated using option pricing models, such as the Black-Scholes model. The fair value estimate is affected by the volatility of the underlying stock, the expected life of the option, the risk-free rate of interest, and expected dividends on the underlying shares during the option term. This model is further explained in Appendix 16C.

[49] In practice, you generally do not have to actually buy and sell the shares to settle the option and realize the gain. You can settle net in cash as previously discussed under non-financial derivatives. This is referred to as the net settlement feature of option contracts.

[50] The decline in value of the time value portion of the options from $400 to $100 reflects both the decreased likelihood that the Laredo shares will continue to increase in value over the option period and the shorter time to maturity of the option contract.

[51] A loss exists due to the decrease in the time value component of the option. As time passes, the time value component declines and is zero at the end of the contract.

Investment—Trading	120,000	
Loss	100	
Cash		100,000
Derivatives—Trading		20,100

A = L + SE
−100   −100

Cash flows: ↓ 100,000 outflow

Abalone could have purchased the Laredo shares directly on January 2 instead of buying an option. To make the initial investment in Laredo shares, Abalone would have had to pay the full cost of the shares upfront and would therefore have had to pay more cash than it did for the option. If the price of the Laredo shares then increased, Abalone would realize a gain; however, Abalone would also be at risk for a loss if the Laredo shares declined in value.

Sometimes companies buy options on their own shares. Assume Abalone paid $400 for the right to buy its own common shares at a present price. Why would Abalone do this? Perhaps Abalone is looking to buy back its own shares to boost share values. Using options is one way to ensure that shares trade at the most favourable price. Should the cost of the option be treated as an investment as noted above? This is a **presentation** issue. **GAAP dictates that this would be treated as a reduction from shareholders' equity and not as an investment.**[52]

We will return to the discussion of options in Appendix 16A. Chapter 17 will also revisit the option framework when looking at the potentially dilutive impact of options in calculating earnings per share.

Forwards

A **forward contract** is another type of derivative. Under a forward contract, the parties to the contract each **commit upfront to do something in the future**. For example, one party commits to buy an item (referred to as the underlying) and the other to sell the item at a specified price on a specified date. The price and time period are locked in under the contract. The contracts are specific to the transacting parties based on their needs. These instruments generally do not trade on exchanges. They are called "over-the-counter"(OTC) contracts since they can be bought and sold "over-the–counter" only, meaning between specific parties to the contract. Usually banks buy and sell these contracts. Forwards are measured at the present value of any future cash flows under the contract—discounted at a rate that reflects risk.

Illustration of a Forward Contract

To illustrate, assume that on January 2, 2007, Abalone Inc. agrees to buy $1,000 in U.S. currency for $1,150 in Canadian currency in 30 days from Baird Bank. The forward contract not only transfers to the holder the right to increases in value of the underlying (in this case, U.S. dollars), it also creates an obligation to pay a fixed amount at a specified date (in this case $1,150). **This is different than the purchased option, which creates a right but not an obligation: with a purchased option, the holder may choose to exercise the option but does not have to.** The forward contract transfers the **currency risk** inherent in the Canada-U.S. exchange rate. In addition, the contract creates credit risk and liquidity risk. The credit risk is the risk that at the end of the contract, the counterparty (Baird in this case) will not deliver the underlying (U.S. $1000). The liquidity risk is the risk that Abalone will not be able to honour its commitment to deliver Canadian $1,150 at the end of the contract.

Upon inception, the contract is priced such that the value of the forward contract is zero. Assume in the example above, that the date on which the transaction is entered into,

---

[52] *CICA Handbook*, Section 3863.07.

U.S. $1 = Canadian $1.10. No journal entry would be recorded at this point because we must consider the fair value of the contract—not just the difference between the spot rate and the forward rate. Like the option, the value of the forward considers both the intrinsic value and the time value component. It is generally valued at the present value of the future net cash flows under the contract.

Under derivatives accounting, subsequently, the forward is remeasured at fair value. The value will vary depending on interest rates as well as on what is happening with the spot prices (the current value) and forward prices (future value as quoted today) for the U.S. dollar. If the U.S. dollar appreciates in value, in general, the contract will have value since Abalone has locked in to pay only $1,150 for the U.S. $1,000. Assuming that the fair value of the contract is $50, on January 5, 2007, Abalone would record the following:

A   = L + SE
+50   +50

Cash flows: No effect

Derivative—Trading	50	
Gain		50

The derivative would be presented as an asset on the balance sheet and measured at fair value with gains and losses, both unrealized and realized, being booked through net income.

Suppose on January 31, there is a negative fair value, i.e., if the contract were settled today, the company would suffer a loss of $30. This might occur for instance if the value of the U.S. currency depreciates. In this case, Abalone is locked in to pay $1,150 for something that is worth less. The following journal entry would be booked:

A   = L   + SE
−50   +30   −80

Cash flows: No effect

Loss	80	
Derivative – Trading		80

The original gain is reversed and the additional loss must be booked.

The forward contract meets the definition of a financial liability as it is a **contractual obligation to exchange financial instruments with another party under conditions that are potentially unfavourable**. The Derivative-Trading account would therefore be presented as a liability on the balance sheet. Since the Derivative contract can sometimes be an asset while at other times it can be a liability, it can be presented as either an asset or a liability on the balance sheet.

Assume that on February 1, the settlement date, the U.S. dollar is worth $1.04 Canadian. The following entry would be booked to settle the contract if it was settled on a net basis:

A   = L   + SE
−110 −30   −80

Cash flows: ↓ 110 outflow

Loss	80	
Derivative—Trading	30 (carrying value)	
Cash		110[a]
[a]U.S. $1,000 × (1.15 − 1.04)		

If Abalone actually took delivery of the U.S. dollars, the following journal entry would be booked:

A   = L   + SE
−110 −30   −80

Cash flows: ↓ 110 outflow

Cash – U.S.$	1,040 (spot/current exchange rate)	
Derivative—Trading	30 (carrying value)	
Loss	80	
Cash—Canadian $		1,150

Futures

Futures contracts, another popular type of derivative, are the same as forwards except for the following:

1. They are standardized as to amounts and dates.

2. Futures contracts are exchange traded and therefore have ready market values.

3. They are settled through clearing houses, which generally removes the credit risk.

4. There is a requirement to put up collateral in the form of a "margin" account. The margin account represents a percentage of the contract's value. Daily changes in the value of the contract are settled daily against the margin account by the clearing house (known as marking to market) and resulting deficiencies in the margin account must be made up daily.

    The initial margin is treated as a deposit account similar to a bank account, and is increased or decreased as the margin amount changes. The gain or loss on the contract, reflected in the daily change in the account, is recognized in income.

    For example, assume Forward Inc. entered into a futures contract to sell grain for $1,000. The exchange/broker requires a $100 initial margin (normally a percentage of the market value of the contract or a fixed amount times the number of contracts). This amount is deposited in cash with the exchange/broker. Like the forward, the futures contract would have a zero value up front.

    At the date when the contract is entered into, the following journal entry would be booked to show the margin that has been deposited with the exchange/broker. The contract is otherwise valued at $0 on inception.

Deposits	100	
Cash		100

A = L + SE
0

Cash flows: ↓ 100 outflow

Assume that the value of the grain increases after the contract has been entered into. The contract is marked to market by the exchange/broker. Assume that the market value of the contract decreases by $50. This is because Forward has agreed to sell the grain for a fixed amount that is lower than the current market value. The $50 loss is removed from Future's margin account by the exchange/broker. The clearing house then requires Forward to restore the margin account by depositing an additional $50. The entries to record the loss and the additional deposit would be:

Loss	50	
Derivative—Trading*		50
Derivative—Trading*	50	
Cash		50
*Alternatively, these amounts can be booked to Deposits.		

A = L + SE
−50   −50

Cash flows: ↓ 50 outflow

If the contract is closed out (settled net without delivering the grain) with no further changes in value, the following entry would be booked.

Cash	100	
Deposits		100

A = L + SE
0

Cash flows: ↑ 100 inflow

Forward suffered a loss of $50, which was booked to net income already through the journal entries above. This is because they had agreed to sell the grain for $1000 when it was worth more. Instead of delivering the grain, Forward paid the difference in cash—thus locking in the loss. Note that the net impact is a loss of $50 on the contract.

STOCK COMPENSATION PLANS

It is generally agreed that effective compensation programs:

1. Motivate employees to high levels of performance.

2. Help retain executives and recruit new talent.

3. Base compensation on employee and company performance.

4. Maximize the employee's after-tax benefit and minimize the employer's after-tax cost.

5. Use performance criteria that the employee can control.

Although straightforward cash compensation plans (salary and, perhaps, a bonus) are an important part of any compensation program, they are oriented to the short run. Many companies recognize that a more long-run compensation plan is often needed in addition to a cash component.

Long-term compensation plans aim to develop a strong loyalty toward the company. An effective way to accomplish this goal is to give the employees an equity interest based on changes in their company's long-term measures, such as increases in earnings per share, revenues, share price, or market share. These plans come in many different forms. Essentially, they provide the executive or employee with the opportunity to receive shares or cash in the future if the company's performance is satisfactory. Stock-based compensation plans also help companies conserve cash. When they are used, the company does not expend any cash. In fact, if options are used to compensate employees, the employees actually pay cash into the company when they exercise the option. Start-up companies find this aspect very useful since they are often cash-poor in that early phase.

Types of Plans

Objective 7
Describe the various types of stock compensation plans.

Many different types of plans are used to compensate employees and especially management. In all these plans, the reward amount depends on future events. Consequently, continued employment is a necessary element in almost all types of plans. The popularity of a particular plan usually depends on prospects in the stock market and tax considerations. For example, if it appears that appreciation will occur in a company's shares, a plan that offers the option to purchase shares is attractive to an executive. Conversely, if it appears that price appreciation is unlikely, then compensation might be tied to some performance measure such as an increase in book value or earnings per share.

Four common compensation plans that illustrate different objectives are:

1. Direct awards of stock

2. Compensatory stock option plans (CSOPs)

3. Stock appreciation rights plans (SARs)

4. Performance-type plans

The main accounting issues relate to **recognition** of the plan (when should the cost of the plan be recognized) and **measurement** (how should the cost be measured). SARs and performance-type plans will be discussed in Appendix 16B.

Underlying Concept

There is no transparency if the costs of compensatory plans are not captured in the income statement.

Direct Awards of Stock

Stock may be awarded directly as compensation for services provided by an employee. This type of transaction is more broadly known as a **non-monetary reciprocal transaction**. The transaction is non-monetary because it involves little or no cash, and it is reciprocal because it is a two-way transaction. The company gives something up (shares) and gets something in return (the employee's services). Almost all business transactions are reciprocal. As a **non-monetary** transaction, direct awards of stock are recorded at the fair value of the item that is given up (the stock).[53] For instance, instead of paying cash salary, the company may offer shares of the company as remuneration. This would be recorded as salary expense at the fair value of the shares.

Stock Options Revisited

Before looking at the accounting for employee stock option plans, it is useful to revisit the earlier discussion about stock options in this chapter. So far, stock options have been discussed in the following context:

> **8 Objective**
> Explain the differences between employee and compensatory option plans and other options.

- as derivatives, used to manage risk (hedge or speculation)

- as debt with detachable warrants (options), used as sweeteners with bonds to access pools of capital and reduce the cost of capital

The above instruments are often **exchange traded options**; that is, they trade on an options or stock exchange. The accounting for these has been dealt with but as you recall, both types of instruments are valued at fair value.

Companies also use stock options for the following reasons:

1. To **give employees an opportunity to own part of the company**, with the issue being made to a wide group of people (e.g., all employees). Another benefit of these plans if they are widely subscribed to is that the company raises cash. These are called **employee stock option plans (ESOPs)**.

2. To **remunerate management or employees**. These are called **compensatory stock option plans (CSOPs)**.

3. As **compensation in a particular purchase or acquisition transaction**, with the stock options being provided instead of paying cash or another asset, or incurring a liability. For instance, a company might buy another company and pay for the investment with stock options. These, like direct awards of stock, are valued at fair value. The accounting is similar to the accounting covered in Chapter 10 under acquisition of assets upon issuance of shares.

Illustration 16-11 reviews the different types of options and option plans. Note that ESOPs and CSOPs are generally not traded on an exchange. As a result, the fair value cannot be measured as readily.

What is the difference between ESOPs and CSOPs in terms of accounting? The answer has to do with the real nature of the transaction. The main difference between the two plans is that with ESOPs, the employee usually pays for the options (either fully or partially). Thus these transactions are seen as **capital** transactions (charged to equity accounts). The employee is investing in the company. CSOPs, on the other hand, are primarily seen as an **alternative way to compensate** the employees for their services, like a barter transaction. The services are rendered by the employee in the act of producing revenues. This information must be recognized in the income statement as an operating transaction (expensed).

Illustration 16-12 summarizes the difference between CSOPs and non-compensatory plans, or ESOPs.

---

[53] *CICA Handbook*, Section 3870.24.

Illustration 16-11

Different Ways of Using Options

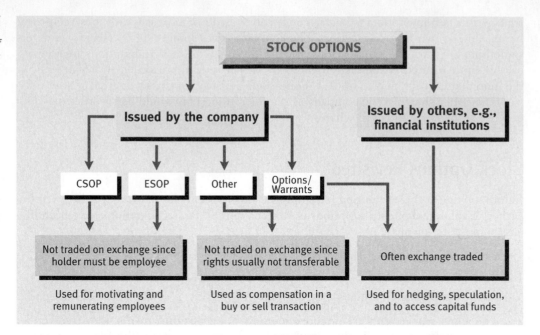

Illustration 16-12

Compensatory versus Non-Compensatory Plans

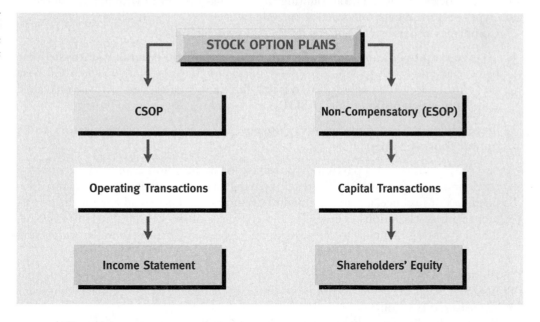

The following factors dictate whether or not the plan is compensatory:

1. **Option terms** (e.g., dealing with enrolment and cancellation). Non-standard terms that give the employees a longer time to enrol and the ability to cancel the option imply that the options are compensatory.

2. **Discount from market price.** A large discount implies that the plan is compensatory.[54]

3. **Eligibility.** Making options available only to certain restricted groups of employees, often management, implies that they are compensatory. Plans that are available to all employees are seen as non-compensatory.[55]

---

[54] Note that a company might offer an option under an ESOP at less than the fair value of the option. As long as this discount is small and effectively represents the issue costs that a company might otherwise have incurred had it done a public offering, this is not seen as compensatory.

[55] *CICA Handbook*, Section 3870.28.

Under an ESOP, when an option or share right is sold to an employee, the Cash account is debited and the Contributed Surplus account is credited for the amount of the premium (i.e., the cost of the option). When the right or option is exercised, the Cash account is again debited for the exercise price, along with the Contributed Surplus account (to reverse the earlier entry) and the Common Shares account is credited to show the issuance of the shares.

To illustrate, assume that Fanco Limited set up an ESOP that gives employees the option to purchase company shares for $10 per share. The option premium is $1 per share and Fanco has set aside 10,000 shares. On January 1, 2008, employees purchase 6,000 options for $6,000. The journal entry is as follows:

Cash	6,000	
Contributed Surplus—Stock Options		6,000

A = L + SE
+6,000   +6,000

Cash flows: ↑ 6,000 inflow

Subsequently, all 6,000 options are exercised, resulting in 6,000 shares being issued. The journal entry is as follows:

Cash	60,000	
Contributed Surplus—Stock Options	6,000	
Common Shares		66,000

A = L + SE
+60,000   +60,000

Cash flows: ↑ 60,000 inflow

If the options are never exercised, any funds that were received by the company on the sale of the options would remain in Contributed Surplus.

Compensatory Stock Option Plans

CSOPs must be measured using **fair value**.[56] The plan has value since many employees accept the stock options in lieu of salary or a bonus. The value, as previously mentioned in the chapter, lies in the potential for future gain. **Recall that an option gets its value from two components: the intrinsic value component and a time value component.** While the intrinsic value may be easy to measure (the fair value of the shares less the exercise price), the time value component is more difficult to measure. The use of options pricing models to value the option helps measure what the option is worth when there is no market value available. **The cost of employee services should be based on the value of the compensation that is paid, which reflects the value of the services provided. The compensation cost that arises from employee stock options should be recognized as the services are being provided.**[57]

9 Objective
Describe the accounting for compensatory stock option plans.

Determining Expense

The total compensation expense is calculated on the date when the options are granted to the employee (the **grant date**) and is based on the fair value of the options that are expected to **vest**.[58] The grant date is the date when the employee and company agree on the value of what is to be exchanged. **The grant date is therefore the measurement**

---

[56] *CICA Handbook*, Section 3870.24.

[57] Stock options that are issued to non-employees in exchange for other goods or services must be measured according to their fair value as non-monetary transactions.

[58] "Vested" means to earn the rights to something. An employee's award becomes vested at the date that the employee's right to receive or retain shares of stock or cash under the award no longer depends on the employee remaining in the employer's service.

date. Fair value for public companies is estimated using an option pricing model, with some adjustments for the unique factors of employee stock options. No adjustments are made after the grant date for any subsequent changes in the share price, either up or down. The option pricing model incorporates several input measures:

1. The exercise price

2. The expected life of the option

3. The current market price of the underlying stock

4. The volatility of the underlying stock

5. The expected dividend during the option life

6. The risk-free rate of interest for the option life

The **measurement date** may be later for plans that have variable terms (i.e., if the number of shares and/or option price are not known) that depend on events after the date of grant. For such variable plans, the compensation expense may have to be estimated based on assumptions about the final number of shares and the option price (usually at the exercise date).

Allocating Compensation Expense

In general, compensation expense is recognized in the periods in which the employee performs the service (the **service period**). Unless something different is specified, the service period is the **vesting period**: the time between the grant date and the vesting date. Thus, the total compensation cost is determined at the grant date and allocated to the periods that benefit from the employee services. Illustration 16-13 presents the relevant dates and time frames.

Illustration 16-13

Key Dates in Accounting for Stock Option Plans

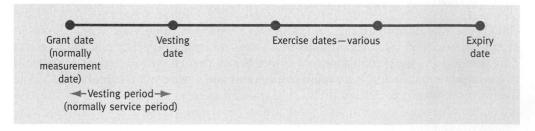

To illustrate the accounting for a stock option plan, assume that on November 1, 2008, the shareholders of Chen Corp. approve a plan that grants options to the company's five executives to purchase 2,000 shares each of the company's common shares. The options are granted on January 1, 2009, and may be exercised at any time within the next 10 years. The option price per share is $60, and the market price at the date of grant is $70 per share.

The total compensation expense is calculated by applying an acceptable fair value option pricing model (such as the Black-Scholes model). To keep this illustration simple, we will assume that the fair value, as determined using an option pricing model, results in a total compensation expense of $220,000.

At grant date   Recall that the option's value is recognized as an expense in the periods in which the employee performs services. In the case of Chen Corp., assume that the documents that are associated with the issuance of the options indicate that the expected period of benefit/service is two years, starting on the grant date. The journal entries to record the transactions related to this option are as follows:

January 1, 2009		
No entry		

December 31, 2009		
Compensation Expense	110,000	
Contributed Surplus—Stock Options ($220,000 ÷ 2)		110,000

A = L + SE
          0
Cash flows: No effect

December 31, 2010		
Compensation Expense	110,000	
Contributed Surplus—Stock Options		110,000

A = L + SE
          0
Cash flows: No effect

The compensation expense is allocated evenly over the two-year service period, assuming that equal service is provided during the entire period.

At exercise date   If 20% or 2,000 of the 10,000 options were exercised on June 1, 2012 (three years and five months after date of grant), the following journal entry would be recorded:

June 1, 2012		
Cash (2,000 × $60)	120,000	
Contributed Surplus—Stock Options (20% × $220,000)	44,000	
Common Shares		164,000

A   = L +   SE
↓ 120,000   ↓ 120,000
Cash flows: ↑ 120,000 inflow

At expiration   If the remaining stock options are not exercised before their expiration date, the balance in the Contributed Surplus account would remain. If the company kept several Contributed Surplus accounts, the balance would be shifted to a specific Contributed Surplus account that is used for options that have expired. The entry to record this transaction at the date of expiration is:

Contributed Surplus—Stock Options	176,000	
Contributed Surplus—Expired Stock Options (80% × $220,000)		176,000

A = L + SE
          0
Cash flows: No effect

Adjustment   The fact that a stock option is not exercised does not make it incorrect to record the costs of the services received from executives that have been attributed to the stock option plan. However, if a stock option is forfeited because an employee fails to satisfy a service requirement (e.g., if the employee leaves the company), the estimate of the compensation expense that has been recorded should be adjusted as a change in estimate (credit Compensation Expense and debit Contributed Surplus) unless the forfeit has already been taken into account in the option pricing model.

Special Issues Associated with Private Companies

Companies whose shares are traded on stock exchanges are able to measure the value of the options more readily since they can measure volatility. Private companies, however, do not have volatility measures. The profession allows these companies to assume a volatility of zero as an input to the option pricing model.

Private companies have another issue. If they issue CSOPs to their employees, how do the employees realize the value? If an employee exercises the option and buys the shares, there is no ready market to sell the shares in and the value is therefore locked in. Often private companies will offer to buy back the shares from the employee. If the company has a policy and past practice of repurchasing the shares, does this create a liability? **This requires professional judgement but a good argument may be made for recognizing a liability instead of equity. In other words, the past practice of repurchasing the shares and the probability that this will be done again (since the employees cannot sell the shares elsewhere) support the recognition of a liability.** The company in substance has an obligation to the employee.[59] The liability would have to be remeasured on an ongoing basis with the difference being charged to income as compensation expense.

Disclosure of Compensation Plans

Full disclosure should be made of the following:

- the accounting policy that is being used

- a description of the plans and modifications

- details of the numbers and values of the options issued, exercised, forfeited, and expired

- a description of the assumptions and methods being used to determine fair values

- the total compensation cost included in net income and contributed surplus

- other[60]

PERSPECTIVES

Analysis

Many complex financial instruments exist and must be accounted for in the company's financial statements. It is important to understand the nature of the instruments from an economic perspective: why would the company issue this type of instrument and why would an investor invest in it? It is also important to understand what creates the instrument's value. This will help in understanding the economic substance of the instrument. The accounting issues relate to presentation (Is it debt or equity, or both?) and measurement.

Derivatives have been the focus of some very negative publicity in the past few years with companies suffering significant losses and perhaps even going bankrupt due to derivative instruments. This is partially due to the complexity of these contracts and the fact that they are not well understood by many who use them. One key complexity is the presence of leverage. Many derivative instruments use the principle of leverage, which magnifies the potential gain or loss. Therefore, while the cost to enter into the contract may be relatively low, the potential for gain or loss is exponentially great and has in the past decade forced long-established companies such as Barings Bank and even governments (Orange County in the United States) into bankruptcy.

Do complex accounting standards add any value in the capital marketplace? They certainly add to the costs of preparing financial statements. Accountants in industry must stay up to date on these standards, as must the auditors. There is a very real risk that investors and creditors do not understand the standards and perhaps may not even have the educational background that is required to be able to work through the complexities.

The new project on financial instruments that the IASB and FASB are working on will hopefully simplify the standards.

---

[59] *CICA Handbook*, Section 3870.03.

[60] *CICA Handbook*, Section 3870.67.

International

Illustration 16-14 compares Canadian GAAP with the international standards on complex financial instruments, providing additional information relative to the information included in the comparison illustrations in Chapters 14 and 15.

Illustration 16-14

Comparison of Canadian and International GAAP

Canada	International
Section 3865: Hedges	IAS 39: Financial instruments—recognition and measurement
	IFRS 7: Financial instruments—disclosures
Section 3870: Stock-Based Compensation and Other Stock-Based Payments	IFRS 2: Share-based payments

Section 3865 and IAS 32 are basically converged except that IAS 32 does not allow for the initial measurement of compound financial instruments using the relative fair value method. As noted earlier, the IASB and FASB are working on a new financial instruments project which will hopefully remove some of the complexity.

Section 3870 and IFRS 2 are converged except for certain transactions with non-employees, and some other issues that are beyond the scope of this text.

Summary of Learning Objectives

 Student Website

Glossary

www.wiley.com/canada/kieso

1 Describe whether an instrument issued for financing purposes represents a liability, equity, or both.

Complex instruments include compound and hybrid instruments where the legal form may differ from the economic substance. The economic substance dictates the accounting. The main issue is that of presentation: should the instrument be presented as debt or equity? The definitions of debt and equity are useful in analyzing this. It is also important to understand what gives the instruments their value from a finance or economic perspective. If an instrument has both debt and equity components, use of the proportional and incremental methods will help in allocating the carrying value between the two components. Related interest, dividends, gains, and losses are treated in a way that is consistent with the balance sheet presentation.

2 Explain the accounting for the issuance, conversion, and retirement of convertible securities.

The method for recording convertible bonds at the date of issuance is different from the method that is used to record straight debt issues. As the instrument is a compound instrument and contains both debt and equity components, these must be measured separately and presented as debt and equity respectively. Any discount or premium that results from the issuance of convertible bonds is amortized, assuming the bonds will be held to maturity. If bonds are converted into other securities, the principal accounting problem is to determine the amount at which to record the securities that have been exchanged for the bond. The book value method is often used in practice.

3 Understand what derivatives are and why they exist.

Derivatives are financial instruments that derive (get) their value from an underlying instrument. They are attractive since they transfer risks and rewards without having to necessarily invest directly in the underlying instrument. They are used for both

KEY TERMS

book value method, 962
call option, 972
compensatory stock option plans (CSOPs), 979
compound financial instruments, 953
convertible bonds, 960
counterparty, 973
credit risk, 967
currency risk, 967
derivative instruments, 965
embedded derivatives, 966
employee stock option plans (ESOPs), 979
equity instrument, 953
exchangeable debentures, 964
exercise period, 956
exercise price, 956
fair value, 971

speculative purposes (to expose a company to increased risks in the hope of increased returns) and for hedging purposes (to reduce existing risk).

4 Explain the various types of financial risks, and how they arise.

Financial risks include credit, currency, interest rate, liquidity, market, and other price risks. Credit risk is the risk that the other party to a financial instrument contract will fail to deliver. Currency and interest rate risk are the risk of a change in value and cash flows due to currency or interest rate changes. Liquidity risk is the risk that the company itself will not be able to honour the contract due to cash problems. Finally, market risk is the risk of a change in value and/or cash flows related to market forces.

5 Understand what options, forwards, and futures are.

All of these instruments are derivatives. Options may be purchased or written. If they are purchased, they give the holder the right but not the obligation to do something. If they are written, the writer is obligated to do something, which results in a liability. Put options carry the right to sell, whereas call options carry the right to purchase. Forward contracts are promises to do something in the future, normally buying or selling something. Futures are similar to forwards except that they trade on organized exchanges. They are therefore easy to value. Futures contracts come in standardized amounts and mature on a limited number of specified dates. Companies that enter into futures contracts are required to deposit a percentage of the value (known as a margin) with their broker.

6 Describe the recognition, measurement, and presentation issues for options, forwards, and futures.

All derivatives are recognized on the balance sheet on the date that the contract is initiated. They are classified as held-for-trading and are remeasured, on each balance sheet date, to their fair value. The related gains and losses are recorded through net income. Written options create liabilities. Futures contracts require the company to deposit a portion of the contracts' value with the broker/exchange. The contracts are marked to market by the broker/exchange daily and the company may have to deposit additional funds to cover deficiencies in the margin account.

7 Describe the various types of stock compensation plans.

Stock compensation includes direct awards of stock (when a company gives the shares to an employee as compensation), compensatory stock option plans whereby an employee is given stock options in lieu of salary, stock appreciation rights, and performance-type plans. The latter are discussed in Appendix 16B.

8 Explain the differences between employee and compensatory option plans and other options.

Employee stock option plans are meant to motivate employees and raise capital for the company. They are therefore capital transactions. Compensatory stock option plans are operating transactions since they are meant to compensate the employee for service provided. Costs relating to the latter are booked as expense.

9 Describe the accounting for compensatory stock option plans.

CSOPs are measured at fair value (using an options pricing model) at the grant date. The cost is then allocated to expense over the period that the employee provides service.

10 Compare current Canadian and international GAAP, and understand which direction international GAAP is headed.

The standards are basically converged except that IAS 39 does not allow compound instruments to be measured using the relative fair value method (proportional method).

Appendix 16A

Hedging

Derivatives Used for Hedging

In the body of the chapter, we discussed basic issues related to derivatives. This appendix will focus on the accounting for **derivatives that are used for hedging**. How does hedging actually reduce risk from an economic perspective and what are the accounting implications?

Companies that are already exposed to financial risks because of existing business transactions that arise from their business models may choose to protect themselves by managing and reducing those risks. For example, most public companies borrow and lend substantial amounts in credit markets and are therefore exposed to significant financial risks. They face substantial risk that the fair values or cash flows of interest-sensitive assets or liabilities will change if interest rates increase or decrease (**interest rate risk**). These same companies often also have cross-border transactions or international operations that expose them to **exchange rate risk**. The borrowing activity creates **liquidity risk** for the company and the lending activity creates **credit risk**.

Because the value and/or cash flows of derivative financial instruments can vary according to changes in interest rates, foreign currency exchange rates, or other external factors, derivatives may be used to offset the associated risks. **Using derivatives or other instruments to offset risks is called hedging.** A properly hedged position should result in no economic loss to the company. It may result in no gain, and there may be costs involved to effect the transactions, but it should limit or eliminate any potential losses. It reduces uncertainty/risk, and therefore volatility, and that is what gives hedging its value.

Separating the Act of Hedging Risks from the Decision to Use Hedge Accounting

It is important to separate the **act of hedging** to reduce economic and financial risks from the **accounting** for these hedges. Hedge accounting is optional and in some cases not even necessary. A company may choose to apply it or not. It is an accounting policy choice.

Why do we need special accounting rules for hedges? They exist in part due to our **mixed measurement model** (fair value, amortized cost, cost) and the **treatment of the related gains and losses where fair value is used**. They also exist because sometimes we **need to hedge future transactions that are not yet recognized on the balance sheet**.

Symmetry in Accounting—No Need for Special Hedge Accounting

Consider the situation where a company has a U.S. $100 receivable that is due in 30 days. The company is exposed to a **foreign currency risk**. Each time the currency rate changes, the economic value of the asset changes. Under existing GAAP, at each balance sheet date, we revalue the asset to reflect the current spot rate for the U.S. dollar. If the U.S. dollar depreciates against the Canadian dollar, the receivable is worth less and the resulting loss gets booked to the income statement. Now let's assume that the company does not want this foreign currency exposure and it enters into a forward contract to sell U.S. dollars for $120 Canadian in 30 days. This provides an **effective (economic) hedge** against changes in the value of the asset. If the U.S. dollar subsequently depreciates in value, then the forward contract increases in value because, under the contract, we can still sell the U.S. $100 for $120 Canadian no matter what happens to the exchange rate. From an **economic perspective**, the gains on the forward offset the losses on the receivable. From an **accounting perspective**, this gain gets booked to the income statement and thus offsets the loss on the receivable. In this case, because the losses on the receivable offset the gains on the forward, **no special hedge accounting is needed**.

No Symmetry in Accounting—Potential Need for Special Hedge Accounting

If instead, the company had an investment in a security classified as available for sale, losses due to decreases in the value of the security would be booked to Other Comprehensive Income. Suppose the company decided to purchase an option to sell the shares at a fixed price. This would protect it against future losses and would therefore be an **effective (economic) hedge**. If the value of the shares declined, the value of the option to sell at a set price would increase, resulting in a gain. This gain would normally be booked to net income since the option is a derivative. In this case, **even though the gains and losses offset from an economic perspective, there is asymmetry in the accounting because the loss is booked to Other Comprehensive Income and the gain to net income**. The company needs to decide whether it wants to use hedge accounting to ensure that the gains and losses will offset in net income. The journal entries for this example will be looked at later in this appendix.

> **Underlying Concept**
>
> Using hedge accounting increases transparency— reflecting the decrease in income volatility.

Hedge accounting divides hedges into two basic groups:

1. Fair value hedges

2. Cash flow hedges

Each will be discussed in further detail below. Because hedge accounting is designed to ensure that the **timing of the recognition** of gains/losses in net income is the same for both the hedged item and the hedging item, **it will result in recognition and measurement that is different than under normal GAAP. Thus, it is important to ensure that the hedge is effective and properly identified and documented** in order to allow it to qualify for special treatment.

Qualifying Hedge Criteria

Hedges may qualify for optional hedge accounting when the following criteria are met:[61]

1. At the inception of the hedge, the entity must do the following:
   (a) **Identify** the exposure.
   (b) **Designate** that hedge accounting will be applied.
   (c) **Document** the risk management objectives and strategies, the hedging relationship, the items being hedged and used to hedge, the methods of assessing the effectiveness of the hedge, and the method of accounting for the hedge.

---

[61] *CICA Handbook*, Section 3865.

2. At the inception and throughout the term, the entity should have reasonable assurance that the relationship is **effective and consistent with the risk management policy**. As a result, all of the following must be respected:

   (a) The effectiveness of the hedge should be reliably measurable.

   (b) The hedging relationship should be reassessed regularly.

   (c) Where the hedge involves forecasted transactions, it should be probable that these transactions will occur.

Fair Value Hedges

Objective 13

Explain the difference between a fair value hedge and cash flow hedge.

Objective 14

Calculate the impact on net income of using hedge accounting for both types of hedges.

In a **fair value hedge**, a derivative may be used to hedge or offset the exposure to changes in the fair value of a **recognized asset or liability** (or of a previously unrecognized firm commitment),[62] and thus **reduce market risk**.[63] In a perfectly hedged position, the economic gain/loss on the fair value of the derivative and that of the hedged asset or liability should be equal and offsetting. A typical fair value hedge is the use of **put options** (options to sell an investment at a preset price) or a forward contract (to sell the investment at a preset price) to hedge the risk that an investment will decline in value. Let's look at an example.

Using Hedge Accounting—Put Options as Fair Value Hedges

To illustrate, assume that Cathay Inc. purchases an investment for $1,000. This exposes the company to a market risk—the risk that the shares will decline in value. If the investment is designated as available for sale, it will be carried at its fair value with gains and losses normally being booked through Other Comprehensive Income. The journal entry to record the initial investment at January 1, 2009, would be as follows:

A = L + SE
0

Cash flows: ↓ 1,000 outflow

Investment—Available for Sale	1,000	
Cash		1,000

Assume that on the same date the company also enters into a derivative contract in which it purchases an option to sell the shares at $1,000 to protect itself against losses in value of the security. The cost of the option is $10. If the value of the shares declines, the company can sell the shares under the option for $1,000—thus limiting any loss. As a derivative, the option will be measured at fair value with subsequent gains and losses booked to net income. The entry would be as follows:

A = L + SE
0

Cash flows: ↓ 10 outflow

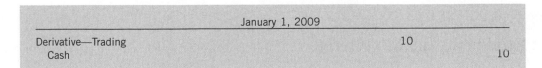

January 1, 2009		
Derivative—Trading	10	
Cash		10

If at December 31, 2009, the fair value of the investment increased by $50, the derivative would decrease in value by $50. (In actual fact, the loss on the option would not exactly offset the gains on the investment as the value of the option incorporates other variables.) The journal entries to record this are as follows:

---

[62] If a firm commitment such as a purchase commitment is hedged, then the commitment itself must be recognized on the balance sheet so that resulting gains and losses offset the gains and losses generated by the hedging item.

[63] Note that the trade-off to reducing market risk with a derivative is an increase in credit, liquidity, and operational risks.

Investment—Available for Sale	50	
Gain/Loss		50
Gain/Loss	50	
Derivative—Trading		50

$$A = L + SE$$
$$+50 \qquad +50$$
Cash flows: No effect

$$A = L + SE$$
$$-50 \qquad -50$$
Cash flows: No effect

As previously mentioned, the derivative is always valued at fair value with the gains/ losses being booked to net income. However, normally the gain on the available-for-sale investment would be booked to Other Comprehensive Income. There is therefore a mismatch. **Hedge accounting allows the gain on the hedged item to be booked through net income so it may be offset by the loss on the derivative as noted in the journal entry above. Hedge accounting allows us to modify the way we would normally account for the available for sale investment.**

Using Hedge Accounting—Purchase Commitments as Hedged Items

What if the exposure to be hedged relates to a **purchase commitment**? For example, what if the company has committed to purchase a certain amount of raw materials at a fixed price in order to secure a stable supply of the raw materials? This would create a **market risk—if the price of the raw material declines, the company has locked in at a higher price and therefore has a potential loss.** Normally, a company would not recognize purchase commitments for which it intends to take delivery of the raw materials unless there was a contingent loss that was measurable and probable.[64]

Would the hedge of a purchase commitment qualify as a fair value hedge? If the purchase commitment were hedged with a derivative instrument, the latter would be recognized on the balance sheet and measured at fair value, with gains and losses being recorded in net income. If the purchase commitment were not recognized on the balance sheet, there would be another mismatch. **Therefore, under hedge accounting, the purchase commitment would also need to be recorded and measured at fair value.**

Cash Flow Hedges

A **cash flow hedge** deals with **transactions that offset the effects of future variable cash flows,** such as future interest payments on variable rate debt. Because the debt is variable rate, the interest to be paid out will fluctuate, and this therefore makes future cash flows uncertain. Since the hedged position (i.e., the potential change in future interest payments) is not yet recognized on the balance sheet, the gains/losses related to changes in value (and hence the cash flows) are not captured. **Thus, under hedge accounting, any gains/losses on the hedging item should not be included in net income either.** They are therefore recognized in Other Comprehensive Income.

In a cash flow hedge, the company is trying to protect itself against variations in future cash flows. Different derivative instruments may be used to effect this. Let's look at an example.

Using Hedge Accounting—Interest Rate Swaps as Cash Flow Hedges

When a company has a series of similar transactions that it wants to hedge, a **swap contract** may be used. A swap is a transaction between two parties in which the first party

---

[64] If the terms of the contract allowed the contract to be settled net in cash (instead of taking delivery of the raw material), it may meet the definition of a derivative and have to be recognized as being such, **unless** the entity documents that it intends to take delivery. If the purchase commitment were recognized as a derivative and it was hedged with a derivative, there would be no need for special hedge accounting.

promises to make a series of payments to the second party. Similarly, the second party promises to make simultaneous payments to the first party. The parties swap payments. **A swap is a series of forward contracts.** The most common type of swap is the **interest rate swap**, in which one party makes payments based on a fixed or floating rate and the second party does just the opposite. In most cases, financial institutions and other intermediaries find the two parties, bring them together, and handle the flow of payments between the two parties, as shown in Illustration 16A-1.

Illustration 16A-1

Swap Transaction

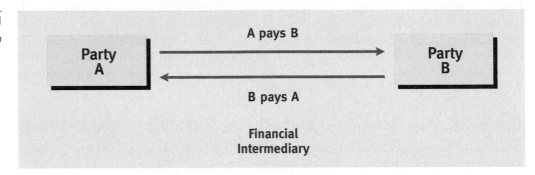

To illustrate the accounting for a cash flow hedge, assume that Jones Corporation issues $1 million of five-year, floating-rate bonds on January 2, 2009. The entry to record this transaction is as follows:

A = L + SE
+1,000,000   +1,000,000

Cash flows: ↑ 1,000,000 inflow

January 2, 2009		
Cash	1,000,000	
Bonds Payable		1,000,000

A floating interest rate was offered to appeal to investors, but Jones is concerned about the cash flow uncertainty associated with the variable rate interest. To protect against the **cash flow uncertainty**, Jones decides to hedge the risk by entering into a five-year interest rate swap. Under the terms of the swap contract, the following will occur:

1. Jones will pay fixed payments at 8% (based on the $1 million amount) to a counterparty.

2. Jones will receive, from the counterparty, variable or floating rates that are based on the market rate in effect throughout the life of the swap contract.

As Illustration 16A-2 shows, by using this swap Jones can change the interest on the bonds payable from a floating rate to a fixed rate. Jones thus swaps the floating rate, assumed to be 9% in the example, for a fixed rate.

Illustration 16A-2

Interest Rate Swap

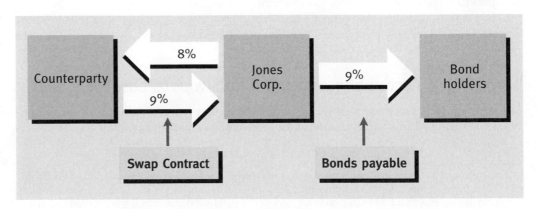

The settlement dates for the swap correspond to the interest payment dates on the debt (December 31). On each interest payment (**settlement date**), Jones and the counterparty will calculate the difference between current market interest rates (9% in the example) and the fixed rate of 8%, and settle the difference.[65] Both parties will also need to value the swap contract on each balance sheet date using a discounted cash flow model. If interest rates rise, the value of the swap contract to Jones increases (Jones has a gain), while at the same time Jones' floating-rate debt obligation becomes larger (Jones has an economic loss). **The swap is an effective risk management tool in this setting because its value is related to the same underlying (interest rates) that will affect the value of the floating-rate bond payable. Thus, if the swap's value goes up, it offsets the loss related to the debt obligation.**

Assuming that the swap was entered into on January 2, 2009 (the same date as the issuance of the debt), the swap at this time has no value and there is therefore no need for a journal entry.

January 2, 2009
No entry required. Memorandum to indicate that the swap contract is signed.

At the end of 2009, the interest payment on the bonds is made. Assume the floating rate is 9%. The journal entry to record this transaction is as follows:

December 31, 2009		
Interest Expense	90,000	
Cash (9% × $1,000,000)		90,000

A = L + SE
−90,000   −90,000

Cash flows: ↓ 90,000 outflow

At the end of 2009, market interest rates have increased substantially to 9%, and the value of the swap contract has therefore increased. Recall (see Illustration 16A-2) that in the swap Jones is to receive a floating rate of 9%, or $90,000 ($1 million × 9%), and pay a fixed rate of 8%, or $80,000. Jones therefore receives $10,000 ($90,000 − $80,000) as a settlement payment on the swap contract on the first interest payment date. The entry to record this transaction is as follows:

December 31, 2009		
Cash	10,000	
Interest Expense		10,000

A = L + SE
+10,000   +10,000

Cash flows: ↑ 10,000 inflow

In addition, assume that the fair value of the interest rate swap has increased by $40,000. This increase in value is recorded as follows:[66]

---

[65] The decision to make an interest rate swap is based on a recognized index of market interest rates. The most commonly used index is the London Interbank Offer Rate, or LIBOR. The prime lending rate is another rate that is commonly referenced in loan agreements and other financial instruments. This rate is set periodically by the Bank of Canada. The interest rates that are attached to various instruments are normally above prime (e.g. P + 1% or P + 2%, etc.).

[66] Theoretically, this fair value change reflects the present value of expected future differences in variable and fixed interest rates and any changes in the counterparty's credit risk.

A = L +   SE
+40,000   +40,000

Cash flows: No effect

December 31, 2009		
Derivative—Trading	40,000	
Other Comprehensive Income— Unrealized Holding Gain or Loss		40,000

As a derivative, as previously noted, this swap contract is recognized in the balance sheet, and the gain in fair value is normally reported in net income. **Under hedge accounting, the gain on the hedging activity is reported in Other Comprehensive Income (as opposed to net income).** This is because there is asymmetry in the accounting under normal GAAP. The losses on the bond payable do not get recognized because the bond is carried at amortized cost. The gains on the swap do get recognized because the swap is a derivative.

The unrealized holding gain will gradually be reflected in net income as the benefit of the locked in (lower) rate is realized as reduced interest expense, as the earlier entries showed. By the end of the swap contract, the value of the contract will be nil and the company will have recorded net interest expense that reflects the fixed rate. Illustration 16A-3 shows the balance sheet presentations of a cash flow hedge.

Illustration 16A-3

Balance Sheet Presentation of Cash Flow Hedge

JONES CORPORATION
Balance Sheet (partial)
December 31, 2009

Held for trading derivatives:	
Swap contract	$ 40,000
Long-term liabilities	
Bonds payable	$1,000,000
Equity	
Other comprehensive income	$ 40,000

The effect on the Jones Corporation balance sheet is the addition of the swap asset. On the income statement, interest expense of $80,000 is reported. Jones has effectively changed the debt's interest rate from variable to fixed (economic substance). That is, by receiving a floating rate and paying a fixed rate on the swap, the floating rate on the bond payable is converted to variable, which results in an effective interest rate of 8% in 2009. The economic gain on the swap offsets the economic loss related to the debt obligation (since interest rates are higher), and therefore the net gain or loss on the hedging activity is zero. **Hedge accounting allows us to record the gain outside of net income since the economic substance is that the risk has been neutralized.**

One last point on interest rate swaps. **As noted above, they may be used as cash flow hedges. They may also be used as fair value hedges.** In the latter case, they would protect against changes in fair value of a recorded asset or liability that would occur when market interest rates change and where the asset or liability has a fixed interest rate. They can be used to offset fixed interest rate payments on a debt obligation to take advantage of lower interest rates or to offset a decline in the value of a bond investment when market interest rates are increasing. Interestingly, while this eliminates **risk** created by fixed interest rates, it exposes the company to **cash flow risk**. Financial instruments are bundles of different types of risks. A company must choose which risks, if any, it wants to eliminate, and always keep in mind that the hedging instrument may carry new risks.

Using Hedge Accounting—Derivatives as Cash Flow Hedges of Anticipated Transactions

Another example of a cash flow hedge is a hedge of an anticipated future transaction, such as a raw material purchase.

To illustrate the accounting for cash flow hedges, assume that in September 2009 Allied Can Co. anticipates purchasing 1,000 metric tonnes of aluminum in January 2010. Allied is concerned that prices for aluminum will increase in the next few months, and it wants to protect against possible price increases for aluminum inventory. To hedge the risk that it might have to pay for higher prices for inventory in January 2010, Allied enters into a cash-settled aluminum forward contract.

The contract requires Allied to pay any difference between $1,550 per tonne and the spot price for aluminum, if lower, to the counterparty. If the price of aluminum increases, the counterparty will make a payment for the difference to Allied.[67] The contract matures on the expected purchase date in January 2010. The underlying for this derivative is the price of aluminum. If the price of aluminum rises above $1,550, the value of the contract to Allied increases because Allied will be able to purchase the aluminum at the lower price of $1,550 per tonne.

Assume that the contract was entered into on September 1, 2009, and that the price to be paid today for inventory to be delivered in January, the forward price, was equal to the current spot price adjusted for the time between September and January. On a net present value basis, the fair value of this contract will be zero. Therefore no entry is necessary.

September 1, 2009
No entry required. Memorandum to indicate that the contract is signed.

Assume that at December 31, 2009, the price for January delivery of aluminum has increased. The fair value of the contract has therefore also increased, with its value now assumed to be $25,000. Allied would make the following entry to record this increase in the value of the forward contract:

December 31, 2009		
Derivative—Trading	25,000	
Other Comprehensive Income—Unrealized Holding Gain or Loss		25,000

A   =   L   +   SE
+25,000   +25,000

Cash flows: No effect

The derivative contract is reported in the balance sheet as an asset. The gain on the contract would normally be recorded through net income. **However, under hedge accounting, it is reported as part of Other Comprehensive Income.** Since Allied has not yet purchased and sold the inventory, this is an **anticipated transaction**. In this type of transaction, gains or losses on the futures contract are accumulated in equity as part of other comprehensive income until the period in which the inventory is sold and earnings is affected.

---

[67] Under the net settlement feature, the actual aluminum does not have to be exchanged. Rather, the parties to the contract may settle by paying the cash difference between the forward price and the price of aluminum on the settlement date.

Assume now that in January 2010 Allied purchases (separately) 1,000 metric tonnes of aluminum for $1,575. It would make the following entry:

A = L + SE
0

Cash flows: ↓ 1,575,000 outflow

January 2010		
Aluminum Inventory	1,575,000	
Cash ($1,575 × 1,000 tonnes)		1,575,000

At the same time, Allied makes final settlement on the derivative contract and makes the following entry:

A = L + SE
0

Cash flows: ↑ 25,000 inflow

January 2010		
Cash	25,000	
Derivative—Trading		25,000
($1,575,000 – $1,550,000)		

Through use of the derivative contract, Allied has been able to fix the cost of its inventory. The $25,000 contract settlement payment offsets the amount paid to purchase the inventory at the prevailing market price of $1,575,000. The result is that the net cash outflow is at $1,550 per metric tonne, as desired. In this way, Allied has hedged the cash flow for the purchase of inventory, as shown in Illustration 16A-4.

Illustration 16A-4

Effect of Hedge on Cash Flows

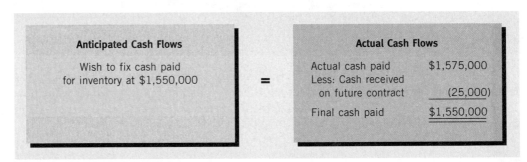

There are no income effects at this point. The gain on the futures contract is accumulated in equity as part of Accumulated Other Comprehensive Income until the period when the inventory is sold and earnings is affected through cost of goods sold.

For example, assume that the aluminum is processed into cans, the finished goods. The total cost of the cans (including the aluminum purchases in January 2010) is $1.7 million. Allied sells the cans in July 2010 for $2 million. The entry to record the sale is as follows:

A   = L + SE
+300,000   +300,000

Cash flows: ↑ 300,000 inflow

July 2010		
Cash	2,000,000	
Sales Revenue		2,000,000
Cost of Goods Sold	1,700,000	
Inventory (Cans)		1,700,000

Since the effect on the anticipated transaction has now affected earnings, Allied makes the following entry related to the hedging transaction:

July 2010		
Other Comprehensive Income—Unrealized Holding Gain or Loss	25,000	
Cost of Goods Sold		25,000

A = L + SE
0

Cash flows: No effect

The gain on the futures contract, which was reported as part of Other Comprehensive Income, now reduces the cost of goods sold. As a result, the cost of aluminum included in the overall cost of goods sold is $1,550,000. The derivative contract has worked as planned to manage the cash paid for aluminum inventory and the amount of cost of goods sold. Note that this entry could also be made at the date when the inventory was acquired, except that the credit would be booked to Inventory. Thus, the cost of goods sold in July 2010 would be $1,675,000.

Disclosures

Current disclosure provisions for all financial instruments including hedges are significant and focus on risks.[68]

Summary of Learning Objectives for Appendix 16A

Student Website

Glossary

www.wiley.com/canada/kieso

KEY TERMS

cash flow hedge, 991
fair value hedge, 990
interest rate swap, 992
settlement date, 993
swap contract, 991

11 Understand how derivatives are used in hedging.

Any company or individual that wants to protect itself against different types of business risks often uses derivative contracts to achieve this objective. In general, where the intent is to manage and reduce risk, these transactions involve some type of hedge. Derivatives are useful tools for this since they have the effect of transferring risks and rewards between the parties to the contract. Derivatives can be used to hedge a company's exposure to fluctuations in interest rates, foreign currency exchange rates, equity, or commodity prices.

12 Explain what hedge accounting is and identify the qualifying hedge criteria.

Hedge accounting is optional accounting that ensures that properly hedged positions will reduce volatility in net income created by hedging with derivatives. It seeks to match gains and losses from hedged positions with those of the hedging items so that they may be offset. Since this is special accounting, companies must ensure that there is in fact a real hedge (i.e., that the contract insulates the company from economic loss or undesirable consequences) and that the hedge remains effective. Proper documentation of the risks and risk management strategy is important.

13 Explain the difference between a fair value hedge and cash flow hedge.

A fair value hedge reduces risks relating to fair value changes of recorded assets and liabilities as well as purchase commitments. Cash flow hedges protect against future losses due to future cash flow changes relating to exposures that are not captured on the balance sheet.

---

[68] *CICA Handbook*, Section 3865.63–.69.

14 **Calculate the impact on net income of using hedge accounting for both types of hedges.**

Properly hedged positions reduce income fluctuations because gains and losses are offset. For cash flow hedges, the gains and losses on the hedging items are booked through Other Comprehensive Income and are brought into net income in the same (future) period that the hedged items are booked to net income.

Appendix 16B

Stock Compensation Plans—Additional Complications

Two common plans (beyond the stock option plans discussed in the chapter) that illustrate different accounting issues are:

1. Stock appreciation rights plans

2. Performance-type plans

Stock Appreciation Rights Plans

One of the main drawbacks of compensatory stock option plans is that in order to realize the stock options benefit, the employees must exercise the options and then sell the shares. This is a somewhat complex process and usually involves incurring transactions costs. One solution to this problem was the creation of **stock appreciation rights (SARs)**. In this type of plan, the executive or employee is given the right to receive compensation equal to the share appreciation, which is defined as the excess of the market price of the shares at the date of exercise over a pre-established price. This share appreciation may be paid in cash, shares, or a combination of both.

The major advantage of SARs is that the employee often does not have to make a cash outlay at the date of exercise, and instead receives a payment for the share appreciation. Unlike shares that are acquired under a stock option plan, the shares that constitute the basis for calculating the appreciation in a SARs plan are not issued. The executive is awarded only cash or shares having a market value equivalent to the appreciation.

As indicated earlier, the usual date for measuring compensation related to stock compensation plans is the date of grant. However, with SARs, the final amount of the cash (or shares, or combination of the two) to be distributed is not known until the date of exercise—the measurement date. Therefore, total compensation expense cannot be measured until this date.

How then should compensation expense be recorded during the interim periods from the date of grant to the date of exercise? This determination is not easy because it is impossible to know what the total compensation cost will be until the date of exercise, and the service period will probably not coincide with the exercise date. The best estimate of

15 Objective
Account for
stock appreciation
rights plans.

total compensation cost for the plan at any interim period is the difference between the current market price of the stock and the option price multiplied by the number of stock appreciation rights outstanding. This total estimated compensation expense is then allocated over the service period, to record an expense (or decrease expense if the market price falls) in each period. At the end of each interim period, the total compensation expense reported to date should equal the percentage of the total service period that has elapsed, multiplied by the estimated compensation cost.

For example, assume that at the end of an interim period the service period is 40% complete and the total estimated compensation is $100,000. At this time, the cumulative compensation expense reported to date should equal $40,000 ($100,000 × 0.40). As a second example, assume the following: In the first year of a four-year plan the company charges one-fourth of the appreciation to date. In the second year, it charges off two-fourths or 50% of the appreciation to date, less the amount that was already recognized in the first year. In the third year, it charges off three-fourths of the appreciation to date, less the amount recognized previously, and in the fourth year it charges off the remaining compensation expense. This method is referred to as the **percentage approach** for allocating compensation expense.

A special problem arises when the exercise date is later than the service period. In the previous example, if the SARs were not exercised at the end of four years, it would be necessary to account for the difference in the market price and the option price in the fifth year. In this case, the compensation expense is adjusted whenever a change in the stock's market price **occurs in subsequent reporting periods until the rights expire or are exercised, whichever comes first.**

Increases or decreases in the market value of those shares between the date of grant and the exercise date, therefore, result in a change in the measure of compensation. Some periods will have credits to compensation expense if the stock's quoted market price falls from one period to the next; the credit to Compensation Expense, however, cannot exceed previously recognized compensation expense. In other words, **cumulative compensation expense cannot be negative**.

To illustrate, assume that Hotels, Inc. establishes a SARs program on January 1, 2009, which entitles executives to receive cash at the date of exercise (anytime in the next five years) for the difference between the shares' market price and the pre-established or stated price of $10 on 10,000 SARs. The shares' market price on December 31, 2009, is $13 and the service period runs for two years (2009 to 2010). Illustration 16B-1 shows the amount of compensation expense to be recorded each period, assuming that the executives exercise their rights after holding the SARs for three years.

In 2009, Hotels would record compensation expense of $15,000 because 50% of the $30,000 total compensation cost estimated at December 31, 2009, is allocable to 2009.

Illustration 16B-1

Compensation Expense, Stock Appreciation Rights

STOCK APPRECIATION RIGHTS
Schedule of Compensation Expense

(1) Date	(2) Market Price	(3) Pre-established Price (10,000 SARs)	(4) Cumulative Compensation Recognizable[a]	(5) Percentage Accrued[b]	(6) Cumulative Compensation Accrued to Date	Expense 2009	Expense 2010	Expense 2011
12/31/09	$13	$10	$30,000	50%	$(15,000)	$15,000		
					$(55,000)		$55,000	
12/31/10	$17	$10	$70,000	100%	$(70,000)			
					$(20,000)			$(20,000)
12/31/11	$15	$10	$50,000	100%	$(50,000)			

[a]Cumulative compensation for unexercised SARs to be allocated to periods of service.
[b]The percentage accrued is based on a two-year service period (2009 to 2010).

In 2010, the market price increased to $17 per share; therefore, the additional compensation expense of $55,000 ($70,000 − $15,000) was recorded. The SARs were held through 2011, during which time the shares decreased to $15. The decrease is recognized by recording a $20,000 credit to Compensation Expense and a debit to Liability under Stock Appreciation Plan. Note that after the service period ends, since the rights are still outstanding, the rights are adjusted to market at December 31, 2011. Any such credit to Compensation Expense cannot exceed previous charges to expense that can be attributed to that plan.

As the compensation expense is recorded each period, the corresponding credit should be to a liability account if the stock appreciation is to be paid in cash. According to GAAP, SARs that call for settlement in cash are indexed liabilities and the measurement date is therefore the settlement date.[69]

If shares are to be issued, then a more appropriate credit would be to Contributed Surplus. The entry to record compensation expense in the first year, assuming that the SARs ultimately will be paid in cash, is as follows:

Compensation Expense	15,000	
Liability under Stock Appreciation Plan		15,000

A = L + SE
+15,000 −15,000
Cash flows: No effect

The liability account would be credited again in 2010 for $55,000 and debited for $20,000 in 2011, when the negative compensation expense is recorded. The entry to record the negative compensation expense is as follows:

Liability under Stock Appreciation Plan	20,000	
Compensation Expense		20,000

A = L + SE
−20,000 +20,000
Cash flows: No effect

At December 31, 2011, the executives receive $50,000; the entry removing the liability is as follows:

Liability under Stock Appreciation Plan	50,000	
Cash		50,000

A = L + SE
−50,000 −50,000
Cash flows: ↓ 50,000 outflow

In general, if the employee has the option of choosing to be paid out in shares or cash, assume that cash will be chosen, and that a **liability** thus exists. If the employer has the choice, an obligation is not necessarily created since the employer is not obligated to pay cash. The SARs may therefore be designated as an **equity instrument**.[70] Since the value of the SARs is equity driven and since no cash will be paid out, it is indeed an equity instrument. **The entity would value the plan like a stock option at the grant date and allocate this fixed amount over the service period. It would not subsequently be changed.**

Either way, if the company is unable to measure the cost at the grant date, the measurement date is the exercise date and the amount is continually re-estimated.

SARs are often issued in combination with compensatory stock options (referred to as **tandem** or **combination plans**) and the executive must then select which of the two sets of terms to exercise and which one to cancel. The existence of alternative plans running concurrently poses additional problems. Based on the facts available each period, it must

---

[69] *CICA Handbook*, Section 3870.39.

[70] *CICA Handbook*, Section 3870.03a. Note, however, that if the number of shares to be issued changes with the amount owed to the employee, this might meet the definition of a liability per Section 3863.12. Having stated this, Section 3860 is not meant to apply to stock compensation plans.

be determined which of the two plans is more likely to be exercised and that plan is then accounted for and the other is ignored.

Performance–Type Plans

Objective 16
Explain what performance-type plans are.

Some executives have become disenchanted with stock compensation plans in which payment depends ultimately on an increase in the common shares' market price. They do not like having their compensation and judgement of performance at the mercy of the stock market's erratic behaviour. As a result, there has been a large increase in the use of **performance-type plans** that award the executives common shares (or cash) if specified performance criteria are attained during the performance period (generally three to five years). Many large companies now have some type of plan that does not rely on share price appreciation. The performance criteria are usually increases in return on assets or equity, growth in sales, growth in earnings per share (EPS), or a combination of these factors.

A performance-type plan's measurement date is the date of exercise because the number of shares that will be issued or the cash that will be paid out when performance is achieved are not known at the date of grant. The company must use its best estimates to measure the compensation cost before the date of exercise. The compensation cost is allocated to the periods involved in the same way as is done with stock appreciation rights; that is, the percentage approach is used.

Tandem or combination awards are popular with these plans. The executive has the choice of selecting between a performance or stock option award. Companies such as **General Electric** and **Xerox** have adopted plans of this nature. In these cases, the executive has the best of both worlds: if either the share price increases or the performance goal is achieved, the executive gains. Sometimes, the executive receives both types of plans, so that the monies received from the performance plan can finance the exercise price on the stock option plan.

Student Website

Glossary

www.wiley.com/canada/kieso

KEY TERMS

combination plan, 1001
percentage approach, 1000
stock appreciation rights (SARs), 999
tandem plan, 1001

Summary of Learning Objectives for Appendix 16B

15 Account for stock appreciation rights plans.

SARs are popular because the employee can share in increases in value of the company's shares without having to purchase them. The increases in value over a certain amount are paid to the employee as cash or shares. Obligations to pay cash represent a liability that must be remeasured. The cost is therefore continually adjusted, with the measurement date being the exercise date. The related expense is spread over the service period. If the SARs are not exercised at the end of the service period, the liability must continue to be remeasured.

16 Explain what performance-type plans are.

Compensation is measured by the market value of shares issued on the exercise date. Compensation expense is allocated by the percentage approach over the service period, and then marked to market.

Appendix 16c

Fair Value Measurement

As we move toward greater use of fair values, the focus on the development of fair value measurement models has intensified for accountants. When there is already a market, **fair value** is easy to determine. It is defined as the amount of consideration that would be agreed upon in an arm's-length transaction between knowledgeable, willing parties who are under no obligation to act.[71]

The best evidence of fair value is from an **active market** where frequent trades are made and prices are published. However, where a **market price** is not available, a **valuation technique** is used. As a general rule, the valuation technique should use all the input variables that are available from external market sources and rely as little as possible on internally generated variables. This allows the model to produce more objective, and more reliable, fair value estimates.

Fair value estimates incorporate one or more of the following variables:[72]

(a) **Risk-free interest rates**, such as government rates. Well publicized rates such as LIBOR are used for some products even though LIBOR is not a risk-free rate and, therefore, the credit risk in the analysis would have to be adjusted to reflect this.

(b) **Credit risk**. This is the premium over the risk-free rate and reflects additional riskiness that relates to the ability to pay the cash flows.

(c) **Foreign currency prices**, based on historical data.

(d) **Equity prices**, based on historical data.

(e) **Marketability**. This is the return that participants demand in cases where there is not a liquid market, and is based on historical data.

(f) **Volatility**. This is the magnitude of future changes in the market price. Volatility of liquid traded options can be observed in the prices for those options but is often estimated from historical price data.

(g) **Prepayment/surrender risk**. This is the expected prepayment or surrender patterns. This factor can be very difficult to estimate.

(h) **Servicing costs**, which are estimated using comparisons with fees that are currently being charged.

---

[71] *CICA Handbook*, Section 3855.19(j),

[72] *CICA Handbook*, Section 3855.A54.

Examples of valuation techniques include discounted cash flows analysis and options pricing models. These will be discussed next.

Option Pricing Models

There are numerous **option pricing models** and they are usually covered in more advanced finance texts and courses. The Black-Scholes and binomial tree option pricing models are two of these models. The Black-Scholes options pricing model will be briefly introduced here as it is often used to estimate fair values of options for companies whose shares are publicly traded.

Recall that financial instrument values have two components—an **intrinsic value** component and a **time value** component. These two components are used in the Black-Scholes model, which requires the following two amounts to be calculated. Note that this model can be used with published tables.

1. The standard deviation of proportionate changes in the fair value of the asset underlying the options, multiplied by the square root of the time to expiry of the option. This amount relates to the time value portion and the potential for the value of the asset underlying the option to change over time. The volatility of the shares as compared with the volatility of the market in general is an important factor here. The more volatile the shares, the greater the fair value of the options. This is because the volatility introduces more risk and the higher the risk, the higher the return.

2. The ratio of the fair value of the asset underlying the option to the present value of the option exercise price. This relates to the intrinsic value.[73]

The following is an example taken from the *CICA Handbook* Section 3863.A9. It illustrates the use of the Black-Scholes option pricing model in the context of splitting a combined instrument into its debt and equity components:

> An entity issues 2,000 convertible bonds at the start of Year 1. The bonds have a three-year term, and are issued at par with a face value of $1,000 per bond, giving total proceeds of $2,000,000. Interest is payable annually in arrears at a nominal annual interest rate of six percent. Each bond is convertible at any time up to maturity into 250 common shares.
>
> > When the bonds are issued, the prevailing market interest rate for similar debt without conversion options is nine percent. At the issue date, the market price of one common share is $3. The dividends expected over the three-year term of the bonds amount to $0.14 per share at the end of each year. The risk-free annual interest rate for a three-year term is five percent.
>
> The following example illustrates the application of a version of the Black-Scholes model that utilizes tables available in finance textbooks and other sources. The steps in applying this version of the model are set out below.
>
> > This model first requires the calculation of two amounts that are used in the option valuation tables:

---

[73] *CICA Handbook*, Section 3863.A9.

(a) Standard deviation of proportionate changes in the fair value of the asset underlying the option multiplied by the square root of the time to expiry of the option.

This amount relates to the potential for favourable (and unfavourable) changes in the price of the asset underlying the option, in this case the common shares of the entity issuing the convertible bonds. The volatility of the returns on the underlying asset is estimated by the standard deviation of the returns. The higher the standard deviation, the greater the fair value of the option. In this example, the standard deviation of the annual returns on the shares is assumed to be 30 percent. The time to expiry of the conversion rights is three years. The standard deviation of proportionate changes in fair value of the shares multiplied by the square root of the time to expiry of the option is thus determined as:

$$0.3 \times \text{square root of } 3 = 0.5196$$

(b) Ratio of the fair value of the asset underlying the option to the present value of the option exercise price.

This amount relates the present value of the asset underlying the option to the cost that the option holder must pay to obtain that asset, and is associated with the intrinsic value of the option. The higher this amount, the greater the fair value of a call option. In this example, the market value of each share on issuance of the bonds is $3. The present value of the expected dividends over the term of the option is deducted from the market price, since the payment of dividends reduces the fair value of the shares and thus the fair value of the option. The present value of a dividend of $0.14 per share at the end of each year, discounted at the risk-free rate of five percent, is $0.3813. The present value of the asset underlying the option is therefore:

$$\$3 - \$0.3813 = \$2.6187 \text{ per share}$$

The present value of the exercise price is $4 per share discounted at the risk-free rate of five percent over three years, assuming that the bonds are converted at maturity, or $3.4554. The ratio is thus determined as:

$$\$2.6187 \div \$3.4554 = 0.7579$$

The bond conversion option is a form of call option. The call option valuation table indicates that, for the two amounts calculated above (i.e., 0.5196 and 0.7579), the fair value of the option is approximately 11.05 percent of the fair value of the underlying asset.

The valuation of the conversion options can therefore be calculated as:

$$0.1105 \times \$2.6187 \text{ per share} \times 250 \text{ shares per bond} \times 2,000 \text{ bonds} = \$144,683$$

The fair value of the debt component of the compound instrument calculated by the present value method plus the fair value of the option calculated by the Black-Scholes option pricing model does not equal the $2,000,000 proceeds from issuance of the convertible bonds (i.e., $1,848,122 + $144,683 = $1,992,805). The small difference can be prorated over the fair values of the two components to produce a fair value for the liability of $1,854,794 and a fair value for the option of $145,206.

Discounted Cash Flows

The **discounted cash flow method** is a very robust, widely accepted tool for dealing with uncertainty and the time value of money. In essence, the entity estimates future cash flows and selects a discount rate to discount the cash flows to today's value.

The net present value calculated needs to reflect all risks inherent in the cash flows including credit quality and currency.[74] The discount rate also needs to reflect the time until the cash flow occurs. Two approaches are possible:

1. Discount rate adjustment approach—the discount rate reflects all risks in the cash flows but the cash flows are assumed to be certain

2. Cash flow adjustment approach—a risk-free discount rate is used to discount cash flows that have been adjusted for uncertainty.

Discount Rate Adjustment Approach

Under the **discount rate adjustment approach**, the stream of contracted cash flows is discounted, and the discount rate is adjusted to accommodate the riskiness of the cash flows. This model is best used where the cash flows are otherwise fairly certain. The discount rate would be adjusted for the credit risk that is associated with the party who is paying the cash flows. This method is useful for instruments where the cash flows are specified in the contract, such as fixed interest and principal payments. It is not very useful for more complex instruments where the cash flows may be variable for other reasons than the credit risk.

Assume that Company A has issued a 10% bond that is due in 10 years and has a face value of $100. Assume further that the risk-adjusted market rate that reflects the credit risk of Company A is 10%. This rate would be the rate that the market would demand of Company A, given the specific credit risk. The present value of the bond would be calculated as follows:

> PV $1 at 10% × Principal + PV of an annuity for 10 years at 10% – All discounted at 10% = $100

Cash Flow Adjustment Approach

Under the **cash flow adjustment approach**, the discount rate is the risk-free rate and the cash flow uncertainty is dealt with by using probabilities. The projected cash flows reflect the uncertainty in terms of amount and timing using probability weighting. This model is more flexible and is useful where the financial instruments have variable cash flows.

In this case, assume that the instrument has a variable cash flow. Assume that there is a 20% chance of a payment in three years of $30 and an 80% chance of a payment in three years of $60. If the risk-free rate were 5%, the expected cash flows (incorporating the credit risk) are as follows:

> 20% × $30 + 80% × $60 = $54
>
> PV $54 at 5% in three years = $54 × 0.86384 = $46.65

---

[74] *CICA Handbook*, Section 3855.A53.

Note that these methods may be used for other purposes than just financial instruments. In fact, they are also used for asset impairment valuations.[75]

International

There is a significant joint initiative regarding fair value measurements between the IASB and FASB. It is felt that all standard setters have been adding in "bits and pieces" regarding how to value financial statement elements over the years. These "bits and pieces" are spread out over a number of topics and are not necessarily consistent. Now is a good time to rationalize the body of knowledge. According to the IASB, the objective of the project is to establish a single source of guidance for all fair value measurements required by IFRS.

The following principles have been agreed on to date:

(i)   The definition of fair value and its measurement objective should be consistent for all fair value measurements required by IFRS. The Board acknowledged this will require consequential amendments to some standards.

(ii) A fair value measurement should reflect market views of the attributes of the asset or liability being measured and should not include views of the reporting entity if those views differ from market expectations.

(iii) A fair value measurement should consider the utility of the asset or liability being measured. As such, the fair value measurement should consider the location, condition, and restrictions on the use of the asset or liability at its measurement date.

In addition a new definition of fair value is emerging as follows:

Fair value is the price that would be received for an asset or paid to transfer a liability in a transaction between market participants at the measurement date (an exit price). This definition is consistent with SFAS 157 on fair value measurements.

Summary of Learning Objective for Appendix 16C

Student Website

Glossary

www.wiley.com/canada/kieso

17 Understand the different fair value measurement options and models.

Fair value is most readily determined where there is an active market with published prices. Where this is not the case, a valuation technique is used. Where possible, valuation techniques should use available external inputs to ensure that they are more objective. Two common valuation techniques are option pricing models and discounted cash flows. Discounted cash flow methods include the more traditional discount rate adjustment approach and the cash flow adjustment approach.

KEY TERMS

cash flow adjustment
   approach, 1006
discount rate adjustment
   approach, 1006
fair value, 1003

---

[75] *CICA Handbook*, Section 3063.A11–A18.

Brief Exercises

Note: All assignment material with an asterisk (*) relates to an appendix to the chapter.

(LO 1)   **BE16-1**   Jamieson Limited issued century bonds that will not be due until 2104. The bonds carry interest at 5%. Explain how this instrument should be presented on the statement of financial position.

(LO 1)   **BE16-2**   Silky Limited has redeemable preferred shares outstanding that carry a dividend of 5%. If the shares are not redeemed within five years, the dividend will double every five years from then on. How should Silky account for this instrument?

(LO 1)   **BE16-3**   Refer to BE 16-2. How should Silky treat the dividends associated with the redeemable preferred shares?

(LO 1)   **BE16-4**   During 2008, Genoa Limited issued retractable preferred shares. The shares may be presented to the company by the holder for redemption after 2010. Explain how these should be presented in the financial statements.

(LO 2)   **BE16-5**   Verbitsky Corporation had 500 $1,900 bonds outstanding, with each one convertible into 20 common shares. The bonds were later converted on December 31, 2007, when the unamortized discount was $39,000, and the shares' market price was $21 per share. Record the conversion using the book value approach.

(LO 2)   **BE16-6**   Selly Corporation issued 3,000 common shares upon conversion of 1,000 preferred shares. The preferred shares were originally issued at $70 per share and the Contributed Surplus—Conversion Rights account for the preferred shares had a balance of $7,000. The common shares were trading at $36 per share at the time of conversion. Record the conversion of the preferred shares.

(LO 2)   **BE16-7**   Divac Corporation issued 900 $1,000 bonds at 101. Each bond was issued with one detachable stock warrant. After issuance, the bonds were selling in the market at 98, and the warrants had a market value of $35. Use the proportional method to record the issuance of the bonds and warrants.

(LO 2)   **BE16-8**   Ceballos Corporation issued 1,000 $1,000 bonds at 102. Each bond was issued with one detachable stock warrant. After issuance, the bonds were selling separately at 98. The warrant's market price without the bonds cannot be determined. Use the incremental method to record the issuance of the bonds and warrants.

(LO 9)   **BE16-9**   On January 1, 2008, Johnson Corporation granted 4,000 options to executives. Each option entitles the holder to purchase one share of Johnson's common shares at $40 per share at any time during the next five years. The shares' market price is $55 per share on the date of grant. The period of benefit is two years. Prepare Johnson's journal entries for January 1, 2008, and December 31, 2008 and 2009. Assume that the options' fair value as calculated using an option pricing model is $106,000.

(LO 6)   **BE16-10**   Pseudo Inc. purchased options to acquire 1,000 common shares of Ego Limited for $20 per share within the next six months. The premium (cost) related to the options was $500. How should this be accounted for in the financial statements of Pseudo?

(LO 6)   **BE 16-11**   Refer to BE16-10. Instead of purchasing the options, assume that Pseudo wrote the options and collected $500 from Alter Limited as the option premium. How would this be accounted for in the financial statements of Pseudo?

(LO 6)   **BE 16-12**   On January 1, 2008, Ginseng Inc. entered into a forward contract to purchase U.S. $1,000 for $1,080 Canadian in 30 days. On January 15, the fair value of the contract was $20 (reflecting the present value of the future cash flows under the contract). Assume that the company would like to update its records on January 15. Prepare only necessary journal entries on January 1 and 15, 2008.

(LO 6)   **BE 16-13**   Refer to BE 16-12. Assume the same facts except that the forward contract is a futures contract that trades on the Futures Exchange. Ginseng was required to deposit $50 with the stockbroker as a margin. On January 15, the broker asked Ginseng to deposit an additional $7. Prepare the journal entries to update the books on January 1 and 15 for the additional margin call as well as the change in value of the futures contract.

(LO 15)   ***BE16-14**   Perkins, Inc. established a stock appreciation rights (SARs) program on January 1, 2008, which entitles executives to receive cash at the date of exercise for the difference between the shares' market price and the pre-established price of $20 on 5,400 SARs. The required service period is two years. The shares' market price is $22 on December 31, 2008, and $34 on December 31, 2009. The SARs are exercised on January 1, 2010. Calculate Perkins' compensation expense for 2008 and 2009.

Exercises

E16-1   **(Issuance and Conversion of Bonds)**   **(LO 2)**

Instructions

Present the required entry(ies) to record each of the following unrelated transactions:

(a) On March 1, 2009, Loma Corporation issued $300,000 of 8% non-convertible bonds at 104, which are due on February 28, 2026. In addition, each $1,000 bond was issued with 25 detachable stock warrants, each of which entitled the bondholder to purchase for $50 one of Loma's no par value common shares. The bonds without the warrants would normally sell at 95. On March 1, 2009, the fair market value of Loma's common shares was $40 per share and the fair market value of each warrant was $2.

(b) Grand Corp. issued $10 million of par value, 9%, convertible bonds at 97. If the bonds had not been convertible, the company's investment banker estimates they would have been sold at 93.

(c) Hussein Limited issued $20 million of par value, 7% bonds at 98. One detachable stock purchase warrant was issued with each $100 par value bond. At the time of issuance, the warrants were selling for $6.

(d) On July 1, 2007, Tien Limited called its 9% convertible debentures for conversion. The $10 million of par value bonds were converted into 1 million common shares. On July 1, there was $75,000 of unamortized discount applicable to the bonds, and the company paid an additional $65,000 to the bondholders to induce conversion of all the bonds. The company records the conversion using the book value method. The balance in the account Contributed Surplus—Conversion Rights was $270,000 at the time of conversion.

(e) On December 1, 2008, Horton Company issued 500 of its $1,000, 9% bonds at 103. Attached to each bond was one detachable stock warrant entitling the holder to purchase 10 of Horton's common shares. On December 1, 2008, the market value of the bonds, without the stock warrants, was 95, and the market value of each stock warrant was $50.

E16-2   **(Conversion of Bonds)** Aubrey Inc. issued $6 million of 10-year, 9%, convertible bonds on June 1, 2007, at 98   **(LO 2)** plus accrued interest. The bonds were dated April 1, 2007, with interest payable April 1 and October 1. Bond discount is amortized semi-annually on a straight-line basis. Bonds without conversion privileges would have sold at 97 plus accrued interest.

On April 1, 2008, $1.5 million of these bonds were converted into 30,000 common shares. Accrued interest was paid in cash at the time of conversion but only to the bondholders whose bonds were being converted.

Instructions

(a) Prepare the entry to record the issuance of the convertible bonds on June 1, 2007.

(b) Prepare the entry to record the interest expense at October 1, 2007. Assume that accrued interest payable was credited when the bonds were issued. (Round to nearest dollar.)

(c) Prepare the entry(ies) to record the conversion on April 1, 2008. (The book value method is used.) Assume that the entry to record amortization of the bond discount using the straight-line method and interest payment has been made.

(d) What do you believe was the likely market value of the common shares as of the date of the conversion of April 1, 2008?

E16-3   **(Conversion of Bonds)** Vargo Limited had $1.9 million of bonds payable outstanding and the unamortized premium   **(LO 2)** for these bonds amounted to $28,500. Each $1,000 bond was convertible into 20 preferred shares. All bonds were then converted into preferred shares. The Contributed Surplus—Conversion Rights account had a balance of $13,200.

Instructions

(a) Assuming that the book value method was used, what entry would be made?

(b) From the perspective of the bondholders, what is the likely motive for the conversion of bonds into preferred shares? What are the advantages of each investment that are given up or obtained by the bondholders who chose to convert their investment?

E16-4   **(Conversion of Bonds and Expired Rights)** Dadayeva Inc. has $3 million of 8% convertible bonds outstand-   **(LO 2)** ing. Each $1,000 bond is convertible into 30 no par value common shares. The bonds pay interest on January 31 and July 31. On July 31, 2009, the holders of $900,000 of these bonds exercised the conversion privilege. On that date, the market price of the bonds was 105, the market price of the common shares was $36, the carrying value of the common shares was $18, and the Contributed Surplus—Conversion Right account balance was $450,000. The total unamortized bond premium at the date of conversion was $210,000. The remaining bonds were never converted and were retired when they reached the maturity date.

Instructions

(a) Assuming that the book value method was used, record the conversion of the $900,000 of bonds on July 31, 2009.

(b) Prepare the journal entry that would be required for the remaining amount in Contributed Surplus—Conversion Right when the maturity of the remaining bonds is recorded.

(LO 2)   **E16-5   (Conversion of Bonds)** On January 1, 2007, when its common shares were selling for $80 per share, Plato Corp. issued $10 million of 8% convertible debentures due in 20 years. The conversion option allowed the holder of each $1,000 bond to convert the bond into five common shares. The debentures were issued for $10.8 million. The bond payment's present value at the time of issuance was $8.5 million and the corporation believes the difference between the present value and the amount paid is attributable to the conversion feature. On January 1, 2008, the corporation's common shares were split 2 for 1, and the conversion rate for the bonds was adjusted accordingly. On January 1, 2009, when the corporation's common shares were selling for $135 per share, holders of 30% of the convertible debentures exercised their conversion option. The corporation uses the ~~straight-line method~~ for amortizing any bond discounts or premiums.

effective interest rate method

Instructions

(a) Prepare in general journal form the entry to record the original issuance of the convertible debentures.

(b) Using the book value method, prepare in general journal form the entry to record the exercise of the conversion option. Show supporting calculations in good form.

(c) How many shares were issued as a result of the conversion?

(d) From the perspective of Plato Corp., what are the advantages and disadvantages of the conversion of the bonds into common shares?

(LO 2)   **E16-6   (Conversion of Bonds)** An excerpt from the December 31, 2008, statement of financial position of Kepler Corp. shows the following balances:

$500,000 Face Value, 10%, Callable, Convertible Bonds Payable (semi-annual interest dates of April 30 and October 31; convertible into six common shares per $1,000 of bond principal; maturity date of April 30, 2012)	$489,760
Contributed Surplus—Conversion Rights	$ 19,000

On March 5, 2009, Kepler Corp. called all of the bonds as of April 30 for the principal plus interest through April 30. By April 30, all bondholders had converted to common shares as of the interest payment date. Consequently, on April 30, Kepler Corp. paid the semi-annual interest and issued common shares for the bonds. The discount is amortized on a straight-line basis. Kepler uses the book value method.

Instructions

Prepare the entry(ies) to record the interest expense and conversion on April 30, 2009. Note that reversing entries were made on January 1, 2009. (Round to the nearest dollar.)

(LO 2)   **E16-7   (Conversion of Bonds)** Shankman Corporation had two issues of securities outstanding: common shares and an 8% convertible bond issue in the face amount of $8 million. Interest payment dates of the bond issue are June 30 and December 31. The conversion clause in the bond indenture entitles the bondholders to receive 40 no par value common shares in exchange for each $1,000 bond. The value of the equity portion of the bond issue is $60,000. On June 30, 2009, the holders of $1.2 million of the face value bonds exercised the conversion privilege. The market price of the bonds on that date was $1,100 per bond and the market price of the common shares was $35. The total unamortized bond discount at the date of conversion was $500,000.

Instructions

Prepare in general journal form the entry to record the exercise of the conversion option, using the book value method.

(LO 2)   **E16-8   (Conversion of Bonds)** On January 1, 2007, Gottlieb Corporation issued $6 million of 10-year, 7%, convertible debentures at 104. Investment bankers believe that the debenture would have sold at 102 without the conversion privilege. Interest is to be paid semi-annually on June 30 and December 31. Each $1,000 debenture can be converted into five common shares of Gottlieb Corporation after December 31, 2008. On January 1, 2009, $400,000 of debentures are converted into common shares, which are then selling at $110. An additional $400,000 of debentures are converted on March 31, 2009. The common shares' market price is then $115. Accrued interest at March 31 will be paid on the next interest date. Bond premium is amortized on a straight-line basis.

Instructions

(a) Make the necessary journal entries for:

1. December 31, 2008   3. March 31, 2009
2. January 1, 2009   4. June 30, 2009

Record the conversions using the book value method.

(b) From the perspective of the debenture holders, why would they be motivated to wait for the conversion of the bonds into common shares? What are the risks involved in waiting and what could the bondholders ultimately give up by waiting too long?

E16-9 **(Issuance of Bonds with Warrants)** Illiad Inc. has decided to raise additional capital by issuing bonds with a **(LO 2)** face value of $170,000 and a coupon rate of 10%. In discussions with Illiad's investment bankers, it was determined that to help the sale of the bonds, detachable stock warrants should be issued at the rate of one warrant for each $100 bond sold. The bonds' value without the warrants is considered to be $130,000, and the warrants' value in the market is $30,000. The bonds sold in the market at issuance for $158,000.

Instructions

(a) What entry should be made at the time of the issuance of the bonds and warrants?

(b) If the warrants were non-detachable, would the entries be different? Discuss.

E16-10 **(Issuance of Bonds with Detachable Warrants)** On September 1, 2008, Sands Corp. sold at 102 (plus accrued **(LO 2)** interest) 5,200 of its $1,000 face value, 10-year, 9%, non-convertible bonds with detachable stock warrants. Each bond carried two detachable warrants; each warrant was for one common share at a specified option price of $10 per share. Shortly after issuance, the warrants were quoted on the market for $5 each. Assume that no market value is available for the bonds. Interest is payable on December 1 and June 1.

Instructions

Prepare in general journal format the entry to record the issuance of the bonds.

(AICPA adapted)

E16-11 **(Issuance of Bonds with Stock Warrants)** On May 1, 2008, Farhad Limited issued 5,500 $1,000 bonds at 101. **(LO 2)** Each bond was issued with one detachable stock warrant. Shortly after issuance, the bonds were selling at 96; the warrants' market value cannot be determined.

Instructions

(a) Prepare the entry to record the issuance of the bonds and warrants.

(b) Assume the same facts as part (a), except that the warrants had a fair value of $40 each. Prepare the entry to record the issuance of the bonds and warrants using the proportional method.

(c) From the perspective of Farhad Limited, what is the motive in adding a stock warrant to the bond issue?

E16-12 **(Derivative Transaction)** On January 2, 2007, Jones Corporation purchased a call option for $200 on **(LO 6)** Merchant common shares. The call option gives Jones the option to buy 1,000 shares of Merchant at a strike price of $40 per share. The market price of a Merchant share was $40 on January 2, 2007 (the intrinsic value was therefore $0). On March 31, 2007, the market price for Merchant stock was $53 per share, and the value of the option was $13,200.

Instructions

(a) Prepare the journal entry to record the purchase of the call option on January 2, 2007.

(b) Prepare the journal entry(ies) to recognize the change in the call option's fair value as of March 31, 2007.

(c) What was the effect on net income of entering into the derivative transaction for the period January 2 to March 31, 2007?

(d) Based on the available facts, explain whether the company is using the option as a hedge or for speculative purposes.

E16-13 **(Issuance and Exercise of Stock Options)** On November 1, 2008, Columbo Corp. adopted a stock option **(LO 9)** plan that granted options to key executives to purchase 32,000 common shares. The options were granted on January 2, 2009, and were exercisable two years after the date of grant if the grantee was still a company employee; the options expire six years from the date of grant. The option price was set at $40 and, using an option pricing model to value the options, the total compensation expense was estimated to be $450,000. Note that the calculation did not take into account forfeitures.

On April 1, 2010, 2,000 options were terminated when some employees resigned from the company. The market value of the shares at that date was $32. All of the remaining options were exercised during the year 2011: 20,000 on January 3 when the market price was $62, and 10,000 on May 1 when the market price was $77 a share.

Instructions

(a) Prepare journal entries relating to the stock option plan for the years 2009, 2010, and 2011. Assume that the employees perform services equally in 2009 and 2010, and that the year end is December 31.

(b) What is the significance of the fact that the pricing model did not take into account forfeitures? Would taking expected forfeitures into account make the estimate of the total compensation expense higher or lower?

(LO 9) **E16-14 (Issuance, Exercise, and Termination of Stock Options)** On January 1, 2009, Titania Inc. granted stock options to officers and key employees to buy 40,000 of the company's common shares at $25 per share. The options were exercisable within a one-year period beginning January 1, 2011, by grantees still employed by the company, and expired December 31, 2011. The service period for this award is two years. Assume that, using an option pricing model, the total compensation expense was estimated to be $450,000.

On March 31, 2011, 12,000 option shares were exercised when the common shares' market value was $40 per share. Assume that the market price was below $20 by December 31, 2011.

Instructions

Prepare journal entries to record the issuance of the stock options, expiry of the stock options, exercise of the stock options, and charges to compensation expense, for the years ended December 31, 2009, 2010, and 2011.

(LO 9) **E16-15 (Issuance, Exercise, and Termination of Stock Options)** On January 1, 2007, Nichols Corporation granted 20,000 options to key executives. Each option allows the executive to purchase one share of Nichols' common shares at a price of $25 per share. The options were exercisable within a two-year period beginning January 1, 2009, if the grantee was still employed by the company at the time of the exercise. On the grant date, Nichols' shares were trading at $20 per share, and a fair value option pricing model determined total compensation to be $400,000.

On May 1, 2009, 8,000 options were exercised when the market price of Nichols' shares was $31 per share. The remaining options lapsed on January 1, 2011, because executives decided not to exercise their options.

Instructions

(a) Prepare the necessary journal entries related to the stock option plan for the years ended December 31, 2007 through 2011.

(b) What is the significance of the $20 market price of the Nichols shares at the date of grant? Would the exercise price normally be higher or lower than the market price of the shares on the date of grant?

(c) What is the significance of the $31 market price of the Nichols shares at May 1, 2009, the date of the exercise of the stock options?

(d) What likely happened to the market price of the shares in 2010?

(e) What motive might an employee have for delaying the exercise of the stock option? What are the risks involved?

(LO 9) **E16-16 (Issuance, Exercise, and Termination of Stock Options)** On January 1, 2003, Sorvino Corp. granted stock options to its chief executive officer. This is the only stock option that Sorvino offers and the details are as follows:

Option to purchase:	5,000 common shares
Option price per share:	$62.00
Market price per common share on date of grant:	$57.00
Stock option expiration:	The earlier of 8 years after issuance or the employee's cessation of employment with Sorvino for any reason other than retirement
Date when options are first exercisable:	The earlier of 4 years after issuance or the date on which an employee reaches the retirement age of 65
Fair value at grant date, as determined by an option pricing model:	$10.00

On January 1, 2008, 4,000 of the options were exercised when the market price of the common shares was $78. The remaining stock options were allowed to expire.

Instructions

Record the journal entries at the following dates:

(a) January 1, 2003

(b) December 31, 2003, the fiscal year end of Sorvino Inc.

(c) January 1, 2008—the exercise date

(d) December 31, 2010—the expiry date of the options

*E16-17 (Cash Flow Hedge) On January 2, 2008, MacCloud Corp. issued a $100,000, four-year note at prime + 1% **(LO 13,14)** variable interest, with interest payable semi-annually. MacCloud now wants to change the note to a fixed rate note. As a result, on January 2, 2008, MacCloud Corp. enters into an interest rate swap where it agrees to pay 6% fixed and receive prime + 1% for the first six months on $100,000. At each six-month period, the variable rate will be reset. The prime interest rate is 5.7% on January 2, 2008, and is reset to 6.7% on June 30, 2008.

Instructions

(a) Calculate the net interest expense to be reported for this note and related swap transaction as of June 30 and December 31, 2008.

(b) Prepare the journal entries relating to the swap for the year ended December 31, 2008.

(c) Explain why this is a cash flow hedge.

*E16-18 (Cash Flow Hedge) On January 2, 2007, Parton Corp. issues a $10 million, five-year note at LIBOR, with **(LO 13,14)** interest paid annually. The variable rate is reset at the end of each year. The LIBOR rate for the first year is 5.8%. Parton later decides that it prefers fixed-rate financing and wants to lock in a rate of 6%. As a result, Parton enters into an interest rate swap to pay 6% fixed and receive LIBOR based on $10 million for the remainder of the term of the note. The variable rate is reset to 6.6% on January 2, 2008.

Instructions

(a) Calculate the net interest expense to be reported for this note and related swap transactions as of December 31, 2007 and 2008.

(b) Prepare the journal entries relating to the swap for the years ended December 31, 2007 and 2008.

(c) Explain why this is a cash flow hedge.

*E16-19 (Fair Value Hedge) Sarazan Corp. purchased a $1-million, four-year, 7.5% fixed-rate interest only, non-pre- **(LO 13,14)** payable bond on December 31, 2007. The bond is actively traded and is held as an available-for-sale security. Sarazan later decided to hedge the interest rate and change from a fixed rate to variable rate, so it entered into a swap agreement with M&S Corp. The swap agreement specified that Sarazan will pay a fixed rate of 7.5% and receive variable rate interest with settlement dates that match the interest payments on the instrument. Assume that interest rates increased during 2008 and that Sarazan received $13,000 as a net settlement on the swap for the settlement at December 31, 2008. The loss related to the investment (due to interest rate changes) was $48,000. The value of the swap contract increased by $48,000.

Instructions

(a) Prepare the journal entry to record the receipt of interest on December 31, 2008, from the company that issued the bond.

(b) Prepare the journal entry to record the receipt of the swap settlement on December 31, 2008.

(c) Prepare the journal entry to record the change in the fair value of the swap contract on December 31, 2008.

(d) Prepare the journal entry to record the change in the fair value of the bond on December 31, 2008. Note how this is different from how the fair value change would have been booked if the bond had not been hedged.

(e) Explain why the interest rate swap is a fair value hedge in this situation.

(f) Explain how an interest rate swap can act as both a fair value hedge and a cash flow hedge.

*E16-20 (Stock Appreciation Rights) Aoun Limited established a stock appreciation rights program that entitled its **(LO 15)** new president, Ashley Murfitt, to receive cash for the difference between the Aoun Limited common shares' market price and a pre-established price of $32 (also market price) on December 31, 2006, on 40,000 SARs. The date of grant is December 31, 2006, and the required employment (service) period is four years. The common shares' market value fluctuated as follows: December 31, 2006, $36; December 31, 2007, $40; December 31, 2008, $45; December 31, 2009, $36; December 31, 2010, $48. Aoun Limited recognizes the SARs in its financial statements. Ashley Murfitt exercised half of the SARs on June 1, 2011.

Instructions

(a) Prepare a five-year (2006 to 2011) schedule of compensation expense pertaining to the 40,000 SARs granted to President Murfitt.

(b) Prepare the journal entry for compensation expense in 2006, 2009, and 2010 relative to the 40,000 SARs.

(c) Prepare the entry at June 1, 2011, for the exercise of the SARs.

(LO 15) ***E16-21** **(Stock Appreciation Rights)** At the end of its fiscal year, December 31, 2006, Beckford Limited issued 200,000 stock appreciation rights to its officers that entitled them to receive cash for the difference between the market price of its stock and a pre-established price of $12. The market price fluctuated as follows: December 31, 2007, $15; December 31, 2008, $11; December 31, 2009, $21; December 31, 2010, $19. The service period is four years and the exercise period is seven years. The company recognizes the SARs in its financial statements.

Instructions

(a) Prepare a schedule that shows the amount of compensation expense that is allocable to each year that is affected by the stock appreciation rights plan.

(b) Prepare the entry at December 31, 2010, to record compensation expense, if any, in 2010.

(c) Prepare the entry at December 31, 2010, assuming that all 200,000 SARs are exercised.

(LO 15) ***E16-22** **(Stock Appreciation Rights)** Chiu Limited established a stock appreciation rights program that entitled its new president, Ben Dan, to receive cash for the difference between the shares' market price and a pre-established price of $32 (also market price) on December 31, 2005, on 50,000 SARs. The date of grant is December 31, 2005, and the required employment (service) period is four years. The president exercised all of the SARs in 2011. The shares' market value fluctuated as follows: December 31, 2006, $36; December 31, 2007, $39; December 31, 2008, $45; December 31, 2009, $36; December 31, 2010, $48. The company recognizes the SARs in its financial statements.

Instructions

(a) Prepare a five-year (2006 to 2011) schedule of compensation expense pertaining to the 50,000 SARs granted to President Dan.

(b) Prepare the journal entry for compensation expense in 2006, 2009, and 2010 relative to the 50,000 SARs.

(c) From the perspective of the employee, contrast the features of a stock appreciation right to the features of compensatory stock options.

Problems

P16-1 The shareholders' equity section of McLean Inc. at the beginning of the current year is as follows:

Common shares, 1,000,000 shares authorized, 300,000 shares issued and outstanding	$3,600,000
Retained earnings	570,000

During the current year, the following transactions occurred:

1. The company issued 100,000 rights to the shareholders. Ten rights are needed to buy one share at $32 and the rights are void after 30 days. The shares' market price at this time was $34 per share.

2. The company sold to the public a $200,000, 10% bond issue at par. The company also issued with each $100 bond one detachable stock purchase warrant, which provided for the purchase of common shares at $30 per share. Shortly after issuance, similar bonds without warrants were selling at 96 and the warrants at $8.

3. All but 10,000 of the rights issued in item 1 were exercised in 30 days.

4. At the end of the year, 80% of the warrants in item 2 had been exercised, and the remaining were outstanding and in good standing.

5. During the current year, the company granted stock options for 5,000 common shares to company executives. The company, using an option pricing model, determined that each option is worth $10. The exercise or strike price is $30. The options were to expire at year end and were considered compensation for the current year.

6. All but 1,000 shares related to the stock option plan were exercised by year end. The expiration resulted because one of the executives failed to fulfill an obligation related to the employment contract.

Instructions

(a) Prepare general journal entries for the current year to record each of the transactions.

(b) Prepare the shareholders' equity section of the statement of financial position at the end of the current year. Assume that retained earnings at the end of the current year is $750,000.

P16-2 Lacroix Inc. issued convertible bonds for the first time on January 1, 2008. The $1 million of five-year, 10% (payable annually on December 31, starting December 31, 2008), convertible bonds were issued at 108, yielding 8%. The bonds would have been issued at 98 without a conversion feature, and yielding a higher rate of return. The bonds are convertible at the investor's option.

The company's bookkeeper recorded the bonds at 108 and, based on the $1,080,000 bond carrying value, recorded interest expense using the effective interest method for 2008. He prepared the following amortization table:

Date	Cash Interest (10%)	Effective Interest (8%)	Premium Amortization	Carrying Amount of Bonds
Jan. 1, 2008				$1,080,000
Dec. 31, 2008	$100,000	$86,400	$13,600	1,066,400

You were hired as an accountant to replace the bookkeeper in November 2009. It is now December 31, 2009, the company's year end, and the CEO is concerned that the company's debt covenant may be breached. The debt covenant requires Lacroix to maintain a maximum debt-to-equity ratio of 2.3. Based on the current financial statements, the debt-to-equity ratio would be 2.6. The CEO recalls hearing that convertible bonds should be reported by separating out the liability and equity components, yet he does not see any equity amounts related to the bonds on the current financial statements. He has asked you to look into the bond transactions recorded and make any necessary adjustments. He would also like you to explain how any adjustments that you make affect the debt-to-equity ratio.

Instructions

(a) Determine the amount that should have been reported in the equity section of the statement of financial position at January 1, 2008, for the conversion right. Prepare the journal entry that should have been recorded on January 1, 2008, and explain the approach that should have been used by the bookkeeper.

(b) Using a financial calculator or computer spreadsheet functions, calculate the effective rate (yield rate) for the bonds. Leave at least four decimal places in your calculation.

(c) Prepare a bond amortization schedule from January 1, 2008, to December 31, 2012, using the effective interest method and the corrected value for the bonds.

(d) Prepare the journal entry(ies) dated January 1, 2009, to correct the bookkeeper's recording errors in 2008. Ignore income tax effects.

(e) Prepare the journal entry at December 31, 2009, for the interest payment on the bonds.

(f) Explain the effect that the error correction prepared in (d) has on the debt-to-equity ratio.

P16-3 On January 1, 2008, Biron Corp. issued $1.2 million of five-year, zero-interest-bearing notes along with warrants to buy 1 million common shares at $20 per share. On January 1, 2008, Biron had 9.6 million common shares outstanding and the market price was $19 per share. Biron Corp. received $1 million for the notes and warrants. If offered alone, on January 1, 2008, the notes would have been issued to yield 12% to the creditor.

Instructions

(a) Prepare the journal entry(ies) to record the issuance of the zero-interest-bearing notes and warrants for the cash consideration that was received.

(b) Prepare an amortization table for the note using the effective interest method.

(c) Prepare adjusting journal entries for Biron Corp. at the end of its fiscal year of December 31, 2008.

P16-4 On September 30, 2008, Gargiola Inc. issued $4 million of 10-year, 8%, convertible bonds. The bonds pay interest on March 31 and September 30 and mature on September 30, 2018. Each $1,000 bond can be converted into 80 no-par value common shares. In addition, each bond included 20 detachable warrants. Each warrant can be used to purchase one common share at an exercise price of $15. Immediately after the bond issuance, the warrants traded at $3 each. Without the warrants and the conversion rights, the bonds would have been expected to sell for $4.3 million.

The proceeds from the issuance of the bonds with conversion rights and with the detachable warrants included the following:

Gross proceeds:	$4,700,000
Underwriting fees	100,000
Net proceeds	$4,600,000

Gargiola Inc. adopted the policy of capitalizing and amortizing the underwriting fees with the bonds' premium, which is accounted for using the effective interest method.

On March 23, 2011, half of the warrants were exercised. The common shares of Gargiola Inc. were trading at $20 each on this day.

Immediately after the payment of interest on the bonds, on September 30, 2013, all bonds outstanding were converted into common shares.

Instructions

(a) Prepare the journal entry to record the issuance of the bonds on September 30, 2008.

(b) Using a financial calculator or computer spreadsheet functions, calculate the effective rate (yield rate) for the bonds. Leave at least four decimal places in your calculation.

(c) Prepare a bond amortization schedule from September 30, 2008, to September 30, 2013, using the effective interest rate.

(d) Prepare the December 31, 2008, year-end adjusting journal entries and the payment of interest on March 31, 2009. Assume that Gargiola Inc. does not use reversing entries.

(e) Prepare the journal entry to account for the exercise of the warrants on March 30, 2011. How many common shares were issued in this transaction?

(f) Prepare the journal entry to account for the bond redemption on September 30, 2013.

(g) How many shares were issued on September 30, 2013? What do you believe was the likely market value of the common shares as of the date of the conversion, September 30, 2013?

P16-5   On February 1, 2005, Parsons Inc. sold its $1,000 par value, five-year, 8% bonds, which were convertible at the investor's option into Parsons Inc. common shares at a ratio of 10 common shares for each bond. The convertible bonds were sold by Parsons at a discount. Interest is payable annually each February 1. On February 1, 2008, Wong Corp., an investor in the Parsons Inc. convertible bonds, tendered 1,000 bonds for conversion into 10,000 shares of Parsons Inc. common shares that had a market value of $120 per share at the date of the conversion.

Instructions

How should Parsons account for the conversion of the convertible bonds into common shares under both the book value and market value methods? Discuss the rationale for each method.

(AICPA adapted)

P16-6   The treasurer of Miller Corp. has read on the Internet that the stock price of Ewing Inc. is about to take off. In order to profit from this potential development, Miller purchased a call option on Ewing common shares on July 7, 2007, for $240. The call option is for 200 shares (notional value), and the strike price is $70. The option expires on January 31, 2008. The following data are available with respect to the call option:

Date	Fair Value of Option	Market Price of Ewing Shares
Sept. 30, 2007	$1,340	$77 per share
Dec. 31, 2007	$825	$75 per share
Jan. 4, 2008	$1,200	$76 per share

Instructions

Prepare the journal entries for Miller for the following dates:

(a) July 7, 2007: Investment in call option on Ewing shares.

(b) September 30, 2007: Miller prepares financial statements.

(c) December 31, 2007: Miller prepares financial statements.

(d) January 4, 2008: Miller settles the call option net on the Ewing shares (i.e., without buying the shares).

P16-7 Refer to P16-6, but assume that Miller wrote (sold) the call option for a premium of $240 (instead of buying it). Assume that the market price of the shares and the value of the options is otherwise the same.

Instructions

Prepare the journal entries for Miller for the following dates:

(a) July 7, 2007: Sale of the call option on Ewing shares.

(b) September 30, 2007: Miller prepares financial statements.

(c) December 31, 2007: Miller prepares financial statements.

(d) January 4, 2008: Miller settles the call option net on the Ewing shares (i.e., without selling the shares).

P16-8 Johnstone Corp. purchased a put option on Ewing common shares on July 7, 2007, for $240. The put option is for 200 shares, and the strike price is $70. The option expires on January 31, 2008. The following data are available with respect to the put option:

Date	Fair Value of Option	Market Price of Ewing Shares
Sept. 30, 2007	$125	$77 per share
Dec. 31, 2007	$50	$75 per share
Jan. 31, 2008	$0	$78 per share

Instructions

Prepare the journal entries for Johnstone Corp. for the following dates:

(a) July 7, 2007: Investment in put option on Ewing shares.

(b) September 30, 2007: Johnstone prepares financial statements.

(c) December 31, 2007: Johnstone prepares financial statements.

(d) January 31, 2008: Put option expires.

P16-9 Warren Corp. purchased a put option on Echo common shares on January 7, 2007, for $360. The put option is for 400 shares, and the strike price is $85. The option expires on July 31, 2007. The following data are available with respect to the put option:

Date	Fair Value of Option	Market Price of Echo Shares
March 31, 2007	$2,200	$80 per share
June 30, 2007	$1,290	$82 per share
July 6, 2007	$3,200	$77 per share

Instructions

Prepare the journal entries for Warren Corp. for the following dates:

(a) January 7, 2007: Investment in put option on Echo shares.

(b) March 31, 2007: Warren prepares financial statements.

(c) June 30, 2007: Warren prepares financial statements.

(d) July 6, 2007: Warren settles the put option net on the Echo shares (i.e., without selling the shares).

P16-10 ISU Corp. adopted a stock option plan on November 30, 2009, that designated 70,000 common shares as available for the granting of options to officers of the corporation at an exercise price of $8 a share. The market value was $12 a share on November 30, 2009.

On January 2, 2010, options to purchase 28,000 shares were granted to President Don Pedro: 15,000 for services to be rendered in 2010, and 13,000 for services to be rendered in 2011. Also on that date, options to purchase 14,000 shares were granted to Vice-President Beatrice Leonato: 7,000 for services to be rendered in 2010, and 7,000 for services to be rendered in 2011. The shares' market value was $14 a share on January 2, 2010. The options were exercisable for a period of one year following the year in which the services were rendered. The value of the options was estimated at $400,000 at that time.

In 2010, neither the president nor the vice-president exercised their options because the shares' market price was below the exercise price. The shares' market value was $7 a share on December 31, 2011, when the options for 2010 services lapsed.

On December 31, 2012, both the president and vice-president exercised their options for 13,000 and 7,000 shares, respectively, when the market price was $16 a share. The company's year end is December 31.

Instructions

Prepare the necessary journal entries in 2009 when the stock option plan was adopted, in 2010 when the options were granted, in 2011 when the options lapsed, and in 2012 when the options were exercised.

*P16-11   On December 31, 2007, Mercantile Corp. had a $10-million floating rate (based in LIBOR) note outstanding that was payable in two years. It decided to enter into a two-year swap with First Bank to convert the floating-rate debt to fixed-rate debt. The terms of the swap specified that Mercantile will pay interest at a fixed rate of 8% and will receive a variable rate equal to the six-month LIBOR rate, based on the $10-million amount. The LIBOR rate on December 31, 2007, was 7%. The LIBOR rate will be reset every six months and will be used to determine the variable rate to be paid for the following six-month period. Mercantile Corp. designated the swap as a fair value hedge. Assume that the hedging relationship meets all the conditions necessary for hedge accounting. The six-month LIBOR rate and the swap and debt fair values were as follows:

Date	6-Month LIBOR Rate	Swap Fair Value	Debt Fair Value
Dec. 31, 2007	7.0%		$10,000,000
June 30, 2008	7.5%	$(200,000)	9,800,000
Dec. 31, 2008	6.0%	60,000	10,060,000

Instructions

(a) Present the journal entries to record the following transactions:

   1. The entry, if any, to record the swap on December 31, 2007.

   2. The entry to record the semi-annual debt interest payment on June 30, 2008.

   3. The entry to record the settlement of the semi-annual swap amount receivable at 8%, less the amount payable at LIBOR, 7%.

   4. The entry, if any, to record the change in the debt's fair value at June 30, 2008.

   5. The entry, if any, to record the change in the swap's fair value at June 30, 2008.

(b) Indicate the amount(s) reported on the statement of financial position and income statement related to the debt and swap on December 31, 2007.

(c) Indicate the amount(s) reported on the statement of financial position and income statement related to the debt and swap on June 30, 2008.

(d) Indicate the amount(s) reported on the statement of financial position and income statement related to the debt and swap on December 31, 2008.

*P16-12   LEW Jewellery Corp. uses gold in the manufacture of its products. LEW anticipates that it will need to purchase 500 ounces of gold in October 2008 for jewellery that will be shipped for the holiday shopping season. However, if the price of gold increases, LEW's cost to produce its jewellery will increase, which could reduce its profit margins.

To hedge the risk of increased gold prices, on April 1, 2008, LEW enters into a gold forward contract and designates this contract as a cash flow hedge of the anticipated gold purchase. The notional amount of the contract is 500 ounces, and the terms of the contract require LEW to purchase gold at a price of $300 per ounce on October 31, 2008 (or settle the contract net on the basis of the difference between the $300 and the gold price at October 31). Assume the following data with respect to the price of gold:

Date	Fair value of forward
Apr. 1, 2008	$ 0
June 30, 2008	$5,000
Sept. 30, 2008	$7,500
Oct. 31, 2008	$7,500

Instructions

Prepare the journal entries for the following transactions:

(a) April 1, 2008: Inception of the forward contract.

(b) June 30, 2008: LEW prepares financial statements.

(c) September 30, 2008: LEW prepares financial statements.

(d) October 31, 2008: LEW purchases 500 ounces of gold at $300 per ounce under the forward contract.

(e) December 20, 2008: LEW sells for $350,000 jewellery containing the gold purchased in October 2008. The cost of the finished goods inventory is $200,000.

(f) Indicate the amount(s) reported on the statement of financial position and income statement related to the futures contract on June 30, 2008.

(g) Indicate the amount(s) reported on the income statement related to the futures contract and the inventory transactions on December 31, 2008.

*P16-13 On November 3, 2008, Sprinkle Corp. invested $2,000 in 40 common shares of Johnstone Corp. Sprinkle classified this investment as an available-for-sale investment. Sprinkle Corp. is considering making a more significant investment in Johnstone Corp. at some point in the future but has decided to wait and see how the stock does over the next several quarters.

To hedge against potential declines in the value of Johnstone shares during this period, Sprinkle also purchased a put option on the Johnstone shares. Sprinkle paid an option premium of $100 for the put option, which gives Sprinkle the option to sell 40 Johnstone shares at a strike price of $50 per share; the option expires on July 31, 2009. The following data are available with respect to the values of the Johnstone shares and the put option:

Date	Market Price of Johnstone Shares	Fair Value of Put Option
Dec. 31, 2008	$50 per share	$100
Mar. 31, 2009	$45 per share	$250
June 30, 2009	$43 per share	$280

Assume the company uses hedge accounting.

Instructions

(a) Prepare the journal entries for Sprinkle Corp. for the following dates:

1. November 3, 2008: Investment in Johnstone shares and the put option on Johnstone shares.
2. December 31, 2008: Sprinkle prepares financial statements.
3. March 31, 2009: Sprinkle prepares financial statements.
4. June 30, 2009: Sprinkle prepares financial statements.
5. July 1, 2009: Sprinkle sells the Johnstone shares for $50 per share under the put option.

(b) Indicate the amount(s) reported on the statement of financial position and income statement related to the Johnstone investment and the put option on December 31, 2008.

(c) Indicate the amount(s) reported on the statement of financial position and income statement related to the Johnstone investment and the put option on June 30, 2009.

Writing Assignments

WA16-1 For various reasons, a corporation may issue warrants/options that give their holder the right to purchase the corporation's common shares at specified prices that, depending on the circumstances, may be less than, equal to, or greater than the current market price. For example, warrants may be issued to:

1. Existing shareholders on a pro rata basis
2. Certain key employees under an incentive stock option plan
3. Purchasers of the corporation's bonds

Instructions

For each of the three examples of whom stock warrants/options may be issued to:

(a) Explain why the warrants are used.

(b) Discuss the significance of the price (or prices) at which the warrants are issued (or granted) in relation to (1) the current market price of the company's shares, and (2) the length of time over which they can be exercised.

(c) Describe the information that should be disclosed in the financial statements or notes that are prepared when stock warrants are outstanding in the hands of the three groups of holders listed above.

(AICPA adapted)

WA16-2   The following excerpt is from a speech given by SEC commissioner J. Carter Beese, Jr.:

"I believe investors will be far better off if the value of stock options is reported in a footnote rather than on the face of the income statement. By allowing footnote disclosures, we will protect shareholders' current and future investments by not raising the cost of capital for the innovative, growth companies that depend on stock options to attract and retain key employees. I've said it before and I'll say it again: the stock option accounting debate essentially boils down to one thing: the cost of capital. And as long as we can adequately protect investors without raising the cost of capital to such a vital segment of our economy, why would we want to do it any other way?

"The FASB has made the assertion that when it comes to public policy, they lack the competence to weigh various national goals. I also agree with the sentiment that, as a general matter, Congress should not be in the business of writing accounting standards. But the SEC has the experience and the capability to determine exactly where to draw the regulatory lines to best serve investors and our capital markets. That is our mandate, and that is what we do, day in and day out.

"But we may have to act sooner rather than later. As we speak, the FASB's proposals are raising the cost of venture capital. That's because venture capitalists are pricing deals based on their exit strategies, which usually include cashing out in public offerings. The FASB's proposals, however, provide incentives for companies to stay private longer, they are able to use options more freely to attract and retain key employees, and they avoid the earnings hit that going public would entail. Even worse, as venture capital deals become less profitable because of the FASB's proposed actions, venture capitalists are starting to look overseas for alternative investment opportunities that lack the investment drag now associated with certain American ventures.

"I acknowledge that the FASB deserves some degree of freedom to determine what they believe is the best accounting approach. At the same time, however, I cannot stand by idly for long and watch venture capital increase in price or even flee this country because of a myopic search for an accounting holy grail. At some point, I believe that the SEC must inject itself into this debate, and help the FASB determine what accounting approach is ultimately in the best interests of investors as a whole.

"We owe it to shareholders, issuers and all market participants, and indeed our country, to make the best decision in accordance with the public good, not just technical accounting theory."

Instructions

Write a response to Commissioner Beese, defending the use of the concept of neutrality in financial accounting and reporting.

WA16-3   Many companies expose themselves to various financial risks—primarily due to their business models (the way they conduct business).

Instructions

Discuss the preceding statement by identifying the various financial risks and giving "real life" examples. In creating shareholder value, why is it important for a company to manage risk?

WA16-4   Many companies use forward contracts to manage price risks, especially for raw material purchases. As derivatives, forwards are recognized on the balance sheet and valued at fair value, and gains and losses related to the forwards are booked to net income. Purchase commitments serve the same business purpose as forwards as they allow companies to lock in a purchase price for raw materials. As executory contracts, however, they are not recognized on the balance sheet except in certain circumstances.

Instructions

Why are these two types of contracts (forwards and purchase commitments) treated differently? Discuss, making reference to the conceptual framework.

WA16-5   Embedded derivatives are derivatives that reside within a host instrument. These combined instruments are often referred to as hybrid or compound instruments.

Instructions

Why is it important to identify embedded derivatives from a financial reporting perspective? Discuss, making reference to the conceptual framework.

*WA16-6   Hedge accounting is optional and in some cases not even necessary.

Instructions

Write a short essay in which you discuss the preceding statement.

Cases

Refer to the Case Primer on the Student Website to help you answer these cases.

CA16-1   In 2009, Sanford Corp. adopted a plan to give additional incentive compensation to its dealers to sell its main product: fire extinguishers. Under the plan, Sanford transferred 9,000 of its common shares to a trust with the provision that Sanford would have to forfeit interest in the trust and no part of the trust fund could ever revert to Sanford. Shares were to be distributed to dealers based on each dealer's portion of the total number of fire extinguishers purchased from Sanford (above certain minimum levels per dealer) over the three-year period ending June 30, 2012.

In 2009, the shares were closely held. The shares' book value was $7.90 per share as of June 30, 2009, and in 2009 additional shares were sold to existing shareholders for $8 per share. Based on available information, the shares' market value was determined to be $8 per share.

In 2009, when the shares were transferred to the trust, Sanford charged Deferred Costs for $72,000 ($8 per share market value) and credited Common Shares for the same amount. The deferred cost was charged to operations over a three-year period ended June 30, 2012. Sanford sold a substantial number of shares to the public in 2006 at $60 per share.

In July 2012, all shares in the trust were distributed to the dealers. The shares' market value at the date of distribution from the trust had risen to $110 per share.

Instructions

Adopt the role of a financial analyst and discuss the financial reporting issues.

*CA16-2   **Air Canada** is Canada's largest domestic and international airline, providing scheduled and charter air transportation for passengers and cargo. The airline industry has suffered many difficulties and financial setbacks in the past decade. The high costs associated with operating an airline have claimed many victims, including Canadian Airlines, which was purchased by Air Canada in 2000 in a highly publicized takeover battle. One of the largest cost components on Air Canada's income statement is aircraft fuel.

Since aircraft fuel is a commodity good, its price is subject to significant fluctuations. The cost of a barrel of aircraft fuel is determined by supply and demand relationships and other global economic conditions that affect production. As a result, Air Canada, like all other airlines, faces a high amount of uncertainty about the cost that it will be required to pay for aircraft fuel. In order to reduce the uncertainty and attempt to limit exposure, Air Canada uses a fuel hedging strategy. The notes to the company's financial statements describe the airline's method for accounting for its fuel hedging strategy and provide additional disclosure as follows:

Fuel Price Risk Management

The Corporation enters into contracts with financial intermediaries to manage its exposure to jet fuel price volatility. As of December 31, 2006, the Corporation had collar option and swap structures in place to hedge a portion of its anticipated jet fuel requirements over the 2007 to 2008 period. Since jet fuel is not traded on an organized futures exchange, liquidity for hedging this commodity is mostly limited to a shorter time horizon. Crude oil and heating oil contracts are effective commodities for hedging jet fuel and the Corporation mainly uses these commodities for medium to longer term hedges.

As of December 31, 2006, approximately 39% of the Corporation's anticipated purchases of jet fuel for 2007 were hedged. The Corporation's contracts to hedge anticipated jet fuel purchases over the 2007 period comprised of jet fuel, heating oil and crude-oil based contract. The Corporation's contracts to hedge anticipated purchases over the 2008 period are all crude oil-based and covered 8% of the first quarter of 2008 anticipated jet fuel purchase requirements.

Hedge accounting was applied prospectively from October 1, 2005. Under hedge accounting, gains or losses on fuel hedging contracts are recognized in earnings as a component of aircraft fuel expense when the underlying jet fuel being hedged is consumed. Prior to the commencement of the Corporation's hedge accounting being applied, an unrealized gain of

$2 was recorded in other non-operating expense during the nine months ended September 30, 2005.

For the year ended December 31, 2006, the Corporation recognized a net loss of $43 as a component of fuel expense on the combined consolidated statement of operations (net loss of $3 for the year ended December 31, 2005) on the settlement of matured contracts and amortization of deferred costs. The fair value of the Corporation's fuel hedging contracts as at December 31, 2006 was $24 (US$21) in favour of counterparties (2005 – $3 in favour of third parties).

During 2006, the Corporation entered into two three-way collar option structures which are composed of one short put option, one long call option and one short call option. This structure creates a ceiling on the potential benefits to be realized by the Corporation if commodity prices increase above the threshold of the short call strike price. Due to the ceiling in these derivative instruments, this type of derivative does not qualify as a hedging instrument under GAAP. As at December 31, 2006, one of the three-way collar option structures remains outstanding, the fair value of this derivative instrument is $1 in favour of the counterparty and is recorded in Accounts payable and accrued liabilities on the combined consolidated statement of financial position.

During 2005, the Corporation de-designated one contract previously under hedge accounting that was combined into a new net-written option. The net-written option has a fair value less than zero at the time of inception and so it does not qualify as a hedging instrument under GAAP. As at December 31, 2006, the fair value of the net written option was $2 in favour of the counterparty (2005 – less than $1 in favour of the counterparty) and is recorded in Accounts payable and accrued liabilities on the combined consolidated statement of financial position.

The Corporation has recognized a net loss of $3 in non-operating expense during the year ended 2006 for these derivative instruments which do not qualify as hedge accounting instruments.

The company also refers to its aircraft fuel hedging operations in its disclosures of significant accounting policies.

Instructions

Discuss the various accounting issues that arise as a result of Air Canada's aircraft fuel hedging strategy. Specifically, discuss whether or not the company should use hedge accounting (which is optional).

CA16-3   The executive officers of Coach Corporation have a performance-based compensation plan that links performance criteria to growth in earnings per share. When annual EPS growth is 12%, the Coach executives earn 100% of a predetermined bonus amount; if growth is 16%, they earn 125%. If EPS growth is lower than 8%, the executives receive no additional compensation.

In 2008, Joanna Becker, the controller of Coach, reviews year-end estimates of bad debt expense and warranty expense. She calculates the EPS growth at 15%. Peter Reiser, a member of the executive group, remarks over lunch one day that the estimate of bad debt expense might be decreased, increasing EPS growth to 16.1%. Becker is not sure she should do this, because she believes that the current estimate of bad debts is sound. On the other hand, she recognizes that a great deal of subjectivity is involved in the calculation.

Instructions

Discuss the financial reporting issues.

Integrated Cases

IC16-1 **Legacy Hotels (LH)** is a real estate investment trust that was created in 1997 to own and operate hotel properties. Real estate investment trusts have become popular in the past decade since they do not pay income taxes on their operating profits. Another factor that makes real estate investment trusts popular is that they are required to pay out substantially all of their income to unitholders as cash flow distributions. This provides unitholders with a steady cash flow from their investment (similar to dividends). Each year, the company must calculate what is known as "distributable income." Distributable income is calculated as net income before amortization, income taxes, and special charges less a capital replacement reserve (in accordance with the company's Declaration of Trust agreement). The capital replacement reserve represents funds set aside or retained by LH in order to keep the assets in good shape and maintain its Fairmont brand. Distributable income, once calculated, is then paid out in cash to unitholders.

LH units are currently listed on the TSX. While many of the units of the company are held by a large group of dispersed investors, 35% is owned by Fairmont Hotels & Resorts Inc. (FHR). LH owns 22 luxury and first class hotels and resorts in Canada and the United States, including the Fairmont Château Frontenac, the Fairmont Royal York, and the Fairmont Empress hotels. FHR manages many of the hotels that LH owns.

According to the annual report, the company's objective is to provide stable and growing distributions while increasing unitholder value over time. The year 2002 was a challenging one for the company. However, the mix of leisure and business travel helped to minimize the impact of a prolonged decrease in business travel. At the end of 2002, the company noted that it had increased revenues by 6.7% and earnings before interest, taxes, depreciation, and amortization by 4.1% over the prior year. In total, 62% of gross revenues are generated from room occupancy and 32% from food and beverage sales. Net income was approximately $55 million.

Expenditures on properties totalling $50.4 million were made in 2002 (down from $60.2 million the prior year). These expenditures included:

- Phase two of the renovation program at the Fairmont Queen Elizabeth. This included guestroom upgrades and upgrades to the lobby.

- Opening of the Willow Stream spa at the Fairmont Empress

In order to finance the expenditures, the company issued 7.75% convertible debentures maturing on April 1, 2007. The debentures are convertible to units of the company and may be redeemed by LH after April 1, 2004. LH may elect to satisfy the principal and interest obligation through issuance of units. The company has accounted for these instruments as equity. Interest and issue costs have been charged directly to retained earnings (as opposed to net income) but have been deducted in arriving at distributable income.

The company has various debentures outstanding that carry restrictive covenants. In addition to these covenants, the Declaration of Trust agreement notes that the company may not incur additional indebtedness if after giving effect to the indebtedness, the total debt of the company would exceed 50% of total assets.

LH has entered into several management agreements with FHR to manage the properties. In return for managing the properties, LH pays FHR management fees. Incentive fees are also paid to FHR to ensure that the properties are efficiently run and that the Fairmont brand image is maintained. The incentive fees are calculated based on net operating income plus amortization less the capital replacement reserve.

The company uses the sinking fund method to amortize its capital assets (resulting in smaller depreciation charges in the earlier years of an asset's life). In 2002, the company signed a long-term incentive contract with FHR for management of a hotel. In return for the contract, FHR agreed to pay a fixed amount to LH over three years. LH has deferred this amount and will amortize it over the life of the management contract. The amortization is applied to reduce management fee expense.

Instructions

Adopt the role of the company's external auditors and evaluate the financial reporting issues. Assume that the 2002 financial statements are still in draft form and that this is a new client for your auditing firm.

IC16-2   Excerpts follow from the 2006 financial statements of **Air Canada**:

20. Special Charge for Aeroplan Miles

In 2001, Air Canada established Aeroplan Limited Partnership as a limited partnership wholly owned by Air Canada. The Aeroplan loyalty program was previously a division of Air Canada.

Under the Commercial Participation and Services Agreement ("CPSA") between Air Canada and Aeroplan, Air Canada retained responsibility for the 103 billion miles to be redeemed from accumulations up to December 31, 2001. Aeroplan assumed responsibility for all miles issued beginning January 1, 2002. On December 31, 2001, there were 171 billion miles outstanding of which, after considering breakage, Management estimated that 103 billion miles would be redeemed.

With the assistance of independent actuaries, Management of Air Canada and Aeroplan re-estimated the number of miles expected to be redeemed from accumulations up to December 31, 2001. Management now expects that 112 billion miles will be redeemed compared to the original estimate of 103 billion. Pursuant to the terms of the CPSA, dated June 9, 2004, as amended, the Management of Air Canada and Aeroplan have agreed to further amend the terms of the CPSA. Effective October 13, 2006, by amendment, Air Canada has assumed responsibility for the redemption of up to 112 billion miles and, as a result, recorded a special charge of $102 for the incremental 9 billion miles against operating revenues in the year ended December 31, 2006 and increased Aeroplan deferred revenues. This charge is referred to as the "special charge for Aeroplan miles" in this MD&A. This amendment to the CPSA represents full and final settlement between the parties in connection with Aeroplan of Air Canada's obligations for the redemption of pre-2002 miles. Aeroplan is responsible for any redemption of miles in excess of the re-estimated 112 billion miles. The amount of the additional liability was determined by valuing the incremental miles at the current fair value.

12. Shareholders' Equity

Special Common Shares and Special Preferred Shares
During the period from January 1, 2006 to the date of the Air Canada IPO:

– 1,000 special common shares were issued to ACE in consideration for the acquisition of ACGHS and certain other general partners as described in Note 1.

– 50,001,101 special common shares and 50,000,000 special preferred shares were converted into 90,475,190 common shares. The carrying value of the special preferred share liability of $50 was reclassified to share capital and the number of common shares deemed to be issued for the special preferred shares is 2,380,952. ACE received a special common share in consideration for the accrued interest on the special preferred share liability.

During 2005, all issued and outstanding common shares were cancelled in exchange for 50,000,000 special common shares and 50,000,000 special preferred shares. As at December 31, 2005, the share capital of Air Canada consisted of 50 million special common shares held by ACE.

Based on the characteristics of the special preferred shares, the 50 million special preferred shares held by a wholly owned subsidiary of ACE as at December 31, 2005 were classified as a liability in these combined consolidated financial statements.

Special Common Shares
Each holder of special common shares was entitled to one vote per special common share held and each special common share had liquidation rights in preference to other common shares of $0.01 per share.

Special Preferred Shares
Each holder of special preferred shares was not entitled to voting rights in respect to the special preferred shares held. The holder of the special preferred shares was entitled to receive cumulative dividends at a fixed rate of 8% per annum payable in money, property or by the issue of fully paid shares of any class of the share capital of Air Canada. A holder

of special preferred shares shall be entitled to require the Corporation to redeem at any time all, or from time to time part, of the special preferred shares at $1 per share.

Exchangeable Distressed Preferred Shares
Each holder of exchangeable distressed preferred ("EDP") shares was not entitled to voting rights in respect to the EDP shares held. The holders of EDP shares were entitled to receive an aggregate amount of $5 by way of reduction of the stated capital of the EDP shares over a period of 5 years. Each EDP share was convertible at any time at the option of the holder into one fully paid and non-assessable common share. During 2005, 23,646,547 EDP shares with a nil carrying value were exchanged into common shares.

Instructions
Discuss the financial reporting issues that the excerpt raises.

Research and Financial Analysis

RA16-1 Intrawest Corporation

Refer to the financial statements and accompanying notes and discussion of Intrawest Corporation, Limited that are presented at the end of this book.

Instructions

(a) The company has several stock-based compensation plans. Compare and contrast these plans, noting such things as who is eligible, whether they have to buy shares to access any benefit, what the benefit or compensation is based on (profits or stock price), and so on. Prepare a chart to present your findings.

(b) Review the financial statements and discuss how the stock plans are accounted for.

(c) Comment on any professional judgement that is used in accounting for the stock plans.

(d) Comment on the impact of the stock plans on quality of earnings. Does the financial reporting of the plans contribute to higher or lower quality of earnings?

RA16-2 Canadian Tire Corporation

Go to the Student Website to access the annual report of Canadian Tire Corporation. According to the annual report, the company operates over 400 retail stores across Canada, selling automotive parts, accessories, and services; sports and leisure products; and home products.

Instructions

(a) Read the Management Discussion and Analysis portion of the annual report.

(b) Identify and summarize the various risks that the company is exposed to. Explain how these risks stem from the underlying nature of the business (i.e., the business model).

(c) How is the company dealing with its financial risks?

(d) Read Note 15 to the financial statements. What derivative instruments are being used by the company to hedge its risks?

(e) In your opinion, explain what the company would have to do in order for hedge accounting to be used in the financial statements.

RA16-3 Canadian Utilities Limited

Access the financial statements of Canadian Utilities Limited for 2006 on the Student Website.

Instructions

Read Note 2 on the deferred electricity and deferred hearing costs and answer the following.

(a) How did these amounts arise?

(b) Discuss the special nature of regulated industries.

(c) Discuss any financial reporting issues that are raised by the note.

RA16-4 Barrick Gold Corporation

Go to the Student Website to access the annual report of Barrick Gold Corporation.

Instructions

(a) Discuss the company's business model—i.e., how it earns income.

(b) Identify and summarize the various risks that the company is exposed to. Explain how these risks stem from the underlying nature of the business (i.e., the business model).

(c) How is the company dealing with its financial risks?

(d) Read Note 16 to the financial statements. What derivative instruments, if any, are being used by the company to hedge its risks related to commodities?

(e) Explain what the company would have to do in order for hedge accounting to be used in its financial statements and be in accordance with GAAP.

Open Earnings

OPEN TEXT CORPORATION

Based in Waterloo, Ontario, Open Text Corporation has been in the software business for more than 15 years and is now the second largest software company in Canada. With 3,000 employees, it is the world's largest independent provider of enterprise content management software.

For the first quarter of its 2007 fiscal year, Open Text reported an adjusted net income of U.S. $12.2 million, or $0.24 per share, on a diluted basis. This is almost double its adjusted net income for the same quarter the previous year. Net income in accordance with U.S. GAAP was U.S. $7.3 million or $0.15 per share on a diluted basis, compared to a net loss for the same quarter in 2006.

"Although we report GAAP-based net income, as required, we also present adjusted net income in our press release and provide reconciliations between GAAP-based net income and adjusted net income," says Greg Secord, Open Text's director of investor relations. "Net income in accordance with GAAP is a defined term with a standardized meaning, whereas adjusted income does not have a standardized meaning."

The reasons for reporting adjusted net income vary from company to company, but most want to provide investors with a snapshot of their core operational performance and a perspective on the business without the impact of unusual or infrequent items, Secord explains. "Technology companies generally operate in growth-oriented industries; market repositioning and acquisitions are common strategies. These activities can result in one-time operational expenses, such as restructuring charges. We articulate adjusted net income because we believe that certain expenses like this do not accurately reflect the company's normal day-to-day operations."

Open Text also reports net income per share on both a basic and diluted basis. The diluted figures take into account outstanding options that are in the money, that is, the options that could be exercised and would affect diluted earnings. "For us, reporting on a diluted basis is not just our preferred method, but also the most conservative approach and a mandatory requirement for GAAP," says Secord. ∎

Earnings per Share

chapter 17

Learning Objectives

After studying this chapter, you should be able to:

1. Understand why earnings per share (EPS) is an important number.
2. Understand when and how earnings per share must be presented.
3. Identify potential common shares.
4. Calculate earnings per share in a simple capital structure.
5. Calculate diluted earnings per share using the if-converted method.
6. Calculate diluted earnings per share using the treasury stock method.
7. Calculate diluted earnings per share using the reverse treasury stock method.
8. Identify antidilutive potential common shares.
9. Compare current Canadian and international GAAP, and understand which direction international GAAP is headed in.

Preview of Chapter 17

Earnings per share data are frequently reported in the financial press and are widely used by shareholders and potential investors in evaluating a company's profitability and value. This chapter examines how basic and diluted earnings per share figures are calculated and what information they contain.

The chapter is organized as follows:

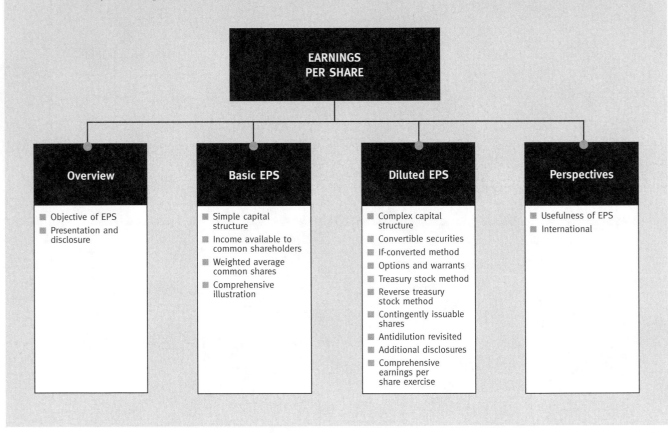

EARNINGS PER SHARE

Overview
- Objective of EPS
- Presentation and disclosure

Basic EPS
- Simple capital structure
- Income available to common shareholders
- Weighted average common shares
- Comprehensive illustration

Diluted EPS
- Complex capital structure
- Convertible securities
- If-converted method
- Options and warrants
- Treasury stock method
- Reverse treasury stock method
- Contingently issuable shares
- Antidilution revisited
- Additional disclosures
- Comprehensive earnings per share exercise

Perspectives
- Usefulness of EPS
- International

OVERVIEW

Objective of EPS

Objective 1
Understand why earnings per share (EPS) is an important number.

Common shareholders need to know how much of a company's available income can be attributed to the shares that they own. This helps them assess future dividend payouts and the value of each share. As noted in Chapter 16, common shares are different from other forms of financing, such as debt and preferred shares. Common shareholders have a residual investment in the company. The return on investment does not depend on the passage of time or a face value (as it does for debt). If the company does well, common shareholders are the ones who gain the most. Similarly, if a company does not do well, common shareholders stand to lose the most. (There may not be anything left after a company covers its costs and obligations.) How big is the common shareholders' part of the profit pie? How is it affected by financial instruments such as convertible debt and options? Earnings per share disclosures help investors (both common shareholders and potential investors) by indicating the amount of income that is earned by each common share: in other words, how big the common shareholders' piece of the earnings pie is. The basic calculation is shown in Illustration 17-1.

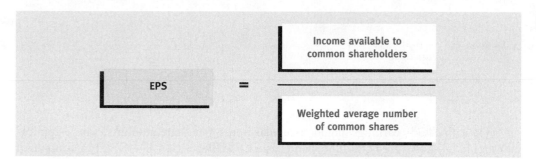

Illustration 17-1

The EPS Formula

Note that EPS is normally only calculated for common shares. The calculation is done for both basic EPS and diluted EPS. **Basic EPS** looks at **actual** earnings and the **actual** number of common shares outstanding (with this number prorated for the amount of time that the shares have been outstanding). **Diluted EPS** is a "**what if**" calculation that takes into account the possibility that financial instruments such as convertible debt and options (and others) might have a negative impact on existing shareholder returns and, therefore, the shares' value. This chapter will deal first with the calculations for basic EPS and then the calculations for diluted EPS.

Presentation and Disclosure

Because of the importance of earnings per share information, most companies are required to report this information on the face of the income statement.[1] The exception is non-public companies: because of cost-benefit considerations, they do not have to report this information.[2] Generally, earnings per share information is reported below net income in the income statement.

When the income statement presents different components of income, earnings per share should be disclosed for each component.[3] **The EPS numbers related to these other components may be disclosed on the face of the statement or in the notes.** The EPS data in Illustration 17-2 are representative of this disclosure, and assume that the EPS numbers for discontinued operations and extraordinary items are presented on the face of the income statement.

2 Objective
Understand when and how earnings per share must be presented.

Earnings per share:	
Income from continuing operations	$4.00
Loss from discontinued operations, net of tax	(0.60)
Extraordinary gain, net of tax	1.00
Net income	$4.40

Illustration 17-2

Income Statement Presentation of EPS Components

[1] *CICA Handbook*, Section 3500.60.

[2] A non-public enterprise is an enterprise other than (1) one whose debt or equity securities are traded in a public market on a foreign or domestic stock exchange or in the over-the-counter market (including securities that are quoted locally or regionally) or (2) one that has made a filing or is in the process of making a filing with a securities commission in preparation for the sale of those securities (*CICA Handbook*, Section 3500.02).

[3] *CICA Handbook*, Section 3500.61.

These disclosures make it possible for users of the financial statements to know the specific impact of income from continuing operations on EPS, rather than have a single EPS number that also includes the impact of a gain or loss from irregular items. If a corporation's capital structure is complex, the earnings per share presentation would be as in Illustration 17-3.

Illustration 17-3

EPS Presentation—Complex Capital Structure

Earnings per common share:	
Basic earnings per share	$3.30
Diluted earnings per share	$2.70

When a period's earnings include irregular items, per share amounts (where applicable) should be shown for both diluted and basic EPS. Illustration 17-4 gives an example of a presentation format that reports an extraordinary item.

Illustration 17-4

EPS Presentation, with Extraordinary Item

Basic earnings per share:	
Income before extraordinary item	$3.80
Extraordinary item	(0.80)
Net income	$3.00
Diluted earnings per share:	
Income before extraordinary item	$3.35
Extraordinary item	(0.65)
Net income	$2.70

GAAP requires the following:

- Earnings per share amounts must be shown for all periods that are presented.

- If there has been a stock dividend or stock split, all per share amounts of prior period earnings should be restated using the new number of outstanding shares.

- If diluted EPS data are reported for at least one period, they should be reported for all periods that are presented, even if they are the same as basic EPS.

- When the results of operations of a prior period have been restated as a result of a prior period adjustment, the corresponding earnings per share data should also be restated. The restatement's effect should then be disclosed in the year of the restatement.

BASIC EPS

Simple Capital Structure

Objective 3

Identify potential common shares.

When a corporation's capital structure consists only of common shares and preferred shares and/or debt without conversion rights, the company is said to have a **simple capital structure**. In contrast, a company is said to have a **complex capital structure** if the structure includes securities that could have a dilutive or negative effect (i.e., a lowering effect) on earnings per common share. In the EPS formula given in Illustration 17-1, any increase in the denominator will result in a decrease in EPS. These other, potentially dilutive securities are called potential common shares. A **potential common share** is a security or other contract that may give its holder the right to obtain a common share during or after the end of the reporting period. Examples are debt and equity instruments (e.g., preferred shares) that are convertible into common shares, warrants, options, and contingently issuable shares.[4] **Contingently issuable shares** are shares that are issuable for little or no consideration once a condition involving uncertainty has been resolved.[5] For instance, in an acquisition of another company, the acquirer may promise to issue some additional shares (at a later date) as part of the purchase consideration if the acquired company performs well.

Companies with simple capital structures only need to calculate and present basic EPS. Those with complex capital structures must calculate and present both basic and diluted EPS. The table in Illustration 17-5 summarizes the reporting requirements.

Illustration 17-5

EPS Reporting Requirements for Different Capital Structures

Capital Structure	Major Types of Equity Instruments	Impact on EPS Calculations
Simple	— Common (residual, voting) shares — Preferred shares	— Need only calculate basic EPS

Complex	— Common shares
	— Potential common shares
	  • Convertible preferred shares
	  • Convertible debt
	  • Options/warrants
	  • Contingently issuable shares
	  • Other
		— Must calculate basic and diluted EPS

The calculation of earnings per share for a simple capital structure involves two items: income available for common shareholders and the weighted average number of common shares outstanding. These are examined separately in the next sections.

Income Available to Common Shareholders

As noted earlier, basic EPS looks at **actual** earnings that are left or available after paying operating costs (including interest) and after paying or setting aside funds for dividends on shares that rank in preference (most often preferred shares) over the common shares.

Illustration 17-6 shows the concept of income available to common shareholders as a residual component of income.

4 Objective
Calculate earnings per share in a simple capital structure.

---

[4] *CICA Handbook*, Section 3500.05.

[5] *CICA Handbook*, Section 3500.05.

Illustration 17-6

Income Available to Common Shareholders (CSH)

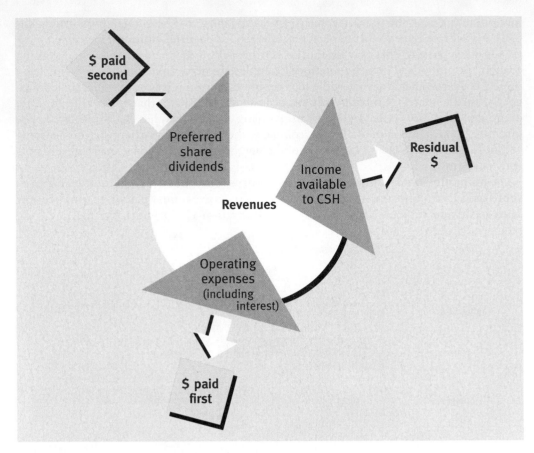

Income available to common shareholders is equal to net income less amounts that have been set aside to cover obligations of other instruments, such as preferred shares that rank in preference over common shares. Preferred shares are actually part of a larger class of financial instruments known as senior equity instruments. **Senior equity instruments** are defined as "preferred shares and other financial instruments that provide their holders with claims on earnings prior to those of the common shareholders and are classified as equity."[6] Since these instruments are senior, they rank in preference in terms of return on investment and these funds must be set aside before looking at how much is available for the common or residual shareholders.

Dividends on Senior Equity Instruments

When a company has both **common and senior equity instruments outstanding, the dividends for the current year** on these senior equity instruments **are subtracted from net income** to arrive at **income available to common shareholders**.

In reporting earnings per share information, dividends declared on preferred shares should be subtracted from income from continuing operations **and** from net income to arrive at income available to common shareholders. If dividends on preferred shares are declared and a net loss occurs, the preferred dividend is added to the loss in calculating the loss per share. If the preferred shares are cumulative and the dividend is **not declared** in the current year, an amount equal to the dividend that should have been declared for the

[6] *CICA Handbook*, Section 3500.05.

current year only should be subtracted from net income or added to the net loss. Dividends in arrears for previous years should have been included in the previous years' calculations.

Assume, for example, that Michael Limited has net income of $3 million and two classes of preferred shares, in addition to common shares. Class A preferred shares are cumulative and carry a dividend of $4 per share. There are 100,000 shares outstanding throughout the year. No dividend declaration has been made and no dividends have been paid during the year. Class B preferred shares are non-cumulative and carry a dividend of $3 per share. There are 100,000 shares outstanding throughout the year and the dividends have not been declared or paid in the current year. The income available for common shareholders would be calculated as follows:

Net Income	$3,000,000
Less:	
Preferred dividends—Class A	(400,000)
Income available to common shareholders	$2,600,000

Note that the Class A share dividends are deducted even though they have not been declared or paid. This is because they are cumulative and will eventually have to be paid. No dividends are set aside for the Class B shares since they are non-cumulative and have not been declared. Because they are non-cumulative, the company never has to make up a lost dividend to the Class B shareholders.

Weighted Average Common Shares

In all calculations of earnings per share, the **weighted average number of shares** outstanding (WACS) during the period is the basis for the per share amounts that are reported. Shares that are issued or purchased during the period affect the amount outstanding and must be weighted by the fraction of the period that they have been outstanding. The rationale for this approach is that the income was generated on the issue proceeds for only part of the year. Accordingly, the number of shares outstanding should be weighted by the same factor. To illustrate, assume that Salomski Inc. has the data in Illustration 17-7 for the changes in its common shares outstanding for the period.

> **International Insight**
>
> Where EPS disclosure is common practice, it is usually based on the weighted average number of shares outstanding.

Date	Share Changes	Shares Outstanding
Jan. 1	Beginning balance	90,000
Apr. 1	Issued 30,000 shares for cash	30,000
		120,000
July 1	Purchased 39,000 shares	39,000
		81,000
Nov. 1	Issued 60,000 shares for cash	60,000
Dec. 31	Ending balance	141,000

Illustration 17-7

Common Shares Outstanding, Ending Balance—Salomski Inc.

To calculate the weighted average number of shares outstanding, the calculation is done as in Illustration 17-8.

Illustration 17-8

Weighted Average Number of Shares Outstanding

Dates Outstanding	(A) Shares Outstanding	(B) Fraction of Year	(C) Weighted Shares (A × B)
Jan. 1–Apr. 1	90,000	3/12	22,500
Apr. 1–July 1	120,000	3/12	30,000
July 1–Nov. 1	81,000	4/12	27,000
Nov. 1–Dec. 31	141,000	2/12	23,500
Weighted average number of shares outstanding			103,000

As illustrated, 90,000 shares were outstanding for three months, which translates to 22,500 whole shares for the entire year. Because additional shares were issued on April 1, the number of shares outstanding changes and these shares must be weighted for the time that they have been outstanding. When 39,000 shares were repurchased on July 1, this reduced the number of shares outstanding and a new calculation again has to be made to determine the proper weighted number of shares outstanding.

Stock Dividends, Splits, and Reverse Splits

When stock dividends or stock splits occur, calculation of the weighted average number of shares requires a restatement of the shares outstanding before the stock dividend or split.[7] For example, assume that a corporation had 100,000 shares outstanding on January 1 and issued a 25% stock dividend on June 30. For purposes of calculating a weighted average for the current year, the additional 25,000 shares outstanding as a result of the stock dividend are assumed to have been outstanding since the beginning of the year. Thus, the weighted average for the year would be 125,000 shares.

The issuance of a stock dividend or stock split requires a restatement (which is applied retroactively), but the issuance or repurchase of shares for cash does not. Why? Stock splits and stock dividends do not increase or decrease the net enterprise's assets; only additional shares are issued. Therefore, the weighted average number of shares must be restated. By restating the number, valid comparisons of earnings per share can be made between periods before and after the stock split or stock dividend. Conversely, the issuance or purchase of shares for cash changes the amount of net assets. The company either earns more or less in the future as a result of this change in net assets. Stated another way, a stock dividend or split does not change the shareholders' total investment; it only increases (unless it is a reverse stock split) the **number** of common shares.

To illustrate how a stock dividend affects the calculation of the weighted average number of shares outstanding, assume that Baiye Limited has the data in Illustration 17-9 for the changes in its common shares during the year.

Illustration 17-9

Shares Outstanding, Ending Balance—Baiye Limited

Date	Share Changes	Shares Outstanding
Jan. 1	Beginning balance	100,000
Mar. 1	Issued 20,000 shares for cash	20,000
		120,000
June 1	60,000 additional shares (50% stock dividend)	60,000
		180,000
Nov. 1	Issued 30,000 shares for cash	30,000
Dec. 31	Ending balance	210,000

---

[7] *CICA Handbook*, Section 3500.58.

Illustration 17-10 shows the calculation of the weighted average number of shares outstanding.

Dates Outstanding	(A) Shares Outstanding	(B) Restatement	(C) Fraction of Year	(D) Shares Weighted (A × B × C)
Jan. 1–Mar. 1	100,000	1.50	2/12	25,000
Mar. 1–June 1	120,000	1.50	3/12	45,000
June 1–Nov. 1	180,000		5/12	75,000
Nov. 1–Dec. 31	210,000		2/12	35,000
Weighted average number of shares outstanding				180,000

Illustration 17-10

Weighted Average Number of Shares Outstanding—Share Issue and Stock Dividend

The shares outstanding before the stock dividend must be restated. The shares outstanding from January 1 to June 1 are adjusted for the stock dividend so that these shares are stated on the same basis as shares issued after the stock dividend. Shares issued after the stock dividend do not have to be restated because they are on the new basis. The stock dividend simply restates existing shares. A stock split is treated in the same way.

If a stock dividend or stock split occurs after the end of the year, but before the financial statements are issued, the weighted average number of shares outstanding for the year (and any other years presented in comparative form) must be restated.[8] For example, assume that Hendricks Corp. calculates its weighted average number of shares to be 100,000 for the year ended December 31, 2008. On January 15, 2009, before the financial statements are issued, the company splits its shares 3 for 1. In this case, the weighted average number of shares used in calculating earnings per share for 2008 would be 300,000 shares. If earnings per share information for 2007 is provided as comparative information, it also must be adjusted for the stock split.

Comprehensive Illustration

Leung Corporation has income of $580,000 before extraordinary items and an extraordinary gain, net of tax, of $240,000. In addition, it has declared preferred dividends of $1 per share on 100,000 preferred shares outstanding. Leung Corporation also has the data shown in Illustration 17-11 for changes in its common shares outstanding during 2008.

Dates	Share Changes	Shares Outstanding
Jan. 1	Beginning balance	180,000
May 1	Purchased 30,000 shares	30,000
		150,000
July 1	300,000 additional shares issued (3-for-1 stock split)	300,000
		450,000
Dec. 31	Issued 50,000 shares for cash	50,000
Dec. 31	Ending balance	500,000

Illustration 17-11

Shares Outstanding, Ending Balance—Leung Corp.

To calculate the earnings per share information, the weighted average number of shares outstanding is first determined as in Illustration 17-12.

___
[8] *CICA Handbook*, Section 3500.58.

Illustration 17-12

Weighted Average Number of Shares Outstanding

Dates Outstanding	(A) Shares Outstanding	(B) Restatement	(C) Fraction of Year	(D) Shares Weighted (A × B × C)
Jan. 1–May 1	180,000	3	4/12	180,000
May 1–Dec. 31	150,000	3	8/12	300,000
Weighted average number of shares outstanding				480,000

In calculating the weighted average number of shares, the shares sold on December 31, 2008, are ignored because they have not been outstanding during the year. The weighted average number of shares is then divided into income before discontinued and extraordinary items and net income to determine the earnings per share. Leung Corporation's preferred dividends of $100,000 are subtracted from income before discontinued and extraordinary items ($580,000) to arrive at income before discontinued and extraordinary items available to common shareholders of $480,000 ($580,000 – $100,000). Deducting the preferred dividends from the income before discontinued and extraordinary items has the effect of also reducing net income without affecting the amount of the extraordinary item. The final amount is referred to as income available to common shareholders. Illustration 17-13 shows the calculation of income available to common shareholders.

Illustration 17-13

Calculation of Income Available to Common Shareholders

	(A) Income Information	(B) Weighted Shares	(C) Earnings per Share (A ÷ B)
Income before discontinued operations and extraordinary items available to common shareholders	$480,000	480,000	$1.00
Extraordinary gain (net of tax)	240,000	480,000	0.50
Income available to common shareholders	$720,000	480,000	$1.50

Disclosure of the per share amount for the extraordinary item (net of tax) must be reported either on the face of the income statement or in the notes to the financial statements. Income and per share information would be reported as in Illustration 17-14.

Illustration 17-14

Earnings per Share, with Extraordinary Item

Income before extraordinary item	$580,000
Extraordinary gain, net of tax	240,000
Net income	$820,000
Earnings per share:	
Income before extraordinary item	$1.00
Extraordinary item, net of tax	0.50
Net income	$1.50

DILUTED EPS

Complex Capital Structure

One problem with a basic EPS calculation is that it fails to recognize the potentially dilutive impact on outstanding shares when a corporation has dilutive securities in its capital structure. **Dilutive securities present a serious problem because their conversion or exercise often decreases earnings per share.** This adverse effect can be significant and, more important, unexpected, unless financial statements call attention to the potential dilutive effect.

A **complex capital structure** exists when a corporation has potential common shares such as convertible securities, options, warrants, or other rights that could dilute earnings per share if they are converted or exercised. **Therefore, as noted earlier, when a company has a complex capital structure, both basic and diluted earnings per share are generally reported.** The calculation of diluted EPS is similar to the calculation of basic EPS. The difference is that diluted EPS includes the effect of all dilutive potential common shares that were outstanding during the period. The formula in Illustration 17-15 shows the relationship between basic EPS and diluted EPS.

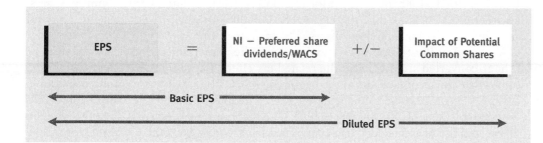

Illustration 17-15

Relationship between Basic and Diluted EPS

Note that companies with complex capital structures will not report diluted EPS if the securities in their capital structure are antidilutive. **Antidilutive securities** are securities that, upon conversion or exercise, increase earnings per share (or reduce the loss per share). **The purpose of presenting both EPS numbers is to inform financial statement users of situations that will likely occur and to provide worst-case dilutive situations.** If the securities are antidilutive, the likelihood of conversion or exercise is considered remote. **Thus, companies that have only antidilutive securities are not permitted to increase earnings per share and are required to report only the basic EPS number.**[9]

The calculation of basic EPS was shown in the previous section. The discussion in the following sections addresses the effects of convertible and other dilutive securities on EPS calculations.

Convertible Securities

At conversion, convertible securities are exchanged for common shares. Convertible securities are therefore potential common shares and may be dilutive. The method that is used to measure the dilutive effects of a potential conversion on EPS is called the **if-converted method.**

If-Converted Method

The if-converted method for convertible debt or preferred shares assumes both of the following:

1. It assumes that the convertible securities are converted at the **beginning of the period** (or at the time of the security issuance, if they are issued during the period).[10]

5 Objective

Calculate diluted earnings per share using the if-converted method.

---

[9] *CICA Handbook*, Section 3500.30.

[10] *CICA Handbook*, Section 3500.35.

2. It assumes **the elimination of related interest, net of tax** or a preferred share dividend. If the debt/equity had been converted at the beginning of the period, there would be no bond interest expense/preferred dividend. No tax effect is calculated, because preferred dividends generally are not tax-deductible.

Thus the denominator—the weighted average number of shares outstanding—is increased by the additional shares that are assumed to be issued. The numerator—net income—is increased by the amount of interest expense, net of tax, that is associated with those potential common shares.

As an example, assume that Field Corporation has net income for the year of $210,000 and a weighted average number of common shares outstanding during the period of 100,000 shares. The basic earnings per share is therefore $2.10 ($210,000 ÷ 100,000). The company has two convertible debenture bond issues outstanding.[11] One is a 6% issue sold at 100 (total $1,000,000) in a prior year and convertible into 20,000 common shares. The other is a 10% issue sold at 100 (total $1,000,000) on April 1 of the current year and convertible into 32,000 common shares. The tax rate is 40%.

As shown in Illustration 17-16, to determine the numerator, we add back the interest on the if-converted securities less the related tax effect. Because the if-converted method assumes that conversion occurs at the beginning of the year, no interest on the convertible securities is assumed to be paid during the year. The interest on the 6% convertible bonds is $60,000 for the year ($1,000,000 × 6%). The increased tax expense is $24,000 ($60,000 × 0.40), and the interest added back net of taxes is $36,000 [$60,000 − $24,000, or simply $60,000 × (1 − 0.40)].

Because the 10% convertible bonds are issued after the beginning of the year, the shares that are assumed to have been issued on that date, April 1, are weighted as outstanding from April 1 to the end of the year. In addition, the interest adjustment to the numerator for these bonds would only reflect the interest for nine months. Thus, the interest added back on the 10% convertible security would be $45,000 [$1,000,000 × 10% × 9/12 year × (1 − 0.40)]. The calculation of earnings (the numerator) for diluted earnings per share is shown in Illustration 17-16.

Net income for the year	$210,000
Add: Adjustment for interest (net of tax)	
6% debentures ($60,000 × [1 − 0.40])	36,000
10% debentures ($100,000 × 9/12 × [1 − 0.40])	45,000
Adjusted net income	$291,000

Illustration 17-16
Calculation of Adjusted Net Income

The calculation of the weighted average number of shares adjusted for dilutive securities—the denominator in a diluted earnings per share calculation—is shown in Illustration 17-17.

Weighted average number of shares outstanding	100,000
Add: Shares assumed to be issued:	
6% debentures (as of beginning of year)	20,000
10% debentures (as of date of issue, April 1; 9/12 × 32,000)	24,000
Weighted average number of shares adjusted for dilutive securities	144,000

Illustration 17-17
Calculation of Weighted Average Number of Shares— Dilutive Securities

[11] To simplify, the consequences of measuring and presenting the debt and equity components of the convertible debentures separately have been ignored for this example. As previously noted in the chapter, part of the proceeds would be allocated to the equity component. The interest expense would be calculated using the market interest rate for straight debt—i.e., without the conversion feature.

Field Corporation would then report earnings per share based on a dual presentation on the face of the income statement: that is, it would present both basic and diluted earnings per share.[12] The presentation is shown in Illustration 17-18.

Illustration 17-18

Earnings per Share Disclosure

Net income for the year	$210,000
Earnings per share:	
Basic earnings per share ($210,000 ÷ 100,000)	$2.10
Diluted earnings per share ($291,000 ÷ 144,000)	$2.02

Other Factors

The example above assumed that Field Corporation's bonds were sold at their face amount. If the bonds were instead sold at a premium or discount, interest expense would have to be adjusted each period to account for this occurrence. Therefore, the amount of interest expense added back, net of tax, to net income is the interest expense reported on the income statement, not the interest paid in cash during the period. Likewise, because the convertible debentures are compound instruments, a portion of the proceeds would actually be allocated to the equity component, and the discount rate on the debt would be the market interest rate on straight debt. (Further discussion of this aspect is beyond the scope of this text.)

The conversion rate on a dilutive security may change over the period that the dilutive security is outstanding. In this situation, for the diluted EPS calculation, the most advantageous conversion rate available to the holder is used.[13] For example, assume that a convertible bond was issued January 1, 2006, with a conversion rate of 10 common shares for each bond starting January 1, 2008; beginning January 1, 2011, the conversion rate is 12 common shares for each bond; and beginning January 1, 2015, it is 15 common shares for each bond. In calculating diluted EPS in 2006, the conversion rate of 15 shares to one bond would be used.

Underlying Concept

Showing both basic and diluted EPS reflects the full disclosure principle. The diluted EPS calculation shows the possible negative impact of conversions.

Options and Warrants

Recall from Chapter 16 that stock options allow the holder to buy or sell shares at a preset price (the **exercise price**). The company may either **write** the options or **purchase** them. The options may also allow the holder to buy the shares (**call options**) or sell the shares (**put options**).

Written Options

When the company writes or sells the options, it gives the holder/purchaser the right to either buy (call) or sell (put) the shares. **Thus, if the holder/purchaser decides to exercise the options, the company will have to deliver (either buy or sell the shares).** Generally speaking, the holder of the options will exercise the right if the options are "**in the money**." They are "in the money" if the holder of the options will benefit from exercising them. If the option is a call option—giving the holder the right to buy the shares at a preset price—the holder will exercise it if the preset/exercise price is lower than the current market price. **Written options and their equivalents must be included in the**

---

[12] The conversion of bonds is dilutive because EPS with conversion ($2.02) is less than basic EPS ($2.10).

[13] *CICA Handbook*, Section 3500.27.

diluted EPS calculations if they are dilutive. Generally speaking, they are dilutive when they are written options that are in the money.

Assume, for example, that Gaddy Limited sold (or wrote) **call options** for $2 that allow the purchaser to buy shares of Gaddy at $10 (the exercise price). At the time, Gaddy shares were trading at $9. Assume further that the market price of Gaddy shares subsequently increases to $15. The options are now in the money since they have value to the holder. If the holder exercises the options, Gaddy will have to issue its own shares for the exercise price ($10). **This will result in dilution for Gaddy and so must be considered in the diluted EPS calculation.** Note that if the shares of Gaddy never go beyond $10, the holder will not exercise them and the options will expire. Expired options as well as options that are not in the money are excluded from the diluted EPS calculation.

If Gaddy had instead sold **put options** that allow the purchaser to sell shares of Gaddy to Gaddy at an exercise price of $8, these might also be dilutive. Assume that when the put options were issued, Gaddy shares were $9, and that the shares subsequently went down to $6. If the put option is exercised, Gaddy will have to buy the shares from the option holder and will have to pay $8—the exercise price. Again, this must be incorporated in the diluted EPS calculation as it is in the money for the holder. The holder can sell the shares for more than their market value. Once again, if the options expire or are not in the money, they are not included in the diluted EPS calculation (since it is assumed that they will not be exercised).

Written put options, where the company may be forced to buy the shares at an unfavourable price, are the same as **forward purchase contracts**. Forward purchase contracts are included in the calculations if they represent a liability, that is, if the forward purchase price is higher than the average market price. Similarly, written call options are the same as **forward sales contracts**. Forward sales contracts are also included in the calculations if they represent a liability, that is, if the forward selling price is lower than the market price. In both cases, the instruments are in the money to the other party.

Purchased Options

Purchased options, on the other hand, do not result in the company having an obligation (as opposed to written options, which do). When the company buys options, it obtains the right but not the obligation to buy (call) or sell (put) its own shares. When will it exercise these options? Like any option holder, it is assumed that the company will exercise the options when they are **in the money**. Thus, when the underlying shares in a purchased call option have a market value that is greater than the exercise price, they are in the money. Alternatively, when the underlying shares in a purchased put option have a market value that is less than the exercise price, the options are in the money and it is assumed that they will be exercised.

Illustration 17-19 summarizes this.

Illustration 17-19

In the Money Options

	Call	Put
Written	In the money when market price is greater than exercise price	In the money when market price is less than exercise price
Purchased	In the money when market price is greater than exercise price	In the money when market price is less than exercise price

Purchased options will always be antidilutive since they will only be exercised when they are in the money and this will always be favourable to the company. They are therefore not considered in the calculation.[14]

Treasury Stock Method

Written options and warrants, and their equivalents, are included in earnings per share calculations through the treasury stock or reverse treasury stock method.

The **treasury stock method** applies to **written call options and equivalents** and assumes both of the following:

1. that the options/warrants or equivalents are exercised **at the beginning of the year** (or on the date of issue if it is later).

2. that the proceeds are used to purchase common shares for the treasury at the **average market price** during the year.

If the exercise price is lower than the average market price, then the proceeds from exercise are not sufficient to buy back all the shares. This will result in more shares being issued than purchased and the effect will therefore be dilutive. **The excess number of the shares issued over the number of shares purchased is added to the weighted average number of shares outstanding in calculating the diluted earnings per share. Note that no adjustment is made to the numerator.**

Assume, for example, that 1,500 (written) call options are outstanding at an exercise price of $30 for a common share. The average common share market price per share is $50. Because the market price is greater than the exercise price, the options are considered in the money and the holder is assumed to exercise them. The holder can buy the shares for a price that is less than market price—a bargain. By applying the treasury stock method, there would be 600 incremental shares outstanding, calculated as in Illustration 17-20.[15]

Proceeds from exercise of 1,500 options (1,500 × $30)	$45,000
Shares issued upon exercise of options	1,500
Treasury shares purchasable with proceeds ($45,000 ÷ $50)	900
Incremental shares outstanding (additional potential common shares)	600

Illustration 17-20

Calculation of Incremental Shares

Thus, if the exercise price of the call option or warrant is lower than the shares' market price, dilution occurs because, on a net basis, more common shares are assumed to be outstanding after the exercise. If the exercise price of the call option or warrant is higher than the shares' market price, the options would not be exercised and would therefore be irrelevant to the EPS calculation.[16] As a practical matter, a simple average of the weekly or monthly prices is adequate, as long as the prices do not fluctuate significantly.

6 Objective

Calculate diluted earnings per share using the treasury stock method.

---

[14] *CICA Handbook*, Section 3500.45.

[15] The incremental number of shares can be calculated in a simpler way: (Market price − Option price) ÷ Market price × Number of options = Number of shares; ($50 − $30) ÷ $50 × 1,500 options = 600 shares

[16] It might be noted that options and warrants have basically the same assumptions and problems of calculation, although the warrants may allow or require the tendering of some other security, such as debt, in lieu of cash upon exercise. In such situations, the accounting becomes quite complex and is beyond the scope of this book.

Comprehensive Illustration—Treasury Stock Method

To illustrate the application of the treasury stock method, assume that Kubitz Industries, Inc. has net income for the period of $220,000. The average number of shares outstanding for the period was 100,000 shares. Hence, basic EPS, ignoring all dilutive securities, is $2.20. The average number of shares that are outstanding under written call options at an option price of $20 per share is 5,000 shares (although the options are not exercisable at this time). The average market price of the common shares during the year was $28. Illustration 17-21 shows the calculation.

Illustration 17-21

Calculation of Earnings per Share—Treasury Stock Method

	Basic Earnings per Share	Diluted Earnings per Share
Average number of shares outstanding under option:		5,000
Option price per share		× $20
Proceeds upon exercise of options		$100,000
Average market price of common shares		$ 28
Treasury shares that could be repurchased with proceeds ($100,000 ÷ $28)		3,571
Excess of shares under option over the treasury shares that could be repurchased (5,000 − 3,571)— potential common incremental shares		1,429
Average number of common shares outstanding	100,000	100,000
Total average number of common shares outstanding and potential common shares	100,000 (A)	101,429 (C)
Net income for the year	$ 220,000 (B)	$ 220,000 (D)
Earnings per share	$2.20 (B ÷ A)	$2.17 (D ÷ C)

Reverse Treasury Stock Method

Objective 7
Calculate diluted earnings per share using the reverse treasury stock method.

The **reverse treasury stock method** is used for (written) put options and forward purchase contracts. It assumes both of the following:

1. that the company will issue enough common shares **at the beginning of the year** in the marketplace (at the average market price) to generate sufficient funds to buy the shares under the option/forward.

2. that the proceeds from the above will be used to buy back the shares under the option/forward at the beginning of the year.

If the options are in the money, the company will have to buy the shares back under the options/forward at a higher price than the market price. Thus, it will have to issue more shares at the beginning of the year to generate sufficient funds to meet the obligation under the option/forward.

Assume, for example, that 1,500 (written) put options are outstanding at an exercise price of $30 for a common share. The average market price per common share is $20. Because the market price is less than the exercise price, the options are considered in the money and the holder is assumed to exercise them. The holder can sell the shares for a price that is higher than market price—again, a bargain. By applying the reverse treasury stock method, there would be 750 additional (incremental) shares outstanding, calculated as in Illustration 17-22.

Amount needed to buy 1,500 shares under put option (1,500 x $30)	$45,000
Shares issued in market to obtain $45,000 ($45,000 ÷ $20)	2,250
Number of shares purchased under the put options	1,500
Incremental shares outstanding (potential common shares)	750

Illustration 17-22

Calculation of Incremental Shares

This is dilutive because there will be 750 more shares outstanding. If the market price were higher than the exercise price, the options would never be exercised (the holder could sell the shares in the marketplace for a higher amount). Thus, options that are not in the money are ignored in the diluted EPS calculation. Likewise, when the forward purchase price of a forward purchase contract is lower than the market price, the forward contract is antidilutive because the company would theoretically have to issue fewer shares in the marketplace in order to generate sufficient money to honour the forward contract. In other words, it would issue fewer shares than it would buy back, resulting in fewer common shares outstanding (not more).

Contingently Issuable Shares

Contingently issuable shares are potential common shares, as mentioned earlier. If these shares are issuable simply with the passage of time, they are not considered contingently issuable since it is certain that time will pass.[17] Instead, these shares would be considered outstanding for basic EPS only once the set period of time has passed and the shares have become issuable. They would then be included in the diluted EPS calculations as at the beginning of the year (or later if the agreement was made during the year).

If instead the shares are issuable upon attaining a certain earnings or market price level, and this level is met at the end of the year, they should be considered as outstanding from the beginning of the year for the calculation of diluted earnings per share.[18] If the conditions have not been met, however, the diluted EPS may still be affected. The number of contingently issuable shares included in the diluted EPS calculation would be based on the number of shares (if any) that would be issuable if the end of the reporting period were the end of the contingency period and if the impact were dilutive.[19]

For example, assume that Walz Corporation purchased Cardella Limited in 2007 and agreed to give the shareholders of Cardella 20,000 additional shares in 2009 if Cardella's net income in 2008 is $90,000. Assume also that in 2007 Cardella's net income is $100,000, which is higher than the $90,000 target for 2008. Because the contingency of stipulated earnings of $90,000 is already being attained in 2007, and because 2007 is treated as though it were the end of the contingency period, Walz's diluted earnings per share for 2007 would include the 20,000 contingent shares in the calculation of the number of shares outstanding.

---

[17] *CICA Handbook*, Section 3500.21.

[18] *CICA Handbook*, Section 3500.49. In addition to contingent issuances of stock, other types of situations that might lead to dilution are the issuance of participating securities and two classes of common shares. The reporting of these types of securities in EPS calculations is beyond the scope of this textbook.

[19] *CICA Handbook*, Section 3500.50 to .52.

Antidilution Revisited

Objective 8
Identify antidilutive potential common shares

In calculating diluted EPS, the combined impact of all dilutive securities must be considered. However, it is necessary to first determine which potentially dilutive securities are in fact individually dilutive and which are antidilutive. As was stated earlier, securities that are antidilutive have to be excluded from EPS calculations; they therefore cannot be used to offset dilutive securities.

Recall that antidilutive securities are securities whose inclusion in earnings per share calculations **would increase earnings per share (or reduce net loss per share)**. Convertible debt is antidilutive if the addition to income of the interest (net of tax) would cause a greater percentage increase in income (the numerator) than a conversion of the bonds would cause a percentage increase in common and potentially dilutive shares (the denominator). In other words, convertible debt is antidilutive if conversion of the security would cause common share earnings to increase by a greater amount per additional common share than the earnings per share amount before the conversion.

To illustrate, assume that Kohl Corporation has a $1-million, 6% debt issue that is convertible into 10,000 common shares. Net income for the year is $210,000, the weighted average number of common shares outstanding is 100,000 shares, and the tax rate is 40%. In this case, assume also that conversion of the debt into common shares at the beginning of the year requires the adjustments to net income and the weighted average number of shares outstanding that are shown in Illustration 17-23.

Illustration 17-23

Test for Antidilution

Net income for year	$210,000	Average number of shares outstanding	100,000
Add: Adjustment for interest (net of tax) on 6% debentures $60,000 × (1 − 0.40)	36,000	Add: Shares issued upon assumed conversion of debt	10,000
Adjusted net income	$246,000	Average number of common and potential common shares	110,000

Basic EPS = $210,000 ÷ 100,000 = $2.10
Diluted EPS = $246,000 ÷ 110,000 = $2.24 (Antidilutive)

As a shortcut, the convertible debt can also be identified as antidilutive by comparing the incremental EPS resulting from conversion, $3.60 ($36,000 additional earnings ÷ 10,000 additional shares), with EPS before inclusion of the convertible debt, $2.10.

With options or warrants, whenever the option or warrant is not in the money, it is irrelevant to the calculations because the holder will not exercise it.

Additional Disclosures

Complex capital structures and a dual presentation of earnings require the following additional disclosures in note form:

1. Adjustments to income before discontinued operations and extraordinary items for returns on senior equity instruments in arriving at income available to common shareholders

2. A reconciliation of the numerators and denominators of basic and diluted per share calculations for income before discontinued operations and extraordinary items (including the individual income and share amounts of each class of securities that affects EPS)

3. Securities that could dilute basic EPS in the future but were not included in the calculations because they have antidilutive features

Illustration 17-24 presents an example of the reconciliation and related disclosure that is needed to meet the standard's disclosure requirements. Assume stock options to purchase 1 million common shares at $85 per share were outstanding during the second half of 2008 but that the options are antidilutive.

	For the Year Ended December 31, 2008		
	Income (Numerator)	Shares (Denominator)	Per Share Amount
Income before extraordinary item and accounting change	$7,500,000		
Less: Preferred stock dividends	(45,000)		
Basic EPS			
Income available to common shareholders	7,455,000	3,991,666	$1.87
Warrants		30,768	
Convertible preferred shares	45,000	308,333	
4% convertible bonds (net of tax)	60,000	50,000	
Diluted EPS			
Income available to common shareholders + assumed conversions	$7,560,000	4,380,767	$1.73

Illustration 17-24

Reconciliation for Basic and Diluted EPS

Related disclosure: Stock options to purchase 1 million common shares at $85 per share were outstanding during the second half of 2008 but were not included in the calculation of diluted EPS because the options' exercise price was greater than the average market price of the common shares. The options were still outstanding at the end of 2008 and expire on June 30, 2018.

Comprehensive Earnings per Share Exercise

The purpose of the following exercise is to show the method of calculating dilution when many securities are involved. Illustration 17-25 presents a section of the balance sheet of Andrews Corporation, our assumed company; assumptions about the company's capital structure follow the illustration.

ANDREWS CORPORATION Selected Balance Sheet Information At December 31, 2008	
Long-term debt:	
Notes payable, 14%	$ 1,000,000
7% convertible bonds payable	2,000,000
9% convertible bonds payable	3,000,000
Total long-term debt	$ 6,000,000
Shareholders' equity:	
$10 cumulative dividend, convertible preferred shares, no par value; 100,000 shares authorized, 20,000 shares issued and outstanding	$ 2,000,000
Common shares, no par value; 5,000,000 shares authorized, 400,000 shares issued and outstanding	400,000
Contributed surplus	2,100,000
Retained earnings	9,000,000
Total shareholders' equity	$13,500,000

Illustration 17-25

Balance Sheet for Comprehensive Illustration

Notes and Assumptions
December 31, 2008

1. Options were granted/written in July 2006 to purchase 30,000 common shares at $15 per share. The average market price of Andrews' common shares during 2008 was $25 per common share. The options expire in 2016 and no options were exercised during 2008.

2. The 7% bonds were issued in 2007 at face value. The 9% convertible bonds were issued on July 1, 2008, at face value. Each convertible bond is convertible into 50 common shares (each bond has a face value of $1,000).

3. The $10 cumulative, convertible preferred shares were issued at the beginning of 2005. Each preferred share is convertible into four common shares.

4. The average income tax rate is 35%.

5. The 400,000 common shares were issued at $1 per share and were outstanding during the entire year.

6. Preferred dividends were not declared in 2008.

7. Net income was $1.2 million in 2008.

8. No bonds or preferred shares were converted during 2008.

Instructions

(a) Calculate basic earnings per share for Andrews for 2008.

(b) Calculate diluted earnings per share for Andrews for 2008, following these steps:
   1. Determine, for each dilutive security, the incremental per share effect if the security is exercised/converted. Where there are multiple dilutive securities, rank the results from the lowest earnings effect per share to the largest; that is, rank the results from least dilutive to most dilutive. The instruments with the lowest incremental EPS calculation will drag the EPS number down the most and are therefore most dilutive.

   2. Beginning with the earnings per share based upon the weighted average number of common shares outstanding, recalculate the earnings per share by adding the smallest per share effects from the first step. If the results from this recalculation are less than EPS in the prior step, go to the next smallest per share effect and recalculate the earnings per share. This process is continued as long as each recalculated earnings per share amount is smaller than the previous amount. The process will end either because there are no more securities to test or because a particular security maintains or increases the earnings per share (i.e., it is antidilutive).

(c) Show the presentation of earnings per share for Andrews for 2008.

Solution to Comprehensive EPS Exercise

(a) **Basic earnings per share**

The calculation of basic earnings per share for 2008 starts with the amount based upon the weighted average number of common shares outstanding, as shown below.

Net income	$1,200,000
Less: $10 cumulative, convertible preferred share dividend requirements	200,000
Income applicable to common shareholders	$1,000,000
Weighted average number of common shares outstanding	400,000
Earnings per common share	$2.50

Note the following points about the above calculation:

1. When preferred shares are cumulative, the preferred dividend is subtracted to arrive at the income that is applicable to common shares, whether or not the dividend is declared.

2. The earnings per share of $2.50 is calculated as a starting point because the per share amount is not reduced by the existence of convertible securities and options.

(b) **Diluted earnings per share**

The steps in calculating diluted EPS are now applied to Andrews Corporation. (Note that net income and income available to common shareholders are not the same if preferred dividends are declared or are cumulative.) Andrews Corporation has four securities (options, 7% and 9% convertible bonds, and the convertible preferred shares) that could reduce EPS.

The first step in the calculation of diluted earnings per share is to determine an incremental per share effect for each potentially dilutive security. Illustrations 17-26 through 17-29 show these calculations. Anything that is less than basic EPS is potentially dilutive.

Number of shares under option	30,000	**Illustration** 17-26
Option price per share	× $15	*Incremental Impact of Options*
Proceeds upon assumed exercise of options	$450,000	
Average 2008 market price of common shares	$ 25	
Treasury shares that could be acquired with proceeds ($450,000 ÷ $25)	18,000	
Excess shares under option over treasury shares that could be repurchased (30,000 − 18,000)	12,000	
Per share effect:		
Incremental numerator effect: None		
Incremental denominator effect: 12,000 shares	$ 0	
Therefore potentially dilutive		

Interest expense for year ($2,000,000 × 7%)	$140,000	**Illustration** 17-27
Income tax reduction due to interest (35% × $140,000)	49,000	*Incremental Impact of 7% Bonds*
Interest expense avoided (net of tax)	$ 91,000	
Number of common shares issued, assuming conversion of bonds (2,000 bonds × 50 shares)	100,000	
Per share effect:		
Incremental numerator effect: $91,000		
Incremental denominator effect: 100,000 shares	$ 0.91	
Therefore potentially dilutive		

Interest expense for year ($3,000,000 × 9%)	$270,000	**Illustration** 17-28
Income tax reduction due to interest (35% × $270,000)	94,500	*Incremental Impact of 9% Bonds*
Interest expense avoided (net of tax)	$175,500	
Number of common shares issued, assuming conversion of bonds (3,000 bonds × 50 shares)	150,000	
Per share effect (outstanding 1/2 year):		
Incremental numerator effect: $175,500 x 0.5 = $87,750		
Incremental denominator effect: 150,000 shares × 0.5 = 75,000	$ 1.17	
Therefore potentially dilutive		

Illustration 17-29

Incremental Impact of Preferred Shares

Dividend requirement on cumulative preferred (20,000 shares × $10)	$200,000
Income tax effect (dividends not a tax deduction): None	0
Dividend requirement avoided	$200,000
Number of common shares issued, assuming conversion of preferred (4 × 20,000 shares)	80,000
Per share effect: Incremental numerator effect: $200,000 Incremental denominator effect: 80,000 shares	$ 2.50
Therefore neutral	

Illustration 17-30 shows the ranking of all four potentially dilutive securities.

Illustration 17-30

Ranking of Potential Common Shares (Most Dilutive First)

	$ Effect Per Share
Options	0
7% convertible bonds	0.91
9% convertible bonds	1.17
$10 convertible preferred	2.50

The next step is to determine earnings per share and, through this determination, to give effect to the ranking in Illustration 17-30. Starting with the earnings per share of $2.50 calculated previously, add the incremental effects of the options to the original calculation, as shown in Illustrations 17-31 to 17-34.

Options*

Income applicable to common shareholders	$1,000,000
Add: Incremental numerator effect of options: None	0
Total	$1,000,000
Weighted average number of common shares outstanding	400,000
Add: Incremental denominator effect of options—Illustration 17-26	12,000
Total	412,000
Recalculated earnings per share ($1,000,000 ÷ 412,000 shares)	$ 2.43

*(From Illustration 17-26)

Since the recalculated earnings per share is reduced (from $2.50 to $2.43), the effect of the options is dilutive. Again, this effect could have been anticipated because the average market price exceeded the option price ($15).

Illustration 17-32 shows the recalculated earnings per share assuming the 7% bonds are converted.

7% Bonds*

Numerator from previous calculation	$1,000,000
Add: Interest expense avoided (net of tax)	91,000
Total	$1,091,000
Denominator from previous calculation (shares)	412,000
Add: Number of common shares assumed issued upon conversion of bonds	100,000
Total	512,000
Recalculated earnings per share ($1,091,000 ÷ 512,000 shares)	$ 2.13

*(From Illustration 17-27)

Since the recalculated earnings per share is reduced (from $2.43 to $2.13), the effect of the 7% bonds is dilutive.

Next, in Illustration 17-33, earnings per share is recalculated assuming the conversion of the 9% bonds.

9% Bonds*	
Numerator from previous calculation	$1,091,000
Add: Interest expense avoided (net of tax)	87,750
Total	$1,178,750
Denominator from previous calculation (shares)	512,000
Add: Number of common shares assumed issued upon conversion of bonds	75,000
Total	587,000
Recalculated earnings per share ($1,178,750 ÷ 587,000 shares)	$ 2.01
*(From Illustration 17-28)	

Illustration 17-33

Step-by-Step Calculation of Diluted EPS, Adding 9% Bonds Next (Next Most Dilutive)

Since the recalculated earnings per share is reduced (from $2.13 to $2.01), the effect of the 9% convertible bonds is dilutive.

The final step (Illustration 17-34) is the recalculation that includes the 10% preferred shares.

Preferred Shares*	
Numerator from previous calculation	$1,178,750
Add: Dividend requirements avoided	200,000
Total	$1,378,750
Denominator from previous calculation (shares)	587,000
Add: Number of common shares assumed issued upon conversion of preferred	80,000
Total	667,000
Recalculated earnings per share ($1,378,750 ÷ 667,000 shares)	$ 2.07
*(From Illustration 17-29)	

Illustration 17-34

Step-by-Step Calculation of Diluted EPS, Adding Preferred Shares Next (Least Dilutive)

The effect of the $10 convertible preferred shares is not dilutive, because the per share effects result in a higher EPS of $2.07. Since the recalculated earnings per share is not reduced, the effects of the convertible preferred shares are not used in the calculation. Diluted earnings per share to be reported is therefore $2.01.

(c) Presentation of EPS

The disclosure of earnings per share on the income statement for Andrews Corporation is shown in Illustration 17-35.

Net Income	$1,200,000
Basic earnings per common share	$ 2.50
Diluted earnings per common share	$ 2.01

Illustration 17-35

Presentation of EPS

PERSPECTIVES

Usefulness of EPS

EPS is one of the most highly visible standards of measurement for assessing management stewardship and predicting a company's future value. It is therefore a very important number and, because of this importance, GAAP is very specific in regard to its calculation.

Recall Illustration 17-6, which showed the common shareholders' claim on only residual income. Earnings per share provides shareholders with information that helps them predict the value of their shareholdings. The diluted EPS calculation is especially useful since there are many potential common shares outstanding through convertible securities, options/warrants, and other financial instruments, and shareholders need to understand how these instruments can affect their holdings. From an economic perspective, it is therefore important to carefully analyze the potential dilutive impact of the various securities instruments, and the AcSB is helping make it possible to do such analyses by continually striving to ensure greater transparency in EPS calculations. Sometimes this is not so easy. Consider the case of Finisar below.

What Do the Numbers Mean?

Finisar Corporation is a public company whose shares trade on NASDAQ. The company provides fibre-optic solutions to its customers. On October 9, 2006, Finisar announced that it was entering into an agreement with certain of its creditors to exchange $100 million worth of 2¹/₂% Convertible Subordinated Notes due in 2010 for new 2¹/₂% Convertible Senior Subordinated Notes due in 2010. What was the difference between the two?

The company noted that the new notes gave it more flexibility in terms of cash flows between now and 2010 and minimized dilution to shareholders. According to the press release, the new notes contain net share settlement provisions which, upon conversion of the notes, require payment in cash up to the principal amount and excess amounts to be settled in shares of the company. The excess amount is only payable if the market value of the shares exceeds a stated share conversion price.

The press release goes on to say that because the current market price of the shares is below the stated share conversion price, the potential common shares are not included in the diluted earnings per share calculation for accounting purposes and the instrument is therefore not dilutive. In essence, the notes contain an embedded call option, which, because it is not "in the money," does not get picked up in the diluted EPS calculation under the treasury stock method. Note that the potential for dilution still exists, however, and may be even more dilutive from an economic perspective since the new notes are convertible into 35 more shares per $1,000 note than the old notes.

In the U.S., in the early 2000s, companies were issuing conditional convertible debt such as Finisar's and not treating it as dilutive if the conditions for conversion had not been met. On the surface, this sounds okay, but sometimes the embedded options were in the money and therefore dilutive from an economic perspective. Often the notes were structured so that the conversion feature did not take effect until the market share price exceeded the conversion price by a certain premium (e.g., the market price would need to be 130% of the conversion price). Thus, there was a grey area where the option was in the money but the conversion feature had not been triggered. Should these financial instruments be treated as contingently issuable shares or as debt with an embedded option?

The FASB issued an Emerging Issue Task Force (EITF) abstract in 2004 noting that the instrument would be considered dilutive if it was in the money regardless of whether the conversion feature took effect or not. The board argued that there was no substantive economic difference between contingently convertible instruments and conventional convertible instruments with a market price conversion premium (per EITF 04-8).

Underlying Concept

This is yet another case of accounting trying to follow economic substance rather than legal form. The problem is that many of these financial instruments are very complex and it is not always easy to break them down into their economic components.

Earnings per share is also useful in valuing companies. When companies or their shares are valued, "earnings" are often discounted to arrive at an estimated value. While there are many different ways of doing this, discounted cash flow calculations (with earnings often used as a substitute for the calculation) or NPV (net present value) calculations are commonly used to estimate company or share value. Ideally, a **normalized or sustainable cash flow or earnings** number should be used in the valuation calculation since earnings or net income may be of higher or lower quality (as noted in Chapter 4). However, since calculating normalized or sustainable cash flows and earnings requires significant judgement, when valuing common shares the EPS number may be used instead since it is felt to be more reliable.

The price earnings ratio provides useful information by relating earnings to the price that the shares are trading at. It is sometimes used to generate a quick estimate of the value of the shares, and therefore the company. It allows an easy comparison with other companies and the information is often readily available. The price earnings ratio divides the price of the share by the earnings per share number. The result is often called the **multiplier**. The multiplier shows the per share value that each dollar of earnings generates. For example, if the share value is $10 and EPS is $1, the multiplier is 10 (10 ÷ 1). **Therefore, each additional dollar of earnings is felt to generate an additional $10 in share price.** This is a very rough calculation only, especially when you think of the judgement that went into calculating that EPS number in the first place. Consider the hundreds of financial reporting choices such as accounting methods, measurement uncertainty, bias, and other judgements. This is one of the major reasons why preparers of financial statements must be aware of the impact of all financial reporting decisions on the bottom line.

9 Objective
Compare current Canadian and international GAAP, and understand which direction international GAAP is headed in.

International

Illustration 17-36 compares Canadian GAAP with international GAAP.

Canada	International
Section 3500: Earnings Per Share	IAS 33: Earnings Per Share

Illustration 17-36

Comparison of Canadian and International GAAP

The standards are converged except for the following three (fairly minor) points:

1. IAS 33 does not require presentation of EPS for income before discontinued operations and extraordinary items.

2. IAS 33 requires that companies assume that contracts that may be settled in shares or cash will be settled in cash (with no rebuttal allowed).

3. IAS 33 does not preclude the presentation of cash flow per share.

Where do we go from here? As derivative accounting takes hold, standard setters are gradually revisiting other areas to determine the impact of the new standards for financial instruments on these other *CICA Handbook* sections. Earnings per share is one such area. The use of the if-converted method is being questioned.

Conversion features embedded in instruments, such as convertible debt and convertible preferred shares, are in substance embedded options. For instance, in many convertible debt instruments, the conversion feature represents a written call option. Why, then, would we not treat these embedded options as we treat stand-alone options? Why not use the treasury stock or reverse treasury stock method?

With respect to financial instruments that are carried at fair value with gains/losses being booked through net income, many feel that the potentially dilutive impact is already captured when the instruments are revalued to their fair value. The IASB and FASB are working toward issuing a new Exposure Draft in 2007 and a revised standard by 2008.

KEY TERMS

antidilutive securities, 1039

basic EPS, 1031

call options, 1041

complex capital structure, 1032

contingently issuable shares, 1033

diluted EPS, 1031

exercise price, 1041

if-converted method, 1039

income available to common shareholders, 1034

in the money, 1041

potential common share, 1033

put options, 1041

reverse treasury stock method, 1044

senior equity instruments, 1034

simple capital structure, 1032

treasury stock method, 1043

weighted average number of shares, 1035

Summary of Learning Objectives

1 Understand why earnings per share (EPS) is an important number.

Earnings per share numbers give common shareholders an idea of the amount of earnings that can be attributed to each common share. This information is often used to predict future cash flows from the shares and to value companies.

2 Understand when and how earnings per share must be presented.

EPS must be presented for all public companies or companies that are intending to go public. The calculations must be presented on the face of the income statement for net income from continuing operations and net income (for both basic EPS and diluted EPS in the case of complex capital structures). When there are discontinued operations or extraordinary items, the per share impact of these items must also be shown, but it can be shown either on the face of the income statement or in the notes. Comparative calculations must also be shown.

3 Identify potential common shares.

Potential common shares include convertible debt and preferred shares, options/warrants, contingently issuable shares, and other instruments that may result in additional common shares being issued by the company. They are relevant because they may cause the present interests of the common shareholders to become diluted.

4 Calculate earnings per share in a simple capital structure.

Basic earnings per share is an actual calculation that takes income available to common shareholders and divides it by the weighted average number of common shares outstanding during the period.

5 Calculate diluted earnings per share using the if-converted method.

Diluted earnings per share is a "what if" calculation that considers the impact of potential common shares. The if-converted method considers the impact of convertible securities such as convertible debt and preferred shares. It assumes that the instruments are converted at the beginning of the year and that any related interest or dividend is thus avoided.

6 Calculate diluted earnings per share using the treasury stock method.

The treasury stock method looks at the impact of written call options on EPS numbers. It assumes that the options are exercised at the beginning of the year and that the money from the exercise is used to buy back shares in the open market at the average common share price.

7 Calculate diluted earnings per share using the reverse treasury stock method.

The reverse treasury stock method looks at the impact of written put options. It assumes that the options are exercised at the beginning of the year and that the company must first issue shares in the market (at the average share price) to obtain sufficient funds to buy the shares under the option.

8 Identify antidilutive potential common shares.

Antidilutive potential common shares are irrelevant since they result in diluted EPS calculations that are higher than the basic EPS; thus, these numbers are antidilutive. Diluted EPS must show the worst possible EPS number. Note that purchased options and written options that are not in the money are ignored for purposes of calculating diluted EPS because they are either antidilutive or will not be exercised.

9 Compare current Canadian and international GAAP, and understand which direction international GAAP is headed in.

Currently, international and Canadian standards are largely converged in this area except for three minor issues. The IASB and FASB are working on a revised Exposure Draft to be issued in the second quarter of 2007. The main issue is the impact of derivatives accounting on the EPS calculations.

Brief Exercises

BE17-1 The 2009 income statement of Schrempf Corporation showed net income of $1,480,000 and an extraordinary loss of $240,000. Schrempf had 60,000 common shares outstanding all year. Prepare Schrempf's income statement presentation of earnings per share. **(LO 2)**

BE17-2 Haley Corporation had 2008 net income of $1.2 million. During 2008, Haley paid a dividend of $6 per share on 100,000 preferred shares. Haley also had 270,000 common shares outstanding during the year. Calculate Haley's 2008 earnings per share. **(LO 4)**

BE17-3 Assume the same information as in BE17-2 except that the preferred shares are non-cumulative and the dividend has not been declared or paid. **(LO 4)**

BE17-4 Assume the same information as in BE17-2 except that the preferred shares are cumulative and the dividends have not yet been declared or paid. **(LO 4)**

BE17-5 Barkley Corporation had 120,000 common shares outstanding on January 1, 2008. On May 1, 2008, Barkley issued 65,000 shares. On July 1, Barkley repurchased and cancelled 22,000 shares. Calculate Barkley's weighted average number of shares outstanding for the year ended December 31, 2008. **(LO 4)**

BE17-6 Lebel Limited had 42,000 common shares outstanding on January 1, 2008. On March 1, 2008, Lebel issued 20,000 shares in exchange for equipment. On July 1, Lebel repurchased and cancelled 10,000 shares. On October 1, 2008, Lebel declared and issued a 10% stock dividend. Calculate the weighted average number of shares outstanding for Lebel for the year ended December 31, 2008. **(LO 4)**

BE17-7 Assume the same information as in BE17-6 except that on October 1, 2008, Lebel declared a 3-for-1 stock split instead of a 10% stock dividend. **(LO 4)**

BE17-8 Assume the same information as in BE17-6 except that on October 1, 2008, Lebel declared a 1-for-2 reverse stock split instead of a 10% stock dividend. **(LO 4)**

BE17-9 Green Corporation had 500,000 common shares outstanding on January 1, 2008. On May 1, Green issued 150,000 shares. (a) Calculate the weighted average number of shares outstanding for the year ended December 31, 2008, if the 150,000 shares were issued for cash. (b) Calculate the weighted average number of shares outstanding for the year ended December 31, 2008, if the 150,000 shares were issued in a stock dividend. **(LO 4)**

BE17-10 Sabonis Corporation reported net income of $1.4 million in 2007 and had 230,000 common shares outstanding throughout the year. Also outstanding all year were 19,000 shares of cumulative preferred shares, with each being convertible into two common shares. The preferred shares pay an annual dividend of $5 per share. Sabonis' tax rate is 40%. Calculate Sabonis' 2007 diluted earnings per share. **(LO 4, 5)**

BE17-11 Strickland Corporation earned net income of $560,000 in 2008 and had 100,000 common shares outstanding throughout the year. Also outstanding all year was $400,000 of 10% bonds that are convertible into 22,000 common shares. Strickland's tax rate is 35%. Calculate Strickland's 2008 diluted earnings per share. **(LO 5)**

BE17-12 Lee Limited has 150,000 common shares outstanding throughout the year. On June 30, Lee issued 28,000 convertible preferred shares that are convertible into one common share each. Calculate the weighted average common shares for purposes of the diluted EPS calculations. Assume that the preferred shares are dilutive. **(LO 5)**

BE17-13 Sarunas Corporation reported net income of $780,000 in 2009 and had 300,000 common shares outstanding throughout the year. Also outstanding all year were 60,000 (written) options to purchase common shares at $11 per share. The average market price for the common shares during the year was $16 per share. Calculate the diluted earnings per share. **(LO 6)**

(LO 6)   BE17-14   Ghenghis Limited purchased $40,000 of call options during the year. The options give the company the right to buy its own common shares for $9 each. The average market price during the year was $12 per share. Calculate the incremental shares outstanding for Ghenghis Limited.

(LO 7)   BE17-15   Use the same information as in BE17-14 and assume that Ghenghis also wrote put options that allow the holder to sell Ghenghis's shares to Ghenghis at $13 per share. Calculate the incremental shares outstanding for Ghenghis Limited.

(LO 8)   BE17-16   Assume the same information as in BE17-14 except that Ghenghis can buy its own common shares for $10 each. How should the options be treated for purposes of the diluted EPS calculation?

(LO 8)   BE17-17   Assume the same information as in BE17-15 except that the put options allow the holder to sell Ghenghis's shares to Ghenghis at $11 each. How should these options be treated for purposes of the diluted EPS calculation?

Exercises

(LO 2, 4)   E17-1   (EPS: Simple Capital Structure) On January 1, 2009, Portmann Corp. had 580,000 common shares outstanding. During 2009, it had the following transactions that affected the common share account:

Feb. 1	Issued 180,000 shares.
Mar. 1	Issued a 10% stock dividend.
May 1	Acquired 200,000 common shares and retired them.
June 1	Issued a 3-for-1 stock split.
Oct. 1	Issued 60,000 shares.

The company's year end is December 31.

Instructions

(a) Determine the weighted average number of shares outstanding as at December 31, 2009.

(b) Assume that Portmann earned net income of $3,456,000 during 2009. In addition, it had 100,000 at 9%, $100 par, non-convertible, non-cumulative preferred shares outstanding for the entire year. Because of liquidity limitations, however, the company did not declare and pay a preferred dividend in 2009. Calculate earnings per share for 2009, using the weighted average number of shares determined in part (a).

(c) Assume the same facts as in part (b), except that the preferred shares were cumulative. Calculate earnings per share for 2009.

(d) Assume the same facts as in part (b), except that net income included an extraordinary gain of $864,000 and a loss from discontinued operations of $432,000. Both items are net of applicable income taxes. Calculate earnings per share for 2009.

(e) What is the reasoning behind using a weighted average calculation for the number of shares outstanding in the EPS ratio?

(LO 2, 4)   E17-2   (EPS: Simple Capital Structure) Valaderez Inc. had 650,000 common shares outstanding on December 31, 2008. During 2009, the company issued 22,000 shares on May 1 and retired 14,000 shares on October 31. For 2009, the company reported net income of $449,690 after an extraordinary gain of $36,600 (net of tax).

Instructions

(a) What earnings per share data should be reported at the bottom of Valaderez Inc.'s income statement?

(b) Is it possible for a corporation to have a simple capital structure one fiscal year and a complex capital structure in another fiscal year? If yes, how could this happen?

(LO 2, 4)   E17-3   (EPS: Simple Capital Structure) Flagstad Inc. presented the following data:

Net income	$5,500,000
Preferred shares: 50,000 shares outstanding, $100 par,	
8% cumulative, not convertible	$5,000,000
Common shares: Shares outstanding, Jan. 1, 2009	650,000
Issued for cash, May 1, 2009	100,000
Acquired treasury stock for cash, Sept. 1, 2009 (shares cancelled)	150,000
2-for-1 stock split, Oct. 1, 2009	

Instructions

(a) Calculate earnings per share for the year ended December 31, 2009.

(b) Discuss what the effect would be on your calculation in (a) if the stock split had been declared on January 30, 2010, instead of on October 1, 2009, assuming the financial statements of Flagstad Inc. for the year ending December 31, 2009, were issued after January 30, 2010.

E17-4 (EPS: Simple Capital Structure) A portion of the combined statement of income and retained earnings of **(LO 2, 4)** Seminole Inc. for the current year ended December 31 follows:

Income before extraordinary item		$ 30,000,000
Extraordinary loss, net of applicable income tax (Note 1)		1,740,000
Net income		28,260,000
Retained earnings at beginning of year		93,250,000
		121,510,000
Dividends declared:		
On preferred shares, $6.00 per share	$ 540,000	
On common shares, $1.75 per share	14,875,000	15,415,000
Retained earnings at end of year		$106,095,000

Note 1. During the year, Seminole Inc. suffered a loss of $1,740,000 after the applicable income tax reduction of $1.2 million. This was booked as an extraordinary item.

At the end of the current year, Seminole Inc. has outstanding 12.5 million common shares and 90,000 shares of 6% preferred.

On April 1 of the current year, Seminole Inc. issued 1 million common shares for $32 per share to help finance the loss.

Instructions

Calculate the earnings per share on common shares for the current year as it should be reported to shareholders.

E17-5 (EPS: Simple Capital Structure) On January 1, 2008, Le Phong Limited had shares outstanding as follows: **(LO 2, 4)**

6% cumulative preferred shares, $100 par value,	
10,000 shares issued and outstanding	$1,000,000
Common shares, 200,000 shares issued and outstanding	2,000,000

To acquire the net assets of three smaller companies, the company authorized the issuance of an additional 260,000 common shares. The acquisitions were as follows:

Date of Acquisition	Shares Issued
Company A: April 1, 2008	190,000
Company B: July 1, 2008	100,000
Company C: October 1, 2008	40,000

On May 14, 2008, Le Phong realized a $97,000 insurance gain (before taxes) on the government expropriation of land that had originally been purchased in 1994.

On December 31, 2008, the company recorded income of $680,000 before tax and not including the expropriation gain, which is considered extraordinary. Le Phong has a 50% tax rate.

Instructions

(a) Calculate the earnings per share data that should appear on the company's financial statements as at December 31, 2008.

(b) What determines that Le Phong has a simple capital structure?

E17-6 (Weighted Average Number of Shares) On January 1, 2008, Sharma Distillers Inc. had 950,000 common **(LO 4)** shares outstanding. On April 1, the corporation issued 95,000 new common shares to raise additional capital. On July 1, the corporation declared and distributed a 20% stock dividend on its common shares. On November 1, the corporation repurchased on the market 90,000 of its own outstanding common shares to make them available for issuances relating to its key executives' outstanding stock options.

Instructions

(a) Calculate the weighted average number of shares outstanding as at December 31, 2008.

(b) Assume that Sharma Distillers Inc. had a 5-for-1 reverse stock split instead of a 20% stock dividend on July 1, 2008. Calculate the weighted average number of shares outstanding as at December 31, 2008.

(LO 4) E17-7 (EPS: Simple Capital Structure) At January 1, 2009, Michael Limited's outstanding shares included the following:

> 280,000 shares of $50 par value, 7%, cumulative preferred shares
> 900,000 common shares

Net income for 2009 was $2,130,000. No cash dividends were declared or paid during 2009. On February 15, 2010, however, all preferred dividends in arrears were paid, together with a 5% stock dividend on common shares. There were no dividends in arrears before 2009.

On April 1, 2009, 550,000 common shares were sold for $10 per share and on October 1, 2009, 310,000 common shares were purchased for $20 per share.

The financial statements for 2009 were issued in March 2010.

Instructions

(a) Calculate earnings per share for the year ended December 31, 2009.

(b) What is the significance of the declaration and payment date of February 15, 2010, for the dividend on preferred shares? What effect, if any, will this transaction have on the December 31, 2009, financial statements?

(c) Would your answer in (b) change if the dividend arrears on preferred shares were for two years as at December 31, 2009?

(LO 4) E17-8 (Weighted Average Number of Shares) Newton Inc. uses a calendar year for financial reporting. The company is authorized to issue 9 million common shares. At no time has Newton issued any potentially dilutive securities. The following list is a summary of Newton's common share activities:

Number of common shares issued and outstanding at December 31, 2007	6,500,000
Shares issued as a result of a 10% stock dividend on September 30, 2008	650,000
Shares issued for cash on March 31, 2009	2,500,000
Number of common shares issued and outstanding at December 31, 2009	9,650,000

A 3-for-1 stock split of Newton's common shares occurred on March 31, 2010.

Instructions

(a) Calculate the weighted average number of common shares to use in calculating earnings per common share for 2008 on the 2009 comparative income statement.

(b) Calculate the weighted average number of common shares to use in calculating earnings per common share for 2009 on the 2009 comparative income statement.

(c) Calculate the weighted average number of common shares to use in calculating earnings per common share for 2009 on the 2010 comparative income statement.

(d) Calculate the weighted average number of common shares to used in calculating earnings per common share for 2010 on the 2010 comparative income statement.

(CMA adapted)

(LO 5) E17-9 (EPS with Convertible Bonds, Various Situations) In 2006, Ben Lo Inc. issued $80,000 of 8% bonds at par, with each $1,000 bond being convertible into 50 common shares. The company had revenues of $47,500 and expenses of $31,600 for 2007, not including interest and taxes (assume a tax rate of 45%). Throughout 2007, 2,600 common shares were outstanding, and none of the bonds were converted or redeemed. (For simplicity, assume that the convertible bond's equity element is not recorded.)

Instructions

(a) Calculate diluted earnings per share for the year ended December 31, 2007.

(b) Repeat the calculation in (a), but assume that the 80 bonds were issued on September 1, 2007 (rather than in 2006), and that none have been converted or redeemed.

(c) Repeat the calculation in (a), but assume that 40 of the 80 bonds were converted on July 1, 2007.

E17-10 (EPS with Convertible Bonds) On June 1, 2006, Mowbray Corp. and Surrey Limited merged to form **(LO 5)** Lancaster Inc. A total of 800,000 shares were issued to complete the merger. The new corporation uses the calendar year as its fiscal year.

On April 1, 2008, the company issued an additional 400,000 shares for cash. All 1.2 million shares were outstanding on December 31, 2008. Lancaster Inc. also issued $600,000 of 20-year, 8% convertible bonds at par on July 1, 2008. Each $1,000 bond converts to 40 shares of common at any interest date. None of the bonds have been converted to date. If the bonds had been issued without the conversion feature, the annual interest rate would have been 10%.

Lancaster Inc. is preparing its annual report for the fiscal year ending December 31, 2008. The annual report will show earnings per share figures based on a reported after-tax net income of $1,540,000 (the tax rate is 40%).

Instructions

(a) Determine for 2008 the number of shares to be used in calculating:

   1. basic earnings per share.

   2. diluted earnings per share.

(b) Determine for 2008 the earnings figures to be used in calculating:

   1. basic earnings per share.

   2. diluted earnings per share.

(CMA adapted)

E17-11 (EPS with Convertible Bonds and Preferred Shares) Shengru Corporation issued $7 million of 10-year, 7% **(LO 5)** callable convertible subordinated debentures at par on January 2, 2008. The debentures have a face value of $1,000, with interest payable annually. The current conversion ratio is 10:1, and in two years it will increase to 14:1. At the date of issue, the bonds were sold at 98. Bond discount is amortized on a straight-line basis. Shengru's effective tax was 35%. Net income in 2008 was $10.5 million, and the company had 2 million shares outstanding during the entire year. For simplicity, ignore the requirement to record the debentures' debt and equity components separately.

Instructions

(a) Prepare a schedule to calculate both basic and diluted earnings per share for the year ended December 31, 2008.

(b) Discuss how the schedule would differ if the security were convertible preferred shares.

(c) Assume that Shengru Corporation experienced a substantial loss instead of income for the fiscal year ending December 31, 2008. How would you respond to the argument made by a friend who states: "The interest expense from the conversion of the debentures is not actually saved; and there are no income taxes to be paid on the additional income that is assumed to have been created from the conversion of the debentures."

E17-12 (EPS with Convertible Bonds and Preferred Shares) On January 1, 2008, Sharif Limited issued $2 million of **(LO 5)** face value, 10-year, 6% bonds at par. Each $1,000 bond is convertible into 15 shares of common. Sharif's net income in 2008 was $300,000, and its tax rate was 40%. The company had 100,000 common shares outstanding throughout 2008. None of the bonds were exercised in 2008. For simplicity, ignore the requirement to record the bonds' debt and equity components separately.

Instructions

(a) Calculate diluted earnings per share for the year ended December 31, 2008.

(b) Calculate diluted earnings per share for 2008, assuming the same facts as above, except that $1 million of 6% convertible preferred shares was issued instead of the bonds. Each $100 preferred share is convertible into five common shares.

E17-13 (EPS with Convertible Bonds and Preferred Shares) Masters Corporation is preparing earnings per share **(LO 5)** data for 2009. The net income for the year ended December 31, 2009, was $400,000 and there were 60,000 common shares outstanding during the entire year. Masters has the following two convertible securities outstanding:

10% convertible bonds (each $1,000 bond is convertible into 25 common shares)	$100,000
5% convertible $100 par value preferred shares (each share is convertible into two common shares)	$ 50,000

Both convertible securities were issued at face value in 2006. There were no conversions during 2009, and Masters' income tax rate is 34%. The preferred shares are cumulative.

Instructions

(a) Calculate Masters' basic earnings per share for 2009.

(b) Calculate Masters' diluted earnings per share for 2009.

(c) Recalculate Masters' basic and diluted earnings per share for 2009, assuming instead that the preferred shares pay a 14% dividend.

(LO 5)   **E17-14   (EPS with Convertible Bond with Conversion and Preferred Shares)** Use the same information as in E17-13, except for the changes in part (c). Assume instead that 40% of the convertible bonds were converted to common shares on April 1, 2009.

Instructions

(a) Calculate Masters' weighted average common shares outstanding.

(b) Calculate Masters' basic earnings per share for 2009.

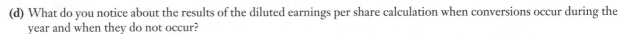

(c) Calculate Masters' diluted earnings per share for 2009.

(d) What do you notice about the results of the diluted earnings per share calculation when conversions occur during the year and when they do not occur?

(LO 6, 8)   **E17-15   (EPS with Options, Various Situations)** Viens Corp.'s net income for 2008 is $90,000. The only potentially dilutive securities outstanding were 1,000 call options issued during 2007, with each option being exercisable for one share at $14. None has been exercised, and 50,000 common shares were outstanding during 2008.

The average market price of the company's shares during 2008 was $20.

Instructions

(a) Calculate diluted earnings per share for the year ended December 31, 2008 (round to nearest cent).

(b) Assuming that the 1,000 call options were instead issued on October 1, 2008 (rather than in 2007), calculate diluted earnings per share for the year ended December 31, 2008 (round to nearest cent). The average market price during the last three months of 2008 was $20.

(c) How would your answers for (a) and (b) change if, in addition to the information for parts (a) and (b), the company issued (wrote) 1,000 put options with an exercise price of $10?

(LO 6)   **E17-16   (EPS with Warrants)** Howat Corporation earned $480,000 during a period when it had an average of 100,000 common shares outstanding. The common shares sold at an average market price of $23 per share during the period. Also outstanding were 18,000 warrants that could each be exercised to purchase one common share for $10.

Instructions

(a) Are the warrants dilutive?

(b) Calculate basic earnings per share.

(c) Calculate diluted earnings per share.

(LO 7)   **E17-17   (EPS with Contingent Issuance Agreement)** Winsor Inc. recently purchased Holiday Corp., a large home-painting corporation. One of the terms of the merger was that if Holiday's income for 2008 were $110,000 or more, 10,000 additional shares would be issued to Holiday's shareholders in 2009. Holiday's income for 2007 was $120,000.

Instructions

(a) Would the contingent shares have to be considered in Winsor's 2007 earnings per share calculations?

(b) Assume the same facts, except that the 10,000 shares are contingent on Holiday achieving a net income of $130,000 in 2008. Would the contingent shares have to be considered in Winsor's earnings per share calculations for 2007?

Problems

P17-1 Fernandez Corporation is a new audit client of yours and has not reported earnings per share data in its annual reports to shareholders in the past. The treasurer, Angelo Balthazar, has asked you to provide information about the reporting of earnings per share data in the current year's annual report in accordance with generally accepted accounting principles.

Instructions

(a) Define the term "earnings per share" as it applies to a corporation with a capitalization structure that is composed of only one class of common shares. Explain how earnings per share should be calculated and how the information should be disclosed in the corporation's financial statements.

(b) Discuss the treatment, if any, that should be given to each of the following items in calculating the earnings per share of common shares for financial statement reporting:

1. Outstanding preferred shares issued at a premium with a par value liquidation right

2. The exercise at a price below market value but above book value of a call option on common shares that was issued during the current fiscal year to officers of the corporation

3. The replacement of a machine immediately before the close of the current fiscal year at a cost that is 20% above the original cost of the replaced machine. The new machine will perform the same function as the old machine, which was sold for its book value.

4. The declaration of current dividends on cumulative preferred shares

5. The existence of purchased call options that allow the company to purchase shares of its own common stock at a price that is lower than the average market price

6. The acquisition of some of the corporation's outstanding common shares during the current fiscal year. The shares were classified as treasury stock.

7. A 2-for-1 stock split of common shares during the current fiscal year

8. A provision created out of retained earnings for a contingent liability related to a possible lawsuit

P17-2 Hillel Corporation is preparing the comparative financial statements for the annual report to its shareholders for the fiscal years ended May 31, 2007, and May 31, 2008. The income from operations was $2.8 million and $3.5 million, respectively, for each year. In both years, the company incurred a 9% interest expense on $2.4 million of debt for an obligation that requires interest-only payments for five years. The company experienced a loss of $400,000 from a fire in its Scotland facility in February 2008, which was determined to be an extraordinary loss. The company uses a 45% effective tax rate for income taxes.

The capital structure of Hillel Corporation on June 1, 2006, consisted of 3 million common shares outstanding and 120,000 $50, par value, 8% cumulative preferred shares. There were no preferred dividends in arrears, and the company had not issued any convertible securities, options, or warrants.

On October 1, 2006, Hillel sold an additional 500,000 common shares at $20 per share. Hillel distributed a 20% stock dividend on the common shares outstanding on January 1, 2007. On December 1, 2007, Hillel was able to sell an additional 800,000 common shares at $22 per share. These were the only common share transactions that occurred during the two fiscal years.

Instructions

(a) Identify whether the capital structure at Hillel Corporation is a simple or complex capital structure, and explain why.

(b) Determine the weighted average number of shares that Hillel Corporation would use in calculating earnings per share for the fiscal year ended:

1. May 31, 2007.

2. May 31, 2008.

(c) Prepare, in good form, a comparative income statement that begins with income from operations for Hillel Corporation for the fiscal years ended May 31, 2007, and May 31, 2008. This statement will be included in Hillel's annual report and should display the appropriate earnings per share presentations.

(CMA adapted)

P17-3 Edmund Halvor of the controller's office of East Aurora Corporation was given the assignment of determining the basic and diluted earnings per share values for the year ending December 31, 2008. Halvor has gathered the following information:

1. The company is authorized to issue 8 million common shares. As of December 31, 2007, 5 million shares had been issued and were outstanding.

2. The per share market prices of the common shares on selected dates were as follows:

	Price per Share
July 1, 2007	$30.00
Jan. 1, 2008	21.00
Apr. 1, 2008	25.00
July 1, 2008	11.00
Aug. 1, 2008	10.50
Nov. 1, 2008	9.00
Dec. 31, 2008	11.00

3. A total of 900,000 shares of an authorized 1.2 million convertible preferred shares had been issued on July 1, 2007. The shares were issued at $25, and have a cumulative dividend of $4 per share. The shares are convertible into common shares at the rate of one convertible preferred share for one common share. The rate of conversion is to be automatically adjusted for stock splits and stock dividends. Dividends are paid quarterly on September 30, December 31, March 31, and June 30.

4. East Aurora Corporation is subject to a 42% income tax rate.

5. The after-tax net income for the year ended December 31, 2008, was $13,550,000.

The following specific activities took place during 2008:

1. January 1: A 5% common stock dividend was issued. The dividend had been declared on December 1, 2007, to all shareholders of record on December 29, 2007.

2. April 1: A total of 200,000 shares of the $4 convertible preferred shares were converted into common shares. The company issued new common shares and retired the preferred shares. This was the only conversion of the preferred shares during 2008.

3. July 1: A 2-for-1 split of the common shares became effective on this date. The board of directors had authorized the split on June 1.

4. August 1: A total of 300,000 common shares were issued to acquire a factory building.

5. November 1: A total of 24,000 common shares were purchased on the open market at $9 per share and cancelled.

6. Cash dividends to common shareholders were declared and paid as follows:

    April 15: $0.40 per share
    October 15: $0.50 per share

7. Cash dividends to preferred shareholders were declared and paid as scheduled.

Instructions

(a) Determine the number of shares to use in calculating basic earnings per share for the year ended December 31, 2008.

(b) Determine the number of shares to use in calculating diluted earnings per share for the year ended December 31, 2008.

(c) Calculate the adjusted net income amount to use as the numerator in the basic earnings per share calculation for the year ended December 31, 2008.

P17-4   Campos Corporation Ltd. has the following capital structure at December 31, 2008, its fiscal year end:

	2008	2007
Number of common shares	375,000	330,000
Number of non-convertible, non-cumulative preferred A shares	10,000	10,000
Amount of 7% convertible bonds	$2,000,000	$2,000,000

The following additional information is available:

1. On July 31, 2008, Campos Corporation exchanged common shares for a large piece of equipment.

2. Income before extraordinary item for 2008 was $950,000, and an extraordinary loss of $150,000 was recorded, net of applicable tax recovery.

3. During 2008, dividends in the amount of $4.00 per share were paid on the preferred A shares.

4. Each $1,000 bond can be converted into 20 common shares.

5. There were unexercised stock options, outstanding since 2005, that allow holders to purchase 20,000 common shares at $40.00 per share.

6. Warrants to purchase 20,000 common shares at $52.00 per share were outstanding at the end of 2009.

7. The average market value of the common shares for 2008 was $50.00

8. Campos' tax rate is 40%.

9. Campos declared and paid a $100,000 dividend to common shareholders on June 1, 2008.

Instructions

(a) Determine the weighted average number of common shares that would be used in calculating earnings per share for the year ending December 31, 2008.

(b) Starting with the caption "Income before extraordinary item," prepare the bottom portion of the income statement for the year ended December 31, 2008, including all necessary earnings per share disclosures.

(AICPA adapted)

P17-5 Diane Leto is the controller at Yaeger Pharmaceutical Industries, a public company. She is currently preparing the calculation for basic and diluted earnings per share and the related disclosure for Yaeger's external financial statements. The following is selected financial information for the fiscal year ended June 30, 2008:

YAEGER PHARMACEUTICAL INDUSTRIES
Selected Statement of Financial Position Information
June 30, 2008

Long-term debt

Notes payable, 10%	$ 1,000,000
7% convertible bonds payable	5,000,000
10% bonds payable	6,000,000
Total long-term debt	$12,000,000

Shareholders' equity

Preferred shares, $4.25 cumulative, 100,000 shares authorized, 25,000 shares issued and outstanding	$ 1,250,000
Common shares, unlimited number of shares authorized, 1,000,000 shares issued and outstanding	4,500,000
Contributed surplus—conversion rights	500,000
Retained earnings	6,000,000
Total shareholders' equity	$12,250,000

The following transactions have also occurred at Yaeger:

1. Options were granted by the company in 2006 to purchase 100,000 shares at $15 per share. Although no options were exercised during 2008, the average price per common share during fiscal year 2008 was $20 per share.

2. Each bond was issued at face value. The 7% convertible debenture will convert into common shares at 50 shares per $1,000 bond. It is exercisable after five years and was issued in 2007. Ignore any requirement to record the bond's debt and equity components separately.

3. The $4.25 preferred shares were issued in 2006.

4. There are no preferred dividends in arrears; however, preferred dividends were not declared in fiscal year 2008.

5. The 1 million common shares were outstanding for the entire 2008 fiscal year.

6. Net income for fiscal year 2008 was $1.5 million, and the average income tax rate was 40%.

Instructions

(a) For the fiscal year ended June 30, 2008, calculate the following for Yaeger Pharmaceutical Industries:

1. Basic earnings per share
2. Diluted earnings per share

(b) Explain how premiums and discounts on outstanding convertible bonds affect the calculation of diluted earnings per share.

P17-6 An excerpt from the balance sheet of Delaware Limited follows:

DELAWARE LIMITED
Selected Balance Sheet Information
At December 31, 2008

Long-term debt

Notes payable, 10%	$ 2,000,000
4% convertible bonds payable	3,000,000
6% convertible bonds payable	4,000,000
Total long-term debt	$ 9,000,000

Shareholders' equity

$0.80 cumulative, no par value, convertible preferred shares (unlimited number of shares authorized, 280,000 shares issued and outstanding)	$ 4,000,000
Common shares, no par value (5,000,000 shares authorized, 1,800,000 shares issued and outstanding)	18,000,000
Contributed surplus	100,000
Retained earnings	5,000,000
Total shareholders' equity	$27,100,000

Notes and Assumptions
December 31, 2008

1. Options were granted/written in 2007 that give the holder the right to purchase 50,000 common shares at $12 per share. The average market price of the company's common shares during 2008 was $18 per share. The options expire in 2016 and no options were exercised in 2008.

2. The 4% bonds were issued in 2007 at face value. The 6% convertible bonds were issued on July 1, 2008, at face value. Each convertible bond is convertible into 80 common shares (each bond has a face value of $1,000).

3. The convertible preferred shares were issued at the beginning of 2008. Each share of preferred is convertible into one common share.

4. The average income tax rate is 42%.

5. The common shares were outstanding during the entire year.

6. Preferred dividends were not declared in 2008.

7. Net income was $1,750,000 in 2008.

8. No bonds or preferred shares were converted during 2008.

Instructions

(a) Calculate basic earnings per share for 2008.

(b) Calculate diluted earnings per share for 2008.

P17-7   Letourneau Limited had net income for the fiscal year ending June 30, 2008, of $16.4 million. There were 2 million common shares outstanding throughout 2008. The average market price of the common shares for the entire fiscal year was $75. Letourneau's tax rate was 40% for 2008.

Letourneau had the following potential common shares outstanding during 2008:

1. Options to buy 100,000 common shares at $60 per share.

2. 800,000 convertible preferred shares entitled to a cumulative dividend of $8 per share. Each preferred share is convertible into two common shares.

3. 5% convertible debentures with a principal amount of $100 million, issued at par. Each $1,000 debenture is convertible into 20 common shares.

Instructions

For the fiscal year ended June 30, 2008, calculate the following for Letourneau Limited:

(a) Basic earnings per share

(b) Diluted earnings per share

P17-8 As auditor for Banquo & Associates, you have been assigned to check Duncan Corporation's calculation of earnings per share for the current year. The controller, Mac Beth, has supplied you with the following calculations:

Net income	$3,374,960
Common shares issued and outstanding:	
Beginning of year	1,285,000
End of year	1,200,000
Average	1,242,500
Earnings per share:	

$$\frac{\$3,374,960}{1,242,500} = \$2.72 \text{ per share}$$

You have gathered the following additional information:

1. The only equity securities are the common shares.

2. There are no options or warrants outstanding to purchase common shares.

3. There are no convertible debt securities.

4. Activity in common shares during the year was as follows:

Outstanding, Jan. 1	1,285,000
Shares acquired, Oct. 1	(250,000)
	1,035,000
Shares issued, Dec. 1	165,000
Outstanding, Dec. 31	1,200,000

Instructions

(a) Based on the information, do you agree with the controller's calculation of earnings per share for the year? If you disagree, prepare a revised calculation.

(b) Assume the same facts except that call options had also been issued for 140,000 shares of common shares at $10 per share. These options were outstanding at the beginning of the year and none had been exercised or cancelled during the year. The average market price of the common shares during the year was $20 and the ending market price was $25. Prepare a calculation of earnings per share.

P17-9 The following information is for Prancer Limited for 2008:

Net income for the year	$2,200,000
8% convertible bonds issued at par ($1,000 per bond), with each bond convertible into	
30 common shares	1,000,000
6% convertible, cumulative preferred shares, $100 par value, with each share convertible into	
3 common shares	3,000,000
Common shares (600,000 shares outstanding)	6,000,000
Stock options (granted in a prior year) to purchase 50,000 common shares at $20 per share	500,000
Tax rate for 2008	42%
Average market price of common shares	$27 per share

There were no changes during 2008 in the number of common shares, preferred shares, or convertible bonds outstanding. For simplicity, ignore the requirement to book the convertible bonds' equity portion separately.

Instructions

(a) Calculate basic earnings per share for 2008.

(b) Calculate diluted earnings per share for 2008.

P17-10 Cordelia Corporation is preparing the comparative financial statements to be included in the annual report to shareholders. Cordelia's fiscal year ends May 31. The following information is available:

1. Income from operations before income taxes for Cordelia was $1.4 million and $660,000, respectively, for the fiscal years ended May 31, 2008 and 2007.

2. Cordelia experienced an extraordinary loss of $500,000 because of an earthquake on March 3, 2008.

3. A 41% combined income tax rate applies to all of Cordelia Corporation's profits, gains, and losses.

4. Cordelia's capital structure consists of preferred shares and common shares. The company has not issued any convertible securities or warrants and there are no outstanding stock options.

5. Cordelia issued 150,000 $100 par value, 6% cumulative preferred shares in 2000. All of these shares are outstanding, and no preferred dividends are in arrears.

6. There were 1.5 million common shares outstanding on June 1, 2006. On September 1, 2006, Cordelia sold an additional 300,000 common shares at $17 per share. Cordelia distributed a 15% stock dividend on the common shares outstanding on December 1, 2007.

7. These were the only common share transactions during the past two fiscal years.

Instructions

(a) Determine the weighted average number of common shares that would be used in calculating earnings per share on the current comparative income statement for:

1. the year ended May 31, 2008.

2. the year ended May 31, 2007.

(b) Starting with income from operations before income taxes, prepare a comparative income statement for the years ended May 31, 2008 and 2007. The statement will be part of Cordelia Corporation's annual report to shareholders and should include an appropriate earnings per share presentation.

(c) A corporation's capital structure is the result of its past financing decisions. Furthermore, the earnings per share data that are presented on a corporation's financial statements depend on the corporation's capital structure.

1. Explain why Cordelia Corporation is considered to have a simple capital structure.

2. Describe how earnings per share data would be presented for a corporation that has a complex capital structure.

(CMA adapted)

P17-11   Larocque Enterprises Ltd. has a tax rate of 40% and reported net income of $8.5 million in 2008. The following details are from the balance sheet of Larocque as at December 31, 2008, the end of its fiscal year:

Long-Term Debt:	
Bonds payable due Dec.31, 2014, 10% (issued at par)	$ 5,000,000
Bonds payable, face value $9,000,000, due Dec. 31, 2018, 7.25%, convertible into	
common shares at the investor's option at the rate of two shares per $100 of bonds:	8,600,000
Shareholders' Equity:	
Preferred shares, $4.50 cumulative, convertible into common shares at the rate of two common	
shares for each preferred share, 120,000 shares outstanding	$ 5,500,000
Preferred shares, $3.00 cumulative, convertible into common shares at the rate of one common	
share for each preferred share, 400,000 shares outstanding	10,000,000
Common shares, 1,700,000 shares outstanding	
Contributed surplus—conversion rights for bonds	750,000
Retained earnings	9,500,000

Other information:

1. Quarterly dividends were declared on March 1, June 1, September 1, and December 1 for the preferred shares and paid 10 days after the date of declaration.

2. Dividends paid on common shares amounted to $980,000 during the year and were paid on December 20, 2008.

3. Interest expense on bonds payable totalled $1,465,000, including bond discount amortization, which is recorded using the straight-line method.

4. There were no issuances of common shares during the 2008 fiscal year, and no conversions.

Instructions

(a) Determine the amount of interest expense incurred in 2008 for each of the bonds outstanding at December 31, 2008.

(b) Calculate basic earnings per share for 2008.

(c) Determine the potential for dilution for each security that is convertible into common shares.

(d) Calculate diluted earnings per share for 2008.

(e) What is the significance of the preferred share dividends being paid quarterly? What impact, if any, does this frequency in payment have on the calculation of diluted earnings per share?

P17-12   The following information is available for Nunez Inc., a company whose shares are traded on the Toronto Stock Exchange:

Net income	$150,000
Average market price of common shares during 2008 (adjusted for stock dividend)	$20
December 31, 2008 (fiscal year end) market price of common shares	$20
Income tax rate for fiscal year 2008	40%

Transactions in common shares during 2008:	Change	Cumulative shares
Jan. 1, 2008, common shares outstanding		90,000
Mar. 1, 2008, issuance of common shares	30,000	120,000
June 1, 2008, 10% stock dividend	12,000	132,000
Nov. 1, 2008, repurchase of common shares	(30,000)	102,000

Other information:

1. For all of the fiscal year 2008, $100,000 of 6% cumulative convertible bonds have been outstanding. The bonds were issued at par and are convertible into a total of 10,000 common shares (adjusted for the stock dividend) at the option of the holder, and at any time after issuance.

2. Stock options for 20,000 common shares have been outstanding for the entire 2008 fiscal year, and are exercisable at the option price of $25 per share (adjusted for the stock dividend).

3. For all of the fiscal year 2008, $100,000 of 4% cumulative convertible preferred shares have been outstanding. The preferred shares are convertible into a total of 15,000 common shares (adjusted for the stock dividend) at the option of the holder, and at any time after January 2013.

Instructions

(a) Determine the weighted average number of common shares that would be used in calculating earnings per share for the year ending December 31, 2008.

(b) Calculate basic earnings per share for 2008.

(c) Determine the potential for dilution for each security that is convertible into common shares.

(d) Calculate diluted earnings per share for 2008.

P17-13   Arncy Inc. has 1 million common shares outstanding as at January 1, 2007. On June 30, 2007, 4% convertible bonds were converted into 100,000 additional shares. Up to that point, the bonds had paid interest of $250,000 after tax. Net income for the year was $1,298,678. During the year, the company issued the following:

June 30: 10,000 call options giving holders the right to purchase shares of the company for $30
Sept. 30: 15,000 put options allowing holders to sell shares of the company for $25

On February 1, Arney also purchased in the open market 10,000 call options on its own shares, allowing it to purchase its own shares for $27. Assume the average market price for the shares during the year was $35.

Instructions

(a) Calculate the required EPS numbers under GAAP. For simplicity, ignore the impact that would result from the convertible debt being a hybrid security.

(b) Show the required presentations on the face of the income statement.

P17-14   Use the same information as in P17-13, but also assume the following:

1. On September 30, 200,000 convertible preferred shares were redeemed. If they had been converted, these shares would have resulted in an additional 100,000 common shares being issued. The shares carried a dividend rate of $3 per share to be paid on September 30. No conversions have ever occurred.

2. There are 10,000 $1,000, 5% convertible bonds outstanding with a conversion rate of three common shares for each bond starting January 1, 2008. Beginning January 1, 2011, the conversion rate is six common shares for each bond; and beginning January 1, 2015, it is nine common shares for each bond. The tax rate is 40%.

Instructions

(a) Calculate the required EPS numbers under GAAP. For simplicity, ignore the impact that would result from the convertible debt being a hybrid security.

(b) Show the required presentations on the face of the income statement.

Writing Assignments

WA17-1   "Earnings per share" (EPS) is the most commonly featured financial statistic about modern corporations. For many securities, the daily published quotations of share prices have recently been expanded to include a "times earnings" figure that is based on EPS. Stock analysts often focus their discussions on the EPS of the corporations that they study.

Instructions

(a) Explain how the calculation of EPS is affected by dividends or dividend requirements on classes of preferred shares that may be outstanding.

(b) One of the technical procedures that applies to EPS calculations is the treasury stock method. Briefly describe the circumstances that can make it appropriate to use the treasury stock method.

(c) Convertible debentures are considered potentially dilutive common shares. Explain how convertible debentures are handled in regard to EPS calculations.

(AICPA adapted)

WA17-2   Matt Kacskos is a shareholder of Howat Corporation and has asked you, the firm's accountant, to explain why his stock warrants were not included in diluted EPS. In order to explain this situation, you must briefly explain what dilutive securities are, why they are included in the EPS calculation, and why some securities are antidilutive and therefore are not included in this calculation.

Instructions

Write Mr. Kacskos a one-and-a-half page letter explaining why the warrants are not included in the calculation. Use the following data to help you explain this situation:
(1) Howat Corporation earned $228,000 during the period, when it had an average of 100,000 shares of common shares outstanding. (2) The common shares sold at an average market price of $25 per share during the period. (3) Also outstanding were 15,000 warrants that could be exercised by the holder to purchase one share of common shares at $30 per warrant.

WA17-3   Stock options are used by companies for various purposes.

Instructions

Write a two-page essay examining the business reasons for using stock options and warrants and the impact that they have on earnings per share calculations. (Hint: Refer to Chapters 16 and 17.)

WA17-4   Cash Flow per Share and Other per Share Amounts
In April 2002, the CICA issued an Exposure Draft relating to proposed revisions to cash flow statements and EPS. Currently, presentation of cash flow per share and other income per share amounts outside of *CICA Handbook* Section 3500 are no longer allowed in Canada, but they are allowed under IFRS.

Instructions

Write a short essay on the pros and cons of allowing companies to include alternate per share amounts in their annual reports.

Case

Refer to the Case Primer on the Student Website to help you answer these cases.

CA17-1   Candelabra Products Inc. (CP) has been in business for quite a while. Its shares trade on a public exchange and it is thinking of expanding onto the NYSE and LSE. Recently, however, the company has run into cash flow difficulties. The CEO is confident that the company can overcome this problem in the longer term as it has a solid business model; however, in the shorter term the company needs to be very careful in managing its cash flows. Of particular concern is the fact that it has multiple potential common shares outstanding that cause the diluted earnings per share numbers to be significantly lower than the company's basic EPS. This in turn has recently caused Candelabra's stock price to decline and is affecting the company's ability to get the best interest rates on its bank loans.

At a recent meeting with the CFO, the CEO decided to exchange the company's convertible senior subordinated notes (the old notes) for new senior subordinated notes (the new notes). The notes were held by a large institutional investor who agreed to the exchange. The old notes were convertible into 25 shares for each $1,000 note. The new notes have a net share settlement provision which requires that, upon conversion, the company will pay the holders up to $1,000 in cash for each note, plus an excess amount which would be settled in shares at a fixed conversion price (30 shares for each $1,000 note in the total consideration). The notes may only be turned in if the share price exceeds 20% of the fixed conversion price.

It is now year end and the share price is trading above the fixed conversion price but well below the 20% premium level. The note therefore cannot be turned in (i.e., converted). The CEO feels that the share price will not exceed the 20% premium for a couple of years.

Instructions
Adopt the role of the auditors and discuss the issues related to the new notes.

Integrated Cases

IC17-1   Canadian Utilities Limited (CUL) is based in Alberta and is involved in power generation, utilities, logistics, and energy services and technologies. The company was incorporated in 1927 and its shares trade on the TSE. PricewaterhouseCoopers is the current auditor.

According to the notes to the 2002 financial statements:

> In December 2000, the Province of Alberta issued regulations providing for the deferral of price and volume variance in excess of forecast amounts in respect of the supply of electricity by distributors to their customers for the year ended December 31, 2000. In June 2002 ... a decision ... was issued approving the collection by ... the company ... of its deferred costs from customers over a period that is expected to end in July 2003, and permitting ... the company ... to sell these deferred costs and related rights.
>
> On August 14, 2002 ... the company ... sold deferred costs of $81 million to an unrelated purchaser for equivalent cash consideration. GAAP requires that this transaction be accounted for as a financing arrangement rather than a sale. Accordingly, the cash received results in the recording of a deferred electricity cost obligation rather than a reduction of deferred electricity costs. The obligation bears interest at 3.3975%, which approximates the interest earned on the deferred costs. The obligation principal and interest incurred will be paid to the purchaser as the deferred costs and interest earned are collected from customers.

The company has Class A and B shares outstanding. The Class A shares are non-voting, whereas the Class B shares are voting. Both shares are entitled to participate equally on a share-for-share basis in all dividends declared on either of the shares as well as remaining property upon dissolution of the company. The company has a stock option plan under which 3,200,000 Class A shares are reserved for issuance. Under the plan, options may be granted to directors, officers, and key employees at an exercise price equal to the weighted average of the trading price of the shares in the TSE for the five trading days immediately preceding the date of the grant.

Instructions
Adopt the role of the auditor and discuss any financial reporting issues.

IC17-2   Toby's Foods Limited (TFL) is in the supermarket business. It is a public company and is thinking of going private (i.e., of buying up all of its shares that are available). The funds will come from a private consortium. The consortium has offered to buy all shares if the share price hits a certain level. Although the company has come through some tough times, things have been looking up recently. This is partially due to a new strategy to upgrade the stores and increase square footage.

TFL obtains revenues from two sources—in-store sales to customers and fees from sales of new franchises and continuing franchise fees. This year was a banner year for sales of new franchises. The company sold and booked revenues for 10 new franchised stores. Most of these new stores have not yet opened but locations have been found and deposits have been taken from each of the franchisees.

Under the terms of the franchise contracts, TFL has agreed to absorb any losses that the stores suffer for the first five years. Based on market research, however, and the location of the new stores, it is highly unlikely that losses will occur. Just in case, TFL has requested that franchisees deposit a certain amount of funds in a trust fund. In addition, TFL has agreed to issue shares of TFL to the franchisees if the stores are profitable in the first two years.

TFL received a substantial amount of cash under a new program under which new suppliers pay an upfront fee for the right to sell groceries to TFL. The amount is non-refundable. Although it is not written down anywhere, there is a tacit understanding that the fee will guarantee that the suppliers will continue to be able to sell a certain amount of product to TFL over the next three years.

During the year, TFL issued long-term debt that is convertible into common shares of the company. The number of common shares varies depending on the share price. Because of the potential for taking the company private, TFL agreed to certain concessions. If the company goes private, TFL must pay back 120% of the face value of the debt.

Instructions
Assume the role of the controller and discuss the financial reporting issues.

Research and Financial Analysis

RA17-1   British Sky Broadcasting Group PLC

British Sky Broadcasting Group PLC (BSkyB) operates the leading pay television broadcast service in the UK and Ireland. Shares of the company trade on the London Stock Exchange and the NYSE. The company produces financial statements in accordance with IFRS and includes a reconciliation to U.S. GAAP. The following excerpts are from the 2006 financial statement notes:

h) Inventories

i. Acquired and commissioned television programme rights

Programme rights are stated at the lower of cost and net realisable value ("NRV"), including, where applicable, estimated subscriber escalation payments, and net of the accumulated expense charged to the income statement to date.

Programme rights are recorded in inventories when the programmes are available for transmission. Contractual obligations for television programme rights not yet available for transmission are not included in inventories and are instead disclosed as contractual commitments (see note 26). Payments made upon receipt of commissioned and acquired programming, but in advance of the legal right to broadcast the programmes, are treated as prepayments.

The cost of television programme rights is recognised in the operating expense line of the income statement, primarily as described below:

Sports—100% of the cost is recognised in the income statement on the first showing or, where the rights are for multiple seasons or competitions, such rights are principally recognised on a straight-line basis across the seasons or competitions.

News—100% of the cost is recognised in the income statement on first showing.

General entertainment—The cost is recognised in the income statement based on the expected profile of transmission.

Movies—The cost is recognised in the income statement on a straight-line basis over the period of transmission rights.

Where programme rights are surplus to the Group's requirements, and no gain is anticipated through a disposal of the rights, or where the programming will not be broadcast for any other reason, a write-down to the income statement is made. Any reversals of inventory writedowns are recognised as reductions in operating expense.

ii Digiboxes and related equipment

Digiboxes (including Sky+ boxes and High Definition boxes) and related equipment are valued at the lower of cost and NRV, the latter of which reflects the value the business expects to realise from the digiboxes and the related equipment in the hands of the customer, and are recognised through the operating expenses line of the income statement. Any subsidy is expensed on enablement, which is the process of activating the viewing card once inserted in the digibox upon installation, so as to enable a viewer to view encrypted broadcast services, and effectively represents the completion of the installation process for new subscribers. The amount recognised in the income statement as the inventories are sold is recognised on a first-in first-out basis ("FIFO").

iii Raw materials, consumables and goods held for resale

Raw materials, consumables and goods held for resale are valued at the lower of cost and NRV. The cost of raw materials, consumables and goods held for resale is recognised through the operating expenses line of the income statement on a FIFO basis.

n) Revenue recognition

Revenue, which excludes value added tax and transactions between Group companies, represents the gross inflow of economic benefit from Sky's operating activities. Revenue is measured at the fair value of the consideration received or receivable. The Group's main sources of revenue are recognised as follows:

- Revenue from the provision of direct-to-home ("DTH") subscription services, including residential broadband services and revenue associated with sale of the customer magazine, is recognised as the goods or services are provided, net of any discount given. Pay-per-view revenue is recognised when the event, movie or football match is viewed.

- Cable revenue is recognised as the services are provided to the cable wholesalers and is based on the number of subscribers taking the Sky channels, as reported to the Group by the cable wholesalers, and the applicable rate card.

- Advertising sales revenue is recognised when the advertising is broadcast. Revenue generated from airtime sales where Sky acts as an agent on behalf of third parties is recognised on a net commission basis.

- Betting and gaming revenues are recognised in accordance with IAS 39 "Financial Instruments: Recognition and Measurement" ("IAS 39"). Sky Bet revenues therefore represent income in the period for betting and gaming activities, defined as amounts staked by customers less betting payouts.

- Sky Active revenues include income from online advertising, email, telephony income from the use of interactive services (e.g. voting), interconnect, text services and digibox subsidy recovery revenues earned through conditional access and access control charges made to customers on the Sky digital platform. All Sky Active revenues are recognised in the income statement when the goods or services are delivered.

- Other revenue principally includes income from installations, digibox sales (including the sales of Sky+, Multiroom boxes and High Definition boxes), Sky Talk, service calls, warranties, customer management service fees, access control fees, SkyCard, Sky Mobile TV and the supply of broadband services to business customers. Other revenues are recognised, net of any discount given, when the relevant goods or service are provided.

---

s) Earnings per share

Basic earnings per share represents the profit for the year, divided by the weighted average number of ordinary shares in issue during the year, excluding the weighted average number of ordinary shares purchased by the Group and held in the Group's ESOP during the year to satisfy employee share awards.

Diluted earnings per share represents the profit for the year, divided by the weighted average number of ordinary shares in issue during the year, excluding the weighted average number of ordinary shares purchased by the Group and held in the Group's ESOP Trust during the year to satisfy employee share awards, plus the weighted average number of dilutive shares resulting from share options and other potential ordinary shares outstanding during the year.

Instructions

(a) For the items noted above, how do the accounting policies differ if at all in terms of Canadian GAAP?

(b) Access the annual report through the Student Website and review note 32 to the financial statements. Then answer the following:

    1. How complex is the note?

    2. Discuss the pros and cons of using reconciliation between the two GAAPs (IFRS and U.S. GAAP) versus preparing two separate sets of financial statements: one under U.S. GAAP for U.S. investors and one under IFRS for European investors.

RA17-2 Molson Coors Brewing Company

Instructions

Go to the Student Website and obtain the annual report for **Molson Coors Brewing Company**. Then answer the following.

(a) Does the company have a complex or simple capital structure?

(b) Identify any potential common shares.

(c) What is the source of the exchangeable common shares? In other words, what created them?

(d) Discuss how the company calculated its diluted earnings per share and explain any choices that it made.

RA17-3 ClubLink Corporation

Instructions

Go to the Student Website and access the annual report for **ClubLink Corporation**. Then do the following.

(a) Comment on the capital structure of the company.

(b) Identify potential common shares.

(c) Even though potential common shares exist, the basic and diluted EPS are the same. Discuss.

RA17-4 EPS Harmonization

As of the time of writing this text, the IASB and FASB were planning to issue an Exposure Draft to revise the EPS GAAP as part of their short-term convergence project.

Instructions

Go to the FASB website (www.fasb.org) and read the Exposure Draft. Discuss the issues raised and comment on whether the changes will result in better financial reporting.

Taxing Changes

EnCana Corporation is a leading natural gas and oil producer whose operations are mainly in Canada and the U.S. Based in Calgary, it has an enterprise value of approximately $50 billion.

In trying to forecast its taxes, Encana faces a number of challenges, simply because of the many unpredictable variables. "Three primary factors influence the amount of tax we can expect to pay," explains Brian Ferguson, EnCana's chief financial officer. "First, the business's cash flow, which is directly impacted by commodity prices; second, the magnitude and type of capital expenditures; and third, unusual events such as a major business transaction or significant changes in tax laws that affect us."

Since EnCana's creation, oil and gas prices have fluctuated significantly. The post-2001 rise in oil and gas prices increased cash flow and, therefore, taxable income. On the capital expenditure side, Ferguson says those same price increases fuelled inflation, which increased the cost of drilling a well. Another factor that affects taxes is the type of work done. Drilling an exploration well results in a full write-off of the costs in the year they are incurred, while the costs of a development well are deducted for tax purposes over a longer period. "Also influencing cash tax expense estimates," says Ferguson, "is where the company invests. The tax rates on income and the treatment of expenditures are specific to and can be quite different in each country where we operate." A major acquisition or sale can also cause changes to an organization's taxable income and cash tax expense.

Summing up, Ferguson says, "Add to those variables the changes in federal and provincial tax rates, and you have a multitude of contributors to the volatility of our cash tax expense." ■

chapter 18

Income Taxes

Learning Objectives

After studying this chapter, you should be able to:

1. Explain the difference between accounting income and taxable income.
2. Identify the difference between timing and permanent differences, and calculate taxable income and current income taxes.
3. Explain what a taxable temporary difference is and why a future tax liability is recognized.
4. Explain what a deductible temporary difference is and why a future tax asset is recognized.
5. Prepare analyses of future income tax balances and record future income tax expense.
6. Explain the effect of various tax rates and tax rate changes on future income tax accounts.
7. Apply accounting procedures for a tax loss carryback.
8. Apply accounting procedures and disclosure requirements for a tax loss carryforward.
9. Explain why the Future Income Tax Asset account is reassessed at the balance sheet date.
10. Identify and apply the reporting and disclosure requirements for corporate income taxes, including intraperiod tax allocation.
11. Compare current Canadian and international GAAP for income taxes.
12. Identify and apply the differential reporting option for income taxes.
13. Identify outstanding issues with the asset-liability method.

Preview of Chapter 18

Careful management means, in part, managing all of a company's costs in ways that maximize shareholder value. For example, to minimize the overall cost of doing business, good managers look for the best prices for the raw materials and supplies that go into making the company's products and are expected to be savvy bargainers in negotiating labour and other service contracts. Since income taxes are a major cost to most corporations, however, prudent managers also devote a large amount of time and effort to minimizing a company's tax payments. For example, by using accelerated amortization methods for capital assets, companies can defer paying taxes. With faster tax write-offs on plant and equipment, companies report lower taxable income and pay lower taxes in the early years of the assets' lives. Good managers therefore pay attention to managing a company's tax costs and, as the opening story about EnCana shows, it is usually the required cash flow—the tax payment—that gets the most attention!

This chapter discusses the standards that companies follow in accounting for and reporting income taxes. It is organized as follows:

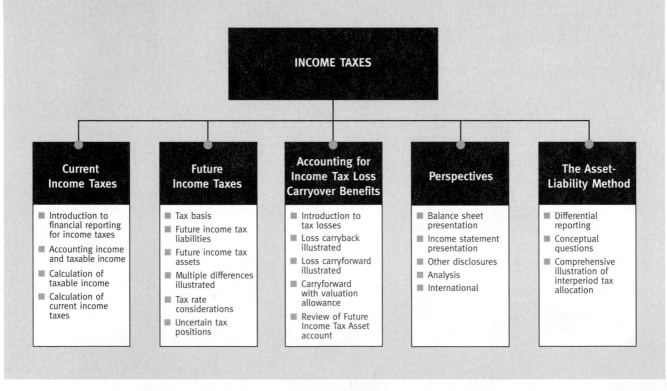

CURRENT INCOME TAXES

Introduction to Financial Reporting for Income Taxes

Up to now in this textbook, you have learned the basic principles that corporations use to report information to investors and creditors. You also recognize that corporations must file income tax returns following the *Income Tax Act* (and related provincial legislation), which is administered by the Canada Revenue Agency or CRA.[1] Because GAAP accounting standards differ in several ways from tax regulations, certain adjustments must be made and recognized on both the balance sheet and the income statement.

For example, the carrying amounts of assets and liabilities on the GAAP **balance sheet** often differ from their tax balances determined by tax legislation. This common situation makes it necessary to recognize the future tax implications of these differences as either future income tax assets or future income tax liabilities on the balance sheet.

At the same time, the current year's pre-tax income on the **income statement** (i.e., the income amount as determined by the company's accounting choices) and the company's taxable income often differ. As a result, the amount that a company reports as total income tax expense on its GAAP income statement often differs from the amount of income taxes that is currently payable to the CRA. This is highlighted in Illustration 18-1.

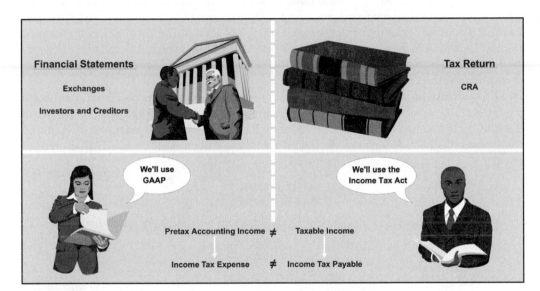

Illustration 18-1

Income Statement Differences between Financial and Tax Reporting

The difference between the total income tax expense on the income statement and the income tax that is currently payable is related to the adjustment for the future tax implications on the balance sheet. To make GAAP more understandable, the chapter analyzes tax implications in two steps:

1. The first step explains why there are differences between accounting income and taxable income, and how to calculate taxable income. The accounting entry for **current income tax expense** and the income tax that is currently payable is based on the amount of taxable income.

2. The second step zeroes in on the balance sheet and explains why there are differences between the book values and tax values of assets and liabilities. The tax consequences of these differences are recognized as future income tax assets or liabilities on the balance sheet, and the adjustment that is needed to the balance sheet future tax account is the accounting entry for **future income tax expense**.

---

[1] Proprietorships and partnerships do not pay income taxes as separate legal entities. Instead, their income is taxed as part of the proprietor's or partners' income as individuals. Organizations that are organized as income trusts also generally do not have their income taxed, because they distribute the income to their unitholders. Taxes that are owed on such distributions are obligations of the unitholders. The favourable tax treatment for most income trusts is scheduled to be phased out by 2011.

The **total income tax expense** that is reported on the income statement is the sum of current income tax expense and future income tax expense. These two steps explain the basics of how to apply current GAAP for income taxes. This approach is known as the **asset-liability method (or liability method)** because of the importance of asset and liability recognition and measurement requirements in determining the total income tax expense.

Accounting Income and Taxable Income

Objective 1

Explain the difference between accounting income and taxable income.

Accounting income is a financial reporting term and is also often referred to as income before taxes, income for financial reporting purposes, or income for book purposes. In this chapter, it is a pre-tax concept. Accounting income is determined according to GAAP and is measured with the objective of providing useful information to investors and creditors. **Taxable income** (income for tax purposes) is a tax accounting term and indicates the amount on which income tax payable is calculated. Taxable income is determined according to the *Income Tax Act and Regulations*, which is designed to raise money to support government operations.

To illustrate how differences in GAAP and tax rules affect financial reporting and taxable income, assume that Chelsea Inc. reported revenues of $130,000 and expenses of $60,000 on its income statement in each of its first three years of operations. Illustration 18-2 shows the (partial) income statements over these three years.

Illustration 18-2

Accounting Income

CHELSEA INC.
GAAP Reporting

	2008	2009	2010	Total
Revenues	$130,000	$130,000	$130,000	
Expenses	60,000	60,000	60,000	
Accounting income	**$ 70,000**	**$ 70,000**	**$ 70,000**	**$210,000**

For tax purposes (following tax regulations), Chelsea reported the same expenses to the CRA in each of the years. However, the $130,000 of revenue that was reported each year was taxed in different accounting periods: taxable revenues were $100,000 in 2008, $150,000 in 2009, and $140,000 in 2010, as shown in Illustration 18-3.

Illustration 18-3

Taxable Income

CHELSEA INC.
Tax Reporting

	2008	2009	2010	Total
Revenues	$100,000	$150,000	$140,000	
Expenses	60,000	60,000	60,000	
Taxable income	**$ 40,000**	**$ 90,000**	**$ 80,000**	**$210,000**

In reality, companies do not submit revised income statements for the tax return that list only taxable revenues and deductible expenses. Instead, they prepare a schedule that begins with accounting income and they then adjust this amount for each area of difference between GAAP income and taxable income; the result is taxable income. Chelsea's schedules would appear as in Illustration 18-4.

CHELSEA INC.			
	2008	2009	2010
Accounting income	$70,000	$70,000	$70,000
Less revenue taxable in a future period	(30,000)		
Add revenue recognized in previous period, taxable in current period		20,000	10,000
Taxable income	$40,000	$90,000	$80,000
Taxes payable (40% assumed rate)	$16,000	$36,000	$32,000

Illustration 18-4

Schedule to Reconcile Accounting Income to Taxable Income

Calculation of Taxable Income

Temporary and Permanent Differences

We will now take a more detailed look at the differences between GAAP income and taxable income. The Chelsea Inc. example above illustrated how to calculate taxable income when there is only one such difference. In reality, many adjustments may be needed. The major reasons for differences between accounting and taxable income follow, along with some examples:[2]

2 Objective

Identify the difference between timing and permanent differences, and calculate taxable income and current income taxes.

1. ***Revenues or gains are taxable after they are recognized in accounting income.*** A sale may be recorded in the current accounting period with a debit to a receivable and a credit to revenue, but the revenue may not be included in taxable income until future years when the receivable is actually collected in cash. There is thus a timing difference. Such a timing difference may also apply to a gain on sale or to holding gains recognized on assets being held, as these amounts too may not be taxable until they have been realized. Examples include:

    - instalment sales that are accounted for on the accrual basis for financial reporting purposes and on the cash basis for tax purposes

    - contracts that are accounted for under the percentage-of-completion method for financial reporting purposes and the completed contract basis for tax purposes—resulting in some or all of the related gross profit being deferred for tax purposes

    - holding gains that are recognized in income on held-for-trading investments and in OCI on available-for-sale investments, which are taxable only when realized

    Note that, in these examples, the GAAP balance sheet reports an asset (from an account receivable, construction in process, or investment account) with a carrying amount that is higher than the tax basis or tax value of the asset, because, for tax purposes, less income (or OCI) has been recognized.[3] It is important to recognize and understand this difference when we discuss future income taxes in the next segment of the chapter.

---

[2] At the risk of oversimplification, it can be said that the *Income Tax Act* follows a principle of having the tax follow the cash flow. While taxable income is based mainly on income reported under GAAP, in cases where the timing of cash flows is significantly different from the timing of GAAP recognition, revenues tend to be taxable as they are received in cash and expenses are allowable as deductions when they are paid.

[3] Note that no one prepares a "tax" balance sheet—it is an artificial construct. However, if there were one, the tax values that are referred to here are what would be on that balance sheet, and they would be based on how the transaction is accounted for tax purposes. If the revenue is not yet recognized for tax purposes, there would be no receivable either. That is, the tax basis of the receivable is $0. Alternatively, there would be a deferred gross profit account for tax purposes, but there would be no such account on the GAAP balance sheet.

2. ***Expenses or losses are deductible for tax purposes after they are recognized in accounting income.*** Some expenses or losses that are recognized for accounting purposes are not allowed to be deducted for tax purposes until a future period. For example, for financial statement purposes, an expense may have to be accrued, but for tax purposes it may not be deductible as an expense until it is paid. Thus, it is only when the liability is eventually settled that the expense or loss is deducted in calculating taxable income. Examples include the following:

   • product warranty liabilities

   • estimated losses and liabilities related to restructurings

   • litigation accruals

   • accrued pension costs

   • holding or impairment losses on investments or other assets

   In all these examples, note that a liability (or contra asset or direct asset reduction) is recognized on the balance sheet when the expense or loss is recognized for financial reporting purposes. For tax purposes, however, the expense is not recognized in the current period and, therefore, neither is the liability or reduction in asset value.

3. ***Revenues or gains are taxable before they are recognized in accounting income.*** A company may recognize cash that it received during the year as unearned revenue if it is an advance payment for goods or services to be provided in future years. For tax purposes, the advance payment may have to be included in taxable income when the cash is received. When the entity recognizes revenue on the income statement in later years as the goods or services are provided to customers, these amounts are deducted in calculating taxable income. This is because they were included in taxable income in the year the cash was received. They cannot be taxed twice. Examples include the following:

   • subscriptions, royalties, and rentals received in advance

   • sales and leasebacks, including a deferral of profit on a sale for financial reporting purposes that would be reported as realized for tax purposes

   Once again, the balance sheet is also affected. There will be a difference between the book value of the liability account Unearned Revenue and its tax basis.

4. ***Expenses or losses are deductible before they are recognized in accounting income.*** The cost of assets such as equipment, for example, is deducted for financial statement purposes according to whichever GAAP amortization method the company uses. However, depending on which amortization method was chosen, its cost may be deducted faster for tax purposes than it is expensed for financial reporting purposes. When this happens, taxable income in the early years of the asset's life is lower than the accounting income. Because the asset's capital cost is the total amount that can be depreciated both on the books and for tax purposes, this means that future taxable incomes will be higher than the accounting incomes. Examples include the following:

   • depreciable property and depletable resources

   • deductible pension funding that exceeds the pension expense that was recognized

   • prepaid expenses that are deducted in calculating taxable income in the period when they are paid

   These too will result in a balance sheet account with a book value that is different than its tax basis.

5. ***Permanent differences.*** Some differences between taxable income and accounting income are permanent. **Permanent differences** are caused by items that (1) are included in accounting income but never in taxable income, or (2) are included in taxable income but never in accounting income. Examples include the following:

- items that are included in accounting income but never in taxable income: **non-tax-deductible expenses** such as fines and penalties, golf and social club dues, and expenses related to the earning of non-taxable revenue; and **non-taxable revenue**, such as dividends from taxable Canadian corporations, and proceeds on life insurance policies carried by the company on key officers or employees

- items that are included in taxable income but never in accounting income: depletion allowances of natural resources that exceed the resources' cost

Since permanent differences affect only the period in which they occur, there are no future tax consequences associated with balance sheet accounts.

The differences identified in numbers 1 to 4 above are known as **timing differences**, and they are directly related to income differences. Their accounting treatment and tax treatment are the same, but **the timing of when they are included in accounting income and when they are included in taxable income differs**. While timing differences also cause the differences between the book value and tax value of assets and liabilities on the balance sheet to change, this aspect of their behaviour will be discussed later in this chapter as part of the discussion of future income taxes.

International Insight

In some countries, taxable income and accounting income are the same. For entities in such countries, accounting for differences between tax and book income is not an issue.

Multiple Differences Illustrated

To illustrate the calculations when there are multiple differences between accounting and taxable income, assume that BT Corporation reports accounting income of $200,000 in each of the years 2007, 2008, and 2009. Assume also that the company is subject to a 30% tax rate in each year, and has the following differences between income reported on the financial statements and taxable income:

1. For tax purposes, the gross profit of $18,000 on an instalment sale made in 2007 is reported over an 18-month period at an equal amount each month as it is collected, beginning January 1, 2008. The entire sale and related profit is recognized for financial reporting purposes in 2007.

2. A premium of $5,000 is paid in each of 2008 and 2009 for life insurance that the company carries on key officers. This is not deductible for tax purposes, but is expensed for accounting purposes.

3. A warranty with an associated expense of $30,000 was provided on sales in 2007 and recognized in the same year. It was expected that $20,000 of the warranty work would be performed in 2008 and $10,000 in 2009, and this is what actually happened. For tax purposes, warranty expenses are not deductible until the costs are actually incurred.

The first and third items are timing differences. The second item is a permanent difference with no future tax consequences. The reconciliation of BT's accounting income to its taxable income for each year is shown in Illustration 18-5.

	2007	2008	2009
Accounting income	$200,000	$200,000	$200,000
Adjustments:			
Instalment sale	(18,000)	12,000	6,000
Warranty expense	30,000	(20,000)	(10,000)
Non-deductible insurance expense		5,000	5,000
Taxable income	$212,000	$197,000	$201,000

Illustration 18-5

Calculation of Taxable Income

The analysis always starts with pre-tax income reported on the income statement. This amount is adjusted to the taxable amount as follows: revenue items that are not taxable until a future period are deducted, and expenses that are not deductible in the year are added back. This explains the $18,000 deduction of instalment gross profit in 2007 as the amount was included in 2007's accounting income but is not taxable in 2007. It will be taxable in 2008 and 2009 as the timing difference reverses, that is, as the receivable is collected. In those years, therefore, it will be added to the accounting incomes that are reported in order to calculate the taxable income for each year.

It also explains why the $30,000 of warranty expense is added back to accounting income in 2007, increasing that year's taxable income. Because BT Corporation did not make any payments under the warranty in 2007, the company cannot deduct any warranty expense. The full amount of $30,000 was deducted in calculating accounting income in 2007, so it is all added back in determining taxable income. The warranty costs are deducted in calculating taxable income in the year they are actually paid by the company (i.e., in 2008 and 2009) even though no warranty expense was deducted in the accounting incomes of those two years.

The terms **originating timing difference** and **reversing timing difference** are often used to refer to these adjustments to taxable income. The originating difference is the cause of the initial difference between the accounting and taxable income amounts for each specific book-versus-tax timing difference. An example is the $30,000 originating difference related to warranty expense in 2007. The reversing difference, on the other hand, causes the opposite effect in subsequent years, such as the $20,000 and $10,000 warranty timing differences in 2008 and 2009.

The $5,000 life insurance premium is added back to 2008 and 2009's accounting income because it was deducted as an expense in calculating accounting income in each of those years. It is a non-deductible expense for tax purposes in both years and the $5,000 will not affect any future year's taxable income. It is a permanent difference.

Calculation of Current Income Taxes

While the calculation of taxable income may sometimes be challenging, for our purposes the calculation of current income tax expense and income taxes payable is straightforward. To arrive at this amount, the current rate of tax is simply applied to the company's taxable income. Continuing with the BT Corporation example above and the taxable incomes determined in Illustration 18-5, the calculation of the company's current income tax expense and income taxes payable for each of the three years is shown in Illustration 18-6.

Illustration 18-6

BT Corporation's Current Income Tax Expense and Taxes Payable

	2007	2008	2009
Taxable income	$212,000	$197,000	$201,000
Tax rate	30%	30%	30%
Income tax payable and current income tax expense	$ 63,600	$ 59,100	$ 60,300

The year-end adjusting entries to record current income tax each year are as follows:

Dec. 31, 2007	Current Income Tax Expense	63,600	
	Income Tax Payable		63,600
Dec. 31, 2008	Current Income Tax Expense	59,100	
	Income Tax Payable		59,100
Dec. 31, 2009	Current Income Tax Expense	60,300	
	Income Tax Payable		60,300

Notice that although BT Corporation reported identical accounting income in each year and the tax rate stayed the same, the current income tax expense differs. This fluctuation is caused mainly by the timing differences created by the instalment sales and warranty expense. However, the income tax expense that is reported on the income statement **should be related to the accounting income that is reported**, not to the amount that is taxable in the period. Therefore an additional adjustment is necessary to capture the effects of any changes in the accumulated timing differences and report them as part of the income tax expense. The calculation of this **future income tax expense** is covered next.

FUTURE INCOME TAXES

As alluded to above, the future income tax accounts on the balance sheet need to be adjusted as a result of the differences between the carrying amount and tax basis of a company's assets and liabilities. The adjustment is the amount of **future** income tax expense to be recognized in the year. The **future income tax expense** and the **current income tax expense** are then both reported on the income statement.

The basic principle that underlies future income taxes is as follows: If the recovery of an asset, or settlement of a liability, that is reported on the balance sheet will result in the company's having to pay income taxes in the future, a future or deferred income tax liability should also be recognized on the current period's balance sheet. Alternatively, if the recovery or settlement results in future income tax reductions (benefits), a future or deferred income tax asset should be recognized on the current balance sheet. This is explained further in the next sections.

Tax Basis

According to the IASB and FASB short-term convergence project on income taxes, the **tax basis** or **tax base** is a measurement attribute, just as historical cost and fair value are measurement attributes. It is "the measurement under existing tax law applicable to a present asset, liability, or equity instrument recognised for tax purposes as a result of one or more past events. That asset, liability, or equity instrument may or may not be recognised for financial reporting."[4] In other words, it is the amount that is attributed for tax purposes to the balance sheet item.

The **tax base of an asset** is described in IAS 12 as "the amount that will be deductible for tax purposes against any taxable economic benefits that will flow to an entity when it recovers the carrying amount of the asset. If those economic benefits will not be taxable, the tax base of the asset is equal to its carrying amount."[5] We will now look at some examples from *Handbook* Section 3465 to see how this is applied.

Example 1 of tax basis of an asset. A capital asset was acquired with an original cost (and tax basis) of $1,000. By the end of Year 3, capital cost allowance of $424 has been deducted for purposes of calculating taxable income in Years 1, 2, and 3. The tax basis of this asset at the end of Year 3 is therefore calculated as $1,000 − $424 = $576, which is its undepreciated capital cost. Going back to the definition above, this is the amount that will be deductible for tax purposes in the future as the asset is used to generate cash flows and recover its carrying amount on the balance sheet.

---

[4] IASB, "Short-Term Convergence: Income Taxes," Project Update, December 2006.

[5] International Accounting Standard 12, *Income Taxes*, para. 7.

Example 2 of tax basis of an asset. A portfolio investment was purchased and carried on the balance sheet at its cost of $1,000. In determining taxable income when the investment is disposed of, this amount is deductible from the proceeds that will be received on its sale. The tax basis of the investment is therefore $1,000.

Example 3 of tax basis of an asset. A company holds a life insurance policy on the company president. The policy has a cash surrender value and carrying amount of $100,000. If the company receives the $100,000 on the president's death, the proceeds are not taxable. Based on the definition above, the tax basis of the policy is the same as its carrying amount. There are no tax consequences.

The **tax basis of a liability** is "its carrying amount less any amount that will be deductible for income tax purposes in respect of that liability in future periods. In the case of revenue that is received in advance, the tax basis of the resulting liability is its carrying amount, less any amount that will not be taxable in future periods. Where a liability can be settled for its carrying amount without tax consequences, the tax basis of the liability is considered to be the same as its carrying amount."[6] Again, let us look at some examples.

Example 1 of tax basis of a liability. Liabilities include an accrued liability with a book value of $1,000. The related expense will be deductible for tax purposes only when it is paid. According to the definition above, the tax basis of the accrued liability is its carrying amount ($1,000) less any amount that will be deductible for tax purposes in future periods ($1,000). Its tax basis is, therefore, $0.

Example 2 of tax basis of a liability. A company receives $1,000 of interest in advance and reports this on its balance sheet as unearned revenue, a liability. The interest was taxed on a cash basis. The tax basis of the revenue received in advance is its carrying amount ($1,000) less any amount that will not be taxable in the future ($1,000), thus, $0.

Example 3 of tax basis of a liability. A company reports an accrued liability of $200 where the related expenses have already been deducted for tax purposes. The company also reports a loan payable of $500. In both cases, there is no income tax consequence when the liability is paid in the future. The tax basis of the accrued liability and of the loan payable is the same as the carrying amount of each liability on the books.

The difference between the tax basis of an asset or liability and its reported amount in the balance sheet is called a **temporary difference**. There are two types. A **taxable temporary difference** will result in taxable amounts in future years when the reported amount of the asset is received or the liability is settled. That is, taxable income, and therefore, taxes will be increased in the future. A **deductible temporary difference** will decrease taxable income and taxes in the future. We will first explain **taxable** temporary differences and then discuss **deductible** temporary differences.

Future Income Tax Liabilities

Objective 3
Explain what a taxable temporary difference is and why a future tax liability is recognized.

In the Chelsea Inc. example discussed earlier in Illustrations 18-2 to 18-4, the company reported revenue of $130,000 on its 2008 income statement. It would also have reported accounts receivable of $130,000 on its balance sheet for these sales. For tax purposes, Chelsea reported only $100,000 of taxable revenue, the amount that was collected in cash in the year. At the end of 2008, the carrying amount of accounts receivable on the balance sheet is $30,000 (i.e., $130,000 – $100,000 collected). What is the tax basis of the accounts receivable? Going back to the definition of the tax base of an asset, it is the amount that

---

[6] *CICA Handbook*, Section 3465.13.

can be deducted for tax purposes from the $30,000 received. In this case, the full $30,000 will be taxable as it is collected—no amount can be deducted from this. Therefore, the tax value of the accounts receivable is $0.

In the future, in the year when Chelsea collects the $30,000 in accounts receivable, the $30,000 will become taxable and the company will have to pay income tax on it. Therefore, the difference between the book and tax value of the accounts receivable is a taxable amount—a taxable temporary difference.

What will happen to this $30,000 temporary difference that originated in 2008 for Chelsea Inc.? Assuming that Chelsea expects to collect $20,000 of the receivable in 2009 and $10,000 in 2010, this will result in taxable amounts of $20,000 in 2009 and $10,000 in 2010. These future taxable amounts will cause taxable income to be greater than accounting income in both of these years, increasing the amount of future tax payable. Illustration 18-7 presents the originating difference, the reversal or turnaround of this temporary difference, and the resulting taxable amounts in future periods.

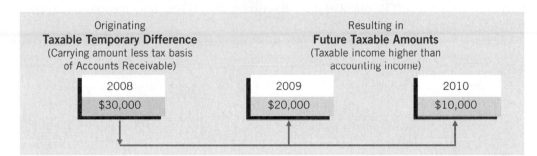

Illustration 18-7

Reversal of Temporary Difference, Chelsea Inc.

An assumption that is inherent in a company's GAAP balance sheet is that the assets and liabilities will be recovered and settled, respectively, at their reported amounts (carrying amounts). This assumption creates a requirement under accrual accounting to recognize the future tax consequences of temporary differences in the current year. In other words, it is necessary to recognize in the current period the amount of income taxes that will be payable, reduced, or refunded when the assets' reported amounts are recovered or the liabilities are settled.

In our example, we have assumed that Chelsea will collect the accounts receivable and report the $30,000 collection as taxable revenue in 2009 and 2010. Based on this, additional income tax will be paid in those years. We therefore record in Chelsea's books in 2008 the future tax that arises from the future collection.

Future Income Tax Liability

A **future income tax liability** or **deferred tax liability** is the future tax consequence of a taxable temporary difference. In other words, a future tax liability represents the increase in taxes payable in future years as a result of a taxable temporary difference existing at the end of the current year. Recall from the Chelsea example that income tax payable is $16,000 ($40,000 × 40%) in 2008 (Illustration 18-4). In addition, there is a future tax liability at the end of 2008 of $12,000, calculated as shown in Illustration 18-8.

Book value of accounts receivable	$30,000
Tax basis of accounts receivable	–0–
Taxable temporary difference at the end of 2008	30,000
Future tax rate	40%
Future income tax liability at the end of 2008	$12,000

Illustration 18-8

Calculation of Future Tax Liability, End of 2008

Another way to calculate the future tax liability is to **prepare a schedule that shows the taxable amounts by year** as a result of existing temporary differences, as is shown in Illustration 18-9. A detailed schedule like this is needed when the tax rates in future years are different and the calculations become more complex.

Illustration 18-9

Schedule of Future Taxable Amounts

	Future Years		Total
	2009	2010	
Future taxable amounts	$20,000	$10,000	$30,000
Future tax rate	40%	40%	
Future income tax liability at the end of 2008	$ 8,000	$ 4,000	$12,000

Because it is the first year of operation for Chelsea, there is no future tax liability at the beginning of the year. The calculation of the current, future, and total income tax expense for 2008 is shown in Illustration 18-10.

Illustration 18-10

Calculation of Income Tax Expense, 2008

Current tax expense, 2008 (from Illustration 18-4)		
Taxable income × tax rate ($40,000 × 40%)		$16,000
Future tax expense, 2008		
Future tax liability, end of 2008	$12,000	
Less: Future tax liability, beginning of 2008	–0–	12,000
Income tax expense (total) for 2008		$28,000

This calculation indicates that income tax expense has two components: current tax expense (the amount of income tax payable or refundable for the period) and deferred or future tax expense. **Future income tax expense** or **deferred tax expense** is **the change in** the balance sheet future income tax asset or liability account from the beginning to the end of the accounting period.

Journal entries are needed to record both the current and future income taxes. Taxes due and payable are credited to Income Tax Payable, while the increase in future taxes is credited to Future Income Tax Liability. These tax entries could be combined into one entry. However, because disclosure is required of both components, using two entries makes it easier to keep track of the current tax expense and the future tax expense. For Chelsea Inc., the following entries are made at the end of 2008:

A =   L   +   SE
    +16,000   −16,000

Cash flows: No effect

Current Income Tax Expense	16,000	
Income Tax Payable		16,000

A =   L   +   SE
    +12,000   −12,000

Cash flows: No effect

Future Income Tax Expense	12,000	
Future Income Tax Liability		12,000

At the end of 2009 (the second year), the taxable temporary difference—the difference between the book value ($10,000) and tax basis ($0) of the accounts receivable—that relates to the 2008 sales is $10,000. This difference is multiplied by the applicable future tax rate to determine the future tax liability of $4,000 ($10,000 × 40%) to be reported at the end of 2009. Both the current and future income tax expense for 2009 are calculated in Illustration 18-11.

Illustration 18-11

Calculation of Income Tax Expense, 2009

Current tax expense, 2009 (from Illustration 18-4)		
Taxable income × tax rate ($90,000 × 40%)		$36,000
Future tax expense, 2009		
Future tax liability, end of 2009 ($10,000 × 40%)	$ 4,000	
Future tax liability, beginning of 2009	12,000	(8,000)
Income tax expense (total) for 2009		$28,000

The journal entries to record income taxes for 2009 are as follows:

Current Income Tax Expense	36,000	
Income Tax Payable		36,000

A = L + SE
    +36,000   −36,000

Cash flows: No effect

Future Income Tax Liability	8,000	
Future Income Tax Expense/Benefit		8,000

A = L + SE
    −8,000   +8,000

Cash flows: No effect

Notice in the second entry that an **income tax expense with a credit balance** is often referred to as an **income tax benefit**.

In the entry to record future income taxes at the end of 2010, the Future Income Tax Liability balance is reduced by another $4,000. Illustration 18-12 shows this ledger account as it appears at the end of 2010.

Illustration 18-12

Future Income Tax Liability Account after Reversals

Future Income Tax Liability

		12,000	2008
2009	8,000		
2010	4,000		
		–0–	Balance

The Future Income Tax Liability account has a zero balance at the end of 2010.

Some analysts dismiss future tax liabilities when they assess a company's financial strength. However, a future tax liability does meet the definition of a liability in *CICA Handbook* Section 1000 "Financial Statement Concepts" for the following reasons:

What Do the Numbers Mean?

1. *It results from a past transaction.* In the Chelsea example, services were performed for customers and revenue was recognized in 2008 for financial reporting purposes but was deferred for tax purposes.

2. *It is a present obligation.* Taxable income in future periods will be higher than accounting income as a result of this temporary difference. Therefore, a present obligation exists.

3. *It represents a future sacrifice.* Increased taxable income and increased taxes will result in future periods from events that have already occurred. Paying these taxes when they come due will require the transfer or use of assets in the future.

A study by B. Ayers[7] found that the market views deferred (i.e., future) tax assets and liabilities in much the same way as it views other assets and liabilities, and that U.S. SFAS No. 109 increased the usefulness of future tax amounts in financial statements. The requirements in *CICA Handbook* Section 3465 are almost identical to those of SFAS 109.

---

[7] B. Ayers, "Deferred Tax Accounting Under *SFAS No. 109*: An Empirical Investigation of Its Incremental Value-Relevance Relative to *APB No. 11*," *The Accounting Review* (April 1998).

It is also important to note that the balance sheet at the end of each accounting period reports the eventual cash impact of recovering each account receivable's book value (of converting it to cash). The following table shows the relationship between the future economic benefits accruing to Chelsea and the net assets reported on its balance sheet:

	End of 2008	End of 2009
Future inflows of cash from transaction:		
Future cash to be collected on the receivable	$30,000	$10,000
Future cash outflow for related income tax	12,000	4,000
Net future cash inflow	$18,000	$ 6,000
Net assets reported on the balance sheet:		
Accounts receivable (in assets)	$30,000	$10,000
Future income tax liability (in liabilities)	12,000	4,000
Net assets reported	$18,000	$ 6,000

If the future tax liability were not recognized at the end of 2008, assets of $30,000 would be reported on the balance sheet but they would generate only $18,000 of future economic benefits. At the end of 2009, net assets would thus be overstated by $4,000.

Income Tax Accounting Objectives

One objective of accounting for income taxes is to recognize the amount of tax that is payable or refundable for the current year. In Chelsea's case, income tax payable is $16,000 for 2008.

A second objective is **interperiod tax allocation**: to recognize future tax liabilities and assets that relate to the future tax consequences of events that have already been recognized in the financial statements and tax returns. In Chelsea's case, this is achieved as follows: A future income tax liability of $12,000 is reported on Chelsea's balance sheet at the end of 2008, representing the increase in taxes that will accrue in future years ($8,000 in 2009 and $4,000 in 2010) as a result of a temporary difference existing at the end of the current year. It is then reduced by $8,000 at the end of 2009 and by another $4,000 at the end of 2010. Accounting for the effect of future income taxes on the balance sheet in this way is what underlies the **asset-liability method**.

In addition to affecting the balance sheet, future taxes affect income tax expense in each of the three years. The expense relates mainly to the revenues and expenses that are reported on each year's income statement as shown in Illustration 18-13 for Chelsea Inc. In some years, total tax expense is greater than taxes payable, and in others it is less. The net result is to report income tax expense that is based on the income statement amounts—in this case 40% of the accounting income, or $28,000. The expense is not based on what is reported on the tax return.

Illustration 18-13

Accounting Income and Total Income Tax Expense

CHELSEA INC.
Financial Reporting of Income Tax Expense

	2008	2009	2010
Revenues	$130,000	$130,000	$130,000
Expenses	60,000	60,000	60,000
Income before income tax	70,000	70,000	70,000

Less income tax expense:			
Current tax expense	16,000	36,000	32,000
Future tax expense	12,000	(8,000)	(4,000)
	28,000	28,000	28,000
Net income	$42,000	$42,000	$42,000

Future Income Tax Assets

To help explain deductible temporary differences and future income tax assets, assume that Cunningham Inc. sells microwave ovens on which it offers a two-year warranty. In 2008, the company estimated its warranty expense related to its 2008 sales of microwave ovens to be $500,000. Cunningham expects that $300,000 of these warranty costs will actually be incurred in 2009, and $200,000 in 2010.

    Cunningham reports the $500,000 of warranty expense on its 2008 income statement and a related estimated liability for warranties of $500,000 on its December 31, 2008, balance sheet. For tax purposes, warranty costs are deductible only when the costs are actually incurred. Therefore, no warranty expense can be deducted in determining 2008's taxable income. Because $500,000 will be deductible in future periods when the warranty obligation is settled, the tax basis of the warranty liability at December 31, 2008 is $0. That is, there is a temporary difference related to the warranty liability.

    Because of this temporary difference, Cunningham Inc. recognizes in 2008 the tax benefits (positive tax consequences) associated with the tax deductions that will result when the liability is settled. These deductible amounts will cause taxable income to be less than accounting income in the future. The future tax benefit is reported in the December 31, 2008, balance sheet as a **future income tax asset**.

    Cunningham's temporary difference originates in one period (2008) and reverses over two periods (2009 and 2010). This situation is diagrammed in Illustration 18-14.

4 Objective

Explain what a deductible temporary difference is and why a future tax asset is recognized.

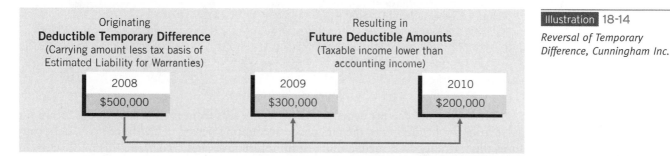

Illustration 18-14

Reversal of Temporary Difference, Cunningham Inc.

A **future income tax asset** or **deferred tax asset** is the future tax consequence of a **deductible temporary difference**. In other words, a future income tax asset represents the reduction in taxes payable or the increase in taxes refundable in future years as a result of a deductible temporary difference that exists at the end of the current year.[8]

    To illustrate the future income tax asset and income tax benefit, we continue with the Cunningham example. The warranty expense recognized on the income statement in 2008 is not deductible for tax purposes until the period when the actual warranty costs are

---

[8] *CICA Handbook* Section 3465.09(d) indicates that future income tax assets also include the income tax benefits that arise through the carryforward of unused tax losses and unused income tax reductions, excluding investment tax credits. These are discussed later in the chapter.

incurred. As a result, a deduction will be allowed for tax purposes in 2009 and again in 2010 as the estimated liability for warranties is settled, causing taxable income in those years to be lower than accounting income. The future income tax asset at the end of 2008 (assuming a 40% tax rate for 2009 and 2010) is calculated in Illustration 18-15.

Illustration 18-15

Calculation of Future Income Tax Asset, End of 2008

Book value of warranty liability	$500,000
Tax basis of warranty liability	–0–
Deductible temporary difference at the end of 2008	500,000
Future tax rate	40%
Future income tax asset at the end of 2008	$200,000

Another way to calculate the future tax asset is to prepare a schedule like the one in Illustration 18-16. It shows the deductible amounts that are scheduled for the future as a result of the deductible temporary difference.

Illustration 18-16

Schedule of Future Deductible Amounts

	Future Years		
	2009	2010	Total
Future deductible amounts	$300,000	$200,000	$500,000
Future tax rate	40%	40%	
Future income tax asset at the end of 2008	$120,000	$ 80,000	$200,000

Assuming that 2008 is Cunningham's first year of operations and that income tax payable for this year is $600,000, income tax expense is calculated as in Illustration 18-17.

Illustration 18-17

Calculation of Income Tax Expense, 2008

Current tax expense, 2008, (given)		
Taxable income × tax rate		$600,000
Future tax expense/benefit, 2008		
Future tax asset, end of 2008	$200,000	
Less: Future tax asset, beginning of 2008	–0–	(200,000)
Income tax expense (total) for 2008		$400,000

The future income tax benefit of $200,000 results from the increase in the future tax asset from the beginning to the end of the accounting period. The future tax benefit captures the warranty costs' deductibility from future taxes and recognizes this in the current period when the expense is reported for financial reporting purposes. The total income tax expense of $400,000 on the 2008 income statement is therefore made up of two elements: a current tax expense of $600,000 and the future tax benefit of $200,000. The following journal entries are therefore made at the end of 2008 to recognize income taxes:

A =   L   +   SE
    +600,000   −600,000

Cash flows: No effect

Current Income Tax Expense	600,000	
Income Tax Payable		600,000

A   = L +   SE
+200,000   +200,000

Cash flows: No effect

Future Income Tax Asset	200,000	
Future Income Tax Expense/Benefit		200,000

Assuming warranty costs were incurred in the same amount that was expected, the estimated liability for warranties at the end of 2009 has a book value of $500,000 less $300,000, which equals $200,000. The tax basis of this liability is still $0 and the future deductible amount is now $200,000. Therefore, the future tax asset at this date is 40% of $200,000, or $80,000. Assuming income tax payable for 2009 is $440,000, the calculation of income tax expense for 2009 is as shown in Illustration 18-18.

Current tax expense, 2009, (given)		
Taxable income × tax rate		$440,000
Future tax expense/benefit, 2009		
Future tax asset, end of 2009	$ 80,000	
Less: Future tax asset, beginning of 2009	(200,000)	120,000
Income tax expense (total) for 2009		$560,000

Illustration 18-18

Calculation of Income Tax Expense, 2009

As expected, a reduction in the tax asset account, as with assets in general, results in an increase in the expense to be recognized. The journal entries to record income taxes in 2009 are as follows:

Current Income Tax Expense	440,000	
Income Tax Payable		440,000

A =   L   +   SE
   +440,000   −440,000

Cash flows: No effect

Future Income Tax Expense	120,000	
Future Income Tax Asset		120,000

A   = L +   SE
−120,000   −120,000

Cash flows: No effect

The total income tax expense of $560,000 on the income statement for 2009 is made up of two parts: a current tax expense of $440,000 and a future tax expense of $120,000.

You may have noticed that the future income tax expense of $120,000 that is recognized in 2009 **is not related to future events at all.** It represents the using up or reversal of a future income tax benefit that was recognized at the end of the preceding year. While it is possible to give separate recognition to a third component of income tax expense for the current year, such as Utilization of Previously Recognized Future Tax Assets or Reduction in Future Income Tax Assets, the authors have instead chosen to include this as a component of future income tax expense or benefit. **In every case, the future income tax expense or benefit measures the change in the future income tax liability or asset account over the period.** As such, it is a combination of increased future tax liabilities, reversals of taxable temporary differences, recognition of future tax assets, and the use of future tax benefits that were recognized in the past.

At the end of 2010, the Future Income Tax Asset balance is further reduced by $80,000, as shown in the T account in Illustration 18-19. Future income tax expense in 2010 is $80,000.

Future Income Tax Asset			
2008	200,000		
		120,000	2009
		80,000	2010
Balance	–0–		

Illustration 18-19

Future Income Tax Asset Account after Reversals

What Do the Numbers Mean?

A key issue in accounting for income taxes is whether or not a future tax asset should be recognized in the accounts. Based on the definition of an asset in *CICA Handbook* Section 1000, a future income tax asset meets the three main conditions for an item to be recognized as an asset:

1. *It will contribute to future net cash flows.* Taxable income for Cunningham is higher than accounting income in the current year (2008). However, in the next year the opposite occurs, with taxable income lower than income reported for financial statement purposes. Because the deductible temporary difference reduces taxes payable in the future, a future benefit exists at the end of the year.

2. *Access to the benefits is controlled by the entity.* Cunningham has the ability to obtain the benefit of existing deductible temporary differences by reducing its taxes payable in the future. The company has the exclusive right to this benefit and can control others' access to it.

3. *It results from a past transaction or event.* In the Cunningham example, the sale of the product with the two-year warranty is the past event that gives rise to a future deductible temporary difference.

The reaction of market analysts to the write-off of future income taxes supports treating them as assets, as does management's treatment of them. When **Air Canada** ran into financial problems in the early part of this decade, it reduced its $400-million balance at the end of one year in its future income tax asset account to zero at the end of the next year. The reason? Because the airline was not sure that it would be able to generate enough taxable income in the future, its ability to realize any benefits from future deductible amounts was questionable. Like other assets with uncertain benefits, this asset had to be written down.

Note that when the future tax asset is recognized, the balance sheet at the end of each accounting period reports the economic resources that will be needed to settle the warranty liability. The following table shows this relationship.

	End of 2008	End of 2009
Economic resources needed to settle the obligation:		
Future resources needed to settle the liability	$500,000	$200,000
Future tax savings as liability is settled	200,000	80,000
Net future economic resources needed	$300,000	$120,000
Net liabilities reported on the balance sheet:		
Warranty liability (in liabilities)	$500,000	$200,000
Future income tax asset (in assets)	200,000	80,000
Net liabilities reported	$300,000	$120,000

If there were no interperiod tax allocation (that is, if the future income tax asset was not recognized at the end of 2008), liabilities of $500,000 would be reported on the balance sheet, yet they would need only $300,000 of economic resources to settle. At the end of 2009, the result would be an $80,000 overstatement of the liability.

In addition to affecting the balance sheet, future taxes affect income tax expense in each of the three years. As a result of recognizing future tax expense/benefit, the total income tax expense on the income statement now bears a reasonable relationship to the accounting income that is reported.

Valuation of Future Income Tax Assets

Like all assets, future income tax assets have to be reviewed to ensure that they are not reported on the balance sheet at more than their recoverable amount. Future income tax assets can only be recognized to the extent that it is **more likely than not** that the future tax asset will be realized. This means that its value to the company depends on whether the company will earn enough taxable income in the future against which the temporary differences can be deducted (recall the Air Canada example from above). The valuation of future tax assets is covered in more detail later in this chapter.

Multiple Differences Illustrated

To illustrate the analysis that is needed to adjust the future income tax accounts on the balance sheet and to record future income tax expense when there are multiple temporary differences, we return to the BT Corporation example used earlier in the chapter where current income tax expense was explained.[9] The details are provided for you again here.

Assume that BT Corporation reports accounting income of $200,000 in each of the years 2007, 2008, and 2009. Assume also that the company is subject to a 30% tax rate in each year, and has the following differences between income reported on the financial statements and taxable income:

1. For tax purposes, the gross profit of $18,000 on an instalment sale made in 2007 is reported over an 18-month period at an equal amount each month as it is collected, beginning January 1, 2008. The entire sale and related profit is recognized for financial reporting purposes in 2007.

2. A premium of $5,000 is paid in each of 2008 and 2009 for life insurance that the company carries on key officers. This is not deductible for tax purposes, but is expensed for accounting purposes.

3. A warranty with an associated expense of $30,000 was provided on sales in 2007 and recognized in the same year. It was expected that $20,000 of the warranty work would be performed in 2008 and $10,000 in 2009, and this is what actually happened.

The calculations of taxable income and current income tax expense are shown in Illustrations 18-5 and 18-6. We will now see how this information affects the balance sheet and future income taxes.

All differences between the accounting income and taxable income are considered in reconciling the income reported on the financial statements to taxable income. However, **only those that are temporary differences are considered when calculating future income tax amounts for the balance sheet**. When there are multiple differences, a schedule is prepared of the balance sheet accounts whose carrying and tax basis amounts are different.

For BT Corporation, the gross profit on its instalment sale resulted in an $18,000 difference between the carrying amount and the tax basis amount of its accounts receivable at the end of 2007. The sale was recognized as revenue (and a receivable) in 2007, but no amounts were paid on the receivable until 2008, and no amounts were included in taxable income in 2007. Its tax value is therefore $0.

The life insurance premium expense is a permanent difference. It has no future tax consequences and therefore is not considered in calculating future income taxes.

BT Corporation ended 2007 with a warranty liability on its books of $30,000 because none of the actual warranty work had been carried out as at the end of the year. For tax purposes, however, no warranty expense has been recognized and the tax value of the warranty liability at December 31, 2007, is therefore $0.

5 Objective

Prepare analyses of future income tax balances, and record future income tax expense.

---

[9] *Financial Reporting in Canada—2006* (CICA) identified 17 reasons for temporary differences that resulted in future income tax assets and liabilities on the financial statements of their 200 surveyed companies in 2005. The two most common temporary differences related to plant and equipment (176 companies) and tax loss carryforwards (157 companies). Other explanations included pensions, share issue costs, intangibles other than goodwill, site restoration and reclamation liabilities, and goodwill.

The company's analysis and calculation of the temporary differences, the net future income tax asset or liability, and the future income tax expense or benefit for 2007 are shown in Illustration 18-20. Because the same tax rate is assumed for all periods, calculating the future tax asset and liability is simplified. If the tax rate for future years has been legislated at different rates, a schedule is needed to determine when the timing differences reverse.

Illustration 18-20

Calculation of Future Income Tax Asset/Liability and Future Tax Expense—2007

Balance Sheet Account	Carrying Amount	−	Tax Basis	=	(Taxable) Deductible Temporary Difference	×	Tax Rate	=	Future Income Tax Asset (Liability)
Accounts receivable	$18,000		$–0–		$(18,000)		.30		$(5,400)
Warranty liability	30,000		–0–		30,000		.30		9,000
Net future income tax asset, December 31, 2007									3,600
Net future income tax asset (liability) before adjustment									–0–
Increase in future income tax asset and future income tax benefit, 2007									$ 3,600

In 2007, BT has two originating timing differences that result in temporary differences. The journal entries to record income taxes for 2007, based on the above analysis and the analysis for current income tax expense in Illustration 18-6, are as follows:

A = L + SE
+63,600   −63,600

Cash flows: No effect

Current Income Tax Expense	63,600	
Income Tax Payable (see Illustration 18-6)		63,600

A = L + SE
+3,600   +3,600

Cash flows: No effect

Future Income Tax Asset	3,600	
Future Income Tax Benefit		3,600

At the end of 2008, the analysis in Illustration 18-21 is made of the temporary differences. The two differences that originated in 2007 have begun to reverse. The account receivable has been reduced to $6,000 at the end of 2008, and the warranty liability outstanding is now only $10,000. Again, as Illustration 18-21 shows, the future tax expense or benefit is determined **by the change in** the future tax asset or liability account on the balance sheet.

Illustration 18-21

Calculation of Future Income Tax Asset/Liability and Future Tax Expense—2008

Balance Sheet Account	Carrying Amount	−	Tax Basis	=	(Taxable) Deductible Temporary Difference	×	Tax Rate	=	Future Income Tax Asset (Liability)
Accounts receivable	$ 6,000		$–0–		$ (6,000)		.30		$(1,800)
Warranty liability	10,000		–0–		10,000		.30		3,000
Net future income tax asset, December 31, 2008									1,200
Net future income tax asset before adjustment									3,600
Decrease in future income tax asset and future income tax expense, 2008									$(2,400)

The journal entries to record income taxes at December 31, 2008, are:

| Current Income Tax Expense | 59,100 | |
| Income Tax Payable (see Illustration 18-6) | | 59,100 |

A =   L   +   SE
        +59,100   −59,100
Cash flows: No effect

| Future Income Tax Expense | 2,400 | |
| Future Income Tax Asset | | 2,400 |

A   = L +   SE
−2,400   −2,400
Cash flows: No effect

As indicated in Illustration 18-22, by the end of 2009 all differences have reversed, leaving no temporary differences between balance sheet amounts and tax values.

Illustration 18-22

Calculation of Future Income Tax Asset/Liability and Future Tax Expense—2009

Balance Sheet Account	Carrying Amount	−	Tax Basis	=	(Taxable) Deductible Temporary Difference	×	Tax Rate	=	Future Income Tax Asset (Liability)
Accounts receivable	$ –0–		$ –0–		$ –0–		n/a		$ –0–
Warranty liability	–0–		–0–		–0–		n/a		–0–
Net future income tax asset, December 31, 2009									–0–
Net future income tax asset before adjustment									1,200
Decrease in future income tax asset and future income tax expense, 2009									$(1,200)

The journal entries at December 31, 2009, reduce the Future Income Tax Asset account to zero and recognize $1,200 in future income tax expense for 2009.

| Current Income Tax Expense | 60,300 | |
| Income Tax Payable (see Illustration 18-6) | | 60,300 |

A =   L   +   SE
        +60,300   −60,300
Cash flows: No effect

| Future Income Tax Expense | 1,200 | |
| Future Income Tax Asset | | 1,200 |

A   = L +   SE
−1,200   −1,200
Cash flows: No effect

Illustration 18-23 provides a summary of the bottom portion of the income statements for BT Corporation for each of the three years.

Illustration 18-23

BT Corporation Income Statements—2007, 2008, and 2009

BT CORPORATION
Income Statements (partial)
for the Years

	2007	2008	2009
Income before income tax expense	$200,000	$200,000	$200,000
Less: income tax expense			
Current expense	63,600	59,100	60,300
Future expense (benefit)	(3,600)	2,400	1,200
	60,000	61,500	61,500
Net income	$140,000	$138,500	$138,500

Total income tax expense reported in 2007, 2008, and 2009 is $60,000, $61,500, and $61,500, respectively. Although the statutory or enacted rate (i.e., the rate set by government act) of 30% applies for all three years, the effective rate is 30% for 2007 ($60,000/$200,000 = 30%) and 30.75% for 2008 and 2009 ($61,500 ÷ $200,000 = 30.75%). The **effective tax rate** is calculated by dividing total income tax expense for the period by the pre-tax income reported on the financial statements. The difference between the enacted and effective rates in 2008 and 2009 of 0.75% in this case is caused by the $5,000 non-deductible life insurance expense ([$5,000 × 0.30] ÷ $200,000).

Objective 6

Explain the effect of various tax rates and tax rate changes on future income tax accounts.

International Insight

IAS 12 also uses the "substantively enacted" rate at the balance sheet date. As part of the short-term convergence project with the FASB, IAS 12 is expected to be amended to indicate that "substantively enacted" occurs when any future steps in the enactment process will not change the outcome. In the U.S., this occurs only when the tax laws are enacted.

Tax Rate Considerations

In the previous illustrations, the enacted tax rate did not change from one year to the next. To calculate the future tax account reported on the balance sheet, the temporary difference was therefore simply multiplied by the current tax rate because it was expected to apply to future years as well. Tax rates do change, however.

Future Tax Rates

What happens if tax rates are different for future years? *CICA Handbook* Section 3465 takes the position that the income tax rates to use in the calculations should be the ones that are expected to apply when the tax liabilities are settled or tax assets are realized. These would normally be the rates that have been enacted at the balance sheet date.[10] The accounting standard does recognize, however, that situations may exist where a substantively enacted rate may be more appropriate.[11] To illustrate the use of different tax rates, we will use the example of Warlen Corp., which at the end of 2007 is assumed to have a temporary difference of $300,000 as calculated in Illustration 18-24.

Illustration 18-24

Calculation of Temporary Difference

Net book value of depreciable assets	$1,000,000
Tax basis of depreciable assets (undepreciated capital cost or UCC)	700,000
Taxable temporary difference	$ 300,000

This is a **taxable** temporary difference because, to date, Warlen has deducted $300,000 more CCA on its tax returns than it has deducted amortization expense on its income statements. This is shown by the fact that the undepreciated capital cost is $300,000 lower than the assets' net book value. When Warlen Corp. calculates taxable income in the future, it will have to add back its depreciation expense and deduct a lower amount of CCA. The result will be a taxable income that is higher than the accounting income.

Continuing with the example, assume that the $300,000 will reverse and that the tax rates that are expected to apply in the following years on the resulting taxable amounts are as shown in Illustration 18-25.

Illustration 18-25

Future Tax Liability Based on Future Rates

	2008	2009	2010	2011	2012	Total
Future taxable amounts	$80,000	$70,000	$60,000	$50,000	$40,000	$300,000
Tax rate	40%	40%	35%	30%	30%	
Future tax liability	$32,000	$28,000	$21,000	$15,000	$12,000	$108,000

---

[10] *CICA Handbook*, Section 3465.56. Note that this covers changes in tax laws as well as tax rates.

[11] *CICA Handbook*, Section 3465.58. In order to use a substantively enacted rate, there must be persuasive evidence that the government is able and committed to enacting the proposed change in the foreseeable future. This usually means that the legislation or regulation has to have been drafted in an appropriate form and tabled in Parliament or presented in Council. *EIC-111* provides more detailed guidance.

As indicated, the future income tax liability is $108,000—the total future tax effect of the temporary difference at the end of 2007.

Because the Canadian tax system provides, as incentives, reductions in the income tax rates that are applied to taxable income, the tax rate that is used to calculate the future tax amounts should include the tax rate reductions, provided it is more likely than not that the company will qualify for the rate reductions in the periods of reversal.[12] The general principle is to use the rates that are expected to apply to the taxable income of the periods when the temporary differences are expected to reverse, provided that the rates are enacted or substantively enacted at the balance sheet date. *CICA Handbook* Section 3465, consistent with the IASB and FASB standards, prohibits the discounting of future income tax assets and liabilities.[13] The issue of discounting remains a contentious one that requires resolution on a broader level.

Revision of Future Tax Rates

When a change in the tax rate is enacted (or substantively enacted) into law, **its effect on the existing future income tax asset and liability accounts is recorded immediately as an adjustment to income tax expense in the period of the change.**

Assume that on September 10, 2008, a new income tax rate is enacted that lowers the corporate rate from 40% to 35%, effective January 1, 2010. To illustrate such a change, we will use the example of Hostel Corp. If Hostel Corp. has one temporary difference at the beginning of 2008 related to $3 million of excess capital cost allowance, then it has a Future Income Tax Liability account with a balance of $1.2 million ($3,000,000 × 40%) at January 1, 2008. If taxable amounts related to this difference are scheduled to increase the taxable income equally in 2009, 2010, and 2011, the future tax liability at September 10, 2008 is now $1.1 million, calculated as shown in Illustration 18-26.

	2009	2010	2011	Total
Future taxable amounts	$1,000,000	$1,000,000	$1,000,000	$3,000,000
Tax rate	40%	35%	35%	
Future tax liability	$ 400,000	$ 350,000	$ 350,000	$1,100,000

Illustration 18-26

Schedule of Future Taxable Amounts and Related Tax Rates

An entry is made on September 10, 2008, to recognize the $100,000 decrease ($1,200,000 − $1,100,000) in the future tax liability:

Future Income Tax Liability	100,000	
Future Income Tax Benefit		100,000

A	=	L	+	SE
		−100,000		+100,000

Cash flows: No effect

Separate disclosure of this component of future income tax expense is suggested, but not required, by the accounting standard.

In mid-2006, the federal government and the Alberta and Saskatchewan provincial governments substantively enacted income tax rate reductions that resulted in tax windfalls in the second-quarter results of many companies in the oil patch. The federal rate was to fall from 21 percent in 2007 to 19 percent in 2010. Companies reporting large future income tax liabilities saw immediate reductions as they remeasured these liabilities. There was a concurrent increase in the earnings reported by the companies as the reduction in

What Do the Numbers Mean?

---

[12] Examples of tax incentives include the small business deduction, the manufacturing and processing profits deduction, and the resource allowance deduction.

[13] *CICA Handbook*, Section 3465.57.

the future tax liability was taken into income through being recognized as a future income tax benefit. **Husky Energy Inc.**, an integrated energy and energy-related company, for example, indicated that the reduction in tax rates increased its profits for the second quarter of 2006 by $328 million, helping its profit more than double to $978 million. **Canadian Natural Resources Ltd.**, Canada's second largest independent petroleum producer, recognized a similar gain from the tax rate change, some $438 million, which brought its reported profit to more than $1 billion!

Basic corporate tax rates do not change often, and the current rate is therefore normally used.[14] However, changes in provincial rates, the small business deduction, foreign tax rates, and surcharges on all levels of income affect the effective rate and may require adjustments to the future tax accounts.

Uncertain Tax Positions

In addition to uncertainties about when temporary differences will reverse and about the tax rates that may apply in the future, a company may also face **uncertain tax positions**—uncertainty about whether a position it has taken on its tax return will be accepted by the tax authorities. The most common example is the question of whether or not the CRA will agree with a deduction that the company has taken.

The IASB, studying this issue with the FASB, has decided on an approach that would measure the current and deferred (future) tax balances based on an expected outcome amount.[15] That is, the account is measured as the probability-weighted average of the possible amounts and possible rates. The AcSB expects to issue proposals that are similar to those of the IASB, but not until they are incorporated in the IFRS, likely by 2009.[16] This situation is not addressed in current Canadian standards.

ACCOUNTING FOR INCOME TAX LOSS CARRYOVER BENEFITS

Introduction to Tax Losses

A **loss for income tax purposes** or **tax loss** occurs when the year's tax-deductible expenses and losses exceed the company's taxable revenues and gains. The tax burden would be unfair if companies were taxed during profitable periods and received no tax relief during periods of losses. Therefore, a company pays no income tax in a year in which it incurs a tax loss. In addition, the tax laws permit taxpayers to use a tax loss of one year to offset taxable income of other years. This is accomplished through the tax loss carryback and carryforward provisions of income tax legislation, which allow taxpayers to benefit from tax losses either by recovering taxes that were previously paid or by reducing taxes that will otherwise be payable in the future.

A corporation can choose to carry a tax loss back against taxable income of the immediately preceding three years. This is a **loss carryback**. Alternatively, it can choose to carry losses that it earned in tax years ending after 2005 forward to the 20 years that immediately follow the loss. This is a **loss carryforward**.[17] Or, it may choose to do both. Illustration 18-27 presents a diagram of the carryover periods, assuming a tax loss is incurred in 2008.

---

[14] The federal general corporate income tax rate has gradually dropped from 28% to 18.5% over the period from 2001 to 2011. Federal budgets after March 2007 could change these rates further.

[15] See Appendix 16C for more information about measurement issues.

[16] As this text goes to print in mid-2007, proposed amendments to IAS 37 ("Provisions, Contingent Liabilities, and Contingent Assets") on recognition and consequential amendments to IAS 12 on income taxes have not yet been finalized.

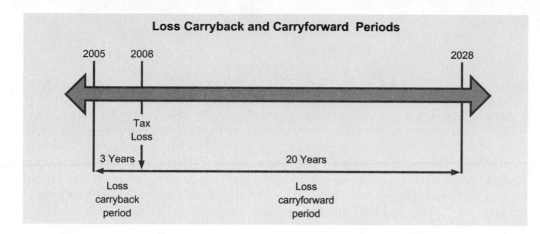

Illustration 18-27

Loss Carryback and Carryforward Procedure

If a loss is carried back, it is usually applied against the earliest available income—2005 in the example above. The **benefit from a loss carryback** is the **recovery of some or all of the taxes** that were paid in those years. The tax returns for the preceding years are refiled; the current year tax loss is deducted from the previously reported taxable income; and a revised amount of income tax payable is determined for each year. This figure is then compared with the taxes that were actually paid for each of the preceding years, and the government is asked to refund the difference.

If a corporation decides to carry the loss forward, or if the full amount of the loss could not be absorbed in the carryback period, **the tax loss can be used to offset taxable income in the future so that taxes that would otherwise be payable in those years are reduced or eliminated**.

The decision on how to use a tax loss depends on factors such as its size, the results of the previous years' operations, past and anticipated future tax rates, and other factors in which management sees the greatest tax advantage.[18]

Tax losses are relatively common and can be large. Companies that have suffered substantial losses are often attractive merger candidates because, in certain cases, the acquirer may use these losses to reduce its taxable income and, therefore, its income taxes. In a sense, a company that has suffered substantial losses may find itself worth more "dead" than "alive" because of the economic value related to the tax benefit that may be had by another company that "acquires" its losses.[19] The following sections discuss the accounting treatment of loss carrybacks and carryforwards.

Loss Carryback Illustrated

To illustrate the accounting procedures for a tax loss carryback, assume that Groh Inc. has no temporary or permanent differences. Groh has the taxable incomes and losses shown in Illustration 18-28.

7 Objective
Apply accounting procedures for a tax loss carryback.

---

[17] The carryforward period has been increasing. The 2004 federal budget increased it from 7 years to 10, and the 2006 budget increased it again to 20 years. Note also that the references in this chapter to tax losses are limited to non-capital losses. Special rules apply to capital losses.

[18] At one time, it was common practice when refiling prior years' returns to reduce the amount of CCA claimed, thus increasing the amount of taxable income in those prior years. The company could then absorb more of a current year tax loss. With the recent extensions of the carryforward period, now at 20 years, this option is now not commonly allowed.

[19] When Sears Canada Inc. bought 19 Eaton's stores for $80 million, $20 million of the price was for approximately $175 million of tax losses accumulated by Eaton's. The $20 million could not be distributed until five years after Sears had benefited from it. This was because the Canada Revenue Agency could legally appeal the company's use of the losses. The $20 million was finally paid out in 2006.

Year	Taxable Income or Loss	Tax Rate	Tax Paid
2004	$ 75,000	30%	$22,500
2005	50,000	35%	17,500
2006	100,000	30%	30,000
2007	200,000	40%	80,000
2008	(500,000)	—	–0–

In 2008, Groh Inc. incurs a tax loss that it decides to carry back. The carryback is applied first to 2005, the third year preceding the loss year. Any unused loss is then carried back to 2006, and then to 2007. Accordingly, Groh files amended tax returns for each of the years 2005, 2006, and 2007, receiving refunds for the $127,500 ($17,500 + $30,000 + $80,000) of taxes paid in those years.

For accounting purposes, the $127,500 represents the **tax benefit of the loss carryback**. The tax benefit is recognized in 2008, the loss year, because the tax loss gives rise to a refund (an asset) that is both measurable and currently realizable.

The following journal entry is prepared in 2008:

A   = L +   SE
+127,500   +127,500

Cash flows: No effect

Income Tax Refund Receivable	127,500	
Current Income Tax Benefit		127,500

The Income Tax Refund Receivable amount is reported on the balance sheet as a current asset at December 31, 2008. The tax benefit is reported on the income statement for 2008 as in Illustration 18-29.

GROH INC.
Income Statement (partial) for 2008

Loss before income taxes	$(500,000)
Income tax benefit	
Current benefit due to loss carryback	127,500
Net loss	$(372,500)

If the tax loss carried back to the three preceding years is less than the taxable incomes of those three years, the only entry that is required is similar to the one above. In the Groh Inc. example, however, the $500,000 tax loss for 2008 exceeds the $350,000 in total taxable income from the three preceding years; **the remaining $150,000 loss can therefore be carried forward**. The accounting for a tax loss carryforward is covered next.

Objective 8

Apply accounting procedures and disclosure requirements for a tax loss carryforward.

International Insight

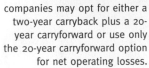

In the United States, companies may opt for either a two-year carryback plus a 20-year carryforward or use only the 20-year carryforward option for net operating losses.

Loss Carryforward Illustrated

If a net operating loss is not fully absorbed through a carryback or if the company decides not to carry the loss back, **the loss can instead be carried forward for up to 20 years**. Because carryforwards are used to offset future taxable income, the tax benefit associated with a loss carryforward is represented by future tax savings: reductions in taxes in the future that would otherwise be payable. Being able to actually realize the future tax benefit depends on there being future taxable income, which may be highly uncertain in some cases.

The accounting issue, then, is whether the tax benefit of a loss carryforward should be recognized **in the loss year when the potential benefits arise**, or **in future years when the benefits are actually realized**. Canadian accounting standards take the position that the potential benefit of unused tax losses meets the definition of an asset and that **the benefit should be recognized in the loss year** to the extent that it is **more likely than not** that there will be future taxable income against which the losses and reductions can be applied. **More likely than not** is defined as a probability of greater than 50 percent.[20]

When a tax loss carryforward is more likely than not to result in future economic benefits, it should be accounted for in the same way as a deductible temporary difference: a future income tax asset is recognized in an amount equal to the expected benefit.

Future Taxable Income More Likely Than Not

To illustrate the accounting for an income tax loss carryforward, we continue with the Groh Inc. example. In 2008, after carrying back as much of the loss as possible to the three preceding years, the company has a $150,000 tax loss available to carry forward. Assuming the company determines **it is more likely than not to generate sufficient taxable income in the future** so that the benefit of the remaining $150,000 loss will be realized, Groh records a future tax asset to recognize the benefit of the loss. If a tax rate of 40% is expected to apply to future years, the amount of the asset recognized is $60,000 ($150,000 × 40%). The journal entries to record the benefits of the carryback and the carryforward in 2008 are as follows:

International Insight

The FASB's SFAS 109 also uses the words "more likely than not." IAS 12 indicates that a deferred tax asset shall be recognized to the extent that it is "probable" that future taxable profit will be available. The IAS has agreed to define "probable" as meaning "more likely than not."

To recognize benefit of loss carryback		
Income Tax Refund Receivable	127,500	
Current Income Tax Benefit		127,500

A = L + SE
+127,500   +127,500
Cash flows: No effect

To recognize benefit of loss carryforward		
Future Income Tax Asset	60,000	
Future Income Tax Benefit		60,000

A = L + SE
+60,000   +60,000
Cash flows: No effect

The income tax refund receivable of $127,500 will be realized immediately as a refund of taxes paid in the past. The Future Income Tax Asset account measures the benefit of the future tax savings. The two accounts that are credited appear on the 2008 income statement as in Illustration 18-30.

GROH INC. Income Statement (partial) for 2008		
Loss before income taxes		$(500,000)
Income tax benefit		
Current benefit due to loss carryback	$127,500	
Future benefit due to loss carryforward	60,000	187,500
Net loss		$(312,500)

Illustration 18-30

Recognition of the Benefit of the Loss Carryback and Carryforward in the Loss Year

The $60,000 **future tax benefit** for the year results from an **increase in the future tax asset account.**

---

[20]*CICA Handbook*, Section 3465.09(i).

For 2009, assume that Groh Inc. returns to profitability and has taxable income of $200,000 from the year's operations, subject to a 40% tax rate. In 2009, Groh Inc. **realizes** the benefits of the entire $150,000 tax loss carryforward that was **recognized** for accounting purposes in 2008. The income tax payable for 2009 is calculated as in Illustration 18-31.

Illustration 18-31

Calculation of Income Tax Payable in the Year the Loss Carryforward Is Realized

Taxable income before loss carryforward, 2009	$ 200,000
Loss carryforward deduction	(150,000)
Taxable income for 2009	50,000
Tax rate	40%
Income tax payable for 2009 and current tax expense	$ 20,000
Future income tax asset, opening balance ($150,000 × .4)	$ 60,000
Future income tax asset, December 31, 2009 ($0 × .4)	–0–
Future income tax expense, 2009	$ 60,000

The journal entries to record income taxes in 2009 are:

A = L + SE
  +20,000   −20,000

Cash flows: No effect

Current Income Tax Expense	20,000	
Income Tax Payable		20,000

A = L + SE
−60,000   −60,000

Cash flows: No effect

Future Income Tax Expense	60,000	
Future Income Tax Asset		60,000

The first entry records income taxes payable for 2009 and, therefore, current income tax expense. The second entry records the use of the tax benefit that was captured in the future income tax asset recognized the previous year.

The 2009 income statement in Illustration 18-32 shows that the 2009 total income tax expense is based on 2009's reported income. The **benefit of the tax loss** is not reported in 2009 as it was already reported in 2008.

Illustration 18-32

Presentation of the Benefit of Loss Carryforward Realized in 2009, Recognized in 2008

GROH INC.		
Income Statement (partial) for 2009		
Income before income taxes		$200,000
Income tax expense		
Current	$20,000	
Future	60,000	80,000
Net income		$120,000

Future Taxable Income Not Likely

Return to the Groh Inc. example and 2008. A tax asset (recorded in Income Tax Refund Receivable) was recognized in 2008 because the ability to carry back the loss and recover income taxes paid in the past provides evidence that $127,500 of benefits from $350,000 of the loss will be realized. Assume now that the company's future is uncertain and, as a result, it is determined at December 31, 2008, that there is not enough evidence that there will be adequate future taxable income to recognize an income tax asset and benefit related to the remaining $150,000 of income tax losses. In this case, the only 2008 income tax entry is:

Income Tax Refund Receivable	127,500	
Current Income Tax Benefit		127,500

A = L + SE
+127,500 +127,500
Cash flows: No effect

The presentation in the 2008 income statement in Illustration 18-33 shows that **only the benefit related to the loss carryback is recognized**. However, the unrecognized potential tax benefit and related unrecognized future income tax asset associated with the remaining $150,000 of tax losses is relevant information for financial statement readers. **Therefore, the amounts and expiry dates of unrecognized (i.e., unbooked) income tax assets related to the carryforward of unused tax losses must be disclosed.** Such information is useful as it makes readers aware of the possibility of future benefits (reduced future income tax outflows) from the loss, even though the likelihood of realizing these benefits at this time is too uncertain for them to be formally recognized in the body of the statements.

Illustration 18-33

Recognition of Benefit of Loss Carryback Only

GROH INC. Income Statement (partial) for 2008	
Loss before income taxes	$(500,000)
Income tax benefit	
Current benefit due to loss carryback	127,500
Net loss	$(372,500)

Assume now that in 2009 the company performs better than expected, generating taxable income of $200,000 from its annual operations. After applying the $150,000 loss carryforward, tax is payable on only $50,000 of income. With a tax rate of 40%, the following entry is made.

Current Income Tax Expense	20,000	
Income Tax Payable ($50,000 × 40%)		20,000

A = L + SE
+20,000 −20,000
Cash flows: No effect

This entry recognizes the taxes currently payable in the year. Because the potential tax benefit associated with the loss carryforward **was not recognized in 2008, the tax benefit is recognized in 2009**, the year it is realized. The $20,000 of current tax expense is actually made up of two components: income taxes of $80,000 accrued on the 2009 income of $200,000, and a $60,000 tax benefit from the realization of the unrecorded loss carryforward. Separate disclosure of these components is suggested by Section 3465, but is not required.[21]

Illustration 18-34 shows the 2009 income statement.

Illustration 18-34

Recognition of Benefit of Loss Carryforward When Realized

GROH INC. Income Statement (partial) for 2009	
Income before income taxes	$200,000
Current income tax expense (note)	20,000
Net income	$180,000

Note to financial statements (not required): Current income tax expense includes a $60,000 benefit from realizing a previously unrecognized tax loss carryforward.

---

[21] *Financial Reporting in Canada-2006* (CICA) indicates that less than half of the 200 companies surveyed in 2005 disclosed the major components of income tax expense. However, six companies did report a component related to recognition of the benefit of a previously unrecognized loss carryforward.

If 2009's taxable income had been less than $150,000, only a portion of the unrecorded and unused tax loss could have been applied. The entry to record 2009 income taxes would have been similar to the entry above. In addition, a note to the financial statements would be provided to disclose the remaining amount and expiry date of the unused loss.

Carryforward with Valuation Allowance

International Insight

In 2007, IAS 12 only recognizes a deferred or future income tax asset if it is probable that it will be realized. The IASB has agreed, however, to move to the SFAS 109 (U.S.) valuation allowance approach, so it is likely that future Canadian practice will also require this approach.

In the Groh Inc. example above, the assumption was made that the company's future was uncertain and there was insufficient evidence that the company would benefit from the remaining $150,000 of 2008 tax losses available to be carried forward. As a result, no future income tax asset was recognized in 2008.

The U.S. accounting standard recommends an alternative approach to this situation. Instead, a future income tax asset is recognized for the full amount of the tax effect on the $150,000 loss carryforward, **along with an offsetting valuation allowance**, a contra account to the future tax asset account. Because the effect on the financial statements is the same, the valuation allowance approach is also permitted in Canada. How does a valuation allowance work?

Assuming that the entry for the loss carryback has already been made, the following entries are required to recognize the tax effect on the full $150,000 loss carryforward and to recognize the valuation allowance to bring the future tax asset account to its realizable value of zero at December 31, 2008:

```
A    =  L  +   SE
+60,000       +60,000

Cash flows: No effect
```

Future Income Tax Asset ($150,000 × 40%)	60,000	
Future Income Tax Benefit (re: loss carryforward)		60,000

```
A    =  L  +   SE
−60,000       −60,000

Cash flows: No effect
```

Future Income Tax Expense (re: loss carryforward)	60,000	
Allowance to Reduce Future Income Tax		
Asset to Expected Realizable Value		60,000

The latter entry, which sets up the allowance account, indicates that there was insufficient evidence that the company would benefit from the tax loss in the future. The effect on the financial statements is the same whether these two entries are made or the future income tax asset is not recognized in the accounts at all. The income statement under the allowance approach is identical to the statement provided in Illustration 18-33 using the current Canadian approach.

Assume again that the company performs better than expected in 2009, generating taxable income of $200,000. After applying the $150,000 loss carryforward, tax is payable on only $50,000 of income. With a tax rate of 40%, the entry for current taxes is:

```
A  =    L   +   SE
    +20,000   −20,000

Cash flows: No effect
```

Current Income Tax Expense	20,000	
Income Tax Payable ($50,000 × 40%)		20,000

Because the amount of tax losses available to carry forward to future years has changed, the Future Income Tax Asset account and its valuation allowance must be adjusted. In this case, no tax losses remain.

```
A    =  L  +   SE
−60,000       −60,000

Cash flows: No effect
```

Future Income Tax Expense (re: loss carryforward)	60,000	
Future Income Tax Asset		60,000

Allowance to Reduce Future Income Tax				
Asset to Expected Realizable Value	60,000			
Future Income Tax Benefit (loss carryforward)		60,000		

A = L +   SE
+60,000   +60,000

Cash flows: No effect

The future income tax expense of $60,000 (from adjusting the tax asset account) cancels out the $60,000 future income tax benefit (from adjusting the allowance account). The effect on the income statement is limited to a current income tax expense of $20,000, the same as reported in Illustration 18-34 when neither the asset nor the allowance was recognized.

To summarize, Canada currently prefers an "affirmative judgement" approach by recognizing future tax assets only for deductible temporary differences, unused tax losses, and income tax reductions that are **expected to be used**, and this is consistent with the 2007 requirements in IAS 12. This approach differs from the "impairment approach" recommended by SFAS 109. The U.S. method recognizes a future income tax asset for all deductible temporary differences, unused tax losses, and income tax reductions and **offsets them by an impairment allowance** for the portion of the asset that is considered more likely than not to *not* be realized. As part of the short-term convergence project between the IASB and the FASB, the IASB has agreed to move to the SFAS 109 valuation allowance approach. It is likely that the Canadian standard will also do so.

Review of Future Income Tax Asset Account

CICA Handbook Section 3465 recommends recognizing a future income tax asset for all deductible temporary differences and for the carryforward of unused tax losses and income tax reductions, **to the extent that it is more likely than not that the future income tax asset will be realized; in other words, as long as taxable income is likely to be available against which the deductible temporary differences, unused tax losses, or income tax reductions can be applied.** Consistent with the reporting for all assets, the Future Income Tax Asset account must be reviewed to ensure that the carrying amount is appropriate.

9 Objective
Explain why the Future Income Tax Asset account is reassessed at the balance sheet date.

Assume that Jensen Corp. has a deductible temporary difference or loss carryforward of $1 million at the end of its first year of operations. Its tax rate is 40% and a future tax asset of $400,000 ($1,000,000 × 40%) is recognized on the basis that it is more likely than not that enough taxable income will be generated in the future. The journal entry to record the future income tax benefit and the change in the future tax asset is:

Future Income Tax Asset	400,000	
Future Income Tax Benefit		400,000

A = L +   SE
+400,000   +400,000

Cash flows: No effect

If, at the end of the next period, the deductible temporary difference or loss carryforward remains at $1 million but now only $750,000 is more likely than not to be used, the future tax asset that is expected to be realized is recalculated at 40% of $750,000, or $300,000. The entry to be made depends on whether the allowance approach is used or not. Both methods of adjusting the asset account are shown in Illustration 18-35.

Direct Adjustment		**Allowance Method**	
Future Income Tax Expense 100,000		Future Income Tax Expense 100,000	
Future Income Tax Asset	100,000	Allowance to Reduce Future	
		Income Tax Asset to	
		Expected Realizable Value	100,000

Illustration 18-35
Revaluation of Future Income Tax Asset Account

If a valuation account is used, it is reported on the balance sheet (or is explained in the notes) as a contra account to the Future Income Tax Asset account. If the adjustment is made directly to the Future Income Tax Asset account, the asset is reported on the balance sheet only as the net amount. The balance sheet reporting is shown in Illustration 18-36.

Illustration 18-36

Balance Sheet Presentation of Remaining Future Income Tax Asset

Direct Adjustment		Allowance Method	
Future Income Tax Asset	$300,000	Future Income Tax Asset	$400,000
		Less: Allowance to Reduce Future Income Tax Asset to Expected Realizable Value	(100,000)
		Future Income Tax Asset (net)	$300,000

The amount of the future income tax asset and its realizable value are evaluated at the end of each accounting period. At the end of the next period, if $350,000 is expected to be realized in the future from the original $1 million of deductible amounts, the entry in Illustration 18-37 is made to adjust the accounts. As can be seen, the net effect of the two approaches is identical. However, the valuation allowance method has the advantage of retaining the relationship between the Future Income Tax Asset account and the future deductible amounts.

Illustration 18-37

Revaluation of Future Income Tax Asset Account

Direct Adjustment			Allowance Method		
Future Income Tax Asset	50,000		Allowance to Reduce Future Income Tax Asset to Expected Realizable Value	50,000	
Future Income Tax Benefit		50,000	Future Income Tax Benefit		50,000

The *CICA Handbook* offers guidance on how to determine whether it is more likely than not that future taxable income will be available, and emphasizes the need to use judgement in weighing the evidence. All available evidence, both positive and negative, should be carefully considered in determining the appropriate value for the future tax account. The following **possible sources of taxable income may be available under the tax law to realize a tax benefit** for deductible temporary differences and tax loss carry-overs. Any one of these sources is sufficient to recognize the future tax asset.

1. Future reversals of existing taxable temporary differences

2. Future taxable income exclusive of reversing temporary differences and loss carry-forwards

3. Taxable income in prior carryback years

4. Tax-planning strategies that would, if necessary, be implemented to realize a future income tax asset. Tax strategies are actions that are prudent and feasible, and that would be applied.[22]

Deciding to recognize a future tax asset is difficult when there is **negative evidence**, such as cumulative losses in recent years. Other examples of negative evidence include the following:

• a history of tax losses or income tax reductions that have expired unused

• losses that are expected in early future years (by a presently profitable entity)

---

[22] *CICA Handbook*, Section 3465.25.

- unsettled circumstances that, if they are unfavourably resolved, would adversely affect future operations and profit levels on a continuing basis in future years

- a carryback or carryforward period that is so brief that it would limit realization of tax benefits, particularly if the enterprise operates in a traditionally cyclical business[23]

Examples of **positive evidence** that might support a conclusion to recognize a future tax asset when there is also negative evidence include the following:

- the existence of enough taxable temporary differences for there to be taxable amounts against which tax losses or reductions can be applied

- the existence of contracts or a firm sales backlog that will produce more than enough taxable income to realize the future tax asset based on existing sale prices and cost structures

- an excess amount of fair value over the tax basis of the entity's net assets that is sufficient to realize the future tax asset

- a strong earnings history, exclusive of the loss that created the future deductible amount, and with evidence indicating that the loss is an aberration rather than a continuing condition[24]

The future tax asset account must also be reviewed to determine whether conditions have changed, because it may now be reasonable to recognize a future tax asset that was previously unrecognized. If so, a future income tax asset is recognized to the extent that it is more likely than not to be realized.[25] The associated tax benefit is recognized in the income statement of the same period. If the entity uses a valuation allowance account, the full future tax asset is already included in the account, and it is the allowance that needs to be adjusted (in this case, reduced).

Agrium Inc., headquartered in Calgary, Alberta, produces and markets agricultural nutrients and industrial products and is a retail supplier of agricultural products and services in both North and South America. As seen in Illustration 18-38, Agrium reports information about its future income tax assets, including loss carryforwards, in Note 5 to its financial statements for its year ended December 31, 2006.

In this excerpt, Agrium provides information about the sources of the temporary differences that resulted in future deductible amounts and future income tax assets. Of the U.S. $175 million of future tax assets at December 31, 2006, a valuation allowance of U.S. $20 million was needed. Valuation allowances are used by a significant number of Canadian public companies, especially by those that are listed on a U.S. exchange.

Illustration 18-38

Future Income Tax Assets and Valuation Allowance

Note 5 (excerpt)		
	December 31	
(in millions of U.S. $)	2006	2005
Future income tax assets		
Loss carry forwards expiring through 2026	46	12
Asset retirement obligations and environmental liabilities	64	59
Receivables, inventories and accrued liabilities	40	22
Employee future benefits	20	17
Other	5	13
Future income tax assets before valuation allowance	175	123
Valuation allowance	(20)	(8)
Total future income tax assets, net of valuation allowance	155	115

---

[23] *CICA Handbook*, Section 3465.27.

[24] *CICA Handbook*, Section 3465.28.

[25] *CICA Handbook*, Section 3465.31(b).

PERSPECTIVES

Balance Sheet Presentation

Objective 10

Identify and apply the reporting and disclosure requirements for corporate income taxes, including intraperiod tax allocation.

International Insight

IAS 1 requires all deferred (future) tax assets and liabilities to be reported as non-current if they are presented in a balance sheet that distinguishes between current and non-current balances. As part of the FASB-IASB short-term harmonization project, the IASB has decided to change this requirement to converge with the U.S. and Canadian standards.

Because income taxes have a unique nature, income tax assets and liabilities have to be reported separately from other assets and liabilities on the balance sheet. In addition, **current** tax assets and liabilities are reported separately from **future** or deferred tax assets and liabilities.[26]

Where an entity classifies its balance sheet into current and non-current amounts, it is common practice to classify and report **future** income tax assets and liabilities as one **net current amount** and one **net non-current amount**, assuming the amounts relate to the same taxable entity and taxing authority. In other words, the current future tax assets and liabilities are netted, as are the long-term accounts, as long as the entity has the legal right to offset them. The classification of an individual future tax liability or asset **as current or non-current** is determined by **the classification of the related asset or liability for financial reporting purposes**.[27]

Most companies have a large number of transactions that give rise to future income taxes. The balances in the future income tax accounts must be analyzed and classified on the balance sheet into two categories: one for current amounts and one for non-current amounts. This procedure is summarized as follows:

1. *Classify the amounts as current or non-current.* If they are related to a specific asset or liability, they are classified in the same way as the related asset or liability. If there is no underlying asset or liability on the balance sheet, they are classified according to the expected reversal date.

2. *Determine the net current amount* by summing the various future tax assets and liabilities that are classified as current. If the net result is an asset, report it on the balance sheet as a current asset; if it is a liability, report it as a current liability.

3. *Determine the net non-current amount* by summing the various future tax assets and liabilities that are classified as non-current. If the net result is an asset, report it on the balance sheet as a non-current asset; if it is a liability, report it as a long-term liability.

To illustrate, assume that K. Scoffi Limited has four future tax items at December 31, 2008. The analysis in Illustration 18-39 shows how each temporary difference and related future tax asset or liability is classified.

Illustration 18-39

Classification of Temporary Differences as Current or Non-Current

Temporary Difference Related To:	Resulting Future Tax Asset	Liability	Related Balance Sheet Account	Classification
1. **Rent collected in advance:** recognized when earned for accounting purposes and when received for tax purposes	$42,000		Unearned Rent	Current
2. Use of **straight-line amortization** for accounting purposes and accelerated amortization for tax purposes		$214,000	Equipment	Non-current
3. Recognition of **profits on instalment sales** during period of sale for accounting purposes and during period of collection for tax purposes		45,000	Instalment Accounts Receivable	Current

[26] *CICA Handbook*, Section 3465.86.

[27] *CICA Handbook*, Section 3465.87–.88.

4. **Warranty liabilities:** recognized for accounting purposes at time of sale; for tax purposes at time paid	12,000		Estimated Liability under Warranties	Current
Totals	$54,000	$259,000		

The future taxes to be classified as current net to a $9,000 asset ($42,000 + $12,000 − $45,000), and the future taxes to be classified as non-current net to a $214,000 liability. Consequently, future income taxes appear on the December 31, 2008, balance sheet as shown in Illustration 18-40.

Current assets	
Future income tax asset	$9,000
Long-term liabilities	
Future income tax liability	$214,000

Illustration 18-40

Balance Sheet Presentation of Future Income Taxes

As indicated earlier, a future tax asset or liability **may not be related to a balance sheet asset or liability**. One example is research costs that, for financial reporting purposes, are recognized as expenses when they are incurred, but may be deferred and deducted in later years for tax purposes. Another example is a tax loss carryforward. In both cases, a future tax asset is recorded, but there is no related, identifiable asset or liability for financial reporting purposes. In these situations, future income taxes are classified according to the expected reversal date of the temporary difference or the date when the tax benefit is expected to be realized.[28] That is, **where there is no related balance sheet asset or liability**, the tax effect of the temporary differences that is expected to reverse or be realized in the next fiscal year is classified as current and the remainder is reported as non-current.

Income taxes currently payable are reported as a current liability on the balance sheet. Because corporations are required to make several instalment payments to the Canada Revenue Agency during the year, there could at times be a debit balance in the Income Tax Payable account. When this occurs, it is reported as a current asset called Prepaid Income Taxes or Income Taxes Receivable. An income tax refund that is the result of carrying a current year's tax loss back against previous years' taxable income is also reported as an income tax receivable and current asset. Current income tax liabilities and current income tax assets are usually netted.[29]

Income Statement Presentation

Intraperiod Tax Allocation

Another key objective of accounting for income taxes is to show the tax cost or benefit in the same place on the financial statements as **the underlying transaction or event that gave rise to the tax asset or liability**.[30] In general, this means that the current and future income tax expense (or benefit) of the current period related to **discontinued operations, extraordinary items, other comprehensive income, adjustments**

---

[28] *CICA Handbook*, Section 3465.87.

[29] *CICA Handbook*, Section 3465.88. Offsetting is only permitted if the amounts relate to the same taxable entity and the same taxation authority. This issue is especially relevant to consolidated financial statements.

[30] *CICA Handbook*, Section 3465.07.

reported in retained earnings, and capital transactions should be reported in the same place as the item that it is related to. This approach to allocating taxes **within** the financial statements of the current period is referred to as **intraperiod tax allocation**. **Interperiod tax allocation**, on the other hand, reflects the appropriate allocation of taxes **between** years, and results in the recognition of future income taxes.

To illustrate **intraperiod** tax allocation, assume that Copy Doctor Inc., with a tax rate of 35%, reports the following pre-tax amounts in 2008:

- a loss from continuing operations of $500,000

- an extraordinary gain of $900,000, of which $210,000 is not taxable

- a holding gain of $25,000 on its available-for-sale investments that is reported in other comprehensive income (assume that this will be taxable as ordinary income when it is realized)

Illustration 18-41 shows the analysis that is needed to determine where the current income tax expense or benefit will be reported.

Illustration 18-41

Analysis, Intraperiod Tax Allocation—Current Income Taxes, 2008

	Continuing operations	Extraordinary items	OCI	Total
Accounting income (loss)	($500,000)	$900,000	$25,000	$425,000
Deduct non-taxable permanent difference		(210,000)		(210,000)
Deduct timing difference: gain taxable when realized			(25,000)	(25,000)
Taxable income	($500,000)	$690,000	$-0-	$190,000
Current income tax expense/ tax payable at 35%	($175,000)	$241,500	$-0-	$66,500

Whenever income tax has to be reported separately so that it appears with a particular component of income or in another statement, prepare your analysis by first setting up a separate column for each component that attracts tax, as shown in the illustration. Note that the CRA is not interested in where the company reports various amounts on the GAAP financial statements—the agency is only interested in the last column of the illustration, that is, in what is taxable and what is not. Based on the analysis, the entry to record current income taxes is as follows:

A = L + SE
   +66,500 −66,500

Cash flows: No effect

Current Income Tax Expense (extraordinary items)	241,500	
Current Income Tax Benefit (continuing operations)		175,000
Income Tax Payable		66,500

Future income taxes also have to be allocated to the financial statement items that attract the tax. In this case, we will assume that the $25,000 temporary difference between the book value of the available-for-sale investments and their tax basis is the only temporary difference in this and previous years. Illustration 18-42 shows the calculations in determining future income taxes.

Illustration 18-42

Analysis, Intraperiod Tax
Allocation—Future Income
Taxes, 2008

	Continuing operations	Extraordinary items	OCI	Total
Taxable temporary difference, Dec. 31, 2008	$–0–	$–0–	$25,000	$25,000
Future income tax liability at 35% future rate, Dec. 31, 2008	$–0–	$–0–	$ 8,750	$ 8,750
Less future income tax liability before adjustment	–0–	–0–	–0–	–0–
Future income tax expense	$–0–	$–0–	$ 8,750	$ 8,750

The calculations are the same as the ones done earlier in the chapter, with added columns for the different parts of the statements that attract tax. In this example, the only temporary difference is related to amounts that are recognized in other comprehensive income. The tax effect must therefore be reported there as well. The entry to record future taxes is:

Future Income Tax Expense (OCI)	8,750	
Future Income Tax Liability		8,750

A	=	L	+	SE
		+8,750		–8,750

Cash flows: No effect

Illustration 18-43 shows how the income taxes calculated above are reported in the financial statements along with the items that attract the tax. The tax amounts can be taken directly from your entries or from the analysis.

Illustration 18-43

Statement Presentation—
Intraperiod Tax Allocation

COPY DOCTOR INC.
Income Statement
Year Ended December 31, 2008

Income (loss) before tax from continuing operations	$(500,000)	
Less: Current income tax benefit	175,000	$(325,000)
Extraordinary item	900,000	
Less: Current income tax expense	(241,500)	658,500
Net income		$ 333,500

Statement of Comprehensive Income
Year Ended December 31, 2008

Net income		$ 333,500
Other comprehensive income:		
Holding gains, AFS investments	$ 25,000	
Less: Future income tax expense	(8,750)	16,250
Comprehensive income		$ 349,750

In terms of real-world examples, we can look to **CGI Group Inc.** and **RONA inc.** For its year ended September 30, 2006, CGI Group Inc. reported income tax expense separately for earnings from continuing operations and for earnings from discontinued operations. The comparative statements provided for 2004 also show that income taxes were deducted from share issue costs in the statement of retained earnings. RONA inc. reported income tax effects in two places on its 2006 financial statements: on the income statement;

and on the statement of contributed surplus, related to a gain on disposal of the company's shares by joint ventures and a subsidiary company.

Other Income Statement Disclosures

In addition to intraperiod tax reporting, the following items also require separate disclosure:

- current income tax expense, and the future income tax expense related to income or loss before discontinued operations and extraordinary items

- income tax expense related to discontinued operations and to extraordinary items[31]

It may be useful to financial statement readers when a company discloses the major components of income tax expense that are included in income or a loss before discontinued operations and extraordinary items, but this disclosure is not required. Such a disclosure might include the amount of future tax expense related to a change in income tax rates or the reduction in tax expense that is due to recognition of a previously unrecorded tax loss, for example.

Other Disclosures

International Insight

After the FASB-IASB short-term convergence project is complete, IAS 12 will require public entities that are not subject to income tax because their income is taxed directly in the hands of their owners to disclose this fact. They will also have to disclose the net difference between the tax basis and carrying amounts of their assets and liabilities.

For all entities, separate disclosure is required of the current and future income taxes that are related to items charged or credited to equity, of the amount and expiry date of unused tax losses and reductions, and of the amount of deductible temporary differences for which no future tax asset has been recognized.[32]

For public and other specified companies, an additional series of disclosures is required:

1. The nature and tax effect of the temporary differences, unused tax losses, and unused tax reductions that give rise to future income tax assets and future income tax liabilities, with disclosure of significant offsetting items that are included in the future tax asset and liability balances

2. The major components of income tax expense that were included in determining the net income or loss for the period before discontinued operations and extraordinary items

3. A reconciliation of the income tax expense (related to net income or loss for the period before discontinued operations and extraordinary items) to the statutory income tax rate or dollar amount, and including the nature and amount of each significant reconciling item using percentages or dollar amounts. Significant offsetting items should be disclosed even if there is no variation from the statutory rate.[33]

Excerpts from the financial statements of **Vector Aerospace Corporation** for its year ended December 31, 2006, appear in Illustration 18-44 and show the reporting of many of these required disclosures.

---

[31] *CICA Handbook*, Section 3465.85 and .93.

[32] *CICA Handbook*, Section 3465.91.

[33] *CICA Handbook*, Section 3465.92. These additional disclosures are required of entities with debt or equity securities traded in a public market (a stock exchange or over-the-counter market) that are required to file financial statements with a securities commission, entities that provide financial statements in connection with the issue of securities in a public market, life insurance companies, deposit-taking institutions, and cooperative business enterprises.

CONSOLIDATED BALANCE SHEETS (excerpts)

Illustration 18-44

Disclosure of Income Taxes— Vector Aerospace Corporation

Student Website

Student Toolkit—Additional Disclosures

www.wiley.com/canada/kieso

As at December 31 (in thousands of Canadian dollars)	2006	2005
Assets (Note 5)		
Current Assets		
Income tax receivable	1,973	942
Future income tax asset (Note 11)	138	191
Liabilities and Shareholders' Equity		
Current Liabilities		
Income tax payable	6,045	198
Other credits (Note 6)	22,589	20,066

CONSOLIDATED STATEMENTS OF OPERATIONS

For the Years Ended December 31 (in thousands of Canadian dollars except per share amounts)	2006	2005	2004
Earnings from continuing operations before income taxes	20,923	14,899	3,547
Income tax expense (recovery) (Note 11)			
Current	3,706	2,069	(2,292)
Future	789	1,289	2,596
	4,495	3,358	304
Earnings from continuing operations	16,428	11,541	3,243
Discontinued operations (Note 13)	—		(250)
Net earnings	$ 16,428	$ 11,541	$ 2,993

NOTES TO THE CONSOLIDATED FINANCIAL STATEMENTS
December 31, 2006, 2005 and 2004 (all tabular amounts in thousands of Canadian dollars, except per share information)

2. Summary of significant accounting policies (continued)

Income taxes

The Company follows the liability method of accounting for income taxes. Under the liability method, future income tax assets and liabilities are determined based on the differences between the financial reporting and tax bases of assets and liabilities, as well as the benefit of losses that will more likely than not be realized and carried forward to future years to reduce income taxes. Assets and liabilities are measured using substantively enacted tax rates and laws that are expected to be in effect in the periods in which the future tax assets or liabilities are expected to be realized or settled. The effect of a change in substantively enacted income tax rates on future income tax assets and liabilities is recognized in income in the period that the change occurs. A valuation allowance is provided to the extent that it is more likely than not that future income tax assets will not be realized.

6. Other credits

	2006	2005	2004
Deferred government assistance, less accumulated amortization of $11,719,000 (2005 – $10,876,000; 2004 – $9,951,000)	$ 7,033	$ 6,696	$ 7,623
Accrued defined benefit pension liability (Note 17)	12,490	10,327	9,406
Future income tax liability (Note 11)	3,066	3,043	2,897
	$ 22,589	$ 20,066	$ 19,926

11. Income taxes

	2006	2005	2004
Canadian statutory income tax rate	35.99%	36.29%	36.00%
Income tax expense calculated at statutory rates	$ 7,530	$ 5,407	$ 1,277
Different tax rates of certain subsidiaries	241	130	(651)
Provincial tax rebate	(434)	(1,219)	(611)
Change in valuation allowance	(1,131)	(2,554)	(2,614)
Change in rates	(345)	(122)	–
Non-taxable portion of capital gains	(29)	(2)	(352)
Difference between rate of expected future reversal of temporary differences and current year rate	(480)	280	2,835
Other non-deductible amounts	(857)	1,438	420
Income tax expense (recovery)	$ 4,495	$ 3,358	$ 304

Income tax expense (recovery) comprises a current income tax expense of $3,706,000 (2005 – expense of $2,069,000; 2004 – recovery of $2,292,000) and future income tax expense of $789,000 (2005 – expense of $1,289,000; 2004 – expense of $2,596,000).

Significant components of the Company's future tax assets and liabilities as at December 31 are as follows:

	2006	2005	2004
Tax deductible amounts related to assets acquired on formation of the Company	$ 7,815	$ 9,013	$ 9,585
Employee pension plan obligations	5,029	3,872	3,588
Warranties and other deductible differences	1,073	1,013	2,030
Loss carry-forwards	13,011	15,350	19,866
	26,928	29,248	35,069
Valuation allowance	(15,896)	(15,564)	(21,004)
Total future tax assets	$ 11,032	$ 13,684	$ 14,065

The valuation allowance relates to potential future benefits in respect of net loss carry forwards of $40,294,000 (2005 – $47,564,000; 2004 – $61,046,000) and in respect of other deductible differences of $27,099,000 (2005 – $25,609,000; 2004 – $30,979,000). The tax value of these assets is approximately $20,958,000 (2005 – $22,850,000; 2004 – $29,745,000) of which $15,896,000 (2005 – $15,564,000; 2004 – $21,004,000) is subject to a valuation allowance. Tax assets subject to the valuation allowance may be recognized in future years when it becomes more likely than not that the benefits will be realized. At December 31, 2006, the Company and its subsidiaries had tax losses of approximately US $11,070,000 in the United States and approximately £12,289,000 in the United Kingdom, which are available to reduce taxable income in those jurisdictions in future years. The Company has recorded a valuation allowance, in aggregate, of $11,759,000 against the future tax asset associated with these losses. Future changes in the valuation allowance will be based on changes in management's assessment of the likelihood of realizing the future tax asset and will directly affect income tax expense and therefore net income of the Company.

	2006	2005	2004
Total future tax assets (cont'd)	$ 11,032	$ 13,684	$ 14,065
Future tax liabilities			
Carrying value in excess of tax bases	$ 11,071	$ 12,875	$ 11,707
Reserves	2,273	2,299	2,399
Deferred costs	376	370	495
Total future tax liabilities	$ 13,720	$ 15,544	$ 14,601
Net future tax liability	$ (2,688)	$ (1,860)	$ (536)
Distributed as follows:			
Current future tax asset	$ 138	$ 191	$ 520
Long-term future tax asset	240	992	1,841
Long-term future tax liability	(3,066)	(3,043)	(2,897)
Net future tax liability	$ (2,688)	$ (1,860)	$ (536)

At December 31, 2006, the Company has net loss carry forwards of $40,294,000 for tax purposes that expire as follows:

2010	$ 2,496
2011	—
Thereafter	12,901
No expiry	24,897
	$ 40,294

13. Discontinued operations

Information relating to discontinued operations is summarized as follows:

	2006	2005	2004
Revenue	$ —	$ —	$ 3,811
Operating loss	—	—	(878)
Gain on sale	—	—	489
Income tax expense (recovery)	—	—	(139)
Net loss	$ —	$ —	$ (250)

Note that Vector Aerospace provides a reconciliation from its statutory tax rate of 35.99% to its effective rate of 21.48% ($4,495/$20,923) in 2006. All items where the tax effect is other than 35.99% are identified along with the effect of each, and, as can be seen, the effects vary considerably from year to year. Interestingly, the higher 36.29% statutory rate in 2005 resulted in a lower effective rate (22.54%) than in 2006. Many companies prepare the reconciliation in percentages instead of dollar amounts, but the same basic information is provided to users.

Analysis

Review the disclosure requirements and how Vector Aerospace complied with them in Illustration 18-44. These disclosures are required for several reasons, some of which are discussed here.

Assessment of Quality of Earnings

In trying to assess the quality of a company's earnings, many investors are interested in the reconciliations between accounting and tax numbers. Earnings that are improved by a favourable tax effect should be examined carefully, particularly if the tax effect is non-recurring. For example, in 2005 Nortel Networks Limited reported net income of U.S. $7 million. This resulted from recognizing a U.S. $55-million income tax benefit on a U.S. $48-million loss before taxes. The reasons for this anomaly are important for anyone analyzing the company's performance and position, and much of the explanatory information was made available in the notes to the financial statements.

**What
Do the
Numbers
Mean?**

An area that requires considerable judgement and that therefore may be open to abuse is the accounting for future tax assets. To justify the recognition of future income tax assets on the balance sheet and tax benefits on the income statement, it takes only a small amount of optimism for management to expect flows of future taxable income against which it will apply tax losses and other future deductible amounts. Valuation of future income tax assets, either directly or through an adjustment of the valuation allowance account, affects bottom-line income on a dollar-for-dollar basis.

Stelco Inc., "Canada's largest and most diversified steel producer," presented an interesting example a short while ago. In one year, the company's loss of $217 million was reduced by $81 million of future income tax benefits, while $139 million of future income tax assets were reported on its balance sheet. In the next year, the company's $9 million of income was increased by an $11-million future tax benefit, and $161 million of net future tax assets were reported on the balance sheet, **with $74 million classified as a current asset**. The future deductible amounts underlying the tax asset accounts were related to the recognition of employee retirement benefit expenses in excess of amounts paid, and income tax losses carried forward.

To have classified $74 million of the future tax asset as a current asset, management must have expected the upcoming year to be an excellent one for the company! As it turned out, sales volume and prices were down, costs increased, and the cash position deteriorated, resulting in Stelco's obtaining an order to initiate a court-supervised restructuring under the *Companies' Creditors Arrangement Act*.

Regardless of management's motivations in assessing the value of future income tax assets, financial statement readers should be aware of how big a part judgement plays in these measurements.

Better Predictions of Future Cash Flows

Examining the future portion of income tax expense provides information about whether taxes payable are likely to be higher or lower in the future. A close examination may provide additional insight into the company's policies on capitalization of costs and recognition of revenue, and on other policies that give rise to a difference between income reported on the financial statements and taxable income. As a result, it may be possible to predict upcoming reductions in future tax liabilities if the cash required for income tax payments in the future exceeds the amount of income tax expense reported on the income statement. This may lead to a loss of liquidity.[34]

Predicting Future Cash Flows from Operating Loss Carryforwards Companies should disclose the amounts and expiration dates of any loss carryforwards for tax purposes. From this disclosure, analysts can determine the type and amount of income that the company may recognize in the future and on which it will pay no income tax. For example, Vector Aerospace, in Illustration 18-44, indicates that the company has

---

[34] R.P. Weber and J.E. Wheeler, "Using Income Disclosures to Explore Significant Economic Transactions," *Accounting Horizons* (September 1992) discuss how deferred (future) tax disclosures can be used to assess the quality of earnings and to predict future cash flows.

$40.294 million of net loss carryforwards that it can use to reduce future income taxes. The company indicates that $24,897 million of this amount has no expiry date, which may mean that the amount is due to capital losses that can only be offset against capital gains. Identifying the specific expiration dates for the remaining losses would have been useful information, as would how much of the valuation allowance of $15,896 million is related specifically to the losses.

Helpful in Setting Government Policy

Understanding the amount that companies currently pay and the effective tax rate is helpful to government policy-makers. In the early 1970s, when oil companies were believed to have earned excess profits, many politicians and other interested parties tried to determine their effective tax rates. Unfortunately, at that time, such information was not available in published annual reports.

International

Comparison of Canadian and International GAAP

With the U.S., Canada, and the international community all using a balance sheet or asset-liability approach to accounting for income taxes, there are few differences among their standards at the level of this textbook. Furthermore, the FASB and IASB are working to eliminate differences at a detailed level as part of their short-term convergence project on income taxes. This will serve to bring the Canadian and international standards even closer. Illustration 18-45 presents the primary source of Canadian GAAP and the corresponding IFRS in this important area.

11 Objective
Compare current Canadian and international GAAP for income taxes.

Canada	International
Section 3465: Income taxes	IAS 12: Income taxes
	SIC-25: Income taxes—changes in the tax status of an enterprise or its shareholders

Illustration 18-45
Primary Sources of GAAP

Terminology. There are minor differences in the terms that are used, but no differences in substance. For example, the IASB uses the terms **deferred income taxes**, deferred tax assets, and deferred tax liabilities, as does the U.S. The Canadian standards refer instead to future income taxes, future tax assets, and future tax liabilities. The meanings are identical. So too is the tax "base" used by the IASB instead of Canada's reference to the tax "basis" of an asset or liability. Also, the IASB has agreed that its use of the term "probable" in terms of recognizing future tax assets should be defined as meaning "more likely than not."

Business combinations and intercompany transactions. There are differences in the recognition and measurement aspects of transactions related to business combinations and transfers of assets within a group of companies that relate to future tax considerations. These differences, which are covered in advanced accounting courses, are being harmonized as part of the Business Combination project.

Balance sheet classification. IAS 1 requires deferred tax assets and liabilities to be classified as non-current in a balance sheet that distinguishes between current and non-current assets and liabilities. The IASB has decided to amend this requirement so that classification of future tax assets and liabilities will be based on the same principles as the Canadian standards and the FASB's SFAS 109.

Change in an entity's tax status. Unlike in Canada, international standards provide guidance (in SIC-25) on how to account for any change in the tax status of an enterprise or its shareholders that may affect the measurement of its tax assets or liabilities. In short, any current or deferred tax consequences of a change are required to be recognized in income in the period of the change, unless the consequences relate to a transaction or event that is a direct charge or credit to equity. This still leaves open the question of what is meant by "the period of the change." This will be important to many income trusts in Canada whose tax status will change in 2011. As part of the short-term convergence project with the FASB, the IASB decided to include guidance on when the change should be recognized: if it is a result of a change in tax law, recognize the effect on the date the tax law is enacted or is substantively enacted; if it is a voluntary change, recognize the effect on the approval date, or the filing date if approval is not necessary.

Disclosures. IAS 12 considers that an adjustment in the current period that relates to the current tax of prior periods qualifies as a significant component of income tax expense that should be disclosed. The IASB will add a requirement to IAS 12 that, where appropriate, public entities that are not subject to income taxes because their income is taxed directly to their owners should disclose this fact as well as any differences between tax bases and carrying amounts. Neither of these disclosures is now required under Section 3465.[35]

The changes referred to above have been agreed upon by the IASB as part of the short-term convergence project on this topic with the FASB. The changes will still be subject to an exposure draft and final standards process that may not be completed and effective until 2008 or later. The AcSB expects to issue a converged standard after completion of the FASB-IASB process.

THE ASSET–LIABILITY METHOD

Differential Reporting

Accounting standard setters have concluded that there are situations where the costs of compiling information and providing extensive disclosures under certain standards exceed the benefits that users derive from that information.

Following from this, the Canadian standard for income taxes allows qualifying entities—those that are non-publicly accountable and whose owners unanimously consent to the application of an approved alternative—to apply a different method and still be in accordance with GAAP. This is known as **differential reporting**, and the allowed alternative for income taxes is known as **the taxes payable method.**[36]

The **taxes payable method** recognizes as income tax expense (or benefit) an amount that is equal to the income taxes that are currently payable (receivable). That is, the expense falls into the period when the revenues and expenses are recognized for tax purposes. No future tax assets and liabilities are recognized. While this approach to accounting for taxes is considerably less complex, companies are still required to provide the following income-tax-specific disclosures:

1. The income tax expense (or benefit) included in the following: income before discontinued operations and extraordinary items, discontinued operations, extraordinary items, and capital transactions reported in equity

---

[35] IASB, "Short-Term Convergence: Income Taxes," Project Update, December 2006.
[36] *CICA Handbook*, Section 1300.06 and 3465.105.

2. A reconciliation of the tax rate (or expense) from the statutory rate to the effective rate (or expense) related to income before discontinued operations and extraordinary items, including the nature and amounts of the reconciling items

3. The amount and expiry date of losses carried forward and unused income tax credits

4. The amount of any capital gain reserves to be included in taxable income in the next five years[37]

Chapter 23 discusses the topic of differential reporting and *CICA Handbook* Section 1300 in more detail.

Conceptual Questions

North American standard setters and the IASB believe that the asset-liability method (sometimes referred to as the liability approach) is the most conceptually sound method of accounting for income taxes. One objective of this approach is to recognize the amount of taxes payable or refundable for the current year. A second objective is to **recognize future tax liabilities and assets for the future tax consequences of events that have been recognized in the financial statements or tax returns**.

Although the asset-liability method is considered to be the most appropriate approach, some conceptual questions remain.

Failure to discount. Without discounting the asset or liability (that is, by not considering its present value), financial statements do not indicate the appropriate benefit of a tax deferral or the burden of a tax prepayment. This impairs the comparability of the financial statements, because a dollar in a short-term deferral is presented as being of the same value as a dollar in a longer-term deferral.

Classification issue. The standards call for future tax assets and liabilities to be classified on the balance sheet based on the classification of the underlying asset or liability that caused the temporary difference. Many observers support the position that future taxes should be classified relative to when the temporary differences will reverse.

Dual criteria for recognition of future tax asset. Many observers believe that future deductible amounts arising from operating loss carryforwards are different from future deductible amounts arising from other causes. One rationale for this view is that a future tax asset arising from normal transactions results in a tax prepayment: a prepaid tax asset. In the case of losses available to carry forward, no tax prepayment has been made. Others argue that realization of a loss carryforward is less likely and thus should require a more severe test than for a net deductible amount arising from normal operations. Some critics have indicated that because of the nature of net operating losses, future tax assets should never be established for these items.

The above controversies exist even within the asset-liability approach. Others argue that completely different types of approaches should be used to report future income taxes.

Comprehensive Illustration of Interperiod Tax Allocation

The example below is a comprehensive illustration of a future income tax problem with several temporary and permanent differences. The illustration follows one company

13 Objective
Identify outstanding issues with the asset-liability method.

Student Website

Student Toolkit—Expanded Discussions

www.wiley.com/canada/kieso

---

[37] *CICA Handbook* Section 3465.106.

through two complete years (2007 and 2008). Study it carefully. It should help cement your understanding of the concepts and procedures presented in the chapter.

First Year—2007

Allman Corporation, which began operations at the beginning of 2007, produces various products on a contract basis. Each contract generates a gross profit of $80,000 and some of Allman's contracts provide for the customer to pay on an instalment basis. In such cases, the customer pays one-fifth of the contract revenue in the year of the sale and in each of the following four years. Gross profit is recognized in the year when the contract is completed for financial reporting purposes (accrual basis) and in the year when cash is collected for tax purposes (instalment basis). Information on Allman's operations for 2007 is as follows:

1. In 2007, the company completed seven contracts that allow the customer to pay on an instalment basis. The related gross profit of $560,000 on instalment sales of $1.5 million (to be collected at a rate of $300,000 per year beginning in 2007) is recognized for financial reporting purposes, but only $112,000 of gross profit on instalment sales was reported on the 2007 tax return. Future collections on the related instalment receivables are expected to result in taxable amounts of $112,000 in each of the next four years.

2. At the beginning of 2007, Allman Corporation purchased depreciable assets with a cost of $540,000. For financial reporting purposes, Allman amortizes these assets using the straight-line method over a six-year service life. For tax purposes, the assets fall into CCA Class 8, permitting a 20% rate, and for the first year the half-year rule is applied. The following table shows the amortization and net asset value schedules for both financial reporting and tax purposes:

	Accounting		Tax	
Year	Amortization	Carrying Amount, End of Year	CCA	Undepreciated Capital Cost, End of Year
2007	$ 90,000	$450,000	$ 54,000	$486,000
2008	90,000	360,000	97,200	388,800
2009	90,000	270,000	77,760	311,040
2010	90,000	180,000	62,208	248,832
2011	90,000	90,000	49,766	199,066
2012	90,000	—	199,066	—
	$540,000		$540,000	

3. The company guarantees its product for two years from the contract completion date. During 2007, the product warranty liability accrued for financial reporting purposes was $200,000, and the amount paid to satisfy the warranty liability was $44,000. The remaining $156,000 is expected to be settled by expenditures of $56,000 in 2008 and $100,000 in 2009.

4. At December 31, 2007, the company accrued non-taxable dividends receivable of $28,000, the only dividend revenue reported for the year.

5. During 2007, non-deductible fines and penalties of $26,000 were paid.

6. Accounting income for 2007 (before the provision for income taxes) amounts to $412,000.

7. The enacted tax rate for 2007 is 50%, and for 2008 and future years it is 40%.

8. Allman Corporation has a December 31 year end.

9. The company is expected to have taxable income in all future years.

Taxable Income, Income Tax Payable, Current Income Tax Expense—2007

The first step in determining the company's income tax payable for 2007 is to calculate its taxable income. The calculation, starting with the income reported on the income statement, is reconciled to taxable income. The taxes that are levied on the taxable amount are the taxes payable and the current income tax expense for the year. Illustration 18-46 shows the results.

Accounting income for 2007	$ 412,000
Permanent differences:	
Non-taxable revenue—dividends	(28,000)
Non-deductible expenses—fines and penalties	26,000
Timing differences:	
Excess gross profit per books ($560,000 – $112,000)	(448,000)
Excess amortization per books ($90,000 – $54,000)	36,000
Excess warranty expense per books ($200,000 – $44,000)	156,000
Taxable income for 2007	$ 154,000
Income tax payable (current income tax expense) for 2007: $154,000 × 50%	$ 77,000

Illustration 18-46

Calculation of Taxable Income and Taxes Payable—2007

Future Income Tax Assets and Liabilities at December 31, 2007, and 2007 Future Income Tax Expense

Because future income tax expense is the difference between the opening and closing balance of the net future income tax asset or liability account, the next step is to calculate the future tax asset and liability amounts. These represent the tax effects of the temporary differences between the carrying amounts and tax basis of related assets and liabilities on December 31, 2007. Illustration 18-47 summarizes the temporary differences, the future tax asset and liability amounts, the correct balance of the future tax liability or asset account at December 31, 2007, and the amount that is needed for the future tax expense entry.

Balance Sheet Account	Carrying Amount	–	Tax Basis	=	(Taxable) Deductible Temporary Difference	×	Tax Rate	=	Future Income Tax Asset (Liability)
Deferred gross profit (contra to A/R)	$ –0–		$448,000		$(448,000)		.40		$(179,200)
Plant & equipment	450,000		486,000		36,000		.40		14,400
Liability for warranties	156,000		–0–		156,000		.40		62,400
Net future income tax liability, December 31, 2007									(102,400)
Net future income tax asset (liability) before adjustment									–0–
Increase in future tax liability account and future income tax expense, 2007									$(102,400)

Illustration 18-47

Determination of Future Income Tax Assets, Liabilities, and Future Income Tax Expense—2007

Let us now review each step in this illustration. Allman Corporation recognized all the profit on the 2007 instalment sales in its 2007 income statement. None of the $560,000 of gross profit was deferred for financial reporting purposes. Therefore, the book value of the deferred gross profit (a contra account to Accounts Receivable) at December 31, 2007, was $0. However, only $112,000 of the gross profit was recognized in taxable income.

Therefore, the remaining $448,000 ($560,000 – $112,000) of gross profit was deferred for tax purposes and it will be included in taxable income in the future as the instalment sales are collected. The tax basis of the deferred gross profit account is $448,000. This temporary difference will result in taxable amounts in the future. At the enacted rate of 40%, this will cause an additional $179,200 of income tax to be payable in the future.

The carrying amount of the depreciable assets is $450,000 at the end of 2007, but their undepreciated capital cost, or tax value, is $486,000. Because the company has taken $36,000 **less CCA** than amortization to the end of 2007, in the future there will be $36,000 **more CCA** deductible for tax purposes than amortization taken on the books. Therefore, the $36,000 is a deductible temporary difference that will cause future taxes to be reduced by $14,400. Comparing the CCA and amortization schedule over the next few years reveals that in some years (2008, 2012, and onwards) excess CCA will be claimed, while in others (2009, 2010, and 2011) less CCA than amortization will be claimed. These net out at December 31, 2007, to $36,000 more CCA than amortization in the future.

Allman reports a warranty liability on its December 31, 2007, balance sheet with a book value of $156,000. This whole amount will be deductible in calculating taxable income in the future as the liability is settled. Because Allman has not yet recognized the $156,000 of expenses for tax purposes, the tax basis of the liability is $0. This third temporary difference, therefore, is a deductible temporary difference and, at a 40% rate, it will result in future tax savings of $62,400.

The key to the analysis is to determine whether taxable income **in a future period will be increased or decreased**. If increased, it is a **taxable** temporary difference; if decreased, it is a **deductible** temporary difference.

The tax effect of each temporary difference is determined by applying the enacted rate for each specific year. In this case, because the tax rates for all future years are identical, the future tax assets and liability can be calculated by simply applying the 40% rate to the temporary differences at the end of 2007 as shown in Illustration 18-47. If the tax rates for each future year were not the same, a schedule of when the temporary differences are expected to reverse is needed. Such a schedule is shown in Illustration 18-48.

Illustration 18-48

Schedule of Reversals of Temporary Differences at December 31, 2007

	Total	2008	2009	2010	2011	2012
				Future Years		
(Taxable) deductible temporary differences						
Deferred gross profit	$(448,000)	$(112,000)	$(112,000)	$(112,000)	$(112,000)	
Plant & equipment	36,000	7,200	(12,240)	(27,792)	(40,234)	$109,066
Warranty liability	156,000	56,000	100,000			
Net (taxable) deductible amount	$(256,000)	$ (48,800)	$ (24,240)	$(139,792)	$(152,234)	$109,066
Tax rate enacted for year		40%	40%	40%	40%	40%
Net future tax asset (liability)	$(102,400)	$ (19,520)	$ (9,696)	$ (55,917)	$ (60,894)	$ 43,627

Income Tax Accounting Entries—2007   The entries to record current and future income taxes for 2007 are as follows:

A = L + SE
+77,000 −77,000

Cash flows: No effect

Current Income Tax Expense	77,000	
Income Tax Payable (Illustration 18-46)		77,000

Future Income Tax Expense	102,400	
Future Income Tax Liability (Illustration 18-47)		102,400

A =   L   +   SE
+102,400   −102,400

Cash flows: No effect

Financial Statement Presentation—2007   Future tax assets and liabilities are classified as current and non-current on the balance sheet based on the classifications of the related assets and liabilities that underlie the temporary differences. They are then summarized into one net current and one net non-current amount. The classification of Allman Corporation's future tax account at the end of 2007 is shown in Illustration 18-49.

Illustration 18-49

Classification of Future Tax Asset/Liability Account

Balance Sheet Account	Balance Sheet Classification	Future Tax Asset (Liability)*	Classification of Future Tax Asset (Liability)	
			Current	Non-current
Deferred gross profit (A/R)	mixed	$(179,200)	$(44,800)	$(134,400)
Plant & equipment	non-current	14,400		14,400
Warranty liability	mixed	62,400	22,400	40,000
		$(102,400)	$(22,400)	$ (80,000)

*From Illustration 18-47

For the first temporary difference, the related account on the balance sheet is the deferred gross profit, a contra account to the accounts receivable. The account receivable is classified partially as a current asset and partially as long-term. Because one-fourth of the gross profit relates to the receivable due in 2008, this portion of the receivable is a current asset and the current portion of the future tax liability is $44,800 ($179,200 × 1/4). The $134,400 remainder ($179,200 − $44,800) of the future tax liability is non-current.

As the plant and equipment are classified as long-term, the resulting future tax asset is classified as non-current. The warranty liability account, like the instalment receivables, is split between the current and long-term categories. Our assumption is that $56,000 of the liability is reported as current and the remaining $100,000 as non-current. The current portion of the future tax asset, therefore, is $22,400 ($56,000 ÷ $156,000 × $62,400). The remainder ($62,400 − $22,400 = $40,000) is non-current.

As indicated in Illustration 18-49, the $102,400 net future tax liability that was previously calculated will be reported on the balance sheet in two parts: a future income tax liability of $22,400 will be reported as a **current liability**, and a future income tax liability of $80,000 will be reported as a **long-term liability**. The financial statement presentation is shown in Illustration 18-50.

Illustration 18-50

Financial Statement Presentation—2007

Balance Sheet, December 31, 2007 (partial)

Current liabilities		
Income tax payable		$ 77,000
Future income tax liability		22,400
Long-term liabilities		
Future income tax liability		$ 80,000

Income Statement, Year Ended December 31, 2007 (partial)

Income before income tax		$412,000
Income tax expense		
Current	$ 77,000	
Future	102,400	179,400
Net income		$232,600

Second Year—2008

1. During 2008, the company collected one-fifth of the original sales price (or one-quarter of the outstanding receivable at December 31, 2007) from customers for the receivables arising from contracts completed in 2007. Recovery of the remaining receivables is still expected to result in taxable amounts of $112,000 in each of the following three years.

2. In 2008, the company completed four new contracts with a total selling price of $1 million (to be paid in five equal instalments beginning in 2008) and had a gross profit of $320,000. For financial reporting purposes, the full $320,000 is recognized in 2008, whereas for tax purposes the gross profit is deferred and taken into taxable income as the cash is received; that is, one-fifth, or $64,000, in 2008 and one-fifth in each of 2009 to 2012.

3. During 2008, Allman continued to amortize the assets acquired in 2007 according to the amortization and CCA schedules that appear on page 1120. Therefore, amortization expense amounted to $90,000 and CCA of $97,200 was claimed for tax purposes.

4. Information about the product warranty liability account and timing of warranty expenditures at the end of 2008 is shown in Illustration 18-51.

Illustration 18-51

Warranty Liability and Expenditure Information

Balance of liability at beginning of 2008	$156,000
Expense for 2008 income statement purposes	180,000
Amount paid for contracts completed in 2007	(62,000)
Amount paid for contracts completed in 2008	(50,000)
Balance of liability at end of 2008	$224,000
Estimated warranty expenditures:	
$ 94,000 in 2009 due to 2007 contracts	
50,000 in 2009 due to 2008 contracts	
80,000 in 2010 due to 2008 contracts	
$224,000	

5. During 2008, non-taxable dividend revenue was $24,000.

6. A loss of $172,000 was accrued for financial reporting purposes because of pending litigation. This amount is not tax-deductible until the period when the loss is realized, which is estimated to be 2013.

7. Accounting income for 2008 is $504,800.

8. The tax rate in effect for 2008 is 40%; at year end, tax rate increases were enacted for 2009 and subsequent years at 42%.

Taxable Income, Income Tax Payable, Current Income Tax Expense—2008
Taxable income, income tax payable, and current income tax expense for 2008 are calculated in Illustration 18-52.

Illustration 18-52

Calculation of Taxable Income and Taxes Payable—2008

Accounting income for 2008	$504,800
Permanent difference:	
Non-taxable revenue—dividends	(24,000)
Timing differences:	
Gross profit on 2007 instalment sales	112,000

Deferred gross profit—2008 contracts ($320,000 − $64,000)	$(256,000)
Excess CCA ($97,200 − $90,000)	(7,200)
Payments on warranties from 2007 contracts	(62,000)
Excess warranty expense per books—2008 contracts ($180,000 − $50,000)	130,000
Loss accrual per books	172,000
Taxable income for 2008	$ 569,600
Income tax payable (current income tax expense) for 2008: $569,600 × 40%	$ 227,840

Future Income Tax Assets and Liabilities at December 31, 2008, and 2008 Future Income Tax Expense   The next step is to determine the correct balance of the net future income tax asset or liability account at December 31, 2008. The amount required to adjust this account to its correct balance is the future income tax expense/benefit for 2008.

Illustration 18-53 summarizes the temporary differences at December 31, 2008, the future tax effects of these differences, the correct ending balance of the balance sheet future tax account, and the entry that is required for the future income tax benefit.

Balance Sheet Account	Carrying Amount	−	Tax Basis	=	(Taxable) Deductible Temporary Difference	×	Tax Rate	=	Future Income Tax Asset (Liability)
Deferred gross profit (A/R)									
–2007 sales	$–0–		$336,000		$(336,000)		.42		$(141,120)
–2008 sales	–0–		$256,000		(256,000)		.42		(107,520)
Plant & equipment	360,000		388,800		28,800		.42		12,096
Liability for warranties									
–2007 sales	94,000		–0–		94,000		.42		39,480
–2008 sales	130,000		–0–		130,000		.42		54,600
Litigation liability	172,000		–0–		172,000		.42		72,240
Net future income tax liability, December 31, 2008									(70,224)
Net future income tax asset (liability) before adjustment									(102,400)
Decrease in future tax liability account and future income tax benefit, 2008									$ 32,176

Illustration 18-53

Determination of Future Income Tax Expense/Benefit—2008

The temporary difference that is caused by deferring the profit on the instalment sales for tax purposes again results in a taxable temporary difference and a future tax liability. For both the 2007 and 2008 sales, the company has no deferred profits in the accounts—it has all been recognized in income. For tax purposes, three-fifths of the 2007 profit of $560,000 (i.e., $336,000) is still deferred at December 31, 2008; while four-fifths of the 2008 profit of $320,000 (i.e., $256,000) is deferred. These amounts will increase taxable income in the future.

To the end of 2008, $28,800 less CCA has been claimed than amortization. This can be seen by comparing the book value of the plant and equipment of $360,000 with its UCC or tax basis of $388,800 at the same date. In the future, there will be $28,800 more CCA deductible for tax purposes than amortization taken on the books, which will reduce future taxable income. The temporary difference due to warranty costs will result in deductible amounts in each of 2009 and 2010 as this difference reverses, and the $172,000 loss that is not deductible for tax purposes this year will be deductible in the future.

Again, because the future tax rates are identical for each future year, the future tax liability can be calculated by applying the 42% rate to the total of each temporary difference.

If instead the rates had been changed to 42% for 2009, 43% for 2010, and 44% thereafter, for example, a schedule similar to the one in Illustration 18-48 would be prepared and the appropriate rate applied to when each temporary difference is expected to reverse.

Income Tax Accounting Entries—2008   The entries to record current and future income taxes for 2008 are as follows:

A =   L   +   SE
    +227,840   −227,840
Cash flows: No effect

Current Income Tax Expense	227,840	
Income Tax Payable (Illustration 18-52)		227,840

A =   L   +   SE
    −32,176   +32,176
Cash flows: No effect

Future Income Tax Liability (Illustration 18-53)	32,176	
Future Income Tax Benefit		32,176

Financial Statement Presentation—2008   The classification of Allman Corporation's future tax account at the end of 2008 is shown in Illustration 18-54.

Illustration 18-54

Classification of Future Tax Asset/Liability Account

Balance Sheet Account	Balance Sheet Classification	Future Tax Asset (Liability)*	Classification of Future Tax Asset (Liability)	
			Current	Non-current
Deferred gross profit (A/R)				
–2007 sales	mixed	$(141,120)	$(47,040)	$(94,080)
–2008 sales	mixed	(107,520)	(26,880)	(80,640)
Plant & equipment	non-current	12,096		12,096
Warranty liability				
–2007 sales	current	39,480	39,480	
–2008 sales	mixed	54,600	21,000	33,600
Litigation liability	non-current	72,240		72,240
		$ (70,224)	$(13,440)	$(56,784)

*From Illustration 18-53

The future tax accounts related to the deferred gross profit (contra account to the instalment receivables) follow the balance sheet classification of the receivables. Of the amounts owed on the 2007 sales, one-third will be collected in 2009, so one-third of the receivable is reported in current assets. One-third of the future tax liability ($1/3 \times$ $141,120 = $47,040) is also classified as a current item, with the remaining two-thirds reported as non-current. The deferred gross profit on the 2008 sales is analyzed the same way—in this case, one-quarter is current and three-quarters non-current. The warranty liability related to the 2007 sales is all expected to be paid within the next year; therefore the liability is reported as a current item on the balance sheet. The related future tax asset must also be designated as current. Of the $130,000 warranty liability related to the 2008 sales, $50,000 is expected to be paid in 2009 and is included in current liabilities. The current portion of the future tax asset is therefore $21,000 ($50,000 ÷ $130,000 × $54,600), and the remainder is long-term.[38] The litigation liability is reported outside current liabilities and so is its related future tax account.

---

[38] If Allman Corporation classifies all warranty liabilities as current because the company defines the operating cycle as including the two-year warranty period, then the entire future tax asset related to the warranties would be reported as a current amount.

The balance sheet at the end of 2008 and the 2008 income statement are shown in Illustration 18-55.

Illustration 18-55
Financial Statement Presentation—2008

Balance Sheet, December 31, 2008 (partial)

Current liabilities	
Income tax payable	$227,840
Future income tax liability	13,440
Long-term liabilities	
Future income tax liability	$56,784

Income Statement, Year Ended December 31, 2008 (partial)

Income before income tax		$504,800
Income tax expense		
Current	$227,840	
Future	(32,176)*	195,664
Net income		$309,136

*Components may be disclosed

As the major components of income tax expense are required to be disclosed in some cases and disclosure, even if not required, is desirable in others, it is possible to do a further analysis which determines how much of the future tax expense is due to a change in the rate of tax that is being used to measure the net future tax liability and how much is due to a change in temporary differences. Because the tax rate for measuring the net future tax **liability** increased from 40% to 42% at the end of the year, the change in rate results in an increase in both the liability and the future tax expense. The analysis to explain the $32,176 benefit is shown in Illustration 18-56.

Illustration 18-56
Analysis of Future Income Tax Benefit—2008

Future income tax expense (benefit) due to:		
• **Increase in tax rate**		
Opening future tax liability at 40%	$102,400	
Opening future tax liability at 42% ($256,000 × .42)	107,520	$ 5,120
• **Originating and reversing temporary differences during 2008**		
Opening future tax liability at 42%	107,520	
Ending future tax liability at 42%	70,224	
Decrease in net future tax liability		(37,296)
Change in future income tax liability, and future income tax expense (benefit) for 2008		$(32,176)

Summary of Learning Objectives

1 Explain the difference between accounting income and taxable income.

Accounting income (income reported on the income statement before income taxes) is calculated in accordance with generally accepted accounting principles. Taxable income is calculated in accordance with prescribed tax legislation and regulations. Because tax legislation and GAAP have different objectives, accounting income and taxable income often differ. To calculate taxable income, companies start with their accounting income and then add and deduct items to adjust the GAAP measure of income to what is actually taxable and tax-deductible in the period.

**Student
Website**

Glossary

www.wiley.com/canada/kieso

KEY TERMS

accounting income, 1078

asset-liability method, 1078

deductible temporary difference, 1084

deferred income taxes, 1117

deferred tax asset, 1089

deferred tax expense, 1086

deferred tax liability, 1085

differential reporting, 1118

effective tax rate, 1096

future income tax asset, 1089

future income tax expense, 1086

future income tax liability, 1085

income tax benefit, 1087

interperiod tax allocation, 1088

intraperiod tax allocation, 1110

liability method, 1078

loss carryback, 1098

loss carryforward, 1098

loss for income tax purposes, 1098

more likely than not, 1101

originating timing difference, 1082

permanent difference, 1080

reversing timing difference, 1082

taxable income, 1078

taxable temporary difference, 1084

tax base/basis, 1083

tax base of an asset, 1083

tax base of a liability, 1084

tax loss, 1098

taxes payable method, 1118

temporary difference, 1084

2 Identify the difference between timing and permanent differences, and calculate taxable income and current income taxes.

In any year, there are usually differences between income reported on the financial statements and taxable income on the tax return. Differences that had no past and have no future tax consequences are known as permanent differences. Their effect is only on the current period. Those that relate to recognizing revenues and expenses in different periods for book and tax purposes are known as timing differences. Current income tax expense and income taxes payable are always based on taxable income, using the current income tax rate.

3 Explain what a taxable temporary difference is and why a future tax liability is recognized.

A taxable temporary difference is the difference between the carrying amount of an asset or liability and its tax basis with the consequence that, when the asset is recovered or the liability is settled in the future for an amount equal to its carrying value, the taxable income of that future period will be increased. Because taxes increase in the future as a result of temporary differences that exist at the balance sheet date, the future tax consequences of these taxable amounts are recognized in the current period as a future tax liability.

4 Explain what a deductible temporary difference is and why a future tax asset is recognized.

A deductible temporary difference is the difference between the carrying amount of an asset or liability and its tax basis with the consequence that, when the asset is recovered or the liability is settled in the future for an amount equal to its carrying value, the taxable income of that future period will be reduced. Because taxes are reduced in the future as a result of temporary differences that exist at the balance sheet date, the future tax consequences of these deductible amounts are recognized in the current period as a future tax asset.

5 Prepare analyses of future income tax balances and record future income tax expense.

The following steps are taken: (1) identify all temporary differences between the book values and tax basis of assets and liabilities at the balance sheet date; (2) calculate the correct net future income tax asset or liability balance at the end of the period; (3) compare the pre-adjusted opening future tax asset or liability with the correct balance at the balance sheet date—the difference is the future tax expense/benefit; (4) prepare the journal entry based on the change in the amount of the net future tax asset or liability.

6 Explain the effect of various tax rates and tax rate changes on future income tax accounts.

Tax rates other than the current rate can only be used when the future tax rates have been enacted into legislation or substantively enacted. When there is a change in the future tax rate, its effect on the future income tax accounts should be recognized immediately. The effects are reported as an adjustment to future income tax expense in the period of the change.

7 Apply accounting procedures for a tax loss carryback.

A company may carry a taxable loss back three years and receive refunds to a maximum of the income taxes paid in those years. Because the economic benefits related to the losses carried back are certain, they are recognized in the period of the loss as a tax benefit on the income statement and as an asset (income tax refund receivable), on the balance sheet.

8 Apply accounting procedures and disclosure requirements for a tax loss carryforward.

A post-2005 tax loss can be carried forward and applied against the taxable incomes of the next 20 years. If the economic benefits related to the tax loss are more likely than not to be realized because of the likelihood of generating sufficient taxable income during the carryforward period, they can be recognized in the period of the loss as a tax benefit in the income statement and as a future tax asset on the balance sheet. Otherwise, they should not be recognized in the financial statements. Alternatively, they may be recognized in the accounts along with a contra valuation allowance account. This alternative approach will probably be required in Canada as we move to adopt IFRS. Disclosure is required of the amounts of tax loss carryforwards and their expiry dates. If previously unrecorded tax losses are subsequently used to benefit a future period, the benefit is recognized in that future period.

9 Explain why the Future Income Tax Asset account is reassessed at the balance sheet date.

Consistent with asset valuation principles in general, every asset must be assessed to ensure that it is not reported at an amount in excess of the economic benefits that are expected to be received from the use or sale of the asset. The economic benefit to be received from the future income tax asset is the reduction in future income taxes payable. If it is unlikely that sufficient taxable income will be generated in the future to allow the entity to benefit from future deductible amounts, the income tax asset may have to be written down. If previously unrecognized amounts are now expected to be realizable, a future tax asset is recognized. These entries may be made directly to the future tax asset account or through a valuation allowance contra account.

10 Identify and apply the reporting and disclosure requirements for corporate income taxes, including intraperiod tax allocation.

Income taxes currently payable or receivable are reported separately as a current liability or current asset on the balance sheet. Assuming a single tax authority, future income tax assets and liabilities are classified as one net current amount and one net non-current amount based on the classification of the asset or liability that the temporary difference relates to. If a future tax account arises from something other than an existing balance sheet account, it is classified according to when the temporary differences are expected to reverse. On the income statement, current and future tax expense is disclosed for income before discontinued operations and extraordinary items. Separate disclosure is required of the amounts and expiry dates of unused tax losses, the amount of deductible temporary differences for which no future tax asset has been recognized, and any tax expense related to items that have been charged or credited to equity. For companies that have outstanding financing from public markets, additional disclosures are required about temporary differences and unused tax losses, about the major components of income tax expense, and the reasons for the difference between the statutory tax rate and the effective rate indicated on the income statement. Because the income statement is classified into "Income before Discontinued Operations and Extraordinary Items," "Discontinued Operations," and "Extraordinary Items," the income taxes that are associated with each component are reported with that component. Taxes that relate to items reported in other comprehensive income and retained earnings, and those associated with share capital should also be reported with the related items in the financial statements.

11 Compare current Canadian and international GAAP for income taxes.

Current Canadian and international standards are very similar as they are both based on the asset-liability method. As the FASB and the IASB work on their short-term convergence project in this area, minor changes are likely to be made in the Canadian standard before the changeover to IFRS in 2011.

12 Identify and apply the differential reporting option for income taxes.

For qualifying companies (i.e., non-publicly accountable entities whose owners all agree), the simpler taxes payable method of accounting is permitted for income taxes. Basically, this results in not accounting for future taxes, although considerable disclosure related to future taxes is still required.

13 Identify outstanding issues with the asset-liability method.

Those who agree with the asset-liability approach to comprehensive tax allocation do not necessarily agree on all the issues. There is disagreement about whether the future tax amounts should be discounted, the basis on which future tax assets and liabilities should be classified, and the degree of certainty that should exist before the benefits of future deductible amounts and tax losses should be given accounting recognition.

Brief Exercises

(LO 2) **BE18-1** In 2008, Gonzales Corporation had accounting income of $248,000 and taxable income of $198,000. The difference is due to the use of different amortization methods for tax and accounting purposes. The tax rate is 40%. Calculate the amount to be reported as income taxes payable at December 31, 2008.

(LO 5) **BE18-2** At December 31, 2007, Serbius Corporation had a future tax liability of $35,000. At December 31, 2008, the future tax liability is $52,000. The corporation's 2008 current tax expense is $53,000. What amount should Serbius report as total 2008 income tax expense?

(LO 2, 5) **BE18-3** Jazman Inc. had accounting income of $156,000 in 2008. Included in the calculation of that amount is insurance expense of $5,000, which is not deductible for tax purposes. In addition, the CCA for tax purposes is $14,000 higher than the accounting amortization amount. Prepare Jazman's journal entry to record 2008 taxes, assuming a tax rate of 25%.

(LO 3, 5) **BE18-4** At December 31, 2008, Thunderforce Inc. owned equipment that had a book value of $145,000 and a tax basis of $114,000 due to the use of different amortization methods for accounting and tax purposes. The enacted tax rate is 30%. Calculate the amount that Thunderforce should report as a future tax liability at December 31, 2008.

(LO 3) **BE18-5** Merridit Corp. began operations in 2008 and reported accounting income of $275,000 for the year. Merridit's CCA exceeded its book amortization by $40,000. Merridit's tax rate for 2008 and years thereafter is 35%. In its December 31, 2008, balance sheet, what amount of future income tax liability should be reported?

(LO 4) **BE18-6** At December 31, 2008, Spacene Corporation had an estimated warranty liability of $155,000 for accounting purposes and $0 for tax purposes. (The warranty costs are not deductible until they are paid.) The tax rate is 40%. Calculate the amount that Spacene should report as a future tax asset at December 31, 2008.

(LO 5) **BE18-7** At December 31, 2007, Next Inc. had a future tax asset of $40,000. At December 31, 2008, the future tax asset is $62,000. The corporation's 2008 current tax expense is $70,000. What amount should Next report as total 2008 tax expense?

(LO 2, 5) **BE18-8** Using the information from BE18-5, and assuming that the $40,000 difference is the only difference between Merridit's accounting income and taxable income, prepare the journal entry(ies) to record the current income tax expense, future income tax expense, income taxes payable, and the future income tax liability.

(LO 5) **BE18-9** Using the information from BE18-3, calculate the effective rate of income tax for Jazman Inc. for 2008. Also make a reconciliation from the statutory rate to the effective rate, using percentages.

(LO 6) **BE18-10** Minator Corporation has a taxable temporary difference related to amortization of $715,000 at December 31, 2008. This difference will reverse as follows: 2009, $47,000; 2010, $334,000; and 2011, $334,000. Enacted tax rates are 37% for 2009 and 2010, and 43% for 2011. Calculate the amount that Minator should report as a future tax asset or liability at December 31, 2008.

BE18-11 At December 31, 2007, Ricks Corporation had a future tax asset of $999,000, resulting from future deductible **(LO 6)** amounts of $2.7 million and an enacted tax rate of 37%. In May 2008, new income tax legislation is signed into law that raises the tax rate to 39% for 2008 and future years. Prepare the journal entry for Ricks to adjust the future tax account.

BE18-12 Valquois Corporation had the following tax information: **(LO 7)**

Year	Taxable Income	Tax Rate	Taxes Paid
2005	$390,000	35%	$136,500
2006	$325,000	30%	$ 97,500
2007	$400,000	30%	$120,000

In 2008, Valquois suffered a net operating loss of $550,000, which it decided to carry back. The 2008 enacted tax rate is 29%. Prepare Valquois' entry to record the effect of the loss carryback.

BE18-13 Zoopler Inc. incurred a net operating loss of $580,000 in 2008. Combined income for 2005, 2006, and 2007 **(LO 7, 8)** was $460,000. The tax rate for all years is 35%. Prepare the journal entries to record the benefits of the carryback and the carryforward, assuming it is more likely than not that the benefits of the loss carryforward will be realized.

BE18-14 Use the information for Zoopler Inc. given in BE18-13, but assume instead that it is more likely than not **(LO 7, 8)** that the entire tax loss carryforward will not be realized in future years. Prepare all the journal entries that are necessary at the end of 2008 assuming (a) that Zoopler does not use a valuation allowance account, and (b) that Zoopler uses a valuation allowance account.

BE18-15 Use the information for Zoopler Inc. given in BE18-14. Assume now that Zoopler earns taxable income of **(LO 7, 8)** $25,000 in 2009 and that at the end of 2009 there is still too much uncertainty to recognize a future tax asset. Prepare all the journal entries that are necessary at the end of 2009 assuming (a) that Zoopler does not use a valuation allowance account, and (b) that Zoopler uses a valuation allowance account.

BE18-16 At December 31, 2008, Stargat Corporation has a future tax asset of $340,000. After a careful review of all **(LO 9)** available evidence, it is determined that it is more likely than not that $85,000 of this future tax asset will not be realized. Prepare the necessary journal entry assuming (a) that Stargat does not use a valuation allowance account, and (b) that Stargat uses a valuation allowance account.

BE18-17 In 2008, Bélanger Limited purchased shares of Killeen Corp. at a cost of $45,000. This was the first time the **(LO 10)** company had ever acquired an available-for-sale investment. At December 31, 2008, the Killeen Corp. shares had a fair value of $41,000. Bélanger Limited's income tax rate is 40%. Assume that any gains that are ultimately realized on the sale of the Killeen Corp. shares will be taxable as ordinary income when the gains are realized. Prepare the necessary journal entries to record the unrealized loss and the related income taxes in 2008. Prepare the statement of comprehensive income for Bélanger Limited, beginning with the line for net income of $55,000.

BE18-18 Steagal Corporation had income before income taxes of $220,000 in 2008. Steagal's current income tax **(LO 10)** expense is $53,000, and future income tax expense is $49,000. Prepare Steagal's 2008 income statement, beginning with income before income taxes.

BE18-19 LePage Inc. reported income from continuing operations of $71,000, a loss from discontinued operations of **(LO 10)** $10,000, and an extraordinary gain of $28,000 in 2008, all before income taxes. All items are fully taxable and deductible for tax purposes. Prepare the bottom of the income statement for LePage Inc., beginning with income from continuing operations before income taxes. Assume a tax rate of 25%.

BE18-20 Vector Corporation has temporary differences at December 31, 2008 that result in the following balance **(LO 10)** sheet future tax accounts:

Future tax liability, current	$38,000
Future tax asset, current	$52,000
Future tax liability, non-current	$96,000
Future tax asset, non-current	$27,000

Indicate how these balances will be presented in Vector's December 31, 2008, balance sheet.

BE18-21 Using the information from BE18-3, prepare Jazman's journal entry to record 2008 taxes. Assume a tax rate of **(LO 12)** 25% and that Jazman's shareholders have decided to use the taxes payable method of accounting for income taxes as a permitted differential accounting option.

Exercises

(LO 3) E18-1   (Identify Temporary or Permanent Differences and Show Effects) The accounting for the items in the lettered list that follows is commonly different for financial reporting purposes than it is for tax purposes:

(a) For financial reporting purposes, the straight-line amortization method is used for plant assets that have a useful life of 10 years; for tax purposes, the CCA declining-balance method is used with a rate of 20% (ignore the half-year rule).

(b) A landlord collects rents in advance. Rents are taxable in the period when they are received.

(c) Non-deductible expenses are incurred in obtaining income that is exempt from taxes.

(d) Costs of guarantees and warranties are estimated and accrued for financial reporting purposes.

(e) Instalment sales are accounted for by the accrual method for financial reporting purposes and the cash basis for tax purposes.

(f) For some assets, straight-line amortization is used for both financial reporting purposes and tax purposes but the assets' lives are shorter for tax purposes.

(g) Pension expense is reported on the income statement before it is funded. Pension costs are deductible only when they are funded.

(h) Proceeds are received from a life insurance company because of the death of a key officer (the company carries a policy on key officers).

(i) The company reports dividends received from taxable Canadian corporations as investment income on its income statement, even though the dividends are non-taxable.

(j) Estimated losses on pending lawsuits and claims are accrued for financial reporting purposes. These losses are tax deductible in the period(s) when the related liabilities are settled.

(k) Held-for-trading security investments are adjusted at the end of the year to their fair value. This is the first year that the company has such investments and the fair value is lower than the cost.

(l) An impairment loss is recorded for goodwill in the current accounting period.

Instructions

(a) Match each item in the preceding list to the number below that best describes it:

1. a timing difference that will result in future deductible amounts and, therefore, will usually give rise to a future income tax asset

2. a timing difference that will result in future taxable amounts and, therefore, will usually give rise to a future income tax liability

3. a permanent difference

(b) For each item in the lettered list, indicate if the amounts that are involved in the current year will be added to or deducted from accounting income to arrive at taxable income.

(LO 3) E18-2   (Terminology, Relationships, Calculations, Entries)

Instructions
Complete the following statements by filling in the blanks.

(a) In a period in which a taxable temporary difference reverses, the reversal will cause taxable income to be _____ (less than, greater than) accounting income.

(b) In a period in which a deductible temporary difference reverses, the reversal will cause taxable income to be _____ (less than, greater than) accounting income.

(c) If a $76,000 balance in the Future Tax Asset account was calculated using a 40% rate, the underlying temporary difference amounts to $_____.

(d) Future taxes _____ (are, are not) recorded to account for permanent differences.

(e) If a taxable temporary difference originates in 2008, it causes taxable income of 2008 to be _____ (less than, greater than) accounting income for 2008.

(f) If total tax expense is $50,000 and future tax expense is $65,000, then the current portion of the expense is referred to as a current tax _____ (expense, benefit) of $_____.

(g) If a corporation's tax return shows taxable income of $100,000 for Year 2 and a tax rate of 40%, how much will appear on the December 31, Year 2 balance sheet for "Income tax payable" if the company has made estimated tax payments of $36,500 for Year 2? $_____

(h) An increase in the Future Tax Liability account on the balance sheet is recorded by a _____ (debit, credit) to the Future Income Tax Expense account.

(i) An income statement that reports current tax expense of $82,000 and future tax benefit of $23,000 will report total income tax expense of $_____.

(j) A valuation account may be used whenever it is judged to be more likely than not that a portion of a future tax asset _____ (will be, will not be) realized.

(k) If the tax return shows total taxes due for the period of $75,000 but the income statement shows total income tax expense of $55,000, the difference of $20,000 is referred to as a future tax_____ (expense, benefit).

E18-3 **(Permanent and Timing Differences, Calculate Taxable Income, Entry for Taxes)** Geneva Inc. reports accounting income of $105,000 for 2008. The following items cause taxable income to be different than income reported on the financial statements: **(LO 2, 3, 4, 5)**

1. Capital cost allowance (on the tax return) is greater than amortization on the income statement by $16,000.

2. Rent reported on the tax return is $24,000 higher than rent earned on the income statement.

3. Non-deductible fines for pollution appear as an expense of $11,000 on the income statement.

4. Geneva's tax rate is 30% for all years and the company expects to report taxable income in all future years. There are no future taxes at the beginning of 2008.

Instructions

(a) Calculate taxable income and income taxes payable for 2008.

(b) Calculate any future income tax balances at December 31, 2008.

(c) Prepare the journal entries to record income taxes for 2008.

(d) Prepare the income tax expense section of the income statement for 2008, beginning with the line "Income before income taxes."

(e) Reconcile the statutory and effective rates of income tax for 2008.

(f) Provide the balance sheet disclosure for any resulting future tax balance sheet accounts at December 31, 2008. Be specific about the classification.

E18-4 **(One Temporary Difference, Future Taxable Amounts, One Rate, No Beginning Future Taxes)** Mattice Limited had held-for-trading (HFT) investments on its balance sheet for the first time at the end of its fiscal year ending December 31, 2009. During 2009, realized losses and gains on the trading of shares and bonds resulted in investment income, which is fully taxable in the year. Mattice also accrued unrealized gains at December 31, 2009, which are not taxable until the investment securities are sold. The portfolio of trading securities had an original cost of $314,450 and a fair value of $318,200. The entry recorded by Mattice on December 31, 2009, was as follows: **(LO 2, 3, 5)**

Investments (HFT)	3,750	
Investment Income/Loss (HFT)		3,750

Income before income taxes for Mattice was $302,000 for the year ended December 31, 2009. There are no other permanent or timing differences in arriving at the taxable income for Mattice Limited for the fiscal year ending December 31, 2009. The enacted tax rate for 2009 and future years is 42%.

Instructions

(a) Explain the tax treatment that should be given to the unrealized gain that Mattice Limited reported on its income statement.

(b) Calculate the future income tax balance at December 31, 2009.

(c) Calculate the current income tax for the year ending December 31, 2009.

(d) Prepare the journal entries to record income taxes for 2009.

(e) Prepare the income statement for 2009, beginning with the line "Income before income taxes."

(f) Provide the balance sheet disclosure for any resulting income tax balance sheet accounts at December 31, 2009. Be clear on the classification you have chosen and explain your choice.

(LO 2, 3, 4, 5) **E18-5** **(One Temporary Difference, Future Taxable Amount Becomes Future Deductible Amount, One Rate, Change in Rate)** Refer to the information for Mattice Limited in E18-4. Following the year ended December 31, 2009, Mattice continued to actively trade its HFT investments until the end of its 2010 fiscal year when it was forced to sell several of its investments at a loss, because of the need for cash for operations. By December 31, 2010, the portfolio of investments contained a single investment in shares, which was purchased in November 2010. Mattice Limited had paid $42,000 for these remaining shares. At December 31, 2010, the market value of the shares was $40,000. Income before income taxes for Mattice was $120,000 for the year ended December 31, 2010. There are no other permanent or timing differences in arriving at the taxable income for Mattice Limited for the fiscal year ending December 31, 2010. The enacted tax rate for 2010 and future years is 42%.

Instructions

(a) Prepare the necessary journal entry for Mattice Limited to accrue the unrealized loss on its HFT investments.

(b) Explain the tax treatment that should be given to the unrealized accrued loss that Mattice Limited reported on its income statement.

(c) Calculate the future income tax balance at December 31, 2010.

(d) Calculate the current income tax for the year ending December 31, 2010.

(e) Prepare the journal entries to record income taxes for 2010. Assume that there have been no entries to the ending balances of future taxes reported at December 31, 2009.

(f) Prepare the income statement for 2010, beginning with the line "Income before income taxes."

(g) Provide the balance sheet disclosure for any resulting future tax balance sheet account at December 31, 2010. Be clear on the classification you have chosen and explain your choice.

(h) Prepare the journal entries in part (e) under the assumption that, late in 2010, the income tax rate changed to 40% for 2011 and subsequent years.

(LO 2, 4, 5) **E18-6** **(One Temporary Difference, Future Taxable Amounts, One Rate, No Beginning Future Taxes)** North River Corporation purchased equipment very late in 2008. Based on generous capital cost allowances rates provided in the *Income Tax Act*, North River Corporation claimed CCA on its 2008 tax return but did not record any amortization as the equipment had not yet been put into use. This temporary difference will reverse and cause taxable amounts of $25,000 in 2009, $30,000 in 2010, and $40,000 in 2011. North River's accounting income for 2008 is $200,000 and the tax rate is 40% for all years. There are no future tax accounts at the beginning of 2008.

Instructions

(a) Calculate the future income tax balance at December 31, 2008.

(b) Calculate taxable income and income taxes payable for 2008.

(c) Prepare the journal entries to record income taxes for 2008.

(d) Prepare the income tax expense section of the income statement for 2008, beginning with the line "Income before income taxes."

(LO 2, 4, 5) **E18-7** **(One Temporary Difference, Future Taxable Amounts, One Rate, Beginning Future Taxes)** Use the information for North River Corporation in E18-6, and assume that the company reports accounting income of $180,000 in each of 2009 and 2010, and no other temporary differences than the one identified in E18-6.

Instructions

(a) Calculate the future income tax balances at December 31, 2009 and 2010.

(b) Calculate taxable income and income taxes payable for 2009 and 2010.

(c) Prepare the journal entries to record income taxes for 2009 and 2010.

(d) Prepare the income tax expense section of the income statements for 2009 and 2010, beginning with the line "Income before income taxes."

(e) What trend do you notice in the amount of net income reported for 2009 and 2010 in part (d)? Is this a coincidence? Explain.

E18-8　(One Temporary Difference, Future Taxable Amounts, No Beginning Future Taxes, Change in Rate) **(LO 2,** Use the information for North River Corporation in E18-6, and assume that the company reports accounting income of **4, 5)** $180,000 in each of 2009 and 2010, and no other temporary differences than the one identified in E18-6. In addition, assume now that North River Corporation was informed on December 31, 2009, that the enacted rate for 2010 and subsequent years is 35%.

Instructions

(a) Calculate the future income tax balances at December 31, 2009 and 2010.

(b) Calculate taxable income and income taxes payable for 2009 and 2010.

(c) Prepare the journal entries to record income taxes for 2009 and 2010.

(d) Prepare the income tax expense section of the income statements for 2009 and 2010, beginning with the line "Income before income taxes."

E18-9　(One Temporary Difference, Future Deductible Amounts, One Rate, No Beginning Future Taxes) South **(LO 2,** Shore Corporation recorded warranty accruals as of December 31, 2008 in the amount of $130,000. This temporary dif- **3, 5)** ference will reverse and cause deductible amounts of $50,000 in 2009, $35,000 in 2010, and $45,000 in 2011. South Shore's accounting income for 2008 is $135,000 and the tax rate is 25% for all years. There are no future tax accounts at the beginning of 2008.

Instructions

(a) Calculate the future income tax balance at December 31, 2008.

(b) Calculate taxable income and current income taxes payable for 2008.

(c) Prepare the journal entries to record income taxes for 2008.

(d) Prepare the income tax expense section of the income statement for 2008, beginning with the line "Income before income taxes."

E18-10　(One Temporary Difference, Future Deductible Amounts, One Rate, Beginning Future Taxes) Use the **(LO 2,** information for South Shore Corporation in E18-9, and assume that the company reports accounting income of $155,000 **3, 5)** in each of 2009 and 2010 and the warranty expenditures occurred as expected. No other temporary differences exist other than the one identified in E18-9.

Instructions

(a) Calculate the future income tax balances at December 31, 2009 and 2010.

(b) Calculate taxable income and income taxes payable for 2009 and 2010.

(c) Prepare the journal entries to record income taxes for 2009 and 2010.

(d) Prepare the income tax expense section of the income statements for 2009 and 2010, beginning with the line "Income before income taxes."

(e) What trend do you notice in the amount of net income reported for 2009 and 2010 in part (d)? Is this a coincidence? Explain.

E18-11　(One Temporary Difference, Future Deductible Amounts, No Beginning Future Taxes, Change in Rate) **(LO 2,** Use the information for South Shore Corporation in E18-9, and assume that the company reports accounting income of **3, 5)** $155,000 in each of 2009 and 2010, and no other temporary differences than the one identified in E18-9. In addition, assume now that South Shore Corporation was informed on December 31, 2009 that the enacted rate for 2010 and subsequent years is 28%.

Instructions

(a) Calculate the future income tax balances at December 31, 2009 and 2010.

(b) Calculate taxable income and income taxes payable for 2009 and 2010.

(c) Prepare the journal entries to record income taxes for 2009 and 2010.

(d) Prepare the income tax expense section of the income statements for 2009 and 2010, beginning with the line "Income before income taxes."

(LO 2, 3, 4, 5)   E18-12   (Two Temporary Differences, Future Taxable and Deductible Amounts, No Beginning Future Taxes, One Tax Rate) Miron Sand and Gravel Ltd. operates a road construction business. In its first year of operations, the company obtained a contract to construct a road for the municipality of Temiskaming Shores, and it is estimated that the project will be completed over a three-year period starting in June 2008. Miron uses the percentage-of-completion method of recognizing revenue on its long-term construction contracts. For tax purposes, and in order to postpone the tax on such revenue for as long as possible, Miron uses the completed-contract method allowed by the CRA. By its first fiscal year end, the accounts related to the contract had the following balances:

Accounts Receivable	$320,000
Construction in Process	500,000
Revenue from Long-Term Contract	500,000
Construction Expense	350,000
Billings on Construction in Process	400,000

The accounts related to the equipment that Miron purchased to construct the road had the following balances at the end of the first fiscal year ending December 31, 2008 for accounting and tax purposes:

Construction Equipment	$1,100,000
Accumulated Amortization—Construction Equipment	170,000
Undepreciated Capital Cost	980,000

Miron's tax rate is 45% for 2008 and subsequent years. Income before income tax for the year ended December 31, 2008, was $195,000.

Instructions

(a) Calculate the future income tax asset or liability balances at December 31, 2008.

(b) Calculate taxable income and income taxes payable for 2008.

(c) Prepare the journal entries to record income taxes for 2008.

(d) Prepare the income statement for 2008, beginning with the line "Income before income taxes."

(e) Provide the balance sheet disclosure for any resulting future tax balance sheet accounts at December 31, 2008. Be specific about the classification.

(LO 2, 3, 4, 5)   E18-13   (Two Temporary Differences, Future Taxable and Deductible Amounts, Beginning Future Taxes, One Tax Rate) Refer to E18-12 for Miron Sand and Gravel Ltd., and assume the same facts for the fiscal year ending December 31, 2008. For the second year of operations, Miron made progress on the construction of the road for the municipality. The account balances at December 31, 2009 for the construction project and the accounting and tax balances of accounts related to the equipment used for construction follow (the balances at December 31, 2008 are also listed):

	2009	2008
Accounts Receivable	$ 105,000	$ 320,000
Construction in Process	940,000	500,000
Revenue from Long-Term Contract	440,000	500,000
Construction Expense	410,000	350,000
Billings on Construction in Process	390,000	400,000
Construction Equipment	1,100,000	1,100,000
Accumulated Amortization—Construction Equipment	460,000	170,000
Undepreciated Capital Cost	620,000	980,000

Miron's tax rate continues to be 45% for 2009 and subsequent years. Income before income tax for the year ended December 31, 2009 was $120,000.

Instructions

(a) Calculate the future income tax asset or liability balances at December 31, 2009.

(b) Calculate taxable income and income taxes payable for 2009.

(c) Prepare the journal entries to record income taxes for 2009.

(d) Prepare a comparative income statement for 2008 and 2009, beginning with the line "Income before income taxes."

(e) Provide the comparative balance sheet disclosure for any resulting future tax balance sheet accounts at December 31, 2008 and 2009. Be specific about the classification.

E18-14 (**Two Temporary Differences, Future Taxable and Deductible Amounts, Beginning Future Taxes, Change in Tax Rate**) Refer to E18-13 for Miron Sand and Gravel Ltd., and assume the same facts as in E18-13 for the fiscal year ending December 31, 2009, except that the enacted tax rate for 2010 and subsequent years has been reduced to 40%. **(LO 2, 3, 4, 5)**

Instructions

(a) Calculate any future income tax balances at December 31, 2009.

(b) Calculate taxable income and income taxes payable for 2009.

(c) Prepare the journal entries to record income taxes for 2009.

(d) Prepare a comparative income statement for 2008 and 2009, beginning with the line "Income before income taxes."

(e) Provide the comparative balance sheet disclosure for any resulting future tax balance sheet accounts at December 31, 2008 and 2009. Be specific about the classification.

E18-15 (**Amortization, Temporary Difference over Five Years, Determine Taxable Income, Taxes Payable Method**) Patrician Corp. purchased depreciable assets costing $600,000 on January 2, 2007. For tax purposes, the company uses CCA in a class that has a 40% rate. For financial reporting purposes, the company uses straight-line amortization over five years. The enacted tax rate is 34% for all years. This amortization difference is the only temporary difference the company has. Assume that Patrician has income before income taxes of $340,000 in each of the years 2007 to 2011. **(LO 3, 5, 12)**

Instructions

(a) Calculate the amount of capital cost allowance and amortization expense from 2007 to 2011, as well as the corresponding balances for net book value and undepreciated capital cost of the depreciable assets at the end of each of the years 2007 to 2011.

(b) Determine the amount of taxable income in each year from 2007 to 2011.

(c) Determine the amount of future income taxes that should be reported in the balance sheet for each year from 2007 to 2011.

(d) Prepare the journal entries to record income taxes for each year from 2007 to 2011.

(e) Prepare the income tax entry(ies) to record income taxes for each year, assuming the shareholders have decided on the differential accounting option (taxes payable basis).

E18-16 (**One Temporary Difference through Three Years, One Rate**) Odessa Corporation reports the following amounts in its first three years of operations: **(LO 3)**

	2008	2009	2010
Taxable income	$160,000	$139,000	$131,000
Accounting income	245,000	121,000	125,000

The difference between taxable income and accounting income is due to one timing difference. The tax rate is 35% for all years and the company expects to continue with profitable operations in the future.

Instructions

(a) For each year, (1) identify the amount of the temporary difference originating or reversing during that year, and (2) indicate the amount of the temporary difference at the end of the year.

(b) Indicate the balance in the related future tax account at the end of each year and identify it as either a future tax asset or liability.

E18-17 (**Timing and Permanent Differences, Future Taxable and Deductible Amounts, No Beginning Future Taxes, Several Tax Rates**) Naud Holding Inc. owns commercial property consisting mainly of strip malls that generate rental revenue. Due to a shift in retail customers' shopping trends, Naud entered into inducement agreements with its existing and new tenants for the first time in 2009. Naud's objective in offering inducements is to secure lease rates that are slightly higher than the market rate for terms of a minimum of three years. Naud offered rent-free periods of up to six months to tenants to induce them to sign new leases or renew existing leases for its properties. **(LO 2, 3, 4, 5)**

Naud's accounting policy related to the rent-free periods consists of allocating the revenue from the leases evenly over all months of the lease. For tax purposes, Naud is allowed to use the cash basis. By using the cash basis for tax purposes, Naud can postpone the tax related to the rent revenue. For financial reporting purposes, the rent revenue is accrued during the rent-free periods in an account called Rent Recoverable. Following the rent-free period, the Rent Recoverable account is amortized to Rent Revenue over the remaining term of each lease.

Naud's lease agreements also call for the tenants to make quarterly rental payments three months in advance. These rental payments are initially recorded as unearned rent revenue for accounting purposes. The CRA requires that Naud report the rental revenue in the accounting period in which the rent is collected.

During the fiscal year ending December 31, 2009, Naud paid pollution fines and interest on late and deficient income tax instalments, and received non-taxable dividends.

At December 31, 2009, Naud had the following balances for the accounts related to the information above:

Rent Recoverable (assume non-current classification)	$440,000
Unearned Rent Revenue (assume current classification and no balance at Dec. 31, 2008)	360,000
Dividend Income	15,000
Fines Expense (non-tax deductible)	34,000
Tax Instalment Interest Expense (non-tax deductible)	4,000

Naud's tax rate is 42% for 2009 and 40% for subsequent years. Income before income tax for the year ended December 31, 2009, was $1,140,000.

Instructions

(a) Calculate the future income tax asset or liability balances at December 31, 2009.

(b) Calculate taxable income and income taxes payable for 2009.

(c) Prepare the journal entries to record income taxes for 2009.

(d) Prepare the income statement for 2009, beginning with the line "Income before income taxes."

(e) Provide the balance sheet disclosure for any resulting future tax balance sheet accounts at December 31, 2009. Be specific about the classification.

(f) Calculate the effective rate of tax. Provide a reconciliation and explanation why this differs from the statutory rate of 42%. Begin the reconciliation with the statutory rate.

(LO 2, 3, 4, 5)   **E18-18   (Timing and Permanent Differences, Future Taxable and Deductible Amounts, Beginning Future Taxes, Several Tax Rates)** Refer to E18-17 for Naud Holding Inc., and assume the same facts for the fiscal year ending December 31, 2009. During the next year of operations, 2010, Naud continued to offer rent-free periods to its tenants as an inducement to renew or sign new leases for its rental properties. The balances for the accounts related to its rental operations and for the payments for interest on late and deficient tax instalments, and the balance for non-taxable dividend income for the year ending December 31, 2010 follow (balances at December 31, 2009, are also listed):

	2010	2009
Rent Recoverable (assume non-current classification)	$350,000	$440,000
Unearned Rent Revenue (assume current classification)	410,000	360,000
Dividend Income	20,000	15,000
Fines Expense		34,000
Tax Instalment Interest Expense	6,000	4,000

Naud's tax rate is 40% for 2010 and subsequent years. Income before income tax for the year ended December 31, 2010 was $1.28 million.

Instructions

(a) Calculate the future income tax asset or liability balances at December 31, 2010.

(b) Calculate taxable income and income taxes payable for 2010.

(c) Prepare the journal entries to record income taxes for 2010.

(d) Prepare a comparative income statement for 2009 and 2010, beginning with the line "Income before income taxes."

(e) Provide the comparative balance sheet disclosure for any resulting future tax balance sheet accounts at December 31, 2009 and 2010. Be specific about the classification.

(f) Calculate the effective rate of tax. Provide a reconciliation and explanation of why this differs from the statutory rate of 40%. Begin the reconciliation with the statutory rate.

(LO 2, 3, 4, 5)   **E18-19   (Timing and Permanent Differences, Future Taxable and Deductible Amounts, No Beginning Future Taxes, Several Tax Rates)** Strand Tools Ltd. operates tool repair outlets and is a tenant in several of Naud Holding Inc.'s strip malls (see E18-17). Strand signed several lease renewals with Naud that each called for a three-month rent-free period. The leases start at various dates and are for three to five years each. As with all of Naud's tenants, Strand pays rent quarterly, three months in advance, and records the payments initially to Prepaid Rent.

The rent-free period obtained in the lease agreement with Naud Holding Inc. reduces the overall rental costs of the outlets over the term of each lease. Strand's accounting policy requires the leasing costs of each outlet to be allocated evenly over the term of the lease to fairly match expenses with revenues. Stand accrues rent expense during the rent-free period to an account called Rent Payable. Following the rent-free period, the Rent Payable account is amortized to Rent Expense over the remaining term of the lease. For tax purposes, Strand must use the cash basis and is unable to deduct the rent expense accrued during the rent-free periods. On its tax return, Strand can only deduct the actual rent payments when they are paid.

By December 31, 2009, its fiscal year end, Strand Tools Ltd. had the following balances related to rent-free periods and its prepaid rent. Details of non-deductible expenses are also provided.

Prepaid Rent (assume current classification and no balance at Dec. 31, 2008)	$ 89,000
Rent Payable (assume non-current classification and no balance at Dec. 31, 2008)	146,000
Golf Dues Expense	13,000
Interest Expense (incurred to earn tax exempt income)	4,000

Strand's tax rate is 43% for 2009 and 42% for subsequent years. Income before income tax for the year ended December 31, 2009, was $884,000.

Instructions

(a) Calculate the future income tax asset or liability balances at December 31, 2009.

(b) Calculate taxable income and income taxes payable for 2009.

(c) Prepare the journal entries to record income taxes for 2009.

(d) Prepare the income statement for 2009, beginning with the line "Income before income taxes."

(e) Provide the balance sheet disclosure for any resulting future tax balance sheet accounts at December 31, 2009. Be specific about the classification.

(f) Calculate the effective rate of tax. Provide a reconciliation and explanation of why this differs from the statutory rate of 43%. Begin the reconciliation with the statutory rate.

E18-20 (Timing and Permanent Differences, Future Taxable and Deductible Amounts, No Beginning Future Taxes, Change in Rates) Refer to E18-19 for Strand Tools Ltd., and assume the same facts for the fiscal year ending December 31, 2009. During 2010, Strand continued to sign leases with Naud Holding Inc. for premises, receiving rent-free periods as inducements to renew leases or sign new ones. Under the terms of the leases, Strand continued to pay rent quarterly, three months in advance. **(LO 2, 3, 4, 5)**

The balances for the accounts related to prepaid rent and rent payable under leases as well as payments for interest to earn tax-exempt income and payments for golf dues for the year ending December 31, 2010 follow (balances at December 31, 2009 are also shown):

	2010	2009
Prepaid Rent (assume current classification)	$ 92,000	$ 89,000
Rent Payable (assume non-current classification)	133,000	146,000
Golf Dues Expense	11,000	13,000
Interest Expense (incurred to earn tax exempt income)	6,000	4,000

During 2010, Strand's tax rate changed to 44% for 2010 and subsequent years. Income before income tax for the year ended December 31, 2010 was $997,000.

Instructions

(a) Calculate the future income tax asset or liability balances at December 31, 2010.

(b) Calculate taxable income and income taxes payable for 2010.

(c) Prepare the journal entries to record income taxes for 2010.

(d) Prepare a comparative income statement for 2009 and 2010, beginning with the line "Income before income taxes."

(e) Provide the comparative balance sheet disclosure for any resulting future tax balance sheet accounts at December 31, 2009 and 2010. Be specific about the classification.

(f) Calculate the effective rate of tax. Provide a reconciliation and explanation of why this differs from the statutory rate of 44%. Begin the reconciliation with the statutory rate.

(LO 2, 3, 4, 5)   **E18-21   (Timing and Permanent Differences, Future Taxable Amount, No Beginning Future Taxes)** Aaron Inc. holds a variety of investments, some of which are classified as held for trading, and some of which are classified as available for sale. On January 1, 2008, the beginning of the fiscal year, Aaron's accounts and records include the following information:

	Cost	Market Value
Held-for-trading investments	$60,000	$60,000
Available-for-sale investments	$71,000	$71,000

Market values for the held-for-trading investments and available-for-sale investments at December 31, 2008 were $58,000 and $75,000, respectively. Computers that are used to track investment performance were purchased during 2008 for $10,000. The CRA places computers in Class 10 with a CCA rate of 30%. Amortization expense for the year was $2,000. Aaron recorded meals and entertainment expenses of $12,000 related to wining and dining clients. The CRA allows 50% of these costs as deductible business expense.

Aaron's income before income taxes for 2008 is $110,000. This amount does not include any entries to adjust investments to market values at December 31, 2008. Aaron's tax rate for 2008 is 40%, although changes enacted in tax legislation before December 31, 2008, result in an increase in this rate to 45% for 2009 and subsequent taxation years. Assume that these rates apply to all income that is reported. There were no future tax accounts at January 1, 2008.

Instructions

(a) Prepare journal entries to reflect the difference between the carrying amount and market value for the above investments at Aaron's year end of December 31, 2008.

(b) Explain the tax treatment that should be given to the unrealized accrued gains or losses reported on Aaron Inc.'s statement of income and statement of comprehensive income.

(c) Calculate the future income tax asset or liability balances at December 31, 2008, and indicate their classification.

(d) Calculate taxable income and income taxes payable for 2008.

(e) Prepare the journal entries to record income taxes for 2008.

(LO 3, 6)   **E18-22   (One Difference, Multiple Rates, Beginning Future Taxes, Change in Rates)** At the end of 2007, McNevil Corporation reported a future tax liability of $31,000. At the end of 2008, the company had $201,000 of temporary differences related to property, plant, and equipment. Amortization expense on this property, plant, and equipment has been lower than the CCA claimed on McNevil's income tax returns. The resulting future taxable amounts are as follows:

2009	$ 67,000
2010	50,000
2011	45,000
2012	39,000
	$201,000

The tax rates enacted as of the beginning of 2007 are as follows: 40% for 2007 and 2008; 30% for 2009 and 2010; 25% for 2011 and later. Taxable income is expected in all future years.

Instructions

(a) Calculate the future tax account balance at December 31, 2008.

(b) Prepare the journal entry for McNevil to record future income taxes for 2008.

(c) Early in 2009, after the 2008 financial statements were released, new tax rates were enacted as follows: 29% for 2009; 27% for 2010 and later. Prepare the journal entry for McNevil to recognize the change in tax rates.

(LO 3, 6)   **E18-23   (Future Tax Liability, Change in Tax Rate)** Notkovich Inc.'s only temporary difference at the beginning and end of 2008 is caused by a $3.3 million deferred gain for tax purposes on an instalment sale of a plant asset. The related receivable (only one-half of which is classified as a current asset) is due in equal instalments in 2009 and 2010. The related future tax liability at the beginning of the year is $1.32 million. In the third quarter of 2008, a new tax rate of 39% is enacted into law and is scheduled to become effective for 2010. Taxable income is expected in all future years.

Instructions

(a) Determine the amount to be reported as a future tax liability at the end of 2008. Indicate its proper classification(s).

(b) Prepare the journal entry (if any) that is necessary to adjust the future tax liability when the new tax rate is enacted into law.

E18-24 **(Loss Carryback)** Beilman Inc. reports the following incomes (losses) for both book and tax purposes (assume **(LO 7)** the carryback provision is used where possible):

Year	Accounting Income (Loss)	Tax Rate
2006	$120,000	40%
2007	90,000	40%
2008	(80,000)	45%
2009	(40,000)	45%

The tax rates listed were all enacted by the beginning of 2006.

Instructions

(a) Prepare the journal entries for each of the years 2006 to 2009 to record income taxes.

(b) Prepare the income tax section of the income statements for each of the years 2006 to 2009, beginning with the line "Income (loss) before income taxes."

E18-25 **(Carryback and Carryforward of Tax Loss)** The accounting income (or loss) figures for Spangler **(LO 7, 8)** Corporation are as follows:

2003	$ 160,000
2004	250,000
2005	80,000
2006	(160,000)
2007	(380,000)
2008	130,000
2009	145,000

Accounting income (or loss) and taxable income (loss) were the same for all years involved. Assume a 45% tax rate for 2003 and 2004, and a 40% tax rate for the remaining years.

Instructions

Prepare the journal entries for each of the years 2005 to 2009 to record income tax expense and the effects of the tax loss carrybacks and carryforwards assuming Spangler Corporation uses the carryback provision first. All income and losses relate to normal operations and it is more likely than not that the company will generate substantial taxable income in the future.

E18-26 **(Loss Carryback and Carryforward)** Spamela Inc. reports the following pre-tax incomes (losses) for both **(LO 7, 8)** financial reporting purposes and tax purposes:

Year	Accounting Income (Loss)	Tax Rate
2006	$ 120,000	34%
2007	90,000	34%
2008	$(280,000)	38%
2009	220,000	38%

The tax rates listed were all enacted by the beginning of 2006.

Instructions

(a) Prepare the journal entries for each of the years 2006 to 2009 to record income taxes, assuming the tax loss is first carried back, and that at the end of 2008, the loss carryforward benefits are judged more likely than not to be realized in the future.

(b) Using the assumption as in (a), prepare the income tax section of the 2008 and 2009 income statements, beginning with the line "Income (loss) before income taxes."

(c) Prepare the journal entries for 2008 and 2009, assuming that it is more likely than not that 25% of the carryforward benefits will not be realized. A valuation allowance is not used by this company.

(d) Using the assumption in (c), prepare the income tax section of the 2008 and 2009 income statements, beginning with the line "Income (loss) before income taxes."

E18-27 **(Loss Carryback and Carryforward Using a Valuation Allowance)** Refer to the information for Spamela **(LO 7,** Inc. in E18-26.   **8, 9)**

Instructions

(a) Assume that Spamela Inc. uses a valuation allowance to account for future tax assets, and also that it is more likely than not that 25% of the carryforward benefits will not be realized. Prepare the journal entries for 2008 and 2009.

(b) Based on your entries in (a), prepare the income tax section of the 2008 and 2009 income statements, beginning with the line "Income (loss) before income taxes."

(c) Indicate how the future tax asset account will be reported on the December 31, 2008 and 2009, balance sheets.

(d) Assume that on June 30, 2009, the enacted tax rates changed for 2009. Should management record any adjustment to the accounts? If yes, which accounts will be involved and when should the adjustment be recorded?

(LO 9)   E18-28   (Future Tax Asset—Different Amounts to Be Realized) Marshall Corp. had a future tax asset account with a balance of $101,500 at the end of 2007 due to a single temporary difference of $290,000 related to warranty liability accruals. At the end of 2008, this same temporary difference has increased to $315,000. Taxable income for 2008 is $887,000. The tax rate is 35% for all years.

Instructions

(a) Calculate and record income taxes for 2008, assuming that it is more likely than not that the future tax asset will be realized.

(b) 1. Assuming that it is more likely than not that $30,000 of the future tax asset will not be realized, prepare the journal entries to record income taxes for 2008. Marshall does not use a valuation allowance account.

  2. In 2009, prospects for the company improved. While there was no change in the temporary deductible differences underlying the future tax asset account, it was now considered more likely than not that the company would be able to make full use of the temporary differences. Prepare the entry, if applicable, to adjust the future tax asset account.

(LO 9)   E18-29   (Future Tax Asset—Different Amounts to Be Realized; Valuation Allowance) Refer to the information provided about Marshall Corp. in E18-28.

Instructions

(a) Assuming that it is more likely than not that $30,000 of the future tax asset will not be realized, prepare the journal entries to record income taxes for 2008. Marshall uses a valuation allowance account.

(b) In 2009, prospects for the company improved. While there was no change in the temporary deductible differences underlying the future tax asset account, it was now considered more likely than not that the company would be able to make full use of the temporary differences. Prepare the entry, if applicable, to adjust the future tax asset and related account(s).

(LO 10)   E18-30   (Three Differences, Classification of Future Taxes) At December 31, 2008, Surya Corporation had a net future tax liability of $375,000. An explanation of the items that make up this balance follows:

Temporary Differences	Resulting Balances in Future Tax Account
1. Excess of accumulated tax amortization over book amortization	$230,000
2. Accrual, for book purposes, of estimated loss contingency from pending lawsuit that is expected to be settled in 2009. The loss will be deducted on the tax return when it is paid.	(80,000)
3. Accrual method (account receivable) used for book purposes and instalment method used for tax purposes for an isolated instalment sale of an investment, due in 2010.	225,000
	$375,000

Instructions

Indicate how future taxes should be presented on Surya Corporation's December 31, 2008, balance sheet.

(LO 3)   E18-31   (Intraperiod Tax Allocation—Other Comprehensive Income) Stratcona Technologies Inc. held a portfolio of shares and bonds that it classified as available-for-sale securities on its balance sheet at December 31, 2008. This was the first year that Stratcona had purchased investments. In part due to Stratcona's inexperience, by December 31, 2008, the market value of the portfolio had dropped below its original cost by $28,000. Stratcona recorded the necessary adjustments at December 31, 2008, and was determined to hold the securities until the unrealized loss of 2008 could be recovered. By December 31, 2009, Stratcona's goals of recovery had been realized and the original portfolio of shares and bonds had a fair market value $5,500 higher than the original purchase costs. Stratcona's income tax rate is 38% for all years. Assume that any gains that will ultimately be realized on the sale of the shares and bonds are taxable as ordinary income when they are realized.

Instructions

(a) Prepare the journal entries at December 31, 2008 to accrue the unrealized loss on available-for-sale securities and the related income taxes.

(b) Prepare the journal entries at December 31, 2009 to accrue the unrealized gain on available-for-sale securities and the related income taxes.

(c) Prepare a comparative statement of comprehensive income for the fiscal years ending December 31, 2008 and 2009. Assume net income of $100,000 in each fiscal year.

E18-32 **(Intraperiod Tax Allocation—Extraordinary Item)** Wang Corp. had a profitable year on its regular operations in 2008, reporting $1,745,000 in income before income taxes. Unfortunately, a major decision was handed down by the courts in late November 2008 that found Wang responsible for environmental damage to prime farmland over the previous 10-year period. Wang is not insured for such a risk and the company expects it will cost approximately $2.2 million to correct this problem. Wang has reported this as an extraordinary item on its 2008 income statement. Part of this estimated loss, $170,000, is a fine levied by the province and it is not a deductible expense for tax purposes. The remainder is deductible, but not until 2009, when the costs will actually be incurred. **(LO 10)**

In completing the tax return for 2008, Wang noted that its accounting income included $100,000 of dividends from taxable Canadian corporations and $12,800 of golf club dues for top management. There were no future income tax assets or liabilities on the December 31, 2007 financial statements. The tax rate applicable to 2008 and future years is 32%.

Instructions

(a) Calculate income taxes payable and the amount of any future income tax asset or liability at the end of 2008.

(b) Prepare the journal entries to record income taxes for 2008.

(c) Indicate how income taxes will be reported on the income statement for 2008 by preparing the bottom portion of the statement, beginning with "Income before taxes and extraordinary items."

E18-33 **(Intraperiod Tax Allocation—Discontinued Operations)** Yining Corp.'s operations in 2008 had mixed results. One division, Vista Group, again failed to earn income at a rate that was high enough to justify its continued operation, and management therefore decided to close the division. Vista Group earned revenue of $118,000 during 2008 and recognized total expenses of $110,500. The remaining two divisions reported revenues of $273,000 and total expenses of $216,000 in 2008. **(LO 10)**

In preparing the annual income tax return, Yining's controller took into account the following information:

1. The CCA exceeded amortization expense by $3,700. There were no amortizable assets in the Vista Group division.

2. Included in Vista's expenses is an accrued litigation loss of $5,100 that is not deductible for tax purposes until 2009.

3. Included in the continuing divisions' expenses are the president's golf club dues of $4,500, and their revenues include $1,700 of dividends from taxable Canadian corporations.

4. There were no future tax account balances for any of the divisions on January 1, 2008.

5. The tax rate for 2008 and future years is 35%.

Instructions

(a) Calculate the taxable income and income taxes payable by Yining Corp. in 2008 and the future income tax asset or liability balances at December 31, 2008.

(b) Prepare the journal entry(ies) to record income taxes for 2008.

(c) Indicate how income taxes will be reported on the income statement for 2008 by preparing the bottom portion of the statement, beginning with "Income before taxes and discontinued operations." Assume that 10,000 common shares were outstanding throughout 2008.

(d) Provide the balance sheet disclosure for any resulting future tax balance sheet accounts at December 31, 2008. Be specific about the classification.

E18-34 **(Taxes Payable Method—Differential Reporting Disclosures)** Refer to the information in E18-4 for Mattice Limited. Assume that the company is not publicly accountable and that its shareholders have agreed that the taxes payable method of accounting will be used for income taxes. **(LO 10, 12)**

Instructions

(a) Prepare the journal entry(ies) to record income taxes at December 31, 2009.

(b) Prepare the income statement for 2009, beginning with the line "Income before income taxes."

(c) Provide the balance sheet disclosure for any resulting income tax balance sheet accounts at December 31, 2009.

(d) Prepare the additional disclosures that become necessary because the taxes payable method is being used.

(e) Now that Mattice Limited has adopted the taxes payable method, what do you believe would be the reaction of creditors to this accounting policy when they read Mattice's financial statements? Explain.

(LO 12)   E18-35   (Taxes Payable Method) Refer to the information in E18-3 for Geneva Inc. Assume that the company is not publicly accountable and that its shareholders have agreed that the taxes payable method of accounting will be used for income taxes. During the year, Geneva Inc. made tax instalment payments of $42,000.

Instructions

(a) Calculate the taxable income and tax expense for the year ended December 31, 2008.

(b) Prepare the journal entry(ies) to record income taxes at December 31, 2008.

(c) Prepare the income statement for 2008, beginning with the line "Income before income taxes."

(d) Provide the balance sheet disclosure for any resulting income tax balance sheet accounts at December 31, 2008.

Problems

P18-1   Silver Ltd. began business on January 1, 2008. At December 31, 2008, it had a $3,000 balance in the future tax liability account that pertains to property, plant, and equipment previously acquired at a cost of $1 million. The tax basis of these assets at December 31, 2008, was $940,000; the accounting basis was $950,000. Silver's income before taxes for 2009 was $80,000.

The following items caused the only differences between accounting income before income taxes and taxable income in 2009:

1. In 2009, the company paid $75,000 for rent; of this amount, $25,000 was expensed in 2009. The other $50,000 will be expensed equally over the year 2010 and 2011 accounting periods. The full $75,000 was deducted for tax purposes in 2009.

2. Silver Ltd. pays $5,000 a year for a membership in a local golf club for the company's president.

3. Silver Ltd. now offers a one-year warranty on all its merchandise sold. Warranty expenses for 2009 were $12,000. Cash payments in 2009 for warranty repairs were $6,000.

4. Meals and entertainment expenses (only 50% of which are ever tax deductible) totalled $10,000 for 2009.

5. Amortization expense was $50,000 and CCA was $55,000 for 2009. No new assets were acquired in the year, and there were no asset disposals.

Income tax rates have not changed over the past five years.

Instructions

(a) Calculate the balance in the Future Income Tax Asset/Liability account at December 31, 2009.

(b) Calculate income taxes payable for 2009.

(c) Prepare the journal entries to record income taxes for 2009.

(d) Prepare the income tax expense section of the income statement for 2009, beginning with the line "Income before income taxes."

(e) Indicate how future income taxes should be presented on the December 31, 2009 balance sheet.

P18-2   At December 31, 2007, Hewlett Corporation had a temporary difference (related to pensions) and reported a related future tax asset of $40,000 on its balance sheet. At December 31, 2008, Hewlett has five temporary differences. An analysis reveals the following:

Temporary Difference	Future (Taxable) Deductible Amounts		
	2009	2010	2011
1. Pension liability: expensed as incurred on the books; deductible when funded for tax purposes	$ 30,000	$ 20,000	$ 10,000
2. Royalties collected in advance: recognized when earned for accounting purposes and when received for tax purposes	76,000	—	—
3. Accrued liabilities: various expenses accrued for accounting purposes and recognized for tax purposes when paid	24,000	—	—
4. Deferred gross profit: profits recognized on instalment sales when sold for book purposes, and as collected for tax purposes	(36,000)	(36,000)	(36,000)
5. Equipment: straight-line amortization for accounting purposes, and CCA for tax purposes	(90,000)	(50,000)	(40,000)
	$ 4,000	$(66,000)	$(66,000)

The enacted tax rate has been 40% for many years. In November 2008, the rate was changed to 38% for all periods after January 1, 2010. Assume that the company has income taxes due of $180,000 on the 2008 tax return.

Instructions

(a) Indicate how future income taxes should be presented on Hewlett Corporation's December 31, 2008 balance sheet.

(b) Calculate taxable income for 2008.

(c) Calculate accounting income for 2008.

(d) Draft the income tax section of the 2008 income statement, beginning with the line "Income before income taxes." Provide as much information as possible about the components of income tax expense.

P18-3 Information about Swanson Corporation's income before taxes of $633,000 for its year ended December 31, 2008 includes the following:

1. CCA reported on the 2008 tax return exceeded amortization reported on the income statement by $100,000. This difference, plus the $150,000 accumulated taxable temporary difference at January 1, 2008, is expected to reverse in equal amounts over the four-year period from 2009 to 2012.

2. Dividends received from taxable Canadian corporations were $10,000.

3. Rent collected in advance and included in taxable income as of December 31, 2007, totalled $60,000 for a three-year period. Of this amount, $40,000 was reported as unearned for book purposes at December 31, 2008. Unearned revenue is reported as a current liability by Swanson if it will be recognized in income within 12 months from the balance sheet date.

4. Swanson paid a $3,500 interest penalty for late income tax instalments. The interest penalty is not deductible for income tax purposes at any time.

5. Equipment was disposed of during the year for $90,000. The equipment had a cost of $105,000 and accumulated amortization to the date of disposal of $37,000. The total proceeds on the sale of these assets reduced the CCA class; in other words, no gain or loss is reported for tax purposes.

6. Swanson recognized a $75,000 loss on impairment of a long-term investment whose value was considered impaired. The *Income Tax Act* only permits the loss to be deducted when the investment is sold and the loss is actually realized. The investment was classified for accounting purposes as held to maturity.

7. The tax rates are 40% for 2008, and 35% for 2009 and subsequent years. These rates have been enacted and known for the past two years.

Instructions

(a) Calculate the balance in the Future Income Tax Asset/Liability account at December 31, 2007.

(b) Calculate the balance in the Future Income Tax Asset/Liability account at December 31, 2008.

(c) Prepare the journal entries to record income taxes for 2008.

(d) Indicate how the Future Income Tax Asset/Liability account(s) will be reported on the comparative balance sheet for 2007 and 2008.

(e) Prepare the income tax expense section of the income statement for 2008, beginning with "Income before income taxes."

(f) Calculate the effective rate of tax. Provide a reconciliation and explanation of why this differs from the statutory rate of 40%. Begin the reconciliation with the statutory rate.

P18-4   The accounting income of Kristali Corporation and its taxable income for the years 2008 to 2011 are as follows:

Year	Accounting Income	Taxable Income	Tax Rate
2008	$460,000	$299,000	35%
2009	420,000	294,000	40%
2010	390,000	304,200	40%
2011	460,000	644,000	40%

The change in the tax rate from 35% to 40% was not enacted until early in 2009.

Accounting income for each year includes an expense of $40,000 that will never be deductible for tax purposes. The remainder of the difference between accounting income and taxable income in each period is due to one timing difference for the amortization of property, plant, and equipment. No future income taxes existed at the beginning of 2008.

Instructions

(a) Calculate the current and future tax expense or benefit for each of the four years. Also calculate the balance of the future income tax balance sheet account at the end of each fiscal year from 2008 to 2011.

(b) Prepare journal entries to record income taxes in all four years.

(c) Prepare the bottom of the income statement for 2009, beginning with the line "Income before income taxes."

P18-5   The following information is for Kerdyk Corporation:

1. Prior to 2007, taxable income and accounting income were identical.

2. Accounting income was $1.7 million in 2007 and $1.4 million in 2008.

3. On January 1, 2007, equipment costing $1 million was purchased. It is being amortized on a straight-line basis over eight years for financial reporting purposes, and is a Class 8—20% asset for tax purposes.

4. Tax exempt interest income of $60,000 was received in 2008.

5. Included in 2008 accounting income is an extraordinary gain of $200,000, which is fully taxable.

6. The tax rate is 35% for all periods.

7. Taxable income is expected in all future years.

8. Kerdyk Corporation had 100,000 common shares outstanding throughout 2008.

Instructions

(a) Calculate the amount of capital cost allowance and amortization expense for 2007 and 2008, and the corresponding net book value and undepreciated capital cost of the depreciable assets at the end of 2007 and 2008.

(b) Determine the amount of current and future income tax expense for 2008.

(c) Prepare the journal entry(ies) to record 2008 income taxes.

(d) Prepare the bottom portion of Kerdyk's 2008 income statement, beginning with the line "Income before income taxes and extraordinary items."

(e) Indicate how future income taxes should be presented on the December 31, 2008 balance sheet.

P18-6   The accounting records of Andronni Corp., a real estate developer, indicated income before taxes of $850,000 for its year ended December 31, 2008, and of $525,000 for the year ended December 31, 2009. The following data are also available:

1. Andronni Corp. pays an annual life insurance premium of $9,000 covering the top management team. The company is the named beneficiary.

2. The net book value of the company's property, plant, and equipment at January 1, 2008 was $1,256,000, and the UCC at that date was $998,000. Andronni recorded amortization expense of $175,000 and $180,000 in 2008 and 2009, respectively. CCA for tax purposes was $192,000 and $163,500 for 2008 and 2009, respectively. There were no asset additions or disposals over the two-year period.

3. Andronni deducted $211,000 as a restructuring charge in determining income for 2007. At December 31, 2007, an accrued liability of $199,500 (reported in current liabilities) remained outstanding relative to the restructuring. This expense is deductible for tax purposes, but only as the actual costs are incurred and paid for. When the actual restructuring of operations took place in 2008 and 2009, the liability was reduced to $68,000 at the end of 2008 and $0 at the end of 2009.

4. In 2008, property held for development was sold and a profit of $52,000 was recognized in income. Because the sale was made with delayed payment terms, the profit is taxable only as Andronni receives payments from the purchaser. A 10% down payment was received in 2008, with the remaining 90% expected in equal amounts over the following three years.

5. Non-taxable dividends of $2,250 in 2008 and of $2,750 in 2009 were received from taxable Canadian corporations.

6. In addition to the income before taxes identified above, Andronni reported a before-tax gain on discontinued operations of $18,800 in 2008.

7. A 30% rate of tax has been in effect since 2006.

Instructions

(a) Determine the balance of any future income tax asset or liability accounts at December 31, 2007, 2008, and 2009.

(b) Determine 2008 and 2009 taxable income and current income tax expense.

(c) Prepare the journal entries to record current and future income tax expense for 2008 and 2009.

(d) Identify how the future income tax asset or liability account(s) will be reported on the December 31, 2008 and 2009 balance sheets.

(e) Prepare partial income statements for the years ended December 31, 2008 and 2009, beginning with the line "Income from continuing operations before income tax."

P18-7 Joe Ali and Merry Madison are discussing accounting for income taxes. They are currently studying a schedule of taxable and deductible amounts that will arise in the future as a result of existing temporary differences. The schedule is as follows:

	Current Year	Future Years			
	2008	2009	2010	2011	2012
Taxable income	$50,000				
Taxable amounts		$75,000	$75,000	$ 75,000	$75,000
Deductible amounts				(2,400,000)	
Enacted tax rate	50%	48%	46%	44%	44%

Instructions

(a) Explain the concept of future taxable amounts and future deductible amounts as shown in the schedule.

(b) Determine the balance of the future income tax asset and future income tax liability accounts on the December 31, 2008, balance sheet. Assuming all temporary differences originated in 2008, prepare the journal entry to recognize income tax expense for 2008.

(c) Assume that this company is not expected to perform well in the future due to a sluggish economy and in-house management problems. Identify any concerns you may have about reporting the future tax asset/liability account as calculated.

(d) Company management determines that it is unlikely that the company will be able to benefit from all of the future deductible amounts. Early in 2009, after the entries in (b) have been made, but before the financial statements have been finalized and released, management estimates that $2 million of the $2.4 million in future deductible amounts will not be used, and that the remaining amount will be deductible in 2011. Prepare the entry that is required to recognize this, assuming the company uses a valuation allowance to adjust the future income tax asset account.

(e) When finalizing the 2009 financial statements, management estimates that, due to the prospects for an economic recovery, it is now more likely than not that the company will benefit from a total of $2.1 million of the future deductible amounts: $600,000 in 2011 and $1.5 million in 2012. Prepare the journal entry that is required, if any, to adjust the allowance account at December 31, 2009.

(f) Indicate how the future income tax accounts will be reported on the December 31, 2008 and 2009 balance sheets after taking into account the information in (d) and (e) above. Explain how these would differ, if at all, if the company did not use a valuation allowance account.

P18-8   Aneke Corp. reported the following differences between balance sheet carrying amounts and tax values at December 31, 2007:

	Book Value	UCC Tax Value
Depreciable assets	$125,000	$93,000
Warranty liability (current liability)	18,500	0
Pension funded status liability (long-term liability)	34,600	0

The differences between the carrying amounts and tax values were expected to reverse as follows:

	2008	2009	After 2009
Depreciable assets	$17,500	$12,500	$2,000
Warranty liability	18,500	0	0
Pension funded status liability	11,000	11,000	12,600

Tax rates enacted at December 31, 2007 were 31% for 2007, 30% for 2008, 29% for 2009, and 28% for 2010 and later years.

During 2008, Aneke made four quarterly tax instalment payments of $8,000 each and reported income before taxes on its income statement of $109,400. Included in this amount were dividends from taxable Canadian corporations of $4,300 (non-taxable income) and $20,000 of expenses related to the executive team's golf dues (non–tax-deductible expenses). There were no changes to the enacted tax rates during the year.

As expected, book depreciation in 2008 exceeded the capital cost allowance claimed for tax purposes by $17,500, and there were no additions or disposals of property, plant, and equipment during the year. A review of the 2008 activity in the warranty liability account in the ledger indicated the following:

Balance, Dec. 31, 2007	$ 18,500
Payments on 2007 product warranties	(18,900)
Payments on 2008 product warranties	(5,600)
2008 warranty accrual	28,300
Balance, Dec. 31, 2008	$ 22,300

All warranties are valid for one year only. The pension funded status liability account reported the following activity:

Balance, Dec. 31, 2007	$ 34,600
Payment to pension trustee	(70,000)
2008 pension expense	59,000
Balance, Dec. 31, 2008	$ 23,600

Pension expenses are deductible for tax purposes, but only as they are paid to the trustee, not as they are accrued for financial reporting purposes.

Instructions

(a) Calculate the future tax asset or liability account at December 31, 2007, and explain how it should be reported on the December 31, 2007 balance sheet.

(b) Calculate the future tax asset or liability account at December 31, 2008.

(c) Prepare all 2008 income tax entries for Aneke Corp. for 2008.

(d) Identify the balances of all income tax accounts at December 31, 2008, and show how they will be reported on the comparative GAAP balance sheets at December 31, 2008 and 2007, and on the income statement for the year ended December 31, 2008.

P18-9   The following are two independent situations related to future taxable and deductible amounts that resulted from temporary differences at December 31, 2008. In both situations, the future taxable amounts relate to property, plant, and equipment amortization, and the future deductible amounts relate to settlements of litigation that were previously accrued in the accounts.

1. Pirates Corp. has developed the following schedule of future taxable and deductible amounts:

	2009	2010	2011	2012	2013
Taxable amounts	$300	$300	$300	$ 200	$100
Deductible amount	—	—	—	(1,800)	—

Pirates reported a net future income tax liability of $500 at January 1, 2008.

2. Eagles Corp. has the following schedule of future taxable and deductible amounts:

	2009	2010	2011	2012
Taxable amounts	$400	$400	$ 400	$400
Deductible amount	—	—	(3,000)	—

Eagles Corp. reported a net future tax asset of $600 at January 1, 2008.

Both Pirates Corp. and Eagles Corp. have taxable income of $4,000 in 2008 and expect to have taxable income in all future years. The tax rates enacted as of the beginning of 2008 are 30% for 2008 to 2011, and 35% for 2012 and subsequent years. All of the underlying temporary differences relate to non-current assets and liabilities.

Instructions

(a) Determine the future income tax assets or liabilities that will be reported on each company's December 31, 2008 balance sheet.

(b) For each of these two situations, prepare journal entries to record income taxes for 2008. Show all calculations.

(c) Provide the balance sheet disclosure of future tax accounts on each company's December 31, 2008 balance sheet, including their correct classification.

P18-10   The following information was disclosed during the audit of Muster Inc.:

1.

Year	Amount Due per Tax Return
2008	$140,000
2009	112,000

2. On January 1, 2008, equipment was purchased for $400,000. For financial reporting purposes, the company uses straight-line amortization over a five-year life, with no residual value. For tax purposes, the CCA rate is 25%.

3. In January 2009, $225,000 was collected in advance for the rental of a building for the next three years. The entire $225,000 is reported as taxable income in 2009, but $150,000 of the $225,000 is reported as unearned revenue on the December 31, 2009 balance sheet. The $150,000 of unearned revenue will be earned equally in 2010 and 2011.

4. The tax rate is 40% in 2008 and all subsequent periods.

5. No temporary differences existed at the end of 2007. Muster expects to report taxable income in each of the next five years. Its fiscal year ends December 31.

Instructions

(a) Calculate the amount of capital cost allowance and amortization expense for 2008 and 2009, and the corresponding net book value and undepreciated capital cost of the depreciable assets at December 31, 2008 and 2009.

(b) Determine the balance of the future income tax asset or liability account at December 31, 2008, and indicate the account's classification on the balance sheet.

(c) Prepare the journal entry(ies) to record income taxes for 2008.

(d) Draft the bottom of the income statement for 2008, beginning with "Income before income taxes."

(e) Determine the balance of the future income tax asset or liability account at December 31, 2009, and indicate the account's classification on the December 31, 2009 balance sheet.

(f) Prepare the journal entry(ies) to record income taxes for 2009.

(g) Prepare the bottom of the income statement for 2009, beginning with "Income before income taxes."

(h) Provide the comparative balance sheet disclosure for the future tax balance sheet accounts at December 31, 2008 and 2009. Be specific about the classification.

(i) Is it possible to have more than two accounts for future taxes reported on a balance sheet? Explain.

P18-11 The following information relates to Kringe Corporation's transactions during 2008, its first year of operations:

1. Income before taxes on the income statement for 2008 was $110,000.

2. In addition, Kringe reported an extraordinary loss of $46,000 for financial reporting purposes.

3. Kringe reported a tax-deductible financing charge of $5,700 on its 2008 statement of retained earnings. The charge is for interest on a financial instrument that is legally debt, but in substance is equity for financial reporting purposes.

4. The tax rate enacted for 2008 and future years is 40%. Since this was Kringe Corporation's first taxation year, no instalments on account of income taxes were required or paid by Kringe.

5. Differences between the 2008 GAAP amounts and their treatment for tax purposes were as follows:

   (a) Warranty expense accrued for financial reporting purposes amounted to $15,000. Warranty payments deducted for taxes amounted to $12,000. Warranty liabilities were classified as current on the balance sheet.

   (b) Of the extraordinary loss of $46,000, 25% will never be tax deductible. The remaining 75% will be deductible for tax purposes evenly over the years from 2009 to 2011. The loss relates to the loss in value of company land due to contamination.

   (c) Gross profit on construction contracts using the percentage-of-completion method for book purposes amounted to $30,000. For tax purposes, gross profit on construction contracts amounted to $0 as the completed-contract method is used and no contracts were completed during the year. Construction costs amounted to $270,000 during the year.

   (d) Amortization of property, plant, and equipment for financial reporting purposes amounted to $60,000. CCA charged on the tax return amounted to $80,000. The related property, plant, and equipment cost $300,000 when it was acquired early in 2008.

   (e) A $3,500 fine paid for a violation of pollution laws was deducted in calculating accounting income.

   (f) Dividend revenue earned on an investment was tax exempt and amounted to $1,400.

6. Taxable income is expected for the next few years.

Instructions

(a) Calculate Kringe Corporation's future income tax asset or liability at December 31, 2008.

(b) Calculate the taxable income for 2008. Show all details of the adjustments to accounting income to arrive at taxable income.

(c) Prepare the journal entry(ies) to record income taxes for 2008.

(d) Prepare a partial 2008 income statement, beginning with "Income before income taxes and extraordinary items."

(e) Prepare a statement of retained earnings for the year ended December 31, 2008, assuming no dividends were declared in the year.

(f) Show how the balance of the future income tax asset or liability account will be reported on the December 31, 2008 balance sheet.

(g) Calculate the effective rate of tax. Provide a reconciliation and explanation of why this differs from the statutory rate of 40%. Begin the reconciliation with the statutory rate.

P18-12 Mearat Inc. reported the following accounting income (loss) and related tax rates during the years 2003 to 2009:

Year	Accounting Income (Loss)	Tax Rate
2003	$ 70,000	30%
2004	25,000	30%
2005	60,000	30%
2006	80,000	40%
2007	(210,000)	45%
2008	70,000	40%
2009	90,000	35%

Accounting income (loss) and taxable income (loss) were the same for all years since Mearat began business. The tax rates from 2006 to 2009 were enacted in 2006.

Instructions

(a) Prepare the journal entries to record income taxes for the years 2007 to 2009. Assume that Mearat uses the carryback provision where possible and expects to realize the benefits of any loss carryforward in the year that immediately follows the loss year.

(b) Indicate the effect of the 2007 entry(ies) on the December 31, 2007 balance sheet.

(c) Show how the bottom portion of the income statement would be reported in 2007, beginning with "Loss before income taxes."

(d) Indicate how the bottom portion of the income statement would be reported in 2008, starting with "Income before income taxes."

(e) Prepare the journal entries for the years 2007 to 2009 to record income taxes, assuming that Mearat uses the carryback provision where possible but is uncertain if it will realize the benefits of any loss carryforward in the future. Mearat does not use a valuation allowance.

(f) Assume now that Mearat uses a valuation allowance account along with its future tax asset account. Identify which entries in (e) would differ and prepare them.

(g) Based on your entries in (e), indicate how the bottom portion of the income statements for 2007 and 2008 would be reported, beginning with "Income (loss) before income taxes."

(h) From a cash flow perspective, can you think of any advantage in using the valuation allowance for financial reporting purposes? Can you think of any advantages in not using it?

Writing Assignments

WA18-1 The amount of income taxes that are due to the government for a period of time is rarely the same as the amount of income tax expense that is reported on the income statement for that same period.

Instructions

(a) Explain the objectives of accounting for income taxes in general purpose financial statements.

(b) Explain the basic principles that are applied in accounting for income taxes at the date of the financial statements to meet the objectives discussed in (a).

(c) Explain how the recognition of future tax accounts on the balance sheet is consistent with the conceptual framework in *CICA Handbook* Section 1000.

WA18-2 The asset-liability approach for recording future income taxes is an integral part of generally accepted accounting principles.

Instructions

(a) Indicate whether each of the following independent situations results in a timing difference or a permanent difference in the year. Explain your answer.

1. Estimated warranty costs (covering a three-year warranty) are expensed for financial reporting purposes at the time of sale but deducted for income tax purposes when they are paid.

2. Held-for-trading investments are adjusted to their fair value at the balance sheet date.

3. The amortization on equipment is different for book and income tax purposes because of different bases of carrying the asset, which was acquired in a trade-in. The different bases are a result of different rules that are used for book and tax purposes to calculate the cost of assets acquired in a trade-in.

4. A company properly uses the equity method to account for its 30% investment in another taxable Canadian corporation. The investee pays non-taxable dividends that are about 10% of its annual earnings.

5. Management determines that an available-for-sale investment that had gradually been losing value over the past three years, was, in fact, impaired. Appropriate entries were made to recognize the impairment.

6. A company reports a contingent loss that it expects will result from an ongoing lawsuit. The loss is not reported on the current year's tax return. Half the loss is a penalty it expects to be charged by the courts. This portion of the loss is not a tax deductible expenditure, even when it is paid.

(b) Discuss the nature of any future income tax accounts that result from the situations in (a) above, including their possible classifications in the company's balance sheet. Indicate how these accounts should be reported.

WA18-3 The following are common items that are treated differently for financial reporting purposes than they are for tax purposes:

1. The excess amount of a charge to the accounting records (allowance method) over a charge to the tax return (direct write-off method) for uncollectible receivables

2. The excess amount of accrued pension expense over the amount paid

3. The receipt of dividends from a taxable Canadian corporation that are treated as income for accounting purposes but are not subject to tax

4. Expenses incurred in obtaining tax exempt income

5. A trademark that is acquired directly from the government and is capitalized and amortized over subsequent periods for accounting purposes and expensed for tax purposes

6. A prepaid advertising expense that is deferred for accounting purposes and deducted as an expense for tax purposes

7. Premiums paid on life insurance of officers (where the corporation is the beneficiary)

8. A penalty paid for filing a late tax return

9. Proceeds of life insurance policies on lives of officers

10. Restructuring costs that are recognized as an unusual item on the income statement and are not deductible until actual costs are incurred

11. Holding gains and losses that are recognized on held-for-trading and available-for-sale investments and are not taxable or deductible until realized for tax purposes

12. Excess depletion for accounting purposes over the amount taken for tax purposes

13. The estimated gross profit on a long-term construction contract that is reported in the income statement, with some of the gross profit being deferred for tax purposes

Instructions

(a) Indicate for each item above if the situation is a permanent difference, or a timing difference resulting in a temporary difference.

(b) Indicate for each item above if the situation will usually create future taxable amounts, resulting in a future tax liability; or future deductible amounts, resulting in a future tax asset; or whether it will have no future tax implications.

WA18-4 Henrietta Aguirre, CGA, is the newly hired director of corporate taxation for Mesa Incorporated, which is a publicly traded corporation. Aguirre's first job with Mesa was to review the company's accounting practices on future income taxes. In doing her review, she noted differences between tax and book amortization methods that permitted Mesa to recognize a sizeable future tax liability on its balance sheet. As a result, Mesa did not have to report current income tax expenses.

Aguirre also discovered that Mesa has an explicit policy of selling off plant and equipment assets before they reversed in the future tax liability account. This policy, together with the rapid expansion of Mesa's capital asset base, allowed Mesa to defer all income taxes payable for several years, at the same time as it reported positive earnings and an increasing EPS. Aguirre checked with the legal department and found the policy to be legal, but she is uncomfortable with the ethics of it.

Instructions

(a) Why would Mesa have an explicit policy of selling assets before they reversed in the future tax liability account?

(b) What are the ethical implications of Mesa's deferral of income taxes?

(c) Who could be harmed by Mesa's ability to defer income taxes payable for several years, despite positive earnings?

(d) In a situation such as this, what are Aguirre's professional responsibilities as a CGA?

WA18-5 At December 31, 2008, Golden Corporation has one temporary difference that will reverse and cause taxable amounts in 2009. In 2008, new tax legislation set taxes equal to 45% for 2008, 40% for 2009, and 34% for 2010 and the years thereafter.

Instructions
Explain what circumstances would require Golden to calculate its future tax liability at the end of 2008 by multiplying the temporary difference by:

(a) 45%.   **(b)** 40%.   **(c)** 34%.

Cases

Refer to the Case Primer on the Student Website to help you answer these cases.

Student Website
www.wiley.com/canada/kieso

CA18-1 Baker Company Limited (BCL) was founded in 2000 and its first year of operations turned out to be a good one, as start-up years go, since the company not only broke even but actually showed a very small profit. Just as the company was getting established in the market, however, a full-fledged recession hit in 2001 and had devastating effects. Demand for BCL's products in retail markets declined as consumers tightened their purse strings. Through tight cost controls, however, BCL managed to hold its own and still recorded a small profit in 2001.

While the recession finally petered out by the end of 2002, BCL did end up feeling its effects as the company was unable to remain profitable and suffered large operating losses that year. In fact, the losses were significantly greater than the profits that were reported in the previous two years. Despite this change, BCL management was not overly alarmed by the losses and had the following comments to make:

> "The losses were expected given the widespread recession. Since the bulk of our sales are in retail markets and with unemployment levels being at record highs, it is not surprising that consumer demand has fallen off. If BCL is compared with the industry, you will see that we did much better than our competitors, some of whom went bankrupt.
>
> Keep in mind that we are a relatively new company and managed to record a profit in two out of our first three years. We attribute this to our strong management team and our ability as a streamlined company to react to the recession with cost control measures and an aggressive, yet flexible sales staff.
>
> We see ourselves positioned for a new growth spurt given that the economy seems to have recovered and a lot of 'dead wood' (i.e., competition) has been cleared out. As a matter of fact, in that regard, the recession will have a positive impact on our short- to mid-term growth potential.
>
> BCL is on the verge of introducing two new products that will revolutionize the industry and assure us a solid earnings base for the future. These products will be introduced in 2003 and we have already lined up sufficient buyers such that we predict we will at least break even in terms of net income in 2003. This is a very conservative forecast."

Although the effects of the recession were lessening, unemployment was still high in early 2003 and consumer spending had not increased significantly. Some economists were predicting that it would take two or three years for consumer confidence and spending to pick up to pre-recession levels.

Instructions
Adopt the role of the company's auditor and determine whether BCL should recognize the benefits of the losses suffered in the 2002 financial statements.

CA18-2 Tomkins PLC is a global engineering and manufacturing company with two major business groups. They operate in the industrial and automotive business and the building products business. Their shares trade on the London Stock Exchange under the trading symbol TOMK. Currently, they file financial statements following International GAAP as set out by the International Accounting Standards Board. In addition, for the year ended December 31, 2006, the company also filed financial statements under UK GAAP and U.S. GAAP.

The following excerpt is from the financial statements of the company and deals with its tax accounting:

R. Taxation

Current tax is the amount of tax payable or recoverable in respect of the taxable profit or loss for the period. Taxable profit differs from accounting profit because it excludes items of income or expense recognised for accounting purposes that are either not taxable or deductible for tax purposes or are taxable or deductible in other periods. Current tax is calculated using tax rates that have been enacted or substantively enacted at the balance sheet date. The Group recognises provisions in respect of uncertain tax positions whereby additional current tax may become payable in future periods following the audit by the tax authorities of previously filed tax returns. Provisions for uncertain tax positions are based upon management's assessment of the likely outcome of issues associated with assumed permanent differences, interest that may be applied to temporary differences, the possible disallowance of tax credits and penalties. Provisions for uncertain tax positions are reviewed regularly and are adjusted to reflect events such as the expiry of limitation periods for assessing tax, administrative guidance given by the tax authorities and court decisions.

Deferred tax is tax expected to be payable or recoverable on differences between the carrying amount of an asset or a liability and its tax base used in the computation of taxable profit. Deferred tax is accounted for using the liability method, whereby deferred tax liabilities are generally recognised for all taxable temporary differences and deferred tax assets are recognised to the extent that it is probable that taxable profits will be available against which deductible temporary differences can be utilised.

Deferred tax assets and liabilities are not recognised if the temporary difference arises from the initial recognition of goodwill or from the initial recognition of other assets and liabilities in a transaction other than a business combination that affects neither accounting profit nor taxable profit.

Deferred tax is provided on temporary differences arising on investments in foreign subsidiaries and associates, except where the Group is able to control the reversal of the temporary difference and it is probable that the temporary difference will not reverse in the foreseeable future.

Deferred tax is calculated using the tax rates that are expected to apply in the period in which the liability is settled or the asset is realised. Tax assets and liabilities are offset when there is a legally enforceable right to set off current tax assets against current tax liabilities and when they relate to income taxes levied by the same taxation authority and the Group intends to settle its current tax assets and liabilities on a net basis.

Current and deferred tax is recognised in the income statement unless it relates to an item recognised directly in equity, in which case it is recognised directly in equity.

J. Taxation

The Group is subject to income tax in each of the jurisdictions in which it operates. Management is required to exercise significant judgement in determining the Group's provision for income taxes.

Estimation is required of taxable profit in order to determine the Group's current tax liability. Management's judgement is required in relation to uncertain tax positions whereby additional current tax may become payable in the future following the audit by the tax authorities of previously filed tax returns. As at 30 December 2006, the Group recognised a provision for uncertain tax positions amounting to £36.3 million. It is possible that the final outcome of these uncertain tax positions may differ from management's estimates.

Estimation is also required of temporary differences between the carrying amount of assets and liabilities and their tax base. Deferred tax liabilities are recognised for all taxable temporary differences, but where there exist deductible temporary differences management's judgement is required as to whether a deferred tax asset should be recognised based on the availability of future taxable profits. As at 30 December 2006, the Group recognised net deferred tax assets amounting to £33.5 million. It is possible that the deferred tax assets actually recoverable may differ from the amounts recognised if actual taxable profits differ from management's estimates.

During 2006, there was a release of provisions for uncertain tax positions of £50.6 million as a result of tax planning, the clarification of tax legislation, the performance of certain studies and the change of views on the likely outcome of challenges by various tax authorities. During 2005, there was a similar release of £58.7 million.

Instructions

Adopt the role of a financial analyst who is trying to look at the impact between differing GAAP. Specifically, compare and contrast the accounting for taxes under Canadian GAAP and international GAAP. (Hint: You do not need to look up the international standard IAS 12. Instead, read the above excerpt from the company's notes and compare what you find there to Canadian GAAP.) Which set of GAAP is more transparent?

Research and Financial Analysis

RA18-1 Stantec Inc.

The complete financial statements of **Stantec Inc.** for the company's year ended December 31, 2005 are presented at the end of this volume. Refer to Stantec's financial statements and accompanying notes and answer the following questions.

Instructions

(a) Identify all income tax accounts reported on the December 31, 2005 balance sheet. Explain clearly what each account represents.

(b) What are the temporary differences that existed at December 31, 2005 and resulted in the future income tax asset(s) that are reported? Which differences do you think related to the future tax account reported in current assets? Which in non-current? Explain the reasons for your answers.

(c) What are the temporary differences that existed at December 31, 2005 and resulted in the future income tax liability(ies) that are reported? Which differences do you think related to the future tax account reported in current liabilities? Which in non-current? Explain the reasons for your answers.

(d) Does Stantec management think it is more likely than not that the benefits related to future deductible amounts will be realized? Explain.

(e) Has Stantec Inc. applied intraperiod tax allocation in 2005? Explain. (Hint: Read Note 12.)

(f) How much income tax did Stantec Inc. pay in 2005? Where did you find this information?

(g) What was the effective tax rate for Stantec Inc. in 2005? In 2004? What were the major causes of the differences between the statutory and effective tax rates? For each reason you give, explain whether the effective rate was made higher or lower than the statutory rate, and why.

RA18-2 Finning International Inc.

Finning International Inc., a Canadian company based in Vancouver, B.C., is the world's largest Caterpillar equipment dealer. The company sells, rents, finances, and provides customer support for Caterpillar equipment and engines in western Canada, the UK, and South America. It also owns Hewden, the largest equipment rental business in Europe.

Instructions

Through SEDAR (www.sedar.com) or Finning's website, obtain a copy of the company's financial statements for its year ended December 31, 2006, and answer the following questions.

(a) Review the Consolidated Statements of Income and Retained Earnings for 2006 and 2005. Determine whether the company applied intraperiod tax allocation in each of these years. Briefly describe your findings.

(b) What was the company's effective tax rate for 2006? For 2005? What was the statutory rate in each of these years? If the rates are significantly different, what caused the differences? Be specific about whether the effective rate was increased or decreased as a result of each cause that you identify.

(c) Identify the total income tax expense reported in the statement of income for each of the last two years. How much of each year's total income tax expense was currently payable? Identify what made up the remainder of the total tax expense.

(d) *CICA Handbook* Section 3465.87 indicates that "the current and noncurrent portions of future income tax liabilities and future income tax assets should … be segregated." Identify how Finning has complied with this requirement.

(e) For each future income tax account reported on the December 31, 2006 balance sheet, explain what underlies the balance that is reported. For each temporary difference, identify the balance sheet asset or liability where the tax basis and book value differ. If there is no recognized book or carrying amount, explain why Finning classified the future tax account as it did (i.e., as current or non-current).

RA18-3 Comparative Analysis

Alimentation Couche-Tard Inc., Metro Inc., and Sobeys Inc. are three companies of similar size. Because all three are in the same industry, the expectation is that their operations and financial positions are also similar.

Instructions

Go to SEDAR (www.sedar.com), the company websites, or the Student Website and, using Alimentation Couche-Tard's financial statements for the year ended April 29, 2006, Metro's financial statements for the year ended September 30, 2006, and Sobeys' financial statements for the year ended May 6, 2006, answer the following questions.

(a) Identify what industry all three companies are in.

(b) Identify all the areas where intraperiod tax allocation was used by the three companies. This requires a careful reading of some of the notes to the financial statements as well as the main statements themselves. Prepare a schedule of the total income tax provision (expense) or recovery (benefit) for each company, and identify where the provision or recovery was reported.

(c) Compare the three companies' future income tax assets and/or future income tax liabilities, and identify, as much as possible, what temporary differences are responsible for these accounts. Would you expect companies in the same industry to have similar types of temporary differences? Do they?

(d) Would you expect the three companies to be subject to similar income tax legislation and tax rates? Are their statutory rates the same? Comment. Compare the companies' statutory and effective rates and explain why there are differences if there are any.

RA18-4 International Comparison

Homburg Invest Inc. is a real estate investment company headquartered in Halifax, Nova Scotia, and operating throughout Canada, Germany, The Netherlands, and in parts of the United States. The company has prepared its financial statements under both Canadian and international accounting standards for many years. With Canadian standards moving to IFRS, it is informative to determine how accounting for income taxes in the future might differ from what is currently being done in Canada.

Instructions
Go to SEDAR (www.sedar.com), Homburg Invest's website, or the Student Website and access the company's financial statements prepared under Canadian GAAP for its year ended December 31, 2006. At the end of the Notes to Canadian GAAP Consolidated Financial Statements, there is a schedule that reconciles these statements to the ones prepared under IFRS. Based on the information provided, prepare a short report in which you explain the causes of all differences that relate to income taxes.

Retirement Woes

Nortel recently announced significant changes to its North American pension program as part of a new business initiative aimed at increasing the company's competitiveness. One of the changes is to eliminate the company's current package of health-care benefits after retirement for all employees who are not 50 years old or more and with five years of service as of July 1, 2006. Nortel specified that all future retirees who do not meet the age and service criteria will still have access to the company's preferred provider health-care coverage, but at their own cost. The pension income benefit will not change for current retirees in Canada and the United States, although the cost-sharing formula for medical benefits may change for some retirees in the United States.

Nortel is among many Canadian organizations that have reduced or are considering reducing the level of post-retirement health-care coverage that they provide. According to a survey of 218 organizations done by the human resources firm Hewitt Associates in 2006, more than half

(57%) plan to reduce the level of benefits that they offer in the coming years. Most companies (95%) said rising health-care costs were one of the top three reasons for reducing post-retirement health-care benefits. Two-thirds (67%) cited accounting costs and 43% listed the large number of employees who will retire in the next decade as reasons to consider reducing benefits.

Organizations will reduce post-retirement health-care benefits in several ways. Some plan to use stricter eligibility requirements, while others plan to reduce medical coverage by eliminating medical services, increasing deductibles/copayments, or capping certain health-care services. Approximately one-third (30%) said they plan to add or increase retiree contributions to their programs. In addition, many companies are now offering flexible retirement benefit programs, which allow them to control their benefit spending by paying for benefits through a monetary allowance instead of funding them directly. ◼

Pensions and Other Employee Future Benefits

Learning Objectives

After studying this chapter, you should be able to:

1. Identify a defined contribution plan, and apply the accounting and disclosure requirements for such plans.
2. Explain what a defined benefit plan is.
3. Identify a defined benefit plan whose benefits do not vest or accumulate, and account for such plans.
4. Identify a defined benefit plan whose benefits vest or accumulate, and explain how such plans are accounted for.
5. Distinguish between accounting for the employer's pension costs and accounting for the pension fund.
6. Explain what the employer's benefit obligation is and identify alternative measures for valuing this obligation.
7. Identify transactions and events that change the amount of the employer's accrued benefit obligation, and calculate the balance of the obligation.
8. Identify transactions and events that change the amount of the plan assets, and calculate the balance of the assets.
9. Explain and calculate a benefit plan's funded status.
10. Identify the possible components of pension benefit cost, and account for a defined benefit pension plan under Canadian GAAP.
11. Explain the usefulness of—and complete—a work sheet to support the employer's pension accounts.
12. Define and account for past service costs.
13. Explain what actuarial gains and losses are, and account for them using the corridor approach to amortization.
14. Identify the financial reporting and disclosure requirements for defined benefit plans.
15. Compare current Canadian and international GAAP.

After studying the Appendix, you should be able to:

16. Explain the basics of what each of current service cost, accrued benefit obligation, and past service cost represent.

Preview of Chapter 19

Since employers are concerned about the current and future well-being of their employees, as are the employees themselves, a variety of future benefit programs have been established for employees. For example, private pension and other post-retirement benefit plans have become common in companies of all sizes. In mid-2006, of the 5.7 million Canadian workers who belong to employer pension plans, about 4.6 million are members of plans whose assets are held in trusteed pension funds. Called trusteed pension funds because they are governed by the provisions of a trust agreement, these funds are impressive in size. The market value of the assets held in trusteed pension funds in Canada peaked at $836.8 billion in the first quarter of 2006, up considerably from $532.0 billion three years earlier.[1]

A pension is part of an employee's overall compensation package. Post-retirement health-care and other benefits are also often part of this package. The substantial growth of these plans, both in how many employees are covered and in the dollar amount of benefits, has made their costs significantly larger in relation to a company's financial position, results of operations, and cash flows. This is made clear in the opening story about Nortel and other companies that are taking steps to reduce such costs. This chapter discusses the accounting issues related to these future benefits.

The chapter is organized as follows:

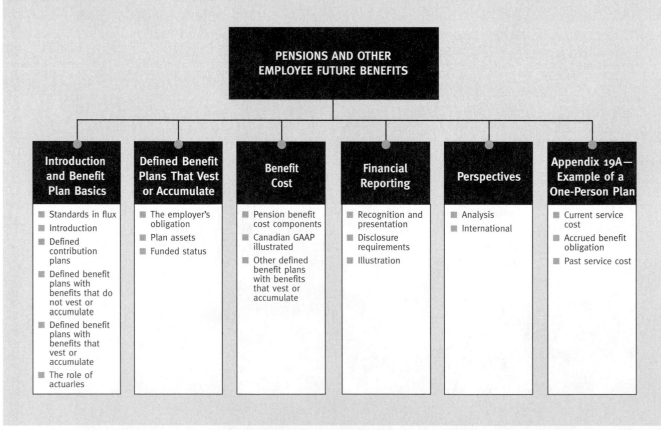

PENSIONS AND OTHER EMPLOYEE FUTURE BENEFITS

Introduction and Benefit Plan Basics	Defined Benefit Plans That Vest or Accumulate	Benefit Cost	Financial Reporting	Perspectives	Appendix 19A— Example of a One-Person Plan
■ Standards in flux ■ Introduction ■ Defined contribution plans ■ Defined benefit plans with benefits that do not vest or accumulate ■ Defined benefit plans with benefits that vest or accumulate ■ The role of actuaries	■ The employer's obligation ■ Plan assets ■ Funded status	■ Pension benefit cost components ■ Canadian GAAP illustrated ■ Other defined benefit plans with benefits that vest or accumulate	■ Recognition and presentation ■ Disclosure requirements ■ Illustration	■ Analysis ■ International	■ Current service cost ■ Accrued benefit obligation ■ Past service cost

[1] Statistics Canada, *The Daily*, September 22, 2006, and January 4, 2007 at http://www.statcan.ca/Daily.

INTRODUCTION AND BENEFIT PLAN BASICS

Standards in Flux

Accounting for such benefits as pensions is almost the same as it was 30 years ago. Although there has been an increase in the range of benefit programs that are covered by standards and the disclosure requirements have improved significantly over this period, the basic approach to calculating the benefit costs and what is reported on the balance sheet has not changed.

In 2007, the Accounting Standards Board (AcSB) released an Exposure Draft to amend *CICA Handbook* Section 3461, Employee Future Benefits. The Exposure Draft proposed new requirements that would have resulted in major changes in what was measured and reported on many companies' balance sheets.[2] In July 2007, however, **the AcSB decided not to proceed with the proposed amendments**. Although the AcSB believed the changes would have improved Canadian financial reporting for employee future benefits, it decided to postpone any changes until IAS 19, Employee Benefits, is adopted on the transition date to international financial reporting standards. The 2007 Exposure Draft proposals were meant only as interim measures that are part of an ongoing evolution, as both the FASB and IASB have begun longer-term and broader projects on this topic. The IASB's phased project is expected to result in an interim standard, probably by 2010, "that would significantly improve pension accounting, pending a fundamental review of all aspects of post-employment benefit accounting."[3] The goal is a converged standard whose requirements will be accepted by Canada when the IFRS are adopted in 2011.

This chapter starts by introducing basic terminology, different categories of benefits, and the accounting for plans that are not too complex. Because the accounting standards now in place may change by the time many current students are writing professional exams and working as practising professionals, the next section explains the key underlying components of defined benefit plans—such as the company obligation and assets of pension plans—and what causes them to change. These components and the changes in them are the basic building blocks for employee future-benefits accounting. By understanding them, students will understand such topics as pension accounting, even when the accounting standards later change.

The remainder of the chapter describes current Canadian GAAP. Appendix 19A provides a simplified example of a single-person pension plan to help students better visualize and understand some of the new concepts that are introduced in this chapter.

Introduction

Chapter 19 covers the accounting and reporting for a variety of employee future benefits that are earned by employees and that are expected to be provided to them **when they are no longer in active service**. Three types of benefit plans are included:

1. Post-retirement plans. These refer to pension and other plans where the benefits are provided after an employee's retirement. Examples include plans that provide post-retirement health care or life insurance benefits.

International Insight

IAS 19, "Employee Benefits," covers short-term compensated absences, profit sharing, and bonus plans in addition to post-employment and post-retirement benefits that are provided when employees are not in active service.

---

[2] The proposed amendments to the Canadian standards were motivated significantly by the release of FASB's *Statement No. 158* the previous year. Stakeholders who responded to the Exposure Draft believed that the focus should be on the implications of adopting IAS 19 and the IASB's current project on employee future benefits.

[3] IASB, "Post-Employment Benefits: Phase 1," Project Update, December 2006.

2. Post-employment benefit plans. Examples of this type of plan are long- and short-term disability benefits, supplemental unemployment insurance benefits, job training and counselling, severance benefits, and other benefits that are paid after employment but before retirement.

3. Compensated absences. This type of benefit includes payments that are made while an employee is absent from work. It includes parental leaves, unrestricted sabbatical leaves, and accumulated sick days that employees can take whether they are ill or not.

Benefits that are provided while employees are actively employed, such as regular vacations and occasional sick days, were discussed in Chapter 13.

Employee future-benefit plans can also be described as (1) defined contribution plans, or (2) defined benefit plans. Defined benefit plans can be further subdivided between (a) those with benefits that vest or accumulate, and (b) those with benefits that do not vest or accumulate. These terms are explained below.

Defined contribution plans are fairly straightforward, as are the defined benefit plans where the benefits do not vest or accumulate, so we will begin with them. We will then focus on what takes up most of the discussion in this chapter, the complexities that are associated with defined benefit plans whose benefits vest or accumulate.

Defined Contribution Plans

Objective 1
Identify a defined contribution plan, and apply the accounting and disclosure requirements for such plans.

A **defined contribution (DC) plan**, such as some pension plans, specifies how contributions or payments into the plan are determined, and also attributes the contributions to specific individuals.[4] It does not state what benefits the individual will receive or what method will be used to determine those benefits. The contributions may be a fixed sum, for example, $1,000 per year, or they may be related to salary, such as 6% of regular earnings plus overtime earnings. Usually, no promise is made about the ultimate benefit that will be paid out to the employees.

For a defined contribution pension plan, the amounts that are contributed are usually turned over to an independent third party or trustee who acts for (i.e., on behalf of) the beneficiaries (the participating employees). The trustee assumes ownership of the pension assets and is responsible for their investment and distribution. The trust is separate and distinct from the employer. The size of the pension benefit that the employee finally collects under the plan depends on the amounts that have been contributed to the pension trust, the income that has accumulated in the trust, and the treatment of forfeitures of funds, which are created by the termination of an employee before his or her retirement.

Because **the contribution is defined**, the accounting for a defined contribution plan is straightforward. The employer's annual benefit cost (i.e., the pension expense) is simply the amount that the company is obligated to contribute to the plan. A liability is only reported on the employer's balance sheet if the contribution has not been made in full, and an asset is only reported if more than the required amount has been contributed. The employer generally has no other obligation and assumes no other risk relative to this plan.

When a defined contribution plan is first established, or when it is later amended, the employer may be obligated to make contributions for employee services that were provided before the start of the plan or its amendment. This obligation is referred to as **prior or past service cost**. Amounts that arise as past service costs are amortized in a rational and systematic way as part of the annual benefit expense over the period that the organization is expected to benefit from the plan change.[5] In addition to the amount of pension or

---

[4] *CICA Handbook*, Section 3461.009(f).

[5] *CICA Handbook*, Section 3461.019.

benefit expense, the employer is also required to disclose the following: the nature and effect of significant matters that affect comparability from period to period, and the total cash amount that was recognized in the period as paid or payable for that period in relation to the future benefits.[6]

Defined Benefit Plans with Benefits That Do Not Vest or Accumulate

A **defined benefit (DB) plan** is any benefit plan that is not a defined contribution plan. It is a benefit plan that "specifies either the benefits to be received by an employee, or the method of determining those benefits."[7] Examples include the entitlement to a lump sum payment of $5,000 on the employee's 10th and 25th anniversaries of employment with the employer company, or an annual pension benefit on retirement equal to 2% of the average of the employee's best three years of salary multiplied by the number of years of employment.

2 Objective
Explain what a defined benefit plan is.

The most complex type of benefit plan provides defined benefits that vest in the employee based on the employee's length of service. Employees' rights to post-retirement medical benefits, for example, usually vest only after the employee has worked a specified number of years. The amount of pension benefit, on the other hand, usually increases with the length of service. **Vesting** means that an employee keeps the rights to the benefit even if the employee no longer works for the entity. That is, if an employee whose benefits have vested leaves the company, the individual will still receive those benefits. If, on the other hand, they are not vested when the employee leaves, the rights to medical benefits on retirement, for example, are lost.

Other defined benefit plans, however, are available to all employees regardless of the length of service that they have provided. **Entitlement to the benefits does not depend on or increase with the employee's length of service, and the benefits do not vest.** Employees are eligible for these benefits simply by virtue of being an employee. Examples include additional compensation and time off for parental (maternity and paternity) leave beyond what the government provides, and some short-term and long-term disability benefits.

3 Objective
Identify a defined benefit plan whose benefits do not vest or accumulate, and account for such plans.

Because the rights to the benefits do not accrue over time with these plans, the liability and expense are recognized only "when the event that obligates the entity occurs."[8] Thus, when an employee applies for parental leave or becomes disabled, the total estimated liability and expense that is associated with the event is recognized at that time. Assume, for example, that Sue Kim applies for a one-year parental leave on April 18. Resource Corp., her employer, provides a benefit plan that promises to pay the employee, for a period of up to one year, an amount equal to the difference between the employee's current salary and the amount paid by employment insurance during the parental leave. Resource Corp. calculates that the benefit payable by the company to Sue Kim will be $200 per week. The company makes the following entry when she begins her leave:

Employee Benefit Expense	10,400	
Parental Leave Benefits Payable		10,400
($200 × 52 weeks = $10,400)		

A = L + SE
+10,400 −10,400

Cash flows: No effect

[6] *CICA Handbook*, Section 3461.153.
[7] *CICA Handbook*, Section 3461.009(e).
[8] *CICA Handbook*, Section 3461.029.

As the compensated absence (i.e., the parental leave) is taken and Sue Kim is paid, the liability is reduced. Assuming a biweekly payroll for Resource Corp., the following entry is made each pay period:

A   =   L   +   SE
−400   −400

Cash flows: ↓ 400 outflow

Parental Leave Benefits Payable	400	
Cash		400
($200 × 2 weeks = $400)		

In theory, the liability for the benefits and their cost should be accrued as the employees provide services. However, there are practical difficulties in measuring the liability and the amounts are often immaterial. Therefore, the accounting standard delays recognition until an event occurs that obligates the company to provide the benefit. This method of accounting is called the **event accrual method**. Because there may be similar measurement problems with sick leave that accumulates but does not vest, the event accrual method may also be appropriate in this circumstance. Discounting is appropriate if the benefit payments extend over the long term.

Defined Benefit Plans with Benefits That Vest or Accumulate

Objective 4

Identify a defined benefit plan whose benefits vest or accumulate, and explain how such plans are accounted for.

As indicated above, the most complex type of benefit plan is one that provides defined benefits that vest in the employee or accumulate to an employee's credit based on his or her length of service. Common types of such plans are those related to pensions or other post-retirement benefits, but they also include other post-employment benefits and compensated absences such as sick leave that accumulates and that is paid out without an illness-related absence, and long-term disability benefits that increase with length of service. All of these benefit plans have something in common: **the entitlement to the benefits increases with the length of the employee's service**. It is reasonable, therefore, for the expense and liability related to these plans to be recognized over the accounting periods in which the related services are provided. Because defined benefit pension plans will be used extensively in this chapter to show how to account for this type of benefit plan, basic information about pensions is provided next.

Nature of Pension Plans

Objective 5

Distinguish between accounting for the employer's pension costs and accounting for the pension fund.

A **pension plan** is an arrangement where an employer provides benefits (payments) to employees after they retire for services that the employees provided while they were working. Pension accounting may refer **either to accounting for the employer** or **accounting for the pension plan. This chapter focuses on the former.** The company or employer is the organization that sponsors the pension plan. It incurs the cost and contributes to the pension fund. The fund is the entity that receives the employer contributions, administers the pension assets, and makes the benefit payments to the pension recipients (the retired employees). Illustration 19-1 shows the three participants in a pension plan and the flow of cash among them.

Illustration 19-1

Flow of Cash among Pension Plan Participants

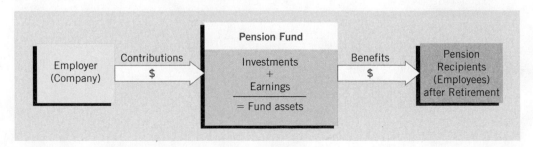

The pension plan in the illustration is being **funded**.[9] This means that the employer (company) sets funds aside for future pension benefits by making payments to a funding agency that is responsible for accumulating the pension plan assets and for making payments to the recipients as the benefits come due. In an insured plan, the funding agency is an insurance company; in a trust fund plan, the funding agency is a trustee. The assets that are transferred are the assets of the pension plan, which is a separate legal entity. They are not company assets.

In **contributory plans**, the employees pay part of the cost of the stated benefits or they voluntarily make payments to increase their benefits. In **non-contributory plans**, the employer bears the entire cost. Companies generally design pension plans in accordance with federal income tax laws that permit deduction of the employer's and employees' contributions to the pension fund and offer tax-free status for earnings from pension fund assets. The pension benefits are taxable when they are received by the pensioner.

The need for proper administration of pension funds, as well as sound accounting, becomes apparent when one appreciates the size of these funds. The following list shows the pension expense, fund assets, and shareholders' equity of a sample of large Canadian companies.

What Do the Numbers Mean?

Company	Year	Pension Expense	Pension Fund Assets	Shareholders' Equity
		in millions	in millions	in millions
Manulife Financial Corporation	2005	$ 85	$3,479	$23,787
Royal Bank of Canada	2006	390	6,407	22,123
Suncor Energy Inc.	2006	80	616	8,952
Bombardier Inc. (U.S. $)	2006	287	3,916	2,425
The Thomson Corporation (U.S. $)	2006	101	2,457	10,481

As the list shows, pension expense can be a substantial amount, and the fund assets are sometimes larger than the shareholders' equity of the company that is sponsoring the plan.

The plan is usually a separate legal and accounting entity for which a set of books is maintained and financial statements are prepared. General purpose financial statements for pension plans are not covered in this chapter but they are prescribed by the *CICA Handbook* in Section 4100. This chapter is devoted to issues that relate to **the employer**, as the sponsor of pension and other future employee benefit plans.

The two most common types of pension plans are defined contribution (DC) plans, discussed earlier, and defined benefit (DB) plans, discussed next.

Defined Benefit Pension Plans

A defined benefit pension plan identifies the pension benefits that an employee will receive after retiring. The formula that the benefit is based on usually relates the benefits to the employee's years of service and compensation level when he or she is close to retirement. In order to ensure that appropriate resources are available to pay the benefits at retirement, there is usually a requirement that funds be set aside during the service life of the employees.

The **employees** are the beneficiaries of a **defined contribution** trust, as described earlier, but the **employer** is the beneficiary of a **defined benefit** trust. The trust's main purpose under a defined benefit plan is to safeguard assets and to invest them so that there will be enough to pay the employer's obligation to the employees when they retire. **In form**, the trust is a separate entity; **in substance**, the trust liabilities belong to the employer. That is, **as long as the plan continues, the employer is responsible for**

International Insight

Outside Canada and the United States, private pension plans are less common because many other nations tend to rely on government-sponsored pension plans. Consequently, accounting for defined benefit pension plans is generally a less important issue in other countries.

---

[9] When it is used as a verb, **fund** means to pay to a funding agency (for example, to fund future pension benefits or to fund pension cost). Used as a noun, it refers to assets that have accumulated in the hands of a funding agency (trustee) for the purpose of meeting pension benefits when they come due.

paying the defined benefits, no matter what happens in the trust. Any shortfall in the accumulated assets being held by the trust must be made up by the employer. If there are excess assets that have accumulated in the trust, it may be possible for the employer to recapture them either through reduced future funding or through a reversion of funds, depending on the trust agreement, plan documents, and provincial legislation.[10]

With a defined benefit plan, the employer assumes the economic risks: the employee is secure because the benefits to be paid on retirement are predefined, but the employer is at risk because the cost is uncertain. The cost depends on factors such as employee turnover, mortality, length of service, and compensation levels, as well as investment returns that are earned on pension assets, inflation, and other economic conditions over long periods of time.

At one time, most employer-sponsored pension plans in Canada were of the defined benefit type. The majority of plans now are defined contribution plans, and the percentage is growing. However, in terms of pension assets, the amount that is in defined benefit plans continues to be disproportionately high in Canada.

Because the cost to the company is affected by a wide range of uncertain future variables, it is not easy to measure the pension cost and liability that have to be recognized each period as employees provide services to earn their pension entitlement. In addition, an appropriate funding pattern must be established to assure that enough funds will be available at retirement to provide the benefits that have been promised. Whatever funding method is decided on, it should provide enough money at retirement to meet the benefits defined by the plan. Note that **the expense to be recognized each period is not the same as the cash funding contribution,** just as amortization expense that is recognized on the use of plant and equipment is not measured in terms of how the asset is financed or paid for.

The accounting issues related to defined benefit plans are complex, but interesting. The discussion in the following sections deals primarily with this type of plan.

The Role of Actuaries

The problems that are associated with many benefit plans involve complicated actuarial considerations. Companies therefore use the services of actuaries to ensure that the plan is appropriate for the particular employee group that is being covered. **Actuaries** are individuals who are trained through a long and rigorous certification program to assign probabilities to future events and their financial effects.[11] The insurance industry employs actuaries to assess risks and to advise the industry on the setting of premiums and other aspects of insurance policies. Employers rely heavily on actuaries for help in developing, implementing, and funding pension plans.

Actuaries make predictions, called **actuarial assumptions**, about mortality rates, employee turnover, interest and earnings rates, early retirement frequency, future salaries, and any other factors that need to be known in order to operate a pension plan. They assist

---

[10] There has been a lot of litigation recently over the ownership of pension fund surpluses. The courts have increasingly determined that pension fund surpluses, or a significant portion of them, should accrue to the benefit of the employee group. Provincial pension legislation increasingly dictates how pension surpluses must be handled.

[11] An actuary's chief purpose in pension accounting is to ensure that the company has established an appropriate funding pattern to meet its pension obligations. This calculation requires a set of assumptions to be established and the continued monitoring of these assumptions to ensure that they are realistic. That the general public has little understanding of what an actuary does is illustrated by the following excerpt from *The Wall Street Journal*: "A polling organization once asked the general public what an actuary was and received among its more coherent responses the opinion that it was a place where you put dead actors."

by calculating the various measures that affect the financial statements, such as the pension obligation, the annual cost of servicing the plan, and the cost of amendments to the plan. In summary, accounting for defined benefit pension plans relies heavily on information and measurements that are provided by actuaries.

DEFINED BENEFIT PLANS THAT VEST OR ACCUMULATE

As mentioned earlier in the chapter, accounting for employee future benefits such as pensions is in a state of change. While both the FASB and the IASB have begun projects that are taking a fresh look at this whole issue, two of the foundations for such plans are not likely to change substantially and pension accounting will therefore continue to be based on them. The first one is the employer's obligation to pay out benefits in the future for the employees' services up to the balance sheet date. This is estimated by the actuary. The second foundation is the plan assets that have been set aside to fund this obligation. Understanding the nature of the **accrued obligation** and **fund assets**, and the transactions and events that affect their measurement, helps clarify the study of accounting for benefit plans, even as the standards change.

The Employer's Obligation

Alternative Measures of the Obligation

Most companies agree that an employer's **pension obligation** is the deferred compensation obligation that it has to its employees for their service under the terms of the pension plan. Measuring that obligation is not so simple, though, because there are different ways of doing so.

One measure of the pension obligation bases it only on the benefits vested to the employees. **Vested benefits** are those that an employee is entitled to receive even if he or she provides no additional services to the company. Most pension plans require a specific minimum number of years of service to the employer before an employee achieves the status of having vested benefits. Companies calculate the **vested benefit obligation** using current salary levels and only vested benefits.

Another way to measure the obligation is to use both vested and non-vested years of service. On this basis, the deferred compensation amount is calculated on all years of service performed by employees under the plan—both vested and non-vested—using current salary levels. This measurement of the pension obligation is called the **accumulated benefit obligation**.

A third method calculates the deferred compensation amount using both vested and non-vested service and **using future salaries**. This measurement of the pension obligation is called the **projected benefit obligation**. Because future salaries are expected to be higher than current salaries, this approach results in the largest measure of the pension obligation.

Deciding which measure to use is critical because it affects the amount of the pension obligation and the annual pension expense that is recognized. The diagram in Illustration 19-2 presents the differences in these three measurements. **Regardless of the approach that is used, the estimated future benefits to be paid are discounted to their present value.**

6 Objective
Explain what the employer's benefit obligation is and identify alternative measures for valuing this obligation.

International Insight
IAS 19, "Employee Benefits," also requires companies to base pension expense on estimated future compensation levels.

Illustration 19-2

*Different Measures of the
Pension Obligation*

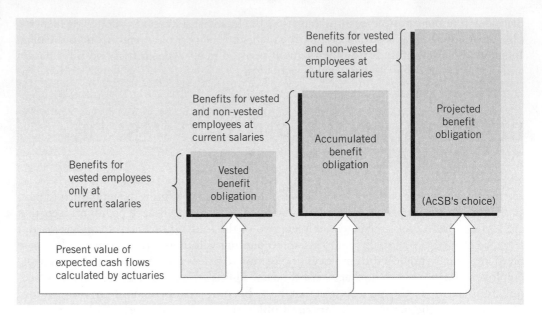

Which of these approaches is generally accepted as the best measure of the obligation? The FASB, IASB, and Canadian Accounting Standards Board have all adopted the projected benefit method. This means that the obligation is the present value of vested and non-vested benefits based on employees' future salary levels.[12] For this chapter, we use the term **accrued benefit obligation (ABO)** throughout, and mean by it the portion of the projected benefit obligation that can be attributed to the services provided to date.[13]

Critics who are against using projected salaries argue that using future salary levels results in future obligations being added to existing ones. Those in favour of the projected benefit obligation counter that a promise by an employer to pay benefits based on a percentage of the employees' future salary is far different from a promise to pay a percentage of their current salary, and that this difference should be reflected in the pension liability and pension expense.

Underlying Concept

Recognizing the smaller benefit obligation ignores the going concern concept. A going concern would not expect to settle the obligation today at current salaries and wages. A going concern would expect to settle the obligation based on future salary levels.

Capitalization versus Non-Capitalization

Another fundamental choice in accounting for pensions and other future benefits is whether a capitalization or non-capitalization approach should be taken. The major issue in this case is whether the full obligation should be recognized as a liability (capitalization), or whether the amount that is recorded should be restricted and related only to the amount of expense that has been recognized (non-capitalization).

Under a **capitalization approach**, pension plan assets and full pension obligations are reported as assets and liabilities on the employer company's balance sheet. This fits the economic substance of the pension plan arrangement, since the employer has a clear obligation to pay pension benefits for employee services that have already been performed. As the employees work, pension costs are incurred and the employer's liability increases. The pension liability and the pension assets are both reduced through the payment of benefits to retired employees. Funding the plan is recognized on the balance sheet by the transfer

---

[12] When the term "present value of benefits" is used throughout this chapter, it really means the **actuarial present value** of benefits. Actuarial present value is the amount payable adjusted to reflect the time value of money and the probability of payment (by means of decreases for events such as death, disability, withdrawals, or retirement) between the present date and the expected date of payment. For simplicity, we will use the term "present value" instead of "actuarial present value" in our discussion.

[13] *CICA Handbook*, Section 3461.024(d).

of company assets into a separate category of asset that is set aside for the pension fund, but the funding has no effect on the liability amount.

A **non-capitalization approach**, on the other hand, is more consistent with the legal form of pension arrangements since **the plan is considered a separate legal and accounting entity**. Cash and investments that are set aside to fund pension obligations are considered assets of the pension plan, not of the employer company; therefore, neither the pension assets nor the obligation are recognized on the employer's balance sheet. Under this approach, the employer accrues a pension liability equal to the pension expense that is recognized, and, as long as the employer's contribution to the fund trustee is the same as the pension expense, the balance sheet reports no asset or liability related to the pension plan.[14] If the funding exceeds the expense that has been recognized, a prepaid expense or other deferred charge is included on the balance sheet; if the funding is less than the expense, a pension liability is reported. When the trustee pays benefits to retirees, **the employer records no entries** since the company's recorded assets and liabilities are not reduced. This approach is often referred to as a method of off–balance sheet financing because any underfunding of the plan itself, for which the employer is ultimately responsible, is not recognized on the company's balance sheet.

The AcSB adopted a noncapitalization approach as a compromise position in *CICA Handbook* Section 3461. In 2006, the FASB moved closer to a capitalization method with the release of its *Statement No. 158*, which requires companies to report the funded status of a defined benefit plan—the difference between the plan assets and the accrued benefit obligation—on the statement of financial position.[15] Canadian changes await further IASB study and discussion.

Changes in the Accrued Benefit Obligation

Although it is not recognized as a liability on the employer's statement of financial position, the accrued benefit obligation is central to the accounting for pension costs.

Illustration 19-3 summarizes the accrued benefit obligation, or **ABO**, from the perspective of the transactions and events that change it. At any point in time, the ABO represents the actuarial present value of the benefits attributed to employee services that have been rendered to date. A simplified example of its measurement is provided in Appendix 19A. The accrued obligation increases as employees provide further services and as interest is added to this discounted liability. The obligation decreases as benefit payments are made to retirees. In addition, the ABO might either increase or decrease as plans are amended to change the future benefits that were promised for prior services, and as the assumptions that are used to calculate the obligation change. Actuaries provide most of the necessary measurements related to the ABO.

7 Objective
Identify transactions and events that change the amount of the employer's accrued benefit obligation, and calculate the balance of the obligation.

```
Accrued benefit obligation (ABO), at beginning of period
+ Current service cost
+ Interest cost
– Benefits paid to retirees
± Past service costs of plan amendments during period
± Actuarial gains (–) or losses (+) during period

= Accrued benefit obligation (ABO), at end of period
```

Illustration 19-3

Accrued Benefit Obligation— Continuity Schedule

[14] For purposes of this chapter, "pension expense" refers to both the portion that is recognized as an expense on the income statement and any amounts capitalized in the year (e.g., a portion of direct or indirect labour charged to an asset such as inventory.)

[15] FASB *Statement No. 158* is "Employers' Accounting for Defined Benefit Pension and Other Post-retirement Plans: An Amendment of FASB Statements No. 87, 88, 106, and 132(R)."

Service Cost   The current **service cost** is the cost of the benefits that are to be provided in the future in exchange for the services that the employees performed in the current period. In measuring the service cost to assign to each period, standard setters had to decide on a method of allocating the estimated cost to the individual years during which the entitlement to the benefits builds. Should the total cost be allocated based on the percentage earned by the employee during the year of the total estimated career compensation (i.e., **prorated on salaries**) or on an equal amount per year of service (i.e., **prorated on service**)? The standard setters decided on the method that accrues a relatively equal charge for each period—the prorated on service approach.

To calculate current service cost, the actuary predicts the additional benefits that must be paid under the plan's benefit formula as a result of the employees' current year of service and then discounts the cost of these benefits to their present value. For example, consider the following pension benefit formula:

> Annual pension benefit on retirement = 2% of salary at retirement × Number of years of service

By working an additional year, the employee earns an entitlement to an increased pension, and the company's pension obligation increases by 2% of the employee's estimated final salary for each year of retirement. Appendix 19A provides a simplified example of this calculation.

For defined benefit plans where future benefits depend on or are increased by the length of service, the actuary bases the calculations on future salary levels and then attributes the cost of the future benefits to the accounting periods between the date of hire and when the employee becomes eligible for full benefits. This is known as the **attribution period**. The obligation to provide benefits is attributed to the periods in which the employee provides the service that gives rise to the benefits. While the date of hire is the most common date for employees to begin earning benefits, it may be a later date, and eligibility for full benefits may occur before the date of retirement.[16]

Interest Cost   Because a pension is a deferred compensation arrangement—it is essentially an element of wages that is deferred and thus creates an obligation—the time value of money has to be considered. As the obligation is not paid until maturity, it is measured on a discounted basis. As time to maturity passes, the **interest accrues on the accrued benefit obligation just as it does on any discounted debt**. The interest for the period is based on the accrued benefit obligation that is outstanding during the period.

What interest rate should be used? Current accounting standards require the use of a current market rate, such as the current yield on high-quality debt instruments or the current **settlement rate**: the rate implied in an insurance contract that could be purchased to effectively settle the pension obligation. The rate that is used should be the rate at the beginning of the period.[17] Note that minor changes in the interest rate that is used to discount pension benefits can dramatically affect the measurement of the employer's obligation. For example, a 1% decrease in the discount rate could increase pension liabilities by 15%. The discount rate that is used to measure the pension liability has to be changed at each measurement date to the current rate.

Benefits Paid to Retirees   The pension fund trustee is responsible for paying the pension benefits to the former employees. Similar to all liabilities, as obligations are met, the balance of the obligation is reduced.

---

[16] *CICA Handbook*, Section 3461.038 and .039.
[17] *CICA Handbook*, Section 3461.050 and .075.

Past Service Costs   When a defined benefit plan is either initiated (begun) or amended, credit is often given to employees for years of service that they provided before the date of initiation or amendment. As a result of these credits for prior services, the actuary remeasures the accrued benefit obligation, and it usually ends up being larger than it was before the change. The increase in the accrued benefit obligation on the date when the plan is initiated or amended is known as **past service cost**, the cost of the retroactive benefits. This increase is often substantial. A simplified illustration of how past service cost is calculated is provided in Appendix 19A.

In recent years, because they want to reduce the very significant costs that are associated with post-retirement plans, many companies have been negotiating reductions in some of their plan benefits. When this happens, there could be a decrease in the accrued benefit obligation at a specific date for past services.

Actuarial Gains and Losses   **Actuarial gains and losses** have two sources: (1) a change in actuarial assumptions, which means a change in the assumptions about the occurrence of future events that affect the measurement of the future benefit costs and obligations; and (2) an **experience gain or loss**, which is the difference between what has actually occurred and the previous actuarial assumptions about what would occur.[18] When later events show that assumptions were inaccurate, adjustments are needed.

In estimating the accrued benefit obligation (the liability), actuaries make assumptions about such variables as mortality rates, retirement rates, turnover rates, disability rates, and rates of salary escalation (increase). Any difference between these assumed rates and the ones that are actually experienced changes the amount of the accrued benefit obligation. Actual experience is rarely exactly the same as actuarial predictions. An unexpected gain or loss that results in a change in the amount of the ABO is referred to as a **liability experience gain or loss**. Actuarial gains and losses also occur when the assumptions that are used by the actuary in calculating the ABO are revised, as this causes a change in the amount of the obligation. An example is the effect on the obligation of a change in the interest rate that is used to discount the pension cash flows. Because experience gains and losses are similar to and affect the ABO in the same way as actuarial gains and losses, **both types are referred to as actuarial gains and losses**.

To illustrate, assume that a company's expected accrued benefit obligation—based on its opening balance and the year's service cost, interest cost, benefits paid, and plan amendments—is $262,000 at December 31, 2008. If the company's actuaries, using December 31, 2008, estimates, calculate an accrued benefit obligation of $275,000, then the company has suffered an actuarial loss of $13,000 ($275,000 – $262,000). If the actuary calculates a reduced obligation, the result is an actuarial gain. Whatever the result, the ABO is adjusted to its most recent actuarial valuation.

Plan settlements and curtailments will also affect the amount of the accrued benefit obligation, but these are outside the scope of this chapter.

Plan Assets

The benefit plan assets are the other major foundation on which pension accounting is based. **Plan assets** are assets that have been set aside in a trust or other legal entity that is separate from the employer company. The assets are restricted and can be used only to settle the related accrued benefit obligation: they cannot be used for meeting the claims of other company creditors. The plan assets are made up mainly of cash and investments in debt and equity securities that are held to earn a reasonable return, generally at a minimum of risk.

Student Website

Expanded Discussion

www.wiley.com/canada/kieso

8 Objective

Identify transactions and events that change the amount of the plan assets, and calculate the balance of the assets.

---

[18] *CICA Handbook*, Section 3461.024(e).

Changes in Plan Assets

As can be seen in Illustration 19-4, the fund assets change as a result of contributions from the employer (and employee, if the plan is contributory) and from the actual return that is generated on the assets that have been invested. The pool of assets is reduced by payments to retirees.

Illustration 19-4

Plan Assets—Continuity Schedule

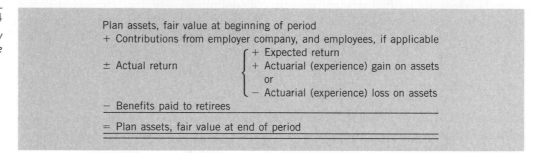

Contributions   The amount of an employer company's contributions to the plan has a direct effect on the plan's ability to pay the accrued obligation. Who and what determines how much a company contributes to the plan? In Canada, pension plans come under either federal or provincial pension legislation as well as regulations of the Canada Revenue Agency (CRA). The CRA stipulates the amount of the contributions that are tax-deductible to the company and the conditions on the payment of benefits out of the plan. Federal and provincial laws dictate the funding requirements.[19]

Actual Return   The **actual return** that is earned on the fund assets is the income generated on the assets that are being held by the trustee, less the cost of administering the fund. The actual return that is earned on these assets increases the fund balance. The return is made up of dividends and interest as well as profits that are generated on any real estate investments. In addition, because the assets are measured at fair value, holding gains and losses on the assets are also included as part of the actual return. Including the holding gains and losses explains why the actual return could increase the plan assets in one year and decrease them in another. In years when stock and/or bond markets decline, the reduction in fair value may be greater than the other forms of income that are reported and the fund will report a loss for the period.

Because the actual return can be highly variable from one year to the next, actuaries ignore short-term fluctuations when they develop a funding pattern to pay expected benefits in the future. Instead, they develop an expected long-term rate of return and apply it to the fair value, or a market-related value, to arrive at an **expected return** on plan assets.[20] As shown in Illustration 19-4, the actual return is made up of two components: (1) the expected return, and (2) the difference between the expected return and the actual return. The plan trustee provides most of this information.

---

[19] In general, the current service cost has to be funded annually. If a plan is in a surplus position (i.e., fund assets are greater than the accrued obligation), the company may be able to take a contribution holiday, in other words, to temporarily not make any contributions. If there is a funding deficiency, the extent of the shortfall is determined by two different valuations: one based on a going concern assumption and one based on a termination assumption. These dictate the additional funding that is required, and that any deficiency must be funded over either a five-year or 15-year period. In 2006, the funding periods were increased for some defined benefit plans. The accumulated benefit obligation (using current salary levels) is most often used to determine the minimum funding requirements.

[20] The **market-related value of plan assets** is a calculated value that recognizes changes in fair value in a systematic and rational way over no more than five years (*CICA Handbook*, Section 3461.076 and .077). Different ways of calculating a market-related value may be used for different asset classes. For example, an employer might use fair value for bonds and a five-year moving average for equities, but the way of determining market-related value should be applied consistently from year to year for each asset class.

Actuarial Gains and Losses The difference between the expected return and the actual return is referred to as an **asset experience gain or loss**. A gain occurs when the actual return is greater than the expected return. A loss occurs when actual returns are less than expected. The amount of the asset gain or loss is determined at the end of each year by comparing the calculated expected return with the actual return that was earned. For example, if the actuary expected a return of $20,000 based on the long-run average rate, and the actual return earned in the year was only $19,000, the records would indicate an actuarial (or experience) loss of $1,000 in the year. The actual return ($19,000) is made up of the expected return ($20,000) and the actuarial loss ($1,000). Asset experience gains and losses are also referred to as actuarial gains and losses.

Benefits Paid The plan trustee pays out benefits to the retirees according to the plan formula and pension agreement.

Funded Status

As indicated in Illustration 19-5, the difference between the accrued benefit obligation and the pension assets' fair value at any point in time is known as the plan's **funded status**. A plan with more liabilities than assets is **underfunded**; a plan with accumulated assets that are greater than the related obligation is **overfunded**.[21] Because the Accounting Standards Board follows a non-capitalization approach, the **funded status liability** or **funded status asset** for defined benefit plans such as pensions is not reported on the statement of financial position.

9 Objective
Explain and calculate a benefit plan's funded status.

Accrued benefit obligation (ABO), end of period
− Fair value of plan assets, end of period

= Plan's funded status

ABO > Plan assets = **underfunded** = a funded status liability
Plan assets > ABO = **overfunded** = a funded status asset

Illustration 19-5
Funded Status

Transitional Asset or Obligation

Amendments to pension accounting standards in the late 1980s and the introduction of *CICA Handbook* Section 3461 in 2000 resulted in significant changes to the accounting for pensions and other employee future benefits. When companies first applied the new requirements, they determined the funded status of their plans at that time. If a company decided to apply the new standards **prospectively**, that is, with the accounting effects assigned to future periods, the company had a net **transitional asset** (if the benefit plan was overfunded) or **transitional obligation or liability** (if the benefit plan was underfunded) that had to be accounted for. The transitional asset or liability is merely the funded status of the plan when the accounting standards were applied for the first time. Many companies still report transitional balances that have not yet been fully amortized to benefit expense.

Now that you have been introduced to all the components that are needed to account for a defined benefit plan with benefits that vest or accumulate, it is time to look

Underlying Concept

Many plans are underfunded but still quite viable. For example, **Canadian Imperial Bank of Commerce** had a $1,043-million pension and other benefit plans shortfall. But CIBC at that time had earnings of $2,063 million and a net worth of $13,778 million. Concern over pensions being underfunded is directly related to the financial position and performance of the employer company—the plan sponsor.

---

[21] When Air Canada filed for protection under the *Companies' Creditors Arrangement Act* on April 1, 2003, a $1.5-billion unfunded pension liability was listed as one of the key factors behind the company's insolvency. The Office of the Superintendent of Financial Institutions had ordered the company to transfer assets to its pension funds in the latter part of March. How to deal with this underfunded plan and unbooked liability was central to Air Canada's restructuring negotiations.

at the actual accounting for such plans. If all the changes in the accrued benefit obligation and in the fund assets (except for the cash contributions made by the employer company to the fund assets) were recognized in accounting entries as part of the benefit expense and as a change in the benefit asset or liability on the balance sheet, pension accounting would be very straightforward. The balance sheet account would have the same balance as the funded status, and the income statement account along with the company contributions into the plan would explain the change in the funded status. For a variety of reasons, however, pension accounting introduces several variations in how these amounts are recognized. These, and the reasons for them, are explained in the next section of the chapter.

BENEFIT COST

Objective 10
Identify the possible components of pension benefit cost, and account for a defined benefit pension plan under Canadian GAAP.

Pension Benefit Cost Components

You have already been introduced to the component parts that make up the pension benefit cost that is recognized on the income statement. These are, for the most part, the events that change the balances of the accrued benefit obligation and the fund assets:

- Service cost
- Interest cost
- Expected return on plan assets
- Past service costs
- Actuarial gains and losses
- Transitional balances

International Insight

The FASB's requirements for calculating defined benefit pension expense are similar to those of *CICA Handbook* Section 3461.

Under current Canadian standards, these events are not all recognized in expense in the same period as when they affect the funded status—i.e., the ABO and plan assets. Some amounts are not recognized in the accounts, but are deferred and recognized in expense only as they are amortized in a later period. Illustration 19-6 summarizes the components of pension expense and what is deferred off–balance sheet—i.e., outside the accounts.

Illustration 19-6

Accounting for Components of Pension Benefit Plans

Component	Pension Expense on Income Statement	Unamortized Pension Benefit Costs: Off–Balance Sheet
Service cost	Service cost	
Interest cost	+ Interest cost	
Expected return on plan assets	− Expected return on plan assets	
Past service cost	± Past service cost amortized in year	± Past service cost for current year amendments ± Past service cost amortized in year
Actuarial gains and losses	± Actuarial gains/losses amortized in year	± Current year actuarial gains/losses ± Actuarial gains/losses amortized in year
Transitional asset or liability	± Transitional asset/liability amortized in year	± New transitional asset/liability recognized ± Transitional asset/liability amortized in year
	= Pension expense	Balance, end of year: reported in notes to the financial statements

While there is general agreement that pension costs should be accounted for on the accrual basis and matched with revenues in the accounting periods that benefit from the employees' service, not everyone agrees on which cost components should be included in current year expense. Current accounting standards recognize the various cost components as expense in the following ways:

1. Service cost and interest cost: Both the service cost for benefits that have been earned by employees in the current year and the interest cost that has accrued on the ABO are recognized and included in pension expense in the period when the costs are incurred. If the plan is a contributory one, the service cost is reduced by the contributions made by employees.

2. Expected return on plan assets. The return earned by the fund assets reduces the cost to the employer of sponsoring an employee pension plan. However, because the actual returns can vary so much from year to year, pension expense is calculated using the expected rate. The actuarial gain or loss amount—the variance between the yearly actual return and the expected return—is accumulated in supplementary files outside the accounts and, as we will see later, it may be included in periodic pension expense, but amortized over future periods.

3. Past service cost. Although plan amendments instantly change the balance of the ABO, the total cost of the amendment is not recognized immediately in pension expense. The rationale is that plan amendments are made with the expectation that the employer will realize economic benefits in future periods from continued employee service. Therefore, past service costs incurred are kept track of outside the accounts initially, and are amortized to pension expense over future periods.

4. Actuarial gains and losses. Actuarial gains and losses, if they were recognized fully in expense in the period when they are incurred, would cause significant fluctuations in the reported expense from year to year. Because they are expected to cancel each other out over time, the amount of these gains and losses incurred in the period is noted outside the accounts. If the accumulated amounts are significant, they are amortized to expense using a "corridor approach," which is described later in the chapter.

5. Transitional asset or obligation. When companies apply the accounting standards for the first time for pension or other defined benefit plans with benefits that vest or accumulate, they must determine the unrecorded funded status of the plan at that time. If the new standards are applied prospectively, the net transitional asset or liability is measured, but not recognized in the accounts initially. The net cost or benefit is later amortized to expense.

Other components of expense for the period are identified in the accounting standard. These include gains and losses on plan settlements and curtailments, and termination benefits. In addition, some part of the change in the valuation allowance related to the funded status asset is also included. These are discussed on the Student Website.

Canadian GAAP Illustrated

Before covering the "amortized" pension expense components in detail, we will illustrate the basic accounting for the first three components: service cost, interest cost, and expected return on plan assets.

Underlying Concept

Together, the definition of a liability and the matching concept justify accounting for pension costs on the accrual basis. This requires recording an expense when the future benefits are earned by the employees and recognizing an existing obligation to pay pensions later based on current services received.

Student Website

Expanded Discussion
www.wiley.com/canada/kieso

Use of a **non-capitalization** approach is an essential part of the accounting for pensions (and other similar future benefits) under current Canadian and international standards. In this context, non-capitalization means that the fund assets and ABO are not recognized on the employer's balance sheet. Instead, the fund assets and ABO—the funded status of the plan—is reported only in the notes to the financial statements, usually with a reconciliation to the asset or liability actually reported on the balance sheet. Because the only differences between what is recorded in the accounts and what affects the funded status relates to **the unamortized balances** of past service cost, actuarial gains and losses, and any transitional asset or liability, these unrecorded balances are needed to complete the reconciliation. This will become clearer as we work through the following examples.

A work sheet that is unique to pension accounting is used to keep track of pension expense and the accrued benefit asset/liability on the balance sheet, as well as the accrued benefit obligation, fund assets, and each off–balance sheet unamortized balance. The work sheet illustrates the relationship among all the components.[22] The work sheet format is shown in Illustration 19-7.

<table>
<tr><td rowspan="2" colspan="3" style="text-align:center">**Illustration 19-7**
Basic Format of Pension Work Sheet</td><td colspan="3" style="text-align:center">General Journal Entries</td><td colspan="3" style="text-align:center">Memo Record</td></tr>
<tr><td>Annual
Pension
Expense</td><td>Cash</td><td>Accrued
Pension
Asset/Liability</td><td>Accrued
Benefit
Obligation</td><td>Plan
Assets</td><td>Unamortized
Balances</td></tr>
<tr><td colspan="3">Items</td><td></td><td></td><td></td><td></td><td></td><td></td></tr>
</table>

Objective 11
Explain the usefulness of—and complete—a work sheet to support the employer's pension accounts.

The left-hand columns of the work sheet under "General Journal Entries" are the source for entries in the general ledger accounts. The right-hand "Memo Record" columns maintain balances on the accrued benefit obligation, the fund assets, and, where applicable, any unamortized balances. On the first line of the work sheet, the beginning balances are recorded. Subsequently, transactions and events that relate to the pension plan are entered, using debits and credits and using both sets of records as if there was just one set for recording the entries. For each transaction or event the debits must equal the credits, and the balance in the Accrued Pension Asset/Liability column must equal the net balance in the Memo Record columns. Notice as we work through the work sheet examples that it is the changes in the ABO and fund assets that lead to most of the work sheet entries. At the end of the period, assuming there are no unamortized amounts, the balance in the balance sheet Accrued Pension Asset/Liability account is equal to the funded status.

The Basics—2007 Work Sheet and Entries

To illustrate the use of a work sheet and how it helps in accounting for a pension plan, assume that on January 1, 2007, Zarle Corporation adopts *CICA Handbook* Section 3461 to account for its defined benefit pension plan. The following facts are for the pension plan for the year 2007:

1. Plan assets at January 1, 2007, are $100,000; and at December 31, 2007, are $111,000.

2. The accrued benefit obligation at January 1, 2007, is $100,000; and at December 31, 2007, is $112,000.

3. The annual service cost for 2007 is $9,000, accrued as of the end of 2007.

---

[22] This pension entry work sheet is taken from Paul B.W. Miller, "The New Pension Accounting (part 2)," *Journal of Accountancy*, February 1987, pp. 86–94.

4. The interest (discount) rate on the liability for 2007 is 10%.

5. The expected and actual earnings on plan assets for 2007 are 10%.

6. The contributions (funding) in 2007 are $8,000, remitted at the end of 2007.

7. Benefits paid to retirees by the trustee during the year are $7,000, paid at the end of 2007.

Using these data, Illustration 19-8 presents the work sheet, including the beginning balances and all the pension entries that Zarle Corporation needs to make for 2007. The beginning balances of the accrued benefit obligation and the pension plan assets are recorded on the work sheet's first line in the memo record. They are not recorded in the accounts and, therefore, are not reported as a liability and an asset in Zarle Corporation's financial statements. Notice that, although they are "off balance sheet," the January 1, 2007, funded status of $0 is the same as the balance of $0 in the Accrued Pension Asset/Liability account on the balance sheet on that date. This will happen only when there are no unamortized balances relating to past service costs, actuarial gains/losses, or transitional amounts at that date.

	General Journal Entries			Memo Record	
Items	Annual Pension Expense	Cash	Accrued Pension Asset/Liability	Accrued Benefit Obligation	Plan Assets
Balance, Jan. 1, 2007			–0–	100,000 Cr.	100,000 Dr.
(a) Service cost	9,000 Dr.			9,000 Cr.	
(b) Interest cost	10,000 Dr.			10,000 Cr.	
(c) Expected return	10,000 Cr.				10,000 Dr.
(d) Contributions		8,000 Cr.			8,000 Dr.
(e) Benefits paid				7,000 Dr.	7,000 Cr.
Expense entry, 2007	9,000 Dr.		9,000 Cr.		
Contribution entry, 2007		8,000 Cr.	8,000 Dr.		
Balance, Dec. 31, 2007			1,000 Cr.	112,000 Cr.	111,000 Dr.

Illustration 19-8

Pension Work Sheet—2007

Entry (a) recognizes the service cost component, which increases the accrued benefit obligation by $9,000 and increases pension expense by $9,000. Entry (b) accrues the interest cost, increasing both the ABO and pension expense by $10,000 (the weighted average balance of the accrued benefit obligation multiplied by the discount rate of 10%). Entry (c) records the expected return on plan assets, which increases the plan assets and decreases pension expense. Entry (d) reflects Zarle Corporation's contribution (funding) of assets to the pension fund; cash is decreased by $8,000 and plan assets are increased by $8,000. Entry (e) records the benefit payments made to retirees, which results in equal $7,000 decreases in the plan assets and the accrued benefit obligation.

The adjusting journal entry on December 31, 2007, to formally record the expense for the year is as follows:

Pension Expense	9,000	
Accrued Pension Asset/Liability		9,000

A =	L	+	SE
	+9,000		–9,000

Cash flows: No effect

When Zarle Corporation issued its $8,000 cheque to the pension fund trustee, it made the following entry:

A = L + SE
−8,000 −8,000
Cash flows: ↓ 8,000 outflow

| Accrued Pension Asset/Liability | 8,000 | |
| Cash | | 8,000 |

The credit balance in the Accrued Pension Asset/Liability account of $1,000 now represents the funded status—the difference between the accrued benefit obligation and the fund assets. Illustration 19-9 shows a reconciliation of the off–balance sheet memo items with the liability reported on the balance sheet.

Illustration 19-9

Pension Reconciliation Schedule—December 31, 2007

Accrued benefit obligation	$112,000
Plan assets	111,000
Funded status—net liability	$ 1,000
Accrued pension liability on balance sheet	$ 1,000

In addition, the balance sheet liability account also represents the excess of the accumulated pension expense recognized to date ($9,000) over the accumulated contributions made to date ($8,000)—a $1,000 liability. Although we are not told what expense was reported and contributions were made in prior years, we can tell that these amounts were equal at January 1, 2007. This is because the Accrued Pension Asset/Liability balance was $0 at that date.

The work sheet is designed to highlight the relationships among the related accounts and amounts—information that is useful later in preparing the notes related to pension disclosures.

Past Service Costs (PSC)—2008 Work Sheet and Entries

Objective 12
Define and account for past service costs.

One question that standards setters have wrestled with is whether the past service costs or credits that are associated with the adoption or amendment of pension plans should be fully recognized in net income when the plan is initiated or amended. The AcSB has taken the position that these costs should not be recognized in expense when the plan is adopted or amended. The board's rationale is that the employer would not provide credit for past years of service unless it expected to receive benefits in the future; based on this reasoning, the past service costs should therefore be deferred.

In line with the AcSB's position, current Canadian standards specify that the past service cost be deferred initially and recognized as an expense on a straight-line basis over the periods that benefit. This is normally the expected period from the time of adoption or amendment until the employee group that is covered by the plan is eligible for the plan's full benefits.[23] As Illustration 19-10 shows, to determine the period of amortization, the affected employees are grouped according to their expected remaining years of service until full eligibility and the expected remaining service period is calculated.

[23] *CICA Handbook*, Section 3461.079. Note that this accounting treatment is consistent with the upper limit of the attribution period (i.e., the expected period to full eligibility) that is used for attributing current service cost to accounting periods.

Group	Number of Employees	Expected Remaining Years of Service to Full Eligibility	Total
A	40	1	40
B	20	2	40
C	40	3	120
D	50	4	200
E	20	5	100
	170		500

Expected period to full eligibility = 500 ÷ 170 = 2.94

Note: FASB prefers a "years-to-service" amortization method similar to a units-of-production calculation. In the first year, for example, 170 service years are worked by employees. Therefore, 170/500 of the past service cost is recognized in the first year.

Illustration 19-10

Calculation of Expected Period until Full Eligibility

International Insight

Under IAS 19, which addresses employee benefits, past service costs are recognized as an expense immediately if they are vested; otherwise, they are amortized on a straight-line basis over the average period until the benefits are vested. The IAS Board is considering immediate recognition for all past service costs, whether vested or not.

Alternatively, a company could conclude that the benefits are received over a shorter period of time if the company has a history of making plan amendments regularly. Regardless, amortization has the effect of smoothing the amount of pension expense over time.

To illustrate the initial amount of past service cost and its subsequent amortization to expense, assume that Zarle Corporation amends its defined benefit pension plan on January 1, 2008, to grant prior service benefits to certain employees. The company's actuaries determine that this causes an increase in the accrued benefit obligation of $80,000. The full $80,000 is initially deferred.

The portion of the past service cost that needs to be recognized in pension expense each year based on Illustration 19-10 is as follows: $27,211 ($80,000 ÷ 2.94) in 2008; $27,211 in 2009; and the remainder of $25,578 in 2010. These amounts reduce the unamortized balance each year as they are recognized as an expense in the income statement. At the end of 2008 and 2009, therefore, a portion of the original past service costs from 2008 remains unrecognized. Such past service costs that have not yet been amortized to income are known as **unamortized past service costs** or **unrecognized past service costs.**

2008 Entries and Work Sheet. Continuing the Zarle Corporation illustration into 2008, we note that the January 1, 2008, amendment to the pension plan grants to employees prior service benefits that have a present value of $80,000. The annual amortization of $27,211 for 2008 that was calculated in the previous section is carried forward in this illustration. The following facts apply to the pension plan for the year 2008:

1. On January 1, 2008, Zarle Corporation grants prior service benefits that have a present value of $80,000.

2. The annual service cost for 2008 is $9,500.

3. Interest on the pension obligation (ABO) is 10%.

4. The expected and actual return on plan assets is 10%.

5. Annual contributions (funding) are $20,000.

6. Benefits paid to retirees in 2008 are $8,000.

7. The amortization of past service costs is $27,211.

8. At December 31, 2008, the ABO is $212,700 and plan assets are $134,100.

Note that in all chapter examples and end-of-chapter problem material, unless we specify otherwise, **it is assumed that current service cost is credited at year end and** that contributions to the fund and benefits paid to retirees are year-end cash flows. Such an assumption is needed in order to determine the average balances outstanding for the interest and expected return calculations.

Illustration 19-11 presents all the pension "entries" and information used by Zarle Corporation in 2008. The work sheet's first line shows the beginning balances of the Accrued Pension Asset/Liability account, and the components of the plan's funded status. Entry (f) records Zarle Corporation's granting of prior service benefits by adding $80,000 to the accrued benefit obligation and to the balance of the unrecognized past service cost. Entries (g), (h), (i), (k), and (l) are similar to the corresponding entries in 2007. Entry (j) recognizes the 2008 amortization of past service cost by transferring $27,211 to Pension Expense.

Illustration 19-11

Pension Work Sheet—2008

	General Journal Entries			Memo Record		
Items	Annual Pension Expense	Cash	Accrued Pension Asset/Liability	Accrued Benefit Obligation	Plan Assets	Unrecognized Past Service Cost
Balance, Dec. 31, 2007			1,000 Cr.	112,000 Cr.	111,000 Dr.	
(f) Past service cost				80,000 Cr.		80,000 Dr.
Balance, Jan. 1, 2008			1,000 Cr.	192,000 Cr.	111,000 Dr.	80,000 Dr.
(g) Service cost	9,500 Dr.			9,500 Cr.		
(h) Interest cost	19,200 Dr.			19,200 Cr.		
(i) Expected return	11,100 Cr.				11,100 Dr.	
(j) Amortization of PSC	27,211 Dr.					27,211 Cr.
(k) Contribution		20,000 Cr.			20,000 Dr.	
(l) Benefits paid				8,000 Dr.	8,000 Cr.	
Expense entry, 2008	44,811 Dr.		44,811 Cr.			
Contribution entry, 2008		20,000 Cr.	20,000 Dr.			
Balance, Dec. 31, 2008			25,811 Cr.	212,700 Cr.	134,100 Dr.	52,789 Dr.

An entry is needed on December 31, 2008 to formally record the pension expense for the year.

A = L + SE
+44,811 −44,811

Cash flows: No effect

Pension Expense	44,811	
Accrued Pension Asset/Liability		44,811
(To recognize pension expense for the year)		

When the company made its contributions to the pension fund during the year, the following entry was recorded:

A = L + SE
−20,000 −20,000

Cash flows: ↓ 20,000 outflow

Accrued Pension Asset/Liability	20,000	
Cash		20,000

Because the expense exceeds the funding, the Accrued Pension Liability account increases during the year by the $24,811 difference ($44,811 less $20,000). In 2008, as in 2007, the balance of the Accrued Pension Liability account ($25,811) is equal to the net of the balances in the memo accounts as shown in the following reconciliation schedule.

	At Dec. 31, 2008
Accrued benefit obligation	$212,700 Cr.
Plan assets	134,100 Dr.
Funded status—net liability (underfunded)	78,600 Cr.
Unrecognized past service cost	52,789 Dr.
Accrued pension liability on balance sheet	$ 25,811 Cr.

Actuarial Gains and Losses—2009 Work Sheet and Entries

Of great concern to companies that have pension plans are the uncontrollable and unexpected swings in pension expense that could be caused by (1) large and sudden changes in the market value of plan assets and (2) changes in actuarial assumptions that affect the amount of the accrued benefit obligation. These two events are the sources of actuarial gains and losses. If these gains or losses were to be fully included in pension expense in the period in which they occurred, substantial fluctuations in pension expense would result. Therefore, the profession decided to reduce the volatility that could be associated with pension expense by using smoothing techniques that dampen and in some cases fully eliminate the fluctuations, as we will see shortly.

Asset Gains and Losses. The return on plan assets is a component of pension expense that normally reduces the expense amount. Because significant changes in the actual return from year to year could result in unacceptable fluctuations in the reported pension expense, accounting standards use a long-term expected rate of return instead of the actual rate of return. This is consistent with the actuary's use of a long-run average rate when developing a funding pattern for an employer to ensure that funds are set aside to pay expected benefits in the future.

> **13 Objective**
> Explain what actuarial gains and losses are, and account for them using the corridor approach to amortization.

To determine the expected return component of pension expense, the fair value (or market-related value) of plan assets at the beginning of the year is adjusted for additional contributions and payments to retirees during the year and then the weighted average balance of the assets is multiplied by the expected long-term rate of return (the actuary's rate). Throughout our Zarle Corporation illustrations, the market-related value and fair value of plan assets are assumed to be equal.

As explained earlier in the chapter, the asset actuarial (experience) gain or loss is determined at the end of each year by comparing the calculated expected return with the actual return that was earned. In the preceding example, the expected return on Zarle's pension fund assets for 2008 was $11,100. If the actual return on the plan assets for the year 2008 was $12,000, there would be an experience gain of $900 ($12,000 – $11,100). Plan assets are increased by $12,000, annual expense is credited with $11,100, and an actuarial gain of $900 is noted but not recognized. The gain is deferred by combining it with actuarial gains and losses accumulated in prior years and the accumulated amount is reported in the notes to the financial statements.

Liability Gains and Losses. Actuarial (experience) gains and losses on plan liabilities, on the other hand, arise from differences between the actuary's assumptions and actual experience, and from changes in the assumptions that are used by the actuary in calculating the ABO.

To illustrate, assume that the expected projected benefit obligation of Zarle Corporation was $212,700 at December 31, 2008. If the company's actuaries, using estimates at December 31, 2008, calculate a projected benefit obligation of $213,500, then the company has suffered an actuarial loss of $800 ($213,500 – $212,700). If the actuary calculates a reduced obligation, the result is an actuarial gain. The ABO is adjusted to its most recent estimate and the difference is deferred with actuarial gains and losses (both asset and liability gains and losses) accumulated in prior years. The balance of the accumulated net actuarial gain or loss is reported in the notes to the financial statements.

Corridor Amortization for Net Actuarial Gains and Losses. Because actuarial gains and losses can and are expected to offset each other over time, the accumulated **unrecognized** or **unamortized net actuarial gain or loss** may not actually grow very large. In fact, this is the reason that is given for not including these gains and losses directly in pension expense each year. But it is possible that no offsetting will occur and that the balance of the accumulated net gain or loss will continue to grow. To limit its growth, the **corridor approach** is used to amortize the balance. The corridor approach amortizes the net gain or loss when its balance is considered too large. It is considered **too large and must be amortized only if it exceeds the arbitrarily selected criterion of 10% of the larger of the accrued benefit obligation and the fair or market-related value of the plan assets at the first of the year**.

Illustration 19-12 presents assumed data on an ABO and plan assets over the six-year period from 2006 to 2011. We will now use this data to explain how the corridor approach works.

Illustration 19-12

Calculation of the Corridor

	Beginning-of-the-Year Balances		
	Accrued Benefit Obligation	Fair or Market-Related Value of Plan Assets	Corridor* +/– 10%
2006	**$1,000,000**	$ 900,000	$100,000
2007	**1,200,000**	1,100,000	120,000
2008	1,300,000	**1,700,000**	170,000
2009	1,500,000	**2,250,000**	225,000
2010	**1,700,000**	1,750,000	175,000
2011	**1,800,000**	1,700,000	180,000

* The corridor is 10% of the larger (in **boldface**) of the accrued benefit obligation and the fair or market-related plan asset value.

If the balance of the accumulated net gain or loss stays within the corridor limits for each year, no amortization is required—the balance is carried forward unchanged. This becomes easier to see when the data are shown in a graph as in Illustration 19-13.

Illustration 19-13

Graphic Illustration of the Corridor

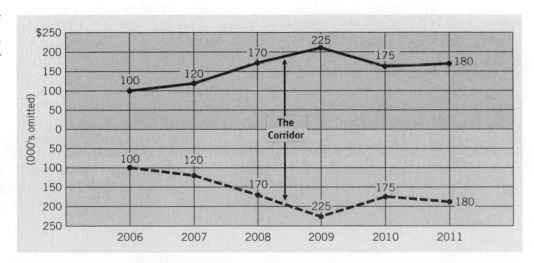

If the accumulated net gain or loss at the first of the year is more than the corridor limit, the amount in excess of the limit must be amortized. The minimum amortization is the accumulated net gain or loss in excess of the corridor amount divided by the **expected average remaining service life** of the employee group that is covered by the plan.[24] The expected average remaining service life of an employee group, known as **EARSL**, is the total number of years of future service that the group is expected to render divided by the number of employees in the group. Any systematic method of amortization may be used instead of the amount determined under this approach, as long as it is greater than the minimum, is used consistently for both gains and losses, and is disclosed.

Illustration of the Corridor Approach. In applying the corridor approach, remember that **all calculations are based on beginning-of-period balances only**. That is, amortization of the excess is included as a component of pension expense only if the unamortized net gain or loss **at the beginning of the year** exceeds the **beginning-of-year corridor**. If there is no accumulated net gain or loss at the beginning of the period, there will be no actuarial gain or loss component of pension expense in the current period.

To illustrate the amortization procedure, assume that a company provides the following information:

	2007	2008	2009
Accrued benefit obligation, January 1	$2,100,000	$2,600,000	$2,900,000
Fair value of fund assets, January 1	2,600,000	2,800,000	2,700,000
Net actuarial loss <gain> in year	400,000	300,000	<170,000>
Corridor: 10% of greater of opening ABO and plan assets	260,000	280,000	290,000

Illustration 19-14 shows how the amortization of the accumulated net loss is determined in each of the three years, assuming the employee group's average remaining service life is five-and-a-half years.

Year	(a) Corridor for Year (see above)	(b) Unrecognized net loss <gain>, first of year	(c) Excess loss <gain> to be amortized (b) − (a)	(d) Amortization (c) ÷ 5.5	(e) Actuarial loss <gain> in year (see above)	(f) Unrecognized net loss <gain>, end of year (b) − (d) + (e)
2007	$260,000	—	—	—	$400,000	$400,000
2008	280,000	$400,000	$120,000	$21,818	300,000	678,182
2009	290,000	678,182	388,182	70,579	<170,000>	437,603

Illustration 19-14

Corridor Test and Gain/Loss Amortization

Note that the unrecognized net actuarial gain or loss is a cumulative number:

	Opening balance of the accumulated net actuarial gain or loss
±	Asset and liability gains and losses in the current year
−	Current year's amortization and transfer to expense, if any
=	Ending balance of the accumulated net actuarial gain or loss

---

[24] *CICA Handbook*, Section 3461.088.

As Illustration 19-14 shows, the $400,000 accumulated loss at the beginning of 2008 increases pension expense in 2008 by $21,818. This amount is small in comparison with the total loss of $400,000 and indicates that the corridor approach dampens the effects (reduces the volatility) of these gains and losses on pension expense. The rationale for the corridor is that gains and losses result from refinements in estimates as well as real changes in economic value and that, over time, some of these gains and losses will cancel each other out. It therefore seems reasonable that gains and losses should not be recognized fully as a component of pension expense in the period in which they arise.[25]

Note that the gains and losses go through three stages of smoothing. First, the asset gain or loss is smoothed by using the expected return. Then the accumulated net actuarial gain or loss at the beginning of the year is not amortized to expense unless it is greater than the corridor. Finally, the excess is spread over the remaining service life of the current employees.

2009 Entries and Work Sheet. Continuing the Zarle Corporation illustration into 2009, the following facts apply to the pension plan:

1. The annual service cost for 2009 is $13,000.

2. Interest on accrued benefits is 10%.

3. The expected return on plan assets is 10%, or $13,410.

4. The actual return on plan assets is $12,000.

5. The fair value of plan assets at December 31, 2009, is $159,600.

6. The amortization of past service cost in 2009 is $27,211.

7. Annual contributions (funding) are $24,000.

8. Benefits paid to retirees in 2009 are $10,500.

9. Changes in actuarial assumptions establish the end-of-year ABO at $265,000.

The work sheet in Illustration 19-15 presents the pension information that Zarle Corporation needs for 2009. The beginning balances that relate to the pension plan are recorded on the work sheet's first line. In this case, the beginning balances for Zarle Corporation are the ending balances from the 2008 pension work sheet in Illustration 19-11.

Entries (m), (n), (o), (p), (q), and (r) are similar to the entries that were explained in 2007 and 2008 for these components. Entries (o) and (t) are related to each other. The recording of the expected return in entry (o) has been illustrated in 2007 and 2008. In both these years, it was assumed that the actual return on plan assets was equal to the expected return. In 2009, the expected return of $13,410 (the expected rate of 10% times the weighted average balance of plan assets of $134,100) is higher than the actual return of $12,000. Entry (t) shows the resulting asset loss of $1,410 ($13,410 − $12,000), which, instead of being recognized in pension expense in 2009, is added to the unrecognized actuarial gains/losses.

[25] There is an exception, however. Gains and losses that arise from a single occurrence that is not directly related to the operation of the pension plan and is not in the ordinary course of the employer's business should be recognized immediately. For example, a gain or loss that is directly related to a plant closing, a disposal of a segment, or a similar event that greatly affects the size of the work force is recognized as a part of the gain or loss associated with that event.

Items	General Journal Entries			Memo Record			
	Annual Pension Expense	Cash	Accrued Pension Asset/Liability	Accrued Benefit Obligation	Plan Assets	Unrecognized Past Service Cost	Unrecognized Actuarial Gain or Loss
Balance, Dec. 31, 2008			25,811 Cr.	212,700 Cr.	134,100 Dr.	52,789 Dr.	
(m) Service cost	13,000 Dr.			13,000 Cr.			
(n) Interest cost	21,270 Dr.			21,270 Cr.			
(o) Expected return	13,410 Cr.				13,410 Dr.		
(p) Amortization of PSC	27,211 Dr.					27,211 Cr.	
(q) Contributions		24,000 Cr.			24,000 Dr.		
(r) Benefits paid				10,500 Dr.	10,500 Cr.		
(s) Liability loss				28,530 Cr.			28,530 Dr.
(t) Asset loss					1,410 Cr.		1,410 Dr.
Expense entry, 2009	48,071 Dr.		48,071 Cr.				
Contribution entry, 2009		24,000 Cr.	24,000 Dr.				
Balance, Dec. 31, 2009			49,882 Cr.	265,000 Cr.	159,600 Dr.	25,578 Dr.	29,940 Dr.

Illustration 19-15

Pension Work Sheet—2009

Entry (s) records the change in the accrued benefit obligation that results from a change in actuarial assumptions. As indicated, the actuary has now calculated the ending balance to be $265,000. Since the memo record balance at December 31 is $236,470 ($212,700 + $13,000 + $21,270 − $10,500), there is a difference of $28,530 ($265,000 − $236,470). This $28,530 increase in the employer's obligation is an actuarial loss that is deferred by including it in the unrecognized actuarial gain/loss balance. No amortization of the net actuarial loss is recognized in 2009 because amortization is based only on the accumulated net actuarial gain or loss **that existed at the first of the year**, which was $0.

The journal entry on December 31, 2009, to formally record pension expense for the year is as follows:

Pension Expense	48,071	
Accrued Pension Asset/Liability		48,071

A = L + SE
     +48,071   −48,071

Cash flows: No effect

The company has already recorded the $24,000 contribution during the year as follows:

Accrued Pension Asset/Liability	24,000	
Cash		24,000

A = L + SE
−24,000   −24,000

Cash flows: ↓ 24,000 outflow

As illustrated previously for the 2007 and 2008 work sheets, the credit balance of the Accrued Pension Liability account reported on the statement of financial position at December 31, 2009 of $49,882 is equal to the net of the balances in the memo accounts at the same date. This is shown in Illustration 19-16. Notice that it is the unrecognized past service costs and unrecognized actuarial loss balances that explain the difference between the actual funded status of the plan and the liability that is reported on the balance sheet.

Illustration 19-16

Reconciliation of Balance Sheet Account with Memo Accounts

		At Dec. 31, 2009
Accrued benefit obligation		$265,000 Cr.
Plan assets		159,600 Dr.
Funded status—net liability (underfunded)		105,400 Cr.
Unrecognized amounts:		
Past service cost	$25,578 Dr.	
Net actuarial losses	29,940 Dr.	55,518 Dr.
Accrued pension liability on balance sheet		$ 49,882 Cr.

Other Defined Benefit Plans with Benefits That Vest or Accumulate

Other Post-Retirement Benefit Plans

In addition to pension plans, companies also provide their employees with other post-employment benefits as part of their compensation package. These may include such benefits as health care, prescription drugs, life insurance, dental and eye care, legal and tax services, tuition assistance, or free or subsidized travel. In the past, companies accounted for the cost of these employee future benefits as an expense in the period when the benefits were provided to the retirees, their spouses, dependents, and beneficiaries; that is, on a pay-as-you-go basis.

The pay-as-you-go basis remained the predominant method for most companies in Canada until the adoption of *CICA Handbook* Section 3461, which took effect in 2000. **This standard requires Canadian companies to account for all defined benefit plans where the benefits vest or accumulate on the same basis as they account for defined benefit pension plans.**

What Do the Numbers Mean?

In 1990 the FASB issued *Statement No. 106*, "Employers' Accounting for Post-Retirement Benefits Other Than Pensions." This standard required a change from the pay-as-you-go method of accounting for these benefits to an accrual basis, similar to pension accounting. When the standard was first applied, the effect on most U.S. companies was significant. For example, General Motors announced a U.S. $20.8-billion charge against its 1992 earnings as a result of adopting the new standard, and this was at a time when the company's net book value before the charge was approximately U.S. $28 billion! The impact of the change in Canada was not as significant as in the United States because of broader health-care coverage paid for by the government. A Financial Executives Institute Canada (FEI) study estimated a total Canadian unreported liability of $52 billion, almost entirely unfunded. In both countries, the requirement to measure the outstanding obligation and related costs resulted in corporate management paying much closer attention to the benefit packages that are offered to employee groups, supporting the credo that "you only control what gets measured and reported."

Unlike pension benefits, companies tend not to prefund (set aside assets in advance) their other post-employment benefit plans. The major reason is that payments to prefund health-care costs are not tax-deductible, unlike contributions to a pension trust. Another reason is that such benefits were once perceived as low-cost employee benefits that could be changed or eliminated at will and therefore were not a legal liability. The accounting definition of a liability now goes beyond the notion of a legally enforceable claim to also include equitable or constructive obligations, making it clear that many future benefit promises are liabilities.

Differences between Pension Benefits and Post-Retirement Health-Care Benefits

Although these two types of retirement benefits appear similar, there are some significant differences, as Illustration 19-17 shows.

Item	Pensions	Health-Care Benefits
Funding	Generally funded	Generally not funded
Benefit	Well-defined and level dollar amount	Generally uncapped and great variability
Beneficiary	Retiree (maybe some benefit to surviving spouse)	Retiree, spouse, and other dependents
Benefit payable	Monthly	As needed and used
Predictability	Variables are reasonably predictable	Utilization difficult to predict; level of cost varies geographically and fluctuates over time

Illustration 19-17

Differences between Pensions and Post-Retirement Health-Care Benefits

Measuring the net cost of the post-retirement benefits for the period is complex. Due to the uncertainties in forecasting health-care costs, rates of usage, changes in government health programs, and the differences in non-medical assumptions (e.g., the discount rate, employee turnover, rate of pre-65 retirement, spouse-age difference, etc.), estimates of post-retirement benefit costs may have a large margin of error. Is the resulting information relevant and reliable? Is it verifiable? The FASB, in adopting *Statement 106*, concluded "that the obligation to provide post-retirement benefits meets the definition of a liability, is representationally faithful, is relevant to financial statement users, and can be measured with sufficient reliability at a justifiable cost."[26] Not accruing an obligation and an expense before paying benefits is considered by the FASB to be an unfaithful representation of what financial statements are supposed to be presenting. The Canadian standard setters agreed. Because this issue was addressed, companies now recognize the magnitude of these costs.

The basic concepts, accounting terminology, and measurement methods that apply to defined benefit pensions **also apply to the requirements for other benefits** that vest or accumulate based on the service provided by employees. The recognition and measurement criteria for the obligation and plan assets are the same, as is the actuarial valuation method, the attribution period, and the calculation of the current cost of benefits.

Transitional Balance. One area where there is a difference is in the existence and relative size of the transitional amount. When companies first applied the recommendations of Section 3461 **on a prospective basis** to such future benefits as post-retirement health care and life insurance, a large transitional liability—underfunded status—was usually seen. This was caused by there being significant liabilities and minimal plan assets since it was common practice to not fund these plans. The net unrecorded obligation is amortized on a systematic and rational basis over an appropriate period of time, which normally is the expected average remaining service life of the employee group that is covered by the plan.[27] The amortization is a component of the current benefit expense.

Many companies adopted the new accounting policy on a retroactive basis, recognizing the net accrued obligation as a liability and the accumulated cost as an adjustment to opening retained earnings. In all other respects, accounting for the benefit costs is similar to the accounting that was illustrated for defined benefit pensions.

---

[26] *FASB Statement No. 106*, par. 163.

[27] *CICA Handbook*, Section 3461.167.

Other Post-Employment Benefits and Compensated Absences

Full accrual accounting is also appropriate for post-employment benefits and compensated absences where the benefits either vest in the employee or accumulate with the length of service that is provided.

Examples of such benefits include sabbaticals where unrestricted time off with pay is granted for past service, service-related long-term disability benefits, or sick days not used that accumulate and are paid out on retirement.[28] Assume, for example, that an employee benefit plan provides a cash bonus of $500 per year of service when an employee retires, or has his or her employment terminated for other reasons, on condition that the employee has been employed for at least 10 years. Because the right to the benefit is earned by rendering service and the benefit increases with the length of service provided, the cost and related liability are accrued starting from the date of employment. The measurement of the obligation and expense takes into consideration the probabilities related to employee turnover. The fact that the benefits do not vest for 10 years does not eliminate the need to recognize the cost and liability over the first 10 years of employment.

Benefits such as sick leave that accumulate with service but do not vest in the employee should, in theory, be accrued as the employee provides service. In practical terms, however, because it is difficult to make a reasonable estimate of such benefit amounts, and since the amounts are relatively immaterial, these costs are usually not accrued.

Comprehensive Illustration with a Transitional Balance

Assume that on January 1, 2006, Quest Limited adopted the new accounting standards to account for its retirement health-care benefit plan and accounted for the change in accounting policy on a prospective basis. Two years later, in 2008, the following facts apply to this plan:

1. Plan assets at fair value on January 1, 2008, are $10,000.

2. ABO, January 1, 2008, is $426,000.

3. The unrecognized (unamortized) transition cost at January 1, 2008, is $336,000 (original amount of $368,000; amortization period of 23 years).

4. The unrecognized net actuarial loss at January 1, 2008, is $48,000.

5. The accrued benefit liability on the balance sheet at January 1, 2008, is $32,000.

6. The actual return on plan assets in 2008 is $600.

7. The expected return on plan assets in 2008 is $800.

8. The discount rate is 8%.

9. There is an increase of $20,000 in the ABO at December 31, 2008, due to a change in actuarial assumptions.

10. The service cost for 2008 is $26,000.

11. Contributions (funding) to the plan in 2008 are $50,000.

12. Benefit payments on behalf of retirees in 2008 are $35,000.

13. The expected average remaining service life (EARSL) at January 1, 2008, is 24 years.

---

[28] Sabbaticals where the employee is expected to use the compensated absence to perform research or provide other activities to benefit the organization do not need to be accrued over the period when the sabbatical is earned. These costs are expensed as the sabbatical is taken.

Illustration 19-18 shows the analysis and information that Quest Limited needs in 2008.

Items	General Journal Entries			Memo Record			
	Annual Expense	Cash	Accrued Benefit Asset/Liability	Accrued Benefit Obligation	Plan Assets	Unrecognized Transition Amount	Unrecognized Net Actuarial Gain or Loss
Balance, Jan. 1, 2008			32,000 Cr.	426,000 Cr.	10,000 Dr.	336,000 Dr.	48,000 Dr.
(a) Service cost	26,000 Dr.			26,000 Cr.			
(b) Interest cost	34,080 Dr.			34,080 Cr.			
(c) Expected return	800 Cr.				800 Dr.		
(d) Experience loss					200 Cr.		200 Dr.
(e) Contributions		50,000 Cr.			50,000 Dr.		
(f) Benefits paid				35,000 Dr.	35,000 Cr.		
(g) Amortization of transition cost	16,000 Dr.					16,000 Cr.	
(h) Increase in ABO—loss				20,000 Cr.			20,000 Dr.
(i) Amortization of unrecognized net actuarial loss	225 Dr.						225 Cr.
Expense entry, 2008	75,505 Dr.		75,505 Cr.				
Contribution entry, 2008		50,000 Cr.	50,000 Dr.				
Balance, Dec. 31, 2008			57,505 Cr.	471,080 Cr.	25,600 Dr.	320,000 Dr.	67,975 Dr.

Illustration 19-18
Quest Limited Work Sheet—2008

Entry (a) records the service cost component, which increases the retirement health benefit expense by $26,000 and the ABO by $26,000. Entry (b) accrues the interest cost, which increases both the accrued obligation and the expense by $34,080—the weighted-average ABO multiplied by the discount rate of 8%. Because the service cost, benefits paid, and actuarial loss are all assumed to take place at the end of the year, the ABO's weighted-average balance for the year is the opening balance of $426,000.

Entries (c) and (d) are related. The expected return of $800 is higher than the actual return of $600. The expected return is calculated by applying the expected long-term rate of return on plan assets to the weighted-average fair value of the plan assets. The payments on behalf of retirees and contributions received from the employer are assumed to be year-end transactions. The weighted-average value for 2008, therefore, is the opening balance at January 1, 2008. The expected return of $800 is given in this case. The experience loss of $200 ($800 − $600) increases (debits) the accumulated balance of the unrecognized net actuarial loss.

Entry (e) records Quest Limited's contribution (funding) of assets to the retirement health-care benefit fund. Entry (f) records the payments made for the benefit of retirees, which results in equal $35,000 decreases in the plan assets and the obligation. Entry (g) records the annual amortization of the **unrecognized transition cost**. It is amortized over the employee group's expected average remaining service life on January 1, 2006, of 23 years. The amortization of $16,000 ($368,000 ÷ 23) increases the expense and decreases the unamortized transition cost balance.

Entry (h) records the change in the ABO that results from a change in actuarial assumptions. This $20,000 increase in the employer's accrued obligation is a current year actuarial loss that is deferred by adding it to the unrecognized net actuarial loss balance. The last adjustment, entry (i), records the amortization of the accumulated net actuarial loss at the beginning of the year. The $225 amortization is determined as follows:

Accumulated net actuarial loss, Jan. 1, 2008	$48,000
Corridor amount: 10% of the greater of the Jan. 1, 2008 balance of the ABO ($426,000) and the fair value of the plan assets ($10,000): $426,000 × 10%	42,600
Excess of accumulated loss over corridor amount, Jan. 1, 2008	$ 5,400
Minimum amortization required: $5,400 ÷ 24	$ 225

Quest Limited could use a different method of amortization, but the minimum amortization in 2008 is $225. This increases the current retirement health-care benefit expense and reduces the balance of the unrecognized net actuarial losses.

During 2008, Quest Limited recorded the cash disbursement to the benefit fund as follows:

A   =   L   + SE
−50,000   −50,000

Cash flows: ↓ 50,000 outflow

Accrued Retirement Health Benefit Asset/Liability	50,000	
Cash		50,000

All that remains is to record the December 31, 2008, adjusting journal entry to recognize the annual retirement health benefit expense as follows:

A =   L   +   SE
    +75,505   −75,505

Cash flows: No effect

Retirement Health Benefit Expense	75,505	
Accrued Retirement Health Benefit Asset/Liability		75,505

The balance of the Accrued Retirement Health Benefit Liability account on the December 31, 2008, balance sheet of $57,505 is equal to the net of the balances in the memo accounts as shown in the reconciliation in Illustration 19-19. Once again, notice that the difference between the actual funded status of the plan and the liability account reported on the statement of financial position is explained by the unamortized balances not yet recognized in pension expense (and the accrued benefit liability) on the books.

Illustration 19-19

Reconciliation of Balance Sheet Account with Memo Accounts

		At Dec. 31, 2008
Accrued benefit obligation		$471,080 Cr.
Plan assets		25,600 Dr.
Funded status—net liability (underfunded)		445,480 Cr.
Unrecognized amounts:		
Transition amount	$320,000 Dr.	
Net actuarial losses	67,975 Dr.	387,975 Dr.
Accrued benefit liability on balance sheet		$ 57,505 Cr.

FINANCIAL REPORTING

Objective 14

Identify the financial reporting and disclosure requirements for defined benefit plans.

Recognition and Presentation

Although the illustrations provided in this chapter result in accrued benefit liabilities being reported on the statement of financial position, accrued benefit assets are also commonly found on corporate balance sheets. The accounting standard provides for an **asset ceiling**

test on the balance of any benefit asset reported on the balance sheet. It is silent, however, on how to classify accrued benefit assets and liabilities as current or long-term.

Limit on the Carrying Amount of an Accrued Benefit Asset

Similar to most assets we have studied, there is also a limit on the carrying amount of an accrued benefit asset resulting from a defined benefit plan. If the accrued benefit asset recognized is greater than the expected future benefits the company is expected to receive from the asset, a valuation allowance is needed to reduce the asset's reported amount.[29]

Although the calculations required are not explained in this text, students should be aware that the change in the valuation allowance in the year is recognized as a component of the benefit expense in income in the year. In addition, the asset is reported net of the allowance.

Balance Sheet Classification of Accrued Benefit Assets/Liabilities

Entities with two or more defined benefit plans are required to separately measure the benefit cost, accrued benefit obligation, and plan assets for each funded benefit plan. If all the plans result in an accrued benefit liability on the balance sheet or all result in an accrued benefit asset, the plans can be reported together in the financial statements. However, because companies generally do not have the legal right to use the assets of one plan to pay for the benefits of other plans, an accrued benefit asset of one plan and an accrued benefit liability of another must be reported separately on the balance sheet.[30]

The accounting standard does not provide any guidance on how to determine whether accrued benefit assets and liabilities are current or long-term, so companies revert to basic underlying principles to determine the classification. As a result, such assets and liabilities are found in both current and long-term classifications on both sides of the balance sheet.

Disclosure Requirements

For a phenomenon as significant and specialized as pensions and other defined benefit plans, it is not surprising that there are extensive reporting and disclosure requirements. *CICA Handbook* Section 3461 requires a high level of accountability from companies for the effect of such plans on their current and future performance, financial position, and risk.

The objective, as always, is to provide better information for users. The information should help users assess the amounts and likelihood of the cash flows that are associated with future benefits, the relationship between cash flows and pension and other benefits expenses, the impact of employee benefits on the income statement, and the reasonableness of the assumptions that underlie the measurement of the accrued obligation, fund assets, and current expense. In addition, information about unrecognized amounts reported in the notes to the financial statements informs readers about how extensively future earnings will be affected by the obligations to employees to date. The accounting standard supports two levels of disclosure. One level applies to all companies. A second, expanded level of disclosure applies to public enterprises, cooperative organizations, deposit-taking institutions, and life insurance enterprises.

All companies are required to provide a description of their plans, and to disclose information about the accounting policies they have applied, the amounts they have

Underlying Concept

The now cancelled 2007 proposals to change the accounting standards for defined benefit plans such as pensions required the reporting of a benefit asset or liability on the balance sheet that corresponded to the funded status of the plan. Standard setters believed that financial information would be more reliable this way because it would be more complete and representationally faithful.

[29] The expected future benefits represent those that the company can realize from a plan surplus through amounts it can withdraw from the plan or reductions it can make in its future contributions.

[30] *CICA Handbook*, Section 3461.096 to .100.

recognized in the financial statements, the off–balance sheet accounts, and the underlying assumptions they have used.

- **Accounting policies applied.** Wherever a company has choices in pension accounting, it is required to disclose the policies that it has adopted.

- **Underlying assumptions.** To help in assessing the reasonableness of the amounts reported, all of the following are required disclosures: the discount rates, the expected long-term rate of return on plan assets, the rate of compensation increase, information about trends, and the rate assumptions that were used to calculate the cost of health-care benefits.

- **Amounts included in the financial statements.** In addition to disclosing the benefit costs that the company has recognized in net income and the benefits paid during the period, disclosure is required of the balance of any accrued benefit assets (separately reporting any related valuation allowance) or liabilities, along with their balance sheet classifications. In addition, the **total cash amount** that was initially recognized in the period as paid or payable for that period for employee future benefits is disclosed.[31]

- **Off–balance sheet accounts.** The amount of the accrued benefit obligation is reported along with the fair value of the plan assets. This funded status position is then reconciled to the accrued benefit asset or liability reported on the balance sheet. The reconciliation must show separately the amounts of unamortized past service costs, unamortized actuarial gains/losses, and the unamortized balance of any transitional obligation or asset. Detail is required about the major asset categories in the plan and the extent to which employer-company securities and related party securities are included in the fund assets.

For financial institutions and public enterprises, there is an **additional level of required information**. These entities must disclose all of the following:

- Additional information about each individual component making up the total expense

- The balance of each unamortized off–balance sheet amount at the balance sheet date that has not yet been recognized in benefit cost

- Reconciliation of the beginning and ending balances of the accrued pension benefit obligation (ABO), with separate disclosure of the contributions made by employees during the period, benefits paid, current service cost, interest cost, actuarial gains/losses, and the effects of material non-routine events

- Reconciliation of the beginning and ending balances of the fair value of plan assets, indicating both employer and employee contributions, the actual return, the benefits paid, and the effects of material non-routine events

- For post-retirement health-care benefit plans, the effect of a 1% increase and a 1% decrease in the assumed health-care cost trend on the total of interest and service costs for the period and on the ending ABO[32]

Additional disclosures for complex issues that are not included as part of the chapter discussion have been left out of the preceding lists. Even without these, it is very evident from the extent of the disclosure requirements that readers must be well-informed because of the significant effect that these plans can have on a company!

---

[31] The "total cash amount" is made up of contributions to funded defined benefit plans (and to defined contribution plans), payments to employees or their beneficiaries or estates, and payments to third-party service providers on behalf of employees.

[32] *CICA Handbook*, Section 3461.150 to .163.

Illustration

Companies organize these disclosures in a variety of acceptable ways. **Winpak Ltd.**, a Winnipeg-based manufacturer and distributor of high-quality packaging materials and packaging machines, provides extensive information in the notes to its financial statements for the 52 weeks ended December 31, 2006. Excerpts from these notes, with amounts reported in thousands of U.S. dollars, are provided in Illustration 19-20.

Illustration 19-20

Illustrative Disclosure—Winpak Ltd.

NOTES TO CONSOLIDATED FINANCIAL STATEMENTS

2. Significant accounting policies

(j) Employee benefit plans:

The Company maintains six funded non-contributory defined benefit pension plans in Canada and the U.S. and one funded non-contributory supplementary income postretirement plan for certain Canadian-based executives. A market discount rate is used to measure the benefit obligations. The expected return on pension plan assets is calculated on the fair value of the assets as of the year-end date. The cost of these non-contributory defined benefit pension plans is actuarially determined using the projected benefits method prorated on years of employee service, final average salary levels during specified years of employment, retirement ages of employees and other actuarial factors, together with the expected rate of return on pension plan assets. Current service costs, interest costs on the benefit obligation, curtailment and settlement costs are charged to earnings as they accrue. Past service costs, plan amendments, changes in assumptions, the net transitional asset amount and the cumulative unrecognized net actuarial gains and losses in excess of 10% of the greater of the benefit obligation or the fair value of plan assets are amortized to earnings on a straight-line basis over the expected average remaining service lives (10-20 years) of active plan members. The Company's funding policy is consistent with statutory regulations and amounts funded are deductible for income tax purposes.

One of the Company's subsidiaries maintains one unfunded contributory defined benefit postretirement plan for health care benefits for a limited group of U.S. individuals. A market discount rate is used to measure the benefit obligation. The cost of the plan is actuarially determined using the per capita claims cost method. Interest costs on the benefit obligation are charged to earnings as they accrue. Past service costs, plan amendments, changes in assumptions and the cumulative unrecognized net actuarial gains and losses are amortized to earnings on a straight-line basis over the expected average future lifetime (11 years) of the retirees.

The Company maintains seven defined contribution pension plans in Canada and the U.S. The pension expense for these plans is the annual funding contribution by the Company.

11. Employee benefit plans:

The Company maintains six funded non-contributory defined benefit pension plans, one funded non-contributory supplementary income postretirement plan for certain Canadian-based executives, one unfunded contributory defined benefit postretirement plan for health care benefits for a limited group of U.S. individuals and seven defined contribution pension plans.

Effective January 1, 2005 three defined benefit pension plans in Canada and the U.S. covering certain salaried employees were frozen. Subsequent to this date, all defined benefit pension plans are frozen and all new employees are required to participate in defined contribution plans upon satisfaction of certain eligibility requirements.

Total amounts paid by the Company on account of all employee benefit plans, consisting of: defined benefit pension plans, supplementary income postretirement plan, direct payments to beneficiaries for the unfunded postretirement plan and defined contribution plans, amounted to $6,477 (2005 - $4,760).

The following presents the financial position of the Company's defined benefit pension plans and other postretirement benefits, which include the supplementary income plan and the postretirement plan for health care benefits:

	Defined Benefit Pension Plans		Other Postretirement Benefits	
	2006	2005	**2006**	2005
Change in benefit obligation				
Benefit obligation, beginning of year	**43,149**	33,749	**6,656**	6,380
Current service cost	**2,456**	2,126	**141**	230
Interest cost	**2,378**	2,019	**347**	386
Prior service cost	**-**	-	**488**	-
Actuarial loss (gain)	**103**	3,829	**(78)**	(147)
Curtailment and settlement	**-**	1,372	**-**	(194)
Benefits paid	**(1,375)**	(984)	**(208)**	(158)
Foreign exchange	**(327)**	1,038	**(71)**	159
Benefit obligation, end of year	**46,384**	43,149	**7,275**	6,656

Change in plan assets

Fair value of plan assets, beginning of year	**31,737**	27,482	**3,092**	2,374
Actual return on plan assets	**4,079**	2,317	**282**	91
Employer contributions	**2,410**	2,093	**2,213**	674
Benefits paid	**(1,375)**	(984)	**(208)**	(158)
Foreign exchange	**(323)**	829	**(100)**	111
Fair value of plan assets, end of year	**36,528**	31,737	**5,279**	3,092

Funded status

Plan assets less than benefit obligation	**(10,131)**	(11,475)	**(1,996)**	(3,564)
Plan assets greater than benefit obligation	**275**	63	**-**	-
Net plan assets less than benefit obligation	**(9,856)**	(11,412)	**(1,996)**	(3,564)
Unrecognized net transition amount	**(1,015)**	(1,198)	**-**	-
Unrecognized prior service cost	**599**	652	**2,133**	1,900
Unamortized actuarial loss	**11,361**	13,673	**586**	912
Accrued asset (liability)	**1,089**	1,715	**723**	(752)

Amounts recognized in the consolidated balance sheet

Accrued asset	**3,302**	3,404	**2,204**	692
Accrued liability	**(2,213)**	(1,689)	**(1,481)**	(1,444)
Accrued asset (liability)	**1,089**	1,715	**723**	(752)

Benefit plans with fair value of plan assets less than benefit obligation

Fair value of plan assets	**33,363**	30,126	**5,279**	3,092
Benefit obligation	**(43,494)**	(41,601)	**(7,275)**	(6,656)
Plan assets less than benefit obligation, end of year	**(10,131)**	(11,475)	**(1,996)**	(3,564)

The defined benefit pension plans do not invest in the shares of the Company. The expected rate of return on the plan assets is based on historical and projected rates of return for each asset category measured over a four-year time period. The objective of the asset allocation policy is to manage the funded status of the plans at an appropriate level of risk, giving consideration to the security of the assets and the potential volatility of market returns. The long-term rate of return is targeted to exceed the return indicated by a benchmark portfolio by at least 1% annually.

The following presents the net benefit plan cost of the Company's defined benefit pension plans and other postretirement benefits, which include the supplementary income plan and postretirement plan for health care benefits:

	Defined Benefit Pension Plans		Other Postretirement Benefits	
	2006	2005	**2006**	2005
Net benefit plan cost				
Current service cost	**2,456**	2,126	**141**	230
Interest cost on accrued benefit obligation	**2,378**	2,019	**347**	386
Actual return on plan assets	**(4,079)**	(2,317)	**(282)**	(91)
Actuarial loss (gain) on accrued benefit obligation	**103**	3,829	**(78)**	(147)
Prior service cost	**-**	-	**488**	-
Benefit plans cost before adjustments to recognize the long-term nature of benefit plans	**858**	5,657	**616**	378
Excess of actual over expected return on plan assets	**1,774**	373	**163**	11
Deferral of amounts arising during the year:				
Actuarial loss on accrued benefit obligation	**(103)**	(3,829)	**78**	147
Prior service cost	**-**	-	**(488)**	-
Amortization of previously deferred amounts:				
Transitional asset	**(190)**	(207)	**132**	132
Net actuarial loss	**610**	415	**69**	13
Prior service cost	**74**	53	**122**	71
Adjustments to recognize the long-term nature of benefit plans	**2,165**	(3,195)	**76**	374
Net benefit plan cost	**3,023**	2,462	**692**	752

Significant assumptions

The following weighted averages were used:

Accrued benefit obligations as of the year-end date:

Discount rate	**5.4%**	5.3%	**5.4%**	5.3%
Rate of compensation increase	**4.2%**	4.2%	**-**	-

Net benefit plan cost for the year:				
Discount rate	5.3%	5.9%	5.3%	5.9%
Expected return on plan assets	7.2%	7.3%	3.5%	3.5%
Rate of compensation increase	4.2%	4.2%	-	-

The postretirement benefit plan assumed health care cost trend rate is 9% with the rate declining to 5% by 2013 and remaining consistent thereafter to 2015. A one-percentage point change in the assumed health care cost trend rate would affect the net benefit plan cost by approximately $8 and the accrued benefit obligation by $145.

Defined contribution pension plans
The Company maintains four defined contribution plans for certain employees in Canada and three savings retirement plans (401(k) Plans) for certain employees in the United States. The Company has recorded a total expense of $1,853 (2005 - $1,815) for these plans.

Winpak's notes provide a schedule of what makes up the benefit plan cost for both the pension and other post-retirement plans. The company also includes a reconciliation of the opening and closing balances of the accrued benefit obligation and the plan assets, and these look almost identical to the schedules that were used in this chapter. The funded status is reported as being underfunded on both the pension plan ($9,856) and other retirement benefit plans ($1,996). It is surprising, therefore, to see Winpak report an accrued pension asset amount of $1,089 and an accrued other post-retirement benefit asset of $723 in the Other Assets section on its December 31, 2006, balance sheet, and no liability!

This situation is precisely why the FASB made recent changes to its employee benefit standards and why the AcSB issued its now-cancelled proposals to change the Canadian standards. Notice that it is the unrecognized transition amounts, past service cost, and actuarial losses that explain the difference between the funded status and the balance sheet amounts that are reported. The new U.S. standards require these previously unrecognized amounts to be recognized in the balance sheet accounts, with the offset to OCI. A review of Illustration 19-20 shows that had the unrecognized amounts been included, the balance sheet accounts would have had liability balances equal to the funded status. The Canadian standards await changes to the international standards.

Student Website

Student Toolkit—
Additional Disclosures
www.wiley.com/canada/kieso

PERSPECTIVES

Analysis

With all the information that is reported in the notes to the financial statements, what should an analysis focus on? The most important elements are the major assumptions that underlie the calculations, the status of the plan, and the company's future cash requirements.

As was indicated earlier in the chapter, the accrued benefit obligation and benefit expense are based on several estimates that, if altered, can significantly change the amounts. Aside from the actuarial assumptions that were used by the actuary and the rate of compensation increase—which are both important—the choice of discount rate that was used to measure the ABO, the current service cost, and the interest cost are also key variables. A one-percentage-point difference in rate could have a 10 to 20% effect on the discounted value. This rate is required to be disclosed so that readers can assess the rate for reasonableness and compare it with the rates used by other companies in the industry.

The expected rate of return on plan assets also has a direct effect on pension expense. Remember that the difference between the expected and actual returns is recognized through the corridor approach, which considerably reduces the effect, if any, of the actual return on the income statement.

An analysis of the past service costs, actuarial gains or losses, and transitional costs remaining unrecognized provides useful information. These amounts were not included in pension expense when they were incurred, but they will gradually be included in pension expense and the balance sheet accrued pension/asset liability account as they are transferred to benefit expense in future periods.

As a company's actual cash flow related to pensions is often very distant from the pension costs that have been recognized on the income statement, analysts try to determine what the company's future cash commitments are. The disclosure requirements of the standards are helpful in this regard. They require that the components of expense for the pension costs that were actually incurred in the period be reported separately from those which are the result of accounting allocation (i.e., amortization) adjustments, and also require companies to report the cash impact of the plans in the current period. This, however, falls short of requiring that companies report their future funding commitments.

What Do the Numbers Mean?

The new U.S. accounting standards for post-retirement benefits that were issued in 2006 require companies to record their previously unrecognized past service costs, actuarial gains and losses, and transition costs in Other Comprehensive Income and to recognize the plans' funded status on the balance sheet. Previously, and as is still the case in Canada, the unrecognized amounts were simply not recorded. As a result, the balance sheet benefit asset or liability did not, therefore, portray the entity's real resource or obligation as measured by the funded status of its plan. Would a similar change have made much difference to Canadian companies?

To some companies, the adjustment to the new requirements would be minor. For others, it would be very significant. The following table shows the benefit asset or liability that was reported on a sample of Canadian companies' balance sheets; the actual funded status of the benefit plans at the same date; and the unrecognized, unamortized balances related to past service costs, actuarial gains and losses, and transition costs. To put the numbers in perspective, the total shareholders' equity at the balance sheet date is also given.

Company	Year End	Benefit Asset (A) or Liability (L) Reported on Balance Sheet	Funded Status of Plan at Balance Sheet Date	Unrecognized, Unamortized, Off–Balance Sheet Amounts	Total Shareholders' Equity at Balance Sheet Date
Norbord Inc. (U.S. $ million)	Dec. 31, 2006	4 (L)	23 (L)	19 (L)	434
Bombardier Inc. (U.S. $ million)	Jan. 31, 2006	493 (L)	2,671 (L)	2,178 (L)	2,425
Finning International Inc. (Cdn. $ million)	Dec. 31, 2006	43 (A)	18 (L)	61 (L)	1,624
Abitibi Consolidated Inc. (Cdn. $ million)	Dec. 31, 2006	166 (A)	858 (L)	1,024 (L)	2,451

The major accomplishment of the FASB changes to the accounting standards was to require recognition of the previously "Unrecognized" amounts in the balance sheet asset or liability account, instead of just in the notes. They required that the amounts brought onto the balance sheet be recognized in OCI. As you can tell from the numbers presented in the table, such a change to the Canadian standards would have had a significant effect on many companies' debt-equity ratios and other provisions that underlie existing debt agreements!

This chapter has presented the basics of accounting for employee future benefits. Further complexities arise from temporary deviations from the benefit plan, valuation of the funded status asset, obligation settlements, benefits provided through insurance contracts or other arrangements, plan curtailments, termination benefits, and multi-employer or multiple-employer plans. The **Winpak Ltd.** note disclosures in Illustration 19-20 refer to some of these issues, as do the expanded discussions on the Student Website.

In the financial press, articles can often be found that analyze the issues related to pension plans. This is hardly surprising given the obligations that companies have and the billions of dollars of assets that are held by Canadian pension funds. While Canadian accounting standards impose a consistent treatment for plans with similar characteristics and clarify many issues, pension accounting reform remains on the agendas of standard-setting bodies. A key outstanding factor is the non-recognition of the funded status on the balance sheet. Another issue relates to the delayed recognition of certain events in income, and the related smoothing of various elements of pension cost. Another relates to the netting of interest expense, investment returns, and compensation cost—items that are reported separately in income for non-pension-related matters. There could even be a debate before 2011, when Canada changes to IFRS, about whether a capitalization approach should be used, which would require that the assets and accrued obligations for such benefits be reported on the balance sheet.

Student Website

Expanded Discussions
www.wiley.com/canada/kieso

International

All major elements in the approach to accounting for employee future benefits are the same for Canadian and international standards. The primary source of GAAP for each is given in Illustration 19-21.

15 Objective
Compare current Canadian and international GAAP.

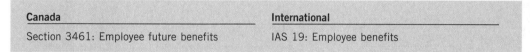

Canada	International
Section 3461: Employee future benefits	IAS 19: Employee benefits

Illustration 19-21
Primary Sources of GAAP

IAS 19 is broader in its coverage than the corresponding *Handbook* Section as IAS 19 also provides accounting standards for short-term benefits such as profit-sharing and bonus plans, and for short-term compensated absences. Other differences relate to the treatment of actuarial gains and losses and the recognition of past service costs.

Actuarial Gains and Losses. The Canadian standard accounts for actuarial gains and losses off–balance sheet when they originate, and only transfers or amortizes amounts to the benefit plan expense in the income statement (and to the balance sheet account) when the balance of the accumulated net actuarial gain or loss is significant. IAS 19 also generally uses the same method, including the corridor approach for amortization. However, there is a provision in the international standard that enables an entity to recognize the entire amount of actuarial gains or losses directly in equity (to OCI) as the gains and losses are incurred. These, though, are not later amortized to the benefit plan expense.

Past Service Costs. The Canadian standard requires past service costs to be deferred off–balance sheet initially and then for these costs to be transferred to the benefit expense (and to the balance sheet account) as they are amortized over the period to full eligibility. IAS 19 recommends that past service costs be recognized over the average period until the amended benefits become vested. Those that are already vested, therefore, are fully recognized in the period of the amendment.

The IASB has tentatively decided as part of its post-employment benefits project that all changes in the post-employment benefit obligation and in the value of the plan assets should be recognized in comprehensive income when they are incurred, similar to the recent FASB changes. In fact, IASB's preliminary view is that all such changes should be recognized in bottom line net income. By 2010, the IASB hopes to issue a Phase I standard that will significantly improve pension accounting.[33] This standard is likely to create other differences between current Canadian standards and IFRS, but will be adopted in its entirety at the changeover date in 2011.

---

[33] *IASB Update*, March 2007, IASB.

Summary of Learning Objectives

1 **Identify a defined contribution plan, and apply the accounting and disclosure requirements for such plans.**

Defined contribution plans are plans that specify how contributions are determined rather than what benefits the individual will receive. They are accounted for close to a cash basis. Companies are required to disclose the expense recognized for the period, the nature and effect of significant matters that affect comparability from period to period, and the total cash amount initially recognized in the period as paid or payable for that period in relation to the future benefits.

2 **Explain what a defined benefit plan is.**

Defined benefit plans specify the benefits that the employee is entitled to. The formula that is typically used provides for the benefits to be a function of the employee's years of service and compensation level.

3 **Identify a defined benefit plan whose benefits do not vest or accumulate, and account for such plans.**

Defined benefit plans whose benefits do not vest or accumulate are plans where the employee is entitled to the benefits simply because he or she is an employee. The cost of the benefits cannot be accrued and matched with employee service, because there is no specified service period over which to accrue the cost of the benefits and the related liability. Instead, the "event accrual" method is applied: when the event that obligates the employer to provide the benefit occurs, the total estimated expense and liability are recognized.

4 **Identify a defined benefit plan whose benefits vest or accumulate, and explain how such plans are accounted for.**

Defined benefit plans whose benefits vest or accumulate are plans where the employee is entitled to the benefits only after a specified term of service and where the amount of the benefit generally increases with the length of service that the employee has provided. In general, the cost of such a plan is accrued as an expense as the employee provides the service. This requires the services of a specialist—an actuary—to determine the cost that should be charged to each period.

5 **Distinguish between accounting for the employer's pension costs and accounting for the pension fund.**

The company or employer is the organization that sponsors the pension plan. It incurs the cost and makes contributions to the pension fund. The fund or plan is the entity that receives the contributions from the employer, administers the pension assets, and makes the benefit payments to the pension recipients (retired employees). The fund should be a separate legal and accounting entity for which a set of books is maintained and financial statements are prepared.

6 **Explain what the employer's benefit obligation is and identify alternative measures for valuing this obligation.**

The employer's benefit obligation is the actuarial present value of the benefits that have been earned by employees for services they have rendered up to the balance sheet date. The vested benefits pension obligation is calculated using current salary levels and includes only vested benefits. Vested benefits are benefits that the employee is entitled to receive even if the employee is no longer employed. Another

Student Website

Glossary

www.wiley.com/canada/kieso

KEY TERMS

accrued benefit
  obligation (ABO), 1168
accumulated benefit
  obligation, 1167
actual return, 1172
actuarial assumptions,
  1166
actuarial gains and
  losses, 1171
actuaries, 1166
asset ceiling test, 1190
asset experience gain
  or loss, 1173
attribution period, 1170
capitalization approach,
  1168
contributory plans, 1165
corridor approach, 1182
defined benefit
  (DB) plan, 1163
defined contribution
  (DC) plan, 1162
EARSL, 1183
event accrual method,
  1164
expected average
  remaining service
  life, 1183
expected return, 1172
experience gain and
  loss, 1171
funded, 1165
funded status, 1173
funded status asset, 1173
funded status liability, 1173
liability experience gain
  or loss, 1171
market-related value of
  plan assets, 1172
non-capitalization
  approach, 1169
non-contributory plans,
  1165
overfunded, 1173

measure of the obligation, the accumulated benefit obligation, bases the calculation of the deferred compensation amount on all years of service performed by employees under the plan, both vested and non-vested, using current salary levels. A third measure, the projected benefit obligation, bases the calculation of the deferred compensation amount on both vested and non-vested service using future salaries. This last measure is GAAP.

7 Identify transactions and events that change the amount of the employer's accrued benefit obligation, and calculate the balance of the obligation.

The balance of the accrued benefit obligation is increased by the cost of the pension benefits earned by employees for services they have provided in the current period, by the interest cost on the outstanding obligation, by plan amendments that usually increase employee entitlements for prior services, and by actuarial losses. The balance is reduced by the payment of pension benefits and by actuarial gains.

8 Identify transactions and events that change the amount of the plan assets, and calculate the balance of the assets.

Plan assets are increased by company and employee contributions and the actual return that is earned on fund assets (that is, the expected return plus the asset experience gain or minus the asset experience loss), and are reduced by pension benefits paid to retirees.

9 Explain and calculate a benefit plan's funded status.

A plan's funded status is the difference between the accrued benefit obligation and the plan assets at a point in time. It tells you the extent to which a company has a net obligation (underfunded) or a surplus (overfunded) relative to the benefits that are promised.

10 Identify the possible components of pension benefit cost, and account for a defined benefit pension plan under Canadian GAAP.

Pension cost is a function of the following components: (1) service cost, (2) interest on the liability, (3) expected return on plan assets, (4) past service costs, (5) net actuarial gain or loss, and (6) transitional balances. Under Canadian GAAP, items (1) to (3) are included in current expense entirely, while items (4) to (6) are recognized only through a process of amortization. The unamortized balances of items (4) to (6) are reported only in the notes to the financial statement.

11 Explain the usefulness of—and complete—a work sheet to support the employer's pension accounts.

A pension work sheet accumulates all the information that is needed to calculate pension expense. It includes continuity schedules for the accrued benefit obligation and fund assets, as well as continuity schedules for the balances of the unamortized (and therefore unrecognized) amounts reported off–balance sheet. By completing the work sheet, year-end balances are determined for the accrued pension benefit asset or liability on the balance sheet, the ABO, fund assets, and each source of unrecognized amounts. A reconciliation is easily prepared between the balance sheet account and the funded status.

12 Define and account for past service costs.

Past service costs arise from giving credit to employees for service they provided before the date of initiating or amending a pension plan and, for defined benefit plans, are measured as the increase in the accrued benefit obligation as a result of such a change. Because the increased pension benefits are expected to benefit the employer as the employee group covered provides service to the company in the future, past service costs are initially deferred and then amortized to pension expense over the expected period until the affected employee group attains full pension eligibility.

13 Explain what actuarial gains and losses are, and account for them using the corridor approach to amortization.

Actuarial gains and losses are (1) the difference between the expected return on plan assets and the actual return that is earned, and (2) the change in the accrued benefit obligation due to the difference between expected variables and actual outcomes and changes in actuarial assumptions. If these changes are taken into pension expense each year in their entirety, reported pension expense fluctuates widely. Because the actuary uses long-term rates to project funding requirements, expected long-term rates are used to calculate pension expense. The net actuarial gain or loss is required to be amortized into pension expense, and therefore recognized, only when it grows to an amount greater than 10% of the larger of the ABO and the fair or market-related value of the fund assets. At a minimum, only the excess over the 10% corridor amount is required to be amortized over the employee group's EARSL.

14 Identify the financial reporting and disclosure requirements for defined benefit plans.

The accounting standards set a ceiling on the value that can be reported as the accrued benefit asset. Unless a right of offset exists, accrued benefit assets and accrued benefit liabilities for different plans must be reported separately. There are two levels of disclosure required by GAAP: (1) all companies are required to report information about the policies they followed, amounts recorded in the financial statements, and underlying assumptions that they used; and (2) public companies and others with broad public accountability have additional requirements. These include reconciliations of both the ABO and plan asset balances from one year to the next and additional information about the unrecognized balances reported in the notes to the financial statements.

15 Compare current Canadian and international GAAP.

Canadian and international GAAP are substantially harmonized; however, IAS 19 permits recognition of actuarial gains and losses in OCI. There are also some differences in how past service costs and actuarial gains and losses are recognized in expense, and in the balance sheet asset or liability. Changes in international accounting for employee future benefits are expected by 2010.

Example of a One-Person Plan

Objective 16

Explain the basics of what each of current service cost, accrued benefit obligation, and past service cost represent.

The following simplified example is provided to help students better visualize and understand some of the new concepts introduced in this chapter.

Assume that Lee Sung, age 30, begins employment with HTSM Corp. on January 1, 2006, at a starting salary of $37,500. It is expected that Lee will work for HTSM Corp. for 35 years, retiring on December 31, 2040, when Lee is 65 years old. Taking into account estimated compensation increases of approximately 4% per year, Lee's salary at retirement is expected to be $150,000. Further assume that mortality tables indicate the life expectancy of someone age 65 in 2040 is 12 years.

The timeline in Illustration 19A-1 provides a snapshot of much of this information.

Illustration 19A-1

Timeline

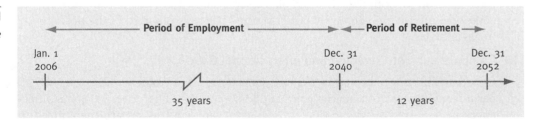

HTSM Corp. sponsors a defined benefit pension plan for its employees with the following **pension benefit formula**:

> Annual pension benefit on retirement = 2% of salary at retirement for each year of service, or
> = 2% × final salary × years of service

In order to measure 2006 pension costs, dollars paid in the future must be discounted to their present values. Assume a **discount rate of 6%**, which is the current yield on high-quality debt instruments.

Current Service Cost

Year 2006

How much pension does Lee Sung earn for the one year of service in 2006? Applying the pension formula **using projected salaries**:

Annual pension benefit on retirement = 2% × $150,000 × 1 year
                                     = $3,000 per year of retirement

That is, by virtue of working one year, Lee Sung has earned an entitlement to a pension of $3,000 per year for life.

To determine the company's expense in 2006 related to this benefit, HTSM must discount these future payments to their present value at December 31, 2006. This is a two-step process. **First**, the pension annuity of $3,000 per year for an estimated 12 years is discounted to its present value on December 31, 2040, the employee's retirement date. Because this is still 34 years in the future at December 31, 2006, the **second** step discounts the annuity's present value at the beginning of retirement to its present value at the end of 2006. The calculations are as follows:

PV of $3,000 annuity ($n = 12$, $i = 6\%$) at Dec. 31, 2040 = $3,000 × 8.38384 (Table A-4)
                                                           = $25,151.52
PV of amount of $25,151.52 ($n = 34$, $i = 6\%$) at Dec. 31, 2006 = $25,151.52 × 0.13791 (TableA-2)
                                                                = $3,469

Therefore the current service cost to HTSM of the pension benefit earned by Lee Sung in 2006 is $3,469. This is a primary component of the period's pension expense.

Year 2007

The calculation of HTSM's current service cost for 2007 is identical to 2006, assuming a continuing discount rate of 6% and no change in the pension formula. The only difference is that the $3,000 of pension benefit earned by Lee Sung in 2007 is discounted back to December 31, 2007, instead of 2006. The calculation is as follows:

Annual pension benefit on retirement = 2% × $150,000 × 1 year
                                     = $3,000 per year of retirement
PV of $3,000 annuity ($n = 12$, $i = 6\%$) at Dec. 31, 2040 = $3,000 × 8.38384 (Table A-4)
                                                           = $25,151.52
PV of amount of $25,151.52 ($n = 33$, $i = 6\%$) at Dec. 31, 2007 = $25,151.52 × 0.14619 (TableA-2)
                                                                = $3,677

Therefore the current service cost to HTSM of the pension benefit earned by Lee Sung in 2007 is $3,677.

Accrued Benefit Obligation

At December 31, 2007

The accrued benefit obligation calculation is similar to the current service cost calculation except that it represents the present value of the pension benefits that have **accumulated for employee services provided to date as determined under the pension benefit formula**. Because 2006 was the first year of employment, we will assume that the ABO at December 31, 2006, is $3,469, the same as the current service cost. At December 31, 2007, the ABO is determined as follows:

$$
\begin{aligned}
\text{Pension benefit earned to Dec. 31, 2007} &= 2\% \times \$150{,}000 \times 2 \text{ years} \\
&= \$6{,}000 \text{ per year of retirement} \\
\text{PV of \$6,000 annuity } (n = 12, i = 6\%) \text{ at Dec. 31, 2040} &= \$6{,}000 \times 8.38384 \text{ (Table A-4)} \\
&= \$50{,}303.04 \\
\text{PV of amount of \$50,303.04 } (n = 33, i = 6\%) \text{ at Dec. 31, 2007} &= \$50{,}303.04 \times 0.14619 \text{ (Table A-2)} \\
&= \$7{,}354
\end{aligned}
$$

The accrued benefit obligation at the end of 2007 is $7,354. Further, we can reconcile the opening ABO at January 1, 2007, with the ending ABO at December 31, 2007:

ABO, January 1, 2007	$3,469
Add interest on the outstanding obligation: $3,469 × 6% × 1 year	208
Add 2007 current service cost	3,677
ABO, December 31, 2007	$7,354

At December 31, 2040

If Lee Sung works for the full 35 years, assuming no change in the $150,000 final salary estimate, pension benefit formula, discount rate, and life expectancy, the ABO on retirement is as follows:

$$
\begin{aligned}
\text{Pension benefit earned to Dec. 31, 2040} &= 2\% \times \$150{,}000 \times 35 \text{ years} \\
&= \$105{,}000 \text{ per year of retirement} \\
\text{PV of \$105,000 annuity } (n = 12, i = 6\%) \text{ at Dec. 31, 2040} &= \$105{,}000 \times 8.38384 \text{ (Table A-4)} \\
&= \$880{,}303
\end{aligned}
$$

At December 31, 2040, HTSM has an obligation with a present value of $880,303. If the company had set aside assets (that is, funded the plan) each year in an amount equal to the current service cost and the funds had earned exactly 6%, the fund assets would have accumulated to $880,303 as well. The company needs to have this amount of cash in order to purchase an annuity that will pay Lee Sung an annual pension of $105,000 for a 12-year life.

Past Service Cost

Now assume that Lee Sung had worked for HTSM's subsidiary company for six years prior to working for HTSM. Further assume that, on December 31, 2010, in determining Lee's pension benefits on retirement, HTSM agrees to give Lee Sung credit for the years that he worked for the subsidiary company before 2006. What is the cost—the past service cost—of this to HTSM? We can determine this by calculating the company's accrued obligation (ABO) before and after the pension amendment:

	Before credit for prior service	After credit for prior service
Pension benefit earned to Dec. 31, 2010:	2% × $150,000 × 5 yrs = $3,000 × 5 = $15,000 per year	2% × $150,000 × 11 yrs = $3,000 × 11 = $33,000 per year

PV of pension earned to date
at Dec. 31, 2040:

(PV factor, annuity: $n = 12$, $i = 6$)	$15,000 × 8.38384 = $125,757.60	$33,000 × 8.38384 = $276,666.72

PV of pension earned to date
at Dec. 31, 2010:

(PV factor, amount: $n = 30$, $i = 6$)	$125,757.60 × 0.17411 = $21,896	$276,666.72 × 0.17411 = $48,170

ABO at Dec. 31, 2010 **after** prior service recognized	$48,170
ABO at Dec. 31, 2010 **before** prior service recognized	21,896
Past service cost incurred	$26,274

Giving credit for prior years of service is not the only event that creates a past service cost. Another common cause of past service cost is a change in the pension benefit formula. For example, if HTSM had agreed to change the formula to 2½% of final salary per year worked, this would have a significant effect on the ABO calculation as soon as the formula was changed. A one-half-percentage-point increase on a base rate of 2% is a 25% increase!

Summary of Learning Objective for Appendix 19A

16 Explain the basics of what each of current service cost, accrued benefit obligation, and past service cost represent.

The current service cost is a calculation of the present value of the benefits earned by employees that is attributable to the current period. The accrued benefit obligation is the present value of the accumulated benefits earned to a point in time, according to the pension formula and using projected salaries. Past service cost is the present value of the additional benefits granted to employees in the case of a plan amendment.

Brief Exercises

Note: All assignment material with an asterisk (*) relates to the appendix to the chapter.

(LO 1) BE19-1   Ditek Corp. provides a defined contribution pension plan for its employees. Under the plan, the company is required to contribute 3% of employees' gross pay to a fund trustee each year. Ditek's total payroll for 2008 was $1,366,432, and the company made all required payments within the year. Prepare a summary journal entry to record Ditek's pension expense for the year.

(LO 3) BE19-2   Laurin Corporation offers parental benefits to its staff as a top-up on employment insurance so that employees end up receiving 100% of their salary for 12 months of parental leave. Ruzbeh Awad, who earns $74,000 per year, announced that he will be taking parental leave for a period of four months starting on December 1, 2008. Assume that employment insurance pays him a maximum of $720 per week for the 12 months. Prepare all entries that Laurin Corporation must make during its 2008 fiscal year related to the parental benefits plan as it applies to Ruzbeh Awad.

(LO 7) BE19-3   Kerr Corp. reports the following information to you about its defined benefit pension plan for 2008 (in thousands):

Actual return on plan assets	11	Current service cost	21
Benefits paid to retirees	8	Interest cost	9
Contributions from employer	20	Opening balance, ABO	92
Cost of plan amendment in year	13	Opening balance, fund assets	100

Provide a continuity schedule for the ABO for the year.

(LO 8) BE19-4   Refer to the information for Kerr Corp. in BE19-3, and provide a continuity schedule for the plan assets for the year. Is the plan overfunded or underfunded?

(LO 8) BE19-5   For Castor Corporation, year-end plan assets were $2 million. At the beginning of the year, plan assets were $1.65 million. During the year, contributions to the pension fund were $130,000, while benefits paid were $170,000. Calculate Castor's actual return on plan assets.

(LO 9) BE19-6   At December 31, 2008, Judy Corporation has the following balances:

Accrued benefit obligation	$3,400,000
Plan assets at fair value	2,420,000
Unrecognized past service cost	990,000

Determine the account and its balance that should be reported on Judy Corporation's December 31, 2008, balance sheet.

(LO 10) BE19-7   The following information is available for Borke Corporation for 2008:

Service cost	$29,000
Interest on ABO	22,000
Expected return on plan assets	20,000
Amortization of unrecognized past service cost	15,200
Amortization of unrecognized net actuarial loss	500

Calculate Borke's 2008 pension expense.

(LO 11) BE19-8   At January 1, 2008, Uddin Corporation had plan assets of $250,000 and an accrued benefit obligation of the same amount. During 2008, the service cost was $27,500, discount rate was 10%, actual and expected return on plan assets was $25,000, contributions were $20,000, and benefits paid were $17,500. Prepare a pension work sheet for Uddin Corporation for 2008.

(LO 11) BE19-9   For 2008, Potts Corporation had pension expense of $32,000 and contributed $25,000 to the pension fund. Prepare Potts Corporation's journal entries to record pension expense and funding.

(LO 12) BE19-10   Tuesbury Corporation amended its pension plan on January 1, 2008, and granted prior service benefits with a cost of $120,000 to its employees. The employees are expected to provide a total of 2,000 service years in the future, with 350 service years in 2008. Calculate the past service cost amortization for 2008.

(LO 12) BE19-11   At December 31, 2008, Conway Corporation had an accrued benefit obligation of $510,000, plan assets of $322,000, and unrecognized past service cost of $127,000. Calculate the balance of the pension asset or liability that will be reported on the December 31, 2008, balance sheet.

BE19-12   Fisher Corporation provides the following information at December 31, 2008.   **(LO 12)**

Accrued benefit obligation	$1,800,000
Plan assets at fair value	1,000,000
Accrued pension liability	450,000

Calculate the amount of the unrecognized past service cost at December 31, 2008. There are no other unrecognized amounts.

BE19-13   Hunt Corporation had an accrued benefit obligation of $3.1 million and plan assets of $3.3 million at January   **(LO 13)**
1, 2008. Hunt's unrecognized net actuarial loss was $475,000 at that time. The average remaining service period of Hunt's employees is 7.5 years. Calculate Hunt's minimum amortization of the unrecognized actuarial loss for 2008.

BE19-14   Legacy Corporation has the following information available concerning its post-retirement benefit plan   **(LO 13)**
for 2008:

Service cost	$40,000
Interest cost	52,400
Expected return on plan assets	26,900
Amortization of transition liability	24,600

Calculate Legacy's 2008 post-retirement expense.

BE19-15   For 2008, Benjamin Inc. calculated its annual post-retirement expense as $240,900. Benjamin's contribution to   **(LO 13)**
the plan during 2008 was $160,000 and amortization of its transition cost was $22,300. Prepare Benjamin's 2008 entry to record post-retirement expense and the entry to record the disbursement for the contribution into the plan.

Exercises

E19-1   **(Defined Contribution Plan)** Jabara Limited provides a defined contribution pension plan for its employees.   **(LO 1)**
The plan requires the company to deduct 5% of each employee's gross pay for each payroll period as the employee contribution. The company then matches this amount by an equal contribution. Both amounts are remitted to the pension trustee within 10 days of the end of each month for the previous month's payroll. At November 30, 2008, Jabara reported $26,300 of combined withheld and matched contributions owing to the trustee. During December, Jabara reported gross salaries and wages of $276,100.

Instructions

(a) Prepare the entry to record the December payment to the plan trustee.

(b) What amount of pension expense will the company report for December 2008?

(c) Determine the appropriate pension account and its balance to be reported on the December 31, 2008, balance sheet.

E19-2   **(Defined Contribution Plan)** Refer to the Stantec Inc. financial statements at the back of this textbook. What   **(LO 1)**
type of pension plan does the company offer its employees? Assume that the company has a December 31, 2004, balance in its pension liability account of $540,000 and a December 31, 2005, balance of $826,000, and that the company matches the employees' contributions to the pension plan. Prepare the journal entries to record the pension-related amounts for the year. How much cash did Stantec pay to the pension plan trustee? What is Stantec's net cash outflow?

E19-3   **(Maternity Benefits)** Goldwing Corporation offers enriched maternity benefits to the women on its staff. While   **(LO 3)**
the government provides compensation based on employment insurance legislation for a period of 12 months, Goldwing increases the amounts received and extends the period of compensation. The benefit program tops up the amount received to 100% of the employee's salary for the first 12 months, and pays the employee 75% of her full salary for another six months after the employment insurance payments have ceased.

Zeinab Jolan, who earns $54,000 per year, announced to her manager in early June 2008 that she was expecting a baby in mid-November. On October 29, 2008, nine weeks before the end of the calendar year and Goldwing's fiscal year, Zeinab began her 18-month maternity leave. Assume that employment insurance pays her a maximum of $720 per week for 52 weeks.

Instructions
Round all answers to the nearest dollar.

(a) Prepare all entries that Goldwing Corporation must make during its 2008 fiscal year related to the maternity benefits plan in regard to Zeinab Jolan. Be sure to include the date of each entry.

(b) Prepare one entry to summarize all entries that the company will make in 2009 relative to Zeinab Jolan's leave.

(c) Calculate the amount of maternity benefits payable at December 31, 2008 and 2009. Explain how these amounts will be shown on the company's balance sheet.

(LO 7, 8, 10, 14)   **E19-4   (Continuity Schedules and Calculation of Pension Expense)** Rebek Corporation provides the following information about its defined benefit pension plan for the year 2008:

Service cost	$ 90,000
Contribution to the plan	105,000
Past service cost amortization	10,000
Actual and expected return on plan assets	64,000
Benefits paid	40,000
Accrued pension liability at Jan. 1, 2008	10,000
Plan assets at Jan. 1, 2008	640,000
Accrued benefit obligation at Jan. 1, 2008	800,000
Unrecognized past service cost balance at Jan. 1, 2008	150,000
Settlement rate	10%

Instructions

(a) Prepare a continuity schedule for 2008 for the accrued benefit obligation.

(b) Prepare a continuity schedule for 2008 for the plan assets.

(c) Calculate pension expense for the year 2008.

(d) Prepare all pension journal entries recorded by Rebek in 2008.

(e) What pension amounts will appear on Rebek's balance sheet at December 31, 2008?

(LO 11)   **E19-5   (Preparation of Pension Work Sheet)** Using the information in E19-4, prepare a pension work sheet: insert the January 1, 2008, balances, and show the December 31, 2008, balances, including the entries recording the pension expense and the funding.

(LO 8)   **E19-6   (Calculation of Actual Return)** Bijan Importers provides the following pension plan information:

Fair value of pension plan assets, Jan. 1, 2008	$2,270,000
Fair value of pension plan assets, Dec. 31, 2008	2,555,000
Contributions to the plan in 2008	340,000
Benefits paid to retirees in 2008	350,000

Instructions

Calculate the actual return on the plan assets for 2008.

(LO 10)   **E19-7   (Pension Expense, Journal Entries)** The following information is available for Huntley Corporation's pension plan for the year 2008:

Actual and expected return on plan assets	$ 15,000
Benefits paid to retirees	40,000
Contributions (funding)	95,000
Discount rate	10%
Past service cost amortization	9,000
Accrued benefit obligation, Jan. 1, 2008	500,000
Service cost	65,000

Instructions

(a) Calculate pension expense for 2008.

(b) Prepare the journal entries to record all pension activity in 2008.

(LO 10, 13)   **E19-8   (Pension Expense)** The following facts apply to the pension plan of Yorke Inc. for the year 2008:

Plan assets, Jan. 1, 2008	$490,000
Accrued benefit obligation, Jan. 1, 2008	490,000
Interest and expected earnings rate	8.5%
Annual pension service cost	40,000
Contributions (funding)	30,000
Actual return on plan assets	49,700
Benefits paid to retirees	33,400

Instructions

Calculate pension expense for the year 2008, and provide the entries to recognize the pension expense and funding for the year.

E19-9   The following information is available for different companies' defined benefit pension plans for 2008:   **(LO 12)**

	A Corp.	B Corp.	C Corp.
Accrued pension liability/asset	$ –0–	$ 45,000 Cr.	$?
Accumulated benefit obligation	260,000	370,000	190,000
Fair value of plan assets	255,000	?	245,000
Projected benefit obligation	350,000	455,000	220,000
Unrecognized past service cost	?	110,000	22,000

Instructions

Determine the missing amounts.

E19-10   (Average Remaining Service Life and Amortization) Valente Company has five employees participating   **(LO 12)**
in its defined benefit pension plan. The expected years of future service for these employees at the beginning of 2008
are as follows:

Employee	Future Years of Service
Ed	3
Yasser	4
Mati	6
Suzanne	6
Alikah	6

On January 1, 2008, the company amended its pension plan, increasing its accrued benefit obligation by $60,000.

Instructions

Calculate the amount of past service cost amortization for the years 2008 through 2013 using the straight-line method.

E19-11   (ABO and Fund Asset Continuity Schedules) The following defined benefit pension data of Doret Corp.   **(LO 7, 8, 9,**
apply to the year 2008:   **10, 12, 13)**

Accrued benefit obligation, 1/1/08 (before amendment)	$560,000
Plan assets, 1/1/08	546,200
Accrued pension liability, 1/1/08	13,800
On January 1, 2008, Doret Corp., through a plan amendment, grants prior service benefits having a present value of	100,000
Discount rate and expected return	9%
Annual pension service cost	58,000
Contributions (funding)	55,000
Actual return on plan assets	52,280
Benefits paid to retirees	40,000
Past service cost amortization for 2008	17,000

Instructions

(a) Prepare a continuity schedule for the ABO for 2008.

(b) Prepare a continuity schedule for the plan assets for 2008.

(c) Calculate pension expense for 2008 and prepare the entry to record the expense.

(d) Identify the year-end balances in all pension-related accounts, both those reported on the balance sheet and those that are off–balance sheet accounts.

(e) Prepare a reconciliation of the plan's funded status to the asset or liability reported on the December 31, 2008, balance sheet.

(f) What would be the cash flow impact of the pension information above?

E19-12   (Application of the Corridor Approach) Dougherty Corp. has the following beginning-of-year present values   **(LO 13)**
for its accrued benefit obligation, and fair values for its pension plan assets:

	Accrued Benefit Obligation	Plan Assets
2006	$2,000,000	$1,900,000
2007	2,400,000	2,500,000
2008	2,900,000	2,600,000
2009	3,600,000	3,000,000

The average remaining service life per employee in 2006 and 2007 is 10 years, and in 2008 and 2009 is 12 years. The net actuarial gain or loss that occurred during each year is as follows: 2006, $280,000 loss; 2007, $90,000 loss; 2008, $10,000 loss; and 2009, $25,000 gain.

Instructions

Using the corridor approach, calculate the minimum amount of net actuarial gain or loss that should be amortized and charged to pension expense in each of the four years.

(LO 14)   E19-13   (Pension Calculations and Disclosures) Mila Enterprises Ltd. provides the following information about its defined benefit pension plan:

BALANCES OR VALUES AT DECEMBER 31, 2008

Accrued benefit obligation	$2,737,000
Accumulated benefit obligation	1,980,000
Vested benefit obligation	1,645,852
Fair value of plan assets	2,278,329
Unrecognized past service cost	205,000
Unrecognized net actuarial loss (1/1/08 balance, $0)	45,680
Accrued Pension liability	207,991
Other pension plan data:	
Service cost for 2008	94,000
Past service cost amortization for 2008	45,000
Actual return on plan assets in 2008	130,000
Expected return on plan assets in 2008	175,680
Interest on Jan. 1, 2008, accrued benefit obligation	253,000
Funding of plan in 2008	92,329
Benefits paid	140,000

Instructions

(a) Prepare the required disclosures for Mila's financial statements for the year ended December 31, 2008, assuming the company is not a public company and does not have broad public accountability.

(b) Prepare the additional disclosures that would be required if Mila's common shares were traded on the Toronto Stock Exchange.

(c) Calculate the January 1, 2008, balances for the pension-related accounts.

(LO 7, 8, 10, 12, 13)   E19-14   (Continuity Schedules, Pension Expense, Reconciliation) Vail Corp. sponsors a defined benefit pension plan for its employees. On January 1, 2008, the following balances relate to this plan:

Plan assets	$480,000
Accrued benefit obligation	625,000
Accrued Pension liability	45,000
Unrecognized past service cost	100,000

As a result of the plan's operation during 2008, the following additional data are provided by the actuary:

Service cost for 2008	$90,000
Discount or settlement rate	9%
Actual return on plan assets in 2008	57,000
Amortization of past service cost	19,000
Expected return on plan assets	52,000
Unexpected loss from change in accrued benefit obligation due to change in actuarial predictions	76,000
Contributions (plan funding) in 2008	99,000
Benefits paid to retirees in 2008	85,000

Instructions

(a) Provide a continuity schedule to explain the change in the ABO from its opening balance to its ending balance.

(b) Provide a continuity schedule to explain the change in the fund assets from its opening balance to its ending balance.

(c) Calculate pension expense for Vail Corp. for 2008. Do not use a work sheet.

(d) Prepare the entry(ies) to record the expense and the funding of the plan in the year.

(e) At December 31, 2008, prepare a schedule reconciling the funded status of the plan with the pension amount reported on the balance sheet.

E19-15 (Pension Expense, Journal Entries, Disclosure) Griseta Limited sponsors a defined benefit pension plan for   **(LO 10, 14)**
its employees. The following data relate to the operation of the plan for the year 2008:

1. The actuarial present value of future benefits earned by employees for services rendered in 2008 amounted to
$56,000.

2. The company's funding policy requires a contribution to the pension trustee of $145,000 for 2008.

3. As at January 1, 2008, the company had an accrued benefit obligation of $1 million and an unrecognized past service
cost of $400,000. The fair value of pension plan assets amounted to $600,000 at the beginning of the year. The actual
and expected return on plan assets was $54,000. The discount rate was 9%.

4. Amortization of past service costs was $40,000 in 2008.

5. No benefits were paid in 2008.

Instructions

(a) Determine the pension expense that should be recognized by the company in 2008.

(b) Prepare all pension related journal entries for 2008.

(c) Determine the plan's funded status and reconcile this to the accrued pension asset/liability on the December 31, 2008
balance sheet.

(d) Assuming Griseta is not a public company and does not have broad public accountability, prepare the required disclosures for the 2008 financial statements.

(e) Calculate the January 1, 2008 balance in accrued pension asset/liability.

E19-16 (Pension Expense, Entries, Statement Presentation) Altom Corporation received the following selected   **(LO 10, 14)**
information from its pension plan trustee concerning the operation of the company's defined benefit pension plan for the
year ended December 31, 2008:

	January 1, 2008	December 31, 2008
Accrued benefit obligation	$2,000,000	$2,077,000
Market-related and fair value of plan assets	800,000	1,130,000
Actuarial gains	–0–	200,000

The service cost component of pension expense for employee services rendered in the current year amounted to $77,000,
and the amortization of unrecognized past service cost was $115,000. The company's actual funding of the plan in 2008
amounted to $250,000. The expected return on plan assets and the actual rate were both 10%; the discount rate was 10%.
No accrued pension asset/liability existed on January 1, 2008. Assume that no benefits were paid in 2008.

Instructions

(a) Determine the pension expense that should be recognized by the company in 2008.

(b) Prepare the journal entries to record pension expense and the employer's contribution to the pension plan in 2008.

(c) Indicate the pension-related amounts that would be reported on the income statement and the balance sheet for
Altom Corporation for the year 2008.

(d) Calculate the balance of any unrecognized amounts at December 31, 2008. Discuss the relationship between the
accrued pension asset/liability account on the balance sheet and the funded status and explain what these amounts
represent.

E19-17 (Calculation of Actual Return, Gains and Losses, Corridor Test, Past Service Cost, Pension Expense,   **(LO 8, 10**
and Reconciliation) Berstler Limited sponsors a defined benefit pension plan. The corporation's actuary provides the   **12, 13, 14)**
following information about the plan:

	January 1, 2008	December 31, 2008
Vested benefit obligation	$1,500	$1,900
Accumulated benefit obligation	1,900	2,730
Accrued benefit obligation	2,800	3,645
Plan assets (fair value)	1,700	2,620
Discount rate and expected rate of return	10%	10%
Accrued pension asset/liability	0	?
Unrecognized past service cost	1,100	?
Service cost for the year 2008		400
Contributions (funding in 2008)		800
Benefits paid in 2008		200

The average remaining service life and period to full eligibility is 20 years.

Instructions

(a) Calculate the actual return on the plan assets in 2008.

(b) Calculate the amount of the unrecognized net actuarial gain or loss as at December 31, 2008 (assume the January 1, 2008, balance was zero).

(c) Calculate the amount of actuarial gain or loss amortization for 2008 using the corridor approach. How will 2009's expense be affected, if at all?

(d) Calculate the amount of past service cost amortization for 2008.

(e) Calculate the pension expense for 2008.

(f) Prepare a schedule reconciling the plan's funded status with the amount reported on the December 31, 2008 balance sheet.

(LO 11) E19-18 (Work Sheet for E19-17) Using the information in E19-17 about Berstler Limited's defined benefit pension plan, prepare (a) a 2008 pension work sheet with supplementary schedules of calculations, and (b) the journal entries at December 31, 2008, to record pension expense and the funding contributions. Also, prepare a schedule reconciling the plan's funded status with the pension amounts reported on the balance sheet.

(LO 13) E19-19 (Corridor Amortization) The actuary for the pension plan of Brush Inc. calculated the following net actuarial gains and losses:

	Net Gain or Loss
Incurred during the Year	(Gain) or Loss
2007	$480,000
2008	300,000
2009	(210,000)
2010	(290,000)

Other information about the company's pension obligation and plan assets is as follows:

As at January 1	Accrued Obligation	Benefit Plan Assets
2007	$4,000,000	$2,400,000
2008	4,520,000	2,200,000
2009	4,980,000	2,600,000
2010	4,250,000	3,040,000

Brush Inc. has a stable labour force of 400 employees who are expected to receive benefits under the plan. Their expected average remaining service life is 12 years. The beginning balance of unrecognized net actuarial gain/loss is zero on January 1, 2007. The plan assets' market-related value and fair value are the same for the four-year period.

Instructions

Prepare a schedule that shows the minimum amount of amortization of the unrecognized net actuarial gain or loss for each of the years 2007, 2008, 2009, and 2010. (Round to the nearest dollar.)

(LO 10, 13) E19-20 (Pension Expense, Reconciliation, Corridor Approach) Lo Limited sponsors a defined benefit pension plan for its 600 employees. The company's actuary provided the following information about the plan:

	January 1, 2008	December 31, 2008
Accrued benefit obligation	$2,800,000	$3,909,000
Plan assets, at fair and market-related value	1,700,000	2,370,000
Net actuarial loss (gain) in the year on the ABO	–0–	401,000
Discount rate		11%
Actual and expected asset return rate		10%
Contributions to fund		500,000

The company anticipates that the employees' expected average remaining service life and expected period to full eligibility is 10.5 years. The service cost component of net periodic pension expense for employee services rendered amounted to $400,000 in 2008. At January 1, 2008, the only unrecognized amounts related to past service costs of $1.1 million. No benefits have been paid.

Instructions

Round all answers to the nearest dollar.

(a) Calculate the pension expense to be reported in 2008.

(b) Prepare continuity schedules for the ABO and the fund assets for 2008.

(c) Reconcile the funded status at December 31, 2008 with the amount recognized on the December 31, 2008, balance sheet.

(d) Calculate the amortization, if any, of the net actuarial gain or loss to be included in pension expense in 2009.

E19-21   (Post-Retirement Benefit Expense Calculation and Entries) Opsco Corp. provides the following informa-   **(LO 13)**
tion about its non-pension post-retirement benefit plan for the year 2008:

Service cost	$ 90,000
Past service cost amortization	3,000
Contribution to the plan	21,000
Actual and expected return on plan assets	63,000
Benefits paid	40,000
Plan assets at Jan. 1, 2008	710,000
Post-retirement benefit obligation at Jan. 1, 2008	810,000
Unrecognized past service cost balance at Jan. 1, 2008	20,000
Amortization of net transition liability	9,000
Unrecognized net transition liability at Jan. 1, 2008	80,000
Discount rate	9%

Instructions

Calculate the post-retirement benefit expense for 2008, and prepare all required journal entries related to the benefit plan that were made by Opsco in 2008.

E19-22   (Post-Retirement Benefit Work Sheet)   **(LO 13)**

Instructions

(a) Using the information in E19-21, complete a post-retirement work sheet for 2008.

(b) Prepare all required journal entries related to the plan made by Opsco in 2008.

E19-23   (Post-Retirement Benefit Reconciliation Schedule) The following is partial information related to Conley   **(LO 13)**
Corp.'s non-pension post-retirement benefit plan at December 31, 2008:

Accrued post-retirement benefit obligation	$950,000
Plan assets (at fair value)	650,000
Past service cost not yet recognized in post-retirement expense	60,000
Net actuarial gains/losses	–0–
Unrecognized transition liability	100,000

Instructions

(a) Prepare a schedule reconciling the funded status with the asset/liability reported on the balance sheet at December 31, 2008.

(b) Repeat (a) assuming the same facts as above except that Conley Corp. has an unrecognized actuarial gain of $20,000 at December 31, 2008, that arose in the current period.

E19-24   (Post-Retirement Benefit Expense, Funded Status, and Reconciliation) Rosek Inc. provides the following   **(LO 13)**
information related to its post-retirement benefits for the year 2008:

Accrued post-retirement benefit obligation at Jan. 1, 2008	$610,000
Plan assets, Jan. 1, 2008	42,000
Unrecognized net transitional loss, Jan. 1, 2008	568,000
Actual and expected return on plan assets, 2008	3,000
Amortization of transition liability, 2008	35,000
Discount rate	10%
Service cost, 2008	57,000
Plan funding during 2008	22,000
Payments from plan on behalf of retirees	6,000
Actuarial loss on accrued benefit obligation, 2008 (end of year)	88,000

The only unrecognized cost related to this plan at January 1, 2008, was the net transition loss.

Instructions

(a) Calculate the post-retirement benefit expense for 2008.

(b) Determine the December 31, 2008, balance of the fund assets, the accrued obligation, and the funded status.

(c) Determine the balance of the accrued post-retirement benefit asset/liability account on the December 31, 2008 balance sheet.

(d) Reconcile the funded status with the amount reported on the balance sheet at December 31, 2008.

(LO 16)   ***E19-25   (Calculation of Current Service Cost and ABO)** Josit Ltd. initiated a one-person pension plan in January 2003 that promises the employee a pension on retirement according to the following formula: pension benefit = 2½% of final salary per year of service after the plan initiation. The employee began employment with Josit early in 2000 at age 33, and expects to retire at the end of 2026, the year in which he turns 60. His life expectancy at that time is 21 years.

Assume that this employee earned an annual salary of $40,000 when he joined Josit, that his salary was expected to increase at a rate of 4% per year, and that this remains a reasonable assumption to date. Josit considers a discount rate of 6% to be appropriate.

Instructions

(a) What is the employee's expected final salary?

(b) What amount of current service cost should Josit recognize in 2008 relative to this plan?

(c) What is the amount of the accrued benefit obligation (ABO) at December 31, 2008?

Problems

P19-1   RWL Limited provides a long-term disability program for its employees through an insurance company. For an annual premium of $18,000, the insurance company is responsible for providing salary continuation to disabled employees on a long-term basis after a three-month waiting period. During the waiting period, RWL continues to pay the employee at full salary. The employees contribute to the cost of this plan through regular payroll deductions that amount to $6,000 for the year. In late October 2008, Tony Hurst, a department manager earning $5,400 per month, was injured and was not expected to be able to return to work for at least one year.

Instructions

Prepare all entries made by RWL in 2008 in connection with the benefit plan, as well as any entries required in 2009.

P19-2   Halifax University recently signed a contract with the bargaining unit that represents full-time professors. The contract agreement begins on April 1, 2007, the start of the university's fiscal year.

The following excerpt outlines the portion of the signed agreement that relates to sabbaticals: *"Professors will receive a one-year sabbatical leave after seven continuous years of employment."*

After completing the required amount of time, any professor may apply for the leave. The contract notes particular types of activities that the sabbatical is intended to promote, including formal research, continued professional development, and independent study and research. Individual professors are left to make their own choices about whichever of these activities to pursue while on sabbatical leave. As part of their agreement, they must continue to work for Halifax University for one year after their sabbatical, or reimburse the university for funds they receive while on leave. Professors may delay, or be asked to delay, their application for sabbatical, in which case it will accumulate and either be taken as leave in the future or as payment upon retirement. The agreement states that professors receive 80% of their salary while on sabbatical leave.

The issue of sabbaticals had long been a point of contention with faculty at Halifax University, which is an independent institution, and they fought vehemently for the right to this paid leave, which had not previously been in their collective agreement. The university is phasing in the unfunded sabbatical plan gradually, which means that the first professors will be eligible to apply for and take their sabbaticals in seven years.

The Controller has put together the following salary information relative to the employee group:

Professors with salaries averaging $60,000	55
Professors with salaries averaging $70,000	40
Professors with salaries averaging $100,000	10

The union agreement calls for a wage increase of 2% per year in each of the next five years. This is consistent with past union agreements for this bargaining unit. Five of the professors with salaries averaging $100,000 are scheduled to retire in four years. Halifax University expects to keep a similar composition of salaried professors in the future. Assume a discount rate of 6%.

Instructions

(a) Prepare any entries that are required at the March 31, 2008, fiscal year end assuming sabbaticals will be granted only if the sabbatical activities proposed by the applicants are expected to benefit the university in some way.

(b) Prepare any entries that are required at the March 31, 2008, fiscal year end assuming sabbaticals will be granted automatically with no restrictions on the professors' activities during the year.

(c) Five employees are granted approval to take sabbatical in the first year that they are eligible under the assumption in (b). Prepare the entry that will be required when the professors are paid, assuming that an amount of $367,000 has correctly been accrued for these employees.

(d) The contract allows employees of the bargaining unit to take up to 10 days of paid sick leave per year. Explain the accounting implications under the following assumptions:

1. The sick leave is allowed to be carried over for up to a one-year period following year end.

2. Any unused sick time is not eligible to be carried over to the following fiscal period.

P19-3 Dayte Corporation reports the following January 1, 2007, balances for its defined benefit pension plan: plan assets, $200,000; accrued benefit obligation, $200,000. Other data relating to three years of operation of the plan are as follows:

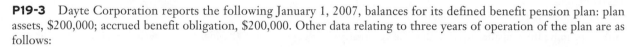

	2007	2008	2009
Annual service cost	$16,000	$ 19,000	$ 26,000
Discount rate and expected rate of return	10%	10%	10%
Actual return on plan assets	17,000	21,900	24,000
Funding of current service cost	16,000	19,000	26,000
Funding of past service cost	—	30,000	35,000
Benefits paid	14,000	16,400	21,000
Unrecognized past service cost (plan amended, 1/1/08)		160,000	
Amortization of unrecognized past service cost		54,400	41,600
Change in actuarial assumptions establishes a Dec. 31, 2009, accrued benefit obligation of			520,000

Instructions

(a) Prepare a continuity schedule of the projected benefit obligation over the three-year period.

(b) Prepare a continuity schedule of the fund assets over the three-year period.

(c) Determine the pension expense for each of 2007, 2008, and 2009.

(d) Prepare the journal entries to reflect the pension plan transactions and events for each year.

(e) Prepare a schedule reconciling the plan's funded status with the pension amounts reported on the balance sheet over the three-year period.

P19-4 On January 1, 2008, Industrial Corporation has the following defined benefit pension plan balances:

Accrued benefit obligation	$5,200,000
Fair value of plan assets	$5,200,000

The interest (settlement) rate applicable to the plan is 10%. On January 1, 2009, the company amended its pension agreement, resulting in the creation of prior service costs of $550,000. Other data related to the pension plan follow:

	2008	2009
Service costs	$160,000	$195,000
Unrecognized past service cost amortization	–0–	95,000
Contributions (funding) to the plan	255,000	285,000
Benefits paid	200,000	680,000
Actual return on plan assets	312,000	405,000
Expected rate of return on assets	6%	8%

Instructions

(a) Prepare a pension work sheet for the pension plan for 2008 and 2009.

(b) As of December 31, 2009, prepare a schedule reconciling the funded status with the accrued pension asset/liability reported on the balance sheet.

P19-5   Stanfield Corporation sponsors a defined benefit plan for its 100 employees. On January 1, 2008, the company's actuary provided the following information:

Unrecognized past service cost	$150,000
Pension plan assets (fair value)	400,000
Accrued benefit obligation	550,000

The participating employees' EARSL and average remaining service period to full eligibility is 10.5 years. All employees are expected to receive benefits under the plan. On December 31, 2008, the actuary calculated that the present value of future benefits earned for employee services rendered in the current year amounted to $82,000; the accrued benefit obligation was $702,000; the fair value of pension assets was $526,000; and the accumulated benefit obligation amounted to $665,000. The expected return on plan assets and the discount rate on the accrued benefit obligation were both 10%. The actual return on plan assets is $31,000. The company funded the current service cost as well as $41,000 of the past service costs in the current year. No benefits were paid during the year.

Instructions

Round all answers to the nearest dollar.

(a) Determine the pension expense that the company will recognize in 2008, identifying each component clearly. (Do not prepare a work sheet.)

(b) Calculate the amount of any 2008 increase/decrease in unrecognized actuarial gains or losses and the amount to be amortized in 2008 and 2009.

(c) Prepare the journal entries to record pension expense and the company's funding of the pension plan in 2008.

(d) Prepare a schedule that reconciles the plan's funded status with the accrued pension asset/liability reported on the December 31, 2008, balance sheet.

(e) Assume that the liability and asset losses on the accrued benefit obligation and plan assets arose because of the disposal of a segment of Stanfield's business. How should these losses be reported on the company's 2008 financial statements?

P19-6   Manon Corporation sponsors a defined benefit pension plan. The following pension plan information is available for 2008 and 2009:

	2008	2009
Plan assets (fair value), Dec. 31	$380,000	$465,000
Accrued benefit obligation, Jan. 1	600,000	700,000
Accrued pension liability, Jan. 1	40,000	?
Unrecognized past service cost, Jan. 1	250,000	240,000
Service cost	60,000	90,000
Actual and expected return on plan assets	24,000	30,000
Amortization of past service cost	10,000	12,000
Funding of current service costs	60,000	90,000
Funding of past service costs	50,000	30,000
Interest/settlement rate	9%	9%

The pension fund paid out benefits in each year. While there was an unrecognized actuarial gain/loss at January 1, 2008, no additional actuarial gains or losses were incurred in the two-year period.

Instructions

(a) Calculate pension expense for 2008 and 2009.

(b) Prepare all journal entries to record the pension expense and the company's pension plan funding for both years.

(c) Assuming that Manon is not a public company and does not have broad public accountability, prepare the required notes to the financial statements at December 31, 2009.

(d) Prepare the complete pension work sheets for Manon for 2008 and 2009.

P19-7   Dubel Toothpaste Corporation initiated a defined benefit pension plan for its 50 employees on January 1, 2007. The insurance company that administers the pension plan provides the following information for the years 2007, 2008, and 2009:

	For Year Ended December 31		
	2007	2008	2009
Plan assets (fair value)	$50,000	$85,000	$170,000
Accrued benefit obligation	63,900	?	?
Net actuarial (gain) loss re: ABO	8,900	(24,500)	84,500
Net actuarial (gain) loss re: fund assets	?	?	(18,200)
Employer's funding contribution (made at end of year)	50,000	60,000	95,000

There were no balances as at January 1, 2007 when the plan was initiated. The long-run expected return on plan assets was 8% throughout the three-year period. The settlement rate that was used to discount the company's pension obligation was 13% in 2007, 11% in 2008, and 8% in 2009. The service cost component of net periodic pension expense amounted to the following: 2007, $55,000; 2008, $85,000; and 2009, $119,000. The average remaining service life per employee is 10 years. No benefits were paid in 2007, but $30,000 was paid in 2008, and $35,000 in 2009 (all benefits were paid at the end of the year).

Instructions

Depending on what your instructor assigns, do either (a), (b), (c), and (e); or only (d) and (e). (Round all answers to the nearest dollar.)

(a) Prepare a continuity schedule for the accrued benefit obligation over the three-year period.

(b) Prepare a continuity schedule for the plan assets over the three-year period.

(c) Calculate the amount of net periodic pension expense that the company will recognize in each of 2007, 2008, and 2009.

(d) Prepare and complete a pension work sheet for each of 2007, 2008, and 2009.

(e) Determine the funded status at December 31, 2009, and the balance of the accrued pension asset or liability that will be reported on the December 31, 2009, balance sheet. Fully explain why these amounts differ.

P19-8   Ekedahl Inc. has sponsored a non-contributory defined benefit pension plan for its employees since 1987. Prior to 2008, the funding of this plan exactly equalled cumulative net pension expense. Other relevant information about the pension plan on January 1, 2008, is as follows:

1. The company has 200 employees who are expected to receive benefits under the plan. The employees' expected period to full eligibility is 13 years with an EARSL of 16 years.

2. The accrued benefit obligation amounted to $5 million and the fair and market-related value of pension plan assets was $3 million. Unrecognized past service cost was $2 million.

On December 31, 2008, the accrued benefit obligation was $4.75 million. The fair value of the pension plan assets amounted to $3.9 million at the end of the year. A 10% discount rate and an 8% expected asset return rate were used in the actuarial present value calculations in the pension plan. The present value of benefits attributed by the pension benefit formula to employee service in 2008 amounted to $200,000. The employer's contribution to the plan assets was $575,000 in 2008. No pension benefits were paid to retirees during this period.

Instructions

Round all answers to the nearest dollar.

(a) What amount of past service cost will be included as a component of pension expense in 2008, 2009, and 2010?

(b) Calculate pension expense for the year 2008.

(c) Determine the amount of any actuarial gains or losses in 2008 and the amount to be amortized to expense in 2008 and 2009.

(d) Prepare the necessary journal entries to account for the company's pension plan for 2008.

(e) Prepare a schedule reconciling the plan's funded status with the pension amounts reported on the December 31, 2008, balance sheet.

(f) Assume that Ekedahl's pension plan is contributory rather than non-contributory. Would any part of your answers above change? What would be the impact on the company's financial statements of a contributory plan?

P19-9   Zen Corp. sponsors a defined benefit pension plan for its employees. On January 1, 2008, the following balances related to this plan:

Plan assets (fair value)	$547,000
Accrued benefit obligation	752,000
Accrued pension liability	26,000
Unrecognized past service cost	83,000
Unrecognized net actuarial gain/loss (debit)	96,000

As a result of the plan's operation during 2008, the actuary provided the following additional data at December 31, 2008:

Service cost for 2008	$110,000
Discount rate, 9%; expected rate of return, 10%	
Actual return on assets in 2008	50,700
Amortization of past service cost	25,000
Current service costs funded in 2008	112,000
Past service costs funded in 2008	27,000
Benefits paid to retirees in 2008	95,000
Average period to full eligibility of employee group	10 years
Average remaining service life of active employees	13 years

Instructions

Calculate the pension expense for Zen Corp. for the year 2008 by completing a pension work sheet. Prepare all the journal entries to record events involving the pension-related accounts.

P19-10   Glesen Corporation sponsors a defined benefit pension plan for its employees. The following data relate to the operation of the plan for the years 2008 and 2009:

	2008	2009
Accrued benefit obligation, Jan. 1	$650,000	
Plan assets (fair value and market-related value), Jan. 1	410,000	
Accrued pension liability, Jan. 1	80,000	
Unrecognized past service cost, Jan. 1	160,000	
Service cost	40,000	$ 59,000
Settlement rate (discount rate)	10%	10%
Expected rate of return	9%	9%
Actual return on plan assets	36,000	61,000
Amortization of past service costs	70,000	55,000
Annual funding per actuary's instructions	72,000	81,000
Benefits paid to retirees	31,500	54,000
Increase in accrued benefit obligation due to changes in actuarial assumptions	87,000	–0–
Average service life and period to full eligibility of employees		20 years
Vested benefit obligation at Dec. 31		464,000

Instructions

(a) Prepare a pension work sheet for both 2008 and 2009.

(b) Prepare the employer journal entries to reflect the pension transactions and events for 2008 and 2009.

(c) At December 31, 2009, prepare a schedule reconciling the pension plan's funded status with the pension amount reported on the company's balance sheet.

P19-11   You are the auditor of Beaton and Gunter Inc., the Canadian subsidiary of a multinational engineering company that offers a defined benefit pension plan to its eligible employees. Employees are permitted to join the plan after two years of employment, and benefits vest two years after joining the plan. You have received the following information from the fund trustee for the year ended December 31, 2008:

Discount rate	5%
Expected long-term rate of return on plan assets	6.5%
Rate of compensation increase	3.5%

Accrued Benefit Obligation

Accrued benefit obligation at Jan. 1, 2008	$18,200,000
Current service cost	680,000
Interest cost	910,000
Benefits paid	1,210,000
Actuarial loss for the period	1,010,000

Plan Assets

Market value of plan assets at Jan. 1, 2008	14,500,000
Actual return on plan assets, net of expenses	1,800,000
Employer contributions	790,000
Employee contributions	130,000
Benefits paid	1,210,000

Other relevant information:

1. The accrued pension liability on January 1, 2008, is $2,563,000.

2. There is an unrecognized past service cost of $3,187,000 on January 1, 2008.

3. There is an unrecognized net actuarial gain of $2,050,000 on January 1, 2008.

4. Employee contributions to the plan are withheld as payroll deductions, and are remitted to the pension trustee along with the employer contributions.

5. The expected period to full eligibility and the EARSL are both 20 years.

Instructions

(a) Prepare a pension work sheet for the company.

(b) Prepare the employer's journal entries to reflect the accounting for the pension plan for the year ended December 31, 2008.

(c) Prepare a schedule reconciling the plan's funded status with the pension amounts reported on the December 31, 2008 balance sheet.

(d) Assume that interest rates in the economy are falling. Explain what effect this is likely to have on the funded status of the plan.

P19-12   Donnie Harpin was recently promoted to assistant controller of Glomski Corporation, having previously served Glomski as a staff accountant. One of her new responsibilities is to prepare the annual pension accrual. Judy Gralapp, the corporate controller, provided Harpin with last year's working papers and information from the actuary's annual report. The pension work sheet for the prior year is as follows:

	General Journal Entries			Memo Records		
	Pension Expense	Cash	Accrued Pension Asset/Liability	Accrued Benefit Obligation	Plan Assets	Unrecognized Past Service Cost
June 1, 2007[1]				$(20,000)	$20,000	
Service cost[1]	$1,800			(1,800)		
Interest[2]	1,200			(1,200)		
Actual return[3]	(1,600)				1,600	
Contribution[1]		$(1,000)			1,000	
Benefits paid[1]				900	(900)	
Past service cost[4]				(2,000)		$2,000
Journal entries	$1,400		($1,400)			
		$(1,000)	1,000			
May 31, 2008, balance			$(400)	($24,100)	$21,700	$2,000

[1]Per actuary's report.

[2]Beginning accrued benefit obligation × discount rate of 6%.

[3]Expected return was $1,600 (beginning plan assets × expected return of 8%).

[4]A plan amendment that granted employees retroactive benefits for work performed in earlier periods took effect on May 31, 2008. The amendment increased the May 31, 2008, accrued benefit obligation by $2,000. No amortization was recorded in the fiscal year ended May 31, 2008.

The actuary's report for the year ended May 31, 2009, indicated no actuarial gains or losses in the fiscal year ended May 31, 2009. Other pertinent information from the report is as follows:

Contribution	$ 425	Actual return on plan assets	$1,736
Service cost	3,000	Benefits paid	500
Discount rate	6%	Average remaining service life	10 years
Expected return	8%		
Average period to full eligibility	8 years		

Instructions

(a) Prepare the pension work sheet for Glomski Corporation for the year ended May 31, 2009.

(b) Prepare the necessary journal entries to reflect the accounting for Glomski Corporation's pension plan for the year ended May 31, 2009.

P19-13   Hass Foods Inc. sponsors a post-retirement medical and dental benefit plan for its employees. The company adopted the provisions of *CICA Handbook* Section 3461 beginning January 1, 2008, and decided to account for any transitional balances on a prospective basis. The following balances relate to this plan on January 1, 2008:

Plan assets	$200,000
Accrued post-retirement benefit obligation	882,000
Past service costs	–0–

As a result of the plan's operation during 2008, the following additional data were provided by the actuary:

1. The service cost for 2008 was $70,000.

2. The discount rate was 9%.

3. Funding payments in 2008 were $60,000.

4. The expected return on plan assets was $9,000.

5. The actual return on plan assets was $15,000.

6. The benefits paid on behalf of retirees from the plan were $44,000.

7. The average remaining service life to full eligibility was 20 years.

8. The average remaining service life to expected retirement was 22 years.

Instructions

(a) Calculate the post-retirement benefit expense for 2008.

(b) Prepare a continuity schedule for the accrued benefit obligation and for the plan assets from the beginning of the year to the end of 2008.

(c) At December 31, 2008, prepare a schedule reconciling the plan's funded status with the post-retirement amount reported on the balance sheet.

(d) Explain in what ways, if any, the accounting requirements for this plan are different from the requirements for a defined benefit pension plan.

*P19-14   Refer to the example of HTSM Corp. in Appendix A and assume it is now 2008, two years after the defined pension plan was initiated. In December 2008, HTSM's actuary provided the company with an actuarial revaluation of the plan. The actuary's assumptions included the following changes:

Estimated final salary on retirement	$145,000
Current settlement/discount rate	7%

Instructions

(a) Calculate the accrued benefit obligation (ABO) at December 31, 2008, and the amount of any actuarial gain or loss.

(b) Based on the revised assumptions at the end of the year, determine what percentage increase or decrease there would be in the ABO for (1) a 1% increase in the discount rate and (2) a 1% decrease in the discount rate.

(c) Determine the effect of the actuarial revaluation on the plan's funded status at December 31, 2008, and on pension expense for 2008 and for 2009.

(d) Based on the revised assumptions, recalculate the past service cost that was incurred by the company in 2010.

Writing Assignments

WA19-1 Shikkiah Corp. tries to attract the most knowledgeable and creative employees it can find. To help accomplish this, the company offers a special group of technology employees the right to a fully paid sabbatical leave after every five years of continuous service. It is the company's objective that the employees will come back renewed and with fresh ideas, but there are no restrictions on what they do during the sabbatical year.

Shikkiah hired three employees in early 2008 who were entitled to this benefit. Each new hire agreed to a starting salary of $80,000 per year.

Instructions

(a) Explain generally how this employee benefit should be accounted for by Shikkiah Corp.

(b) Assume that you are the assistant to the company controller. In response to the controller's request, list all the information you need in order to calculate the amounts and prepare the adjusting entry that is required at December 31, 2008, relative to this plan.

(c) Assume that the activities of the employees during the sixth (the sabbatical) year are specified by the company: the employees must work on research and promotion activities that will benefit the company. Would your answer to (a) change? If yes, explain why and how it would be accounted for. If not, explain why not.

WA19-2 Many business organizations have been concerned with providing for employee retirement since the late 1800s. During recent decades, a marked increase in this concern has resulted in the establishment of private pension and other post-retirement benefit plans in most companies of any size.

The substantial growth of these plans, both in the numbers of employees that they cover and in the types and value of retirement benefits, has increased the significance of the cost of these benefit plans in relation to the financial position, results of operations, and cash flows of many companies. In working with the benefit plans, accountants encounter a variety of terms. Each benefit plan component must be dealt with appropriately if generally accepted accounting principles are to be reflected in the financial statements of entities that offer these plans.

Instructions

(a) What is a private benefit plan? How does a contributory plan differ from a non-contributory plan?

(b) Differentiate between accounting for the employer and accounting for the benefit plan.

(c) Explain the terms "funded" and "benefit liability" as they relate to the employer and the benefit plan itself.

(d) **1.** Explain the theoretical justification for accrual recognition of future benefit costs.

    2. Explain the theoretical justification for "event accrual" accounting for future benefit costs.

    3. In terms of the reliability concept, discuss the measurement process that is used for full accrual accounting, versus event accrual accounting, versus cash (pay-as-you-go) accounting for annual benefit costs.

(e) Distinguish between each of the following sets of terms as they relate to pension plans:

    1. Current service cost and past service cost

    2. Asset experience gain/loss and liability experience gain/loss

    3. Capitalization and non-capitalization approaches to pension accounting

(f) Explain how the accounting for other post-retirement benefit plans with benefits that vest or accumulate differs from the accounting for defined benefit pension plans, if there is any difference.

WA19-3 Philip Regan, chief executive officer of Relief Dynamics Inc., a large defence contracting firm, is considering ways to improve the company's financial position after several years of sharply declining profitability. One way to do this is to reduce or completely eliminate Relief's non-contractual commitment to present and future retirees who have full prescription drug and dental benefits coverage. Regan is considering making this recommendation to the board of directors as he has read many recent articles in the financial press about companies cutting back on such post-retirement benefits. Despite financial problems, the company has always been committed to providing excellent pension benefits.

Instructions

Answer the following questions.

(a) Does the requirement for reporting liabilities on the balance sheet only apply to liabilities that are contractual obligations? Explain. Include in your answer a reference to any relevant IFRS as well as the Canadian position.

(b) What factors should Regan consider in developing his recommendation for the board of directors?

(c) Would your answer to the above question change if Relief Dynamics were paying Philip Regan, CEO, a salary of $30 million per year? Explain.

(d) Research what Canadian companies have been doing in recent years in response to rising post-retirement health-care costs and the risks that are associated with defined benefit pension plans. Write a short report on your findings that would be suitable to present to Philip Regan.

WA19-4 Ruth Moore and Carl Nies have to lead a class discussion on employee future benefits, particularly the benefits that relate to pensions and other post-retirement benefits. In preparing for their presentation, they decided to give the class a series of questions related to these benefits and then to discuss the answers in class. Since the students are up to date on the most recent Canadian standards, Ruth and Carl felt that this approach would lead to an interesting class. Here are the situations and questions they have suggested to stimulate discussion:

1. In an article in *The Globe and Mail* that appeared before the adoption of Section 3461, it was reported that the discount rates used by the largest 200 companies for pension reporting ranged from 5% to 11%. What problem would this cause? Does Section 3461 remedy this problem?

2. A recent article noted that while "smoothing" is not necessarily an accounting virtue, pension accounting has long been recognized as an exception—an area of accounting in which at least some dampening of market swings is appropriate. Where does smoothing take place under existing standards, and what reasons are given to justify it in each case?

3. Changes to U.S. standards effective in 2007 finally brought the benefit asset or liability reported on the balance sheet in line with the funded status of the benefit plans, although Canadian standard setters agreed not to change until Canadian companies adopt international standards. How can the benefit asset or liability reported on the balance sheet be the same as the funded status?

4. In order to understand how post-retirement benefit accounting affects a company, detailed information is needed about the company's benefit plans and an analysis must be done of the relationship between many factors. How does each of the following factors affect a company's financial statements?

    (a) the transition amount, the date of initial application, and the method of accounting for the change in accounting policy

    (b) the type(s) of plan(s) and any significant amendments

    (c) the plan participants

    (d) the funding status

    (e) the actuarial funding method and assumptions currently being used

Instructions

Prepare answers to the questions and issues that Ruth and Carl have raised as a basis for their presentation.

Cases

Refer to the Case Primer on the Student Website to help you answer these cases.

CA19-1 Pablo Ltd. (PL) reproduces fine works of art as posters. The company was started 10 years ago with used equipment. Demand for the posters increased recently when PL began to glue the posters onto a wood backing and laminate them. The old equipment has become very expensive to maintain and keeps breaking down, disrupting production. Pietro Pablo, the owner, has decided to go to the bank for a loan to buy new equipment. In preliminary talks with the bank, the manager indicated that financial statements are needed from PL for the year ended December 31, 2008.

While the statements have now been drafted, Pietro is not happy with the net income figure, which is lower than he had expected. Pietro calls you, his accounting manager, and asks if the net income has been correctly calculated. He points to the large payroll expense, which has increased over last year. You note that the main cause of the increase is that pension expense increased for the following two reasons:

1. The pension plan with the employees was renegotiated at the beginning of the year and a key change was to increase the amount of pension benefits for each employee for each hour worked. The plan is a defined benefit plan and the amendment provided for retroactive application, so that most of the employees, who were older, would benefit from the plan. The increase in the pension obligation arising from this amendment is being amortized to net income over 14 years, beginning with 2008.

2. The actuary has recently prepared a new actuarial valuation of the pension obligation. In doing so, she suggested that the interest rate used for discounting be changed to reflect recent reductions in interest rates. Short-term interest

rates have declined but many economists predict that the mid- to long-term rates will remain more stable at the higher rate. The reduction in the interest rate for discounting has resulted in an increase in the pension obligation. The increase is also being amortized to net income over 14 years, beginning with 2008.

Pietro asks you to go back and read the *CICA Handbook* and determine whether there is any flexibility in applying the rules.

Instructions

Discuss the issues.

CA 19-2   In February 2008, Beaton's Limited (BL) filed for protection under the Companies' Creditors Arrangement Act due to liquidity problems. The act gives troubled companies time to restructure their debt and to hopefully avoid bankruptcy. As part of the restructuring process, BL approached its employees and pensioners to split the surplus in the pension plan and allow BL to withdraw a portion of the surplus in cash to help lessen the liquidity problems.

In note 9 to the unaudited financial statements, the following was disclosed with respect to the company's pension plan for the year ended December 31, 2008 (in thousands of dollars):

Plan assets at market	$735,501
Plan assets—four-year moving average market basis	$600,662
Projected benefit obligations	$327,101
Pension surplus	$273,561
Unrecognized actuarial experience adjustment	$119,181
Pension surplus per financial statements	$154,380

The company further notes that, effective January 1, 2008, the interest rate assumption changed from 9% to 8% to reflect more conservative long-term interest rate expectations.

Instructions

Adopt the role of the pensioners as well as the role of company management and discuss the financial reporting issues related to management's desire to split and withdraw from the pension plan surplus.

CA 19-3   Farquar Inc. (FI) is in the process of going public. The company is in the Canadian oil and gas industry but has decided that it would like to list its shares on a U.S. stock exchange or on the London Stock Exchange and therefore follow U.S. or International Accounting Standards. Currently, the company follows Canadian GAAP.

The controller of the company, Perry Plank, is concerned about all the changes in GAAP lately—especially as they relate to pension accounting. FI has a significant pension plan that is currently underfunded (i.e., there is a large deficit). For the year ended December 31, 2006, the company (under Canadian GAAP) did not recognize this amount as a liability since it related to past service costs. Perry has on his desk the new U.S. accounting standard and the almost identical proposed Canadian Exposure Draft on employee future benefits. Under the new U.S. standard, companies will have to recognize such unfunded amounts through Other Comprehensive Income.

Perry also has on his desk some information about the differences between Canadian and international GAAP.

Instructions

Adopt the role of the controller and discuss the relative strengths and weaknesses of the three differing views of accounting for the unfunded costs. Perry is very concerned about the impact on the company's debt to equity ratio and the earnings per share numbers.

Integrated Case

IC 19-1   **Stelco Inc.** (Stelco) is a Canadian steel manufacturing company. In 2004, the company filed for bankruptcy protection citing the following reasons for declining profits and viability problems:

- Costs have risen dramatically for inputs such as natural gas and electricity and raw materials, such as coal, coke, and scrap.

- The cost of employee future benefits—pensions and health care—are also increasing due to improved pension benefits negotiated in contracts with unionized employees, increasing health care costs, lower returns on pension plan assets, and the effect of lower interest rates on the discount factors that are used to determine the Corporation's liabilities under the pension and other benefit plans.

- Global steelmaking overcapacity has created downward pressure on selling prices due to significant and continued import penetration of the Canadian market by steel products offered, in management's opinion, at unfairly low prices over the last several years.

- The appreciation in the value of the Canadian dollar during 2003 further negatively affected selling prices. Selling prices strengthened in the early part of 2004, due in part to increased demand, particularly in China. However, the Corporation believes that these price increases are not sustainable and therefore are not expected to be sufficient to offset growing cost issues.

- Several North American steel producers have emerged from court-supervised bankruptcy protection with a cost structure that is more competitive than that of the Corporation. The Corporation cannot compete effectively in this new environment unless it takes steps to reduce its liabilities and lower its overall costs.

- In addition, the Corporation requires additional funding to complete strategically critical capital projects at its Hamilton and Lake Erie business units. The Corporation is unable to raise additional funds to complete these projects.

The protection afforded by the Companies' Creditors Arrangement Act (CCAA) was challenged by the United Steel Workers of America (USWA). The president of USWA Local 1005 was quoted in the newspapers as saying, "We are not going to allow them to blackmail us by using CCAA as a way to convince us to give up our wages and benefits. It amounts to legalized corruption. In my opinion, the CCAA process is an abuse of power." The USWA challenged the courts as to whether Stelco should be protected by CCAA.

Stelco's assets had a book value of $2.74 billion and liabilities of $2.09 billion in the bankruptcy documents. The following is an excerpt from the 2003 financial statements:

Note 18. Employee Future Benefits (continued)

Accrued benefit obligation and plan assets

Information about the Corporation's defined benefit plans, other than the multiemployer defined benefit plan, in aggregate, is as follows:

	2003		2002	
(in millions)	Pension benefit plans	Other benefit plans	Pension benefit plans	Other benefit plans
Accrued benefit obligation				
Balance at beginning of year	$ 3,263	$ 1,082	$ 2,748	$ 924
Increase (decrease) in ownership of joint venture	(18)	(8)	11	2
Current service cost	53	15	49	14
Interest cost	200	72	192	62
Benefits paid	(195)	(55)	(181)	(52)
Actuarial losses	244	156	189	135
Plan curtailments	6	(2)	–	–
Plan amendments	1	2	255	(1)
Other	2	2	–	(2)
Balance at end of year	3,556	1,264	3,263	1,082
Plan assets				
Fair value at beginning of year	2,613	9	2,822	9
Increase (decrease) in ownership of joint venture	(13)	–	11	–
Actual return on plan assets	342	1	(76)	(1)
Administrative expenses paid	(8)	–	(6)	–
Employer contributions	62	1	41	1
Benefits paid	(195)	(1)	(181)	–
Other	3	–	2	–
Fair value at end of year	2,804	10	2,613	9
Funded status – plan surplus (deficit)	(752)	(1,254)	(650)	(1,073)
Unamortized net actuarial loss	773	328	679	186
Unamortized past service costs	253	2	272	–
Accrued benefit asset (liability)	274	(924)	301	(887)
Valuation allowance	–	–	(2)	–
Accrued benefit asset (liability) net of valuation allowance	$ 274	$ (924)	$ 299	$ (887)

The accrued benefit asset (liability) is reflected in the Consolidated Statement of Financial Position as follows:

| | 2003 | | | 2002 | |
| | Pension benefit plans | Other benefit plans | | Pension benefit plans | Other benefit plans |
(in millions)					
Deferred pension cost	$ 274	$ –		$ 299	$ –
Employee future benefits liability – current	–	(49)		–	(47)
Employee future benefits liability – non-current	–	(875)		–	(840)
Total	$ 274	$ (924)		$ 299	$ (887)

In 2002, when the company was first experiencing the cash flow difficulties that led to the current situation, it issued $90 million of 9.5% convertible unsecured subordinated debentures that were due in 2007. The effective interest rate on the debentures was 16.65% and they were convertible into common shares at the option of the holder. They were also redeemable by the corporation after February 2005 and the company had the option of paying the interest in cash or by issuing shares to a trustee, with the proceeds being used to settle the interest. The principal could also be paid in shares.

Although the *CCAA* proceedings have triggered defaults under virtually all debt obligations, the *CCAA* generally protects companies from attempts by creditors to collect the loans.

Instructions

Adopt the role of the company and analyze the financial reporting issues.

Research and Financial Analysis

RA19-1 RONA Inc.

RONA Inc. is one of Canada's leading retailers and distributors of home improvement, hardware, and gardening products. The company's 2006 annual report indicates that, as of February 2007, RONA had 642 corporate, franchised, and affiliated stores and seven distribution centres. It also reports that as at December 31, 2006, the company had nine defined contribution pension plans and four defined benefit pension plans.

Instructions

Refer to the 2006 financial statements of RONA inc. that are found on the Student Website or at www.sedar.com. Then answer the following questions.

 (a) Determine what the funded status is of the defined benefit plans and what the dollar amount of the over- or underfunding is at December 31, 2006. Has the status improved or deteriorated since the end of the preceding year? What is the major reason for the change in RONA's funded status?

 (b) Identify the balance of any defined benefit pension asset or liability reported by RONA on its December 31, 2006 balance sheet. Prepare a reconciliation of the funded status of these plans at December 31, 2006 to the amounts reported on the balance sheet.

 (c) Referring to your results in parts (a) and (b), write a short explanation of why the U.S. accounting standards changed in 2007, and why the Canadian standard setters were looking at changing the standards to require that the funded status be reflected on the balance sheet. The unrecognized amounts currently reported in the notes would also be recognized through other comprehensive income. (Note that the Canadian Exposure Draft that was later withdrawn would have brought Canadian standards in line with the new U.S. requirements.)

 (d) If the Canadian Exposure Draft, explained in (c) above, had been approved and RONA changed the accounting for its defined benefit pension plans on January 1, 2007, to the new standard, what would the balance of the balance sheet pension account be on that date? What else in the balance sheet would have been affected? By how much?

 (e) What was the expected return on the plan assets in 2006? What amount of actuarial gains and losses, if any, were amortized to pension expense in 2006?

(f) What is the reason for the significant difference between the net pension costs that were recognized in income in 2005 and in 2006?

RA19-2 Research Topic

The CICA publication *Financial Reporting in Canada—2006* provides interesting information and insights into the Canadian companies that it surveys.

Instructions

Write a brief report on the employee future benefits that are reported by the Canadian companies in the publication's sample and note any trends that are especially evident. Include in this report such information as the types of benefits offered, the types of plans, whether most companies report balance sheet asset or liability balances, whether defined benefit pension plans are over- or underfunded, whether other types of defined benefit plans are over- or underfunded, and the reasons for major differences between the funded status and the amounts reported on the balance sheet.

RA19-3 Research Topic

Choose three companies that report defined benefit pension plans and access their annual financial statements.

Instructions

Analyze the notes to the financial statements of each of the three companies, and provide answers to the following questions.

(a) For each company, identify the following three assumptions: (1) the discount rate, (2) the rate of compensation increase that was used to measure the projected benefit obligation, and (3) the expected long-run rate of return on plan assets.

(b) Comment on any significant differences between the assumptions that are used by each firm.

(c) Did any of the companies change their assumptions during the period covered by the notes? If yes, what was the effect on each of the following: the current year's accrued benefit obligation, the plan assets, and the pension expense? Explain.

(d) Identify the types of plans and the assumptions that underlie any future benefit plans other than pensions. Are these similar across the three companies? Comment on how any differences would affect an intercompany analysis.

RA19-4 International Reporting Case: Michelin

Compagnie Générale des Établissements Michelin (CGEM) and its subsidiaries, otherwise known as **The Michelin Group**, manufacture, distribute, and sell tires all around the world. Based in France, its two best-known brands are Michelin and BFGoodrich tires. Since 2005, its consolidated financial statements have been prepared in accordance with International Financial Reporting Standards (IFRS) as adopted by the European Union.

Refer to the 2006 financial statements of The Michelin Group that are found on the company's website at www.michelin.com.

Instructions

Referring to Notes 3 and 26 to the financial statements, answer the following questions.

(a) Review the company's accounting policy for "Pension and other post-employment benefits" in Note 3 to the financial statements. Identify the ways in which the policies that Michelin follows differ from Canadian GAAP.

(b) Are Michelin's defined benefit plans underfunded or overfunded at December 31, 2006? Explain, providing information on the size of the over- or underfunding.

(c) What does the company report about these defined benefit plans on its statement of financial position? If there is a difference between what is reported on the balance sheet and the funded status, explain why there is a difference.

(d) The company reports detailed information about its defined benefit pension plans, including the changes in the ABO and plan assets by geographic segment. Prepare a summary of what transactions and events caused the total ABO and the total plan assets to change during 2006. Use a format similar to the one used in the chapter.

(e) Which was higher in 2006: the expected return on plan assets or the actual return? Provide numbers to support your answer.

(f) Note 26 also provides information about the assumptions that were used to measure the accrued benefit pension obligation. Explain why different rates are used for the company's North American, European, and other plans. Are the measurements sensitive to a small change in the discount rate, for example? Discuss. What would be the effect on the funded status of a 1% variation in the discount rate?

RA19-5 Research Topic

Because of the importance of pension and other post-retirement benefit plans to Canadian companies' financial results, users scrutinize the calculations that underlie the measurement of the accrued benefit obligation. Even a small change in some of the underlying assumptions can make a significant difference to balance sheets, income statements, and ratios that rely on the values that are reported. The expectation is that companies in the same industry, in the same country, and over the same period of time, should have similar experiences and therefore use underlying assumptions that are almost the same.

Locate financial statements that cover a similar period of time for three Canadian companies in the same industry. Try to locate companies that sponsor both defined benefit pension plans and other post-retirement benefit plans.

Instructions

Part A

(a) Locate information in each of the three companies' financial statements that indicates the underlying assumptions that were used in measuring the accrued pension and other post-retirement obligations and annual costs. Prepare a table of all the variables that were used over the latest two-year period.

(b) Compare the rates and assumptions that were used by all three companies in the most recent year. Identify any significant differences. Repeat the analysis for the preceding year.

(c) In cases where the rates changed in the current year, did they change in the same direction for all companies? Would you expect them to? Comment.

(d) For each assumption that is identified, indicate which accounting measurements would be affected if the rate changed.

(e) Comment on what you have found out, if anything, about each of the three companies. Does one company seem particularly conservative with the rates that it uses (i.e., do they result in higher obligation, service cost, and benefit expense)? Does any company appear to use rates that result in "better" numbers on the financial statements (i.e., lower obligation, service cost, and benefit expense)?

Part B

Use the financial statements for the same companies as in Part A.

(a) Choose the most recent fiscal year and prepare a schedule for that year that reports each company:
- the balance of the accrued benefit asset/liability reported on the balance sheet
- the funded status
- the total of the unrecognized (unamortized) past service costs, net actuarial gains/losses, and transition balances at the balance sheet date
- total liabilities
- total shareholders' equity

(b) Calculate the total debt/equity ratio for each of the three companies at the balance sheet date.

(c) Determine revised balances for the total liabilities and total shareholders' equity, assuming companies are required instead to recognize the funded status balance on the balance sheet and the unamortized past service costs, net actuarial gains/losses, and transition amounts in accumulated other comprehensive income (loss).

(d) Recalculate the total debt/equity ratios using the revised balances from part (c), and comment on your findings.

Leasing and Dealing

Casino Regina
Always Entertaining

With its impressive location in a grand old train station, Casino Regina is Saskatchewan's biggest tourist attraction, drawing some two million people each year.

As a Treasury Board Crown Corporation regulated by the Saskatchewan Liquor and Gaming Authority, the casino's operator—the Saskatchewan Gaming Corporation (SGC)—must hand all profits over to the government, says controller Wendy Hutchison, CA. This requires some careful accounting and purchasing arrangements. For example, as part of a major expansion in 2002, SGC entered into a sale-leaseback arrangement with a Saskatchewan-based leasing company for 473 new slot machines and other equipment.

SGC purchased the specific equipment it wanted, then sold it to the leasing company, which then leased it back. The casino got what it needed, but didn't incur the huge financial drain of buying. "The cash wasn't available to do an outright purchase," Hutchison explains. "So this was a means of financing."

The equipment leases were for 36 to 43 months with an option to buy at the end. The leases' terms ended in the period from June 2005 to December 2006. "SGC purchased the assets at the end of each individual lease arrangement," Hutchison says. Since the leases were operating leases, they had not been included as capital expenditures on the casino's balance sheet. There was simply a charge to the income statement for the lease expense in each year. However, after the purchase, Hutchison explains, the assets were treated as any capital purchase would be, which means they were recorded as a capital asset at the buyback amount on the balance sheet.

SGC also has a capital lease for the Art Deco building housing its second casino in Moose Jaw. Without the cash available to buy, SGC leased the building in September 2002, when the casino opened. The lease includes an option to buy for $1 at the end of its 25-year term. ∎

Leases

Learning Objectives

After studying this chapter, you should be able to:

1. Explain the nature, economic substance, and advantages of lease transactions.

2. Identify and apply the criteria that are used to determine the type of lease for accounting purposes for a lessee.

3. Account for a lessee's basic capital lease.

4. Explain the accounting and identify the disclosure requirements for an operating lease for a lessee.

5. Contrast the operating and capitalization methods of accounting for leases.

6. Calculate the lease payment that is required for a lessor to earn a specific return.

7. Identify and apply the criteria that are used to determine the type of lease for a lessor.

8. Account for basic direct financing and sales-type leases by the lessor.

9. Explain the accounting and identify the disclosure requirements for an operating lease for a lessor.

10. Determine the effect of residual values in a lessee's capital lease, and account for them.

11. Determine the effect of residual values for a lessor, and account for them.

12. Determine the effect of bargain purchase options for the lessee and lessor, and account for such options.

13. Explain how a lessor accounts for initial direct costs for each type of lease.

14. Determine the current and long-term portions of a lease receivable and lease obligation.

15. Identify the lessee's disclosure requirements for capital leases.

16. Identify the lessor's disclosure requirements for non-operating leases.

17. Compare current Canadian and international GAAP for leases.

After studying Appendix 20A, you should be able to:

18. Describe and apply the lessee's accounting for sale-leaseback transactions.

19. Explain the classification and accounting treatment for leases that involve land as well as buildings and equipment.

Preview of Chapter 20

Leasing continues to grow in popularity as a form of asset-based financing.[1] Instead of borrowing money to buy an airplane, a computer, a nuclear core, or a satellite, a company leases the item. Airlines and railroads lease huge amounts of equipment, many hotel and motel chains lease their facilities, most retail chains lease the bulk of their retail premises and warehouses, and, as indicated in the opening vignette, some casinos lease their slot machines! The popularity of leasing is shown by the fact that 174 of 200 companies surveyed in *Financial Reporting in Canada—2006* disclosed lease data.[2] Small and medium-sized enterprises also use leases as an important form of debt financing.

Because of the significance and popularity of lease arrangements, consistent accounting and complete reporting of these transactions are crucial. In this chapter, we look at the accounting issues related to leasing.

The chapter is organized as follows:

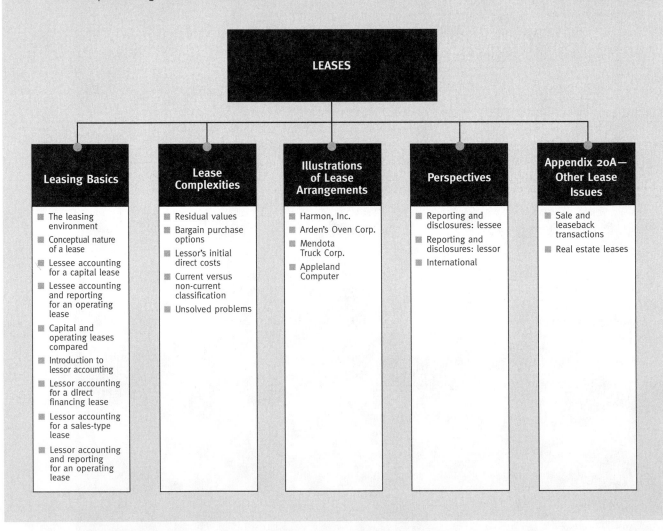

LEASES

Leasing Basics	Lease Complexities	Illustrations of Lease Arrangements	Perspectives	Appendix 20A— Other Lease Issues
■ The leasing environment ■ Conceptual nature of a lease ■ Lessee accounting for a capital lease ■ Lessee accounting and reporting for an operating lease ■ Capital and operating leases compared ■ Introduction to lessor accounting ■ Lessor accounting for a direct financing lease ■ Lessor accounting for a sales-type lease ■ Lessor accounting and reporting for an operating lease	■ Residual values ■ Bargain purchase options ■ Lessor's initial direct costs ■ Current versus non-current classification ■ Unsolved problems	■ Harmon, Inc. ■ Arden's Oven Corp. ■ Mendota Truck Corp. ■ Appleland Computer	■ Reporting and disclosures: lessee ■ Reporting and disclosures: lessor ■ International	■ Sale and leaseback transactions ■ Real estate leases

---

[1] Asset-based financing is the financing of equipment through a secured loan, conditional sales contract, or lease.

[2] CICA, *Financial Reporting in Canada—2006*, p. 301.

LEASING BASICS

The Leasing Environment

Aristotle once said, "Wealth does not lie in ownership but in the use of things"! Many Canadian companies have clearly come to agree with Aristotle as, rather than owning assets, they now are heavily involved in leasing them.

A **lease** is a contractual agreement between a **lessor** and a **lessee** that gives the lessee, for a specified period of time, the right to use specific property owned by the lessor in return for specified, and generally periodic, cash payments (rents). An essential element of the lease agreement is that the lessor transfers less than the total interest in the property. Because of the financial, operating, and risk advantages that the lease arrangement provides, many businesses and other types of organizations lease substantial amounts of property as an alternative to ownership. Any type of equipment or property can be leased, such as rail cars, helicopters, bulldozers, schools, golf club facilities, barges, CT scanners, computers, and so on. The largest class of leased equipment is information technology equipment. Next are assets in the transportation area, such as trucks, aircraft, and rail cars.

Because a lease is a contract, the provisions that the lessor and lessee agree to can vary widely from lease to lease. Indeed, they are limited only by the ingenuity of the two parties to the contract and their advisors.[3] The lease's duration—lease term—may be anything from a short period of time to the entire expected economic life of the asset. The **rental payments** may be the same amount from year to year, or they may increase or decrease; further, they may be predetermined or may vary with sales, the prime interest rate, the consumer price index, or some other factor. In many cases, the rent is set at an amount that enables the lessor to recover the asset's cost plus a fair return over the life of the lease.

The obligations for taxes, insurance, and maintenance (executory costs) may be the responsibility of either the lessor or the lessee, or they may be divided. In order to protect the lessor from default on the rents, the lease may include restrictions—comparable to those in bond indentures—that limit the lessee's activities in making dividend payments or incurring further debt. In addition, the lease contract may be non-cancellable or may grant the right to early termination on payment of a set scale of prices plus a penalty. In case of default, the lessee may be liable for all future payments at once, and receive title to the property in exchange; or the lessor may have the right to sell the asset to a third party and collect from the lessee all or a portion of the difference between the sale price and the lessor's unrecovered cost.

At termination of the lease, different alternatives may be available to the lessee: these may range from simple termination with no further options to the right to purchase the leased asset at its fair market value, or the right to renew or buy it at a nominal price.

Who Are the Players?

Who are the lessors that are referred to above? In Canada, lessors are usually one of three types of company:

1. Manufacturer finance companies

2. Independent finance companies

3. Traditional financial institutions

1 Objective
Explain the nature, economic substance, and advantages of lease transactions.

---

[3] See *EIC-150*, "Determining Whether an Arrangement Contains a Lease," for further discussion about arrangements that do not take the legal form of a lease, but which are, in substance, lease arrangements to which *CICA Handbook* Section 3065 applies.

Manufacturer finance companies, or captive leasing companies as they are also called, are subsidiaries whose main business is to perform leasing operations for the parent company. **General Motors Acceptance Corporation of Canada, Limited** is an example of a captive leasing company. As soon as the parent company receives a possible order, its leasing subsidiary can quickly develop a lease-financing arrangement that facilitates the parent company's sale of its product.

An **independent finance company** acts as a financial intermediary by providing financing for transactions for manufacturers, vendors, or distributors. Your dentist, for example, when acquiring specialized equipment for his or her practice, may order the equipment through the manufacturer or distributor, who in turn may outsource the financing to a lessor such as an independent finance company.

Subsidiaries of domestic and foreign banks are examples of **traditional financial institutions** that provide leasing as another form of financing to their customers.[4]

Advantages of Leasing

Although leasing does have disadvantages, the growth in its use suggests that it often has a genuine advantage over owning property. Some of the advantages are as follows:

1. *100% financing at fixed rates*   Leases are often signed without requiring any money down from the lessee, which helps to conserve scarce cash—an especially desirable feature for new and developing companies. In addition, lease payments often remain fixed (i.e., unchanging), which protects the lessee against inflation and increases in the cost of money. The following comment about a conventional loan is typical: "Our local bank finally agreed to finance 80 percent of the purchase price but wouldn't go any higher, and they wanted a floating interest rate. We just couldn't afford the down payment and we needed to lock in a payment we knew we could live with."

   Turning to the lessor's point of view, financial institutions and leasing companies find leasing profitable because it provides attractive interest margins.

2. *Protection against obsolescence*   Leasing equipment reduces the risk of obsolescence to the lessee, and in many cases passes the risk of residual value to the lessor. For example, a company that leases computers may have a lease agreement that permits it to turn in an old computer for a new model at any time, cancelling the old lease and writing a new one. The cost of the new lease is added to the balance due on the old lease, less the old computer's trade-in value. As one treasurer remarked, "Our instinct is to purchase." But when new computers come along in a short time, "then leasing is just a heck of a lot more convenient than purchasing."

   On the other hand, the lessor can benefit from the property reversion (i.e., the return of the asset) at the end of the lease term. Residual values can produce very large profits. For example, **Citicorp** at one time assumed that the commercial aircraft it was leasing to the airline industry would have a residual value of 5 percent of their purchase price. As it turned out, however, the planes were worth 150 percent of their cost—a handsome price appreciation. Three years later these same planes slumped to 80 percent of their cost, but this was still a far greater residual value than the projected 5 percent.

3. *Flexibility*   Lease agreements may contain less restrictive provisions than other debt agreements. Innovative lessors can tailor a lease agreement to the lessee's special needs. For instance, a ski lift operator using equipment for only six months of the year can arrange rental payments that fit well with the operation's revenue streams. In

---

[4] The Centre for Spatial Economics, *Asset-based Financing, Investment and Economic Growth in Canada*, prepared for the Canadian Finance & Leasing Association, December 15, 2004.

addition, because the lessor retains ownership and the leased property is the collateral, it is usually easier to arrange financing through a lease.

4. *Less costly financing for lessee, tax incentives for lessor*   Some companies find leasing cheaper than other forms of financing. For example, start-up companies in depressed industries or companies in low tax brackets may lease as a way of claiming tax benefits that might otherwise be lost. Investment tax credits and capital cost allowance deductions offer no benefit to companies that have little or no taxable income. Through leasing, these tax benefits are used by the leasing companies or financial institutions. They can then pass some of these tax benefits back to the asset's user through lower rental payments.

5. *Off–balance sheet financing*   Certain leases do not add debt on a balance sheet or affect financial ratios, and may add to borrowing capacity.[5] **Off–balance sheet financing** is critical to some companies. For example, airlines use lease arrangements extensively, which results in a great deal of off–balance sheet financing. Illustration 20-1 indicates that debt levels are understated by **WestJet Airlines Ltd.**, **Air Canada**, and **Helijet International Inc.**, a sample of Canadian companies in the transportation industry.

International Insight

Some companies "double-dip" at the international level. The leasing rules of the lessor's and lessee's countries may differ, permitting both parties to own the asset. In such cases, both the lessor and lessee can receive the tax benefits related to amortization.

	WestJet December 31, 2006 ($ thousands)	Air Canada December 31, 2006 ($ millions)	Helijet August 31,2006 ($ thousands)
Long-term liabilities, excluding future income taxes and deferred credits	$1,292,619	$5,544	$ 754
Shareholders' equity	806,027	1,852	(497)
Unrecognized future minimum lease payments under existing operating leases	1,237,791	2,957	13,517

Illustration 20-1

Reported Debt and Unrecognized Operating Lease Obligations

Conceptual Nature of a Lease

If an airline borrows $80 million on a 10-year note from the bank to purchase a Boeing 787 jet plane, it is clear that an asset and related liability should be reported on the company's balance sheet at that amount. If the airline purchases the 787 for $80 million directly from Boeing through an instalment purchase over 10 years, it is equally clear that an asset and related liability should be reported (i.e., the instalment purchase transaction should be "capitalized"). However, if the Boeing 787 is leased for 10 years through a non-cancellable lease transaction with payments of the same amount as the instalment purchase, there are differences of opinion about how this transaction should be reported. The various views on accounting for leases can be summarized as follows:

Underlying Concept

The issue of how to report leases is the classic case of substance versus form. Although legal title does not technically pass in lease transactions, the benefits from the use of the property do transfer.

Do not capitalize any leased assets—an executory contract approach.   Because the lessee does not own the property, it is inappropriate to capitalize the lease. Furthermore, a lease is an **executory contract** that requires continuing performance by both parties. Because other executory contracts (such as purchase commitments and employment contracts) are not currently capitalized, leases should not be capitalized either. The lessor should continue to recognize the leased item as an asset.

---

[5] As is shown later in this chapter, certain types of lease arrangements are not capitalized on the balance sheet. This keeps the liabilities section free from large lease commitments that, if they were recorded, would have a negative impact on the debt-to-equity ratio. The reluctance to record lease obligations as liabilities is one of the main reasons that some companies resist capitalized lease accounting.

Capitalize leases that are similar to instalment purchases—a whole asset approach.   Accountants should report transactions according to their economic substance; therefore, since instalment purchases are capitalized, leases that have similar characteristics to instalment purchases should also be capitalized. In the earlier airline example, the airline is committed to the same payments over a 10-year period for either a lease or an instalment purchase; lessees simply make rental payments, whereas owners make mortgage payments. The financial statements should report these transactions in the same way, which means recognizing the physical asset on the lessee's balance sheet where appropriate.

Capitalize all leases—a right of use approach.   Under the right of use approach, the asset that is acquired is not the physical property that is leased; rather, it is the right to use the property that is conveyed under the lease agreement. The liability is the contractual obligation to make lease payments. Under this property rights approach, it is justifiable to capitalize the fair value of the rights and obligations associated with a broad range of leases.[6]

In short, the various viewpoints range from no capitalization to capitalization of all leases.[7] The CICA standard is consistent with the approach that capitalizes leases that are similar to an instalment purchase, as it requires that **a lease that transfers substantially all of the benefits and risks of property ownership should be capitalized**. This view implies three basic conclusions: (1) the characteristics that indicate that substantially all of the benefits and risks of ownership have been transferred must be identified; (2) the same characteristics should apply consistently to the lessee and the lessor; and (3) leases that do **not** transfer substantially all the benefits and risks of ownership should not be capitalized.

By capitalizing the present value of the future rental payments, the **lessee** records an asset and a liability at an amount that is generally representative of the asset's fair value or purchase price. The **lessor**, having transferred substantially all the benefits and risks of ownership, removes the asset from its balance sheet, and replaces it with a receivable. The typical journal entries for the lessee and the lessor, assuming equipment is leased and is capitalized, are shown at the top of Illustration 20-2. If the benefits and risks of ownership **are not transferred** from one party to the other, the rents are accounted for by the lessee and lessor as shown in the bottom of Illustration 20-2.

Illustration 20-2

Journal Entries for Capital and Operating Leases

	Lessee		Lessor	
Capitalized— Capital Lease	Leased Equipment	xx	Lease Receivable (net)	xx
	Lease Obligation	xx	Equipment	xx
	Amortization Expense	x		
	Accumulated Amortization	x		
	Lease Obligation	x	Cash	x
	Interest Expense	x	Interest Income	x
	Cash	x	Lease Receivable	x
Not Capitalized— Operating Lease	Rent Expense	x	Cash	x
	Cash	x	Rental Income	x

Having capitalized the asset, the lessee recognizes the amortization. The lessor and lessee treat the lease rentals as the receipt and the payment of interest and principal. If the lease is not capitalized, no asset is recorded by the lessee and no asset is removed from the

---

[6] The property rights approach was originally recommended in *Accounting Research Study No. 4* (New York: AICPA, 1964), pp. 10–11. Recently, this view has received additional support. See Warren McGregor, "Accounting for Leases: A New Approach," Special Report (Norwalk, Conn.: FASB, 1996).

[7] While the CICA, FASB, and IASB standards are all currently consistent with the approach that capitalizes leases that are similar to an instalment purchase, a new converged standard that may be based on the right of use approach is likely, perhaps by 2010.

lessor's books. When a lease payment is made, the lessee records rent or lease expense and the lessor recognizes rental or lease income.

Before we discuss the accounting for specific types of leases and the disclosures that are required by the accounting standards, we will begin by looking at how it is decided if a particular lease agreement should be capitalized or not.

Capitalization Criteria

From the lessee's standpoint, all leases are classified for accounting purposes as either operating leases or capital leases. When the risks and benefits of ownership are transferred from the lessor to the lessee, the lease is accounted for as a capital lease (**capitalization method**); otherwise, it is accounted for as an operating lease (**non-capitalization method**).

What are the risks and benefits (or rewards) of ownership? *CICA Handbook* Section 3065.05 identifies the benefits as "the expectation of profitable operations over the property's economic life and of gain from appreciation in value or realization of a residual value." Alternatively, the risks "include possibilities of losses from idle capacity or technological obsolescence and of variation in return due to changing economic conditions."

Rather than simply leaving the standard to be expressed as a general principle, *Handbook* Section 3065.06 provides additional application guidance. It specifies that if, at the beginning of the lease, **any one of** the following criteria is met, the risks and benefits of ownership **are assumed to be transferred to the lessee**, and the lessee should classify and account for the arrangement as a **capital lease**:

1. There is reasonable assurance that the lessee will obtain ownership of the leased property by the end of the lease term. If there is a bargain purchase option[8] in the lease, it is assumed that the lessee will exercise it and obtain ownership.

2. The lease term is long enough that the lessee will receive substantially all of the economic benefits that are expected to be derived from the use of the leased property over its life. This is usually assumed to occur if the lease term is 75 percent or more of the leased property's economic life.

3. The lease allows the lessor to recover its investment in the leased property and to earn a return on the investment. This is assumed to occur if the present value of the minimum lease payments (excluding executory costs) is equal to substantially all (usually 90 percent or more) of the fair value of the leased property.

If none of the three criteria is met, the lease is classified and accounted for by the lessee as an **operating lease**. The flowchart in Illustration 20-3 illustrates this decision, and the **capitalization criteria** are discussed in more detail below.

2 Objective
Identify and apply the criteria that are used to determine the type of lease for accounting purposes for a lessee.

International Insight
IAS 17 on leases also identifies two types of leases in the same way as the Canadian standard. However, the international standard uses the term "finance" lease instead of "capital" lease.

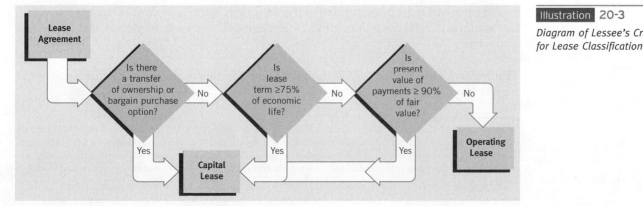

Illustration 20-3

Diagram of Lessee's Criteria for Lease Classification

---

[8] Bargain purchase options will be defined in the next section.

Transfer of Ownership Test   If the lease transfers ownership of the asset to the lessee, it is a **capital lease**. This criterion is not controversial and is easily followed in practice.

The transfer of ownership may occur at the end of the lease term with no additional payment or through a bargain purchase option. A **bargain purchase option** is a provision that allows the lessee to purchase the leased property for a price that is significantly lower than the property's expected fair value at the date when the lessee gains the right to exercise the option. At the beginning of the lease, the difference between the option price and the expected fair value must be large enough to make it reasonably sure that the option will be exercised.[9] The opening story indicates a bargain purchase option of $1 at the end of the casino building's lease, but the option price does not need to be this low to be considered a bargain.

For example, assume that you were to lease a car for $599 per month for 40 months with an option to purchase it for $100 at the end of the 40-month period. If the car's estimated fair value is $3,000 at the end of the 40 months, the $100 option to purchase is clearly a bargain and, therefore, capitalization is required. In other cases, it is not so clearly evident whether the option price is a bargain.

Economic Life Test   If the lease period is equal to or greater than 75 percent of the asset's economic life, it follows that most of the risks and rewards of ownership are going to accrue to the lessee. However, determining the lease term and the asset's economic life may be troublesome.

The **lease term** is **generally considered the fixed, non-cancellable term of the lease**. However, this period can be extended if a bargain renewal option is provided in the lease agreement. A **bargain renewal option** is a provision that allows the lessee to renew the lease for a rental amount that is lower than the expected fair rental at the date when the option becomes exercisable. At the beginning of the lease, the difference between the renewal rental and the expected fair rental must be large enough to provide reasonable assurance that the option to renew will be exercised. With bargain renewal options, as with bargain purchase options, it is sometimes difficult to determine what is a bargain.[10]

Estimating the economic life can also be a problem, especially if the leased item is a specialized item or has been used for a long period of time. For example, determining the economic life of a nuclear core is extremely difficult because it is affected by much more than normal wear and tear.

Recovery of Investment by Lessor Test   If the present value of the minimum lease payments is equal to or greater than 90 percent of the asset's fair value, then the leased asset is capitalized. The rationale for this test is that if the present value of the payments is reasonably close to the asset's market price, the lessor is recovering its investment in the asset plus a return on the investment through the lease. In effect, therefore, the lessee is purchasing the asset.

In calculating the present value of the minimum lease payments, three important factors are involved: (1) the minimum lease payments, (2) any executory costs, and (3) the discount rate.

Minimum Lease Payments. **Minimum lease payments** are defined in the accounting standard as comprising:

---

[9] The Emerging Issues Committee of the CICA, in *EIC 30*, concluded that the ultimate test is whether there is reasonable assurance that the lessee will obtain ownership by the end of the lease. A situation where there is no bargain purchase option, but other lease provisions make it probable that the lessee will acquire the leased property for its fair value at the end of the lease term is sufficient to classify the transaction as a capital lease.

[10] The original lease term is also extended for leases that have the following: substantial penalties for non-renewal; periods for which the lessor has the option to renew or extend the lease; renewal periods that precede the date when a bargain purchase option becomes exercisable; and renewal periods in which the lessee guarantees the lessor's debt related to the leased property.

1. *Minimum rental payments:* The minimum payments that the lessee is obligated to make to the lessor under the lease agreement, excluding executory costs (defined below). The minimum lease payments may also include any of the following three items if these are included in the agreement.

2. *Residual value:* The **residual value** is the asset's estimated fair value at the end of the lease term. The lessor often transfers the risk of loss in value to the lessee or to a third party by requiring a guarantee of the estimated residual value. The **guaranteed residual value** is (1) the amount that the lessor can require the lessee to purchase the asset for; or (2) the amount that the lessee or a third-party guarantor guarantees the lessor will realize from the asset at the end of the lease. The **unguaranteed residual value** is the portion of the residual value that is not guaranteed or is guaranteed solely by a party that is related to the lessor. Often, no part of the residual is guaranteed.

   From the **lessee's perspective**, only any residual value guaranteed by the lessee, or a third party related to the lessee, is included in the definition of minimum lease payments.

   From the **lessor's perspective**, any residual value guaranteed by the lessee, or a third party related to the lessee, or a third party that is unrelated to either the lessee or lessor is included in the definition of minimum lease payments. Therefore, the definition of minimum lease payments is different for the lessor, as it includes in addition any residual value guaranteed by an independent third party.

3. *Penalty for failure to renew or extend the lease:* The amount that is payable by the lessee if the agreement specifies that the lease must be extended or renewed and the lessee does not do so.

4. *Bargain purchase option:* An option given to the lessee to purchase the equipment at the end of the lease at a price that is sufficiently below the expected fair value so that, at the lease's inception, the purchase appears to be reasonably assured. If a bargain purchase option is included in the lease agreement, only the minimum rental payments and the bargain purchase option are included in the definition of the minimum payments.[11]

Executory Costs. Like most assets, leased property needs to be insured and maintained, and it may require the payment of property tax. These ownership-type expenses are called **executory costs**. If the lessor stays responsible for these costs, any portion of each lease payment that represents the recovery of executory costs from the lessee **is excluded** from the rental payment amount when the present value of the minimum lease payments is calculated. This portion of the payment does not represent a reduction of the capitalized obligation. Even if the amount that represents executory costs cannot be determined from the lease contract, an estimate of the amount of executory costs must be made. Many lease agreements, however, require the lessee to pay the executory costs directly. In these cases, the rental payments can be used without any adjustment in the present value calculations.

Discount Rate. The lessee calculates the present value of the minimum lease payments using its own **incremental borrowing rate**. This is defined as the interest rate that, at the beginning of the lease, the lessee would have incurred to borrow the necessary funds to purchase the leased asset, assuming a similar term and using similar security for the borrowing.[12] Determining that rate often requires judgement because it is based on a hypothetical property purchase.

   There is one exception to the use of this rate. If (1) the lessee knows the **implicit interest rate** that is used by the lessor in calculating the amount of the lease payments, and (2) the implicit interest rate is less than the lessee's incremental borrowing rate, **then**

International Insight

IAS 17 requires the lessee to use the interest rate that is implicit in the lease whenever it is reasonably determinable. Otherwise, the lessee's incremental borrowing rate is used.

---

[11] *CICA Handbook*, Section 3065.03(q).

[12] *CICA Handbook*, Section 3065.03(p).

the lessee must use the lessor's implicit rate. The interest rate implicit in the lease is the discount rate that corresponds to the lessor's internal rate of return on the lease.[13]

There are two reasons for this exception. First, the lessor's implicit rate is generally a more realistic rate to use in determining the amount, if any, to report as the asset and related liability for the lessee. Second, the guideline is provided to ensure that the lessee does not use an artificially high incremental borrowing rate **that would cause the present value of the minimum lease payments to be less than 90 percent of the property's fair value. This might make it possible to avoid capitalization of the asset and related liability!** Remember that the higher the discount rate that is used, the lower the discounted value. The lessee may argue that it cannot determine the implicit rate of the lessor and therefore the higher rate should be used. However, in many cases, the implicit rate that is used by the lessor is disclosed or can be estimated. Determining whether or not a reasonable estimate could be made requires judgement, particularly when using the incremental borrowing rate comes close to meeting the 90-percent test. Because the leased property cannot be capitalized at more than its fair value, the lessee is prevented from using an excessively low discount rate.

The next two segments of this chapter explain the accounting for a basic capital lease and an operating lease **by the lessee**.

Lessee Accounting for a Capital Lease

Asset and Liability Recorded

Objective 3
Account for a lessee's basic capital lease.

In a capital lease transaction, the lessee is using the lease **as a source of financing**. The lessor provides the leased asset to the lessee and finances the transaction by accepting instalment payments. The lessee accounts for the transaction as if an asset is purchased and a long-term liability is created. Over the life of the lease, the rental payments made by the lessee are basically a repayment of principal plus interest.

The lessee recognizes the asset and liability at the lower of (1) the present value of the minimum lease payments as defined above and (2) the fair value of the leased asset at the lease's inception. The reason for this is that, like other assets, a leased asset cannot be recorded at more than its fair value.

Amortization Period and Method

One decision to be made in accounting for the capitalized asset is identifying the **amortization period**. If the lease agreement transfers ownership of the asset to the lessee or contains a bargain purchase option (criterion 1), the leased asset is amortized **over the asset's useful or economic life** to the lessee, just as the company does for its owned assets.

On the other hand, if the asset is expected to be returned to the lessor at the end of the lease, the asset is amortized **over the term of the lease**. The lessee amortizes the leased asset by applying conventional amortization methods such as straight-line, declining-balance, or units-of-production methods.

Effective Interest Method

Although the amount that is capitalized as an asset and recorded as an obligation is initially calculated at the same present value, **the subsequent amortization of the asset and the accounting for the obligation are independent processes**.

Over the term of the lease, the **effective interest method** is used to allocate each lease payment between principal and interest. In this way, the periodic interest expense is

---

[13] *CICA Handbook*, Section 3065.03(m).

equal to a constant percentage of the obligation's outstanding balance. The lessee uses the same discount rate in applying the effective interest method as it used in calculating the present value of the minimum lease payments.

Capital Lease Method Illustrated

To illustrate the accounting for a capital lease, we will use the example of a lease agreement between Lessor Corporation and Lessee Corporation. The contract calls for Lessor Corporation to lease equipment to Lessee Corporation beginning January 1, 2008. The lease agreement's terms and provisions and other pertinent data are given in Illustration 20-4.

1. The lease term is five years, the lease agreement is non-cancellable, and it requires equal rental payments of $25,981.62 at the beginning of each year (annuity due basis), beginning January 1, 2008.
2. The equipment has a fair value on January 1, 2008, of $100,000, an estimated economic life of five years, and no residual value.
3. Lessee Corporation pays all executory costs directly to third parties except for the property taxes of $2,000 per year, which are included in the annual payments to the lessor.
4. The lease contains no renewal options; the equipment reverts to Lessor Corporation at the termination of the lease.
5. Lessee Corporation's incremental borrowing rate is 11% per year.
6. Lessee Corporation uses straight-line amortization for similar equipment that it owns.
7. Lessor Corporation set the annual rental to earn a rate of return on its investment of 10% per year; this fact is known to Lessee Corporation.

Illustration 20-4
Lease Agreement Terms and Conditions

The lease meets the criteria for classification as a capital lease for two reasons: (1) the lease term of five years is equal to more than 75 percent of the equipment's estimated economic life of five years, which satisfies criterion 2; and (2) the present value of the minimum lease payments ($100,000 as calculated below) exceeds 90 percent of the property's $100,000 fair value, satisfying criterion 3. Only one of the three criteria has to be met to require capitalization.

The **minimum lease payments** amount to $119,908.10 ($23,981.62 × 5), and the present value of the minimum lease payments is $100,000 as calculated in Illustration 20-5.[14] This is the amount that is capitalized as the leased asset and lease obligation.

P.V. of minimum   = ($25,981.62 − $2,000) × present value of an annuity due of $1 for
lease payments   5 periods at 10% (Table A-5)
                  = $23,981.62 × 4.16986
                  = $100,000

Illustration 20-5
Present Value of Minimum Lease Payments

The lessor's implicit interest rate of 10 percent is used instead of the lessee's incremental borrowing rate of 11 percent because (1) it is lower and (2) the lessee has knowledge of it.[15]

---

[14] Alternatively, using Excel or another spreadsheet program, enter the following series of key strokes: INSERT/FUNCTION/PV. Fill in the required variables that the program asks for. Note that the interest rate must be provided with the % sign or in decimal form.

[15] If Lessee Corporation had an incremental borrowing rate of 9% (lower than the 10% rate used by Lessor Corporation) or it did not know the rate used by Lessor, the present value calculation yields a capitalized amount of $101,675.35 ($23,981.62 × 4.23972). Because this amount exceeds the equipment's $100,000 fair value, Lessee Corporation capitalizes the $100,000 and uses 10% as its effective rate for amortization of the lease obligation.

The entry to record the lease on Lessee Corporation's books on January 1, 2008, is:

A   =   L   + SE
+100,000   +100,000

Cash flows: No effect

| Equipment under Capital Leases | 100,000 | |
| Obligations under Capital Leases | | 100,000 |

The journal entry to record the first lease payment on January 1, 2008, is:

A   =   L   +   SE
−25,981.62 −23,981.62 −2,000.00

Cash flows: ↓ 25,981.62 outflow

Property Tax Expense	2,000.00	
Obligations under Capital Leases	23,981.62	
Cash		25,981.62

Each lease payment of $25,981.62 consists of three elements: (1) a reduction in the principal of the lease obligation, (2) a financing cost (interest expense), and (3) executory costs (property taxes). The total financing cost or interest expense over the lease's term is the difference between the present value of the minimum lease payments ($100,000) and the actual cash that is disbursed excluding the executory costs ($119,908.10), which is $19,908.10. These amounts, along with the annual interest expense, are shown in Illustration 20-6 where the effective interest method is used to prepare a lease amortization schedule for the lessee.[16]

Illustration 20-6

Lease Amortization Schedule for Lessee—Annuity Due Basis

LESSEE CORPORATION
Lease Amortization Schedule
(Annuity due basis)

Date	Annual Lease Payment	Interest (10%) on Unpaid Obligation	Reduction of Lease Obligation	Balance of Lease Obligation
	(a)	(b)	(c)	(d)
1/1/08				$100,000.00
1/1/08	$ 23,981.62	$ −0−	$ 23,981.62	76,018.38
1/1/09	23,981.62	7,601.84	16,379.78	59,638.60
1/1/10	23,981.62	5,963.86	18,017.76	41,620.84
1/1/11	23,981.62	4,162.08	19,819.54	21,801.30
1/1/12	23,981.62	2,180.32*	21,801.30	−0−
	$119,908.10	$19,908.10	$100,000.00	

(a) Lease payment as required by lease, excluding executory costs.
(b) 10% of the preceding balance of (d) except for 1/1/08; since this is an annuity due, no time has elapsed at the date of the first payment and no interest has accrued.
(c) (a) minus (b).
(d) Preceding balance minus (c).
*Rounded by 19 cents.

Accrued interest is recorded at Lessee Corporation's fiscal year end, December 31, 2008, as follows:

A =   L   +   SE
   +7,601.84 −7,601.84

Cash flows: No effect

| Interest Expense | 7,601.84 | |
| Interest Payable | | 7,601.84 |

---

[16] This is a perfect task for Excel or other spreadsheet programs. Set up the schedule headings, and use formulas to perform the calculations for you.

Using Lessee Corporation's normal amortization policy, the following entry is made on December 31, 2008, to record the current year's amortization of the leased equipment:

Amortization Expense—Leased Equipment	20,000	
Accumulated Amortization—Leased Equipment		20,000
($100,000 ÷ 5 years)		

A = L + SE
−20,000   −20,000

Cash flows: No effect

At December 31, 2008, the assets that are recorded under capital leases are identified separately on the lessee's balance sheet, or in a note cross-referenced to the balance sheet. Similarly, the related obligations are identified separately. The principal portion that is due within one year or the operating cycle, whichever is longer, is classified with current liabilities and the remainder is reported with non-current liabilities. For example, the current portion of the December 31, 2008, total obligation of $76,018 **is the amount of the principal of the obligation that will be paid off within the next 12 months**. Therefore, the current portion is $16,379.78, as indicated on the amortization schedule. Illustration 20-7 shows the liability section of the December 31, 2008, balance sheet for the lease obligation and related accrued interest.

Current liabilities	
Interest payable	$ 7,601.84
Obligations under capital leases	16,379.78
Non-current liabilities	
Obligations under capital leases	$59,638.60

Illustration 20-7

Reporting Current and Non-Current Lease Liabilities

The journal entry to record the lease payment on January 1, 2009, is as follows:

Property Tax Expense	2,000.00	
Interest Payable[17]	7,601.84	
Obligations under Capital Leases	16,379.78	
Cash		25,981.62

A = L + SE
−25,981.62 −23,981.62 −2,000.00

Cash flows: ↓ 25,981.62 outflow

Entries through to the year 2012 follow the same pattern as above. Other executory costs (insurance and maintenance) that are assumed by Lessee Corporation are recorded the same way as the company records operating costs incurred on other assets that it owns.

At the end of the lease, the amount capitalized as leased equipment is fully amortized and the lease obligation is fully discharged. If the equipment is not purchased, the lessee returns it to the lessor and removes the equipment and related accumulated amortization accounts from the books. If instead the lessee purchases the equipment at the end of the lease for $5,000, and expects to use it for another two years, the following entry is made:

Equipment ($100,000 + $5,000)	105,000	
Accumulated Amortization—Leased Equipment	100,000	
Equipment under Capital Leases		100,000
Accumulated Amortization—Equipment		100,000
Cash		5,000

A = L + SE
0   0   0

Cash flows: ↓ 5,000 outflow

---

[17] This entry assumes that the company does not prepare reversing entries. If reversing entries are used, Interest Expense is debited for this amount.

Lessee Accounting and Reporting for an Operating Lease

Accounting

Objective 4

Explain the accounting and identify the disclosure requirements for an operating lease for a lessee.

In a lease agreement where the risks and benefits of ownership of the leased asset are not transferred to the lessee, a non-capitalization method is appropriate. Under this type of lease, **neither the leased asset nor the obligation to make lease payments is recognized in the accounts.** Instead, the lease payments are treated as rent expense, with the expense assigned to the accounting periods that benefit from use of the leased asset.[18] Appropriate accruals or deferrals are made if the accounting period ends between cash payment dates.

Assume now that the capital lease described in Illustration 20-4, and accounted for above, does not qualify as a capital lease and, by default, is therefore an operating lease. The charge to the income statement for rent expense each year is $25,981.62, the amount of the rental payment. The journal entry to record the payment each January 1 is as follows:

A = L + SE
0   0   0

Cash flows: ↓ 25,981.62 outflow

Prepaid Rent	25,981.62	
Cash		25,981.62

Assuming that adjusting entries are prepared only annually, the following entry is made at each December 31 fiscal year end:

A   = L +   SE
−25,981.62   −25,981.62

Cash flows: No effect

Rent Expense	25,981.62	
Prepaid Rent		25,981.62

Reporting

Lessees are required to disclose the following for operating leases:

1. The future minimum lease payments, in total and for each of the next five years

2. A description of the nature of other commitments under such leases[19]

These disclosures allow readers to evaluate the impact of such agreements on the organization. An example of how **Transforce Income Fund** reported this information in Note 14 of its December 31, 2006, financial statements is provided in Illustration 20-18, later in the chapter.

In particular circumstances, other information may be useful as well. This might include the amount of operating lease rentals charged against income, and details about any contingent rentals or sub-lease revenue. Any guarantees of residual values in operating leases are reported under the standards that cover guarantees.

Capital and Operating Leases Compared

Objective 5

Contrast the operating and capitalization methods of accounting for leases.

As indicated above, if the lease in Illustration 20-4 had been accounted for as an operating lease, the first-year charge to operations would have been $25,981.62, the amount of the

---

[18] *EIC-21*, "Accounting for Lease Inducements by the Lessee" (CICA: January 21, 1991) provides guidance on accounting for the benefits of lease inducements such as an upfront cash payment to the lessee, initial rent-free periods, etc. It is recommended that such benefits be taken into income over the lease's term on a straight-line or other basis that is representative of the pattern of benefits from the leased property.

[19] *CICA Handbook*, Section 3065.31–.33.

rental payment. Treating the transaction as a capital lease, however, resulted in a first-year charge of $29,601.84: straight-line amortization of $20,000, interest expense of $7,601.84, and executory expenses of $2,000. Illustration 20-8 shows that, while the total charges to operations are the same over the lease term whether the lease is accounted for as a capital lease or as an operating lease, the charges are higher in the earlier years and lower in the later years under the capital lease treatment. The higher expense in the early years, along with the increase in debt that is reported, are two reasons that lessees are reluctant to classify leases as capital leases. Lessees, especially when real estate leases are involved, claim that it is no more costly to operate the leased asset in the early years than in the later years; thus, they prefer an even charge like what the operating method offers.

LESSEE CORPORATION
Schedule of Charges to Operations
Capital Lease versus Operating Lease

| | Capital Lease | | | | Operating | |
Year	Amortization	Executory Costs	Interest	Total Expense	Lease Expense	Difference
2008	$ 20,000	$ 2,000	$ 7,601.84	$ 29,601.84	$ 25,981.62	$ 3,620.22
2009	20,000	2,000	5,963.86	27,963.86	25,981.62	1,982.24
2010	20,000	2,000	4,162.08	26,162.08	25,981.62	180.46
2011	20,000	2,000	2,180.32	24,180.32	25,981.62	(1,801.30)
2012	20,000	2,000	—	22,000.00	25,981.62	(3,981.62)
	$100,000	$10,000	$19,908.10	$129,908.10	$129,908.10	$ –0–

Illustration 20-8

Comparison of Charges to Operations—Capital vs. Operating Leases

If an accelerated amortization method is used, the difference between the amounts that are charged to operations under the two methods is even larger in the earlier and later years.

The most important and significant difference between the two approaches, however, is the effect on the balance sheet. The capital lease approach initially reports an asset and related liability of $100,000 on the balance sheet, **whereas no such asset or liability is reported under the operating method**. Refer back to Illustration 20-1 to understand the significance of the amounts that are left off the statement of financial position for WestJet, Air Canada, and Helijet. It is not surprising that the business community resists capitalizing leases, as the resulting **higher debt-to-equity ratio**, **reduced total asset turnover**, and **reduced rate of return on total assets** are seen as having a detrimental effect on the company.

What Do the Numbers Mean?

And resist this they have! The intention of the Canadian standard was to have the accounting for leases based on whether or not the risks and benefits of ownership were transferred. However, because the standard specifies 75 percent of useful life and 90 percent of the fair value of the asset, management often interprets these numbers as "rates to beat." That is, leases have been and continue to be specifically engineered to ensure that ownership is not transferred and to have them come in just under the 75- and 90-percent hurdles so that the capitalization criteria are not met.

The Canadian experience with companies' responses to this standard remains one of the key reasons why the Accounting Standards Board shies away from identifying specific numerical criteria in its standards. It prefers to rely on principles-based, rather than rules-based, guidance.

Whether this resistance is reasonable is a matter of opinion. From a cash flow point of view—and excluding any cash flow effects that are associated with income tax differences—the company is in the same position whether the lease is accounted for as an operating or a capital lease. Illustration 20-9 identifies the effects on Lessee Company's cash flows, including how the cash flows are reported on the company's cash flow statement.

Illustration 20-9

Comparison of Cash Flow Reporting—Capital vs. Operating Leases

LESSEE CORPORATION
Reporting of Cash Flows on the Statement of Cash Flows
Capital Lease versus Operating Lease

| Year | Capital Lease Cash Outflows | | | | Operating Lease Cash Outflows | |
	Operating	Investing	Financing	Total	Operating	Difference
Lease signed		Note 1	Note 1	—	—	—
Payments:						
2008	$ 2,000.00	—	$ 23,981.62	$ 25,981.62	$ 25,981.62	$ —
2009	9,601.84	—	16,379.78	25,981.62	25,981.62	—
2010	7,963.86	—	18,017.76	25,981.62	25,981.62	—
2011	6,162.08	—	19,819.54	25,981.62	25,981.62	—
2012	4,180.32	—	21,801.30	25,981.62	25,981.62	—
	$29,908.10	—	$100,000.00	$129,908.10	$129,908.10	$ —

Note 1: The new $100,000 investment in the leased capital asset and the new $100,000 financing through a lease arrangement are non-cash transactions. They are not included on the cash flow statement, but are required to be reported elsewhere in the financial statements

Under the capital lease scenario, the operating cash outflows are made up of the portion of the lease payment that represents executory costs ($2,000) plus the portion that represents interest expense. The financing outflows are the decreases in the principal balance of the lease obligation. As you can see, although the cash outflows are identical each period and in total under the two methods, they are reported very differently on the cash flow statement. Each presentation, however, is consistent with the underlying substance of the transaction.

The reasons that managers often give when they argue against capitalization are that capitalization can more easily lead to violation of loan covenants; can affect the amount of compensation that is received (for example, a stock compensation plan tied to earnings); and can lower rates of return and increase debt-to-equity relationships, thus making the company less attractive to present and potential investors.[20]

Introduction to Lessor Accounting

Calculation of Lease Payments

Objective 6
Calculate the lease payment that is required for a lessor to earn a specific return.

The lessor determines the rental amount to charge based on the rate of return—the implicit rate—that the lessor needs to receive in order to justify leasing the asset.[21] The key variables that the lessor must consider in deciding the rate of return are the lessee's credit standing, the length of the lease, and the status of the residual value (guaranteed or

---

[20] One study indicates that management's behaviour did change as a result of the profession's requirements to capitalize certain leases. Many companies restructured their leases to avoid capitalization; others increased their purchases of assets instead of leasing; and others, faced with capitalization, postponed their debt offerings or issued shares instead. It is interesting to note that the study found no significant effect on share or bond prices as a result of capitalization of leases. A. Rashad Abdel-khalik, "The Economic Effects on Lessees of *FASB Statement No. 13*, Accounting for Leases," Research Report (Stamford, Conn.: FASB, 1981).

[21] In lease-versus-buy decisions and in determining the lessor's implicit rate, income tax consequences must be factored in. A major variable is whether the CRA requires the lease to be accounted for as a conditional sale: this is usually established based on whether the title is transferred by the end of the lease term or the lessee has a bargain purchase option. Tax shields that relate to the rental payment and capital cost allowance significantly affect the return and an investment's net present value.

unguaranteed). In the Lessor Corporation/Lessee Corporation example in Illustration 20-4, the lessor wants a 10-percent return on its investment of $100,000. Illustration 20-10 shows how Lessor Corporation determines the amount of the rental payment, assuming there is no bargain purchase option or residual value at the end of the lease.[22]

Investment to be recovered	$100,000.00
Less: Present value of the amount to be recovered through a bargain purchase option or residual value at end of lease term	–0–
Present value of amount to be recovered through lease payments	$100,000.00
Five beginning-of-the-year lease payments to yield a 10% return: ($100,000 ÷ 4.16986[a])	$ 23,981.62

[a]PV of an annuity due (Table A-5); $i = 10\%$, $n = 5$

Illustration 20-10

Calculation of Lease Payments by Lessor

If there is a bargain purchase option or some other residual value, the lessor does not have to recover as much through the rental payments. In such cases, the present value of these other recoveries is deducted before determining the lease payment. This is illustrated later in the chapter in more detail.

Classification of Leases by the Lessor

From the **lessor's** standpoint,[23] all leases are classified for accounting purposes as either of the following:

(a) Operating lease

(b) Direct financing lease or sales-type lease

Recalling what the lessee must consider in accounting for a lease, the lessor accounts for a lease contract as an operating lease if the risks and benefits of ownership that relate to the leased property are retained mostly by the lessor.[24] If instead the risks and benefits of ownership are transferred to the lessee, the lessor accounts for the lease as either a direct financing lease or a sales-type lease.

Whether a lease is a direct financing or a sales-type lease depends on the specific situation. Some manufacturers enter into lease agreements either directly or through a subsidiary captive leasing company as a way of facilitating the sale of their product. These transactions are usually sales-type lease arrangements. Other companies are in business mainly to finance a variety of assets in order to generate financing income. They usually enter into direct financing leases. The next section identifies how the classification decision is made between whether a lease is a sales-type or a direct financing lease.

Capitalization Criteria

Illustration 20-11 presents the criteria for deciding how to classify a lease. If, at the beginning of the lease, **one or more** of the Group I criteria and **both** of the Group II criteria

7 Objective

Identify and apply the criteria that are used to determine the type of lease for a lessor.

International Insight

IAS 17 does not use the terms "direct financing" and "sales-type," but refers to them both as "financing" leases. The standard instead makes this distinction by having specific requirements for manufacturer and dealer lessors.

---

[22] Alternatively, use Excel or some other spreadsheet program to calculate the required payments. With Excel, use the following series of keystrokes: INSERT/FUNCTION/PMT. Fill in the variables that you are prompted to enter.

[23] Not surprisingly, there are fewer lessors than lessee companies. *Financial Reporting in Canada—2006* (CICA) reports that only 4.5% of its 200 survey companies in 2005 provided information about their roles as lessors, while 87% had disclosures related to their activities as lessees.

[24] *CICA Handbook*, Section 3065.09-.10.

are met, the lessor classifies and accounts for the arrangement as either a direct financing lease or a sales-type lease.[25] Otherwise, it is an operating lease. Note that **the Group I criteria are identical** to the criteria that must be met for a lease to be classified as a capital lease by a lessee.

Illustration 20-11

*Capitalization Criteria
for the Lessor*

Group I

1. There is reasonable assurance that the lessee will obtain ownership of the leased property by the end of the lease term. If there is a bargain purchase option in the lease, it is assumed that the lessee will exercise it and obtain ownership.
2. The lease term is long enough that the lessee will receive substantially all of the economic benefits expected to be derived from the use of the leased property over its life. This is usually assumed to occur if the lease term is 75 percent or more of the leased property's economic life.
3. The lease allows the lessor to recover its investment in the leased property and to earn a return on the investment. This is assumed to occur if the present value of the minimum lease payments (excluding executory costs) is equal to substantially all (usually 90 percent or more) of the fair value of the leased property.

Group II

1. The credit risk associated with the lease is normal when compared with the risk of collection of similar receivables.
2. The amounts of any unreimbursable costs that are likely to be incurred by the lessor under the lease can be reasonably estimated.

Why are the Group II criteria required? The answer is that the profession wants to make sure that the lessor has really transferred the risks and benefits of ownership. If collectibility of the amounts that are due under the contract is not reasonably assured or if the lessor still has to absorb an uncertain amount of additional costs associated with the agreement, then it is not appropriate to remove the asset from the lessor's books and recognize revenue. In short, the Group II criteria are **standard revenue recognition criteria**.

Computer leasing companies at one time used to buy IBM equipment, lease it out, and remove the assets from their balance sheets. In leasing the asset, the computer lessors stated that they would substitute new IBM equipment if obsolescence occurred. However, when IBM introduced a new computer line, IBM refused to sell it to the computer leasing companies. As a result, some of these lessors could not meet their contracts with their customers and were forced to take back the old equipment. What the computer leasing companies had taken off the books now had to be reinstated. This situation demonstrates one reason for the requirements in Group II.

How do you distinguish between a sales-type and a direct financing lease? The difference between these classifications **is the presence or absence of a manufacturer's or dealer's profit (or loss)**. A **sales-type lease** includes in the rental amount the recovery of a **manufacturer's or dealer's profit** as well as the asset's cost. The profit (or loss) to this lessor is the difference between the fair value of the leased property at the beginning of the lease, and the lessor's cost or carrying amount (book value). As indicated above, sales-type leases normally arise when manufacturers or dealers use leasing as a way of marketing their products. The present value of the payments that will be received **is the sales price**, which is normally higher than the cost of the asset to the company. A profit is thus earned on the "sale," in addition to interest income on the financing of the sale.

Direct financing leases, on the other hand, generally result from arrangements with lessors that are engaged mostly in financing operations, such as lease-finance companies and a variety of financial intermediaries, such as banks or their finance subsidiaries. These lessors acquire the specific assets that lessees have asked them to acquire. Their business model is to earn interest income on the financing arrangement with the lessee.

---

[25] *CICA Handbook*, Section 3065.07.

All leases that do not qualify as direct financing or sales-type leases are classified and accounted for by the lessor as operating leases. The flowchart in Illustration 20-12 shows the circumstances for a lease to be classified by the lessor as operating, direct financing, or sales-type.

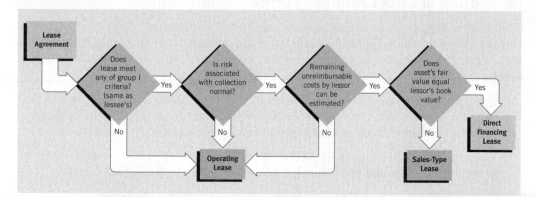

Illustration 20-12

Flowchart of Lessor's Criteria for Lease Classification

When both Group II criteria are not met, it is possible that a lessor that will classify a lease as an **operating** lease while the lessee will classify the same lease as a **capital** lease. When this happens, both the lessor and lessee carry the asset on their books and both amortize the capitalized asset.

Lessor Accounting for a Direct Financing Lease

Direct financing leases are, in substance, the financing of an asset purchase by the lessee. In this type of lease, the lessor removes the asset from its books and replaces it with a receivable. The accounts and information that are needed to record a direct financing lease are as follows:

8 Objective
Account for basic direct financing and sales-type leases by the lessor.

DIRECT FINANCING LEASE TERMINOLOGY		
Term	**Account**	**Explanation**
Gross investment in lease	Lease Payments Receivable	The undiscounted rental/lease payments (excluding executory costs) plus any guaranteed or unguaranteed residual value that accrues to the lessor at the end of the lease term or any bargain purchase option.[a]
Unearned finance or interest income	Unearned Interest Income (contra account to Lease Payments Receivable)	The difference between the undiscounted Lease Payments Receivable and the carrying amount of the leased property.
Net investment in lease	Net of the two accounts above	The gross investment (the Lease Payments Receivable account) less the Unearned Interest Income, i.e., the gross investment's present value.

[a] This is equal to the lessor's minimum lease payments, as defined, plus any unguaranteed residual value.

The net investment is the present value of the items that make up the gross investment. The difference between these two accounts is the unearned interest. The unearned interest income is amortized and taken into income over the lease term by applying the effective interest method. This results in a constant rate of return being produced on the net investment in the lease.

Illustration of Direct Financing Lease (Annuity Due)

The following direct financing lease example uses the same data as the Lessor Corporation/Lessee Corporation example in Illustration 20-4. In accounting for this lease transaction, the relevant information for Lessor Corporation from the illustration is as follows:

1. The lease is for a **five-year term** that begins January 1, 2008, is non-cancellable, and requires equal **rental payments of $25,981.62** at the beginning of each year. Payments include **$2,000 of executory costs** (property taxes).

2. The equipment has a **cost of $100,000** to Lessor Corporation, a **fair value of $100,000**, an estimated **economic life of five years**, and **no residual value**.

3. No initial direct costs are incurred in negotiating and closing the lease contract.

4. The lease contains no renewal options and the **equipment reverts to Lessor Corporation** at the end of the lease.

5. **Collectibility is reasonably assured** and **no additional costs** (with the exception of the property taxes being reimbursed by the lessee) are to be incurred by Lessor Corporation.

6. Lessor Corporation set the annual lease payments to ensure a **rate of return of 10 percent** on its investment, shown previously in Illustration 20-10.

The lease meets the criteria for classification as a direct financing lease because (1) the lease term exceeds 75 percent of the equipment's estimated economic life, **or** (2) the present value of the minimum lease payments exceeds 90 percent of the equipment's fair value, **and** (3) the credit risk is normal compared to similar receivables (collectibility of the payments is reasonably assured), **and** (4) there are no further unreimbursable costs to be incurred by Lessor Corporation. It is not a sales-type lease, because **there is no dealer profit** between the equipment's fair value and the lessor's cost.

Illustration 20-13 calculates the initial gross investment in the lease—which is the amount to be recognized in Lease Payments Receivable.

Illustration 20-13

Calculation of Lease Payments Receivable

Lease Payments Receivable = Total lease payments (excluding executory costs) plus residual value or bargain purchase option
= [($25,981.62 − $2,000) × 5] + $0
= $119,908.10

The interest income that will be earned over the term of the lease is the difference between the lease payments receivable amount and the lessor's cost or carrying amount of the leased asset, as shown in Illustration 20-14.

Illustration 20-14

Calculation of Unearned Interest Income

Unearned Interest Income = Lease Payments Receivable minus asset cost or carrying amount
= $119,908.10 − $100,000
= $19,908.10

The net investment in this direct financing lease is $100,000—the gross investment of $119,908.10 minus the unearned interest income of $19,908.10.

The acquisition of the asset by the lessor, its transfer to the lessee, the resulting receivable, and the unearned interest income are recorded on January 1, 2008, as follows:

Equipment Purchased for Lease	100,000		A = L + SE
Cash[26]		100,000	0 0 0

Cash flows: ↓ 100,000 outflow

Lease Payments Receivable	119,908.10		A = L + SE
Equipment Purchased for Lease		100,000.00	0 0 0
Unearned Interest Income—Leases		19,908.10	

Cash flows: No effect

The Unearned Interest Income account is classified on the balance sheet as a contra account to the receivable account. Generally, the lease payments receivable amount, although it is **recorded** at the gross investment amount, is **reported** in the balance sheet at the "net investment" amount and entitled "Net investment in capital leases."[27]

In its books, Lessor Corporation replaces its investment in the asset that it acquired for Lessee Corporation at a cost of $100,000, with a net lease receivable of $100,000. Similar to Lessee's treatment of interest, Lessor Corporation applies the effective interest method and recognizes interest income according to the unrecovered net investment balance, as shown in Illustration 20-15.

LESSOR CORPORATION
Lease Amortization Schedule
(Annuity due basis)

Date	Annual Lease Payment	Interest (10%) on Net Investment	Net Investment Recovery	Net Investment
	(a)	(b)	(c)	(d)
1/1/08				$100,000.00
1/1/08	$ 23,981.62	$ –0–	$ 23,981.62	76,018.38
1/1/09	23,981.62	7,601.84	16,379.78	59,638.60
1/1/10	23,981.62	5,963.86	18,017.76	41,620.84
1/1/11	23,981.62	4,162.08	19,819.54	21,801.30
1/1/12	23,981.62	2,180.32*	21,801.30	–0–
	$119,908.10	$19,908.10	$100,000.00	

(a) Annual rental that provides a 10% return on net investment (exclusive of executory costs).
(b) Ten percent of the preceding balance of (d) except for 1/1/08.
(c) (a) minus (b).
(d) Preceding balance minus (c).
*Rounded by 19 cents.

Illustration 20-15

Lease Amortization Schedule for Lessor—Annuity Due Basis

On January 1, 2008, the journal entry to record the receipt of the first year's lease payment is as follows:

---

[26]The lessor usually finances the purchase of this asset over a term that generally coincides with the term of the lease. Because the lessor's cost of capital is lower than the rate that is implicit in the lease, the lessor earns a profit represented by the interest spread.

[27] While lessees may record and report the lease obligation on a net basis, lessors tend to recognize the gross amount in receivables. Unlike the lessee, lessors may have hundreds or thousands of lease contracts to administer and the amounts to be collected are the gross receivables. Therefore, for administrative simplicity, the amounts that are received are a direct reduction of the receivable, and the interest is determined and adjusted for separately.

A = L + SE
+2,000   +2,000

Cash flows: ↑ 25,981.62 inflow

Cash	25,981.62	
Lease Payments Receivable		23,981.62
Property Tax Expense		2,000.00

On December 31, 2008, the interest income that was earned during the first year is recognized through the following entry:

A = L + SE
+7,601.84   +7,601.84

Cash flows: No effect

Unearned Interest Income—Leases	7,601.84	
Interest Income—Leases		7,601.84

T accounts for the receivable and its unearned interest contra account, and the effect on the net investment after these entries are posted are shown in Illustration 20-16.

Illustration 20-16

General Ledger Lease Asset Accounts

	Lease Payments Receivable		Unearned Interest Income		Net Investment in Lease
Jan. 1/08	$119,908.10			$19,908.10	$100,000.00
Jan. 1/08		23,981.62			(23,981.62)
	95,926.48			19,908.10	76,018.38
Dec. 31/08			7,601.84		7,601.84
	95,926.48			12,306.26	83,620.22

At December 31, 2008, the net investment in capital leases is reported in Lessor Corporation's balance sheet among current and non-current assets, as appropriate. The portion that is due within one year or the operating cycle, whichever is longer, is classified as a current asset and the remainder is reported with non-current assets.

The net investment at December 31, 2008, is $83,620.22, which is the balance at January 1, 2008, of $76,018.38 plus interest earned up to the balance sheet date of $7,601.84. The **current portion** is determined as follows:

Recovery of net investment within 12 months from Dec. 31, 2008	$16,379.78
Interest accrued to Dec. 31, 2008	7,601.84
Current portion of net investment	$23,981.62

The **long-term portion** is the $59,638.60 remainder. The lease amortization schedule in Illustration 20-15 indicates that this is the net investment that will still have to be recovered after 12 months from the balance sheet date.

Illustration 20-17 shows how the lease assets appear on the December 31, 2008, balance sheet.

Illustration 20-17

Balance Sheet Reporting by Lessor

Current assets	
Net investment in capital leases	$23,981.62
Non-current assets (investments)	
Net investment in capital leases	$59,638.60

The following entries record the receipt of the second year's lease payment and recognition of the interest earned in 2009:

Jan. 1, 2009	Cash	25,981.62	
	Lease Payments Receivable		23,981.62
	Property Tax Expense		2,000.00

$$A = L + SE$$
$$+2,000 \qquad +2,000$$
Cash flows: ↑ 25,981.62 inflow

| Dec. 31, 2009 | Unearned Interest Income—Leases | 5,963.86 | |
| | Interest Income—Leases | | 5,963.86 |

$$A = L + SE$$
$$+5,963.86 \qquad +5,963.86$$
Cash flows: No effect

Journal entries through to 2012 follow the same pattern except that no entry is recorded in 2012 (the last year) for earned interest. Because the receivable is fully collected by January 1, 2012, there is no outstanding investment balance during 2012 for Lessor Corporation to earn interest on. When the lease term is completed, the gross receivable and the unearned interest have been fully written off. Note that Lessor Corporation records no amortization. If the equipment is sold to Lessee Corporation for $5,000 when the lease expires, Lessor Corporation recognizes the disposition of the equipment as follows:

| Cash | 5,000 | |
| Gain on Sale of Leased Equipment | | 5,000 |

$$A = L + SE$$
$$+5,000 \qquad +5,000$$
Cash flows: ↑ 5,000 inflow

Lessor Accounting for a Sales-Type Lease

Accounting for a sales-type lease is very similar to accounting for a direct financing lease. The major difference is that the lessor in the sales-type lease has usually manufactured or acquired the leased asset in order to sell it and is looking, through the lease agreement, to recover the asset's selling price through the lease payments. The cost or carrying amount on the lessor's books is usually less than the asset's fair value to the customer. The lessor, therefore, records a sale and the related cost of goods sold for the asset that is being "sold."

The following terminology is relevant for a sales-type lease:

SALES-TYPE LEASE TERMINOLOGY		
Term	**Account**	**Explanation**
Gross investment in lease	Lease Payments Receivable	The undiscounted rental/lease payments (excluding executory costs) plus any guaranteed or unguaranteed residual value that accrues to the lessor at the end of the lease term or any bargain purchase option (the same as for a direct financing lease).[a]
Unearned finance or interest income	Unearned Interest Income (contra account to Lease Payments Receivable)	The difference between the undiscounted amounts making up the Lease Payments Receivable and the present values of the same amounts.
Net investment in lease	Net of the two accounts above	The gross investment (the Lease Payments Receivable account) less the Unearned Interest Income, i.e., the gross investment's present value (the same as for a direct financing lease).

| Selling price of the asset | Sales | The present value of the Lease Payments Receivable account reduced by the present value of any unguaranteed residual.[b] |
| Cost of the leased asset being sold | Cost of Goods Sold | The cost of the asset to the lessor, reduced by the present value of any unguaranteed residual. |

[a] This is equal to the lessor's minimum lease payments, as defined, plus any unguaranteed residual value.
[b] This is equal to the present value of the minimum lease payments.

The same data from the earlier Lessor Corporation/Lessee Corporation example, summarized below, are used to illustrate the accounting for a sales-type lease. There is one exception: instead of the leased asset having a cost of $100,000 to Lessor Corporation, the assumption is that Lessor Corporation manufactured the asset and that it is in Lessor's inventory at a cost of $85,000. Lessor's regular selling price for this asset—its fair value— is $100,000, and Lessor wants to recover this amount through the lease payments.

1. Lease term: five years, beginning January 1, 2008

2. Rental payments: $25,981.62, including $2,000 of executory costs, beginning January 1, 2008

3. Manufactured cost and carrying amount of leased asset on Lessor's books: $85,000. Leased asset's regular selling price and fair value: $100,000

4. No lease renewal options; equipment reverts to Lessor at end of lease; no residual value.

5. Lessor sets the lease payment to ensure a 10% rate of return on its investment

The lessor's accounting entries to record the lease transactions are the same as the entries illustrated earlier for a direct financing lease, except for the entry at the lease's inception. **Sales and cost of goods sold are recorded in a sales-type lease.** The entries are as follows:

	January 1, 2008		

A   =   L   +   SE
+100,000   +100,000
 	
Cash flows: No effect
	Lease Payments Receivable ($23,981.62 × 5)
	    Unearned Interest Income—Leases
	    Sales
		119,908.10	19,908.10
			100,000.00

| A   =   L   +   SE
−85,000   −85,000

Cash flows: No effect | Cost of Goods Sold
    Inventory | 85,000.00 | 85,000.00 |

| A   =   L   +   SE
+2,000   +2,000

Cash flows: ↑ 25,981.62 inflow | Cash
    Lease Payments Receivable
    Property Tax Expense | 25,981.62 | 23,981.62
2,000.00 |

	December 31, 2008		
A = L + SE +7,601.84 +7,601.84 Cash flows: No effect	Unearned Interest Income—Leases Interest Income—Leases	7,601.84	7,601.84

Compare the January 1, 2008, entries above with the entries for the direct financing lease. The sales-type lease recognizes that what is being recovered is the asset's selling price, so a sale is therefore recorded. The cost of the inventory is transferred to cost of goods sold. With a sales-type lease, the lessor recognizes **a gross profit from the sale**, which is reported at the lease's inception, and also recognizes **interest** or **finance income** over the period of the lease until the receivable is no longer outstanding. A lessor with a direct financing lease reports **only financing income**.

Lessor Accounting and Reporting for an Operating Lease

Accounting

With an operating lease, the lessor records each rental receipt as rental income. The leased asset remains on the lessor's books and is amortized in the normal manner, with the amortization expense of the period matched against the rental income. An equal (straight-line) amount of rental income is recognized in each accounting period regardless of the lease provisions, unless another systematic and rational basis better represents the pattern in which the leased asset provides benefits. In addition to the amortization charge, maintenance and other operating costs that were incurred during the period are also charged to expense.

9 Objective
Explain the accounting and identify the disclosure requirements for an operating lease for a lessor.

To illustrate the accounting for an operating lease, assume that the Lessor Corporation/Lessee Corporation lease agreement above does not meet the capitalization criteria and is therefore classified as an operating lease. The entry to record the cash rental receipt, assuming the $2,000 is to cover the lessor's property tax expense, is as follows:

Cash	25,981.62	
Rental Income		25,981.62

A = L + SE
+25,981.62   +25,981.62

Cash flows: ↑ 25,981.62 inflow

Lessor records amortization as follows, assuming the straight-line method, a cost basis of $100,000, and a five-year life:

Amortization Expense—Leased Equipment	20,000	
Accumulated Amortization—Leased Equipment		20,000

If property taxes, insurance, maintenance, and other operating costs during the year are the lessor's obligation, they are recorded as expenses that are chargeable against the gross rental revenues.

Reporting

The objective of the required disclosures for **operating leases** is to enable users to assess how much of the company's resources are committed to this activity and the amount of cash flows that they generate. Lessors, therefore, report the cost and related accumulated amortization of property that is held for leasing purposes and the amount of rental income from such leases.

If, in addition to the assets that it leases to others, the lessor also owns plant assets for its own use, the leased equipment and accompanying accumulated amortization are separately classified in an account such as Equipment Leased to Others or Investment in Leased Property. If they are significant in amount or in terms of activity, the rental income and accompanying expenses are identified and reported on the income statement. Management may include additional information about minimum future rentals and contingent rentals, but this is not required.[28]

LEASE COMPLEXITIES

The following are special features of lease arrangements that need accounting solutions:

1. Residual values

2. Bargain purchase options

3. Initial direct costs of the lessor

4. The classification between current and non-current

Residual Values

Objective 10
Determine the effect of residual values in a lessee's capital lease, and account for them.

Up to this point, we have generally ignored residual values so that we could focus on the basic accounting issues related to lessee and lessor accounting. Residual values add some complexity to the accounting for leases, but the requirements are relatively straightforward.

The **residual value** is the leased asset's estimated fair value at the end of the lease term. Frequently, there is a significant residual value, especially when the leased asset's economic life is longer than the lease term. If title does not pass to the lessee and there is no bargain purchase option (criterion 1), the lessee returns the leased asset to the lessor at the end of the lease.[29]

Guaranteed versus Unguaranteed

The residual value may be unguaranteed or guaranteed by the lessee. If the lessee agrees to pay for any loss in value below a stated amount at the end of the lease, the stated amount is the **guaranteed residual value**.

The guaranteed residual value is used in lease arrangements for two reasons. The first is a business reason: It protects the lessor against any loss in estimated residual value, and so ensures that the lessor will get its desired rate of return on its investment. The second, discussed more fully later in the chapter, relates to how the lease is classified by the lessor and lessee.

In the case of an **operating lease**, the guarantee of a residual value by the lessee meets the definition of a financial liability that entities are required to recognize and measure at fair value.[30] Accounting Guideline 14 on "Disclosure of Guarantees" requires companies to **disclose** information about the nature of such guarantees, the maximum potential amount of future payments that are payable under such guarantees, and the current carrying amount of the liability covering such obligations. This information is required even if it is unlikely that any payments will have to be made. As Illustration 20-18 shows, **Transforce Income Fund** reports this type of guarantee, along with its lease commitments, in its 2006 financial statements.

---

[28] *CICA Handbook*, Section 3065.57–.59.

[29] When the lease term and the economic life are not the same, the asset's residual value and salvage value will probably differ. Salvage value refers to the estimated value at the end of the asset's economic life and is normally small.

[30] *CICA Handbook* Section 3855.A38 indicates that the fair value would be determined by referring to the premium that the company would need to charge to provide that same guarantee in a stand-alone transaction. This aspect of accounting for financial instruments is beyond the scope of this text.

Illustration 20-18

Disclosure of Operating Lease Commitments and Guarantees

TRANSFORCE INCOME FUND (excerpt)

Notes to Consolidated Financial Statements
Year Ended December 31, 2006

(A) The Fund entered into operating leases expiring on various dates through to March 2026, which call for lease payments of $220,118,000 with respect to rolling stock, real estate and others. Minimum lease payments for the upcoming years are as follows:

2007	$62,084
2008	48,502
2009	32,556
2010	16,615
2011	10,368
2012 to 2026	49,993

(D) Significant guarantees the Fund has provided to third parties include the following:

14. Commitments, Contingencies and Guarantees

Operating Leases

The Fund has guaranteed a portion of the residual values of certain of its assets under operating leases with expiry dates between January 2007 and April 2010, for the benefit of the lessor. If the fair value of the assets, at the end of their respective lease term, is less than the residual value, the Fund must, under certain conditions, compensate the lessor for a portion of the shortfall up to a maximum amount. As at December 31, 2006, the maximum exposure in respect of these guarantees is $4,627,000 (2005 – $5,271,000), and no provisions were necessary nor recorded associated with these guarantees.

In the case of **capital leases**, residual values may affect the amounts that are recognized on the financial statements of the lessor and lessee.

Effect on Lease Payments

A guaranteed residual value—by definition—is more likely to be realized than an unguaranteed residual value. As the certainty of recovery is higher, the lessor may decide to reduce the required rate of return, and therefore the rental rate. It makes no difference from an accounting point of view whether the residual value is guaranteed or unguaranteed since, once the rate is set, the net investment that is recorded by the lessor will be the same.

Assume the same data as in the Lessee Corporation/Lessor Corporation illustrations: Lessor wants to recover its net investment of $100,000 in the leased asset and earn a 10-percent return.[31] The asset reverts to Lessor at the end of the five-year lease term. Now assume that the asset is expected to have a residual value of $5,000 at the end of the lease. Whether the residual value is guaranteed or not, Lessor Corporation calculates the lease payments in the way that was described earlier in the chapter. Illustration 20-19 shows the calculations when the residual value is included.

Illustration 20-19

Lessor's Calculation of Lease Payments

LESSOR'S CALCULATION OF LEASE PAYMENTS (10% ROI)
Guaranteed or Unguaranteed Residual Value
(Annuity due basis)

Investment in leased equipment to be recovered	$100,000.00
Amount to be recovered through residual value, end of year 5:	
Present value of residual value ($5,000 × 0.62092, Table A-2)	3,104.60
Amount to be recovered by lessor through lease payments	$ 96,895.40
Five periodic lease payments ($96,895.40 ÷ 4.16986, Table A-5)	$ 23,237.09

Contrast this lease payment with the lease payment of $23,981.62 that was calculated in Illustration 20-10 when there was no residual value. The payments are lower because a

[31] Technically, the rate of return that is demanded by the lessor would differ depending on whether the residual value was guaranteed or unguaranteed. To simplify the illustrations, we are ignoring this difference in later sections of this chapter.

portion of the lessor's net investment of $100,000 is recovered through the residual value. The **present value** of the residual is used in the calculation because it will not be received for five years.

Lessee Accounting for Residual Value

Whether the estimated residual value is guaranteed by the lessee or not has both economic and accounting consequences **for the lessee**. The accounting difference is that the lease payments to be capitalized **include the guaranteed** residual value but **exclude an unguaranteed** residual value. If the residual value is not guaranteed by the lessee, the lessee has no responsibility or obligation for the asset's condition at the end of the lease; and the residual value, therefore, is not included in the calculation of the lease obligation.

Guaranteed Residual Value　A guaranteed residual value affects the amounts that the lessee capitalizes as a leased asset and a lease obligation. In effect, it is similar to an additional lease payment that will be paid in property or cash, or both, at the end of the lease term. Using the rental payments as calculated by the lessor in Illustration 20-19, the lessee's **minimum lease payments** are $121,185.45 ([$23,237.09 × 5] + $5,000). Illustration 20-20 shows the calculation of the present value of the minimum lease payments. This amount is capitalized as the leased asset and lease obligation.

Illustration 20-20

Calculation of Lessee's Capitalized Amount— Guaranteed Residual Value

LESSEE'S CAPITALIZED AMOUNT (10% RATE) (Annuity due basis; guaranteed residual value)	
Present value of five annual rental payments of $23,237.09, *i* = 10% ($23,237.09 × 4.16986, Table A-5)	$ 96,895.40
Present value of guaranteed residual value of $5,000 due at end of five-year lease term: ($5,000 × 0.62092, Table A-2)	3,104.60
Lessee's capitalized amount	$100,000.00

As Illustration 20-21 shows, Lessee Corporation's schedule of interest expense and amortization of the $100,000 lease obligation results in a $5,000 guaranteed residual value payment at the end of five years, on December 31, 2012.

Illustration 20-21

Lease Amortization Schedule for Lessee—Guaranteed Residual Value

LESSEE CORPORATION
Lease Amortization Schedule
(Annuity due basis, guaranteed residual value)

Date	Lease Payment	Interest (10%) on Unpaid Obligation	Reduction of Lease Obligation	Lease Obligation
	(a)	(b)	(c)	(d)
1/1/08				$100,000.00
1/1/08	$ 23,237.09	$ –0–	$ 23,237.09	76,762.91
1/1/09	23,237.09	7,676.29	15,560.80	61,202.11
1/1/10	23,237.09	6,120.21	17,116.88	44,085.23
1/1/11	23,237.09	4,408.52	18,828.57	25,256.66
1/1/12	23,237.09	2,525.67	20,711.42	4,545.24
12/31/12	5,000.00*	454.76**	4,545.24	–0–
	$121,185.45	$21,185.45	$100,000.00	

(a) Annual lease payment as required by lease, excluding executory costs.
(b) Preceding balance of (d) × 10%, except 1/1/08.　　*Represents the guaranteed residual value.
(c) (a) minus (b).　　**Rounded by 24 cents.
(d) Preceding balance minus (c).

The journal entries in the first column of Illustration 20-26 that record the leased asset and obligation, and the amortization, interest, property tax, and lease payments are based on a **guaranteed residual value**. The format of these entries is the same as illustrated earlier, but the amounts are different because of the capitalized residual value. As you might expect, the guaranteed residual value is subtracted from the cost of the leased asset in determining the amortization amount. Assuming the straight-line method is used, the amortization expense each year is $19,000 ([$100,000 − $5,000] ÷ 5). Note that the **undiscounted residual value is used** in this calculation, consistent with Chapter 11 and your introductory accounting course.

Illustration 20-22 shows how the leased asset and obligation are reported on the December 31, 2012, balance sheet, just before the lessee transfers the asset back to the lessor.

Property, plant, and equipment		Current liabilities	
Equipment under capital leases	$100,000.00	Interest payable	$ 454.76
Less: Accumulated amortization—		Obligations under capital leases	4,545.24
capital leases	95,000.00		
	$ 5,000.00		$5,000.00

Illustration 20-22

Account Balances on Lessee's Books at End of Lease— Guaranteed Residual Value

If the fair value of the equipment is less than $5,000 at the end of the lease, Lessee Corporation records a loss. For example, assume that Lessee Corporation amortized the leased asset down to its residual value of $5,000 but the asset's fair value at December 31, 2012 is only $3,000. In this case, Lessee Corporation records the following entry, assuming cash is paid to make up the residual value deficiency:

Loss on Capital Lease	2,000.00	
Interest Payable	454.76	
Obligations under Capital Leases	4,545.24	
Accumulated Amortization—Capital Leases	95,000.00	
Equipment under Capital Leases		100,000.00
Cash		2,000.00

A	=	L	+	SE
−7,000		−5,000		−2,000

Cash flows: ↓ 2,000 outflow

If the fair value is greater than $5,000, a gain may or may not be recognized. Gains on guaranteed residual values are shared between the lessor and lessee in whatever ratio the parties initially agreed to.

Unguaranteed Residual Value   From the lessee's viewpoint, an **unguaranteed residual value** has the same effect as no residual value on the lessee's calculation of the minimum lease payments and the capitalization of the leased asset and lease obligation. Assume the same facts as those above except that the $5,000 residual value is **unguaranteed**. The annual lease payment is the same ($23,237.09) because, whether the residual is guaranteed or unguaranteed, Lessor Corporation's amount to be recovered through lease rentals is the same: $96,895.40. Lessee Corporation's minimum lease payments are $116,185.45 ($23,237.09 × 5). Illustration 20-23 calculates the capitalized amount for the lessee.

LESSEE'S CAPITALIZED AMOUNT (10% RATE)	
(Annuity due basis, unguaranteed residual value)	
Present value of five annual rental payments of $23,237.09, *i* = 10%	
$23,237.09 × 4.16986 (Table A-5)	$96,895.40
Present value of unguaranteed residual value of $5,000 (not capitalized by lessee)	–0–
Lessee's capitalized amount	$96,895.40

Illustration 20-23

Calculation of Lessee's Capitalized Amount— Unguaranteed Residual Value

Assuming an unguaranteed residual value, Lessee Corporation's lease amortization table for the $96,895.40 obligation is provided in Illustration 20-24.

LESSEE CORPORATION
Lease Amortization Schedule (10%)
(Annuity due basis, unguaranteed residual value)

Date	Lease Payment	Interest (10%) on Unpaid Obligation	Reduction of Lease Obligation	Lease Obligation
	(a)	(b)	(c)	(d)
1/1/08				$96,895.40
1/1/08	$ 23,237.09	$ –0–	$23,237.09	73,658.31
1/1/09	23,237.09	7,365.83	15,871.26	57,787.05
1/1/10	23,237.09	5,778.71	17,458.38	40,328.67
1/1/11	23,237.09	4,032.87	19,204.22	21,124.45
1/1/12	23,237.09	2,112.64*	21,124.45	–0–
	$116,185.45	$19,290.05	$96,895.40	

(a) Annual lease payment as required by lease, excluding executory costs.
(b) Preceding balance of (d) × 10%, except Jan. 1, 2008.
(c) (a) minus (b).
(d) Preceding balance minus (c).
*Rounded by 19 cents.

Based on the residual value being unguaranteed, the journal entries that are needed to record the lease agreement and subsequent amortization, interest, property tax, and payments are reported in the right-hand column of Illustration 20-26. The format of these entries is the same as illustrated earlier. Note that the leased asset is recorded at $96,895.40 and is amortized over five years. Using straight-line amortization, the amortization expense each year is $19,379.08 ($96,895.40 ÷ 5). Illustration 20-25 shows how the asset and obligation are reported on the December 31, 2012, balance sheet, just before the lessee transfers the asset to the lessor.

Property, plant, and equipment		Current liabilities	
Equipment under capital leases	$96,895	Obligations under capital leases	$ –0–
Less: Accumulated amortization— capital leases	96,895		
	$ –0–		

Whether the asset's fair value at the end of the lease is $3,000 or $6,000, the only entry that is required is the one to remove the asset and its accumulated amortization from the books. There is no entry to report a gain or loss.

Lessee Entries Involving Residual Values   The entries by Lessee Corporation for both a guaranteed and an unguaranteed residual value are shown side by side in Illustration 20-26.

Guaranteed Residual Value			Unguaranteed Residual Value		
Capitalization of Lease (January 1, 2008):					
Equipment under Capital Leases	100,000.00		Equipment under Capital Leases	96,895.40	
Obligations under Capital Leases		100,000.00	Obligations under Capital Leases		96,895.40
First Payment (January 1, 2008):					
Property Tax Expense	2,000.00		Property Tax Expense	2,000.00	
Obligations under Capital Leases	23,237.09		Obligations under Capital Leases	23,237.09	
Cash		25,237.09	Cash		25,237.09
Adjusting Entry for Accrued Interest (December 31, 2008):					
Interest Expense	7,676.29		Interest Expense	7,365.83	
Interest Payable		7,676.29	Interest Payable		7,365.83
Entry to Record Amortization (December 31, 2008):					
Amortization Expense—Capital Leases	19,000.00		Amortization Expense—Capital Leases	19,379.08	
Accumulated Amortization—			Accumulated Amortization—		
Capital Leases		19,000.00	Capital Leases		19,379.08
([$100,000 − $5,000] ÷ 5 years)			($96,895.40 ÷ 5 years)		
Second Payment (January 1, 2009):					
Property Tax Expense	2,000.00		Property Tax Expense	2,000.00	
Obligations under Capital Leases	15,560.80		Obligations under Capital Leases	15,871.26	
Interest Payable	7,676.29		Interest Payable	7,365.83	
Cash		25,237.09	Cash		25,237.09

Illustration 20-26

Comparative Entries for Guaranteed and Unguaranteed Residual Values, Lessee Corporation

Lessor Accounting for Residual Value

Direct Financing Lease   As stated earlier, whether or not the residual value is guaranteed, the lessor assumes that the residual value will be realized at the end of the lease term. The lease payments that are needed by the lessor to earn a particular return on investment are the same under both assumptions. As you can see from the Lessee Corporation/Lessor Corporation example, the lease payment was $23,237.09, both with the guarantee and without it.

Illustration 20-27 provides the calculations that are the basis for the lessor's accounting for a direct financing lease, whether the residual value of $5,000 is guaranteed or unguaranteed. The example again uses the Lessee Corporation/Lessor Corporation data.

11 Objective

Determine the effect of residual values for a lessor, and account for them.

Gross investment	= ($23,237.09 × 5) + $5,000	= $121,185.45
Net investment:		
PV of lease payments +	= $23,237.09 × 4.16986 (Table A-5) +	
PV of residual value	$5,000 × 0.62092 (Table A-2)	= 100,000.00
Unearned interest income		$ 21,185.45

Illustration 20-27

Calculation of Direct Financing Lease Amounts by Lessor

Illustration 20-28 shows the lessor's amortization schedule, which is the same whether the residual value is guaranteed or unguaranteed.

Illustration 20-28

Lease Amortization Schedule for Lessor—Guaranteed or Unguaranteed Residual Value

LESSOR CORPORATION
Lease Amortization Schedule
(Annuity due basis, guaranteed or unguaranteed residual value)

Date	Lease Payment Received	Interest (10%) on Net Investment	Net Investment Recovery	Net Investment
	(a)	(b)	(c)	(d)
1/1/08				$100,000.00
1/1/08	$ 23,237.09	$ –0–	$ 23,237.09	76,762.91
1/1/09	23,237.09	7,676.29	15,560.80	61,202.11
1/1/10	23,237.09	6,120.21	17,116.88	44,085.23
1/1/11	23,237.09	4,408.52	18,828.57	25,256.66
1/1/12	23,237.09	2,525.67	20,711.42	4,545.24
12/31/12	5,000.00*	454.76**	4,545.24	–0–
	$121,185.45	$21,185.45	$100,000.00	

(a) Lease payment as required by lease, excluding executory costs.
(b) Preceding balance of (d) × 10%, except January 1, 2008.
(c) (a) minus (b).
(d) Preceding balance minus (c).
*Represents the residual value.
**Rounded by 24 cents.

Lessor Corporation's entries during the first year for this direct financing lease are shown in Illustration 20-29. Note the similarity between these entries and those of Lessee Corporation in Illustration 20-26.

Illustration 20-29

Entries for Either Guaranteed or Unguaranteed Residual Value, Lessor Corporation

Inception of Lease (January 1, 2008):		
Lease Payments Receivable	121,185.45	
Equipment Purchased for Lease		100,000.00
Unearned Interest Income—Leases		21,185.45
First Payment Received (January 1, 2008):		
Cash	25,237.09	
Lease Payments Receivable		23,237.09
Property Tax Expense		2,000.00
Adjusting Entry for Accrued Interest (December 31, 2008):		
Unearned Interest Income—Leases	7,676.29	
Interest Income—Leases		7,676.29

Sales-Type Lease The gross investment and the original amount of unearned interest income are the same for a sales-type lease and a direct financing lease, whether or not the residual value is guaranteed.

When recording **sales revenue** and **cost of goods sold**, however, there is a difference in accounting for guaranteed and unguaranteed residual values. A guaranteed residual value can be considered part of sales revenue because the lessor knows that the entire amount will be realized. There is less certainty, however, that any unguaranteed residual will be realized; therefore, **sales and cost of goods sold are only recognized for the portion of the asset that is sure to be realized**. The gross profit amount that is reported on the asset's sale **is the same**, however, whether the residual value is guaranteed or not. This is because the present value of any unguaranteed residual is not included in the calculation **of either the sales amount or the cost of goods sold**.

To illustrate a sales-type lease with and without a guaranteed residual value, assume the same facts as in the preceding examples: the estimated residual value is $5,000 (the present value of which is $3,104.60); the annual lease payments are $23,237.09 (the present value of which is $96,895.40); and the leased equipment has an $85,000 cost to the manufacturer, Lessor Corporation. At the end of the lease, assume that the leased asset's fair value is $3,000.

Illustration 20-30 provides the calculations that are needed to account for this sales-type lease.

	Sales-Type Lease	
	Guaranteed Residual Value	Unguaranteed Residual Value
Gross investment	$121,185.45 ([$23,237.09 × 5] + $5,000)	Same
Unearned interest income	$21,185.45 ($121,185.45 − [$96,895.40 + $3,104.60])	Same
Sales	$100,000 ($96,895.40 + $3,104.60)	$96,895.40
Cost of goods sold	$85,000	$81,895.40 ($85,000 − $3,104.60)
Gross profit	$15,000 ($100,000 − $85,000)	$15,000 ($96,895.40 − $81,895.40)

Illustration 20-30

Calculation of Lease Amounts by Lessor Corporation—Sales-Type Lease

The $15,000 gross profit that is recorded by Lessor Corporation at the point of sale is the same whether the residual value is guaranteed or unguaranteed, but the amounts of **sales revenue** and **cost of goods sold** that are reported are **different**.

The 2008 and 2009 entries and the entry to record the asset's return at the end of the lease are provided in Illustration 20-31. The only differences are in the original entry that recognizes the lease and the final entry to record the asset's return to the lessor.

Illustration 20-31

Entries for Guaranteed and Unguaranteed Residual Values, Lessor Corporation—Sales-Type Lease

Guaranteed Residual Value			Unguaranteed Residual Value		
To record sales-type lease at inception (January 1, 2008):					
Cost of Goods Sold	85,000.00		Cost of Goods Sold	81,895.40	
Lease Payments Receivable	121,185.45		Lease Payments Receivable	121,185.45	
Sales Revenue		100,000.00	Sales Revenue		96,895.40
Unearned Interest Income		21,185.45	Unearned Interest Income		21,185.45
Inventory		85,000.00	Inventory		85,000.00
To record receipt of the first lease payment (January 1, 2008):					
Cash	25,237.09		Cash	25,237.09	
Lease Payments Receivable		23,237.09	Lease Payments Receivable		23,237.09
Property Tax Expense		2,000.00	Property Tax Expense		2,000.00
To recognize interest income earned during the first year (December 31, 2008):					
Unearned Interest Income	7,676.29		Unearned Interest Income	7,676.29	
Interest Income		7,676.29	Interest Income		7,676.29
(See lease amortization schedule, Illustration 20-28)					
To record receipt of the second lease payment (January 1, 2009):					
Cash	25,237.09		Cash	25,237.09	
Lease Payments Receivable		23,237.09	Lease Payments Receivable		23,237.09
Property Tax Expense		2,000.00	Property Tax Expense		2,000.00
To recognize interest income earned during the second year (December 31, 2009):					
Unearned Interest Income	6,120.21		Unearned Interest Income	6,120.21	
Interest Income		6,120.21	Interest Income		6,120.21
To record receipt of residual value at end of lease (December 31, 2012):					
Inventory	3,000		Inventory	3,000	
Cash	2,000		Loss on Capital Lease	2,000	
Lease Payments Receivable		5,000	Lease Payments Receivable		5,000

The estimated unguaranteed residual value in a sales-type lease (and in a direct financing-type lease) needs to be reviewed periodically by the lessor. If the estimate of the unguaranteed residual value declines, the accounting for the transaction must be revised using the changed estimate. The decline represents a reduction in the lessor's net investment and is recognized as a loss in the period when the residual estimate is reduced. Upward adjustments in estimated residual value are not recognized.

Bargain Purchase Options

Objective 12

Determine the effect of bargain purchase options for the lessee and lessor, and account for such options.

A bargain purchase option allows the lessee to purchase the leased property for a future price that is substantially less than the property's expected fair value in the future. The price is so favourable when the lease is entered into that it is reasonably sure that the option will be exercised in the future. If there is a bargain purchase option, the lessee's accounting **assumes that the option will be exercised** and that the title to the leased property will therefore be transferred to the lessee. As a result, the lessee **includes the present value of the option price when calculating the amount to capitalize and recognize as a liability**.

For example, assume that Lessee Corporation in our continuing illustration had an option to buy the leased equipment for $5,000 at the end of the five-year lease term when the fair value is expected to be $18,000. The significant difference between the option price and the estimated fair value indicates that this is a bargain, and there is reasonable assurance that the option will be exercised. The following calculations are affected by a bargain purchase option **in the same way as they were by a guaranteed residual value**:

1. The amount of the five lease payments that are necessary for the lessor to earn a 10-percent return on the net investment

2. The amount of the minimum lease payments

3. The amount that is capitalized as leased assets and lease obligation

4. The amortization of the lease obligation

There is **no difference** between the lessee's calculations and the amortization schedule for the lease obligation for a $5,000 **bargain purchase option** and those shown previously for the $5,000 **guaranteed residual value**. The only accounting difference is the calculation of the **annual amortization of the asset**. In the case of a guaranteed residual value, the lessee amortizes the asset over the lease term because the asset will be returned to the lessor. In the case of a bargain purchase option, the lessee uses the asset's economic life and its estimated residual value at that time because it is assumed that the lessee will acquire title to the asset by exercising the option, and will then continue to use it.

The lessor includes the bargain purchase option in calculating the lease payments receivable amount and the present value of the bargain purchase option in determining the net investment in the lease. The accounting is the same as that for a guaranteed residual value, regardless of whether the lease is a direct financing or a sales-type lease.

Lessor's Initial Direct Costs

Objective 13

Explain how a lessor accounts for initial direct costs for each type of lease.

Initial direct costs are defined in Section 3065.03(l) of the *CICA Handbook* as:

> those costs incurred by the lessor that are directly associated with negotiating and executing a specific leasing transaction. Such costs include commissions, legal fees and costs of preparing and processing documents for new leases. Such costs do not include

supervisory and administrative costs, promotion and lease design costs intended for recurring use, costs incurred in collection activities and provisions for uncollectible rentals.

The costs that directly relate to the time that an employee spent on a specific lease transaction may also be considered initial direct costs.

In a **direct financing lease**, the initial direct costs are expensed as they are incurred and the lessor offsets this expense by taking into income an equal amount of the unearned interest income. At the lease's inception, therefore, the net effect on income of the direct costs is zero; however, the amount of the net investment in the lease (the gross investment less the unearned interest income) is increased as a result of reducing the asset contra account.

For example, if the Lease Payments Receivable account is $600,000, with Unearned Interest Income at the lease's inception of $200,000, the net investment is $400,000. If initial direct costs of $35,000 are incurred and expensed and $35,000 of the unearned interest is recognized as earned, the net investment is increased to $435,000 ($600,000 − [$200,000 − $35,000]).

Because the finance income that is earned on the net investment should be recognized at a constant rate of return each period, the lessor has to recalculate the effective rate (it will be lower) for purposes of amortizing the net investment.[32] In this way, the initial costs are recognized over the lease term in the form of reduced interest income each period.

In a **sales-type lease** transaction, the lessor expenses the initial direct costs in the year that the costs are incurred; that is, they are expensed in the same period that the gross profit on the sale is recognized.

For **operating leases**, the lessor defers initial direct costs and allocates them over the lease term in proportion to the amount of rental income that is recognized.

Underlying Concept

The accounting treatment for the lessor's initial direct costs applies the matching concept.

International Insight

The effect of applying the provisions of IAS 17 that deal with initial direct costs is exactly the same as the effect of applying the Canadian standards, although the specific requirements are somewhat different.

Current versus Non-Current Classification

The classification of the lease obligation/net investment was presented earlier for an **annuity due** situation. As indicated in Illustration 20-7, the lessee's current portion of the lease obligation is the reduction in its principal balance within 12 months from the balance sheet date **plus** interest accrued to the balance sheet date. Coincidentally, the total of these two amounts in the example is the same as the rental payment of $23,981.62 that will be made one day later on January 1 of the next year. Similarly, as shown in Illustration 20-17, the lessor's current asset is the amount collected ($23,981.62) one day later on January 1, 2009. In both these examples, the balance sheet date is December 31 and the due date of the lease payment is January 1, so the total of the principal reduction on January 1 and the interest accrued to December 31 is the same as the rental payment ($23,981.62). **Note that this will happen only when the payment is due the day following the fiscal year end.** Understandably, this is not a common situation.

The following questions might now be asked. What happens if the lease payments fall as an **ordinary annuity** rather than an annuity due, and what if the lease payment dates do not coincide with the company's fiscal year? To illustrate, assume that the lease in our original example from Illustration 20-4 was signed and effective on September 1, 2008, with

14 Objective

Determine the current and long-term portions of a lease receivable and lease obligation.

---

[32] To calculate the effective or implied rate of interest in a lease when it is not given, students are referred to the Student Website's coverage of present values or to the Finance function in an Excel work sheet. In short, i is the internal rate of return. It is a matter of solving for i when the present value amount, the annuity amount, and n are all known. The interest rate is the rate that equates the present value amount (in this case the net investment) with the annuity payments. It can also be calculated using a trial and error method.

the first lease payment to be made on September 1, 2009—an ordinary annuity situation. Assume also that we continue to use the other facts of the Lessee Corporation/Lessor Corporation example, excluding the executory costs. Because the rents are paid at the end of the lease periods instead of at the beginning, the five rents are set at $26,379.73 to earn the lessor an interest rate of 10 percent.[33] With both companies having December 31 year ends, Illustration 20-32 provides the appropriate lease amortization schedule for this lease, based on the September 1 lease anniversary date each year.

Illustration 20-32

Lease Amortization Schedule—Ordinary Annuity Basis, Mid-Year Lease Date

LESSEE CORPORATION/LESSOR CORPORATION
Lease Amortization Schedule
(Ordinary annuity basis)

Date	Annual Lease Payment	Interest (10%)	Reduction of Principal	Balance of Lease Obligation/ Net Investment
1/9/08				$100,000.00
1/9/09	$ 26,379.73	$10,000.00	$ 16,379.73	83,620.27
1/9/10	26,379.73	8,362.03	18,017.70	65,602.57
1/9/11	26,379.73	6,560.26	19,819.47	45,783.10
1/9/12	26,379.73	4,578.31	21,801.42	23,981.68
1/9/13	26,379.73	2,398.05*	23,981.68	–0–
	$131,898.65	$31,898.65	$100,000.00	

*Rounded by 12 cents.

At December 31, 2008, the lease obligation/net investment in the lease is still $100,000. How much should be reported in current liabilities on the December 31, 2008, balance sheet and how much in long-term liabilities? The answer here is the same as in earlier chapters: **the current portion is the principal that will be repaid within 12 months from the balance sheet date** (i.e., $16,379.73). **In addition, any interest that has accrued up to the balance sheet date** (i.e., 10% of $100,000 × 4/12 = $3,333) is reported in current liabilities. The long-term portion of the obligation or net investment is the principal that will **not** be repaid within 12 months from the balance sheet date, or $83,620.27. It helps if you can first correctly describe in words what makes up the current portion, then determine the numbers that correspond.

On December 31, 2009, the long-term portion of the lease is $65,602.57. The principal due within 12 months from December 31, 2009, or $18,017.70, is included as a current liability along with interest accrued to December 31, 2009, of $2,787 (10% of $83,620.27 × 4/12).

Unsolved Problems

International Insight

The U.S. standards for leases are consistent with *CICA Handbook* Section 3065 but, as is the case with many of the standards, the U.S. rules are much more prescriptive and detailed.

As indicated at the beginning of this chapter, lease accounting is an area of accounting that is much abused through great efforts to circumvent the provisions of *CICA Handbook* Section 3065. In practice, the accounting rules for capitalizing leases have been rendered partly ineffective by the strong motivation of lessees to resist capitalization. Leasing generally involves large dollar amounts that, if capitalized, materially increase reported liabilities and weaken debt-to-equity and other ratios. Lease capitalization is also resisted because charges to expense in the early years of the lease are higher when leases are capitalized than when they are treated as operating leases, often with no corresponding tax

---

[33] The rent is now calculated as $100,000 ÷ 3.79079 = $26,379.73. The denominator is the factor for $n = 5$ and $i = 10$ for an ordinary annuity (Table A-4).

benefit. As a consequence, much effort has been devoted to "beating" the profession's lease capitalization rules.

To avoid asset capitalization, lease agreements are designed, written, and interpreted so that none of the three criteria is satisfied from the lessee's viewpoint. Devising such lease agreements is not too difficult as one simply has to use the following specifications:

1. Make certain that the lease does not transfer title of the asset to the lessee and that it does not include a bargain purchase option.

2. Set the lease term at something less than 75 percent of the leased property's estimated economic life.

3. Arrange for the present value of the minimum lease payments to be less than 90 percent of the leased property's fair value.

But the real challenge lies in disqualifying the lease as a capital lease to the lessee **while having the same lease qualify as a capital (sales or financing) lease to the lessor**. Unlike lessees, lessors try to avoid having lease arrangements classified as operating leases.[34]

Avoiding the first two criteria is relatively simple, but it takes a little ingenuity to avoid the 90-percent recovery test for the lessee while satisfying it for the lessor. Two of the factors that help accomplish this are (1) use of the incremental borrowing rate by the lessee when it is higher than the lessor's implicit interest rate, and making information about the implicit rate unavailable to the lessee; and (2) residual value guarantees.

The lessee's use of the higher interest rate is probably the more popular strategy. While lessees are knowledgeable about the fair value of the leased property and, of course, the rental payments, they generally are not aware of the estimated residual value used by the lessor. Therefore, not knowing exactly what the lessor's implicit interest rate is, the lessee can use its own incremental borrowing rate.

The residual value guarantee is the other popular device that is used by lessees and lessors. In fact, a whole new industry has emerged to help parties to a lease avoid symmetry in the lessee's and lessor's accounting for a lease. The residual value guarantee has spawned numerous companies whose main function is to guarantee the residual value of leased assets. For a fee, these third-party guarantors (insurers) assume the risk of deficiencies in the leased asset's residual value.

Because the (guaranteed) residual value is included in the minimum lease payments for the lessor, the 90-percent recovery of fair value test is satisfied and the lease is not an operating lease to the lessor. Because the residual value is guaranteed by an independent third party, the lessee's minimum lease payments **do not** include the guarantee. Thus, by merely transferring some of the risk to a third party, lessees can substantially alter the accounting treatment by converting what would otherwise be capital leases to operating leases.

Much of this getting around the rules is encouraged by the nature of the criteria that are used in the standard, and accounting standard-setting bodies continue to have poor experience with size and percentage criteria that are arbitrary, such as "90 percent of" and "75 percent of." This situation provided much of the motivation for further study of the topic and the subsequent publication of papers on new approaches to lease accounting.

The AcSB has decided not to pursue changes to its lease accounting standards until conceptual issues have been reviewed and dealt with internationally. The IASB and FASB, through a Joint International Working Group, are currently looking at a variety of conceptual models, and they intend to choose a model that will rely on asset and liability definitions in the conceptual framework, which is being revised at the same time. As this

---

[34] The reason is that most lessors are financial institutions, which do not want these types of rental assets on their balance sheets. Furthermore, the capital lease transaction from the lessor's standpoint provides higher income flows in the lease's earlier periods.

text went to print, the model that appears to have the most support proposes that lease accounting should be based on whether the lessee has obtained an asset defined in terms of "the right of use," and incurred an obligation to make payments for the lease period.[35] This is a very different concept than the "transfer of risks and benefits" approach that recognizes a physical asset on the balance sheet. Under the right-of-use approach, the capital and operating lease distinction would disappear and most leases would qualify for recognition as assets and liabilities by the lessee.

ILLUSTRATIONS OF LEASE ARRANGEMENTS

This next section illustrates a number of concepts that were discussed in the chapter, and uses Morgan Bakeries as an example of a lessee that is involved in four different leases. These leases are non-cancellable and none of the lease agreements automatically transfers title of the leased properties to the lessee during or at the end of the lease term. All leases start on January 1, 2008, and make the first rental payment due at the beginning of the year. Additional information is given in Illustration 20-33.

Illustration 20-33

Illustrative Lease Situations

	Harmon, Inc.	Arden's Oven Corp.	Mendota Truck Corp.	Appleland Computer
Type of property	Cabinets	Oven	Truck	Computer
Yearly rental	$6,000	$15,000	$5,582.62	$3,557.25
Lease term	20 years	10 years	3 years	3 years
Estimated economic life	30 years	25 years	7 years	5 years
Purchase option	None	$75,000 at end of 10 years $4,000 at end of 15 years	None	$3,000 at end of 3 years, which approximates fair value
Renewal option	None	5-year renewal option at $15,000 per year	None	1 year at $1,500; no penalty for non-renewal; standard renewal clause
Fair value at inception of lease	$60,000	$120,000	$20,000	$10,000
Cost of asset to lessor	$60,000	$120,000	$15,000	$10,000
Residual value				
Guaranteed	–0–	–0–	$7,000	–0–
Unguaranteed	$5,000	–0–	–0–	$3,000
Incremental borrowing rate of lessee	12%	12%	12%	12%
Executory costs paid by	Lessee $300 per year	Lessee $1,000 per year	Lessee $500 per year	Lessor Estimated to be $500 per year
Present value of minimum lease payments				
Using incremental borrowing rate of lessee	$50,194.68	$115,153.35	$20,000	$8,224.16
Using implicit rate of lessor	Not known	Not known	Not known	Known by lessee, $8,027.48
Estimated fair value at end of lease	$5,000	$80,000 at end of 10 years $60,000 at end of 15 years	Not available	$3,000
Credit risk of lease	Normal	Normal	Normal	Normal
Lessor's unreimbursable costs can be estimated	Yes	Yes	Yes	Yes

---

[35] *IASB Update*, IASB, March 2007.

Harmon, Inc.

The following is an analysis of the Harmon, Inc. lease.

1. **Transfer of title.** In lease? No. Bargain purchase option? No.

2. **Economic life test (75% test).** The lease term is 20 years and the estimated economic life is 30 years. It therefore does not meet the 75% test.

3. **Recovery of investment test (90% test):**

Rental payments	$ 6,000
PV factor for an annuity due, 20 years at 12%	× 8.36578
PV of rental payments	$50,194.68
90% of fair value: $60,000 × 90% =	$54,000.00

Because the minimum lease payments' present value is less than 90% of the fair value, the 90% test is not met either. Both Morgan and Harmon account for this lease as an operating lease, as indicated by the January 1, 2008, entries shown in Illustration 20-34.

Morgan Bakeries (Lessee)		Harmon, Inc. (Lessor)	
Rent Expense	6,000	Cash	6,000
Cash	6,000	Rental Income	6,000

Illustration 20-34
Comparative Entries for Operating Lease

Alternatively, Morgan might debit Prepaid Rent (and Harmon might credit Unearned Rent Income) and charge (credit) the $6,000 to income at $500 per month. Harmon continues to carry the leased cabinets in its books, amortizing them over their economic life.

Arden's Oven Corp.

The following is an analysis of the Arden's Oven Corp. lease.

1. **Transfer of title.** In lease? No. Bargain purchase option? The $75,000 option at the end of 10 years does not appear to be sufficiently lower than the expected fair value of $80,000 to make it reasonably assured that it will be exercised. However, the $4,000 at the end of 15 years when the fair value is $60,000 does appear to be a bargain. From the information given, criterion 1 is therefore met. Note that both the guaranteed and the unguaranteed residual values are assigned zero values because the lessee does not expect to return the asset to the lessor.

2. **Economic life test (75% test).** Because there is a bargain purchase option, the lease term is the initial lease period of 10 years plus the five-year renewal option since it precedes a bargain purchase option. Even though the lease term is now considered to be 15 years, this test is still not met because 15 years is only 60% of the asset's 25-year economic life.

3. **Recovery of investment test (90% test):**

Rental payments	$ 15,000.00
PV factor for an annuity due, 15 years at 12%	× 7.62817
PV of rental payments	114,422.55
PV of bargain purchase option: $4,000(PVF$_{15,12\%}$) = $4,000(0.18270) =	730.80
PV of minimum lease payments	$115,153.35
90% of fair value: $120,000 × 90% =	$108,000.00

The present value of the minimum lease payments is greater than 90% of the fair value; therefore, the 90% test is met. Morgan Bakeries accounts for this as a capital lease because at least one of the three criteria is met. Assuming that Arden's implicit rate is the same as Morgan's incremental borrowing rate, the entries in Illustration 20-35 are made on January 1, 2008.

Illustration 20-35

Comparative Entries for Capital Lease—Bargain Purchase Option

Morgan Bakeries (Lessee)		Arden's Oven Corp. (Lessor)		
Leased Asset—Oven 115,153.35		Lease Payments		
Obligation under		Receivable	229,000*	
Capital Lease	115,153.35	Unearned Interest		
		Income		109,000
		Asset—Oven		120,000
		*([$15,000 × 15] + $4,000)		

Morgan Bakeries amortizes the leased asset over its economic life of 25 years because it is assumed that the lessee will acquire title to the asset through the bargain purchase option. Arden uses the direct financing method and not sales-type lease accounting because the asset's fair value and cost are the same at the lease's inception.

Mendota Truck Corp.

The following is an analysis of the Mendota Truck Corp. lease.

1. **Transfer of title.** In the lease? No. Bargain purchase option? No.

2. **Economic life test (75% test).** The lease term is three years and the estimated economic life is seven years. It therefore does not meet the 75% test.

3. **Recovery of investment test (90% test):**

Rental payments	$ 5,582.62
PV factor for an annuity due, 3 years at 12%	× 2.69005
PV of rental payments	15,017.54
PV of guaranteed residual value: $7,000(PVF$_{3,12\%}$) = $7,000(0.71178) =	4,982.46
PV of minimum lease payments	$20,000.00
90% of fair value: $20,000 × 90% =	$18,000.00

The minimum lease payments' present value is greater than 90% of the fair value; therefore, the 90% test is met. Assuming that Mendota's implicit rate is the same as Morgan's incremental borrowing rate, the entries in Illustration 20-36 are made on January 1, 2008.

Illustration 20-36

Comparative Entries for Capital Lease

Morgan Bakeries (Lessee)		Mendota Truck Corp. (Lessor)		
Leased Asset—Truck	20,000.00	Lease Payments		
Obligation under		Receivable	23,747.86*	
Capital Lease	20,000.00	Cost of Goods Sold	15,000.00	
		Inventory—Truck		15,000.00
		Sales		20,000.00
		Unearned Interest		
		Income		3,747.86

*([$5,582.62 × 3] + $7,000)

The leased asset is amortized by Morgan over three years to its guaranteed residual value. The annual amortization on a straight-line basis is $4,333 ([$20,000 − $7,000] ÷ 3).

Appleland Computer

The following is an analysis of the Appleland Computer lease.

1. **Transfer of title.** In lease? No. Bargain purchase option? No. The option to purchase at the end of three years at fair value is clearly not a bargain.

2. **Economic life test (75% test).** The lease term is three years and there is no bargain renewal period. It therefore does not meet the 75% test.

3. **Recovery of investment test (90% test):**

Rental payments	$ 3,557.25
Less executory costs	500.00
	3,057.25
PV factor for an annuity due, 3 years at 12%	× 2.69005
PV of minimum lease payments using incremental borrowing rate	$ 8,224.16
90% of fair value: $10,000 × 90% =	$ 9,000.00

The present value of the minimum lease payments using the incremental borrowing rate is $8,224.16; using the implicit rate, it is $8,027.48 (see Illustration 20-33). The lessor's implicit rate must, therefore, be higher than the lessee's incremental borrowing rate. Given this situation, the lessee uses the $8,224.16 (the lower interest rate when discounting) for deciding on criterion 3. Because the minimum lease payments' present value is lower than 90% of the fair value, the recovery of investment test is not met.

This lease is an operating lease because not one of the three capitalization criteria is met. The entries in Illustration 20-37 are made on January 1, 2008, to recognize this transaction.

Illustration 20-37

Comparative Entries for Operating Lease

Morgan Bakeries (Lessee)			Appleland Computer (Lessor)		
Rent Expense	3,557.25		Cash	3,557.25	
Cash		3,557.25	Rental Income		3,557.25

Note that if the lease payments had been $3,557.25 with no executory costs included, this lease would qualify for capital lease accounting treatment. If the renewal option of $1,500 for Year 4 is considered a bargain renewal option, the minimum lease payments' present value (as shown below) is closer, but still below the 90% cut-off, and operating lease treatment would therefore still be appropriate.

PV of minimum lease payments, years 1 to 3 (as above)	$8,224.16
Add PV of beginning-of-year-4 payment	
$1,500 − $500 = $1,000 × 0.71178	711.78
PV of minimum lease payments	$8,935.94

PERSPECTIVES

Reporting and Disclosures: Lessee

Objective 15
Identify the lessee's disclosure requirements for capital leases.

International Insight

IAS 17 also requires disclosure of renewal options, purchase options, contingent rentals, and other contingencies.

Because a capital lease recognizes the leased property, plant, and equipment and a long-term liability, most of the required disclosures are similar to those required in *CICA Handbook* Sections 3061 and 3210 for property, plant, and equipment and long-term liabilities, respectively. The standard for leases requires the following disclosures:

1. The gross amount of assets recorded under capital leases and related accumulated amortization

2. Amortization expense on leased assets, either disclosed separately or as part of amortization expense for fixed assets, and the methods and rates of amortization

3. Separate disclosure of lease obligations and related details about interest rates, expiry dates, and any significant restrictions imposed as a result of the lease agreements

4. Future minimum lease payments, in the aggregate and for each of the next five fiscal years, with a separate deduction for amounts included in the minimum lease payments that represent executory costs and imputed interest. (The resulting net amount is the total lease obligation reported on the balance sheet.)

5. Interest expense related to lease obligations, either disclosed separately or included in interest on long-term indebtedness

Although not required, it may be appropriate to disclose separately total contingent rentals (rentals based on a factor other than the passage of time) as well as the amount of future minimum rentals receivable from non-cancellable sub-leases.[36]

Illustration of Capital Lease Disclosure by a Lessee

The excerpts from the financial statements of **Canadian Pacific Railway Limited** (CPR) for the year ended December 31, 2006 in Illustration 20-38 show how this lessee company met the disclosure requirements for its capital leases.

---

[36] *CICA Handbook* Section 3065.21 to .28.

NOTES TO CONSOLIDATED FINANCIAL STATEMENTS (excerpts)

December 31, 2006

1. Summary of Significant Accounting Policies

Net Properties

Equipment under capital lease is included in properties and depreciated over the period of expected use.

14. Net Properties

(in millions)	Cost	Accumulated depreciation	Net book value
2006			
Track and roadway	$ 8,615.1	$ 2,770.5	$ 5,844.6
Buildings	344.8	154.1	190.7
Rolling stock	3,548.3	1,450.9	2,097.4
Other	1,625.6	635.4	990.2
Total net properties	$ 14,133.8	$ 5,010.9	$ 9,122.9
2005			
Track and roadway	$ 8,180.0	$ 2,614.2	$ 5,565.8
Buildings	329.7	143.0	186.7
Rolling stock	3,448.5	1,395.7	2,052.8
Other	1,610.5	624.9	985.6
Total net properties	$ 13,568.7	$ 4,777.8	$ 8,790.9

At December 31, 2006, software development costs of $609.8 million (2005 – $608.7 million) and accumulated depreciation of $239.8 million (2005 – $230.0 million) were included in the category "Other". Additions during 2006 were $37.6 million (2005 – $39.6 million; 2004 – $30.3 million) and depreciation expense was $53.2 million (2005 – $52.3 million; 2004 – $53.6 million).

At December 31, 2006, net properties included $522.5 million (2005 – $401.0 million) of assets held under capital lease at cost and related accumulated depreciation of $112.4 million (2005 – $98.7 million).

During 2006, capital assets were acquired under the Company's capital program at an aggregate cost of $818.6 million (2005 – $906.0 million; 2004 – $686.3 million), $21.6 million of which were acquired by means of capital leases (2005 – $0.6 million; 2004 – nil). Cash payments related to capital purchases were $793.7 million in 2006 (2005 – $884.4 million; 2004 – $673.8 million). At December 31, 2006, $3.5 million (2005 – $9.4 million; 2004 – $0.2 million) remained in accounts payable related to the above purchases.

16. Long-term Debt

(in millions)	Currency in which payable	2006	2005
6.250 % Notes due 2011	US$	$ 466.2	$ 465.2
7.125 % Debentures due 2031	US$	407.9	407.1
9.450 % Debentures due 2021	US$	291.4	290.7
5.750 % Debentures due 2033	US$	291.4	290.7
4.90 % Medium Term Notes due 2010	CDN$	350.0	350.0
5.41 % Senior Secured Notes due 2024	US$	160.3	163.6
6.91 % Secured Equipment Notes due 2007 – 2024	CDN$	223.2	229.3
7.49 % Equipment Trust Certificates due 2007 – 2021	US$	134.9	137.6
Secured Equipment Loan due 2007	US$	141.6	143.1
Secured Equipment Loan due 2007 – 2015	CDN$	149.6	154.0
Obligations under capital leases due 2007 – 2022 (6.85 % – 7.65 %)	US$	317.0	320.8
Obligations under capital leases due 2007 (7.88 % – 10.93 %)	CDN$	21.9	0.3
Bank loan payable on demand due 2010 (5.883 %)	CDN$	4.7	4.5
Other	US$	–	0.2
		2,960.1	2,957.1
Perpetual 4 % Consolidated Debenture Stock	US$	35.7	35.6
Perpetual 4 % Consolidated Debenture Stock	GB£	9.0	8.1
		3,004.8	3,000.8
Less: Long-term debt maturing within one year		191.3	30.0
		$ 2,813.5	$ 2,970.8

At December 31, 2006, capital lease obligations included in long-term debt were as follows:

(in millions)	Year	Capital leases
Minimum lease payments in:	2007	$ 49.7
	2008	30.7
	2009	32.1
	2010	43.8
	2011	21.3
	Thereafter	380.2
Total minimum lease payments		557.8
Less: Imputed interest		(218.9)
Present value of minimum lease payments		338.9
Less: Current portion		(27.0)
Long-term portion of capital lease obligations		$ 311.9

Capital lease obligations include $2.8 million owing to a VIE for which the Company is not the primary beneficiary.

The carrying value of the assets securing the capital lease obligations was $410.1 million at December 31, 2006.

Reporting and Disclosures: Lessor

For direct financing and sales-type leases, the lessor discloses on the balance sheet the net investment in leases, with the investment appropriately segregated between current and long-term assets, and reports how the investment in leases has been calculated for income recognition purposes. In addition, the amount of finance income from these leases must be provided.[37]

The list of desirable disclosures is longer, with the AcSB suggesting that all of the following would be useful information: the total future minimum lease payments receivable, unguaranteed residual values, unearned finance income, executory costs included in minimum lease payments, contingent rentals taken into income, lease terms, and the amounts of minimum lease payments receivable for each of the next five years.[38] Few companies report this level of detail.

> **16 Objective**
> Identify the lessor's disclosure requirements for non-operating leases.

Illustration of Lease Disclosures by a Lessor

Excerpts from the financial statements of **Bombardier Inc.** for its year ended January 31, 2007, are reproduced in Illustration 20-39 to provide an example of the disclosures provided by a lessor for direct financing or sales-type leases. Headquartered in Montreal, Bombardier is a worldwide manufacturer of transportation-related assets, from regional aircraft and business jets to rail transportation equipment, systems, and services. The company uses sales-type leases and loans to facilitate the marketing of the aircraft it manufactures.

> **Illustration 20-39**
>
> *Non-Operating Lease Disclosures by a Lessor— Bombardier*

CONSOLIDATED BALANCE SHEETS
(in millions of U.S. dollars)

AS AT JANUARY 31	NOTES	2007	2006
Assets			
Cash and cash equivalents		$ 2,648	$ 2,917
Invested collateral	8	1,129	–
Receivables	1	1,789	1,684
Aircraft financing	2	1,042	1,457

SUMMARY OF SIGNIFICANT ACCOUNTING POLICIES

For the fiscal years ended January 31, 2007 and January 31, 2006

Lease receivables
Aircraft leased under terms which transfer substantially all of the benefits and risks of ownership to customers are accounted for as sales-type leases and are presented in Aircraft financing.

Revenue recognition
Aerospace programs– Revenues from the sale of regional aircraft and narrow-body business aircraft (*Learjet* Series) are recognized upon final delivery of products and presented in Manufacturing revenues.

Wide-body business aircraft (*Challenger* and *Global* Series) contracts are segmented between green aircraft (i.e. before exterior painting and installation of customer-selected interiors and optional avionics) and completion. Revenues are recognized based on green aircraft deliveries (when certain conditions are met), and upon final acceptance of interiors and optional avionics by customers. Revenues for green aircraft delivery and completion are presented in Manufacturing revenues.

Other– Interest income related to aircraft financing is recognized over the terms of the applicable loans or leases in a manner that produces a constant rate of return on the investment and is included in Financing income.

---

[37] *CICA Handbook*, Section 3065.54.

[38] *CICA Handbook*, Section 3065.54.

NOTE 2.
AIRCRAFT FINANCING

Aircraft financing was as follows as at January 31:

		2007					2006		
		WEIGHTED-AVERAGE					WEIGHTED-AVERAGE		
	TOTAL	MATURITY (IN MONTHS)	RATE[1] (%)	FIXED/ VARIABLE RATE[1]	TOTAL		MATURITY (IN MONTHS)	RATE[1] (%)	FIXED/ VARIABLE RATE[1]
Commercial aircraft									
Interim financing[2]									
Loans	$ 206	56	8.4	Variable	$ 435		79	7.1	Variable
Lease receivables	254	212	8.8	Variable	388		211	7.3	Variable
	460				823				
Long-term financing									
Loans	362	127	7.8	Fix./var.	278		107	6.2	Fix./var.
Lease receivables[3]	55	20	8.0	Fix./var.	104		21	6.0	Fix./var.
	417				382				
Business aircraft loans[4]	36	36	7.8	Fix./var.	58		41	5.7	Fix./var.
Total loans and lease receivables	913				1,263				
Allowance for credit losses	(111)				(84)				
	802				1,179				
Assets under operating leases	185				230				
Investment in financing structures	55				48				
	$1,042				$1,457				

1 Interest rates are before giving effect to the related hedging derivative financial instruments.
2 The commercial aircraft interim financing portfolio consists of bridge financing to customers until third-party permanent financing is put in place.
3 Includes $8 million of lease receivables related to consolidated VIEs as at January 31, 2007 ($67 million as at January 31, 2006).
4 This portfolio is being wound down.

Loans and lease receivables – Financing with three airlines represents approximately 45% of the total loans and lease receivables as at January 31, 2007 (three airlines represented 41% as at January 31, 2006). Loans and lease receivables are generally collateralized by the related assets. The value of the collateral is closely related to commercial airline industry performance and aircraft-specific factors (age, type-variant and seating capacity), as well as other factors. The value of the collateral also fluctuates with economic cycles.

Lease receivables consist of the following, before allowance for credit losses, as at January 31:

	2007	2006
Total minimum lease payments	$ 825	$ 978
Unearned income	(518)	(538)
Unguaranteed residual value	2	52
	$ 309	$ 492

Allowance for credit losses – Changes in the allowance for credit losses were as follows as at January 31:

	2007	2006
Balance at beginning of year	$ 84	$ 94
Provision for credit losses	29	(7)
Amounts charged off, net of recoveries	(2)	(4)
Effect of foreign currency exchange rate changes	–	1
Balance at end of year	$ 111	$ 84

Impaired loans and lease receivables amounted to $49 million as at January 31, 2007 ($237 million as at January 31, 2006).

NOTE 15.
FINANCING INCOME AND FINANCING EXPENSE (in part)

The Corporation's financing income and financing expense were as follows for fiscal years:

	2007	2006
Financing income		
Cash and cash equivalents	$ (71)	$ (55)
Loans and lease receivables – after effect of hedges	(65)	(93)
Dividends on preferred shares	(7)	–
Invested collateral	(4)	–
Other	(10)	(8)
	$(157)	$(156)

The capital leases are evidenced by the lease receivables included in the Aircraft Financing account on the balance sheet. Although the company does not classify its balance sheet into current and non-current categories, Bombardier provides information over and above the minimum required by Section 3065. The financing income from the loans and leases is reported in a note to the financial statements and additional information is provided in the notes about rates of return and major associated costs.

International

Comparison of Canadian and International GAAP

In lease accounting, as with many of the other topics covered in previous chapters, we find there are no substantial differences between the Canadian standards and those of the IFRS. Illustration 20-40 identifies the primary source of GAAP for each.

17 Objective
Compare current Canadian and international GAAP for leases.

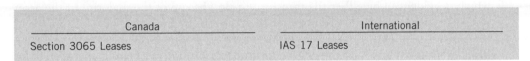

Canada	International
Section 3065 Leases	IAS 17 Leases

Illustration 20-40
Primary Sources of GAAP

In addition to the primary standards, there are numerous EICs in Canada and pronouncements of the IASB's Standing Interpretations Committee (SIC) and International Financial Reporting Interpretations Committee (IFRIC) dealing with lease-related issues.

Three examples where there are minor differences between IAS 17 and Section 3065 relate to classification and terminology, capitalization criteria, and disclosures.

Classification and terminology. Under the international standards, leases are classified only as either finance leases or operating leases. In Canada, a clear distinction is made between sales-type and direct financing sub-classifications within the capital lease category.

Classification criteria. The classification criteria to determine whether a transaction is a capital lease or an operating lease in IAS 17 are not as prescriptive as in the Canadian standard. There is no mention made of 75-percent or 90-percent hurdles, often referred to as "bright lines" in North America. The international lease standard is therefore more principles-based than Section 3065.

Disclosures. IAS 17 requires a lessor to disclose the gross investment in and unearned income from finance leases, and to report its operating lease assets on the balance sheet according to the nature of the assets. The Canadian standard requires information only about the net investment in a lessor's non-capital leases, and does not require the additional detail about its investment in operating lease assets.

As indicated, the lease accounting standards in Canada and internationally, as well as in the U.S., are basically converged. While convergence is expected to continue, it is not likely that it will be with the same lease standards that are now being used. The FASB and IASB have begun a joint project to fundamentally reconsider all aspects of lease accounting. The early indications are that a "right of use" approach will gather the most support: that is, the asset acquired by the lessee is the right to use the asset benefits, not the physical asset itself. With this approach, the current distinction between operating and capital leases would disappear. The first step is the publication of a discussion paper in 2008, after which new harmonized standards will be developed, perhaps by 2010. Canada will adopt the new standards at that time or in 2011 when the IFRS are fully adopted here in Canada.

Student
Website

Glossary
www.wiley.com/canada/kieso

KEY TERMS

amortization period, 1238

asset-based financing,
    1230

bargain purchase option,
    1236

bargain renewal option,
    1236

capital lease, 1235

capitalization criteria,
    1235

capitalization method,
    1235

direct financing leases,
    1246

effective interest
    method, 1238

executory contract, 1233

executory costs, 1237

gross investment in
    lease, 1237

guaranteed residual
    value, 1237

implicit interest rate, 1237

incremental borrowing
    rate, 1237

initial direct costs, 1262

lease, 1231

lease term, 1236

lessee, 1231

lessor, 1231

manufacturer's or dealer's
    profit, 1246

minimum lease
    payments, 1236

net investment in
    lease, 1247

non-capitalization
    method, 1235

off-balance sheet
    financing, 1233

operating lease, 1235

rental payments, 1231

residual value, 1237

Summary of Learning Objectives

**1 Explain the nature, economic substance, and advantages of
    lease transactions.**

A lease is a contract between two parties that gives the lessee the right to use property
that is owned by the lessor. In situations where the lessee obtains the use of the
majority of the economic benefits inherent in a leased asset, the transaction is similar
in substance to acquiring an asset. Therefore, the lessee recognizes the asset and associated liability and the lessor transfers the asset. The major advantages of leasing for
the lessee relate to the cost and flexibility of the financing, and protection against
obsolescence. For the lessor, the finance income is attractive.

**2 Identify and apply the criteria that are used to determine the type of lease
    for accounting purposes for a lessee.**

Where the risks and benefits of owning the leased asset are transferred to the lessee—
which is evidenced by either the transfer of title, the use of the majority of the asset
services inherent in the leased asset, or the recovery by the lessor of substantially all
of its investment in the leased asset plus a return on that investment—the lease is classified as a capital lease. If none of the three criteria is met, the lease is classified as an
operating lease.

3 Account for a lessee's basic capital lease.

As a capital lease, the asset is capitalized on the lessee's balance sheet and a liability is
recognized for the obligation owing to the lessor. The amount capitalized is the present value of the minimum lease payments (in effect the payments, excluding executory costs) that the lessee has agreed to take responsibility for. The asset is then
amortized in the same way as other capital assets owned by the lessee. Payments to
the lessor are divided into an interest portion and a principal payment, using the
effective interest method.

**4 Explain the accounting and identify the disclosure requirements for
    an operating lease for a lessee.**

A lessee recognizes the lease payments that are made as rent expense in the period
that is covered by the lease, usually based on the proportion of time. The lessee must
disclose the future minimum lease payments in total and for each of the next five
years, and the nature of any other commitments under such leases. Information about
any guarantees of residual values is required to be disclosed, and could result in a liability needing to be recognized on the balance sheet.

5 Contrast the operating and capitalization methods of accounting for leases.

Over the term of a lease, the total amount that is charged to expense is the same
whether the lease has been treated as a capital lease or as an operating lease. The difference relates to the timing of recognition for the expense (more is charged in the
early years for a capital lease), the type of expense that is charged (amortization and
interest expense for a capital lease versus rent expense for an operating lease), and
the recognition of an asset and liability on the balance sheet for a capital lease versus
non-recognition for an operating lease. Aside from any income tax differences, the
cash flows for a lease are the same whether it is classified as an operating or capital
lease. However, the cash flows are described differently on the cash flow statement.
All payments in an operating lease are classified as operating cash outflows, whereas
they are split between operating (for interest) and financing (for principal payments)
in a capital lease.

6 Calculate the lease payment that is required for the lessor to earn a specific return.

The lessor determines the investment that it wants to recover from a leased asset. If the lessor has acquired an asset for the purpose of leasing it, the lessor usually wants to recover the asset's cost. If the lessor participates in leases as a way of selling its product, it usually wants to recover the sales price. The lessor's investment in the cost or selling price can be recovered in part through the asset's estimated residual value if the asset will be returned to the lessor, or through a bargain purchase price that it expects the lessee to pay, if a bargain purchase is part of the lease agreement. In addition to these sources, the lessor recovers its investment through the lease payments. The periodic lease payment, therefore, is the annuity amount whose present value exactly equals the amount to be recovered through lease payments.

7 Identify and apply the criteria that are used to determine the type of lease for a lessor.

If a lease, in substance, transfers the risks and benefits of ownership of the leased asset to the lessee (decided in the same way as for the lessee) and revenue recognition criteria related to collectibility and ability to estimate any remaining unreimbursable costs are met, the lessor accounts for the lease as either a direct financing or a sales-type lease. The existence of a manufacturer's or dealer's profit on the amount to be recovered from the lessee is the difference between the sales-type lease and a direct financing lease, as the objective is only to generate finance income in the latter. If any one of the capitalization or revenue recognition criteria is not met, the lessor accounts for the lease as an operating lease.

8 Account for basic direct financing and sales-type leases by the lessor.

For both types of lease, the lessor removes the leased asset from its books and replaces it with its net investment in the lease. This is made up of two accounts: (1) the gross investment or lease payments receivable, which captures the dollars to be received through lease payments (excluding executory costs) plus estimated residual values or bargain purchase options, offset by (2) the portion of these amounts that represents unearned interest. The net investment, therefore, represents the present value of the lease payments and the residual value or bargain purchase option amounts. For a direct financing lease, this also represents the cost of the leased asset to the lessor. For a sales-type lease, this represents the selling price, and the lessor recognizes the sale and also the cost of goods sold. As the lease payments are received, the receivable is reduced. As time passes, the unearned interest is taken into income based on the implicit rate of return that applies to the net investment.

9 Explain the accounting and identify the disclosure requirements for an operating lease for a lessor.

The lessor records the lease payments received from the lessee as rental income in the period covered by the lease payment. Because the leased asset remains on the lessor's books, the lessor records amortization expense. Separate disclosure is required of the cost and accumulated amortization of property held for leasing purposes, and the amount of rental income earned

10 Determine the effect of residual values in a lessee's capital lease, and account for them.

When a lessee guarantees a residual value, it is obligated to return either the leased asset or cash, or a combination of both, in an amount that is equal to the guaranteed value. The lessee includes the guaranteed residual in the lease obligation and leased asset value. The asset is amortized to this value by the end of the lease term. If the

right-of-use approach, 1234

sales-type lease, 1246

unguaranteed residual value, 1237

1278 CHAPTER 20 Leases

residual is unguaranteed, the lessee takes no responsibility for the residual and it is excluded from the lessee's calculations.

11 Determine the effect of residual values for a lessor, and account for them.

From the lessor's viewpoint in a direct financing lease, it makes no difference whether or not the residual is guaranteed. The expected residual is included in the lessor's calculations as the best estimate of what will be returned at the end of the lease. In a sales-type lease, the gross investment, net investment, and unearned finance income are not affected by whether or not the residual is guaranteed. There is a minor difference when the residual is unguaranteed. The uncertainty that is associated with whether or not the full sales amount will be realized dictates that the sales revenue and cost of goods sold amounts that are recognized must be reduced by the unguaranteed residual's present value. There is no difference, however, in the amount of gross profit that is recognized on the sales-type lease.

12 Determine the effect of bargain purchase options for the lessee and lessor, and account for such options.

In a lease with a bargain purchase option, it is assumed that the lessee will exercise the option and that the title to the leased asset will be transferred to the lessee. The bargain purchase option's present value is therefore included in the amount capitalized as the asset and lease liability. The asset is amortized over its economic life. Whether the lease is a direct financing lease or a sales-type lease, the lessor includes the bargain purchase option in the gross investment and its present value in the net investment in the leased asset.

13 Explain how a lessor accounts for initial direct costs for each type of lease.

In all cases, the initial direct costs are matched with the revenue that is generated from the incurrence of the costs. For an operating lease, they are deferred and recognized over the same period during which the rental income is recognized; for a sales-type lease, they are deducted in the same period during which the gross profit on sale is recognized; and for a direct financing lease, they are amortized over the term of the lease.

14 Determine the current and long-term portions of a lease receivable and lease obligation.

In both cases, the current portion of the obligation or net investment is the principal that will be repaid within 12 months from the balance sheet date. The current portion also includes the amount of interest that has accrued up to the balance sheet date. The long-term portion of the obligation or net investment is the principal balance that will not be paid within 12 months of the balance sheet date.

15 Identify the lessee's disclosure requirements for capital leases.

Lessees must disclose information similar to the required disclosures for capital assets and long-term debt in general. In addition, the total future minimum lease payments and those required in each of the next five years must be reported, along with a separate deduction for executory and interest costs so that the total owing can be reconciled to the obligation that is reported on the balance sheet.

16 Identify the lessor's disclosure requirements for non-operating leases.

For direct financing and sales-type leases, the lessor must disclose its net investment in the leases, with the investment segregated according to current and non-current asset categories, and how the investment was calculated for income recognition. The amount of finance income that has been recognized must also be disclosed.

17 Compare current Canadian and international GAAP for leases.

Current GAAP in Canada is substantially harmonized with the international requirements.

Appendix 20A

OTHER LEASE ISSUES

Sale and Leaseback Transactions

Sale-leaseback describes a transaction in which the property owner (the seller-lessee) sells the property to another party (the purchaser-lessor) and immediately leases it back from the new owner. The property generally continues to be used without any interruption. This type of transaction is fairly common.[39]

For example, a company buys land, constructs a building to its specifications, sells the property to an investor, and then immediately leases it back. From the seller's viewpoint, the advantage of a sale and leaseback usually has to do with financing. If an equipment purchase has already been financed, and rates have subsequently decreased, a sale-leaseback can allow the seller to refinance the purchase at lower rates. Alternatively, a sale-leaseback can also provide additional working capital when liquidity is tight.

To the extent that, after the sale, the seller-lessee continues to use the asset it has sold, **the sale-leaseback is really a form of financing**, and therefore no gain or loss is recognized on the transaction. In substance, the seller-lessee is simply borrowing funds. On the other hand, if the seller-lessee gives up the right to use the asset that was sold, the transaction is clearly a sale, and gain or loss recognition is appropriate. Trying to determine when the lessee has given up the use of the asset is sometimes difficult, however, and complex rules have been formulated to identify this situation.[40] The profession's basic position in this area is that the lease should be accounted for as a capital, direct financing, or operating lease, as appropriate, by the seller-lessee and by the purchaser-lessor.[41]

18 **Objective**
Describe and apply the lessee's accounting for sale-leaseback transactions.

Underlying Concept

A sale-leaseback may be similar in substance to the parking of inventories discussed in Chapter 8. As the ultimate economic benefits remain under the control of the "seller," the definition of an asset is satisfied.

Lessee Accounting

If the lease meets one of the three criteria for being classified as a capital lease, **the seller-lessee accounts for the transaction as a sale, and the lease as a capital lease**. Any profit or loss experienced by the seller-lessee from the sale of the assets that are leased back under a capital lease **are deferred and amortized over the lease term** (or the economic life if criterion 1 is satisfied) on the same basis as the amortization of the leased assets. If the leased asset is land only, the amortization is on a straight-line basis over the lease term.[42] For example, if Lessee Inc. sells equipment having a book value of $580,000 and a

---

[39] *Financial Reporting in Canada—2006* (CICA, 2006) reports that out of 200 companies surveyed, 6 companies in 2005, 10 companies in 2004, 13 in 2003, and 9 in 2002 disclosed information about one or more sale and leaseback transactions.

[40] Guidance is provided in *EIC-25* (CICA, April 22, 1991) for situations where the leaseback relates to only a portion of the property sold by the seller-lessee. A discussion of the issues related to these transactions is beyond the scope of this textbook.

[41] *CICA Handbook*, Section 3065.66.

[42] *CICA Handbook*, Section 3065.68

fair value of $623,110 to Lessor Inc. for $623,110 and leases the equipment back for $50,000 a year for 20 years, the profit of $43,110 (i.e., $623,110 − $580,000) is deferred and amortized over the 20-year period using the same rate that is used to amortize the $623,110 leased asset's cost. The $43,110 is credited originally to a Deferred Profit on Sale-Leaseback account.

If none of the capital lease criteria are satisfied, **the seller-lessee accounts for the transaction as a sale, and the lease as an operating lease**. Under an operating lease, the profit or loss on sale is deferred and amortized in proportion to the rental payments over the period of time that it is expected the lessee will use the assets.[43]

The accounting standard requires, however, that when there is a legitimate loss on the sale of the asset—that is, when the asset's **fair value is less than its carrying amount**— the loss be recognized immediately. For example, if Lessee Inc. sells equipment that has a book value of $650,000 and a fair value of $623,110, the difference of $26,890 is charged directly to a loss account.[44]

Lessor Accounting

If the lease meets one of the criteria in Group I and both the criteria in Group II (see Illustration 20-11), **the purchaser-lessor records the transaction as a purchase and a direct financing lease**. If the lease does not meet the criteria, the purchaser-lessor records the transaction as a purchase and an operating lease. The criteria for a sales-type lease would not be met in a sale-leaseback transaction.

Sale-Leaseback Illustration

To illustrate the accounting treatment for a sale-leaseback transaction, assume that on January 1, 2008, Lessee Inc. sells a used Boeing 767, having a cost of $85.5 million and a carrying amount on Lessee's books of $75.5 million, to Lessor Inc. for $80 million, and then immediately leases the aircraft back under the following conditions:

1. The term of the non-cancellable lease is 15 years, and the agreement requires equal annual rental payments of $10,487,443, beginning January 1, 2008.

2. The aircraft has a fair value of $80 million on January 1, 2008, and an estimated economic life of 15 years.

3. Lessee Inc. pays all executory costs.

4. Lessee Inc. amortizes similar aircraft that it owns on a straight-line basis over 15 years.

5. The annual payments assure the lessor a 12% return, which is the same as Lessee's incremental borrowing rate.

6. The present value of the minimum lease payments is $80 million, or $10,487,443 × 7.62817 (Table A-5: $i = 12$, $n = 15$).

This lease is a capital lease to Lessee Inc. because the lease term exceeds 75 percent of the aircraft's estimated remaining life or because the minimum lease payments' present

---

[43] *CICA Handbook*, Section 3065.69.

[44] *CICA Handbook*, Section 3065.70. There can be two types of losses in sale-leaseback arrangements. One is a real economic loss that results when the asset's carrying amount is higher than its fair value. In this case, the loss should be recognized. An artificial loss results when the sale price is below the asset's carrying amount but the fair value is above the carrying amount. In this case, the loss is more in the form of prepaid rent and should be deferred and amortized in the future.

value exceeds 90 percent of the aircraft's fair value. Assuming that collectibility of the lease payments is reasonably assured and that there are no important uncertainties about unreimbursable costs yet to be incurred by the lessor, Lessor Inc. classifies this lease as a direct financing lease.

Illustration 20A-1 shows the journal entries to record the transactions related to this lease for both Lessee Inc. and Lessor Inc. for the first year.

Illustration 20A-1

Comparative Entries for Sale-Leaseback for Lessee and Lessor

Lessee Inc.			Lessor Inc.		
Sale of Aircraft by Lessee Inc. to Lessor Inc., January 1, 2008, and leaseback transaction:					
Cash	80,000,000		Aircraft	80,000,000	
Accumulated Amortization	10,000,000		Cash		80,000,000
Aircraft		85,500,000			
Deferred Profit on					
Sale-Leaseback		4,500,000			
Aircraft under Capital Leases	80,000,000		Lease Payments Receivable	157,311,645	
Obligations under Capital Leases		80,000,000	Aircraft		80,000,000
			Unearned Interest Income		77,311,645
			($10,487,443 × 15 = $157,311,645)		
First Lease Payment, January 1, 2008:					
Obligations under			Cash	10,487,443	
Capital Leases	10,487,443		Lease Payments		
Cash		10,487,443	Receivable		10,487,443
Incurrence and Payment of Executory Costs by Lessee Inc. throughout 2008:					
Insurance, Maintenance,				(No entry)	
Taxes, etc., Expense	XXX				
Cash or Accounts Payable		XXX			
Amortization Expense for 2008 on the Aircraft, December 31, 2008:					
Amortization Expense	5,333,333			(No entry)	
Accumulated Amortization—					
Leased Aircraft		5,333,333			
($80,000,000 ÷ 15)					
Amortization of Deferred Profit on Sale-Leaseback by Lessee Inc., December 31, 2008:					
Deferred Profit on				(No entry)	
Sale-Leaseback	300,000				
Amortization Expense*		300,000			
($4,500,000 ÷ 15)					
*A case might be made for crediting a gain account instead of Amortization Expense.					
Interest for 2008, December 31, 2008:					
Interest Expense	8,341,507[a]		Unearned Interest Income	8,341,507	
Interest Payable		8,341,507	Interest Income		8,341,507[a]

[a] **Partial Lease Amortization Schedule:**

Date	Annual Rental Payment	Interest 12%	Reduction of Balance	Balance
1/1/08				$80,000,000
1/1/08	$10,487,443	$ –0–	$10,487,443	69,512,557
1/1/09	10,487,443	8,341,507	2,145,936	67,366,621

Looking ahead to expected changes in the lease accounting standards, it is likely that the standards on sale-leasebacks will also change. One area of controversy is the reporting of a deferred gain as a liability when there is no obligation to a creditor or other party. As recent AcSB decisions support an asset-liability approach to income measurement, deferred charges and deferred credits that do not meet the definitions of assets and liabilities, respectively, are not likely to remain. Also, the international lease standard considers an issue that the current Canadian standard does not. IAS 17 recognizes that if the lease-back is an operating lease, the sale has actually transferred the risks and benefits of ownership to the purchaser. The international standard therefore allows a gain to be recognized, but only if the transaction takes place at fair value.

Although there are no specific disclosure requirements for a sale-leaseback transaction other than the ones that are required for leases in general, Illustration 20A-2 provides an example of how British Columbia–based **Helijet International Inc.** reported its sale-leaseback transaction.

Illustration 20A-2

*Example of
Sale-Leaseback
Disclosure*

HELIJET INTERNATIONAL INC.
NOTES TO CONSOLIDATED FINANCIAL STATEMENTS
AUGUST 31, 2006 AND 2005

4. Deferred Gain on Sale and Leaseback

Effective April, 2004, and August, 2006, the Company completed sale and leaseback transactions involving seven helicopters. The proceeds received under the agreements were $1,867,344 (2005 – $1,667,086) in excess of the net book values of the helicopters (the "deferred gain"). The deferred gain is being amortized over the terms of the leases as a reduction of the related lease expense.

The transactions are represented by:

	2006	2005
Original deferred gain	$1,867,344	$1,667,086
Less, cumulative amount amortized as a reduction of helicopter lease expense	794,036	481,234
	$1,073,308	$1,185,852
Less, current portion	388,097	333,417
Non-current portion	$ 685,211	$ 852,435

Included in deferred gain on sale leaseback is $224,512 arising on the sale of two airraft (see Note 5) to DAS Leasing Inc., a related company.

Real Estate Leases

Objective 19

Explain the classification and accounting treatment for leases that involve land as well as buildings and equipment.

When a capital lease involves land, and ownership of the land will not be transferred to the lessee, capitalizing the land on the lessee's balance sheet would result in no amortization or other similar expense being recognized over the term of the lease. Then, a loss equal to the capitalized value of the land would have to be recognized when the land reverts to the lessor. This is why there is **special guidance for leases that involve land**.

Land

If land is the only leased asset, the **lessee** accounts for the lease as a capital lease only if criterion 1 is met; that is, if the lease transfers ownership of the property or contains a bargain purchase option. Otherwise, it is accounted for as an operating lease. The **lessor** accounts for a land lease either as a sales-type or direct financing lease, whichever is appropriate, as long as the lease transfers ownership or contains a bargain purchase option and meets both the collectibility and future cost uncertainty tests—otherwise the operating method is used.

Land and Building

If both land and a building are leased, and the lease transfers ownership or contains a bargain purchase option, the **lessee** capitalizes the land and the building separately. The present value of the minimum lease payments is allocated between land and building in proportion to their fair values at the beginning of the lease. The **lessor** accounts for the leased assets as a single unit, and as a sales-type, direct financing, or operating lease, as appropriate.

When a lease covering both land and a building does not transfer ownership or contain a bargain purchase option, the accounting treatment depends on the relative proportions of land and building. **If the fair value of the land is minor** compared to the total value of the leased property, both the lessee and lessor consider the land and the building as a single unit. **Otherwise, the land and building are considered separately** by both the lessee and lessor. If one of criteria 2 and 3 is met, the lessee accounts for the building as a capital lease and the land as an operating lease. If none of the criteria are met, both are accounted for as operating leases. The lessor accounts for the building as a sales-type or direct financing lease as appropriate, and treats the land element separately as an operating lease.

Real Estate and Equipment

If a lease involves both real estate and equipment, the portion of the lease payments that applies to the equipment is estimated by whatever method is appropriate and reasonable. The equipment is then treated separately for purposes of applying the criteria and accounted for separately according to its classification by both the lessee and lessor.

Summary of Learning Objectives for Appendix 20A

Student Website

Glossary

www.wiley.com/canada/kieso

KEY TERM

Sale-leaseback, 1279

18 Describe and apply the lessee's accounting for sale-leaseback transactions.

A sale and leaseback is accounted for by the lessee as if the two transactions are related. Any gain or loss, with the exception of an economic loss, must be deferred by the lessee and recognized in income over the lease term. If it is an operating lease, the seller-lessee takes the deferred gain or loss into income in proportion to the rental payments made; if it is a capital lease, the deferred gain or loss is taken into income over the same period and basis as the amortization of the leased asset.

19 Explain the classification and accounting treatment for leases that involve land as well as buildings and equipment.

Because the capitalization of land by the lessee in a capital lease that does not transfer title results in an unwanted and unintended effect on the lessee's financial statements, the portion of such leases that relates to land is accounted for as an operating lease. If the relative value of the land is minor, however, the minimum lease payments are fully capitalized as building and/or equipment.

Brief Exercises

Note: All assignment material with an asterisk (*) relates to the appendix to the chapter.

(LO 2)   BE20-1   WarpSpeed Corporation recently signed a lease for equipment from Photon Inc. The lease term is five years and requires equal rental payments of $30,000 at the beginning of each year. The equipment has a fair value at the lease's inception of $138,000, an estimated useful life of eight years, and no residual value. WarpSpeed pays all executory costs directly to third parties. Photon set the annual rental to earn a rate of return of 10%, and this fact is known to WarpSpeed. The lease does not transfer title or contain a bargain purchase option. How should WarpSpeed classify this lease?

(LO 3)   BE20-2   Waterworld Corporation recently signed a lease for equipment from Costner Ltd. The lease term is four years and requires equal rental payments of $48,755 at the beginning of each year. The equipment has a fair value at the lease's inception of $170,000, an estimated useful life of four years, and no residual value. Waterworld pays all executory costs directly to third parties. The appropriate interest rate is 10%. Prepare Waterworld's journal entries at the inception of the lease.

(LO 6)   BE20-3   Use the information for Waterworld and Costner from BE20-2. Explain, using numbers, how Costner determined the amount of the lease payment of $48,755.

(LO 3)   BE20-4   Beckner Corporation recorded a capital lease at $250,000 on June 1, 2008. The interest rate is 12%. Beckner Corporation made the first lease payment of $44,934 on June 1, 2008. The lease requires a total of eight annual payments. The equipment has a useful life of eight years with no residual value. Prepare Beckner Corporation's December 31, 2008, adjusting entries.

(LO 3)   BE20-5   Use the information for Beckner Corporation from BE20-4. Assume that at December 31, 2008, Beckner made an adjusting entry to accrue interest expense of $14,355 on the lease. Prepare Beckner's June 1, 2009, journal entry to record the second lease payment of $44,934. Assume that no reversing entries are made.

(LO 4)   BE20-6   Jana Corporation enters into a lease with Sharda Inc, a lessor, on January 1, 2008, that does not transfer ownership or contain a bargain purchase option. It covers three years of the equipment's eight-year useful life, and the present value of the minimum lease payments is less than 90% of the fair market value of the equipment. Prepare Jana's journal entry to record its January 1, 2008, annual lease payment of $37,500.

(LO 9)   BE20-7   Use the information for Jana Corporation and Sharda Inc. from BE20-6. Assume that Sharda, the lessor, has a June 30 year end. Prepare Sharda's entry on January 1, 2008, and any adjusting entry needed on June 30, 2008.

(LO 7, 8)   BE20-8   Fadhil Corporation leased equipment that was carried at a cost of $180,000 to Swander Inc., the lessee. The term of the lease is six years, beginning January 1, 2008, with equal rental payments of $36,813 at the beginning of each year. Swander pays all executory costs directly to third parties. The equipment's fair value at the lease's inception is $180,000. The equipment has a useful life of six years with no residual value. The lease has an implicit interest rate of 9%, no bargain purchase option, and no transfer of title. Collectibility is reasonably assured, with no additional costs to be incurred by Fadhil. Prepare Fadhil Corporation's January 1, 2008, journal entries at the inception of the lease.

(LO 8)   BE20-9   Use the information for Fadhil Corporation from BE20-8. Assume that the direct financing lease was recorded at a present value of $180,000. Prepare Fadhil's December 31, 2008, entry to record interest.

(LO 7, 8)   BE20-10   Use the information for Fadhil Corporation from BE20-8. Assume that instead of costing Fadhil $180,000, the equipment was manufactured by Fadhil at a cost of $142,000 and the equipment's regular selling price is $180,000. Prepare Fadhil Corporation's January 1, 2008, journal entries at the inception of the lease, and the entry at December 31, 2008, to record interest.

(LO 10)   BE20-11   Estey Corporation enters into a six-year lease of machinery on September 13, 2008, that requires six annual payments of $30,000 each, beginning September 13, 2008. In addition, Estey guarantees the lessor a residual value of $20,000 at lease end. The machinery has a useful life of six years. Prepare Estey's September 13, 2008, journal entries, assuming an interest rate of 10%.

(LO 10)   BE20-12   Use the information for Estey Corporation from BE20-11. Assume that a residual value of $20,000 is expected at the end of the lease, but that Estey does not guarantee the residual value. Prepare Estey's September 13, 2008, journal entries, assuming an interest rate of 10%.

(LO 11)   BE20-13   Use the information for Estey Corporation from BE20-11. Assume that for Moxey Corporation, the lessor, collectibility is reasonably predictable, there are no important uncertainties concerning costs, and the machinery's carrying amount is $155,013. Prepare Moxey's September 13, 2008, journal entries.

BE20-14   Arbeau Corporation manufactures replicators. On January 29, 2008, it leased to Barnes Limited a replicator **(LO 11)** that cost $130,000 to manufacture and usually sells for $205,000. The lease agreement covers the replicator's five-year useful life and requires five equal annual rentals of $47,965 each, beginning January 29, 2008. The equipment reverts to Arbeau at the end of the lease, at which time it is expected that the replicator will have a residual value of $20,000, which has been guaranteed by Barnes, the lessee. An interest rate of 12% is implicit in the lease agreement. Collectibility of the rentals is reasonably assured, and there are no important uncertainties concerning costs. Prepare Arbeau's January 29, 2008, journal entries.

BE20-15   Use the information for Arbeau Corporation from BE20-14. Assume instead that the residual value is not **(LO 11)** guaranteed. Prepare Arbeau's January 29, 2008, journal entries.

*BE20-16   On January 1, 2008, Ryan Animation sold a truck to Coyne Finance for $65,000 and immediately leased it **(LO 18)** back. The truck was carried on Ryan Animation's books at $53,000, net of $16,000 of accumulated amortization. The term of the lease is five years, and title transfers to Ryan Animation at lease end. The lease requires five equal rental payments of $17,147, with each payment made at year end. The appropriate rate of interest is 10%, and the truck has a useful life of five years with no salvage value. Prepare Ryan Animation's 2008 journal entries.

*BE20-17   Lessee Corp. agreed to lease property from Lessor Corp. effective January 1, 2008, for an annual payment of **(LO 19)** $23,576.90, beginning January 1, 2008. The property is made up of land with a fair value of $100,000 and a two-storey office building with a fair value of $150,000 and a useful life of 20 years. The implicit interest rate is 8%, the lease term is 20 years, and title to the property is transferred to Lessee at the end of the lease term. Prepare the required entries made by Lessee Corp. on January 1, 2008, and at its year end of December 31, 2008.

*BE20-18   Use the information provided in BE20-17 about Lessee Corp. Assume that title to the property will not be **(LO 19)** transferred to Lessee by the end of the lease term and that there is also no bargain purchase option, but that the lease does meet other criteria to qualify as a capital lease. Prepare the required entries made by Lessee Corp. on January 1, 2008, and at its year end of December 31, 2008.

Exercises

E20-1   **(Type of Lease and Amortization Schedule)** Maroscia Leasing Corporation leases a new machine that has a **(LO 2, 6)** cost and fair value of $95,000 to Sharrer Corporation on a three-year, non-cancellable contract. Sharrer Corporation agrees to assume all risks of normal ownership, including such costs as insurance, taxes, and maintenance. The machine has a three-year useful life and no residual value. The lease was signed on January 1, 2008, and Maroscia Leasing Corporation expects to earn a 9% return on its investment. The annual rentals are payable on each December 31, beginning December 31, 2008.

Instructions

(a) Discuss the nature of the lease arrangement and the accounting method that each party to the lease should apply.

(b) Use a computer spreadsheet to prepare an amortization schedule that would be suitable for both the lessor and the lessee and that covers all the years involved.

E20-2   **(Lessee Entries and Capital Lease with Unguaranteed Residual Value)** On January 1, 2008, Burke **(LO 2,** Corporation signed a five-year, non-cancellable lease for a machine. The terms of the lease called for Burke to make **3, 10)** annual payments of $13,668 at the beginning of each year, starting January 1, 2008. The machine has an estimated useful life of six years and a $9,000 unguaranteed residual value. The machine reverts back to the lessor at the end of the lease term. Burke uses the straight-line method of amortization for all of its plant assets. Burke's incremental borrowing rate is 10%, and the lessor's implicit rate is unknown.

Instructions

(a) Explain why this is a capital lease to Burke.

(b) Using time value of money tables, a financial calculator, or computer spreadsheet functions, calculate the present value of the minimum lease payments for the lessee.

(c) Prepare all necessary journal entries for Burke for this lease through January 1, 2009.

E20-3   **(Lessee Entries, Operating Lease, Comparison)** Refer to the data and other information provided in E20-2. **(LO 4,** Assume that the machine has an estimated economic life of seven years and that its fair value on January 1, 2008, is **5, 14)** $50,000.

Instructions

(a) Explain why this lease is now considered an operating lease.

(b) Prepare all necessary journal entries for Burke Corporation for this lease through January 1, 2009.

(c) Identify what accounts will appear on Burke's December 31, 2008, statement of financial position and income statement relative to this lease.

(d) How would Burke's December 31, 2008, statement of financial position and income statement differ from your answer to (c) if the lease were a capital lease as described in E20-2?

(e) What major financial statement ratios would be different if Burke accounted for this lease as an operating lease rather than as a capital lease? Explain.

(LO 2, 3, 14, 15) **E20-4** **(Lessee Calculations and Entries; Capital Lease; Disclosure)** On December 31, 2008, Nishida Ltd. entered into an eight-year lease agreement for a conveyor machine. Annual lease payments are $28,500 at the beginning of each lease year, which ends December 31, and Nishida made the first payment on January 1, 2009. At the end of the lease, the machine will revert to the lessor. However, conveyor machines are only expected to last for eight years and have no residual value. At the time of the lease agreement, conveyor machines could be purchased for approximately $166,000 cash. Equivalent financing for the machine could have been obtained from Nishida's bank at 10.5%. Nishida's fiscal year coincides with the calendar year and Nishida uses straight-line amortization for its conveyor machines.

Instructions

(a) Calculate the present value of the minimum lease payments using a financial calculator or worksheet functions.

(b) Explain why this is a capital lease to Nishida Ltd. Document your calculations in arriving at your explanation.

(c) Prepare an amortization schedule for the term of the lease to be used by Nishida Ltd. Use a computer spreadsheet.

(d) Prepare the journal entries on Nishida Ltd.'s books to reflect the signing of the lease agreement and to record the payments and expenses related to this lease for the years 2009 and 2010 as well as any adjusting journal entries at its fiscal year ends of December 31, 2009 and 2010.

(e) Prepare a partial comparative statement of financial position at December 31, 2010 and 2009, for all of the accounts related to this lease for Nishida Ltd. Be specific about the classifications that should be used.

(f) Provide Nishida Ltd.'s required note disclosure concerning the lease for the fiscal year ending December 31, 2010.

(g) What is the significance of the difference between the amount of the present value of the minimum lease payments calculated in part (a) and the approximate selling price of the machine of $166,000?

(LO 2, 3, 10) **E20-5** **(Lessee Calculations and Entries; Capital Lease with Guaranteed Residual Value)** Delaney Corporation leases an automobile with a fair value of $8,725 from Simon Motors, Inc. on the following lease terms:

1. It is a non-cancellable term of 50 months.

2. The rental is $200 per month at the end of each month (the present value at 1% per month is $7,840).

3. The estimated residual value after 50 months is $1,180 (the present value at 1% per month is $715). Delaney Corporation guarantees the residual value of $1,180.

4. The estimated economic life of the automobile is 60 months.

5. Delaney Corporation's incremental borrowing rate is 12% a year (1% a month). Simon's implicit rate is unknown.

Instructions

(a) Explain why this is a capital lease to Delaney Corporation.

(b) What is the present value of the minimum lease payments for Delaney?

(c) Record the lease on Delaney Corporation's books at the date of inception.

(d) Record the first month's amortization on Delaney Corporation's books (assume straight-line).

(e) Record the first month's lease payment.

(LO 2, 3, 10, 15) **E20-6** **(Lessee Entries; Capital Lease with Executory Costs and Unguaranteed Residual Value)** On January 1, 2008, Lahey Paper Corp. signs a 10-year, non-cancellable lease agreement to lease a storage building from Sheffield Storage Corporation. The following information concerns the lease agreement:

1. The agreement requires equal rental payments of $73,580, beginning on January 1, 2008.

2. The building's fair value on January 1, 2008, is $450,000.

3. The building has an estimated economic life of 12 years, with an unguaranteed residual value of $12,000. Lahey Paper Co. amortizes similar buildings on the straight-line method.

4. The lease is non-renewable. At the termination of the lease, the building reverts to the lessor.

5. Lahey Paper's incremental borrowing rate is 12% per year. The lessor's implicit rate is not known by Lahey Paper Co.

6. The yearly rental payment includes $2,470.29 of executory costs related to taxes on the property.

Instructions

(a) Prepare an amortization schedule for the term of the lease to be used by Lahey. Use a computer spreadsheet.

(b) Prepare the journal entries on Lahey Paper Corp.'s books to reflect the signing of the lease agreement and to record the payments and expenses related to this lease for the years 2008 and 2009 as well as any adjusting journal entries at its fiscal year ends of December 31, 2008 and 2009.

(c) Prepare Lahey Paper Corp.'s required note disclosure on the lease for the fiscal year ending December 31, 2009.

E20-7   (Lessee Entries; Capital Lease with Executory Costs and Unguaranteed Residual Value—Lease and Fiscal Years Differ)   **(LO 2, 3, 10)**

Instructions

Refer to the data and other information provided in E20-6, but now assume that Lahey Paper's fiscal year end is May 31. Prepare the journal entries on Lahey Paper Corp.'s books to reflect the lease signing and to record payments and expenses related to this lease for the calendar years 2008 and 2009. Lahey Paper does not prepare reversing entries.

E20-8   (Amortization Schedule and Journal Entries for Lessee) Jodrey Leasing Corporation signs an agreement on January 1, 2008, to lease equipment to LeBlanc Limited. The following information relates to the agreement.   **(LO 2, 3, 6, 15)**

1. The term of the non-cancellable lease is five years, with no renewal option. The equipment has an estimated economic life of six years.

2. The asset's fair value at January 1, 2008, is $80,000.

3. The asset will revert to the lessor at the end of the lease term, at which time the asset is expected to have a residual value of $7,000, which is not guaranteed.

4. LeBlanc Limited assumes direct responsibility for all executory costs, which include the following annual amounts: $900 to Rocky Mountain Insurance Corporation for insurance and $1,600 to Laclede County for property taxes.

5. The agreement requires equal annual rental payments of $18,142.95 to the lessor, beginning on January 1, 2008.

6. The lessee's incremental borrowing rate is 12%. The lessor's implicit rate is 10% and is known to the lessee.

7. LeBlanc Limited uses the straight-line amortization method for all equipment.

8. LeBlanc uses reversing entries when appropriate.

Instructions

Answer the following, rounding all numbers to the nearest cent.

(a) Use a computer spreadsheet to prepare an amortization schedule for Leblanc Limited for the lease term.

(b) Prepare all of Leblanc's journal entries for 2008 and 2009 to record the lease agreement, the lease payments, and all expenses related to this lease. Assume that the lessee's annual accounting period ends on December 31.

(c) Provide the required note disclosure for Leblanc Limited concerning the lease for the fiscal year ending December 31, 2009.

E20-9   (Accounting for an Operating Lease) On January 1, 2008, Novac Corp. leased a building to Wisen Inc. The relevant information on the lease is as follows: **(LO 4, 9)**

1. The lease arrangement is for 10 years.

2. The leased building cost $4.5 million and was purchased by Novac for cash on January 1, 2008.

3. The building is amortized on a straight-line basis. Its estimated economic life is 50 years.

4. Lease payments are $325,000 per year and are made at the end of the year.

5. Property tax expense of $87,000 and insurance expense of $11,000 on the building were incurred by Novac in the first year. Payment on these two items was made at the end of the year.

6. Both the lessor and the lessee have their fiscal years on a calendar-year basis.

Instructions

(a) Prepare the journal entries made by Novac Corp. in 2008.

(b) Prepare the journal entries made by Wisen Inc. in 2008.

(c) If Novac paid $30,000 to a real estate broker on January 1, 2008, as a fee for finding the lessee, how much should Novac Corp. report as an expense for this fee item in 2008?

(LO 4, 9) E20-10 (Accounting and Disclosure for an Operating Lease—Lessee and Lessor) On February 1, 2008, a machine was purchased for $1.15 million by Pomeroy Corp. The machine is expected to have an eight-year life with no salvage value and is to be amortized on a straight-line basis. The machine was leased to St. Leger Inc. on February 1, 2008, at an annual rental of $290,000. Other relevant information is as follows:

1. The lease term is three years.

2. Pomeroy Corp. incurred maintenance and other executory costs of $60,000 in 2008 related to this lease.

3. The machine could have been sold by Pomeroy Corp. for $1.2 million instead of leasing it.

4. St. Leger is required to pay a rent security deposit of $35,000 and to prepay the last month's rent of $17,500 on signing the lease.

Instructions

(a) How much should Pomeroy Corp. report as income before income tax on this lease for 2008?

(b) What amount should St. Leger Inc. report for rent expense for 2008 on this lease?

(c) What financial statement disclosures relative to this lease are required for each company's December 31, 2008, year end?

(LO 4, 9, 13) E20-11 (Operating Lease for Lessee and Lessor with Initial Costs) On February 20, 2008, Sigouin Inc. purchased a machine for $1.5 million for the purpose of leasing it. The machine is expected to have a 10-year life with no residual value, and will be amortized on the straight-line basis. The machine was leased to Roudy Corporation on March 1, 2008, for a four-year period at a monthly rental of $24,500. There is no provision for the renewal of the lease or purchase of the machine by the lessee at the expiration of the lease term. Sigouin paid $36,000 to a third party for commissions associated with negotiating the lease in February 2008.

Instructions

(a) What expense should Roudy Corporation record based on the above facts for the year ended December 31, 2008? Show supporting calculations in good form.

(b) What income or loss before income taxes should Sigouin record based on the above facts for the year ended December 31, 2008?

(AICPA adapted)

(LO 5) E20-12 (Operating Lease vs. Capital Lease) You are auditing the December 31, 2008, financial statements of Shamess, Inc., a manufacturer of novelties and party favours. During your inspection of the company garage, you discovered that a 2007 Shirk automobile is parked in the company garage but is not listed in the equipment subsidiary ledger. You ask the plant manager about the vehicle, and she tells you that the company did not list the automobile because the company was only leasing it. The lease agreement was entered into on January 1, 2008, with Yablon New and Used Cars. You decide to review the lease agreement to ensure that the lease should be given operating lease treatment, and you discover the following lease terms:

1. It is a non-cancellable term of 50 months.

2. The rental is $180 per month at the end of each month (the present value at 1% per month is $7,055).

3. The estimated residual value after 50 months is $1,100 (the present value at 1% per month is $699). Shamess guarantees the residual value of $1,100.

4. The estimated economic life of the automobile is 60 months.

5. Shamess's incremental borrowing rate is 12% per year (1% per month).

Instructions

You are a senior auditor writing a memo to your supervisor, the audit partner in charge of this audit, to discuss the situation. Be sure to include (a) why you inspected the lease agreement, (b) what you determined about the lease, and (c) how you advised your client to account for this lease. Explain every journal entry that you believe is necessary to record this lease properly on the client's books.

E20-13 **(Lease Payment Calculation and Lessee-Lessor Entries—Capital/Sales-Type Lease)** On January 1, 2008, Garcin Corporation leased equipment to Flynn Corporation. The following information pertains to this lease: **(LO 2, 6, 7, 8)**

1. The term of the non-cancellable lease is six years, with no renewal option. The equipment reverts to the lessor at the termination of the lease, at which time it is expected to have a residual value (not guaranteed) of $10,000. Flynn Corporation amortizes all its equipment on a straight-line basis.

2. Equal rental payments are due on January 1 of each year, beginning in 2008.

3. The equipment's fair value on January 1, 2008, is $150,000 and its cost to Garcin is $120,000.

4. The equipment has an economic life of eight years.

5. Garcin set the annual rental to ensure an 11% rate of return. Flynn's incremental borrowing rate is 12% and the lessor's implicit rate is unknown to the lessee.

6. Collectibility of lease payments is reasonably predictable and there are no important uncertainties about any costs that have not yet been incurred by the lessor.

Instructions

(a) Explain clearly why this lease is a capital lease to Flynn and a sales-type lease to Garcin.

(b) Using time value of money tables, a financial calculator, or computer spreadsheet functions, calculate the amount of the annual rental payment.

(c) Prepare all necessary journal entries for Flynn for 2008.

(d) Prepare all necessary journal entries for Garcin for 2008.

E20-14 **(Lessor Entries, Direct Financing Lease with Option to Purchase, Lessee Capitalizable Amount)** Castle Leasing Corporation signs a lease agreement on January 1, 2008, to lease electronic equipment to Jan Wai Corporation. The term of the non-cancellable lease is two years and payments are required at the end of each year. The following information relates to this agreement: **(LO 3, 6, 8, 11)**

1. Jan Wai Corporation has the option to purchase the equipment for $16,000 upon the termination of the lease.

2. The equipment has a cost and fair value of $160,000 to Castle Leasing Corporation. The useful economic life is two years, with a residual value of $16,000.

3. Jan Wai Corporation is required to pay $5,000 each year to the lessor for executory costs.

4. Castle Leasing Corporation wants to earn a return of 10% on its investment.

5. Collectibility of the payments is reasonably predictable, and there are no important uncertainties surrounding the costs that have not yet been incurred by the lessor.

Instructions

(a) Using time value of money tables, a financial calculator, or computer spreadsheet functions, calculate the lease payment that Castle would require from Jan Wai Corporation.

(b) Prepare the journal entries on Castle Leasing's books to reflect the payments received under the lease and to recognize income for the years 2008 and 2009.

(c) Assuming that Jan Wai Corporation exercises its option to purchase the equipment on December 31, 2009, prepare the journal entry to reflect the sale on Castle's books.

(d) What amount would Jan Wai Corporation capitalize and recognize as a liability on signing the lease? Explain.

E20-15 **(Rental Amount Calculation, Lessor Entries, Disclosure—Financing Lease with Unguaranteed Residual Value)** On January 1, 2008, Vick Leasing Inc., a lessor, signed an agreement with Sanders Corporation, a lessee, for the use of a compression system. The system cost $415,000 and was purchased from Manufacturing Solutions Ltd. specifically for Sanders Corporation. Annual payments are made each January 1 by Sanders. In addition to making the lease payment, Sanders also reimburses Vick $4,000 each January 1 for a portion of the maintenance expenditures, which cost Vick Leasing a total of $6,000 per year. At the end of the five-year agreement, the compression equipment will revert to Vick and is expected to have a residual value of $25,000, which is not guaranteed. Collectibility of the rentals is reasonably predictable, and there are no important uncertainties surrounding the costs that have not yet been incurred by Vick Leasing Inc. **(LO 6, 8, 11)**

Instructions

(a) Assume that Vick Leasing Inc. has a required rate of return of 8%. Calculate the amount of the lease payments that would be needed to generate this return on the agreement if payments were made each:

1. January 1
2. December 31

(b) Use a computer spreadsheet to prepare an amortization table that shows how the lessor's net investment in the lease receivable will be reduced over the lease term if payments are made each:

1. January 1
2. December 31

(c) Assume that the payments are due each January 1. Prepare all journal entries and adjusting journal entries for 2008 and 2009 for the lessor, assuming that Vick has a calendar year end. Include the payment for the purchase of the equipment for leasing in your entries and the annual payment for maintenance.

(d) Provide the note disclosure concerning the lease that would be required for Vick Leasing Inc. at December 31, 2009. Assume that payments are due each January 1.

(LO 7, 8) E20-16 (Lessor Entries—Sales-Type Lease) Crosley Corporation, a machinery dealer, leased a machine to Ernst Corporation on January 1, 2008. The lease is for an eight-year period and requires equal annual payments of $38,514 at the beginning of each year. The first payment is received on January 1, 2008. Crosley had purchased the machine during 2007 for $170,000. Collectibility of lease payments is reasonably predictable, and no important uncertainties exist about costs that have not yet been incurred by Crosley. Crosley set the annual rental amount to ensure an 11% rate of return. The machine has an economic life of eight years, with no residual value, and reverts to Crosley at the termination of the lease.

Instructions

(a) Using time value of money tables, a financial calculator, or computer spreadsheet functions, calculate the amount of each of the following:

1. Gross investment
2. Unearned interest income
3. Net investment in the lease

(b) Prepare all necessary journal entries for Crosley for 2008.

(LO 2, 3, 12) E20-17 (Type of Lease, Lessee Entries with Bargain Purchase Option) The following facts are for a non-cancellable lease agreement between Hebert Corporation and Ibrahim Corporation, a lessee:

Inception date	May 1, 2008
Annual lease payment due at the beginning of each year, starting May 1, 2008	$21,227.65
Bargain purchase option price at end of lease term	$ 4,000.00
Lease term	5 years
Economic life of leased equipment	10 years
Lessor's cost	$65,000.00
Fair value of asset at May 1, 2008	$91,000.00
Lessor's implicit rate	10%
Lessee's incremental borrowing rate	10%

The collectibility of the lease payments is reasonably predictable, and there are no important uncertainties about costs that have not yet been incurred by the lessor. The lessee assumes responsibility for all executory costs.

Instructions

Answer the following, rounding all numbers to the nearest cent.

(a) Discuss the nature of this lease to Ibrahim Corporation, the lessee.

(b) Discuss the nature of this lease to Hebert Corporation, the lessor.

(c) Prepare a lease amortization schedule using a computer spreadsheet for Ibrahim Corporation for the five-year lease term.

(d) Prepare the journal entries on the lessee's books to reflect the signing of the lease and to record the payments and expenses related to this lease for the years 2008 and 2009. Ibrahim's annual accounting period ends on December 31, and Ibrahim does not use reversing entries.

(LO 7, 8, 12) E20-18 (Lessor Entries with Bargain Purchase Option) A lease agreement between Hebert Corporation and Ibrahim Corporation is described in E20-17.

Instructions

Provide the following for Hebert Corporation, the lessor, rounding all numbers to the nearest cent.

(a) Calculate the amount of gross investment at the inception of the lease.

(b) Calculate the amount of net investment at the inception of the lease.

(c) Prepare a lease amortization schedule using a computer spreadsheet for Hebert Corporation for the five-year lease term.

(d) Prepare the journal entries to reflect the signing of the lease and to record the receipts and income related to this lease for the years 2008, 2009, and 2010. The lessor's accounting period ends on December 31, and Hebert Corporation does not use reversing entries.

E20-19 **(Calculation of Rental, Amortization Table, Journal Entries for Lessor)** Jamil Leasing Corporation **(LO 6,** signs an agreement on January 1, 2008, to lease equipment to Irvine Limited. The following information relates to the **7, 8)** agreement:

1. The term of the non-cancellable lease is six years, with no renewal option. The equipment has an estimated economic life of eight years.

2. The asset's cost to Jamil, the lessor, is $305,000. The asset's fair value at January 1, 2008, is $305,000.

3. The asset will revert to the lessor at the end of the lease term, at which time the asset is expected to have a residual value of $45,626, which is not guaranteed.

4. Irvine Limited, the lessee, assumes direct responsibility for all executory costs.

5. The agreement requires equal annual rental payments, beginning on January 1, 2008.

6. Collectibility of the lease payments is reasonably predictable. There are no important uncertainties about costs that have not yet been incurred by the lessor.

Instructions

Answer the following, rounding all numbers in parts (b) and (c) to the nearest cent.

(a) Assuming that Jamil Leasing desires a 10% rate of return on its investment, use time value of money tables, a financial calculator, or computer spreadsheet functions to calculate the amount of the annual rental payment that is required. Round to the nearest dollar.

(b) Prepare an amortization schedule using a computer spreadsheet that would be suitable for the lessor for the lease term.

(c) Prepare all of the journal entries for the lessor for 2008 and 2009 to record the lease agreement, the receipt of lease payments, and the recognition of income. Assume that the lessor's annual accounting period ends on December 31.

E20-20 **(Lessor Entries, Determination of Type of Lease, Lease Payment Calculation, Spreadsheet** **(LO 6, 7,** **Application, Financial Statement Amounts)** Cadette Corp. leases a car to Jaimme DeLory on June 1, 2008. The term **8, 11)** of the non-cancellable lease is 48 months. The following information is provided about the lease:

1. The lessee is given an option to purchase the automobile at the end of the lease term for $5,000.

2. The automobile's fair value on June 1, 2008, is $29,500. It is carried in Cadette's inventory at $21,200.

3. The car has an economic life of seven years, with a $1,000 residual value at the end of that time. The car's estimated fair value is $10,000 after four years, $7,000 after five years, and $2,500 after six years.

4. Cadette wants to earn a 12% rate of return (1% per month) on any financing transactions.

5. Jaimme DeLory represents a reasonable credit risk and no future costs are anticipated in relation to this lease.

6. The lease agreement calls for a $1,000 down payment on June 1, 2008, and 48 equal monthly payments on the first of each month, beginning June 1, 2008.

Instructions

(a) Determine the amount of the monthly lease payment using present value tables, a financial calculator, or computer spreadsheet functions.

(b) What type of lease is this to Cadette Corp.? Explain.

(c) Prepare a lease amortization schedule for the 48-month lease term using a computer spreadsheet.

(d) Prepare the entries that are required, if any, on December 31, 2008, Cadette's fiscal year end.

(e) How much income will Cadette report on its 2008 income statement relative to this lease?

(f) What is the net investment in the lease to be reported on the December 31, 2008, statement of financial position? How much is reported in current assets? In non-current assets?

(LO 18) *E20-21   (Sale-Leaseback—Lessee and Lessor Entries) On January 1, 2008, Hein Do Corporation sells equipment to Liquidity Finance Corp. for $720,000 and immediately leases the equipment back. Other relevant information is as follows:

1. The equipment's carrying value on Hein Do's books on January 1, 2008, is $640,000.

2. The term of the non-cancellable lease is 10 years. Title will transfer to Hein Do at the end of the lease.

3. The lease agreement requires equal rental payments of $117,176.68 at the end of each year.

4. The incremental borrowing rate of Hein Do Corporation is 12%. Hein Do is aware that Liquidity Finance Corp. set the annual rental to ensure a rate of return of 10%.

5. The equipment has a fair value of $720,000 on January 1, 2008, and an estimated economic life of 10 years, with no residual value.

6. Hein Do pays executory costs of $11,000 per year directly to appropriate third parties.

Instructions

(a) Prepare the journal entries for both the lessee and the lessor for 2008 to reflect the sale and leaseback agreement. No uncertainties exist and collectibility is reasonably certain.

(b) What is Hein Do's primary objective in entering a sale-leaseback arrangement with Liquidity Finance Corp.? Would you consider this transaction to be a red flag to creditors, demonstrating that Hein Do is in financial difficulty?

(LO 18) *E20-22   (Lessee-Lessor, Sale-Leaseback) Presented below are four independent situations.

1. On December 31, 2008, Zarle Inc. sold equipment to Daniell Corp. and immediately leased it back for 10 years. The equipment's selling price was $520,000, its carrying amount $400,000, and its estimated remaining economic life 12 years.

2. On December 31, 2008, Wasicsko Corp. sold a machine to Cross Ltd. and simultaneously leased it back for one year. The machine's selling price was $480,000, its carrying amount was $420,000, and it had an estimated remaining useful life of 14 years. The rental payments' present value for one year is $35,000.

3. On January 1, 2008, McKane Corp. sold an airplane with an estimated useful life of 10 years. At the same time, McKane leased back the plane for 10 years. The airplane's selling price was $500,000, the carrying amount $379,000, and the annual rental $73,975.22. McKane Corp. intends to amortize the leased asset using the sum-of-the-years'-digits amortization method.

4. On January 1, 2008, Sondgeroth Corp. sold equipment with an estimated useful life of five years. At the same time, Sondgeroth leased back the equipment for two years under a lease classified as an operating lease. The equipment's selling price (fair value) was $212,700, the carrying amount was $300,000, the monthly rental under the lease $6,000, and the rental payments' present value was $115,753.

Instructions

(a) For situation 1: Determine the amount of deferred profit to be reported by Zarle Inc. from the equipment sale on December 31, 2008.

(b) For situation 2: At December 31, 2008, how much should Wasicsko report as deferred profit from the sale of the machine?

(c) For situation 3: Discuss how the gain on the sale should be reported by McKane at the end of 2008 in the financial statements.

(d) For situation 4: For the year ended December 31, 2008, identify the items that would be reported on Sondgeroth's income statement related to the sale-leaseback transaction.

(LO 18) *E20-23   (Land Lease, Lessee and Lessor) On September 15, 2008, Metro Camping Products Limited, the lessee, entered into a 20-year lease with Sullivan Corp. to rent a parcel of land at a rate of $15,000 per year. The annual rental is due in advance each September 15, beginning in 2008. The land has a current fair value of $95,000. The land reverts to Sullivan at the end of the lease. Metro Camping's incremental borrowing rate and Sullivan's implicit interest rate are both 8%.

Instructions

(a) Prepare Metro Camping Products' required journal entries on September 15, 2008, and at December 31, 2008, its year end.

(b) Explain how and why these entries might differ if Metro were leasing equipment instead of land.

(c) Prepare the entries required on Sullivan's books at September 15, 2008, and at December 31, 2008, its year end.

*E20-24   (Real Estate Lease) Rancour Ltd. recently expanded its operations into an adjoining municipality and, on March 30, 2008, signed a 15-year lease with its Municipal Industrial Commission (MIC). The property has a total fair value of $150,000 on March 30, 2008, with one-third of the amount attributable to the land and two-thirds to the building. The land is expected to double in value over the next 15 years, while the building will depreciate by 60%. The lease includes a purchase option at the end of the lease that allows Rancour to receive title to the property for a payment of $90,000.   **(LO 18, 19)**

Rancour is required to make rental payments of $10,000 annually, with the first payment due March 30, 2008. The MIC's implicit interest rate, known to all, is 7%. The building's economic life is estimated at 20 years, at which time it will have a small residual value of $10,000.

Instructions

(a) Prepare the entries required by Rancour on the signing of the lease and the payment of the first lease payment.

(b) Assuming that Rancour's year end is December 31, prepare the entries that are required on December 31, 2008, March 30, 2009, and December 31, 2009. Rancour does not use reversing entries.

Problems

P20-1   Interior Design Inc. (ID) is a privately owned business that produces interior decorating options for consumers. The software that it purchased 10 years ago to present clients with designs that are unique to their offices is no longer state-of-the-art, and ID is faced with making a decision on the replacement of its software. The company has two options:

1 Enter into a lease agreement with Precision Inc. whereby ID makes an upfront lease payment of $12,000 on January 1, 2009, and annual payments of $4,500 over the next five years on each December 31. At the end of the lease, ID has the option to buy the software for $5,000. The first annual lease payment is on December 31, 2009.

2. Enter into a lease agreement with Graphic Design Inc. on January 1, 2009, whereby ID makes five annual lease payments of $6,500, beginning on January 1, 2009. ID may purchase the software at the end of the lease period for $200. This is considered a bargain price compared with the offer of $5,000 in the proposal from Precision Inc.

Under both options, the software will require annual upgrades that are expected to cost $1,500 per year. These upgrade costs are in addition to the lease payments that are required under the two independent options. As this additional cost is the same under both options, ID has decided to ignore it in making its choice.

The Precision agreement requires a licensing fee of $1,000 to be renewed on an annual basis. If ID decides on the Precision option, the licensing fee will be included in the annual lease payment of $4,500. Both Precision Inc. and Graphic Design Inc. offer software programs of similar quality and ease in use, and both provide adequate support. The software under each offer is expected to be used for up to eight years, although this depends to some extent on technological advances in future years. Both offers are equivalent in terms of the product and service.

It is now early October 2008, and ID hopes to have the software in place by its fiscal year end of December 31, 2008. ID is currently working on preparing its third-quarter financial statements, which its bank is particularly interested in seeing in order to ensure that ID is respecting its debt-to-equity ratio covenant in its loan agreement with the bank. The interest rate on the bank loan, which is ID's only source of external financing, is 10% per year. ID would have preferred to be in a position where it could buy rather than lease the software, but the anticipated purchase price of $30,000 exceeds the limits that the bank set for ID's borrowing.

Instructions

(a) Discuss the nature of the lease arrangement under each of the two lease options offered to Interior Design and the corresponding accounting treatment that should be applied.

(b) Prepare all necessary journal entries and adjusting journal entries for Interior Design under the Precision Inc. option, from lease inception on January 1, 2009, through to December 31, 2009.

(c) Prepare an amortization schedule using a computer spreadsheet that would be suitable for the lease term in the Graphic Design option.

(d) Prepare all necessary journal entries and adjusting journal entries for Interior Design under Graphic Design's option, from lease inception on January 1, 2009, through to January 1, 2010.

(e) Summarize and contrast the effects on Interior Design's financial statements for the year ending December 31, 2009, using the entries prepared in parts (b) and (d) above. Include in your summary the total cash outflows that would be made by Interior Design during 2009 under each option.

(f) Discuss the qualitative considerations that should enter into Interior Design's decision on which lease to sign. Which lease do you think will most likely be chosen by Interior Design? Why?

(g) What are the long-term and short-term implications of the choice between these two options? How do these implications support the direction in which GAAP is likely headed in the future concerning the accounting for leases?

P20-2   On January 1, 2008, Hunter Ltd. entered into an agreement to lease a truck from Murray Ltd. The details of the agreement are as follows:

Carrying value of truck for Murray Ltd.	$20,691
Fair value of truck	$20,691
Economic life of truck	5 years
Lease term	3 years
Rental payments (at beginning of each month)	$ 620
Executory costs included in rental payments each month for insurance	$ 20
Incremental borrowing rate for Hunter Ltd.	12%
Hunter Ltd. guarantees Murray Ltd. that at the end of the lease term Murray Ltd. will realize $3,500 from selling the truck.	

Additional information:

1. There are no abnormal risks associated with the collection of lease payments from Hunter.

2. There are no additional unreimbursable costs to be incurred by Murray in connection with the leased truck.

3. At the end of the lease term, Murray sold the truck to a third party for $3,200, which was the truck's fair value at December 31, 2010. Hunter paid Murray the difference between the guaranteed residual value of $3,500 and the proceeds obtained on the resale.

4. Hunter knows the interest rate that is implicit in the lease.

5. Hunter knows the amount of executory costs included in the minimum lease payments.

6. Hunter uses straight-line amortization for its trucks.

Instructions

(a) Discuss the nature of this lease for both Hunter Ltd. (the lessee) and Murray Ltd. (the lessor).

(b) Assume that the effective interest of 12% had not been provided in the data. Prove the effective interest rate of 12% using a financial calculator or computer spreadsheet function.

(c) Prepare a lease amortization schedule for the full term of the lease using a computer spreadsheet.

(d) Prepare the journal entries that Hunter would make on January 1, 2008 and 2009, and any year-end adjusting journal entries at December 31, 2008, related to the lease arrangement, assuming that Hunter does not use reversing entries.

(e) Identify all accounts that will be reported by Hunter Ltd. on its comparative statement of financial position at December 31, 2009 and 2008, and comparative income statement for the fiscal years ending December 31, 2009 and 2008. Include all the necessary note disclosures on the transactions related to this lease for Hunter and be specific about the classifications in each statement.

(f) Prepare the journal entry for Hunter's payment on December 31, 2010, to Murray to settle the guaranteed residual value deficiency. Assume that no accruals for interest have been recorded as yet during 2010, but that the 2010 amortization expense for the truck has been recorded.

(g) Prepare Hunter's partial comparative statement of cash flows for the years ended December 31, 2009 and 2008, for all transactions related to the above information. Be specific about the classifications in the financial statement.

P20-3   Refer to the information in P20-2.

Instructions

(a) Prepare the journal entries that Murray would make on January 1, 2008, and the adjusting journal entries at December 31, 2008, to record the annual interest income from the lease arrangement, assuming that Murray has a December 31 fiscal year end.

(b) Identify all accounts that will be reported by Murray Ltd. on its comparative income statement for the fiscal years ending December 31, 2009 and 2008, and its comparative statement of financial position at December 31, 2009 and 2008. Be specific about the classifications in each statement.

(c) Prepare a partial comparative statement of cash flows for Murray for the years ended December 31, 2009 and 2008, for all transactions related to the information in P20-2. Be specific about the classifications in the financial statement.

P20-4   LePage Manufacturing Ltd. agrees to lease machinery to Morand Corporation on July 15, 2008. The following information relates to the lease agreement:

1. The lease term is seven years, with no renewal option, and the machinery has an estimated economic life of nine years.

2. The machinery's cost is $420,000 and the asset's fair value on July 15, 2008, is $560,000.

3. At the end of the lease term, the asset reverts to LePage, the lessor. The asset is expected to have a residual value of $80,000 at this time, and this value is guaranteed by Morand. Morand amortizes all of its equipment on a straight-line basis.

4. The lease agreement requires equal annual rental payments, beginning on July 15, 2008.

5. LePage usually sells its equipment to customers who buy the product outright, but Morand was unable to get acceptable financing for an outright purchase. LePage's credit investigation on Morand revealed that the company's financial situation was deteriorating. Because Morand had been a good customer many years ago, LePage agreed to enter into this lease agreement, but used a higher than usual 15% interest rate in setting the lease payments. Morand is aware of this rate.

6. LePage is uncertain about what additional costs it might have to incur in connection with this lease during the lease term, although Morand has agreed to pay all executory costs directly to third parties.

7. LePage incurred legal costs of $4,000 in early July 2008 in finalizing the lease agreement.

Instructions

(a) Discuss the nature of this lease for both the lessee and the lessor.

(b) Using time value of money tables, a financial calculator, or computer spreadsheet functions, calculate the amount of the annual rental payment that is required.

(c) Prepare the journal entries that Morand would make in 2008 and 2009 related to the lease arrangement, assuming that the company has a December 31 fiscal year end and that it does not use reversing entries.

(d) From the information you have calculated and recorded, identify all balances related to this lease that would be reported on Morand's December 31, 2008, statement of financial position and income statement, and where each amount would be reported.

(e) Prepare the journal entries that LePage would make in 2008 and 2009 related to the lease arrangement, assuming that the company has a December 31 fiscal year end and does not use reversing entries.

(f) From the information you have calculated and recorded, identify all balances related to this lease that would be reported on LePage's December 31, 2008, statement of financial position and income statement, and where each amount would be reported.

(g) Comment briefly on the December 31, 2008, reported results in (d) and (f) above.

P20-5   Synergetics Inc. leased a new crane to Gumowski Construction under a five-year, non-cancellable contract starting September 1, 2008. The lease terms require payments of $22,000 each September 1, starting September 1, 2008. Synergetics will pay insurance, taxes, and maintenance charges on the crane, which has an estimated life of 12 years, a fair value of $160,000, and a cost to Synergetics of $160,000. The crane's estimated fair value is $45,000 at the end of the lease term. No bargain purchase or renewal options are included in the contract. Both Synergetics and Gumowski adjust and close books annually at December 31. Collectibility of the lease payments is reasonably certain and there are no uncertainties about unreimbursable lessor costs. Gumowski's incremental borrowing rate is 10% and Synergetics' implicit interest rate of 9% is known to Gumowski.

Instructions

(a) Identify the type of lease that is involved and give reasons for your classification. Also discuss the accounting treatment that should be applied by both the lessee and the lessor.

(b) Prepare all the entries related to the lease contract and leased asset for the year 2008 for the lessee and lessor, assuming the following executory costs: insurance of $500 covering the period September 1, 2008, to August 31, 2009; taxes of $200 for the remainder of calendar year 2008; and a six-month maintenance contract beginning September 1, 2008, costing $650. Straight-line amortization is used for similar leased assets. The crane is expected to have a residual value of $10,000 at the end of its useful life.

(c) Identify what will be presented on the statement of financial position and income statement, and in the related notes, of both the lessee and the lessor at December 31, 2008.

P20-6   Brayes Corporation is a diversified company with nationwide interests in commercial real estate development, banking, copper mining, and metal fabrication. The company has offices and operating locations in major cities throughout Canada. With corporate headquarters located in a metropolitan area of a western province, company executives must travel extensively to stay connected with the various phases of operations. In order to make business travel more efficient to areas that are not adequately served by commercial airlines, corporate management is currently evaluating the feasibility of acquiring a business aircraft that can be used by Brayes executives. Proposals for either leasing or purchasing a suitable aircraft have been analyzed, and the leasing proposal was considered more desirable.

The proposed lease agreement involves a twin-engine turboprop Viking that has a fair value of $1 million. This plane would be leased for a period of 10 years, beginning January 14, 2008. The lease agreement is cancellable only upon accidental destruction of the plane. An annual lease payment of $141,780 is due on January 14 of each year, with the first payment to be made on January 14, 2008. Maintenance operations are strictly scheduled by the lessor, and Brayes will pay for these services as they are performed. Estimated annual maintenance costs are $6,900. The lessor will pay all insurance premiums and local property taxes, which amount to a combined total of $4,000 annually and are included in the annual lease payment of $141,780. Upon expiration of the 10-year lease, Brayes can purchase the Viking for $44,440. The plane's estimated useful life is 15 years, and its value in the used plane market is estimated to be $100,000 after 10 years. The residual value probably will never be less than $75,000 if the engines are overhauled and maintained as prescribed by the manufacturer. If the purchase option is not exercised, possession of the plane will revert to the lessor; there is no provision for renewing the lease agreement beyond its termination on December 31, 2017.

Brayes can borrow $1 million under a 10-year term loan agreement at an annual interest rate of 12%. The lessor's implicit interest rate is not expressly stated in the lease agreement, but this rate appears to be approximately 8% based on 10 net rental payments of $137,780 per year and the initial market value of $1 million for the plane. On January 14, 2008, the present value of all net rental payments and the purchase option of $44,440 is $886,215 using the 12% interest rate. The present value of all net rental payments and the $44,440 purchase option on January 14, 2008, is $1,019,061 using the 8% interest rate implicit in the lease agreement. The financial vice-president of Brayes Corporation has established that this lease agreement is a capital lease as defined in *CICA Handbook* Section 3065 on "Leases."

Instructions

(a) *CICA Handbook* Section 3065 indicates that the crucial accounting issue is whether the risks and rewards (or benefits) of ownership are transferred from one party to the other, regardless of whether ownership is transferred. What is meant by "the risks and benefits of ownership," and what factors are general indicators of such a transfer?

(b) Have the risks and benefits of ownership been transferred in the lease described above? What evidence is there?

(c) What is the appropriate amount for Brayes Corporation to recognize for the leased aircraft on its statement of financial position after the lease is signed?

(d) Independent of your answer in part (c), assume that the annual lease payment is $141,780 as stated above, that the appropriate capitalized amount for the leased aircraft is $1 million on January 14, 2008, and that the interest rate is 9%. How will the lease be reported in the December 31, 2008, statement of financial position and related income statement? (Ignore any income tax implications.)

(CMA adapted, in part)

P20-7   The following facts pertain to a non-cancellable lease agreement between Alschuler Leasing Corporation and McKee Electronics Ltd., a lessee, for a computer system:

Inception date	October 1, 2008
Lease term	6 years
Economic life of leased equipment	6 years
Fair value of asset at October 1, 2008	$150,690
Residual value at end of lease term	–0–
Lessor's implicit rate	8.5%
Lessee's incremental borrowing rate	8.5%
Annual lease payment due at the beginning of each year, beginning October 1, 2008	$ 30,500

The collectibility of the lease payments is reasonably predictable, and there are no important uncertainties about costs that have not yet been incurred by the lessor. McKee Electronics Ltd., the lessee, assumes responsibility for all executory costs, which amount to $2,500 per year and are to be paid each October 1, beginning October 1, 2008. (This $2,500 is not included in the rental payment of $30,500.) The asset will revert to the lessor at the end of the lease term. The straight-line amortization method is used for all equipment.

The following amortization schedule has been prepared correctly for use by both the lessor and the lessee in accounting for this lease. The lease is accounted for properly as a capital lease by the lessee and as a direct financing lease by the lessor.

Date	Annual Lease Payment/ Receipt	Interest (8.5%) on Unpaid Obligation/ Net Investment	Reduction of Lease Obligation/ Net Investment	Balance of Lease Obligation/ Net Investment
10/01/08				$150,690
10/01/08	$ 30,500	–0–	$ 30,500	120,190
10/01/09	30,500	$10,216	20,284	99,906
10/01/10	30,500	8,492	22,008	77,898
10/01/11	30,500	6,621	23,879	54,019
10/01/12	30,500	4,592	25,908	28,111
10/01/13	30,500	2,389	28,111	–0–
	$183,000	$32,310	$150,690	

Instructions

Answer the following questions, rounding all numbers to the nearest dollar.

(a) Assuming that McKee Electronics' accounting period ends on September 30, answer the following questions with respect to this lease agreement:

1. What items and amounts will appear on the lessee's income statement for the year ending September 30, 2009?

2. What items and amounts will appear on the lessee's statement of financial position at September 30, 2009?

3. What items and amounts will appear on the lessee's income statement for the year ending September 30, 2010?

4. What items and amounts will appear on the lessee's statement of financial position at September 30, 2010?

(b) Assuming that McKee Electronics' accounting period ends on December 31, answer the same questions as in (a) above for the years ending December 31, 2008 and 2009.

P20-8 Assume the same information as in P20-7.

Instructions

Answer the following questions, rounding all numbers to the nearest dollar.

(a) Assuming that Alschuler Leasing Corporation's accounting period ends on September 30, answer the following questions with respect to this lease agreement:

1. What items and amounts will appear on the lessor's income statement for the year ending September 30, 2009?

2. What items and amounts will appear on the lessor's statement of financial position at September 30, 2009?

3. What items and amounts will appear on the lessor's income statement for the year ending September 30, 2010?

4. What items and amounts will appear on the lessor's statement of financial position at September 30, 2010?

(b) Assuming that Alschuler Leasing Corporation's accounting period ends on December 31, answer the same questions as in (a) above for the years ending December 31, 2008 and 2009.

P20-9 In 2005, Yin Trucking Corporation negotiated and closed a long-term lease contract for newly constructed truck terminals and freight storage facilities. The buildings were erected to the company's specifications on land owned by the company. On January 1, 2006, Yin Trucking Corporation took possession of the leased properties. On January 1, 2006 and 2007, the company made cash payments of $1,048,000 that were recorded as rental expenses.

Although the useful life of each terminal is 40 years, the non-cancellable lease runs for 20 years from January 1, 2006, with a purchase option available upon expiration of the lease.

The 20-year lease is effective for the period January 1, 2006, through December 31, 2025. Advance rental payments of $900,000 are payable to the lessor on January 1 of each of the first 10 years of the lease term. Advance rental payments of $320,000 are due on January 1 for each of the last 10 years of the lease. The company has an option to purchase all of these leased facilities for $1 million on December 31, 2025, although their fair value at that time is estimated at $3 million. At the end of 40 years, the terminals and facilities will have no remaining value. Yin Trucking must also make annual payments to the lessor of $125,000 for property taxes and $23,000 for insurance. The lease was negotiated to assure the lessor a 6% rate of return.

Instructions

Answer the following questions, rounding all numbers to the nearest dollar.

(a) Using time value of money tables, a financial calculator, or computer spreadsheet functions, calculate for Yin Trucking Corporation the amount, if any, that should be capitalized on its January 1, 2006, statement of financial position.

(b) Assuming a capital lease and a capitalized value of terminal facilities at January 1, 2006, of $8.7 million, prepare journal entries for Yin Trucking Corporation to record the following:

1. The cash payment to the lessor on January 1, 2008

2. Amortization of the cost of the leased properties for 2008 using the straight-line method

3. The accrual of interest expense at December 31, 2008

P20-10 Lee Industries and Lor Inc. enter into an agreement that requires Lor Inc. to build three diesel-electric engines to Lee's specifications. Upon completion of the engines, Lee has agreed to lease them for a period of 10 years and to assume all costs and risks of ownership. The lease is non-cancellable, becomes effective on January 1, 2008, and requires annual rental payments of $620,956 each January 1, starting January 1, 2008.

Lee's incremental borrowing rate is 10%, and the implicit interest rate used by Lor Inc. is 8% and is known to Lee. The total cost of building the three engines is $3.9 million. The engines' economic life is estimated to be 10 years, with residual value expected to be zero. Lee amortizes similar equipment on a straight-line basis. At the end of the lease, Lee assumes title to the engines. Collectibility of the lease payments is reasonably certain and there are no uncertainties about unreimbursable lessor costs.

Instructions

Answer the following questions, rounding all numbers to the nearest dollar.

(a) Discuss the nature of this lease transaction from the viewpoints of both the lessee (Lee Industries) and lessor (Lor Inc.).

(b) Prepare the journal entry or entries to record the transactions on January 1, 2008, on the books of Lee Industries.

(c) Prepare the journal entry or entries to record the transactions on January 1, 2008, on the books of Lor Inc.

(d) Prepare the journal entries for both the lessee and lessor to record interest expense (income) at December 31, 2008. (Prepare a lease amortization schedule for two years using a computer spreadsheet.)

(e) Show the items and amounts that would be reported on the statement of financial position (ignore the notes) at December 31, 2008, for both the lessee and the lessor.

(f) Identify how the lease transactions would be reported on each company's statement of cash flows in 2008.

(g) Provide the note disclosure concerning the lease that would be required for the lessee, Lee Industries.

(h) Provide the note disclosure concerning the lease that would be required for the lessor, Lor Inc.

P20-11 Hilary Steel Corporation, as lessee, signed a lease agreement for equipment for five years, beginning December 31, 2007. Annual rental payments of $32,000 are to be made at the beginning of each lease year (December 31). The taxes, insurance, and maintenance costs are the lessee's obligation. The interest rate used by the lessor in setting the payment schedule is 10%; Hilary's incremental borrowing rate is 12%. Hilary is unaware of the rate being used by the lessor. At the end of the lease, Hilary has the option to buy the equipment for $1,000, which is considerably below its estimated fair value at that time. The equipment has an estimated useful life of seven years with no residual value. Hilary uses straight-line amortization on similar equipment that it owns.

Instructions

Answer the following questions, rounding all numbers to the nearest dollar.

(a) Prepare the journal entry or entries, with explanations, that should be recorded on December 31, 2007, by Hilary.

(b) Prepare the journal entry or entries, with explanations, that should be recorded on December 31, 2008, by Hilary. (Prepare the lease amortization schedule using a computer spreadsheet for the minimum lease payments.)

(c) Prepare the journal entry or entries, with explanations, that should be recorded on December 31, 2009, by Hilary.

(d) What amounts would appear on Hilary's December 31, 2009, statement of financial position relative to the lease arrangement?

(e) What amounts would appear on Hilary's statement of cash flows for 2007 relative to the lease arrangement? Where would the amounts be reported?

(f) Assume that the leased equipment had a fair value of $150,000 at the inception of the lease, and that no bargain purchase option is available at the end of the lease. Determine what amounts would appear on Hilary's December 31, 2009, statement of financial position and what amounts would appear on the 2009 statement of cash flows relative to the leasing arrangements.

P20-12 Thomash Corporation manufactures specialty equipment with an estimated economic life of 12 years and leases it to Provincial Airlines Corp. for a period of 10 years. The equipment's normal selling price is $210,482 and its unguaranteed residual value at the end of the lease term is estimated to be $15,000. Provincial Airlines will pay annual payments of $25,000 at the beginning of each year and all maintenance, insurance, and taxes. Thomash incurred costs of $105,000 in manufacturing the equipment and $7,000 in negotiating and closing the lease. Thomash has determined that the collectibility of the lease payments is reasonably predictable, that no additional costs will be incurred, and that the implicit interest rate is 8%.

Instructions

Answer the following questions, rounding all numbers to the nearest dollar.

(a) Discuss the nature of this lease in relation to the lessor and calculate the amount of each of the following items:

1. Gross investment
2. Unearned interest income
3. Sales price
4. Cost of sales

(b) Prepare a 10-year lease amortization schedule using a computer spreadsheet.

(c) Prepare all of the lessor's journal entries for the first year of the lease, assuming the lessor's fiscal year end is five months into the lease. Reversing entries are not used.

(d) Determine the current and non-current portion of the net investment at the lessor's fiscal year end, which is five months into the lease.

(e) Assuming that the $15,000 residual value is guaranteed by the lessee, what changes are necessary to parts (a) to (d)?

P20-13 Assume the same data as in P20-12 and that Provincial Airlines Corp. has an incremental borrowing rate of 8%.

Instructions

Answer the following questions, rounding all numbers to the nearest dollar.

(a) Discuss the nature of this lease in relation to the lessee. Using time value of money tables, a financial calculator, or computer spreadsheet functions, calculate the amount of the initial obligation under capital leases.

(b) Prepare a 10-year lease amortization schedule using a computer spreadsheet.

(c) Prepare all of the lessee's journal entries for the first year, assuming that the lease year and Provincial Airlines' fiscal year are the same.

(d) Prepare the entries in (c) again, assuming that the residual value of $15,000 was guaranteed by the lessee.

(e) Prepare the entries in (c) again, assuming a residual value at the end of the lease term of $45,000 and a purchase option of $15,000.

P20-14 Jennings Inc. manufactures an X-ray machine with an estimated life of 12 years and leases it to Gocker Medical Centre for a period of 10 years. The machine's normal selling price is $343,734, and the lessee guarantees a residual value at the end of the lease term of $15,000. The hospital will pay rents of $50,000 at the beginning of each year and all maintenance, insurance, and taxes. Jennings incurred costs of $210,000 in manufacturing the machine and $14,000 in negotiating and closing the lease. Jennings has determined that the collectibility of the lease payments is reasonably predictable, that there will be no additional costs incurred, and that its implicit interest rate is 10%.

Instructions

Answer the following questions, rounding all numbers to the nearest dollar.

(a) Discuss the nature of this lease in relation to the lessor and calculate the amount of each of the following items:

1. Gross investment	3. Sales price
2. Unearned interest income	4. Cost of sales

(b) Prepare a 10-year lease amortization schedule.

(c) Prepare all of the lessor's journal entries for the first year.

(d) Identify the amounts to be reported on Jennings' statement of financial position, income statement, and statement of cash flows one year after signing the lease, and prepare any required note disclosures.

(e) Assume that Gocker Medical Centre's incremental borrowing rate is 12% and that the Centre knows that 10% is the rate implicit in the lease. Determine the amortization expense that Gocker will recognize in the first full year that it leases the machine.

(f) Assuming instead that the residual value is not guaranteed, what changes, if any, are necessary in parts (a) to (d) for the lessor and in part (e) for the lessee?

P20-15   Lanier Dairy Ltd. leases its milking equipment from Zeff Finance Corporation under the following lease terms:

1. The lease is dated May 30, 2008, with a lease term of 10 years. It is non-cancellable and requires equal rental payments of $25,250 due each May 30, beginning in 2008.

2. The equipment has a fair value and cost at the inception of the lease of $185,078, an estimated economic life of 11 years, and a residual value (which is guaranteed by Lanier Dairy) of $20,000.

3. The lease contains no renewal options and the equipment reverts to Zeff Finance Corporation on termination of the lease.

4. Lanier Dairy's incremental borrowing rate is 9% per year; the implicit rate is also 9%.

5. Lanier Dairy uses straight-line amortization for similar equipment that it owns.

6. Collectibility of the payments is reasonably predictable, and there are no important uncertainties about costs that have not yet been incurred by the lessor.

Instructions

(a) Describe the nature of the lease and, in general, discuss how the lessee and lessor should account for the lease transaction.

(b) Prepare the journal entries for the lessee and lessor at May 30, 2008, and at December 31, 2008, which are the lessee's and lessor's year ends, respectively.

(c) Prepare the journal entries at May 30, 2009, for the lessee and lessor. Assume reversing entries are not used.

(d) What amount would have been capitalized by the lessee upon inception of the lease if:
   1. the residual value of $20,000 had been guaranteed by a third party, not the lessee?
   2. the residual value of $20,000 had not been guaranteed at all?

(e) On the lessor's books, what amount would be recorded as the net investment at the inception of the lease, assuming:
   1. Zeff Finance had incurred $1,200 of direct costs in processing the lease?
   2. the residual value of $20,000 had been guaranteed by a third party?
   3. the residual value of $20,000 had not been guaranteed at all?

(f) Assume that the milking equipment's useful life is 20 years. How large would the residual value have to be at the end of 10 years in order for the lessee to qualify for the operating method? Assume that the residual value would be guaranteed by a third party. (Hint: The lessee's annual payments will be appropriately reduced as the residual value increases.)

P20-16   Fram Fibreglass Corp. (FFC) is a New Brunswick company that manufactures a variety of fibreglass products for the fishing and food services industry. With the traditional fishery in decline over the past few years, FFC found itself in a tight financial position in early 2008. Revenues had levelled off, inventories were overstocked, and most operating costs were increasing each year.

The Royal Montreal Bank, which FFC has dealt with for 20 years, was getting anxious as FFC's loans and line of credit were at an all-time high, the most recent loan carrying an interest rate of 15%. In fact, the bank had just recently imposed stipulations on FFC that prevented the company from paying out any dividends or increasing its debt-to-equity ratio above current levels without the bank's prior approval.

The vice-president of Finance, Joe Blowski, CMA, knew that with aggressive investment in new equipment the company could go after new markets in the construction industry. He had investigated the cost of the necessary equipment and found that $50,000 of new capital investment would allow the company to get started. All it needed was the financing. Joe set up appointments with Kirk Cullen, the loans officer at the provincial Industrial Development Bank (IDB), and with Heidi Hazen, the manager of the local office of Municipal Finance Corp. (MFC).

Kirk Cullen was very receptive to Joe's request. He indicated that the IDB would be interested in working with FFFC, and could provide him with a lease on the equipment he identified. Heidi Hazen also welcomed the business, suggesting a lease arrangement between MFC and FFC as well. Two days later, Joe had proposals from both the IDB and MFC on his desk.

You are an accounting major and co-op student placed with FFC for your final work term. On his way out of the office for a meeting, Joe provides you with the two proposals and asks, just before the elevator door closes, "Would you please review these and give me your analysis and recommendation on which proposal to accept, if either?" The details of the two proposals are as follows:

	IDB Proposal	MFC Proposal
Selling price of equipment	$50,000	$50,000
Lease term	April 23, 2008 to April 22, 2013	May 1, 2008 to April 30, 2013
Economic life of equipment	7 years	7 years
Residual value, end of lease term	$10,000	$10,000
Residual value guaranteed	no	by lessee
Annual rental payment	$12,000 in advance	$11,681 in advance
Executory costs	$1,020 per year included in rent	$300 per year in addition to rent
Interest rate implicit in lease	12%	unknown
Equipment returned at end of lease	yes	yes

Instructions

Prepare the required report.

P20-17 Mulholland Corp., a lessee, entered into a non-cancellable lease agreement with Stewiacke Manufacturing Ltd., a lessor, to lease special purpose equipment for a period of seven years. The following information relates to the agreement:

Lease inception	May 2, 2008
Annual lease payment due at the beginning of each lease year	$?
Residual value of equipment at end of lease term, guaranteed by an independent third party	$100,000
Economic life of equipment	10 years
Usual selling price of equipment	$415,000
Manufacturing cost of equipment on lessor's books	$327,500
Lessor's implicit interest rate, known to lessee	12%
Lessee's incremental borrowing rate	12? %
Executory costs per year to be paid by lessee, estimated	$ 14,500

The leased equipment reverts to Stewiacke Manufacturing at the end of the lease, although Mulholland has an option to purchase it at its expected fair value at that time.

Instructions

(a) Using time value of money tables, a financial calculator, or computer spreadsheet functions, calculate the lease payment determined by the lessor to provide a 12% return.

(b) Prepare a lease amortization table for Stewiacke Manufacturing, the lessor, covering the entire term of the lease.

(c) Assuming that Stewiacke Manufacturing has a December 31 year end, and that reversing entries are not made, prepare all entries made by the company up to and including May 2, 2010.

(d) Identify the balances and classification of amounts that Stewiacke Manufacturing will report on its December 31, 2008, statement of financial position, and the amounts on its 2008 income statement and statement of cash flows related to this lease.

(e) Assuming that Mulholland has a December 31 year end, and that reversing entries are not made, prepare all entries made by the company up to and including May 2, 2010. Assume payments of executory costs of $14,000, $14,400, and $14,950 covering fiscal years 2008, 2009, and 2010, respectively.

(f) Identify the balances and classification of amounts that Mulholland will report on its December 31, 2008, statement of financial position, and the amounts on its 2008 income statement and statement of cash flows related to this lease.

(g) On whose statement of financial position should the equipment appear? On whose statement of financial position does the equipment currently get reported?

*P20-18   The head office and main branch of North Central Credit Union has operated in the central business district for almost 50 years. In 1992, new offices were constructed on the same site at a cost of $9.5 million. The new building was opened on January 4, 1993, and was expected to be used for 35 years, at which time it would have a value of approximately $2 million.

In 2008, as the conventional banks again began to consider merger strategies among themselves, North Central felt that the time was right to expand the number of its community branches throughout the province. The development and construction of more branches required significant financing and, as a source of cash, North Central looked into selling the building that housed its head office and main branch. On June 29, 2008, Rural Life Insurance Company Ltd. purchased the building (but not the land) for $8 million and immediately entered into a 20-year lease with North Central to lease back the occupied space. The terms of the lease were as follows:

1. It is non-cancellable, with an option to purchase the building at the end of the lease for $1 million.

2. The annual rental is $838,380, payable on June 29 each year, beginning on June 29, 2008.

3. Rural Life expects to earn a return of 10% on its net investment in the lease, the same as North Central's incremental borrowing rate.

4. North Central is responsible for maintenance, insurance, and property taxes.

5. Estimates of useful life and residual value have not changed significantly since 1990.

Instructions

(a) Prepare all entries for North Central Credit Union from June 29, 2008, to December 31, 2009. North Central has a calendar year fiscal period.

(b) Assume instead that there was no option to purchase, that $8 million represents the building's fair value on June 29, 2008, and that the lease term was 12 years. Prepare all entries for North Central Credit Union from June 29, 2008, to December 31, 2009.

(c) Besides the increase in cash that it needs from the sale of the building, what effect should North Central Credit Union expect to see on the net assets appearing on its statement of financial position immediately after the sale and leaseback?

*P20-19   Akbari Ltd. is a private corporation whose operations rely considerably on a group of technology companies that experienced operating difficulties from 2005 to 2007. As a result, Akbari suffered temporary cash flow problems that required it to look for innovative means of financing. In 2008, Akbari's management therefore decided to enter into a sale and leaseback agreement with a major Canadian leasing company, Intranational Leasing.

Immediately after its September 30, 2008, year end, Akbari sold one of its major manufacturing sites to Intranational Leasing for $1.75 million, and entered into a 15-year agreement to lease back the property for $175,000 per year. The lease payment is due October 1 of each year, beginning October 1, 2008.

Akbari's carrying amount of the property when sold was $250,000. The lease agreement gives Akbari the right to purchase the property at the end of the lease for its expected fair value at that time of $2.5 million. In 2008, the land is estimated to be worth 40% of the total property value, and the building, 60%. Akbari uses a 10% declining-balance method of amortizing its buildings, and has a 7% incremental borrowing rate.

Instructions

(a) Prepare all entries that are needed by Akbari to recognize the sale and leaseback transaction on October 1, 2008; any adjusting entries that are required on September 30, 2009; and the October 1, 2009, transaction. Reversing entries are not used.

(b) Prepare all necessary note disclosures and amounts that are to be reported on Akbari's September 30, 2009, statement of financial position, income statement, and statement of cash flows for its year ended September 30, 2009.

(CICA adapted)

Writing Assignments

WA20-1   Cuby Corporation entered into a lease agreement for 10 photocopy machines for its corporate headquarters. The lease agreement qualifies as an operating lease in all ways except that there is a bargain purchase option. After the five-year lease term, the corporation can purchase each copier for $1,000, when the anticipated market value of each machine will be $2,500.

Glenn Beckert, the financial vice-president, thinks the financial statements must recognize the lease agreement as a capital lease because of the bargain purchase clause. The controller, Tareek Koba, disagrees: "Although I don't know much about the copiers themselves, there is a way to avoid recording the lease liability." She argues that the corporation might claim that copier technology advances rapidly and that by the end of the lease term—five years in the future—the machines will most likely not be worth the $1,000 bargain price.

Instructions

Answer the following questions.

(a) Is there an ethical issue at stake? Explain.

(b) Should the controller's argument be accepted if she does not really know much about copier technology? Would it make a difference if the controller were knowledgeable about how quickly copier technology changes?

(c) What should Beckert do?

WA20-2   Sporon Corp. is a fast-growing Canadian company in the IT industry, selling software solutions to a variety of large private and public companies. Sporon has recently moved into a new state-of-the-art building designed specifically for its needs, and signed a 20-year lease with PPS Pension Inc., the owner. Because Sporon accounts for this lease as an operating lease, it expenses both the monthly rental and the annual payment that it agreed on with PPS to cover property tax increases above the 2007 base property tax cost. The tax increase amount is determined by PPS and is payable by September 30 each year.

The small group of individuals who own the company is very interested in the company's annual financial statements as they expect, if all goes well, to take the company public by 2011. For this and other reasons, Sporon's chief financial officer, Louise Bren, has been very interested in the move to IFRS expected in 2011 and she has begun a process of determining what has to be done to prepare for this change. The current topic of interest to her is the leasing standards.

Louise tells you that she has been reading about a joint FASB-IASB group that is studying lease accounting with a view to issuing new harmonized standards that might be very different from current GAAP.

Instructions

(a) Explain to Louise Bren to what extent, if any, adjustments will be needed to Sporon's financial statements for the lease described above, based on **existing** Canadian and international accounting standards.

(b) Assume that the joint FASB-IASB study group supports the right-of-use approach for leases. Prepare a short report for the CFO that explains the conceptual basis for this approach and that identifies how Sporon Corp.'s balance sheet, income statement, and cash flow statement will likely differ under revised leasing standards based on this approach.

(c) Prepare a short, but informative, appendix to your report in (b) that addresses how applying such a revised standard might affect a financial analyst's basic ratio analysis of Sporon Corp.'s profitability (profit margin, return on assets, return on equity); risk (debt-to-equity, times interest earned); and solvency (operating cash flows to total debt).

WA20-3   As the IASB/FASB joint international working group began its study of lease accounting in late 2006 and early 2007, it had a number of staff documents prepared to help observers at their meetings follow the working group's discussions. These documents are available on the IASB website (www.iasb.org) by following the "Projects" link for "Leases." They cover a wealth of information, including the results of prior academic research on lease accounting and its potential implications for the lease accounting project.

Obtain a copy of the "Information for Observers" for the March 22, 2007, meeting of the IASB/FASB joint committee that deals with academic research on lease accounting. Alternatively, research and read up on the academic accounting literature on lease accounting.

Instructions

(a) Summarize the issues that have been addressed by academic research on lease accounting.

(b) In general, what were the findings of this research on each issue?

(c) Identify what the implications are of the research findings for the development of new accounting standards for leases.

WA20-4   On January 1, Shinault Corporation, a lessee, entered into three non-cancellable leases for brand new equipment: Lease L, Lease M, and Lease N. None of the three leases transfers ownership of the equipment to Shinault at the end of the lease term. For each of the three leases, the present value at the beginning of the lease term of the minimum lease payments (excluding the portion of the payments representing executory costs, such as insurance, maintenance, and taxes to be paid by the lessor) is 75% of the equipment's fair value. The following information is provided about each lease:

1. Lease L does not contain a bargain purchase option; the lease term is equal to 80% of the equipment's estimated economic life.

2. Lease M contains a bargain purchase option; the lease term is equal to 50% of the equipment's estimated economic life.

3. Lease N does not contain a bargain purchase option; the lease term is equal to 50% of the equipment's estimated economic life.

Instructions

(a) What is the theoretical basis for the accounting standard that requires certain long-term leases to be capitalized by the lessee? Do not discuss the specific criteria for classifying a specific lease as a capital lease.

(b) How should Shinault Corporation classify each of the three leases? Give the reasons for your answer.

(c) Assuming that the rental payments are made on a straight-line basis, how should Shinault record each rental payment for each of the leases?

(AICPA adapted)

*WA20-5   On October 30, 2008, Truttman Corp. sold six-month-old equipment at its fair value and leased it back. There was a loss on the sale. Truttman pays all insurance, maintenance, and taxes on the equipment. The lease provides for eight equal annual payments, beginning October 30, 2009, with a present value equal to 85% of the equipment's fair value and sales price. The lease's term is equal to 80% of the equipment's useful life. There is no provision for Truttman to reacquire ownership of the equipment at the end of the lease term.

Instructions

(a) Why would Truttman have entered into such an agreement?

(b) In reaching a decision on how to classify a lease, why is it important to compare the equipment's fair value with the present value of the lease payments, and its useful life to the lease term? What does this information tell you?

(c) How should Truttman account for the sale portion of the sale-leaseback transaction on its financial statements for the year ended December 31, 2008?

(d) How should Truttman report the leaseback portion of the sale-leaseback transaction on its financial statements for the year ended December 31, 2008?

Cases

Student Website

www.wiley.com/canada/kieso

Refer to the Case Primer on the Student Website to help you answer these cases.

CA20-1   Crown Inc. (CI) is a public company that manufactures a special type of cap that fits on a bottle. At present, it is the only manufacturer of this cap and therefore enjoys market security. The machinery that makes the cap has been in use for 20 years and is due for replacement. CI has the option of buying the machine or leasing it. Currently, CI is leaning toward leasing the machine since it is expensive to buy and funds would have to be borrowed from the bank. The company's debt-to-equity ratio is currently marginal, and if the funds were borrowed, the debt-to-equity ratio would surely worsen. CI's top management is anxious to maintain the ratio at its present level.

The dilemma for CI is that if it leases the machine, it may have to set up a long-term obligation under the lease and this would also affect the debt-to-equity ratio. Since this is clearly unacceptable, CI decided to see if the leasing company, Anchor Limited (AL), could do anything to help with the situation. After much negotiation, the following terms were agreed upon and written into the lease agreement:

- AL would manufacture and lease to CI a unique machine for making caps.

- The lease would be for a period of 12 years.

- The lease payments of $150,000 would be paid at the end of each year.

- CI would have the option to purchase the machine for $850,000 at the end of the lease term, which is equal to the expected FMV at that time; otherwise, the machine would be returned to the lessor.

- CI also has the option to lease the machine for another eight years at $150,000 per year.

- The rate that is implicit in the lease is 9%.

The new machine is expected to last 20 years. Since it is a unique machine, AL has no other use for it if CI does not either purchase it at the end of the lease or renew the lease. If CI had purchased the asset, it would have cost $1.9 million. Although it was purposefully omitted from the written lease agreement, there was a tacit understanding that CI would either renew the lease or exercise the purchase option.

Instructions

Assume the role of CI's auditors and discuss the nature of the lease, noting how it should be accounted for. The controller of the company has confided in you that the machine will likely be purchased. Assume that you are aware of top management's position on adding debt to the balance sheet.

CA20-2   Kelly's Shoes Limited (KSL) used to be a major department store in Canada before it went bankrupt and was bought by Bears Shoes Limited (BSL). Many of the stores were anchor tenants in medium- to large-sized retail shopping malls. This space was primarily leased under non-cancellable real estate leases as disclosed in note 16 to the consolidated financial statements. Aggregate commitments under both capital and operating leases amounted to over $1.3 million.

As part of KSL's restructuring and downsizing plans prior to its bankruptcy, the company announced at the beginning of the year that it planned to close down 31 of its 85 stores by June 30. Subsequently, it announced that it might keep certain stores open until February in the following year if the landlords were prepared to provide an appropriate level of financial support. KSL also announced that landlords who allowed the stores to close June 30 (the earlier date) would be given a bonus of three months of rent.

Instructions

Assume the role of management and discuss the financial reporting issues that the company had to deal with before its bankruptcy.

Integrated Cases

IC20-1   Air Canada (AC) is Canada's largest airline, operating domestic and international flights on a full-service basis. During 2003, the company ran into financial difficulty and took steps to reorganize its operations and rethink its business model. The company needed to obtain significant additional financing and was looking to undergo a financial reorganization under which control of the company would likely change hands.

In March 2004, the company set up voluntary separation programs, which allowed for up to 300 non-unionized employees to "retire" with severance payments. Unionized employees were covered by a separate similar plan. In addition, it was planned that certain employees would be terminated and receive severance payments under pre-existing contracts.

Many lease contracts were renegotiated and/or terminated. While operating under bankruptcy protection court orders, the company had ceased to pay its lessors. GE Capital Corporation and its subsidiaries (GE), leased, managed the leases of, or had an interest in 108 aircraft—the bulk of Air Canada's aircraft. GE's lawyers notified the airline that it must either pay the back rent or return the planes, noting that the company should not be allowed to hide behind the bankruptcy protection and use the planes for free. The company had many of its leased planes recorded as operating leases. Aircraft operating lease rentals over the lease term were amortized to operating expense on a straight-line basis. The difference between the straight-line aircraft rent expense and the payments as stipulated under the lease agreement was included in deferred charges and deferred credits ($1.8 billion).

The following is an excerpt from the financial statements:

11. Convertible Subordinated Debentures

In December 1999, the Corporation issued $150 convertible subordinated debentures which have an annual interest rate of 7.25%, payable quarterly, and are convertible at $16.00, at the holder's option, into Air Canada common shares and Class A non-voting common shares ("Class A shares") at any time up to and including maturity in December 2009. This equals a rate of 6.25 shares per $100.00 principal amount of convertible subordinated debentures. There are no principal payments until maturity in 2009. The Corporation can force conversion into common shares and Class A shares at any time following the seventh anniversary of the issue if the weighted average closing price of the shares of the Corporation for the 20 trading days prior to the date of the redemption provides the holder an internal rate of return of at least 12% for the period commencing from the date of issuance of the convertible subordinated debentures and ending on the redemption date. The internal rate of return calculation includes interest payments made by the Corporation under the convertible subordinated debentures and the excess of the weighted average closing price above $16.00.

The company entered into a new cobranding agreement with CIBC regarding Aeroplan points and the Aerogold Visa card. The agreement revised a prior agreement with CIBC increasing the amount that CIBC would pay for the Aeroplan points (by 24%). As a result of revising the old agreement, CIBC is seeking damages of $209 million. In addition, the new CIBC contract also provides the Company with a borrowing facility under which the Company received financing of $315. During the year, at CIBC's option, the principal portion of the loan was reduced through the offset of amounts owing from CIBC for Aeroplan miles purchased.

Instructions

Adopt the role of the company's auditors and discuss the financial reporting issues.

IC20-2   Imax Corporation (Imax) is a Canadian company whose shares trade on the TSX and NASDAQ. The company files its statements in U.S. GAAP (as allowed by the Ontario Securities Commission) and provides a reconciliation from U.S. GAAP to Canadian GAAP. The company is one of the world's leading entertainment technology companies, specializing in large-format and three-dimensional film presentations. It designs, manufactures, sells, and leases projection systems. Most IMAX theatres are operated by third parties under lease and licensing agreements. The company also produces films.

The following excerpts from various documents that were issued by the company (including SEC filings and the December 31, 2005, financial statements) explain various transactions that have been entered into:

Theater system leases and sales. The Company's system leases generally have 10 to 20-year initial terms and are typically renewable by the customer for one or more additional 10-year terms. As part of the lease agreement, the Company advises the customer on theater design, custom assemblies and supervises the installation of the theater system, provides training in using the equipment to theater personnel, and for a separate fee, provides ongoing maintenance to the system. Prospective theater owners are responsible for providing the theater location, the design and construction of the theatre building, the installation of the system and any other necessary improvements as well as the marketing and programming at the theater. Under the terms of the typical lease agreement, the title to all theater system equipment (including the projection screen, the projector and the sound system) remains with the Company. The Company has the right to remove the equipment for non-payment or other defaults by the customer. The contracts are generally not cancelable by the customer unless the Company fails to perform its obligations. In certain circumstances, the Company enters into sale agreements with their customers. In these instances, the title to the theater system equipment remains with the customer, however, the Company retains the first right to purchase the systems back at the end of the trademark license term. Recently the Company has entered into joint profit-sharing arrangements, where the Company receives a large portion of a theatre's box office revenue in exchange for a contributing the projection system to the venue. The contracts are generally denominated in U.S. dollars, except in Canada, Japan and parts of Europe, where contracts are denominated in local currency.

The typical lease agreement provides for three major sources of revenue for the Company: initial rental fees; ongoing minimum and additional rental payments; and ongoing maintenance fees. Ongoing minimum and additional rental payments and maintenance fees are generally received over the life of the contract and are usually adjusted annually based on changes in the local consumer price index. The terms of each lease agreement vary according to the system technology provided and the geographic location of the customer.

Sales backlog. Signed contracts for theater system installations are listed as sales backlog prior to the time of revenue recognition. The value of sales backlog represents the total value of all signed system sales and sales-type lease agreements that are expected to be recognized as revenue in the future. Sales backlog includes initial rental fees along with the present value of contractual minimum rents due over the lease term, but excludes maintenance revenues as well as rents in excess of contractual minimums that might be received in the future. Sales backlog does not include revenues from theaters in which the Company has an equity-interest, agreements covered by letters of intent or conditional theater commitments.

(1) The Company generally enters into multi-year system lease agreements with customers that typically contain customer payment obligations prior to the scheduled installation of the system. During the period of time between lease signing and system installation, certain customers each year generally are unable, or elect not, to proceed with system installation for a number of reasons including business considerations, or the inability to obtain certain consents, approvals or financing. Once the determination is made that the customer will not proceed with installation, the customer and the Company may enter into a consensual lease buyout, whereby the parties are released from all their future obligations under the lease, the initial lease payments that the customer previously made to the Company are recognized as revenue and the geographic territory granted to the customer reverts to the Company. In addition, since the introduction of its new IMAX MPX theater system in 2003, the Company has agreed with several customers to modify their lease agreements to substitute MPX systems for the systems for which the customers previously contracted, which were in the Company's backlog. Included in IMAX systems revenue are: $0.6 million related to MPX backlog upgrades, $11.7 million related to consensual lease buyouts and $2.0 million related to terminations due to customer defaults (an aggregate of $14.3 million for 2005, $19.1 million for 2004, $9.5 million for 2003, $5.1 million for 2002 and $5.5 million for 2001).

Film Production, Distribution and Post-Production

Films produced by the Company are typically financed through third parties, whereby the Company will generally receive a film production fee in exchange for producing the film and will be a distributor of the film. The ownership rights to such films may be held by the film sponsors, the film investors and/or the Company. In the past, the Company often internally financed film production, but has increasingly moved towards a model utilizing third-party funding for the large-format films it distributes.

The Company is a significant distributor of 15/70-format films. The Company generally distributes films which it has produced or for which it has acquired distribution rights from independent producers. As a distributor, the Company generally receives a percentage of the theater box office receipts.

(f) Film assets

Costs of producing films, including capitalized interest, and costs of acquiring film rights are recorded as film assets and accounted for in accordance with AICPA Statement of Position 00-2, "Accounting by Producers or Distributors of Films". Production financing provided by third parties that acquire substantive rights in the film is recorded as a reduction of the cost of the production. Film assets are amortized and participation costs are accrued using the individual-film-forecast method in the same ratio that current gross revenues bear to anticipated total ultimate revenues. Estimates of ultimate revenues are prepared on a title-by-title basis and reviewed regularly by management and revised where necessary to reflect most current information. Ultimate revenue for films includes estimates of revenue over a period not to exceed ten years following the date of initial release.

Film exploitation costs, including advertising costs, are expensed as incurred.

Costs of digitally re-mastering films where the copyright is owned by a third party are recorded as film assets. These costs are amortized over the period of benefit using the individual-film-forecast method in the same ratio that current gross revenues bear to anticipated ultimate revenues from the re-mastered film.

The recoverability of film costs is dependent upon commercial acceptance of the films. If events or circumstances indicate that the fair value of a film is less than the unamortized film costs, the film is written down to fair value by a charge to earnings. The Company determines the fair value of its films using a discounted cash flow model.

The company had total liabilities of $266 million and total shareholders' deficit of $23 million as at December 31, 2005. According to the notes to the financial statements, there were debt covenants that impose certain restrictions on the company including restrictions on incurring additional debt, paying dividends, selling certain assets, and entering into certain transactions with affiliates.

Instructions

Adopt the role of a potential investor and analyze the financial reporting issues.

Research and Financial Analysis

RA20-1 Stantec Inc.

Refer to the 2005 financial statements and accompanying notes of Stantec Inc. presented at the back of this text, and then answer the following questions about the company.

Instructions

(a) What business is Stantec in? Where did you find this information?

(b) Identify all balance sheet and income statement accounts, along with their dollar amounts, that relate to any lease agreements that the company is a party to. Explain briefly what each lease agreement covers.

(c) Identify the line account(s) on the Consolidated Statements of Cash Flows where the cash lease payments are reported. Explain your answer.

(d) Calculate Stantec's return on total assets and total debt-to-equity ratios for the company's most recent year that is reported.

(e) Assume the IASB develops a revised lease accounting standard using the right-of-use approach, and that Canadian public companies are required to follow it in 2011 when our accounting standards are harmonized with the IFRS. (Assume any gain on a sale-leaseback transaction continues to be deferred.) Apply the effects of this revised approach to the 2005 financial statements of Stantec by identifying which balance sheet numbers are likely to change, and by how much. Justify your approach to estimating the revised balance sheet amounts.

(f) Using the estimates developed in part (e), recalculate Stantec's return on assets and total debt-to-equity ratios and compare them with the ratios in part (d). Comment.

RA20-2 Canadian National Railway Company and Canadian Pacific Railway Limited

The accounting for operating leases is a controversial issue. Many observers argue that firms that use operating leases are using significantly more assets and are more highly leveraged than their balance sheets indicate. As a result, analysts often use footnote disclosures to reconstruct and then capitalize operating lease obligations. One way to do so is to increase a firm's assets and liabilities by the present value of all its future minimum rental payments.

Instructions

Go to the SEDAR website (www.sedar.com) or the websites of the companies and access the financial statements of Canadian National Railway Company and Canadian Pacific Railway Limited for their years ended December 31, 2006. Refer to the financial statements and notes to the financial statements and answer the following questions.

(a) Identify all lease arrangements that are indicated in each company's financial statements and notes. For each lease arrangement, give the title and balances of the related lease accounts that are included on the financial statements.

(b) Have CN and CP provided all the lease disclosures as required by the accounting standards?

(c) What are the terms of these leases?

(d) What amount did each company report as its future minimum annual rental commitments under capital leases? Under operating leases? Are there significant differences between the two companies and the way they provide for their physical operating capacity, or are they basically similar?

(e) Calculate the debt-to-equity ratio for each company at December 31, 2006.

(f) Using an 8% discount rate, estimate the capitalized value of the off–balance sheet operating leases for each company.

(g) Recalculate the ratios in part (e), incorporating the capitalized values from part (f). Comment on your results.

RA20-3 Indigo Books & Music Inc.

Indigo Books & Music Inc., operating under *Indigo Books, Music & More*; *Chapters*; *Coles*; *The World's Biggest Bookstore*; *SmithBooks*; *The Book Company*, and *chapters.indigo.ca*, employs an estimated 6,000 people across Canada. Through the SEDAR website (www.sedar.com) or another source of your choice, access the financial statements of Indigo Books & Music Inc. for its 52 weeks ending April 1, 2006. Refer to the financial statements and notes to the financial statements and answer the following questions.

Instructions

(a) Identify all lease arrangements that are indicated in the company's financial statements, including the notes. Indicate any balances related to these leases that are reported on the income statement and balance sheet.

(b) Calculate the following ratios for Indigo based on the 2006 published financial statements:

1. Debt-to-equity ratio

2. Capital asset turnover ratio

3. Total asset turnover ratio

4. Return on investment (net income to total assets)

(c) Assume that you would like to compare Indigo's financial statements with those of competitors who purchase both the buildings that their businesses are in and all the equipment that they use. To make this comparison, you would need to capitalize the operating lease obligations that are reported by Indigo.

1. What information do you need to capitalize operating lease commitments?

2. Provide an estimate of the amount that would have to be capitalized for Indigo, and state your assumptions.

3. Using your estimate of the amount to capitalize for Indigo, recalculate the ratios in (b) above.

4. Compare the recalculated ratios with the original results and comment on the differences.

RA20-4 Research an Automobile Lease

Instructions

Contact an automobile dealership and find out the full out-of-pocket cost of purchasing a specific model of car if you were to pay cash for it. Also find out the details of the costs that are associated with leasing the same model car. Answer the following questions.

(a) What terms and conditions are associated with the lease? In other words, specify the lease term, residual values and whether they are guaranteed by the lessee or not, the lessor's implicit interest rate, any purchase options, etc.

(b) What cash flows are associated with the lease?

(c) Which do you think is the better deal? Briefly explain.

RIM Requires Restatement?

Sometimes companies have to go back and correct their financial statements of past years, perhaps because of an accounting error or some misrepresentation or manipulation. Take, for example, Research In Motion Limited, which is based in Waterloo, Ontario, and produces the famous BlackBerry. In the fall of 2006, RIM management initiated a voluntary review of the company's stock option grants.

Early results of the review showed that GAAP accounting errors had been made with the administration of stock options that were granted from fiscal 1998 to 2006, and that RIM's historical financial statements would therefore need to be restated.

During the review, the company also identified a technical error that will likely lead to further adjustments to the historical financial statements and was caused by a difference in the historical application of U.S. GAAP and Canadian GAAP. This technical error relates to a "net settlement" feature that existed in RIM's stock option plan before February 2002 and was designed to make it easier for employees who were short of cash to fund the exercise price for their stock options.

One result of the audit committee review was that RIM had to delay filing its interim financial statements for the three months ended September 2, 2006. The company was also unable to provide its restated historical financial statements or its interim financial statements before its December 2006 deadline. As a result of these delays, a management cease-trade order issued by the Ontario Securities Commission (OSC) then came into effect and RIM had to provide the OSC with an update on the status of its continuous disclosure obligations.

In the end, the company decided that the accounting impact on its most recently filed Canadian GAAP statements did not result in a material adjustment and therefore it did not restate the previously filed Canadian GAAP financial statements. The impact of the restatement on RIM's fiscal 2007 results was not material either. Earnings according to U.S. GAAP (fully diluted) for the fiscal year ended March 3, 2007, were $3.31 per share instead of the previously reported $3.33 per share. RIM expected the cease-trade order to be lifted in May 2007. ■

Source: Research In Motion press releases.May 17, 2007, Oct. 13 and Dec. 21, 2006.

chapter 21

Accounting Changes and Error Analysis

Learning Objectives

After studying this chapter, you should be able to:

1. Identify and differentiate among the types of accounting changes.

2. Identify and explain alternative methods of accounting for accounting changes.

3. Identify the accounting standards for each type of accounting change.

4. Apply the retrospective application method of accounting for a change in accounting policy.

5. Identify the disclosure requirements for a change in accounting policy.

6. Apply retrospective restatement for the correction of an accounting error.

7. Identify the disclosure requirements for the correction of an accounting error.

8. Apply the prospective application method for an accounting change.

9. Identify the disclosure requirements for a change in an accounting estimate.

10. Identify economic motives for changing accounting methods.

11. Compare current Canadian and international GAAP for accounting changes.

12. Correct the effects of errors and prepare restated financial statements.

Preview of Chapter 21

This chapter discusses the accounting and disclosure requirements for accounting changes set out in *CICA Handbook* Section 1506.[1] Whether companies are dealing with new or revised AcSB accounting standards, with errors such as those described in the opening vignette for Research In Motion Limited, or with having to make revisions to estimates that are a fundamental part of accounting measurements, they need clear standards to follow to account for these changes. This chapter provides a framework for the analysis of accounting changes and for the reporting and disclosure requirements that are designed to ensure that companies' financial statements remain relevant, reliable, and comparable.

The chapter is organized as follows:

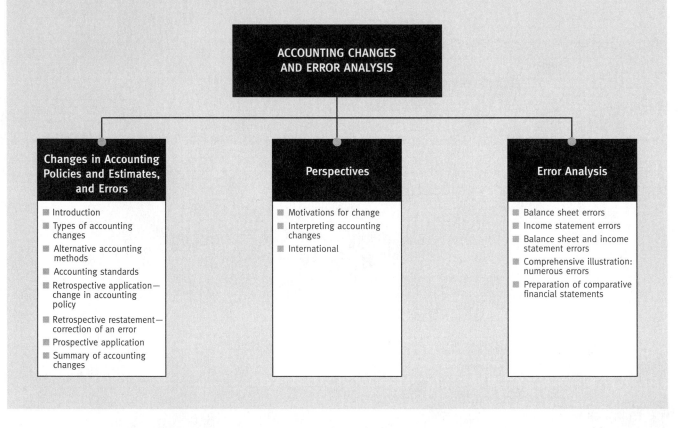

ACCOUNTING CHANGES AND ERROR ANALYSIS

Changes in Accounting Policies and Estimates, and Errors
- Introduction
- Types of accounting changes
- Alternative accounting methods
- Accounting standards
- Retrospective application—change in accounting policy
- Retrospective restatement—correction of an error
- Prospective application
- Summary of accounting changes

Perspectives
- Motivations for change
- Interpreting accounting changes
- International

Error Analysis
- Balance sheet errors
- Income statement errors
- Balance sheet and income statement errors
- Comprehensive illustration: numerous errors
- Preparation of comparative financial statements

CHANGES IN ACCOUNTING POLICIES AND ESTIMATES, AND ERRORS

Introduction

Financial press readers regularly see headlines about companies that report accounting changes and related events. Why do these accounting changes occur?

---

[1] *CICA Handbook* Section 1506, "Accounting Changes," has recently been revised and the new standards became effective for fiscal years that begin on or after January 1, 2007.

First, the accounting profession may mandate a new accounting method or standard. For example, the AcSB issued significant new accounting standards for financial instruments and for hedging and comprehensive income that apply to fiscal years that began on or after October 1, 2006. The board also issued revisions to inventory standards that are effective January 1, 2008—with earlier application encouraged—and even to the accounting standard for accounting changes itself, effective a year earlier. Second, changing economic conditions may cause a company to revise its methods of accounting. Third, changes in technology and in operations may require a company to revise estimates of the service lives, amortization method, or expected residual value of amortizable assets. Many Canadian companies, for example, have recently changed their estimates of service lives as well as their amortization methods due to changes in their regulatory environment or the speed of technological change. Lastly, corrections are needed when accounting errors are discovered. How should all these changes be accounted for and disclosed so that the financial information's usefulness is maintained and enhanced?

Before the existence of a standard for accounting changes, companies had considerable flexibility and were able to use alternative accounting treatments for what were basically equivalent situations. The overall objectives of accounting and disclosure standards for accounting changes, therefore, are to limit the types of changes permitted, standardize the reporting for each type of change, and ensure that readers of accounting reports have the necessary information to understand the effects of such changes on the financial statements. Section 1506 clearly states that its standards are "intended to enhance the relevance and reliability of an entity's financial statements over time and with the financial statements of other entities."

Underlying Concept

While the qualitative characteristic of usefulness may be improved by changes in accounting methods, the characteristics of comparability and consistency may be weakened by such changes.

International Insight

Section 1506 is now based, with few differences, on international standard IAS 8, "Accounting Policies, Changes in Accounting Estimates and Errors." The FASB standard, FAS 154, has also been significantly converged with IAS 8.

Types of Accounting Changes

The AcSB has established a reporting framework that covers three types of accounting changes:

1. **A change in accounting policy.** Changes in the choice of "specific principles, bases, rules, and practices applied by an entity in preparing and presenting financial statements" are all changes in accounting policies.[2] The initial adoption of a new accounting standard and a change from a weighted average cost flow formula to one based on FIFO are both examples of a change in policy.

2. **A change in accounting estimate.** A change in an accounting estimate is an adjustment in the carrying amount of an asset or a liability or the amount of an asset's periodic consumption, and is the result either of an assessment of the present status of the asset or liability, or of the expected future benefits and obligations associated with the asset.[3] Examples include a change in the estimate of the service life of an asset that is subject to amortization, and a change in the estimate of the net realizable value of accounts receivable.

3. **Correction of a prior period error. Prior period errors** are omissions from or misstatements in the financial statements of one or more prior periods, and are caused by the misuse of, or failure to use, reliable information that existed when those financial statements were completed and could reasonably have been found and used in their preparation and presentation.[4] An example is the failure to recognize amortization on a group of capital assets that are used in operations for a specific prior period.

1 Objective

Identify and differentiate among the types of accounting changes.

---

[2] *CICA Handbook*, Section 1506.05(a).

[3] *CICA Handbook*, Section 1506.05(b).

[4] *CICA Handbook*, Section 1506.05(c).

Each of these classifications is discussed separately below.[5]

CICA Handbook Sections 1581 on "Business Combinations" and 3475 on "Disposal of Long-Lived Assets and Discontinued Operations" require specific accounting and reporting when the components that comprise the reporting entity change. These are not included in the types of changes covered in Section 1506. Discontinued operations were explained in Chapter 4 and business combinations and other reporting entity changes are covered in most advanced accounting courses.

Changes in Accounting Policies

The recent revisions to *CICA Handbook* Section 1506 became necessary in part because the **GAAP hierarchy** was updated. *CICA Handbook* Section 1100 on "Generally Accepted Accounting Principles," which was introduced and took effect in 2003, redefined GAAP and the hierarchy or "pecking order" of the evidence that supports decisions about which principles and methods determine accepted accounting practice at a particular time. This means that before determining when a change might be appropriate, it is essential to first understand the issues related to the initial choice of accounting policy.

Section 1100 identifies two main levels or sources of GAAP:

1. Primary sources of GAAP

2. Policies that are consistent with the primary sources of GAAP, and are developed by exercising professional judgement and applying concepts in *CICA Handbook* Section 1000, "Financial Statement Concepts"

The first level, the **primary sources of GAAP**, lists these sources, from most authoritative to least, as follows:

(a) *CICA Handbook* Sections 1300 to 4460, including appendices and Board notices;

(b) Accounting Guidelines, including appendices and Board notices;

(c) Abstracts of issues discussed by the Emerging Issues Committee (EIC), including appendices;

(d) Background Information and Basis for Conclusions documents associated with (a) and (b) above, including appendices;

(e) Illustrative material such as decision trees and examples provided with (a) to (d) above; and

(f) Implementation Guides authorized by the Board.[6]

The second source—policies consistent with the primary sources, applying professional judgement and the concepts in *CICA Handbook* Section 1000—is used only when primary sources of GAAP do not deal with the specific issue. Section 1100 provides additional guidance on applying secondary sources.

Section 1100 also addresses the topic of consistency in accounting policies. It indicates that similar transactions, events, and circumstances are to be "recognized, measured and

---

[5] *Financial Reporting in Canada—2006* (CICA) reports that only 113 of the 200 companies surveyed in 2005 reported a change in accounting policy, as compared with 180 companies three years earlier. This reflects the large number of major revisions to *CICA Handbook* recommendations effective from 2002 to 2004 and fewer changes effective in 2005. Although a change in accounting estimate did not have to be disclosed before the Section 1506 revisions, four of the 200 companies reported such a change in 2005. Identifying a change as the correction of an error is less common, with only one of the surveyed companies in 2005 reporting this type of accounting change.

[6] *CICA Handbook*, Section 1100.02(c).

presented in a consistent manner in an entity's financial statements." However, if the source of GAAP specifically requires or permits categorization of items and different policies to be used, different methods may be used; but once an appropriate method is chosen from among those that are allowable, this method must then be applied consistently within the category.[7]

Having now been introduced to the original choice of policy, we can now ask what conditions must exist in order for an entity to be allowed to change its policy. One of the following two situations must occur for a change in an accounting policy to be allowed:

1. The change is required by a primary source of GAAP.

2. The change results in the financial statements presenting reliable and more relevant information about the effects of the transactions, events, or conditions on the financial position, financial performance, or cash flows of the entity.[8]

Specific transitional provisions that indicate how any changes are to be accounted for are often identified in new or revised standards and other documents that qualify as a primary source of GAAP. The second situation permitting a change in policy—a **voluntary change**—underscores one of the principles underlying Section 1506: for a change in accounting policy to be acceptable, the new standard that is chosen must result in financial information that **remains reliable** and is **more relevant**. In other words, the change would be unacceptable if it produces more reliable but less relevant information. The assumption, therefore, is also that the use of another method that remains reliable and is equally relevant would not meet the criterion for being an acceptable change. The onus is on management to explain why a different method is more relevant than the method that is currently being applied. An example of a change in accounting policy that would be acceptable is the change made by a company that constructs its own long-lived assets if the company moves from expensing all interest charges as they are incurred to capitalizing interest during construction. Another acceptable change in policy is a change in the measurement basis applied, such as moving to a fair value measurement for a financial asset from measuring it at historic cost.[9] In both cases, management can substantiate that the resulting financial information has become more relevant and remains reliable.

The requirement based on relevance and reliability links back to the two primary qualitative characteristics of accounting information that make it useful, as outlined in *CICA Handbook* Section 1000. The main purpose of the qualitative characteristics in the conceptual framework is their use as evaluative criteria in choosing among accounting alternatives. Any new or revised standard that is issued as a primary source of GAAP has been evaluated against these characteristics as part of the process of its development.

It is not always obvious whether an accounting change is, in fact, a change in accounting policy. It is clearly **not a change in policy** if either one of the following two situations occurs:

1. A different policy is applied to transactions, events, or conditions that differ in substance from those that were previously occurring.

2. A different policy is applied to transactions, events, or conditions that did not occur previously or that were previously immaterial.[10]

Underlying Concept

Relevance and reliability are used in Section 1506 as criteria in the choice of accounting methods.

---

[7] *CICA Handbook*, Section 1100.31A. An example is the choice between the three inventory cost formulas permitted in Section 3031.23 to .27.

[8] *CICA Handbook*, Section 1506.14. If an entity changes its accounting policy by following a source other than a primary source of GAAP, this is treated as a voluntary change in policy (1506.21).

[9] *CICA Handbook*, Section 1506.35.

[10] *CICA Handbook*, Section 1506.16.

Consider, for example, a company that begins to capitalize interest during the construction of its own long-lived assets. If the company was not involved in any self-construction activities previously, the new policy of capitalizing interest would not be considered a change in accounting policy. Another example would be if marketing expenditures were previously immaterial and therefore expensed in the period when they were incurred, but the expenditures have since become material and the company now defers and amortizes them. In this case, because there has been a change in materiality, the switch to the "defer and amortize" policy would not be treated as a change in policy. A third example would be the case of a company that changes from the direct write-off method to the allowance method of accounting for bad debts because the company has moved from primarily cash-based sales to sales on account: this situation also is not recognized as a change in accounting policy. In each of these three examples, the method that was used previously was appropriate for the circumstances that existed then; the new policy is appropriate for the changed circumstances.

What happens if the accounting policy that was previously followed was not acceptable, or if the policy was applied incorrectly? Rather than being a change in accounting policy, these changes to a generally accepted accounting policy are considered corrections of an error. A switch from the cash basis of accounting to the accrual basis is considered an error correction. If a company incorrectly deducted residual values when calculating double-declining amortization on tangible capital assets and later recalculates the amortization without deducting the estimated residual value, the change is considered the correction of an error.

Finally, companies often change how they allocate or group items within categories on the financial statements. When an item is reclassified on the financial statements of the prior period(s) in order to make the statements comparable, this is considered a change in presentation only and not, in itself, a change in accounting policy.[11]

Changes in Accounting Estimates

In preparing financial statements, estimates of the effects of future conditions and events are often made. As future conditions and events and their effects cannot be known with certainty, estimation requires the use of judgement. The following are examples of items that require estimates:

1. Uncollectible receivables

2. Inventory obsolescence

3. Fair value of financial assets or financial liabilities

4. Useful lives of, the pattern of consumption of the future economic benefits that are embodied in, and the residual values of depreciable assets

5. Liabilities for warranty costs

6. Asset retirement obligations

7. Recoverable mineral reserves

The use of reasonable estimates is considered an essential part of the accounting process. And it is normal to expect that accounting estimates will change over time as new events occur, circumstances change, more experience is acquired, or additional information is obtained. By its very nature, a change in estimate does not relate to past periods. Instead, and as its definition reinforces, the change is brought about by assessing the present status and future expectations that are associated with assets and liabilities.

---

[11] *CICA Handbook*, Section 1400.13A.

It is sometimes difficult to differentiate between a change in an estimate and a change in an accounting policy. Assume, for example, that a company changes its method of amortizing its property, plant, and equipment. At first glance, this clearly appears to be a change in an accounting policy. Or does the new method result from a change in the estimate of the pattern in which the assets' benefits will be consumed by the entity? Assume that a company changes from deferring and amortizing certain marketing costs to recording them as expenses as they are incurred because the future benefits associated with these costs have become doubtful. Is this a change in policy or a change in estimate?

The definition of a change in accounting estimate includes both of these scenarios. Further, in cases where it is unclear whether a change in policy or a change in estimate has occurred, the change is treated as a change in estimate.[12] A revision of an estimate, such as a prior year's tax assessment not caused by errors, for example, is given "change in estimate" treatment. It is clearly not the same thing as a correction of an error, which is discussed next.

Correction of an Error in Prior Period Financial Statements

No business, large or small, is immune from errors. The risk of material errors, however, may be reduced by installing good internal controls and applying sound accounting procedures. The accounting standard defines prior period errors and makes a distinction between errors and changes in accounting estimates. Estimates, by their nature, are approximations whose values change as circumstances and conditions change and more information becomes available. Errors, on the other hand, are omissions or mistakes, either intentional or through oversight, that are not discovered until after the financial statements for a period have been issued.

The following are examples of accounting errors and their correction:

1. A change from an accounting policy that is not generally accepted to an accounting policy that is acceptable. The rationale adopted is that the prior periods were incorrectly presented because an improper accounting policy was applied. Example: a change from the cash basis of accounting to the accrual basis.

2. Arithmetic mistakes that result from adding, subtracting, and so on. Example: the incorrect totalling of the inventory count sheets in calculating total inventory cost.

3. Changes in estimates that occur because previous estimates were not prepared in good faith. Example: Based on information that was available when an amortization rate was determined, an entity used a clearly unrealistic rate.

4. An oversight. Example: the failure to accrue or defer certain expenses or revenues at the end of the period.

5. An incorrect classification. Example: the classification of a cost as an asset instead of as an expense.

6. A misappropriation of assets. Example: the correction of a previous year's financial statements because inventory theft was discovered.

A problem may arise in distinguishing between the **correction of an accounting error** and a change in estimate. What is the correct treatment of the settlement of litigation (not previously accrued) related to a reassessment of a prior year's income taxes? How do we determine whether the information was overlooked in earlier periods (an error) or whether it results from new information, more experience, or subsequent developments

---

[12] *CICA Handbook*, Section 1506.32(d) and .35.

(a change in estimate)? This decision is important because, depending on the answer, a different accounting treatment is applied. The general rule is that when a careful estimate later proves to be incorrect, the change is considered a change in estimate. This is the case with most unaccrued tax litigation settlements. Only when the estimate was obviously calculated incorrectly because of lack of expertise or it was done in bad faith should the adjustment be considered an error correction. There is no clear separating line here, and good judgement must therefore be used in light of all the circumstances.

Objective 2

Identify and explain alternative methods of accounting for accounting changes.

International Insight

Until recently, the Canadian and U.S. standards used the term "retroactive" instead of the IAS 8 term "retrospective." All three now use the IAS 8 term but acknowledge that the two terms have identical meanings.

Alternative Accounting Methods

Three approaches have been suggested for reporting changes in the accounts:

1. **Retrospective**. **Retrospective application** (also known as **retroactive application**) requires applying a new accounting policy in the accounts as if the new method had always been used. The cumulative effect of the change on the financial statements at the beginning of the period is calculated and an adjustment is made to the financial statements. In addition, all prior years' financial statements that are affected are restated on a basis that is consistent with the newly adopted policy. Advocates of this position argue that only by restating prior periods can accounting changes lead to comparable information. If this approach is not used, the years before the change will be on one method and the current and following years will present financial statements on a different basis. Consistency is considered essential in providing meaningful earnings-trend data and other financial relationships that are necessary to evaluate a business.

2. **Current**. The cumulative effect of the change on the financial statements at the beginning of the period is calculated. This "catch-up" adjustment is then reported in the current year's income statement. Advocates of this position argue that restating financial statements for prior years results in a loss of confidence by investors in financial reports. How will a present or prospective investor react when told that the earnings reported five years ago are now entirely different? Restatement, if permitted, might also upset many contractual and other arrangements that were based on the old figures. For example, profit-sharing arrangements based on the old policy might have to be recalculated and completely new distributions made, which might create numerous legal problems. Many practical difficulties also exist: the cost of restatement may be excessive, or restatement may be impossible based on the data available.

3. **Prospective** (in the future). With **prospective application**, previously reported results remain; no change is made. Opening balances are not adjusted, and no attempt is made to correct or change past periods. Instead, the new policy or estimate is applied to balances existing at the date of the change, with effects of the change reported in current and future periods. Supporters of this position argue that once management presents financial statements based on acceptable accounting principles, methods, and estimates, they are final; management cannot change prior periods by adopting new methods and calculations. According to this line of reasoning, a cumulative adjustment in the current year is not appropriate, because such an approach includes amounts that have little or no relationship to the current year's income or economic events.

Objective 3

Identify the accounting standards for each type of accounting change.

Accounting Standards

Illustration 21-1 identifies the accounting standards for each type of accounting change. These are more fully explained and illustrated afterwards.

Type of Accounting Change	Accounting Method Applied
Change in accounting policy—on adoption of a primary source of GAAP	Apply the method that is approved in the transitional provisions of the primary source.
	If there is none, use retrospective application to the extent that it is practicable.
	If retrospective application is impracticable, apply prospectively.
Change in accounting policy—voluntary	Use retrospective application to the extent practicable.
	If impracticable, apply prospectively.
Change in accounting estimate	Apply prospectively.
Correction of an error	Use retrospective restatement.

Illustration 21-1

Accounting Changes—GAAP Accounting Methods

As indicated, only two of the general approaches are permitted: retrospective and prospective treatment. When new or revised primary sources of GAAP are adopted, recommendations are usually included that specify how an entity should handle the transition. The **transitional provisions** are sometimes complex. Those involving new disclosures (e.g., Section 3862 on financial instruments—disclosures) tend to be applied prospectively. Those that require existing balance sheet items to be remeasured (e.g., Section 3855 on financial instruments—recognition and measurement) tend to require retroactive application by adjusting the opening asset and liability measurements and retained earnings balance. Some particularly major changes (e.g., parts of Section 3461 on employee future benefits) permit a choice of either prospective or retroactive application. The transitional provisions also set out specific disclosures that are required when the new or revised primary sources are adopted.

For all accounting changes, the requirements apply to each incident—it is inappropriate to net the effects of two or more changes when considering materiality. Let's turn now to how these methods are applied. Retrospective application is discussed first, followed by prospective treatment.

International Insight

Up until the United States harmonized its policies with the IASB in 2004, the FASB required the current or "catch-up" method to be used for changes in accounting principles. The cumulative effect was recognized on the income statement between extraordinary items and net income.

Retrospective Application—Change in Accounting Policy

Introduction

Retrospective application is considered the most informative method of accounting for and reporting the effects on the financial statements when an entity voluntarily changes one of its accounting policies. This method is often recommended in the specific transitional provisions of a new or revised primary source of GAAP as well.

The underlying principle is that all comparative periods should be presented as if the new accounting policy had always been used. This outcome provides the best information to users who assess trends in financial information for prediction purposes. Specifically, retrospective application means that the opening balance of each affected component of equity is adjusted for the earliest prior period that is presented, and all other affected comparative amounts that are disclosed for each prior period that is provided are presented as if the new accounting policy had always been in use.[13]

Faced with having to retrospectively restate its financial statements of prior periods, an entity may find that data from specific prior periods may not be available, or may only

4 Objective

Apply the retrospective application method of accounting for a change in accounting policy.

Underlying Concept

The cost-benefit constraint is always considered by the AcSB in determining appropriate accounting policies.

---

[13] *CICA Handbook*, Section 1506.22.

be available at too high a cost. If it is impracticable to do the restatements—i.e., when the entity cannot determine the specific effects on a prior period or the cumulative effect of the change in policy for all comparative prior periods after making all reasonable efforts to do so—a limited version of retrospective application may be applied.

The accounting standard clearly explains what is meant by **impracticable**. It is considered impracticable to apply a change to a particular prior period if any of the following situations are true:

1. The effects of the retrospective application cannot be determined.

2. Assumptions are needed about what management's intents were in that prior period.

3. Significant estimates must be made that need to take into account circumstances that existed in that prior period, and it is no longer possible to do this.[14]

Partial retrospective application is permitted only when one or more of these three limitations exist. If the cumulative effect cannot be determined **even on the opening balances of the current period**, then a change in accounting policy is accounted for prospectively.

Retrospective Application with Full Restatement of Comparative Information

Retrospective application with full restatement of all comparative information is applied as follows:

1. An accounting entry is made to recognize the effects of the new accounting policy that is being applied retrospectively, along with any related income tax effects.

2. Financial statement amounts for prior periods that are included for comparative purposes are restated to give effect to the new accounting policy.

3. Disclosures are made that enable users of the financial statements to understand the effects of any changes on the financial statements so that the statements remain comparable to those of other years and of other entities.

To illustrate **full retrospective application**, assume that Denson Ltd. has expensed all interest costs incurred on self-constructed assets since beginning its major capital upgrading project in 2006. In 2008, the company changes its accounting policy to one of capitalizing all avoidable interest costs related to the self-constructed assets because management believes that this approach provides a more relevant measure of income earned. Shareholders and financial analysts are better able to assess a period's operating performance and prospects for the future with information that is reported under this changed accounting policy. The company is subject to a 40% tax rate. Denson has expensed interest for tax purposes and plans to continue using this method in the future.

Illustration 21-2 provides the information for analysis.

Illustration 21-2

Data for Full Retrospective Application Example

	Interest Expensed Policy Reported in Prior Years		
	2008	2007	2006
Income Statement			
Income before income tax	$190,000	$160,000	$400,000
Income tax—40%	76,000	64,000	160,000
Net income	$114,000	$96,000	$240,000

[14] *CICA Handbook*, Section 1506.05(f).

Statement of Retained Earnings

Opening balance	$1,696,000	$1,600,000	$1,360,000
Net income	114,000	96,000	240,000
Closing balance	$1,810,000	$1,696,000	$1,600,000

	Incomes if **Interest Capitalization Policy** Had Been Used		
	2008	2007	2006
Income Statement			
Income before income tax	$200,000	$180,000	$600,000
Income tax—40%	80,000	72,000	240,000
Net income	$120,000	$108,000	$360,000

	Differences in Income, Income Tax, and Net Income Using Interest Capitalization Policy		
	2008	2007	2006
Increase in income before tax	$10,000	$20,000	$200,000
Increase in income tax expense	4,000	8,000	80,000
Increase in net income	$ 6,000	$12,000	$120,000

Accounting entry to recognize the change   The first step is to prepare the accounting entry to recognize this change in accounting policy. Because the 2008 accounts have not yet been closed, any adjustments that are needed to 2008's income are made to the income statement and balance sheet accounts themselves, while any changes to prior years must be made through retained earnings.

The entry to record the change effective January 1, 2008, is:

Property, Plant, and Equipment (net)	220,000	
Future Income Tax Liability		88,000
Retained Earnings—Change in Accounting Policy		132,000

A	=	L	+	SE
+220,000		+88,000		+132,000

Cash flows: No effect

The Property, Plant, and Equipment account, net of its accumulated amortization is increased by $220,000. This amount represents the additional costs charged to the capital asset accounts for interest, less the related increase in the accumulated amortization account from the increased amortization expense since the assets were completed and used in operations ($200,000 + $20,000). The $220,000 adjustment brings these accounts to what the January 1, 2008 balances would have been if the revised policy had been in effect since the beginning of construction. In reality, both the asset account and its contra account—the accumulated amortization—are affected. The adjustment is shown as a net amount so you can focus on the other balance sheet effects. The Future Income Tax Liability credit recognizes the tax effects of the taxable temporary difference; that is, the difference between the carrying amount and tax basis of the capital asset account. In future periods, because taxable income will be higher than accounting income as a result of this temporary difference at January 1, 2008, a future tax liability is recognized. The adjustment to Retained Earnings is the accumulated after-tax effect of the new policy up to the beginning of the current year and represents all changes to prior years' incomes ($120,000 + $12,000 = $132,000). The entry corrects the accounts to January 1, 2008, as the revised policy is applied to the current year's operations.

The next step is to prepare the comparative financial statements by restating them as if the new policy had been in use from the beginning of 2006, the first year that Denson Ltd. incurred interest costs on self-constructed assets.

Financial statement presentation   Illustration 21-3 shows what the bottom portion of the income statement for Denson Ltd. looks like after giving effect to the retrospective change in accounting policy. It also presents the statements of retained earnings as if the interest capitalization policy had been used from the beginning.

<table>
<tr><td></td><td colspan="3">Denson Ltd.
Statement of Income
Year Ended December 31</td></tr>
<tr><td></td><td>2008</td><td>2007
(restated)</td><td>2006
(restated)</td></tr>
<tr><td>Income before income tax</td><td>$200,000</td><td>$180,000</td><td>$600,000</td></tr>
<tr><td>Income tax—40%</td><td>80,000</td><td>72,000</td><td>240,000</td></tr>
<tr><td>Net income</td><td>$120,000</td><td>$108,000</td><td>$360,000</td></tr>
</table>

<table>
<tr><td></td><td colspan="3">Denson Ltd.
Statement of Retained Earnings
Year Ended December 31</td></tr>
<tr><td></td><td>2008
(restated)</td><td>2007
(restated)</td><td>2006
(restated)</td></tr>
<tr><td>Opening balance</td><td>$1,828,000</td><td>$1,720,000</td><td>$1,360,000</td></tr>
<tr><td>Net income</td><td>120,000</td><td>108,000</td><td>360,000</td></tr>
<tr><td>Closing balance</td><td>$1,948,000</td><td>$1,828,000</td><td>$1,720,000</td></tr>
</table>

Illustration 21-3

Comparative Income Statements and Statements of Retained Earnings

Underlying Concept

Applying full retrospective treatment and providing the related disclosures that are required is an attempt to restore the comparability of the income statements.

The accounts on the financial statements, including the Property, Plant, and Equipment (and Accumulated Amortization) and Future Income Tax Liability accounts on the comparative balance sheet, appear as if the new accounting policy had always been used, and this is the objective of retrospective application. However, it is important for the reader to be alerted to the fact that Denson did change a key policy in the year. The disclosure requirements are identified after our next illustration.

Retrospective Application with Partial Restatement of Comparative Information

Impracticability   As indicated earlier, retrospectively restating the financial statements of a prior year requires information that may, in many cases, be impracticable to obtain, even though the cumulative effect can be determined. For example, when companies adopted the accounting standards for post-retirement benefits other than pensions (Section 3461) for the first time, most companies accounted for the change retroactively. Before the new standard took effect, companies recognized payments that they made for medical premiums for retirees as an expense as the payments were made—a pay-as-you-go method. Under the revised standard, the expense was required to be estimated and charged to the period in which the employees earn the entitlement to the future benefit—an accrual approach. For many reasons, however, it was not practicable for some companies to retroactively determine the effect of the new standard on specific prior years—a necessary condition for restatement. Section 3461's transitional provisions therefore permitted a **partial retrospective application**.

Thus, if the effect of a change in policy can be determined for some of the prior periods, the change in policy is applied retrospectively with restatement to the carrying amounts of assets, liabilities, and affected components of equity at the beginning of the earliest period for which restatement is possible. This could even be the current year. An adjustment is then made to the opening balances of the equity components for that earliest period, similar to the adjustments in the full restatement that was illustrated above.[15]

While estimates can be used to allow some restatements to be made retrospectively, estimates should not be made for this purpose after the fact if it is impossible to objectively assess circumstances and conditions in prior years that need to be known in order to develop those estimates. Hindsight is not applied in developing measurements that need to be used. Instead, measurements should be based on conditions that existed in the prior period.

If it is not practicable to determine the cumulative effect of the change even at the beginning of the current period, retrospective treatment cannot be applied. Instead, the new accounting policy is applied **prospectively** from the earliest date that is practicable.[16] This may occur if the necessary data were not collected and it is impracticable to recreate them.

Example   In the Denson Ltd. example in Illustrations 21-2 and 21-3, the company was able to determine the effect of the change in accounting policy on each prior year affected. What would happen if the company had been using a policy of expensing interest on self-constructed assets for many years and management concluded that it was impracticable to determine the effects on specific years any further back than 2007? It knows what the effect is on the January 1, 2007, capital assets, future income tax liability, and retained earnings, but it does not know the income effects on specific years prior to that date.

Management, therefore, is only able to determine the information provided in Illustration 21-4.

	Interest Expensed Policy Reported in Prior Years		
	2008	2007	2006
Income Statement			
Income before income tax	$190,000	$160,000	$400,000
Income tax—40%	76,000	64,000	160,000
Net income	$114,000	$96,000	$240,000
Statement of Retained Earnings			
Opening balance	$1,696,000	$1,600,000	$1,360,000
Net income	114,000	96,000	240,000
Closing balance	$1,810,000	$1,696,000	$1,600,000
	Incomes if Interest Capitalization Policy Had Been Used		
	2008	2007	2006
Income Statement			
Income before income tax	$200,000	$180,000	Unknown
Income tax—40%	80,000	72,000	
Net income	$120,000	$108,000	
	Differences in Income, Income Tax, and Net Income Using Interest Capitalization Policy		
	2008	2007	2006
Increase in income before tax	$10,000	$20,000	Unknown
Increase in income tax expense	4,000	8,000	
Increase in net income	$ 6,000	$12,000	

Illustration 21-4

Data for Partial Retrospective Application Example

---

[15] *CICA Handbook*, Section 1506.24.

[16] *CICA Handbook*, Section 1506.25.

When it is impracticable to determine the effects on a specific period that is presented for comparative purposes, the accounting standard indicates that the relevant assets and liabilities of the earliest prior period for which the effect is known should be adjusted, along with the opening balances of that period's equity accounts.

The journal entry to record the change in accounting policy is the same as the one that was made for the full restatement above:

$$A = L + SE$$
$$+220,000 \quad +88,000 \quad +132,000$$

Cash flows: No effect

Property, Plant, and Equipment (net)	220,000	
Future Income Tax Liability		88,000
Retained Earnings—Change in Accounting Policy		132,000

Illustration 21-5 shows how the comparative financial statements are presented when only partial retrospective restatement is possible.

Illustration 21-5

Partial Retrospective Application: Comparative Income Statements and Statements of Retained Earnings

Denson Ltd.
Statement of Income
Year Ended December 31

	2008	2007 (restated)	2006
Income before income tax	$200,000	$180,000	$400,000
Income tax—40%	80,000	72,000	160,000
Net income	$120,000	$108,000	$240,000

Denson Ltd.
Statement of Retained Earnings
Year Ended December 31

	2008 (restated)	2007 (restated)	2006
Opening balance, as previously reported		$1,600,000	
Change in capitalization of interest accounting policy		120,000	
Opening balance, as restated	$1,828,000	1,720,000	$1,360,000
Net income	120,000	108,000	240,000
Closing balance	$1,948,000	$1,828,000	$1,600,000

As the illustration shows, the 2006 financial statements are not restated. Instead, the effect of the policy change is carried back only to January 1, 2007, and the retained earnings amount at that date is adjusted for the cumulative effect of the change to that date. The new policy is applied in the 2007 and 2008 comparative income statements and balance sheets, and is supported by the required disclosures.

An expanded retained earnings statement is included in this presentation to show the type of adjustment that is needed to restate the beginning balance of retained earnings for the earliest prior period that is presented. In 2007, the beginning balance is adjusted for the excess of the "capitalization of interest" incomes over the "interest expensed" incomes prior to 2007 ($120,000). The restated balance is the amount that the opening balance would have been if the new policy had always been in effect. In 2008, the restated opening balance is what would have been in the accounts if the new policy had always been applied.

This adjustment process might appear complicated at first. It may be helpful at this point for you to try to develop the revised income and retained earnings statements on your own assuming the interest capitalization policy had always been used. You should end up with the results in Illustrations 21-3 and 21-5.

Is there any effect **on the statement of cash flows**? As you might expect, past cash flows for prior periods do not change just because we change an accounting policy in 2008. However, the category of cash flow will change in our example. Instead of all the interest paid being reported as an operating outflow, the restated financial statements report the capitalized interest as an investing outflow, thereby increasing the cash flow from operations above the amount previously reported. In other situations the cash flow from operations does not change. In the Shaw Communications Inc. example in Illustration 21-6, the type of cash flow changes between the financing and operating categories, but the cash flow amount does not change in total.

Continuing with our Denson Ltd. example, if the company had been unable to determine the effect on 2007's income, the adjustment would have been made instead to the opening balance of 2008's retained earnings. In the most limited circumstances, if it were not practicable to determine the cumulative effect even at the beginning of the 2008 year, retrospective application would not be possible and Denson would apply the new accounting policy on a **prospective basis** from the earliest possible date in the current year. The prospective method is explained later in the chapter where it is applied to changes in estimates.

Changes in accounting policy, whether they are mandated or voluntary, can have a significant effect on reported incomes and therefore on trend data for analysis.

Consider the following data about Canadian companies from an article in *Canadian Business* magazine after the AcSB approved an accounting standard that required companies to charge the cost of stock options to expense based on their fair values rather than their lower intrinsic values.

What Do the Numbers Mean?

Company	Earnings before Change in Policy*	Earnings after Change in Policy*	Percentage Drop
QLT	$ 12,405	$ −13,120	205.8
Certicom	−4,900	−11,922	143.3
Cott	3,900	−1,500	138.5
Imax	11,972	−1,207	110.1
Pivotal	−27,646	−42,135	52.4
Shaw Communications	−47,828	−68,664	43.6
Cognos	73,144	46,005	37.1
Open Text	27,757	19,397	30.1
Nortel Networks	−3,585,000	−4,537,000	26.6
Zarlink Semiconductor	−57,900	−73,100	26.3

Source: John Gray, "Out of Options," *Canadian Business*, Jan. 19–Feb. 1, 2004.
*All figures in U.S. dollars, except Shaw

Application of the new standard, however, did not have such a dramatic effect on other companies, such as the Canadian banks, which began expensing options before being required to do so.

The expense is measured using an option pricing model that requires several assumptions, including the expected option life, stock volatility, dividends, and a risk-free rate of return. Because each of these variables is an estimate, companies have some latitude in the expense calculation.

Objective **5**

Identify the disclosure requirements for a change in accounting policy.

Disclosures Required for a Change in Accounting Policy

Whether the change in accounting policy is due to the initial application of a primary source of GAAP or to a voluntary change, considerable information must be reported so that readers can determine why the change was made and what its effects are on previous financial statements, as well as what they might be on future periods. The following information is required to be disclosed, if practicable, regardless of whether it was accounted for retrospectively or currently or only affects future periods:

1. The nature of the change in accounting policy

2. The amount of the adjustment for each financial statement line item that is affected and the basic and fully diluted EPS, if applicable, for the current period and each prior period that is presented

3. The amount of the adjustment that relates to periods before those that are presented

4. The reasons why retrospective application was not practicable for restatement to particular prior periods, along with a description of how the change has been applied and from what date

When the change is due to the initial **application of a primary source of GAAP**, the entity also discloses the title of the primary source, and, if the change is made in accordance with the source's transitional provisions, the entity provides a description of the transitional provisions, including any that might have an effect on future periods. For a **voluntary change** in accounting policy, the entity is also required to explain why the new policy provides reliable and more relevant information. None of these disclosures has to be repeated in subsequent years.

Finally, disclosure is also required of **new primary sources of GAAP that are not yet effective and have not been applied**. At a minimum, the entity discloses the fact that a new primary source has been issued, and it discloses any reasonably reliable information that would be useful in assessing the possible impact that the new primary source will have on the entity's financial statement in the period in which it will first be applied.[17]

Example of Disclosures

Shaw Communications Inc. is a diversified Canadian communications company whose shares are listed on both the Toronto and New York stock exchanges. Illustration 21-6 provides excerpts from Shaw Communications' financial statements for its year ended August 31, 2006. These provide a good example of the retrospective application of a change in a primary source of GAAP, the effects on previously reported retained earnings (in this case, deficits), and the effects on numerous balance sheet accounts. As revisions to the standards for accounting changes were not effective until 2007, some of the disclosures that are required by the most recent standard have not yet been applied.

Illustration 21-6

Example of Disclosure of a Change in Accounting Policy

Student Website

Student Toolkit— Additional Disclosures

www.wiley.com/canada/kieso

CONSOLIDATED STATEMENTS OF INCOME AND DEFICIT (excerpts)			
Years ended August 31			
[thousands of Canadian dollars except per share amounts]	2006 $	2005 $	2004 $
		(Restated – note 1)	(Restated – note 1)
Net income	458,250	153,221	70,870
Deficit beginning of year, as previously reported	(471,488)	(369,194)	(336,695)
Adjustment for change in accounting policy *[note 1]*	42,633	36,403	16,257
Deficit, beginning of year, restated	(428,855)	(332,791)	(320,438)
	29,395	(179,570)	(249,568)

---

[17] *CICA Handbook*, Section 1506.28–.31.

Reduction on Class B Non-Voting Shares purchased for cancellation *[note 11]*	**(97,056)**	(175,575)	(46,313)
Amortization of opening fair value loss on a foreign currency forward contract *[note 7]*	**(1,705)**	(3,195)	–
Dividends – Class A and Class B Non-Voting Shares	**(103,335)**	(70,515)	(36,910)
Deficit, end of year	**(172,701)**	(428,855)	(332,791)

Earnings per share *[note 11]*			
Basic	**$2.11**	$0.67	$0.31
Diluted	**$2.09**	$0.67	$0.31

NOTES TO CONSOLIDATED FINANCIAL STATEMENTS

August 31, 2006, 2005 and 2004

[all amounts in thousands of Canadian dollars except share and per share amounts]

1.   SIGNIFICANT ACCOUNTING POLICIES (excerpts)
Adoption of recent Canadian accounting pronouncements

(i)   Equity Instruments

Effective September 1, 2006, the Company retroactively adopted the amended Canadian standard, Financial Instruments – Disclosure and Presentation, which requires obligations that may be settled at the issuer's option by a variable number of the issuer's own equity instruments to be presented as liabilities, which is consistent with US standards. As a result, the Company's Canadian Originated Preferred Securities ("COPrS") and Zero Coupon Loan have been classified as debt instead of equity and the dividend entitlements thereon are treated as interest expense instead of dividends. In addition, such US denominated instruments are translated at period-end exchange rates and to the extent they are unhedged, the resulting gains and losses are included in the Consolidated Statements of Income and Deficit. The impact on the Consolidated Balance Sheets as at August 31, 2006 and 2005 and on the Consolidated Statements of Income and Cash flows for each of the years in the three year period ended August 31, 2006 is as follows:

	Increase (decrease)	
	2006 $	2005 $
Consolidated balance sheets:		
Deferred charges	**793**	13,247
Long-term debt	**100,000**	454,775
Future income taxes	**267**	14,033
Share capital	**(98,467)**	(498,194)
Deficit	**1,007**	(42,633)
Decrease in deficit:		
Adjusted for change in accounting policy	**(42,633)**	(36,403)
Decrease in equity entitlements (net of income taxes)	**(16,788)**	(31,318)
Decrease in gain on redemption of COPrS	**40,484**	12,803
Decrease in gain on settlement of Zero Coupon Loan	**–**	4,921
Decrease in net income	**19,944**	7,364
	1,007	(42,633)

	Increase (decrease) in net income		
	2006 $	2005 $	2004 $
Consolidated statements of income:			
Increase in amortization of deferred charges	**(206)**	(258)	(312)
Increase in interest on long-term debt	**(25,341)**	(48,541)	(62,302)
Increase in foreign exchange gain on unhedged long-term debt	**2,881**	34,258	24,559
Increase in debt retirement costs	**(12,248)**	(6,311)	–
Decrease in fair value loss on foreign currency forward contract	**2,415**	–	–
Decrease in income tax expense	**12,555**	13,488	18,016
Decrease in net income	**(19,944)**	(7,364)	(20,039)
Increase (decrease) in earnings per share:	**(0.01)**	0.03	0.09

	Increase (decrease)		
	2006 $	2005 $	2004 $
Statement of cash flows:			
Operating activities	**(20,724)**	(41,468)	(38,343)
Financing activities	**20,724**	41,468	38,343

Retrospective Restatement—Correction of an Error

Introduction

Although the general approach to accounting for an error correction is similar to accounting for a change in accounting policy, the accounting standard makes a distinction between the two: prior financial statements with material errors were never prepared in accordance with GAAP, unlike those which used a different, but acceptable, accounting policy. The standard uses the term **retrospective restatement** in the case of an error correction. The result is the correction of amounts that were reported in the financial statements of prior periods as if the error had never occurred.[18] Specifically, retrospective restatement takes place in the first set of financial statements that is completed after the error's discovery by doing either of the following:

- restating the comparative amounts for the prior period(s) presented in which the error occurred

- restating the opening balances of assets, liabilities, and equity for the earliest period presented if the error took place before that period[19]

Because an accounting error, by its definition and nature, can be traced to a specific prior year, full retrospective changes to all prior years that are affected is required. Management cannot make a case that it is impracticable to do so.

Retrospective Restatement—Affecting One Prior Period

As soon as they are discovered, errors are corrected retrospectively by proper entries in the accounts and are reflected in the financial statements. In the year in which the error is discovered, the correction is reported in the financial statements as an adjustment to the beginning balance of retained earnings. **If comparative statements are presented, the prior statements that are affected are restated to correct the error so that they appear as if the error had never occurred.** Because error correction requires retrospective restatement of all prior periods that are affected, the accounting is similar to the above example of retrospective application for a voluntary change in accounting policy.

To illustrate, assume that the bookkeeper for Selectric Corporation discovered in 2008 that in 2007 the company had failed to record in the accounts $20,000 of amortization expense on a newly constructed building. Selectric's tax rate is 40%.

As a result of the $20,000 amortization error in 2007, the following balances are incorrect:

Amortization expense (2007) was understated by:	$20,000
Accumulated amortization at December 31, 2007/January 1, 2008, is understated by:	20,000
Future income tax expense (2007) was overstated by ($20,000 × 40%):	8,000
Net income (2007) was overstated by ($20,000 − $8,000):	12,000
Future income tax liability at December 31, 2007/January 1, 2008, is overstated by ($20,000 × 40%):	8,000

The entry that is needed in 2008 to correct the omission of $20,000 of amortization in 2007, assuming the books for 2007 have been closed, is:

---

[18] *CICA Handbook*, Section 1506.05(e).

[19] *CICA Handbook*, Section 1506.42.

Retained Earnings	12,000	
Future Income Tax Asset/Liability	8,000	
Accumulated Amortization—Buildings		20,000

A	=	L	+	SE
−20,000		−8,000		−12,000

Cash flows: No effect

The retained earnings account is adjusted because all 2007 income statement accounts were closed to retained earnings at the end of 2007. The journal entry to record the error correction is the same whether single-period or comparative financial statements are prepared; however, presentation on the financial statements will differ. If single-period financial statements are presented, the error is reported as an adjustment to the opening balance of retained earnings of the period in which the error is discovered, as Illustration 21-7 shows.

Illustration 21-7

*Reporting an Error—
Single-Period Financial
Statements*

Retained earnings, January 1, 2008		
As previously reported (assumed)		$350,000
Correction of an error (amortization)	**$(20,000)**	
Less: Applicable income tax reduction	**8,000**	**(12,000)**
Restated balance of retained earnings, January 1, 2008		338,000
Add: Net income 2008 (assumed)		400,000
Retained earnings, December 31, 2008		$738,000

If comparative financial statements are prepared, adjustments are made to correct the amounts of all affected accounts in the statements of all periods that are reported. The data for each year that is being presented are restated to the correct amounts. In addition, the opening balance of retained earnings for the earliest period being reported is adjusted for any cumulative change in amounts that relates to periods that are prior to the reported periods. In the case of Selectric Corporation, the error of omitting the amortization of $20,000 in 2007, which was discovered in 2008, results in restating the 2007 financial statements when they are presented for comparison with those of 2008. Illustration 21-8 shows the restated amounts.

Illustration 21-8

*Reporting an Error
Correction—Comparative
Financial Statements*

Comparative Balance Sheet (restated)
December 31, 2007

Accumulated amortization, buildings	+$20,000	Future income tax liability	−$ 8,000
		Retained earnings	− 12,000

Comparative Income Statement (restated)
Year ended December 31, 2007

Amortization expense	+$20,000
Future income tax expense	− 8,000
Net income	− 12,000

Comparative Statement of Retained Earnings
Years ended December 31

	2008	2007 changes
	(restated)	(restated)
Opening balance, January 1 ($350,000 − $12,000)	$338,000	N/C*
Net income	400,000	−$12,000
Ending balance, December 31	$738,000	−$12,000

*No change

As the illustration shows, Selectric's 2008 financial statements presented in comparative form with those of 2007 are prepared as if the error had not occurred; the only exception to this is the correction to the opening balance of the retained earnings amount at January 1, 2008, that was previously reported. In addition, a note to the 2008 financial statements that provides all appropriate disclosures is also included.

Retrospective Restatement—Affecting Multiple Prior Periods

Assume that when preparing the financial statements for the year ended December 31, 2008, the controller of Shilling Corp. discovered that a property purchased in mid-2005 for $200,000 had been charged entirely to the Land account in error. The $200,000 cost should have been allocated between Land ($50,000) and Building ($150,000). The building was expected to be used for 20 years and then sold for $70,000 (not including the land). Prior to discovery of this error, Shilling Corp.'s accounting records reported the information in Illustration 21-9.

Illustration 21-9

Accounting Records before Restatement

	2008 (books not closed)	2007
Revenues	$402,000	$398,000
Expenses	329,000	320,000
Income before tax	73,000	78,000
Income tax expense (30%)	21,900	23,400
Net income	$ 51,100	$ 54,600
Retained earnings, January 1	$294,000	$242,000
Net income for year	51,100	54,600
Dividends declared	(2,100)	(2,600)
Retained earnings, December 31	$343,000	$294,000

Retrospective restatement is required, so the first step is to determine the effect of this error on all prior periods. Preparing an appropriate analysis provides backup for the required correcting entry and helps in the restatement of the financial statements. The specific analysis differs for each situation encountered. However, each analysis requires identifying two things: first, what is in the books and records now; and second, what would have been in the accounts if the error had not occurred. The correcting entry then adjusts what is there now to what should be there. Illustration 21-10 shows the analysis that underlies the correcting entry to Shilling's accounts. Assume that the tax records were not updated for the building acquisition and therefore no CCA was claimed on the building over the years. Go through each line, making sure that you understand the source of each number.

Illustration 21-10

Analysis of Error on Shilling's Records

	2008	2007	2006	2005
Income statement effects:				
Correct amortization expense ($150,000 − $70,000) ÷ 20 = $4,000 per year	$ 4,000	$ 4,000	$ 4,000	$ 2,000
Correct tax benefit related to amortization = 30% of amortization expense	1,200	1,200	1,200	600
Income overstated each year by:	$ 2,800	$ 2,800	$ 2,800	$ 1,400

Balance sheet effects, end of each year:				
Land reported	$200,000	$200,000	$200,000	$200,000
Correct land balance	50,000	50,000	50,000	50,000
Building reported	–0–	–0–	–0–	–0–
Correct building balance	150,000	150,000	150,000	150,000
Accumulated amortization reported	–0–	–0–	–0–	–0–
Correct accumulated amortization	14,000	10,000	6,000	2,000
Future tax asset reported re building	–0–	–0–	–0–	–0–
Correct future tax asset balance				
(= 30% of accumulated amortization				
at year end)	4,200	3,000	1,800	600

The correcting entry needed at the 2008 year end when the error is discovered is taken directly from the analysis in Illustration 21-10.

Building (150,000 − 0)	150,000	
Amortization Expense (4,000 − 0)	4,000	
Future Tax Asset (4,200 − 0)	4,200	
Retained Earnings (Jan. 1, 2008: 2,800 + 2,800 + 1,400)	7,000	
Land (200,000 − 50,000)		150,000
Accumulated Amortization (14,000 − 0)		14,000
Income Tax Expense (1,200 − 0)		1,200

A   = L +   SE
−9,800   −9,800

Cash flows: No effect

Let's review this entry. The objective is to correct the accounts so the amounts in the records are the same as they would have been if there had been no error. The Building account would have had a $150,000 balance, but now stands at $0, so it is necessary to debit $150,000 to Building. Amortization expense should have been taken on the building in 2008 but was not, so the current year's expense needs to be recognized. However, with income statement items, because all accounts get closed out each year to Retained Earnings, the correction to amortization expense for 2005 to 2007 must be to Retained Earnings. The expense for 2008 has not yet been closed out, so the adjustment is made directly to the expense. The same explanation applies to the adjustment to Income Tax Expense. In 2008, the adjustment is made to the expense account but for 2005 to 2007, it is made to Retained Earnings. In effect, the $7,000 adjustment to decrease the January 1, 2008, Retained Earnings balance represents the 2005 to 2007 Amortization Expense correction of $10,000 net of the related 2005 to 2007 Income Tax Expense correction of $3,000.

Three other balance sheet accounts need correcting. The Land account, now at $200,000, must be reduced to $50,000. The Accumulated Amortization now stands at $0 but should be $14,000. Lastly, the Future Tax Asset account related to the temporary deductible difference between the tax basis (UCC) of the building and its revised carrying amount is recognized.

Now that the records have been adjusted, the accounting error has to be reported on the comparative statements for 2007, assuming that only one year's comparative statements are being provided. These financial statements must be presented "as if the error had never occurred." If the error occurred before the earliest period that is presented, the error should be corrected by "restating the opening balances of assets, liabilities and equity for the earliest prior period presented."[20] The required income statements and statements of retained earnings, but without any note disclosures, are presented in Illustration 21-11.

---

[20] *CICA Handbook*, Section 1506.42(b).

Income Statement	2008	2007 (restated)
Revenues	$402,000	$398,000
Expenses	333,000[a]	324,000[b]
Income before tax	69,000	74,000
Income tax expense	20,700[c]	22,200[d]
Net income	$ 48,300	$ 51,800

[a]$329,000 + $4,000   [b]$320,000 + $4,000
[c]$21,900 − $1,200   [d]$23,400 − $1,200

Statement of Retained Earnings		
Retained earnings, January 1, as previously reported		$242,000
Cumulative effect of accounting error, net of tax benefit of $1,800		(4,200)
Retained earnings, January 1, as restated	$287,000	237,800
Net income	48,300	51,800
Less: Dividends declared	(2,100)	(2,600)
Retained earnings, December 31	$333,200	$287,000

The adjustments to the income statement are relatively straightforward as the expenses and income tax lines are simply changed to the corrected amounts. The earliest retained earnings balance that is reported now has to be restated to what it would have been if the error had never occurred.

For the 2007 statement of retained earnings, the previously reported opening retained earnings balance (i.e., the 2006 ending balance) is adjusted for the effects on income (and therefore retained earnings) prior to January 1, 2007. The cumulative adjustment at this date is $4,200. This reflects the $6,000 of additional amortization expense ($2,000 + $4,000) reduced by the $1,800 of related income tax benefit ($600 + $1,200) to January 1, 2007. If the error had not been made, the balance of retained earnings at January 1, 2007, would have been $237,800. The revised 2007 net income of $51,800 is added to this and the 2007 dividends are deducted in determining the corrected December 31, 2007, balance of retained earnings.

For 2008, the restated opening retained earnings for 2008 of $287,000 is the balance that would have been reported if the error had never occurred. The correct income for 2008 is added to this and the 2008 dividends are deducted to give the retained earnings at the end of 2008. It is not an accounting error in the current year as it has been corrected.

The comparative balance sheet for 2007 is designated as "restated" and information is disclosed about the effect on each financial statement line item that has been affected.

Disclosures Required for the Correction of an Accounting Error

Objective 7
Identify the disclosure requirements for the correction of an accounting error.

The disclosures required when a company corrects an error in a prior period are few, but informative. The following information is required to be disclosed in the year of the correction, but is not necessary in subsequent periods:

1. The nature of the error

2. The amount of the correction to basic and fully diluted earnings per share and to each line item on the financial statements presented for comparative purposes

3. The amount of the correction made at the beginning of the earliest prior period presented

Example of Disclosures

Illustration 21-12 presents **Inco Limited**'s note to its December 31, 2005, financial statements that describes the effects of its retrospective restatements for an error in calculating minority (non-controlling) interest.

Notes to Consolidated Financial Statements

Note 2. Changes in accounting policies and restatements

Restatements

Effective January 1, 2005, on a retroactive basis, we restated our minority interest and current deferred income taxes to correct an error in the allocation of net earnings to minority interests. The impact of the correction for our December 31, 2004 balance sheet was a decrease in minority interest of $59 million (2003 - $38 million), a decrease in current deferred taxes of $21 million (2003 - $14 million) and an increase in retained earnings of $38 million (2003 - $24 million). The net impact on 2004 net earnings was an increase of $14 million (2003 - $10 million), or 7 cents per share (2003 – 5 cents per share).

Illustration 21-12

Example of Disclosure of the Effects of an Error Correction

Student Website

Student Toolkit—
Additional Disclosures

www.wiley.com/canada/kieso

Prospective Application

Introduction

As explained above, the effects of changes in estimates are handled prospectively. That is, **no changes are made to previously reported results, but instead they are made forward from the time of the change in estimate.** Changes in estimates are viewed as normal recurring corrections and adjustments—the natural result of the accounting process and retrospective treatment is therefore not appropriate. Opening balances are not adjusted, and no attempt is made to "catch up" for prior periods. The financial statements of prior periods are not restated.

Instead, the effect of a change in estimate is accounted for by including it in net income or comprehensive income, as appropriate, in (1) the period of change if the change affects that period only, or (2) the period of change and future periods if the change affects both. If the estimate relates to the balance of an asset, liability, or equity item, the item's carrying amount is changed.[21]

The circumstances related to a change in estimate are different from those related to a change in accounting policy. If changes in estimates were handled on a retroactive basis, continual adjustments of prior years' income would occur. It seems proper to accept the view that, because new conditions or circumstances exist, the revision fits the new situation and should be handled in the current and future periods only.

As indicated earlier in the chapter, **it is also appropriate to apply prospective treatment to a change in accounting policy** if it is impracticable to determine the effect of the change even as far back as the beginning of the current period. In such a situation, the new accounting policy is only applied to transactions and events that occur after the accounting policy is changed.

Illustration—Change in Estimate

To illustrate the accounting for a change in estimate, assume that Underwriter Labs Inc. purchased a building for $300,000 that was originally estimated to have a useful life of

8 Objective

Apply the prospective application method for an accounting change.

---

[21] *CICA Handbook*, Section 1506.36 and .37.

15 years and no residual value. Amortization of $20,000 per year has been recorded for five years on a straight-line basis. In 2008, the total useful life estimate is revised to 25 years. The accounts at the beginning of the sixth year are as follows:

Building	$300,000
Less accumulated amortization at end of 2007: 5 × $20,000 =	100,000
Carrying amount of building, January 1, 2008	$200,000

Assuming no entry has yet been made in 2008, the entry to record amortization for 2008 is:

A = L + SE
−10,000   −10,000

Cash flows: No effect

Amortization Expense	10,000	
Accumulated Amortization—Building		10,000

The $10,000 amortization charge is calculated in Illustration 21-13.

Illustration 21-13
Amortization after Change in Estimate

$$\text{Amortization charge} = \frac{\text{Carrying amount of asset} - \text{Residual value}}{\text{Remaining service life}} = \frac{\$200,000 - \$0}{25 \text{ years} - 5 \text{ years}} = \$10,000$$

Prospective treatment applied to a change in accounting policy simply means that the new policy is applied to the current balance of the related asset, liability, and/or equity item after the date of change.

Disclosure Requirements for a Change in an Accounting Estimate

Objective 9
Identify the disclosure requirements for a change in an accounting estimate.

Disclosures for changes in estimates have the same objective as other types of changes: to provide information that is useful in assessing the effects of the change on the financial statements. The minimum disclosures, therefore, are as follows:

1. The nature of the change in estimate

2. The amount of the change in estimate that affects the current period or is expected to affect future periods, unless it is not practicable to estimate that effect. If impracticable, this fact is disclosed.[22]

Materiality plays an important role here, as it does with other accounting standards.

Example of disclosure of a change in estimate Celestica Inc., headquartered in Toronto, operates a global manufacturing network for the computer, communications, industrial, and consumer markets in Asia, the Americas, and Europe. Illustration 21-14 captures Celestica's note about a recent change in accounting estimate that was reported in its financial statements for the year ended December 31, 2006.

[22] *CICA Handbook*, Section 1506.39–.40.

Illustration 21-14

*Example of Disclosure
of a Change in
Accounting Estimate*

**CELESTICA INC.
NOTES TO THE CONSOLIDATED FINANCIAL STATEMENTS**
(in millions of U.S. dollars)

2. SIGNIFICANT ACCOUNTING POLICIES

(g) Capital assets:

We carry capital assets at cost and amortize these assets over their estimated useful lives or lease terms on a straight-line basis. The estimated useful lives for our principal asset categories are as follows:

Buildings	25 years
Buildings/leasehold improvements	Up to 25 years or term of lease
Office equipment	5 years
Machinery and equipment	3 to 7 years
Software	1 to 10 years

We expense maintenance and repair costs as incurred.

Effective October 1, 2005, we changed the estimated useful lives of certain machinery and equipment from five years to seven years based on our experience and the extended use of these assets. As a result of this change in estimated useful life, depreciation expense included in cost of sales was lower by approximately $16 in 2006 and approximately $6 in 2005.

Summary of Accounting Changes

Developing recommendations for reporting accounting changes has helped resolve several significant and long-standing accounting problems. Yet, because of the diversity of situations and of characteristics of the items that are encountered in practice, applying professional judgement is still highly important. The primary objective is to serve the user of the financial statements. Achieving this requires full disclosure and the avoidance of any misleading inferences. The main distinctions and treatments that were presented in the earlier discussion are summarized in Illustration 21-15.

Illustration 21-15

*Flowchart—Accounting
Changes*

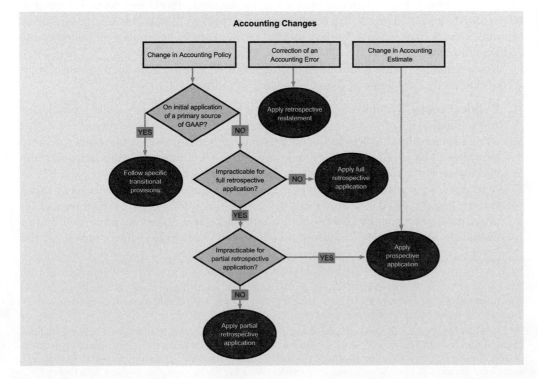

1336 CHAPTER 21 Accounting Changes and Error Analysis

Changes in accounting policies are considered appropriate only when they are dictated by a primary source of GAAP or the enterprise demonstrates that an alternative generally accepted accounting policy or its method of application is preferable to the existing one. The decision of whether one policy should be preferred over another is based on **whether the new policy results in a more relevant presentation in the financial statements**. Standard setters make this assessment when they are formulating or revising primary sources of GAAP, and the same test is required for voluntary changes.[23] But determining what is "more relevant" is not always obvious in financial reporting. How is relevance measured? One enterprise might argue that a change in accounting policy from FIFO to an average cost formula better matches current costs and current revenues, providing more predictive, and therefore more relevant, information. Conversely, another enterprise might change from an average cost formula to FIFO because it wants to report a more current and relevant ending inventory amount that also has better predictive value. How do you determine which is the better of these two arguments? The revised standards are an improvement over the previous ones because they provide a context for the decision; they relate the decision to qualitative characteristics that have been agreed upon as financial statement concepts in *CICA Handbook* Section 1000. Applying the standards, however, will continue to require the use of professional judgement.

PERSPECTIVES

Motivations for Change

Objective 10
Identify economic motives for changing accounting methods.

Understanding how an entity chooses its accounting methods and procedures is complex. The complexity is due to the fact that managers (and others) have an interest in how the financial statements make the company look. Managers naturally want to show their financial performance in the best light. A favourable profit picture can influence investors, and a strong liquidity position can influence creditors. Too favourable a profit picture, however, can provide union negotiators with ammunition during bargaining talks. Also, if the federal government has established price controls, managers might believe that a trend of lower profits might persuade the regulatory authorities to grant their company a price increase. Hence, managers might have varying profit motives, depending on the economy and who they want to impress.

Research has provided additional insights into why companies may prefer certain accounting methods.[24] Some of these reasons are as follows.

1. **Political costs.** As companies become larger and more politically visible, politicians and regulators devote more attention to them. The larger the firm, the more likely it is to become subject to legislation such as anti-competition regulations and the more likely it is to be required to pay higher taxes. Therefore, companies that are politically visible may try to report income numbers that are low in order to avoid the scrutiny of regulators. By reporting low income numbers, companies hope to reduce their exposure to being viewed as a monopoly power.[25] This practice can have an impact on other concerned parties as well. For example, labour unions may be less willing to demand wage increases if reported income is low. Researchers have found that the

---

[23] CICA, "Accounting Changes—Background Information and Basis for Conclusions," July 2006, par. 14.

[24] See Ross L. Watts and Jerold L. Zimmerman, "Positive Accounting Theory: A Ten-Year Perspective," *The Accounting Review* (January 1990) for an excellent review of research findings related to management incentives in selecting accounting methods.

[25] "There's an old saw on Bay Street that the Royal Bank earned a billion dollars three years before it told the world," indicates Kim Shannon of Sionna Investment Managers Inc. Although the comment was made in the context of a discussion on income smoothing, the authors believe that this was directly related to the appearance of the situation at a time when banks were heavily under fire for "gouging" consumers with fees and closing branches. "A Beautiful Find," *Globe and Mail* on-line, Jan. 30, 2004, http://www.globeandmail.com.

larger a company is, the more likely it is to adopt approaches that decrease income when it selects its accounting methods.

2. **Capital structure.** Several studies have found that a company's capital structure can affect the selection of accounting methods. For example, a company with a high debt-to-equity ratio is more likely to be constrained by debt covenants. That is, a company may have a debt covenant that indicates that it cannot pay any dividends if retained earnings fall below a certain level. As a result, this type of company is more likely to select accounting methods that will increase net income—such as capitalizing interest instead of expensing it, or using the full cost method instead of the successful efforts approach.

3. **Bonus payments.** Studies have found that if compensation plans tie managers' bonus payments to income, management will select accounting methods that maximize bonus payments.

4. **Smooth earnings.** Substantial increases in earnings attract the attention of politicians, regulators, and competitors. In addition, large increases in income create problems for management because the same results are difficult to achieve in subsequent years. Compensation plans may adjust to these higher numbers as a baseline and make it difficult for management to achieve its profit goals and receive bonuses in the following years. On the other hand, decreases in earnings might signal that the company is in financial trouble. Furthermore, significant decreases in income raise concerns on the part of shareholders, lenders, and other interested parties about the competency of management. For all these reasons, companies have an incentive to "manage" or "smooth" their earnings. Management typically believes that steady growth of 10 percent per year is much better than 30-percent growth one year followed by a 10-percent decline the next. In other words, management usually prefers to report gradually increasing income and sometimes changes accounting methods to ensure such a result.

Management pays careful attention to the accounting it follows and often changes accounting methods, not for conceptual reasons, but rather for economic reasons. As indicated throughout this textbook, such arguments have come to be known as economic consequences arguments, since they focus on the supposed impact of accounting on the behaviour of investors, creditors, competitors, governments, and the managers of the reporting companies themselves, rather than address the conceptual justification for accounting standards.[26]

To counter these pressures, standard setters have declared, as part of their conceptual framework, that they will assess the merits of proposed standards from a position of neutrality. That is, the soundness of standards should not be evaluated on the grounds of their possible impact on behaviour. It is not the Accounting Standards Board's place to choose standards according to the kinds of behaviour that the Board's members want to promote or discourage. At the same time, it must be admitted that some standards often have the effect of influencing behaviour. Nonetheless, their justification should be conceptual, and not viewed in terms of their economic impact.

Interpreting Accounting Changes

What effect do accounting changes have on financial statement analysis? Not surprisingly, they often make it difficult to develop meaningful trend data, which undermines one of the major reasons that accounting information has been found useful in the past.

---

[26] Economic consequences arguments—and there are many of them—constitute manipulation through the use of lobbying and other forms of pressure brought on standard setters. We have seen examples of these arguments in the oil and gas industry about successful efforts versus full cost, in the technology area with the issue of mandatory expensing of research and most development costs, and with stock options, and so on.

What Do the Numbers Mean?

Alliance Atlantis Communications Inc. reported numerous accounting changes recently. In one year, the company adopted three revised accounting policies, and during the next fiscal period, it adopted three more. All but one of the six changes were initial applications of a primary source of GAAP. The voluntary change transferred what had been classified as investing expenditures to the operating classification, reducing previously reported cash from operations by hundreds of millions of dollars!

Another note to the financial statements indicates that the company changed its method of accounting for its "investment in the two *CSI* television series," but fails to adequately explain the reason. Was this an error? What may not be clear to readers is that while certain income (revenues of $77.1 million and income of $32.8 million) was reported in the financial statements of the two prior years, these amounts were pulled out of retained earnings in the current year, and, one assumes, were or will again be reported in revenue and income at a later date.

International Hi-Tech Industries Inc., based in Vancouver, provides another example. In a recent year, the company announced it was restating its aggregate revenue for the previous seven years by more than $6 million and reducing its income over the past two and a half years by about $3 million. At issue was the fact that the company had determined that revenue related to non-refundable fees and deposits had been recognized earlier than it should have been. Here, too, the restatement cancelled out previously reported earnings, leaving them available to be reported on the income statement again in the future! To be fair, the new revenue recognition policy appears to be a more appropriate policy.

These situations highlight the difficulty that investors may experience when they are trying to identify trend data for analysis and the challenge that standard setters have in determining best practice for reporting accounting changes. The new accounting standard covering these issues attempts to limit the changes to situations where they are well warranted.

In general, financial statement readers should look closely at all accounting changes and adjust any trend data appropriately. Although most changes have no cash effect on the statements, some can end up converting previously reported operating cash flows to investment or financing flows. Most changes tend to shift earnings from one accounting period to another.

Consider the case of Quebec-based giant **Quebecor Inc.** when it applied the revised recommendations on accounting for goodwill in 2002. Under the old standard, goodwill was amortized over its useful life; under the new standard, goodwill is kept on the books but, instead of being amortized, is tested for impairment each year. The transitional provisions required companies to account for this change prospectively, but permitted them to carry out a transitional impairment test at the effective date of the new standard. Any transitional impairment loss on goodwill was treated as the effect of a change in accounting policy and accounted for retroactively without restatement. Quebecor Inc., which reported goodwill of $10.2 billion on its prior year's balance sheet, used the transitional provision to write off $2.2 billion of goodwill one day later. It was reported as an adjustment to opening retained earnings at that date, relieving future income statements of $2.2 billion of costs! **BCE Inc.** similarly revised its goodwill policy at this time, retroactively adjusting its previously reported opening retained earnings balance of $712 million downward **by almost $8.2 billion**.

International

Objective 11
Compare current Canadian and international GAAP for accounting changes.

Comparison of Canadian and International GAAP

The Canadian standard for accounting changes, effective for fiscal years beginning on or after January 1, 2007, is based on the relevant parts of the related international standard.

Therefore, there are few differences between these two primary sources of GAAP identified in Illustration 21-16.

Illustration 21-16

Canadian and International Primary Sources of GAAP

Canada	International
Section 1506: Accounting changes	IAS 8: Accounting policies, changes in accounting estimates and errors
Section 1100: Generally accepted accounting principles	IFRS 1: First-time adoption of international reporting standards

Although it is based on IAS 8, and uses the same paragraph numbers and terminology, the Canadian standard did not adopt certain paragraphs of the IFRS. The following differences are noted:

Selection of accounting policies. IAS 8 includes a section on the general selection of accounting policies. Because this topic is included in *CICA Handbook* Section 1100, "Generally Accepted Accounting Principles," and it has recently been revised and is widely referenced, this section was not incorporated in Section 1506.

Retrospective restatement and impracticability. Under the Canadian standard, there are no exceptions to the requirement to provide a full retrospective restatement in the case of an accounting error. IAS 8, on the other hand, indicates that if full retrospective restatement is not practicable, then an entity is permitted to restate information for the earliest period for which it is practicable.

Prospective application guidance. While both the Canadian and international standards use the same definition of the term "prospective" and use the term in the same way, Section 1506 allows a primary source of GAAP to override the definition. IAS 8 does not.

When international standards are adopted by publicly accountable enterprises in Canada, expected in 2011, all differences from IAS 8 will be eliminated.

Adoption of IFRSs

The most significant accounting change looming on the Canadian accounting horizon is the move to adopt IFRSs in 2011. How will this change be applied?

IFRS 1, "First-time Adoption of International Financial Reporting Standards," is the standard for an entity's preparation of its first IFRS financial statements. IAS 8 **does not deal with changes in accounting policies** for this first-time adoption. The document's objective is to ensure that these first statements contain high-quality, cost-effective information that is comparable for all periods presented, is transparent for users, and provides the appropriate base for application of IFRSs in the future.[27]

If the changeover date to international standards is identified as January 1, 2011, and an entity's first **reporting date** is December 31, 2011, its **date of transition to IFRSs** is actually the beginning of business on January 1, 2010. The reason for the earlier date of transition is that at least one full year of comparative information is required in the first reporting period. An **opening IFRS balance sheet** is needed for the entity one year before the effective date announced by the Canadian Accounting Standards Board.[28]

In general, the accounting policies to be used in reporting the assets, liabilities, and equity items on an entity's opening IFRS balance sheet and in all periods covered by its

---

[27] IFRS 1, par. 1.

[28] As this text went to print, the Accounting Standards Board planned to announce the changeover date to IFRS by March 31, 2008. Note also that for an entity reporting in a jurisdiction that requires two years' comparative balance sheets to be provided, the date of transition would be January 1, 2009.

first set of statements are required to comply with the IFRSs that are in effect on the first reporting date. The adjustments that are needed to bring the entity's previous GAAP measures in line with IFRS balance sheet recognition and measurement standards are recognized directly in retained earnings (or some other category of equity, if applicable). Retrospective application to prior periods is not applied.

The remainder of IFRS 1 identifies various exemptions from some IFRS requirements, prohibits retrospective application of certain aspects of other IFRSs, and provides presentation and disclosure requirements. It also allows some one-time opportunities to reconsider accounting decisions, such as the classification and revaluation of certain assets.

ERROR ANALYSIS

Objective 12
Correct the effects of errors and prepare restated financial statements.

In the past, it was unusual to see the correction of material errors in the financial statements of large corporations. Internal control procedures and the diligence of the accounting staff were normally sufficient to find and correct any major errors in the system before the statements were released. However, in the first half of this decade, there have been a number of well-publicized cases of major companies restating past results. As this text was written, numerous companies in the U.S. and Canada, including **Research In Motion** (see the chapter-opening vignette), were in the midst of restating past financial statements for a number of years due to improper dating of stock option grants, and **Nortel Networks** continues to grapple with restatements after issuing revised statements at least twice in the recent past. Whether these and other similar situations are true errors or overly aggressive choices of accounting methods remains to be seen. Smaller businesses may face a different problem. These enterprises may not be able to afford an internal audit staff or to implement the necessary control procedures to ensure that accounting data are recorded accurately.

What Do the Numbers Mean?

Investor research firm Glass, Lewis & Co. recently reported that the number of error restatements made by U.S. public companies in 2006 was 12 times higher than in 1997. The top categories they identified were as follows:

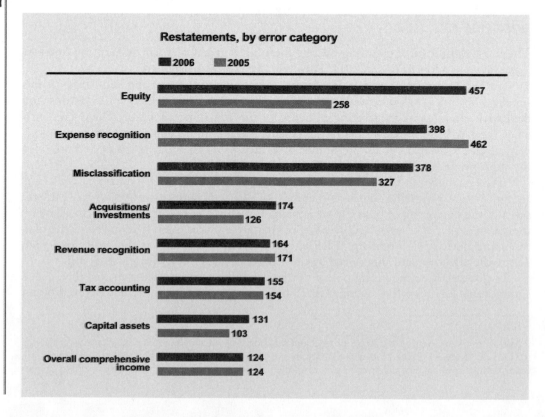

Restatements, by error category

2006   2005

Category	2006	2005
Equity	457	258
Expense recognition	398	462
Misclassification	378	327
Acquisitions/Investments	174	126
Revenue recognition	164	171
Tax accounting	155	154
Capital assets	131	103
Overall comprehensive income	124	124

Many of these errors were found through regulatory investigations into accounting misrepresentations, and others were turned up through the examination of internal controls that was mandated by the *Sarbanes-Oxley Act* of 2002. Others came to light as companies implemented or adapted comprehensive enterprise-resource-planning software. But what caused these restatements in the first place?

The complexity of corporate transactions themselves—especially increasingly sophisticated financing techniques—provides fertile ground for making errors. In addition, the increased number and complexity of accounting standards and other regulations, low budgets for the internal audit function, and reduced levels of spending on external audit fees all contributed to the need for restatements. Trent Gazzaway, the U.S. national managing partner of corporate governance for audit firm Grant Thornton, LLP, suggested that "[c]ompanies are in business to produce their product and sell it at a profit, and the reporting of the processes around that is a secondary goal. In some cases, it's become too secondary." And, of course, some errors are due to "just plain dumb mistakes."

Source: Roy Harris, "Say Again? An Explosion in Accounting Errors—in Part Reflecting the Difficulties of Today's Complex Rules—Has Forced Nearly a Quarter of U.S. Companies to Learn the Art of the Restatement," CFO.com (*CFO Magazine*, April 2007).

In practice, firms do not correct errors that are discovered if they do not have a significant effect on the financial statements. For example, the failure to record accrued wages of $5,000 when the total payroll for the year is $1,750,000 and net income is $940,000 is not considered significant, and no correction is made. Obviously, defining materiality is difficult, and experience and judgement are used to determine whether adjustment is necessary for a given error. All errors that are discussed in this section are assumed to be material and to require adjustment. For simplicity, we have chosen to ignore the tax effects initially so that you can focus instead on the direct effects of the errors themselves.

The accountant must answer three questions in error analysis:

1. What type of error is involved?

2. What entries are needed to correct the error?

3. How are financial statements to be restated once the error is discovered?

As indicated earlier, the profession requires that errors be corrected retrospectively with restatement, meaning that the elements of the financial statements are adjusted as if the error had never occurred. Three types of errors can occur. Because each type has its own peculiarities, it is important to understand their differences.

Balance Sheet Errors

These errors affect only the presentation of an asset, liability, or shareholders' equity account. Examples are classifying a short-term receivable as part of the investment section, a note payable as an account payable, or plant assets as inventory. Reclassification of the item to its proper position is needed when the error is discovered. If comparative statements that include the error year are prepared, the balance sheet for the error year is restated correctly. No further corrections are needed.

Income Statement Errors

These errors affect only income statement accounts. Errors involve the improper classification of revenues or expenses, such as recording interest revenue as part of sales, purchases as bad debt expense, or amortization expense as interest expense. An income statement classification error has no effect on the balance sheet or on net income. If a reclassification error is discovered in the year the error is made, an entry is needed to correct it. If the error occurred in prior periods, no entry is needed at the date of discovery because the accounts for the year of the misclassification have all been closed to retained earnings and the current year is correctly stated. If comparative statements that include the error year are prepared, the income statement for the error year is restated correctly.

Balance Sheet and Income Statement Errors

The third type of error involves both the balance sheet and the income statement. For example, assume that accrued wages were overlooked by the bookkeeper at the end of the accounting period. The error's effect is to understate expenses and liabilities, and overstate net income for that accounting period. **This type of error affects both the balance sheet and the income statement** and is determined to be either a counterbalancing or a non-counterbalancing error.

Counterbalancing errors are errors that will be offset or that will self-correct over two periods. In the previous illustration, the failure to record accrued wages is considered a counterbalancing error because, after a two-year period, the error will no longer be present. In other words, the failure to record accrued wages in year one means that (1) wages expense for the first period is understated, (2) net income for the first period is overstated, (3) accrued wages payable (a liability) at the end of the first period is understated, and (4) retained earnings at the end of the first period is overstated. In period two, wages expense is overstated and net income is understated, but both accrued wages payable (a liability) and retained earnings at the end of the second period **are now correct. For the two years combined**, both wages expense and net income are correct, as are the ending balance sheet amounts of wages payable and retained earnings. Most errors in accounting that affect both the balance sheet and income statement are counterbalancing errors.

Non-counterbalancing errors are errors that are not offset in the next accounting period. An example is the failure to capitalize equipment that has a useful life of five years. If we expense this asset immediately, expenses will be overstated in the first period but understated in the next four periods. At the end of the second period, the error's effect is not fully offset. Net income is only correct overall at the end of five years, because the asset will have been fully amortized at this point, assuming it has no residual value. Thus, **non-counterbalancing errors are those that take longer than two periods to correct themselves**.

Only in rare instances is an error never reversed. This would occur, for example, if land were initially expensed. Because land is not subject to amortization, the error is not offset until the land is sold.

Counterbalancing Errors

The usual types of counterbalancing errors are illustrated on the following pages. In studying these illustrations, several points should be remembered. **First**—and this is key—**the entries will differ depending on whether or not the books have been closed for the period in which the error is found.**

1. When **the books have been closed**:
    (a) If the error is already counterbalanced, no entry is necessary.
    (b) If the error is not yet counterbalanced, an entry is necessary to adjust the present balance of retained earnings and the other affected balance sheet account(s).

2. When **the books have not been closed**:
    (a) If the error is already counterbalanced and the company is in the second year, an entry is necessary to correct the current period income statement account(s) and to adjust the beginning balance of retained earnings.

(b) If the error is not yet counterbalanced, an entry is necessary to adjust the beginning balance of retained earnings and correct the affected current period income statement account(s) and balance sheet account(s).

Second, if comparative statements are presented, it is necessary to restate the amounts for comparative purposes. **Restatement is necessary even if a correcting journal entry is not required.** To illustrate, assume that Sanford Cement Ltd. failed to accrue revenue in 2006 when it was earned, but recorded the revenue in 2007 when it was received. The error is discovered in 2009. No entry is necessary to correct this error, because the effects have been counterbalanced by the time the error is discovered in 2009. However, if comparative financial statements for 2006 through to 2009 are presented, the accounts and related amounts for the years 2006 and 2007 are restated correctly for financial reporting purposes.

The following are examples of counterbalancing errors. **Income tax effects have been ignored for now.** Do not memorize these. Rather, you should work with them until you understand each one.

1. **Failure to record accrued wages.** On December 31, 2008, accrued wages of $1,500 were not recognized. The entry in 2009 to correct this error, assuming that the books have not been closed for 2009, is:

Retained Earnings	1,500	
Wages Expense		1,500

A = L + SE
0   0   0
Cash flows: No effect

The rationale for this entry is as follows: When the accrued wages relating to 2008 were paid in 2009, an additional debit of $1,500 was made to 2009 Wages Expense, overstating this account by $1,500. Because 2008 accrued wages were not recorded as Wages Expense for 2008, net income for 2008 was overstated by $1,500. Because 2008 net income was overstated by $1,500, the 2009 opening Retained Earnings were also overstated by $1,500.

If the books have been closed for 2009, no entry is made, because the error is counterbalanced.

2. **Failure to record prepaid expenses.** In January 2008, a two-year insurance policy costing $1,000 was purchased; Insurance Expense was debited, and Cash was credited. No adjusting entries were made at the end of 2008. The entry on December 31, 2009, to correct this error, assuming that the books have not been closed for 2009, is:

Insurance Expense	500	
Retained Earnings		500

A = L + SE
0   0   0
Cash flows: No effect

If the books are closed for 2009, no entry is made, because the error is counterbalanced.

3. **Understatement of unearned revenue.** On December 31, 2008, cash of $50,000 was received as a prepayment for renting office space for the following year. The entry that was made when the rent payment was received was a debit to Cash and a credit to Rent Revenue. No adjusting entry was made as at December 31, 2008. The entry on December 31, 2009, to correct this error, assuming that the books have not been closed for 2009, is:

Retained Earnings	50,000	
Rent Revenue		50,000

A = L + SE
0   0   0
Cash flows: No effect

If the books are closed for 2009, no entry is made, because the error is counterbalanced.

4. **Overstatement of accrued revenue.** On December 31, 2008, interest income of $8,000 was accrued that applied to 2009. The entry made on December 31, 2008, was to debit Interest Receivable and credit Interest Income. The entry on December 31, 2009, to correct this error, assuming that the books have not been closed for 2009, is:

A = L + SE
0   0   0

Cash flows: No effect

Retained Earnings	8,000	
Interest Income		8,000

If the books have been closed for 2009, no entry is made, because the error is counterbalanced.

5. **Overstatement of purchases.** The accountant recorded a purchase of merchandise for $9,000 in 2008 that applied to 2009. The physical inventory for 2008 was correctly stated. The company uses the periodic inventory method. The entry on December 31, 2009, to correct this error, assuming that the books have not been closed for 2009, is:

A = L + SE
0   0   0

Cash flows: No effect

Purchases	9,000	
Retained Earnings		9,000

If the 2009 books have been closed, no entry is made, because the error is counterbalanced.

6. **Understatement of ending inventory.** On December 31, 2008, the physical inventory count was understated by $25,000 because the inventory crew failed to count one section of a merchandise warehouse. The entry on December 31, 2009, to correct this error, assuming the 2009 books have not yet been closed and the ending inventory has not yet been adjusted to the inventory account, is:

A   = L + SE
+25,000   +25,000

Cash flows: No effect

Inventory (beginning)	25,000	
Retained Earnings		25,000

If the books are closed for 2009, no entry would be made, because the error has been counterbalanced.

7. **Overstatement of purchases and inventories.** Sometimes, both the physical inventory and the purchases are incorrectly stated. Assume that 2009 purchases of $9,000 were incorrectly recorded as 2008 purchases and that 2008 ending inventory was overstated by the same amount. The entry on December 31, 2009, to correct this error before the 2009 books are closed and the correct ending inventory is adjusted to the inventory account is:

A   = L + SE
−9,000   −9,000

Cash flows: No effect

Purchases	9,000	
Inventory (beginning)		9,000

The net income for 2008 is correct because the overstatement of purchases was offset by the overstatement of ending inventory in cost of goods sold. As with the other examples of counterbalancing errors, no entry is required if the 2009 books have already been closed.

Non-Counterbalancing Errors

Because non-counterbalancing errors do not self-correct over a two-year period, the entries for them are more complex, and correcting entries are needed even if the books have been closed. The best approach is to identify what the relevant account balances **are** in the accounts, what they **should be**, and then bring them to the correct balances through correcting entries. Examples follow.

1. **Failure to record amortization.** Assume that a machine with an estimated five-year useful life was purchased on January 1, 2008, for $10,000. The accountant incorrectly expensed this machine in 2008 and the error was discovered in 2009. If we assume that the company uses straight-line amortization on similar assets, the entry on December 31, 2009, to correct this error, given that the 2009 books are not yet closed, is:

Machinery	10,000	
Amortization Expense (2009)	2,000	
Retained Earnings		8,000
Accumulated Amortization		4,000

Retained Earnings:

Expense reported in 2008	$10,000
Correct amortization for 2008 (20% × $10,000)	(2,000)
Retained earnings understated as at Dec. 31, 2008, by	$ 8,000

Accumulated Amortization, Dec. 31, 2009:

Accumulated amortization (20% × $10,000 × 2)	$ 4,000

A = L + SE
+6,000   +6,000

Cash flows: No effect

If the books are closed for 2009, the entry is:

Machinery	10,000	
Retained Earnings		6,000
Accumulated Amortization		4,000

Retained Earnings:

Retained earnings understated as at Dec. 31, 2008, by	$ 8,000
Correct amortization for 2009 (20% × $10,000)	(2,000)
Retained earnings understated as at Dec. 31, 2009, by	$ 6,000

A = L + SE
+6,000   +6,000

Cash flows: No effect

2. **Failure to adjust for bad debts.** Assume that a company has inappropriately been using the direct write-off method when the allowance method should have been applied. Thus, the following bad debt expense has been recognized as the debts have actually become uncollectible.

	2008	2009
From 2008 sales	$550	$690
From 2009 sales		700

The company estimates that an additional $1,400 will be written off in 2010, of which $300 applies to 2008 sales and $1,100 to 2009 sales. The entry on December 31, 2009, to correct the accounts for bad debt expense, assuming that the books have not been closed for 2009, is:

A = L + SE
−1,400   −1,400

Cash flows: No effect

Bad Debt Expense	410	
Retained Earnings	990	
Allowance for Doubtful Accounts		1,400

Allowance for doubtful accounts:
Additional $300 for 2008 sales and $1,100 for 2009
sales = $1,400.

Bad debt expense corrections needed:	2008	2009
Accounts written off by year of sale ($550 + $690 = $1,240)	$1,240	$ 700
Additional bad debts anticipated (total of $1,400)	300	1,100
Correct amount of bad debt expense each year	1,540	1,800
Bad debt expense previously recorded	(550)	(1,390)
Bad debt expense adjustment needed	$ 990	$ 410

If the books have been closed for 2009, the entry is:

A = L + SE
−1,400   −1,400

Cash flows: No effect

Retained Earnings	1,400	
Allowance for Doubtful Accounts		1,400

Income Tax Effects

As mentioned earlier, the income tax effects were not reported with the above correcting entries in order to make it easier for you to focus on the effects of the errors themselves. Once you understand the correcting entries, you can then add the income tax effects, as we will do now.

If a correction **increases a previous year's income** (either by an increase in revenue or a decrease in expense), the income tax expense for that period will usually be increased: more income, more tax. If the correction **reduces a previous year's income** (either by a decrease in revenue or an increase in expense), the income tax expense for that period will usually be reduced: less income, less tax. The net correction to retained earnings, therefore, is made net of tax. Note that for counterbalancing errors, the income tax effects also offset each other over the two-year period, assuming tax rates have not changed.

Because the tax return for the previous period has already been filed, any adjustment of the previous year's balance sheet accounts and income for financial reporting purposes creates a temporary difference between tax values and the corrected book values. The tax effect, therefore, is captured in the Future Income Tax Asset/Liability account.

Illustration 21-17 identifies the correcting entries that are needed, including the tax effects for the counterbalancing and non-counterbalancing examples provided on pages 1342 to 1346. A 40% income tax rate is assumed for all years.

Illustration 21-17

Correcting Entries with Income Tax Effects

	BOOKS FOR 2009		
Error	Not Closed		Closed
COUNTERBALANCING ERRORS			
1. Accrued Wages			
Retained Earnings	900		–No Entry–
Future Tax Asset/Liability	600		
Wages Expense		1,500	

2. Prepaid expenses

Insurance Expense	500		–No Entry–
Retained Earnings		300	
Future Tax Asset/Liability		200	

3. Unearned Revenue

Retained Earnings	30,000		–No Entry–
Future Tax Asset/Liability	20,000		
Rent Revenue		50,000	

4. Accrued Revenue

Retained Earnings	4,800		–No Entry–
Future Tax Asset/Liability	3,200		
Interest Income		8,000	

5. Overstatement of Purchases

Purchases	9,000		–No Entry–
Retained Earnings		5,400	
Future Tax Asset/Liability		3,600	

6. Understatement of Ending Inventory

Inventory (beginning)	25,000		–No Entry–
Retained Earnings		15,000	
Future Tax Asset/Liability		10,000	

7. Overstatement of Purchases and Inventories

Purchases	9,000		–No Entry–
Inventory (beginning)		9,000	

NON-COUNTERBALANCING ERRORS

1. Amortization

Machinery	10,000		Machinery	10,000	
Amortization Expense	2,000		Accumulated Amortization		4,000
Accumulated Amortization		4,000	Retained Earnings		3,600
Retained Earnings		4,800	Future Tax Asset/Liability		2,400
Future Tax Asset/Liability		3,200			

2. Bad Debts

Bad Debt Expense	410		Retained Earnings	840	
Retained Earnings	594		Future Tax Asset/Liability	560	
Future Tax Asset/Liability	396		Allowance for Doubtful		1,400
Allowance for Doubtful		1,400	Accounts		
Accounts					

Comprehensive Illustration: Numerous Errors

In some circumstances, a combination of errors occurs, and a work sheet is therefore prepared to help with the analysis. To demonstrate the use of a work sheet, the following problem is presented for solution. The mechanics of how the work sheet is prepared should be clear from the format of the solution. The tax effects are omitted.

The income statements of Hudson Corporation for the three years ended December 31, 2007, 2008, and 2009, show the following net incomes:

2007	$17,400
2008	20,200
2009	11,300

An examination of the company's accounting records for these years revealed that several errors were made in arriving at the net income amounts that were reported. The following errors were discovered:

1. Wages earned by workers but not paid at December 31 were consistently omitted from the records. The amounts omitted were:

December 31, 2007	$1,000
December 31, 2008	1,400
December 31, 2009	1,600

These amounts were recorded as expenses when they were paid, that is, in the year following the year when they were earned by the employees.

2. The merchandise inventory on December 31, 2007, was overstated by $1,900 as a result of errors made in the footings and extensions on the inventory sheets.

3. Insurance of $1,200 that is applicable to 2009 was expensed on December 31, 2008.

4. Interest receivable in the amount of $240 was not recorded on December 31, 2008.

5. On January 2, 2008, a piece of equipment costing $3,900 was sold for $1,800. At the date of sale, the equipment had accumulated amortization of $2,400. The cash received was recorded in Miscellaneous Income in 2008. In addition, amortization was recorded for this equipment in both 2008 and 2009 at the rate of 10% of cost.

The **first step** in preparing the work sheet is to prepare a schedule showing the corrected net income amounts for each of the years ended December 31, 2007, 2008, and 2009. Each correction of the amount that was originally reported is clearly labelled. The **next step** is to indicate the balance sheet accounts affected as at December 31, 2009, if any. The completed work sheet for Hudson Corporation is provided in Illustration 21-18.

Illustration 21-18

Work Sheet to Correct Income and Balance Sheet Errors

HUDSON CORPORATION
Work Sheet to Correct Income and Balance Sheet Errors

	Work Sheet Analysis of Changes in Net Income				Balance Sheet Correction at December 31, 2009		
	2007	2008	2009	Totals	Debit	Credit	Account
Net income as reported	$17,400	$20,200	$11,300	$48,900			
Wages unpaid, 12/31/07	(1,000)	1,000		–0–			
Wages unpaid, 12/31/08		(1,400)	1,400	–0–			
Wages unpaid, 12/31/09			(1,600)	(1,600)		$1,600	Wages Payable
Inventory overstatement, 12/31/07	(1,900)	1,900		–0–			
Unexpired insurance, 12/31/08		1,200	(1,200)	–0–			
Interest receivable, 12/31/08		240	(240)	–0–			
Correction for entry made on sale of equipment, 1/2/08[a]		(1,500)		(1,500)	$2,400	3,900	Accumulated Amortization Machinery
Overcharge of amortization, 2008		390		390	390		Accumulated Amortization
Overcharge of amortization, 2009			390	390		390	Accumulated Amortization
Corrected net income	$14,500	$22,030	$10,050	$46,580			

aCalculations		
Cost	$ 3,900	
Accumulated amortization	2,400	
Book value	1,500	
Proceeds from sale	1,800	
Gain on sale	300	
Income reported	1,800	
Adjustment	$ (1,500)	

Correcting entries **if the books have not been closed for 2009** are as follows:

Retained Earnings	1,400	
Wages Expense		1,400

(To correct wages expense charged to 2009 that should have been charged to prior year.)

Wages Expense	1,600	
Wages Payable		1,600

(To record proper wages expense and accrual for wages at 2009 year end.)

Insurance Expense	1,200	
Retained Earnings		1,200

(To correct insurance expense charged to 2008 that should have been charged to 2009.)

Interest Income	240	
Retained Earnings		240

(To correct interest income recognized in 2009 that should have been reported in 2008.)

Retained Earnings	1,500	
Accumulated Amortization	2,400	
Machinery		3,900

(To record write-off of machinery and correction of the gain reported in 2008.)

Accumulated Amortization	780	
Amortization Expense		390
Retained Earnings		390

(To correct improper charges to amortization expense in 2008 and 2009.)

If instead the books have been closed for 2009, the correcting entries are as follows:

Retained Earnings	1,600	
Wages Payable		1,600

(To correct the cumulative effect of accrued wages errors to December 31, 2009.)

Retained Earnings	1,500	
Accumulated Amortization	2,400	
Machinery		3,900

(To record write-off of machinery and correction of the gain reported in 2008.)

Accumulated Amortization	780	
Retained Earnings		780

(To correct improper charges to amortization expense in 2008 and 2009.)

Preparation of Comparative Financial Statements

Up to now, our discussion of error analysis has been concerned with identifying the type of error involved and then accounting for its correction **in the accounting records**. Equally important is how the corrections are presented on comparative financial statements. In addition, five- or 10-year summaries are often provided for the interested financial statement reader. Illustration 21-19, explained below, shows how a typical year's financial statements are restated, assuming that many different errors have been corrected.

Dick & Wally's Outlet Ltd. is a small retail outlet in the town of Priestly Sound. Lacking expertise in accounting, its management does not keep adequate records. As a result, numerous errors occurred in recording accounting information:

1. The bookkeeper, by mistake, failed to record a cash receipt of $1,000 on the sale of merchandise in 2009.

2. Accrued wages at the end of 2008 were $2,500; at the end of 2009, $3,200. The company does not accrue for wages; all wages are charged to administrative expense.

3. The 2009 beginning inventory was understated by $5,400 because goods in transit at the end of last year were not counted. The purchase entry was made early in 2009.

4. No allowance had been set up for estimated uncollectible receivables. Dick and Wally decided to set up such an allowance for the estimated probable losses as at December 31, 2009, for 2008 accounts of $700, and for 2009 accounts of $1,500. They also decided to correct the charge against each year so that it shows the losses (actual and estimated) relating to that year's sales. Accounts have been written off to bad debt expense (selling expense) as follows:

	In 2008	In 2009
2008 accounts	$400	$2,000
2009 accounts		1,600

5. Unexpired insurance not recorded at the end of 2008 was $600, and at the end of 2009, $400. All insurance is charged to Administrative Expense.

6. An account payable at the end of 2009 of $6,000 should have been a note payable.

7. During 2008, an asset that cost $10,000 and had a book value of $4,000 was sold for $7,000. At the time of sale, Cash was debited and Miscellaneous Revenue was credited for $7,000.

8. As a result of transaction 7, the company overstated amortization expense (an administrative expense) in 2008 by $800 and in 2009 by $1,200.

9. In a physical count, the company determined the 2009 ending inventory to be $40,000.

Illustration 21-19 presents a work sheet that begins with the unadjusted trial balance of Dick & Wally's Outlet. The correcting entries and their effect on the financial statements can be determined by examining the work sheet. The numbers in parentheses show which transaction number the correction relates to.

Illustration 21-19

Work Sheet to Adjust Financial Statements

DICK & WALLY'S OUTLET
Work Sheet Analysis to Adjust Financial Statements for the Year 2009

	Trial Balance Unadjusted		Adjustments		Income Statement Adjusted		Balance Sheet Adjusted	
	Debit	Credit	Debit	Credit	Debit	Credit	Debit	Credit
Cash	3,100		(1) 1,000				4,100	
Accounts Receivable	17,600						17,600	
Notes Receivable	8,500						8,500	
Inventory, Jan. 1, 2009	34,000		(3) 5,400		39,400			
Property, Plant, and Equipment	112,000			(7) 10,000ᵃ			102,000	
Accumulated Amortization		83,500	(7) 6,000ᵃ					75,500
			(8) 2,000					
Investments	24,300						24,300	
Accounts Payable		14,500	(6) 6,000					8,500
Notes Payable		10,000		(6) 6,000				16,000
Share Capital		43,500						43,500
Retained Earnings		20,000	(4) 2,700ᵇ	(3) 5,400				
			(7) 4,000ᵃ	(5) 600				
			(2) 2,500	(8) 800				17,600
Sales		94,000		(1) 1,000		95,000		
Purchases	21,000				21,000			
Selling Expenses	22,000			(4) 500ᵇ	21,500			
Administrative Expenses	23,000		(2) 700	(5) 400	22,700			
			(5) 600	(8) 1,200				
Totals	265,500	265,500						
Wages Payable				(2) 3,200				3,200
Allowance for Doubtful Accounts				(4) 2,200ᵇ				2,200
Unexpired Insurance			(5) 400				400	
Inventory, Dec. 31, 2009						(9) 40,000	(9) 40,000	
Net Income					30,400			30,400
Totals			31,300	31,300	135,000	135,000	196,900	196,900

Calculations:

ᵃMachinery		ᵇBad Debts	For Sales in	
			2008	2009
Proceeds from sale	$7,000	Bad debts charged	$2,400	$1,600
Book value of machinery	4,000	Additional bad debts anticipated	700	1,500
Gain on sale	3,000		3,100	3,100
Income credited	7,000	Charges currently made to each year	400	3,600
Retained earnings adjustment	$(4,000)	Bad debt adjustment	$2,700	$ (500)

Summary of Learning Objectives

1 Identify and differentiate among the types of accounting changes.

There are three different types of accounting changes. (1) Change in accounting policy: a change in the specific principles, bases, rules, or practices that an entity applies in the preparation of its financial statements. This could be imposed by the transitional provisions in a new primary source of GAAP, or it could be a voluntary change. (2) Change in an accounting estimate: a change in the carrying amount of an asset or liability or the amount of an asset's periodic consumption from reassessing the current status of the asset or liability or the expected future benefits or obligations associated with it. This usually results from new information, more experience, or subsequent developments. (3) Correction of a prior period error: a change caused by an omission from or misstatement in prior years' financial statements from the misuse of or failure to use reliable information that existed at the time the statements were completed and that could have been used in their preparation and presentation.

2 Identify and explain alternative methods of accounting for accounting changes.

Accounting changes could be accounted for retrospectively (retroactively), currently, or prospectively. The retrospective method requires restatement of prior periods as if the accounting change had been used from the beginning, and includes corrections of the opening retained earnings balances that were previously reported. The current method calculates a catch-up adjustment related to the effect on all prior years, with this cumulative effect recognized in the current period. Prospective treatment requires making no adjustment for cumulative effects, but instead, beginning to use the new method in the current and future periods.

3 Identify the accounting standards for each type of accounting change.

A change in accounting policy due to the initial application of a new primary source of GAAP is accounted for according to the transitional provisions of that standard. If none is provided, or if it is a voluntary change, full retrospective application is used. If it is impracticable to determine the effect on all prior years that are presented, partial retrospective application is applied. If it is not even possible to determine the effect at the beginning of the current period, prospective application is used. A change in an accounting estimate is accounted for prospectively. Errors are corrected through full retrospective restatement.

4 Apply the retrospective application method of accounting for a change in an accounting policy.

All comparative periods should be presented as if the new accounting policy had always been applied. This means that the opening balance of each affected component of equity is adjusted for the earliest prior period that is presented, and all other affected comparative amounts for each prior period that is provided are restated to what they would have been if the policy had been in use in that period. When the effects on particular prior periods of a change in accounting policy are impracticable to determine, the cumulative effect of the change (net of tax) is shown as an adjustment to the beginning retained earnings of the earliest prior period possible and comparative financial statements of periods before this are not restated.

5 Identify the disclosure requirements for a change in an accounting policy.

The objective of disclosure for all changes is to ensure that users of financial statements can determine the effect of the change on those financial statements. Required disclosures therefore include identifying the nature of the change, the effect on each financial statement item affected, the amounts relating to periods prior to those that are presented, and why full retrospective application was not applied, if applicable. If the change resulted from applying transitional provisions, information about the standards and the provisions is provided, including the effects on future periods. If it is a voluntary change, the reasons why the new policy results in more relevant information are disclosed. Information about the future effect of changes in primary sources of GAAP that are issued but not yet effective is also required.

6 Apply retrospective restatement for the correction of an accounting error.

The goal is to correct prior financial statements and report them as if the error had never been made. All comparative amounts for the prior periods that are affected are restated, and, if the error is in a period before the earliest comparative statements that are provided, then the opening balances of the earliest comparative period are restated.

7 Identify the disclosure requirements for the correction of an accounting error.

The nature of the error, the amount of the adjustment to each comparative financial statement line item and to EPS, and the amount of the correction made at the beginning of the earliest prior period that is presented are all required disclosures.

8 Apply the prospective application method for an accounting change.

Prospective treatment affects only the current and future fiscal periods. There is no adjustment of current year opening balances and no attempt is made to "catch up" for prior periods.

9 Identify the disclosure requirements for a change in an accounting estimate.

The nature and amount of a change in an accounting estimate that affects the current period or is expected to affect future periods are required disclosures.

10 Identify economic motives for changing accounting methods.

Managers might have varying motives underlying the change in an accounting method, depending on economic circumstances. Some of the aspects that affect decisions about the choice of accounting methods are (1) political costs, (2) the capital structure, (3) bonus payments, and (4) the desire to smooth earnings.

11 Compare current Canadian and international GAAP for accounting changes.

The current accounting standard for accounting changes is based directly on the international standard, IAS 8. Minor differences exist, such as IAS 8's permitting partial retrospective treatment for the correction of an accounting error. The Canadian standard does not.

12 Correct the effects of errors and prepare restated financial statements.

Three types of errors can occur: (1) Balance sheet errors that affect only the presentation of an asset, liability, or shareholders' equity account. (2) Income statement errors that affect only the presentation of the nominal accounts in the income statement. (3) Errors that affect both the balance sheet and the income statement. This last type of error is classified into two sub types: (a) counterbalancing errors, where the effects are offset or corrected over two periods, and (b) non-counterbalancing errors, where the effects are not offset in the next accounting period but take longer than two periods to correct themselves.

Brief Exercises

(LO 4) **BE21-1** Marko Corporation decided at the beginning of 2008 to change from the capital cost allowance method of amortizing its capital assets (a declining-balance method) to straight-line amortization because the straight-line method will result in more relevant financial information. The company will continue to use the capital cost allowance method for tax purposes. For years prior to 2008, total amortization expense under the two methods is as follows: capital cost allowance, $128,000; and straight-line, $80,000. The tax rate is 35%. Prepare Marko's 2008 journal entry to record the change in accounting policy.

(LO 3) **BE21-2** Use the information in BE21-1, but assume instead that the change to the straight-line method was made because straight-line better represents the pattern of benefits provided by the capital assets. Prepare Marko's 2008 journal entry, if any, to record the change in estimate.

(LO 4) **BE21-3** Bytown Corp. changed amortization methods in 2008 from straight-line to double-declining-balance because management argued that the change would improve the relevance of the information to financial statement readers. The assets involved were acquired early in 2005 for $175,000 and had an estimated useful life of eight years, with no residual value. The 2008 income using the straight-line method was $550,000. Bytown had 10,000 common shares outstanding all year. What is the effect of the accounting policy change on the reported income and EPS for 2008? Ignore income taxes.

(LO 4) **BE21-4** Boey, Inc. changed from the average cost formula to the FIFO cost formula in 2008. The increase in the prior years' income before taxes as a result of this change is $525,000. The tax rate is 40%. Prepare Boey's 2008 journal entry to record the change in accounting principle, assuming that the company's financial statements were determined to have better predictive value as a result of the change.

(LO 3) **BE21-5** Castle Corporation purchased a computer system for $60,000 on January 1, 2007. It was amortized based on a seven-year life and an $18,000 residual value. On January 1, 2009, Castle revised these estimates to a total useful life of four years and a residual value of $10,000. Prepare Castle's entry to record 2009 amortization expense. Assume straight-line amortization.

(LO 6) **BE21-6** In 2009, Dalida Corporation discovered that equipment purchased on January 1, 2007, for $85,000 was expensed in error at that time. The equipment should have been amortized over five years, with no residual value. The tax rate is 36%. Prepare Dalida's 2009 journal entry to correct the error and record 2009 amortization.

(LO 6, 12) **BE21-7** At January 1, 2008, Monat Corp. reported retained earnings of $2 million. In 2008, Monat discovered that 2007 amortization expense was understated in error by $500,000. In 2008, net income was $900,000 and dividends declared were $250,000. The tax rate is 40%. Prepare a 2008 retained earnings statement for Monat Corp.

(LO 12) **BE21-8** Indicate the effect—Understated (U), Overstated (O), No Effect (NE)—that each of the following errors has on 2008 net income and 2009 net income:

	2008	2009
Wages payable were not recorded at Dec. 31, 2008.	___	___
Equipment purchased in 2007 was expensed.	___	___
Equipment purchased in 2008 was expensed.	___	___
Ending inventory at Dec. 31, 2008, was overstated.	___	___
Patent amortization was not recorded in 2009.	___	___

Exercises

(LO 12) **E21-1** **(Accounting for Accounting Changes)** The following are various types of accounting changes:

_____ 1. Change in a plant asset's residual value

_____ 2. Change due to an overstatement of inventory

_____ 3. Change from sum-of-the-years'-digits to straight-line method of amortization because of a change in the pattern of benefits received

_____ 4. Change in a primary source of GAAP

_____ 5. Change from not capitalizing interest during construction to capitalizing because the change increases the relevance of the resulting information

_____ **6.** Change in the rate used to calculate warranty costs

_____ **7.** Change from an unacceptable accounting principle to an acceptable accounting principle

_____ **8.** Change in a patent's amortization period

_____ **9.** Change from the completed-contract to percentage-of-completion method on construction contracts because the company now accepts longer commercial contracts rather than shorter residential contracts

_____ **10.** Recognition of additional income taxes owing from three years ago as a result of improper calculations by the accountant, who was not familiar with income tax legislation and income tax returns

Instructions

(a) For each change or error, use the following code letters to indicate how it would be accounted for:

> Accounted for in the current year only (CY)
> Accounted for prospectively (P)
> Accounted for retrospectively (R)
> None of the above, or unable to tell. Explain. (NA)

(b) Identify the type of change for each of the situations numbered 1 to 10.

E21-2 (Error and Change in Policy—Amortization) Mekong Ltd. purchased a machine on January 1, 2006, for $1.35 **(LO 4, 6)** million. At that time, it was estimated that the machine would have a 10-year life and no residual value. On December 31, 2009, the firm's accountant found that the entry for amortization expense had been omitted in 2007. In addition, management informed the accountant that it planned to switch to straight-line amortization, starting with the year 2009. At present, the company uses the double-declining-balance method for amortizing equipment.

Instructions

(a) Assuming that this is a change in accounting policy and that the change will result in information that is more relevant to users, prepare the general journal entries the accountant should make at December 31, 2009. (Ignore tax effects.)

(b) Assume the same information as above, but factor in tax effects. The company has a 34% tax rate for 2006 to 2009.

E21-3 (Change in Policy and Change in Estimate—Amortization) Kato Inc. acquired the following assets in **(LO 4, 8)** January 2005:

Equipment: estimated service life, 5 years; residual value, $15,000	$525,000
Building: estimated service life, 30 years; no residual value	$693,000

The equipment was amortized using the double-declining-balance method for the first three years for financial reporting purposes. In 2008, the company decided to change the method of calculating amortization to the straight-line method for the equipment, but no change was made in the estimated service life or residual value. Management determined that this change would result in financial statements that would provide more relevant information to the users. It was also decided to change the building's total estimated service life from 30 years to 40 years, with no change in the estimated residual value. The building is amortized on the straight-line method.

The company has 100,000 common shares outstanding, and the results of operations for 2008 and 2007 are as follows:

	2008	2007
Net income (amortization for 2008 has been calculated on the straight-line basis for both the equipment and building[a])	$385,000	$380,000
Earnings per share	$3.85	$3.80

[a]Note that the calculation for amortization expense for 2008 and 2007 for the building was based on the original estimate of a 30-year service life.

Instructions

(a) Assume that the change to the straight-line method for the equipment is a change in accounting principle. Calculate the effect of the change to be reported in the restated statement of retained earnings for 2008, and prepare the journal entry to record the change. (Ignore tax effects.)

(b) Calculate the amount of income and EPS reported on the comparative financial statements presented in 2008. (Ignore tax effects.)

(c) Assume that Kato had retained earnings of $1.25 million at January 1, 2007, and $1.63 million at January 1, 2008, and that no dividends were declared during either year. Prepare the statement of retained earnings on a comparative basis. (Ignore tax effects.)

(LO 4, 8) E21-4   (Change in Policy and in Accounting Estimate) On January 1, 2004, Zhang Corporation purchased a building and equipment that have the following useful lives, residual values, and costs:

> Building: 40-year estimated useful life, $50,000 residual value, $800,000 cost
> Equipment: 12-year estimated useful life, $10,000 residual value, $100,000 cost

The building and equipment have been amortized under the double-declining-balance method through 2007. In 2008, the company decided to switch to the straight-line method of amortization. In 2009, Zhang decided to change the equipment's total useful life to nine years, with a residual value of $5,000 at the end of that time.

Instructions
Answer the following, ignoring income taxes.

(a) Assuming that the change to the straight-line method qualifies for a change in accounting policy, what is the amount of the adjustment to opening retained earnings as of January 1, 2008?

(b) What is the amount of the adjustment to opening retained earnings as of January 1, 2007, for purposes of the comparative statements?

(c) Prepare the necessary journal entry(ies) to record the changes made in 2008.

(d) Calculate amortization expense on the equipment for 2009.

(LO 4) E21-5   (Change in Policy and Accounting Estimate with Tax Effect) Refer to the information in E21-4. Assume that Zhang Corporation's tax rate is 25% and that this rate is expected to stay the same.

Instructions

(a) Assuming that the change to the straight-line method qualifies for a change in accounting policy, what is the amount of the adjustment to opening retained earnings as of January 1, 2008?

(b) What is the amount of the adjustment to opening retained earnings as of January 1, 2007, for purposes of the comparative statements?

(c) Prepare the necessary journal entry(ies) to record the changes made in 2008.

(LO 4, 8) E21-6   (Change in Policy, Change in Estimate—Amortization) Inglewood Corp. changed from the straight-line method of amortization on its plant assets acquired early in 2006 to the double-declining-balance method in 2008 (before finalizing its 2008 financial statements). The assets had an eight-year life and no expected residual value. Information related to both methods follows:

Year	Double-Declining-Balance Amortization	Straight-Line Amortization	Difference
2006	$250,000	$125,000	$125,000
2007	187,500	125,000	62,500
2008	140,625	125,000	15,625

Net income for 2007 was reported at $270,000; net income for 2008 before amortization and income tax is $300,000. Assume an income tax rate of 30%.

Instructions

(a) Assume that the change from the straight-line method to the double-declining-balance method is accepted as a change in accounting policy.

   1. What net income is reported for 2008?
   2. What is the amount of the adjustment to opening retained earnings as of January 1, 2008?
   3. What is the amount of the adjustment to opening retained earnings as of January 1, 2007?
   4. Prepare the journal entry(ies) to record the adjustment in the accounting records, assuming that the accounting records for 2008 are not yet closed.

(b) Repeat (a) assuming that the change from the straight-line method to the double-declining-balance method is considered a change in estimate.

E21-7 **(Determine Type of Change and Method of Accounting; Prepare Journal Entries)** Godot Corp. began **(LO 2,** operations in January 2005 and is subject to a 40% income tax rate. In 2008, the following events took place: **4, 6)**

1. The company switched from the completed-contract to the percentage-of-completion method of accounting for its long-term construction projects. This change was a result of hiring an experienced estimator that made it possible to estimate costs of completion.

2. Due to a change in maintenance policy, the estimated useful life of the fleet of trucks was lengthened.

3. It was discovered that a machine with an original cost of $100,000, residual value of $10,000, and useful life of four years, was expensed in error on January 23, 2007, when it was acquired. This situation was discovered after preparing the 2008 adjusting entries but prior to calculating income tax expense and closing the accounts. Godot uses straight-line amortization, and takes a full year in the year of acquisition. The asset's cost had been appropriately added to the CCA class in 2007 before the CCA was calculated and claimed.

4. As a result of an inventory study early in 2008 after the accounts for 2007 had been closed, management decided that the average costing method would provide a more relevant presentation in the financial statements than does FIFO cost. In making the change to average cost, Godot determined the following:

Date	Inventory—FIFO Cost	Inventory—Average Cost
Dec. 31, 2007	$ 90,000	$ 80,000
Dec. 31, 2006	$130,000	$100,000
Dec. 31, 2005	$200,000	$150,000

Instructions

(a) Analyze each of the four 2008 events described above. For each event, identify the type of accounting change that has occurred, and indicate whether it should be accounted for with full retrospective application, partial retrospective application, or prospectively.

(b) Prepare any necessary journal entries that would be recorded in 2008 to account for events 3 and 4.

(ASCA adapted)

E21-8 **(Change in Policy—Long-Term Contracts)** Talos Construction Company Ltd. changed from the completed- **(LO 1, 4)** contract to the percentage-of-completion method of accounting for long-term construction contracts during 2008. For tax purposes, the company uses the completed-contract method and will continue this approach in the future. The appropriate information related to this change is as follows:

	Pre-Tax Income Using:		
	Percentage-of-Completion	Completed-Contract	Difference
2007	$820,000	$620,000	$200,000
2008	700,000	480,000	220,000

Instructions

(a) Assuming that the change qualifies as a change in accounting policy and that the tax rate is 35%, calculate the net income to be reported in 2008.

(b) Provide the necessary entry(ies) to adjust the accounting records for the change in accounting policy.

(c) If this change was made to reflect changed circumstances, how should the change be accounted for?

E21-9 **(Various Changes in Policy—Inventory Methods)** Anita Instrument Corp. began operations on January 1, **(LO 4, 5)** 2005, and uses a periodic inventory system. The following net income amounts were calculated for Anita under three different inventory methods:

	FIFO	Average Cost	LIFO
2005	$26,000	$24,000	$20,000
2006	30,000	25,000	21,000
2007	28,000	27,000	24,000
2008	34,000	30,000	26,000

Instructions
Answer the following, ignoring tax considerations.

(a) Assume that in 2008 Anita changed from the average cost method to the FIFO method of costing inventories and it was agreed that the FIFO method provided more relevant financial statement information. Prepare the necessary journal entry for the change that took place during 2008, and provide all the information that is needed for reporting on a comparative basis.

(b) Assume that in 2008 Anita, which had been using the LIFO method since incorporation in 2005, changed to the FIFO method of costing inventories in order to comply with new *CICA Handbook* Section 3031. The company applies the new policy retrospectively in accordance with the transitional provisions of the new section. Prepare the necessary journal entry for the change, and provide all the information that is needed for reporting on a comparative basis.

(LO 6, 7 8, 9) **E21-10** **(Change in Estimate, Error Correction)** Hébert Co.'s controller was preparing the year-end adjusting entries for the company's year ended December 31, 2008, when the V.P. Finance called him into her office.

"Bob," she said, "I've been considering a couple of matters that may require different treatment this year. First, the patent we acquired in early January 2006 for $410,000 will now likely be used until the end of 2010 and then be sold for $110,000. We previously thought that we'd use it for 10 years in total and then be able to sell it for $50,000. We've been using straight-line amortization on the patent."

"Secondly, I just discovered that the property we bought midway through 2005 for $135,000 was charged entirely to the Land account instead of being allocated between Land ($33,750) and Building ($101,250). The building should be of use to us for a total of 20 years. At that point, it'll be sold and we should be able to realize at least $37,000 from the sale of the building."

"Please let me know how these changes should be accounted for and what effect they will have on the financial statements."

Instructions

(a) Briefly identify the accounting treatment that should be applied to each accounting change that is required.

(b) Assuming that no amortization has been recorded as yet for the patent for 2008, prepare the December 31, 2008, entries that are necessary to make the accounting changes and to record patent amortization expense for 2008.

(c) Identify, and calculate where possible, the required disclosures for each change.

(d) Discuss the timing of applying the change in the patent's useful life and residual value. Since the determination of the change was done as part of the year-end process, should the change be applied to 2008 going forward, or to 2009 going forward? What are the implications of either approach?

(e) Could Hébert's controller consider the patent to be impaired instead of revising its useful life and residual value? What criteria should the controller look at to determine the appropriate treatment?

(ASCA adapted)

(LO 1, 6) **E21-11** **(Error Correction Entries)** The first audit of the books of Gensing Limited was recently carried out for the year ended December 31, 2008. In examining the books, the auditor found that certain items had been overlooked or might have been incorrectly handled in the past:

1. At the beginning of 2006, the company purchased a machine for $510,000 (residual value of $51,000) that had a useful life of six years. The bookkeeper used straight-line amortization, but failed to deduct the residual value in calculating the amortization base for the three years.

2. At the end of 2007, the company accrued sales salaries of $45,000 in excess of the correct amount.

3. A tax lawsuit that involved the year 2006 was settled late in 2008. It was determined that the company owed an additional $85,000 in taxes related to 2006. The company did not record a liability in 2006 or 2007, because the possibility of losing was considered remote. The company charged the $85,000 to retained earnings in 2008 as a correction of a prior year's error.

4. Gensing purchased another company early in 2004 and recorded goodwill of $450,000. Gensing amortized $22,500 of goodwill in 2004, and $45,000 in each subsequent year.

5. In 2008, the company changed its basis of inventory costing from FIFO to weighted average cost. The change's cumulative effect was to decrease net income of prior years by $71,000. The company debited this cumulative effect to Retained Earnings. The average cost method was used in calculating income for 2008.

6. In 2008, the company wrote off $87,000 of inventory that it discovered, in 2008, had been stolen from one of its warehouses in 2007. This loss was charged to a loss account in 2008.

Instructions

(a) Prepare the journal entries in 2008 to correct the books where necessary, assuming that the 2008 books have not been closed. Assume that the change from FIFO to weighted average cost can be justified as resulting in more relevant financial information. Disregard the effects of corrections on income tax.

(b) Identify the type of change for each of the six items.

(c) Redo part (a) but include the effects of income tax, assuming the company has a tax rate of 25%.

E21-12 **(Change in Principle and Error, Financial Statements)** The comparative statements for Habbe Inc. follow: **(LO 4, 6)**

	2008	2007
Sales	$340,000	$270,000
Cost of sales	200,000	142,000
Gross profit	140,000	128,000
Expenses	88,000	50,000
Net income	$ 52,000	$ 78,000
Retained earnings (Jan. 1)	$125,000	$ 72,000
Net income	52,000	78,000
Dividends	(30,000)	(25,000)
Retained earnings (Dec. 31)	$147,000	$125,000

The following additional information is provided:

1. In 2008, Habbe decided to change its amortization method from sum-of-the-years'-digits to straight-line. The differences in the two amortization methods for the affected assets are as follows:

	2008	2007
Sum-of-the-years'-digits	$30,000[a]	$40,000
Straight-line	25,000	25,000

[a]The 2008 income statement contains amortization expense of $30,000.

2. In 2008, the company discovered that the ending inventory for 2007 was overstated by $24,000; ending inventory for 2008 is correctly stated.

Instructions

(a) Prepare the revised income and retained earnings statements for 2007 and 2008, assuming full retrospective treatment (ignore income tax effects). Do not prepare footnotes.

(b) Prepare the revised income and retained earnings statements for 2007 and 2008, assuming partial retrospective treatment (ignore income tax effects). Do not prepare footnotes.

(c) Identify the proper accounting treatment for the change in amortization method if Habbe cannot justify the change as resulting in more relevant information for statement users.

E21-13 **(Political Motivations for Policies)** Ever since the unethical actions of some employees of Enron Corp. first **(LO 10)** came to light, ethics in accounting has been in the news with increasing frequency. The unethical actions of the employees essentially involved their selection of certain accounting policies for the company.

In many instances, GAAP does allow firms some flexibility in their choice of legitimate accounting policies. This is true, for example, in choosing an inventory cost formula. However, the company's choice of policies may ultimately be influenced by several specific factors.

Instructions

State three of these factors and explain why each of them may influence an accounting policy choice.

(CGA adapted)

E21-14 **(Error Analysis and Correcting Entries)** Management at YEF Corporation is concerned about the following **(LO 12)** business transactions that the company conducted during 2008:

1. The company decided to switch from the direct write-off method of accounting for bad debt expense to the allowance approach. Assume that YEF has been recognizing bad debt expense on an ongoing basis as the receivables actually become uncollectible, with the following results:

	2007	2008
Bad debt expense—		
From 2007 sales	$63,600	$24,000
From 2008 sales		90,000

The controller estimates that an additional $130,800 will be recorded in 2009, with $22,800 of this amount applicable to 2007 sales and $108,000 applicable to 2008 sales.

2. Inventory that was shipped on consignment was recorded as ordinary credit sales. At December 31, 2008, inventory at a selling price of $960,000 was in the hands of consignees, with a 20% markup on cost. Assume that consigned inventory is sold in the following year and that the company uses the perpetual inventory system.

3. During 2008, the company sold $1.8 million of goods on instalments. The cost of goods sold associated with these sales was $1.35 million. The company inadvertently recorded these sales and related costs as part of the regular sales transactions. Cash of $516,000, including a down payment of $180,000, was collected on these instalment sales during the current year. Due to questionable collectibility, the instalment method was considered appropriate.

Instructions
Prepare the journal entries at December 31, 2008, assuming that the books have been closed.

(CGA adapted)

(LO 12) **E21-15** **(Error Analysis and Correcting Entry)** You have been engaged to review the financial statements of Linette Corporation. In the course of your examination, you conclude that the bookkeeper hired during the year that just ended is not doing a good job. You noticed a number of irregularities for the past fiscal year:

1. Year-end wages payable of $3,400 were not recorded, because the bookkeeper thought that "they were immaterial."

2. Accrued vacation pay for the year of $31,100 was not recorded, because the bookkeeper "never heard that you had to do it."

3. Insurance that covers a 12-month period and was purchased on November 1 was charged to insurance expense in "the amount of $2,640 because the amount of the cheque is about the same every year."

4. Reported sales revenue for the year was $2.12 million and included all sales taxes charged for the year. The sales tax rate is 6%. Because the sales tax is forwarded to the provincial ministry of revenue, the bookkeeper thought that "the sales tax is a selling expense" and therefore debited the Sales Tax Expense account. At the end of the fiscal year, the balance in the Sales Tax Expense account was $103,400.

Instructions
Prepare the necessary correcting entries, assuming that Linette uses a calendar-year basis and that the books for the fiscal year that just ended are not yet closed.

(LO 12) **E21-16** **(Error Analysis)** Henning Tool Corporation's December 31 year-end financial statements contained the following errors:

	December 31, 2007	December 31, 2008
Ending inventory	$9,600 overstated	$8,100 understated
Amortization expense	$2,300 overstated	—

An insurance premium of $66,000 and covering the years 2007, 2008, and 2009 was prepaid in 2007, with the entire amount charged to expense that year. In addition, on December 31, 2008, fully amortized machinery was sold for $15,000 cash, but the entry was not recorded until 2009. There were no other errors during 2007 or 2008, and no corrections have been made for any of the errors.

Instructions
Answer the following, ignoring income tax considerations.

(a) Calculate the total effect of the errors on 2008 net income.

(b) Calculate the total effect of the errors on the amount of Henning's working capital at December 31, 2008.

(c) Calculate the total effect of the errors on the balance of Henning's retained earnings at December 31, 2008.

(d) Assume that the company has retained earnings on January 1, 2007 and 2008, of $1,250,000 and $1,607,000 respectively; net income for 2007 and 2008 of $422,000 and $375,000 respectively; and cash dividends declared for 2007 and 2008 of $65,000 and $45,000, before adjustment for the above items. Prepare a revised statement of retained earnings for 2007 and 2008.

(e) Outline the accounting treatment required by GAAP in this situation and explain how these requirements help investors.

(CGA adapted)

E21-17 **(Error Analysis and Correcting Entries)** A partial trial balance of Kamil Corporation at December 31, 2008, **(LO 12)** follows:

	Dr.	Cr.
Supplies on hand	$ 4,100	
Accrued salaries and wages		$ 3,900
Interest receivable on investments	5,500	
Prepaid insurance	93,000	
Unearned rent		–0–
Accrued interest payable		15,000

Additional adjusting data:

1. A physical count of supplies on hand on December 31, 2008, totalled $2,100. Through oversight, the Accrued Salaries and Wages account was not changed during 2008. Accrued salaries and wages on December 31, 2008, amounted to $5,100.

2. The Interest Receivable on Investments account was also left unchanged during 2008. Accrued interest on investments amounted to $4,750 on December 31, 2008.

3. The unexpired portions of the insurance policies totalled $65,000 as of December 31, 2008.

4. A cheque for $44,000 was received on January 1, 2008, for the rent of a building for both 2008 and 2009. The entire amount was credited to rental income.

5. Amortization for the year was recorded in error as $5,350 rather than the correct figure of $53,500.

6. A further review of prior years' amortization calculations revealed that amortization of $13,500 had not been recorded. It was decided that this oversight should be corrected by adjusting prior years' income.

Instructions

(a) Assuming that the books have not been closed, what adjusting entries are necessary at December 31, 2008? Ignore income tax considerations.

(b) Assuming that the books have been closed, what adjusting entries are necessary at December 31, 2008? Ignore income tax considerations.

(c) Discuss the nature of the adjustments that are needed and how the situations could have occurred. Are they all accounting errors, or are they part of the normal accounting cycle? (Hint: Revisit adjusting entries from Chapter 3.) How should management present the adjustments for these items on its financial statements and in the notes?

E21-18 **(Error Analysis)** The before-tax income for Lonnie Holland Corp. for 2007 was $101,000; it was $77,400 for **(LO 12)** 2008. However, the accountant noted that the following errors had been made:

1. Sales for 2007 included amounts of $38,200 that had been received in cash during 2007, but for which the related products were delivered in 2008. Title did not pass to the purchaser until 2008.

2. The inventory on December 31, 2007, was understated by $8,640.

3. The bookkeeper, in recording interest expense for both 2007 and 2008 on bonds payable, made the following entry each year:

Interest Expense	15,000	
Cash		15,000

The bonds have a face value of $250,000 and pay a stated interest rate of 6%. They were issued at a discount of $15,000 on January 1, 2007, to yield an effective interest rate of 7%. (Use the effective interest method.)

4. Ordinary repairs to equipment had been charged in error to the Equipment account during 2007 and 2008. In total, repairs in the amount of $8,500 in 2007 and $9,400 in 2008 were charged in this way. The company applies a rate of 10% to the balance in the Equipment account at year end in determining its amortization charges.

Instructions

(a) Prepare a schedule showing the calculation of corrected income before taxes for 2007 and 2008.

(b) Prepare the journal entries that the company's accountant would prepare in 2008, assuming the errors are discovered while the 2008 books are still open. Ignore income taxes.

(LO 12)   E21-19   (Error Analysis) When the records of Haida Corporation were reviewed at the close of 2008, the following errors were discovered.

	2007			2008		
	Over-statement	Under-statement	No Effect	Over-statement	Under-statement	No Effect
1. Failure to record amortization of patent in 2008						
2. Failure to record the correct amount of ending 2007 inventory (the amount was understated because of a calculation error)						
3. Failure to record merchandise purchased in 2007 (it was also omitted from ending inventory in 2007 and remained unsold at the end of 2008)						
4. Failure to record accrued interest on notes payable in 2007 (the amount was recorded when paid in 2008)						
5. Failure to reflect supplies on hand on balance sheet at end of 2007						

Instructions

For each item, indicate by a check mark in the appropriate column whether the error resulted in an overstatement or understatement, or had no effect on net income for the years 2007 and 2008.

Problems

P21-1   Siew Kim Enterprises Ltd. reported income before income taxes of $176,000, $180,000, and $198,000 in each of the years 2006, 2007, and 2008, respectively. The following information is also available:

1. In 2008, Siew Kim lost a court case in which it was the defendant. The case was a patent infringement suit, and Siew Kim must now pay a competitor $35,000 to settle the suit. No previous entries had been recorded in the books relative to this case as Siew Kim management felt the company would win.

2. A review of the company's provision for uncollectible accounts during 2008 resulted in a determination that 1% of sales is the appropriate amount of bad debt expense to be charged to operations, rather than the 1.5% used for the preceding two years. Bad debt expense recognized in 2007 and 2006 was $25,000 and $17,500, respectively. The company would have recorded $22,500 of bad debt expense under the old rate for 2008. No entry has yet been made in 2008 for bad debt expense.

3. Siew Kim acquired land on January 1, 2005, at a cost of $45,000. The land was charged to the equipment account in error and has been amortized since then on the basis of a five-year life with no residual value.

4. During 2008, the company changed from the double-declining-balance method of amortization for its building to the straight-line method. Siew Kim changed to the straight-line method because its parent company uses straight-line, and making the change therefore results in more relevant information for users of the consolidated statements in their decision-making. Total amortization under both methods for the past three years is as follows. Double-declining-balance amortization has been used in 2008.

	Straight-Line	Double-Declining-Balance
2006	$32,000	$60,000
2007	32,000	57,000
2008	32,000	54,150

5. Late in 2008, Siew Kim determined that a piece of specialized equipment purchased in January 2005 at a cost of $54,000 with an estimated life of five years and residual value of $4,000 is now expected to continue in use until the end of 2012 and have a residual value of $2,000 at that time. The company has been using straight-line amortization for this equipment, and amortization for 2008 has already been recognized based on the original estimates.

6. The company has determined that a $225,000 note payable that it issued in 2006 has been incorrectly classified on its balance sheet. The note is payable in annual instalments of $25,000, but the full amount of the note has been shown as a long-term liability with no portion shown in current liabilities. Interest expense relating to the note has been properly recorded.

Instructions

(a) For each of the accounting changes, errors, or transactions, present the journal entry(ies) that Siew Kim needs to make to correct or adjust the accounts, assuming the accounts for 2008 have not yet been closed. If no entry is required, write "none" and briefly explain why. Ignore income tax considerations.

(b) Prepare the entries required in (a) but assume an income tax rate of 25% throughout the fiscal periods that are identified.

(c) For each of the accounting changes, identify the type of change involved and whether retrospective or prospective treatment is required.

P21-2   As at December 31, 2008, Orleans Corporation is having its financial statements audited for the first time ever. The auditor has found the following items that might have an effect on previous years:

1. Orleans purchased equipment on January 2, 2005, for $130,000. At that time, the equipment had an estimated useful life of 10 years, with a $10,000 residual value. The equipment is amortized on a straight-line basis. On January 2, 2008, as a result of additional information, the company determined that the equipment had a total useful life of seven years with a $6,000 residual value.

2. During 2008, Orleans changed from the double-declining-balance method for its building to the straight-line method because the company thinks the straight-line method now more closely follows the benefits received from using the assets. In case the following information was needed, the auditor provided calculations that present amortization on both bases. The building had originally cost $1.2 million when purchased at the beginning of 2006 and has a residual value of $120,000. It is amortized over 20 years. The original estimates of useful life and residual value are still accurate.

	2008	2007	2006
Straight-line	$54,000	$ 54,000	$ 54,000
Double-declining-balance	97,200	108,000	120,000

3. Orleans purchased a machine on July 1, 2005, at a cost of $160,000. The machine has a residual value of $16,000 and a useful life of eight years. Orleans's bookkeeper recorded straight-line amortization during each year but failed to consider the residual value.

4. Prior to 2008, staff training costs were immediately expensed because they were immaterial, even though the company would benefit for at least three years because of improved worker efficiency. With the spurt in growth, these costs have now become material and management has decided to amortize them over three years. Amounts expensed in 2005, 2006, and 2007 were $300, $500, and $1,000, respectively. During 2008, $4,500 was spent and the amount was debited to Deferred Training Costs (an asset account).

Instructions

Answer the following, ignoring income tax considerations.

(a) Prepare the necessary journal entries to record each of the changes or errors. The books for 2008 have not been closed.

(b) Calculate the 2008 amortization expense on the equipment.

(c) Calculate the comparative net incomes for 2007 and 2008, starting with income before the effects of any of the changes identified above. Income before amortization expense was $600,000 in 2008 and $420,000 in 2007.

P21-3 On December 31, 2008, before the books were closed, management and the accountant at Keltner Inc. made the following determinations about three amortizable assets:

1. Capital asset A was purchased on January 2, 2005. It originally cost $495,000 and the straight-line method was chosen for amortization. The asset was originally expected to be useful for 10 years and have no residual value. In 2008, the decision was made to change the amortization method from straight-line to double-declining-balance, and the estimates relating to useful life and residual value remained unchanged (assume that this change in policy is appropriate).

2. Capital asset B was purchased on January 3, 2004. It originally cost $120,000 and the straight-line method was chosen for amortization. The asset was expected to be useful for 15 years and have no residual value. In 2008, the decision was made to shorten this asset's total life to nine years and to estimate the residual value at $3,000.

3. Capital asset C was purchased on January 5, 2004. The asset's original cost was $140,000 and this amount was entirely expensed in 2004 in error. This particular asset has a 10-year useful life and no residual value. The straight-line method is appropriate.

Additional data:

1. Income in 2008 before amortization expense amounted to $400,000.

2. Amortization expense on assets other than A, B, and C totalled $55,000 in 2008.

3. Income in 2007 was reported at $370,000.

4. In both 2007 and 2008, 100,000 common shares were outstanding. No dividends were declared in either year.

Instructions

Answer the following questions, ignoring all income tax effects.

(a) Prepare all necessary entries in 2008 to record these determinations.

(b) Calculate the adjusted net income and earnings per share for 2007 and 2008.

(c) Prepare comparative retained earnings statements for Keltner Inc. for 2007 and 2008. The company reported retained earnings of $200,000 at December 31, 2006.

(d) Prepare the required note disclosures for each of these changes.

(e) How would the changes to Keltner's amortizable assets be reflected on the statement of cash flows?

P21-4 Both the management of Kreiter Instrument Corporation and its independent auditors recently concluded that the company's results of operations will have greater predictive value in future years if Kreiter changes its method of costing inventory from FIFO to average cost. The following data are a five-year income summary and a schedule of what the inventories might have been if they had been stated on the average cost method:

KREITER INSTRUMENT CORPORATION
Statement of Income and Retained Earnings for the Years Ended May 31

	2004	2005	2006	2007	2008
Sales—net	$13,964	$15,506	$16,673	$18,221	$18,898
Cost of goods sold					
Beginning inventory	1,000	1,100	1,000	1,115	1,237
Purchases	13,000	13,900	15,000	15,900	17,100
Ending inventory	(1,100)	(1,000)	(1,115)	(1,237)	(1,369)
Total	12,900	14,000	14,885	15,778	16,968
Gross profit	1,064	1,506	1,788	2,443	1,930
Administrative expenses	700	763	832	907	989
Income before taxes	364	743	956	1,536	941
Income taxes (50%)	182	372	478	768	471
Net income	182	371	478	768	470
Retained earnings—beginning	1,206	1,388	1,759	2,237	3,005
Retained earnings—ending	$ 1,388	$ 1,759	$ 2,237	$ 3,005	$ 3,475
Earnings per share	$ 1.82	$ 3.71	$ 4.78	$ 7.68	$ 4.70

SCHEDULE OF INVENTORY BALANCES USING AVERAGE COST METHOD
Year Ended May 31

2003	2004	2005	2006	2007	2008
$950	$1,124	$1,091	$1,270	$1,480	$1,699

Instructions

(a) Prepare comparative statements for the five years that would be suitable for inclusion in the historical summary portion of Kreiter's annual report, assuming that Kreiter had changed its inventory costing method to average cost in 2008. Indicate the effects on net income and earnings per share for the years involved. (All amounts except EPS are rounded up to the nearest dollar.)

(b) Prepare the statement of retained earnings for 2008, with comparative statements for 2007 and 2006 to be issued to shareholders, assuming retrospective treatment.

(c) Identify all balance sheet accounts that require restatement on the comparative May 31, 2007 and 2006, balance sheets issued to shareholders in 2008.

(d) Prepare the statement of retained earnings for 2008, with a comparative statement for 2007 to be issued to shareholders, assuming that the data for the years 2003 to 2007 was not available and Kreiter used partial retrospective treatment.

P21-5 McInnes Corporation has decided that in preparing its 2008 financial statements, two changes should be made from the methods used in prior years:

1. **Amortization.** McInnes has always used the CCA method for tax and financial reporting purposes but has decided to change during 2008 to the straight-line method for financial reporting purposes. Prior to 2008, the company's only investors were members of the McInnes family and the CCA method was more efficient in preparing financial information. During 2008, however, the company obtained financing through a share issuance, and with the larger number of investors now using its financial statements, the company believes that changing its amortization method will provide more relevant information. The effect of this change is as follows:

	Excess of CCA over Straight-Line Amortization
Prior to 2007	$1,365,000
2007	106,050
2008	103,950
	$1,575,000

Amortization is charged to cost of sales and to selling, general, and administrative expenses on the basis of 75% and 25%, respectively.

2. **Bad debt expense.** In the past, McInnes recognized bad debt expense equal to 1.5% of net sales. After careful review, it has been decided that a rate of 1.75% is more appropriate for 2008. Bad debt expense is charged to selling, general, and administrative expenses. The following information is taken from preliminary financial statements, which were prepared before including the effect of the two changes:

MCINNES CORPORATION
Condensed Balance Sheet
December 31, 2008

Assets	2008	2007
Current assets^a	$43,561,000	$43,900,000
Plant assets, at cost	45,792,000	43,974,000
Less: Accumulated amortization	23,761,000	22,946,000
	$65,592,000	$64,928,000
Liabilities and Shareholders' Equity		
Current liabilities	$21,124,000	$23,650,000
Long-term debt	15,154,000	14,097,000
Share capital	11,620,000	11,620,000
Retained earnings	17,694,000	15,561,000
	$65,592,000	$64,928,000

^aIncludes future income tax asset of $225,000 (2008) and $234,000 (2007), with the latter amount being the result of deductible temporary differences that occurred before 2007.

MCINNES CORPORATION
Income Statement
Year Ended December 31, 2008

	2008	2007
Net sales	$80,520,000	$78,920,000
Cost of goods sold	54,847,000	53,074,000
	25,673,000	25,846,000
Selling, general, and administrative expenses	19,540,000	18,411,000
	6,133,000	7,435,000
Other income (expense), net	(1,198,000)	(1,079,000)
Income before income taxes	4,935,000	6,356,000
Income taxes	2,220,750	2,860,200
Net income	$ 2,714,250	$ 3,495,800

There have been no temporary differences between any book and tax items prior to the above changes except for those that involve the allowance for doubtful accounts. For tax purposes, bad debts are deductible only when they are written off. The tax rate is 45%.

Instructions

(a) For each of the items that follow, calculate the amounts that would appear on the comparative (2008 and 2007) financial statements of McInnes Corporation after adjustment for the two accounting changes. Show amounts for both 2008 and 2007, and prepare supporting schedules as necessary.

   1. Accumulated amortization

   2. Future tax asset/liability

   3. Selling, general, and administrative expenses

   4. Current portion of income tax expense

   5. Future portion of income tax expense

(b) Prepare the comparative financial statements that will be issued to shareholders for McInnes' year ended December 31, 2008.

P21-6 The founder, president, and major shareholder of Horne Corp. recently sold his controlling interest in the company to a national distributor in the same line of business. The change in ownership was effective June 30, 2008, halfway through Horne's current fiscal year.

   During the due diligence process of acquiring the company and over the last six months of 2008, the new senior management team had a chance to review the company's accounting records and policies. By the end of 2008, the following decisions had been made:

   1. Horne's policy of expensing all interest as incurred will be changed to correspond to the policy of the controlling shareholder whereby interest on self-constructed assets is capitalized. This policy will be applied retrospectively, and going forward will simplify the consolidation process for the parent company. The major effect of this policy is to reduce interest expense in 2006 by $9,200 and to increase the cost of equipment by the same amount. The equipment was put into service early in 2007. Horne uses straight-line amortization for equipment and a five-year life. Because the interest has already been deducted for tax purposes, the change in policy results in a taxable temporary difference.

   2. Deferred charges of $12,000 remained in long-term assets at December 31, 2007. These were being written off on a straight-line basis with another three years remaining at that time. On reviewing the December 31, 2008, balances (after an additional year of amortization), management decided that there were no further benefits to be received from these deferrals and there likely had not been any benefits for the past two years. The original costs were tax deductible when incurred.

   3. A long-term contract with a preferred customer was completed in December 2008. When discussing payment with the client, it came to light that a down payment of $30,000 made by the customer on the contract at the end of 2006 had been taken into revenue (and into taxable income) when received. The revenue should have been recognized in 2008 on completion of the contract.

Horne's financial statements (summarized) were as follows at December 31, 2007 and 2008, before any corrections related to the information above. The December 31, 2008, statements are in draft form only and the 2008 accounts have not yet been closed.

Statement of Financial Position
December 31

Assets	2008	2007	Liabilities & Equity	2008	2007
Current assets	$192,300	$168,400	Current liabilities	$117,000	$103,000
Long-term assets	322,000	311,000	Long-term liabilities	166,000	153,000
			Share capital (10,000 shares)	50,000	50,000
			Retained earnings	181,300	173,400
	$514,300	$479,400		$514,300	$479,400

Income Statement
Year Ended December 31

	2008	2007
Revenues	$475,000	$460,000
Expenses	378,000	376,000
	97,000	84,000
Income tax (30% effective rate)	29,100	25,200
Net income	$ 67,900	$ 58,800
Earnings per share	$ 6.79	$ 5.88
Dividends declared, per share	$ 6.00	$ 2.50

Instructions

(a) Prepare any December 31, 2008, journal entries that are necessary to put into effect the decisions made by senior management.

(b) Prepare the comparative statement of financial position, income statement, and statement of retained earnings that will be issued to shareholders for the year ended December 31, 2008.

(c) Prepare the required note disclosures for the accounting changes.

P21-7 Plato Corporation performs year-end planning in November each year before its fiscal year ends in December. The preliminary estimated net income is $3 million. The CFO, Mary Shito, meets with the company president, Sam Plato, to review the projected numbers. She presents the following projected information:

PLATO CORPORATION
Projected Income Statement
Year Ended December 31, 2008
($000s)

Sales		$29,000
Cost of goods sold	$14,000	
Amortization	2,600	
Operating expenses	6,400	23,000
Income before income taxes		6,000
Provision for income taxes		3,000
Net income		$ 3,000

SELECTED BALANCE SHEET INFORMATION
December 31, 2008
($000s)

Estimated cash balance	$ 5,000
Available-for-sale securities (at cost)	10,000

Security	Cost	Estimated Market
A	$ 2,000	$ 2,200
B	4,000	3,900
C	3,000	3,000
D	1,000	2,800
Total	$10,000	$11,900

Other information ($000s) at December 31, 2008:

Equipment	$3,000
Accumulated amortization (5 years, straight-line)	1,200
New robotic equipment (purchased 1/1/08)	5,000
Accumulated amortization (5 years, double-declining-balance)	2,000

The corporation has never used robotic equipment before, and Shito assumed an accelerated method because of the rapidly changing technology in robotic equipment. The company normally uses straight-line amortization for production equipment. The investments held at year end were purchased during 2008.

Plato explains to Shito that it is important for the corporation to show an $8-million net income before taxes because Plato receives a $1-million bonus if the income before taxes and bonus reaches $8 million. He also cautions that he will not pay more than $3 million in income taxes to the government.

Instructions

(a) What can Shito do within GAAP to accommodate the president's wishes to achieve $8 million of income before taxes and bonus? Present the revised income statement based on your decision.

(b) Are the actions ethical? Who are the stakeholders in this decision, and what effect does Shito's actions have on their interests?

(c) Are there any cash flow implications to the choices made to achieve the president's wishes?

P21-8 Kolb Corporation is in the process of negotiating a loan for expansion purposes. Kolb's books and records have never been audited and the bank has requested that an audit be performed. Kolb has prepared the following comparative financial statements for the years ended December 31, 2008 and 2007:

KOLB CORPORATION
Statement of Financial Position
as of December 31, 2008 and 2007

	2008	2007
Assets		
Current assets		
Cash	$163,000	$ 82,000
Accounts receivable	392,000	296,000
Allowance for doubtful accounts	(37,000)	(18,000)
Investments (held-for-trading), at cost	78,000	78,000
Merchandise inventory	207,000	202,000
Total current assets	803,000	640,000
Plant assets		
Property, plant, and equipment	167,000	169,500
Accumulated amortization	(121,600)	(106,400)
Plant assets (net)	45,400	63,100
Total assets	$848,400	$703,100

Liabilities and Shareholders' Equity

Liabilities		
Accounts payable	$121,400	$196,100
Shareholders' equity		
Common shares, no par value,		
50,000 authorized, 20,000 issued and		
outstanding	260,000	260,000
Retained earnings	467,000	247,000
Total shareholders' equity	727,000	507,000
Total liabilities and shareholders' equity	$848,400	$703,100

KOLB CORPORATION
Statement of Income
for the Years Ended December 31, 2008 and 2007

	2008	2007
Sales	$1,000,000	$900,000
Cost of sales	430,000	395,000
Gross profit	570,000	505,000
Operating expenses	210,000	205,000
Administrative expenses	140,000	105,000
	350,000	310,000
Net income	$ 220,000	$195,000

During the audit, the following additional facts were determined:

1. An analysis of collections and losses on accounts receivable during the past two years indicates a drop in anticipated bad debts losses. After consulting with management, it was agreed that the loss experience rate on sales should be reduced from the recorded 2% to 1.5%, beginning with the year ended December 31, 2008.

2. An analysis of the held-for-trading investments revealed that the total market valuation for these investments as of the end of each year was as follows:

Dec. 31, 2007	$78,000
Dec. 31, 2008	$65,000

3. The merchandise inventory at December 31, 2007, was overstated by $8,900 and the merchandise inventory at December 31, 2008, was overstated by $13,600.

4. On January 2, 2007, equipment costing $30,000 (estimated useful life of 10 years and residual value of $5,000) was incorrectly charged to operating expenses. Kolb records amortization on the straight-line basis. In 2008, fully amortized equipment (with no residual value) that originally cost $17,500 was sold as scrap for $2,800. Kolb credited the $2,800 in proceeds to the equipment account.

5. An analysis of 2007 operating expenses revealed that Kolb charged to expense a four-year insurance premium of $4,700 on January 15, 2007.

6. The analysis of operating expenses also revealed that operating expenses were incorrectly classified as part of administrative expenses in the amount of $15,000 in 2007 and $35,000 in 2008.

Instructions

(a) Prepare the journal entries to correct the books at December 31, 2008. The books for 2008 have not been closed. Ignore income taxes.

(b) Beginning with reported net income, prepare a schedule showing the calculation of corrected net income for the years ended December 31, 2008 and 2007, assuming that any adjustments are to be reported on comparative statements for the two years. Ignore income taxes. (Do not prepare financial statements.)

(c) Prepare a schedule showing the calculation of corrected retained earnings at January 1, 2008.

(AICPA adapted)

P21-9   You have been assigned to examine the financial statements of Pecco Corporation for the year ended December 31, 2008. You discover the following situations:

1. The physical inventory count on December 31, 2007, improperly excluded merchandise costing $29,000 that had been temporarily stored in a public warehouse. Pecco uses a periodic inventory system.

2. The physical inventory count on December 31, 2008, improperly included merchandise with a cost of $18,500 that had been recorded as a sale on December 27, 2008, and was being held for the customer to pick up on January 4, 2009.

3. A collection of $7,600 on account from a customer received on December 31, 2008, was not recorded until January 2, 2009.

4. Amortization of $6,400 for 2008 on delivery vehicles was not recorded.

5. In 2008, the company received $6,700 on a sale of fully amortized equipment that originally cost $22,000. The company credited the proceeds from the sale to the Equipment account.

6. During November 2008, a competitor company filed a patent infringement suit against Pecco, claiming damages of $720,000. The company's legal counsel has indicated that an unfavourable verdict is probable and a reasonable estimate of the court's award to the competitor is $525,000. The company has not reflected or disclosed this situation in the financial statements.

7. A large piece of equipment was purchased on January 3, 2008, for $48,000 and was charged in error to Repairs Expense. The equipment is estimated to have a service life of eight years and no residual value. Pecco normally uses the straight-line amortization method for this type of equipment.

8. Pecco has a portfolio of temporary investments reported as trading investments at fair value. No adjusting entry has been made yet in 2008. Information on carrying amounts and fair value is as follows:

	Carrying Amount	Fair value
Dec. 31, 2007	$95,000	$95,000
Dec. 31, 2008	$94,000	$82,000

9. At December 31, 2008, an analysis of payroll information showed accrued salaries of $12,200. The Accrued Salaries Payable account had a balance of $18,000 at December 31, 2008, which was unchanged from its balance at December 31, 2007.

10. A $21,000 insurance premium paid on July 1, 2007, for a policy that expires on June 30, 2010, was charged to insurance expense.

11. A trademark was acquired at the beginning of 2007 for $50,000. Through an oversight, no amortization has been recorded since its acquisition. Pecco expected the trademark to benefit the company for a total of approximately 15 years.

Instructions
Assume that the trial balance has been prepared, the ending inventory has not yet been recorded, and the books have not been closed for 2008. Assuming also that all amounts are material, prepare journal entries showing the adjustments that are required. Ignore income tax considerations.

P21-10   Voga Company is adjusting and correcting its books at the end of 2008. In reviewing its records, the following information is compiled:

1. Voga has failed to accrue sales commissions payable at the end of each of the last three years, as follows:

Dec. 31, 2006	$11,300
Dec. 31, 2007	$4,000
Dec. 31, 2008	$2,500

2. In reviewing the December 31, 2008, inventory, Voga discovered errors in its inventory-taking procedures that have caused inventories for the last three years to be incorrect, as follows:

Dec. 31, 2006	Overstated	$16,000
Dec. 31, 2007	Understated	$21,000
Dec. 31, 2008	Overstated	$ 6,700

Voga has already made an entry that established the incorrect December 31, 2008, inventory amount.

3. At December 31, 2008, Voga changed the amortization method on its office equipment from double-declining-balance to straight-line. Assume that this qualifies as a change in accounting policy, and that tax amortization is higher than the double-declining-balance amortization taken for each period. The following information is available (the tax rate is 40%):

	Double-Declining-Balance	Straight-Line	Pre-Tax Difference	Tax Effect	Difference, Net of Tax
Prior to 2008	$70,000	$40,000	$30,000	$12,000	$18,000
2008	12,000	10,000	2,000	800	1,200

Voga has already recorded the 2008 amortization expense using the double-declining-balance method.

4. Before 2008, Voga accounted for its income from long-term construction contracts on the completed-contract basis because it was unable to reliably measure the degree of completion or the estimated costs to complete. Early in 2008, Voga's growth permitted the company to hire an experienced cost accountant and the company changed to the percentage-of-completion basis for financial accounting purposes. The completed-contract method will continue to be used for tax purposes. Income for 2008 has been recorded using the percentage-of-completion method. The income tax rate is 40%. The following information is available:

	Pre-Tax Income	
	Percentage-of-Completion	Completed-Contract
Prior to 2008	$150,000	$95,000
2008	60,000	20,000

Instructions

(a) Prepare the necessary journal entries at December 31, 2008, to record the above corrections and changes as appropriate. The books are still open for 2008. As Voga has not yet recorded its 2008 income tax expense and payable amounts, tax effects for the current year may be ignored. Prior-year tax effects must be considered in items 3 and 4.

(b) If there are alternative methods of accounting for any items listed above, explain what the options are and why you chose the particular alternative.

P21-11 On May 5, 2009, you were hired by Gower Inc., a closely held company, as a staff member of its newly created internal auditing department. While reviewing the company's records for 2007 and 2008, you discover that no adjustments have yet been made for the items listed below:

1. Interest income of $28,200 was not accrued at the end of 2007. It was recorded when received in February 2008.

2. Equipment costing $18,000 was expensed when purchased on July 1, 2007. It is expected to have a four-year life with no residual value. The company typically uses straight-line amortization for all fixed assets.

3. Research costs of $36,000 were incurred early in 2007. They were capitalized and were to be amortized over a three-year period. Amortization of $12,000 was recorded for 2007 and $12,000 for 2008. For tax purposes, the research costs were expensed as incurred.

4. On January 2, 2007, Gower leased a building for five years at a monthly rental of $9,000. On that date, the company paid the following amounts, which were expensed when paid for both financial reporting and tax purposes:

Security deposit	$35,000
First month's rent	9,000
Last month's rent	9,000
	$53,000

5. The company received $45,000 from a customer at the beginning of 2007 for services that it is to perform evenly over a three-year period beginning in 2007. None of the amount received was reported as unearned revenue at the end of 2007. The $45,000 was included in taxable income in 2007.

6. Merchandise inventory costing $18,200 was in the warehouse at December 31, 2007, but was incorrectly omitted from the physical count at that date. The company uses the periodic inventory method.

Instructions

Using the table that follows, enter the appropriate dollar amounts in the appropriate columns to indicate the effect of any errors on the net income figure reported on the income statement for the year ending December 31, 2007, and the retained earnings figure reported on the balance sheet at December 31, 2008. Assume that all amounts are material and that an income tax rate of 25% is appropriate for all years. Assume also that each item is independent of the other items. It is not necessary to total the columns on the grid.

	Net Income for 2007		Retained Earnings at Dec. 31, 2008	
Item	Understated	Overstated	Understated	Overstated
	————	————	————	————
	————	————	————	————

(CIA adapted)

P21-12   Kipawa Corporation has used the accrual basis of accounting for several years. A review of the records, however, indicates that some expenses and revenues have been handled on a cash basis because of errors made by an inexperienced bookkeeper. Income statements prepared by the bookkeeper reported $29,000 net income for 2007 and $37,000 net income for 2008. Further examination of the records reveals that the following items were handled improperly:

1. Rent of $1,300 was received from a tenant in December 2007, but the full amount was recorded as income at that time even though the rental related to 2008.

2. Wages payable on December 31 have been consistently omitted from the records of that date and have been entered instead as expenses when paid in the following year. The amounts of the accruals that were recorded in this way were as follows:

Dec. 31, 2006	$1,100
Dec. 31, 2007	1,500
Dec. 31, 2008	940

3. Invoices for office supplies purchased have been charged to expense accounts when received. Inventories of supplies on hand at the end of each year have been ignored, and no entry has been made for them. The inventories were as follows:

Dec. 31, 2006	$1,300
Dec. 31, 2007	740
Dec. 31, 2008	1,420

Instructions

(a) Prepare a schedule that shows the corrected net income for the years 2007 and 2008. All listed items should be labelled clearly. Ignore income tax considerations.

(b) Prepare the required journal entries to correct the 2008 net income. Assume that the books are open and ignore income tax considerations.

(c) Assume that Kipawa had unadjusted retained earnings of $95,000 at January 1, 2007, and of $124,000 at January 1, 2008. Prepare a schedule that shows the corrected opening retained earnings balances.

P21-13   You have been asked by a client to review the records of Ashok Corporation, a small manufacturer of precision tools and machines. Your client is interested in buying the business, and arrangements were made for you to review the accounting records. Your examination reveals the following:

1. Ashok Corporation commenced business on April 1, 2005, and has been reporting on a fiscal year ending March 31. The company has never been audited, but the annual statements prepared by the bookkeeper reflect the following income before closing and before deducting income taxes:

Year Ended March 31	Income Before Taxes
2006	$ 71,600
2007	111,400
2008	103,580

2. A relatively small number of machines have been shipped on consignment. These transactions have been recorded as ordinary sales and billed in this way, with the gross profit on each sale being recognized when the machine was shipped. On March 31 of each year, the amounts for machines billed and in the hands of consignees were as follows:

2006	$6,500
2007	none
2008	5,590

The sales price was determined by adding 30% to cost. Assume that the consigned machines are sold the following year.

3. On March 30, 2007, two machines were shipped to a customer on a C.O.D. basis. The sale was not entered until April 5, 2007, when $6,100 cash was received. The machines were not included in the inventory at March 31, 2007. (Title passed on March 30, 2007.)

4. All machines are sold subject to a five-year warranty. It is estimated that the expense ultimately to be incurred in connection with the warranty will amount to 0.5% of sales. The company has charged an expense account for actual warranty costs incurred. Sales per books and warranty costs were as follows:

| Year Ended March 31 | Sales | Actual Warranty Costs Incurred for Sales Made in | | | |
		2006	2007	2008	Total
2006	$ 940,000	$760			$ 760
2007	1,010,000	360	$1,310		1,670
2008	1,795,000	320	1,620	$1,910	3,850

5. A review of the corporate minutes reveals that the manager is entitled to a bonus of 0.5% of the income before deducting income taxes and the bonus. The bonuses have never been recorded or paid.

6. Bad debts have been recorded on a direct write-off basis. Experience of similar enterprises indicates that losses will approximate 0.25% of sales. Bad debts written off and expensed were as follows:

| | Bad Debts Incurred on Sales Made in | | | |
	2006	2007	2008	Total
2006	$750			$ 750
2007	800	$ 520		1,320
2008	350	1,800	$1,700	3,850

7. The bank deducts 6% on all contracts that it finances. Of this amount, 0.5% is placed in a reserve to the credit of Ashok Corporation and is refunded to Ashok as financed contracts are paid in full. The reserve established by the bank has not been reflected in Ashok's books. On the books of the bank for each fiscal year, the excess of credits over debits (the net increase) to the reserve account for Ashok were as follows:

2006	$ 3,000
2007	3,900
2008	5,100
	$12,000

8. Commissions on sales have been entered when paid. Commissions payable on March 31 of each year were as follows:

2006	$1,400
2007	800
2008	1,120

Instructions

(a) Present a schedule showing the revised income before income taxes for each of the years ended March 31, 2006, 2007, and 2008. Make calculations to the nearest dollar.

(b) Prepare the journal entry or entries that you would give the bookkeeper to correct the books. Assume that the books have not yet been closed for the fiscal year ended March 31, 2008. Disregard corrections of income taxes.

(AICPA adapted)

P21-14 You are the auditor of Varion Services Inc., a privately owned full service cleaning company that is undergoing its first audit for the period ending September 30, 2008. The bank has requested that Varion have its statements audited this year to satisfy a condition of its debt covenant. It is currently October 1, 2008, and the company's books have been closed. As part of the audit, you have found the following situations:

1. Despite having high receivables, Varion has no allowance for doubtful accounts and cash collections have slowed dramatically. Unfortunately, Varion is owed $5,000 from Ben's Fast Foods at the end of fiscal 2008. Ben's has received substantial media attention during the past year due to Department of Health investigations that ultimately resulted in the closure of the company's operations, and the owner has apparently moved to the Bahamas. No adjustment has been made for this balance. Company management estimates that an allowance for doubtful accounts of $47,000 is required. During the 2008 fiscal year, the company wrote off $38,000 in receivables, and it estimates that its September 30, 2007, allowance for doubtful accounts should have been $30,000.

2. Varion's only capital asset on its books is an advanced cleaning system that has a cost of $35,000 and a net book value of $20,825. Varion has been depreciating this asset using the capital cost allowance used for tax purposes for the two years prior to the 2008 fiscal year, at the rate of 30%. Useful life at the time of purchase was estimated to be 10 years. Varion would like to change to a straight-line approach to provide more relevant information to its statement users. Management anticipates that the asset will continue to be of use for the next four years and will have no residual value. Since the company's accountant was uncertain about how to deal with the change in policy, amortization expense has not been recorded for the fiscal year.

3. Varion purchased a computer at the beginning of the fiscal year and immediately expensed its $3,000 cost. Upon questioning, one of the owners said he thought the computer would likely not need to be replaced for at least two more years.

4. You notice that there are no supplies on the statement of financial position. Company management explains that it expenses all supplies when purchased. The company had $1,500 of cleaning supplies on hand at the end of September 2008, which is about $500 higher than the balance that was on hand at the end of the previous year.

5. Varion started this year to keep a small amount of excess cash in available-for-sale investments. At the end of September 2008, the fair value of this portfolio was $15,000 and the cost of the investments was $12,000.

Instructions

(a) Assuming that the company's books are closed, prepare any journal entries that are required for each of the transactions. Ignore income tax considerations.

(b) For each of the items, discuss the type of change that is involved and how it is accounted for on the current and comparative financial statements.

(c) If Varion elected to employ differential reporting, discuss how this might change your answers to (a).

(d) Repeat part (a) assuming that the books are open.

Writing Assignments

WA21-1   Cranmore Inc. recently hired a new accountant, Jodie Larson, who has proposed the following accounting changes in connection with Cranmore Inc.'s 2008 financial statements:

1. At December 31, 2007, Cranmore had a receivable of $820,000 from Michael Inc. on its balance sheet that had been owed since mid-2006. Michael Inc. has recently been declared bankrupt, and no recovery is expected. Jodie proposes to write off the receivable in 2008 against retained earnings as a correction of a 2006 error.

2. Jodie proposes to change from double-declining-balance to straight-line amortization for the company's manufacturing assets because of a change in the pattern in which the assets provide benefits to the company. If straight-line amortization had been used for all prior periods, retained earnings would have been $380,800 higher at December 31, 2007. The change's effect just on 2008 income is a reduction of $48,800.

3. For equipment in the leasing division, Jodie proposes to adopt the sum-of-the-years'-digits amortization method, which the company has never used before. Cranmore began operating its leasing division in 2008. If straight-line amortization were used, 2008 income would be $110,000 higher.

4. In the past, the company has spread preproduction costs in its furniture division over five years. Because its latest furniture is of the "fad" type and it appears that the largest volume of sales will now occur during the first two years after introduction, Jodie proposes to amortize preproduction costs on a per-unit basis. This will result in expensing most of such costs during the first two years after the furniture's introduction. If the new accounting method had been used prior to 2008, retained earnings at December 31, 2007, would have been $375,000 less.

5. To achieve a better measure of the performance of its building construction division, Jodie proposes to switch from the completed-contract method of accounting to the percentage-of-completion method. If the percentage-of-completion method had been used in all prior years, retained earnings at December 31, 2007, would have been $1,175,000 higher and current year income would have been $400,000 lower.

Instructions

(a) For each of the changes described above, identify whether the situation is a change in policy, a change in estimate, or the correction of an error. Justify your answer.

(b) For each of the changes described above, determine whether a restatement of January 1, 2008, retained earnings is required. What is the amount of the adjustment, if any?

(c) Identify what disclosures are required in the notes to the financial statements as a result of each of these changes. Include the appropriate numerical amounts, if applicable.

WA21-2 Various types of accounting changes can affect the financial statements of a business enterprise differently. Assume that each item on the following list would have a material effect on the financial statements of your business in the current year:

1. A change from the completed-contract method to the percentage-of-completion method of accounting for long-term construction contracts because of increased sophistication of your costing department and a move to longer contracts in the current year than in prior years.

2. A change in the estimated useful life of previously recorded capital assets.

3. A change from deferring and amortizing preproduction costs to expensing the costs as incurred. The new accounting method was adopted in recognition of the change in estimated future benefits.

4. A change from including the employer share of CPP premiums with Payroll Tax Expenses to including it with Salaries and Wages Expense on the income statement.

5. The correction of a mathematical error in inventory costing that was made in a prior period.

6. A change from straight-line amortization to a double-declining method in recognition of the effect that technology has on the pattern of benefits received from the asset's use.

7. A change from presenting unconsolidated statements to presenting consolidated statements for the company and its two long-held subsidiaries.

8. A change in the method of accounting for leases for tax purposes to conform with the financial accounting method; as a result, both future and current taxes payable changed substantially.

9. A change from the periodic inventory method to the perpetual method with the introduction of scanning equipment and updated computer software.

10. A change in an accounting method due to a change in a primary source of GAAP.

Instructions

Identify the type of accounting change that is described in each item, and indicate whether the prior years' financial statements must be restated when they are presented in comparative form with the current year's statements.

WA21-3 Ali Reiners, controller of Luftsa Corp., is aware that there is a revised *CICA Handbook* section on accounting changes that became effective in 2007. After reading the section, she is not clear about what action to take on the following items related to Luftsa Corp. for the year 2007:

1. In 2007, Luftsa decided to change its policy on accounting for certain marketing costs. Previously, the company deferred and amortized all marketing costs over a period of at least five years because management believed that a return on these expenditures did not occur immediately. Recently, however, the returns are earned over a much shorter period, and Luftsa is now expensing the marketing costs as incurred.

2. In 2007, the company examined its entire policy relating to the amortization of plant equipment. Plant equipment had normally been amortized over a 15-year period, but recent experience indicated that the assets should be amortized over a 20-year period. In addition, because the benefits from use of the assets are received relatively evenly over their useful life, the company is changing from a declining-balance to the straight-line method.

3. One division of Luftsa Corp., Rosentiel Co., has consistently shown an increasing net income from period to period. On closer examination of its operating statement, Ali Reiners noted that bad debt expense and inventory obsolescence charges are much lower than in other divisions. In discussing this with the division's controller, Ali learned that the controller knowingly makes low estimates related to the write-off of receivables and inventory in order to manage his bottom line.

4. In 2007, the company purchased new machinery that is expected to increase production dramatically, particularly in the early years. The company has decided to amortize this machinery on an accelerated basis, even though other machinery is amortized on a straight-line basis.

5. All equipment sold by Luftsa is subject to a three-year warranty. It has been estimated that the expense ultimately to be incurred on these machines is 1% of sales. In 2007, because of a production breakthrough, it is now estimated that 0.5% of sales is sufficient. In 2005 and 2006, warranty expense was calculated as $64,000 and $70,000, respectively. The company now believes that warranty costs should be reduced by 50%.

6. Another division, Usher Division, is a fast-growing business in the commercial construction industry. In reviewing the capital asset ledger, Ali found a series of unusual accounting changes in which the useful lives of assets were substantially reduced when half-way through the original life estimate. For example, the useful life of one dump truck was changed from 10 to 6 years during its fifth year of service. The divisional manager, who is compensated in large part by bonuses, indicated on investigation, "It's perfectly legal to change an accounting estimate. We always have better information after time has passed."

Instructions

Ali Reiners has come to you for advice about each of the situations. Prepare a memorandum to the controller, indicating the appropriate accounting treatment that should be given to each situation. For any situations where there might be ethical considerations, identify and assess the issues and suggest what should be done.

WA21-4 Rydell Manufacturing Ltd. is preparing its year-end financial statements. The controller, Theo Kimbria, is confronted with several decisions about statement presentation for the following items:

1. The vice-president of sales indicated that one product line has lost its customer appeal and will be phased out over the next three years. Therefore, a decision has been made to lower the estimated lives on related production equipment from the remaining five years to three years.

2. Estimating the lives of new products in the Leisure Products Division has become very difficult because of the highly competitive conditions in this market. Therefore, the practice of deferring and amortizing preproduction costs has been abandoned in favour of expensing these costs as they are incurred.

3. The Hightone Building was converted from a sales office to offices for the accounting department at the beginning of this year. Therefore, the expense related to this building will now appear as an administrative expense rather than a selling expense on the current year's income statement.

4. When the year-end physical inventory adjustment was made for the current year, the controller discovered that the prior year's physical inventory sheets for an entire section of warehouse had been mislaid and left out of last year's count.

5. The method of accounting that is used for financial reporting purposes for certain receivables has been approved for tax purposes during the current tax year by the CRA. This change for tax purposes will cause both current taxes payable and future tax liabilities to change substantially.

6. Management has decided to switch from the FIFO inventory valuation method to the average cost inventory valuation method for all inventories.

Instructions

For each of the six changes that Rydell Manufacturing Ltd. made in the current year, advise Theo on whether the change is a change in accounting policy, a change in estimate, the correction of an error, of none of these. Provide a short explanation for your choice. If the information that is provided is insufficient for you to determine the nature of the change, identify what additional information you need and how this might affect your response.

(CMA adapted)

WA21-5 The new Canadian standard for accounting changes does not permit the correction of an error to be accounted for using partial retrospective restatement. However, IAS 8, on which *Handbook* Section 1506 is based, does allow partial retrospective restatement for error corrections.

Instructions

(a) Write a short memorandum that is suitable for being presented to your class in support of the Canadian position.

(b) Write a short memorandum suitable for presentation to your class in support of the international position.

WA21-6 At a recent conference on financial accounting and reporting, three participants provided examples of similar accounting changes that they had encountered in the last few months. They all involved the current portion of long-term debt.

The first participant explained that it had just recently come to her attention that the current portion of long-term debt was incorrectly calculated in the last three years of her company's financial statements due to an error in an accounting software product. The second participant explained that his company had just decided to change its definition of what is "current" to make it closer to the "operating cycle," which is approximately 18 months. The company had been using "twelve months from the balance sheet date." The third participant also acknowledged that her company has decided to change from a "twelve months from the balance sheet date" definition to one based on the company's operating cycle, which is now close to two years. She explained that the company's strategic plan over the last three years had moved the company into bidding on and winning significant longer-term contracts and that the average life of these contracts has now grown to about two years.

Instructions

As a panellist at this conference who is expected to respond to the participants, prepare a brief report on the advice you would give on how each situation should be handled under GAAP. Identify what steps each participant should take and what disclosures, if any, each would be required to report.

Cases

Refer to the Case Primer on the Student Website to help you answer these cases.

Student Website

www.wiley.com/canada/kieso

CA21-1 Harvey's Hotels Limited (HHL) uses the sinking fund method to depreciate its hotel buildings. It has used this method for the past 20 years on the advice of accountants who no longer audit the company. Originally, the company was seen as being in the real estate business, and having the operation of hotels as a sideline business. But HHL gradually changed its emphasis such that its main business is now hotel operations.

Recently, HHL received a letter from the securities commission, which reviews financial statements of companies whose shares trade on the stock exchange. The letter pointed out that the use of the sinking fund method of depreciation for buildings was not really acceptable in Canada any more, except for the real estate industry. The securities commission requested that the matter be brought to the attention of the company's auditors and suggested a response within three weeks.

HHL had also recently received a research report from a local university that corroborated the observation of the securities commission. There had not been any such study available previously in Canada. HHL had been considering switching from sinking fund to straight-line, since it was now at the point where the depreciation charges under the sinking fund method were quite large and growing. In fact, the increasing depreciation charges under the sinking fund method were causing net income to decrease.

The *CICA Handbook* states that the amortization method and estimates of the remaining lives of assets should be reviewed on a regular basis as part of the ongoing annual assessment of the financial statements. For this reason, HHL had had its hotels appraised. The appraiser noted that due to a strong demand, in many cases the residual value at the end of the expected life of the hotels would likely be about five times higher than the original estimates.

HHL would like to know whether the change to straight-line amortization would be accounted for prospectively or retroactively, and how to incorporate the information from the appraisal.

Instructions

Respond to HHL's concerns by noting all relevant points as well as any other issues.

CA21-2 Andy Frain is an audit senior of a large public accounting firm who has just been assigned to the Usher Corporation's annual audit engagement. Usher has been a client of Frain's firm for many years. Usher is a fast-growing business in the commercial construction industry. In reviewing the fixed asset ledger, Frain discovered a series of unusual accounting changes, in which the useful lives of assets, depreciated using the straight-line method, were substantially lowered near the mid-point of the original estimate. For example, the useful life of one dump truck was changed from 10 to 6 years during its fifth year of service. Upon further investigation, Andy was told by Vince Lloyd, Usher's accounting manager, "I don't really see your problem. After all, it's perfectly legal to change an accounting estimate. Besides, our CEO likes to see big earnings!"

Instructions

Discuss the issues.

Integrated Cases

IC 21-1   Temple Limited (TL) is in the real estate business. After several years of economic growth, most of the company's assets are now worth significantly more than the amount that is recognized on the financial statements. Wanting to capitalize on this positive trend, the company is ready to expand and is looking at developing a new property in the Bahamas that will cost $300 million. Currently, the debt to equity ratio of the company is 5:1 and the company needs to raise funds for the expansion. Lendall Bank (LB), the company's primary lender, understands that there is hidden value in the balance sheet and is willing to finance the project.

TL is now concerned about how the capital markets will react to this increase in debt. The company's shares list on the TSX and, therefore, Canadian GAAP is a constraint. Terry Temple, the company's CEO, recently attended a conference on international GAAP where the speakers noted that Canadian companies that are publicly accountable will move to International GAAP for years beginning on or after January 1, 2011.

Under international accounting, fair value accounting is permitted and gains/losses are booked to shareholders' equity in a revaluation account. Terry understands that Canadian companies are currently not allowed early adoption of the international standards but he is definitely interested in being able to revalue the real estate assets. As part of the conference deliverables, the following handout was given to conference attendees. It represents a tentative timeline for the rollout of international standards in Canada for Canadian companies and comes from the CICA document "Implementation Plan for Incorporating IFRSs into Canadian GAAP" that is dated March 31, 2007.

The following is a tentative timeline of key events for reporting enterprises in adopting IFRSs, based on current assumptions in the Strategic Plan and an assumed changeover of January 1, 2011. For illustrative purposes, this timeline assumes an enterprise with a calendar year end.

2006-2008	Obtain training and thorough knowledge of IFRS. Commence assessment of accounting policies with reference to IFRS and development of a plan for convergence.
By early 2008	Progress review by AcSB
By March 31, 2008	Changeover timing to be announced by the AcSB following progress review
2008	Finalize assessment of accounting policies with reference to IFRSs and plan for convergence
December 31, 2008	Possible disclosure of an enterprise's plan for convergence and what effects the enterprise anticipates will arise with the change to IFRS (see paragraph 32)
December 31, 2009	Same disclosure required as in 2008, but with a greater degree of quantification of the effects of the change to IFRSs (see paragraph 29 of this document)
January 1, 2010	First year for collection of comparative information for inclusion with 2011 financial statements under new IFRS-based requirements. Opening balance sheet for 2010 on IFRS basis required. Valuations on certain items may be advisable for the opening balance sheet preparation, depending on accounting policy choices under IFRS, especially since IFRS 1, First-time Adoption of International Financial Reporting Standards.
December 31, 2010	Last year of reporting under current Canadian GAAP
January 1, 2011	Changeover. First year reporting under new IFRS-based standards. Opening balance sheet for 2011 on IFRS basis required.
March 31, 2011	Enterprises issuing interim financial statements prepare their first IFRS-based statements for the three months ended March 31, 2011
December 31, 2011	End of first annual reporting period in accordance with new IFRS-based requirements including IFRS-based comparatives for 2010

Instructions

Adopt the role of the controller of the company and write a memo to address Terry's concerns. Hint: review Chapters 10 and 11 regarding asset valuation.

IC 21-2   Sunlight Equipment Manufacturers (SEM) manufactures barbeque equipment. The company has historically been very profitable; however, in the last year and a half, things have taken a turn for the worse due to higher consumer interest rates and a slowdown in the economy. On its 2008 draft year-end statements the company is currently showing a break-even position before any final year-end adjustments. The company had fired its CEO, Sam Gloom, at the beginning of the year and a turnaround specialist was hired—Theo Sunshine. Theo has a reputation of being able to come into companies that are suffering and make them profitable within two years. Theo has agreed with the board of directors of the company that he will be paid a $1 million bonus if the company has a combined two-year profit of $5 million by the end of 2009.

Among other things, Theo instituted a more aggressive sales policy in 2008 as well as a new remuneration policy for sales staff. Theo attributed the company's poor performance to untrained sales staff whose remuneration and bonus scheme was not properly aligned to maximize sales. Under the new remuneration policy, sales staff is paid salary as well as a bonus, which is a percent of gross sales as at year end. The sales staff has responded well and sales have increased by 20%.

The new sales policy is as follows:

- Cash down payment of 20% with remaining payment for shipment once the barbeques are sold by the customer to a third party.

- If the customers order double their normal order, no down payment is required.

- The barbeques may be stored on the premises of SEM. Many customers have taken the company up on this offer in order to double the size of their purchase.

- Any unsold barbeques are allowed to be returned after year end.

Under the new policy, sales have increased dramatically with many customers taking advantage of the new terms. As at year end, legal title to all barbeques has passed to the customers. Only customers with excellent credit history have been allowed to purchase under the new policy. The company has accrued bonuses for almost all its sales staff.

The increased profits from these sales have been offset by the accrual of $500,000 of Theo's bonus. He is very confident that he will be able to turn the company around and so has accrued part of his bonus. He has also decided to change several accounting policies, including the following:

- Depreciation on machinery switched to straight-line from double-declining balance. Note that the equipment is about 2 years old with an estimated life of 10 years. Theo felt that the double-declining balance method was arbitrary and noted that several of their competitors used the straight-line method. Machinery is most useful when new since it requires less downtime for fixing.

Another problem that Theo had identified was in inventory management. Theo was convinced that inventory was being stolen and/or "lost" due to poor tracking. The company had therefore hired a company, Software Limited ("SL") to install a new inventory tracking system during the year. Midway through the year, SL had gone bankrupt and was not able to finish the installation. The installation was a customized job and as at year end, the system was not functioning yet. SEM has not been able to find a software company to replace SL. To date, $2 million has been spent on the new system. Theo had capitalized the costs and noted he was confident that he would be able to find a company who could successfully complete the installation.

Instructions

Adopt the role of the company's auditors and discuss the financial reporting issues for the 2008 year end.

Research and Financial Analysis

RA21-1 Stantec Inc.

Refer to the 2005 financial statements and accompanying notes of **Stantec Inc.** that have been reproduced and included at the end of this volume. Assume that in preparing its 2005 financial statements, Stantec discovered an error in the 2004 calculation of depreciation expense on its engineering equipment. The company's policy is to take a full year's amortization on the assets on hand at the beginning of the year at a rate of 25%, but, because of an oversight, a 5% rate was instead used. Stantec uses a declining-balance method of amortization for this equipment.

At December 31, 2003, the engineering equipment had a cost of $27,257 thousand and accumulated depreciation of $12,257 thousand.

Instructions

(a) Prepare the entry that Stantec's accountants would have made in 2005 to correct this error, assuming the same effective tax rate that was reported in 2005.

(b) Prepare the comparative consolidated statements of income and retained earnings that Stantec would have presented if this error had in fact occurred. (Assume that the 2005 amortization expense reported on the income statement is the corrected amount for 2005.)

(c) Prepare all the 2005 required disclosures associated with this correction.

(d) Identify any actual accounting changes that Stantec reported for its fiscal year ending December 31, 2005. These financial statements were prepared before the effective date of revised *Handbook* Section 1506. Compare the accounting and disclosures made by the company with those that are now required under the revised standards. Identify any additional information, if any, that would now need to be disclosed.

RA21-2 Wenzel Downhole Tools Ltd.

According to an announcement in November, 2006, Wenzel Downhole Tools Ltd., headquartered in Alberta, agreed to pay a fine to the Alberta Securities Commission (ASC) to settle allegations of filing false and misleading financial statements in 2002. Looking back at how the 2003 and 2002 financial statements were restated provides interesting information about several areas where accounting changes can occur.

Through the SEDAR website (www.sedar.com) gain access to Wenzel Downhole Tools' 2003 comparative financial statements released on October 14 , 2005.

Instructions

(a) Carefully review the notes to the December 31, 2003, consolidated financial statements. Identify all accounting changes made in 2003.

(b) For the accounting changes noted, identify whether each one is a change in accounting policy, a change in accounting estimate, or the correction of an accounting error according to the definitions of recently revised *Handbook* Section 1506. If the change is a change in accounting policy, was it the result of initial adoption of a primary source of GAAP, or was it a voluntary change?

(c) For each accounting change that you identified, explain whether it was accounted for retrospectively, currently, or prospectively. For any that were adopted retroactively, did Wenzel use full or partial retrospective application?

(d) For each accounting change that you identified, list all the balance sheet and income statement accounts that were affected by the adjustments made.

RA21-3 EnCana Corporation

According to EnCana Corporation's 2006 Annual Report, EnCana is an integrated North American resource company focused on creating long-term value by developing unconventional natural gas and in-situ oilsands resources. We have to go back to the company's 2003 Annual Report, however, to find interesting material related to accounting changes, a situation that is true for many companies. EnCana reports several accounting changes in its financial statements for its year ended December 31, 2003, which were released March 5, 2004. Access the financial statements of EnCana for its year ended December 31, 2003, through www.sedar.com or another source, and answer the following questions.

Instructions

(a) Identify each type of accounting change that was reported by EnCana in 2003 as being one of the following:

    1.   A change in accounting policy mandated by a change in a primary source of GAAP

    2.   A voluntary change in accounting policy

    3.   A change in estimate

    4.   A correction of an error

(b) For each change reported in (a) above, identify the *CICA Handbook* recommendation on how the change should be accounted for.

(c) Were each of the actual changes identified by EnCana accounted for as recommended by the CICA? Explain.

(d) The company adjusted the opening balance of retained earnings at January 1, 2003 by $66 million. How much of this change related to 2002? To 2001? To before 2001? What revenue and expense accounts do you think were affected in the prior years? Explain briefly.

RA21-4 Research Case

In January 2006, the CICA's Accounting Standards Board (AcSB) adopted a new strategic plan. The plan indicated that accounting standards in Canada for public companies are expected to converge with International Financial Reporting Standards (IFRS) by the end of 2011. The AcSB has been actively communicating with Canadian public companies since then, stressing the importance of looking ahead to prepare for the change to IFRS and to determine what effect the changeover is likely to have on each company.

Choose a sample of three public Canadian companies that you are interested in. Locate a copy of each company's financial statements for its years ending in 2006, 2007, and 2008, if possible.

Instructions

(a) Summarize what each company disclosed about this upcoming change to IFRS in its 2006 financial statements.

(b) Compare the disclosures in the companies' 2007 financial reports with those from one year earlier. Is this change expected to have much of an effect on each company? Summarize, to the extent possible, what each company identifies as being its greatest challenge as a result of this change.

(c) If the 2008 financial statements have been released, review the note disclosures related to the change to IFRS. Have the companies made much progress in determining the potential effects on their financial position and performance? Write a short summary of what the major issues appear to be.

RA21-5 Research Case—Transitional Provisions 1

Canadian accounting standards now require companies to provide information about new primary sources of GAAP that have been issued but that are not yet required to be applied.

Instructions

From the SEDAR website (www.sedar.com) or another source, obtain the financial statements of EnCana Corporation or some other large public Canadian company for the company's year ended in 2006.

(a) List all new, but not yet effective, changes in primary GAAP identified by the company in its notes to the financial statements.

(b) For each new or revised primary source of GAAP, determine whether the new standards have identified specific transitional provisions. Briefly explain what the provisions are, if there are any. Also identify when each change will be applied by your specific company, and whether the company expects that the accounting change will have a significant effect on the company's financial statements.

(c) If the company's 2007 financial statements have been released, explain how the company did actually account for each accounting change. Was the significance of the change consistent with what was reported in the 2006 financial statement notes? Comment.

RA21-6 Research Case—Transitional Provisions 2

With the Accounting Standards Board of the CICA working more closely with the FASB and IASB in recent years, the pace of change in primary sources of Canadian GAAP has accelerated. In almost every case, the AcSB includes transitional provisions to ensure that there is uniformity of practice between companies that are changing to the new or revised standards. Some of the more significant changes include the following:

Topic	*CICA Handbook* Section
Impairment of long-lived assets	3063
Asset retirement obligations	3110
Generally accepted accounting principles	1100
Inventories	3031
Accounting Changes	1506

Instructions

Review the transitional provisions, if any, for each of the topics identified above. Write a short report on the accounting requirements for each change in the year when it becomes effective. Briefly discuss whether the requirements seem reasonable, and whether they are consistent from one standard to another.

Cash Flow Is Key

Clearwater Seafoods Limited

Partnership has continued to thrive and provide quality seafood products for more than 30 years, and has done so in part because it knows about cash flows. "The ability to sustain and grow cash flows is key," says Tyrone Cotie, director of corporate finance and investor relations at the Bedford, Nova Scotia–based company. A vertically integrated company, Clearwater operates a large fleet of vessels in Canada and Argentina and owns several processing plants throughout Eastern Canada.

"The statement of cash flows ties together the information contained on the balance sheet and income statement," Cotie explains. "It provides an accurate picture of the cash flows of the business by removing the non-cash items from the earnings statement and by adding the investments noted on the balance sheet to cash outflows. It shows you the cash that was generated during the year and where it was used." For Clearwater, 2006 was a strong year as a stronger product mix and lower costs led to a large increase in profitability, despite the impact of a weakening U.S. dollar as compared with the Canadian dollar.

As an income fund, Clearwater has distributed a significant amount of cash to unit holders since it went public in July 2002. Since 2002, the company has paid distributions of $170 million. "Users of our financial statements look to the operations section of the cash flow statement in order to understand the cash flows that the business is generating, which in turn, after deducting certain items, is the basis for the payment of distributions," Cotie says.

The cash flows generated from operations are a key indicator of the company's health. "The sustainability of a business is ultimately linked to your ability to generate cash," Cotie says. ∎

Statement of Cash Flows

Learning Objectives

After studying this chapter, you should be able to:

1. Describe the purpose and uses of the statement of cash flows.
2. Define cash and cash equivalents.
3. Identify the major classifications of cash flows and explain the significance of each classification.
4. Contrast the direct and indirect methods of calculating net cash flow from operating activities.
5. Differentiate between net income and cash flows from operating activities.
6. Prepare a statement of cash flows using the direct method.
7. Prepare a statement of cash flows using the indirect method.
8. Identify the financial reporting and disclosure requirements for the statement of cash flows.
9. Read and interpret a statement of cash flows.
10. Compare current Canadian and international GAAP for the statement of cash flows.

After studying Appendix 22A, you should be able to:

11. Use a work sheet to prepare a statement of cash flows.

Preview of Chapter 22

Examining a company's income statement may provide insights into its profitability, but it does not provide much information about its liquidity and financial flexibility. The purpose of this chapter is to highlight the requirements of *CICA Handbook* Section 1540, "Cash Flow Statements;" explain the main components of a statement of cash flows and the type of information it provides; and demonstrate how to prepare, report on, and interpret such a statement. The chapter ends with a comparison of current Canadian and international GAAP.

The chapter is organized as follows:

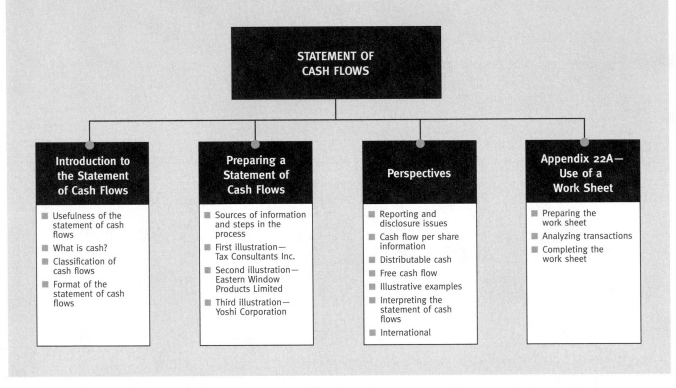

STATEMENT OF CASH FLOWS

Introduction to the Statement of Cash Flows
- Usefulness of the statement of cash flows
- What is cash?
- Classification of cash flows
- Format of the statement of cash flows

Preparing a Statement of Cash Flows
- Sources of information and steps in the process
- First illustration—Tax Consultants Inc.
- Second illustration—Eastern Window Products Limited
- Third illustration—Yoshi Corporation

Perspectives
- Reporting and disclosure issues
- Cash flow per share information
- Distributable cash
- Free cash flow
- Illustrative examples
- Interpreting the statement of cash flows
- International

Appendix 22A—Use of a Work Sheet
- Preparing the work sheet
- Analyzing transactions
- Completing the work sheet

INTRODUCTION TO THE STATEMENT OF CASH FLOWS

Objective 1
Describe the purpose and uses of the statement of cash flows.

Will the company be able to continue to pay dividends? How did the company finance the acquisition of the new subsidiary? Will the company have sufficient cash to meet the significant amount of debt that is maturing next year? How did cash increase when there was a net loss for the period? How were the proceeds of the bond issue used? How was the expansion in plant and equipment financed? Or, as the opening story alludes to, how sustainable are the company's operations? These questions cannot be answered by reviewing the balance sheet and income statement alone. A statement of cash flows is needed.

The primary purpose of the **statement of cash flows** is to provide information about an entity's cash receipts and cash payments during a period. A secondary objective is to provide information on a cash basis about its operating, investing, and financing activities.

The statement of cash flows therefore reports cash receipts, cash payments, and the net change in cash resulting from an enterprise's operating, investing, and financing activities during a period, and does so in a format that reconciles the beginning and ending cash balances.

Usefulness of the Statement of Cash Flows

The information in a statement of cash flows enables investors, creditors, and others to assess the following:

Underlying Concept

The statement of cash flows is another example of relevant information—information that is useful in assessing and predicting future cash flows.

1. **Liquidity and solvency of an entity—its capacity to generate cash and its needs for cash resources.** In regard to the entity's requirements for cash to pay maturing debt, to maintain and increase productive capacity, and to distribute a return to owners, it is important to determine both the timing and degree of certainty of expected cash inflows. [1]

2. **Amounts, timing, and uncertainty of future cash flows.** Historical cash flows are often useful in helping to predict future cash flows. By examining the relationships between items such as sales and net income and the cash flow from operating activities, or cash flow from operating activities and increases or decreases in cash, it is possible to make better predictions of the amounts, timing, and uncertainty of future cash flows than is possible using accrual basis data alone.

3. **Reasons for the difference between net income and cash flow from operating activities.** The net income number is important because it provides information on an enterprise's success or failure from one period to another. But some people are critical of accrual basis income because many estimates are required in its calculation. As a result, the number's reliability is often challenged—which usually does not occur with cash. Readers of the financial statements benefit from knowing the reasons for the difference between net income and cash flow from operating activities. It allows them to make their own assessment of the income number's reliability.

What Is Cash?

As part of a company's cash management system, short-term investments are often held instead of cash because this allows the company to earn a return on cash balances that are greater than its immediate needs. It is also common for an organization to have an agreement with the bank that permits the entity's account to fluctuate between a positive balance and an overdraft. Because a company's cash activity and position are more appropriately described by including these other cash management activities, the AcSB recommends that **cash flows** be defined as inflows and outflows of cash and cash equivalents.

2 Objective

Define cash and cash equivalents.

International Insight

Early in 2007, both the FASB and the IASB tentatively decided to erase the term "cash equivalents" from financial statements. Instead, they suggest that cash equivalents should be classified in the same way as other short-term investments, and the statement of cash flows should report only on the change in "cash."

     Cash is defined as cash on hand and demand deposits. **Cash equivalents** are short-term, highly liquid investments that are readily convertible to known amounts of cash and have an insignificant risk of change in value. [2] Both **non-equity investments** that are acquired with short maturities and **bank overdrafts** that are repayable on demand and fluctuate often between positive and negative balances are included in cash and cash equivalents if they result from and are an integral part of an organization's cash management policies. [3]

---

[1] *CICA Handbook*, Section 1540.01.

[2] *CICA Handbook*, Section 1540.06(a), (b), and (c).

[3] *CICA Handbook*, Section 1540.08–.10. For an investment to qualify as a cash equivalent, a maturity date "of, say three months or less from the date of acquisition" is required. Examples of cash equivalents are treasury bills, commercial paper, and money-market funds purchased with cash that is in excess of immediate needs.

Throughout this chapter, the use of the term "cash" should be interpreted to mean "cash and cash equivalents."

Classification of Cash Flows

The statement of cash flows classifies cash receipts and cash payments according to whether they result from an operating, investing, or financing activity. The transactions and other events that are characteristic of each kind of activity and the significance of each type of cash flow are as follows:

1. **Operating activities** are the enterprise's principal revenue-producing activities and other activities that are not investing or financing activities.[4] Operating flows generally involve the cash effects of transactions that determine net income, such as collections from customers on the sale of goods and services, and payments to suppliers for goods and services acquired, to the CRA for income taxes, and to employees for salaries and wages.

   The level of cash that is provided by or used in operations is key information for financial statement users. Like blood flowing through the veins and arteries of our bodies, operating cash flows—derived mainly from receipts from customers—are needed to maintain the organization's systems: to meet payrolls, to pay suppliers, to cover rentals and insurance, and to pay taxes. In addition, surplus cash flows from operations are needed to repay loans, to take advantage of new investment opportunities, and to pay dividends without having to seek new external financing.

2. **Investing activities** involve the acquisition and disposal of long-term assets and other investments that are not included in cash equivalents.[5] Investing cash flows are a result of such activities as making and collecting loans and acquiring and disposing of investments and productive long-lived assets.

   The use of cash in investing activities tells the financial statement reader whether the entity is ploughing cash back into additional long-term assets that will generate profits and increase cash flows in the future, or whether the stock of long-term productive assets is being decreased by conversion into cash.

3. **Financing activities** result in changes in the size and composition of the enterprise's equity capital and borrowings.[6] Financing cash flows include obtaining cash through the issuance of debt and repaying amounts borrowed, and obtaining capital from owners and providing them with a return on, and a return of, their investment.

   Details of the cash flows related to financing activities allow readers to assess the potential for future claims to the organization's cash and to identify major changes in the form of financing, especially between debt and equity.

   Illustration 22-1 identifies a business enterprise's typical cash receipts and payments and classifies them according to whether they are a result of operating, investing, or financing activities. Note that the *operating* cash flows are related almost entirely to **working capital accounts (i.e., current asset and current liability accounts)**, the *investing* cash flows generally involve **long-term asset items**, and the *financing* flows are derived mainly from changes in **long-term liability and equity accounts**.

---

[4] *CICA Handbook*, Section 1540.06(d).

[5] *CICA Handbook*, Section 1540.06(e).

[6] *CICA Handbook*, Section 1540.06(f).

Illustration 22-1

Classification of Typical Cash Inflows and Outflows

OPERATING
  Cash inflows
    From cash sales and collections from customers on account
    From returns on loans (interest) and equity securities (dividends)
    From receipts for royalties, rents, and fees
  Cash outflows
    To suppliers on account
    To, and on behalf of, employees for services
    To governments for taxes
    To lenders for interest
    To others for expenses

> Generally related to changes in non-cash current assets and current liabilities

INVESTING
  Cash inflows
    From proceeds on the sale of property, plant, and equipment
    From proceeds on the sale of debt or equity securities of other entities
    From the collection of principal on loans to other entities
  Cash outflows
    For purchases of property, plant, and equipment
    For purchases of debt or equity securities of other entities
    For loans to other entities

> Generally related to changes in long-term assets

FINANCING
  Cash inflows
    From proceeds on the issuance of equity securities
    From proceeds on the issuance of debt (bonds and notes)
  Cash outflows
    For payments of dividends to shareholders
    For redemptions of long-term debt or reacquisitions of share capital
    For reductions of capital lease obligations

> Generally related to changes in long-term liabilities and equity

Some transactions that you might think are investing or financing activities are classified on the statement of cash flows as operating cash flows. For example, dividends and interest received and paid **that are included in determining net income** are classified as **operating** flows. Any dividends or interest paid **that are charged against retained earnings, however,** are reported as **financing** flows.[7]

Although they are reported on the income statement, some items are the result of an investing or financing activity. For example, the sale of property, plant, and equipment is an investing activity even though the gain or loss on sale is reported on the income statement. In this case, the cash proceeds received on the sale are properly classified as an investing cash inflow. The gain or loss on the income statement, therefore, must be **excluded** in determining cash flows from operating activities. Similarly, the repayment (extinguishment) of debt is not an operating activity, and the gain or loss on repayment is not an operating cash flow. The cash paid to redeem the debt, not the amount of the gain or loss, is the actual cash flow and the repayment is clearly a financing activity.

The outflows to purchase investments and loans that are acquired specifically for trading purposes, and the proceeds on their sale, are treated the same as flows that relate to inventories acquired for resale—that is, as operating cash flows. If investments are acquired for other purposes, the cash flows are investing flows.

Income taxes present another complexity. While income tax expense can be identified with specific operating, investing, and financing transactions, the related cash payments for taxes usually cannot. For this reason, income tax payments are classified as

International Insight

IAS 7 permits interest and dividends that are received to be reported as either operating or investing flows, and interest and dividends that are paid to be reported as either operating or financing flows, but requires consistent application from period to period.

Underlying Concept

By rejecting the requirement to allocate taxes to the various activities, the Accounting Standards Board invoked the cost-benefit constraint. While the information is beneficial, the cost of providing it exceeds the benefits.

---

[7] Dividend payments that are recognized in the income statement relate to equity securities that are determined to be liabilities in substance; and interest payments that are charged to retained earnings relate to debt securities that are judged to be equity instruments in substance. The statement of cash flows, therefore, treats returns to in-substance equity holders as financing outflows and to those designated as creditors as operating outflows.

operating cash flows unless they can be specifically identified with financing and investing activities.[8]

How should **significant non-cash transactions** that affect an organization's assets and capital structure be handled? The following are examples of such non-cash transactions:

1. An acquisition of assets by assuming directly related liabilities (including capital lease obligations) or by issuing equity securities

2. Exchanges of non-monetary assets

3. A conversion of debt or preferred shares to common shares

4. An issuance of equity securities to retire debt

Because the statement of cash flows reports only the cash effect of activities, significant investing and financing transactions that do not affect cash are excluded from the statement. They are required to be disclosed elsewhere in the financial statements.[9]

In order to evaluate a company's overall cash flow, one must understand what point the company is at in its product life cycle. Generally, companies move through several stages of development, and each stage has implications for cash flow. As the following graph shows, the pattern of cash flows from operating, financing, and investing activities will vary depending on the stage of the cycle.

What Do the Numbers Mean?

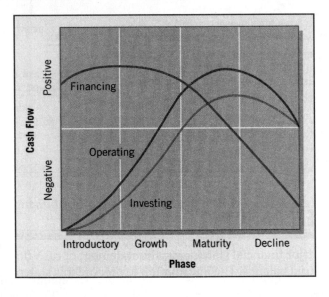

In the introductory phase, the product is likely not generating much revenue so operating cash flow is negative. Because the company is making heavy investments to get a product off the ground, the cash flow associated with investing activities is also negative. Financing cash flows are positive as funds are raised to pay for the investments and cover the operating shortfall.

As the product moves to the growth and maturity phases, these cash flow relationships reverse. The product generates more cash from operations, which can be used to cover investments that are needed to support the product, and less cash is needed from financing. So is a negative operating cash flow bad? Not always. It depends to a great extent on the product life cycle.

Source: Adapted from Paul D. Kimmel, Jerry J. Weygandt, and Donald E. Kieso, *Financial Accounting: Tools for Business Decision Making,* 4th ed. (New York: John Wiley & Sons, 2006), p. 591.

---

[8] *CICA Handbook*, Section 1540.38.

[9] *CICA Handbook*, Section 1540.46 and .47. Note that an asset that is acquired and financed through a third party when the lender pays the seller directly is considered a cash inflow (financing) followed by a cash outflow (investing).

Format of the Statement of Cash Flows

The three activities discussed in the preceding section guide the general format of the statement of cash flows. The operating activities section usually appears first, and is followed by the investing and financing activities sections. The individual inflows and outflows from investing and financing activities are reported separately; that is, they are reported gross, not netted against one another. Thus, a cash outflow from the purchase of property is reported separately from the cash inflow from the sale of property. Similarly, the cash inflow from issuing debt is reported separately from the cash outflow for the retirement of debt. If they are not reported separately, it is harder to see how extensive the enterprise's investing and financing activities are and therefore it is more difficult to assess future cash flows.[10]

The skeleton format of a statement of cash flows is provided in Illustration 22-2. Note that the statement also provides a reconciliation between the beginning-of-the-period cash amount and the end-of-the-period cash amount that are reported in the comparative balance sheets.

COMPANY NAME
Statement of Cash Flows
Period Covered

Cash flows from operating activities		
Net income		XXX
Adjustments to reconcile net income to cash provided by (used in)		
operating activities: (List of individual items)	XX	XX
Net cash provided by (used in) operating activities		**XXX**
Cash flows from investing activities		
(List of individual inflows and outflows)	XX	
Net cash provided by (used in) investing activities		**XXX**
Cash flows from financing activities		
(List of individual inflows and outflows)	XX	
Net cash provided by (used in) financing activities		**XXX**
Net increase (decrease) in cash		**XXX**
Cash at beginning of period		XXX
Cash at end of period		XXX

Illustration 22-2
Format of the Statement of Cash Flows

Illustration 22-2 determines the net cash flow from operating activities indirectly by making the necessary adjustments to the net income reported on the income statement. This is referred to as the **indirect method** (or reconciliation method). The cash flow from operating activities could be calculated directly by identifying the sources of the operating cash receipts and payments. This approach, explained in Illustration 22-3, is referred to as the **direct method**.

4 Objective
Contrast the direct and indirect methods of calculating net cash flow from operating activities.

Cash flows from operating activities	
Cash receipts from customers	XX
Cash receipts from other revenue sources	XX
Cash payments to suppliers for goods and services	(XX)
Cash payments to and on behalf of employees	(XX)
Cash payments of income taxes	(XX)
Net cash provided by (used in) operating activities	**XXX**

Illustration 22-3
Cash Flows from Operating Activities—Direct Method

---

[10] Netting is permitted in limited circumstances. See *CICA Handbook* Section 1540.25–.27.

There has been much discussion by standard setters about which method should be recommended for use. The AcSB encourages use of the direct method because it provides additional information, but its use is not mandatory.[11]

Direct versus Indirect

In general, public companies tend to prefer the indirect method, although commercial lending officers and other investors tend to express a preference for the direct method because of the additional information that it provides.

International Insight

IAS 7 expresses a preference for the direct method, with a separate reconciliation of operating income and cash flows from operations.

In favour of the direct method   The main advantage of the direct method is that it shows operating cash receipts and payments. That is, it is more consistent with the objective of a statement of cash flows—to provide information about cash receipts and cash payments—than the indirect method, which does not report operating cash receipts and payments.

Supporters of the direct method argue that knowing the specific sources of operating cash receipts and the purposes that operating cash payments were made for in past periods is useful in estimating future operating cash flows. Furthermore, information about the amounts of major classes of operating cash receipts and payments is more useful than information only about their arithmetic sum (the net cash flow from operating activities). Such information is more revealing of an enterprise's ability to generate sufficient cash from operating activities to pay its debts, reinvest in its operations, and make distributions to its owners.[12]

Many corporate providers of financial statements say that they do not currently collect information in a manner that allows them to determine amounts, such as cash received from customers or cash paid to suppliers. But supporters of the direct method believe that the incremental cost of assimilating such operating cash receipts and payments data is not significant, especially with sophisticated database accounting systems underlying companies' financial reporting modules.

International Insight

The FASB also encourages use of the direct rather than the indirect method. If the direct method is used, there is a requirement to also provide a reconciliation between net income and cash flow from operating activities.

In favour of the indirect method   The main advantage of the indirect method is that it focuses on the differences between net income and cash flow from operating activities. That is, it provides a useful link between the statement of cash flows and the income statement and balance sheet.

Many providers of financial statements argue that it is less costly to adjust net income to net cash flow from operating activities (indirect) than it is to report gross operating cash receipts and payments (direct). Supporters of the indirect method also state that the direct method, which effectively reports income statement information on a cash rather than an accrual basis, may suggest incorrectly that net cash flow from operating activities is as good as, or better than, net income as a measure of performance.

As the indirect method has been used almost exclusively in the past, both preparers and users are more familiar with it and this helps perpetuate its use. Each method provides different but useful information. The best solution may lie in mandating the direct method, which comes closer to meeting the statement's stated objectives, and requiring supplementary disclosure of the differences between net income and cash flow from operations.

---

[11] Unfortunately, use of the direct method is the exception in Canada. The AcSB stated its preference for the direct method in 1997, two years after *Financial Reporting in Canada—1995* reported that one of 300 surveyed companies in 1994 used the direct method. In 2005, only one company out of 200 surveyed used the direct method. Why no change? It seems in large part to be due to the fact that instructors tend to teach the indirect method because that is what is used, and the indirect method is used because that is what accountants have been taught!

[12] "The Statement of Cash Flows," *Statement of Financial Accounting Standards No. 95* (Stamford, Conn.: FASB, 1987), paras. 107 and 111.

PREPARING A STATEMENT OF CASH FLOWS

Sources of Information and Steps in the Process

The statement of cash flows was previously called the Statement of Changes in Financial Position.[13] By analyzing the changes in all non-cash accounts on the statement of financial position or balance sheet from one period to the next, it is possible to identify and summarize the sources of all cash receipts and all cash disbursements. Illustration 22-4 explains why this is true.

$$A = L + OE$$
$$\Delta A = \Delta(L + OE)$$
$$\Delta A = \Delta L + \Delta OE$$
$$\Delta (Cash + non\text{-}cash\ A) = \Delta L + \Delta OE$$
$$\Delta Cash + \Delta non\text{-}cash\ A = \Delta L + \Delta OE$$
$$\Delta Cash = \Delta L + \Delta OE - \Delta non\text{-}cash\ A$$

Note: Δ is a symbol meaning "change in."

Illustration 22-4

Relationship of Changes in Cash to Other Balance Sheet Accounts

Therefore, unlike the other major financial statements that are prepared directly from the adjusted trial balance, the statement of cash flows is usually based on an analysis of the changes in the accounts on the balance sheet over the accounting period. Information to prepare this statement comes from the following three sources.

Comparing **two successive statements of financial position** provides the amount of the change in each asset, liability, and equity account from the period's beginning to end.

The **current income statement** provides details about the most significant change in the balance sheet retained earnings account. It is also the starting point to determine the amount of cash provided by or used in operations during the period, and provides specific information about some expenses that did not use cash, and revenues that did not generate cash inflows.

Selected transaction data from the general ledger combined with the other two sources provide the remaining details needed to determine how cash was generated or used during the period.

The preparation of the cash flow statement by manually accumulating these three sources of information is still very common today in small and medium-sized enterprises, in spite of the advances made in technology. Alternatively, some companies have unique spreadsheet programs that generate the cash flow statement from a combination of their income statement data, changes in balance sheet accounts, and other cash flow details provided as input. Larger organizations with sophisticated enterprise resource planning systems and multi-dimensional databases have created template-based cash flow reports utilizing their financial statement reporting modules, or have the ability to generate server-based cash flow calculations in real time.

Whether you are preparing a cash flow statement manually, developing a spreadsheet template for use in its preparation, or interpreting a completed statement that has been presented to you, familiarity with the following manual steps involved in the statement's preparation as explained below will enhance your understanding of this important financial statement.

---

[13] Prior to the current standard on cash flows, significant non-cash transactions **were included** in the statement because of their effect on the entity's asset and capital structure. This difference shows the change in focus from a statement of changes in financial position (old terminology) to a statement of cash flows (new terminology), where only cash effects are reported.

Step 1: **Determine the change in cash.** This procedure is straightforward because the difference between the beginning and ending balances of cash and cash equivalents can easily be calculated by examining the comparative balance sheets. **Explaining this change is the objective of the analysis that follows.**

Step 2: **Record information from the income statement on the statement of cash flows.** This is the starting point for calculating cash flows from operating activities. **Whenever subsequent analyses indicate that the actual operating cash flow and the amount reported on the income statement are different, the income statement number is adjusted.**

Most adjustments fall into one of three categories:

Category 1. Amounts that are reported as revenues and expenses on the income statement are not the same as cash received from customers and cash paid to the suppliers of goods and services. Companies receive cash from customers for revenue reported in a previous year, and do not receive cash for all the revenue reported as earned in the current period. Similarly, cash payments are made in the current period to suppliers for goods and services acquired, used, and recognized as expense in a preceding period. In addition, not all amounts that are recognized as expenses in the current year are paid for by year end. Most of the adjustments for these differences are related to receivables, payables, and other working capital accounts.

Category 2. Some expenses, such as amortization, represent deferred costs that were incurred and paid for in a previous period. While there was a cash flow associated with the original acquisition of the asset (an investing flow), there is no cash flow associated with the amortization of these assets over the periods they are used.

Category 3. Amounts that are reported as gains or losses on the income statement are not usually the same as the cash flow from the transaction and, in many cases, the underlying activity is not an operating transaction. For example, gains and losses on the disposal of long-term assets and on the early retirement of long-term debt are reported on the income statement. The first results from an investing transaction and the second from a financing transaction—neither is from an operating activity. Also, the cash flow amounts are the **proceeds on disposal** of the asset and the **payment to retire the debt**, **not the amount of the reported gain or loss**.

Step 3: **Analyze the change in each balance sheet account, identify all cash flows associated with changes in the account balance, and record the effect on the statement of cash flows.** This analysis identifies all investing and financing cash flows, and all adjustments that are needed to convert income reported on the income statement to cash flows from operations. Analyze the accounts on the statement of financial position one at a time until the changes in all accounts have been explained and the related cash flows identified.

Step 4: **Complete the statement of cash flows.** Calculate subtotals for the operating, investing, and financing categories and ensure that the change in cash that is determined by doing the subtotals is equal to the actual change in cash for the period.[14]

On the following pages, we work through these four steps in the process of preparing the statement of cash flows for three different companies of increasing complexity.

---

[14] On occasion, even experienced accountants get to this step and find that the statement does not balance! Don't despair. Determine the amount of your error and review your analysis until you find it.

First Illustration—Tax Consultants Inc.

To illustrate the basic steps in preparing a statement of cash flows, we will use the first year of operations for Tax Consultants Inc. The company started on January 1, 2008, when it issued 60,000 common shares for $60,000 cash. The company rented its office space and furniture and equipment, and performed tax consulting services throughout the first year. The comparative balance sheets at the beginning and end of 2008 and the income statement and additional information for 2008 are presented in Illustration 22-5.

6 Objective
Prepare a statement of cash flows using the direct method.

7 Objective
Prepare a statement of cash flows using the indirect method.

Illustration 22-5

Comparative Balance Sheets and Income Statement—Tax Consultants Inc., 2008

COMPARATIVE BALANCE SHEETS

Assets	Dec. 31, 2008	Jan. 1, 2008	Change Increase/Decrease
Cash	$49,000	$-0-	$49,000 increase
Accounts receivable	36,000	-0-	36,000 increase
	$85,000	$-0-	

Liabilities and Shareholders' Equity

Accounts payable	$ 5,000	$-0-	5,000 increase
Common shares	60,000	-0-	60,000 increase
Retained earnings	20,000	0	20,000 increase
	$85,000	$-0-	

INCOME STATEMENT
For the Year Ended December 31, 2008

Revenues	$125,000
Operating expenses	85,000
Income before income taxes	40,000
Income tax expense	6,000
Net income	$ 34,000

Additional information:
An examination of selected data indicates that a dividend of $14,000 was declared during the year.

Step 1: Determine the change in cash. This first step is a straightforward calculation. Tax Consultants Inc. had no cash on hand at the beginning of 2008, and $49,000 was on hand at the end of 2008; thus, the change in cash for 2008 was an increase of $49,000.

Step 2: Record information from the income statement on the statement of cash flows. Most cash activity in any organization is related to operations, so the second step takes information from the statement of operations (the income statement) and reports it on the statement of cash flows under the heading "Cash flows from operating activities." The specific information that is taken from the income statement and reported on the statement of cash flows in this step **depends on whether the indirect or the direct approach is used**. Regardless of the approach, this information will be converted from the accrual basis to the cash basis through adjustments in Step 3.

Indirect Method The indirect approach begins by transferring the amount of net income reported on the income statement to the operating section of the statement of cash flows, as indicated in Illustration 22-6. Whenever the analysis in Step 3 indicates an operating cash inflow or outflow that differs from the amount of revenue or expense that is captured in the net income figure, an adjustment is made to the net income number to correct it to the operating cash effect.

Illustration 22-6

Indirect Approach

INDIRECT APPROACH

Cash flows from operating activities	
Net income	+34,000
Adjustments:	
Cash flows from investing activities	
Cash flows from financing activities	

Direct Method Under this approach, skeleton headings similar to the ones in Illustration 22-3 are set up under "Cash flows from operating activities." The number and descriptions of these headings vary from company to company. Amounts reported on the income statement are then transferred on a line-by-line basis to the heading that comes closest to representing the type of cash flow, until all components of net income have been transferred.

The three headings in Illustration 22-7 are appropriate for Tax Consultants Inc. Because all income statement amounts are transferred to the Operating Activities section, the numbers that are transferred are equal to the amount of net income, and are the same amount as under the indirect approach.

Illustration 22-7

Direct Approach

DIRECT APPROACH

Cash flows from operating activities	
Cash received from customers	+125,000
Cash paid to suppliers	−85,000
Income taxes paid	−6,000
	+34,000
Cash flows from investing activities	
Cash flows from financing activities	

In Step 3, adjustments are made to the appropriate line item within the Operating Cash Flow section whenever the analysis indicates an operating cash flow that is not equal in amount to the revenue or expense that is reported on the income statement. Revenues of $125,000 will be converted into the amount of cash received from customers; operating expenses of $85,000 will be adjusted to the amount of cash payments made to suppliers; and income tax expense of $6,000 will become income tax payments remitted to the government. Under this approach, the specific revenue and expense lines are adjusted. Under the indirect method discussed above, it is only the bottom-line net income number that is adjusted.

Step 3: Analyze the change in each balance sheet account, identify all cash flows associated with changes in the account balance, and record the effect on the statement of cash flows. By analyzing the change in each balance sheet account, transactions that involve cash can be identified and their effects can be recorded on the statement of cash flows.

Because the change in each account on the statement of financial position has to be explained, begin with the first non-cash asset and work down one after the other through each asset, liability, and equity account. The results of Step 3 are provided in Illustration 22-8, where each item is referenced to the analysis that follows.

Illustration 22-8

Preparation of Statement of Cash Flows—Tax Consultants Inc.

CASH FLOWS FROM OPERATING ACTIVITIES

Indirect Method

Net income			+34,000
Adjustments: Increase in accounts receivable			**−36,000(a)**
Increase in accounts payable			**+ 5,000(b)**
			+ 3,000

Direct Method

Cash received from customers	+125,000	**−36,000(a)**	+89,000
Cash paid to suppliers	− 85,000	**+ 5,000(b)**	−80,000
Income taxes paid	− 6,000		− 6,000
	+ 34,000		+ 3,000

CASH FLOWS FROM INVESTING ACTIVITIES   –0–

CASH FLOWS FROM FINANCING ACTIVITIES

Proceeds from issue of common shares	**+60,000(c)**
Dividends paid	**−14,000(d)**
	+46,000
Increase in cash	+49,000

(a) **Accounts Receivable.** During the year, Tax Consultants' receivables increased by $36,000. Because the Accounts Receivable account is increased by the amount of revenue that is recognized and decreased by the cash received from customers, the cash received from customers must have been $36,000 less than the revenue reported on the 2008 income statement. Therefore, an adjustment is needed to the income statement numbers in the Operating Activities section of the statement of cash flows. Under the indirect method, $36,000 is deducted from the net income number because $36,000 less cash came in than is included in the revenue component of the net income that is reported. Using the direct method, the revenue number is reduced directly.

(b) **Accounts Payable.** Accounts Payable is increased by purchases of goods and services on account and decreased by payments on account. Tax Consultants' purchases must have exceeded cash payments by $5,000 during 2008. An adjustment of $5,000 is required to convert the purchases included in net income to the amount paid to suppliers.

Under the indirect method, $5,000 is added back to net income to reflect the fact that the amounts previously deducted as expense did not use an equivalent amount of cash. Under the direct approach, the $5,000 adjustment is made to the operating expense line where the cost of the goods and services purchased was charged.

(c) **Common Shares.** The increase in this account resulted from the issue of shares that was recorded in this entry:

Cash	60,000	
Common Shares		60,000

The $60,000 inflow of cash is reported on the statement of cash flows as a financing inflow.

(d) **Retained Earnings.** In this account, $34,000 of the increase is explained by net income. This has already been recognized on the statement as the starting point in calculating cash flows from operations. The remaining change in the account is explained by the entry:

Retained Earnings	14,000	
Cash		14,000

The cash outflow of $14,000 to pay dividends is reported as a financing outflow. The entire dividend must have been paid in cash because the company does not report a Dividends Payable account that increased.

The changes in all balance sheet accounts have been explained and their cash effects have been reported appropriately on the statement of cash flows. The statement can now be completed.

Step 4:   ***Complete the statement of cash flows.*** Calculate subtotals for each of the operating, investing, and financing sections of the statement, and then the change in cash for the year. This should agree with the change identified in Step 1. The $49,000 increase in Tax Consultants' cash balance during 2008 has been explained.

The completed statement illustrating both the indirect and the direct method is shown in Illustration 22-9.

Illustration 22-9

Completed Statement of Cash Flows—Tax Consultants Inc.

STATEMENT OF CASH FLOWS
Year Ended December 31, 2008

Indirect Method		Direct Method		
Cash flows from operating activities		**Cash flows from operating activities**		
Net income	$34,000	Cash received from customers		$89,000
Less: Increase in		Less cash payments:		
accounts receivable	(36,000)	To suppliers	$80,000	
Add: Increase in accounts payable	5,000	For income taxes	6,000	86,000
	3,000			3,000
Cash flows from investing activities	–0–	**Cash flows from investing activities**		–0–
Cash flows from financing activities		**Cash flows from financing activities**		
Proceeds on issue of common shares	60,000	Proceeds on issue of common shares		60,000
Payment of dividends	(14,000)	Payment of dividends		(14,000)
	46,000			46,000
Increase in cash during year	49,000	**Increase in cash during year**		49,000
Opening cash balance	–0–	Opening cash balance		–0–
Cash, December 31, 2008	$49,000	Cash, December 31, 2008		$49,000

The $49,000 increase in cash was generated by a combination of net operating inflows of $3,000 and net financing inflows (primarily from the sale of common shares) of $46,000. Note that net cash provided by operating activities is the same whether the direct or indirect method is used. The indirect method explains how the company could report a healthy income of $34,000 yet have an operating cash inflow of only $3,000. The main reason is that $36,000 of the revenue reported has not yet been collected. The direct method provides different insights into operating cash flows. The reason for the $3,000 contribution to cash from operations is because cash collections from customers ($89,000) were only slightly more than the operating cash outflows to suppliers ($80,000) and to the government for taxes ($6,000).

Second Illustration—Eastern Window Products Limited

To illustrate the preparation of a more complex statement of cash flows, we will use the operations of Eastern Window Products Limited (EWPL) for its 2009 year. EWPL has been operating for several years, and the company's comparative balance sheets at December 31, 2009 and 2008, its statement of income and retained earnings for the year ended December 31, 2009, and other information are provided in Illustration 22-10.

Illustration 22-10

Comparative Balance Sheets, and Statement of Income and Retained Earnings—EWPL

BALANCE SHEETS – DECEMBER 31

	2009 $	2008 $	Change Increase/Decrease $
Cash	37,000	59,000	22,000 decrease
Accounts receivable	46,000	56,000	10,000 decrease
Inventory	82,000	73,000	9,000 increase
Prepaid expenses	6,000	7,500	1,500 decrease
Land	70,000	—	70,000 increase
Building	200,000	—	200,000 increase
Accumulated amortization—building	(6,000)	—	6,000 increase
Equipment	68,000	63,000	5,000 increase
Accumulated amortization—equipment	(19,000)	(10,000)	9,000 increase
	484,000	248,500	
Accounts payable	70,000	59,100	10,900 increase
Income taxes payable	4,000	1,000	3,000 increase
Wages payable	2,000	2,700	700 decrease
Mortgage payable	152,400	—	152,400 increase
Bonds payable	50,000	40,000	10,000 increase
Common shares	80,000	72,000	8,000 increase
Retained earnings	125,600	73,700	51,900 increase
	484,000	248,500	

STATEMENT OF INCOME AND RETAINED EARNINGS
Year Ended December 31, 2009

Sales revenue		$592,000
Less: Cost of goods sold		355,000
Gross profit		237,000
Salaries and wages expense	$55,000	
Interest expense	16,200	
Amortization expense	15,000	
Other operating expenses	51,000	137,200
Income before income tax		99,800
Income tax expense		39,900
Net income		59,900
Retained earnings, January 1		73,700
Dividends declared		(8,000)
Retained earnings, December 31		$125,600

Additional information:
The company assumed an existing mortgage of $155,000 on acquiring a building and land during 2009.

Step 1: **Determine the change in cash.** Cash decreased by $22,000 from a balance of $59,000 at the first of the year to $37,000 at the end of the year.

Step 2:   ***Record information from the income statement on the statement of cash flows.*** Under the **indirect approach**, record the $59,900 net income in the Operating Activities section of the statement of cash flows.

Under the **direct approach**, set up skeleton headings for the types of operating cash flows involved. Illustration 22-11 suggests that six headings are likely appropriate for EWPL, including an "Other expenses/losses" section that includes items such as amortization expense that do not fall under the other headings. Because all income statement amounts are transferred to the Operating Activities section, the amount transferred is equal to net income, which is the same amount as under the indirect approach.

As you proceed through Step 3 using the direct approach, sales revenue of $592,000 will be converted into cash received from customers, cost of goods sold of $355,000 and other operating expenses of $51,000 will be adjusted to an amount that represents cash payments to suppliers for goods and services acquired, salaries and wages expense of $55,000 will become cash payments made to and on behalf of employees, interest expense of $16,200 becomes interest payments made, and income tax expense of $39,900 becomes income tax payments remitted to the government.

Step 3:   ***Analyze the change in each balance sheet account, identify any cash flows associated with a change in the account balance, and record the effect on the statement of cash flows.*** The results of this step are provided in Illustration 22-11, where each item is referenced to the analysis that follows.

Illustration 22-11

Statement of Cash Flows Working Paper—EWPL

CASH FLOWS FROM OPERATING ACTIVITIES
Indirect Method

Net income		+ 59,900
Adjustments: Decrease in accounts receivable		+ 10,000(a)
Increase in inventory		− 9,000(b)
Decrease in prepaid expenses		+ 1,500(c)
Amortization expense—building		+ 6,000(e)
Amortization expense—equipment		+ 9,000(g)
Increase in accounts payable		+ 10,900(h)
Increase in income taxes payable		+ 3,000(i)
Decrease in wages payable		− 700(j)
		+ 90,600

Direct Method

Cash received from customers	+592,000	+ 10,000(a)	+602,000
Cash paid to suppliers for goods and services	−355,000	− 9,000(b)	
	− 51,000	+ 1,500(c)	−402,600
		+10,900(h)	
Cash paid to employees	− 55,000	− 700(j)	− 55,700
Cash interest paid	− 16,200		− 16,200
Income taxes paid	− 39,900	+ 3,000(i)	− 36,900
Other expenses/losses—amortization	− 15,000	+ 6,000(e)	—
		+ 9,000(g)	
	+ 59,900		+ 90,600

CASH FLOWS FROM INVESTING ACTIVITIES

Purchase of land and building	−115,000(d)
Purchase of equipment	− 5,000(f)
	−120,000

CASH FLOWS FROM FINANCING ACTIVITIES	
Mortgage payable	− 2,600(k)
Bonds issued	+ 10,000(l)
Shares issued	+ 8,000(m)
Dividends paid	− 8,000(n)
	+ 7,400
CHANGE IN CASH	− 22,000

(a) **Accounts Receivable.** During the year, EWPL's receivables decreased by $10,000. Because the Accounts Receivable account is increased by revenue that is recognized and decreased by cash received from customers, the cash inflow from customers must have been $10,000 more than the revenue reported on the 2009 income statement. Under the indirect method, $10,000 is added to the net income number. Under the direct method, the revenue number is increased directly.

(b) **Inventory.** Inventory increased by $9,000 in 2009. Because the Inventory account is increased by the purchase of goods and is reduced by transferring costs to cost of goods sold, EWPL must have purchased $9,000 more inventory than it sold and, therefore, $9,000 more than the costs included in cost of goods sold on the income statement. The first part of this analysis does not tell us how much cash was paid for the purchases; it only converts cost of goods sold to the cost of purchases in the year. The analysis of accounts payable (see item [h] below) converts the amount purchased to the cash payments to suppliers.

  Cost of goods sold of $355,000 was deducted on the income statement in calculating net income. Under the indirect method, net income must be further reduced by $9,000 to adjust for the additional $9,000 of goods purchased that are still in inventory. Under the direct method, the $9,000 adjustment is made directly to cost of goods sold to adjust it to the cost of goods purchased.

(c) **Prepaid Expenses.** Prepaid Expenses decreased by $1,500 during 2009. Because this account is increased by the acquisition of goods and services in advance of when they are used and decreased by transferring the cost of the goods and services used up to expense—the same as for inventory—EWPL must have recognized $1,500 more expense than the amount purchased. The expenses reported on the income statement, therefore, are reduced by $1,500 to adjust them to the cost of goods and services purchased. Under the indirect method, $1,500 is added back to the income reported. Under the direct method, the appropriate expense is reduced directly for the $1,500. When the Accounts Payable account is analyzed below, the purchases will be adjusted to cash paid to suppliers.

(d) **Land, Building.** The balance sheets indicate an increase in Land of $70,000 and an increase in the Building account of $200,000, suggesting an investing cash outflow of $270,000. The investment in real property, however, is often financed by directly assuming a mortgage note payable that results in a lower net cash outlay. As a review of the records indicates that EWPL assumed a $155,000 mortgage in acquiring the land and building, the actual investing cash outflow is only $115,000 (the $270,000 cost of the land and building less the financing provided by the mortgage of $155,000).

It is often useful to prepare the underlying journal entry:

Land	70,000	
Building	200,000	
Mortgage Payable		155,000
Cash		115,000

This entry explains the change in the Land and the Building accounts on the statement of financial position. It also explains part of the change in the Mortgage Payable account (see item [k] below), and it identifies the actual outflow of cash of $115,000. This is reported as an investing cash flow on the statement.

(e) **Accumulated Amortization—Building.** The $6,000 increase in this account is due entirely to the recognition of amortization expense for the year, which was recorded by this entry:

| Amortization Expense | 6,000 | |
| Accumulated Amortization—Building | | 6,000 |

The entry records a non-cash event. Under the indirect approach, $6,000 is added back to net income because amortization expense did not require the use of cash. Under the direct approach, amortization expense is adjusted directly.

(f) **Equipment.** EWPL purchased $5,000 of equipment during 2009. This resulted in an investing outflow of cash of $5,000.

(g) **Accumulated Amortization—Equipment.** The $9,000 increase in this account is due to amortization expense for the year. As explained in item (e), the statement's operating activities section must be adjusted for this non-cash expense.

(h) **Accounts Payable.** The Accounts Payable account is increased by the cost of purchases and decreased by payments on account. EWPL's cash payments to suppliers, therefore, must have been $10,900 less than the goods and services purchased during 2009. In steps (b) and (c) above, cost of goods sold and other expenses were adjusted to convert them to the cost of goods and services purchased during the year. A further adjustment of $10,900 is required to adjust the purchases to the amount of cash that was actually paid.

Under the indirect method, $10,900 is added back to net income to reflect the fact that the amounts deducted for purchases did not use an equivalent amount of cash. Under the direct approach, the $10,900 adjustment reduces the cost of goods and services purchased to the cash outflow for these purchases.

(i) **Income Taxes Payable.** This liability account is increased by the current income tax expense that is reported and is decreased by payments to the government. Income tax expense, therefore, exceeded payments by $3,000. Under the indirect method, the $3,000 difference is added back to net income. Under the direct method, an adjustment is made to the income tax expense line.

(j) **Wages Payable.** Similar to other current payables, this account is increased by amounts that are recognized as expense and decreased by payments, in this case, to employees. The $700 decrease in this account indicates that cash outflows were $700 more than wages expense. Under the indirect method, an additional $700 is deducted from the reported income. Salaries and wages expense is adjusted under the direct approach.[15]

(k) **Mortgage Payable.** The cash flow associated with part of the change in this account was identified above in item (d). If the account increased by $155,000 when the property was acquired, principal payments of $2,600 must have been made to reduce the balance to $152,400. The entry underlying this transaction is:

Mortgage Payable	2,600	
Cash		2,600

The payment of $2,600 is a financing outflow.

(l) **Bonds Payable.** The increase in this account is explained by the following entry:

Cash	10,000	
Bonds Payable		10,000

The $10,000 in cash received from the bond issue is a financing cash inflow.

(m) **Common Shares.** The $8,000 increase in this account resulted from the issue of shares.

Cash	8,000	
Common Shares		8,000

The $8,000 cash received is a financing inflow.

(n) **Retained Earnings.** Net income is the reason for $59,900 of the increase in retained earnings. This has been recognized on the statement of cash flows already as the starting point in calculating cash flows from operations. The remainder of the change is explained by the entry for dividends:

Retained Earnings	8,000	
Cash		8,000

The payment of dividends that is charged to retained earnings is classified as a financing outflow.

As the changes in all balance sheet accounts have now been explained and all cash flows have been identified, the statement can be completed.

---

[15] For all current asset and current liability account changes that adjust accrual basis net income to cash flows from operations, a simple check can be made. The adjustment for all increases in current asset accounts should have the same effect within the Operating Activities section of the statement of cash flows. All decreases in current asset accounts should have the same effect. All increases and decreases in current liability accounts should have the opposite effect of increases and decreases, respectively, in current asset accounts. This is a useful mechanical procedure to double-check your adjustments.

Step 4: **Complete the statement of cash flows.** Subtotals are calculated for each section of the statement and the change in cash that this reveals is then compared with the change calculated in Step 1. Both indicate a $22,000 decrease in EWPL's cash balance during 2009.

A statement in good form is then prepared from the working paper developed in Illustration 22-11, using more appropriate descriptions and explanations. Illustration 22-12 shows what the final statement might look like if the indirect method is chosen. The additional disclosures that are provided are discussed in a later section of the chapter.

Illustration 22-12

EWPL Statement of Cash Flows, 2009—Indirect Method

EASTERN WINDOW PRODUCTS LIMITED
Statement of Cash Flows
Year Ended December 31, 2009

Cash provided by (used in) operations		
Net income		$ 59,900
Add back non-cash expense—amortization		15,000
Add (deduct) changes in non-cash working capital*		
– accounts receivable	$10,000	
– inventory	(9,000)	
– prepaid expenses	1,500	
– accounts payable	10,900	
– income taxes payable	3,000	
– wages payable	(700)	15,700
		90,600
Cash provided by (used in) investing activities		
Purchase of property, plant, and equipment		(120,000)
Cash provided by (used in) financing activities		
Payment on mortgage payable	(2,600)	
Proceeds on issue of bonds	10,000	
Dividends paid	(8,000)	
Proceeds on issue of common shares	8,000	7,400
Decrease in cash		(22,000)
Cash balance, beginning of year		59,000
Cash balance, end of year		$37,000

Notes:
1. Cash consists of cash on hand and balances with banks.
2. Cash payments during the year for interest and income taxes were $16,200 and $36,900, respectively.
3. During the year, property was acquired at a total cost of $275,000 (land $70,000; building $200,000; equipment $5,000), of which $155,000 was financed directly by the assumption of a mortgage.

*Many companies provide only the subtotal on the statement of cash flows and report the details in a note to the financial statements.

Illustration 22-13 presents the Operating Activities section of the statement of cash flows under the direct method.

Illustration 22-13

Operating Activities Section, Direct Method—EWPL

Cash provided by (used in) operations	
Received from customers	$ 602,000
Payments to suppliers	(402,600)
Payments to and on behalf of employees	(55,700)
Interest payments	(16,200)
Income taxes paid	(36,900)
	90,600

Third Illustration—Yoshi Corporation

The next step is to see how the same principles are applied to more complex situations. Some of these complexities are illustrated through our next example, Yoshi Corporation, as we use the same approach as in the two previous examples. If you prefer a more structured method of accumulating the information for the statement of cash flows than what we will show here, we recommend that you refer to the work sheet approach in Appendix 22A or the T-account method illustrated on the Student Website.

Illustrations 22-14, 22-15, and 22-16 provide the comparative balance sheets of Yoshi Corporation at December 31, 2009 and 2008; the statements of income and retained earnings, comprehensive income, and accumulated other comprehensive income for the year ended December 31, 2009; and selected additional information.

Illustration 22-14

Comparative Balance Sheets—Yoshi Corporation

YOSHI CORPORATION
Comparative Balance Sheets
December 31, 2009 and 2008

	2009 $	2008 $	Change Increase/Decrease $
Assets			
Cash	20,000	32,000	12,000 decrease
Short-term investments	14,000	4,000	10,000 increase
Investments held for trading	25,000	30,000	5,000 decrease
Accounts receivable	106,500	52,700	53,800 increase
Allowance for doubtful accounts	(2,500)	(1,700)	800 increase
Inventories	303,000	311,000	8,000 decrease
Prepaid expenses	16,500	17,000	500 decrease
Investment in shares of Porter Corp.	18,500	15,000	3,500 increase
Investment in shares of Hyco Ltd.	17,500	13,000	4,500 increase
Deferred development costs	190,000	30,000	160,000 increase
Land	131,500	82,000	49,500 increase
Equipment	187,000	142,000	45,000 increase
Accumulated amortization—equipment	(29,000)	(31,000)	2,000 decrease
Buildings	262,000	262,000	—
Accumulated amortization—buildings	(74,100)	(71,000)	3,100 increase
Goodwill	7,600	10,000	2,400 decrease
Total assets	1,193,500	897,000	
Liabilities			
Accounts payable	130,000	131,000	1,000 decrease
Dividends payable, term preferred shares	2,000	—	2,000 increase
Accrued liabilities	43,000	39,000	4,000 increase
Income taxes payable	3,000	16,000	13,000 decrease
Bonds payable	100,000	100,000	—
Discount on bonds payable	(2,200)	(2,500)	300 decrease
Term preferred shares	60,000	—	60,000 increase
Future income tax liability	9,000	6,000	3,000 increase
Total liabilities	344,800	289,500	
Shareholders' Equity			
Common shares	247,000	88,000	159,000 increase
Retained earnings	613,200	518,500	94,700 increase
AOCI	5,500	1,000	4,500 increase
Treasury shares	(17,000)	—	17,000 increase
Total shareholders' equity	848,700	607,500	
Liabilities and shareholders' equity	1,193,500	897,000	

YOSHI CORPORATION
Statement of Income and Retained Earnings
Year Ended December 31, 2009

Net sales		$923,200
Equity in earnings of Porter Corp.		5,500
Investment income, held-for-trading investments		1,300
		930,000
Expenses		
Cost of goods sold	$395,400	
Salaries and wages	200,000	
Selling and administrative	134,600	
Amortization	14,600	
Interest and dividend expense	11,300	
Impairment loss—goodwill	2,400	
Other expenses and losses	12,000	770,300
Income before income tax and extraordinary item		159,700
Income tax: Current	47,000	
Future	3,000	50,000
Income before extraordinary item		109,700
Extraordinary item: Gain on expropriation of land, net of tax of $2,500		8,000
Net income		117,700
Retained earnings, January 1, 2009		518,500
Less: Cash dividends, common shares	6,000	
Stock dividends, common shares	15,000	
Excess of cost of treasury shares over reissue price	2,000	(23,000)
Retained earnings, December 31, 2009		$613,200

Statement of Comprehensive Income
Year Ended December 31, 2009

Net income	$117,700
Add: Other comprehensive income	4,500
Comprehensive income	$122,200

Statement of Accumulated Other Comprehensive Income
Year Ended December 31, 2009

AOCI, January 1, 2009	$ 1,000
Add: Other comprehensive income for the year	4,500
AOCI, December 31, 2009	$ 5,500

Illustration 22-16

Additional Information—
Yoshi Corporation

YOSHI CORPORATION
Additional Information

1. Short-term investments represent money-market instruments with original maturity dates of less than 90 days. They are considered to be cash equivalents.
2. The investments that had been purchased for trading purposes at January 1, 2009, were sold during the year for $32,300. Additional investments, acquired at a cost of $26,000, had a fair value of $25,000 at year end.
3. During 2009, bad debts of $1,450 were written off.
4. Yoshi accounts for its 22% interest in Porter Corp. using the equity method. Porter Corp. paid a dividend in 2009.
5. The investment in shares of Hyco Ltd. was purchased in 2008 for $12,000 and classified for accounting purposes as available for sale.

6. During 2009, Yoshi incurred $200,000 of market development costs that met the criteria for deferral. During the year, $40,000 of deferred costs were amortized.
7. Land in the amount of $54,000 was purchased by issuing term preferred shares. In addition, the municipality expropriated a parcel of land, resulting in a gain of $10,500 before tax.
8. An analysis of the Equipment account and related accumulated amortization indicates the following:

Equipment:

Balance, January 1, 2009	$142,000
Cost of equipment purchased	53,000
Cost of equipment sold (sold at a loss of $1,500)	(8,000)
Balance, December 31, 2009	$187,000

Accumulated amortization:

Balance, January 1, 2009	$ 31,000
Accumulated amortization on equipment sold	(2,500)
Amortization expense, 2009	11,500
Major repair charged to accumulated amortization	(11,000)
Balance, December 31, 2009	$ 29,000

9. An analysis of the common shares account discloses the following:

Balance, January 1, 2009	$ 88,000
Issuance of a 2% stock dividend	15,000
Sale of shares for cash	144,000
Balance, December 31, 2009	$247,000

10. During 2009, Yoshi purchased its own common shares in the market at a cost of $34,000, holding them as treasury shares. Later in the year, half of these shares were reissued for proceeds of $15,000.
11. Changes in other balance sheet accounts resulted from usual transactions and events.

Step 1:   **Determine the change in cash.** Yoshi's cash and cash equivalents include temporary holdings of money-market instruments as well as cash balances, with a decrease in cash of $2,000 that needs to be explained. This is the difference between the opening cash and cash equivalents of $36,000 ($32,000 + $4,000) and the ending cash and cash equivalents of $34,000 ($20,000 + $14,000).

Step 2:   **Record information from the income statement on the statement of cash flows.** Under the **indirect method**, the net income of $117,700 is inserted as the starting point, as shown in Illustration 22-17.

Using the **direct method**, skeleton headings that cover each type of cash flow—from customer receipts to the extraordinary gain—are set up within the Operating Activities section of the statement of cash flows working paper, as shown in Illustration 22-17. The income statement provides clues about the types of operating cash flows and how they should be described. For example, the equity basis income from the investment in Porter Corp. is not a cash flow, but it will be replaced after adjustment with any dividends received from the investment.

Each amount that helps make up the net income of $117,700 is transferred to the most appropriate skeleton heading on the work sheet. Amounts reported as cost of goods sold, selling and administrative expense, and other expenses and losses form the base for what will eventually be "Cash paid to suppliers for goods and services." Income tax expense on both the ordinary income and on the extraordinary gain are included on the line that will be adjusted to "Income taxes paid." The extraordinary item is handled on a before-tax basis because the tax is reported separately.

Illustration 22-17

Statement of Cash Flows Working Paper—Yoshi Corporation

CASH FLOWS FROM OPERATING ACTIVITIES

Indirect Method

Net income	+117,700
Adjustments: Decrease in trading investments	+ 5,000(a)
Increase in accounts receivable, net of write-offs	− 55,250(b)
Bad debt expense	+ 2,250(c)
Decrease in inventories	+ 8,000(d)
Decrease in prepaid expenses	+ 500(e)
Equity method investment income	− 5,500(f)
Dividend from equity method investment	+ 2,000(f)
Amortization of market development costs	+ 40,000(h)
Extraordinary gain on expropriation of land	− 10,500(i)
Loss on disposal of equipment	+ 1,500(j)
Amortization expense—equipment	+ 11,500(j)
Amortization expense—buildings	+ 3,100(k)
Impairment loss—goodwill	+ 2,400(l)
Decrease in accounts payable	− 1,000(m)
Increase in dividends payable on term preferred shares	+ 2,000(n)
Increase in accrued liabilities	+ 4,000(o)
Decrease in income taxes payable	− 13,000(p)
Amortization of bond discount	+ 300(q)
Increase in future income tax liability	+ 3,000(s)
	+118,000

Direct Method

Receipts from customers	+923,200	−55,250(b)	+867,950
Received from investment in Porter Corp.	+ 5,500	− 5,500(f) + 2,000(f)	+ 2,000
Received from trading investments	+ 1,300	+ 5,000(a)	+ 6,300
Payments for goods and services	− 395,400 − 134,600 − 12,000	+ 2,250(c) + 8,000(d) + 500(e) +40,000(h) + 1,500(j) − 1,000(m)	− 490,750
Payments to employees	− 200,000	+ 4,000(o)	− 196,000
Interest and dividend payments	− 11,300	+ 2,000(n) + 300(q)	− 9,000
Income taxes paid	− 50,000 − 2,500	−13,000(p) + 3,000(s)	− 62,500
Other items:			
Amortization expense	− 14,600	+11,500(j) + 3,100(k)	—
Impairment loss	− 2,400	+ 2,400(l)	—
Extraordinary gain, before tax	+ 10,500	−10,500(i)	—
	+117,700		+118,000

CASH FLOWS FROM INVESTING ACTIVITIES

Market development costs incurred	−200,000(h)
Proceeds on expropriation of land (extraordinary item)	+ 15,000(i)
Purchase of equipment	− 53,000(j)
Proceeds on sale of equipment	+ 4,000(j)
Major repair costs incurred	− 11,000(j)
	−245,000

CASH FLOWS FROM FINANCING ACTIVITIES

Proceeds on issue of term preferred shares	+ 6,000(r)
Proceeds on issue of common shares	+144,000(t)
Dividends paid on common shares	− 6,000(u)
Proceeds on reissue of treasury shares	+ 15,000(u)
Payment to acquire treasury shares	− 34,000(v)
	+125,000

CHANGE IN CASH	− 2,000

Step 3: *Analyze the change in each balance sheet account, identify any cash flows associated with a change in the account balance, and record the effect on the statement of cash flows.* The analysis begins with the investments held for trading purposes, because the short-term investments are considered cash equivalents.

(a) **Investments Held for Trading.** During the year, investments were sold for $32,300 cash and additional securities were purchased for cash of $26,000. The net cash flow—an **operating** flow because the securities were acquired for trading purposes—is $32,300 – $26,000, which is a $6,300 net inflow. If we look at the income statement, we see that $1,300 of investment income is already included for these trading securities, so an adjustment is needed in the operating section only for an additional $5,000. Another way to determine the adjustment is to compare the opening and closing balance sheet amounts. The $5,000 decrease tells you that $5,000 more **cash was generated** than the amount reported on the income statement. If the investment balance had increased, this would have indicated that $5,000 of additional cash was **used** to acquire more investments.

What makes up the $1,300 investment income? This can be explained by the $2,300 gain on the securities sold ($32,300 – $30,000) and the $1,000 holding loss on the investments still on hand ($26,000 – $25,000). However, although related, these are not the cash flows.

Under the indirect method, $5,000 is added to the net income number to increase the cash inflow from the trading security transactions from the $1,300 included in net income to the actual $6,300 net cash inflow that was generated. Under the direct approach, the $5,000 adjustment is made to the line item identifying the trading investment activity.

(b) **Accounts Receivable.** Unlike in the illustrations for the two previous companies, Yoshi reports both the receivable and its contra allowance account. The receivable control account is increased by sales on account and reduced by the total of cash received from customers and accounts written off. During 2009, the receivable account increased by $53,800, indicating that the sales reported on the income statement were larger by $53,800 than the total of cash received on account and the accounts written off. Because accounts written off explain $1,450 of the difference, the actual cash inflow from customers must have been $55,250 less than the sales revenue reported (i.e., $53,800 + $1,450). Prepare a T account to verify this reasoning.

	Accounts Receivable		
Jan.1	52,700		
Sales	923,200	1,450	Accounts written off (given)
		?	Cash receipts
Dec. 31	106,500		

The cash received must have been $867,950. This is $55,250 less than the revenue reported on the income statement. Using the indirect approach, $55,250 is deducted from the net income reported. Under the direct method, the revenue of $923,200 is adjusted directly to convert it to cash received from customers.

(c) **Allowance for Doubtful Accounts.** This account had an opening balance of $1,700, was increased by bad debt expense, reduced by accounts written off, and ended the year at $2,500. With accounts written off of $1,450, bad debt expense must have been $2,250 ($1,700 + bad debt expense – $1,450 = $2,500; or prepare a T account to determine this). Because bad debt expense does not use cash, the net income number in the Operating Activities section must be adjusted.

Under the indirect method, $2,250 is added back to net income. Under the direct method, the $2,250 adjustment reduces the expense line that includes bad debt expense. In this example, it is assumed to be in selling expenses.

The only time it is necessary to analyze the Accounts Receivable and the Allowance account separately is when the direct method is used. This is because two adjustments are needed: one to adjust the revenue reported ($55,250) and the other to adjust the non-cash bad debt expense ($2,250). When the indirect method is used, both adjustments correct the net income number. The analysis is easier, therefore, if you focus on the change in the net accounts receivable and make one adjustment to the net income number.[16]

(d) **Inventories.** Because the Inventory account is increased by the cost of goods purchased and decreased by the transfer of costs to cost of goods sold, the $8,000 decrease in the Inventory account indicates that cost of goods sold exceeded purchases by $8,000. Using the indirect approach, $8,000 is added back to the net income number. The direct approach adjusts cost of goods sold directly to convert it to the cost of goods purchased. The analysis of Accounts Payable in step (m) will convert the purchases to cash paid to suppliers.

(e) **Prepaid Expenses.** This account decreased by $500 because the costs that were charged to the income statement were $500 more than the costs of acquiring prepaid goods and services in the year. For reasons similar to the inventory analysis in step (d), $500 is either added back to net income under the indirect approach, or used to adjust the expense line associated with the prepaid expense under the direct approach. It is assumed in this case that the prepaid expenses were charged to selling and administrative expenses when they were used.

(f) **Investment in Shares of Porter Corp.** The journal entries that explain the increase of $3,500 in this account are:

Investment in Porter Corp.	5,500	
Equity in Earnings of Porter Corp.		5,500
(To record investment income in Porter Corp. using the equity method.)		
Cash	2,000	
Investment in Porter Corp.		2,000
(To record the dividend received from Porter Corp.)		

The investment income amount is reported on the income statement and the dividend amount is determined from the change in the account balance. Cash did not change as a result of the investment income; therefore, an adjustment is needed to reduce net income. Under the indirect method, the $5,500 is deducted to offset the $5,500 reported; under the direct approach, the $5,500 adjustment is made to the specific revenue line.

The second entry indicates an operating cash inflow of $2,000. An adjustment is needed to the net income reported because it does not include the dividend. Using the indirect method, $2,000 is added to net income. Under the direct approach, $2,000 is added to the same line as the $5,500 deduction above as this completes the adjustment of equity-basis income to cash received from the investment in Porter.

---

[16] For Yoshi Corporation, net receivables increased $53,000, from $51,000 ($52,700 − $1,700) at the beginning of the year to $104,000 ($106,500 − $2,500) at year end. The increase means that $53,000 of income was recognized that did not result in a corresponding cash flow. On the statement of cash flows under the indirect method, one adjustment to reduce net income by $53,000 is all that is needed.

(g) **Investment in Shares of Hyco Ltd.** The entry that explains the change in this investment classified as available for sale is:

Investment in Shares of Hyco Ltd.	4,500	
Holding Gain on Investment (OCI)		4,500
(To adjust AFS investment to fair value at year end.)		

The entry explains the change in the investment account and the source of the $4,500 of other comprehensive income. No cash flow is involved and no income statement amount is affected. Therefore, no amounts are reported on the statement of cash flows and no adjustment is needed in the operating section.

    If available-for-sale investments had been acquired or sold in the year, there would be investing cash flows to capture on the statement. In the case of a disposal, the realized holding gain or loss transferred from OCI to net income would also need to be eliminated in the operating activities section.

(h) **Deferred Development Costs.** The two transactions that affected this account in the current year are summarized in the following journal entries:

Deferred Development Costs	200,000	
Cash		200,000
(To record capitalized development costs.)		
Market Development Expenses	40,000	
Deferred Development Costs		40,000
(To record the amortization of deferred development costs.)		

    The first entry indicates a cash outflow of $200,000. This is an investing outflow and is recognized in the statement's Investing Activities section.

    The second entry did not affect cash. As explained earlier, it is important to be alert to non-cash amounts that are included in net income. This $40,000 expense did not use any cash; an adjustment to net income is therefore needed under the indirect approach. Under the direct method, the adjustment is made to the specific expense: in this case, to the selling and administrative expense line.

(i) **Land.** This account increased by $49,500 during 2009. Because you know that land was purchased at a cost of $54,000 during the year, there must have been a disposal of land that cost $4,500. The entries that affect this account in 2009 were therefore as follows:

Land	54,000	
Term Preferred Shares		54,000
(To record purchase of land through issue of term preferred shares.)		
Cash	15,000	
Land		4,500
Gain on Disposal of Land		10,500
(To record appropriation by municipality of land costing $4,500.)		

    The first entry indicates that there were no cash flows associated with this transaction. Although this investment and financing transaction is not reported on the statement of cash flows, information about such non-cash transactions is a required disclosure elsewhere in the financial statements.

The second entry identifies a cash inflow of $15,000 on land disposal, an extraordinary item. This is an investing inflow because it affects the company's stock of non-current assets. It is included on the statement of cash flows, separately disclosed as the cash effect of an extraordinary item.

The second transaction also results in a gain of $10,500 on the income statement. By starting with "net income" in the statement's Operating Cash Flow section in Step 2, the $10,500 gain is included in income as if the gain had generated $10,500 of operating cash flows. This is incorrect for two reasons. First, the cash inflow was $15,000, not $10,500. Second, the cash flow was an investing, not an operating, flow. An adjustment is needed, therefore, to deduct $10,500 from the income reported using the indirect method or from the extraordinary item if the direct method is used.

(j) **Equipment and Accumulated Amortization—Equipment.** All the information that is needed to reproduce the entries made to both these accounts in 2009 was provided in Illustrations 22-14, 22-15, and 22-16.

Equipment	53,000	
Cash		53,000
Cash	4,000	
Loss on Disposal of Equipment	1,500	
Accumulated Amortization—Equipment	2,500	
Equipment		8,000
Amortization Expense	11,500	
Accumulated Amortization—Equipment		11,500
Accumulated Amortization—Equipment	11,000	
Cash		11,000

The first entry explains a cash outflow of $53,000 due to the purchase of equipment, an investing activity.

The second entry records the disposal of an asset that cost $8,000 and has accumulated amortization of $2,500; that is, a carrying amount of $5,500. To be sold at a loss of $1,500, the proceeds on disposal must have been $4,000. The analysis of this item is similar to the land disposal in step (i). The cash effect is an inflow of $4,000. This is an investing receipt because it affects the stock of investment in non-current assets. The transaction results in a loss of $1,500 that is reported in 2009 income. Because the cash effect was not a $1,500 payment and because it was not an operating flow, an adjustment is needed in the Operating Cash Flow section. The $1,500 loss is added back to net income under the indirect method, or to the appropriate line (other expenses and losses) under the direct approach.

The third entry reflects the annual amortization expense. Amortization does not use cash, so an adjustment is needed to add this amount back to net income. Under the direct method, the amortization line itself is corrected.

The fourth entry reflects the payment of $11,000 for major repairs.[17] The $11,000 expenditure is an investing outflow.

(k) **Buildings and Accumulated Amortization—Buildings.** There was no change in the asset account during the year and, having no additional information, the increase in the accumulated amortization account must have been due entirely to the amortization recorded for the year. The $3,100 non-cash expense is an adjustment in the Operating Activities section.

---

[17] Because the repairs result in recouping past amortization, the company charged them to accumulated amortization instead of the asset account.

(l) **Goodwill.** The $2,400 decrease in Goodwill is the result of the following entry:

Impairment Loss—Goodwill	2,400	
Goodwill		2,400

There was no effect on cash. Under the indirect method, $2,400 is added back to net income; under the direct approach, the impairment loss line itself is reduced.

(m) **Accounts Payable.** Because the Accounts Payable account is increased by purchases on account for operations and decreased by payments to suppliers, cash outflows to suppliers must have exceeded purchases by $1,000 in 2009. Previous adjustments to the work sheet in (d) and (e) converted expenses reported on the income statement to the cost of goods and services purchased. The analysis of accounts payable completes this by converting the purchases' amount to the cash paid for purchases. The indirect method deducts an additional $1,000 from the net income reported, while the direct method adjusts the expense line.

(n) **Dividends Payable on Term Preferred Shares.** The $2,000 increase indicates that dividends paid were $2,000 less than the dividends declared on these shares. Because the term preferred shares are liabilities in substance, the dividends on these shares are treated the same as interest on debt: they were deducted as dividend expense on the income statement. Under the indirect approach, $2,000 is added back to net income because the cash outflow was less than the dividend expense reported. Under the direct approach, the line item that includes the dividend expense is reduced.

(o) **Accrued Liabilities.** This account is increased by accrued expenses and decreased by payments of the accrued amounts. During 2009, the payments must have been $4,000 less than the expenses reported: $4,000 is therefore added back to net income under the indirect method. Using the direct approach, you must determine which expenses should be adjusted. If it was interest expense that was accrued and paid, the interest expense line is adjusted; if it was wages and salaries payable, the salaries and wages expense is adjusted. In Illustration 22-17, it is assumed that the accruals relate to accrued payroll costs.

(p) **Income Taxes Payable.** This account is increased by current tax expense and decreased by payments to the tax authorities. The $13,000 reduction indicates that the cash outflows were $13,000 more than the expense recognized. Net income is adjusted downward by $13,000 under the indirect approach and the income tax line is adjusted under the direct method.

(q) **Bonds Payable, and Discount on Bonds Payable.** Although there was no change in the Bonds Payable account, the Discount account was reduced through amortization with the following entry:

Interest Expense	300	
Discount on Bonds Payable		300

The entry results in an expense with no corresponding use of cash. An adjustment of $300 is added back to net income under the indirect method, or to the interest expense line under the direct method.[18] The adjustment would be identical if Yoshi carried its bonds directly at the net amount instead of using a discount account.

---

[18] *EIC-47*, "Interest Discount or Premium in the Statement of Changes in Financial Position," (CICA, October 15, 1993) explains how debt issued at a premium or discount is reported on the statement of cash flows at issuance, as it is amortized, and when it is redeemed. The complexity is beyond intermediate coverage. Those interested should refer to the EIC.

(r) **Term Preferred Shares.** Term preferred shares of $60,000 were issued during the year, with $54,000 of this amount issued in exchange for land. This transaction was analyzed in (i) above. Without information to the contrary, the remaining issue of shares must have been for cash and recorded with this entry:

Cash	6,000	
Term Preferred Shares		6,000

This is reported as a financing inflow.

(s) **Future Income Tax Liability.** The increase in this account's credit balance was a result of the following entry:

Future Income Tax Expense	3,000	
Future Income Tax Liability		3,000

This portion of income tax expense did not use cash, so $3,000 is added back to net income under the indirect approach and to the income tax expense line under the direct method.

(t) **Common Shares.** The following entries summarize the changes to this account in 2009:

Retained Earnings	15,000	
Common Shares		15,000
Cash	144,000	
Common Shares		144,000

The first entry records the stock dividend, which neither used nor provided cash. The issue of a stock dividend is not a financing and/or investing transaction, and therefore, is **not** required to be reported. The second entry records a $144,000 inflow of cash as a result of issuing shares, a financing activity. This is reported as a financing inflow on the work sheet.

(u) **Retained Earnings.** The statement of income and retained earnings explains the $94,700 change in this account. The $117,700 increase due to net income and the cash flows associated with it was already included in the Operating Activities section of the statement of cash flows. The $6,000 decrease due to dividends paid on the common shares is a financing outflow. The $15,000 decrease due to the stock dividend was analyzed above as having no effect on cash flow.

The remaining $2,000 decrease due to the excess of cost of treasury shares over the issue price needs to be examined more closely. The entry underlying this transaction is:

Cash	15,000	
Retained Earnings	2,000	
Treasury Shares ($34,000 × 1/2)		17,000

The $15,000 cash inflow on the reissue of treasury shares is reported as a financing activity.

(v) **Treasury Shares.** The $17,000 increase during the year resulted from the company's purchase of its common shares as recorded in the following entry, and the subsequent sale of treasury shares as analyzed in step (u) above:

Treasury Shares	34,000	
Cash		34,000

The purchase is a $34,000 financing outflow of cash. The cash inflow from the reissue of half of these shares was recognized in part (u).

The changes in all balance sheet accounts have now been analyzed and those that affect cash have been recorded on the statement of cash flows working paper. **The following general statements summarize the approach to the analysis:**

1. For most current asset and current liability accounts, focus on what increases and what decreases each account. Compare the effect on the income statement to the amount of the related cash flow, and then adjust the income number(s) in the Operating Activities section of the statement accordingly.

2. For non-current asset and non-current liability accounts in general, reconstruct summary journal entries that explain how and why each account changed. Then analyze each entry as follows:

   (a) The cash effect is the amount of the debit or credit to cash in the entry. Include each investing and financing cash flow or operating flow adjustment on the statement of cash flows.

   (b) Identify all debits or credits to income statement accounts where the operating cash flow is not equal to the amount of revenue, gain, expense, or loss that is reported. Each of these requires an adjustment to the net income number(s) that were originally reported in the Operating Activities section.

While the transactions entered into by Yoshi Corporation represent a good cross-section of common business activities, they do not cover all possible situations. The general principles and approaches used in the above analyses, however, can be applied to most other transactions and events.

Step 4. *Complete the statement of cash flows.* Determine subtotals for each major classification of cash flow and ensure that the statement reconciles to the actual change in cash identified in Step 1.

The working paper prepared in Illustration 22-17 should be presented with more appropriate descriptions and complete disclosure to comply with GAAP and to enable readers to better interpret the information. Illustration 22-18 presents the completed statement of cash flows for Yoshi Corporation, using the direct method to explain the operating flows.

YOSHI CORPORATION
Statement of Cash Flows
Year Ended December 31, 2009

Cash provided by (used in) operations	
Received from customers	$ 867,950
Dividends received on equity method investment	2,000
Received on trading investment transactions	6,300
Payments to suppliers	(490,750)
Payments to and on behalf of employees	(196,000)

Illustration 22-18

Statement of Cash Flows—
Yoshi Corporation
(Direct Method)

Payments for interest, and dividends on term preferred shares		(9,000)
Income taxes paid		(62,500)
		118,000
Cash provided by (used in) investing activities		
Investment in development costs	($200,000)	
Purchase of equipment	(53,000)	
Major repairs incurred	(11,000)	
Proceeds on expropriation of land, an extraordinary item	15,000	
Proceeds on sale of equipment	4,000	(245,000)
Cash provided by (used in) financing activities		
Proceeds on issue of common shares	144,000	
Proceeds on issue of term preferred shares	6,000	
Purchase of treasury shares	(34,000)	
Proceeds on reissue of treasury shares	15,000	
Dividends paid on common shares	(6,000)	125,000
Decrease in cash and cash equivalents (Note 1)		(2,000)
Cash and cash equivalents, January 1		36,000
Cash and cash equivalents, December 31		$ 34,000

Note 1: Cash and cash equivalents are defined as cash on deposit and money-market instruments included as short-term investments.

Note 2: Preferred shares valued at $54,000 were issued during the year as consideration for the purchase of land.

For those who prefer the indirect method of reporting operating cash flows, Illustration 22-19 indicates how the statement's Operating Activities section might look.

Illustration 22-19

Cash Provided by Operations— Yoshi Corporation (Indirect Method)

Cash provided by (used in) operations		
Net income		$117,700
Add back non-cash expenses:		
Amortization expense	$ 14,600	
Impairment loss—goodwill	2,400	
Amortization of bond discount	300	
Amortization of development costs	40,000	57,300
Equity in income of Porter Corp. in excess of dividends received		(3,500)
Deduct non-operating gains (net):		
Extraordinary gain on land	(10,500)	
Loss on disposal of equipment	1,500	(9,000)
Deferral of income tax liability to future periods		3,000
Changes in non-cash working capital accounts (see Note A)		(47,500)
		$118,000
Note A—changes in non-cash working capital:		
Investments held for trading	$ 5,000	
Accounts receivable	(53,000)	
Inventory	8,000	
Prepaid expenses	500	
Accounts payable	(1,000)	
Dividends payable, term preferred shares	2,000	
Accrued liabilities	4,000	
Income taxes payable	(13,000)	
	($47,500)	

PERSPECTIVES

Reporting and Disclosure Issues

In addition to requiring that cash flows be reported according to operating, investing, and financing classifications, *CICA Handbook* Section 1540 requires separate disclosure of the following:

1. Cash flows (before tax) that are associated with extraordinary items; classified as operating, investing, or financing, as appropriate

2. Cash outflows for interest and dividends paid and included as a component of net income (as operating flows), as well as those charged to retained earnings (as financing flows)

3. Cash flows related to income taxes; classified as operating cash flows unless they are specifically identifiable with investing or financing activities

4. Cash flows and other specified information from business combinations and disposals of business units (both as investing flows)

5. The components of cash and cash equivalents, with a reconciliation of the amounts reported on the statement of cash flows with the amounts reported on the balance sheet; the policy for determining cash and cash equivalents; and the amount of cash and cash equivalents with restricted use[19]

The recommendations leave the choice between the direct and indirect method up to the preparer, although the AcSB encourages reporting operating cash flows using the direct approach. The standard requires the reporting of gross cash inflows and outflows from investing and financing activities rather than netted amounts, and separate disclosure in the financial statements about investing and financing transactions that did not generate or use cash resources. Other requirements related to financial institutions, foreign currency cash flows, and business combinations and disposals are left to a course in advanced financial accounting.

> **8 Objective**
> Identify the financial reporting and disclosure requirements for the statement of cash flows.

Cash Flow per Share Information

Because some companies had been reporting **cash flow per share** data in their financial statements, the Accounting Standards Board originally issued an EIC to ensure that readers were adequately informed about this statistic. The Emerging Issues Committee concluded that when companies provide cash flow per share information, it should not be reported as part of the income statement, where it might be given more attention than it deserved and where it might be confused with earnings per share. Later, the EIC was replaced by a recommendation in *CICA Handbook* Section 1540 that specifies that cash flow per share (or per unit) **should not be reported in financial statements,** except for amounts that are payable to owners.

Cash distributions to owners expressed on a per-share or per-unit basis may be disclosed on the face of the statement of cash flows or in a note to the statements. When such a distribution is made on an equity instrument and the amount distributed is determined according to a contract or other agreement, supplementary information needs to be reported about the amount of the total distribution, how the amount is determined, and the extent to which the distribution is non-discretionary.[20]

> **International Insight**
> There is no IAS standard dealing with cash flow per share.

---

[19] *CICA Handbook*, Section 1540.32–.50.

[20] *CICA Handbook*, Section 1540.53–.55.

Distributable Cash

With the growth in income trusts as a form of corporate entity over the past ten years or so, there has been increased concern about what exactly a trust means when it refers to its **distributable cash**, a non-GAAP performance measure that is used extensively by such businesses.[21] The value at which the units trade in capital markets is directly related to the level of expected distributions from each income trust. Therefore, how an entity defines and determines the amount of its distributable cash—even if it is not all paid out—is a major issue. What is its relationship to cash flow from operations? Does it include amounts generated by borrowing or the sale of assets? To what extent should it allow for the maintenance of productive capacity?

Until recently, there was no guidance on how distributable cash should be calculated, and income trusts used a variety of procedures, methods, and principles in calculating this performance measure. The CICA recently issued an Interpretive Release that provides guidance for such flow-through entities on how to determine distributable income and what disclosures are appropriate.[22] The purpose of this document is to increase consistency, comparability, and transparency by setting out guidance for the measurement and disclosure of distributable cash measures in each flow-through entity's management discussion and analysis (MD&A).

A fuller discussion is beyond the scope of this text, but students should be aware that guidance is now available that identifies the components of distributable cash, sets out principles for its measurement, and suggests meaningful disclosures.

Free Cash Flow

Introduced in Chapter 5 and publicized by many companies in recent years, another non-GAAP performance measure is **free cash flow (FCF)**. As the name suggests, this is an indicator of financial flexibility that uses information provided on the statement of cash flows. Free cash flow is net operating cash flows reduced by the capital expenditures that are needed to sustain the current level of operations, and in this respect, is similar to the **distributable cash** measure above. The resulting cash flow is the amount of discretionary cash that a company has available for increasing its capacity and acquiring new investments, paying dividends, retiring debt, purchasing treasury shares, or simply adding to its liquidity.

The calculation of this measure varies by company as some entities deduct all capital expenditures on the basis that it is impossible to separate sustaining expenditures from the total. Others also deduct current dividends. FCF measures are more useful to investors if information is also provided about how they are calculated.

In general, companies with significant free cash flow have a strong degree of financial flexibility. They are able to take advantage of new opportunities or cope well during poor economic times without jeopardizing current operations.

---

[21] Income trusts differ from the usual form of incorporated business in a very important way: income trusts eliminate income taxation at the entity level by distributing (flowing through) their taxable income to unitholders as the income is earned. The distribution is then taxable in the hands of the recipient. Disclosure issues related to distributable cash are even more important with the 2006 announcement by the federal government that this ability to eliminate tax at the entity level will be phased out for many flow-through entities in 2011.

[22] CICA, "Distributable Cash in Income Trusts and Other Flow-Through Entities: Guidance on Preparation and Disclosure in Management's Discussion and Analysis," *Draft Interpretive Release*, November 2006. Because this guidance was not finalized when this text went to printing, the discussion in the chapter is based on the draft release.

Illustrative Examples

Pacific Safety Products Inc.'s Consolidated Statements of Cash Flow for its years ended June 30, 2006 and 2005, are provided in Illustration 22-20. Note that this company uses the direct method to present its operating cash flows. Much of the additional disclosures that are required are presented on the face of the statement itself, although most companies tend to provide it in notes to the financial statements. It is also interesting to note that the company incorporates bank indebtedness as part of its cash and cash equivalents. Review the statement for the differences in cash activity from one year to the next.

Illustration 22-20

Statement of Cash Flows— Pacific Safety Products Inc.

Student Website

Student Toolkit—Additional Disclosures

www.wiley.com/canada/kieso

Consolidated Statements of Cash Flow

For the years ended June 30th	2006	2005
Operating Activities		
Cash receipts from customers	$ 32,804,301	$ 14,573,489
Cash paid to suppliers and employees	(28,979,222)	(17,954,365)
Interest paid	(724,671)	(496,555)
Interest received	41,206	44,822
Cash Flow Provided (Used) by Operating Activities	**3,141,614**	**(3,832,609)**
Investing Activities		
Purchase of property, plant and equipment	(361,569)	(1,102,413)
Investment in new product development	(173,342)	(43,118)
Investment in intangible assets	(80,441)	(356,639)
Cash Flow Used by Investing Activities	**(615,352)**	**(1,502,170)**
Financing Activities		
Proceeds from the issue of long-term debt	—	109,397
Repayment of long-term debt	(1,172,111)	(263,890)
Proceeds from the issue of equity instruments	143,763	8,057,574
Costs related to the issue of equity instruments	(76,590)	(735,674)
Cash Flow from (Used by) Financing Activities	**(1,104,938)**	**7,167,407**
Increase in Cash and Cash Equivalents	**1,421,324**	**1,832,628**
Cash and Cash Equivalents (Bank Indebtedness), Beginning	711,562	(1,121,066)
Cash and Cash Equivalents, Ending	**$2,132,886**	**$711,562**
Represented by:		
Cash and cash equivalents	$ 2,132,886	$ 855,922
Bank indebtedness	—	(144,360)
Cash and cash equivalents	**$ 2,132,886**	**$ 711,562**
Non-Cash Transactions		
Stock-based financing costs	$ —	$ (303,758)
Stock-based compensation	(175,710)	(224,343)
Increase in contributed surplus	175,710	528,101
Expenses related to abandoned projects	—	676,768
Reduction of other assets due to write-down of abandoned projects	—	(676,768)
	$ —	$ —

The accompanying notes are an integral part of these financial statements.

In contrast, the Operating Activities section of **Canadian Pacific Railway Limited**'s Statement of Consolidated Cash Flows for its years ended December 31, 2006, 2005, and 2004, is provided in Illustration 22-21, along with Note 12 to CPR's financial statements. Canadian Pacific uses the indirect method to determine its operating cash flows. Compare the information provided with that of Pacific Safety Products above. It is surprising that the cash flow from operations determined under two such different approaches actually has the same meaning!

Illustration 22-21

Cash Flow from Operations—
Canadian Pacific Railway
Limited

Statement of Consolidated Cash Flows (in part)

Year ended December 31 (in millions)	2006	2005 Restated (see Note 2)	2004 Restated (see Note 2)
Operating activities			
Net income	$ 796.3	$ 543.0	$411.1
Add (deduct) items not affecting cash:			
Depreciation and amortization	464.1	445.1	407.1
Future income taxes (Note 9)	75.3	258.0	131.5
Environmental remediation charge (Notes 4 and 20)	—	(30.9)	90.9
Restructuring and impairment charge (Notes 5 and 20)	—	44.2	(19.0)
Foreign exchange gain on long-term debt	0.1	(44.7)	(94.4)
Amortization of deferred charges	16.5	19.5	24.7
Restructuring and environmental payments (Note 20)	(96.3)	(69.0)	(88.8)
Other operating activities, net	(103.4)	(91.2)	(113.8)
Change in non-cash working capital balances related to operations (Note 12)	(101.6)	(23.3)	33.2
Cash provided by operating activities	$1,051.0	$1,050.7	$782.5

Note 12. Change in Non-Cash Working Capital Balances Related to Operations

(in millions)	2006	2005	2004
(Use) source of cash:			
Accounts receivable and other current assets	$ (101.0)	$ (61.8)	$ (39.0)
Materials and supplies	(15.8)	(14.6)	(35.5)
Accounts payable and accrued liabilities	(0.4)	39.1	112.3
Income and other taxes payable	15.6	14.0	(4.6)
Change in non-cash working capital	**$ (101.6)**	**$ (23.3)**	**$ 33.2**

Interpreting the Statement of Cash Flows

Objective 9
Read and interpret a statement of cash flows.

International Insight

Consolidated statements of cash flows may be of limited use to analysts evaluating multinational companies. With so much data brought together, users of the statements are not able to determine "where in the world" the funds are sourced and used.

Companies have some flexibility in how information is reported in the statement of cash flows. The way in which information is summarized and described can enhance the information content and help users interpret and understand the significance of the cash flow data.

A good approach to begin an analysis of the statement is to focus first on the three subtotals and determine what they tell you about which activities (operating, investing, and financing) generated cash for the company and which used cash. After this general assessment, delve deeper into the details within each section.

As an example, the statement of cash flows of Pacific Safety Products (PSP) in Illustration 22-20 indicates that, **in 2006**, excess operating cash flows of over $3.1 million allowed PSP to internally finance all of its investment activities during the year of $0.6 million, meet all of the company's financing commitments of $1.1 million, and increase its cash balances by $1.4 million. This is a very different story from the one told in the prior year. **In 2005**, operations ate up $3.8 million cash, and investing activities required an additional $1.5 million. On top of that, there was a cash deficiency of over $1.1 million at the beginning of the 2005 fiscal year. Where did PSP get the $5.3 million cash to spend in operations and on new investments? The statement of cash flows indicates very clearly where the cash came from: $7.2 million—enough to replenish its cash reserves—was generated through financing activities.

Compare the pattern of cash flows in these two years to the graph on page 1388. PSP's year 2005 appears to be a classic example of a company in a growth stage, and this is exactly what happened to PSP that year. On the other hand, 2006 is illustrative of the effects on cash in periods following substantial growth.

Operating Activities

Further analysis indicates that PSP was preparing for and working on meeting the delivery requirements of significant contracts during 2005; and, although 2006 sales were down, the cash collections from 2005's sales provided the cash to meet 2006's commitments. Whether the 2006 operating cash flows can be repeated in future years—which is of great interest to investors—depends on PSP's order book for new and recurring contracts. Obviously, the statement of cash flows must be read and interpreted in conjunction with the other financial statements and the MD&A.

Whether a company uses the direct or indirect method, the net **operating cash flows tell you the same thing—the extent to which cash receipts from customers and other operating sources were able to cover cash payments to suppliers of goods and services, to employees, and for other operating expenditures**. This is how the $1,051.0 million cash provided by operating activities at Canadian Pacific Railway Limited (CPR) in 2006 is interpreted. CPR's situation is very different from that of Pacific Safety Products. CPR is a mature company in a mature industry. It has recurring positive operating cash flows, and, although the remainder of the statement of cash flows has not been provided to you, it shows that these cash flows are used for continued investment, repayment of long-term debt, and returns to shareholders.

While the direct method provides more detail about the specific sources and uses of cash and is particularly useful in comparisons with previous years, the indirect method explains the relationship between the accrual-based net income and the cash from operations. CPR's largest adjustment between these two numbers, as is the case with many companies, is the add-back of depreciation and amortization expense. Future income taxes and a variety of other expenses are adjusted because their cash effects are felt in different periods than their income statement effects. A positive adjustment in the current year often means that the related cash outflow will fall in a subsequent year.[23] In CPR's case, it would also be useful to have more information about the "Other operating activities, net" adjustment, as it is significant in each year provided.

An adjustment for the "changes in non-cash working capital balances" is found in the operating activities section of almost every statement of cash flows prepared under the indirect method. The details should be reviewed. Consider the case of **Axcan Pharma Inc.**, which reported cash flow from operating activities of more than U.S. $56.5 million in a recent year, up substantially from U.S. $35.3 million in the previous year. Almost U.S. $12.8 million of the increase, however, came from changes in working capital made up of higher than usual collections of accounts receivable and lower than usual payments on its payables. In that case, the operating cash flows in the period under review are not indicative of operating cash flows that are likely to be replicated; that is, repeated in subsequent years.

Users of financial statements need to look beyond the amount of cash generated or used in operations, and analyze the reasons for the operating cash flows. The objective of the analysis is to assess whether the operating cash flows are sustainable and likely to be repeated in the future, or whether they are the result of payment deferrals and one-time events.

---

[23] A good example of this type of adjustment that one should be aware of is the adjustment for unfunded pension and other post-employment benefits expense. The current year adjustment has a positive effect—it increases operating cash flows above the net income reported as no cash was paid out. However, very large amounts of operating cash outflows will be required in the future when these claims are eventually paid.

Investing Activities

Pacific Safety Products Inc. reports $1.5 million of new investment spending in 2005 and another $0.6 million in 2006. Because investments in new assets are the source of future operating cash flows, it is important to understand whether the new investment just maintains the existing capacity, or whether the investment increases the potential for higher levels of operating cash flows in the future. How do the amounts compare with the stock of existing property, plant, and equipment, and with the depreciation charges for the year? Also, what types of assets have been purchased? Are they tangible productive resources or passive investments in other companies? Are they investments in new technologies and development expenditures? Or are existing assets being disposed of, reducing the potential for future operating flows in the future?

PSP appears to be investing in the future by increasing its stock of productive and intangible assets, as well as engaging in future product development.

Financing Activities

Pacific Safety Products Inc. generated almost $7.2 million of cash from external financing sources in 2005 in order to meet the company's needs for operating and investing cash deficiencies and the negative cash balance at the first of that year. A review of the details indicates that it was all equity capital that was raised, as the small amount of additional debt financing in the year ($0.1 million) was less than the repayment of debt (of $0.3 million). Thus, the debt-equity ratio was reduced in 2005. The type of financing is often related to the type of assets acquired. For example, purchases of intangibles and development expenditures are often difficult to use as collateral and, therefore, they may have to be financed internally from operating cash flows or externally through new equity.

In 2006, PSP continued to lower its debt-equity ratio by making payments of $1.2 million to reduce its long-term debt. A small amount of new share capital was also issued in 2006, and the high costs of issuing new equity in both 2006 and 2005 should probably be investigated.

Details of cash flows related to financing activities allow readers to assess the potential for future claims to the organization's cash and, as indicated above, to identify major shifts in the form of financing, especially between debt and equity. Will there be increased demand for future cash for interest claims and debt repayment? Companies in a growth stage will usually report significant amounts of cash generated from financing activities—financing that is needed to handle the significant investment activity. As growth levels off and operations begin to generate positive cash flows, financing flows tend to reverse as debt is repaid and, if appropriate, shares are redeemed. The required disclosure of long-term debt repayments over the next five years is an excellent source of information about upcoming demands on an organization's cash.

What Do the Numbers Mean?

Due to recent concerns about a decline in the quality of earnings, some investors have been focusing more on cash flow. Management has an incentive to make cash flow look good, because the capital markets pay a premium for companies that generate a lot of cash from operations rather than through borrowings. However, as they can with earnings, companies have ways to pump up cash flow from operations.

One way that companies can boost their operating cash flow is by securitizing receivables. Chapter 7 discussed how companies can speed up cash collections by selling their receivables. For example, **Oxford Industries**, an apparel company, recently reported a $74-million increase in cash flow from operations. This seemed impressive until you read the fine print, which indicated that a significant portion of the increase was due to the sale of receivables. While it originally appeared that the company's core operations had improved, Oxford did little more than accelerate collection of its receivables. In fact, operating cash flow would have been negative without the securitization.

Operating cash flows can also be manipulated by having too liberal a policy of capitalizing expenditures as property, plant, and equipment instead of expensing them as incurred. Such a policy leads to these costs not being deducted in determining net income or cash from operations. They get treated as investment cash outflows. Even when amortized, the costs end up having no effect on operating cash flow. **WorldCom** was able to conceal almost U.S. $4 billion of decline in its operations this way; **Adelphia Communications** overstated its 2002 cash flow by U.S. $102 million this way; and closer to home, **Atlas Cold Storage** later reported a similar situation, although on a smaller scale.

The moral: Operating cash flow, like earnings, can be of high or low quality.

Caution should also be exercised in comparing companies' operating cash flows, even if they are in the same industry. Consider the different effect on operating cash flow of one company that rents its premises under operating leases with another that owns its property or has capital lease arrangements. Or compare one company that capitalizes interest and overhead as part of self-constructed assets to another that expenses these costs, or one company that capitalizes internal-use computer software versus another that absorbs the costs as they are incurred. In all cases, one set of policies results in investing outflows of cash, while the other set reports reduced operating cash flows. And, unlike revenue and expense accruals and deferrals that are reported on an income statement, where the effect reverses over time, the effects on the classifications in the statement of cash flows are permanent.[24]

International

Comparison of Canadian and International GAAP

When the most recent Canadian standard on the statement of cash flows was developed in the late 1990s, the Accounting Standards Board based it on the international document on the same topic. As a result, there are few differences between them. Illustration 22-22 sets out the primary source of GAAP for Canada and the corresponding IFRS.

10 Objective
Compare current Canadian and international GAAP for the statement of cash flows.

Canada	International
Section 1540: Cash flow statements	IAS 7: Cash flow statements

Illustration 22-22
Primary Sources of GAAP

The following minor differences exist between these standards.

Classification of dividends and interest. In order to enhance the comparability of companies' financial statements, Section 1540 requires that dividends and interest received and paid that are included in the determination of net income should be reported as operating cash flows, and dividends and interest paid that are charged against retained earnings should be financing outflows. IAS 7, on the other hand, allows a choice: interest and dividends received may be classified as either operating or investing cash flows; and dividends and interest paid may be included as either financing or operating cash flows.

Supplementary disclosures. IAS 7 encourages, but does not require, disclosure of the following supplementary information: the amount of available but unused borrowing

---

[24] Gerald I. White, Ashwinpaul C. Sondhi, and Dov Fried, *The Analysis and Use of Financial Statements*, 3rd ed. (New York: John Wiley & Sons, Inc., 2003), p. 96.

facilities, cash flows from joint ventures, cash flows required to maintain operating capacity, and cash flows of each reportable segment. These are not addressed in Section 1540.

The categories and display of information on each financial statement, including the statement of cash flows, are being examined as part of a joint FASB/IASB project on financial statement presentation referred to previously in Chapters 4 and 5 in Volume 1 of this text. When Volume 2 went to print, the joint project's anticipated completion date was 2009. The AcSB is committed to harmonization with the FASB and IASB, and expects to issue exposure drafts and final standards as soon as possible after the U.S. and international bodies release theirs.

KEY TERMS

cash, 1385
cash equivalents, 1385
cash flow per share, 1415
cash flows, 1385
direct method, 1389
distributable cash, 1416
financing activities, 1386
free cash flow (FCF), 1416
indirect method, 1389
investing activities, 1386
operating activities, 1386
significant non-cash transactions, 1388
statement of cash flows, 1384

Summary of Learning Objectives

1 Describe the purpose and uses of the statement of cash flows.

The primary purpose of the statement of cash flows is to provide information about an entity's cash receipts and cash payments during a period. A secondary objective is to report the entity's operating, investing, and financing activities during the period. The statement's objective is to provide information about historical changes in an enterprise's cash so that investors and creditors can assess the amount, timing, and degree of certainty associated with an entity's future cash flows, as well as the organization's needs for cash and how cash will be used.

2 Define cash and cash equivalents.

The definition of cash is related to an organization's cash management activities. Cash and cash equivalents include cash on hand, demand deposits, and short-term, highly liquid non-equity investments that are convertible to known amounts of cash with insignificant risk of changes in value, and these amounts are reduced by bank overdrafts that fluctuate from positive to negative balances and that are repayable on demand.

3 Identify the major classifications of cash flows and explain the significance of each classification.

Cash flows are classified into those resulting from operating, investing, and financing activities. A company's ability to generate operating cash flows affects its capacity to pay dividends to shareholders, to take advantage of investment opportunities, to provide internal financing for growth, and to meet obligations when they fall due. The amount of cash that is spent in investing activities affects an organization's potential for future cash flows. Cash invested in increased levels of productive assets forms the basis for future operating cash inflows. Financing cash activities affect the firm's capital structure and, therefore, the requirements for future cash outflows.

4 Contrast the direct and indirect methods of calculating net cash flow from operating activities.

Both methods summarize adjustments in a schedule of changes from the accrual to the cash basis income statement. The direct approach of reporting net cash flow from operating activities is presented in a condensed cash basis income statement format. The indirect method begins with the net income reported and adjusts this number whenever the cash received and paid out for activities related to operations differs from the revenues, gains, expenses, and losses included in net income.

5 Differentiate between net income and cash flows from operating activities.

The calculation of net income is a result of the accrual-based accounting model, which recognizes revenues when they are earned and relates expenses to those revenues. Cash flow from operations differs from this in three ways: (1) cash inflows from customers and outflows to suppliers do not necessarily fall in the same accounting period as the associated revenues and expenses; (2) some expenses, such as amortization, do not have corresponding operating cash outflows but result instead from investing outflows of previous periods; and (3) net income includes gains and losses on the disposal and retirement of non-current assets and liabilities that do not represent the cash flows of the underlying transaction and that are investing and financing rather than operating in nature.

6 Prepare a statement of cash flows using the direct method.

Preparing the statement involves determining the change in cash and cash equivalents during the period, inserting line items from the income statement as the starting point within the statement's Operating Activities section, and analyzing the changes in all accounts on the statement of financial position to identify all transactions that have an impact on cash. Transactions with a cash impact are recorded on the statement of cash flows. To ensure that all cash flows have been identified, the results recorded on the statement are compared with the change in cash during the period. The formal statement is then prepared, complete with appropriate descriptions and disclosures.

7 Prepare a statement of cash flows using the indirect method.

The steps in preparing a statement of cash flows using the indirect method are the same as identified in Objective 6, above, with one exception. Rather than starting with line items from the income statement in the Operating Activities section, the net income amount is the beginning point. All of the adjustments identified in Objective 6 are then used to adjust the net income to a cash basis.

8 Identify the financial reporting and disclosure requirements for the statement of cash flows.

Separate disclosure is required of cash flows associated with extraordinary items, interest and dividends received and paid, the components of cash and cash equivalents reconciled to the amounts reported on the balance sheet, and the amount of and explanation for cash and cash equivalents not available for use. All income tax cash flows are reported as operating flows unless they can be linked directly to investing or financing flows. Gross amounts should be reported except in specifically permitted circumstances, and non-cash investing and financing transactions are excluded from the statement of cash flows, but details about these are reported elsewhere on the financial statements.

9 Read and interpret a statement of cash flows.

The first step is to look at the subtotals for the three classifications of activities and the overall change in cash. This provides a high level summary of the period's cash flows. Next, analyze the items within each section for additional insights, keeping alert for accounting policies that affect the type of cash flow reported.

10 Compare current Canadian and international GAAP for the statement of cash flows.

There are very few differences between Canadian and international GAAP for the statement of cash flows. One difference relates to the choice that is permitted under IAS 7 for the reporting of interest and dividend receipts and payments.

Use of a Work Sheet

When many adjustments are necessary, or there are other complicating factors, a work sheet is often used to assemble and classify the data that will appear on the statement of cash flows. The work sheet (a spreadsheet when using computer software) is merely a device that aids in the preparation of the statement; using one is optional. The skeleton format of the work sheet for preparing the statement of cash flows using the indirect method is shown in Illustration 22A-1.

Illustration 22A-1

Format of Work Sheet for Preparing Statement of Cash Flows

STATEMENT OF CASH FLOWS FOR THE YEAR ENDED...

Balance Sheet Accounts	End of Last Year Balances	Reconciling Items		End of Current Year Balances
		Debits	Credits	
Debit balance accounts	XX	XX	XX	XX
	XX	XX	XX	XX
Totals	XX			XX
Credit balance accounts	XX	XX	XX	XX
	XX	XX	XX	XX
Totals	XX			XX
Cash Flows				
Operating activities				
Net income		XX		
Adjustments		XX	XX	
Investing activities				
Receipts (dr.) and payments (cr.)		XX	XX	
Financing activities				
Receipts (dr.) and payments (cr.)		XX	XX	
Totals		XX	XX	
Increase (cr.) or decrease (dr.) in cash		XX or	XX	
Totals		XX	XX	

The following guidelines are important in using a work sheet:

1. In the Balance Sheet Accounts section, accounts with debit balances are listed separately from those with credit balances. This means, for example, that Accumulated

Amortization is listed under credit balances and not as a contra account under the debit balances. The beginning and ending balances of each account are entered. As the analysis proceeds, each line that relates to a balance sheet account should balance. That is, the beginning balance plus or minus the reconciling item(s) must equal the ending balance. When all balance sheet accounts agree in this way, all changes in account balances have been identified and reconciled and the analysis is complete.

2. The bottom portion of the work sheet is an area to record the operating, investing, and financing cash flows. This section provides the detail for the change in the cash balance during the period—information that is used to prepare the formal statement of cash flows. Inflows of cash are entered as debits in the reconciling columns and outflows of cash are entered as credits in the reconciling columns. Thus, in this section, the sale of equipment for cash at book value is entered as a debit under inflows of cash from investing activities. Similarly, the purchase of land for cash is entered as a credit under outflows of cash from investing activities.

3. The reconciling items shown in the work sheet are not entered in any journal or posted to any account. They do not represent either adjustments or corrections of the balance sheet accounts. They are only used to make it easier to prepare the statement of cash flows.

Preparing the Work Sheet

The preparation of a work sheet involves a series of steps:

Student Website

Student Toolkit—
Expanded Discussions

www.wiley.com/canada/kieso

Step 1.   Enter the balance sheet accounts and their beginning and ending balances in the appropriate Balance Sheet Accounts section.

Step 2.   Enter the debits and credits from the summary entries that explain the changes in each balance sheet account (other than cash); identify all entries that affect cash, and enter these amounts in the reconciling columns at the bottom of the work sheet.

Step 3.   After the analysis is complete and the changes in all balance sheet accounts have been explained, enter the increase or decrease in cash on the balance sheet cash line (or lines, if cash equivalents) and at the bottom of the work sheet. The totals of the reconciling columns should balance.

To illustrate the procedure for preparing the work sheet, we will use the same comprehensive illustration for Yoshi Corporation that was used in the chapter. The indirect method serves initially as the basis for calculating net cash provided by operating activities. An illustration of the direct method is also provided. The financial statements and other data related to Yoshi Corporation for its year ended December 31, 2009, are presented in Illustrations 22-14, 22-15, and 22-16. Most of the analysis was discussed earlier in the chapter and additional explanations related to the work sheet are provided throughout the discussion that follows.

Analyzing Transactions

Before the analysis begins, Yoshi's balance sheet accounts are transferred to the work sheet's opening and ending balance columns. The following discussion explains the individual adjustments that appear on the work sheet in Illustration 22A-2. The discussion assumes that you are familiar with the analysis of the Yoshi illustration earlier in the chapter.

Illustration 22A-2

Work Sheet for Preparation of Statement of Cash Flows— Yoshi Corporation

WORK SHEET FOR PREPARATION OF STATEMENT OF CASH FLOWS
Year Ended December 31, 2009

	Balance 12/31/08	Reconciling Items—2009 Debits		Reconciling Items—2009 Credits		Balance 12/31/09
Debits						
Cash	32,000			(25)	12,000	20,000
Short-term investments	4,000	(25)	10,000			14,000
Investments held for trading	30,000			(2)	5,000	25,000
Accounts receivable	52,700	(3)	55,250	(3)	1,450	106,500
Inventories	311,000			(4)	8,000	303,000
Prepaid Expenses	17,000			(5)	500	16,500
Investment in shares of Porter Corp.	15,000	(6)	5,500	(6)	2,000	18,500
Investment in shares of Hyco Ltd.	13,000	(7)	4,500			17,500
Deferred development costs	30,000	(8)	200,000	(8)	40,000	190,000
Land	82,000	(9)	54,000	(9)	4,500	131,500
Equipment	142,000	(10)	53,000	(10)	8,000	187,000
Buildings	262,000					262,000
Goodwill	10,000			(11)	2,400	7,600
Discount on bonds payable	2,500			(12)	300	2,200
Treasury shares	—	(13)	34,000	(13)	17,000	17,000
Total debits	1,003,200					1,318,300
Credits						
Allowance for doubtful accounts	1,700	(3)	1,450	(14)	2,250	2,500
Accumulated amortization— equipment	31,000	(10) (15)	2,500 11,000	(15)	11,500	29,000
Accumulated amortization— buildings	71,000			(16)	3,100	74,100
Accounts payable	131,000	(17)	1,000			130,000
Dividends payable, term preferred shares	—			(18)	2,000	2,000
Accrued liabilities	39,000			(19)	4,000	43,000
Income taxes payable	16,000	(20)	13,000			3,000
Bonds payable	100,000					100,000
Term preferred shares	—			(9) (21)	54,000 6,000	60,000
Future income tax liability	6,000			(22)	3,000	9,000
Common shares	88,000			(23) (23)	15,000 144,000	247,000
Retained earnings	518,500	(13) (23) (24)	2,000 15,000 6,000	(1)	117,700	613,200
Accumulated other comprehensive income	1,000			(7)	4,500	5,500
Total credits	1,003,200					1,318,300
Cash Flows						
Operating activities:						
Net income		(1)	117,700			
Decrease in HFT investments		(2)	5,000			
Increase in accounts receivable				(3)	55,250	
Decrease in inventories		(4)	8,000			
Decrease in prepaid expenses		(5)	500			
Equity in earnings of Porter Corp.				(6)	5,500	
Dividend from Porter Corp.		(6)	2,000			

Amortization, deferred development costs	(8)	40,000			
Gain on expropriation of land			(9)	10,500	
Loss on disposal of equipment	(10)	1,500			
Impairment loss—goodwill	(11)	2,400			
Amortization of bond discount	(12)	300			
Bad debt expense	(14)	2,250			
Amortization expense—equipment	(15)	11,500			
Amortization expense—buildings	(16)	3,100			
Decrease in accounts payable			(17)	1,000	
Dividend, term preferred shares	(18)	2,000			
Increase in accrued liabilities	(19)	4,000			
Decrease in income taxes payable			(20)	13,000	
Future income tax liability	(22)	3,000			
Investing activities:					
Development costs incurred			(8)	200,000	
Proceeds on disposal of land	(9)	15,000			
Purchase of equipment			(10)	53,000	
Proceeds on sale of equipment	(10)	4,000			
Major repair costs incurred			(15)	11,000	
Financing activities:					
Purchase of treasury shares			(13)	34,000	
Proceeds on reissue of treasury shares	(13)	15,000			
Proceeds on issue of term preferred shares	(21)	6,000			
Proceeds on sale of common shares	(23)	144,000			
Dividend on common shares			(24)	6,000	
Decrease in cash	(25)	2,000			
		857,450		857,450	

1. **Net Income.** Because so much of the analysis requires adjustments to convert accrual basis income to the cash basis, the net income number is usually the first reconciling item put in the work sheet. The entry to reflect this and the balance sheet account affected is:

Net Income (operating cash inflow)	117,700	
Retained Earnings		117,700

The credit to Retained Earnings explains part of the change in that account. We know that net income did not generate $117,700 of cash, so this number is considered a temporary one that will be adjusted whenever the subsequent analysis identifies revenues and expenses whose cash impact is different from the revenue and expense amounts that are included in the net income number. It is a starting point only.[25]

---

[25] Some accountants prefer to slot in "income before discontinued operations and extraordinary items" within the Operating Activities section, the income or loss from discontinued operations separately in the Operating section, the gain or loss on disposal of the discontinued operations in the Investing section, and the "extraordinary item" within the Investing or Financing Activity section, as appropriate. In the Yoshi example, the extraordinary item is an investing activity. Regardless, the transaction underlying the extraordinary item must be revisited in the subsequent analysis and be further adjusted. For this reason, and because there are no discontinued operations, the authors begin with net income and adjust for the extraordinary item later in the analysis.

2. **Investments Held for Trading.** Based on the activity and adjustments in this account during 2009, the entry to explain the net change in its balance is as follows:

Cash ($32,300 – $26,000)	6,300	
Investments Held for Trading		5,000
Investment Income, HFT Investments ($2,300 – $1,000)		1,300

Because the cash flows related to securities and loans held for trading purposes are all operating cash flows, the Operating Activities section should report $6,300 of net cash inflows. However, all that is reported so far is the $1,300 of investment income. Therefore, an adjustment of $5,000 is needed to adjust the investment income number to the cash flows from trading investments. This explains the $5,000 decrease in this account's balance during the year.

3. **Accounts Receivable.** The following two entries summarize the net change in this account and identify the other accounts that are affected:

Accounts Receivable	55,250	
Revenue		55,250
Allowance for Doubtful Accounts	1,450	
Accounts Receivable		1,450

Accounts Receivable increased by $53,800 during the year after writing off accounts totalling $1,450. The increase due to reporting revenue in excess of cash receipts therefore must have been $55,250. This requires an adjustment to the net income reported in the work sheet's Operating Activities section. The other entry explains changes in two balance sheet accounts with no cash impact. Enter these on the work sheet.

4. **Inventories.** The entry to explain the net change in the Inventory account is as follows:

Cost of Goods Sold	8,000	
Inventories		8,000

The credit to inventories explains the change in that account. The debit is an expense of $8,000 that was deducted in calculating net income, but which did not use cash. This requires a debit column adjustment to the net income in the Operating Activities section.[26]

5. **Prepaid Expenses.** Assuming the prepaid expenses were selling and administrative expenses, the following entry summarizes the change in this account during the year:

Selling and Administrative Expense	500	
Prepaid Expenses		500

---

[26] This is consistent with the analysis earlier in the chapter. If $8,000 of cost of goods sold came from a reduction in inventory levels, purchases for the year must have been $8,000 less than cost of goods sold. Therefore both analyses equally well convert the cost of goods sold to the level of purchases in the year.

The credit entry explains the change in the Prepaid Expenses account. The debit represents a non-cash expense deducted on the income statement, requiring an adjustment to the net income reported in the Operating Activities section.

6. **Investment in Shares of Porter Corp.** Entries explaining the change in this account are:

Investment in Shares of Porter Corp.	5,500	
Equity in Earnings of Porter Corp.		5,500
Cash	2,000	
Investment in Shares of Porter Corp.		2,000

The first entry explains part of the change in the investment account and identifies a non-cash revenue included in net income. The entry to adjust net income for this is a $5,500 credit. The second entry credit explains the remainder of the change in the balance sheet account. The debit portion of the entry represents an operating inflow of cash that has not been included in net income. The Operating Activities section is adjusted to reflect this $2,000 operating cash inflow.

7. **Investment in Shares of Hyco Ltd.** A single entry explains the change in this investment classified as available for sale:

Investment in Shares of Hyco Ltd.	4,500	
Holding Gain on Investment (OCI/AOCI)		4,500

The entry explains the change in two balance sheet accounts. This is not a cash transaction.

8. **Deferred Development Costs.** Noting that the development costs relate to marketing activities, the entries to summarize the changes in this account are as follows:

Deferred Development Costs	200,000	
Cash		200,000
Selling and Administrative Expense	40,000	
Deferred Development Costs		40,000

The first entry identifies an outflow of cash related to the investment in this non-current asset—an investing flow. The second entry recognizes the amortization of these deferred costs—a non-cash expense—reported in net income. The adjustment adds back (debits) $40,000 to the net income number. Remember to enter the transactions that explain changes in the balance sheet accounts as you proceed.

9. **Land.** The entries affecting the Land account are:

Land	54,000	
Term Preferred Shares		54,000
Cash	15,000	
Land		4,500
Gain on Disposal of Land (extraordinary item)		10,500

The first entry explains changes in both the Land and Term Preferred Shares accounts—a non-cash transaction. The second entry identifies a $15,000 investing inflow of cash, a reduction of $4,500 in the Land account, and a gain reported in net income that does not correspond to the actual cash flow, and which results from an investing transaction. Net income is adjusted.

10. **Equipment.** The entries that affect the Equipment account are as follows:

Equipment	53,000	
Cash		53,000
Cash	4,000	
Loss on Disposal of Equipment	1,500	
Accumulated Amortization—Equipment	2,500	
Equipment		8,000

The first entry identifies a $53,000 investing outflow of cash. The second entry explains the remainder of the change in the asset account and part of the change in the Accumulated Amortization account, and identifies a $4,000 investing inflow of cash and a $1,500 non-cash loss that is reported in net income and needs to be adjusted.

11. **Goodwill.** The decrease in Goodwill is an impairment loss, recreated with this entry:

Impairment Loss—Goodwill	2,400	
Goodwill		2,400

The impairment loss is a non-cash charge to the income statement. It therefore requires an adjustment to the net income included in the Operating Activities section.

12. **Discount on Bonds Payable.** The entry to record discount amortization is:

Interest Expense	300	
Discount on Bonds Payable		300

Again, a non-cash expense was deducted in determining income and must be adjusted.

13. **Treasury Shares.** The change in this account is explained in two entries:

Treasury Shares	34,000	
Cash		34,000
Cash	15,000	
Retained Earnings	2,000	
Treasury Shares ($34,000 × 1/2)		17,000

The first entry identifies a $34,000 financing outflow of cash to acquire the company's own shares. The second entry explains the remainder of the change in the Treasury Shares account and part of the change in Retained Earnings, and identifies a $15,000 inflow of cash from the reissue of the shares—a financing transaction.

14. **Allowance for Doubtful Accounts.** Part of the change in this account was explained previously in item 3 above. The remaining entry to this account recognized bad debt expense:

| Bad Debt Expense | 2,250 | |
| Allowance for Doubtful Accounts | | 2,250 |

This completes the explanation of changes to the allowance account. In addition, it identifies a non-cash expense of $2,250, which requires an adjustment to net income in the Operating Activities section.

15. **Accumulated Amortization—Equipment.** One of the changes in the Accumulated Amortization account was explained previously in item 10. The other entries affecting this account are:

Amortization Expense	11,500	
Accumulated Amortization—Equipment		11,500
Accumulated Amortization—Equipment	11,000	
Cash		11,000

The first entry identifies an $11,500 non-cash expense requiring an adjustment to net income and the cash flows from operations. The second entry explains the remainder of the change in the account—an investing outflow of cash.

16. **Accumulated Amortization—Buildings.** With no change in the Buildings account during the year, the only entry needed to explain the change in the Accumulated Amortization account is:

| Amortization Expense | 3,100 | |
| Accumulated Amortization—Buildings | | 3,100 |

This $3,100 non-cash expense requires an adjustment to the net income number in the Operating Activities section.

17. **Accounts Payable.** The summary entry to explain the net change in this account is:

| Accounts Payable | 1,000 | |
| Cash | | 1,000 |

The reduction in the payables balance resulted from paying out $1,000 more cash than was recorded in purchases. Cost of goods sold and other expenses have already been adjusted to represent the goods and services purchased, so a $1,000 credit adjustment is needed to convert the purchases to the amount paid; that is, to the operating cash outflow.

18. **Dividends Payable on Term Preferred Shares.** The summary entry explaining the net change in this account is as follows:

| Dividend Expense (income statement expense) | 2,000 | |
| Dividends Payable on Term Preferred Shares | | 2,000 |

The increase in the liability account is due to recognizing more dividends as an expense (these shares are a financial liability in substance) than dividends that were paid in the year. Therefore, $2,000 is added back to net income to adjust the operating cash flows to equal cash dividends paid in 2009.

19. **Accrued Liabilities.** The $4,000 increase in this account was caused by recognizing $4,000 more expense than payments on accrued liabilities in the year. The entry is as follows:

Salaries and Wages Expense (assumed)	4,000	
Accrued Liabilities		4,000

To adjust, $4,000 is added back (debited) to the cash provided by net income as reported.

20. **Income Taxes Payable.** The decrease in this account occurred because Yoshi Corporation paid out more cash than the expense reported, reflected by this entry:

Income Taxes Payable	13,000	
Cash		13,000

Because the expense reported has been deducted in determining the income number, an additional $13,000 outflow must be deducted or credited on the work sheet.

21. **Term Preferred Shares.** For the increase in this account, $54,000 has already been explained. The remaining increase is assumed to have resulted from the following entry, a $6,000 financing inflow:

Cash	6,000	
Term Preferred Shares		6,000

22. **Future Income Tax Liability.** The increase in this account is due to the deferral of the tax liability to future periods, reflected in this entry:

Future Income Tax Expense	3,000	
Future Income Tax Liability		3,000

The change in the balance sheet account is explained, and the non-cash portion of income tax expense is adjusted by adding back $3,000 to net income.

23. **Common Shares.** Two entries explain the change in this account over the year:

Retained Earnings	15,000	
Common Shares		15,000
Cash	144,000	
Common Shares		144,000

The first entry records the stock dividend. As discussed earlier, this is a non-cash activity that, although explaining the change in two balance sheet accounts, is not part of the statement of cash flows. The second entry records the inflow of cash for shares sold—a financing activity.

24. **Retained Earnings.** Most of the changes in this account have already been dealt with above. One additional entry is needed to explain the remainder of the change:

Retained Earnings (dividends)	6,000	
Cash		6,000

This entry records a financing outflow of cash for dividends on common shares.

Completing the Work Sheet

All that remains to complete the balance sheet portion of the work sheet is to credit the Cash account by $12,000 and debit the Short-Term Investments by $10,000, netting to a $2,000 credit or decrease in cash. The $2,000 debit to balance this work sheet entry is inserted at the bottom of the work sheet. The debit and credit columns of the reconciling items are then totalled and balanced.

If the direct method of determining cash flows from operating activities is preferred, one change is needed to the above procedures. Instead of debiting the net income of $117,700 and using this as the starting point to represent cash inflows from operations, the individual revenues, expenses, gains, and losses (netting to $117,700) are transferred to the Operating Activities section on a line-by-line basis. When income statement items differ from the actual cash generated or used, adjustments are made to the specific line item that is involved.

The analysis is simplified if items that will be reported together on the final statement are grouped together, and if all income tax amounts are grouped as well. This step and the adjustments that are needed in the Operating Activities section are shown in Illustration 22A-3. The adjustments in the Operating Activities section are exactly the same as the ones that were made using the indirect approach, except that they are made to a specific line item instead of net income.

Illustration 22A-3

Operating Activities Work Sheet—Direct Method

DIRECT METHOD				
		Debits (inflow)		Credits (outflow)
Cash Flows				
Operating activities:				
Receipts from customers	(1)	923,200	(3)	55,250
Received from investment in Porter Corp.	(1)	5,500	(6)	5,500
	(6)	2,000		
Received from trading investments	(1)	1,300		
	(2)	5,000		
Payments for goods and services	(4)	8,000	(1)	395,400
	(5)	500	(1)	134,600
	(8)	4,000	(1)	12,000
	(10)	1,500	(17)	1,000
	(14)	2,250		
Payments to employees	(19)	4,000	(1)	200,000
Interest and dividend payments	(12)	300	(1)	11,300
	(18)	2,000		
Impairment loss—goodwill	(11)	2,400	(1)	2,400
Income taxes paid	(22)	3,000	(1)	50,000
			(1)	2,500
			(20)	13,000
Amortization expense	(15)	11,500	(1)	14,600
	(16)	3,100		
Cash received, extraordinary item	(1)	10,500	(9)	10,500

The bottom part of the work sheet provides the necessary information to prepare the formal statement of cash flows shown in Illustrations 22-18 (direct method) and 22-19 (indirect method).

Summary of Learning Objective for Appendix 22A

11 Use a work sheet to prepare a statement of cash flows.

A work sheet can be used to organize the analysis and cash flow information that is needed to prepare a statement of cash flows. This method accounts for all changes in the balances of non-cash balance sheet accounts from the period's beginning to the end, identifying all operating, investing, and financing cash flows in the process. The statement of cash flows is prepared from the cash flow information accumulated at the bottom of the work sheet.

Brief Exercises

All assignment material with an asterisk (*) relates to the appendix to the chapter.

(LO 2)   BE22-1   Chrystali Corp. reported the following items on its June 30, 2008, trial balance and on its comparative trial balance one year earlier:

	June 30, 2008	June 30, 2007
Cash in bank	$12,100	$ 9,460
Petty cash	100	125
Investment in shares of GTT Ltd. (to be sold within 60 days)	6,500	–0–
Investment in Canada 60-day treasury bills	22,000	29,300
Accounts payable	44,300	69,225
Temporary bank overdraft, chequing account	13,800	–0–

Determine the June 30, 2008 cash and cash equivalents amount for the 2008 statement of cash flows, and calculate the change in cash and cash equivalents since June 30, 2007.

(LO 3, 8)   BE22-2   In 2008, Mufosta Inc. issued 1,000 common shares for land worth $49,000.

(a) Prepare Mufosta's journal entry to record the transaction.

(b) Indicate the effect that the transaction has on cash.

(c) Indicate how the transaction is reported on the statement of cash flows.

(LO 3, 8)   BE22-3   Vignault Textiles Ltd. entered into a capital lease obligation during 2009 to acquire a cutting machine. The amount recorded to the Equipment under Capital Lease account and the corresponding Capital Lease Obligation account was $85,000 at the date of signing the lease. Vignault paid the first annual lease payment of $2,330 at the date of signing, and by the end of 2009 had recorded amortization of $1,100 for the machine. Using the direct format, provide the necessary disclosure for these transactions on the statement of cash flows.

(LO 3)   BE22-4   Gladhanders Corporation had the following activities in 2008:

1. Sold land for $110,000.

2. Purchased trading securities (HFT) for $15,000.

3. Purchased inventory for $845,000.

4. Received $33,000 cash from bank borrowings.

5. Retired $72,000 of bonds payable.

6. Purchased equipment for $495,000.

7. Issued common shares for $320,000.

8. Purchased long-term investments (HTM) for $61,000.

Calculate the amount that Gladhanders should report as net cash provided (used) by investing activities in its statement of cash flows.

BE22-5   Chrono Corporation had the following activities in 2008:   (LO 3)

1. Paid $770,000 of accounts payable.

2. Paid $2,000 of bank loan interest.

3. Issued common shares for $300,000.

4. Paid $270,000 in dividends (charged to retained earnings).

5. Collected $100,000 in notes receivable.

6. Issued $510,000 of bonds payable.

7. Paid $20,000 on bank loan principal.

8. Received $5,000 on trading investment transactions.

9. Purchased $47,000 of company's own shares.

Calculate the amount that Chrono should report as net cash provided (used) by financing activities in its 2008 statement of cash flows.

BE22-6   Ryker Corporation is using the indirect method to prepare its 2008 statement of cash flows. A list of items that   (LO 3) may affect the statement follows:

_____ **(a)** Increase in accounts receivable

_____ **(b)** Decrease in accounts receivable

_____ **(c)** Issue of shares

_____ **(d)** Amortization expense

_____ **(e)** Sale of land at book value

_____ **(f)** Sale of land at a gain

_____ **(g)** Payment of dividends charged to retained earnings

_____ **(h)** Purchase of land and building

_____ **(i)** Purchase of long-term investment (HTM)

_____ **(j)** Increase in accounts payable

_____ **(k)** Decrease in accounts payable

_____ **(l)** Loan from bank by signing note payable

_____ **(m)** Purchase of equipment by issuing a note payable

_____ **(n)** Increase in inventory

_____ **(o)** Issue of bonds

_____ **(p)** Retirement of bonds

_____ **(q)** Sale of equipment at a loss

_____ **(r)** Purchase of company's own shares

_____ **(s)** Acquisition of equipment using a capital lease

_____ **(t)** Conversion of bonds into common shares

_____ **(u)** Impairment loss on goodwill

Match each code in the list that follows to the items above to show how each item will affect Ryker's 2008 statement of cash flows. Unless stated otherwise, assume that the transaction was for cash.

Code Letter	Effect
A	Added to net income in the operating section
D	Deducted from net income in the operating section
R-I	Cash receipt in investing section
P-I	Cash payment in investing section
R-F	Cash receipt in financing section
P-F	Cash payment in financing section
N	Non-cash investing and/or financing activity disclosed in notes to the financial statement

(LO 6)   BE22-7   At January 1, 2008, Cyberslider Inc. had accounts receivable of $72,000. At December 31, 2008, the accounts receivable balance was $59,000. Sales for 2008 were $420,000. Sales returns and allowances for the year were $10,000. Calculate Cyberslider's 2008 cash receipts from customers.

(LO 6)   BE22-8   Ciao Corporation had January 1 and December 31 balances as follows:

	1/1/08	12/31/08
Inventory	$90,000	$113,000
Accounts payable	61,000	69,000

For 2008, the cost of goods sold was $450,000. Calculate Ciao's 2008 "Cash paid to suppliers of merchandise."

(LO 6)   BE22-9   Hanahan Inc. had the following balances and amounts appear on its comparative financial statements at year end:

	Dec. 31 2009	Dec. 31 2008
Income taxes payable	$1,200	$1,400
Future income tax asset—current	300	0
Future income tax liability—non-current	1,950	1,600
Income tax expense	2,500	2,100
Future Income tax benefit	(600)	(200)

Calculate the amount that should appear as "Cash paid for income taxes."

(LO 6)   BE22-10   Azure Corporation had the following 2008 income statement data:

Sales	$200,000
Cost of goods sold	120,000
Gross profit	80,000
Operating expenses (includes amortization of $21,000)	50,000
Net income	$ 30,000

The following accounts increased during 2008 by the amounts shown: Accounts Receivable, $17,000; Inventory, $11,000; Accounts Payable, $13,000; Mortgage Payable $40,000. Prepare the cash flows from operating activities section of Azure's 2008 statement of cash flows using the direct method.

(LO 7)   BE22-11   Using the information from BE22-10 for Azure Corporation, prepare the cash flows from operating activities section of Azure's 2008 statement of cash flows using the indirect method.

(LO 6, 7)   BE22-12   Tool Time Corporation had the following 2008 income statement data:

Revenues	$100,000
Expenses	60,000
	$ 40,000

In 2008, Tool Time had the following activity in selected accounts:

Accounts Receivable				Allowance for Doubtful Accounts			
1/1/08	20,000					1,200	1/1/08
Revenues	100,000	1,000	Write-offs	Write-offs	1,000	1,540	Bad debt expense
		90,000	Collections				
12/31/08	29,000					1,740	12/31/08

Prepare Tool Time's cash flows from operating activities section of the statement of cash flows using (a) the direct method, and (b) the indirect method.

BE22-13 October Corporation reported net income of $56,000 in 2009. Amortization expense was $17,000. The following accounts changed as indicated in 2009:   **(LO 7)**

Accounts Receivable	$11,000 increase
Long-Term Investments, HTM	16,000 increase
Future Income Tax Assets	2,000 decrease
Inventory	7,400 increase
Non-Trade Note Payable	15,000 decrease
Accounts Payable	9,300 increase

Calculate the net cash provided by operating activities.

BE22-14 In 2008, Izzy Corporation reported a net loss of $56,000. Izzy's only net income adjustments were amortization expense of $87,000 and an increase in accounts receivable of $8,100. Calculate Izzy's net cash provided (used) by operating activities.   **(LO 7)**

*BE22-15 Indicate in general journal form how the following items would be entered in a work sheet to prepare the statement of cash flows: **(LO 11)**

(a) Net income is $317,000.

(b) Cash dividends declared (charged to retained earnings) and paid totalled $120,000.

(c) Equipment was purchased for $114,000.

(d) Equipment that originally cost $40,000 and had accumulated amortization of $32,000 was sold for $13,000.

Exercises

E22-1 **(Classification of Major Transactions and Events)** Doge Industries Ltd. had the following transactions during its most recent fiscal year: **(LO 3)**

(a) Acquired raw materials.

(b) Declared a cash dividend on common shares.

(c) Collected cash dividends from HTM investments.

(d) Acquired a 4% interest in a supplier company's shares.

(e) Made the annual contribution to the employees' pension plan.

(f) Leased new equipment under a capital lease.

(g) Leased additional office space under an operating lease.

(h) Paid the semi-annual interest on outstanding debentures and amortized the associated discount.

(i) Paid the supplier for the acquisition in (a) above.

(j) Acquired land by issuing preferred shares.

(k) Paid the car dealership for a new fleet of vehicles for the sales staff.

(l) Collected a dividend on the investment made in (d) above.

(m) Sold the old fleet of sales vehicles at an amount in excess of their book value.

(n) Granted compensatory stock options to top executives.

(o) Distributed additional shares following a declaration of a 5% stock dividend.

Instructions

Identify each transaction listed above as (1) an operating activity, (2) an investing activity, (3) a financing activity, (4) a significant non-cash investing or financing activity, or (5) none of these options.

(LO 3) E22-2 (Classification of Transactions) Hot Chili Corp. had the following activity in its most recent year of operations:

(a) Purchase of equipment

(b) Redemption of bonds

(c) Conversion of bonds into common shares

(d) Sale of building

(e) Amortization of equipment

(f) Exchange of equipment for furniture

(g) Issue of common shares

(h) Amortization of intangible assets

(i) Purchase of company's own shares

(j) Issue of bonds for land

(k) Impairment loss on goodwill

(l) Holding loss on available-for-sale investment

(m) Payment of dividends on common shares

(n) Increase in interest receivable on notes receivable

(o) Pension expense in excess of amount funded

(p) Signing of a capital lease agreement for equipment

(q) Payment of a capital lease obligation

(r) Purchase of a treasury bill as a cash equivalent

(s) Payment on an operating lease agreement

Instructions

Using the indirect method, classify the items as (1) an operating activity, added to net income; (2) an operating activity, deducted from net income; (3) an investing activity; (4) a financing activity; (5) a significant non-cash investing or financing activity; or (6) none of these options.

(LO 3) E22-3 (Statement Presentation of Transactions—Indirect Method) Each of the following items must be considered in preparing a statement of cash flows (indirect method) for Sage Inc. for the year ended December 31, 2008:

1. Plant assets that cost $20,000 six years before and were being amortized on a straight-line basis over 10 years with no estimated residual value were sold for $5,300.

2. During the year, 10,000 common shares were issued for $43 cash per share.

3. Uncollectible accounts receivable in the amount of $27,000 were written off against the allowance for doubtful accounts.

4. The company sustained a net loss for the year of $50,000. Amortization amounted to $22,000. A gain of $9,000 was reported on the sale of land for $39,000 cash.

5. A three-month Canadian treasury bill was purchased for $100,000 on November 13, 2008. The company uses a cash and cash-equivalent basis for its statement of cash flows.

6. Patent amortization for the year was $20,000.

7. The company exchanged common shares for a 70% interest in Tabaco Corp. for $900,000.

Instructions

Identify where each item is reported in the statement of cash flows, if at all.

E22-4 **(Statement Presentation of Transactions—Equity Accounts)** The following selected account balances are **(LO 3)** taken from the financial statements of Mandrich Inc. at year end:

	2009	2008
Preferred shares	$125,000	$125,000
Common shares: 9,000 shares in 2009, 10,000 shares in 2008	122,000	140,000
Contributed surplus—reacquisition of common shares	1,500	0
Cash dividends—preferred	6,250	6,250
Stock dividends—common	14,000	0
Retained earnings (balance after closing entries)	300,000	240,000

At December 31, 2009, the following information is available:

1. Mandrich Inc. repurchased 2,000 common shares during 2009. The repurchased shares had a weighted average cost of $32,000.

2. During 2009, 1,000 common shares were issued as a stock dividend.

Instructions

(a) Calculate net income for the fiscal year ending December 31, 2009.

(b) Provide the necessary disclosure for all of Mandrich Inc.'s transactions on the statement of cash flows. Also state the section of the cash flow statement in which each item is reported.

E22-5 **(Statement Presentation of Transactions—Investment using Equity Method)** The following selected **(LO 3, 4)** account balances were taken from the financial statements of Bloomberg Inc. concerning its long-term investment in shares of Backfire Inc. over which it has had significant influence since 2006:

	Dec. 31 2009	Dec. 31 2008
Investment in Backfire Inc.	$129,600	$101,000
Investment Income on Backfire	5,200	3,800

At December 31, 2009, the following information is available:

1. Bloomberg purchased additional common shares in Backfire Inc. on January 2, 2009, for $25,000. As a result of this purchase, Bloomberg's ownership interest in Backfire increased to 40%.

2. Backfire reported income of $13,000 for the year ended December 31, 2009.

3. Backfire declared and paid total dividends of $4,000 on its common shares for the year ended December 31, 2009.

Instructions

(a) Prepare a reconciliation of the Investment in Backfire Inc. account from December 31, 2008, to December 31, 2009, assuming Bloomberg Inc. uses the equity method for this investment.

(b) Prepare a table that contrasts the direct and indirect methods for presenting all transactions related to the Backfire Inc. investment on Bloomberg's statement of cash flows. Be specific about the classification in the statement for each item that is reported.

E22-6 **(Classification of Transactions, and Calculation of Cash Flows)** The following are selected balance sheet **(LO 3)** accounts of Aliman Corp. at December 31, 2007 and 2008, and the increases or decreases in each account from 2007 to 2008. Also presented is selected income statement and other information for the year ended December 31, 2008.

Balance Sheet (selected accounts)

	2008	2007	Increase (Decrease)
Assets			
Accounts receivable	$ 84,000	$ 74,000	$10,000
Property, plant, and equipment	277,000	247,000	30,000
Accumulated amortization	(178,000)	(167,000)	11,000

Liabilities and shareholders' equity			
Bonds payable	249,000	246,000	3,000
Dividends payable	8,000	5,000	3,000
Common shares	31,000	22,000	9,000
Retained earnings	104,000	91,000	13,000

Income Statement (selected information)
For the Year Ended December 31, 2008

Sales revenue	$255,000
Amortization expense	33,000
Gain on sale of equipment	14,500
Net income	31,000

Additional information:

1. During 2008, equipment costing $45,000 was sold for cash.

2. Accounts receivable relate to sales of merchandise.

3. During 2008, $20,000 of bonds payable were issued in exchange for property, plant, and equipment. There is no discount or premium on any bonds.

Instructions

Determine the category (operating, investing, or financing) and the amount that should be reported in the statement of cash flows for the following items:

(a) Cash received from customers

(b) Payments for purchases of property, plant, and equipment

(c) Proceeds from the sale of equipment

(d) Cash dividends paid

(e) The redemption of bonds payable

(LO 3,7) E22-7 (Partial Statement of Cash Flows—Indirect Method) The following accounts appear in the ledger of Lazic Limited:

Retained Earnings		Dr.	Cr.	Bal.
Jan. 1, 2008	Credit balance			$ 42,000
Aug. 15	Dividends (cash)	$15,000		27,000
Dec. 31	Net income for 2008		$40,000	67,000

Machinery		Dr.	Cr.	Bal.
Jan. 1, 2008	Debit balance			$140,000
Aug. 3	Purchase of machinery	$62,000		202,000
Sept. 10	Cost of machinery constructed	48,000		250,000
Nov. 15	Machinery sold		$56,000	194,000

Accumulated Amortization—Machinery		Dr.	Cr.	Bal.
Jan. 1, 2008	Credit balance			$ 84,000
Apr. 8	Extraordinary repairs	$21,000		63,000
Nov. 15	Accum. amortization on machinery sold	25,200		37,800
Dec. 31	Amortization for 2008		$16,800	54,600

Instructions

Show how the information posted in the accounts is reported on a statement of cash flows by preparing a partial statement of cash flows using the indirect method. The loss on sale of machinery (November 15) was for $5,800.

(LO 3, 7) E22-8 (Analysis of Changes in Capital Asset Accounts and Related Cash Flows) MacAskill Mills Limited engaged in the following in 2008:

1. The Land account increased by $28,000 over the year: Land that originally cost $10,000 was exchanged for another parcel of land valued at $20,000 and a lump sum cash receipt of $10,000. Additional land was acquired later in the year in a cash purchase.

2. The Furniture and Fixtures account had a balance of $67,500 at the beginning of the year and $62,000 at the end. The related accumulated amortization account decreased over the same period from a balance of $24,000 to $15,200. Fully amortized office furniture that cost $10,000 was sold to employees during the year for $1,000. In addition, fixtures that cost $3,000 and had a net book value of $700 were written off; and new fixtures were acquired and paid for.

3. A five-year capital lease for specialized machinery was entered into halfway through the year; under the terms of the lease the company agreed to make five annual payments (in advance) of $25,000, after which the machinery will revert to the lessor. The present value of these lease payments at the 10% rate that is implicit in the lease was $104,247. The first payment was made as agreed.

Instructions

For each listed item:

(a) Prepare the underlying journal entries that were made by MacAskill Mills during 2008 to record all information related to the changes in each capital asset account and associated accounts over the year.

(b) Identify the amount(s) of the cash flows that result from the transactions and events recorded, and determine the classification of each one.

(c) Identify all charges (debits) or credits to the 2008 income statement that did not generate or use identical amounts of operating cash flows and that, therefore, require adjustments to the net income number(s) reported in the operating activities section of the statement of cash flows.

E22-9 (Accounting Cycle, Financial Statements, Cash Account, and Statement of Cash Flows) The following **(LO 6, 7)** are transactions of Isao Aoki, an interior design consultant, for the month of September 2008:

Sept.	1	Isao Aoki begins business as an interior design consultant, investing $30,000 for 5,000 common shares of the company, I.A. Design Limited.
	2	Purchased furniture and display equipment from Green Jacket Co. for $17,280.
	4	Paid rent for office space for the next three months at $680 per month.
	7	Employed a part-time secretary, Michael Bradley, at $300 per week.
	8	Purchased office supplies on account from Mann Corp. for $1,142.
	9	Received cash of $1,690 from clients for services performed.
	10	Paid miscellaneous office expenses, $430.
	14	Invoiced clients for consulting services, $5,120.
	18	Paid Mann Corp. on account, $600.
	19	Paid a dividend of $1.00 per share on the 5,000 outstanding shares.
	20	Received $980 from clients on account.
	21	Paid Michael Bradley two weeks of salary, $600.
	28	Invoiced clients for consulting services, $2,110.
	29	Paid the September telephone bill of $135 and miscellaneous office expenses of $85.

At September 30, the following information is available:

1. The furniture and display equipment has a useful life of five years and an estimated residual value of $1,500. Straight-line amortization is appropriate.

2. One week's salary is owing to Michael Bradley.

3. Office supplies of $825 remain on hand.

4. Two months of rent has been paid in advance.

5. The invoice for electricity for September of $195 has been received, but not paid.

Instructions

(a) Prepare journal entries to record the transaction entries for September. Set up a T account for the Cash account and post all cash transactions to the account. Determine the balance of cash at September 30, 2008.

(b) Prepare any required adjusting entries at September 30, 2008.

(c) Prepare an adjusted trial balance at September 30, 2008.

(d) Prepare a statement of financial position and income statement for the month ended September 30, 2008.

(e) Prepare a statement of cash flows for the month of September 2008. Use the indirect method for the cash flows from operating activities.

(f) Recast the cash flow from operating activities section using the direct method.

(g) Compare the statement of cash flows in (e) and (f) with the Cash account prepared in item (a) above.

(LO 6) **E22-10** **(Preparation of Operating Activities Section—Direct Method)** The income statement of Vincus Distributing follows:

VINCUS DISTRIBUTING
Income Statement
for the Year Ended December 31, 2008

Sales		$6,900,000
Cost of goods sold		
Beginning inventory	$1,900,000	
Purchases	4,400,000	
Goods available for sale	6,300,000	
Ending inventory	1,600,000	
Cost of goods sold		4,700,000
Gross profit		2,200,000
Operating expenses		
Selling expenses	450,000	
Administrative expenses	700,000	1,150,000
Net income		$1,050,000

Additional information:

1. Accounts receivable increased by $350,000 during the year.

2. Prepaid expenses increased by $170,000 during the year.

3. Accounts payable to suppliers of merchandise decreased by $260,000 during the year.

4. Accrued salaries payable increased by $19,000 during the year.

5. Administrative expenses include amortization expense of $60,000.

6. Selling expenses include commissions and salaries of $300,000; administrative expenses include salaries of $525,000.

Instructions

(a) Prepare the operating activities section of the statement of cash flows for the year ended December 31, 2008, for Vincus Distributing using the direct method.

(b) Why are there so few captions in the operating activities section of the statement of cash flows? What is the difference between this business and others that you have been dealing with in the exercises so far?

(LO 7) **E22-11** **(Preparation of Operating Activities Section—Indirect Method)** Data for Vincus Distributing are presented in E22-10.

Instructions

(a) Prepare the operating activities section of the statement of cash flows using the indirect method.

(b) As a creditor, what would you consider to be an alarming trend that is revealed by the statement that you have prepared? Is this trend as easy to notice under the direct method, as in E22-10?

(LO 6) **E22-12** **(Statement of Cash Flows—Direct Method)** El Lobos Corp. uses the direct method to prepare its statement of cash flows. El Lobos' trial balances at December 31, 2008 and 2007, were as follows:

	Dec. 31, 2008	Dec. 31, 2007
Debits		
Cash	$ 35,000	$ 32,000
Accounts Receivable	33,000	30,000
Inventory	31,000	47,000
Property, Plant, and Equipment	100,000	95,000
Unamortized Bond Discount	4,500	5,000
Cost of Goods Sold	253,000	380,000
Selling Expenses	138,000	172,000
General and Administrative Expenses	140,000	151,300
Interest Expense	20,600	2,600
Income Tax Expense	20,200	61,200
	$775,300	$976,100

Credits

Allowance for Doubtful Accounts	$ 1,300	$ 1,100
Accumulated Amortization	16,500	15,000
Accounts Payable	25,000	15,500
Income Taxes Payable	21,000	29,100
Future Income Tax Liability	5,300	4,600
8% Callable Bonds Payable	45,000	20,000
Common Shares	59,100	47,500
Retained Earnings	44,700	64,600
Sales	557,400	778,700
	$775,300	$976,100

Additional information:

1. El Lobos purchased $5,000 of equipment during 2008.

2. El Lobos allocated one-third of its amortization expense to selling expenses and the remainder to general and administrative expenses.

3. Bad debt expense for 2008 was $5,000 and write-offs of uncollectible accounts totalled $4,800.

Instructions

Determine what amounts El Lobos should report in its statement of cash flows for the year ended December 31, 2008, for the following:

(a) Cash collected from customers

(b) Cash paid to suppliers of goods and services (excluding interest and income taxes)

(c) Cash paid for interest

(d) Cash paid for income taxes

E22-13 **(Preparation of Operating Activities Section—Direct Method)** Krauss Corp.'s income statement for the **(LO 6)** year ended December 31, 2008, had the following condensed information:

Revenue from fees		$860,000
Operating expenses (excluding amortization)	$605,000	
Amortization expense	55,000	
Investment loss on held-for-trading securities	6,000	
Loss on sale of equipment	20,000	686,000
Income before income taxes		174,000
Income tax expense		38,000
Net income		$136,000

There were no purchases or sales of held-for-trading securities during 2008.
Krauss' statement of financial position included the following comparative data at December 31:

	2008	2007
Held-for-trading securities	$20,000	$26,000
Accounts receivable	37,000	54,000
Accounts payable	41,000	31,000
Income taxes payable	4,000	8,500

Instructions

Prepare the operating activities section of the statement of cash flows using the direct method.

E22-14 **(Preparation of Operating Activities Section—Indirect Method)** Data for Krauss Corp. are presented in **(LO 7)** E22-13.

Instructions

Prepare the operating activities section of the statement of cash flows using the indirect method.

E22-15 **(Statement of Cash Flows—Indirect and Direct Methods)** Condensed financial data of Quan Limited for **(LO 6, 7)** 2008 and 2007 follow:

QUAN LIMITED
Comparative Statement of Financial Position
December 31

	2008	2007
Cash	$ 1,800	$ 1,150
Receivables	1,750	1,300
Inventory	1,600	1,900
Plant assets	1,900	1,700
Accumulated amortization	(1,200)	(1,170)
Long-term investments (held-to-maturity)	1,300	1,420
	$ 7,150	$ 6,300
Accounts payable	$ 1,200	$ 900
Accrued liabilities	200	250
Bonds payable	1,400	1,550
Share capital	1,900	1,700
Retained earnings	2,450	1,900
	$ 7,150	$ 6,300

QUAN LIMITED
Income Statement
Year Ended December 31, 2008

Sales	$ 6,900
Cost of goods sold	4,700
Gross margin	2,200
Selling and administrative expense	930
Income from operations	1,270
Other revenues and gains	
Gain on sale of investments	80
Income before tax	1,350
Income tax expense	540
Net income	$ 810

Additional information:
During the year, $70 of common shares were issued in exchange for plant assets. No plant assets were sold in 2008.

Instructions

(a) Prepare a statement of cash flows using the indirect method.

(b) Prepare a statement of cash flows using the direct method.

(c) What would you consider to be an alarming trend that is revealed by the statements that you have prepared? Is it as easy to notice this trend using the direct method, as in part (b)?

(LO 6, 7) E22-16   (Statement of Cash Flows—Direct and Indirect Methods) Tuit Inc., a greeting card company, had the following statements prepared as of December 31, 2009:

TUIT INC.
Comparative Statement of Financial Position
December 31

	2009	2008
Cash and cash equivalents	$ 41,000	$ 25,000
Accounts receivable	68,000	51,000
Inventories	40,000	60,000
Prepaid rent	5,000	4,000
Printing equipment	154,000	130,000
Accumulated amortization—equipment	(35,000)	(25,000)

Goodwill	30,000	50,000
Total assets	$303,000	$295,000
Accounts payable	$ 46,000	$ 40,000
Income taxes payable	4,000	6,000
Wages payable	8,000	4,000
Short-term loans payable	8,000	10,000
Long-term loans payable	60,000	69,000
Common shares	130,000	130,000
Retained earnings	47,000	36,000
Total liabilities and shareholders' equity	$303,000	$295,000

TUIT INC.
Income Statement
Year Ending December 31, 2009

Sales		$338,150
Cost of goods sold		165,000
Gross margin		173,150
Operating expenses		120,000
Operating income		53,150
Interest expense	$ 11,400	
Impairment loss—goodwill	20,000	
Gain on sale of equipment	(2,000)	29,400
Income before tax		23,750
Income tax expense		6,750
Net income		$ 17,000

Additional information:

1. Dividends on common shares in the amount of $6,000 were declared and paid during 2009.

2. Amortization expense is included in operating expenses, as are salaries and wages expense of $69,000.

3. Equipment with a cost of $20,000 that was 70% amortized was sold during 2009.

Instructions

(a) Prepare a statement of cash flows using the direct method.

(b) Prepare a statement of cash flows using the indirect method.

E22-17 (Statement of Cash Flows—Direct and Indirect Methods) Ivan Inc., a major retailer of bicycles and acces- **(LO 6,** sories, operates several stores and is a publicly traded company. The company is currently preparing its statement of cash **7, 9)** flows. The comparative statement of financial position and income statement for Ivan as of May 31, 2009, are as follows:

IVAN INC.
Statement of Financial Position
May 31, 2009 and May 31, 2008

	2009	2008
Current assets		
Cash	$ 33,250	$ 20,000
Accounts receivable	80,000	58,000
Merchandise inventory	210,000	250,000
Prepaid expenses	9,000	7,000
Total current assets	332,250	335,000
Plant assets		
Plant assets	600,000	502,000
Less: Accumulated amortization	150,000	125,000
Net plant assets	450,000	377,000
Total assets	$782,250	$712,000

Current liabilities		
Accounts payable	$123,000	$115,000
Salaries payable	47,250	72,000
Interest payable	27,000	25,000
Total current liabilities	197,250	212,000
Long-term debt		
Bonds payable	70,000	100,000
Total liabilities	267,250	312,000
Shareholders' equity		
Common shares	370,000	280,000
Retained earnings	145,000	120,000
Total shareholders' equity	515,000	400,000
Total liabilities and shareholders' equity	$782,250	$712,000

IVAN INC.
Income Statement
for the Year Ended May 31, 2009

Sales	$1,255,250
Cost of merchandise sold	722,000
Gross margin	533,250
Expenses	
Salary expense	252,100
Interest expense	75,000
Other expenses	8,150
Amortization expense	25,000
Total expenses	360,250
Operating income	173,000
Income tax expense	43,000
Net income	$ 130,000

The following is additional information about Ivan's transactions during the year ended May 31, 2009:

1. Plant assets costing $98,000 were purchased by paying $48,000 in cash and issuing 5,000 common shares.

2. The "other expenses" relate to prepaid items.

3. In order to supplement its cash, Ivan issued 4,000 additional common shares.

4. There were no penalties assessed for the retirement of bonds.

5. Cash dividends of $105,000 were declared and paid at the end of the fiscal year.

Instructions

(a) Compare and contrast the direct method and the indirect method for reporting cash flows from operating activities.

(b) Prepare a statement of cash flows for Ivan Inc. for the year ended May 31, 2009, using the direct method. Support the statement with appropriate calculations, and provide all required disclosures.

(c) Using the indirect method, calculate only the net cash flow from operating activities for Ivan Inc. for the year ended May 31, 2009.

(LO 7)   E22-18   (Convert Net Income to Operating Cash Flow—Indirect Method) Leung Limited reported net income of $32,000 for its latest year ended March 31, 2009.

Instructions

For each of the five different situations involving the balance sheet accounts that follow, calculate the cash flow from operations:

	Accounts Receivable March 31		Inventory March 31		Accounts Payable March 31	
	2009	2008	2009	2008	2009	2008
(a)	$20,000	$21,500	$16,500	$17,900	$ 9,000	$ 9,300
(b)	$23,000	$20,000	$17,300	$20,500	$14,600	$10,200
(c)	$20,000	–0–	$12,000	–0–	$ 7,000	–0–
(d)	$19,500	$21,000	$19,500	$15,600	$10,200	$14,100
(e)	$21,500	$24,000	$12,900	$14,000	$13,300	$11,300

E22-19   (Cash Provided by Operating, Investing, and Financing Activities) Data from the statement of financial **(LO 7)** position of Bruin Corporation at the end of 2008 and 2007 follow:

	2008	2007
Cash	$ 80,000	$ 35,000
Accounts receivable (net)	55,000	45,000
Merchandise inventory	65,000	45,000
Prepaid expenses	15,000	25,000
Equipment	90,000	75,000
Accumulated amortization—equipment	(18,000)	(8,000)
Land	170,000	140,000
	$457,000	$357,000
Accounts payable	$ 65,000	$ 52,000
Accrued expenses	15,000	18,000
Notes payable—bank, long-term	–0–	23,000
Bonds payable	80,000	–0–
Common shares	189,000	159,000
Retained earnings	108,000	105,000
	$457,000	$357,000

Land with a fair value of $30,000 was exchanged for common shares; all equipment purchased was for cash. Equipment costing $10,000 was sold for $3,000; the book value of the equipment was $6,000. Cash dividends of $10,000 were declared and paid during the year.

Instructions

Calculate net cash provided (used) by:

(a) Operating activities

(b) Investing activities

(c) Financing activities

E22-20   (Transactions, Statement of Cash Flows—Indirect Method, and Statement of Financial Position) Jobim **(LO 7)** Inc. had the following condensed statement of financial position at the end of operations for 2008:

JOBIM INC.
Statement of Financial Position
December 31, 2008

Cash	$ 8,500	Current liabilities	$ 15,000
Current assets other than cash	29,000	Long-term notes payable	25,500
Investments, held to maturity	20,000	Bonds payable	25,000
Plant assets (net)	67,500	Share capital	75,000
Land	40,000	Retained earnings	24,500
	$165,000		$165,000

During 2009 the following occurred:

1. A tract of land was purchased for $9,000.

2. Bonds payable in the amount of $15,000 were retired at par.

3. An additional $10,000 of common shares were issued.

4. Dividends totalling $9,375 were paid to shareholders.

5. Net income for 2009 was $35,250 after allowing amortization of $13,500.

6. Land was purchased in exchange for $22,500 of bonds.

7. Jobim Inc. sold part of its investment portfolio of held-to-maturity bond investments for $12,875, resulting in a gain of $2,000.

8. Both current assets (other than cash) and current liabilities remained at the same amount.

Instructions

(a) Prepare a statement of cash flows for 2009 using the indirect method.

(b) Prepare the condensed statement of financial position for Jobim Inc. as it would appear at December 31, 2009.

(LO 7, 9) E22-21 (Prepare Statement from Transactions, and Explain Changes in Cash Flow) Ellwood House, Inc. had the following condensed statement of financial position at the end of operations for 2007:

ELLWOOD HOUSE, INC.
Statement of Financial Position
December 31, 2007

Cash	$ 10,000	Current liabilities	$ 14,500
Current assets (non-cash)	34,000	Long-term notes payable	30,000
Investments, held to maturity	40,000	Bonds payable	32,000
Plant assets	57,500	Share capital	80,000
Land	38,500	Retained earnings	23,500
	$180,000		$180,000

During 2008, the following occurred:

1. Ellwood House, Inc. sold part of its held-to-maturity investment portfolio in bonds for $15,500, resulting in a gain of $500.

2. Dividends totalling $19,000 were paid to shareholders.

3. A parcel of land was purchased for $5,500.

4. Common shares with a fair value of $20,000 were issued.

5. Bonds payable of $10,000 were retired at par.

6. Heavy equipment was purchased through the issuance of $32,000 of bonds.

7. Net income for 2008 was $42,000 after allowing for amortization on Ellwood House's plant assets of $13,550.

8. Both current assets (other than cash) and current liabilities remained at the same amount.

Instructions

(a) Prepare a statement of cash flows for 2008 using the indirect method.

(b) Draft a one-page letter to Mr. Gerald Brauer, president of Ellwood House, Inc., in which you briefly explain the changes within each major cash flow category. Refer to the statement of cash flows whenever necessary.

(c) Prepare a statement of financial position at December 31, 2008, for Ellwood House, Inc.

(d) Comment briefly about why the statement of cash flows used to be called a statement of changes in financial position.

(LO 11) *E22-22 (Work Sheet Analysis of Selected Transactions) The following transactions took place during the year 2008:

1. Convertible bonds payable with a book value of $300,000 were exchanged for unissued no par value common shares.

2. The net income for the year was $410,000.

3. Amortization charged on the building was $90,000.

4. An Appropriations for Bond Indebtedness amount of $300,000 was returned to Retained Earnings during the year because the bonds were retired during the year.

5. Old office equipment was traded in on the purchase of new equipment, resulting in the following entry:

Office Equipment	50,000	
Accumulated Amortization—Office Equipment	30,000	
Office Equipment		40,000
Cash		34,000
Gain on Disposal of Plant Assets*		6,000

*The gain on disposal of plant assets was credited to current operations as ordinary income.

6. Dividends in the amount of $123,000 were declared. They are payable in January 2009.

Instructions

For each item, use journal entries to show the adjustments and reconciling items that would be made on a work sheet for a statement of cash flows:

*E22-23 **(Work Sheet Preparation)** The comparative statement of financial position for McKinley Corporation **(LO 11)** follows:

	Dec. 31, 2009	Dec. 31, 2008
Cash	$ 16,500	$ 21,000
Short-term investments—available for sale	25,000	19,000
Accounts receivable	43,000	45,000
Allowance for doubtful accounts	(1,800)	(2,000)
Prepaid expenses	4,200	2,500
Inventories	81,500	65,000
Land	50,000	50,000
Buildings	125,000	73,500
Accumulated amortization—buildings	(30,000)	(23,000)
Equipment	53,000	46,000
Accumulated amortization—equipment	(19,000)	(15,500)
Delivery equipment	39,000	39,000
Accumulated amortization—delivery equipment	(22,000)	(20,500)
Patents	15,000	–0–
	$379,400	$300,000
Accounts payable	$ 26,000	$ 16,000
Short-term notes payable (trade)	4,000	6,000
Accrued payables	3,000	4,600
Mortgage payable	73,000	53,400
Bonds payable	50,000	62,500
Share capital	150,000	106,000
Retained earnings	73,400	51,500
	$379,400	$300,000

Additional information:

1. Dividends of $15,000 were declared and paid in 2009.

2. There were no unrealized gains or losses on the available-for-sale securities.

Instructions

Based on the information, prepare a work sheet for a statement of cash flows. Make reasonable assumptions as appropriate.

Problems

P22-1 Gousseva Holdings Inc.'s statement of financial position contained the following comparative data at December 31:

Balance sheet accounts:

	2008	2007
Available-for-sale investments	$20,200	$23,500
Accumulated other comprehensive income (loss)	800	(2,000)

Partial statement of income and comprehensive income, 2008:

Investment income		$ 200
Loss on sale of available-for-sale investment		3,200
Net income		XXX
Other comprehensive income		
Net holding loss on available-for-sale investments during the year	($400)	
Reclassification adjustment for loss included in net income	3,200	2,800
Comprehensive income		$ XXX

At December 31, 2008, the following information is available:

1. Gousseva Holdings had a single investment in shares at December 31, 2007. The investment cost $25,500 and was sold during 2008 for $22,300.

2. During 2008, dividends of $200 were received on shares classified as available-for-sale investments.

3. Another AFS investment was purchased at a cost of $19,400. The fair value of this new investment at December 31, 2008, was $20,200.

Instructions

(a) Calculate and reconcile the transactions that were recorded to the accounts Available-For-Sale Investments and Accumulated Other Comprehensive Income.

(b) Using the direct and the indirect methods, prepare a table that contrasts the presentation of all transactions related to the above financial statements and related investment transactions on Gousseva's statement of cash flows. Be specific about the classification within the statement for each item that is reported.

P22-2   The unclassified balance sheet accounts for Sorkin Corporation for the year ended December 31, 2008, and its statement of income and comprehensive income and statement of cash flows for the year ended December 31, 2009, are as follows:

SORKIN CORPORATION
Balance Sheet Accounts
December 31, 2008
($ in millions)

Cash	$ 21
Accounts receivable	194
Inventory	200
Prepaid expenses	12
Long-term investment in shares of Stokes Inc.	125
Land	150
Buildings and equipment	400
Accumulated amortization	(120)
Patents	32
Goodwill	60
Total assets	$1,074
Accounts payable	$ 65
Salaries and wages payable	11
Bond interest payable	4
Income taxes payable	14
Future income tax liability	8
Bonds payable	275
Discount on bonds payable	(25)
Common shares	495
Retained earnings	227
Total liabilities and shareholders' equity	$1,074

SORKIN CORPORATION
Comprehensive Income Statement
Year Ended December 31, 2009
($ in millions)

Revenues:		
Sales revenue	$410	
Investment income	11	$421
Expenses and losses:		
Cost of goods sold	158	
Administrative expenses	22	
Salaries and wages expense	65	
Amortization expense	21	
Bond interest expense	28	
Loss on impairment of goodwill	20	314
Income before income taxes and extraordinary item		107
Income taxes		45
Income before extraordinary item		62
Extraordinary loss of equipment from flood	18	
Less applicable current tax savings	(6)	12
Net income		50
Other comprehensive income		
Holding gain on available-for-sale investments during the year		5
Comprehensive income		$ 55

SORKIN CORPORATION
Statement of Cash Flows (Indirect Method)
For the Year Ended December 31, 2009

Cash flows from operating activities		
Net income		$50
Add back (deduct) non-cash revenues and expenses:		
Investment revenue from equity investment in Stokes Inc.	(11)	
Dividends received from equity investment in Stokes Inc.	6	
Extraordinary loss	18	
Amortization expense	21	
Amortization of bond discount	3	
Loss on impairment of goodwill	20	57
Add (deduct) changes in non-cash working capital:		
Decrease in accounts receivable	4	
Increase in inventories	(5)	
Decrease in prepaid expenses	2	
Decrease in accounts payable	(15)	
Decrease in salaries and wages payable	(5)	
Increase in future income tax liability	3	
Increase in bond interest payable	4	
Decrease in income taxes payable	(2)	(14)
Net cash provided by operating activities		93
Cash flows from investing activities:		
Proceeds from disposal of damaged equipment	10	
Purchase of land (note 1)	(23)	
Purchase of available-for-sale long-term investments	(25)	
Net cash used by investing activities		(38)
Cash flows from financing activities:		
Dividends paid	(7)	
Redemption of serial bonds	(60)	
Issuance of preferred shares	75	
Repurchase of common shares	(9)	

Net cash used by financing activities	(1)
Net increase in cash	54
Cash, January 1, 2009	21
Cash, December 31, 2009	$75

Note 1. Non-cash investing and financing activities

(a) During the year, land was acquired for $46 million in exchange for cash of $23 million and a $23-million, four-year, 15% note payable to the seller.

(b) Equipment was acquired through a lease that was capitalized initially at $82 million.

Additional information from the accounting records:

1. The investment income represents Sorkin's reported income in its 35% owned, significantly influenced investment in Stokes Inc. Sorkin received a dividend from Stokes during the year.

2. Early in 2009, Sorkin purchased shares for $25 million as a long-term available-for-sale investment. There were no purchases or sales of these shares during 2009, nor were there any dividends received from this investment.

3. A machine that originally cost $70 million became unusable due to a rare flood. Most major components of the machine were unharmed and were sold together for $10 million. Sorkin had no insurance coverage for the loss because of the nature of this casualty. This loss was deductible for tax purposes.

4. Timing differences in the year between pre-tax accounting income and taxable income resulted in an increase in future taxable amounts, causing the future income tax liability to increase by $3 million.

5. On December 30, 2009, land costing $46 million was acquired by paying $23 million cash and issuing a $23-million, four-year, 15% note payable to the seller.

6. Equipment was acquired through a 15-year capital lease. The present value of minimum lease payments was $82 million when signing the lease on December 31, 2008. Sorkin made the initial lease payment of $2 million on January 1, 2010.

7. Serial bonds with a face value of $60 million were retired at maturity on June 20, 2009. In order to finance this redemption and have additional cash available for operations, Sorkin issued preferred shares for $75 million cash.

8. In February, Sorkin issued a 4% stock dividend (four million shares). The market price of the common shares was $7.50 per share at that time.

9. There were no purchases or disposals of patents during 2009, and the amortization recorded on patents was $2 million during the year.

10. In April 2009, one million common shares were repurchased for $9 million. The weighted average original issue price of the repurchased shares was $12 million.

Instructions

(a) Prepare the unclassified balance sheet accounts for Sorkin Corporation for the year ended December 31, 2009, as a check on the statement of cash flows. Add whichever accounts you consider necessary.

(b) Prepare the operating activities section of the statement of cash flows for Sorkin Corporation using the direct method.

(c) How would the statement of cash flows differ if the terms on the purchase of land had been essentially the same except that the financing for the note payable had been negotiated with a mortgage company instead of the seller of the land?

P22-3   Jeopardy Inc.'s CFO has just left the office of the company president after a meeting about the draft statement of financial position at April 30, 2008, and income statement for the year ended. (Both are reproduced below.) "Our liquidity position looks healthy," the president had remarked. "Look at the current and acid-test ratios, and the amount of working capital we have. And between the goodwill write-off and amortization, we have almost $23 million of non-cash expenses. I don't understand why you've been complaining about our cash situation."

The CFO turns the draft financial statements over to you, the newest member of the accounting staff, along with extracts from the notes to the financial statements:

JEOPARDY INC.
Consolidated Statement of Financial Position
April 30, 2008 and 2007
(in $000s)

	2008	2007
Assets		
Cash and 60-day treasury bills	$ 3,265	$ 3,739
Accounts receivable	23,744	18,399
Inventories	26,083	21,561
Income taxes recoverable	145	—
Prepaid expenses	1,402	1,613
	54,639	45,312
Investments (Note 1)	5,960	6,962
Property, plant, and equipment (Note 2)	37,332	45,700
Future income tax asset	4,875	2,245
Goodwill	—	12,737
Development costs (Note 3)	4,391	1,911
	$107,197	$114,867
Liabilities		
Current		
Bank overdraft (temporary)	$ 6,844	$ 6,280
Accounts payable and accrued (Note 4)	3,243	4,712
Current portion of long-term debt	1,800	1,200
	11,887	12,192
Long-term debt (Note 5)	14,900	14,500
Shareholders' Equity		
Share capital (Note 6)	79,257	62,965
Retained earnings	1,153	25,210
	80,410	88,175
	$107,197	$114,867

Consolidated Statement of Income and Retained Earnings
Year ended April 30, 2008 and 2007
(in $000s)

	2008	2007
Revenue		
Operating	$ 89,821	$ 68,820
Interest and other	1,310	446
	91,131	69,266
Expenses		
Operating*	76,766	62,455
General and administrative*	13,039	12,482
Amortization	10,220	11,709
Goodwill write-off	12,737	—
Interest	1,289	1,521
Loss on sale of capital assets	394	—
	114,445	88,167
Loss before equity loss and income taxes	(23,314)	(18,901)
Equity income (loss) (Note 1)	(2,518)	100
Loss before income taxes	(25,832)	(18,801)
Income taxes	2,775	5,161
Net loss	(23,057)	(13,640)
Retained earnings, beginning of year	25,210	38,850

	2,153	25,210
Stock dividend	(1,000)	—
Retained earnings, end of year	$ 1,153	$ 25,210

*The operating and general and administrative expenses for 2008 include salaries and wages of $37,509 and $9,115, respectively.

Draft Notes to the Financial Statements
For the Year Ended April 30, 2008

Note 1. Investments
The company's investments at April 30 are as follows (in $000s):

	2008	2007
Compuco Ltd. (market value 2008, $4.3 million)		
Shares, opening balance at equity	$ 6,962	$ 5,862
Equity income (loss)	(2,518)	100
Shares, ending balance at equity	3,444	5,962
Other investments (held to maturity)	2,516	1,000
	$ 5,960	$ 6,962

Note 2. Property, Plant, and Equipment
Additions to property, plant, and equipment for the current year amounted to $2.29 million. Proceeds from the disposal of property, plant, and equipment amounted to $250,000.

Note 3. Development Costs
Development costs for a product are amortized once the product is ready for market. The rate depends on the expected life of the product.

Note 4. Accounts Payable and Accrued (in $000s)

	2008	2007
Accounts payable—suppliers	$ 3,102	$ 4,562
Accrued salaries and wages payable	141	150
	$ 3,243	$ 4,712

Note 5. Long-Term Debt (in $000s)

	2008	2007
Debentures	$12,500	$12,500
Bank term loans, due April 30, 2012, principal repayable at $150,000 a month (2007, at $100,000 a month)	4,200	3,200
	16,700	15,700
Current maturities	(1,800)	(1,200)
	$14,900	$14,500

Debentures bear interest at 12% per annum and are due in 2011. Bank term loans bear interest at 8% and the bank advanced $2.2 million during the year.

Note 6. Share Capital
On September 14, 2007, Jeopardy Inc. issued 3.8 million shares with special warrants. Net proceeds from issuing 3.8 million shares amounted to $14,393,000. Net proceeds from issuing 3.8 million warrants amounted to $899,000. On April 30, 2008, a stock dividend of $1 million was issued.

Instructions

(a) Prepare a statement of cash flows for the year ended April 30, 2008, on a non-comparative basis from the information provided. The CFO wants to use the direct method to report the company's operating cash flows this year. Include all required disclosures.

(b) Prepare a reconciliation of the 2008 net loss to cash provided from (used in) operations. This reconciliation is to be included in a note to the financial statements.

(c) Write a memo to the president of Jeopardy Inc. that explains why the company is experiencing a cash crunch when its liquidity ratios look acceptable and it has significant non-cash expenses.

(CICA adapted)

P22-4 The following is Mann Corp.'s comparative balance sheet at December 31, 2008 and 2007, with a column showing the increase (decrease) from 2007 to 2008:

COMPARATIVE STATEMENT OF FINANCIAL POSITION

	2008	2007	Increase (Decrease)
Cash	$ 807,500	$ 700,000	$107,500
Accounts receivable	128,000	168,000	(40,000)
Inventories	850,000	715,000	135,000
Property, plant, and equipment	3,307,000	2,967,000	340,000
Accumulated amortization	(1,165,000)	(1,040,000)	125,000
Investment in Bligh Corp.	305,000	275,000	30,000
Loan receivable	262,500	—	262,500
Total assets	$4,495,000	$3,785,000	
Accounts payable	$1,015,000	$ 955,000	$ 60,000
Income taxes payable	30,000	50,000	(20,000)
Dividends payable	80,000	100,000	(20,000)
Capital lease obligation	400,000	—	400,000
Share capital, common	1,000,000	1,000,000	—
Retained earnings	1,970,000	1,680,000	290,000
Total liabilities and shareholders' equity	$4,495,000	$3,785,000	

Additional information:

1. On December 31, 2007, Mann acquired 25% of Bligh Corp.'s common shares for $275,000. On that date, the carrying value of Bligh's assets and liabilities was $1.1 million, which approximated their fair values. Bligh reported income of $120,000 for the year ended December 31, 2008. No dividend was paid on Bligh's common shares during the year.

2. During 2008, Mann loaned $300,000 to TLC Corp., an unrelated company. TLC made the first semi-annual principal repayment of $37,500, plus interest at 10%, on December 31, 2008.

3. On January 2, 2008, Mann sold equipment costing $60,000, with a carrying amount of $35,000, for $40,000 cash.

4. On December 31, 2008, Mann entered into a capital lease for an office building. The present value of the annual rental payments is $400,000, which equals the building's fair value. Mann made the first rental payment of $60,000 when due on January 2, 2009.

5. Net income for 2008 was $370,000.

6. Mann declared and paid cash dividends for 2008 and 2007 as follows:

	2008	2007
Declared	Dec. 15, 2008	Dec. 15, 2007
Paid	Feb. 28, 2009	Feb. 28, 2008
Amount	$80,000	$100,000

Instructions

Prepare a statement of cash flows for Mann Corp. for the year ended December 31, 2008, using the indirect method.

(AICPA adapted)

P22-5 Seneca Corporation has contracted with you to prepare a statement of cash flows. The controller has provided the following information:

	December 31	
	2008	2007
Cash	$ 38,500	$13,000
Accounts receivable	12,250	10,000
Inventory	12,000	9,000
Investments—available for sale	–0–	3,000
Building	–0–	29,750
Equipment	40,000	20,000
Patent	5,000	6,250
	$107,750	$91,000
Allowance for doubtful accounts	$ 3,000	$ 4,500
Accumulated amortization—equipment	2,000	4,500
Accumulated amortization—building	–0–	6,000
Accounts payable	5,000	3,000
Dividends payable	–0–	6,000
Notes payable, short-term (non-trade)	3,000	4,000
Long-term notes payable	31,000	25,000
Share capital	43,000	33,000
Retained earnings	20,750	5,000
	$107,750	$91,000

Additional data related to 2008 are as follows:

1. Equipment that cost $11,000 and was 40% amortized at the time of disposal was sold for $2,500.

2. Common shares were issued to pay $10,000 of the long-term note payable.

3. Cash dividends paid were $6,000.

4. On January 1, 2008, a flood destroyed the building. Insurance proceeds on the building were $33,000 (net of $4,000 taxes).

5. Long-term investments (available-for-sale) were sold at $2,500 above their cost. The fair value of these investments at December 31, 2007, equalled their original cost.

6. Cash of $15,000 was paid to acquire equipment.

7. A long-term note for $16,000 was issued in exchange for equipment.

8. Interest of $2,000 and income taxes of $5,000 were paid in cash.

Instructions

(a) Use the indirect method to analyze the above information and prepare a statement of cash flows for Seneca. Flood damage is unusual and infrequent in that part of the country. Ensure all required disclosures are provided.

(b) Prepare a short analysis of Seneca's cash flow activity for 2008. The analysis is to be given to the controller.

(c) What kind of company would you expect to be revealed by the operating, investing, and financing sections of Seneca's statement of cash flows:
   1. A company that is severely troubled financially?
   2. A recently formed company that is experiencing rapid growth?

P22-6 Ballard Corp. reported $145,000 of net income for 2008. In preparing the statement of cash flows, the accountant noted several items that might affect cash flows from operating activities. These items follow:

1. During 2008, Ballard reported a sale of equipment for $7,000. The equipment had a carrying amount of $23,500.

2. During 2008, Ballard sold 100 Lontel Corporation common shares at $200 per share. The acquisition cost of these shares was $145 per share. This investment was shown on Ballard's December 31, 2007, balance sheet as an available-for-sale investment.

3. During 2008, Ballard changed from the straight-line method to the double-declining-balance method of amortization for its machinery. The debit to opening retained earnings was $14,600.

4. During 2008, Ballard revised its estimate for bad debts. Before 2008, Ballard's bad debt expense was 1% of its net sales. In 2008, this percentage was increased to 2%. Net sales for 2008 were $500,000, and net accounts receivable decreased by $15,000 during 2008.

5. During 2008, Ballard issued 500 common shares for a patent. The shares' market value on the transaction date was $23 per share.

6. Amortization expense for 2008 was $38,000.

7. Ballard Corp. holds 40% of Nirvana Corporation's common shares as a long-term investment and exercises significant influence. Nirvana reported $27,000 of net income for 2008.

8. Nirvana Corporation paid a total of $2,800 of cash dividends to all shareholders in 2008.

9. During 2008, Ballard declared a 10% stock dividend, distributing 1,000 no par value common shares. The market price at the date of issuance was $20 per share.

10. Ballard Corp. paid $10,000 in dividends: $2,500 of this amount was paid on term preferred shares classified as a long-term liability.

Instructions

Prepare a schedule that shows the net cash flow from operating activities using the indirect method. Assume that no items other than the ones listed affected the calculation of 2008 cash flow from operating activities.

P22-7   Cabanza Corporation has not yet prepared a formal statement of cash flows for the 2008 fiscal year. Comparative statements of financial position as of December 31, 2007 and 2008, and a statement of income and retained earnings for the year ended December 31, 2008, follow:

CABANZA CORPORATION
Statement of Income and Retained Earnings
Year Ended December 31, 2008
($000)

Sales		$3,800
Expenses		
Cost of goods sold	$1,200	
Salaries and benefits	725	
Heat, light, and power	75	
Amortization—buildings and equipment	80	
Property taxes	19	
Patent amortization	25	
Travel expenses	10	
Interest	30	2,164
Income before income taxes		1,636
Income taxes		818
Net income		818
Retained earnings—January 1, 2008		310
		1,128
Stock dividend declared and issued		600
Retained earnings—December 31, 2008		$ 528

CABANZA CORPORATION
Comparative Statement of Financial Position
December 31
($000)

Assets	2008	2007
Current assets		
Cash	$ 383	$ 100
Canada T-Bills (60-day)	–0–	50
Accounts receivable	740	500
Inventory	720	560
Total current assets	1,843	1,210

Long-term assets		
Land	150	70
Buildings and equipment	910	600
Accumulated amortization	(200)	(120)
Patents (net of amortization)	105	130
Total long-term assets	965	680
Total assets	$2,808	$1,890
Liabilities and Shareholders' Equity		
Current liabilities		
Accounts payable	$ 420	$ 340
Income taxes payable	35	20
Notes payable (trade)	325	320
Total current liabilities	780	680
Long-term notes payable—due 2010	200	200
Total liabilities	980	880
Shareholders' equity		
Common shares	1,300	700
Retained earnings	528	310
Total shareholders' equity	1,828	1,010
Total liabilities and shareholders' equity	$2,808	$1,890

Instructions

(a) Prepare a statement of cash flows using the direct method.

(a) Prepare a short analysis that summarizes the year's cash flow activity.

(CMA adapted)

P22-8   Ashley Limited had the following information available at the end of 2008:

ASHLEY LIMITED
Comparative Statement of Financial Position
December 31, 2008 and 2007

	2008	2007
Cash	$ 15,000	$ –0–
Accounts receivable	17,500	16,950
Held-for-trading investments	20,000	30,000
Inventory	42,000	35,000
Prepaid rent	3,000	12,000
Prepaid insurance	2,100	900
Office supplies	1,000	750
Land	125,000	175,000
Building	350,000	350,000
Accumulated amortization	(105,000)	(87,500)
Equipment	525,000	400,000
Accumulated amortization	(130,000)	(112,000)
Patent	45,000	50,000
Total assets	$ 910,600	$ 871,100
Temporary bank overdraft	$ –0–	$ 12,000
Accounts payable	22,000	20,000
Income taxes payable	5,000	4,000
Wages payable	5,000	3,000
Short-term notes payable (trade)	10,000	10,000
Long-term notes payable (non-trade)	60,000	70,000
Future income tax liability	30,000	25,000

Bonds payable	375,000	375,000
Common shares	260,000	237,500
Retained earnings	143,600	114,600
Total liabilities and shareholders' equity	$ 910,600	$ 871,100

ASHLEY LIMITED
Income Statement
Year Ended December 31, 2008

Sales revenue		$1,160,000
Cost of goods sold		(748,000)
Gross margin		412,000
Operating expenses		
Selling expenses	$ 19,200	
Administrative expenses	124,700	
Salaries and wages expense	92,000	
Amortization expense	40,500	
Total operating expenses		(276,400)
Income from operations		135,600
Other revenues/expenses		
Gain on sale of land	8,000	
Investment income HFT (Note 1)	6,400	
Interest expense	(51,750)	(37,350)
Income before taxes		98,250
Income tax expense		(39,400)
Net income		$ 58,850

Note 1: Investment income for the held for trading investment includes dividend income of $2,400 and unrealized holding gains of $4,000.

Instructions

(a) Prepare a statement of cash flows for Ashley Limited using the direct method, accompanied by all required disclosures and a schedule that reconciles net income to cash flow from operations.

(b) Prepare a memo for top management that summarizes and comments on the cash activities of Ashley in 2008.

(c) Management wants to provide more captions (headings) in the section for cash flow from operating activities. Recommend one additional caption that would help achieve this goal.

P22-9   You have completed the field work in connection with your audit of Casar Corporation for the year ended December 31, 2008. The following schedule shows the balance sheet accounts at the beginning and end of the year:

	Dec. 31, 2008	Dec. 31, 2007	Increase or (Decrease)
Cash	$ 270,969	$ 298,000	$ (27,031)
Accounts receivable	479,424	353,000	126,424
Inventory	731,700	610,000	121,700
Prepaid expenses	12,000	8,000	4,000
Investment in Amarill Ltd.	110,500	–0–	110,500
Machinery	207,000	190,000	17,000
Buildings	535,200	407,900	127,300
Land	52,500	52,500	–0–
Patents	69,000	65,800	3,200
Goodwill	50,000	50,000	–0–
Bond discount	3,737	–0–	3,737
	$2,522,030	$2,035,200	

Income taxes payable	$ 90,250	$ 79,600	$ 10,650
Accounts payable	299,280	280,000	19,280
Dividends payable	70,000	–0–	70,000
Bonds payable—8%	125,000	–0–	125,000
Bonds payable—12%	–0–	100,000	(100,000)
Allowance for doubtful accounts	35,300	40,000	(4,700)
Accumulated amortization—buildings	424,000	400,000	24,000
Accumulated amortization—machinery	173,000	130,000	43,000
Common shares—no par value	1,285,200	1,455,600	(170,400)
Retained earnings	20,000	(450,000)	470,000
	$2,522,030	$2,035,200	

STATEMENT OF RETAINED EARNINGS

Jan. 1, 2008	Balance (deficit)	$(450,000)
Mar. 31, 2008	Net income for first quarter of 2008	25,000
Apr. 1, 2008	Transfer from contributed capital	425,000
	Balance	–0–
Dec. 31, 2008	Net income for last three quarters of 2008	90,000
Dec. 31, 2008	Dividend declared payable January 21, 2009	(70,000)
	Balance	$ 20,000

Your working papers contain the following additional information:

1. On April 1, 2008, the existing deficit was written off against contributed capital (common shares).

2. On November 1, 2008, new common shares were sold for cash.

3. A patent was purchased for $15,000.

4. During the year, machinery that cost $16,400 and on which there was accumulated amortization of $5,200 was sold for $7,000. No other plant assets were sold during the year.

5. The 20-year, 12% bonds were dated and issued on January 2, 1996. Interest was payable on June 30 and December 31. They were sold originally at par. These bonds were retired at 102 plus accrued interest on March 31, 2008.

6. The 40-year, 8% bonds were dated January 1, 2008, and were sold at 97. Interest is payable semi-annually on June 30 and December 31.

7. Casar Corporation acquired a 40% interest in Amarill Ltd. on January 2, 2008, for $100,000. The income statement of Amarill Ltd. for 2008 shows a net income of $26,250, and no dividends were paid in the current year. Casar accounts for this investment using the equity method.

8. Extraordinary repairs to buildings of $7,200 were charged to Accumulated Amortization—Buildings.

9. Interest paid in 2008 was $10,500, and income taxes paid were $34,000.

Instructions

(a) Prepare a statement of cash flows using the indirect method. Details of the principal calculations should be supported by schedules or skeleton ledger accounts. Include all required disclosures.

(b) Prepare a summary report that explains the $27,031 reduction in cash during the year and would be suitable for presenting to Casar's president.

P22-10   Davis Inc. had the following information available at March 31, 2009:

DAVIS INC.
Income Statement
For the Year Ended March 31, 2009

Sales	$450,000
Cost of goods sold	260,000
Gross profit	190,000

Operating expenses		
Salaries and wages	$64,500	
Amortization expense	7,500	
Rent expense	18,000	
Other general and administrative expenses	21,000	
Amortization of patents	1,500	112,500
Operating income		77,500
Other revenues and expenses		
Bond interest expense	(6,750)	
Investment income	12,500	
Gain on retirement of bonds	16,600	22,350
		99,850
Income tax expense—current	19,900	
Income tax expense—future	10,300	30,200
Net income		$69,650

Davis Inc.'s partial list of comparative account balances as of March 31, 2009 and 2008, is as follows:

	March 31		
	2009	2008	Change
Cash	$ 5,200	$ 4,400	$ 800
Temporary investment in 30-day T bills	20,000	6,200	13,800
Accounts receivable	46,400	43,600	2,800
Inventory	35,800	29,600	6,200
Prepaid expenses	2,650	2,800	(150)
Marketable equity securities (AFS)	5,230	2,230	3,000
Deferred rent charges	4,000	0	4,000
Accounts payable, trade	22,800	24,200	(1,400)
Salaries and wages payable	500	1,300	(800)
Income taxes payable	13,000	29,500	(16,500)
Interest payable	3,000	1,500	1,500
Accrued pension cost liability	8,500	6,900	1,600
Future income tax liability	12,900	2,600	10,300

Additional data:

1. Bond interest expense includes $750 of bond discount amortized.

2. The investment income represents Davis' reported income in its 40% owned, significantly influenced investment in Jessa Ltd. Davis received a $2,000 dividend from Jessa on February 15, 2009.

3. During the year, the company retired $500,000 of its outstanding bonds payable, paying out $16,600 less than the price at which the bonds were carried on the books.

4. In early January 2009, Davis renewed and signed a four-year operating lease, agreeing to pay $4,000 each month in rent. The lessor required the payment of the rent for the first and last months of the lease at that time.

5. The change in available-for-sale equity securities is from the change in the market value of the securities for the fiscal year 2009. There were no purchases or sales of these securities during the 2009 fiscal year. Unrealized gains in 2009 were recorded in Other Comprehensive Income.

Note: There is insufficient information to allow you to prepare a complete statement of cash flows.

Instructions

(a) What is the amount of Davis Inc.'s change in cash to be explained on the statement of cash flows for the year ended March 31, 2009?

(b) Prepare the "Cash provided by (used in) operations" section of the statement of cash flows, assuming that the indirect method is used and all necessary information has been provided.

(c) The accounting standard in the *CICA Handbook* prefers the use of the direct method for the cash flows from operations section of the statement. Identify the amounts that would be reported within this section if the direct method were used for the following items:

1. Cash paid to and on behalf of employees

2. Cash received from customers

3. Income taxes paid

4. Cash paid to suppliers for goods and services

5. Interest paid

(d) Calculate the sum of the cash flows in part (c). Should the sum of the cash flows in the direct format equal the amount arrived at in part (a) for "Cash provided by (used in) operations"? If not, why not? If it should, do the amounts equal each other? Why not?

P22-11 Comparative balance sheet accounts of Secada Inc. follow:

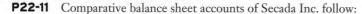

SECADA INC.
Comparative Balance Sheet Accounts
December 31, 2008 and 2007

	December 31	
Debit Accounts	2008	2007
Cash	$ 45,000	$ 33,750
Accounts Receivable	67,500	60,000
Merchandise Inventory	30,000	24,000
Long-Term Investments (available-for-sale)	23,250	40,500
Machinery	30,000	18,750
Buildings	67,500	56,250
Land	7,500	7,500
	$270,750	$240,750
Credit Accounts		
Allowance for Doubtful Accounts	$ 2,250	$ 1,500
Accumulated Amortization—Machinery	5,625	2,250
Accumulated Amortization—Buildings	13,500	9,000
Accounts Payable	30,000	24,750
Accrued Payables	2,375	1,125
Income Taxes Payable	1,000	1,500
Long-Term Note Payable—Non-Trade	26,000	31,000
Common Shares	150,000	125,000
Retained Earnings	39,000	42,625
Accumulated Other Comprehensive Income	1,000	2,000
	$270,750	$240,750

Additional data:

1. Cash dividends declared during the year were $21,125.

2. A 20% stock dividend was declared during the year; and $25,000 of retained earnings was capitalized.

3. Available-for-sale investments that cost $20,000 and had a fair value at December 31, 2007, of $22,500 were sold during the year for $23,750.

4. Machinery that cost $3,750 and had $750 of amortization accumulated was sold for $2,200.

Secada's 2008 statement of income and comprehensive income included the following:

Sales		$640,000
Less cost of goods sold		380,000
Gross margin		260,000
Less: Operating expenses (includes $8,625 amortization, and $5,400 bad debts)		180,450
Income from operations		79,550
Other: Gain on sale of AFS investments	$3,750	
Loss on sale of machinery	(800)	2,950
Income before taxes		82,500

Income tax expense		40,000
Net income		42,500
Other comprehensive income		
Holding gain on available-for-sale investments during the year	2,750	
Reclassification adjustment for gains included in net income	(3,750)	(1,000)
Comprehensive income		$41,500

Instructions

(a) Calculate net cash flow from operating activities using the direct method.

(b) Prepare a statement of cash flows using the indirect method.

(c) Assume that your investment club is considering investing in Secada Inc. Write a memo to the other members of the club about the company's cash activities during 2008.

(d) Management wants to provide more captions (headings) in the section on cash flow from operating activities. Recommend one additional caption that would help achieve that goal.

P22-12 Comparative balance sheet accounts of Laflamme Inc. and its statement of income for the year ending December 31, 2009, follow:

Comparative Balance Sheet Data:

	December 31		
	2009	2008	Change
Cash	$46,000	$56,000	($10,000)
Short-Term Investments (note 1)	36,000	45,000	(9,000)
Accounts Receivable	348,000	271,000	77,000
Prepaid Insurance	16,000	35,000	(19,000)
Inventory	398,000	350,000	48,000
Supplies	13,000	17,000	(4,000)
Long-Term Investment (note 7)	418,000	400,000	18,000
Land	640,000	500,000	140,000
Building (note 3)	1,310,000	1,280,000	30,000
Accumulated Amortization—Building	(400,000)	(360,000)	(40,000)
Equipment (note 4)	632,000	640,000	(8,000)
Accumulated Amortization—Equipment	(160,000)	(135,000)	(25,000)
Patent	60,000	65,000	(5,000)
	$3,357,000	$3,164,000	$ 193,000
Bank Overdrafts	–0–	$93,000	($93,000)
Accounts Payable	$165,000	150,000	15,000
Taxes Payable	26,000	35,000	(9,000)
Accrued Liabilities	57,000	41,000	16,000
Dividends Payable	20,000	50,000	(30,000)
Long-Term Notes Payable	440,000	450,000	(10,000)
Bonds Payable	1,040,000	1,070,000	(30,000)
Discount on Bonds Payable	(61,000)	(65,000)	4,000
Preferred Shares	504,000	380,000	124,000
Common Shares	746,000	666,000	80,000
Retained Earnings	420,000	294,000	126,000
	$3,357,000	$3,164,000	$ 193,000

Income Statement:

Revenues		
Sales revenue	$999,000	
Investment income	90,000	$1,089,000
Expenses and Losses		
Cost of goods sold	314,000	
Commissions expense	108,000	

Operating expenses (note 5)	166,000	
Wages expense	104,000	
Interest expense	95,000	
Loss on sale of equipment (note 4)	11,000	
Income tax expense	96,000	894,000
Net Income		$195,000

The following is additional information about Laflamme's transactions during the year ended December 31, 2009:

1. The short-term investments are typically term deposits that are very liquid and mature on average in 60 days. The bank overdrafts are temporary and reverse within a few days. Laflamme has opted to show these as cash and cash equivalents on its statement of cash flows.

2. A stock dividend on common shares for $18,000 was declared and distributed during the year.

3. There were no disposals of buildings during the year 2009.

4. Equipment with an original cost of $46,000 and book value of $14,000 was sold at a loss during the year.

5. All amortization expense is included in operating expenses.

6. During the year, Laflamme obtained land with a fair market value of $100,000 in exchange for its preferred shares.

7. Investment income includes the equity earnings of $62,000 from a long-term investment accounted for using the equity method and from interest revenue on the short-term investments referred to in item 1 above.

Instructions

(a) Prepare the statement of cash flows for the year ended December 31, 2009, for Laflamme Inc. using the indirect method. Prepare any additional disclosure notes that are required, including a table that shows the details of the cash and cash equivalents accounts at the end of each period.

(b) Prepare the operating activities section of the statement using the direct format.

(c) If Laflamme Inc. chose to not treat the short-term investments and the temporary bank overdrafts as cash and cash equivalents, how would transactions related to these accounts be reported on the statement of cash flows?

P22-13 Comparative balance sheet accounts of Jensen Limited follow:

JENSEN LIMITED
Balance Sheet Accounts
December 31, 2008 and 2007

Debit Balances	2008	2007
Cash	$ 80,000	$ 51,000
Accounts Receivable	138,500	119,000
Merchandise Inventory	75,000	61,000
Long-Term Investments (available-for-sale)	59,000	80,000
Future Income Tax Asset	6,500	11,000
Equipment	70,000	48,000
Building	145,000	145,000
Land	40,000	25,000
	$614,000	$540,000

Credit Balances	2008	2007
Allowance for Doubtful Accounts	$ 10,000	$ 8,000
Accumulated Amortization—Equipment	21,000	14,000
Accumulated Amortization—Building	37,000	28,000
Accounts Payable	72,500	60,000
Income Taxes Payable	12,000	10,000
Long-Term Notes Payable	62,000	70,000
Accrued Pension Liability	7,500	10,000
Common Shares	300,000	250,000
Retained Earnings	88,000	95,000
Accumulated Other Comprehensive Income (Loss)	4,000	(5,000)
	$614,000	$540,000

Data from Jensen's 2008 income statement and statement of comprehensive income follow:

Sales		$950,000
Less: Cost of goods sold		600,000
Gross profit		350,000
Less: Operating expenses (includes amortization and bad debt expense)		250,000
Income from operations		100,000
Other revenues and expenses		
Gain on sale of investments (AFS)	$ 15,000	
Loss on sale of equipment	(3,000)	12,000
Income before taxes		112,000
Income taxes		45,000
Net income		67,000
Other comprehensive income		
Holding gain on available-for-sale investments during the year	24,000	
Reclassification adjustment for gains included in net income	(15,000)	9,000
Comprehensive income		$76,000

Additional data:

1. Equipment that cost $10,000 and was 40% amortized was sold in 2008.

2. Cash dividends were declared and paid during the year.

3. Common shares were issued in exchange for land.

4. Investments that cost $35,000 and had a fair value of $37,000 at December 31, 2007, were sold during the year.

5. Cost of goods sold includes $115,000 of direct labour and benefits and $11,700 of pension costs. Operating expenses include $76,000 of wages and $8,000 of pension expense.

Instructions

(a) Prepare a statement of cash flows using the indirect method, including all required disclosures.

(b) Prepare the "cash provided by (or used in) operating activities" section under the direct method.

(c) Comment on the company's cash activities during the year.

(d) Assume that you are a shareholder of Jensen Limited. What do you think of the dividend payout ratio that is highlighted in the statement of cash flows? Do you see any reasons that would help explain Jensen's dividend policy? If yes, what are they?

Writing Assignments

WA22-1   HTM Limited is a young and growing producer of electronic measurement instruments and technical equipment. You have been retained by HTM to advise it in preparing a statement of cash flows using the indirect method. For the fiscal year ended October 31, 2008, you have obtained the following information about certain HTM events and transactions.

1. Earnings reported for the fiscal year were $800,000, which includes a deduction for an extraordinary loss of $110,000 (see item 5 below).

2. Amortization expense of $315,000 was included in the earnings reported.

3. Uncollectible accounts receivable of $40,000 were written off against the allowance for doubtful accounts. Also, $51,000 of bad debt expense was included in determining income for the year and was added to the allowance for doubtful accounts.

4. A gain of $9,000 was realized on the sale of a machine; it originally cost $75,000, of which $30,000 was amortized to the date of sale.

5. On April 1, 2008, lightning caused an uninsured building loss of $110,000 ($180,000 loss, less income tax benefit of $70,000). This extraordinary loss was included in determining income, as indicated in item 1 above.

6. On July 3, 2008, a building and land were purchased for $700,000; HTM gave in exchange a payment of $75,000 cash, previously unissued common shares with a $200,000 market value, and a $425,000 mortgage note payable for the remainder.

7. On August 3, 2008, $800,000 in face value of HTM's 10% convertible debentures were converted into common shares. The bonds were originally issued at face value.

8. Bonds payable with a par value of $100,000, on which there was an unamortized bond discount of $2,000, were redeemed at 99.5.

9. On September 21, 2008, a new issue of $500,000 par value, 8% convertible bonds was issued at 101. Without the conversion feature, the bonds would have been issued at 99.

10. HTM's employees accrue benefits related to the company's unfunded post-retirement medical plan each year. At October 31, 2008, HTM recognized $49,000 of accrued expense for the current year.

Instructions

(a) Explain whether each of the 10 numbered items is a source of cash, a use of cash, or neither.

(b) Explain how each item that is a source or use of cash should be reported in HTM's statement of cash flows for the fiscal year ended October 31, 2008, assuming HTM uses the indirect approach for the Operating Activities section.

(c) For items that are neither a source nor use of cash, explain why this is true, and indicate the disclosure, if any, that should be made of the item in the company's statement of cash flows for the year ended October 31, 2008.

WA22-2   The past few years have seen numerous changes in Canadian accounting standards, such as for investments, asset retirement obligations, and stock options.

Instructions

For each accounting situation listed below, identify any related cash flows, and explain how the statement of cash flows is affected for companies with this type of transaction:

(a) Temporary investments of securities purchased for trading are held by a company. The investments do not meet the definition of cash equivalents, but are used to earn a return on excess cash until the cash is needed for operations. Small amounts of gains and losses on disposal, interest and dividends received, and changes in their fair values are reported in income.

(b) A company holds long-term investments that are classified as available for sale. One security was disposed of at a gain during the year and the others have fair values that are higher than they were at the previous year end. Dividends have been received and reported in income.

(c) An investment in another company's bonds is classified as held to maturity. The investment was acquired at a premium because the bond pays a higher rate of interest than the market rate.

(d) A company began development activities for a new mine site. As a result, it incurred an obligation related to the mine's eventual retirement, reporting it as an asset retirement liability and as a portion of the mine's cost on its balance sheet. The following year, the obligation was increased due to expanded mine activity as well as the accretion of the amount that was recognized in the preceding year representing interest.

(e) Stock options with a two-year vesting period were issued to the top executive team at the beginning of the current fiscal period. The options' fair value exceeds the option price.

(f) Stock options that were granted three years ago were exercised in the current year when the fair value of the company's shares was at an all-time high. The option or strike price was approximately half of the fair value of the shares when the options were exercised.

WA22-3   Durocher Guitar Corp. is in the business of manufacturing top-quality, steel-string folk guitars. In recent years, the company has experienced working capital problems resulting from investments in new factory equipment, the unanticipated buildup of receivables and inventories, and the payoff of a mortgage on one of its manufacturing plants. The founder and president of the company, Laraine Durocher, has tried to raise cash from various financial institutions, but she has been unsuccessful because of the company's poor performance in recent years. In particular, the company's lead bank, First Provincial, is especially concerned about Durocher's inability to maintain a positive cash position. The commercial loan officer from First Provincial told Laraine Durocher, "I can't even consider your request for capital financing unless I see that your company is able to generate positive cash flows from operations."

Thinking about the banker's comment, Laraine Durocher came up with what she believes is a good plan: with a more attractive statement of cash flows, the bank might be willing to provide long-term financing. To "window dress" cash flows, the company can sell its accounts receivables to factors, liquidate its raw material inventories, and arrange a sale and leaseback for major components of its equipment. These rather costly transactions would generate lots of cash. As the chief accountant for Durocher Guitar, it is your job to advise Laraine Durocher on this plan.

Instructions

(a) Explain how each of these "solutions" would affect Durocher Guitar Corp.'s statement of cash flows. Be specific.

(b) Are there any ethical issues related to Laraine Durocher's idea?

(c) What would you advise Laraine Durocher to do?

WA22-4 *CICA Handbook* Section 1540, "Cash Flow Statements," is the latest in a series of revisions to what was once called the Statement of Source and Application of Funds and the Statement of Changes in Financial Position. Harmonized with IAS 7 on Cash Flow Statements, the changes to Section 1540 completed the move from a statement that explained the changes in financial position to one that is clearly focused on cash flows.

Instructions

(a) Explain what the purpose is of the statement of cash flows, and identify at least three reasons for its development.

(b) Identify and describe the three categories of activities that must be reported in the statement of cash flows. What is the relationship between these activities and a company's balance sheet?

(c) Identify two methods of reporting cash flows from operations. Are both permitted under GAAP? Explain. Which method do you prefer? Why?

(d) Provide two examples of a non-cash investing and financing transaction, and describe the financial reporting requirements for such transactions.

(e) Assume that you overhear the following comment made by an investor in the stock market: "You can't always trust the net income number reported, because of all the estimates and judgement that go into its determination. That's why I only look at the cash flow from operations in analyzing a company." Comment.

WA22-5   Since 2004, the FASB and IASB have been partners in researching and analyzing various ways in which financial information could be displayed on a company's primary financial statements. This "Financial Statement Presentation" project (formerly known as "Reporting Financial Performance") is of great interest to the Canadian AcSB, and it expects to issue exposure drafts and release final standards on each phase of the project as soon as possible after the IASB and FASB have done so.

International Insight

Considerable information about this project is available on the FASB (www.fasb.org) and IASB (www.iasb.org.uk) websites.

Instructions

Locate and read the "Financial Statement Presentation" project summaries and updates on both the FASB and IASB websites. Write a short report that you can present to your class on the decisions that have been made to date on this project that will affect the statement of cash flows. Describe how the statement will be different from what is now reported, and identify any areas where it appears that the FASB and IASB have come to different conclusions.

Case

Refer to the Case Primer on the Student Website to help you answer these cases.

Student Website

www.wiley.com/canada/kieso

CA22-1   Papadopoulos Limited (PL) sells retail merchandise in Canada. The company was incorporated last year and is now in its second year of operations. PL is owned and operated by the Papadopoulos family, and Iris Papadopoulos, the president of the company, has decided to expand the company into the American market- place. In order to do this, bank financing will be necessary.

The books have always been kept by Iris' daughter Tonya, who is presently studying accounting in university. Financial statements had only been prepared for tax purposes in the past. For the year ended December 31, 2008, Tonya prepared the following statement showing cash inflows and cash outflows:

Sources of cash:	
From shareholder loan	$150,000
From sales of merchandise	350,000
From truck financing	50,000
From term deposit cashed in	100,000
From interest income	10,000
Total sources of cash	660,000

Uses of cash:	
For fixed asset purchases	$100,000
For inventory purchases	250,000
Operating expenses, including depreciation of $70,000	160,000
For purchase of investment	55,000
For purchase of truck	50,000
For interest on debt	30,000
Total uses of cash	645,000
Net increase in cash	$15,000

Tonya showed the statement to her mother, noting that the bank was sure to give them a loan, especially since they were profitable in their second year and since cash had increased over the year, which shows that it had been a good year. Iris was not convinced, however, and decided to have the statement looked at by a "real" accountant.

Instructions

Adopt the role of the accountant and redraft the statement, if necessary, in good form for the bank. Discuss the financial position of the company.

Integrated Case

IC 22-1   Earthcom Inc. (EI) is in the telecommunications industry. The company builds and maintains telecommunication lines which are buried in the ground and often lie on the bottom of the ocean. The company is a public company and recently has been having some bad luck. One of its main undersea telecommunications lines was cut by accident and the company cannot determine the exact location of the problem. As a result, many of the company's customers have lost service. Because EI did not have a backup plan, it is uncertain about how long it will take to restore service. The affected customers are not happy and are threatening to sue. In order to try to calm them down, EI has managed to purchase some capacity from a competitor. Unfortunately, the cost of the service is much higher than the revenues from EI's customers. EI is also currently spending quite a bit on consulting fees (on lawyers and damage control consultants).

In addition, EI is spending a significant amount of money trying to track down the problem with its line, and although it has had no luck so far the company recently announced that it was confident that services would be restored imminently. As a result of the work being done, which includes mapping the ocean floor, EI feels that it will be in a better position to restore service if this ever happens again.

The company has also been spending a significant amount of money on many of its very old telecommunications lines that were beginning to degrade due to age. It has capitalized these amounts and they are therefore showing up as investing activities on the cash flow statement. The company's auditors have questioned this as they feel that the amounts should be expensed.

As a result of all this, EI's share price has plummeted, making its stock options worthless. Management has historically been remunerated solely based on these stock options, however. The company's CFO meanwhile has just announced that he is leaving and is demanding severance pay for what he is calling constructive dismissal. He feels that because the stock options are worthless, he is working for free—which he cannot afford to do—and that the company has effectively fired him.

Instructions

Adopt the role of the company controller and discuss the financial reporting issues.

Research and Financial Analysis

RA22-1 Stantec Inc.

Instructions

Refer to the financial statements and accompanying notes and discussion of Stantec Inc. presented at the end of this volume, or access the company's financial statements for its year ended December 31, 2005, from SEDAR (www.sedar.com), and answer the following questions.

(a) How does Stantec Inc. define cash and cash equivalents? Do the cash and cash equivalents reported on the statement of cash flows reconcile to the balance sheet amounts that are reported? Provide details of the reconciliation.

(b) Prepare a summary analysis of Stantec's sources and uses of cash at the level of operating, investing, and financing subtotals only, for 2003, 2004, and 2005. Based on this, comment on the similarities and differences in the company's needs for cash and how they were met over the past three years.

(c) What method of reporting operating cash flows does Stantec use in the statement of cash flows? Now refer to Note 16 to the financial statements. Review this note and prepare an explanation of what the $57,314 total represents. Which approach do you think provides more useful information to a potential investor? Explain briefly.

(d) Using the information provided in Note 16, determine the balances of the Accounts Receivable, Prepaid Expenses, and Accounts Payable and Accrued Liabilities that would have been reported on the December 31, 2003, balance sheet.

(e) In Note 16, it appears that stock-based compensation expense provided $1,814 thousand of cash from operations and that self-insurance activity provided an additional $9,764 thousand. Explain.

(f) Based only on the information in the Financing Activities section of the statement of cash flows, can you tell whether the debt-to-equity ratio increased or decreased during the years ended December 31, 2005 and 2004? Explain.

(g) Is Stantec's operating capability expanding or contracting? What type of assets is the company investing in? What is the likely effect of these investments on Stantec's future operating and financing cash flows?

(h) Comment briefly on the company's solvency and financial flexibility.

RA22-2 Clearwater Seafoods Income Fund

The opening vignette to this chapter discusses the importance of cash flow to Clearwater Seafoods Limited, a Nova Scotia-based vertically integrated company in the fishing industry. In January 2005, Clearwater Seafoods Income Fund announced that it was reducing, and in some cases suspending, cash distributions to its unitholders. In August 2006, distributions to unitholders were reinstated at a rate of $0.05 per unit per month.

Instructions

Review Clearwater Seafoods Income Fund's website, information filed on SEDAR, and/or press reports on this company. Write a short report that explains why the company's cash distributions were suspended, why it was possible to reinstate the distributions one and a half years later, and how the company generates cash needed for continuing investment purposes.

RA22-3 Abitibi-Consolidated Inc.

In 2003, Abitibi-Consolidated Inc. significantly reduced its dividend, hoping to conserve its cash resources. The company was working in difficult market conditions, including having to contend with lower Canadian dollar inflows from forestry product sales priced in U.S. dollars as the Canadian dollar strengthened. The company declared annual dividends of $0.10 per share in 2004 and 2005, $0.05 in fiscal 2006, and suspended dividend payments on July 25, 2006.

Instructions

Access the Canadian GAAP financial statements of Abitibi-Consolidated Inc. for its year ended December 31, 2006, either through the Student Website or SEDAR at www.sedar.com. Analyze the Consolidated Statements of Cash Flows and notes to the financial statements and answer the following questions.

(a) Review the statements of cash flows for the three-year period ending December 31, 2006. What indication is there, if any, that the company might be experiencing cash flow problems?

(b) The company reported $54 million in net income in 2006 compared to a $350-million loss the previous year, even though 2006 sales were lower. Operating cash flows also appear to have improved. What effect did the countervailing and anti-dumping duties described in Note 4 have on 2006 income and on operating cash flows? For the "changes in non-cash operating working capital components," what caused the reduction in continuing operating activities cash flows?

(c) How did Abitibi generate the cash that it needed in 2005 to cover its financing cash needs? How do you think this will affect future operating cash flows?

(d) Note 29C to the financial statements provides condensed consolidated statements of cash flows under both Canadian and U.S. GAAP. What explains the difference between these two sets of statements?

RA22-4 Medicure Inc. versus Biomira Inc. Comparative Analysis

Medicure Inc. and Biomira Inc. are both incorporated under the *Canada Business Corporations Act* and both are involved in the discovery, research, and development of therapeutic products. Manitoba-based Medicure focuses mainly on discovering and developing cardiovascular therapeutics, while Alberta-based Biomira researches and develops therapeutic products for the treatment of cancer.

Instructions

From the SEDAR website (www.sedar.com) or the company websites, obtain the comparative financial statements of Medicure for its year ended May 31, 2006, and of Biomira for its year ended December 31, 2006. Review the financial statements and answer the following questions.

(a) Compare the companies' statements of operations and comment on their results over the past two fiscal periods. What is the major reason for the results that are reported?

(b) How would you expect companies in this industry and stage of development to be financed? Why? Is this consistent with what is reported on their balance sheets? Comment.

(c) For the two most recent years reported by each company, write a brief explanation of their cash activities at the sub-total level of operating, investing, and financing flows. Note any similarities and differences.

(d) How do the investments that Medicure and Biomira make differ from the investments made by companies in other industries? Describe the difference in general, and then specifically explain how it affects each of the financial statements.

(e) Are the companies liquid? Explain. On what does the solvency and financial flexibility of companies in this industry depend?

RA22-5 Cadbury Schweppes plc

According to Cadbury Schweppes plc's 2006 Annual Report, the company is the world's largest confectionery company and it has strong regional beverages businesses in North America and Australia. Locate a copy of the company's comparative financial statements for the 52 weeks ending December 31, 2006, on the website of Cadbury Schweppes (CS).

Instructions

(a) Prepare a summary report of CS's cash activities during its year ended December 31, 2006, at the sub-total level of operating, investing, and financing activities, and a comparative report for the preceding fiscal year. Are there major differences at this level between the two periods? Explain.

(b) Identify what major differences there are between the company's accrual-based income and its cash flow from operating activities over the past two years.

(c) Prepare a short report summarizing CS's investing cash transactions and its financing cash transactions for 2006.

(d) Compare the general presentation and disclosures provided in Cadbury Schweppes's 2006 statement of cash flows with the presentation and disclosures required under Canadian GAAP. Comment on your findings.

The Importance of the Auditor's Opinion

![PRICEWATERHOUSECOOPERS logo]

Following financial scandals in the United States and the subsequent increase in legislative and regulatory initiatives, full disclosure in financial reporting has become highly important for pubic companies. There is now more focus at the audit committee level, there has been increased effort in management's discussion and analysis, and, with the increased responsibility laid on directors, full disclosure has been received more readily.

Two members of the Audit and Assurance Group of professionals at Pricewaterhouse-Coopers LLP in Toronto have commented on the changes. "GAAP has evolved to the point where the disclosures are massive," says Gino Scapillati, partner and Greater Toronto Area (GTA) leader of the Audit and Assurance Group. "Statements disclose a lot more than they used to."

Laurie Woodruff, partner and national leader of the Audit and Assurance Group, adds that the role of the auditor is "to provide an opinion on the financial statements of a company and comment on whether or not the financial statements are prepared in accordance with GAAP." For certain U.S. registrants, an auditor must also attest to the effectiveness of internal controls.

While questionable financial reporting has come under increased media scrutiny, instances of actual fraud are rare. "There is a big distinction between fraudulent financial reporting and errors in financial statements that get caught at a later date," clarifies Lisa Simeoni, another Audit and Assurance Group partner. While there are deliberate acts where the intent is to get a certain financial result, more common are the other instances where there has been a judgement call on an interpretation of GAAP, and a different view is later taken that results in changes to past financials.

For public companies, a qualified opinion is not an option, says Scapillati. When auditors identify a problem, they work with management to address it. They then meet with the Audit Committee to explain how problems have been resolved and adjusted for. ∎

Other Measurement and Disclosure Issues

Learning Objectives

After studying this chapter, you should be able to:

1. Review the full disclosure principle and describe problems of implementation.
2. Explain the use of accounting policy notes in financial statement preparation.
3. Describe the disclosure requirements for major segments of a business.
4. Describe the accounting problems associated with interim reporting.
5. Discuss the accounting issues for related-party transactions.
6. Identify the difference between the two types of subsequent events.
7. Identify issues related to financial forecasts and projections.
8. Identify the major disclosures found in the auditor's report.
9. Compare current Canadian and international GAAP, and understand which direction international GAAP is headed.

Preview of Chapter 23

It is very important to read not only a company's financial statements and related information, but also the president's letter and management discussion and analysis (MD&A). In this chapter, we cover several disclosures that must accompany the financial statements to ensure that the statements are not misleading.

The chapter is organized as follows:

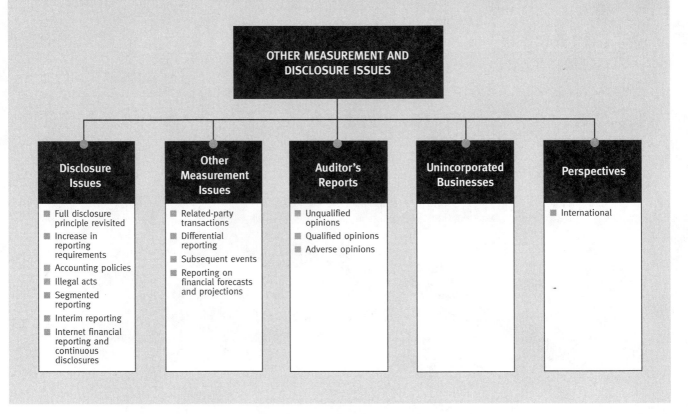

DISCLOSURE ISSUES

Full Disclosure Principle Revisited

Some information is provided best in the financial statements and some is provided better by other means of financial reporting. For example, earnings and cash flows are readily available in financial statements, but investors might do better to look at comparisons with other companies in the same industry, which can be found in news articles or brokerage house reports.

Financial statements, notes to the financial statements, and supplementary information are all areas that are directly affected by GAAP. Other types of information that are found in the annual report, such as management's discussion and analysis, are not subject to GAAP. Illustration 23-1 shows the various types of financial information.

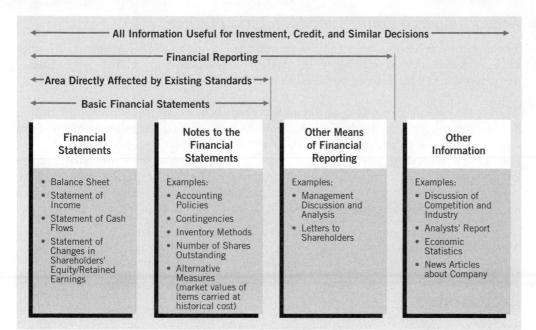

Illustration 23-1

Types of Financial Information

As indicated in Chapter 2, the accounting profession has adopted a **full disclosure principle** that calls for financial reporting of any financial facts that are significant enough to influence the judgement of an informed reader. In some situations, the benefits of disclosure may be apparent while the costs are uncertain. In other instances, the costs may be certain but the benefits of disclosure are less apparent. How much information is enough information? This is a difficult question to answer. While not enough information is clearly problematic, sometimes too much—often referred to as information overload—is equally as problematic.

Different users want different information, and it becomes exceedingly difficult to develop disclosure policies that meet their varied objectives.

Underlying Concept

This is a good example of the trade-off between the cost-benefit constraint and the full disclosure principle.

Increase in Reporting Requirements

Disclosure requirements have increased substantially over the past several decades. As illustrated throughout this textbook, the accounting profession has issued many standards in the last two decades that have substantial disclosure provisions. The reasons for this increase in disclosure requirements are varied. Some of them are as follows.

1 Objective
Review the full disclosure principle and describe problems of implementation.

Complexity of the Business Environment

The difficulty of distilling economic events into summarized reports has been magnified by the increasing complexity of business operations in such areas as derivatives, leasing, business combinations, pensions, financing arrangements, and revenue recognition. As a result, notes to the financial statements are used extensively to explain these transactions and their future effects.

Necessity for Timely Information

Today, more than ever before, users are demanding information that is current and predictive. For example, more complete interim data are required. Published financial forecasts, which have long been avoided and even feared by management, are now recommended.

Accounting as a Control and Monitoring Device

The government has recently sought more information and public disclosure of such phenomena as management compensation, environmental pollution, related-party transactions, errors and irregularities, and illegal activities.

What Do the Numbers Mean?

The biggest overall change in annual reports recently is that companies are now disclosing debt-rating triggers that are buried in their financing arrangements. These triggers can require a company to pay off a loan immediately if the debt rating folds; indeed, they are one of the reasons that **Enron** crumbled as quickly as it did—and few Enron shareholders knew about them, unfortunately, until the gun had gone off. Companies are also telling more about their bank credit lines, liquidity, and any special purpose entities, which were major villains in the Enron drama.

Source: Gretchen Morgenson, "Annual Reports: More Pages, But Better?" *New York Times*, March 17, 2002.

Accounting Policies

Objective 2
Explain the use of accounting policy notes in financial statement preparation.

As mentioned previously, notes are an integral part of a business enterprise's financial statements. However, they are often overlooked because they are highly technical and often appear in small print. Notes are the accountant's means of amplifying or explaining items that are presented in the main body of the statements. Information that is relevant to specific financial statement items can be explained in qualitative terms in notes, and additional quantitative data can be provided to expand the information in the financial statements. Notes can also be used to give information about restrictions that are imposed by financial arrangements or basic contractual agreements. Although notes may be technical and difficult to understand, they provide meaningful information for the financial statement user.

The **accounting policies** of any particular entity are the specific accounting principles and methods that are currently employed and considered most appropriate to present fairly the enterprise's financial statements. Information about the accounting policies that have been adopted and followed by a reporting entity is essential for financial statement users in making economic decisions. The accounting policies disclosure should be given either as the first note or in a separate Summary of Significant Accounting Policies section that immediately precedes the notes to the financial statements. The Summary of Significant Accounting Policies answers such questions as the following: What method of amortization is used on plant assets? What valuation method is employed on inventories? What amortization policy is followed in regard to intangible assets? How are marketing costs handled for financial reporting purposes?

Refer to the audited financial statements of **Stantec Inc.** found in Chapter 5 for an illustration of a note disclosure of accounting policies and other notes. Analysts examine carefully the summary of accounting policies section to determine whether the company is using conservative or liberal accounting practices. For example, recognizing revenues prior to delivery of products would be considered liberal or aggressive. On the other hand, using the successful efforts method for an oil and gas company would generally be viewed as following a conservative practice.

Illegal Acts

Accounting errors are defined as unintentional mistakes, whereas irregularities are intentional distortions of financial statements. As indicated in this textbook, when errors are discovered, the financial statements should be corrected. The same treatment should be given to irregularities. When an accountant or auditor discovers irregularities, however, a whole different set of suspicions, procedures, and responsibilities comes into play.

Illegal acts are defined by the CICA as "a violation of a domestic or foreign statutory law or government regulation attributable to the entity… or to management or employees acting on the entity's behalf."[1] The term "illegal act" is not meant to include personal misconduct by the entity's management or employees, which may be unrelated to the enterprise's business activities. The accountant or auditor must evaluate the adequacy of disclosure in the financial statements and may have to assess whether the item should be recognized in the balance sheet or income statement. For example, if revenue is derived from an illegal act that is considered material in relation to the financial statements, this information should be disclosed. Furthermore, if the illegal act creates a liability to pay a fine, this would need to be reflected in the balance sheet and income statement.

Segmented Reporting

In the last several decades, business enterprises have at times had a tendency to diversify their operations by investing in various other businesses. As a result of such diversification efforts, investors and investment analysts have sought more information about the details behind conglomerate financial statements. Particularly, they want income statement, balance sheet, and cash flow information on the individual segments that together result in the total business income figure. Illustration 23-2 presents **segmented (disaggregated) financial information** for **Torstar Corporation.**

3 Objective
Describe the disclosure requirements for major segments of a business.

Illustration 23-2

Segmented Information Note—Torstar Corporation

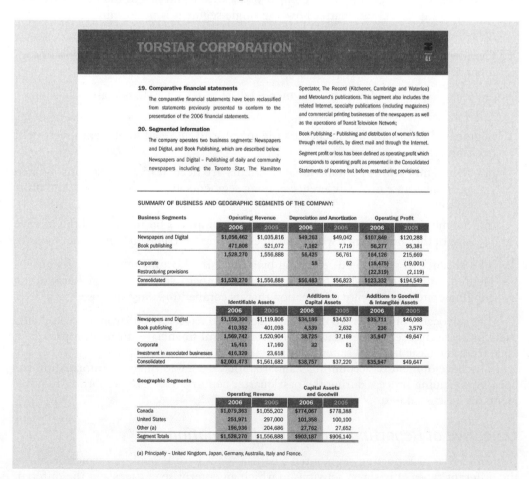

TORSTAR CORPORATION

19. Comparative financial statements

The comparative financial statements have been reclassified from statements previously presented to conform to the presentation of the 2006 financial statements.

20. Segmented information

The company operates two business segments: Newspapers and Digital, and Book Publishing, which are described below.

Newspapers and Digital – Publishing of daily and community newspapers including the Toronto Star, The Hamilton

Spectator, The Record (Kitchener, Cambridge and Waterloo) and Metroland's publications. This segment also includes the related Internet, specialty publications (including magazines) and commercial printing businesses of the newspapers as well as the operations of Transit Television Network;

Book Publishing – Publishing and distribution of women's fiction through retail outlets, by direct mail and through the Internet.

Segment profit or loss has been defined as operating profit which corresponds to operating profit as presented in the Consolidated Statements of Income but before restructuring provisions.

SUMMARY OF BUSINESS AND GEOGRAPHIC SEGMENTS OF THE COMPANY:

Business Segments	Operating Revenue		Depreciation and Amortization		Operating Profit	
	2006	2005	2006	2005	2006	2005
Newspapers and Digital	$1,056,462	$1,035,816	$49,263	$49,042	$107,849	$120,288
Book publishing	471,808	521,072	7,162	7,719	56,277	95,381
	1,528,270	1,556,888	56,425	56,761	164,126	215,669
Corporate			58	62	(18,475)	(19,001)
Restructuring provisions					(22,319)	(2,119)
Consolidated	$1,528,270	$1,556,888	$56,483	$56,823	$123,332	$194,549

	Identifiable Assets		Additions to Capital Assets		Additions to Goodwill & Intangible Assets	
	2006	2005	2006	2005	2006	2005
Newspapers and Digital	$1,159,390	$1,119,806	$34,186	$34,537	$35,711	$46,068
Book publishing	410,352	401,098	4,539	2,632	236	3,579
	1,569,742	1,520,904	38,725	37,169	35,947	49,647
Corporate	15,411	17,160	32	51		
Investment in associated businesses	416,320	23,618				
Consolidated	$2,001,473	$1,561,682	$38,757	$37,220	$35,947	$49,647

Geographic Segments

	Operating Revenue		Capital Assets and Goodwill	
	2006	2005	2006	2005
Canada	$1,079,363	$1,055,202	$774,067	$778,388
United States	251,971	297,000	101,358	100,100
Other (a)	196,936	204,686	27,762	27,652
Segment Totals	$1,528,270	$1,556,888	$903,187	$906,140

(a) Principally – United Kingdom, Japan, Germany, Australia, Italy and France.

---

[1] *CICA Handbook*, Section 5136.03.

If the analyst only has access to the consolidated figures, information about the composition of these figures is hidden in aggregated totals. There is no way to tell from the consolidated data how much each different product line contributes to the company's profitability, risk, and growth potential. For example, in the case of Torstar, the segmented data reveal that the newspaper segment yields 87% of the operating profit while contributing 69% of the revenues, whereas the book publishing segment generates 31% of revenues yet 45% of profits.

Companies have always been somewhat hesitant to disclose segmented data for several reasons, including the following:

1. Without a thorough knowledge of the business and an understanding of such important factors as the competitive environment and capital investment requirements, the investor may find the segmented information meaningless or may even draw improper conclusions about the segments' reported earnings.

2. Additional disclosure may harm reporting firms because it may be helpful to competitors, labour unions, suppliers, and certain government regulatory agencies.

3. Additional disclosure may discourage management from taking intelligent business risks because segments that report losses or unsatisfactory earnings may cause shareholder dissatisfaction with management.

4. The wide variation among firms in the choice of segments, cost allocation, and other accounting problems limits the usefulness of segmented information.

5. The investor is investing in the company as a whole and not in the particular segments, and it should not matter how any single segment is performing if the overall performance is satisfactory.

6. Certain technical problems, such as classification of segments and allocation of segment revenues and costs (especially "common costs"), are challenging.

On the other hand, the advocates of segmented disclosures offer these reasons in support of the practice:

1. Segmented information is needed by the investor to make an intelligent investment decision regarding a diversified company:
   (a) Sales and earnings of individual segments are needed to forecast consolidated profits because of the differences among segments in growth rate, risk, and profitability.
   (b) Segmented reports disclose the nature of a company's businesses and the relative size of the components, which aids in evaluating the company's investment worth.

2. The absence of segmented reporting by a diversified company may put its unsegmented, single product-line competitors at a competitive disadvantage because the conglomerate may obscure information that its competitors must disclose.

The advocates of segmented disclosures appear to have a much stronger case. Many users indicate that segmented data are the most useful financial information provided, aside from the basic financial statements.

The development of accounting standards for segmented financial information has been a continuing process during the past quarter century. The basic reporting requirements are discussed next.

Objective of Reporting Segmented Information

The objective of reporting segmented financial data is to provide information about the different types of business activities in which an enterprise engages and the different economic environments in which it operates so that users of financial statements can

1. better understand the enterprise's performance,

2. better assess its prospects for future net cash flows, and

3. make more informed judgements about the enterprise as a whole.[2]

Basic Principles

A company might meet the segmented reporting objective by providing complete sets of financial statements that are disaggregated in several ways: for example, by products or services, by geography, by legal entity, or by type of customer. However, it is not feasible to provide all that information in every set of financial statements. CICA instead requires that general purpose financial statements include selected information on a single basis of segmentation. The method chosen is referred to as the management approach.[3] The **management approach** is based on the way that management segments the company for making operating decisions, which is made evident by the company's organization structure. As this approach focuses on information about the components of the business that management looks at in making its decisions about operating matters, the components are referred to as **operating segments**.

Identifying Operating Segments

An operating segment is a component of an enterprise that has all of the following characteristics:

1. It engages in business activities from which it earns revenues and incurs expenses.

2. Its operating results are regularly reviewed by the company's chief operating decision-maker to assess segment performance and allocate resources to the segment.

3. There is discrete financial information available on it.[4]

Information about two or more operating segments may only be aggregated if the segments have the same basic characteristics in all of the following areas:

1. The nature of the products and services provided

2. The nature of the production process

3. The type or class of customer

4. The methods of product or service distribution

5. If applicable, the nature of the regulatory environment

After the company decides on the segments for possible disclosure, a quantitative materiality test is made to determine whether the segment is significant enough to warrant actual disclosure. An operating segment is regarded as significant, and is therefore identified as a **reportable segment**, if it satisfies one or more of the following quantitative thresholds:[5]

1. Its revenue (including both sales to external customers and intersegment sales or transfers) is 10% or more of the combined revenue of all the enterprise's operating segments.

2. The absolute amount of its profit or loss is 10% or more of the greater, in absolute amount, of either

---

[2] *CICA Handbook*, Section 1701.02.

[3] *CICA Handbook*, Section 1701.03.

[4] *CICA Handbook*, Section 1701.10.

[5] *CICA Handbook*, Section 1701.19.

(a) the combined operating profit of all operating segments that did not incur a loss, or

(b) the combined loss of all operating segments that did report a loss.

3. Its assets are 10% or more of the combined assets of all operating segments.

In applying these tests, two additional factors must be considered. First, segment data must explain a significant portion of the company's business. Specifically, the segmented results must equal or exceed 75% of the combined sales to unaffiliated customers for the entire enterprise. This test prevents a company from providing limited information on only a few segments and lumping all the rest into one category.[6]

Second, as the profession recognizes that reporting too many segments may overwhelm users with detailed information, it has therefore proposed 10 segments as an upper limit benchmark for the number of segments that a company should be required to disclose.[7]

To illustrate these requirements, assume that a company has identified the six possible reporting segments shown in Illustration 23-3 (amounts in 000s).

Illustration 23-3

Data for Different Possible Reporting Segments

Segments	Total Revenue (Unaffiliated)	Operating Profit (Loss)	Assets
A	$100	$10	$60
B	50	2	30
C	700	40	390
D	300	20	160
E	900	18	280
F	100	(5)	50
	$2,150	$85	$970

The respective tests may be applied as follows:

Revenue test:
10% × $2,150 = $215; C, D, and E meet this test.

Operating profit (loss) test:
10% × $90 = $9 (note that the $5 loss is ignored);
A, C, D, and E meet this test.

Assets tests:
10% × $970 = $97; C, D, and E meet this test.

The reportable segments are therefore A, C, D, and E, assuming that these four segments have enough sales to meet the test of 75% of combined sales. The 75% test is calculated as follows:

75% of combined sales test: 75% × $2,150 = $1,612.50; the sales of A, C, D, and E total $2,000 ($100 + $700 + $300 + $900); therefore, the 75% test is met.

Measurement Principles

The accounting principles that an entity uses for segment disclosure do not need to be the same principles that are used to prepare the consolidated statements. This flexibility may

---

[6] *CICA Handbook*, Section 1701.22.
[7] *CICA Handbook*, Section 1701.27.

at first appear inconsistent. But preparing segment information in accordance with generally accepted accounting principles would be difficult because some principles are not expected to apply at a segment level. Examples include accounting for the cost of company-wide employee benefit plans and accounting for income taxes in a company that files one overall tax return.

Allocations of joint, common, or company-wide costs solely for external reporting purposes are not required. **Common costs** are defined as any costs that are incurred for the benefit of more than one segment and whose interrelated nature prevents a completely objective division of the costs among the segments. For example, the company president's salary is difficult to allocate to various segments. Allocations of common costs are inherently arbitrary and may not be meaningful if they are not used for internal management purposes. There is a presumption instead that allocations to segments are either directly attributable to the segment or reasonably allocable to it. There should be disclosure of the choices that were made in measuring segmented information.

Segmented and Enterprise-Wide Disclosures

CICA requires that an enterprise report the following:[8]

1. **General information** about its reportable segments. This includes factors that management considers most significant in determining the company's reportable segments, and the types of products and services from which each operating segment derives its revenues.

2. **Segment profit and loss, assets, and related information.** This states total profit or loss and total assets for each reportable segment. In addition, the following specific information about each reportable segment must be reported if the amounts are regularly reviewed by management:

    (a) Revenues from external customers

    (b) Revenues from transactions with other operating segments of the same enterprise

    (c) Interest revenue

    (d) Interest expense

    (e) Amortization of capital assets and goodwill

    (f) Unusual items

    (g) Equity in the net income of investees that are subject to significant influence

    (h) Income tax expense or benefit

    (i) Extraordinary items

    (j) Significant non-cash items other than amortization expense

    Note that the amount that is reported should be the amount reviewed by management (otherwise referred to as the chief operating decision-maker). Information about the basis of accounting and other details should be disclosed.

3. **Reconciliations.** An enterprise must provide a reconciliation of the total of the segments' revenues to total revenues; a reconciliation of the total of the operating segments' profits and losses to its income before income taxes, discontinued operations, and extraordinary items; and a reconciliation of the total of the operating segments' assets to total assets. Other reconciliations for other significant items that are disclosed should also be presented and all reconciling items should be separately identified and described for all of the above.

---

[8] *CICA Handbook*, Section 1701.28 to .43.

4. **Products and services.** The amount of revenues from external customers.

5. **Geographic areas.** Revenues from external customers (Canada versus foreign) and capital assets and goodwill (Canada versus foreign) should be stated. Foreign information must be disclosed by country if the amounts are material.

6. **Major customers.** If 10% or more of the revenues are derived from a single customer, the enterprise must disclose the total amount of revenues from each of these customers by segment.

Interim Reporting

One further source of information for the investor is interim reports. As noted earlier, **interim reports** cover periods of less than one year. While, at one time, annual reporting was considered sufficient in terms of providing timely information, demand quickly grew for quarterly information and now capital markets are moving rapidly to even more frequent disclosures. Illustration 23-4 presents the disclosure of selected quarterly data for Torstar. The company also disclosed a balance sheet, statement of comprehensive income, statement of changes in shareholders' equity, and statement of changes in cash flows (along with the related notes). The statements were accompanied by a management discussion of the operations, liquidity and capital resources, outlook, and recent developments. With such comprehensive coverage, the report gives a significant amount of information.

Illustration 23-4

Disclosure of Selected
Quarterly Data

Torstar Corporation
Consolidated Statements of Income
(Dollars in Thousands)
(Unaudited)

	Three months ended March 31	
	2007	2006
Operating revenue		
Newspapers and digital	**$252,986**	$238,764
Book publishing	**124,456**	118,349
	$377,442	$357,113
Operating profit		
Newspapers and digital	**$19,948**	$14,247
Book publishing	**19,123**	15,062
Corporate	**(4,686)**	(4,891)
Restructuring provisions (*note 10*)		(3,700)
	34,385	20,718
Interest	**(8,734)**	(2,819)
Foreign exchange	**(15)**	52
Income (loss) of associated businesses	**501**	(476)
Income before taxes	**26,137**	17,475
Income and other taxes	**(10,400)**	(7,700)
Net income	**$15,737**	$$9,775
Earnings per Class A and Class B share (*note 6 (b)*):		
Net income – Basic	**$0.20**	$0.13
Net income – Diluted	**$0.20**	$012

Because of the short-term nature of the information in these reports, however, there is considerable controversy about the general approach that should be taken. Supporters of the **discrete view** believe that each interim period should be treated as a separate accounting period. Deferrals and accruals would therefore follow the same principles that are used for annual reports. Accounting transactions should be reported as they occur, and expense recognition should not change with the period of time covered. Proponents of the **integral view**, on the other hand, believe that the interim report is an integral part of the annual report and that deferrals and accruals should take into consideration what will happen for the entire year. In this approach, estimated expenses are assigned to parts of a year based on the sales volume or some other activity base. **The current *CICA Handbook* section on interim reporting, Section 1751, favours the discrete view, with a few exceptions.**

One notable exception is in calculating tax expense. Normally a company would prepare its tax return at year end and assess taxes payable and related tax balances. It is neither cost effective nor feasible (since tax rates are often graduated and therefore increase with increasing taxable income) to do this for each interim period, so annual estimates are instead made. Specifically, an estimate is made of interim taxable income and temporary differences and then the annual estimated tax rate is applied. **Another exception relates to the employer's portion of payroll taxes.** Although these taxes may be remitted by the employer early in the year (as required by law), they are assessed by the government on an annual basis. Therefore, for interim reporting periods, the total estimated annual amount is allocated to the interim periods, which means that the expense is recognized on an accrual basis as opposed to a cash basis. **Exceptions for inventory are noted in the next section.**

Interim Reporting Requirements

As a general rule, the profession indicates that the same accounting principles that are used for annual reports should be used for interim reports. Revenues should be recognized in interim periods on the same basis as they are for annual periods. For example, if the instalment sales method is used as the basis for recognizing revenue on an annual basis, then the instalment basis should be applied to interim reports as well. Also, costs that are directly associated with revenues (product costs), such as materials, labour and related fringe benefits, and manufacturing overhead should be treated in the same manner for interim reports as for annual reports.

Companies should also generally use the same inventory cost formulas (FIFO, weighted average, etc.) for interim reports that they use for annual reports. However, the following exception is appropriate at interim reporting periods: planned variances under a standard cost system that are expected to be absorbed by year end should ordinarily be deferred.[9]

Costs and expenses other than product costs, often referred to as period costs, are often charged to the interim period as they are incurred. But they may also be allocated among interim periods based on an estimate of time expired, benefit received, or activity associated with the periods.

At a minimum, the balance sheet, income statement, statement of retained earnings, statement of cash flows, and notes are required.[10] The balance sheet should be presented as at the end of the current interim period with a comparative balance sheet as of the end of the immediately preceding fiscal year. The income statement should be presented for the current interim period and interim year to date with like comparatives (i.e., comparable information for the previous period or year). For the statement of retained earnings, the information should be presented cumulatively for the current fiscal year to date with comparatives. Finally, for the cash flow statements, information should be presented for the

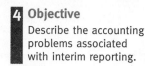

4 Objective
Describe the accounting problems associated with interim reporting.

International Insight

International GAAP requires that interim financial statements use the discrete method, except for tax charges.

Underlying Concept

For information to be relevant, it must be available to decision-makers before it loses its capacity to influence their decisions (timeliness). Interim reporting is an excellent example of this concept.

---

[9] *CICA Handbook*, Section 1751.26.

[10] *CICA Handbook*, Section 1751.16.

current interim period, and cumulatively for the current fiscal year to date with like comparatives.[11] Earnings per share (EPS) information is also required if an enterprise must present this information in its annual information.[12]

Regarding disclosure, the following interim data should be reported as a minimum:[13]

1. If the statements do not comply with GAAP for the annual statements, disclosure that this is the case; disclosure also that the statements should be read in conjunction with the annual statements

2. A statement that the company follows the same accounting policies and methods as the most recent annual financial statements, except for any new policy or method, any policies adopted to address the preparation of interim statements, or any special accounting methods adopted to address temporary costing fluctuations

3. A description of any seasonality or cyclicality of interim period operations

4. The nature and amount of changes in estimates

5. Information about reportable segments

6. Events subsequent to the interim period

7. Specific information about business combinations; plans to exit an activity, restructure, integrate, or reorganize; discontinued operations; and extraordinary items

8. Information about contingencies

9. Any other information that is required for fair presentation

Unique Problems of Interim Reporting

Changes in Accounting   What happens if a company decides to change an accounting principle in the third quarter of a fiscal year? Should the adjustment for the cumulative effect of the change be charged or credited to that quarter? Presentation of a cumulative effect in the third quarter may be misleading because of the inherent subjectivity that is associated with the reported income of the first two quarters. In addition, a question arises as to whether such a change might not be used to manipulate a particular quarter's income. These changes should therefore be reflected by retroactive application to prior interim periods unless the data are not available. The comparable interim periods of prior fiscal years should also be restated.[14]

Earnings Per Share   Interim reporting of earnings per share numbers has all the problems that are inherent in calculating and presenting annual earnings per share figures, and more. If shares are issued in the third period, EPS for the first two periods will not be indicative of year-end EPS. If an extraordinary item is present in one period and new equity shares are sold in another period, the EPS figure for the extraordinary item will change for the year. On an annual basis, only one EPS figure is associated with an extraordinary item and that figure does not change; the interim figure, however, is subject to change. For purposes of calculating earnings per share and making the required disclosure determinations, each interim period should stand alone. That is, all applicable tests should be made for that single period.[15]

---

[11] *CICA Handbook*, Section 1751.10 to .16.

[12] *CICA Handbook*, Section 1751.12.

[13] *CICA Handbook*, Section 1751.13 to .15.

[14] *CICA Handbook*, Section 1751.31.

[15] *CICA Handbook*, Section 1751. B35 and B36.

Seasonality   Seasonality occurs when sales are compressed into one short period of the year while certain costs are fairly evenly spread throughout the year. For example, the natural gas industry has its heavy sales in the winter, while the beverage industry has its heavy sales in the summer.

In a seasonal business, wide fluctuations in profits occur because off-season sales do not absorb the company's fixed costs (for example, manufacturing, selling, and administrative costs that tend to remain fairly constant regardless of sales or production). Revenues and expenses should be recognized and accrued when they are earned or incurred according to GAAP. This also holds for interim periods. Thus, a company would only defer recognition of costs or revenues if it would be appropriate to do so at year end (i.e., the same tests are applied). As mentioned earlier in the text, deferral of costs is not appropriate unless the costs meet the definition of an asst.

Continuing Controversy   The profession has developed the stringent standards noted above for interim reporting and this has alleviated much of the controversy that existed regarding the discrete and integral perspectives.

There is still controversy, however, in regard to the independent auditor's involvement in interim reports. Many auditors are reluctant to express an opinion on interim financial information, arguing that the data are too tentative and subjective. Conversely, an increasing number of individuals are arguing for some type of examination of interim reports. A compromise may be a limited review of interim reports that provides some assurance that an examination has been conducted by an outside party and that the published information appears to be in accord with generally accepted accounting principles.

Analysts want financial information as soon as possible, before it becomes old news. We may not be far from a continuous database system in which corporate financial records can be accessed by computer. Investors might be able to access a company's financial records via computer whenever they wish and put the information in the format they need. Thus, they could learn about sales slippage, cost increases, or earnings changes as they happen, rather than waiting until after the quarter has ended.[16]

A steady stream of information from the company to the investor could be very positive because it might alleviate management's continual concern with short-run interim numbers. It would also alleviate much of the allocation problems that plague current GAAP.

Internet Financial Reporting and Continuous Disclosures

How can companies improve the usefulness of their financial reporting practices? Many companies are using the Internet's power and reach to provide more useful information to financial statement readers. Recent surveys indicate that more than 80% of large companies have Internet sites, and a large proportion of these companies' websites contain links to their financial statements and other disclosures. The increased popularity of such reporting is not surprising, since the costs of printing and disseminating paper reports are reduced.

How does Internet financial reporting improve the overall usefulness of a company's financial reports? First, dissemination of reports via the Internet can allow firms to communicate with more users than is possible with traditional paper reports. In addition, Internet reporting allows users to take advantage of tools such as search engines and hyperlinks to quickly find information about the firm and, sometimes, to download the information for analysis, perhaps in computer spreadsheets. Finally, Internet reporting can

---

[16] A step in this direction is the OSC's mandate for companies to file their financial statements electronically through SEDAR (similar to the SEC requirement to use EDGAR in the United States). SEDAR provides interested parties with computer access to financial information such as periodic filings, corporate prospectuses, and proxy materials.

help make financial reports more relevant by allowing companies to report expanded disaggregated data and more timely data than is possible through paper-based reporting. For example, some companies voluntarily report weekly sales data and segment operating data on their websites.

Given these benefits and ever-improving Internet tools, will it be long before electronic reporting entirely replaces paper-based financial disclosure? The main obstacles to achieving complete electronic reporting are **equality of access to electronic financial reporting and the reliability of the information that is distributed** via the Internet. Although companies may practise Internet financial reporting, they must still prepare traditional paper reports because some investors may not have Internet access. These investors would receive differential (less) information relative to wired investors if companies were to eliminate paper reports. In addition, at present, Internet financial reporting is a voluntary means of reporting. As a result, there are no standards for the completeness of reports on the Internet, nor is there the requirement that these reports be audited. One concern in this regard is that computer hackers could invade a company's website and corrupt the financial information that is there.

A great example of the use of technology and continuous reporting is the current practice of releasing quarterly results via the company website through video and live streaming. Investors and analysts can visit the company website and hear the earnings announcements first-hand.

While Internet financial reporting is gaining in popularity, until issues related to differential access to the Internet and the reliability of web-based information are addressed, we will continue to see traditional paper-based reporting.

OTHER MEASUREMENT ISSUES

Related-Party Transactions

Related-party transactions present especially sensitive and difficult problems. The accountant or auditor who has responsibility for reporting on these types of transactions has to be extremely careful that the rights of the reporting company and the needs of financial statement users are properly balanced.

Objective 5
Discuss the accounting issues for related-party transactions.

Related-party transactions arise when a business engages in transactions in which one of the transacting parties has the ability to significantly influence the policies of the other, or in which a non-transacting party has the ability to influence the policies of the two transacting parties. Related parties include but are not limited to the following:

(a) Companies or individuals who control, or are controlled by, or are under common control with the reporting enterprise

(b) Investors and investees where there is significant influence or joint control

(c) Company management

(d) Members of immediate family of the above

(e) The other party when a management contract exists[17]

Transactions among related parties cannot be presumed to be carried out at arm's length since there may not be the required conditions of competitive, free-market dealings. Transactions such as borrowing or lending money at abnormally low or high interest rates, real estate sales at amounts that differ significantly from appraised values, exchanges

---

[17] *CICA Handbook*, Section 3840.04.

of non-monetary assets, and transactions involving enterprises that have no economic substance ("shell corporations") suggest that related parties may be involved. **In each case, there is a measurement issue.** A basic assumption about financial information is that it is based on transactions that are between arm's-length parties. **Consequently, if this condition is not met, the transactions should at least be disclosed as being between related parties. Furthermore, special measurement principles exist for related-party transactions and these may require a transaction to be remeasured.**

The accountant is expected to report the **economic substance rather than the legal form** of these transactions and to make adequate disclosures. The following disclosures are recommended:[18]

1. The nature of the relationship(s) involved

2. A description of the transactions

3. The recorded amounts of transactions

4. The measurement basis that was used

5. Amounts due from or to related parties and the related terms and conditions

6. Contractual obligations with related parties

7. Contingencies involving related parties

Certain related-party transactions must be remeasured to the carrying amount of the underlying assets or services that were exchanged. **Carrying amount** is defined as the amount of the item transferred as recorded in the books of the transferor. **This is the case if the transaction is not in the normal course of business, there is no substantive change in ownership, and/or the exchange amount is not supported by independent evidence.** The argument to support remeasurement rests on the premise that if the transaction is not an ordinary transaction for the enterprise, there might not be a reasonable measure of fair value. Furthermore, if there is no change in ownership, then no bargaining has taken place and, therefore, the price that is arrived at for the exchange may not represent a value that would have been arrived at had the transaction been at arm's length.

Transactions that are in the normal course of business that have no commercial substance must also be remeasured. This argument rests on the premise that, if the transaction is not bona fide or authentic, there is no real exchange of risks and rewards of ownership and, therefore, no gain or loss should be recognized. **This is only an issue where the transaction is also a non-monetary transaction.** A transaction has **commercial substance** when the entity's cash flows are expected to be significantly different after the transaction and as a result of the transaction. In making this determination, consider the risk, timing, and amount of cash flows.

Where transactions are remeasured to their carrying value, the difference between the carrying amounts of the items that have been exchanged is booked as a charge or credit to equity.[19] To illustrate, assume that Hudson Limited, a manufacturing company, sells land worth $20,000 to Bay Limited. The companies are related because the same shareholder has a 90% equity interest in each company (the rest of the shares are publicly traded). The land has a carrying value of $15,000 on Hudson's books. In exchange, Bay Limited, also a manufacturing company, transfers to Hudson a building that has a net book value of $12,000. This transaction is not in the **ordinary (normal) course of business** since both companies are manufacturers and would not normally be selling capital

---

[18] *CICA Handbook*, Section 3840.46.

[19] *CICA Handbook*, Section 3840.09.

assets such as land and buildings. Based on this assessment, therefore, the transaction merits further analysis.

Illustration 23-5 is a decision tree[20] of the judgement that is necessary when determining how to treat related-party transactions.

Illustration 23-5

Related-Party Transactions— Decision Tree

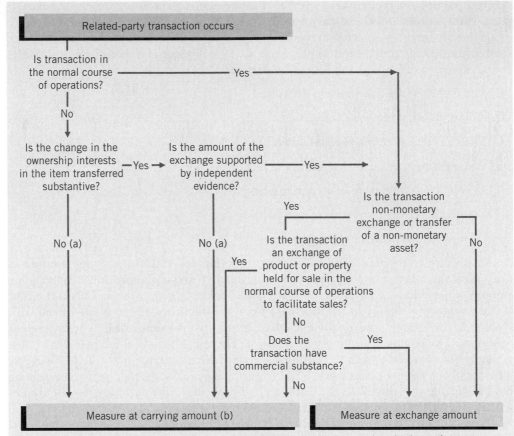

(a) Carrying amount is used for both monetary and non-monetary transactions in these circumstances.
(b) In rare circumstances, when the carrying amount of the item received is not available, a reasonable estimate of the carrying amount, based on the transferor's original cost, may be used to measure the exchange.

Looking at the decision tree, the next question is **whether there has been a substantive change in ownership**. Do different parties own the exchanged items after the transaction? Since the same controlling shareholder owns both assets before and after the transaction (even if indirectly through the companies), there is no substantive change in ownership.[21] The transaction would therefore be remeasured to carrying values with the following journal entry on the Hudson books:

---

[20] *CICA Handbook*, Section 3840 DT.

[21] As a benchmark, a substantive change in ownership may be deemed to have occurred if an unrelated party has gained or given up more than a 20% interest in the exchanged items (*CICA Handbook*, Section 3840.35). In the example above, if the controlling shareholder only owned, say, 70% of both companies and the shares were publicly traded, then one might argue substantive change in ownership may be evident—i.e., the other 30% of the shareholders now own (indirectly, through their shareholdings) part of the asset where they did not before the transaction. This is not so clear cut, however, since the majority shareholders still have controlling interest, and no real bargaining would have happened between the minority shareholders and the majority shareholders. The resolution of this issue would be a matter of judgement. EIC Abstract 103 deals with this issue in further detail.

Property, Plant, and Equipment	12,000		A	= L	+	SE
Retained Earnings	3,000		−3,000			−3,000
Land		15,000	Cash flows: No effect			

Bay would record the land at $15,000 and take the building off its books. The resulting credit would be booked to Contributed Surplus. Note that the difference between the carrying values is generally viewed as an equity contribution or distribution and is therefore booked through equity.

If on the other hand, the transaction had been in the normal course of business, and the transaction had commercial substance, it would have been recorded at the exchange value. The exchange value is defined as the amount of consideration paid or received and agreed to by the related parties.[22] In this case, assume that the agreed exchange value is $20,000. Note that the exchange value is not necessarily equal to the fair value but it could be. It is whatever value the two parties agree on. The *CICA Handbook* notes that it is possible that the transaction value may approximate fair value but it is not necessary to establish what fair value would be if the transaction value is not an approximation. If cash were exchanged, this would determine the exchange value.

In this case, the transaction would be treated like a sale for both parties and Hudson would recognize a gain of $5,000 ($20,000 − 15,000). Likewise, Bay would also recognize a gain of $8,000 ($20,000 − 12,000).

Differential Reporting

The increasing amount and complexity of disclosures and measurement in financial reporting carries a significant cost. For companies whose financial instruments are publicly traded, the benefits of this additional information presumably exceed these costs since users of the financial statements need this information for decision-making. For private companies, however, where the owners of the company have greater access to information about the company, is the cost justified?

CICA has dealt with this issue by creating some relief for **non-publicly accountable enterprises**; that is, those that do not have financial instruments that are traded in a public market.[23] Where the owners of these companies unanimously consent to the application of different accounting principles, **differential reporting** applies.

Differential reporting relates to the following financial reporting areas:

1. Subsidiaries: Management may elect to use the cost or equity methods for accounting for subsidiaries that would otherwise be consolidated. (This is beyond the scope of this text.)

2. Long-term investments: Management may elect to use the cost method rather than the equity method for investments where significant influence exists.

3. Interests in joint ventures: Management may elect to use the cost or equity methods to account for joint ventures that would otherwise be consolidated using the proportionate consolidation method. (This is beyond the scope of this text.)

---

[22] *CICA Handbook*, Section 3840.03.

[23] *CICA Handbook* Section 1300.02 defines this more broadly to include any enterprises other than public enterprises, co-operative business enterprises, regulated financial institutions (and related holding companies), rate regulated enterprises, government business enterprises, and government business-type enterprises.

4. Goodwill and other intangible assets: Rather than test goodwill annually, management may elect to only test goodwill for impairment when an event occurs that might signal potential impairment.

5. Share capital: Management may elect to provide fewer details in terms of disclosures.

6. Income taxes: Management may elect to use the taxes payable method to account for taxes.

7. Financial instruments: Management may elect to treat certain preferred shares as equity rather than debt, and report reduced disclosures. Management may also elect to measure at cost or amortized cost certain financial assets that are available for sale.

Subsequent Events

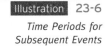

Objective 6

Identify the difference between the two types of subsequent events.

Events that take place after the formal balance sheet date but before the financial statements are approved for release must be considered. These events are referred to as **subsequent events** since they occur subsequent to the balance sheet date. The subsequent events period is time-diagrammed in Illustration 23-6.

Illustration 23-6

Time Periods for Subsequent Events

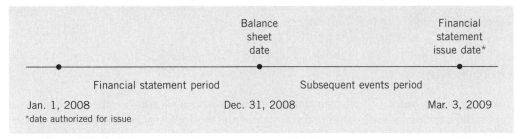

A period of several weeks, and sometimes months, may lapse after the end of the year before the financial statement completion date. Taking and pricing the inventory, reconciling subsidiary ledgers with controlling accounts, preparing necessary adjusting entries, assuring that all transactions for the period have been entered, obtaining an audit of the financial statements by independent public accountants, and printing the annual report all take time. **During the period between the balance sheet date and distribution of the financials to shareholders and creditors, important transactions or other events may occur that materially affect the company's financial position or operating situation.**

Many readers of a recent balance sheet believe that the balance sheet condition is constant and they therefore project it into the future. Readers therefore need to be made aware if the company has sold one of its plants, acquired a subsidiary, suffered extraordinary losses, settled significant litigation, or experienced any other important event in the post-balance sheet period. Without an explanation in a note, the reader might be misled and draw inappropriate conclusions.

Two types of events or transactions that occur after the balance sheet date may have a material effect on the financial statements or may need to be considered to interpret these statements accurately:

1. **Events that provide additional evidence about conditions that existed at the balance sheet date, affect the estimates used in preparing financial statements, and, therefore, result in needed adjustments.** All information that is available prior to the issuance of the financial statements is used to evaluate previously made estimates. To ignore these subsequent events is to skip an opportunity to improve the financial statements' accuracy. This first type of event encompasses information that would have been recorded in the accounts if it had been known at the balance sheet

date. For example, if a loss on an account receivable results from a customer's bankruptcy subsequent to the balance sheet date, the financial statements are adjusted before their issuance. The bankruptcy stems from the customer's poor financial health that existed at the balance sheet date.

The same criterion applies to settlements of litigation. The financial statements must be adjusted if the events that gave rise to the litigation, such as personal injury or patent infringement, took place prior to the balance sheet date. If the event giving rise to the claim took place subsequent to the balance sheet date, no adjustment is necessary, but the event must still be disclosed. Thus, a loss resulting from a customer's fire or flood after the balance sheet date is not indicative of conditions that existed at that date. Accordingly, adjustment of the financial statements is not necessary.

2. **Events that provide evidence about conditions that did not exist at the balance sheet date but arise subsequent to that date and do not require adjustment of the financial statements.** Some of these events may have to be disclosed to keep the financial statements from being misleading. These disclosures take the form of notes, supplemental schedules, or even pro forma "as if" financial data prepared as if the event had occurred on the balance sheet date. The following are examples[24] of such events that require disclosure (but do not result in adjustment):

(a) Events such as a fire or flood that results in a loss

(b) A decline in the market value of investments

(c) A purchase of a business

(d) A commencement of litigation where the cause of action arose subsequent to the balance sheet date

(e) Changes in foreign currency rates

(f) An issuance of shares or debt

Underlying Concept

The periodicity or time period assumption implies that an enterprise's economic activities can be divided into artificial time periods for purposes of analysis.

Illustration 23-7 presents an example of subsequent events disclosure from the 2005 annual report of **ClubLink**.

---

20. Subsequent Events

On February 7, 2006, ClubLink Corporation completed a $65,000,000 mortgage with Pacific Life Insurance Company. The facility bears interest at 6.194%, is fully amortizing over its 20 year term and is secured by the assets of three of ClubLink's unencumbered golf clubs. ClubLink will use the proceeds to redeem on March 14, 2006, an aggregate principal amount of $65,000,000 of the outstanding 6% convertible unsecured subordinated debentures due May 15, 2008.

Many subsequent events or developments are not likely to require either adjustment of the financial statements or disclosure. Typically, these are non-accounting events or conditions that management normally communicates by other means. These events include legislation, product changes, management changes, strikes, unionization, marketing agreements, and loss of important customers. What to include in the financial statements is a matter of professional judgement since all changes to the business will eventually affect performance one way or another.

Sometimes subsequent events are so pervasive—such as a rapid deterioration of the entity's financial health—that they call into question the going concern assumption.[25] Recall from earlier chapters that the going concern assumption presumes that an entity will continue to operate and will be able to realize its assets and discharge its liabilities in

---

[24] *CICA Handbook*, Section 3820.09.

[25] *CICA Handbook*, Section 3820.04.

an orderly manner. This supports the use of the mixed fair value/historical cost measurement model. If the subsequent event calls the going concern assumption into question, the measurement model would perhaps change. The company would have to make a decision as to whether it should include additional note disclosures or whether the assets and liabilities should be remeasured to reflect net realizable values in a liquidation market.

Illustration 23-8 presents an excerpt from **Stem Cell Sciences PLC** (which lists on the London Stock Exchange). This note illustrates the concept of going concern. In this case the company is short on cash and may not be able to continue to operate. It has chosen to take the first step and disclose the problem only. As noted, it has not yet taken the next step, which would be to revalue the assets and liabilities.

Illustration 23-8

Potential Going Concern Issues—Stem Cell Sciences PLC

The Group's current cash resources are forecast by the directors as being sufficient to enable it to continue to trade until August 2007. The Group is proposing a flotation on the Australian Stock Exchange to raise up to AUS$10 million which will be used to fund the start up costs of its manufacturing facility, develop its presence in the US and begin pre-trials into neural and other cell therapies in addition to supporting its ongoing research and development activities. The proposed flotation, which has received the approval of shareholders of the company in a general meeting, is at an advanced stage and has been announced publicly. Costs of £230,000 are held in prepayments in relation to work carried out by professional advisers in relation to the flotation to the extent that these are costs which will be treated as issue costs in relation to the new shares to be issued on the proposed flotation.

While there can be no certainty either that the proposed flotation will be successful or that it will raise the required funds, the Directors are of the opinion that, taking into account existing facilities available to the Group and the expected proceeds from the Australian flotation, the funds available to the Group will be sufficient for the Group's trading requirements for at least twelve months from the date of these financial statements.

However, as noted there can be no certainty in relation to these matters, which may cast significant doubt on the Group's ability to continue as a going concern. The Group may, therefore, be unable to continue realising its assets and is charging its liabilities in the normal course of business but the financial statements do not include any adjustments that would result from either its planned flotation not taking place or raising insufficient funds.

Reporting on Financial Forecasts and Projections

In recent years, the investing public's demand for more and better information has focused on disclosure of corporate expectations for the future.[26] These disclosures take one of two forms, as explained next.[27]

Financial Forecast

A financial forecast consists of prospective financial statements that present, to the best of the responsible party's knowledge and belief, an entity's expected financial position, results of operations, and cash flows. A **financial forecast** is based on the responsible party's assumptions about conditions that it expects to exist and the course of action it expects to take.

Financial Projection

Objective 7
Identify issues related to financial forecasts and projections.

A financial projection consists of prospective financial statements that present—to the best of the responsible party's knowledge and belief, given one or more hypothetical assumptions—an entity's expected financial position, results of operations, and cash flows. A

---

[26] Some areas in which companies are using financial information about the future are equipment lease-versus-buy analysis, analysis of a company's ability to successfully enter new markets, and an examination of merger and acquisition opportunities. In addition, forecasts and projections are also prepared for use by third parties in public-offering documents (which require financial forecasts), tax-oriented investments, and financial feasibility studies. Use of forward-looking data has been enhanced by the increased capability of computers to analyze, compare, and manipulate large quantities of data.

[27] *CICA Handbook*, Section 4250.03 to .05.

financial projection is based on the responsible party's assumptions about conditions that it expects would exist and the course of action it expects would be taken, if one or more hypothetical assumptions occurred.

The difference between a financial forecast and a financial projection is that a forecast attempts to provide information on what is expected to happen, whereas a projection provides information on what is not necessarily expected to happen, but might.

Financial forecasts are the subject of intensive discussion among journalists, corporate executives, securities commissions, financial analysts, accountants, and others. Predictably, there are strong arguments on either side. Listed below are some of the arguments.

Arguments for requiring published forecasts:

1. Investment decisions are based on future expectations; therefore, information about the future facilitates better decisions.

2. Forecasts are already circulated informally, but are uncontrolled, frequently misleading, and not available equally to all investors. This confused situation should be brought under control.

3. Circumstances now change so rapidly that historical information is no longer adequate for prediction.

Arguments against requiring published forecasts:

1. No one can foretell the future. Therefore, forecasts, while conveying an impression of precision about the future, will inevitably be wrong.

2. Organizations will strive only to meet their published forecasts, not to produce results that are in the shareholders' best interest.

3. When forecasts are not proved to be accurate, there will be recriminations and probably legal actions.[28]

4. Disclosure of forecasts will be detrimental to organizations because it will fully inform, not only investors, but also competitors (foreign and domestic).

CICA has issued a statement on standards for accountants' services on prospective financial information. This statement establishes procedures and reporting standards for presenting financial forecasts and projections.[29] It requires all of the following:

1. The use of appropriate assumptions

2. That the time period not extend beyond the point in time for which such information can be reasonably estimated

3. That the information be presented in accordance with the accounting policies that are expected to be used in the historical financial statements

4. That the statements include at least an income statement

5. That there be a cautionary note attached

6. That the information be clearly labelled as being a forecast or projection

7. Various other disclosures, including, among others, assumptions, accounting policies, and the extent to which actual results versus estimated results are incorporated.

---

[28] This issue is serious. Over a recent three-year period, 8% of the companies on the NYSE were sued because of an alleged lack of financial disclosure. Companies complain that they are subject to lawsuits whenever the stock price drops. As one executive noted, you can even be sued if the stock price goes up because you did not disclose the good news fast enough. Nortel Networks was the subject of numerous lawsuits alleging that it misled investors and shareholders.

[29] *CICA Handbook*, Section 4250.

To encourage management to disclose this type of information, securities law has a **safe harbour rule**. This rule gives protection to an enterprise that presents an inaccurate forecast as long as the forecast is prepared on a reasonable basis and is disclosed in good faith. However, many companies note that the safe harbour rule does not actually work in practice, since it does not cover oral statements and it has not kept them out of court.

The United States has permitted financial forecasts for years, and the results have been fairly successful. There are some significant differences between the British and North American business and legal environments, but these could probably be overcome if influential interests in Canada cooperated to produce an atmosphere that supports quality forecasting. Illustration 23-9 shows a typical British forecast that has been adapted from a construction company's report to support a public offering of shares.

Illustration 23-9

Financial Forecast of a British Company

Profits have grown substantially over the past 10 years and directors are confident of being able to continue this expansion... While the rate of expansion will be dependent on the level of economic activity in Ireland and England, the group is well structured to avail itself of opportunities as they arise, particularly in the field of property development, which is expected to play an increasingly important role in the group's future expansion.

Profits before taxation for the half year ended 30th June 2008 were £402,000. On the basis of trading experiences since that date and the present level of sales and completions, the directors expect that in the absence of unforeseen circumstances, the group's profits before taxation for the year to 31st December 2008 will be not less than £960,000.

No dividends will be paid in respect of the year December 31, 2008. In a full financial year, on the basis of above forecasts (not including full year profits) it would be the intention of the board, assuming current rates of tax, to recommend dividends totalling 40% (of after-tax profits), of which 15% payable would be as an interest dividend in November 2009 and 25% as a final dividend in June 2010.

Questions of Liability

What happens if a company does not meet its forecasts? Are the company and the auditor going to be sued? If a company, for example, projects an earnings increase of 15% and achieves only 5%, should the shareholder be allowed to sue the company? One court case involving **Monsanto Chemical Corporation** has provided some guidelines. In this case, Monsanto predicted that sales would increase by 8% to 9% and that earnings would rise by 4% to 5%. In the last part of the year, however, the demand for Monsanto's products dropped as a result of a business turndown, and instead of increasing, the company's earnings declined. The company was sued because the projected earnings figure was erroneous, but the judge dismissed the suit, ruling that the forecasts were the best estimates of qualified people whose intents were honest.

Safe harbour rules are intended to protect enterprises that provide good-faith projections. However, much concern exists as to how securities commissions and the courts will interpret such terms as "good faith" and "reasonable assumptions" when inaccurate forecasts mislead users of this information.

AUDITOR'S REPORTS

Objective 8
Identify the major disclosures found in the auditor's report.

Another important source of information that is often overlooked is the **auditor's report**. An auditor is an accounting professional who conducts an independent examination of the accounting data presented by a business enterprise. If the auditor is satisfied that the financial statements present the financial position, results of operations, and cash flows fairly in accordance with generally accepted accounting principles, an unqualified opinion is expressed, as shown in Illustration 23-10.

Illustration 23-10

Example of Auditors' Report for ClubLink Corporation

AUDITORS' REPORT TO THE SHAREHOLDERS OF CLUBLINK CORPORATION

We have audited the consolidated balance sheets of ClubLink Corporation as at December 31, 2005 and 2004 and the consolidated statements of operations and retained earnings and cash flows for the years then ended. These financial statements are the responsibility of the company's management. Our responsibility is to express an opinion on these financial statements based on our audits.

We conducted our audits in accordance with Canadian generally accepted auditing standards. Those standards require that we plan and perform an audit to obtain reasonable assurance whether the financial statements are free of material misstatement. An audit includes examining, on a test basis, evidence supporting the amounts and disclosures in the financial statements. An audit also includes assessing the accounting principles used and significant estimates made by management, as well as evaluating the overall financial statement presentation.

In our opinion, these consolidated financial statements present fairly, in all material respects, the financial position of the company as at December 31, 2005 and 2004 and the results of its operations and its cash flows for the years then ended in accordance with Canadian generally accepted accounting principles.

Ernst & Young LLP
Chartered Accountants

Toronto, Ontario
February 28, 2006

In preparing a report, an auditor follows these reporting standards in accordance with the reporting standard articulated in the *CICA Handbook* under section 5100.02:

1. The report should identify the financial statements (i.e., the name of the company and the reporting period) and distinguish between the responsibilities of management and the responsibilities of the auditor.

2. The report should describe the scope of the auditor's examination (i.e., what the auditor did).

3. The report should contain either an expression of opinion on the financial statements or an assertion that an opinion cannot be expressed (in which case a reason should be given).

4. Where an opinion is given, it should state whether the financial statements present fairly, in all material respects, the financial position, results of operations, and cash flows in accordance with Canadian GAAP.[30] If there is a reservation, the report should explain it.

Unqualified Opinions

In most cases, the auditor issues a standard **unqualified** or **clean opinion**; that is, the auditor expresses the opinion that the financial statements present fairly, in all material respects, the entity's financial position, results of operations, and cash flows in conformity with generally accepted accounting principles. Certain circumstances, although they do not affect the auditor's unqualified opinion, may require the auditor to add an explanatory paragraph to the audit report.

Qualified Opinions

In some situations, however, the auditor is required to express a qualified opinion. A **qualified opinion** contains an exception to the standard opinion. Ordinarily the exception is

---

[30] As noted earlier, the OSC allows Canadian companies that file in the U.S. to file their statements using U.S. GAAP, even in Canada. In such cases, the audit report would make reference to U.S. GAAP.

not significant enough to invalidate the statements as a whole; if it were, an adverse opinion would be rendered. The usual circumstances in which the auditor may deviate from the standard unqualified short-form report on financial statements are when there is a departure from GAAP.

A qualified opinion states that, except for the effects of the matter related to the qualification, the financial statements present fairly, in all material respects, the financial position, results of operations, and cash flows in conformity with generally accepted accounting principles.

A qualified opinion might also be given where there is a scope limitation; that is, where the auditor has not been able to obtain sufficient and appropriate audit evidence, which might happen for instance if there has been an inadvertent destruction by fire of company records. In this case, there would be a denial of opinion that would note that the auditor is unable to give an opinion.

Adverse Opinions

An **adverse opinion** is required in any report in which the exceptions to fair presentation are so material that in the independent auditor's judgement a qualified opinion is not justified. In such a case, the financial statements taken as a whole are not presented in accordance with generally accepted accounting principles. Adverse opinions are rare, because most enterprises change their accounting to conform to the auditor's desires.

UNINCORPORATED BUSINESSES

Throughout this text, the primary emphasis has been on incorporated businesses. Partnerships are another significant business form. These businesses are unincorporated and thus do not have share capital. This form of business has in the past decade become very popular as a tax shelter in the form of income trusts or investment trusts. Interestingly enough, while ownership of partnerships is generally private, ownership of income and investment trusts is often public. The partnership or trust units trade on various stock exchanges.

The accounting issues related to these types of entities are generally similar to those of incorporated companies, with a few exceptions:

1. It is critical to define the economic entity since unincorporated businesses are not separate legal entities. The financial statements should indicate clearly the name under which the business is conducted and it should be clear that the business is unincorporated and that the statements do not include the assets and liabilities of the owners.[31]

2. Salaries, interest, or similar items accruing to owners should be clearly indicated.[32]

3. No provision for income taxes should be made. Since the businesses are not separate legal entities, the income is taxed in the hands of the unitholders.[33]

Note that the owners' equity section would also include different terminology—e.g., owners' equity versus share capital, and withdrawals versus dividends.

---

[31] *CICA Handbook*, Section 1800.04 and .05.

[32] *CICA Handbook*, Section 1800.07.

[33] *CICA Handbook*, Section 1800.10.

PERSPECTIVES

Throughout this textbook, we have stressed the need to provide information that is useful to predict the amounts, timing, and uncertainty of future cash flows. To achieve this objective, judicious choices of alternative accounting concepts, methods, and means of disclosure must be made. You are probably surprised by the large number of choices among acceptable alternatives that accountants are required to make.

You should be aware, however, as Chapter 1 indicated, that accounting is greatly influenced by its environment. Because it does not exist in a vacuum, it seems unrealistic to assume that alternative presentations of certain transactions and events will be eliminated entirely. Nevertheless, we are hopeful that through developing a conceptual framework the profession will be able to focus on the needs of financial statement users and eliminate diversity where appropriate. The profession must continue its efforts to develop a sound foundation upon which financial standards and practice can be built. As Aristotle said, "The correct beginning is more than half the whole."

> **9 Objective**
> Compare current Canadian and international GAAP, and understand which direction international GAAP is headed.

International

Illustration 23-11[34] compares Canadian GAAP with the international standards on complex financial instruments. It also provides additional information to the information included in the comparison illustrations in Chapters 14 and 15.

> **Illustration 23-11**
> *Comparison of Canadian and International GAAP/GAAS*

Canada	International	
Section 1300: Differential Reporting	None	
Section 1505: Disclosure of Accounting Policies	IAS 1:	Presentation of Financial Statements
Section 1701: Segment Disclosures	IFRS 8:	Operating Segments
Section 1751: Interim Financial Statements	IAS 34:	Interim Financial Reporting
Section 1800: Unincorporated Businesses	None	
Section 3820: Subsequent Events	IAS 10:	Events after the Balance Sheet Date
Section 3840: Related Party Transactions	IAS 24:	Related Party Transactions
Section 5100: Generally Accepted Auditing Standards	CAS 200:	Overall Objective of the Independent Auditor, and the Conduct of an Audit in Accordance with Canadian Auditing Standards

Much of the above is converged except for the following:

Differential reporting: The IASB has issued an Exposure Draft on small and mid-sized firms. The Canadian AcSB has also issued an Exposure Draft relating to private enterprise GAAP, which proposes three alternatives:

1. Adopt the IFRS standard on small and mid-sized entities—possibly with some modification.

2. Adopt IFRS for public enterprises but provide for differences in a number of topics (much like our current differential reporting model).

3. Use an independently developed set of standards.

Disclosure of Accounting Policies: IAS 1 requires disclosure of judgements made in the process of applying accounting policies.

---

[34] Much of the illustration's content is taken from CICA's "Comparison of Canadian GAAP and IFRSs" as updated to March 31, 2007.

Segment Disclosures: IFRS 8 only applies to listed companies and those in the process of filing or listing (i.e., on an exchange or market). In addition, IFRS 8 requires disclose or segment liabilities.

Interim Financial Statements: IAS 34 allows preparing a condensed set of statements, does not require presentation of a cash flow statement for the current interim period, precludes deferral of manufacturing cost variances that are expected to be absorbed by year end, and treats the initial recognition of previously unrecognized income tax assets as an adjustment to the estimated average annual effective income tax rate rather than as a separate item.

Subsequent Events: IAS 10 requires reporting of subsequent events to the date of authorization for issue of the statements and requires disclosure of the date of authorization for issue and who gave the authorization.

Related-Party Transactions: IAS 24 does not contain requirements for measuring related-party transactions nor give any guidance on related gains/losses. It also does not exclude the following from its scope: management compensation arrangements, expense allowances, and similar payments to individuals in the normal course of operations.

Auditing Standards: There is a significant, large project to converge Canadian generally accepted auditing standards (GAAS) with those of the International Auditing and Assurance Standards Board. The new GAAS will likely be in place in 2009. Much of the body of knowledge will be similar—but reorganized and renumbered.

Student Website

Glossary

www.wiley.com/canada/kieso

KEY TERMS

accounting errors, 1476

accounting policies, 1476

adverse opinion, 1496

auditor's report, 1494

clean opinion, 1495

commercial substance, 1487

common costs, 1481

differential reporting, 1489

disaggregated financial information, 1477

discrete view, 1483

financial forecast, 1492

financial projection, 1493

full disclosure principle, 1475

illegal acts, 1477

integral view, 1483

interim reports, 1482

Summary of Learning Objectives

1 Review the full disclosure principle and describe problems of implementation.

The full disclosure principle calls for financial reporting of any financial facts that are significant enough to influence the judgement of an informed reader. Implementing the full disclosure principle is difficult because the cost of disclosure can be substantial and the benefits difficult to assess. Disclosure requirements have increased because of (1) the growing complexity of the business environment, (2) the necessity for timely information, and (3) the use of accounting as a control and monitoring device.

2 Explain the use of accounting policy notes in financial statement preparation.

Notes are the accountant's means of amplifying or explaining the items presented in the main body of the statements. Information that is pertinent to specific financial statement items can be explained in qualitative terms, and supplementary quantitative data can be provided to expand the information in the financial statements. Accounting policy notes explain the accounting methods and policies chosen by the company, thus allowing greater comparability between companies.

3 Describe the disclosure requirements for major segments of a business.

If only the consolidated figures are available to the analyst, much information regarding the composition of these figures is hidden in aggregated figures. There is no way to tell from the consolidated data how much each product line contributes to the company's profitability, risk, and growth potential. As a result, segment information is required by the profession in certain situations.

4 Describe the accounting problems associated with interim reporting.

Interim reports cover periods of less than one year. There are two viewpoints regarding interim reports. The discrete view holds that each interim period should be treated as a separate accounting period. In contrast, the integral view holds that the interim report is an integral part of the annual report and that deferrals and accruals should take into consideration what will happen for the entire year. GAAP encourages the discrete view approach with a few exceptions. The same accounting principles that are used for annual reports should generally be employed for interim reports; however, there are several unique reporting problems.

5 **Discuss the accounting issues for related-party transactions.**

Related-party transactions pose special accounting issues. Since the transactions are not arm's length, they may have to be remeasured as the exchange value is not necessarily representative of the market or fair value. In the absence of reliable information, the transaction may have to be remeasured to reflect historical values or costs.

6 **Identify the difference between the two types of subsequent events.**

Type 1 events provide additional evidence about an event that existed at the balance sheet date. These events should be reflected in the balance sheet and income statement. Type 2 events provide evidence about events or transactions that did not exist at the balance sheet date. These should be disclosed in notes if they will have a material impact on the future of the company.

7 **Identify issues related to financial forecasts and projections.**

There is a concern that companies will be sued if the forecasts are not met. To encourage management to disclose this type of information, securities commissions have issued "safe harbour" rules. The safe harbour rule generally provides protection to an enterprise that presents an inaccurate forecast as long as the projection was prepared on a reasonable basis and was disclosed in good faith. However, the safe harbour rule has not worked well in practice.

8 **Identify the major disclosures found in the auditor's report.**

If the auditor is satisfied that the financial statements present the financial position, results of operations, and cash flows fairly in accordance with generally accepted accounting principles, an unqualified opinion is expressed. A qualified opinion contains an exception to the standard opinion; ordinarily the exception is not significant enough to invalidate the statements as a whole. An adverse opinion is required in any report in which the exceptions to fair presentation are so material that a qualified opinion is not justified. A disclaimer of an opinion is appropriate when the auditor has gathered so little information on the financial statements that no opinion can be expressed.

9 **Compare current Canadian and international GAAP, and understand which direction international GAAP is headed.**

These standards are largely converged, with the differences noted in the chapter. The major differences at the time of writing this text related to auditing standards and GAAP for private enterprises.

management approach, 1479
non-publicly accountable enterprises, 1489
operating segments, 1479
qualified opinion, 1479
related-party transactions, 1486
reportable segment, 1479
safe harbour rule, 1494
segmented financial information, 1477
subsequent events, 1490
unqualified opinion, 1495

Brief Exercises

(LO 1)   **BE23-1**   An annual report of D. Robillard Industries states: "The company and its subsidiaries have long-term leases expiring on various dates after December 31, 2007. Amounts payable under such commitments, without reduction for related rental income, are expected to average approximately $5,711,000 annually for the next three years. Related rental income from certain subleases to others is estimated to average $3,094,000 annually for the next three years." What information is provided by this note?

(LO 1)   **BE23-2**   An annual report of Ford Motor Company states: "Net income a share is computed based upon the average number of shares of capital stock of all classes outstanding. Additional shares of common stock may be issued or delivered in the future on conversion of outstanding convertible debentures, exercise of outstanding employee stock options, and for payment of defined supplemental compensation. Had such additional shares been outstanding, net income a share would have been reduced by 10¢ in the current year and 3¢ in the previous year.

"As a result of capital stock transactions by the company during the current year (primarily the purchase of Class A Stock from Ford Foundation), net income a share was increased by 6¢." What information is provided by this note?

(LO 1)   **BE23-3**   What type of disclosure or accounting is necessary for each of the following items?

(a) Because of a general increase in the number of labour disputes and strikes, both within and outside the industry, there is more chance that a company will suffer a costly strike in the near future.

(b) A company reports an extraordinary item (net of tax) correctly on the income statement. No other mention is made of this item in the annual report.

(c) A company expects to recover a substantial amount in connection with a pending refund claim for a prior year's taxes. Although the claim is being contested, the company's lawyers have confirmed that they expect their client to recover the taxes.

(LO 3)   **BE23-4**   Bess Marvin, a student of Intermediate Accounting, was heard to remark after a class discussion on segmented reporting: "All this is very confusing to me. First we are told that there is merit in presenting the consolidated results and now we are told that it is better to show segmented results. I wish they would make up their minds." Evaluate this comment.

(LO 3)   **BE23-5**   Psuikoden Corporation has seven industry segments with total revenues as follows:

	(thousands)		(thousands)
Genso	$600	Sergei	$225
Konami	650	Takuhi	200
RPG	250	Nippon	700
Red Moon	375		

Based only on the revenues test, which industry segments are reportable?

(LO 3)   **BE23-6**   Operating profits and losses for the seven industry segments of Psuikoden Corporation are as follows:

	(thousands)		(thousands)
Genso	$ 90	Sergei	$(20)
Konami	(40)	Takuhi	34
RPG	25	Nippon	100
Red Moon	50		

Based only on the operating profit (loss) test, which industry segments are reportable?

(LO 3)   **BE23-7**   Assets for the seven industry segments of Psuikoden Corporation are as follows:

	(thousands)		(thousands)
Genso	$500	Sergei	$200
Konami	550	Takuhi	150
RPG	400	Nippon	475
Red Moon	400		

Based only on the assets test, which industry segments are reportable?

BE23-8   What are the accounting problems related to the presentation of interim data?   **(LO 4)**

BE23-9   How does seasonality affect interim reporting and how should companies overcome the seasonality problem?   **(LO 4)**

BE23-10   Minos Limited purchases land from its president for $440,000. The land was purchased by the president 20   **(LO 5)** years ago for $50,000. Prepare the journal entry to record the purchase of the land. Use the decision tree in Illustration 23-5 to explain the basis for your answer. What information should be disclosed for this transaction?

BE23-11   Textile manufacturer Peloso Corp. exchanges computer software having a book value of $11,000 with the real   **(LO 5)** estate company Francis Corp. The software that is received in exchange from Francis Corp. has a book value of $15,100, performs different functions, and has a fair value of $20,800. Both companies are 100% owned by the same individual. Discuss how this transaction should be measured and prepare the journal entries for both companies to record the exchange. Use the decision tree in Illustration 23-5 to explain the reasoning for your answer.

BE23-12   How would the transaction in BE23-11 be recorded if the transaction were arm's length?   **(LO 5)**

BE23-13   How would the transaction in BE23-11 be recorded if the individual shareholder only owned 40% of the   **(LO 5)** shares of each company? Assume that there is independent evidence to support the value of the computer software. Discuss and prepare journal entries. Use the decision tree in Illustration 23-5 to explain the reasoning for your answer.

BE23-14   The following information was described in a note of Cedar Packing Co.:   **(LO 5)**

"During August, A. Belew Products Corporation purchased 311,003 shares of the Company's common shares, which constitutes approximately 35% of the shares outstanding. A. Belew has since obtained representation on the Board of Directors.

"An affiliate of A. Belew Products Corporation acts as a food broker for Cedar packing in the Toronto marketing area. The commissions for such services after August amounted to approximately $20,000."

Why is this information disclosed?

BE23-15   Tosca Corporation is preparing its December 31, 2007, financial statements. The following two events   **(LO 6)** occurred between December 31, 2007, and March 10, 2008, when the statements were issued:

1. A liability, estimated at $140,000 at December 31, 2007, was settled on February 26, 2008, at $190,000.

2. A flood loss of $80,000 occurred on March 1, 2008.

What effect do these subsequent events have on 2007 net income?

BE23-16   What are the major types of subsequent events? Indicate how each of the following "subsequent events"   **(LO 6)** would be reported:

(a) Collection of a note written off in a prior period

(b) Issuance of a large preferred share offering

(c) Acquisition of a company in a different industry

(d) Destruction of a major plant in a flood

(e) Death of the company's chief executive officer

(f) Additional wage costs associated with the settlement of a four-week strike

(g) Settlement of a federal income tax case at considerably more tax than was anticipated at year end

(h) Change in the product mix from consumer goods to industrial goods

Exercises

E23-1   **(Segmented Reporting)** Lancers Inc. is involved in five separate industries. The following information is avail-   **(LO 3)** able for each of the five industries:

Operating Segment	Total Revenue	Operating Profit (Loss)	Assets
A	$140,000	$25,000	$240,000
B	40,000	8,000	11,000
C	26,000	(5,000)	36,000
D	190,000	(2,000)	49,000
E	2,000	500	15,000
	$398,000	$26,500	$351,000

Instructions

Determine which of the operating segments are reportable based on each of the following:

(a) Revenue test

(b) Operating profit (loss) test

(c) Assets test

(LO 5)   E23-2   (Related-Party Transaction)   Midas Corp. owns 75% of Gold Inc. Both companies are in the mining industry. During 2008, Midas Corp. purchased a building from Gold Inc. for $1,000. The building's carrying amount in Gold Inc.'s financial statements is $700. Midas' contributed surplus account contains a credit balance of $200 from previous related party transactions. Gold's contributed surplus account is nil. There is no available independent evidence of the value of the building as it is a unique building in a remote part of the country. Midas subsequently sold the building, during 2009, to an unrelated party for $1,100.

Instructions

Using the related-party decision tree in Illustration 23-5, answer the following:

(a) How would both Midas and Gold record the purchase and sale of the building during 2008?

(b) Record the subsequent sale of the building by Midas during 2009.

(c) Assume that Midas purchased the building from Gold for $500. How would your answer to part (a) change?

(d) Assume that the transaction is in the normal course of operations for both Midas and Gold and that it has commercial substance. How would your answers to (a) and (b) change?

(e) Calculate the total impact on income of the purchase and sale of the building for 2008 and 2009 for the consolidated reporting unit of the two companies. What can you conclude from your calculation?

(LO 5)   E23-3   (Related-Party Transaction) Vertigo Limited owns 90% of Centennial Inc. During 2008, Vertigo acquired a machine from Centennial in exchange for its own used machine. Both companies are in the consulting business. The agreed exchange amount is $1,000, although the transaction is non-monetary. Centennial Inc. carries its machine on its books at a carrying amount of $700, whereas Vertigo carries its machine on its books at a carrying amount of $900. Neither company has a balance in the contributed surplus account relating to previous related-party transactions.

Instructions

Using the related-party decision tree in Illustration 23-5, prepare the journal entries to record the exchange for both Vertigo and Centennial under the following assumptions:

(a) The transaction is not in the normal course of operations for either company, and the transaction has commercial substance.

(b) The transaction is not in the normal course of operations for either company, and the transaction does not have commercial substance.

(c) The transaction is in the normal course of operations for each company, and the transaction has commercial substance.

(d) The transaction is in the normal course of operations for each company, and the transaction does not have commercial substance.

(LO 6)   E23-4   (Post–Balance Sheet Events) Millennium Corporation issued its financial statements for the year ended December 31, 2008, on March 10, 2009. The following events took place early in 2009:

1. On January 10, 19,000 common shares were issued at $45 per share.

2. On March 1, Millennium determined after negotiations with the Canada Revenue Agency that income taxes payable for 2008 should be $1.2 million. At December 31, 2008, income taxes payable were recorded at $1 million.

Instructions

Discuss how these post–balance sheet events should be reflected in the 2008 financial statements.

E23-5   (Post–Balance Sheet Events) For each of the following subsequent (post–balance sheet) events, indicate **(LO 6)** whether a company should (a) adjust the financial statements, (b) disclose the event in notes to the financial statements, or (c) neither adjust nor disclose.

_____ **1.** Settlement of a federal tax case at a cost considerably higher than the amount expected at year end

_____ **2.** Introduction of a new product line

_____ **3.** Loss of an assembly plant due to fire

_____ **4.** Sale of a significant portion of the company's assets

_____ **5.** Retirement of the company president

_____ **6.** Prolonged employee strike

_____ **7.** Loss of a significant customer

_____ **8.** Issuance of a significant number of common shares

_____ **9.** Material loss on a year-end receivable because of a customer's bankruptcy

_____ **10.** Hiring of a new president

_____ **11.** Settlement of a prior year's litigation against the company

_____ **12.** Merger with another company of similar size

Problems

P23-1   Your firm has been engaged to examine the financial statements of Sabrina Corporation for the year 2008. The bookkeeper who maintains the financial records has prepared all the unaudited financial statements for the corporation since its organization on January 2, 2002. The client provides you with the information that follows:

SABRINA CORPORATION
Balance Sheet
As of December 31, 2008

Assets		Liabilities	
Current assets	$1,881,100	Current liabilities	$ 962,400
Other assets	5,121,900	Long-term liabilities	1,390,000
		Capital	4,650,600
	$7,003,000		$7,003,000

An analysis of current assets discloses the following:

Cash (restricted in the amount of $400,000 for plant expansion)	$ 571,000
Investments in land	185,000
Accounts receivable less allowance of $30,000	480,000
Inventories (FIFO flow assumption)	645,100
	$1,881,100

Other assets include:

Prepaid expenses	$ 47,400
Plant and equipment less accumulated amortization of $1,430,000	4,130,000
Cash surrender value of life insurance policy	84,000
Notes receivable (short-term)	162,300
Goodwill	252,000
Land	446,200
	$5,121,900

Current liabilities include:

Accounts payable	$ 510,000
Notes payable (due 2010)	157,400
Estimated income taxes payable	145,000
Premium on common shares	150,000
	$ 962,400

Long-term liabilities include:

Unearned revenue	$ 489,500
Dividends payable (cash)	200,000
8% bonds payable (due May 1, 2013)	700,500
	$1,390,000

Capital includes:

Retained earnings	$2,810,600
Common shares; 200,000 authorized, 184,000 issued	1,840,000
	$4,650,600

The following supplementary information is also provided:

1. On May 1, 2008, the corporation issued at 93.4, $750,000 of bonds to finance plant expansion. The long-term bond agreement provided for the annual payment of interest every May 1. The existing plant was pledged as security for the loan. Use the effective interest method for discount amortization.

2. The bookkeeper made the following mistakes:

   (a) In 2006, the ending inventory was overstated by $183,000. The ending inventories for 2007 and 2008 were correctly calculated.

   (b) In 2008, accrued wages in the amount of $275,000 were omitted from the balance sheet and these expenses were not charged on the income statement.

   (c) In 2008, a gain of $175,000 (net of tax) on the sale of certain plant assets was credited directly to retained earnings.

3. A major competitor has introduced a line of products that will compete directly with Sabrina's primary line, which is now being produced in a specially designed new plant. Because of manufacturing innovations, the competitor's line will be of similar quality but priced 50% below Sabrina's line. The competitor announced its new line on January 14, 2009. Sabrina indicates that the company will meet the lower prices; the lower prices are still high enough to cover Sabrina's variable manufacturing and selling expenses, but will permit only partial recovery of fixed costs.

4. You learned on January 28, 2009, prior to completion of the audit, of heavy damage from a recent fire at one of Sabrina's two plants and that the loss will not be reimbursed by insurance. The newspapers described the event in detail.

Instructions

(a) Analyze the above information to prepare a corrected balance sheet for Sabrina in accordance with standard accounting and reporting principles. Prepare a description of any notes that might need to be prepared. The books are closed and adjustments to income are to be made through retained earnings.

(b) "The financial statements of a company are management's responsibility, not the accountant's." Discuss the implications of this statement.

P23-2   In an examination of Kimmel Corporation Ltd. as of December 31, 2008, you have learned that the following situations exist. No entries have been made in the accounting records for these items.

1. The corporation erected its present factory building in 1993. Amortization was calculated by the straight-line method, using an estimated life of 35 years. Early in 2008, the board of directors conducted a careful survey and estimated that the factory building had a remaining useful life of 25 years as of January 1, 2008.

2. An additional assessment of 2007 income taxes was levied and paid in 2008.

3. When calculating the accrual for officers' salaries at December 31, 2008, it was discovered that the accrual for officers' salaries for December 31, 2007, had been overstated.

4. On December 15, 2008, Kimmel Corporation Ltd. declared a stock dividend of 1,000 common shares per 100,000 of its common shares outstanding, payable February 1, 2009, to the common shareholders of record on December 31, 2008.

5. Kimmel Corporation Ltd., which is on a calendar-year basis, changed its inventory method as of January 1, 2008. The inventory for December 31, 2007, was costed by the LIFO method, and the inventory for December 31, 2008, was costed by the FIFO method. Kimmel is changing its inventory method due to the change in GAAP for inventories.

6. Kimmel has guaranteed the payment of interest on the 20-year first mortgage bonds of Boss Inc., an affiliate. Outstanding bonds of Boss Inc. amount to $150,000 with interest payable at 10% per annum, due June 1 and December 1 of each year. The bonds were issued by Boss Inc., on December 1, 2004, and all interest payments have been met by the company with the exception of the payment due December 1, 2008. Kimmel states that it will pay the defaulted interest to the bondholders on January 15, 2009.

7. During the year 2008, Kimmel Corporation Ltd. was named as a defendant in a suit for damages by Ann Short Corporation for breach of contract. The case was decided in favour of Ann Short Corporation, which was awarded $80,000 damages. At the time of the audit, the case was under appeal to a higher court.

Instructions

Describe fully how each of the items should be reported in the financial statements of Kimmel Corporation Ltd. for the year 2008.

P23-3   Three independent situations follow:

Situation 1

A company offers a one-year warranty for the product that it manufactures. A history of warranty claims has been compiled and the probable amount of claims on sales for any particular period can be determined.

Situation 2

Subsequent to the date of a set of financial statements, but before the date of authorization for issuing the financial statements, a company enters into a contract that will probably result in a significant loss to the company. The loss amount can be reasonably estimated.

Situation 3

A company has adopted a policy of recording self-insurance for any possible losses resulting from injury to others by the company's vehicles. The premium for an insurance policy for the same risk from an independent insurance company would have an annual cost of $4,000. During the period covered by the financial statements, there were no accidents involving the company's vehicles that resulted in injury to others.

Instructions

Discuss the accrual or type of disclosure that is necessary (if any) and the reason(s) why the disclosure is appropriate for each of the three independent situations.

(AICPA adapted)

P23-4   Lion Corporation is currently preparing its annual financial statements for the fiscal year ended April 30, 2008. The company manufactures plastic, glass, and paper containers for sale to food and drink manufacturers and distributors. Lion maintains separate control accounts for its raw materials, work-in-process, and finished goods inventories for each of the three types of containers. The inventories are valued at the lower of cost or market.

The company's property, plant, and equipment are classified in the following major categories: land, office buildings, furniture and fixtures, manufacturing facilities, manufacturing equipment, and leasehold improvements. All fixed assets are carried at cost. The depreciation methods that are used depend on the type of asset (its classification) and when it was acquired.

Lion plans to present the inventory and fixed asset amounts in its April 30, 2008, balance sheet as follows:

Inventories	$4,814,200
Property, plant, and equipment (net of amortization)	$6,310,000

Instructions

What information regarding inventories and property, plant, and equipment must be disclosed by Lion Corporation in the audited financial statements issued to shareholders, either in the body or the notes, for the 2007–2008 fiscal year?

(CMA adapted)

P23-5   Rem Inc. produces electronic components for sale to manufacturers of radios, television sets, and digital sound systems. In connection with her examination of Rem's financial statements for the year ended December 31, 2008, Maggie Zeen, CA, completed field work two weeks ago. Ms. Zeen now is evaluating the significance of the following items prior to preparing her auditor's report. Except as noted, none of these items has been disclosed in the financial statements or notes.

Item 1

A 10-year loan agreement that the company entered into three years ago provides that, subsequent to the date of the agreement, dividend payments may not exceed net income earned after taxes. The balance of retained earnings at the date of the loan agreement was $420,000. From that date through December 31, 2008, net income after taxes has totalled $570,000 and cash dividends have totalled $320,000. Based on these data, the staff auditor who was assigned to this review concluded that there was no retained earnings restriction at December 31, 2008.

Item 2

Recently, Rem interrupted its policy of paying cash dividends quarterly to its shareholders. Dividends were paid regularly through 2007, discontinued for all of 2008 to finance the purchase of equipment for the company's new plant, and resumed in the first quarter of 2009. In the annual report, dividend policy is to be discussed in the president's letter to shareholders.

Item 3

A major electronics firm has introduced a line of products that will compete directly with Rem's primary line, which is now being produced in Rem's specially designed new plant. Because of manufacturing innovations, the competitor's line will be of similar quality but priced 50% below Rem's line. The competitor announced its new line during the week following the completion of Ms. Zeen's field work. Ms. Zeen read the announcement in the newspaper and discussed the situation by telephone with Rem executives. Rem will meet the lower prices as they are still high enough to cover variable manufacturing and selling expenses, although they will permit only partial recovery of fixed costs.

Item 4

The company's new manufacturing plant building, which cost $2.4 million and has an estimated life of 25 years, is leased from Ancient National Bank at an annual rental of $600,000. The company is obligated to pay property taxes, insurance, and maintenance. At the conclusion of its 10-year non-cancellable lease, the company has the option of purchasing the property for $1. In Rem's income statement, the rental payment is reported on a separate line.

Instructions

For each of the items, discuss any additional disclosures in the financial statements and notes that the auditor should recommend to her client. (The cumulative effect of the four items should not be considered.)

P23-6   You have completed your audit of Keesha Inc. and its consolidated subsidiaries for the year ended December 31, 2008, and are satisfied with the results of your examination. You have examined the financial statements of Keesha for the past three years. The corporation is now preparing its annual report to shareholders. The report will include the consolidated financial statements of Keesha and its subsidiaries, and your short-form auditor's report. During your audit, the following matters came to your attention:

1. A vice-president who is also a shareholder resigned on December 31, 2008, after an argument with the president. The vice-president is soliciting proxies from shareholders and expects to obtain sufficient proxies to gain control of the board of directors so that a new president will be appointed. The president plans to have a note prepared that would include information of the pending proxy fight, management's accomplishments over the years, and an appeal by management for the support of shareholders.

2. The corporation decides in 2008 to adopt the straight-line method of depreciation for plant equipment. The straight-line method will be used for new acquisitions and for previously acquired plant equipment that was being depreciated on an accelerated basis. The new policy will result in more relevant financial reporting as it will be more consistent with the new standards.

3. The Canada Revenue Agency is currently examining the corporation's 2006 federal income tax return and is questioning the amount of a deduction claimed by the corporation's domestic subsidiary for a loss sustained in 2006. The examination is still in process, and any additional tax liability is indeterminable at this time. The corporation's tax counsel believes that there will be no substantial additional tax liability.

Instructions

(a) Prepare the notes, if any, that you would suggest for each of the items.

(b) For each item that you decided did not require note disclosure, explain your reasons for not making the disclosure.

(AICPA adapted)

P23-7   Friendly Corporation is a diversified company that operates in five different industries: A, B, C, D, and E. The following information relating to each segment is available for 2008. Sales of segments B and C included intersegment sales of $20,000 and $100,000, respectively.

	A	B	C	D	E
Sales	$40,000	$ 80,000	$580,000	$35,000	$55,000
Cost of goods sold	19,000	50,000	270,000	19,000	30,000
Operating expenses	10,000	40,000	235,000	12,000	18,000
Total expenses	29,000	90,000	505,000	31,000	48,000
Operating profit (loss)	$11,000	$(10,000)	$ 75,000	$ 4,000	$ 7,000
Assets	$35,000	$ 60,000	$500,000	$65,000	$50,000

Instructions

(a) Determine which of the segments are reportable based on each of the following:

1. Revenue test
2. Operating profit (loss) test
3. Assets test

(b) Prepare the necessary disclosures.

(c) The corporation's accountant recently commented, "If I have to disclose our segments individually, the only people who will gain are our competitors and the only people that will lose are our present shareholders." Evaluate this comment.

P23-8 You are compiling the consolidated financial statements for Vender Corporation International (VCI). The corporation's accountant, Vincent Jones, has provided you with the following segment information:

Note 7: Major Segments of Business

VCI conducts funeral service and cemetery operations in Canada and the United States. Substantially all revenues of VCI's major segments of business are from unaffiliated customers. Segment information for fiscal 2008, 2007, and 2006 follows:

(thousands)

	Funeral	Floral	Cemetery	Corporate	Dried Whey	Limousine	Consolidated
Revenues:							
2008	$302,000	$10,000	$ 83,000	$ —	$7,000	$14,000	$416,000
2007	245,000	6,000	61,000	—	4,000	8,000	324,000
2006	208,000	3,000	42,000	—	1,000	6,000	260,000
Operating Income:							
2008	$ 79,000	$ 1,500	$ 18,000	$(36,000)	$ 500	$ 2,000	$ 65,000
2007	64,000	200	12,000	(28,000)	200	400	48,800
2006	54,000	150	6,000	(21,000)	100	350	39,600
Capital Expenditures:[a]							
2008	$ 26,000	$ 1,000	$ 9,000	$ 400	$ 300	$ 1,000	$ 37,700
2007	28,000	2,000	60,000	1,500	100	700	92,300
2006	14,000	25	8,000	600	25	50	22,700
Depreciation and Amortization:							
2008	$ 13,000	$ 100	$ 2,400	$ 1,400	$ 100	$ 200	$ 17,200
2007	10,000	50	1,400	700	50	100	12,300
2006	8,000	25	1,000	600	25	50	9,700
Identifiable Assets:							
2008	$334,000	$ 1,500	$162,000	$114,000	$ 500	$ 8,000	$620,000
2007	322,000	1,000	144,000	52,000	1,000	6,000	526,000
2006	223,000	500	78,000	34,000	500	3,500	339,500

[a]Includes $4,520,000, $111,480,000, and $1,294,000 for the years ended April 30, 2008, 2007, and 2006, respectively, for purchases of businesses.

Instructions

Determine which of the segments must be reported separately and which can be combined under the category "Other." Then write a one-page memo to the company's accountant, Vincent Jones, that explains all of the following:

(a) Which segments must be reported separately and which ones can be combined

(b) Which criteria you used to determine the reportable segments

(c) What major items must be disclosed for each segment

P23-9 The following excerpt is from the financial statements of **H. J. Heinz Company** and provides segmented geographic data:

> The company is engaged principally in one line of business—processed food products—that represents more than 90% of consolidated sales. Information about the company business by geographic area is presented in the table below.
> There were no material amounts of sales or transfers between geographic areas or between affiliates, and no material amounts of United States export sales.

(in thousands of U.S. dollars)	Domestic	United Kingdom	Canada	Western Europe	Other	Total	Worldwide
			Foreign				
Sales	$2,381,054	$547,527	$216,726	$383,784	$209,354	$1,357,391	$3,738,445
Operating income	246,780	61,282	34,146	29,146	25,111	149,685	396,465
Identifiable assets	1,362,152	265,218	112,620	294,732	143,971	816,541	2,178,693
Capital expenditures	72,712	12,262	13,790	8,253	4,368	38,673	111,385
Depreciation expense	42,279	8,364	3,592	6,355	3,606	21,917	64,196

Instructions

(a) Why does H. J. Heinz not prepare segment information on its products or services?

(b) Why are revenues by geographic area important to disclose?

P23-10 At December 31, 2008, Brandt Corp. has assets of $10 million, liabilities of $6 million, common shares of $2 million (representing 2 million common shares of $1.00 par), and retained earnings of $2 million. Net sales for the year 2008 were $18 million, and net income was $800,000. As one of the auditors of this company, you are making a review of subsequent events on February 13, 2009, and you find the following:

1. On February 3, 2009, one of Brandt's customers declared bankruptcy. At December 31, 2008, this company owed Brandt $300,000, of which $40,000 was paid in January 2009.

2. On January 18, 2009, one of the client's three major plants burned.

3. On January 23, 2009, a strike was called at one of Brandt's largest plants and halted 30% of production. As of today (February 13), the strike has not been settled.

4. A major electronics enterprise has introduced a line of products that would compete directly with Brandt's primary line, now being produced in a specially designed new plant. Because of manufacturing innovations, the competitor has been able to achieve quality similar to that of Brandt's products, but at a price 50% lower. Brandt officials say they will meet the lower prices, which are high enough to cover variable manufacturing and selling costs but permit recovery of only a portion of the fixed costs.

5. Merchandise traded in the open market is recorded in the company's records at $1.40 per unit on December 31, 2008. This price held for two weeks after the release of an official market report that predicted vastly excessive supplies; however, no purchases were made at $1.40. The price throughout the preceding year had been about $2.00, which was the level experienced over several years. On January 18, 2009, the price returned to $2.00 after public disclosure of an error in the official calculations of the prior December—the correction erased the expectations of excessive supplies. Inventory at December 31, 2008, was on a lower of cost or net realizable value basis.

6. On February 1, 2009, the board of directors adopted a resolution to accept the offer of an investment banker to guarantee the marketing of $1.2 million of preferred shares.

7. The company owns investments classified as trading securities. The investments have been adjusted to market value as of December 31, 2008. On January 21, 2009, the annual report of one of the investment companies has been issued for its year ended November 30, 2008. The investee company did not meet its earnings forecasts and the market price of the investment has dropped from $49 per share at December 31, 2008, to $27 per share on January 21, 2009.

Instructions

For each event, state how it will affect the 2008 financial statements, if at all.

Writing Assignments

WA23-1 The following article appeared in *The Wall Street Journal*.

WASHINGTON—The Securities and Exchange Commission staff issued guidelines for companies grappling with the problem of dividing up their business into industry segments for their annual reports.

An industry segment is defined by the Financial Accounting Standards Board as a part of an enterprise engaged in providing a product or service or a group of related products or services primarily to unaffiliated customers for a profit.

Although conceding that the process is a "subjective task" that to a considerable extent, depends on the judgement of management, the SEC staff said companies should consider the nature of the products, the nature of their production and their markets and marketing methods to determine whether products and services should be grouped together or in separate industry segments.

Instructions

(a) What does financial reporting for segments of a business enterprise involve?

(b) What are the reasons for requiring financial data to be reported by segments?

(c) What are the possible disadvantages of requiring financial data to be reported by segments?

(d) What accounting difficulties are inherent in segment reporting?

WA23-2 J. J. Kersee Corporation is a publicly traded company and is currently preparing the interim financial data that it will issue to its shareholders and the Securities Commission at the end of the first quarter of the 2008–2009 fiscal year. Kersee's financial accounting department has compiled the following summarized revenue and expense data for the first quarter of the year:

Sales	$60,000,000
Cost of goods sold	36,000,000
Variable selling expenses	2,000,000
Fixed selling expenses	3,000,000

Included in the fixed selling expenses was the single lump sum payment of $2 million for television advertisements for the entire year.

Instructions

(a) J. J. Kersee Corporation must issue its quarterly financial statements in accordance with generally accepted accounting principles regarding interim financial reporting.

  1. Explain whether Kersee should report its operating results for the quarter as if the quarter were an entirely separate reporting period or as if the quarter were an integral part of the annual reporting period.

  2. State how the sales, cost of goods sold, and fixed selling expenses would be reflected in Kersee Corporation's quarterly report prepared for the first quarter of the 2008 – 2009 fiscal year. Briefly justify your presentation.

(b) What financial information, as a minimum, must Kersee Corporation disclose to its shareholders in its quarterly reports?

(CMA adapted)

WA23-3 The following statement is an excerpt from a document on interim financial reporting:

Interim financial information is essential to provide investors and others with timely information about the progress of the enterprise. The usefulness of such information rests on the relationship that it has to the annual results of operations. Accordingly, the Board has concluded that each interim period should be viewed primarily as an integral part of an annual period.

In general, the results for each interim period should be based on the accounting principles and practices used by an enterprise in the preparation of its latest annual financial statements unless a change in an accounting practice or policy has been adopted in the current year. The Board has concluded, however, that certain accounting principles and practices followed for annual reporting purposes may require modification at interim reporting dates so that the reported results for the interim period may better relate to the results of operations for the annual period.

Instructions

Listed below are six independent cases on how accounting facts might be reported on an individual company's interim financial reports. For each case, state whether the method that is proposed for interim reporting would be acceptable under generally accepted accounting principles for interim financial data. Support each answer with a brief explanation.

(a) King Limited takes a physical inventory at year end for annual financial statement purposes. Inventory and cost of sales reported in the interim quarterly statements are based on estimated gross profit rates because a physical inventory would require a stoppage of operations. The company does have reliable perpetual inventory records.

(b) Florence Limited is planning to report one-fourth of its pension expense each quarter.

(c) Lopez Corp. wrote inventory down to reflect lower of cost or market in the first quarter. At year end, the market exceeds the original acquisition cost of this inventory. Consequently, management plans to write the inventory back up to its original cost as a year-end adjustment.

(d) Witt Corp. realized a large gain on the sale of investments at the beginning of the second quarter. The company wants to report one-third of the gain in each of the remaining quarters.

(e) Marble Limited has estimated its annual audit fee. It plans to prorate this expense equally over all four quarters.

(f) McNeil Inc. was reasonably certain that it would have an employee strike in the third quarter. As a result, it shipped heavily during the second quarter but plans to defer the recognition of the sales in excess of the normal sales volume. The deferred sales will be recognized as sales in the third quarter when the strike is in progress. McNeil management thinks this better represents normal second- and third-quarter operations.

WA23-4   An article in *Barron's* noted:

> Okay. Last fall, someone with a long memory and an even longer arm reached into that bureau drawer and came out with a mouldy cheese sandwich and the equally mouldy notion of corporate forecasts. We tried to find out what happened to the cheese sandwich—but, rats!, even recourse to the Freedom of Information Act didn't help. However, the forecast proposal was dusted off, polished up and found quite serviceable. The SEC, indeed, lost no time in running it up the old flagpole—but no one was very eager to salute. Even after some of the more objectionable features—compulsory corrections and detailed explanations of why the estimates went awry—were peeled off the original proposal.
>
> Seemingly, despite the Commission's smiles and sweet talk, those craven corporations were still afraid that an honest mistake would lead down the primrose path to consent decrees and class action suits. To lay to rest such qualms, the Commission last week approved a "Safe Harbor" rule that, providing the forecasts were made on a reasonable basis and in good faith, protected corporations from litigation should the projections prove wide of the mark (as only about 99% are apt to do).

Instructions

Answer the following.

(a) What are the arguments for preparing profit forecasts?

(b) What is the purpose of the safe harbour rule?

(c) Why are corporations concerned about presenting profit forecasts?

Cases

Student Website

www.wiley.com/canada/kieso

Refer to the Case Primer on the Student Website to help you answer these cases.

CA23-1   Patty Gamble, who is the financial vice-president of Castle Manufacturing Corporation, and Victoria Maher, the controller, are currently reviewing the company's financial ratios for the years 2008 and 2009. The financial vice-president notes that the profit margin on sales ratio has increased from 6% to 12%, a hefty gain for the two-year period. Gamble is in the process of issuing a media release that emphasizes the efficiency of Castle Manufacturing in controlling costs. Victoria Maher knows that the difference in ratios is due primarily to an earlier company decision to reduce the estimates of warranty and bad debt expense for 2009. The controller, not sure of her supervisor's motives, hesitates to suggest to Gamble that the company's improvement is unrelated to efficiency in controlling costs. To complicate matters, the media release is scheduled in a few days.

Instructions

Adopt the role of Victoria Maher and discuss the financial reporting issues.

CA23-2 In June 2009, the board of directors for Holtzman Enterprises Inc. authorized the sale of $10 million of corporate bonds. Michelle Collins, treasurer for Holtzman Enterprises Inc., is concerned about the date when the bonds are issued. The company really needs the cash, but she is worried that if the bonds are issued before the company's year end (December 31, 2009), the additional liability will have an adverse effect on several important ratios. In July, she explains to company president Kenneth Holtzman that if they delay issuing the bonds until after December 31, the bonds will not affect the ratios until December 31, 2010. They will have to report the issuance as a subsequent event, which requires only footnote disclosure. Collins predicts that with expected improved financial performance in 2009, the ratios should be better.

Instructions

Adopt the role of Michelle Collins and discuss any issues.

CA23-3 The following is an excerpt from the 1989 financial statements of **Exxon Corporation** and deals with a large oil spill caused by one of the company's oil tankers:

Note 14 to the 1989 annual financial statements of Exxon Corporation.

On March 24, 1989, The Exxon Valdez, a tanker owned by Exxon Shipping Company, a subsidiary of Exxon Corporation, ran aground on Bligh Reef in Prince William Sound off the port of Valdez, Alaska, and released approximately 260,000 barrels of crude oil. More than 170 lawsuits including class actions have been brought in various courts against Exxon Corporation and some of its consolidated subsidiaries. Most of these lawsuits seek unspecified compensatory and physical damages; several lawsuits seek damages in varying specified amounts. Some of the lawsuits seek injunctive relief.

The State of Alaska has filed a suit in Superior Court in Alaska against Exxon Shipping Company, Exxon Corporation and others seeking substantial civil penalties and unspecified damages arising from the oil spill. On February 27, 1990, an indictment was returned in the United States District Court in Anchorage Alaska, charging Exxon Shipping Company and Exxon Corporation with violation of the Refuse Act, the Migratory Bird Treaty Act, the Clean Water Act, the Ports and Waterways Safety Act and the Dangerous Cargo Act.

The potential total costs relating to the matters described above are difficult to predict and are not expected to be resolved for a number of years. It is believed that the ultimate outcome net of reserves already provided, will not have a materially adverse effect upon the corporation's operations or financial condition.

Instructions

(a) Why would the company want to disclose all the details when they reflect negatively on the company?

(b) How much disclosure is necessary in this case, and what level of detail is required?

Integrated Case

IC23-1 Penron Limited (PL) is in the energy business of buying and selling gas and oil and related derivatives. It is a public company whose shares are widely held. It recently underwent a tremendous expansionary period over the past decade, and revenues quadrupled and continue to climb. Executives are remunerated using stock options, and the employee pension plan invests heavily in the company's stock. It is currently October 2008. The year end is December 31, 2008. Many of the benefit plans of the top executives vest at the end of the year (i.e., the executives will have legal entitlement to the benefits even if they leave the company). As a matter of fact, there is a concern that several of these top executives will announce that they plan to leave the company right after the year-end financial statements are released.

PL was seen as a "hot stock" by the marketplace. Numerous analysts followed the stock carefully and had been advising their clients to buy the stock as long as revenues and profits kept increasing. The third quarter results had shown steadily increasing revenues and profits. The company had been signalling that this trend would continue through the fourth quarter.

During the fourth quarter, PL sold some of its pipelines to LPL Corporation. The pipelines had not been in use for some time and were seen as non-essential assets. Over the past two years, PL has steadily been divesting itself of non-essential assets. PL had not written the pipelines down in the financial statements since they were able to sell them and recover twice their cost. This one deal was responsible for substantially all of the fourth quarter profits. Under the terms of the deal, the pipelines were sold for $15 million cash.

LPL Corporation was owned by the president of PL. The company had been established just before the pipeline deal was signed. Since LPL was a new company and otherwise had very few assets, it borrowed the money for the deal from the bank. The bank had requested that PL guarantee the loan, which it did.

During the year, PL issued Class A shares to certain executives of the company. The shares participate in the earnings of the entity much like the common shares of the company (i.e., dividends accrue to the shareholders out of the residual earnings after the preferred dividends have been paid). They are mandatorily redeemable if a triggering event occurs, such as the resignation or termination of the shareholder. The shares are otherwise similar to common shares in that they have no preferential rights.

During the year, the company also began the planning stages for development of a new website that will allow customers to transact with the company over the website interface. A significant amount of time was spent in this planning phase to determine the feasibility and desirability of this type of customer interface. Toward the end of the year, after lengthy discussion about whether or not to go down this path, the company began to acquire software and hardware to facilitate the new website. A large amount was spent on the site's graphic design and on its content.

Instructions

Assume the role of the auditors and discuss the financial reporting issues for the year ended December 31, 2008.

Research and Analysis

RA23-1 Thomson Corporation

In response to the investing public's demand for greater disclosure of corporate expectations for the future, safe harbour rules and legislation have been passed to encourage and protect corporations that issue financial forecasts and projections.

Instructions

Go to the Student Website and review the Management Discussion and Analysis for **Thomson Corporation**.

(a) What general expectation did the company have for the industry in 2006? How did the company plan to react to this expectation?

(b) Give examples of hard data forecasts (if any) that the company disclosed for the upcoming year (2007). Give some examples of soft data forecasts. ("Hard" means concrete or definite, and "soft" means open to judgement, interpretation, or change.)

(c) What limitations or other qualifying statements did the company apply to its forecasts?

(d) What is the difference between a financial forecast and a financial projection?

RA23-2 Air Canada and British Airways

Instructions

Access the annual reports for the above companies on the Student Website and answer the following questions.

(a) What specific items do the companies discuss in their Accounting Policies notes? (Prepare a list of the headings only.)

(b) Note the similarities and differences in regard to these. Comment on these and relate them to the nature of the two businesses.

(c) For what lines of business or segments do the companies present segmented information?

(d) Note and comment on the similarities and differences between the auditors' reports submitted by the independent auditors.

RA23-3 Canadian Financial Reporting

In his article "Easy Prey" (*Canadian Business*, April 16, 2001), the prominent Canadian forensic accountant Al Rosen comments that Canadian investors are being swindled.

Instructions

Read the article and argue in support of this statement and against it.

RA23-4 GAAP

In an article entitled "Mind the GAAP," which appeared in *Canadian Business* on May 14, 2001, Al Rosen argues that generally accepted accounting principles are not generally accepted. In the article, he compares the differences between profit and loss for seven companies' interpretation of Canadian GAAP versus U.S. GAAP.

Instructions

Obtain the financial statements of at least two of the companies mentioned in the article and look at the note to the financial statements where the companies reconcile net income under Canadian GAAP to net income under U.S. GAAP. What are the major differences? Which earnings number is more useful to users? Why?

RA23-5 GAAP for Private Companies

As mentioned in the chapter, CICA has issued an "Invitation to Comment on Financial Reporting by Private Enterprises."

Instructions

Research the merits of the three alternatives that are proposed for financial reporting by private enterprises, drawing on the IFRS Exposure draft on Small and Mid-Sized Firms and the existing differential reporting model (Section 1300 of the current *CICA Handbook*).

RA23-6 GAAP Convergence

The CICA Accounting Standards Board has committed itself to international convergence of accounting standards.

Instructions

Go to the CICA website and note which major standards have been harmonized in the past few years. Also identify convergence initiatives that remain unfinished and comment generally on the success of the convergence mandate.

Specimen Financial Statements

The following pages contain the financial statements and accompanying notes from the 2005 annual report of **Stantec Inc.** (Stantec). The full text of the annual report in PDF format, can be found on the Student Website. Stantec provides design and consulting services in planning, engineering, architecture, interior design, landscape architecture, surveying, and project management. The company offers consulting services through all phases of business, starting with the idea or concept stage and focusing on providing sustainable solutions that have a positive impact on the world. Stantec has 5,500 employees with offices throughout North America and the Caribbean. In 2005, the company completed its acquisition of The Keith Companies, adding 800 employees and many new offices. The company also listed on the NYSE in 2005.

The Business

The company's business model focuses on continuing growth and profitability while controlling risk. Its goal is to become a top 10 global design firm. Stantec operates in five areas: buildings, environment, industrial and project management, transportation, and urban land. Its projects include the following, among others:

1. Creation of environmentally friendly building designs that minimize the impact on the surrounding areas, including wetlands

2. Design of a water treatment plant needed to clean up acid mine drainage from a large former copper mine

3. Development of wind farms

4. Conversion of landfill gas into useable energy

We do not expect that you will understand everything in the company's financial statements and accompanying notes when you first read them. Instead, we expect that by the time you complete the material in this text, your level of understanding and ability to interpret will have grown significantly.

At this point, we recommend that you take 20 to 30 minutes to scan the statements and notes to familiarize yourself with the contents and accounting elements. Throughout the following chapters, when you are asked to refer to specific parts of Stantec's financials, do so. Then, when you have completed reading this book, we challenge you to reread Stantec's financials to see how much greater and more sophisticated your understanding of them has become.

Management Report

The annual report, including the consolidated financial statements, is the responsibility of the management of the Company. The consolidated financial statements were prepared by management in accordance with Canadian generally accepted accounting principles. Where alternative accounting methods exist, management has chosen those it considers most appropriate in the circumstances. The significant accounting policies used are described in note 1 to the consolidated financial statements. Certain amounts in the financial statements are based on estimates and judgments relating to matters not concluded by year-end. The integrity of the information presented in the financial statements is the responsibility of management. Financial information presented elsewhere in this annual report has been prepared by management and is consistent with the information in the consolidated financial statements.

Management is responsible for the development and maintenance of systems of internal accounting and administrative controls of high quality. Such systems are designed to provide reasonable assurance that the financial information is accurate, relevant, and reliable and that the Company's assets are appropriately accounted for and adequately safeguarded.

The Board of Directors is responsible for ensuring that management fulfills its responsibilities and for final approval of the annual consolidated financial statements. The Board has appointed an Audit Committee comprising three Directors, none of whom is an officer or employee of the Company or its subsidiaries. The Audit Committee meets at least four times each year to discharge its responsibilities under a written mandate from the Board of Directors. The Audit Committee meets with management and with the external auditors to satisfy itself that they are properly discharging their responsibilities, reviews the consolidated financial statements and the Auditors' Report, and examines other auditing and accounting matters. The Audit Committee has reviewed the audited consolidated financial statements with management, including a discussion of the quality of the accounting principles as applied and significant judgments affecting the Company's consolidated financial statements. The Audit Committee has discussed with the external auditors the external auditors' judgments of the quality of those principles as applied and judgments noted above. The consolidated financial statements and Management's Discussion and Analysis have been reviewed by the Audit Committee and approved by the Board of Directors of Stantec Inc.

The consolidated financial statements have been examined by the shareholders' auditors, Ernst & Young LLP, Chartered Accountants. The Auditors' Report outlines the nature of their examination and their opinion on the consolidated financial statements of the Company. The external auditors have full and unrestricted access to the Audit Committee, with or without management being present.

Tony Franceschini P.Eng.
President & CEO
February 10, 2006

Don Wilson CA
Vice President & CFO
February 10, 2006

Auditors' Report

To the Shareholders of
Stantec Inc.

We have audited the consolidated balance sheets of **Stantec Inc.** as at December 31, 2005 and 2004 and the consolidated statements of income and retained earnings and cash flows for each of the years in the three-year period ended December 31, 2005. These financial statements are the responsibility of the Company's management. Our responsibility is to express an opinion on these financial statements based on our audits.

We conducted our audits in accordance with Canadian generally accepted auditing standards. Those standards require that we plan and perform an audit to obtain reasonable assurance whether the financial statements are free of material misstatement. An audit includes examining, on a test basis, evidence supporting the amounts and disclosures in the financial statements. An audit also includes assessing the accounting principles used and significant estimates made by management, as well as evaluating the overall financial statement presentation.

In our opinion, these consolidated financial statements present fairly, in all material respects, the financial position of the Company as at December 31, 2005 and 2004 and the results of its operations and its cash flows for each of the years in the three-year period ended December 31, 2005 in accordance with Canadian generally accepted accounting principles.

Ernst & Young LLP

Chartered Accountants
Edmonton, Canada
February 10, 2006

Stantec Inc.
Consolidated Balance Sheets

	As at December 31	
	2005 $	2004 $
	(In thousands of Canadian dollars)	

ASSETS [note 8]
Current

Cash and cash equivalents	28,143	37,890
Restricted cash [note 2]	21,312	–
Accounts receivable, net of allowance for doubtful accounts of $16,053 in 2005 ($21,095 – 2004)	137,928	112,476
Costs and estimated earnings in excess of billings	66,172	40,861
Prepaid expenses	5,420	4,165
Future income tax assets [note 14]	14,827	8,532
Other assets [note 6]	6,569	4,831
Total current assets	280,371	208,755
Property and equipment [note 3]	58,519	48,262
Goodwill [note 4]	242,674	84,694
Intangible assets [note 5]	27,304	6,278
Future income tax assets [note 14]	6,814	6,357
Other assets [note 6]	13,097	7,754
Total assets	628,779	362,100

LIABILITIES AND SHAREHOLDERS' EQUITY
Current

Accounts payable and accrued liabilities [note 7]	106,757	78,718
Billings in excess of costs and estimated earnings	24,251	18,832
Income taxes payable	4,441	5,732
Current portion of long-term debt [note 8]	4,813	12,820
Future income tax liabilities [note 14]	17,552	10,653
Total current liabilities	157,814	126,755
Long-term debt [note 8]	81,886	21,155
Other liabilities [note 9]	24,764	16,818
Future income tax liabilities [note 14]	16,262	8,316
Total liabilities	280,726	173,044

Commitments and contingencies [notes 2, 8, 10, and 11]

Shareholders' equity

Share capital [note 12]	210,604	87,656
Contributed surplus [note 12]	5,522	2,544
Cumulative translation account [note 13]	(25,575)	(19,018)
Deferred stock compensation	(833)	–
Retained earnings	158,335	117,874
Total shareholders' equity	348,053	189,056
Total liabilities and shareholders' equity	628,779	362,100

See accompanying notes

On behalf of the Board:

Director   Director

Stantec Inc.
Consolidated Statements of Income and Retained Earnings

	Years Ended December 31		
	2005 $	2004 $	2003 $
	(In thousands of Canadian dollars, except per share amounts)		
Income			
Gross revenue	618,020	520,879	459,942
Less subconsultant and other direct expenses	93,468	71,728	68,546
Net revenue	524,552	449,151	391,396
Direct payroll costs	234,553	205,513	183,471
Gross margin	289,999	243,638	207,925
Administrative and marketing expenses	212,633	183,739	154,788
Depreciation of property and equipment	12,389	11,986	9,912
Amortization of intangible assets	2,542	927	925
Net interest expense *[note 8]*	571	2,805	2,637
Share of income from associated companies	(187)	(385)	(580)
Foreign exchange (gains) losses	(449)	(94)	615
Income before income taxes	62,500	44,660	39,628
Income taxes *[note 14]*			
Current	21,735	18,065	10,050
Future	143	(3,595)	4,508
Total income taxes	21,878	14,470	14,558
Net income for the year	40,622	30,190	25,070
Retained earnings, beginning of the year	117,874	88,266	64,240
Shares repurchased *[note 12]*	(161)	(582)	(1,044)
Retained earnings, end of the year	158,335	117,874	88,266
Earnings per share *[note 15]*			
Basic	2.04	1.63	1.37
Diluted	1.98	1.59	1.31

See accompanying notes

Stantec Inc.
Consolidated Statements of Cash Flows

	Years Ended December 31		
	2005	2004	2003
	$	$	$
	(In thousands of Canadian dollars)		
CASH FLOWS FROM (USED IN) OPERATING ACTIVITIES			
Cash receipts from clients	**637,391**	568,897	465,114
Cash paid to suppliers	**(200,445)**	(169,573)	(156,460)
Cash paid to employees	**(355,621)**	(313,321)	(274,444)
Dividends from equity investments	**550**	300	–
Interest received	**6,531**	6,426	2,710
Interest paid	**(6,551)**	(8,639)	(4,462)
Income taxes paid	**(28,882)**	(10,530)	(18,142)
Income taxes recovered	**4,341**	3,791	2,577
Cash flows from operating activities *[note 16]*	**57,314**	77,351	16,893
CASH FLOWS FROM (USED IN) INVESTING ACTIVITIES			
Business acquisitions, including cash acquired and bank indebtedness assumed *[note 2]*	**(100,383)**	(18,845)	(6,046)
Cash of joint venture held for sale	**–**	–	(369)
Restricted cash used for acquisitions *[note 2]*	**9,000**	–	–
Increase in investments held for self-insured liabilities	**(7,295)**	(9,562)	–
Proceeds on disposition of investments	**522**	55	195
Collection of notes receivable from disposition of Technology and Design Build segments	**406**	1,014	–
Purchase of property and equipment	**(17,005)**	(17,488)	(28,713)
Proceeds on disposition of property and equipment	**155**	34,672	1,444
Cash flows used in investing activities	**(114,600)**	(10,154)	(33,489)
CASH FLOWS FROM (USED IN) FINANCING ACTIVITIES			
Repayment of long-term debt	**(46,875)**	(35,546)	(20,592)
Proceeds from long-term borrowings	**95,929**	13,960	–
Net change in bank indebtedness financing	**–**	(17,151)	17,151
Repurchase of shares for cancellation *[note 12]*	**(195)**	(720)	(1,392)
Share issue costs *[note 12]*	**(1,969)**	–	–
Proceeds from issue of share capital *[note 12]*	**961**	3,490	651
Cash flows from (used in) financing activities	**47,851**	(35,967)	(4,182)
Foreign exchange loss on cash held in foreign currency	**(312)**	(683)	(1,081)
Net increase (decrease) in cash and cash equivalents	**(9,747)**	30,547	(21,859)
Cash and cash equivalents, beginning of the year	**37,890**	7,343	29,202
Cash and cash equivalents, end of the year	**28,143**	37,890	7,343

See accompanying notes

Stantec Inc.
Notes to the Consolidated Financial Statements

1. Summary of Significant Accounting Policies

Stantec Inc. (the Company) is a provider of comprehensive professional services in the area of infrastructure and facilities for clients in the public and private sectors. The Company's services include planning, engineering, architecture, interior design, landscape architecture, surveying and geomatics, environmental sciences, and project economics.

Generally accepted accounting principles

The Company prepares its consolidated financial statements in accordance with Canadian generally accepted accounting principles (GAAP). These financial statements have, in management's opinion, been properly prepared within reasonable limits of materiality and within the framework of the accounting policies summarized below. The effects of differences between the application of Canadian and United States GAAP on the financial statements of the Company are described in note 20.

Effective January 1, 2005, the Company adopted Accounting Guideline 15 (AcG-15)—"Consolidation of Variable Interest Entities" (VIEs) of the Canadian Institute of Chartered Accountants (CICA) Handbook. VIEs are those entities that are subject to control on a basis other than ownership of voting interests. AcG-15 provides guidance for identifying VIEs and requires the primary beneficiary of a VIE to consolidate the VIE. These consolidated financial statements include all VIEs for which the Company is the primary beneficiary. The initial adoption of this accounting guideline on a prospective basis did not have an impact on the Company's consolidated financial statements.

Effective January 1, 2004, the Company adopted the recommendations of Section 1100 of the CICA Handbook, "Generally Accepted Accounting Principles." This section establishes standards for financial reporting in accordance with GAAP. It describes what constitutes GAAP and its sources and states that an entity should apply every primary source of GAAP that deals with the accounting and reporting in financial statements of transactions or events it encounters. The initial adoption of these recommendations on a prospective basis on January 1, 2004, did not have an impact on the Company's consolidated financial statements.

Use of estimates

The preparation of financial statements in conformity with GAAP requires management to make estimates and assumptions that affect the reported amounts of assets and liabilities at the date of the financial statements and the reported amounts of revenues and expenses during the reporting period. Significant estimates used in the preparation of these consolidated financial statements include the percentage of completion of fixed fee and variable fee with ceiling contracts, provisions for losses on incomplete contracts, allowances for doubtful accounts receivable, provision for legal claims, provision for self-insured liabilities, the fair value of stock-based awards, the fair value of identifiable intangible assets acquired in business acquisitions, liabilities for lease exit activities, and future cash flows used to estimate the fair value of reporting units for goodwill impairment purposes. Actual results may differ from these estimates.

During the 2005 fiscal year, management revised its estimate of the allowance for doubtful accounts based on improved information available on historical loss experience. This revision was applied prospectively and reduced the allowance for doubtful accounts and administrative and marketing expenses at the time of the revision by $4,000,000.

Principles of consolidation

The consolidated financial statements include the accounts of the Company, its subsidiary companies, and all VIEs for which the Company is the primary beneficiary. All significant intercompany accounts and transactions have been eliminated. The results of the operations of subsidiaries acquired during the year are included from their respective dates of acquisition.

Joint ventures and partnerships are accounted for on the proportionate consolidation basis, which results in the Company recording its pro rata share of the assets, liabilities, revenues, and expenses of each of these entities.

Cash and cash equivalents

Cash and cash equivalents include cash and unrestricted investments with initial maturities of three months or less. Such investments are carried at the lower of cost or market value.

Investments

Investments in associated companies over which the Company is able to exercise significant influence, but not control, are accounted for using the equity method, which reflects the Company's investment at original cost plus its share of earnings (losses) net of dividends received. These investments include Teshmont Consultants Inc. (50%), SSBV Consultants Inc. (33.3%), and Planning & Stantec Limited (50%).

Other investments, including investments held for self-insured liabilities, are recorded at cost. When a loss in the value of such investments occurs that is other than temporary, the investment is written down to recognize the loss.

Property and equipment

Property and equipment is recorded at cost less accumulated depreciation. Depreciation is calculated at annual rates designed to write off the costs of assets over their estimated useful lives as follows:

Engineering equipment	20–30%	declining balance
Business information systems		straight-line over 3–5 years
Office equipment	20–30%	declining balance
Automotive equipment	30%	declining balance
Leasehold improvements		straight-line over term of lease plus one renewal period to a maximum of 15 years or the improvement's economic life
Buildings	4–5%	declining balance

Leases

Leases that transfer substantially all the risks and benefits of ownership of assets to the Company are accounted for as capital leases. Assets under capital leases are recorded at the inception of the lease together with the related long-term obligation to reflect the purchase and financing thereof. Rental payments under operating leases are expensed as incurred.

From time to time, the Company enters into or renegotiates premises operating leases that result in the receipt of lease inducement benefits. These benefits are accounted for as a reduction of rental expense over the terms of the associated leases.

Goodwill and intangible assets

The cost of intangible assets with finite lives is amortized over the period in which the benefits of such assets are expected to be realized, principally on a straight-line basis. The Company's policy is to amortize client relationships with determinable lives over periods ranging from 10 to 15 years. Contract backlog is amortized over estimated contractual lives of generally less than one and a half years. Other intangible assets include technology, non-compete agreements, and advantageous leasehold commitments, which are amortized over estimated lives of one to five years. Goodwill is not amortized but is evaluated annually for impairment by comparing the fair value of the reporting unit, determined on a discounted after-tax cash flow basis, to the carrying value. An impairment loss would be recognized if the carrying value of the goodwill were to exceed its fair value.

Long-lived assets

The Company monitors the recoverability of long-lived assets, including property and equipment and intangible assets with finite lives, using factors such as expected future asset utilization, business climate, and future undiscounted cash flows expected to result from the use of the related assets. An impairment loss would be recognized if the carrying value of the long-lived asset were to exceed its fair value.

Accrual and investments held for self-insured liabilities

The Company self-insures certain risks related to professional liability and automobile physical damages. The accrual for self-insured liabilities includes estimates of the costs of reported claims (including potential claims that are probable of being asserted) and is based on estimates of loss using assumptions made by management, including consideration of actuarial projections. The accrual for self-insured liabilities does not include unasserted claims where assertion by a third party is not probable.

The Company invests funds to support the accrual for self-insured liabilities. These investments are classified in other assets as investments held for self-insured liabilities.

Forward contracts

The Company may enter into forward currency exchange contracts to manage risk associated with net operating assets denominated in US dollars. The Company's policy is to not utilize derivative financial instruments for trading or speculative purposes. These derivative contracts, which are not accounted for as hedges, are marked to market, and any changes in the market value are recorded in income or expense when the changes occur. The fair value of such instruments is recorded as either accounts receivable or payable.

Non-interest-bearing debt

Non-interest-bearing debt is carried at its present value using discount rates based on the bank prime rate prevailing at the time the debt was issued. The discount is applied over the term of the debt and is charged to interest expense.

Fair value of financial instruments

The carrying amounts of cash and cash equivalents, restricted cash, accounts receivable, bank loans, and accounts payable and accrued liabilities approximate their fair values because of the short-term maturity of these instruments. The carrying amount of bank loans approximates its fair value because the applicable interest rate is based on variable reference rates. The carrying values of other financial assets and financial liabilities approximate their fair values except as otherwise disclosed in the financial statements.

Credit risk

Financial instruments that subject the Company to credit risk consist primarily of cash and cash equivalents, investments held for self-insured liabilities, and accounts receivable. The Company maintains an allowance for estimated credit losses and mitigates the risk of its investment in bonds through the overall quality and mix of its bond portfolio. The Company provides services to diverse clients in various industries and sectors of the economy, and its credit risk is not concentrated in any particular client, industry, economic, or geographic sector.

Interest rate risk

The Company is subject to interest rate risk to the extent that its credit facilities are based on floating rates of interest. In addition, the Company is subject to interest rate pricing risk to the extent that its investments held for self-insured liabilities contain fixed rate government and corporate bonds. The Company has not entered into any derivative agreements to mitigate these risks.

Revenue recognition

In the course of providing its services, the Company incurs certain direct costs for subconsultants and other expenditures that are recoverable directly from clients. These direct costs are included in the Company's gross revenue. Since such direct costs can vary significantly from contract to contract, changes in gross revenue may not be indicative of the Company's revenue trends. Accordingly, the Company also reports net revenue, which is gross revenue less subconsultant and other direct expenses.

Revenue from fixed fee and variable fee with ceiling contracts is recognized using the percentage of completion method. Contract revenue is recognized on the ratio of contract costs incurred to total estimated costs. Provisions for estimated losses on incomplete contracts are made in the period in which the losses are determined. Revenue from time and material contracts without stated ceilings and from short-term projects is recognized as costs are incurred. Revenue is calculated based on billing rates for the services performed. Costs and estimated earnings in excess of billings represents work in progress that has been recognized as revenue but not yet invoiced to clients. Billings in excess of costs and estimated earnings represents amounts that have been invoiced to clients but not yet recognized as revenue.

Employee benefit plans

The Company contributes to group retirement savings plans and an employee share purchase plan based on the amount of employee contributions subject to maximum limits per employee. The Company accounts for such defined contributions as an expense in the period in which the contributions are made. The expense recorded in 2005 was $8,436,000 (2004 – $7,311,000; 2003 – $5,980,000). The Company does not provide postemployment or postretirement benefits.

Foreign currency translation

Transactions denominated in a foreign currency and the financial statements of foreign subsidiaries (excluding US-based subsidiaries) included in the consolidated financial statements are translated as follows: monetary items at the rate of exchange in effect at the balance sheet date; non-monetary items at historical exchange rates; and revenue and expense items (except depreciation and amortization, which are translated at historical exchange rates) at the average exchange rate for the year. Any resulting gains or losses are included in income in the year incurred.

The Company's US-based subsidiaries are designated as self-sustaining operations. The financial statements of these subsidiaries are translated using the current rate method. Under this method, assets and liabilities are translated at the rate of exchange in effect at the balance sheet date, and revenue and expense items (including depreciation and amortization) are translated at the average rate of exchange for the year. The resulting exchange gains and losses are deferred and included as a separate component of shareholders' equity in the cumulative translation account.

Stock-based compensation and other stock-based payments
The Company has one share option plan, which is described in note 12, and accounts for grants under this plan in accordance with the fair value-based method of accounting for stock-based compensation. Compensation expense for stock options awarded under the plan is measured at the fair value at the grant date using the Black-Scholes valuation model and is recognized over the vesting period of the options granted. In years prior to January 1, 2002, the Company recognized no compensation expense when shares or stock options were issued.

Investment tax credits
Investment tax credits arising from qualifying scientific research and experimental development efforts are recorded as a reduction of the applicable administrative and marketing expenses when there is reasonable assurance of their ultimate realization. Investment tax credits of $1,239,000 (2004 – $426,000; 2003 – $237,000) were recorded and reduced administrative and marketing expenses in 2005.

Income taxes
The Company uses the liability method to account for income taxes. Under this method, future income tax assets and liabilities are determined based on differences between financial reporting and the tax bases of assets and liabilities and measured using the substantively enacted tax rates and laws that will be in effect when these differences are expected to reverse.

Earnings per share
Basic earnings per share is computed based on the weighted average number of common shares outstanding during the year. Diluted earnings per share is computed using the treasury stock method, which assumes that the cash that would be received on the exercise of options is applied to purchase shares at the average price during the year and that the difference between the shares issued on the exercise of options and the number of shares obtainable under this computation, on a weighted average basis, is added to the number of shares outstanding. The impact of outstanding restricted shares, on a weighted average basis, is also added to the number of shares outstanding. Antidilutive options are not considered in computing diluted earnings per share.

Allowance for doubtful accounts
The Company maintains an allowance for doubtful accounts for estimated losses resulting from the inability to collect on its accounts receivable. The Company uses estimates in arriving at its allowance for doubtful accounts that are based, primarily, on the age of the outstanding accounts receivable and on its historical collection and loss experience.

Recent accounting pronouncements
In January 2005, the CICA released the new handbook Section 1530, "Comprehensive Income," and Section 3251, "Equity," effective for annual and interim periods beginning on or after October 1, 2006. These pronouncements further aligned Canadian GAAP with US GAAP (note 20). Section 1530 establishes standards for the reporting and display of comprehensive income. Comprehensive income is defined to include revenues, expenses, gains, and losses that, in accordance with primary sources of GAAP, are recognized in comprehensive income but excluded from net income. Section 1530 does not address issues

of recognition or measurement for comprehensive income and its components. Section 3251, "Equity," establishes standards for the presentation of equity and changes in equity during the reporting period. The requirements set out in Section 3251 are in addition to those established in Section 1530 and require that an enterprise present separately the components of equity: retained earnings, accumulated other comprehensive income, the total for retained earnings and accumulated other comprehensive income, contributed surplus, share capital, and reserves. Upon initial adoption of these recommendations in fiscal 2007, unrealized losses on the translation of self-sustaining foreign operations will be included in comprehensive income. Currently, these unrealized losses are reflected in the Company's cumulative translation account.

In January 2005, the CICA released the new handbook Section 3855, "Financial Instruments—Recognition and Measurement," effective for annual and interim periods beginning on or after October 1, 2006. This pronouncement further aligned Canadian GAAP with US GAAP (note 20). The section provides standards for the classification of financial instruments and related interest, dividends, gains, and losses. It prescribes when a financial instrument should be stated at fair value and when it would be valued using cost-based measures. Financial instruments are defined to include accounts receivable and payable, loans, investments in debt and equity securities, and derivative contracts. Upon initial adoption of these recommendations in fiscal 2007, the Company's investments held for self-insured liabilities will be reflected as investments held for sale, and the resulting unrealized gains or losses will be reflected through other comprehensive income until realized, at which time the gains or losses will be recognized in net income. This new standard is not expected to have a material effect on the results of the Company's operations.

2. Business Acquisitions

Acquisitions are accounted for under the purchase method of accounting, and the results of operations since the respective dates of acquisition are included in the consolidated statements of income. From time to time, as a result of the timing of acquisitions in relation to the Company's reporting schedule, certain of the purchase price allocations may not be finalized at the initial time of reporting. Purchase price allocations are completed after the vendors' final financial statements and income tax returns have been prepared and accepted by the Company. Such preliminary purchase price allocations are based on management's best estimates of the fair value of the acquired assets and liabilities. Upon finalization, adjustments to the initial estimates may be required, and these adjustments may be material. The purchase prices of acquisitions are generally subject to price adjustment clauses included in the purchase agreements. Such purchase price adjustments generally result in an increase or reduction to the promissory note consideration recorded at acquisition to reflect either more or less non-cash working capital realized than was originally expected. These purchase price adjustments, therefore, have no net effect on the original purchase price allocations. In the case of some acquisitions, additional consideration may be payable based on future performance parameters. As at December 31, 2005, the maximum contingent consideration that may be payable in 2006 and future years is approximately $9,000. This additional consideration is recorded as additional goodwill in the period in which the contingency is resolved.

Acquisitions in fiscal 2005

On August 3, 2005, the Company acquired the shares and business of CPV Group Architects & Engineers Ltd. for cash consideration. This acquisition strengthens the Company's architecture and interior design presence in Canada.

On September 15, 2005, the Company acquired the shares and business of The Keith Companies, Inc. (Keith) for a combination of cash consideration and Stantec common shares. Under the terms of the agreement, the number of common shares issued (3,328,776) as consideration was based on the average sale price of the Stantec common stock on the Toronto Stock Exchange for each of the 20 trading days ending on the second trading day prior to the closing of the merger, converted to US dollars for each trading day at the noon buying rate quoted by the Federal Reserve Bank of New York on such trading day. In order for the Keith transaction to qualify as a reorganization under the provisions of Section 368(a) of the U.S. Internal Revenue Code of 1986, a portion of Keith's cash, at the time of acquisition, is subject to restrictions on its use. Generally, the restricted cash can be used to fund further acquisitions as well as future capital expenditures. The acquisition of Keith supplements the Company's urban land development services group and increases the breadth and depth of the Company's multidiscipline engineering and consulting services by adding employees and offices throughout the western and midwestern United States.

On October 1, 2005, the Company acquired the shares and business of Keen Engineering Co. Ltd. for cash consideration and promissory notes. This acquisition supplements the Company's building design services in Canada and the western United States.

The purchase price allocations for the CPV Group Architects & Engineers Ltd., Keith, and Keen Engineering Co. Ltd. acquisitions have not yet been finalized. The Company expects to finalize the purchase price allocations for the CPV Group Architects & Engineers Ltd. and Keith acquisitions during the first quarter of 2006 and for the Keen Engineering Co. Ltd. acquisition during the second quarter of 2006.

During 2005, the Company paid additional contingent consideration in connection with the Cosburn Patterson Mather Limited (2002) acquisition and finalized the purchase price allocations for The Sear-Brown Group, Inc. (2004), GBR Architects Limited (2004), and Dunlop Architects Inc. (2004) acquisitions. In addition, the Company adjusted the purchase price on the Ecological Services Group Inc. (2003), GBR Architects Limited (2004), and Dunlop Architects Inc. (2004) acquisitions pursuant to price adjustment clauses included in the purchase agreements.

Acquisitions in fiscal 2004

During 2004, the Company acquired the shares and business of The Sear-Brown Group, Inc. (April 2, 2004), GBR Architects Limited (May 31, 2004), and Dunlop Architects Inc. (October 8, 2004) and the assets and business of Shaflik Engineering (November 26, 2004). The Sear-Brown Group, Inc. acquisition opened up a new geographic market for the Company in the northeastern United States and a new service in the bio/pharmaceuticals industry. The acquisition of GBR Architects Limited and of Dunlop Architects Inc. supplemented the Company's architecture and interior design practice while increasing its presence in Winnipeg and the Greater Toronto Area, respectively. The Shaflik Engineering acquisition strengthened the Company's capabilities for upcoming Olympic projects in British Columbia with its strong involvement in sports facilities and transportation systems.

During 2004, the Company also adjusted the purchase price in connection with the Cosburn Patterson Mather Limited (2002), The Spink Corporation (2001), the APAI Architecture Inc. and Mandalian Enterprises Limited (2003), the Graeme & Murray Consultants Ltd. (2002), the Ecological Services Group Inc. (2003), and The RPA Group (2002) acquisitions pursuant to price adjustment clauses included in the purchase agreements.

Aggregate consideration paid

Details of the aggregate consideration given and of the fair values of net assets acquired or adjusted for are as follows:

	Keith 2005 $000s	Other 2005 $000s	Total 2005 $000s	Total 2004 $000s
Cash consideration	107,062	11,200	118,262	12,432
Share consideration	125,540	–	125,540	–
Promissory notes	–	2,753	2,753	1,487
Purchase price	232,602	13,953	246,555	13,919
Assets and liabilities acquired at fair values				
Cash acquired (bank indebtedness assumed)	22,075	(4,196)	17,879	(6,413)
Restricted cash acquired	30,882	–	30,882	–
Non-cash working capital	9,747	3,929	13,676	6,057
Property and equipment	5,751	991	6,742	3,211
Investments	32	–	32	87
Goodwill	149,844	12,218	162,062	18,425
Other long-term assets	554	–	554	–
Intangible assets				
Client relationships	17,476	947	18,423	1,357
Contract backlog	3,995	1,053	5,048	301
Other	669	(139)	530	500
Other long-term liabilities	(1,380)	243	(1,137)	(1,642)
Long-term debt	–	(745)	(745)	(8,414)
Future income taxes	(8,226)	(348)	(8,574)	450
Deferred stock compensation	1,183	–	1,183	–
Net assets acquired	232,602	13,953	246,555	13,919

All of the goodwill is non-deductible for income tax purposes.

At the time of acquisition, management estimates the exit costs to downsize or close offices occupied by the acquired entity. These costs are accrued in other long-term liabilities as part of the purchase price allocation (note 9).

Pro forma data

The following unaudited pro forma data presents information as if the acquisitions of The Sear-Brown Group, Inc., GBR Architects Limited, Dunlop Architects Inc., Shaflik Engineering Ltd., CPV Group Architects & Engineers Ltd., Keith, and Keen Engineering Co. Ltd. had occurred on January 1, 2004. This unaudited pro forma data is provided for information purposes only and is based on historical information. This unaudited pro forma data does not necessarily reflect the actual results of operations that would have occurred had these acquired entities and Stantec Inc. comprised a single entity during the periods, nor is it necessarily indicative of the future results of the operations of the combined entities.

	2005 $000s	2004 $000s
		(Unaudited)
Pro forma gross revenue	753,291	726,827
Pro forma net revenue	646,614	628,844
Pro forma net income	49,098	39,563
Basic pro forma earnings per share	2.20	1.81
Diluted pro forma earnings per share	2.15	1.77

3. Property and Equipment

	2005		2004	
	Cost $000s	Accumulated Depreciation $000s	Cost $000s	Accumulated Depreciation $000s
Engineering equipment	42,560	22,736	33,622	19,058
Business information systems	11,475	4,237	9,681	1,796
Office equipment	23,030	10,071	19,953	7,519
Automotive equipment	5,263	2,867	4,254	2,578
Leasehold improvements	14,226	2,053	11,994	2,031
Buildings	4,204	704	1,901	594
Land	429	–	433	–
	101,187	42,668	81,838	33,576
Net book value	58,519		48,262	

In 2004 the Company completed the sale of its Edmonton office building (included in buildings and land) for cash proceeds of $34,500,000. Concurrent with the sale, the Company leased the property back for a period of 15 years. The lease is accounted for as an operating lease. The resulting gain of $7,103,000 was deferred and is being amortized over the lease term (note 9).

Included in leasehold improvements is construction work in progress in the amount of $337,000 (2004 – buildings – $89,000) on which depreciation has not started.

4. Goodwill

	2005 $000s	2004 $000s
Goodwill, beginning of the year	84,694	69,696
Current year acquisitions	160,840	18,006
Additional purchase price payments	700	–
Other purchase price adjustments	522	419
Impact of foreign exchange	(4,082)	(3,427)
Goodwill, end of the year	242,674	84,694

5. Intangible Assets

	2005		2004	
	Gross Carrying Amount $000s	Accumulated Amortization $000s	Gross Carrying Amount $000s	Accumulated Amortization $000s
Client relationships	**24,914**	**2,232**	6,859	1,195
Contract backlog	**4,900**	**1,219**	339	290
Other	**1,218**	**277**	750	185
	31,032	**3,728**	7,948	1,670
Carrying amount	**27,304**		6,278	

Once an intangible asset is fully amortized, the gross carrying amount and related accumulated amortization are removed from the accounts. Other than goodwill, the Company has not recognized any intangible assets with indefinite lives. For intangible assets held as of December 31, 2005, the estimated aggregate amortization expense for each of the next five years is as follows:

	$000s
2006	5,762
2007	3,154
2008	2,609
2009	2,541
2010	2,403
Thereafter	10,835
	27,304

6. Other Assets

	2005 $000s	2004 $000s
Investments held for self-insured liabilities	**16,857**	9,562
Investments in associated companies	**1,545**	1,909
Investments – other	**710**	1,114
Other	**554**	–
	19,666	12,585
Less current portion of investments held for self-insured liabilities	**6,569**	4,831
	13,097	7,754

The investments held for self-insured liabilities consist of government and corporate bonds of $14,013,000 (2004 – $8,740,000) and equity securities of $2,844,000 (2004 – $822,000). The bonds bear interest at rates ranging from 3.0 to 6.8% per annum (2004 – 3.5 to 8.6%). The estimated fair value of the bonds at December 31, 2005, was $13,721,000 (2004 – $8,761,000) and of the equities was $3,406,000 (2004 – $839,000). The term to maturity of the bond portfolio is $373,000 due within one year and $13,640,000 due from one to 10 years.

7. Accounts Payable and Accrued Liabilities

	2005 $000s	2004 $000s
Trade accounts payable	26,784	21,651
Employee and payroll liabilities	52,314	37,188
Accrued liabilities	27,659	19,879
	106,757	78,718

8. Long-Term Debt

	2005 $000s	2004 $000s
Non-interest-bearing note payable	122	111
Other non-interest-bearing notes payable	5,643	7,862
Bank loan	79,035	23,997
Mortgages payable	1,706	1,765
Other	193	240
	86,699	33,975
Less current portion	4,813	12,820
	81,886	21,155

The non-interest-bearing note payable is due November 1, 2027, in the amount of $933,000. The note's carrying value of $122,000 is determined using a discount rate of 9.75%. If the non-interest-bearing note payable were discounted at interest rates in effect at December 31, 2005, the fair value of the note would be $184,000 (2004 – $177,000).

The carrying values of the other non-interest-bearing notes payable have been calculated using a weighted average rate of interest of 5.58% and are supported by promissory notes. The notes are due at various times from 2006 to 2008. The aggregate maturity value of the notes is $5,985,000 (2004 – $8,336,000). As at December 31, 2005, there were no US-dollar non-interest-bearing notes outstanding. As at December 31, 2004, $47,000 of the notes' carrying value was payable in US funds (US$39,000). The carrying value of the other non-interest-bearing notes payable approximates their fair value based on interest rates in effect at December 31, 2005.

During 2005, the Company replaced its existing revolving credit facility with a revolving credit facility in the amount of $160 million due on August 31, 2008. This facility is available for acquisitions, working capital needs, capital expenditures, and general corporate purposes. At December 31, 2005, the facility was accessed to finance a portion of the Keith acquisition. Depending on the form under which the credit facility is accessed, rates of interest will vary between Canadian prime, US base rate, or LIBOR rate or bankers acceptance rates plus 65 or 85 basis points. As at December 31, 2005, $29,075,000 of the bank loan was payable in US funds (US$25,000,000). Repayment of loans under the credit facility may be made from time to time at the option of the Company. The average interest rate applicable at December 31, 2005, was 4.34% (2004 – 3.47%). The credit facility agreement contains restrictive covenants, including, but not limited to, debt to earnings ratio and earnings to debt service ratio. The Company was in compliance with all covenants under this agreement as at December 31, 2005. All assets of the Company are held as collateral under a general security agreement for the bank loan.

The mortgages payable bear interest at a weighted average rate of 7.67% and are supported by first mortgages against land and buildings. Subsequent to the year-end, the mortgages payable were paid out in full.

Other long-term debt bears interest at a weighted average rate of 3.5% and is due at dates ranging from 2006 to 2007. No assets are pledged in support of this debt.

Principal repayments required on long-term debt in each of the next five years and thereafter are as follows:

	$000s
2006	4,813
2007	1,661
2008	80,103
2009	–
2010	–
Thereafter	122
	86,699

The interest incurred on long-term debt in 2005 was $2,000,000 (2004 – $2,219,000; 2003 – $2,681,000). In 2005 total interest expense, net of interest income, was $571,000 (2004 – $2,805,000; 2003 – $2,637,000). At December 31, 2005, the Company had issued and outstanding letters of credit totaling $1,070,000.

9. Other Liabilities

	2005 $000s	2004 $000s
Provision for self-insured liabilities	12,866	5,236
Deferred gain on sale leaseback	6,624	7,073
Lease inducement benefits	7,997	4,742
Liabilities on lease exit activities	2,251	2,817
Other	1,021	–
	30,759	19,868
Less current portion included in accrued liabilities	5,995	3,050
	24,764	16,818

Provision for self-insured liabilities
Effective August 1, 2003, the Company began self-insuring a portion of its estimated liabilities that may arise in connection with reported legal claims (note 11). This provision is based on the results of an actuarial review performed in 2005 and 2004, with the current and long-term portion determined based on the actuarial estimate provided. At December 31, 2005, the long-term portion was $10,288,000 (2004 – $4,731,000).

	2005 $000s	2004 $000s
Provision, beginning of the year	5,236	2,410
Current year provision	9,764	2,826
Payment for claims settlement	(2,134)	–
Provision, end of the year	12,866	5,236

The self-insured liability increased during 2005, primarily due to new claims incurred and reported since the end of 2004. Claim settlements of $2,134,000 were made in 2005. The timing of such settlement payments is dependent upon the resolution of case-specific matters and may extend over several months or years.

Liabilities on lease exit activities

Charges are accrued when management closes offices in existing operations or finalizes plans to downsize offices in locations assumed from an acquiree upon a business acquisition. Included in the liability is the present value of the remaining lease payments, reduced by estimated sublease rentals that can reasonably be obtained.

	2005 $000s	2004 $000s
Liability, beginning of the year	2,817	–
Current year provision:		
Established for existing operations	609	936
Resulting from acquisitions	276	3,465
Payment or reductions:		
Impacting net income	(1,103)	(1,375)
Impacting the purchase price allocation	(325)	–
Impact of foreign exchange	(23)	(209)
Liability, end of the year	2,251	2,817

10. Commitments

Commitments for annual basic premises rent under long-term leases and for equipment and vehicle operating leases for the next five years are as follows:

	$000s
2006	34,794
2007	31,248
2008	25,240
2009	21,936
2010	18,910
Thereafter	79,585
	211,713

The premise rental expense for the year ended December 31, 2005, was $29,282,000 (2004 – $25,116,000; 2003 – $19,321,000).

11. Contingencies

In the normal conduct of operations, various legal claims are pending against the Company alleging, among other things, breaches of contract or negligence in connection with the performance of consulting services. The Company carries professional liability insurance, subject to certain deductibles and policy limits, and has a captive insurance company that provides insurance protection against such claims. In some cases, parties are seeking damages that substantially exceed the Company's insurance coverage. Based on advice and information provided by legal counsel, the Company's previous experience with the settlement of similar claims, and the results of the annual actuarial review, management believes that the Company has recognized adequate provisions for probable and reasonably estimable liabilities associated with these claims and that their ultimate resolutions will not materially exceed insurance coverages or have a material adverse effect on the Company's consolidated financial position or annual results of operations. Management cannot estimate the extent to which losses exceeding those already recorded in the financial statements may be incurred.

12. Share Capital

Authorized

Unlimited	Common shares, with no par value
Unlimited	Preferred shares issuable in series with attributes designated by the Board of Directors

Common shares issued and outstanding

	Capital Stock						Contributed Surplus		
	2005		2004		2003		2005	2004	2003
	Shares		Shares		Shares				
	#	$000s	#	$000s	#	$000s	$000s	$000s	$000s
Balance, beginning of the year	18,871,085	87,656	18,327,284	84,281	18,282,720	83,973	2,544	1,842	1,247
Share options exercised for cash	120,070	961	573,101	3,490	119,264	651			
Stock-based compensation expense							963	725	600
Shares repurchased under normal course issuer bid.	(6,800)	(33)	(29,300)	(134)	(74,700)	(343)	(1)	(4)	(5)
Reclassification of fair value of stock options previously expensed		159		19		–	(159)	(19)	–
Shares issued on acquisition	3,328,776	123,365	–	–	–	–			
Restricted shares issued on acquisition							2,175	–	–
Share issue costs ..		(1,504)		–		–			
Balance, end of the year	**22,313,131**	**210,604**	18,871,085	87,656	18,327,284	84,281	**5,522**	2,544	1,842

During 2005, 6,800 common shares (2004 – 29,300; 2003 – 74,700) were repurchased for cancellation pursuant to an ongoing Normal Course Issuer Bid at a cost of $195,000 (2004 – $720,000; 2003 –

$1,392,000). Of this amount, $33,000 and $1,000 (2004 – $134,000 and $4,000; 2003 – $343,000 and $5,000) reduced the share capital and contributed surplus accounts, respectively, with $161,000 (2004 – $582,000; 2003 – $1,044,000) being charged to retained earnings.

During 2005, the Company incurred share issue costs of $1,969,000 less a future tax recovery of $465,000.

During 2005, the Company recognized a stock-based compensation expense of $1,814,000 (2004 – $1,014,000; 2003 – $706,000) in administrative and marketing expenses. Of the amount expensed, $963,000 related to the fair value of the options granted (2004 – $725,000; 2003 – $600,000); $519,000 related to deferred share unit compensation (2004 – $289,000; 2003 – $106,000), and $332,000 related to the restricted shares issued on the Keith acquisition. The fair value of the options granted was reflected through contributed surplus; the deferred share unit compensation was reflected through accrued liabilities; and the restricted shares were reflected through deferred stock compensation. Upon the exercise of share options for which a stock-based compensation expense has been recognized, the cash paid together with the related portion of contributed surplus is credited to share capital. Upon the vesting of restricted shares for which a stock-based compensation expense has been recognized, the related portion of contributed surplus is credited to share capital.

Share options

Under the Company's share option plan, options to purchase common shares may be granted by the Board of Directors to directors, officers, and employees. Options are granted at exercise prices equal to or greater than fair market value at the issue date, generally vest evenly over a three-year period, and have contractual lives that range from five to 10 years. The aggregate number of common shares reserved for issuance that may be purchased upon the exercise of options granted pursuant to the plan shall not exceed 996,003 common shares. At December 31, 2005, 57,739 options were available for issue.

The Company has granted share options to directors, officers, and employees to purchase 938,264 shares at prices between $3.50 and $27.10 per share. These options expire on dates between March 14, 2006, and January 2, 2013.

	2005		2004		2003	
	Shares #	Weighted Average Exercise Price $	Shares #	Weighted Average Exercise Price $	Shares #	Weighted Average Exercise Price $
Share options, beginning of the year	1,071,333	13.34	1,479,100	9.28	1,296,200	6.09
Granted	–	–	167,000	24.50	307,500	21.29
Exercised	(120,070)	8.00	(573,101)	6.09	(119,264)	5.46
Cancelled	(12,999)	23.69	(1,666)	18.40	(5,336)	12.62
Share options, end of the year	938,264	13.88	1,071,333	13.34	1,479,100	9.28

The Company had issued options to directors, officers, and employees at December 31, 2005, as follows:

	Options Outstanding			Options Exercisable	
Range of Exercise Prices $	Outstanding #	Weighted Average Remaining Contractual Life in Years	Weighted Average Exercise Price $	Shares Exercisable #	Weighted Average Exercise Price $
3.50 – 3.60	347,500	0.8	3.56	347,500	3.56
5.20 – 7.00	40,550	0.8	6.05	40,550	6.05
14.50 – 18.85	159,400	4.1	15.62	159,400	15.62
21.00 – 27.10	390,814	5.8	23.17	148,654	22.22
3.50 – 27.10	938,264	3.4	13.88	696,104	10.45

The fair value of options granted subsequent to January 1, 2002, is determined at the date of grant using the Black-Scholes option-pricing model. The Black-Scholes option valuation model was developed for use in estimating the fair value of traded options that have no vesting restrictions and are fully transferable. In addition, option valuation models require the input of highly subjective assumptions, including expected stock price volatility. Because the Company's employee stock options have characteristics that are significantly different from those of traded options, and because changes in subjective input assumptions can materially affect the fair value estimate, in management's opinion the existing models do not necessarily provide a reliable single measure of the fair value of the Company's employee stock options.

The estimated fair value of options granted both at the share market price on the grant date and in excess of the share market price on the grant date was determined using the weighted average assumptions indicated below. No options were granted in 2005.

	2004	2003	
	Granted at Market	Granted at Market	Granted in Excess of Market
Risk-free interest rate (%)	4.07	4.48	5.04
Expected hold period to exercise (years)	6.0	6.2	9.1
Volatility in the price of the Company's shares (%) ...	26.1	27.4	28.5
Weighted average fair value per option ($)	8.46	7.40	6.04

13. Cumulative Translation Account

The foreign currency cumulative translation account represents the unrealized gain or loss on the Company's net investment in self-sustaining US-based operations. The change in the cumulative translation account during the year relates to the fluctuation in the value of the Canadian dollar relative to the US dollar. Balance sheet accounts denominated in US dollars have been translated to Canadian dollars at the rate of 1.1630 (2004 – 1.2020; 2003 – 1.2965).

	2005 $000s	2004 $000s	2003 $000s
Cumulative translation account, beginning of the year	(19,018)	(13,861)	1,966
Current year deferred translation adjustment	(6,557)	(5,157)	(15,827)
Cumulative translation account, end of the year	(25,575)	(19,018)	(13,861)

14. Income Taxes

The effective income tax rate in the consolidated statements of income differs from statutory Canadian tax rates as a result of the following:

	2005 %	2004 %	2003 %
Income tax expense at statutory Canadian rates	34.8	34.7	36.8
Increase (decrease) resulting from:			
Income from associated companies	(0.1)	(0.3)	(0.6)
Rate differential on foreign income	0.7	(2.0)	0.6
Non-deductible expenses:			
Meals and entertainment	1.1	1.4	1.4
Stock compensation	0.5	0.6	0.6
Non-taxable foreign income net of non-creditable			
withholding taxes	(1.6)	(1.3)	(1.6)
Other	(0.4)	(0.7)	(0.5)
	35.0	32.4	36.7

Since the Company operates in several tax jurisdictions, its income is subject to various rates of taxation. The details of income before income taxes are as follows:

	2005 $000s	2004 $000s	2003 $000s
Domestic	61,323	48,111	36,583
Foreign	1,177	(3,451)	3,045
Total income before income taxes	62,500	44,660	39,628

Details of the income tax expense (recovery) are as follows:

		2005 $000s	2004 $000s	2003 $000s
Current:	Domestic	21,172	17,724	9,474
	Foreign	563	341	576
Total current expense		21,735	18,065	10,050
Future:	Domestic	5	(566)	3,532
	Foreign	138	(3,029)	976
Total future expense		143	(3,595)	4,508
Total:	Domestic	21,177	17,158	13,006
	Foreign	701	(2,688)	1,552
Total income tax expense		21,878	14,470	14,558

Significant components of the Company's future income tax assets and liabilities are as follows:

Future income tax assets	2005 $000s	2004 $000s
Differences in timing of deductibility of expenses	13,470	9,434
Loss carryforwards	4,670	2,316
Share issue and other financing costs	519	237
Tax cost of property and equipment in excess of carrying value	357	684
Deferred gain on sale of building	1,513	1,518
Other	1,112	700
	21,641	14,889
Less current portion	14,827	8,532
	6,814	6,357

Future income tax liabilities	2005 $000s	2004 $000s
Cash to accrual adjustments on acquisitions of US subsidiaries	–	2,091
Differences in timing of taxability of revenues	15,287	7,702
Carrying value of property and equipment in excess of tax cost	7,304	5,025
Carrying value of intangible assets in excess of tax cost	10,625	2,016
Other	598	2,135
	33,814	18,969
Less current portion	17,552	10,653
	16,262	8,316

At December 31, 2005, loss carryforwards of approximately $3,374,000 are available to reduce the taxable income of certain Canadian subsidiaries. These losses expire as set out below:

	$000s
2007	194
2008	1,454
2009	66
2010	978
2014	664
2015	18
	3,374

In addition, the Company has loss carryforwards of approximately $10,625,000 available to reduce the taxable income of certain US subsidiaries that expire at varying times over the next 20 years.

The potential income tax benefits that will result from the application of Canadian and US tax losses have been recognized in these financial statements.

15. Earnings Per Share

The number of basic and diluted common shares outstanding, as calculated on a weighted average basis, is as follows:

	2005 #	2004 #	2003 #
Basic shares outstanding	19,920,117	18,499,598	18,329,960
Share options (dilutive effect of 938,264 options; 2004 – 1,041,333; 2003 – 1,419,100)	533,792	507,691	788,056
Restricted shares (dilutive effect of 58,696 restricted shares)	17,207	–	–
Diluted shares outstanding	20,471,116	19,007,289	19,118,016

16. Cash Flows From (Used In) Operating Activities

Cash flows from operating activities determined by the indirect method are as follows:

	2005 $000s	2004 $000s	2003 $000s
CASH FLOWS FROM OPERATING ACTIVITIES			
Net income for the year	40,622	30,190	25,070
Add (deduct) items not affecting cash:			
Depreciation of property and equipment	12,389	11,986	9,912
Amortization of intangible assets	2,542	927	925
Future income tax	143	(3,595)	4,508
Loss (gain) on dispositions of investments and property and equipment	562	(504)	57
Stock-based compensation expense	1,814	894	706
Provision for self-insured liability	9,764	2,826	–
Other non-cash items	(1,332)	(1,065)	–
Share of income from equity investments	(187)	(385)	(580)
Dividends from equity investments	550	300	–
	66,867	41,574	40,598
Change in non-cash working capital accounts:			
Accounts receivable	15,748	(1,542)	(1,252)
Costs and estimated earnings in excess of billings	(19,572)	30,218	(35,239)
Prepaid expenses	487	496	113
Accounts payable and accrued liabilities	(2,697)	(6,350)	13,944
Billings in excess of costs and estimated earnings	1,664	1,600	4,951
Income taxes payable/recoverable	(5,183)	11,355	(6,222)
	(9,553)	35,777	(23,705)
Cash flows from operating activities	57,314	77,351	16,893

17. Joint Ventures

The Company participates in joint ventures with other parties as follows:

	Percentage Owned		
	2005 %	2004 %	2003 %
yyC.T. Joint Venture	20	20	20
Stantec – S&L Partnership	50	50	50
Colt Stantec Joint Venture	n/a	50	50
Edmonton International Airports Joint Venture	33	33	33
Pine Creek Consultants Joint Venture	33	33	33
Dunlop Joint Ventures	33–80	33–80	n/a
Stantec Architecture Ltd./J.L. Richards & Associates Joint Venture	50	n/a	n/a

As part of the acquisition of Dunlop Architects Inc. (Dunlop), the Company acquired the interests of 13 joint ventures entered into by Dunlop. The interest held in these joint ventures ranges from 33 to 80%, and each is project specific.

A summary of the assets, liabilities, revenues, expenses, and cash flows included in the consolidated financial statements related to joint ventures is as follows:

	2005 $000s	2004 $000s	2003 $000s
Statement of income			
Gross revenue	5,941	1,186	11,949
Subconsultant and other direct expenses	5,072	894	9,611
Administrative and marketing expenses	147	217	776
Net income for the year	722	75	1,562
Balance sheets			
Current assets	3,743	3,445	1,547
Current liabilities	2,842	2,822	1,583
Statement of cash flows			
Cash flows used in operating activities	(488)	(274)	(86)

18. Segmented Information

The Company provides comprehensive professional services in the area of infrastructure and facilities throughout North America and internationally. The Company considers the basis on which it is organized, including geographic areas and service offerings, in identifying its reportable segments. Operating segments of the Company are defined as components of the Company for which separate financial information is available that is evaluated regularly by the chief operating decision maker in allocating resources and assessing performance. The chief operating decision maker is the Chief Executive Officer (CEO) of the Company, and the Company's operating segments are based on its regional geographic areas.

During 2003, the Company had seven operating segments, of which five were aggregated into the Consulting Services reportable segment. The two remaining operating segments (Design Build and Technology), which were below the quantitative thresholds in the recommendations of the CICA, were disclosed in the Other reportable segment. In addition to the above-noted operating segments, corporate administration groups reported to the CEO and were included in the Other reportable segment. In the second quarter of 2004, an additional operating segment was added upon the acquisition of The Sear-Brown Group, Inc. This new segment has been aggregated into the Consulting Services reportable segment.

The Design Build operating segment consisted of the operations of the Company's 50% share of Lockerbie Stanley Inc. that, at December 31, 2003, was reflected as assets held for sale pending the finalization of an agreement to sell the Company's interest. The sale was completed in 2004. In addition, during 2004, the Company sold the operations related to its Technology segment. Operations sold during the year have not been presented as discontinued operations, because the amounts are not material.

Effective 2004, because the operations that comprised the Company's Design Build and Technology segments were sold and because the Company's corporate administration groups are not material, all operations of the Company are included in one reportable segment as Consulting Services.

Geographic information

	Property and Equipment, Goodwill, Intangible Assets	
	2005 $000s	2004 $000s
Canada	104,463	86,731
United States	223,593	52,032
International	441	471
	328,497	139,234

Geographic information

	Gross Revenue		
	2005 $000s	2004 $000s	2003 $000s
Canada	380,471	325,844	290,413
United States	233,428	190,362	161,655
International	4,121	4,673	7,874
	618,020	520,879	459,942

Gross revenue is attributed to countries based on the location of work performed.

Practice area information

	Gross Revenue		
	2005 $000s	2004 $000s	2003 $000s
Consulting Services			
Environment	104,437	105,471	91,758
Buildings	159,233	107,465	89,943
Transportation	92,146	92,631	80,519
Urban Land	208,903	168,876	159,941
Industrial	53,301	45,371	33,304
	618,020	519,814	455,465
Other	–	1,065	4,477
	618,020	520,879	459,942

Customers

The Company has a large number of clients in various industries and sectors of the economy. Gross revenue is not concentrated in any particular client.

19. Forward Contracts

The Company had no forward contracts outstanding at December 31, 2005. As at December 31, 2004, the Company had entered into foreign currency forward contracts that provided for the sale of US$10.0 million at rates ranging from 1.2050 to 1.2386 per US dollar. The fair values of these contracts, estimated using market rates at December 31, 2004, were $229,000. During 2004, net unrealized gains of $229,000 relating to derivative financial instruments were recorded in foreign exchange (gains) losses.

20. United States Generally Accepted Accounting Principles

The consolidated financial statements of the Company are prepared in Canadian dollars in accordance with accounting principles generally accepted in Canada (Canadian GAAP) that, in most respects, conform to accounting principles generally accepted in the United States (US GAAP). The following adjustments and disclosures would be required in order to present these consolidated financial statements in accordance with US GAAP. Investments in joint ventures are accounted for using the equity method under US GAAP, whereas Canadian GAAP requires the proportionate consolidation method. As permitted by the Securities and Exchange Commission, no disclosure of the effect of this difference is required.

a) Net income and comprehensive income

There are no identifiable material items that would result in a change in net income presented under Canadian and US GAAP.

The Company accounts for leases in accordance with Statement of Financial Accounting Standards No. 13, "Accounting for leases" (SFAS 13). SFAS 13 requires leasehold improvements in an operating lease to be amortized over the shorter of their economic lives or the lease term, as defined in SFAS 13. As a result, SFAS 13 requires the amortization period for leasehold improvements to be shorter than that applied by the Company under Canadian GAAP. The incremental amortization has been determined to be immaterial to the years presented.

Under US GAAP, the Company's investments held for self-insured liabilities would be classified as investments available for sale and recorded at fair value (note 6). The difference between the recorded and fair value of these investments has been determined to be immaterial to the years presented.

Comprehensive income is measured in accordance with Statement of Financial Accounting Standards No. 130, "Reporting Comprehensive Income" (SFAS 130). This standard defines comprehensive income as all changes in equity other than those resulting from investments by owners and distributions to owners and includes adjustments arising on the translation of self-sustaining foreign operations. Canadian GAAP does not yet require similar disclosure.

Statement of Comprehensive Income

	2005 $000s	2004 $000s	2003 $000s
Net income under Canadian and US GAAP	**40,622**	30,190	25,070
Other comprehensive income, net of tax:			
Unrealized foreign exchange loss on translation			
of self-sustaining foreign operations	**(6,557)**	(5,157)	(15,827)
Comprehensive Income	**34,065**	25,033	9,243
Accumulated other comprehensive income,			
beginning of year	**(19,018)**	(13,861)	1,966
Unrealized foreign exchange loss on translation			
of self-sustaining foreign operations	**(6,557)**	(5,157)	(15,827)
Accumulated other comprehensive income, end of the year	**(25,575)**	(19,018)	(13,861)

b) Other disclosure requirements

i) Allowance for doubtful accounts

	2005 $000s	2004 $000s	2003 $000s
Balance, beginning of the year	**21,095**	16,952	17,316
Acquired balances	**7,298**	5,294	651
Provision for doubtful accounts	**73**	6,632	4,544
Deductions	**(12,164)**	(7,152)	(4,221)
Impact on foreign exchange	**(249)**	(631)	(1,338)
Balance, end of the year	**16,053**	21,095	16,952

ii) Long-term contracts

Included in accounts receivable are holdbacks on long-term contracts of $1,431,000 in 2005 and of $3,653,000 in 2004.

21. Comparative Figures

Certain comparative figures have been reclassified to conform to the presentation adopted for the current year.

Table A-1

FUTURE VALUE OF 1
(FUTURE VALUE OF A SINGLE SUM)

$$FVF_{n,i} = (1+i)^n$$

(n) periods	2%	2½%	3%	4%	5%	6%	8%	9%	10%	11%	12%	15%
1	1.02000	1.02500	1.03000	1.04000	1.05000	1.06000	1.08000	1.09000	1.10000	1.11000	1.12000	1.15000
2	1.04040	1.05063	1.06090	1.08160	1.10250	1.12360	1.16640	1.18810	1.21000	1.23210	1.25440	1.32250
3	1.06121	1.07689	1.09273	1.12486	1.15763	1.19102	1.25971	1.29503	1.33100	1.36763	1.40493	1.52088
4	1.08243	1.10381	1.12551	1.16986	1.21551	1.26248	1.36049	1.41158	1.46410	1.51807	1.57352	1.74901
5	1.10408	1.13141	1.15927	1.21665	1.27628	1.33823	1.46933	1.53862	1.61051	1.68506	1.76234	2.01136
6	1.12616	1.15969	1.19405	1.26532	1.34010	1.41852	1.58687	1.67710	1.77156	1.87041	1.97382	2.31306
7	1.14869	1.18869	1.22987	1.31593	1.40710	1.50363	1.71382	1.82804	1.94872	2.07616	2.21068	2.66002
8	1.17166	1.21840	1.26677	1.36857	1.47746	1.59385	1.85093	1.99256	2.14359	2.30454	2.47596	3.05902
9	1.19509	1.24886	1.30477	1.42331	1.55133	1.68948	1.99900	2.17189	2.35795	2.55803	2.77308	3.51788
10	1.21899	1.28008	1.34392	1.48024	1.62889	1.79085	2.15892	2.36736	2.59374	2.83942	3.10585	4.04556
11	1.24337	1.31209	1.38423	1.53945	1.71034	1.89830	2.33164	2.58043	2.85312	3.15176	3.47855	4.65239
12	1.26824	1.34489	1.42576	1.60103	1.79586	2.01220	2.51817	2.81267	3.13843	3.49845	3.89598	5.35025
13	1.29361	1.37851	1.46853	1.66507	1.88565	2.13293	2.71962	3.06581	3.45227	3.88328	4.36349	6.15279
14	1.31948	1.41297	1.51259	1.73168	1.97993	2.26090	2.93719	3.34173	3.79750	4.31044	4.88711	7.07571
15	1.34587	1.44830	1.55797	1.80094	2.07893	2.39656	3.17217	3.64248	4.17725	4.78459	5.47357	8.13706
16	1.37279	1.48451	1.60471	1.87298	2.18287	2.54035	3.42594	3.97031	4.59497	5.31089	6.13039	9.35762
17	1.40024	1.52162	1.65285	1.94790	2.29202	2.69277	3.70002	4.32763	5.05447	5.89509	6.86604	10.76126
18	1.42825	1.55966	1.70243	2.02582	2.40662	2.85434	3.99602	4.71712	5.55992	6.54355	7.68997	12.37545
19	1.45681	1.59865	1.75351	2.10685	2.52695	3.02560	4.31570	5.14166	6.11591	7.26334	8.61276	14.23177
20	1.48595	1.63862	1.80611	2.19112	2.65330	3.20714	4.66096	5.60441	6.72750	8.06231	9.64629	16.36654
21	1.51567	1.67958	1.86029	2.27877	2.78596	3.39956	5.03383	6.10881	7.40025	8.94917	10.80385	18.82152
22	1.54598	1.72157	1.91610	2.36992	2.92526	3.60354	5.43654	6.65860	8.14028	9.93357	12.10031	21.64475
23	1.57690	1.76461	1.97359	2.46472	3.07152	3.81975	5.87146	7.25787	8.95430	11.02627	13.55235	24.89146
24	1.60844	1.80873	2.03279	2.56330	3.22510	4.04893	6.34118	7.91108	9.84973	12.23916	15.17863	28.62518
25	1.64061	1.85394	2.09378	2.66584	3.38635	4.29187	6.84847	8.62308	10.83471	13.58546	17.00000	32.91895
26	1.67342	1.90029	2.15659	2.77247	3.55567	4.54938	7.39635	9.39916	11.91818	15.07986	19.04007	37.85680
27	1.70689	1.94780	2.22129	2.88337	3.73346	4.82235	7.98806	10.24508	13.10999	16.73865	21.32488	43.53532
28	1.74102	1.99650	2.28793	2.99870	3.92013	5.11169	8.62711	11.16714	14.42099	18.57990	23.88387	50.06561
29	1.77584	2.04641	2.35657	3.11865	4.11614	5.41839	9.31727	12.17218	15.86309	20.62369	26.74993	57.57545
30	1.81136	2.09757	2.42726	3.24340	4.32194	5.74349	10.06266	13.26768	17.44940	22.89230	29.95992	66.21177
31	1.84759	2.15001	2.50008	3.37313	4.53804	6.08810	10.86767	14.46177	19.19434	25.41045	33.55511	76.14354
32	1.88454	2.20376	2.57508	3.50806	4.76494	6.45339	11.73708	15.76333	21.11378	28.20560	37.58173	87.56507
33	1.92223	2.25885	2.65234	3.64838	5.00319	6.84059	12.67605	17.18203	23.22515	31.30821	42.09153	100.69983
34	1.96068	2.31532	2.73191	3.79432	5.25335	7.25103	13.69013	18.72841	25.54767	34.75212	47.14252	115.80480
35	1.99989	2.37321	2.81386	3.94609	5.51602	7.68609	14.78534	20.41397	28.10244	38.57485	52.79962	133.17552
36	2.03989	2.43254	2.88928	4.10393	5.79182	8.14725	15.96817	22.25123	30.91268	42.81808	59.13557	153.15185
37	2.08069	2.49335	2.98523	4.26809	6.08141	8.63609	17.24563	24.25384	34.00395	47.52807	66.23184	176.12463
38	2.12230	2.55568	3.07478	4.43881	6.38548	9.15425	18.62528	26.43668	37.40434	52.75616	74.17966	202.54332
39	2.16474	2.61957	3.16703	4.61637	6.70475	9.70351	20.11530	28.81598	41.14479	58.55934	83.08122	232.92482
40	2.20804	2.68506	3.26204	4.80102	7.03999	10.28572	21.72452	31.40942	45.25926	65.00087	93.05097	267.86355

Table A-2

PRESENT VALUE OF 1

(PRESENT VALUE OF A SINGLE SUM)

$$PVF_{n,i} = \frac{1}{(1+i)^n} = (1+i)^{-n}$$

(n) periods	2%	2½%	3%	4%	5%	6%	8%	9%	10%	11%	12%	15%
1	.98039	.97561	.97087	.96156	.95238	.94340	.92593	.91743	.90909	.90090	.89286	.86957
2	.96117	.95181	.94260	.92456	.90703	.89000	.85734	.84168	.82645	.81162	.79719	.75614
3	.94232	.92860	.91514	.88900	.86384	.83962	.79383	.77218	.75132	.73119	.71178	.65752
4	.92385	.90595	.88849	.85480	.82270	.79209	.73503	.70843	.68301	.65873	.63552	.57175
5	.90583	.88385	.86261	.82193	.78353	.74726	.68058	.64993	.62092	.59345	.56743	.49718
6	.88797	.86230	.83748	.79031	.74622	.70496	.63017	.59627	.56447	.53464	.50663	.43233
7	.87056	.84127	.81309	.75992	.71068	.66506	.58349	.54703	.51316	.48166	.45235	.37594
8	.85349	.82075	.78941	.73069	.67684	.62741	.54027	.50187	.46651	.43393	.40388	.32690
9	.83676	.80073	.76642	.70259	.64461	.59190	.50025	.46043	.42410	.39092	.36061	.28426
10	.82035	.78120	.74409	.67556	.61391	.55839	.46319	.42241	.38554	.35218	.32197	.24719
11	.80426	.76214	.72242	.64958	.58468	.52679	.42888	.38753	.35049	.31728	.28748	.21494
12	.78849	.74356	.70138	.62460	.55684	.49697	.39711	.35554	.31863	.28584	.25668	.18691
13	.77303	.72542	.68095	.60057	.53032	.46884	.36770	.32618	.28966	.25751	.22917	.16253
14	.75788	.70773	.66112	.57748	.50507	.44230	.34046	.29925	.26333	.23199	.20462	.14133
15	.74301	.69047	.64186	.55526	.48102	.41727	.31524	.27454	.23939	.20900	.18270	.12289
16	.72845	.67362	.62317	.53391	.45811	.39365	.29189	.25187	.21763	.18829	.16312	.10687
17	.71416	.65720	.60502	.51337	.43630	.37136	.27027	.23107	.19785	.16963	.14564	.09293
18	.70016	.64117	.58739	.49363	.41552	.35034	.25025	.21199	.17986	.15282	.13004	.08081
19	.68643	.62553	.57029	.47464	.39573	.33051	.23171	.19449	.16351	.13768	.11611	.07027
20	.67297	.61027	.55368	.45639	.37689	.31180	.21455	.17843	.14864	.12403	.10367	.06110
21	.65978	.59539	.53755	.43883	.35894	.29416	.19866	.16370	.13513	.11174	.09256	.05313
22	.64684	.58086	.52189	.42196	.34185	.27751	.18394	.15018	.12285	.10067	.08264	.04620
23	.63416	.56670	.50669	.40573	.32557	.26180	.17032	.13778	.11168	.09069	.07379	.04017
24	.62172	.55288	.49193	.39012	.31007	.24698	.15770	.12641	.10153	.08170	.06588	.03493
25	.60953	.53939	.47761	.37512	.29530	.23300	.14602	.11597	.09230	.07361	.05882	.03038
26	.59758	.52623	.46369	.36069	.28124	.21981	.13520	.10639	.08391	.06631	.05252	.02642
27	.58586	.51340	.45019	.34682	.26785	.20737	.12519	.09761	.07628	.05974	.04689	.02297
28	.57437	.50088	.43708	.33348	.25509	.19563	.11591	.08955	.06934	.05382	.04187	.01997
29	.56311	.48866	.42435	.32065	.24295	.18456	.10733	.08216	.06304	.04849	.03738	.01737
30	.55207	.47674	.41199	.30832	.23138	.17411	.09938	.07537	.05731	.04368	.03338	.01510
31	.54125	.46511	.39999	.29646	.22036	.16425	.09202	.06915	.05210	.03935	.02980	.01313
32	.53063	.45377	.38834	.28506	.20987	.15496	.08520	.06344	.04736	.03545	.02661	.01142
33	.52023	.44270	.37703	.27409	.19987	.14619	.07889	.05820	.04306	.03194	.02376	.00993
34	.51003	.43191	.36604	.26355	.19035	.13791	.07305	.05340	.03914	.02878	.02121	.00864
35	.50003	.42137	.35538	.25342	.18129	.13011	.06763	.04899	.03558	.02592	.01894	.00751
36	.49022	.41109	.34503	.24367	.17266	.12274	.06262	.04494	.03235	.02335	.01691	.00653
37	.48061	.40107	.33498	.23430	.16444	.11579	.05799	.04123	.02941	.02104	.01510	.00568
38	.47119	.39128	.32523	.22529	.15661	.10924	.05369	.03783	.02674	.01896	.01348	.00494
39	.46195	.38174	.31575	.21662	.14915	.10306	.04971	.03470	.02430	.01708	.01204	.00429
40	.45289	.37243	.30656	.20829	.14205	.09722	.04603	.03184	.02210	.01538	.01075	.00373

Table A-3

FUTURE VALUE OF AN ORDINARY ANNUITY OF 1

$$FVF-OA_{n,\,i} = \frac{(1+i)^n - 1}{i}$$

(n) periods	2%	2½%	3%	4%	5%	6%	8%	9%	10%	11%	12%	15%
1	1.00000	1.00000	1.00000	1.00000	1.00000	1.00000	1.00000	1.00000	1.00000	1.00000	1.00000	1.00000
2	2.02000	2.02500	2.03000	2.04000	2.05000	2.06000	2.08000	2.09000	2.10000	2.11000	2.12000	2.15000
3	3.06040	3.07563	3.09090	3.12160	3.15250	3.18360	3.24640	3.27810	3.31000	3.34210	3.37440	3.47250
4	4.12161	4.15252	4.18363	4.24646	4.31013	4.37462	4.50611	4.57313	4.64100	4.70973	4.77933	4.99338
5	5.20404	5.25633	5.30914	5.41632	5.52563	5.63709	5.86660	5.98471	6.10510	6.22780	6.35285	6.74238
6	6.30812	6.38774	6.46841	6.63298	6.80191	6.97532	7.33592	7.52334	7.71561	7.91286	8.11519	8.75374
7	7.43428	7.54743	7.66246	7.89829	8.14201	8.39384	8.92280	9.20044	9.48717	9.78327	10.08901	11.06680
8	8.58297	8.73612	8.89234	9.21423	9.54911	9.89747	10.63663	11.02847	11.43589	11.85943	12.29969	13.72682
9	9.75463	9.95452	10.15911	10.58280	11.02656	11.49132	12.48756	13.02104	13.57948	14.16397	14.77566	16.78584
10	10.94972	11.20338	11.46338	12.00611	12.57789	13.18079	14.48656	15.19293	15.93743	16.72201	17.54874	20.30372
11	12.16872	12.48347	12.80780	13.48635	14.20679	14.97164	16.64549	17.56029	18.53117	19.56143	20.65458	24.34928
12	13.41209	13.79555	14.19203	15.02581	15.91713	16.86994	18.97713	20.14072	21.38428	22.71319	24.13313	29.00167
13	14.68033	15.14044	15.61779	16.62684	17.71298	18.88214	21.49530	22.95339	24.52271	26.21164	28.02911	34.35192
14	15.97394	16.51895	17.08632	18.29191	19.59863	21.01507	24.21492	26.01919	27.97498	30.09492	32.39260	40.50471
15	17.29342	17.93193	18.59891	20.02359	21.57856	23.27597	27.15211	29.36092	31.77248	34.40536	37.27972	47.58041
16	18.63929	19.38022	20.15688	21.82453	23.65749	25.67253	30.32428	33.00340	35.94973	39.18995	42.75328	55.71747
17	20.01207	20.86473	21.76159	23.69751	25.84037	28.21288	33.75023	36.97371	40.54470	44.50084	48.88367	65.07509
18	21.41231	22.38635	23.41444	25.64541	28.13238	30.90565	37.45024	41.30134	45.59917	50.39593	55.74972	75.83636
19	22.84056	23.94601	25.11687	27.67123	30.53900	33.75999	41.44626	46.01846	51.15909	56.93949	63.43968	88.21181
20	24.29737	25.54466	26.87037	29.77808	33.06595	36.78559	45.76196	51.16012	57.27500	64.20283	72.05244	102.44358
21	25.78332	27.18327	28.67649	31.96920	35.71925	39.99273	50.42292	56.76453	64.00250	72.26514	81.69874	118.81012
22	27.29898	28.86286	30.53678	34.24797	38.50521	43.39229	55.45676	62.87334	71.40275	81.21431	92.50258	137.63164
23	28.84496	30.58443	32.45288	36.61789	41.43048	46.99583	60.89330	69.53194	79.54302	91.14788	104.60289	159.27638
24	30.42186	32.34904	34.42647	39.08260	44.50200	50.81558	66.76476	76.78981	88.49733	102.17415	118.15524	184.16784
25	32.03030	34.15776	36.45926	41.64591	47.72710	54.86451	73.10594	84.70090	98.34706	114.41331	133.33387	212.79302
26	33.67091	36.01171	38.55304	44.31174	51.11345	59.15638	79.95442	93.32398	109.18177	127.99877	150.33393	245.71197
27	35.34432	37.91200	40.70963	47.08421	54.66913	63.70577	87.35077	102.72314	121.09994	143.07864	169.37401	283.56877
28	37.05121	39.85990	42.93092	49.96758	58.40258	68.52811	95.33883	112.96822	134.20994	159.81729	190.69889	327.10408
29	38.79223	41.85630	45.21885	52.96629	62.32271	73.63980	103.96594	124.13536	148.63093	178.39719	214.58275	377.16969
30	40.56808	43.90270	47.57542	56.08494	66.43885	79.05819	113.28321	136.30754	164.49402	199.02088	241.33268	434.74515
31	42.37944	46.00027	50.00268	59.32834	70.76079	84.80168	123.34587	149.57522	181.94343	221.91317	271.29261	500.95692
32	44.22703	48.15028	52.50276	62.70147	75.29883	90.88978	134.21354	164.03699	201.13777	247.32362	304.84772	577.10046
33	46.11157	50.35403	55.07784	66.20953	80.06377	97.34316	145.95062	179.80032	222.25154	275.52922	342.42945	644.66553
34	48.03380	52.61289	57.73018	69.85791	85.06696	104.18376	158.62667	196.98234	245.47670	306.83744	384.52098	765.36535
35	49.99448	54.92821	60.46208	73.65222	90.32031	111.43478	172.31680	215.71076	271.02437	341.58955	431.66350	881.17016
36	51.99437	57.30141	63.27594	77.59831	95.83632	119.12087	187.10215	236.12472	299.12681	380.16441	484.46312	1014.34568
37	54.03425	59.73395	66.17422	81.70225	101.62814	127.26812	203.07032	258.37595	330.03949	422.98249	543.59869	1167.49753
38	56.11494	62.22730	69.15945	85.97034	107.70955	135.90421	220.31595	282.62978	364.04343	470.51056	609.83053	1343.62216
39	58.23724	64.78298	72.23423	90.40915	114.09502	145.05846	238.94122	309.06646	401.44778	523.26673	684.01020	1546.16549
40	60.40198	67.40255	75.40126	95.02552	120.79977	154.76197	259.05652	337.88245	442.59256	581.82607	767.09142	1779.09031

Table A-4

PRESENT VALUE OF AN ORDINARY ANNUITY OF 1

$$PVF\text{-}OA_{n,\,i} = \frac{1 - \dfrac{1}{(1+i)^n}}{i}$$

(n) periods	2%	2½%	3%	4%	5%	6%	8%	9%	10%	11%	12%	15%
1	.98039	.97561	.97087	.96154	.95238	.94340	.92593	.91743	.90909	.90090	.89286	.86957
2	1.94156	1.92742	1.91347	1.88609	1.85941	1.83339	1.78326	1.75911	1.73554	1.71252	1.69005	1.62571
3	2.88388	2.85602	2.82861	2.77509	2.72325	2.67301	2.57710	2.53130	2.48685	2.44371	2.40183	2.28323
4	3.80773	3.76197	3.71710	3.62990	3.54595	3.46511	3.31213	3.23972	3.16986	3.10245	3.03735	2.85498
5	4.71346	4.64583	4.57971	4.45182	4.32948	4.21236	3.99271	3.88965	3.79079	3.69590	3.60478	3.35216
6	5.60143	5.50813	5.41719	5.24214	5.07569	4.91732	4.62288	4.48592	4.35526	4.23054	4.11141	3.78448
7	6.47199	6.34939	6.23028	6.00205	5.78637	5.58238	5.20637	5.03295	4.86842	4.71220	4.56376	4.16042
8	7.32548	7.17014	7.01969	6.73274	6.46321	6.20979	5.74664	5.53482	5.33493	5.14612	4.96764	4.48732
9	8.16224	7.97087	7.78611	7.43533	7.10782	6.80169	6.24689	5.99525	5.75902	5.53705	5.32825	4.77158
10	8.98259	8.75206	8.53020	8.11090	7.72173	7.36009	6.71008	6.41766	6.14457	5.88923	5.65022	5.01877
11	9.78685	9.51421	9.25262	8.76048	8.30641	7.88687	7.13896	6.80519	6.49506	6.20652	5.93770	5.23371
12	10.57534	10.25776	9.95400	9.38507	8.86325	8.38384	7.53608	7.16073	6.81369	6.49236	6.19437	5.42062
13	11.34837	10.98319	10.63496	9.98565	9.39357	8.85268	7.90378	7.48690	7.10336	6.74987	6.42355	5.58315
14	12.10625	11.69091	11.29607	10.56312	9.89864	9.29498	8.24424	7.78615	7.36669	6.98187	6.62817	5.72448
15	12.84926	12.38138	11.93794	11.11839	10.37966	9.71225	8.55948	8.06069	7.60608	7.19087	6.81086	5.84737
16	13.57771	13.05500	12.56110	11.65230	10.83777	10.10590	8.85137	8.31256	7.82371	7.37916	6.97399	5.95424
17	14.29187	13.71220	13.16612	12.16567	11.27407	10.47726	9.12164	8.54363	8.02155	7.54879	7.11963	6.04716
18	14.99203	14.35336	13.75351	12.65930	11.68959	10.82760	9.37189	8.75563	8.20141	7.70162	7.24967	6.12797
19	15.67846	14.97889	14.32380	13.13394	12.08532	11.15812	9.60360	8.95012	8.36492	7.83929	7.36578	6.19823
20	16.35143	15.58916	14.87747	13.59033	12.46221	11.46992	9.81815	9.12855	8.51356	7.96333	7.46944	6.25933
21	17.01121	16.18455	15.41502	14.02916	12.82115	11.76408	10.01680	9.29224	8.64869	8.07507	7.56200	6.31246
22	17.65805	16.76541	15.93692	14.45112	13.16800	12.04158	10.20074	9.44243	8.77154	8.17574	7.64465	6.35866
23	18.29220	17.33211	16.44361	14.85684	13.48857	12.30338	10.37106	9.58021	8.88322	8.26643	7.71843	6.39884
24	18.91393	17.88499	16.93554	15.24696	13.79864	12.55036	10.52876	9.70661	8.98474	8.34814	7.78432	6.43377
25	19.52346	18.42438	17.41315	15.62208	14.09394	12.78336	10.67478	9.82258	9.07704	8.42174	7.84314	6.46415
26	20.12104	18.95061	17.87684	15.98277	14.37519	13.00317	10.80998	9.92897	9.16095	8.48806	7.89566	6.49056
27	20.70690	19.46401	18.32703	16.32959	14.64303	13.21053	10.93516	10.02658	9.23722	8.45780	7.94255	6.51353
28	21.28127	19.96489	18.76411	16.66306	14.89813	13.40616	11.05108	10.11613	9.30657	8.60162	7.98442	6.53351
29	21.84438	20.45355	19.18845	16.98371	15.14107	13.59072	11.15841	10.19828	9.36961	8.65011	8.02181	6.55088
30	22.39646	20.93029	19.60044	17.29203	15.37245	13.76483	11.25778	10.27365	9.42691	8.69379	8.05518	6.56598
31	22.93770	21.39541	20.00043	17.58849	15.59281	13.92909	11.34980	10.34280	9.47901	8.73315	8.08499	6.57911
32	23.46833	21.84918	20.38877	17.87355	15.80268	14.08404	11.43500	10.40624	9.52638	8.76860	8.11159	6.59053
33	23.98856	22.29188	20.76579	18.14765	16.00255	14.23023	11.51389	10.46444	9.56943	8.80054	8.13535	6.60046
34	24.49859	22.72379	21.13184	18.41120	16.19290	14.36814	11.58693	10.51784	9.60858	8.82932	8.15656	6.60910
35	24.99862	23.14516	21.48722	18.66461	16.37419	14.49825	11.65457	10.56682	9.64416	8.85524	8.17550	6.61661
36	25.48884	23.55625	21.83225	18.90828	16.54685	14.62099	11.71719	10.61176	9.67651	8.87859	8.19241	6.62314
37	25.96945	23.95732	22.16724	19.14258	16.71129	14.73678	11.77518	10.65299	9.70592	8.89963	8.20751	6.62882
38	26.44064	24.34860	22.49246	19.36786	16.86789	14.84602	11.82887	10.69082	9.73265	8.91859	8.22099	6.63375
39	26.90259	24.73034	22.80822	19.58448	17.01704	14.94907	11.87858	10.72552	9.75697	8.93567	8.23303	6.63805
40	27.35548	25.10278	23.11477	19.79277	17.15909	15.04630	11.92461	10.75736	9.77905	8.95105	8.24378	6.64178

Time Value of Money

Table A-5

PRESENT VALUE OF AN ANNUITY DUE OF 1

$$PVF-AD_{n,\,i} = 1 + \frac{1 - \dfrac{1}{(1+i)^{n-1}}}{i}$$

(n) periods	2%	2½%	3%	4%	5%	6%	8%	9%	10%	11%	12%	15%
1	1.00000	1.00000	1.00000	1.00000	1.00000	1.00000	1.00000	1.00000	1.00000	1.00000	1.00000	1.00000
2	1.98039	1.97561	1.97087	1.96154	1.95238	1.94340	1.92593	1.91743	1.90909	1.90090	1.89286	1.86957
3	2.94156	2.92742	2.91347	2.88609	2.85941	2.83339	2.78326	2.75911	2.73554	2.71252	2.69005	2.62571
4	3.88388	3.85602	3.82861	3.77509	3.72325	3.67301	3.57710	3.53130	3.48685	3.44371	3.40183	3.28323
5	4.80773	4.76197	4.71710	4.62990	4.54595	4.46511	4.31213	4.23972	4.16986	4.10245	4.03735	3.85498
6	5.71346	5.64583	5.57971	5.45182	5.32948	5.21236	4.99271	4.88965	4.79079	4.69590	4.60478	4.35216
7	6.60143	6.50813	6.41719	6.24214	6.07569	5.91732	5.62288	5.48592	5.35526	5.23054	5.11141	4.78448
8	7.47199	7.34939	7.23028	7.00205	6.78637	6.58238	6.20637	6.03295	5.86842	5.71220	5.56376	5.16042
9	8.32548	8.17014	8.01969	7.73274	7.46321	7.20979	6.74664	6.53482	6.33493	6.14612	5.96764	5.48732
10	9.16224	8.97087	8.78611	8.43533	8.10782	7.80169	7.24689	6.99525	6.75902	6.53705	6.32825	5.77158
11	9.98259	9.75206	9.53020	9.11090	8.72173	8.36009	7.71008	7.41766	7.14457	6.88923	6.65022	6.01877
12	10.78685	10.51421	10.25262	9.76048	9.30641	8.88687	8.13896	7.80519	7.49506	7.20652	6.93770	6.23371
13	11.57534	11.25776	10.95400	10.38507	9.86325	9.38384	8.53608	8.16073	7.81369	7.49236	7.19437	6.42062
14	12.34837	11.98319	11.63496	10.98565	10.39357	9.85268	8.90378	8.48690	8.10336	7.74987	7.42355	6.58315
15	13.10625	12.69091	12.29607	11.56312	10.89864	10.29498	9.24424	8.78615	9.36669	7.98187	7.62817	6.72448
16	13.84926	13.38138	12.93794	12.11839	11.37966	10.71225	9.55948	9.06069	8.60608	8.19087	7.81086	6.84737
17	14.57771	14.05500	13.56110	12.65230	11.83777	11.10590	9.85137	9.31256	8.82371	8.37916	7.97399	6.95424
18	15.29187	14.71220	14.16612	13.16567	12.27407	11.47726	10.12164	9.54363	9.02155	8.54879	8.11963	7.04716
19	15.99203	15.35336	14.75351	13.65930	12.68959	11.82760	10.37189	9.75563	9.20141	8.70162	8.24967	7.12797
20	16.67846	15.97889	15.32380	14.13394	13.08532	12.15812	10.60360	9.95012	9.36492	8.83929	8.36578	7.19823
21	17.35143	16.58916	15.87747	14.59033	13.46221	12.46992	10.81815	10.12855	9.51356	8.96333	8.46944	7.25933
22	18.01121	17.18455	16.41502	15.02916	13.82115	12.76408	11.01680	10.29224	9.64869	9.07507	8.56200	7.31246
23	18.65805	17.76541	16.93692	15.45112	14.16300	13.04158	11.20074	10.44243	9.77154	9.17574	8.64465	7.35866
24	19.29220	18.33211	17.44361	15.85684	14.48857	13.30338	11.37106	10.58021	9.88322	9.26643	8.71843	7.39884
25	19.91393	18.88499	17.93554	16.24696	14.79864	13.55036	11.52876	10.70661	9.98474	9.34814	8.78432	7.43377
26	20.52346	19.42438	18.41315	16.62208	15.09394	13.78336	11.67478	10.82258	10.07704	9.42174	8.84314	7.46415
27	21.12104	19.95061	18.87684	16.98277	15.37519	14.00317	11.80998	10.92897	10.16095	9.48806	8.89566	7.49056
28	21.70690	20.46401	19.32703	17.32959	15.64303	14.21053	11.93518	11.02658	10.23722	9.54780	8.94255	7.51353
29	22.28127	20.96489	19.76411	17.66306	15.89813	14.40616	12.05108	11.11613	10.30657	9.60162	8.98442	7.53351
30	22.84438	21.45355	20.18845	17.98371	16.14107	14.59072	12.15841	11.19828	10.36961	9.65011	9.02181	7.55088
31	23.39646	21.93029	20.60044	18.29203	16.37245	14.76483	12.25778	11.27365	10.42691	9.69379	9.05518	7.56598
32	23.93770	22.39541	21.00043	18.58849	16.59281	14.92909	12.34980	11.34280	10.47901	9.73315	9.08499	7.57911
33	24.46833	22.84918	21.38877	18.87355	16.80268	15.08404	12.43500	11.40624	10.52638	9.76860	9.11159	7.59053
34	24.98856	23.29188	21.76579	19.14765	17.00255	15.23023	12.51389	11.46444	10.56943	9.80054	9.13535	7.60046
35	25.49859	23.72379	22.13184	19.41120	17.19290	15.36814	12.58693	11.51784	10.60858	9.82932	9.15656	7.60910
36	25.99862	24.14516	22.48722	19.66461	17.37419	15.49825	12.65457	11.56682	10.64416	9.85524	9.17550	7.61661
37	26.48884	24.55625	22.83225	19.90828	17.54685	15.62099	12.71719	11.61176	10.67651	9.87859	9.19241	7.62314
38	26.96945	24.95732	23.16724	20.14258	17.71129	15.73678	12.77518	11.65299	10.70592	9.89963	9.20751	7.62882
39	27.44064	25.34860	23.49246	20.36786	17.86789	15.84602	12.82887	11.69082	10.73265	9.91859	9.22099	7.63375
40	27.90259	25.73034	23.80822	20.58448	18.01704	15.94907	12.87858	11.72552	10.75697	9.93567	9.23303	7.63805

COMPANY INDEX

SUBJECT INDEX

PHOTO CREDITS

Page 770: Sears Canada.
Page 834: Great Canadian Gaming Corporation.
Page 892: Sleep Country Canada.
Page 950: TD Securities Inc.
Page 1028: Open Text Corporation.
Page 1074: EnCana Corporation.
Page 1158: PhotoDisc, Inc.
Page 1228: Saskatchewan Gaming Corporation.
Page 1310: Reuters/CORBIS.
Page 1382: Clearwater Seafoods.
Page 1472: George Pchemyan.